# The New Penguin Dictionary of
# Modern
# Quotations

**Robert Andrews**
With the assistance of Kate Hughes

PENGUIN BOOKS

PENGUIN BOOKS

Published by the Penguin Group
Penguin Books Ltd, 80 Strand, London WC2R ORL, England
Penguin Putnam Inc., 375 Hudson Street, New York, New York 10014, USA
Penguin Books Australia Ltd, 250 Camberwell Road, Camberwell, Victoria 3124, Australia
Penguin Books Canada Ltd, 10 Alcorn Avenue, Toronto, Ontario, Canada M4V 3B2
Penguin Books India (P) Ltd, 11, Community Centre, Panchsheel Park, New Delhi – 110 017, India
Penguin Books (NZ) Ltd, Cnr Rosedale and Airborne Roads, Albany, Auckland, New Zealand
Penguin Books (South Africa) (Pty) Ltd, 24 Sturdee Avenue, Rosebank 2196, South Africa

Penguin Books Ltd, Registered Offices: 80 Strand, London WC2R ORL, England

www.penguin.com

First published by Allen Lane The Penguin Press 2000
Published in Penguin Books 2001

1

Copyright © Robert Andrews, 2001

The moral right of the editor has been asserted

Printed in Finland by WS Bookwell

...GU... ...TIONARY OF

... ews is an experienced quotations sleuth. Among other works, he has edited the *Routledge Dictionary of Quotations* and the *Cassell Dictionary of Contemporary Quotations* as well as the monumental *Columbia Dictionary of Quotations*. He has also written travel guides on Britain and Southern Italy. He lives in Bristol.

From early *I-Spy* days Kate Hughes has indulged her researcher tendencies, first in Victorian Studies at Leicester University and later for travel guides and dictionaries of quotations.

# Contents

To Carolyn and Mark and Joyce and Gordon, with love

'Certain brief sentences are peerless in their ability to give one the feeling that nothing remains to be said.'

Jean Rostand's observation could refer to many of the entries in this collection which, taken in isolation, seem to defy improvement. However, the further one reads, the more it becomes clear that there is no 'final word'.

The era which began in 1914 – this book's point of departure – has witnessed a mighty deluge of words: the rampant growth of journalism in all its forms, the outpourings of the evolving film and television industries, popular song, techno-speak and sound bite – all have contributed to the great, unruly ocean of verbiage in which we swim today. It is part of the purpose of the present collection to help salvage the most original, memorable and significant sayings from among these garrulous effusions, and to provide an outline of their original context.

To this end, short biographies of the speakers or writers have been supplied in addition to the relevant details regarding the quotations themselves, enabling a more complete understanding of the circumstances and importance of each entry. Without context, an anthology of quotations can ossify into a mere catalogue of pointless or cryptic fragments which ignores the peculiar milieu that gave birth to them. So rather than a miscellaneous jumble of flotsam, lustrous and intriguing perhaps, but ultimately rootless and unconnected, this work sets out to be a gallery of the vital personalities of our recent history, depicting them through the speeches and phrases with which they are most identified. Cohabiting within the same century, these figures influence each other and interract organically, as indicated by the copious cross-references. The dictionary is, in short, a continuous conversation edited down to its choicest excerpts.

Such is the power of quotations that they preserve a vital residue of a persona, standing for a complex of associations and memories. It is difficult to read the words of Marlon Brando or Camille Paglia without hearing their voices, or those of Marilyn Monroe or Winston Churchill without conjuring up a precise visual image. Although authors are listed alphabetically in the dictionary, the order of quotations under each entry is chronological, a scheme which allows an insight into their authors' lives and the evolution of their philosophies and convictions. The entries by Salman Rushdie, for example, reveal how much of his writing has been a commentary on the theme of belief, and how the infamous fatwa with its death sentence in the middle of his literary career was not just a personal blow but also a poignant and bitterly ironic one in the context of his other major preoccupation: the interplay between literature, faith and society. Similarly, in the entries for George Orwell, Virginia Woolf and Picasso, one can trace the same themes recurring, the enthusiasms and obsessions that ultimately distinguish their careers and systems of thought.

Not all the quotes collected here are familiar. Where people are not particularly known for any specific saying, the essence of their message or achievements has been captured in a significant extract. Hence, alongside the most famous selections, the book includes a substantial element which has never before been anthologized, but while these quotes themselves may be unfamiliar, they encapsulate attitudes or philosophies which are integral to our perceptions of these individuals. Ernest Hemingway, Marcus Garvey, Ezra Pound and Andrea Dworkin are examples of people rarely quoted, yet frequently invoked, their names synonymous with distinct positions and outlooks. Malcolm X and Carl Jung are known to us for their stances: here you will find the words which back these up. There are also numerous entries in the book which appear to contradict the stereotypes. Quotations do not always do what we expect – Walter Benjamin called them 'wayside robbers who leap out armed and relieve the stroller of his conviction' – but untypical pronouncements can be as eloquent and insightful of a character as the most predictable, adding new dimensions to our images of some of the icons of the age.

As a rule, quotations have been ascribed to the person with whom they are most commonly associated. Although this produces occasional anomalies, usually in the fields of music and film, I believe that this approach is the most faithful, in the sense that we do not usually think of a screenwriter or speechwriter when we encounter quotes by an actor or a politician – though screenwriters in films and speechwriters (where known) are specified in the citation. 'Hasta la vista, baby' is indelibly linked to the name of Arnold Schwarzenegger, and 'Here's looking at you, kid' could only be Humphrey Bogart. In some cases, however, where the author is better known – for example Woody Allen or Nora Ephron – the words are credited to their originator. Lyrics of popular songs are entered under the writers where these are best known, such as Irving Berlin or Lennon/McCartney, or to the performer when a singer of the likes of Elvis Presley, Edith Piaf or Frank Sinatra has appropriated a song as his or her own.

Advertising slogans and political slogans are represented in separate sections. These do not aspire to be in any way exhaustive: quotations are primarily individual emanations of a single voice, not manufactured by committees for short-term effect, and slogans will therefore be found more comprehensively listed elsewhere. Nonetheless, they cannot be ignored, since advertising and propaganda are now as integrated in the common parlance as popular song, and a small selection is given here, as is a choice of graffiti. Catch-phrases, equally manufactured but clearly more 'personal', are included under those names with which they are linked.

As mentioned above, quotations are listed chronologically, according to the original date of composition, performance or publication, whichever is known to be earlier. Dates of translations are given only when these were made significantly later than the original composition, or when they are specific versions among many. Translators are named when they are well known. In letters, addressees are mentioned when they are members of the writer's family, or otherwise well known. Specific quotations can be traced by means of the keyword index, while the thematic index allows readers to find quotes on particular subjects.

This project has by no means been a corporate, 'in-house' job, and while we have attempted to embrace as many different viewpoints and influences as possible, the dictionary remains a largely subjective résumé of the most eminent quotations of the modern era. As such, there is always scope for improvement, and any suggestions, amendments and corrections will be gratefully received, addressed to Penguin at 27 Wrights Lane, London w8 5tz.

At the same time, the book has been very much a collective labour, the fruit of the enthusiasms and explorations of a dedicated band, chief amongst whom is Kate Hughes, whose inspired reading and hard-nosed detective work have been crucial ingredients in all aspects of the work's evolution. Her perseverance and passion for accuracy has ensured that the dictionary has attained its main function: that of a reliable reference tool. Philip Krynsky's input has been eclectic and thorough; his insight, experience and instinct for research have been invaluable in a variety of areas. Richard Davoll's erudition combined with his eye for detail has been an essential resource, and I am particularly grateful for his availability at short notice for burrowing among the library's more arcane sections. Esther McLean, whose formidable efficiency and acuity have met every challenge, has been an indispensable member of the team. Margaret Jones lent her broad knowledge and considerable abilities to the editing and research of the material, and her advice and suggestions have been greatly appreciated.

I am also indebted to Lesley Rose, Martin Chester, Dominique Delight, Evelyn Ellworthy, Lucille Smith, Julie Taylor and Emma Brooks, whose meticulous efforts in all areas of research have been hugely appreciated. And heartfelt thanks to Agata Scamporrino for rambling readings during her own difficult pregnancy, and to Joyce Murray for coming up trumps, as ever.

At Penguin, I thank Nigel Wilcockson for his faith in initiating this project, Martin Toseland for his steadfast calm support and encouragement, and Mark Handsley for his editorial expertise. I gratefully acknowledge, too, the constructive copy-editing of Gordon Smith. Deep thanks are also due to the staff at Bristol's University Library and Central Library – the latter has been particularly helpful; to Fiona and Verity for helping me through the nights, and to Quincy and Evelina for being best friends and overall brilliant kids.

## Diane Abbott (b. 1953)

BRITISH POLITICIAN

After working for the National Council for Civil Liberties, the GLC and Lambeth Council, she became the first black woman MP when she was elected to the seat of Hackney North and Stoke Newington for Labour in 1987.

1 The honest truth is that if this Government were to propose a massacre of the first-born, it would still have no difficulty in getting it through the Commons.

Quoted in the *Independent on Sunday* 12 July 1998

## Mumia Abu-Jamal (b. 1954)

US JOURNALIST AND ENVIRONMENTALIST

America's most celebrated prisoner on Death Row was convicted of the murder of a police officer in Philadelphia in 1981. His case has been championed by NORMAN MAILER, WHOOPI GOLDBERG and Paul Newman, among others, though in July 1999 it emerged that Abu-Jamal had previously confessed his guilt to a journalist.

1 Prison is a second-by-second assault on the soul, a day-to-day degradation of the self, an oppressive steel and brick umbrella that transforms seconds into hours and hours into days.

*Live from Death Row*, pt 1, 'Nightraiders meet rage' (1995)

## Chinua Achebe (b. 1930)

NIGERIAN NOVELIST

Originally Albert Chinualumogo. His books deal with the impact of European colonialism on Africa, and with post-colonial African politics. Among the most notable are his first, *Things Fall Apart* (1958), one of the first African novels to make an international impact, and *Anthills of the Savanna* (1987).

1 For I do honestly believe that in the fat-dripping, gummy, eat-and-let-eat régime just ended – a régime which inspired the common saying that a man could only be sure of what he had put away safely in his gut or, in language ever more suited to the times; 'you chop, me self I chop, palaver finish'; a régime in which you see a fellow cursed in the morning for stealing a blind man's stick and later in the evening saw him again mounting the altar of the new shrine in the presence of all the people to whisper into the ear of the chief celebrant – in such a régime, I say, you died a good death if your life had inspired someone to come forward and shoot your murderer in the chest – without asking to be paid.

*A Man of the People*, ch. 13 (1966). In this closing sentence of the book, the narrator (Odili Samalu) refers to the end of the repressive régime of Chief Nanga.

## Dean Acheson (1893–1971)

US DEMOCRATIC POLITICIAN

Advisor to four presidents and Secretary of State to President TRUMAN (1949–53), he was instrumental in implementing the Marshall Aid Plan to Europe and the Truman Doctrine (1947), and in the formation of NATO (1949). According to *Time*, 'his career was a text book example of the rise of a patrician in the snug embrace of the American establishment'.

1 Great Britain has lost an Empire and has not yet found a role.

Speech at US Military Academy, West Point, 5 December 1962, publ. in *Vital Speeches*

2 The first requirement of a statesman is that he be dull. This is not always easy to achieve.

Quoted in the *Observer* 21 June 1970

3 A memorandum is written not to inform the reader but to protect the writer.

Quoted in the *Wall Street Journal* 8 September 1977

## Gilbert Adair (b. 1944)

BRITISH AUTHOR AND CRITIC

He is principally known as a cultural critic, his essays collected in *Myths and Memories* (1986) and *Hollywood's Vietnam* (1989). He has also published novels and translations from the French.

1 The earth is mankind's ultimate haven, our blessed *terra firma*. When it trembles and gives way beneath our feet, it's as though one of God's cheques has bounced.

Quoted in the *Sunday Correspondent* 24 December 1989

2 Postmodernism is, almost by definition, a transitional cusp of social, cultural, economic and ideological history when modernism's high-minded principles and preoccupations have ceased to function, but before they have been replaced with a totally new system of values. It represents a moment of suspension before the batteries are recharged for the new millennium, an acknowledgment that preceding the future is a strange and hybrid interregnum that might be called the last gasp of the past.

*Sunday Times* 21 April 1991

3 The arts in this country exist primarily to fuel the culture industry.

*The Post-Modernist Always Rings Twice*, title essay (1992)

## Douglas Adams (b. 1952)

BRITISH AUTHOR

He attracted legions of fans with *The Hitch Hiker's Guide to the Galaxy,* a pseudo-science fiction series originally broadcast on radio in 1978. It subsequently became a book and was adapted for television, stage and a computer game.

1 Don't panic.

*The Hitch Hiker's Guide to the Galaxy*, Preface and *passim* (1979). The words are inscribed in 'large friendly letters' on the cover of the (fictional) book, 'The Hitch Hiker's Guide to the Galaxy'. The same words were also a catch-phrase of the excitable Corporal Jones (played by Clive Dunn) in the TV series *Dad's Army* (1968–77).

2 I think you ought to know I'm feeling very depressed.

Marvin the robot, in ibid. ch. 11. The first words in the book spoken by this prototype for a new generation of robots with 'Genuine People Personalities'. Adams claims he based Marvin's character on Andrew Marshall, the comedy writer, though he also acknowledges the influence of Eeyore in Winnie-the-Pooh.

3 Life . . . don't talk to me about Life.

ibid.

4 I've been ordered to take you down to the bridge. Here I am, brain the size of a planet and they ask me to take you down to the bridge. Call that *job satisfaction*? 'Cos I don't.

ibid.

5 The Answer to the Great Question . . . Of Life, the Universe and Everything . . . Is . . . Forty-two.

The computer Deep Thought, in ibid. ch. 27

6 So long, and thanks for all the fish.

The dolphins' farewell message to humanity, in *So Long, and Thanks for All the Fish*, ch. 31 (fourth book in the *Hitch Hiker's Guide to the Galaxy* series, 1984)

## Franklin Pierce Adams (1881–1960)

US JOURNALIST AND HUMORIST

A byword from the 1930s for wit and erudition, Adams set a precedent for the modern newspaper column with 'The Conning Tower', in the *Herald Tribune* 1913–37. He said of himself: 'I am easily influenced. Compared with me a weather vane is Gibraltar.'

1 Years ago we discovered the exact point, the dead center of middle age. It occurs when you are too young to take up golf and too old to rush up to the net.

*Nods and Becks*, 'Valentine' (1944)

2 Too much *Truth*
Is uncouth.

ibid. 'From the New England Primer'

3 The trouble with this country is that there are too many politicians who believe, with a conviction based on experience, that you can fool all of the people all of the time.

ibid. 'Baseball Note'. The allusion is to the famous saying credited to both Abraham Lincoln and Phineas Barnum: 'You may fool all the people some of the time; you can even fool some of the people all the time; but you can't fool all of the people all the time.'

## Gerry Adams (b. 1948)

IRISH POLITICIAN

President of Sinn Féin ('We Ourselves'), he was elected to the Northern Ireland Assembly in 1982 and became MP for Belfast West in 1983, though refusing to take his seat at Westminster. He was principal negotiator in the IRA ceasefire (1994–6) and the Good Friday peace agreement (1999).

1 The IRA aren't the cause of violence in Ireland. They are a symptom of it. If this was a normal society, we wouldn't have the violence we are now having to endure.

Column as 'Brownie' in the *Belfast Republican News*, 1976, repr. in *Man of War, Man of Peace* (1997) by David Sharrock and Mark Devenport. Adams, then in prison in Long Kesh, maintained that the 'Brownie' articles were not written solely by him, but were the work of a number of prisoners.

2 Hunger strike is unlike any other form of struggle. An IRA volunteer does not go out to get killed; if he or she gets killed it is because he or she makes a mistake or some circumstance arises. But a hunger striker embarks on a process which, from day one, is designed to end in his or her death.

*Selected Writings*, 'Political Status' (1994)

3 He [David Trimble] is a man I can do business with; he is a man I have to do business with; and he is a man who I will do business with. This is more important than the personalities involved.

Quoted in the *Guardian* 11 September 1998. Referring to his meeting with the Ulster Unionist leader, the first time Unionist and Sinn Féin leaders had met since 1922.

## Harold Adamson (1906–80)

US SONGWRITER

He provided Broadway and Hollywood musicals with a number of successful songs, working with celebrated jazz composers to produce such standards as 'Manhattan Serenade' (1948) and 'My Resistance is Low' (1951). He wrote lyrics for films including *Gentlemen Prefer Blondes* (1953).

1 Comin' in on a wing and a pray'r.

'Comin' in on a Wing and a Pray'r' (song, 1943). The phrase is said to have originated from a pilot's radio-ed words while attempting a landing with a damaged plane.

## Fleur Adcock (b. 1934)

NEW ZEALAND POET AND EDITOR

Based in England since 1963, she is known for the unsentimental, often ironic style of her verse, collected in *The Eye of the Hurricane* (1964), *In Focus* (1977), *The Incident Book* (1986) and *Time Zones* (1991), among other volumes.

1 I write in praise of the solitary act:
of not feeling a trespassing tongue
forced into one's mouth, one's breath

smothered, nipples crushed against the
ribcage, and that metallic tingling
in the chin set off by a certain odd nerve:
unpleasure.
'Against Coupling', publ. in *High Tide in the Garden* (1971)

## Alfred Adler (1870–1937)
AUSTRIAN PSYCHIATRIST

A founder member of the Vienna Psychoanalytic Society, he introduced the concept of the inferiority complex in 1907 and developed
his own school of Individual Psychology from 1911. *The Neurotic
Character* (1912) was his first and most significant book.

1 **The truth is often a terrible weapon of aggression. It is
possible to lie, and even to murder, for the truth.**
*The Problems of Neurosis*, ch. 2 (1929)

2 **It is always easier to fight for one's principles than to live
up to them.**
Quoted in *Alfred Adler: Apostle of Freedom*, ch. 5 (1939) by Phyllis
Bottome. The quote was used by ADLAI STEVENSON in a speech
in New York, 27 August 1952.

## Polly Adler (1900–62)
US BROTHEL-KEEPER AND AUTHOR

A New York 'madam' in the 1920s and 1930s, she retired for good
in 1945. Her memoirs were filmed in 1964.

1 **A house is not a home.**
*A House is Not a Home* (memoirs, 1954)

2 **What it comes down to is this: the grocer, the butcher,
the baker, the merchant, the landlord, the druggist, the
liquor dealer, the policeman, the doctor, the city father
and the politician – these are the people who make money
out of prostitution, these are the real reapers of the wages
of sin.**
ibid. ch. 9

## Theodor W. Adorno (1903–69)
GERMAN PHILOSOPHER, SOCIOLOGIST AND
MUSICOLOGIST

A member of the Frankfurt School of philosophy, he was associated
with the Frankfurt Institute for Social Research from 1928 before
fleeing the Nazis to the USA. He returned to Frankfurt to assume
the post of Director of the Institute (1958–69). His publications
include *The Dialectic of Enlightenment* (1947) and *The Philosophy
of Modern Music* (1949).

1 **Technology is making gestures precise and brutal, and
with them men. It expels from movements all hesitation,
deliberation, civility.**
*Minima Moralia*, pt 1 (dated 1944), 'Do Not Knock' (1951, transl.
G.F.N. Jephcott, 1978)

2 **True thoughts are those alone which do not understand
themselves.**
ibid. pt 3 (dated 1946–7), 'Monograms'

3 **Culture is only true when implicitly critical, and the mind
which forgets this revenges itself in the critics it breeds.
Criticism is an indispensable element of culture.**
*Prisms*, 'Cultural Criticism and Society' (1967)

## Advertising slogans See also SAATCHI AND SAATCHI.

1 **Access – your flexible friend.**
Access credit card, 1980s

2 **American Express? . . . That'll do nicely, sir.**
American Express credit card, 1970s

3 **Can you tell Stork from butter?**
Stork margarine, 1950s

4 **Even your closest friends won't tell you.**
Listerine mouthwash (US), 1920s. The campaign, which focused
on halitosis, ran from 1922 mainly in women's magazines. It hugely
boosted sales of the product, and was an early demonstration of
the power of advertising, also giving birth to the technique of
playing on people's neuroses by inventing unheard-of complaints.
It was subsequently widely copied, and the 'halitosis influence'
became part of standard advertising jargon (discussed in *The Mirror
Makers: A History of American Advertising*, 1984, by Stephen Fox).

5 **Full of Eastern promise.**
Fry's Turkish Delight, from 1950s

6 **Go to work on an egg.**
British Egg Marketing Board, from 1957. Claimed to have been
written by FAY WELDON.

7 **Guinness is good for you.**
Guinness beer, credited to Oswald Greene in 1929 in *The Book of
Guinness Advertising*, ch. 4 (1985) by Brian Sibley. Other slogans
famously associated with Guinness include 'Guinness Gives You
Strength' (also from 1929), which first appeared as 'Guinness is So
Strengthening' and was accompanied by an image of a workman
carrying a girder on his fingertips, and 'My Goodness, My Guinness', which was devised by DOROTHY L. SAYERS, then an advertising copywriter.

8 **Heineken refreshes the parts other beers cannot reach.**
Heineken lager, from 1970s

9 **I'm Mandy, fly me.**
TWA 1975. The words, spoken by an air hostess, were a target of
feminists and the title of a hit song by 10cc in 1976.

10 **I'm only here for the beer.**
Double Diamond beer, from 1971, credited to Ros Levenstein

11 **It could be you.**
British National Lottery, from November 1994

12 **It's finger lickin' good.**
Kentucky Fried Chicken, from 1950s

13 **Just when you thought it was safe to go back in the water.**
Publicity for *Jaws 2* (film, 1978)

14 **Let the train take the strain.**
British Rail, from 1970s

15 **Let your fingers do the walking.**
Yellow Pages telephone book, from 1960s in USA and Britain

16 **A Mars a day helps you work, rest and play.**
Mars bar, from 1960s

17 **A million housewives every day
Pick up a tin of beans and say
*Beanz Meanz Heinz!***
Heinz Baked Beans, from 1967, credited to Maurice Drake

18 **Nice one, Cyril.**
Wonderloaf bread, 1972. The phrase was adopted by supporters of
Tottenham Hotspur football club referring to Cyril Knowles, and
was the title of a song recorded by the 'Cockerel Chorus' in 1973.

19 **Snap! Crackle! Pop!**
Kellogg's Rice Krispies, from 1920s

20 **Things go better with Coke.**
Coca Cola, from 1960s

21 **Top people take *The Times*.**
*The Times*, from 1959

22 ***Vorsprung durch Technik.*
(Progress through technology.)**
Audi cars, from 1980s

23 **We are the Ovaltineys,
Happy girls and boys.**
'We are the Ovaltineys' (song), promoting the drink Ovaltine, 1930s

24 **Wouldn't it be nice if all cities were like Milton Keynes?**
For the town of Milton Keynes, 1990s

25 **You're never alone with a Strand.**
Strand cigarettes, 1960. The music was later released as a record
called 'The Lonely Man Theme'.

## Æ (1867–1935)

IRISH POET AND ESSAYIST

Real name George William Russell. He was a prominent figure in the Irish literary revival and edited the newspapers *Irish Homestead* (1905–23) and *Irish Statesman* (1923–30). His poems, plays and writings, among them *The Divine Vision* (1902), *The Candle of Vision* (1918) and *Midsummer Eve* (1928), were inspired by mysticism and magic.

1 In ancient shadows and twilights
  Where childhood had strayed,
  The world's great sorrows were born
  And its heroes were made.
  In the lost boyhood of Judas
  Christ was betrayed.

'Germinal' (1931), repr. in *Selected Poems by Æ* (1935)

## James Agate (1877–1947)

BRITISH DRAMA CRITIC

An exacting drama critic of the *Sunday Times* from 1923 until his death, he was also an assiduous diary-writer. His journals were published in the nine-part *Ego* (1935–49) and his criticism in *Red-Letter Nights* (1944) among other volumes.

1 The Englishman can get along with sex quite perfectly so long as he can pretend that it isn't sex but something else.

Journal entry, 14 October 1932, publ. in *Ego* (1935)

2 Shaw's plays are the price we pay for Shaw's prefaces.

Journal entry, 10 March 1933, publ. in ibid.

3 Don't pity me now,
  Don't pity me never;
  I'm going to do nothing
  For ever and ever.

A 'charwoman's epitaph', in journal entry 14 March 1933, publ. in ibid. The subject of Agate's verse was a 'self-deceiver', he claimed. 'At least I will lay odds that anybody meeting her in Heaven will find her scrubbing marble and dusting porphyry with a new-born gleam in her old eye.'

4 I was asked to-night why I refuse to have truck with intellectuals after business hours. But of course I won't. 1. I am not an intellectual. Two minutes' talk with Aldous Huxley, William Glock, or any of the *New Statesman* crowd would expose me utterly. 2. I am too tired after my day's work to man the intellectual palisade. 3. When my work is finished I want to eat, drink, smoke, and relax. 4. I don't know very much, but what I do know I know better than anybody, and I don't want to argue about it. I know what I think about an actor or an actress, and am not interested in what anybody else thinks. My mind is not a bed to be made and re-made.

Journal entry, 9 June 1943, publ. in *Ego 6* (1946)

## Spiro T. Agnew (1918–96)

US POLITICIAN, VICE-PRESIDENT

Elected Governor of Maryland in 1966 on a Republican ticket, he was RICHARD NIXON's running mate in 1968, serving as Vice-President in 1969 and again in 1972. His earlier liberal and anti-racist stance hardened into a more conservative position, though his credibility was dented in 1973 when, charged with tax evasion while Governor of Maryland, he was forced to resign.

1 I didn't say I wouldn't go into ghetto areas. I've been in many of them and to some extent I would have to say this: If you've seen one city slum you've seen them all.

Speech in Detroit, 18 October 1968, quoted in *Detroit Free Press* 19 October 1968

2 A spirit of national masochism prevails, encouraged by an effete corps of impudent snobs who characterize themselves as intellectuals.

Speech in New Orleans, 19 October 1969, publ. in *Collected Speeches of Spiro Agnew* (1971)

3 Ultraliberalism today translates into a whimpering isolationism in foreign policy, a mulish obstructionism in domestic policy, and a pusillanimous pussyfooting on the critical issue of law and order.

Speech at Springfield, Illinois, 10 September 1970, publ. in ibid.

## Ama Ata Aidoo (b. 1942)

GHANAIAN SCHOLAR AND AUTHOR

Her work is characterized by the dilemmas of the 'been-to' (an African educated abroad) in reconciling Western influence with traditional African culture, as in the semi-autobiographical *Our Sister Killjoy* (1966). She has written plays, novels, short stories and poems.

1 From all around the Third World,
  You hear the same story;
  Rulers
  Asleep to all things at
  All times –
  Conscious only of
  Riches, which they gather in a
  Coma –
  Intravenously.

'The Plum', publ. in *Our Sister Killjoy: Reflections from a Blackeyed Squint* (1966)

2 It's a sad moment, really, when parents first become a bit frightened of their children.

'The Message', publ. in *Fragment from a Lost Diary and Other Stories* (ed. Naomi Katz and Nancy Milton, 1973)

## Jonathan Aitken (b. 1942)

BRITISH BUSINESSMAN AND POLITICIAN

Formerly a journalist, he was elected a Conservative MP in 1974 and rose to be Chief Secretary to the Treasury (1994–5). Allegations about his business dealings led to a court case in 1998 and a conviction for perjury and perverting the course of justice, for which he served a prison sentence the following year.

1 If it falls to me to start a fight to cut out the cancer of bent and twisted journalism in our country with the simple sword of truth and the trusty shield of British fair play, so be it, I am ready for the fight.

Remark 10 April, 1995, quoted in *Guardian* 11 April 1995. Referring to libel writs issued against the *Guardian* and the *World in Action* television programme over allegations of fraudulent business dealings with the Saudi royal family.

2 As far as the physical miseries go, I am sure I will cope. I lived at Eton in the 1950s and I know all about life in uncomfortable quarters.

Quoted in the *Daily Express* 19 January 1999. On his probable imprisonment.

## Anna Akhmatova (1889–1966)

RUSSIAN POET

Originally named Anna Andreyevna Gorenko. Regarded as the greatest Russian woman poet, she was a member of the Acmeist group, which, in reaction to the Symbolists, favoured precision and concrete detail. Silenced for the predominantly Christian tone of *Anno Domini* (1922), she was rehabilitated in 1956. Later works include *Requiem* (1940) and *Poem without a Hero* (1940–62).

1 It was a time when only the dead
smiled, happy in their peace.

*Requiem*, introduction (written 1935–40, transl. Richard McKane, 1985). Akhmatova's long poem about the Stalinist purges – during which her only son was arrested – was not published until 1963 in West Germany, and not in its entirety in the Soviet Union until 1987.

2 Stars of Death stood over us,
and innocent Russia squirmed
under the bloody boots,
under the wheels of black Marias.

ibid. Final words of introduction.

3 The triumphs of a mysterious non-meeting are desolate ones; unspoken phrases, silent words.

*Two Poems*, no. 2 (1956; transl. Dimitri Obolensky, 1965)

## Zoë Akins (1886–1958)

US PLAYWRIGHT

Although she also wrote screenplays, she is best known for her work for the theatre, winning the Pulitzer Prize for her dramatization of *The Old Maid* by Edith Wharton (1935). Among her other plays are the comedies *Daddy's Gone A-Hunting* (1921) and *The Greeks Had a Word For It* (1930).

1 The Greeks Had a Word for It.

Title of play (1930). The word in question is said to have been *hetaera* ('strumpet'). In a passage deleted from the play's final script, one of the characters states: 'Even the Anglo-Saxons have a word for her sort, and it's usually spelt with a dash.' The words of the play's title do not appear in the final version.

## Alain (1868–1951)

FRENCH PHILOSOPHER

Real name Émile-Auguste Chartier. Taking his pen-name from a medieval French poet, he wrote over 5,000 essays, or *Propos*, written in a lucid, terse style with a strong anti-idealist theme. Among his many other works are *Mars, or the Truth about War* (1921) and *History of My Thoughts* (1936).

1 It is the human condition to question one god after another, one appearance after another, or better, one apparition after another, always pursuing the truth of the imagination, which is not the same as the truth of appearance.

*The Gods*, Introduction (1934; transl. 1988)

2 Nothing is more dangerous than an idea, when you have only one idea.

*Propos sur la Religion*, no. 74 (1938)

## Damon Albarn (b. 1967)

BRITISH ROCK MUSICIAN

Singer and co-writer with the London art school band Blur, he has a laddish, photogenic appeal which smoothed the band's transition from Indie obscurity to spearheading the Britpop scene.

1 Whenever I don't know what to write about, I just close my eyes and think of Essex.

Interview in *Blah Blah Blah* April 1996

## Edward Albee (b. 1928)

US PLAYWRIGHT

Though such early plays as *The Zoo Story* (1959) labelled him as an exponent of the Theatre of the Absurd, he is chiefly known for the naturalistic *Who's Afraid of Virginia Woolf?* (1962, filmed 1966), a harsh portrayal of married life. Later works such as *A Delicate Balance* (1966) and *Seascape* (1975), both Pulitzer Prize-winners, were more abstract.

1 What I wanted to get at is the value difference between pornographic playing-cards when you're a kid, and pornographic playing-cards when you're older. It's that when you're a kid you use the cards as a substitute for a real experience, and when you're older you use real experience as a substitute for the fantasy.

Jerry, in *The Zoo Story* (1959)

2 Who's Afraid of Virginia Woolf?

Title of play (1962). The words are sung by Martha to the tune of 'Who's Afraid of the Big Bad Wolf?' See also FRANK E. CHURCHILL 1.

3 I have a fine sense of the ridiculous, but no sense of humor.

Martha, in *Who's Afraid of Virginia Woolf?*, act 1 (1962)

4 Martha, won't you show her where we keep the . . . euphemism?

George, in ibid. after a guest, Honey, states: 'I want to put some powder on my nose.'

## Richard Aldington (1892–1962)

BRITISH AUTHOR

A leading Imagist poet, translator, critic and editor, he established his name with *Death of a Hero* (1929), a novel which drew on his experiences of the horrors of the First World War. He also produced controversial biographies of D.H. LAWRENCE (1950) and T.E. LAWRENCE (1955), and his autobiography *Life for Life's Sake* was published in 1941.

1 Patriotism is a lively sense of collective responsibility. Nationalism is a silly cock crowing on its own dunghill and calling for larger spurs and brighter beaks. I fear that nationalism is one of England's many spurious gifts to the world.

Purfleet, in *The Colonel's Daughter*, pt 1, ch. 6 (1931)

2 Pure scholarship, like pure science and art, is entirely useless. That is why it is admirable, a demonstration that civilized man is neither an animal nor a savage nor a peasant, for whom nothing exists but what is immediately useful.

*Life for Life's Sake*, ch. 5 (1941)

3 Certainly, truth prevails in the long run, but only when it is too late to have any real influence on affairs.

ibid. ch. 10

## Brian Aldiss (b. 1925)

BRITISH SCIENCE FICTION WRITER

A prolific writer of 'classic' as well as experimental science fiction, he has also published the bawdy fictionalized autobiographies *The Hand-Reared Boy* (1970) and *A Soldier Erect* (1971). *The Helliconia Trilogy* (1982–5) is among the most prominent of his science fiction works, and *Billion-Year Spree* (1973, rev. 1986 as *Trillion-Year Spree*) is a history of the genre.

1 Science fiction is no more written for scientists than ghost stories are written for ghosts.

*Penguin Science Fiction*, Introduction (1962)

2 The bombs were only
In his head
On his memorial tree
A joker wrote
KEEP VIOLENCE IN THE MIND
WHERE IT BELONGS

*Barefoot in the Head*, 'Charteris' (1969). Closing lines of book, in which Colin Charteris is the main character.

## Nelson Algren (1909–81)

US NOVELIST

Trained as a journalist, he was the 'poet of the Chicago slums' for such uncompromising works as *The Man with the Golden Arm*

(1949) and *A Walk on the Wild Side* (1956), both of which were filmed. His affair with SIMONE DE BEAUVOIR inspired her novel *The Mandarins* (1956).

1 **A walk on the wild side.**

Title of novel (1956, filmed 1962). 'Take a Walk on the Wild Side' was the title of one of the biggest-selling records of LOU REED, in 1973.

2 **Never play cards with a man called Doc. Never eat at a place called Mom's. Never sleep with a woman whose troubles are worse than your own. Never let nobody talk you into shaking another man's jolt. And never you cop another man's plea. I've tried 'em all and I know. They don't work.**

Cross-Country Kline advising Dove Linkhorn, in *A Walk on the Wild Side*, pt 3 (1956)

3 **The avocation of assessing the failures of better men can be turned into a comfortable livelihood, providing you back it up with a Ph.D.**

Interview in *Writers at Work* (first series, ed. Malcolm Cowley, 1958)

4 **I went out there [Hollywood] for a thousand a week, and I worked Monday, and I got fired Wednesday. The guy that hired me was out of town Tuesday.**

ibid.

5 **The hard necessity of bringing the judge on the bench down into the dock has been the peculiar responsibility of the writer in all ages of man.**

Preface added to his prose-poem *Chicago: City on the Make* (1961; original work publ. 1951)

## Muhammad Ali (b. 1942)

US BOXER

Original name Cassius Clay, changed in 1964 when he joined the Nation of Islam. He was winner of the World Heavyweight title in 1964, 1974 and 1978 (the only boxer to be world champion three times), though he was stripped of his title in 1967 for refusing to be drafted to the Vietnam War. He was diagnosed with Parkinson's disease in 1981.

1 **I am the greatest.**

Slogan used from 1961, quoted in *The Greatest*, ch. 4 (autobiography, 1975). He describes the origin of his famous brag in Las Vegas in June 1961: 'Before the fight, for the first time I'd talk openly about beating my opponent . . . I kept calling out "I'm the Greatest! I can't be beat!" I'd seen good fighters carry on bloody brawls with hardly anybody caring which one won or lost. At least now they were interested in my fight, even if they wanted me to lose.'

2 **At home I am a nice guy: but I don't want the world to know. Humble people, I've found, don't get very far.**

*Sunday Express* 13 January 1963

3 **Float like a butterfly, sting like a bee.**

Quoted in *The Story of Cassius Clay*, ch. 8 (1964) by George Edward Sullivan. Ali's catchphrase is said to have originated with his aide Drew 'Bundini' Brown.

4 **It's just a job. Grass grows, birds fly, waves pound the sand. I beat people up.**

*The New York Times* 6 April 1977

## Tariq Ali (b. 1943)

PAKISTANI-BORN BRITISH ACTIVIST AND AUTHOR

A left-wing journalist, he became a leading member of Fourth International. He published *The Coming British Revolution* in 1972, collaborated on theatre scripts in the 1980s and 1990s, and was recruited as a commissioning editor for Channel 4 television.

1 **The logic of war dictated that the Americans *should* win, but this logic had been superseded by one superior and infinitely more powerful: the logic of revolution. It remains a logic which can never be properly understood: its**

richness and diversity always excludes the minds of its opponents.

*1968 and After: Inside the Revolution*, ch. 1 (1978). Referring to the Vietnam War.

2 **The idea that a revolution in the West could be based on a small minority, however active and militant, is totally absurd. It is a view of revolution advanced only by those who fear the masses. Or by those products of 1968 who, despairing of the mass parties and their domination of working-class politics, have abandoned politics and picked up sub machine-guns and bombs.**

ibid. ch. 7

## Saul Alinsky (1909–72)

US RADICAL ACTIVIST

Believing that the solution for social ills lay in organization, not charity, he devoted much of his life to setting up community groups, the prototype of which was the Back of the Yards Council (1938) in his home town of Chicago. Among his writings is *Rules for Radicals* (1971).

1 **History is a relay of revolutions.**

*Rules for Radicals*, 'Of Means and Ends' (1971)

2 **Life is a corrupting process from the time a child learns to play his mother off against his father in the politics of when to go to bed; he who fears corruption fears life.**

ibid.

## Fred Allen (1894–1957)

US RADIO COMIC

Original name John Florence Sullivan. Influencing a generation of radio and television performers with his dry wit and laconic style, he is most remembered for *The Fred Allen Show* (1939–49), for which he wrote almost all of the episodes. JAMES THURBER said of him: 'You can count on the thumb of one hand the American who is at once a comedian, a humorist, a wit and a satirist, and his name is Fred Allen.'

1 **California is a fine place to live – if you happen to be an orange.**

*American Magazine* December 1945

2 **The American arrives in Paris with a few French phrases he has culled from a conversational guide or picked up from a friend who owns a beret.**

Quoted in *Paris After Dark*, Introduction (1954) by Art Buchwald

3 **An advertising agency is 85 per cent confusion and 15 per cent commission.**

*Treadmill to Oblivion*, pt 2 (1954)

4 **We are living in the machine age. For the first time in history the comedian has been compelled to supply himself with jokes and comedy material to compete with the machine. Whether he knows it or not, the comedian is on a treadmill to oblivion.**

ibid. pt 4

5 **I have just returned from Boston, it is the only sane thing to do if you find yourself up there.**

Quoted in *The Groucho Letters*, 'Touching on Television' (1967) by Groucho Marx

6 **Hollywood is a place where people from Iowa mistake each other for stars.**

Quoted in *No People Like Show People*, ch. 8 (1951) by Maurice Zolotow

7 **Committee – a group of men who individually can do nothing but as a group decide that nothing can be done.**

Attributed

## Hervey Allen (1889–1949)

US AUTHOR

He won critical acclaim and popularity with his first novel, the complex and historical *Anthony Adverse* (1933) set in the Napoleonic era. He also wrote poetry and biography.

1 The only time you really live fully is from thirty to sixty . . . The young are slaves to dreams; the old servants of regrets. Only the middle-aged have all their five senses in the keeping of their wits.
*Anthony Adverse*, ch. 31 (1933, filmed 1936)

## Woody Allen (b. 1935)

US FILM-MAKER AND ACTOR

Original name Allen Stewart Konigsberg. Stand-up comedian and TV scriptwriter turned film-maker, he is star of most of his own films, which developed from wacky farce to convoluted tales of sexual neurosis set in New York. *Annie Hall* (1977) and *Hannah and Her Sisters* (1986) were awarded Oscars, while *Husbands and Wives* (1992) ironically coincided with the end of his relationship with actress Mia Farrow. See also DIANE KEATON 1.

1 Some guy hit my fender the other day, and I said unto him, 'Be fruitful, and multiply.' But not in those words.
Comedy routine at Chicago night-club, March 1964, recorded on *Woody Allen*, 'Private Life' (album, 1964). Woody Allen's first live recorded monologue describes an acting class rehearsing a play where Allen takes the part of God, and, as he recounts, 'it was method acting, so two weeks beforehand I started to live the part offstage'.

2 I had a rough marriage . . . It was partially my fault that we got a divorce. I had a lousy attitude toward her. For the first year of our marriage, I tended to place my wife underneath a pedestal all the time. We used to argue and fight and finally we decided we should either take a vacation or get a divorce. We discussed it very maturely and we decided on the divorce because we felt we had a limited amount of money to spend. A vacation in Bermuda is over in two weeks but a divorce is something that you always have.
ibid. 'My Marriage'. Allen's accounts of the break-up of his first marriage to Harlene Rosen in 1962 and the repeated jokes at her expense in his comedy acts eventually led her to sue him for a million dollars in 1967; they settled out of court and did not meet again, according to *The Woody Allen Companion*, ch. 4 (1993) by Stephen Spignesi.

3 Is sex dirty? Only if it's done right.
'Chapter' title, in *Everything You Always Wanted to Know About Sex (But Were Afraid to Ask)* (film, 1972, written and directed by Woody Allen). See also DAVID REUBEN 1.

4 I'm not the heroic type. I was beaten up by Quakers.
Miles Monroe (Woody Allen), in *Sleeper* (film, 1973, screenplay by Woody Allen and Marshall Brickman, directed by Woody Allen)

5 [My brain . . . ] it's my second favorite organ.
ibid.

6 I don't want to achieve immortality through my work . . . I want to achieve it through not dying.
Quoted in *Woody Allen and his Comedy*, ch. 12 (1975) by Eric Lax

7 The important thing, I think, is not to be bitter. If it turns out that there is a God, I don't think that he's evil. But the worst thing you can say about him is that he's basically an underachiever. After all, you know, there are worse things in life than death.
Boris Grushenko (Woody Allen), in *Love and Death* (film, 1975, written and directed by Woody Allen)

8 Some men are heterosexual, and some men are homosexual, and some men don't think about sex at all. They become lawyers.
ibid.

9 To me nature is . . . spiders and bugs, and big fish eating little fish, and plants eating plants, and animals eating . . . It's like an enormous restaurant, that's the way I see it.
ibid.

10 I want to tell you a terrific story about oral contraception. I asked this girl to sleep with me and she said 'no'.
Quoted in *Woody Allen: Clown Prince of American Humor*, ch. 2 (1975) by B. Adler and J. Feinman

11 It [bisexuality] immediately doubles your chances for a date on Saturday night.
*The New York Times* 1 December 1975

12 It's not that I'm afraid to die, I just don't want to be there when it happens.
Kleinman, in 'Death (A Play)' publ. in *Without Feathers* (1976)

13 The chief problem about death, incidentally, is the fear that there may be no afterlife – a depressing thought, particularly for those who have bothered to shave. Also, there is the fear that there is an afterlife but no one will know where it's being held.
'The Early Essays', publ. in ibid. In the film *Love and Death*, there is the line, 'I don't believe in an afterlife although I'm bringing a change of underwear.'

14 Money is better than poverty, if only for financial reasons.
ibid.

15 If only God would give me some clear sign! Like making a large deposit in my name at a Swiss bank.
'Selections from the Allen Notebooks', publ. in ibid.

16 Hey, don't knock masturbation! It's sex with someone I love.
Alvy Singer (Woody Allen), in *Annie Hall* (film, 1977, screenplay by Woody Allen and Marshall Brickman, directed by Woody Allen)

17 I don't wanna live in a city where the only cultural advantage is that you can make a right turn on a red light.
ibid. Comparing Los Angeles unfavourably to Manhattan.

18 I was depressed . . . I was suicidal; as a matter of fact, I would have killed myself but I was in analysis with a strict Freudian and if you kill yourself they make you pay for the sessions you miss.
ibid. The gag can also be heard on *The Nightclub Years*, 'Second Marriage' (1968), a live recording of a stand-up routine in San Francisco, August 1968.

19 I was thrown out of NYU my freshman year . . . for cheating on my metaphysics final. You know, I looked within the soul of the boy sitting next to me.
ibid. Alvy is performing in front of a college audience.

20 In Beverly Hills . . . they don't throw their garbage away. They make it into television shows.
ibid.

21 Life is divided up into the horrible and the miserable.
ibid.

22 A relationship, I think, is like a shark, you know? It has to constantly move forward or it dies. And I think what we got on our hands is a dead shark.
ibid. On the end of his affair with Annie Hall (played by Diane Keaton).

23 That [sex] was the most fun I've ever had without laughing.
ibid.

24 I finally had an orgasm and my doctor told me it was the wrong kind.
Polly (Tisa Farrow), in *Manhattan* (film, 1979, screenplay by Woody Allen and Marshall Brickman, directed by Woody Allen)

25 Why is life worth living? That's a very good question. Ummm . . . Well there are certain things, I guess, that make it worthwhile. Uh, like what? Okay. Um, for me . . . oh, I would say . . . what, Groucho Marx, to name one

thing, and . . . Willie Mays, and . . . the second movement of the Jupiter Symphony, and . . . Louis Armstrong's recording of 'Potatohead Blues' . . . Swedish movies, naturally . . . *Sentimental Education* by Flaubert . . . and Marlon Brando, Frank Sinatra . . . those incredible apples and pears by Cézanne.

Isaac Davis (Woody Allen), in ibid.

26 More than any other time in history, mankind faces a crossroads. One path leads to despair and utter hopelessness. The other, to total extinction. Let us pray we have the wisdom to choose correctly.

Side Effects, 'My Speech to the Graduates' (1980)

27 You can't control life. It doesn't wind up perfectly. Only . . . only art you can control. Art and masturbation. Two areas in which I am an absolute expert.

Sandy Bates (Woody Allen), in *Stardust Memories* (film, 1980, written and directed by Woody Allen)

28 Child molestation is a touchy subject . . . Read the papers! Half the country's doing it!

Mickey Sachs (Woody Allen), in *Hannah and Her Sisters* (film, 1986, written and directed by Woody Allen). Allen caused controversy in 1993 when a relationship with Soon-Yi Previn, the adopted daughter of Mia Farrow, led to accusations of child abuse and a court case over custody of his and Farrow's children. He married Soon-Yi in 1997.

29 Life doesn't imitate art, it imitates bad television.

Rain ( Juliette Lewis), in *Husbands and Wives* (film, 1992, written and directed by Woody Allen)

## Isabel Allende (b. 1942)
PERUVIAN-BORN CHILEAN NOVELIST

A writer associated with the 'magic realist' school, she wrote her first and best-selling novel, *The House of the Spirits* (1982, filmed 1993), in exile from Chile following the overthrow (1973) of her uncle SALVADOR ALLENDE. Other books include *Of Love and Shadows* (1984) and *Eva Luna* (1987).

1 Misfortune had spiritualized her [Clara Trueba].

The House of the Spirits, ch. 5 (1985)

2 Charity, like Socialism, is an invention of the weak to exploit the strong and bring them to their knees.

Esteban Trueba, in ibid. ch. 10

3 Photographs deceive time, freezing it on a piece of cardboard where the soul is silent.

Irene Beltran, in *Of Love and Shadows*, pt 1 (1987)

## Salvador Allende (1908–73)
CHILEAN STATESMAN AND PRESIDENT

A founder of the Chilean Socialist Party, he became President in 1970. His nationalization of American-owned copper mines was the prelude to CIA involvement in the coup of 1973, which replaced him with General Pinochet. He died during the assault on the presidential palace.

1 Our Vietnam is neither in Moscow, nor in Peking, Havana or Belgrade. It is in Chile.

Quoted in the *Observer* 1 November 1970

## Svetlana Alliluyeva (b. 1925)
RUSSIAN AUTHOR

Stalin's only daughter, she defected to the United States in the spring of 1967. *Twenty Letters to a Friend* (1967) and *Only One Year* (1969) recall her life, and *The Faraway Music* (1984) records her disenchantment with the West.

1 Moscow, breathing fire like a human volcano with its smouldering lava of passion, ambition and politics, its hurly-burly of meetings and entertainment. . . . Moscow seethes and bubbles and gasps for air. It's always thirsting for something new, the newest events, the latest sensation. Everyone wants to be the first to know. It's the rhythm of life today.

Twenty Letters to a Friend, Introduction (written 1963, publ. 1967)

2 He [Stalin] is gone, but his shadow still stands over all of us. It still dictates to us and we, very often, obey.

ibid. ch. 2

3 As a result of half a century of Soviet rule people have been weaned from a belief in human kindness.

Only One Year, 'The Journey's End' (1969)

## Lisa Alther (b. 1944)
US NOVELIST

Her ribald feminist tales include *Kinflicks* (1976), *Original Sins* (1981) and *Bedrock* (1990).

1 I happen to feel that the degree of a person's intelligence is directly reflected by the number of conflicting attitudes she can bring to bear on the same topic.

Ginny Babcock, in *Kinflicks*, ch. 7 (1976)

## Robert Altman (b. 1925)
US FILM-MAKER

One of Hollywood's most highly regarded directors despite an inconsistent career, he made his name with the antiwar comedy *M\*A\*S\*H* (1970) and went on to direct *McCabe and Mrs Miller* (1971) and *Nashville* (1976) among other films. Neglected in the 1980s, he re-established his reputation with *The Player* (1992).

1 What's a cult? It just means not enough people to make a minority.

Interview in the *Guardian* 11 April 1981

## A. Alvarez (b. 1929)
BRITISH CRITIC, POET AND NOVELIST

Full name Alfred Alvarez. Though he later focused on writing poetry and novels, for example *Day of Atonement* (1991), he is chiefly noted for his criticism, including *The Shaping Spirit* (1958) and *The School of Donne* (1961).

1 Despair, in short, seeks its own environment as surely as water finds its own level.

The Savage God, pt 3, 'Theories' (1971)

2 There is something . . . not quite right about night life, something shadowy in every sense. However efficiently artificial light annihilates the difference between night and day, it never wholly eliminates the primitive suspicion that night people are up to no good.

Night, Preface (1995)

## Leo Amery (1873–1955)
BRITISH POLITICIAN

He became a Conservative MP in 1911 and served as a minister in imperial departments, creating in 1925 the Dominions Office (later the Commonwealth Relations Office). A critic of the Munich Agreement, he was instrumental in bringing down the government of NEVILLE CHAMBERLAIN in 1940. Between 1940 and 1945 he was Secretary of State for India and Burma.

1 Speak for England.

Said in House of Commons, 2 September 1939, quoted in *My Political Life*, vol. 3 (1955). The exhortation was addressed to MP Arthur Greenwood, Deputy Leader of the Labour Party, who was about to speak on the situation in Europe, a day after the Nazi invasion of Poland and on the eve of the declaration of war on Germany by Britain and France. The MP Robert Boothby is also credited with the words.

2 I will quote certain other words. I do it with great reluctance, because I am speaking of those who are old friends and associates of mine, but they are words which, I think, are applicable to the present situation. This is what Cromwell said to the Long Parliament when he thought it was no longer fit to conduct the affairs of the nation: 'You have sat too long here for any good you have been doing. Depart, I say, and let us have done with you. In the name of God, go.'

Speech to House of Commons, publ. in *Hansard* 7 May 1940. Amery was addressing Neville Chamberlain's government, blamed for the failed policy of appeasement to Germany and now faced with the German invasion of Norway. CHAMBERLAIN resigned 10 May, to be replaced by CHURCHILL. Cromwell's words were uttered 20 April 1653, shortly before becoming Lord Protector of England.

## (Sir) Kingsley Amis (1922–95)
BRITISH NOVELIST AND POET

He won great success with his first novel, *Lucky Jim* (1954, filmed 1957), a satire on provincial academic life. Later novels included *The Old Devils* (1986), for which he won the Booker Prize. His work became increasingly caustic in later years; as he commented, 'If you can't annoy somebody, there's little point in writing.' He also published short stories and poetry, and is the father of novelist MARTIN AMIS.

1 We men have got love well weighed up; our stuff
   Can get by without it.
   Women don't seem to think that's good enough;
   They will write about it.

'A Bookshop Idyll', publ. in *A Case of Samples* (1956)

2 Women are really much nicer than men:
   No wonder we like them.

ibid.

3 More will mean worse.

*Encounter* July 1960. On the expansion of higher education in the UK, attacking the notion that 'there are thousands of young people about who are capable of benefiting from university training, but have somehow failed to find their way there'.

4 Outside every fat man there was an even fatter man trying to close in.

Roger Micheldene, in *One Fat Englishman*, ch. 3 (1963). Micheldene, the book's protagonist, is 'a shortish fat Englishman of forty', here musing over a particularly heavy lunch. Earlier versions of the remark exist. See also CYRIL CONNOLLY 18 and GEORGE ORWELL 7.

5 He [Roger Micheldene] was of the faith chiefly in the sense that the church he currently did not attend was Catholic.

ibid. ch. 8

6 Growing older, I have lost the need to be political, which means, in this country, the need to be left. I am driven into grudging toleration of the Conservative Party because it is the party of non-politics, of resistance to politics.

*Sunday Telegraph* 2 July 1967

7 Death has got something to be said for it:
   There's no need to get out of bed for it;
   Wherever you may be,
   They bring it to you, free.

'Delivery Guaranteed' (1979), publ. in *Collected Poems (1944–79)*. In his novel *Money* (1984), Kingsley's son MARTIN AMIS wrote: 'Addictions do come in handy sometimes: at least you have to get out of bed for them.'

8 If there's one word that sums up everything that's gone wrong since the War, it's Workshop.

Jake, in *Jake's Thing*, ch. 14 (1979). '. . . After Youth, that is,' Jake added.

9 Alun's life was coming to consist more and more exclusively of being told at dictation speed what he knew.

*The Old Devils*, ch. 7, sect. 1 (1986). Of author and 'professional Welshman' Alun Weaver.

10 The fact that it is not a sensual or sexy beauty does not make it a less sexual beauty, and that sexuality is still, I believe, an underrated factor in her appeal (or repellence). Envy of it among women, consciousness of its unavailability among men, retains power even when advancing age should have disposed of it.

Of MARGARET THATCHER in *Memoirs*, 'Margaret Thatcher' (1991). Amis referred to her as his 'dream-girl. . .who, more than any other, tends to recur in my dreams'.

11 It is not extraordinary that the extraterrestrial origin of women was a recurrent theme of science fiction, though I have never seen their imperfect grasp of their native language put forward as one more piece of evidence.

*The King's English: A Guide to Modern English Usage*, 'Womanese' (1997)

## Martin Amis (b. 1949)
BRITISH AUTHOR

Son of KINGSLEY AMIS, he writes novels in which, in his words, 'everyone has a bad time'. His scabrous wit and American literary influences are evident in such works as *The Rachel Papers* (1973, filmed 1989), *Money* (1984) and *The Information* (1995).

1 Only one writer has ever written convincingly about happiness and that's Tolstoy. Nobody else seems to make it swing on the page.

Interview in *Time Out* 27 March – 2 April 1981

2 Making lots of money – it's not that hard, you know. It's overestimated. Making lots of money is a breeze. You watch.

*Money* (1984)

3 And being rich is about acting too, isn't it? A style, a pose, an interpretation that you force upon the world? Whether or not you've made the stuff yourself, you have to set about pretending that you merit it, that money chose right in choosing you, and that you'll do right by money in your turn. Moneymad or just moneysmug, you have to pretend it's the natural thing.

ibid.

4 Weapons are like money; no one knows the meaning of *enough*.

*Einstein's Monsters*, Introduction (1987)

5 For myself and my loved ones, I want the heat, which comes at the speed of light. I don't want to have to hang about for the blast, which idles along at the speed of sound.

ibid.

6 The literary interview won't tell you what a writer is *like*. Far more compellingly, to some, it will tell you what a writer is *like to interview*.

*Observer* 30 August 1987, repr. in *Visiting Mrs Nabokov*, 'John Updike' (1993)

7 And meanwhile time goes about its immemorial work of making everyone look and feel like shit.

*London Fields*, ch. 2 (1989)

8 Class! Yes, it's still here. Terrific staying power, and against the historical odds. What *is* it with that old, *old* crap? The class system just doesn't know when to call it a day. Even a nuclear holocaust, I think, would fail to make that much of a dent in it.

ibid.

9 You can't be consumed by another person if you're a writer because your relationship is basically with yourself. You're being intimate with your abilities, with your talent. This means in some very viable sense that for a lot of the time you're just having a wank.

Interview in the *Guardian* 18 March 1995

10 Why do the men cry? Because of fights and feats and marathon preferment, because they want their mothers, because they are blind in time, because of all the hard-ons they have to whistle up out of the thin blue yonder, because of all that men have done. Because they can't be happy or sad any more – only smashed or nuts. And because they don't know how to do it when they're awake.

*The Information*, pt 1 (1995)

11 These days he [Richard Tull] smoked and drank largely to solace himself for what drinking and smoking had done to him – but smoking and drinking had done a lot to him, so he drank and smoked a lot.

ibid.

12 Never trust a poet who can drive. Never trust a poet at the wheel. If he *can* drive, distrust the poems.

ibid.

13 Sunday morning, and everyone was staggering around with their personal burden of prolixity, of fantastic garrulity, of uncontainable communicativeness: the *Sunday Times*.

*Heavy Water*, 'The Coincidence of the Arts' (1998)

14 It is not youth alone that attracts the paedophile. The paedophile, for some reason, wants carnal knowledge of the carnally ignorant: a top-heavy encounter, involving lost significance. So far as the child is concerned, of course, that lost significance doesn't stay lost, but lingers, for ever.

ibid. 'The Janitor on Mars'

15 The [football] crowd. . .is asking something of you; the surrender of your identity. And it will not be opposed. It cannot be opposed. The crowd is a wraparound millipede of rage and yearning, with the body heat of 180,000 torched armpits, with its ear-hurting roars, and that incensed whistling like a billion babies joined in one desperate scream.

Quoted in the *Observer* 30 May 1999

## Cleveland Amory (b. 1917)
US AUTHOR

He wrote social histories, such as *Who Killed Society?* (1958), and a series of animal books including *The Cat Who Came for Christmas* (1987). He was founder (1967) and President of the Fund for Animals, the main US organization campaigning against cruelty to animals.

1 The New England conscience . . . does not stop you from doing what you shouldn't – it just stops you from enjoying it.

*New Yorker* 5 May 1980

## Brett Anderson (b. 1947)
BRITISH ROCK MUSICIAN

He is the androgynous vocalist of the pre-Britpop band Suede, which he formed in 1990 and which released its eponymous debut album amid much media attention in 1993.

1 I see myself as a bisexual man who has never had a homosexual experience.

Quoted in *Arena* May/June 1993. Anderson's comments provoked accusations of hijacking gay imagery. He defended himself: 'If you are asking am I insincere to pose as a sodomite when I've never had someone's cock up my arse, then no, I'm not. The sexuality you express is not limited to the things you've experienced. I mean, if you're a virgin, does that make you asexual?'

2 Pop is all about doing something that connects really easily, and that's why I've never had any time for classical music . . . It just bores me because it's too easy. Anyone can be that complicated. Three notes is far cleverer than

three hundred if they''re arranged in the right way, and that's what pop music is all about.

Interview in *i-D* October 1994

## Gerry Anderson (b. 1929)
BRITISH PROGRAMME-MAKER FOR CHILDREN'S TV

Together with his wife Silvia Anderson, he created some of the classic puppet programmes for children's TV of the 1960s, including *Supercar* (1960), *Thunderbirds* (1965–6) and *Captain Scarlet* (1967). He later made programmes with live actors.

1 Thunderbirds are go!

*Thunderbirds* (TV puppet series, 1965–6, created by Gerry and Silvia Anderson, written by the Andersons et al.)

## Ian Anderson (b. 1947)
BRITISH ROCK MUSICIAN

He was singer and leader of the blues and heavy rock band Jethro Tull, whose albums *Stand Up* (1969), *Aqualung* (1971) and *Thick as a Brick* (1972) gained them a huge following.

1 A lot of pop music is about stealing pocket money from children.

*Rolling Stone* 30 November 1989

## Maxwell Anderson (1888–1959)
US PLAYWRIGHT

He was a writer of verse-plays, including *Elizabeth the Queen* (1930), and of the screenplay for *All Quiet on the Western Front* (1930), receiving the Pulitzer Prize for *Both Your Houses* in 1933.

1 But it's a long, long while
From May to December;
And the days grow short
When you reach September.

'September Song' (song, written with Kurt Weill) from the stage musical *Knickerbocker Holiday* (1938). Among the singers associated with the number are BING CROSBY, FRANK SINATRA, and, most famously, MAURICE CHEVALIER, in the musical *Pepe* (1960).

## Maxwell Anderson (1888–1959) and
## Laurence Stallings (1894–1968)
US PLAYWRIGHTS

Stallings worked on numerous film screenplays from 1925 to 1954, but achieved greatest success for his collaboration with Anderson in the play *What Price Glory?* (1924).

1 What price glory?

Title of anti-First World War play (1924, filmed 1926 and 1952)

## Robert Anderson (b. 1917)
US PLAYWRIGHT

His first and most successful play, *Tea and Sympathy* (1953, filmed 1956), was followed by lesser Broadway hits such as *You Know I Can't Hear You When the Water's Running* (1967).

1 All you're supposed to do is every once in a while give the boys a little tea and sympathy.

Bill, in *Tea and Sympathy*, act 1 (1957). Giving advice about not getting too involved with schoolchildren.

## (Sir) James Anderton (b. 1932)
BRITISH SENIOR POLICE OFFICER

Chief Constable of Greater Manchester Police 1976–91, he has been involved in a range of Christian and philanthropic causes though has often attracted criticism for his outspoken comments.

1 Everywhere I go I see increasing evidence of people swirling about in a human cesspit of their own making.

On AIDS, quoted in the *Guardian* 12 December 1986

2 God works in mysterious ways. Given my love of God and my belief in God and in Jesus Christ, I have to accept that I may well be used by God in this way.

Radio interview, 18 January 1987, quoted in the *Daily Telegraph* 19 January 1987. Referring to the possibility that he may have prophetic powers.

## Giulio Andreotti (b. 1919)
ITALIAN POLITICIAN

A leading member of the Christian Democrat party throughout the post-Second World War period, he was several times Prime Minister between 1972 and 1992, and initiated austere economic measures in the mid-1970s. He was indicted for Mafia association in 1995 but was cleared in 1999.

1 At times, we who live in a world of active politics make the mistake of believing that political facts are the only ones with a true meaning and a resonance.

*The USA Up Close: From the Atlantic Pact to Bush*, ch. 24 (1992 )

2 Power tires only those who do not have it.

Quoted in the *Independent on Sunday* 5 April 1992. Reply when asked how his party had endured in government for so long.

## (Dame) Julie Andrews (b. 1935)
BRITISH ACTRESS AND SINGER

Having starred in Broadway musicals including *My Fair Lady* (1956) and *Camelot* (1960), she made an impact in a series of successful films, starting with *Mary Poppins* (1964) for which she won an Oscar. She later shook off her typecast, wholesome image in films such as *S.O.B.* (1981) and *Victor/Victoria* (1982). For Christopher Plummer, her co-star in *The Sound of Music* (1965), working with her was like 'being hit over the head by a Valentine's card'.

1 Just a spoonful of sugar helps the medicine go down.

'A Spoonful of Sugar' (song written by Richard and Robert Sherman), in *Mary Poppins* (film musical, 1964, screenplay by Bill Walsh and Don Da Gradi based on the Mary Poppins books by P.L. Travers, directed by Robert Stevenson). Julie Andrews played the title role in the film.

2 Supercalifragilisticexpialidocious!
Even though the sound of it is something quite atrocious!
If you say it loud enough you'll always sound precocious.
Supercalifragilisticexpialidocious!

'Supercalifragilisticexpialidocious!' ibid.

## Maya Angelou (b. 1928)
US AUTHOR AND POET

Active in the Black civil rights movement of the 1950s and 1960s, she chronicled her 'roller coaster of a life' in several volumes of autobiography, the first part of which, *I Know Why the Caged Bird Sings* (1969), was an instant success. She is also a prolific poet, and read her poem 'On the Pulse of the Morning' at the inauguration of President CLINTON.

1 I know why the caged bird sings.

Title of book (1969). The line is taken from the poem 'Sympathy' by US poet H. Lawrence Dunbar (1872–1906). 'Caged Bird', a poem from Angelou's 1983 collection *Shaker, Why Don't You Sing?*, contains the lines: 'The caged bird sings/with a fearful trill/of things unknown/but longed for still/and his tune is heard/on the distant hill/for the caged bird/sings of freedom.'

2 Children's talent to endure stems from their ignorance of alternatives.

*I Know Why the Caged Bird Sings*, ch. 17 (1969)

3 The quality of strength lined with tenderness is an unbeat-

able combination, as are intelligence and necessity when unblunted by formal education.

ibid. ch. 29

4 At fifteen life had taught me undeniably that surrender, in its place, was as honorable as resistance, especially if one had no choice.

ibid. ch. 31

5 The fact that the adult American Negro female emerges a formidable character is often met with amazement, distaste and even belligerence. It is seldom accepted as an inevitable outcome of the struggle won by survivors, and deserves respect if not enthusiastic acceptance.

ibid. ch. 34

6 My life has been one great big joke,
A dance that's walked
A song that's spoke,
I laugh so hard I almost choke
When I think about myself.

'When I Think About Myself', publ. in *Just Give Me a Cool Drink of Water 'fore I Diiie* (1971)

7 For Africa to me . . . is more than a glamorous fact. It is a historical truth. No man can know where he is going unless he knows exactly where he has been and exactly how he arrived at his present place.

Quoted in *The New York Times* 16 April 1972. Angelou lived and worked in Ghana and Egypt 1962–6.

8 Life loves the liver of it.

Interview in *Black Scholar* January/February 1977, repr. in *Conversations with Maya Angelou* (ed. Jeffrey M. Elliot, 1989)

9 You may write me down in history
With your bitter, twisted lies,
You may trod me in the very dirt
But still, like dust, I'll rise.

'Still I Rise', publ. in *And Still I Rise* (1978)

10 I love to see a young girl go out and grab the world by the lapels. Life's a bitch. You've got to go out and kick ass.

Interview in *Girl About Town* 13 October 1986, repr. in *Conversations with Maya Angelou* (ed. Jeffrey M. Elliot, 1989)

11 We allow our ignorance to prevail upon us and make us think we can survive alone, alone in patches, alone in groups, alone in races, even alone in genders.

Address at Centenary College of Louisiana, March 1990, publ. in *The New York Times* 11 March 1990

12 A rose by any other name may smell as sweet, but a woman called by a devaluing name will only be weakened by the misnomer.

*Wouldn't Take Nothing for my Journey Now*, 'In All Ways a Woman' (1993)

## Paul Anka See FRANK SINATRA 3.

## Anne, Princess Royal of Great Britain and Northern Ireland (b. 1950)

Only daughter of ELIZABETH II, she is patron of over eighty charities, including the Save the Children Fund, of which she has been President since 1971. She is also a skilled horsewoman, representing Britain in the 1976 Olympics.

1 It could be said that the AIDS pandemic is a classic own-goal scored by the human race against itself.

Quoted in the *Daily Telegraph* 27 January 1988

2 The very idea that all children want to be cuddled by a complete stranger I find utterly amazing.

Quoted in the *Observer* 27 December 1998. Referring to her public duties visiting children.

# Anonymous

1 *Arbeit macht frei.*
(Work liberates.)

Inscribed on the gates of Dachau concentration camp, 1933

2 **Careless talk costs lives.**

Ministry of Information slogan, July 1940, quoted in *Keep Smiling Through: The Home Front 1939–1945*, 'Don't Fence Me In' (1976) by Susan Briggs. The government's poster campaign to persuade people not to betray the war effort through gossip was illustrated with memorable cartoons by Fougasse. Other slogans included 'Tittle-tattle lost the battle' and 'Walls have ears'. According to Jonathon Green in *Says Who?* (1988), the campaign was toned down 'when the over-patriotic began denouncing their more verbose but innocent acquaintances to the authorities'. The equivalent slogan in the USA was 'Loose talk costs lives'.

3 **The difficult we do immediately; the impossible takes a little longer**

US Armed Forces slogan. The words are said to be an interpretation of a remark ascribed to Charles Alexandre de Calonne (1734–1802) during the French Revolution: '*Madame, si c'est possible, c'est fait; impossible? cela se fera*' ('Madam, if it is possible, consider it done; the impossible? that will be done').

4 **I don't like the family Stein.**
**There is Gert, there is Ep, there is Ein.**
**Gert's writings are punk,**
**Ep's statues are junk,**
**Nor can anyone understand Ein.**

A 'low-brow American limerick current in the 20s', according to *The Long Weekend:A Social History of Great Britain 1918–1939*, ch.12 (1940) by Robert Graves and Alan Hodge. Another version, noted in *Einstein*, ch. 18 (1973) by R.W. Clark, runs, 'Three wonderful people called Stein;/There's Gert and there's Ep and there's Ein./Gert writes in blank verse,/Ep's sculptures are worse,/And nobody understands Ein.' Clark is unable to find a source for this, though suggests it may have been inspired by 'Precious Steins', a piece of verse which appeared in *Punch* 11 September 1929. ALBERT EINSTEIN sat for the sculptor Jacob Epstein in September 1933 prior to leaving for the USA. Neither, as far as is known, had any dealings with GERTRUDE STEIN.

5 **If you can remember the 1960s you can't have been there.**

Origin untraced

6 **In the great department store of life, baseball is the toy department.**

Quoted in the *Independent* 28 September 1991. George F. Will, in the conclusion to his book *Men at Work: the Craft of Baseball* (1990), quotes 'sport is the toy department of life'.

7 **It became necessary to destroy the town to save it.**

Unnamed US army major, quoted in *The New York Times* 8 February 1968. The report concerned the battle for Ben Tre during the Tet offensive, South Vietnam.

8 **It's not the bullet with my name on it that worries me.**
**It's the one that says 'To whom it may concern'.**

Belfast resident, quoted in the *Guardian* 16 October 1991

9 **A liberal is a socialist with a wife and two children.**

Thought to have been coined in the 1930s, quoted in Alistair Cooke's *Letter From America*, BBC Radio 4, 8 April 1990

10 *Nil carborundum illegitimi.*
(Don't let the bastards grind you down.)

British army motto 1939–45, in *A Dictionary of Catchphrases* (2nd edn, 1983) by Eric Partridge. The expression was current among army intelligence, gradually becoming more widespread in the army, chiefly among officers.

11 **Not So Much A Programme, More A Way Of Life.**

Comedy series title (BBC, 1964–5). The programme was a successor to the satirical series *That Was The Week That Was* (1962–3), using a similar format and with DAVID FROST as anchorman. It consisted of interviews and discussion around topical subjects.

12 **O Death, where is thy sting-a-ling-a-ling,**
**O Grave, thy victor-ee?**
**The bells of hell go ting-a-ling-a-ling,**
**For you but not for me.**

'The Bells of Hell' (song, 1914–18). Sung to the tune of 'She Only Answered "Ting-a-ling-a-ling"' which itself is believed to be founded on an old Salvation Army song, discussed in *The Long Trail: What the British Soldier Sang and Said 1914–1918*, pt 1, ch. 2 (4th edn, 1965) by John Brophy and Eric Partridge. The words are taken from 1 Corinthians 15:55.

13 **Once again we silence the mighty roar of London's traffic . . .**

Introduction to *In Town Tonight* (BBC radio series, 1933–60), quoted in *The Golden Age of Radio* (1985) by Denis Gifford. The words opened each episode of this live outside-broadcast in which Lionel Gamlin gave spot interviews to passers-by in central London on a Saturday night.

14 **The only reason I might go to the funeral is to make absolutely sure that he's dead.**

An 'eminent editor', of press baron Lord Beaverbrook, quoted in *Anatomy of Britain Today*, ch. 9 (1965) by Anthony Sampson

15 **The opera ain't over till the fat lady sings.**

There is no agreed origin for this modern proverb. Both *The Concise Oxford Dictionary of Proverbs* (ed. John Simpson, 1982) and *Bartlett's Familiar Quotations* (16th edn, 1992) cite sports commentator Dan Cook in the *Washington Post* 13 June 1978, but it was probably already current then. *Bartlett's* notes another version in *Southern Words and Sayings* (ed. Fabia Rue Smith and Charles Rayford Smith, 1976): 'Church ain't out till the fat lady sings.'

16 **Rest in peace. The mistake shall not be repeated.**

Inscription on the cenotaph at Hiroshima, Japan

17 **She was poor, but she was honest,**
**Victim of the squire's whim:**
**For he wooed and he seduced her,**
**And she had a child by him.**

'She Was Poor, But She Was Honest', soldiers' song in the First World War, sung to a pre-1914 melody, publ. in *The Long Trail:What the British Soldier Sang and Said 1914–1918*, pt 1, ch. 3 (4th edn, 1965) by John Brophy and Eric Partridge

18 **There is no such thing as a free lunch.**

Popularized in the 1960s, the words have no known source, though have been ascribed to an Italian immigrant outside New York's Grand Central Station in ALISTAIR COOKE's *America* (epilogue, 1973). 'Free lunches' appeared in the USA in the 1840s with the advent of the new saloons which sold lager beer when it first became widely available, chiefly in Milwaukee. The expression appears in *The Moon is a Harsh Mistress*, ch. 11 (1966) by Robert A. Heinlein, but has become most closely associated with economist MILTON FRIEDMAN, who made it the title of a book in 1975.

19 **Today he plays jazz; tomorrow he betrays his country.**

Stalinist propaganda slogan in the Soviet Union, 1920s

20 **We're here**
**Because**
**We're here**
**Because**
**We're here**
**Because we're here.**

'We're Here Because', First World War soldiers' marching song, sung to the tune of 'Auld Lang Syne', publ. in *The Long Trail:What the British Soldier Sang and Said 1914–1918*, pt 1, ch. 1 (4th edn, 1965) by John Brophy and Eric Partridge

21 **What we've got is passion. All they've got is four quid an hour.**

Anonymous anti-roads protester, referring to the hired security at the Newbury roads protest, quoted in the *Guardian* 6 April 1996

22 **Who Dares Wins.**

Motto of the Special Air Services from 1941. In *The S.A.S. at War: 1941–1945*, ch. 1 (1991) by Anthony Kemp, the motto is ascribed to David Sterling (b. 1915) who created the SAS in 1941.

# Jean Anouilh (1910–87)
FRENCH PLAYWRIGHT

His plays, which, as he declared, present a 'great thirst for purity', made him a leading dramatist of his time. Technically versatile, he grouped his works according to whether they were *pièces noires* (dark plays), *brillantes* (sparkling), *grinçantes* (grating), *costumées* (costumed) or *roses* (rose-coloured). The principal ones are the fantasy *Thieves' Carnival* (1938), the historical drama *Becket* (1959) and reworkings of Greek myths, *Antigone* (1944) and *Medea* (1946).

1 However tight I shut my eyes, there will always be a stray dog somewhere in the world who'll stop me being happy.
Thérèse Tard, in *Restless Heart* (*La Sauvage*), act 3 (1938). Thérèse's last speech in the play.

2 It is restful, tragedy, because one knows that there is no more lousy hope left. You know you're caught, caught at last like a rat with all the world on its back. And the only thing left to do is shout – not moan, or complain, but yell out at the top of your voice.
The Chorus, in *Antigone* (1944)

3 To say yes, you have to sweat and roll up your sleeves and plunge both hands into life up to the elbows. It's easy to say no, even if it means dying.
Creon, in ibid.

4 It takes a certain courage and a certain greatness to be truly base.
Le Général, in *Ardèle*, act 1 (1947)

5 There is love of course. And then there's life, its enemy.
ibid.

6 Poor little men, poor little cocks! As soon as they're old enough, they swell their plumage to be conquerors . . . If they only knew that it's enough to be just a little bit wounded and sad in order to obtain everything without fighting for it.
Araminthe, in *Cécile* (1951)

7 Everything ends this way in France. Weddings, christenings, duels, burials, swindlings, affairs of state – everything is a pretext for a good dinner.
Monsieur Orlas, in ibid.

8 Every man thinks God is on his side. The rich and powerful know he is.
Charles, in *The Lark* (1953, adapted by Lillian Hellman, 1955). The words echo those of soldier and writer Comte de Bussy-Rabutin (1618–93), in a letter of 1677: 'As you know, God is generally on the side of the big squadrons against the small ones.'

9 Saintliness is also a temptation.
Thomas à Becket, in *Becket*, act 3 (1959)

## Bryan Appleyard (b. 1951)
BRITISH JOURNALIST AND AUTHOR

A freelance journalist, he is a regular columnist for the *Sunday Times*. He has written widely on society and the arts, as in *The Pleasures of Peace* (1989) and *Understanding the Present* (1992), a polemic against the spiritual damage caused by science.

1 Modernism may be seen as an attempt to reconstruct the world in the absence of God.
*The Culture Club: Crisis in the Arts*, ch. 6 (1984)

## Yasser Arafat (b. 1929)
PALESTINIAN LEADER

He helped found the Palestine resistance group Al Fatah in the late 1950s and gained control of the Palestine Liberation Organization in 1969. He controversially signed a peace agreement with Israel in 1993, granting limited autonomy to the West Bank and Gaza Strip. He shared the Nobel Peace Prize with Shimon Perez and Yitzhak Rabin in 1994, and was elected President of the Palestinian National Council in 1996.

1 Palestine is the cement that holds the Arab world together, or it is the explosive that blows it apart.
*Time* 11 November 1974

## Louis Aragon (1897–1982)
FRENCH POET AND AUTHOR

Originally named Louis Andrieux. With ANDRÉ BRETON he founded the Surrealist review *Littérature* (1919) to promote the same 'passionate and unruly use of stupefying images' as found in his poetry. He became a Communist after visiting Russia in 1930, and devoted himself to journalism and social-realistic novels, in addition to his patriotic and love poetry.

1 No more painters, no more scribblers, no more musicians, no more sculptors, no more religions, no more royalists, no more radicals, no more imperialists, no more anarchists, no more socialists, no more communists, no more proletariat, no more democrats, no more republicans, no more bourgeois, no more aristocrats, no more arms, no more police, no more nations, an end at last to all this stupidity, nothing left, nothing at all, nothing, nothing.
'Manifesto of the Dada Movement' read out at the second Dada event, 5 February 1920, Salon des Indépendents, Paris, publ. in *Littérature* May 1920, repr. in *The History of Surrealism*, ch. 3 (1964) by Maurice Nadeau

2 There are strange flowers of reason to match each error of the senses.
*Paris Peasant*, 'Preface to a Modern Mythology' (1926)

3 We know that the nature of genius is to provide idiots with ideas twenty years later.
*Treatise on Style*, pt 1, 'The Pen' (1928)

4 O months of blossoming, months of transfigurations,
May without cloud and June stabbed to the heart,
I shall not ever forget the lilacs or the roses
Nor those the spring has kept folded away apart.
'Les Lilas et les Roses', publ. in *Le Crève-Coeur* (1940)

## Diane Arbus (1923–71)
US PHOTOGRAPHER

She is best remembered for her monochrome images of strange or unusual subjects from the streets of New York and other US cities in the 1960s, for example transvestites and midgets. In the year following her death by suicide, she became the first US photographer to be exhibited at the Venice Biennale. In the view of NORMAN MAILER, 'Giving a camera to Diane Arbus is like putting a live grenade in the hands of a child.'

1 There's a quality of legend about freaks. Like a person in a fairy tale who stops you and demands that you answer a riddle. Most people go through life dreading they'll have a traumatic experience. Freaks were born with their trauma. They've already passed their test in life. They're aristocrats.
From classes given in 1971, publ. in *Diane Arbus: An Aperture Monograph* (1972)

2 A photograph is a secret about a secret. The more it tells you the less you know.
Quoted in *Diane Arbus: A Biography*, Preface (1985) by Patricia Bosworth

## Jeffrey Archer (b. 1940)
BRITISH AUTHOR, BUSINESSMAN AND POLITICIAN

Baron Archer of Weston-super-Mare. Nicknamed Lord Archer of Rebound, he has led a colourful career characterized by impressive achievements and sudden downfalls. He was a world-class sprinter while a student at Oxford, served as a Conservative MP (1969–74) and Deputy Chairman of the Conservative Party (1985), and was created a life peer in 1992. He has also written bestselling novels including *Not a Penny More, Not a Penny Less* (1976) and *First Among Equals* (1984). The writer and politician Gyles Brandreth called him 'a modern day Toad of Toad Hall . . . historic, but disaster-prone'.

1 I was unemployed with debts of £400,000. I know what unemployment is like and a lot of it is getting off your backside and finding a job.
Quoted in the *Observer* 13 October 1985

2 I was allowed to ring the bell for five minutes until everyone was in assembly. It was the beginning of power.
On his schooldays, in the *Daily Telegraph* 16 March 1988

3 If I am given the privilege of becoming the first democratically elected Lord Mayor I'll never write another book.
*Independent* 21 March 1998. Although a front-runner to be Conservative candidate for Mayor of London, Archer was forced to withdraw his name in December 1999 in the wake of revelations of perjury.

4 I'm down to my last hundred million.
Quoted in the *Guardian* 28 September 1998. On selling his Andy Warhol collection.

## The Archers
BRITISH SOAP OPERA BROADCAST ON BBC RADIO

1 An everyday story of country folk.
Introduction to each episode, publ. in *The Archers: The First Thirty Years* (ed. William Smethurst, 1980). After a trial week's broadcast in 1950, the series began on 1 January 1951 with this preamble. It continued: 'The Archers are country folk – farmers . . . children of the soil, and like most work-a-day folk they have their joys and troubles, their ups and downs . . .' All episodes were first written by Edward J. Mason and Geoffrey Webb. John Keir Cross took over Webb's place on the latter's death in 1962, and different writers were later used.

## Hannah Arendt (1906–75)
GERMAN-BORN US POLITICAL PHILOSOPHER

A refugee from the Nazis, she was active in Jewish organizations in New York from the 1940s, and in 1951 published *The Origins of Totalitarianism* (1951), one of the first books to relate the development of totalitarianism to the anti-Semitism, nationalism and imperialism of the nineteenth century. In 1959 she became the first woman to be a professor at Princeton University.

1 Totalitarianism is never content to rule by external means, namely, through the state and a machinery of violence; thanks to its peculiar ideology and the role assigned to it in this apparatus of coercion, totalitarianism has discovered a means of dominating and terrorizing human beings from within.
*The Origins of Totalitarianism*, ch. 10, sect. 1 (1951)

2 The human condition is such that pain and effort are not just symptoms which can be removed without changing life itself; they are the modes in which life itself, together with the necessity to which it is bound, makes itself felt. For mortals, the 'easy life of the gods' would be a lifeless life.
*The Human Condition*, ch. 16, 'Labor' (1958)

3 The fearsome, word-and-thought-defying *banality of evil*.
*Eichmann in Jerusalem*, ch. 15 (1963)

4 What makes it so plausible to assume that hypocrisy is the vice of vices is that integrity can indeed exist under the cover of all other vices except this one. Only crime and the criminal, it is true, confront us with the perplexity of radical evil; but only the hypocrite is really rotten to the core.
*On Revolution*, ch. 2, sect. 5 (1963)

5 It is well known that the most radical revolutionary will become a conservative the day after the revolution.
*New Yorker* 12 September 1970

6 Under conditions of tyranny it is far easier to act than to think.
Quoted in *A Certain World*, 'Tyranny' (1970) by W.H. AUDEN

7 The Third World is not a reality but an ideology.
*Crises of the Republic*, 'On Violence', sect. 1 (1972)

## Giorgio Armani (b. 1934)
ITALIAN FASHION DESIGNER

Presenting collections from the mid-1970s, he is known for his elegant, mimimalist style, favoured by both men and women and by such celebrities as Jodie Foster, Eric Clapton and Annette Bening. In his own words, 'I was the first to soften the image of men, and harden the image of women.'

1 I would like to be remembered as the person who created a modern elegance.
Interview in the *Guardian* 4 February 1995

## Simon Armitage (b. 1963)
BRITISH POET

Coming to prominence with *Zoom* (1989), he has subsequently published *Kid* (1992) and *The Dead Sea Poems* (1995), and worked as a freelance writer and broadcaster. A public poet with a colloquial style, he makes use of Northern vernacular in his poetry.

1 And a well-shod president walks to the camera to say
    why
  we should put in the boot,
  and when that happens, a well-dressed prime minister
  usually follows suit.
'Killing Time' (1999)

2 Then the Chinese whisper of a countdown spreads
    across the crowd,
  first to be lit by a century's morning,
  mad to say they were there and then when the moment
    came,
  wild for the starlight that passes for meaning.
ibid.

## Louis Armstrong (1900–71)
US JAZZ MUSICIAN

Nicknamed Satchmo ('Satchel Mouth'), he was the leading trumpeter of his time, famous for his improvisatory solos with his 'Hot Five' and 'Hot Seven' ensembles (1925–8). He is said to have invented the 'scat' style of singing, and he also had chart-topping hits such as 'Hello Dolly' (1964) and 'What a Wonderful World' (1968).

1 Hello, Dolly, well, hello Dolly
  It's so nice to have you back where you belong.
'Hello, Dolly' (song, written by Jerry Herman) in *Hello, Dolly* (stage musical 1964, filmed 1969). In the original stage production, the number was sung by Carol Channing, though it is most associated with Armstrong, who won a Grammy award for Song of the Year in 1964 and later performed it in the film version.

2 And I think to myself
  What a wonderful world.
'What a Wonderful World' (song, written by George David Weiss and George Douglas) on the album *What a Wonderful World* (1967)

3 If you still have to ask . . . shame on you.
On being asked what jazz is, quoted in *Louis*, 'Ambassadors of Jazz' (1971, rev. 1975) by Max Jones and John Chilton. Many versions of the riposte exist, along the lines of 'If you have to ask what jazz is, you'll never know', and variously attributed.

4 All music is folk music, I ain't never heard no horse sing a song.
Quoted in *The New York Times* 7 July 1971. The words have also been attributed to blues guitarist Big Bill Broonzy.

## Neil Armstrong (b. 1930)

US ASTRONAUT

Commander of the Apollo 11 moon mission in 1969, he was the first person to set foot on the moon. He recounted the tale in his autobiography, *First on the Moon* (1970).

1 **Houston, Tranquility Base here. The Eagle has landed.**

Radio message to earth announcing the first manned moon landing, 20 July 1969, quoted in the *Washington Post* 21 July 1969. The message was transmitted as the lunar module 'Eagle' touched down in the Sea of Tranquillity. The words have also been attributed to 'Buzz' Aldrin (Edwin Eugene Aldrin Jnr), a fellow crew-member and the second man on the moon.

2 **That's one small step for a man, one giant leap for mankind.**

Quoted in *The New York Times* 21 July 1969. On his first steps on the moon's surface, 10.56 p.m. (EDT), 20 July 1969. Armstrong's actual message – possibly garbled or obscured by static – was originally reported 'one small step for man, one giant leap for mankind'.

## Robert Armstrong (1890–1973)

US SCREEN ACTOR

Real name Donald Robert Smith. A character actor associated with action roles, he is mostly remembered as the film producer who brought the ape to New York in *King Kong* (1932).

1 **Oh no, it wasn't the aviators, it was beauty that killed the beast.**

Carl Denham (Robert Armstrong), in *King Kong* (film, 1933, screenplay by James Creelman and Ruth Rose based on a story by Merian Cooper and Edgar Wallace, directed by Merian Cooper and Ernest Schoedsack). Last lines of the movie, which are often misquoted 'airplanes' instead of 'aviators'.

## (Sir) Robert Armstrong (b. 1927)

BRITISH CIVIL SERVANT

Baron Armstrong of Ilminster. Secretary of the Cabinet (1979–87) and Head of the Civil Service (1981–7) in the Thatcher government, he played a prominent role during the 'Spycatcher' affair in 1987.

1 **It contains a misleading impression, not a lie. It was being economical with the truth.**

Remark to Supreme Court, New South Wales, 18 November 1986, quoted in the *Daily Telegraph* 19 November 1986. Referring to a letter written by Armstrong when the British government was attempting to suppress publication of the book *Spycatcher* by ex-secret service agent Peter Wright. As Armstrong made clear, he was quoting Edmund Burke in *Two Letters on Proposals for Peace* (1796): 'Falsehood and delusion are allowed in no case whatsoever: But, as in the exercise of all the virtues, there is an economy of truth.' Mark Twain harked back to this notion in *Following the Equator* (1897): 'Truth is the most valuable thing we have. Let us economize it', while Tory minister ALAN CLARK also echoed the words when he admitted he had been 'economical with the actualités' when discussing his role in the Matrix Churchill arms-to-Iraq affair in 1990.

## Peter Arno (1904–68)

US CARTOONIST

Original name Curtis Arnoux Peters. From the 1920s until his death he was associated with the *New Yorker* magazine, satirizing New York's café society in his cartoons. Among his cartoon collections are *Man in the Shower* (1944) and *Sizzling Platter* (1949).

1 **Well, back to the old drawing board.**

Caption to cartoon in the *New Yorker*, repr. in *Peter Arno's Cartoon Revue* (1942). The words are spoken by the designer of a plane just crashed.

## Jean Arp (1887–1966)

FRENCH-GERMAN ARTIST AND POET

Also known as Hans Arp. One of the founders of the Dada movement (1916) and associated with the Surrealists during the 1920s, he produced organic abstract sculpture, including his *papiers déchirés* (torn papers) and *papiers froissés* (crumpled papers). After the Second World War he also wrote poems and essays.

1 **Soon silence will have passed into legend. Man has turned his back on silence. Day after day he invents machines and devices that increase noise and distract humanity from the essence of life, contemplation, meditation ... Tooting, howling, screeching, booming, crashing, whistling, grinding, and trilling bolster his ego. His anxiety subsides. His inhuman void spreads monstruously like a grey vegetation.**

*On My Way*, 'Sacred Silence' (ed. Robert Motherwell, 1948)

## Antonin Artaud (1896–1948)

FRENCH THEATRE PRODUCER, ACTOR AND THEORIST

The anarchistic principles of his Theatre of Cruelty, which aimed to attack the compacency of the audience, were expounded in his *Manifesto of the Theatre of Cruelty* (1932 and 1933) and *The Theatre and Its Double* (1938). His best known acting role was as Marat in Abel Gance's film *Napoléon* (1927).

1 **If I commit suicide, it will not be to destroy myself but to put myself back together again. Suicide will be for me only one means of violently reconquering myself, of brutally invading my being, of anticipating the unpredictable approaches of God. By suicide, I reintroduce my design in nature, I shall for the first time give things the shape of my will.**

'On Suicide', first publ. in *Le Disque vert* no. 1 (1925), repr. in *Artaud Anthology* (ed. Jack Hirschman, 1965)

2 ***Theatre of cruelty*** **means a theatre difficult and cruel for myself first of all. And, on the level of performance, it is not the cruelty we can exercise upon each other by hacking at each other's bodies, carving up our personal anatomies, or, like Assyrian emperors, sending parcels of human ears, noses, or neatly detached nostrils through the mail, but the much more terrible and necessary cruelty which things can exercise against us. We are not free. And the sky can still fall on our heads. And the theatre has been created to teach us that first of all.**

*The Theatre and Its Double*, ch. 1 (1938; transl. 1958)

3 **All true language
is incomprehensible,
Like the chatter
of a beggar's teeth.**

'Ci-Gît' (1947), repr. in *Selected Writings*, pt 36 (ed. Susan Sontag, 1976)

4 **Where there is a stink of shit
there is a smell of being.**

*To Have Done with the Judgment of God*, 'The Pursuit of Fecality' (1947)

5 **No one has ever written, painted, sculpted, modeled, built, or invented except literally to get out of hell.**

*Van Gogh, the Man Suicided by Society* (1947)

6 **Tragedy on the stage is no longer enough for me, I shall bring it into my own life.**

Quoted in the memoirs of Jean-Louis Barrault, *Memories for Tomorrow*, pt 2, 'The Grenier des Grands-Augustins' (1972)

## George Asaf (1880–1951)

BRITISH SONGWRITER

1 **What's the use of worrying?
It never was worth while,**

So, pack up your troubles in your old kit-bag,
And smile, smile, smile.

'Pack up your Troubles' (song, 1915, with music by Felix Powell)

# Neal Ascherson (b. 1932)
BRITISH JOURNALIST

Formerly a foreign correspondent and a regular columnist for the *Observer* and *Independent on Sunday*, he has also published books on central and eastern Europe, for example *Struggle for Poland* (1987) and *Black Sea* (1995).

1 The use of the word 'heritage' as a term of obligation, binding people not only to respect relics of the past but also to understand them in one prescribed way as 'national symbols', is not spontaneous. It is a form of manipulation, devised by politicians and quangocrats to make the tatty, dishevelled building-site of the present look more imposing.

*Independent on Sunday* 19 February 1995

2 War is also the day after the war, when the noise stops. It's the day when what looks like a bald old beggar is helped down from the train returning from the prison camps and the small boy asks his mother: 'Is that my dad? Does he live with us?'

*Observer* 6 September 1998

3 Childhood, long worshipped as a separate secret garden of innocence, has become inconvenient and embarrassing, and is now rapidly collapsing into Youth. Wired-up children as defined by advertisers and journalists haranguing working mums, are now little more than young people under five feet high.

*Observer* 15 November 1998

# (Sir) Paddy Ashdown (b. 1941)
BRITISH LIBERAL DEMOCRAT POLITICIAN

Full name Jeremy John Durham Ashdown. Having served in Borneo, Northern Ireland and the Persian Gulf with the Royal Marines and after a brief diplomatic career, he was elected as a Liberal MP in 1983. He became leader of the amalgamated Liberal and Social Democrat (later Liberal Democrat) Party in 1988, and stepped down as party leader in 1999.

1 Politics is about putting yourself in a state of grace.

*Daily Telegraph* 16 September 1992

2 Lord, make my words sweet and reasonable. For some day I may have to eat them.

Speech at Liberal Party Conference, Brighton, broadcast on *Radio 5 Live* 24 September 1998

# Isaac Asimov (1920–92)
RUSSIAN-BORN US AUTHOR

A pioneering figure in scientific fiction and also a distinguished biochemist, he is principally known for his collection of short stories *I, Robot* (1950), and *The Foundation Trilogy* (1951–3). He has also published accessible books on scientific topics and two volumes of autobiography (1979 and 1980).

1 Let's start with the three fundamental Rules of Robotics . . . We have: one, a robot may not injure a human being, or, through inaction, allow a human being to come to harm. Two, a robot must obey the orders given it by human beings except where such orders would conflict with the First Law. And three, a robot must protect its own existence as long as such protection does not conflict with the First or Second Laws.

Powell, in 'Runaround', a story first publ. in *Astounding Science Fiction* March 1942, repr. in *I, Robot* (1950). According to Asimov, who called the formulation his most important contribution to

science fiction, these three laws have been generally adopted by writers on robots. Asimov also claimed that this passage contains the first recorded use of the term, 'Robotics' (discussed in his essay 'My Robots' in *Robot Visions*, 1993).

2 Science fiction writers foresee the inevitable, and although problems and catastrophes may be inevitable, solutions are not.

'How Easy to See the Future', first publ. in *Natural History* April 1975, repr. in *Asimov on Science Fiction* (1981)

3 It is change, continuing change, inevitable change, that is the dominant factor in society today. No sensible decision can be made any longer without taking into account not only the world as it is, but the world as it will be . . . This, in turn, means that our statesmen, our businessmen, our everyman must take on a science fictional way of thinking.

'My Own View', publ. in *The Encyclopedia of Science Fiction* (ed. Robert Holdstock, 1978)

# Elizabeth Asquith (1897–1945)

The daughter of Herbert Asquith, she married Prince Antoine Bibesco, a Romanian diplomat, in 1919 and subsequently wrote novels, plays and poetry.

1 Kitchener is a great poster.

Quoted by Herbert Asquith, in *More Memories*, ch. 6 (1933) by Margot Asquith. The quote is often misattributed to MARGOT ASQUITH, as in *Kitchener: Portrait of an Imperialist*, ch. 14 (1980) by Sir Philip Magnus, where the quote appears in the form, 'If Kitchener was not a great man, he was, at least, a great poster.'

# Herbert Asquith (1852–1928)
BRITISH STATESMAN

Soon after entering parliament as a Liberal MP in 1886, he served in the government as Home Secretary and then Chancellor of the Exchequer. He was Prime Minister 1908–16 but was ousted as leader of the wartime coalition by LLOYD GEORGE's wing of the party.

1 Youth would be an ideal state if it came a little later in life.

Quoted in the *Observer* 15 April 1923

2 It is fitting that we should have buried the Unknown Prime Minister by the side of the Unknown Soldier.

Quoted in *The Unknown Prime Minister*, ch. 32, sect. 2 (1955) by Robert Blake. Referring to Andrew Bonar Law, Prime Minister 1922–3. Bonar Law (died 30 October 1923) was the first prime minister to be buried in Westminster Abbey since Gladstone in 1898, though it was contrary to his own wishes. Blake comments, 'Asquith certainly intended no compliment by this remark, but Bonar Law would not have resented it. He cared little enough for fame in his own lifetime, still less for the verdict of posterity.'

# Margot Asquith (1864–1945)
BRITISH SOCIALITE

Second wife of HERBERT ASQUITH, she was a renowned wit and society hostess. She published three volumes of revelatory autobiography (1920–43) and an autobiographical novel *Octavia* (1928). As DOROTHY PARKER quipped, 'The affair between Margot Asquith and Margot Asquith will live as one of the prettiest love stories in all literature.'

1 From the happy expression on their faces you might have supposed that they welcomed the war. I have met with men who loved stamps, and stones, and snakes, but I could not imagine any man loving war.

On the crowds outside Downing Street 3 August 1914, the eve of the declaration of the First World War, in *The Autobiography of Margot Asquith* vol. 2, ch. 7 (1922)

2 He could not see a belt without hitting below it.

Of former Prime Minister DAVID LLOYD GEORGE, quoted by Mark Bonham Carter in Introduction to Margot Asquith's *Autobiography* (1962 edn; first publ. 1920)

3 No, no, Jean. The *t* is silent, as in *Harlow*.

Quoted in *Great Tom: Notes Towards a Definition of T.S. Eliot*, ch. 7 (1973) by T. S. Matthews. Said to the actress Jean Harlow, who had been mispronouncing her name. The anecdote is remembered by Emily Hale, a friend of T.S. ELIOT.

## Nancy Astor (1879–1964)
US-BORN BRITISH POLITICIAN

Viscountess Astor of Hever Castle. In 1919 she was the first woman to sit in the House of Commons, succeeding her husband as Conservative MP for Plymouth. She principally concerned herself with temperance issues, and children's and womens' rights. Generally considered a wit, she was portrayed as a 'sort of V-2 rocket' by her husband.

1 I married beneath me – all women do.

Attributed, speech at Oldham, 1951, also quoted in *Dictionary of National Biography*

2 The penalty of success is to be bored by people who snub you.

Quoted in the *Sunday Express* 12 January 1956

## Brooks Atkinson (1894–1984)
US CRITIC AND ESSAYIST

Drama critic of *The New York Times* (1925–42 and 1946–60), he won the Pulitzer Prize for journalism in 1947. His publications include collections of essays and articles, notably *Once Around the Sun* (1951) and *Brief Chronicle* (1966), as well as histories of the theatre.

1 After each war there is a little less democracy to save.

*Once Around the Sun*, '7 January' (1951)

2 The virtue of the camera is not the power it has to transform the photographer into an artist, but the impulse it gives him to keep on looking.

ibid. '28 August'

## Charles Atlas (1893–1972)
ITALIAN-BORN US BODYBUILDER

Original name Angelo Siciliano. With his partner Charles P. Roman, he devised and ran a highly successful mail-order body-building programme, which during the 1920s caused him to be dubbed 'America's Most Perfectly Developed Man'.

1 You too can have a body like mine.

Quoted in *The Life and Times of Charles Atlas*, pt 1 (1942) by Charles Gaines. The slogan was coined by Atlas's partner, Charles Roman c. 1929.

## (Sir) David Attenborough (b. 1926)
BRITISH NATURALIST AND BROADCASTER

Inspired by the 'splendour and fecundity of the natural world', he began filming wildlife in exotic locations for the BBC series *Zoo Quest* (1954–64), hardly stopping since except 1965–72 when he worked as controller of BBC2 and Director of Programmes. His documentary series which have been seen all round the world include *Life on Earth* (1979) and *The Private Life of Plants* (1995).

1 It is more than likely that if men were to disappear from the face of the earth, for whatever reason, there is a modest, unobtrusive creature somewhere that would develop into a new form and take our place.

*Life On Earth*, 'The Compulsive Communicators' (1979)

2 We can now manipulate images to such an extraordinary degree that there is no lie you can't tell.

Quoted in the *Observer* 18 October 1998

## Clement Attlee (1883–1967)
BRITISH POLITICIAN AND PRIME MINISTER

He was the first Labour prime minister to hold an absolute majority in the House of Commons. His premiership (1945–51) saw the initiation of the welfare state, nationalization of major industries, a speeding-up of decolonization and support for NATO. ANEURIN BEVAN remarked: 'He brings to the fierce struggle of politics the tepid enthusiasm of a lazy summer afternoon at a cricket match.' See also ANEURIN BEVAN 12 and WINSTON CHURCHILL 46, 55 and 56.

1 Few thought he was even a starter
There were many who thought themselves smarter
But he ended PM
CH and OM
An earl and a knight of the garter.

Quoted in *Attlee*, ch. 29 (1982) by Kenneth Harris. Describing himself in a letter to his brother Tom Attlee, 8 April 1956, shortly before being enrolled as a Knight of the Garter.

2 [Russian Communism is] the illegitimate child of Karl Marx and Catherine the Great.

Speech at Aarhus University, Denmark, 11 April 1956, quoted in *The Times* 12 April 1956

3 Democracy means government by discussion, but it is only effective if you can stop people talking.

Speech at Oxford, 14 June 1957, quoted in *The Times* 15 June 1957

## Margaret Atwood (b. 1939)
CANADIAN NOVELIST, POET AND CRITIC

Described by MICHAEL ONDAATJE as 'the quiet Mata Hari, the mysterious violent figure. . .who pits herself against the ordered, too-clean world like an arsonist', she is regarded as Canada's leading contemporary writer. Her feminist-influenced novels include *The Edible Woman* (1969), *The Handmaid's Tale* (1985, filmed 1990) and *Cat's Eye* (1989).

1 Everyone thinks writers must know more about the inside of the human head, but that is wrong. They know less, that's why they write. Trying to find out what everyone else takes for granted.

*Dancing Girls*, 'Lives of the Poets' (1977)

2 The beginning of Canadian cultural nationalism was not 'Am I really that oppressed?' but 'Am I really that boring?'

Interview with Joyce Carol Oates in *Ontario Review* Fall/Winter 1978, repr. in *Conversations*, 'Dancing On the Edge Of the Precipice' (ed. Earl G. Ingersoll, 1990)

3 Gardening is not a rational act. What matters is the immersion of the hands in the earth, that ancient ceremony of which the Pope kissing the tarmac is merely a pallid vestigial remnant. In the spring, at the end of the day, you should smell like dirt.

*Bluebeard's Egg*, 'Unearthing Suite' (1983)

4 We yearned for the future. How did we learn it, that talent for insatiability?

*The Handmaid's Tale*, ch. 1 (1986)

5 As all historians know, the past is a great darkness, and filled with echoes. Voices may reach us from it; but what they say to us is imbued with the obscurity of the matrix out of which they come; and try as we may, we cannot always decipher them precisely in the clearer light of our day.

ibid. 'Historical Note'

6 All fathers . . . are invisible in daytime; daytime is ruled by mothers. But fathers come out at night. Darkness brings home the fathers, with their real, unspeakable power. There is more to them than meets the eye.

*Cat's Eye*, ch. 31 (1989)

# W.H. Auden (1907–73)

ANGLO-AMERICAN POET AND CRITIC

One of the most influential poets of the twentieth century, 'an intellectual jackdaw', and, according to PERCY WYNDHAM LEWIS, 'all ice and woodenfaced acrobatics', he was one of the wave of left-wing *literati* of the 1930s. Having established his reputation with *Look Stranger!* (1936) and *Spain* (1937), he emigrated to the USA in 1939 where he was awarded the Pulitzer Prize for his collection *The Age of Anxiety* (1947). He also wrote plays, libretti and literary criticism.

1  Let us honour if we can
The vertical man,
Though we value none
But the horizontal one.
*Poems*, Epigraph (1930), repr. in *Collected Shorter Poems 1927–1957*, 'Shorts' (1966)

2  Harrow the house of the dead; look shining at
New styles of architecture, a change of heart.
'Sir, No Man's Enemy', publ. in *Poems* (1930)

3  Private faces in public places
Are wiser and nicer
Than public faces in private places.
Epigraph to 'The Orators' (1932), repr. in *Collected Shorter Poems 1927–1957*, 'Shorts' (1966)

4  This is the Night Mail crossing the border,
Bringing the cheque and the postal order,
Letters for the rich, letters for the poor,
The shop at the corner, the girl next door.

Pulling up Beattock, a steady climb:
The gradient's against her, but she's on time.
Past cotton-grass and moorland border,
Shovelling white steam over her shoulder.
'Night Mail', sect. 1 (1936), repr. in ibid. Opening lines of poem written as a commentary for a Post Office documentary film.

5  None will hear the postman's knock
Without a quickening of the heart.
For who can bear to feel himself forgotten?
Concluding lines of ibid.

6  And make us as Newton was, who in his garden watching
The apple falling towards England, became aware
Between himself and her of an eternal tie.
'O Love, the Interest Itself', publ. in *Look, Stranger!* (1936). The words 'falling towards England' provided CLIVE JAMES with the title for his second volume of 'unreliable memoirs' in 1985.

7  A shilling life will give you all the facts.
Title and first line of poem (c. 1934), publ. in ibid.

8  The desires of the heart are as crooked as corkscrews
Not to be born is the best for man.
'Death's Echo', publ. in *Spain* (1937). The second line quoted echoes a line by W.B. YEATS in 'From "Oedipus at Colonus"' (1928): 'Never to have lived is best, ancient writers say / Never to have drawn the breath of life, never to have looked into the eye of day'; which in turn recalls a line from Sophocles.

9  To-morrow for the young the poets exploding like bombs,
The walks by the lake, the weeks of perfect communion;
To-morrow the bicycle races
Through the suburbs on summer evenings. But to-day
the struggle.
'Spain', st. 23, publ. in ibid.

10  The stars are dead. The animals will not look.
We are left alone with our day, and the time is short, and
History to the defeated
May say Alas but cannot help nor pardon.
ibid. st. 26. Auden later commented on these lines, which he disliked because they 'equate goodness with success': 'It would have been bad enough if I had ever held this wicked doctrine, but that I should have stated it simply because it sounded to me rhetorically effective is quite inexcusable.'

11  'I'll love you, dear, I'll love you
Till China and Africa meet
And the river jumps over the mountain
And the salmon sing in the street,

'I'll love you till the ocean
Is folded and hung up to dry
And the seven stars go squawking
Like geese about the sky.'
'As I Walked Out One Evening', publ. in *Another Time* (1940)

12  'O plunge your hands in water,
Plunge them in up to the wrist;
Stare, stare in the basin
And wonder what you've missed.

'The glacier knocks in the cupboard,
The desert sighs in the bed,
And the crack in the tea-cup opens
A lane to the land of the dead.'
ibid.

13  When he laughed, respectable senators burst with
laughter,
And when he cried the little children died in the streets.
'Epitaph on a Tyrant' (1940), publ. in ibid. The lines may have been inspired by a description of William of Orange in *The Rise of the Dutch Republic* (1856) by John Lothrop Motley: 'As long as he lived, he was the guiding-star of a whole brave nation, and when he died the little children cried in the streets.'

14  He was my North, my South, my East and West,
My working week and my Sunday rest,
My noon, my midnight, my talk, my song;
I thought that love would last for ever: I was wrong.
'Funeral Blues', publ. in ibid. The poem was recited during the funeral scene in the film *Four Weddings and a Funeral* (1994).

15  For one who lived among enemies so long:
If often he was wrong and at times absurd,
To us he is no more a person
Now but a whole climate of opinion.
'In Memory of Sigmund Freud', st. 17, publ. in ibid.

16  Mad Ireland hurt you into poetry.
Now Ireland has her madness and her weather still.
'In Memory of W.B. Yeats', pt 2, written February 1939, publ. in ibid.

17  For poetry makes nothing happen: it survives
In the valley of its saying where executives
Would never want to tamper.
ibid.

18  Earth, receive an honoured guest:
William Yeats is laid to rest.
Let the Irish vessel lie
Emptied of its poetry.
ibid. pt 3

19  In the nightmare of the dark
All the dogs of Europe bark,
And the living nations wait,
Each sequestered in its hate;
Intellectual disgrace
Stares from every human face.
ibid.

20  Lay your sleeping head, my love,
Human on my faithless arm.
'Lay your sleeping head, my love', publ. in ibid. Opening lines.

21  But in my arms till break of day
Let the living creature lie,
Mortal, guilty, but to me
The entirely beautiful.
ibid.

22  About suffering they were never wrong,
The Old Masters: how well they understood

Its human position; how it takes place
While someone else is eating or opening a window or
  just walking dully along.

'Musée des Beaux Arts', publ. in ibid. Opening lines.

23  I and the public know
What all schoolchildren learn,
Those to whom evil is done
Do evil in return.

'September 1, 1939', st. 2, publ. in ibid.

24  We must love one another or die.

ibid., st. 8. Auden later repudiated the line, insisting that it be
altered for a 1955 anthology to 'We must love one another and die.'
He referred to the poem as 'the most dishonest poem I have ever
written'.

25  Blessed Cecilia, appear in visions
To all musicians, appear and inspire:
Translated Daughter, come down and startle
Composing mortals with immortal fire.

'Anthem for St Cecilia's Day', pt 1, publ. in *New Year Letter*, in USA
*The Double Man* (1941)

26  At Dirty Dick's and Sloppy Joe's
We drank our liquor straight,
Some went upstairs with Margery,
And some, alas, with Kate.

*The Sea and the Mirror*, pt 2, 'Master and Boatswain', publ. in *For
the Time Being* (1944)

27  Thou shalt not sit
With statisticians nor commit
A social science.

'Under Which Lyre', st. 27, written 1946, publ. in *Nones* (1951)

28  Criticism should be a casual conversation.

*The Table Talk of W.H. Auden*, 'November 16, 1946' (comp. Alan
Ansen, ed. Nicholas Jenkins, 1990)

29  Sob, heavy world,
Sob as you spin
Mantled in mist, remote from the happy.

'The Dirge', publ. in *The Age of Anxiety* (1947)

30  The detective must be either the official representative of
the ethical or the exceptional individual who is in a state
of grace.

'The Guilty Vicarage', first publ. in *Harper's Magazine* May 1948,
repr. in *The Dyer's Hand*, pt 3 (1962)

31  Routine, in an intelligent man, is a sign of ambition.

'The Life of That-There Poet' (1958), publ. in the *New Yorker* 26
April 1958

32  To the man-in-the-street, who, I'm sorry to say,
Is a keen observer of life,
The word 'Intellectual' suggests straight away
A man who's untrue to his wife.

'New Year Letter', note to l. 1277 in *Collected Poems* (1976)

33  It is a sad fact about our culture that a poet can earn much
more money writing or talking about his art than he can
by practising it.

*The Dyer's Hand*, Foreword (1962). Opening words.

34  Some books are undeservedly forgotten; none are undeservedly remembered.

ibid. pt 1, 'Reading'

35  It takes little talent to see clearly what lies under one's
nose, a good deal of it to know in which direction to point
that organ.

ibid. 'Writing'

36  No poet or novelist wishes he were the only one who ever
lived, but most of them wish they were the only one alive,
and quite a number fondly believe their wish has been
granted.

ibid.

37  When I find myself in the company of scientists, I feel like

a shabby curate who has strayed by mistake into a drawing
room full of dukes.

ibid. pt 2, 'The Poet and the City'. Auden had specialized in science
studies before switching to English at Oxford.

38  A man has his distinctive personal scent which his wife,
his children and his dog can recognize. A crowd has a
generalized stink. The public is odourless.

ibid.

39  Between friends differences in taste or opinion are irritating in direct proportion to their triviality.

ibid. pt 3, 'Hic et Ille', sect. D

40  Among those whom I like or admire, I can find no
common denominator, but among those whom I love, I
can: all of them make me laugh.

ibid. pt 7, 'Notes on the Comic'

41  A verbal art like poetry is reflective; it stops to think.
Music is immediate, it goes on to become.

ibid. pt 8, 'Notes on Music and Opera'

42  God bless the USA, so large,
So friendly, and so rich.

'On the Circuit', written 1963, publ. in *Collected Poems* (1976)

43  Some thirty inches from my nose
The frontier of my Person goes,
And all the untilled air between
Is private *pagus* or demesne.

Stranger, unless with bedroom eyes
I beckon you to fraternize,
Beware of rudely crossing it:
I have no gun, but I can spit.

'Prologue: the Birth of Architecture: Postscript', publ. in *About the
House* (1965)

44  Healing,
Papa would tell me,
'is not a science,
but the intuitive art
of wooing Nature.'

'The Art of Healing', written 1969, publ. in *Collected Poems*: (1976).

45  Of course, Behaviourism 'works.' So does torture. Give
me a no-nonsense, down-to-earth behaviourist, a few
drugs, and simple electrical appliances, and in six months
I will have him reciting the Athanasian Creed in public.

*A Certain World*, 'Behaviourism' (1970)

46  All sin tends to be addictive, and the terminal point of
addiction is what is called damnation.

ibid. 'Hell'

47  As a poet there is only one political duty, and that is to
defend one's language against corruption. When it is
corrupted, people lose faith in what they hear and this
leads to violence.

Quoted in the *Observer* 31 October 1971

48  You will be a poet because you will always be humiliated.

Quoted by Stephen Spender in his *Journals 1939–1983* (1985), entry
for 11 April 1979. Spender was reminiscing on his first meeting with
Auden at Oxford.

49  My face looks like a wedding-cake left out in the rain.

Quoted in *W.H. Auden*, pt 2, ch. 6 (1981) by Humphrey Carpenter.
On the subject of faces, Auden wrote (in *The Dyer's Hand*, 1962):
'Every European visitor to the United States is struck by the comparative rarity of what he would call a face . . . To have a face, in
the European sense of the word, it would seem that one must not
only enjoy and suffer but also desire to preserve the memory of
even the most humiliating and unpleasant experiences of the past.'

# Daw Aung San Suu Kyi (b. 1945)

BURMESE OPPOSITION LEADER

The daughter of General Aung San, the architect of Burmese
independence, she co-founded in 1988 the National League for

Democracy, the main opposition to the military junta in Burma (re-named Myanmar). Although her party won the 1990 elections, she was placed under house arrest. She was awarded the Nobel Peace prize in 1991.

1 **It may take time and it won't be easy. But what's ten years?**

Sunday Telegraph 4 April 1999. Referring to her persecution by the Burmese government, and her hopes to re-establish democracy in Burma.

## Paul Auster (b. 1947)
US AUTHOR

The New York Trilogy (1987) established his name for experimental story-telling on the themes of modern city life. Other works include The Invention of Solitude (1982), Moon Palace (1989) and Leviathan (1992), and he has also published poems and essays.

1 **We construct a narrative for ourselves, and that's the thread that we follow from one day to the next. People who disintegrate as personalities are the ones who lose that thread.**

Interview in the Sunday Times 16 April 1989

2 **Our lives don't really belong to us, you see – they belong to the world, and in spite of our efforts to make sense of it, the world is a place beyond our understanding.**

Interview 1989/90, publ. in The Red Notebook (1995)

## Tex Avery (1907–80)
US ANIMATOR

Originally named Frederick Bean. He was famous for creating such cartoon characters as Bugs Bunny and Daffy Duck, which appeared on television and in the films King Size Canary (1947) and Bad Luck Blackie (1949), among other classics. He later worked on The Flintstones (1979).

1 **Th-th-th-th-that's all, folks!**

Porky Pig, who appeared in the Warner Brothers Looney Tunes/Merrie Melodies cartoons from 1935 to 1965. The sign-off line (created and voiced by Mel Blanc from 1938) was also used to close various other Warner Brothers cartoons, and was affectionately reprised at the end of the 1972 film What's Up Doc? (see below). Porky Pig first appeared in the Looney Tunes cartoon I Haven't Got a Hat (1935).

2 **Eh, what's up Doc?**

Bugs Bunny's running gag in the Warner Brothers Looney Tunes/Merrie Melodies cartoons from 1938 to 1964. The rabbit made his first appearance in a Looney Tunes cartoon in 1937, voiced by Mel Blanc. In 1940 Tex Avery gave him his name (after West Coast mobster Bugsy Siegel) and his famous catchphrase, and directed the first official Bugs Bunny cartoon, A Wild Hare (1940). What's Up Doc? was also the title of Peter Bogdanovich's screwball comedy with Barbra Streisand and Ryan O'Neal (1972).

## Reverend W. Awdry (1911–97)
BRITISH WRITER OF CHILDREN'S BOOKS

Wilbert Vere Awdry, a country clergyman 1936–65, wrote the Thomas the Tank Engine series of stories for children, the first of which appeared in 1945. They have since gathered a huge following among all ages.

1 **You've a lot to learn about trucks, little Thomas. They are silly things and must be kept in their place. After pushing them about here for a few weeks you'll know almost as much about them as Edward. Then you'll be a Really Useful Engine.**

The Fat Director, in Thomas the Tank Engine, 'Thomas and the Trucks' (1946)

## Hoyt Axton (b. 1938)
US ROCK MUSICIAN

A respected composer of songs for Glen Campbell, RINGO STARR and the group Steppenwolf, among many others, he also recorded his own material with some success in the 1970s. His mother co-wrote 'Heartbreak Hotel' (1955), a hit for ELVIS PRESLEY.

1 **God damn the pusher man.**

'The Pusher' (song) on the album Steppenwolf (1968) by Steppenwolf. The anti-drug anthem featured in Dennis Hopper's film Easy Rider (1969), though was banned on the radio.

## (Sir) Alan Ayckbourn (b. 1939)
BRITISH PLAYWRIGHT

Prolific and master farceur of what he terms 'inspired nonsense', he depicts middle-class suburban life with increasingly acid wit. His plays, which often involve convoluted plots and ingenious sets, as in The Norman Conquests trilogy (1974), are premiered in Scarborough, where he lives and directs the Stephen Joseph theatre.

1 **The only thing for old age is a brave face, a good tailor and comfortable shoes.**

Reg, in Table Manners, act 2, sc. 1, first of the trilogy The Norman Conquests (1975)

2 **Where's the romance gone? Destroyed by cynics and liberationalists. . . . Forget the flowers, the chocolates, the soft word – rather woo her with a self-defence manual in one hand and a family planning leaflet in the other.**

Norman, in Round and Round the Garden, act 1, sc. 1, third of the trilogy The Norman Conquests (1975)

3 **This place, you tell them you're interested in the arts, you get messages of sympathy.**

Dafydd, in Chorus of Disapproval, act 2 (1986)

## (Sir) A.J. Ayer (1910–89)
BRITISH PHILOSOPHER

Full name Alfred Jules Ayer. His first book, Language, Truth and Logic (1936), which expounded the theory of logical positivism as associated with the Vienna Circle, proved one of the most popular philosophical works of the times. He was Wykeham Professor of Logic at Oxford (1959–78).

1 **The traditional disputes of philosophers are, for the most part, as unwarranted as they are unfruitful.**

Language, Truth and Logic, ch. 1 (1936). Opening sentence of book.

2 **No moral system can rest solely on authority.**

Humanist Outlook, Introduction (1968). In a later essay, Ayer wrote, 'To say that authority, whether secular or religious, supplies no ground for morality is not to deny the obvious fact that it supplies a sanction.' ('The Meaning of Life', 1990)

3 **There never comes a point where a theory can be said to be true. The most that one can claim for any theory is that it has shared the successes of all its rivals and that it has passed at least one test which they have failed.**

Philosophy in the Twentieth Century, ch. 4 (1982)

## Pam Ayres (b. 1947)
BRITISH WRITER OF HUMOROUS VERSE

Composer of comic verse since the 1970s, she also writes books for children, is a BBC Radio 2 presenter and gives readings.

1 **I'm glad tomorrow's Thursday,**
   **'Cause with a bit of luck,**
   **As far as I remember,**
   **That's the day they pass the buck.**

'The Bunny Poem', publ. in Some of Me Poetry (1976)

2 **Oh, I wish I'd looked after me teeth,**
   **And spotted the perils beneath,**

All the toffees I chewed,
And the sweet sticky food,
Oh, I wish I'd looked after me teeth.

'Oh, I wish I'd looked after me teeth', publ. in ibid.

3 I see the Time and Motion clock,
Is sayin' nearly noon,
I 'spec me squirt of water,
Will come flyin' at me soon,
And then me spray of pellets,
Will nearly break me leg,
And I'll bite the wire nettin'
And lay one more bloody egg.

'The Battery Hen', publ. in ibid.

4 Medicinal discovery,

It moves in mighty leaps,
It leapt straight past the common cold
And gave it us for keeps.

'Oh no, I got a cold', publ. in ibid.

## Dan Aykroyd (b. 1950)

CANADIAN ACTOR, DIRECTOR AND WRITER

Born Daniel Agraluscarsacra. He developed his writing and performing skills on the TV show *Saturday Night Live* before co-starring in *The Blues Brothers* (1980) and *Trading Places* (1983).

1 They're not going to catch us. We're on a mission from God.

Elwood (Dan Aykroyd), in *The Blues Brothers* (film, 1980, screenplay by John Landis and Dan Aykroyd, directed by John Landis)

## Lauren Bacall (b. 1924)

US ACTRESS

Billed as 'slinky, sultry and sensational', she was also known for her husky voice. She co-starred with her husband HUMPHREY BOGART in a succession of hit films including *The Big Sleep* (1946), *Key Largo* (1948) and *To Have and Have Not* (1953). She made a well-received return to the stage with *Applause* in 1970.

1 **Anybody got a match?**

Marie Browning (Lauren Bacall), in *To Have and Have Not* (film, screenplay by Jules Furthman and William Faulkner, based on Ernest Hemingway's 1937 novel of the same name, produced and directed by Howard Hawks, 1944). Lauren Bacall's screen-debut line, in a film best remembered for the on- and offscreen romance between Bogart and Bacall which resulted in marriage the following year.

2 **You know you don't have to act with me, Steve. You don't have to say anything, and you don't have to do anything. Not a thing. Oh, maybe just whistle. You know how to whistle, don't you, Steve? You just put your lips together, and blow.**

ibid. Spoken to Harry Morgan (Humphrey Bogart).

3 **I think your whole life shows in your face and you should be proud of that.**

*Daily Telegraph* 2 March 1988

## Gaston Bachelard (1884–1962)

FRENCH SCIENTIST, PHILOSOPHER AND LITERARY THEORIST

He belonged to the 'criticism of science' school, believing that reverie and imagination were as important as observation and analysis for the understanding of reality. Among his works are *The Psychoanalysis of Fire* (1938) and *The Right to Dream* (1970).

1 **Man is a creation of desire, not a creation of need.**

*The Psychoanalysis of Fire*, ch. 2, 'Fire and Reverie' (1938)

2 **Reverie is not a mind vacuum. It is rather the gift of an hour which knows the plenitude of the soul.**

*The Poetics of Reverie*, ch. 2, sect. 3 (1960, transl. 1969)

3 **The words of the world want to make sentences.**

ibid. ch. 5, sect. 4

## Joan Baez (b. 1941)

US SINGER

Prominent in the American folk revival of the early 1960s, she was also associated with the protest movement, performing frequently at rallies and festivals. Her albums include *Any Day Now* (1968) and *Diamonds and Rust* (1975).

1 **To sing is to love and to affirm, to fly and soar, to coast into the hearts of the people who listen, to tell them that life is to live, that love is there, that nothing is a promise, but that beauty exists, and must be hunted for and found.**

*Daybreak*, 'Singing' (1970)

2 **The only thing that's been a worse flop than the organization of nonviolence has been the organization of violence.**

ibid. 'What Would You Do If?'

3 **Instead of getting hard on ourselves and trying to compete, women should try and give their best qualities to men – bring them softness, teach them how to cry.**

Quoted in the *Los Angeles Times* 26 May 1974

4 **I've never had a humble opinion in my life. If you're going to have one, why bother to be humble about it?**

*International Herald Tribune* 2 December 1992

## Enid Bagnold (1889–1981)
BRITISH NOVELIST AND PLAYWRIGHT

She adapted several of her novels into plays, the best-known of which, the horseracing tale *National Velvet* (1935), was also filmed in 1944, starring a young Elizabeth Taylor. Her last play, *The Chalk Garden* (1956), was also her most successful on both sides of the Atlantic.

1 Judges don't age. Time decorates them.
Judge, in *The Chalk Garden*, act 2 (1953)

2 The theatre is a gross art, built in sweeps and over-emphasis. Compromise is its second name.
*Autobiography*, ch. 3 (1969)

3 Sex – the great inequality, the great miscalculator, the great Irritator.
ibid. ch. 6

## David Bailey (b. 1938)
BRITISH PHOTOGRAPHER

The 'personification of the photographer as pop hero', in the words of GEORGE MELLY, he specialized in fashion pictures, making the model Jean Shrimpton an icon of the time. His photographic portraits encapsulated the spirit of the 1960s, and his collection *Goodbye Baby and Amen* (1969) was a bitter-sweet farewell to that decade. He has also directed TV commercials and documentaries.

1 All that Swinging Sixties nonsense, we all thought it was passé at the time.
Interview in *The Face* December 1984

2 It takes a lot of imagination to be a good photographer. You need less imagination to be a painter, because you can invent things. But in photography everything is so ordinary; it takes a lot of looking before you learn to see the ordinary.
ibid.

3 I never cared for fashion much, amusing little seams and witty little pleats: it was the girls I liked.
*Independent* 5 November 1990

## (Dame) Beryl Bainbridge (b. 1934)
BRITISH AUTHOR

She has reproduced the milieu of her childhood in post-war Liverpool in many of her richly ironic comedies, which she calls 'horror stories told like everyday gossip', for example *Young Adolf* (1978) and *An Awfully Big Adventure* (1989, filmed 1995). Other novels include *The Dressmaker* (1973, filmed 1979). She has also written plays, short stories and essays, achieving the distinction of being the author most often shortlisted for the Booker Prize, without having won it.

1 And life was war in a more subtle form, that lasted for ever, and only discipline and careful entrenchment would see you through until your own great Armistice Day.
Lionel, in *Another Part of the Wood*, ch. 5 (1968)

2 Emotions weren't like washing. There was no call to peg them out for all the world to view.
Uncle Vernon, in *An Awfully Big Adventure*, ch. 1 (1989)

3 It never ceases to puzzle me that, while men and women's bodies fit jigsaw tight in an altogether miraculous way their minds remain wretchedly unaligned.
Evans, in *The Birthday Boys*, 'Petty Officer (Taff) Evans, June 1910' (1991)

4 There is nothing more guaranteed to reduce a man to the essentials than to live beneath the sky.
*Master Georgie*, plate 3, 'August 1854: Tug-of-war Beside the Sweet Waters of Europe' (1998)

5 When passion is mutual, there is always the danger of the fire burning to ashes.
ibid. plate 4, 'August 1854: Concert Party at Varna'

6 Women are programmed to love completely, and men are programmed to spread it around. We are fools to think it's any different.
*Sunday Times* 1 November 1998

7 The older one becomes the quicker the present fades into sepia and the past looms up in glorious technicolour.
Quoted in the *Observer* 27 December 1998

8 You've got to learn to speak properly. You don't take people seriously who speak badly.
ibid. 7 March 1999. Bainbridge renounced her own Liverpool accent.

## James Baker (b. 1930)
US POLITICIAN

A shrewd political manager for the Republican party, he was REAGAN's Chief of Staff (1981–5) and successfully oversaw GEORGE BUSH's presidential campaign. Appointed Secretary of State in 1989 he played a prominent part in the reunification of East with West Germany in 1990, and the 1990–91 Gulf crisis. In 1992 he once again served as White House Chief of Staff and directed Bush's unsuccessful re-election campaign.

1 Who could not be moved by the sight of that poor, demoralized rabble, outwitted, outflanked, outmanoeuvred by the US military? Yet, given time, I think the press will bounce back.
Quoted in the *Guardian* 26 March 1991. Referring to the media pack during the second Gulf War.

## Kenneth Baker (b. 1934)
BRITISH POLITICIAN

Elected Conservative MP in 1968, he rose to become Secretary of State for the Environment (1985–6) and Education (1986–9) during the Thatcher government. He introduced educational reforms, his name being synonymous with in-service training days for teachers (Baker days). He was Chairman of the Conservative Party (1989–90) and, under John Major, Home Secretary (1990–92).

1 Socialists make the mistake of confusing individual worth with success. They believe you cannot allow people to succeed in case those who fail feel worthless.
Quoted in the *Observer* 13 July 1986

2 He [SDP leader Dr David Owen] has conferred on the practice of vacillation the aura of statesmanship.
*Daily Telegraph* 11 October 1989

## Nicholson Baker (b. 1957)
US AUTHOR

He said of his books, 'I got rid of the plot.' As well as lacking much narrative, his off-beat fiction also eschews action, dialogue and character analysis in favour of close observation. His novels include *The Mezzanine* (1988) and *Room Temperature* (1990), and his essays *The Size of Thoughts* (1996). The critic Barbara Fisher Williamson described his work as 'verbal ballets of incredible delicacy'.

1 Shoes are the first adult machines we are given to master.
*The Mezzanine*, ch. 1 (1988)

2 In my case, adulthood itself was not an advance, although it was a useful waymark.
ibid. ch. 3

3 Footnotes are the finer-suckered surfaces that allow tentacular paragraphs to hold fast to the wider reality of the library.
ibid. ch. 14, footnote

4 When the excessively shy force themselves to be forward,

they are frequently surprisingly unsubtle and overdirect and even rude: they have entered an extreme region beyond their normal personality, an area of social crime where gradations don't count. Unavailable to them are the instincts and taboos that booming extroverts, who know the territory of self-advancement far better, can rely on.

*U And I: A True Story*, ch. 9 (1991)

## Russell Baker (b. 1925)
US JOURNALIST

Known for his 'Observer' column in *The New York Times,* he has satirized politicians, bureaucrats and the excesses of America. He has written the memoirs *Growing Up* (1982) and *The Good Times* (1989) and published collections of his pieces, such as *Baker's Dozen* (1964). *Time* summarized him as 'funny, but full of the pain and absurdity of the age'.

1 Inanimate objects are classified scientifically into three major categories – those that don't work, those that break down and those that get lost.

*The New York Times* 18 June 1968

2 So there he is at last. Man on the moon. The poor magnificent bungler! He can't even get to the office without undergoing the agonies of the damned, but give him a little metal, a few chemicals, some wire and twenty or thirty billion dollars and, vroom! there he is, up on a rock a quarter of a million miles up in the sky.

*The New York Times* 21 July 1969. On the first manned moon landing.

## Jim Bakker (b. 1940)
US EVANGELIST

One-time President of the Inspirational and Praise the Lord television networks, in 1987 he resigned due to sexual scandal and in 1989 was sentenced to five years' imprisonment for fraud. He said after his release, 'If money is a gift from God, we ought to make Michael Jackson the Pope.'

1 I started out by believing God for a newer car than the one I was driving. I started out believing God for a nicer apartment than I had. Then I moved up.

Quoted in the *New Yorker* 23 April 1990. Bakker was explaining the large sums of money needed to finance his luxury religious centre, Heritage USA. As he said, 'Why should I apologize because God throws in crystal chandeliers, mahogany floors, and the best construction in the world?'

## James Baldwin (1924–87)
US AUTHOR

Brought up in poverty in Harlem where most of his works are set, he later lived in Paris, an increasingly marginalized spokesman on black and gay issues. His autobiographical first novel, *Go Tell It on the Mountain* (1953), and others such as *Giovanni's Room* (1956) and *Another Country* (1962) were bleak depictions of sexual and racial relationships. He also published numerous essays and wrote plays, notably *Blues for Mr Charlie* (1964).

1 The American ideal, after all, is that everyone should be as much alike as possible.

'The Harlem Ghetto', first publ. in *Commentary* February 1948, repr. in *Notes of a Native Son*, pt 2 (1955)

2 It is only in his music, which Americans are able to admire because a protective sentimentality limits their understanding of it, that the Negro in America has been able to tell his story.

'Many Thousands Gone', first publ. in *Partisan Review* November/December 1951, repr. in ibid. pt 1

3 Any writer, I suppose, feels that the world into which he

was born is nothing less than a conspiracy against the cultivation of his talent.

*Notes of a Native Son*, 'Autobiographical Notes' (1955)

4 Children have never been very good at listening to their elders, but they have never failed to imitate them. They must, they have no other models.

'Fifth Avenue, Uptown: a letter from Harlem', first publ. in *Esquire* July 1960, repr. in *Nobody Knows My Name* (1961)

5 American history is longer, larger, more various, more beautiful, and more terrible than anything anyone has ever said about it.

'A Talk To Teachers', 16 October 1963, publ. in *The Price of the Ticket* (1985)

6 It comes as a great shock around the age of five, six or seven to discover that the flag to which you have pledged allegiance, along with everybody else, has not pledged allegiance to you. It comes as a great shock to see Gary Cooper killing off the Indians and, although you are rooting for Gary Cooper, that the Indians are you.

Speech to Cambridge Union, Cambridge University, 17 February 1965, quoted in *The New York Times* 7 March 1965

7 If they take you in the morning, they will be coming for us that night.

'Open Letter to my Sister, Angela Davis', publ. in the *New York Review of Books* 7 January 1971

8 You know, it's not the world that was my oppressor, because what the world does to you, if the world does it to you long enough and effectively enough, you begin to do to yourself.

In conversation with Nikki Giovanni, London, 4 November 1971, publ. in *A Dialogue* (1973)

9 [Of the police] He may be a very nice man. But I haven't got the time to figure that out. All I know is, he's got a uniform and a gun and I have to relate to him that way. That's the only way to relate to him because one of us may have to die.

ibid.

10 Whereas England may have been doomed to civilize the world, no power under heaven can civilize England.

*The Devil Finds Work*, ch. 2 (1976)

11 The condition that is now called gay was then called queer. The operative word was *faggot* and, later, pussy, but those epithets really had nothing to do with the question of sexual preference: You were being told simply that you had no balls.

'Freaks and the American Ideal of Manhood', first publ. in *Playboy* January 1985, repr. in *The Price of the Ticket*, 'Here Be Dragons' (1985)

## Stanley Baldwin (1867–1947)
BRITISH POLITICIAN AND PRIME MINISTER

First Earl of Bewdley. As Conservative Prime Minister (1923–4, 1924–9 and 1935–7) he led the country through the General Strike of 1926, the Ethiopian crisis of 1935, and the following year the abdication of EDWARD VIII. Fearing lack of public support, he opposed the rearmament of Britain against the rise of HITLER, which precipitated his resignation. Lord Beaverbrook called him a 'well-meaning man of indifferent judgement'. See also LORD CURZON 2 and RUDYARD KIPLING 7.

1 A platitude is simply a truth repeated until people get tired of hearing it.

Speech to House of Commons, 29 May 1924, quoted in the *Observer* 1 June 1924

2 I hate elections, but you have got to have them; they are medicine.

Quoted in the *Observer* 11 October 1931

3 I think it is well also for the man in the street to realize

that there is no power on earth that can protect him from being bombed. Whatever people may tell him, the bomber will always get through. The only defence is in offence, which means that you have to kill more women and children more quickly than the enemy if you want to save yourselves.

Speech to House of Commons, 10 November 1932, publ. in *The Penguin Book of Twentieth-Century Speeches* (ed. Brian MacArthur, 1999). Baldwin's ambiguous speech strengthened the public mood against rearmament.

4  Let us never forget this – since the day of the air the old frontiers are gone. When you think of the defence of England you no longer think of the chalk cliffs of Dover; you think of the Rhine. That is where our frontier lies.

Speech to House of Commons, 30 July 1934, publ. in *Hansard*

5  Do not run up your nose dead against the Pope or the NUM!

Quoted in *The Art of Memory*, 'Iain Macleod' (1982) by Lord [R.A.B.] Butler

## Arthur James Balfour (1848–1930)
BRITISH POLITICIAN AND PRIME MINISTER

First Earl of Balfour. He entered parliament as a Conservative MP in 1874. While Prime Minister (1902–5) he established the Committee of Imperial Defence and initiated the entente cordiale with France. As Foreign Secretary (1916–19) he was responsible for the Balfour Declaration (1917), which promised a Jewish homeland in Palestine.

1  His Majesty's Government view with favour the establishment in Palestine of a national home for the Jewish people, and will use their best endeavours to facilitate the achievement of this object, it being clearly understood that nothing shall be done which may prejudice the civil and religious rights of existing non-Jewish communities in Palestine, or the rights and political status enjoyed by Jews in any other country.

Letter to Lord Rothschild, 2 November 1917, publ. in *The Middle East Conflict: Notes and Documents (1915–1967)*. The document, which became known as the 'Balfour Declaration', represented a commitment of British support for a Jewish national home in Palestine, though the original wording suggested by Chaim Weizmann, on behalf of the Political Committee of the Zionist Organization (which Rothschild represented), was that the government should recognize Palestine as 'the national home of the Jewish people'.

2  The General Strike has taught the working classes more in four days than years of talking could have done.

Speech 7 May 1926, quoted in the *Observer* 14 November 1926. Five days after the speech, the Trades Unions Congress was forced to call off the General Strike, which, though bringing the country to a virtual standstill, was unable to prevent volunteers from manning essential services.

3  Biography should be written by an acute enemy.

Quoted in the *Observer* 30 January 1927

## Hugo Ball (1886–1927)
GERMAN POET

Along with RICHARD HUELSENBECK he was in 1916 the co-founder of Dada in Zurich, where he performed the first 'sound poem' dressed in cardboard tubes and a cape. He later turned to political journalism and gnostic Catholicism. He published his Dada diary *Flight out of Time* in 1927.

1  We should burn all libraries and allow to remain only that which everyone knows by heart. A beautiful age of the legend would then begin.

Journal entry, 9 January 1917, in *Flight out of Time: A Dada Diary* (1927)

2  The symbolic view of things is a consequence of long

absorption in images. Is sign language the real language of Paradise?

Journal entry, 8 April 1917, in ibid.

## J.G. Ballard (b. 1930)
BRITISH AUTHOR

Full name James Graham Ballard. His science fiction typically portrays apocalyptic visions, as in the dystopian *The Drowned World* (1962). His experimental novel *Crash* (1973) was made into a controversial film in 1996, and he became familiar to a mainstream readership with the autobiographical novel *Empire of the Sun* (1984, filmed 1988).

1  A car crash harnesses elements of eroticism, aggression, desire, speed, drama, kinaesthetic factors, the stylizing of motion, consumer goods, status – all these in one event. I myself see the car crash as a tremenduous sexual event really: a liberation of human and machine libido (if there is such a thing).

Interview in *Penthouse* September 1970

2  Everything is becoming science fiction. From the margins of an almost invisible literature has sprung the intact reality of the twentieth century.

'Fictions of Every Kind', publ. in *Books and Bookmen* February 1971. Ballard continued: 'Even the worst science fiction is better . . . than the best conventional fiction. The future is a better key to the present than the past.'

3  The car as we know it is on the way out. To a large extent, I deplore its passing, for as a basically old-fashioned machine, it enshrines a basically old-fashioned idea: freedom. In terms of pollution, noise and human life, the price of that freedom may be high, but perhaps the car, by the very muddle and confusion it causes, may be holding back the remorseless spread of the regimented, electronic society.

'The Car, The Future', publ. in *Drive* autumn 1971

4  Science and technology multiply around us. To an increasing extent they dictate the languages in which we speak and think. Either we use those languages, or we remain mute.

*Crash*, Introduction to French edn (1974)

5  A widespread taste for pornography means that nature is alerting us to some threat of extinction.

*Myths of the Near Future*, 'News from the Sun' (1982)

6  I would sum up my fear about the future in one word: *boring*. And that's my one fear: that everything has happened; nothing exciting or new or interesting is ever going to happen again . . . the future is just going to be a vast, conforming *suburb of the soul*.

Interview, 30 October 1982, publ. in *Re/Search* no. 8/9 1984

7  'Responsible' TV is far more dangerous than the most mindless entertainment. At its worst, American TV merely trivializes the already trivial, while British TV consistently trivializes the serious.

*The Atrocity Exhibition: With Author's Annotations*, 'Love and Napalm: Export USA', annotation (1993, original text published 1970, rev. 1990)

## Whitney Balliet (b. 1926)
US AUTHOR

He was a long-serving jazz critic for the *New Yorker* and published collections of pieces on jazz musicians including *The Sound of Surprise* (1959) and *American Musicians* (1986).

1  The Sound of Surprise.

Title of book on jazz (1959)

2 A critic is a bundle of biases held loosely together by a sense of taste.

*Dinosaurs in the Morning*, Introductory Note (1962)

## Lester Bangs (1948–82)

US ROCK JOURNALIST

A gentle yet acerbic critic of the 1970s, he was the first to popularize the term 'heavy metal' and his magazine *Creem* became the model for punk-rock and heavy-metal fanzines. From 1976 he worked in New York, contributing to *Village Voice*, and in the 1980s published biographies of Blondie and (with Paul Nelson) Rod Stewart.

1 The ultimate sin of any performer is contempt for the audience.

*Village Voice* 29 August 1977

2 At its best New Wave/punk represents a fundamental and age-old Utopian dream: that if you give people the license to be as outrageous as they want in absolutely any fashion they can dream up, *they'll be creative about it*, and do something good besides.

*New Musical Express* 24 December 1977

3 I think that if most guys in America could somehow get their fave-rave poster girl in bed and have total license to do whatever they wanted with this legendary body for one afternoon, at least 75 percent of the guys in the country would elect to beat her up.

Quoted in *Sound Effects: Youth, Leisure and the Politics of Rock*, ch. 10 (1979) by Simon Frith

## Tallulah Bankhead (1903–68)

US ACTRESS

Notorious for her extravagant personality, 'more of an act that an actress' in the words of one critic, she appeared in plays (*The Little Foxes*, 1939), on radio and in films, most famously in HITCHCOCK's *Lifeboat*, 1944. See also LILLIAN HELLMAN 7.

1 There is less in this than meets the eye.

Quoted in *Shouts and Murmurs*, ch. 4 (1922) by Alexander Woollcott. Remark to Woollcott, referring to a revival of Maeterlinck's play *Aglavaine and Selysette*.

2 I'm as pure as the driven slush.

Quoted in the *Saturday Evening Post* 12 April 1947

3 Let's not quibble! I'm the foe of moderation, the champion of excess. If I may lift a line from a die-hard whose identity is lost in the shuffle, 'I'd rather be strongly wrong than weakly right.'

*Tallulah* (1952), ch.4

4 Cocaine habit-forming? Of course not. I ought to know. I've been using it for years.

ibid. This was, she said, the riposte she used to shock people when taking throat-lozenges: apart from on one occasion, she claimed never to have used cocaine 'except medicinally'. However, LILLIAN HELLMAN, writer of *The Little Foxes* in which Bankhead starred, witnessed her habit – eliciting the actress's stock rejoinder – as described in her *Pentimento* (1973).

5 I've tried several varieties of sex. The conventional position makes me claustrophobic and the others give me a stiff neck or lockjaw.

Quoted in *Miss Tallulah Bankhead* (1972) by Lee Israel

## Tony Banks (b. 1943)

BRITISH POLITICIAN

Elected a Labour MP in 1983, he established a reputation as a forthright and lippy left-winger. He won the seat for West Ham in 1997 and became sports minister in TONY BLAIR's new cabinet, a post he resigned in 1999 to act as special envoy for the 2006 World Cup.

1 [On William Hague] They have elected a foetus as party leader. I bet there's a lot of Tory MPs who wish they hadn't voted against abortion now.

Speech at Labour Party Conference, Brighton, 30 September 1997, quoted in the *Daily Telegraph* 2 October 1997

## Nancy Banks-Smith

BRITISH COLUMNIST

She is a TV reviewer for the *Guardian* of many years standing, known for her idiosyncratic critiques and wry digressions.

1 In my experience, if you have to keep the lavatory door shut by extending your left leg, it's modern architecture.

*Guardian* 20 February 1979

## [Imamu] Amiri Baraka (b. 1934)

US POET AND PLAYWRIGHT

Known as LeRoi Jones until 1967, when he converted to Islam. A confrontational writer of verse collections including *The Dead Lecturer* (1964) and plays such as *The Dutchman* (1964), he founded the Black Arts Repertory Theater in Harlem in 1965 and the Muslim Black Community Development and Defense Organization in 1968.

1 Lately, I've become accustomed to the way
The ground opens up and envelops me
Each time I go out to walk the dog.

'Preface to a Twenty Volume Suicide Note', publ. in *Preface to a Twenty Volume Suicide Note* (1961). Opening lines.

2 You can't steal nothing from a white man, he's already stole it, he owes you anything you want, even his life. All the stores will open if you will say the magic words. The magic words are: Up against the wall motherfucker this is a stick-up!

'Black People!', publ. in *Evergreen Review* summer 1967, repr. in *Black Magic* (1969). The poem/manifesto was read out by the judge at Baraka's trial for illegal arms possesion in Newark, July 1967, with the obscenities omitted. Baraka was involved with the anarchist group Up Against the Wall Motherfucker.

3 When I die, the consciousness I carry I will to black people. May they pick me apart and take the useful parts, the sweet meat of my feelings. And leave the bitter bullshit rotten white parts alone.

'leroy', publ. in *Black Magic* (1969)

4 James Brown and Frank Sinatra are two different quantities in the universe. They represent two different experiences of the world.

Interview in *The Americans*, 'Is Democracy a White Man's Word?' (1970) by David Frost

## Lynn Barber (b. 1944)

BRITISH JOURNALIST

A feature writer for the Sunday press and magazines including *Penthouse*, where she was assistant editor 1967–72, she is renowned as a celebrity interviewer. Her collected interviews include *Mostly Men* (1991) and *Demon Barber* (1998). She has also published handbooks on sex.

1 The best interviews – like the best biographies – should sing the strangeness and variety of the human race.

*Independent on Sunday* 24 February 1991

## Brigitte Bardot (b. 1934)

FRENCH ACTRESS

Original name Camille Javal. The archetypal 'sex kitten' was already establishing herself as a movie starlet when, at the age of 18, she married ROGER VADIM, who directed her in *And God Created Woman* (1956). As the publicity of the time declared, 'God Created Woman, but the devil made Bardot.' Starring in a succession of light sex comedies in the 1960s, she later became an ardent supporter of animal rights. See also ROGER VADIM 1.

1 I leave before being left. I decide.
   Quoted in *Newsweek* 5 March 1973

2 I really am a cat transformed into a woman.
   Quoted in *B,b,: The Films of Brigitte Bardot*, 'The BBeginning' (1975) by Tony Crawley

3 If I could do anything about the way people behave towards each other, I would, but since I can't I'll stick to the animals.
   Quoted in *Bardot*, ch. 15 (1984) by Glenys Roberts

4 I am leaving the town [Saint Tropez] to the invaders: increasingly numerous, mediocre, dirty, badly behaved, shameless tourists.
   Quoted in the *International Herald Tribune* 10 Aug. 1989. On moving out of her long-time home.

## Daniel Barenboim (b. 1942)
ARGENTINIAN-BORN ISRAELI PIANIST, CONDUCTOR

He gained his reputation with the English Chamber Orchestra from 1964, going on to be Conductor of the New York Philharmonic Orchestra in 1970, Director of the Chicago Symphony Orchestra in 1991 and the Berlin Staatskapelle in 1992. He specialized as a pianist in Mozart and Beethoven, and as a conductor extended the nineteenth- and twentieth-century repertoire. He was married to the cellist Jacqueline du Pré.

1 Every great work of art has two faces, one toward its own time and one toward the future, toward eternity.
   *International Herald Tribune* 20 January 1989

## Pat Barker (b. 1943)
BRITISH NOVELIST

She gained her reputation with spare and unsentimental novels of working class women in industrial England, such as *Blow Your House Down* (1984), but achieved greater success with the First World War trilogy *Regeneration* (1991), *The Eye in the Door* (1993) and *The Ghost Road* (1995).

1 Poor Siegfried's rebellion hadn't counted for much, though he reminded himself that he couldn't know that. It had been a completely honest action, and such actions are seeds carried on the wind. Nobody can tell where, or in what circumstances, they will bear fruit.
   W. H. R. Rivers, in *Regeneration*, ch. 23 (1991). The army psychologist reflects on SIEGFRIED SASSOON, having discharged him from Craiglockhart War Hospital from which he was to return to the front in the First World War.

2 Even the living were only ghosts in the making.
   Lieutenant Billy Prior, in *The Ghost Road*, pt 1, ch. 3 (1995)

3 First-person narrators can't die, so long as we keep telling the story of our own lives we're safe. Ha bloody fucking Ha.
   Lieutenant Billy Prior, in ibid. pt 2, ch. 7

## Ronnie Barker (b. 1929)
BRITISH COMIC ACTOR

A hugely popular but intensely private figure in British comedy, he is mainly known for his radio and TV appearances as in the sitcom *Porridge* (1974–7) and, with Ronnie Corbett, *The Two Ronnies* (1971–86). His films include *Robin and Marian* (1976) and *Porridge* (1979).

1 The marvellous thing about a joke with a double meaning is that it can only mean one thing.
   *Sauce*, 'Daddie's Sauce' (1977)

## Djuna Barnes (1892–1982)
US AUTHOR, POET AND COLUMNIST

An established figure of literary Paris in the 1920s and 1930s, she published influential works of Modernist fiction including *Ladies Almanack* (1928), a satire of literary lesbians, and her masterpiece, the dark *Nightwood* (1936). She was admired by T.S. ELIOT, who jibed, 'She's always pissing on the parade.' She returned to New York in the 1940s to live as a recluse.

1 After all, it is not where one washes one's neck that counts but where one moistens one's throat.
   'Greenwich Village As It Is', publ. in *Pearson's Magazine* October 1916, repr. in *Djuna Barnes's New York* (1989)

2 The heart of the jealous knows the best and most satisfying love, that of the other's bed, where the rival perfects the lover's imperfections.
   Doctor, in *Nightwood*, ch. 5 (1936)

## Julian Barnes (b. 1946)
BRITISH NOVELIST

He worked as a journalist and lexicographer before winning acclaim for *Metroland* (1981), his first novel, and *Flaubert's Parrot* (1984), an ironic and witty tribute to his acknowledged influence Flaubert. Later works include *A History of the World in 10½ Chapters* (1989) and *Cross Channel* (1996), a collection of short stories.

1 Why does the writing make us chase the writer? Why can't we leave well alone? Why aren't the books enough?
   The narrator (Geoffrey Braithwaite), in *Flaubert's Parrot*, ch. 1 (1984)

2 I don't care much for coincidences. There's something spooky about them: you sense momentarily what it must be like to live in an ordered, God-run universe, with Himself looking over your shoulder and helpfully dragging coarse hints about a cosmic plan.
   ibid. ch. 5. The narrator adds, 'One way of legitimising coincidences, of course, is to call them ironies. That's what smart people do.'

3 Do not imagine that Art is something which is designed to give gentle uplift and self-confidence. Art is not a *brassière*. At least not in the English sense. But do not forget that *brassière* is the French for life-jacket.
   ibid. ch. 10

4 The greatest patriotism is to tell your country when it is behaving dishonourably, foolishly, viciously.
   ibid.

5 The writer must be universal in sympathy and an outcast by nature: only then can he see clearly.
   ibid.

6 Books are where things are explained to you; life is where things aren't. I'm not surprised some people prefer books. Books make sense of life. The only problem is that the lives they make sense of are other people's lives, never your own.
   ibid. ch. 13

7 We must still believe that objective truth is obtainable; or we must believe that it is 99 per cent obtainable; or if we can't believe this we must believe that 43 per cent objective truth is better than 41 per cent. We must do so because if we don't we're lost, we fall into beguiling relativity, we value one liar's version as much as another liar's.
   *History of the World in 10½ Chapters*, 'Parenthesis' (1989)

8 Imagine the organ of recollection as a left-luggage clerk at some thrumming terminus who looks after your picayune possessions until you next need them. Now consider what you're asking him to take care of. And for so little money! And for so little thanks! It's no wonder the counter isn't manned half the time.
   Oliver, in *Talking It Over*, ch. 1 (1991)

9 It's a sort of primitive law of survival – find someone worse off than yourself and beside them you will blossom.
Stuart, in ibid. ch. 2

10 As you go on living with someone, you slowly lose the power to make them happy, while your capacity to hurt them remains undiminished. And vice versa, of course.
Mme Wyatt, in ibid. ch. 15

11 Love is only what people agree exists, what they agree to put a notional value on. Nowadays it's prized as a commodity by almost everyone. Only not by me. If you ask me, I think love is trading artificially high. One of these days the bottom is going to fall out of love.
Stuart, in ibid. ch. 16

12 We have moved into an era when 'character' is a misleading concept. Character has been replaced by ego, and the exercise of authority as a reflection of character has been replaced by the psychopathic retention of power by all possible means and in mockery of all implausibilities.
Solinsky, in *Porcupine* (1992)

13 If you're an old geezer in his rocker on the porch, you don't play basketball with kids. Old geezers don't jump. You sit and make a virtue of what you have. And what you also do is this; you make the kids think that anyone, *anyone* can jump, but it takes a wise old buzzard to know how to sit there and rock.
Jerry, in *England, England*, pt 1, 'Dream a Little' (1998)

14 Women have traditionally accommodated themselves to men's needs. Men's needs being, of course, double. You put us on a pedestal in order to look up our skirts.
Martha, in ibid. 'Others May Like'

15 I only said the English weren't famous for sex, that's all. Like the Boat Race, in out, in out, then everyone collapsed over their oars.
Martha, in ibid. 'Do You Think?'

16 R–eality is r–ather like a r–abbit, if you'll forgive the aphorism. The great public . . . want reality to be a pet bunny. They want it to lollop along and thump its foot picturesquely in its home-made hutch and eat lettuce out of their hand. If you gave them the real thing, something wild that bit, and, if you'll pardon me, shat, they wouldn't know what to do with it. Except strangle it and cook it.
Dr Max, in ibid. pt 2, 'Did you make that story up?'

## Ann Barr (b. 1929) and
## Peter York (b. 1950)
BRITISH JOURNALISTS

Ann Barr was features editor on *Harper's and Queen* and women's editor of the *Observer*. She co-authored the 1980s bestseller *The Sloane Ranger Handbook* (1982) with PETER YORK, a cultural commentator and so-called 'style guru'.

1 Sloane minds are undeveloped but intuitive, wild places where they go out to bag an idea or see how things are going. They do *not* like theory, unless it produces a joke.
*The Official Sloane Ranger Handbook*, 'Sloane Language' (1982). See also PETER YORK 1.

## Roseanne Barr (b. 1952)
US STAND-UP COMEDIENNE AND ACTRESS

Originally an actress, she is famous for her outspoken personality and appearance in the ABC television series *Roseanne* (1988–97) and *The Roseanne Show* (from 1998). She has also appeared in films such as *Unzipped* (1995).

1 I hate the word housewife; I don't like the word homemaker either. I want to be called – domestic goddess.
*Roseanne* (TV sitcom), quoted in *Funny Business*, 'Roseanne Barr' (1992) by David Housham and John Frank-Keyes

2 You may marry the man of your dreams, ladies, but 14 years later you're married to a couch that burps.
ibid.

## (Sir) J.M. Barrie (1860–1937)
BRITISH PLAYWRIGHT AND NOVELIST

Full name James Matthew Barrie. Described by MRS PATRICK CAMPBELL as 'a little child whom the Gods have whispered to', he continually returned to the themes of childhood and disenchantment with the adult world. He achieved success with his plays *Quality Street* (1901) and *The Admirable Crichton* (1902), but is best remembered for *Peter Pan* (1904).

1 Someone said that God gave us memory so that we might have roses in December.
Rectorial address at St Andrew's University, 3 May 1922, publ. in *Courage* (1922)

2 Never ascribe to an opponent motives meaner than your own.
ibid.

3 We are all failures – at least, all the best of us are.
ibid.

4 You must have been warned against letting the golden hours slip by. Yes, but some of them are golden only because we let them slip.
ibid.

## Ethel Barrymore (1897–1959)
US ACTRESS

As the sister of actors John and Lionel Barrymore she was one of the 'Fabulous Barrymores'. Her stage roles in *The Second Mrs Tanqueray* (1924) and *The Corn is Green* (1942) helped to establish her as 'the first lady of the American theater', and she won an Oscar for her part in the film *None But the Lonely Heart* (1944).

1 For an actress to be a success, she must have the face of Venus, the brains of a Minerva, the grace of Terpsichore, the memory of a Macaulay, the figure of Juno, and the hide of a rhinoceros.
Quoted in *The Theatre in the Fifties* (1953) by George Jean Nathan

2 I never let them [audiences] cough. They wouldn't dare.
*New York Post* 7 June 1956

## Don Barthelme (1931–89)
US AUTHOR

He called cutting up and pasting together pictures his 'secret vice', and this collage effect is evident in his minimalist short stories, as collected in *Come Back, Dr Caligari* (1964) and *City Life* (1970), and his novels, for example *Snow White* (1967).

1 The distinction between children and adults, while probably useful for some purposes, is at bottom a specious one, I feel. There are only individual egos, crazy for love.
The narrator (Joseph), in 'Me And Miss Mandible', first publ. in *Come Back, Dr Caligari* (1964)

## Roland Barthes (1915–80)
FRENCH SEMIOLOGIST

He was one of France's leading post-war critics whose writings on literature and semiotics demystified the language of mass culture and helped to establish structuralism and the New Criticism. *Mythologies* (1957), *Death of the Author* (1968) and *S/Z* (1970) number among his most influential publications.

1 What I claim is to live to the full the contradiction of my time, which may well make sarcasm the condition of truth.
*Mythologies*, Preface (1957, transl. 1972)

2 What the public wants is the image of passion, not passion itself.
ibid. 'The World of Wrestling'

3 The face of Garbo is an Idea, that of Hepburn an Event.
ibid. 'The Face of Garbo'

4 Through the mythology of Einstein, the world blissfully regained the image of knowledge reduced to a formula.
ibid. 'The Brain of Einstein'

5 I think that cars today are almost the exact equivalent of the great Gothic cathedrals: I mean the supreme creation of an era, conceived with passion by unknown artists, and consumed in image if not in usage by a whole population which appropriates them as a purely magical object.
ibid. 'The New Citroën'

6 Myth is neither a lie nor a confession: it is an inflexion.
ibid. 'Myth Today: Reading and Deciphering Myth'

7 Once the Author is removed, the claim to decipher a text becomes quite futile. To give a text an Author is to impose a limit on that text, to furnish it with a final signifier, to close the writing.
*Image-Music-Text*, 'The Death of the Author' (1966, transl. 1978)

8 There is only one way left to escape the alienation of present day society: *to retreat ahead of it.*
*The Pleasure of the Text*, 'Modern' (1975)

9 The bastard form of mass culture is humiliated repetition . . . always new books, new programmes, new films, news items, but always the same meaning.
ibid.

10 Language is legislation, speech is its code. We do not see the power which is in speech because we forget that all speech is a classification, and that all classifications are oppressive.
Inaugural lecture, Collège de France, 7 January 1977, publ. in *Leçon* (1978), repr. in *Barthes: Selected Writings* (ed. Susan Sontag, 1982)

11 Literature is *without proofs.* By which it must be understood that it cannot prove, not only *what* it says, but even that it is worth the trouble of saying it.
'Deliberation', first publ. in *Tel Quel* winter 1979, repr. in ibid.

# Bernard Baruch (1870–1965)
US FINANCIER

He amassed a fortune by his thirties, and through his friendship with President WOODROW WILSON was instrumental in drafting the economic sections of the Treaty of Versailles (1919). An adviser to President FRANKLIN D. ROOSEVELT and WINSTON CHURCHILL during the Second World War, he later served on the UN Atomic Energy Commission (1946–51).

1 Let us not be deceived – we are today in the midst of a cold war. Our enemies are to be found abroad and at home.
Speech to South Carolina Legislature, 16 April 1947, quoted in *The New York Times* 17 April 1947. A year later Baruch told the Senate War Investigating Committee, 'We are in the midst of a cold war which is getting warmer.' Baruch claimed the expression had been suggested to him by his speechwriter, the former editor of the *New York World* Herbert Bayard Swope.

2 To me, old age is always fifteen years older than I am.
Quoted in the *Observer* 21 August 1955

3 A political leader must keep looking over his shoulder all the time to see if the boys are still there. If they aren't still there, he's no longer a political leader.
Quoted in obituary, *The New York Times* 21 June 1965

# Jacques Barzun (b. 1907)
US EDUCATOR AND AUTHOR

Influential in the development of higher education in America, he advocated a broad approach rather than specialization. He published widely on the Humanities, including *Pleasures of Music* (1951), *The House of the Intellect* (1959), *Science: The Glorious Entertainment* (1964) and *The Use and Abuse of Art* (1974).

1 Whoever wants to know the heart and mind of America had better learn baseball, the rules and realities of the game.
*God's Country and Mine*, ch. 8 (1954)

2 Teaching is not a lost art, but the regard for it is a lost tradition.
*Newsweek* 5 December 1955

# Augusto Roa Bastos (b. 1917)
PARAGUAYAN NOVELIST

From 1947–70 he lived in exile in Buenos Aires. His works, including the novel *Son of Man* (1960) and his masterpiece *I the Supreme* (1974), deal largely with Paraguayan history.

1 The things that have come into being change continually. The man with a good memory remembers nothing because he forgets nothing.
*I The Supreme* (1974, transl. 1986)

2 Anyone who attempts to relate his life loses himself in the immediate. One can only speak of another.
ibid.

# H.E. Bates (1905–74)
BRITISH WRITER

Full name Herbert Ernest Bates. A master of the short story and prolific novelist, he wrote of rural England, as in *The Darling Buds of May* (1958, televised 1980s). He also wrote *Fair Stood the Wind for France* (1944), a story of a bomber crew in the Second World War.

1 Perfick!
Pop Larkin, in *A Breath of French Air*, ch. 1 (1959)

# Kathy Bates (b. 1948)
US ACTRESS

On the stage she made an impact with *Frankie and Johnny in the Clair de Lune* (1987), while her films have included *Misery* (1990), for which she won an Oscar for her part as the disturbed fan, and *Diabolique* (1996).

1 I'm your number-one fan.
Annie Wilkes (Kathy Bates), in *Misery* (film, screenplay by William Goldman based on 1987 short story by Stephen King, directed and co-produced by Rob Reiner, 1990)

# Georges Bataille (1897–1962)
FRENCH NOVELIST AND CRITIC

He founded the influential journal *Critique* in 1946 and remained its editor until his death. His themes are atheism, mysticism, and freedom through excess rather than self-denial. His works include *The Birth of Art* (1955), *Death and Sensuality* (1957) and *Eroticism* (1957). He wrote in English under the name of Lord Auch.

1 Intellectual despair results in neither weakness nor dreams, but in violence. . . . It is only a matter of knowing how to give vent to one's rage; whether one only wants to wander like madmen around prisons, or whether one wants to overturn them.
'The "Lugubrious Game"', first publ. in *Documents* December 1929, repr. in *Visions of Excess: Selected Writings 1927–1939* (ed. Allan Stoekl, 1985)

2 Eroticism is assenting to life even in death.
*Eroticism*, Introduction (1957)

3 Beauty is desired in order that it may be befouled; not for

its own sake, but for the joy brought by the certainty of profaning it.

ibid. ch. 13

4 I believe that truth has only one face: that of a violent contradiction.

*The Deadman*, Preface (1967)

## Jean Baudrillard (b. 1929)

FRENCH SEMIOLOGIST

Known as the high priest of postmodernism, his theories on the consumer society, media, art and metaphysics are laid out in *In the Shadow of Silent Majorities* (1978) and *Simulations and Simulacra* (1981) among other titles. *The New York Times* called him 'the sharp-shooting Lone Ranger of the post-Marxist left'.

1 Driving is a spectacular form of amnesia. Everything is to be discovered, everything to be obliterated.

*America*, 'Vanishing Point'

2 What you have to do is enter the fiction of America, enter America as fiction. It is, indeed, on this fictive basis that it dominates the world.

ibid. 'Astral America' (1986)

3 It is always the same: once you are liberated, you are forced to ask who you are.

ibid.

4 The skylines lit up at dead of night, the air-conditioning systems cooling empty hotels in the desert and artificial light in the middle of the day all have something both demented and admirable about them. The mindless luxury of a rich civilization, and yet of a civilization perhaps as scared to see the lights go out as was the hunter in his primitive night.

ibid. Referring to the US, which Baudrillard called 'deep down . . . the *only remaining primitive society*'.

5 The Yuppies are not defectors from revolt, they are a new race, assured, amnestied, exculpated, moving with ease in the world of performance, mentally indifferent to any objective other than that of change and advertising.

ibid. 'The End of US Power?'

6 With the truth, you need to get rid of it as soon as possible and pass it on to someone else. As with illness, this is the only way to be cured of it. The person who keeps truth in his hands has lost.

*Cool Memories*, ch. 1 (1987)

7 The sad thing about artificial intelligence is that it lacks artifice and therefore intelligence.

ibid. ch. 4

8 Information can tell us everything. It has all the answers. But they are answers to questions we have not asked, and which doubtless don't even arise.

ibid. ch. 5

## Vicki Baum (1888–1960)

AUSTRIAN-BORN US NOVELIST

Originally named Vicki Hedvig. Her principal achievement was the novel *Grand Hotel* (1930), whose success as a play in New York (1931) allowed her to emigrate to America. It was later filmed with GRETA GARBO in the main role. She published many later novels, all of them first written in German.

1 The events that happen to people in a big hotel do not constitute entire human destinies, complete and rounded off. They are fragments merely, scraps, pieces. The people behind its doors may signify much or little. They may be rising or falling in the scale of life. Prosperity and disaster may be parted by no more than the thickness of a wall. The revolving door twirls around, and what passes between arrival and departure is nothing complete in itself.

*Grand Hotel* (1930)

2 Marriage always demands the greatest understanding of the art of insincerity possible between two human beings.

*Results of an Accident* (1932)

## Stephen Bayley (b. 1951)

BRITISH DESIGN CRITIC

Founder and Chief Executive (1981–90) of the Design Museum, he left his job as Creative Director of the Millennium Dome in 1999 after political disagreements. He is a regular columnist and cultural commentator, and author of *Sex, Drink and Fast Cars* (1986) and *Taste: The Secret Meaning of Things* (1991) among other titles.

1 Where *do* architects and designers get their ideas? The answer, of course, is mainly from other architects and designers, so is it mere casuistry to distinguish between tradition and plagiarism?

*Commerce and Culture*, ch. 3 (1989)

2 Everyone has taste, yet it is more of a taboo subject than sex or money. The reason for this is simple: claims about your attitudes to or achievements in the carnal and financial arenas can be disputed only by your lover and your financial advisers, whereas by making statements about your taste you expose body and soul to terrible scrutiny. Taste is a merciless betrayer of social and cultural attitudes. Thus, while anybody will tell you as much (and perhaps more than) you want to know about their triumphs in bed and at the bank, it is taste that gets people's nerves tingling.

*Taste*, pt 1, 'Taste: The Story of an Idea' (1991)

3 Viewed holistically, interior design is a travesty of the architectural process and a frightening condemnation of the credulity, helplessness and gullibility of the most formidable consumers – the rich.

ibid. pt 2, 'Interiors: Vacuums of Taste'

4 Alas, in a culture that encourages feeble-minded political correctness, great monuments and great works of art are not to be expected.

*Independent* 17 January 1998. Referring to the influence of focus groups on the Millennium Dome project.

5 Design is the great adventure of the twentieth century; it's led . . . to the aestheticization of the everyday object, to the democratization of luxury. Today, you, me and even young Peter Mandelson can buy a disposable Bic razor for next to nothing and get a better shave than ever Augustus Caesar or the Sun King could.

Quoted in the *Guardian* 21 November 1998

## André Bazin (1918–58)

FRENCH FILM CRITIC

As a proponent of the *auteur* theory of film-making and co-founder in 1951 of Europe's most influential film periodical, *Les Cahiers du cinéma*, he was called the 'spiritual father of the New Wave'. Four volumes of his writings were published after his death, condensed into one volume in English, *What is Cinema?* (1967).

1 The cinema gives us a substitute world which fits our desires.

Quoted in *The New Wave*, ch. 7 (1976) by James Monaco. The words appear in the closing credits of Jean-Luc Godard's film *Le Mépris* (1963).

## BBC (British Broadcasting Corporation)

1 Nation shall speak peace unto nation.

Motto from 1927. Devised by Montague John Rendall (1862–1950), a schoolmaster and member of the first BBC Board of Governors, it was probably inspired by Isaiah 2:4, 'They shall beat their swords into plowshares, and their spears into pruninghooks: nation shall not lift up sword against nation, neither shall they learn war any more' (also Micah 4:3, Joel 3:10).

## Warren Beatty (b. 1937)
US SCREEN ACTOR AND FILM-MAKER

Originally Henry Warren Beaty. Steeped in Hollywood culture and famed for his powers of seduction, the younger brother of SHIRLEY MACLAINE has worked in many different roles in the movie business. His greatest successes have been *Bonnie and Clyde* (1967) and *Reds* (1981), both of which he produced and starred in; he also directed the second of these, for which he won an Oscar.

1 I don't think there's anything to be admired in lying, cheating or philandering. But there might be something to be admired in not burning people at the stake because they have those weaknesses.
*Observer* 7 February 1999. Referring to 'Monica-gate', the revelations about President CLINTON's adultery.

## Ernest Becker (1924–74)
US PSYCHOLOGIST AND CULTURAL ANTHROPOLOGIST

His premise was that mortality, not sexuality as propounded by Freud, was the basis of man's primary repression. He published *The Revolution in Psychiatry* (1964) and won a Pulitzer Prize for *The Denial of Death* (1973).

1 When we understand that man is the only animal who must *create* meaning, who must open a wedge into neutral nature, we already understand the essence of love. Love is the problem of an animal who must *find* life, *create* a dialogue with nature in order to experience his own being.
*The Structure of Evil*, pt 2, ch. 9, 'A Brief Ontology of Love' (1968)

## Samuel Beckett (1906–89)
IRISH PLAYWRIGHT AND NOVELIST

A major influence on absurdist and postmodern literature, he presented a simultaneously comic and bleakly pessimistic portrayal of the human condition, as in the plays *Waiting for Godot* (1953) and *Endgame* (1957). From 1932 he lived mainly in Paris, and composed most of his later works in both French and English. He won the Nobel Prize for Literature in 1969. See also JAMES FENTON 3.

1 I shall state silences more competently than ever a better man spangled the butterflies of vertigo.
Belacqua, in *Dream of Fair to Middling Women* (written 1932, publ. 1992)

2 Nothing to be done.
Estragon, in *Waiting for Godot*, act 1 (1952). The opening words are repeated in the play.

3 There's man all over for you, blaming on his boots the fault of his feet.
Vladimir, in ibid.

4 Estragon: Let's go.
Vladimir: We can't.
Estragon: Why not?
Vladimir: We're waiting for Godot.
ibid. The exchange is repeated several times during the play.

5 The tears of the world are a constant quality. For each one who begins to weep, somewhere else another stops. The same is true of the laugh.
Pozzo, in ibid.

6 Let us not then speak ill of our generation, it is not any unhappier than its predecessors. Let us not speak well of it either. Let us not speak of it at all.
ibid.

7 Nothing happens, nobody comes, nobody goes, it's awful!
Estragon, in ibid.

8 Don't touch me! Don't question me! Don't speak to me! Stay with me!
ibid. act 2

9 We always find something, eh Didi, to give us the impression we exist?
ibid.

10 We all are born mad. Some remain so.
ibid.

11 But we breathe, we change! We lose our hair, our teeth! Our bloom! Our ideals!
Hamm, in *Endgame* (1957)

12 Nothing is funnier than unhappiness, I grant you that. . . . Yes, yes, it's the most comical thing in the world. And we laugh, we laugh, with a will, in the beginning. But it's always the same thing. Yes, it's like the funny story we have heard too often, we still find it funny, but we don't laugh any more.
Nell, in ibid.

13 The bastard! He doesn't exist!
Hamm, after attempting to pray, in ibid. Clov replies, 'Not yet.'

14 Let me go to hell, that's all I ask, and go on cursing them there, and them look down and hear me, that might take some of the shine off their bliss.
The narrator speaking of his parents, in *From an Abandoned Work* (1958), repr. in *Six Residua* (1978)

15 Just under the surface I shall be, all together at first, then separate and drift, through all the earth and perhaps in the end through a cliff into the sea, something of me. A ton of worms in an acre, that is a wonderful thought, a ton of worms, I believe it.
ibid.

16 To find a form that accommodates the mess, that is the task of the artist now.
Conversation with Tom Driver in 1961, quoted in *Samuel Beckett, a Biography*, ch. 21 (1978) by Deirdre Bair

17 What do I know of man's destiny? I could tell you more about radishes.
'Enough', first publ. in *No's Knife* (1967), repr. in *Six Residua* (1978)

18 Personally I have no bone to pick with graveyards, I take the air there willingly, perhaps more willingly than elsewhere, when take the air I must.
*First Love* (1970)

19 I couldn't have done it otherwise. Gone on, I mean. I could not have gone through the awful wretched mess of life without having left a stain upon the silence.
Quoted in *Samuel Beckett, a Biography*, ch. 26 (1978) by Deirdre Bair. Variations of this remark were made on different occasions.

20 Birth was the death of him.
'A Piece of Monologue', publ. in *Three Occasional Pieces* (1982)

21 Ever tried. Ever failed. No matter. Try again. Fail again. Fail better.
*Worstward Ho* (1983)

22 Make sense who may. I switch off.
Bam, in *What Where* (1984)

## Sybille Bedford (b. 1911)
BRITISH AUTHOR

Born into the German aristocracy, she drew on her observations of the upper classes to produce autobiographical novels such as *A Legacy* (1956), a biography of ALDOUS HUXLEY (1973–4), and books on travel and legal trials.

1 A part, a large part, of travelling is an engagement of the ego v. the world. . . . The world is hydra headed, as old as

the rocks and as changing as the sea, enmeshed inextricably in its ways. The ego wants to arrive at places safely and on time.

'The Quality of Travel', first publ. in *Esquire* November 1961, repr. in *As It Was* (1990)

## (Sir) Thomas Beecham (1879–1961)

BRITISH CONDUCTOR

A leading conductor of his time, he introduced Diaghilev's Ballets Russes to London (1911) and founded the Royal Philharmonic Orchestra (1947). He was famous for his 'Lollipop' encores as well as his forthright pronouncements. 'I am not the greatest conductor in this country,' he asserted. 'On the other hand I'm better than any other damned foreigner.' Sir John Barbirolli remarked that he 'conducted like a dancing dervish'.

1 All the arts in America are a gigantic racket run by unscrupulous men for unhealthy women.

Quoted in the *Observer* 5 May 1946

2 Great music is that which penetrates the ear with facility and leaves the memory with difficulty. Magical music never leaves the memory.

Speech, c. 1950, quoted in the *Sunday Times* 16 September 1962

3 Composers should write tunes the chauffeurs and errand boys can whistle.

Quoted in *The New York Times* 9 March 1961

4 The English may not like music, but they absolutely love the noise it makes.

Quoted in the *New York Herald Tribune* 9 March 1961

5 Like two skeletons copulating on a corrugated tin roof.

Quoted in *Beecham Stories* (1978) by Harold Atkins and Archie Newman. Referring to the sound of the harpsichord. Another version likens it to 'a bird-cage played with toasting forks'.

6 Madam, you have between your legs an instrument capable of giving pleasure to thousands – and all you can do is scratch it.

Attributed remark to a cellist. Also quoted '. . . the most sensitive instrument known to man . . .'

## Max Beerbohm (1872–1956)

BRITISH ESSAYIST AND CARICATURIST

He succeeded GEORGE BERNARD SHAW as drama critic of the *Saturday Review*. The author of numerous witty collections of essays and caricatures, he is best remembered for his one novel *Zuleika Dobson* (1911), a parody of Oxford life. Shaw called him 'the incomparable Max', but VITA SACKVILLE-WEST remembered him as a 'shallow, affected, self-conscious fribble'.

1 One might well say that mankind is divisible into two great classes: hosts and guests.

'Hosts and Guests', essay written 1918, repr. in *And Even Now* (1920)

2 To say that a man is vain means merely that he is pleased with the effect he produces on other people. A conceited man is satisfied with the effect he produces on himself.

'Quia Imperfectum', ibid.

3 It seems to be a law of nature that no man, unless he has some obvious physical deformity, ever is loth to sit for his portrait.

ibid.

## Brendan Behan (1923–64)

IRISH PLAYWRIGHT

A supporter of Irish nationalism from an early age, he began writing while in prison, an experience incorporated in his first play, *The Quare Fellow* (1954, filmed 1962). His heavy drinking limited his creative output, though his play *The Hostage* (1958) and autobiographical novel *Borstal Boy* (1958) were acclaimed.

1 He was born an Englishman and remained one for years.

Pat, in *The Hostage*, act 1 (1958). Referring to Monsewer, who later 'found out he was an Irishman'.

2 Pat: He was an Anglo-Irishman.
Meg: In the blessed name of God, what's that?
Pat: A Protestant with a horse.

ibid. Referring to Monsewer.

3 When I came back to Dublin, I was court-martialled in my absence, and sentenced to death in my absence, so I said they could shoot me in my absence.

Pat, on his experiences in the IRA., in ibid.

4 All publicity is good, except an obituary notice.

Quoted in the *Sunday Express* 5 January 1964

5 I am a daylight atheist.

Quoted by Rae Jeffs, publicist and assistant to Behan, in *Sacred Monsters*, 'Rousting in Dublin' (1988) by Daniel Farson

6 One drink is too many for me and a thousand not enough.

ibid.

## Harry Belafonte (b. 1927)

US SINGER AND CIVIL RIGHTS ACTIVIST

Known as the 'King of Calypso' in the late 1950s, he had hits with 'Banana Boat Song' (1956) and 'Mary's Boy Child' (1957), which was the first single to sell a million copies in Britain. Committed to the advancement of black culture, he played a central part in organizing the USA for Africa charity recording 'We Are the World' (1985).

1 You can cage the singer but not the song.

*International Herald Tribune* 3 October 1988. Referring to the suppression of the arts in South Africa.

## Gertrude Bell (1868–1926)

BRITISH ARCHAEOLOGIST AND DIPLOMAT

Her explorations in Palestine and the Syrian desert on the eve of the First World War led to her appointment to the Mesopotamia Expeditionary Force in Basra and Baghdad, where she played a crucial role during and after the war. While Oriental Secretary to the British High Commission there, she continued her archaeological research and contributed to the inception of the modern state of Iraq.

1 When you have drunk the milk of the naga [mother camel] over the camp fire of Abu Tayyi you are baptized of the desert and there is no other salvation for you.

Letter to her father, Hugh Bell, 4 February 1914, publ. in *The Letters of Gertrude Bell*, vol. 1 (ed. Lady Florence Bell, 1927)

2 When people talk of our muddling through it throws me into a passion. Muddle through! why yes so we do – wading through blood and tears that need never have been shed.

Letter to her stepmother, Florence Bell, 27 April 1916, publ. in ibid. Referring to 'the co-ordinating of Arab politics and the creation of an Arabian policy', which Bell believed had been poorly managed by the War Office.

3 The real difficulty under which we labour here is that we don't know, and I suppose can't know till the end of the war, exactly what we intend to do in this country. You are continually confronted with that uncertainty. Can you persuade people to take your side when you are not sure in the end whether you'll be there to take theirs?

Letter to Hugh and Florence Bell, 15 July 1916, publ. in ibid. Speaking of Iraq, from which British forces had expelled the Ottoman administration during the First World War. In 1920 the country was placed under a League of Nations mandate to be administered by the British, which continued until 1932.

4 It is almost impossible to believe that a few years ago the human race was more or less governed by reason and considered consequences, before it did things. . . . At the

back of my mind I have a feeling that we people of the war can never return to complete sanity. The shock has been too great; we're unbalanced.

Letter to her father, 16 January 1923, publ. in ibid. vol. 2. Speaking of the excavation at Niffar (ancient Nippur): 'You see in section age after age of civilization extending over a period of three or four thousand years. It's amazing and rather horrible to be brought face to face with millenniums of human effort and then to consider what a mess we've made of it.'

## Martin Bell (b. 1938)

BRITISH JOURNALIST AND POLITICIAN

Before he was elected Independent MP for Tatton in 1997, he was a correspondent for the BBC and reported on the Gulf War (1990– 91). He was Journalist of the Year in 1992.

1 I am not a saint. I never claimed to be a saint. My suits are not white, they're off-white.

*Independent* 24 May 1997. Said after his election; during and after the campaign Bell continued to don the white suits he previously wore while reporting for television as a foreign correspondent.

## (Sir) Tim Bell (b. 1941)

BRITISH ADVERTISING EXECUTIVE

As a specialist in public relations, he was the original 'spin doctor' and midwife of the general election victory by MARGARET THATCHER in 1979, when he was the Managing Director at SAATCHI AND SAATCHI, the Conservative Party's publicity agency.

1 I'd rather be called a spin doctor than a hidden persuader. Actually I rather like the term. After all, doctors are qualified professionals, and putting the right spin on things is exactly what we do.

*PR Week* 13 October 1995. *The Hidden Persuaders* (1973) was a book by Vance Packard about the manipulative methods of the advertising industry.

2 Don't write a press release when a good leak will do.

Remark at Marketing Society lunch, 8 December 1995, quoted in *Campaign* 5 January 1996. Bell added, 'The truth is that a strong story placed in the newspaper, picked up by everybody else will actually have more impact than an advertising campaign.'

## Hilaire Belloc (1870–1953)

BRITISH AUTHOR

A devout Roman Catholic, he was the author of travel books, historical studies and satirical novels, though is probably best known for his children's nonsense verse *Cautionary Tales* (1907). He was a lifelong friend of G.K. CHESTERTON, who illustrated his books, the pair said to be 'two buttocks of one bum'.

1 It is sometimes necessary to lie damnably in the interests of the nation.

Letter to G.K. Chesterton, 12 December 1917, quoted in *Life of Hilaire Belloc* (1957), ch. 16, by Robert Speaight. Belloc was a zealous propagandist during the First World War.

2 When I am dead, I hope it may be said:
'His sins were scarlet, but his books were read.'

'On His Books', publ. in *Sonnets and Verse* (1923). The reference is to Isaiah 1:18: 'Though your sins be as scarlet, they shall be as white as snow.'

3 The Devil, having nothing else to do,
Went off to tempt My Lady Poltagrue.
My Lady, tempted by a private whim,
To his extreme annoyance, tempted him.

'On Lady Poltagrue', publ. in ibid.

4 I'm tired of Love; I'm still more tired of Rhyme.
But Money gives me pleasure all the time.

'Fatigue', publ. in ibid.

5 Do you remember an Inn,

Miranda?
Do you remember an Inn?
And the tedding and the spreading
Of the straw for a bedding,
And the fleas that tease in the High Pyrenees
And the wine that tasted of the tar?

'Tarantella', publ. in *Sonnets and Verse* (1923). Opening lines.

6 Strong brother in God and last companion, Wine.

'Heroic Poem upon Wine', publ. in *Short Talks with the Dead* (1926)

7 Like many of the Upper Class
He liked the Sound of Broken Glass.

'About John', publ. in *New Cautionary Tales* (1930)

8 Pale Ebenezer thought it wrong to fight,
But Roaring Bill (who killed him) thought it right.

'The Pacifist', publ. in *Sonnets and Verse* (2nd edn, 1938)

9 Believing Truth is staring at the sun
Which but destroys the power that could perceive.
So naught of our poor selves can be at one
With burning Truth, nor utterly believe.

'De Fide: To Lady Diana Cooper', no. 2, publ. in ibid.

## Saul Bellow (b. 1915)

CANADIAN-BORN US NOVELIST

A leading figure in post-Second World War American fiction, winner of a Nobel Prize in 1976, he typically set his novels and short stories in Chicago with Jewish intellectuals as protagonists. Notable works are *Herzog* (1964) and *Humboldt's Gift* (1975), which won the Pulitzer Prize in 1976.

1 Everybody knows there is no fineness or accuracy of suppression; if you hold down one thing, you hold down the adjoining.

*The Adventures of Augie March*, ch. 1 (1953)

2 As for types like my own, obscurely motivated by the conviction that our existence was worthless if we didn't make a turning point of it, we were assigned to the humanities, to poetry, philosophy, painting – the nursery games of humankind, which had to be left behind when the age of science began. The humanities would be called upon to choose a wallpaper for the crypt, as the end drew near.

*The Adventures of Augie March*, ch. 6 (1953)

3 I think that New York is not the cultural centre of America, but the business and administrative centre of American culture.

BBC radio interview, publ. in the *Listener* 22 May 1969

4 There are evils . . . that have the ability to survive identification and go on for ever . . . money, for instance, or war.

Albert Corde, in *The Dean's December*, ch. 13 (1982)

5 Psycho-analysis pretends to investigate the Unconscious. The Unconscious by definition is what you are not conscious of. But the Analysts already know what's in it – they should, because they put it all in beforehand.

ibid. ch. 18

6 In the greatest confusion there is still an open channel to the soul. It may be difficult to find because by midlife it is overgrown, and some of the wildest thickets that surround it grow out of what we describe as our education. But the channel is always there, and it is our business to keep it open, to have access to the deepest part of ourselves.

*The Closing of the American Mind*, Foreword (1987) by Allan Bloom

7 There were two varieties of truth, one symbolized by the Tree of Knowledge, the other by the Tree of Life, one the truth of striving and the other the truth of receptivity. Knowledge divorced from life equals sickness.

*More Die of Heartbreak*, ch. 1 (1987)

8 If you think that historical forces are sending everybody straight to hell you can either go resignedly with the procession or hold out, and hold out not from pride or other personal motives, but from admiration and love for human abilities and powers to which, without exaggeration, the words 'miracle' and 'sublimity' can be applied.

ibid. ch. 2

9 Everything has to be tried out. Funnily enough, the same mind that takes in 'Dallas' or rap music is also accessible to Homer and Shakespeare.

It All Adds Up, 'Mozart: an Overture' (1994)

10 Wedding invitations now are apt to bring to mind divorce statistics, sexual instability, reflections on the sexual revolution and on venereal disease, on the effects of herpes and AIDS on marital infidelity. . . . Your contemporary wedding guest has been transported by modern forces of malign magic into a sphere of distraction where instead of hearing village musicians he is blasted by a great noise – the modern noise.

ibid. 'The Distracted Public'

11 Human character is smaller now, people don't have durable passions; they've replaced passions with excitement. But this won't give you love as strong as death.

Quoted in the Guardian 10 September 1997

## John Belushi (1949–82)

US COMEDIAN, SINGER AND ACTOR

An anti-Establishment comic who rose to fame with NBC's *Saturday Night Live*, he reached an international audience as the overweight slob Bluto in *National Lampoon's Animal House* (1978), and attained cult status with another film, *The Blues Brothers* (1980). He died from a drugs overdose.

1 It's all false pressure; you put the heat on yourself, you get it from the networks and record companies and movie studios, and then you put more pressure on yourself to make everything that much harder because work is no longer challenging. You say, 'Well, I'll get all screwed up and then it'll be a real challenge again.' So stupid – I've often wondered why people do these things. You're so much happier if you don't, but I guess happiness is not a state you want to be in all the time.

Interview in *Cosmopolitan* December 1981

2 In your twenties, you feel like you're indestructible, that nothing can kill you and you laugh at death. You go on and stay up for days and do as many things as you can and then, in your thirties, you think, well, maybe I'll be around here a little longer, so I'm going to maybe take better care of myself.

Interview in *Rolling Stone* 21 January 1982. Belushi died of an overdose of cocaine and heroin two months later.

3 I give so much pleasure to so many people. Why can I not get some pleasure for myself? Why do I have to stop?

Quoted in *Wired: The Short Life and Fast Times of John Belushi*, pt 1, ch. 7 (1984) by Bob Woodward. Referring to his drugs addiction.

## Robert Benchley (1889–1945)

US HUMOROUS WRITER

A drama critic, sketchwriter and editor for *Vanity Fair* and the *New Yorker*, among other publications, he was a founder member of the Algonquin Round Table, a New York dinner club of literati and wits. He also wrote and appeared in short films, notably *How to Sleep* (1935), which won him an Academy Award. See also DOROTHY PARKER.

1 One square foot less and it would be adulterous.

Quoted in the *New Yorker* 5 January 1946. On the office he shared

with DOROTHY PARKER, who echoed this remark in an interview in 1956: 'He [Robert Benchley] and I had an office so tiny that an inch smaller and it would have been adultery.'

2 A dog teaches a boy fidelity, perseverance, and to turn around three times before lying down.

Quoted in *Artemus Ward, His Book*, Introduction (1964 edn)

3 In America there are two classes of travel – first class and with children.

Quoted in *The Algonquin Wits* (ed. Robert E. Drennan, 1968)

4 I do most of my work sitting down. That's where I shine.

ibid.

5 Anyone can do any amount of work, provided it isn't the work he is supposed to be doing.

ibid.

6 Streets flooded. Please advise.

ibid. Telegram on arrival in Venice.

7 It took me fifteen years to discover that I had no talent for writing, but I couldn't give it up because by that time I was too famous.

Quoted in *Robert Benchley*, ch. 1 (1955) by Nathaniel Benchley

## Ruth Benedict (1887–1948)

US ANTHROPOLOGIST

Her studies of primitive societies led her to argue for cultural relativity and against the imposition of cultural values. *Patterns of Culture* (1934) is regarded as her most important work.

1 No man ever looks at the world with pristine eyes. He sees it edited by a definite set of customs and institutions and ways of thinking.

*Patterns of Culture*, ch. 1 (1934)

2 Racism is an *ism* to which everyone in the world today is exposed; for or against, we must take sides. And the history of the future will differ according to the decision which we make.

*Race: Science and Politics*, ch. 1 (1940)

## Stephen Vincent Benét (1898–1943)

US POET AND AUTHOR

He published numerous novels and short stories on themes of American history, but is chiefly known for his long poem on the Civil War, *John Brown's Body* (1928), which won the Pulitzer Prize in 1929 and was dramatized by Charles Laughton in 1953.

1 I have fallen in love with American names,
The sharp, gaunt names that never get fat,
The snakeskin titles of mining claims,
The plumed war-bonnet of Medicine Hat,
Tucson and Deadwood and Lost Mule Flat.

'American Names', st. 1, first publ. in the *Yale Review*, vol. 17 (1927), repr. in *America in Poetry* (ed. Charles Sullivan, 1988)

2 I shall not rest quiet in Montparnasse.
I shall not lie easy at Winchelsea.
You may bury my body in Sussex grass,
You may bury my tongue at Champmédy.
I shall not be there, I shall rise and pass.
Bury my heart at Wounded Knee.

ibid. st. 7. Wounded Knee, a creek in South Dakota, was site of the last major battle of the Indian Wars, 1890. *Bury My Heart at Wounded Knee* was the title of a history of the Indian wars by Dee Brown (1970).

## David Ben-Gurion (1886–1973)

ISRAELI STATESMAN

Born in Poland, he became an active Zionist and emigrated to Palestine in 1906, but was banished by the Ottomans during the First World War, subsequently settling in the USA. In 1930 he was elected leader of the Mapai (Labour) party, and in 1948 became the first Israeli prime minister, serving two terms 1948–63. He was honoured during his lifetime as 'Father of the Nation'.

1 In Israel, in order to be a realist you must believe in miracles.
Interview on CBS-TV, 5 October 1956

## Walter Benjamin (1892–1940)
GERMAN CRITIC AND PHILOSOPHER

Considered one of Germany's most original critics of the first half of the twentieth century, he wove themes of Marxism and Jewish mysticism into his essays and aphorisms, which are collected in *One-Way Street* (1928) and *Illuminations* (1961). He moved to Paris in 1933, and committed suicide after a failed attempt to escape the Nazi occupation.

1 Work on good prose has three steps: a musical stage when it is composed, an architectonic one when it is built, and a textile one when it is woven.
*One-Way Street*, 'Caution: Steps' (1928)

2 Genuine polemics approach a book as lovingly as a cannibal spices a baby.
ibid. 'Post No Bills: The Critic's Technique in Thirteen Theses'

3 The art of the critic in a nutshell: to coin slogans without betraying ideas. The slogans of an inadequate criticism peddle ideas to fashion.
ibid.

4 Books and harlots have their quarrels in public.
ibid. 'No. 13'

5 Truth wants to be startled abruptly, at one stroke, from her self-immersion, whether by uproar, music or cries for help.
ibid. 'Technical Aid'

6 Quotations in my work are like wayside robbers who leap out armed and relieve the stroller of his conviction.
ibid. 'Hardware'

7 Of all the ways of acquiring books, writing them oneself is regarded as the most praiseworthy method. . . . Writers are really people who write books not because they are poor, but because they are dissatisfied with the books which they could buy but do not like.
'Unpacking my Library' (1931), repr. in *Illuminations* (ed. Hannah Arendt, 1968)

8 The destructive character lives from the feeling, not that life is worth living, but that suicide is not worth the trouble.
'The Destructive Character', first publ. in the *Frankfurter Zeitung* 20 November 1931, repr. in *One-Way Street and Other Writings* (1978)

9 Opinions are a private matter. The public has an interest only in judgments.
'Karl Kraus', first publ. in the *Frankfurter Zeitung* no. 76, 1931, repr. in *Illuminations* (ed. Hannah Arendt, 1968)

10 Boredom is the dream bird that hatches the egg of experience. A rustling in the leaves drives him away.
'The Storyteller', sect. 9 (1936), repr. in ibid.

11 Death is the sanction of everything the story-teller can tell. He has borrowed his authority from death.
ibid. sect. 11

## Tony Benn (b. 1925)
BRITISH POLITICIAN

Originally named Anthony Wedgwood Benn. A deeply committed parliamentary radical who is also a staunch traditionalist, he has been a Labour MP since 1950, apart from the interval between inheriting his father's title and consequently being debarred

from the House of Commons in 1960, and renouncing the title in 1963, to be re-elected to parliament the same year. He held various government posts under HAROLD WILSON and JAMES CALLAGHAN, though was consistently defeated in bids for leadership of the party. HAROLD MACMILLAN thought that he 'immatures with age'.

1 The House of Lords is the British Outer Mongolia for retired politicians.
Quoted in the *Observer* 4 February 1962. Comment made during his campaign to disclaim his hereditary peerage. In his *Diaries 1963–67*, Benn states that the words came from a speech made in San Francisco in 1961, and were also used by the Russian former prime minister Molotov. Benn was always relieved to have escaped the Lords, though he was, he said, 'not a reluctant peer but a persistent commoner'.

2 Britain today is suffering from galloping obsolescence.
Speech 31 January 1963, quoted in the *Observer* 2 February 1963

3 We thought we could put the economy right in five years. We were wrong. It will probably take ten.
Speech at Bristol, 18 April 1968, quoted in *The Times* 19 April 1968. Benn was then Minister of Technology.

4 The Marxist analysis has got nothing to do with what happened in Stalin's Russia: it's like blaming Jesus Christ for the Inquisition in Spain.
Quoted in the *Observer* 27 April 1980

5 A holy war with atom bombs could end the human family for ever. I say this as a socialist whose political commitment owes much more to the teachings of Jesus – without the mysteries within which they are presented – than to the writings of Marx whose analysis seems to lack an understanding of the deeper needs of humanity.
*Arguments for Democracy*, ch. 7 (1981)

6 For those without personal wealth or political authority a trade union card and a ballot paper are the only two routes to political power.
ibid. ch. 9

7 I did not enter the Labour Party forty-seven years ago to have our manifesto written by Dr Mori, Dr Gallup and Mr Harris.
*Guardian* 13 June 1988

8 A faith is something you die for, a doctrine is something you kill for. There is all the difference in the world.
BBC television broadcast, 11 April 1989

9 It's the same each time with progress. First they ignore you, then they say you're mad, then dangerous, then there's a pause and then you can't find anyone who disagrees with you.
Quoted in the *Observer* 6 October 1991

10 Mr Tony Benn welcomes compulsory homework for pensioners.
*Sunday Telegraph* 8 November 1998. Illustrating the kind of New Labour press briefing to which he takes exception.

## Alan Bennett (b. 1934)
BRITISH PLAYWRIGHT

At the heart of the satire boom of the 1960s, he was a contributor to the revue *Beyond the Fringe* (1960–61) and achieved further success with his first stage play *Forty Years On* (1969). Later plays include *An Englishman Abroad* (for TV, 1983), *Kafka's Dick* (1986) and *The Madness of George III* (1991, filmed 1995).

1 Life, you know, is rather like opening a tin of sardines. We are all of us looking for the key.
'Sermon', in *Beyond the Fringe* (revue, 1960–61), publ. in *From Fringe to Flying Circus*, ch. 1 (1980) by Roger Wilmut. Bennett first wrote the sketch in 1956 for a concert organized with Russell Harty at Oxford University. 'It took about half an hour to write, and was, I suppose, the most profitable half-hour's work I've ever done.

Once I had hit on the form I used to be able to run up sermons for all sorts of occasions.'

2 Never read the Bible as if it means something. Or at any rate don't *try* and mean it. Nor prayers. The liturgy is best treated and read as if it's someone announcing the departure of trains.

Journal entry, 30 June 1984, publ. in *Writing Home*, 'Diaries 1980–1990' (1994)

3 The majority of people perform well in a crisis and when the spotlight is on them; it's on the Sunday afternoons of this life, when nobody is looking, that the spirit falters.

Journal entry, 13 October 1984, ibid.

4 It's a good job Mrs T. isn't Archbishop of Canterbury, or we would just be left with the cathedrals and a few other 'viable places of worship'.

Journal entry, 20 May 1985, ibid.

5 When people are on their best behaviour they aren't always at their best.

'Dinner at Noon', broadcast April 1988 in BBC TV series *Byline*, publ. in ibid.

6 Biography is all about cutting people down to size. Getting an unruly quart into a pint pot.

Quoted in *Beyond the Fringe . . . and Beyond*, pt 4 (1989) by Ronald Bergan

7 Definition of a classic: a book everyone is assumed to have read and often thinks they have.

*Independent on Sunday* 27 January 1991

8 I generally assume that childhoods more or less ended with the First World War.. . . . Anyone born after 1940 got the Utility version, childhood according to the Authorized Economy Standard.

*Writing Home*, 'Bad John' (1994)

9 Language is balls coming at you from every angle.

Miss Fozzard quoting Mr Clarkson-Hall in *Talking Heads 2*, 'Miss Fozzard Finds Her Feet' (1998)

## Arnold Bennett (1867–1931)

BRITISH NOVELIST, PLAYWRIGHT AND CRITIC

Influenced by the French Realists, he set much of his best work in the Potteries region of his boyhood, notably *Anna of the Five Towns* (1902), *The Old Wives' Tale* (1908), and the *Clayhanger* series (1902–8). He also wrote for the theatre and was an influential reviewer, called by WYNDHAM LEWIS the 'Hitler of the book-racket.'

1 A cause may be inconvenient, but it's magnificent. It's like champagne or high heels, and one must be prepared to suffer for it.

Hildegarde Culver, in *The Title*, act 1 (1918)

2 Being a husband is a whole-time job. That is why so many husbands fail. They cannot give their entire attention to it.

Arthur Culver, in ibid.

3 Examine the Honours List and you can instantly tell how the Government feels in its inside. When the Honours List is full of rascals, millionaires, and – er – chumps, you may be quite sure that the Government is dangerously ill.

ibid.

4 Journalists say a thing that they know isn't true, in the hope that if they keep on saying it long enough it will be true.

ibid. act 2

5 Literature's always a good card to play for Honours. It makes people think that Cabinet ministers are educated.

Hildegarde Culver, in the Title, act 3 (1918)

6 A test of a first-rate work, and a test of your sincerity in calling it a first-rate work, is that you finish it.

*Things That Have Interested Me*, 'Finishing Books' (first series, 1921)

7 The price of justice is eternal publicity.

*Things That Have Interested Me*, 'Secret Trials' (second series, 1923)

8 Good taste is better than bad taste, but bad taste is better than no taste, and men without individuality have no taste – at any rate no taste that they can impose on their publics.

*Evening Standard* 21 August 1930

## Jill Bennett (1931–90)

BRITISH ACTRESS

Comfortable in both classical and contemporary roles, she gained her first success in Anouilh's *Dinner with the Family* (1957). She performed in many plays by her husband JOHN OSBORNE, such as *West of Suez* (1971) and *Watch It Come Down* (1976) as well as in his version of Ibsen's *Hedda Gabler* (1972).

1 Never marry a man who hates his mother, because he'll end up hating you.

Quoted in the *Observer* 12 September 1982 See also JOHN OSBORNE 14.

## Connie Bensley (b. 1929)

BRITISH POET

In her sharp and often satirical poems she focuses on the preoccupations of everyday life and social pretension. Her collections include *Moving In* (1984) and *Choosing to be a Swan* (1994).

1 I sing the love homeopathic:
it cures you before very long.
You just take a speck
of that pain-in-the-neck
and let it dissolve on your tongue.

'A Cure for Love', publ. in *Choosing to be a Swan* (1994). The first line is a parody of Walt Whitman's poem 'I Sing the Body Electric' (1885).

## Stella Benson (1892–1933)

BRITISH AUTHOR

Themes of loneliness and alienation are found in her novels and short stories, reflecting her own isolation after her marriage and move to China in 1922. Her most successful work *Tobit Transplanted* (1930) tells the story of White Russians exiled in China.

1 Family jokes, though rightly cursed by strangers, are the bond that keeps most families alive.

*Pipers and a Dancer*, ch. 9 (1924)

## Lloyd Bentsen (b. 1921)

US DEMOCRATIC POLITICIAN

A member of the House of Representatives (1948–55) and the Senate (1971–93), he was the Democratic vice-presidential candidate in 1988 and Secretary of the Treasury (1993–94) under President CLINTON.

1 Senator, I served with Jack Kennedy. I knew Jack Kennedy. Jack Kennedy was a friend of mine. Senator, you're no Jack Kennedy.

TV vice-presidential debate, 6 October 1988, publ. in *Lend Me Your Ears*, pt 4 (ed. Willaim Safire, 1992). Bentsen was responding to the assertion by DAN QUAYLE that he possessed 'as much experience in the Congress as Jack Kennedy had when he sought the presidency'. Safire calls the riposte, 'the most effective single punch in the history of televised presidential debates'.

## Nikolai A. Berdyaev (1874–1948)

RUSSIAN PHILOSOPHER

He was dismissed from his post as Professor of Philosophy in Moscow in 1922 for defending Orthodox Christianity, and went on to found the Academy of Philosophy and Religion in Berlin (transferred in 1924 to Paris). As a leader of the Christian existentialist school, he was a consistent critic of Russian communism. His books include *The Meaning of History* (1923) and *The Destiny of Man* (1931).

1 In sex we have the source of man's true connection with the cosmos and of his servile dependence. The categories of sex, male and female, are cosmic categories, not merely anthropological categories.
*The Meaning of the Creative Act* (1916)

2 We find the most terrible form of atheism, not in the militant and passionate struggle against the idea of God himself, but in the practical atheism of everyday living, in indifference and torpor. We often encounter these forms of atheism among those who are formally Christians.
*Truth and Revelation* (1953)

## Candice Bergen (b. 1946)
US SCREEN ACTRESS

Known for her film roles in *Carnal Knowledge* (1971) and *Starting Over* (1979), she has also appeared in the late-1980s TV comedy series *Murphy Brown*. She married film director Louis Malle in 1980.

1 I may not be a great actress but I've become the greatest at screen orgasms. Ten seconds of heavy breathing, roll your head from side to side, simulate a slight asthma attack and die a little.
*Daily Mirror*, 1971, quoted in *Halliwell's Filmgoer's Companion* (1984)

## John Berger (b. 1926)
BRITISH AUTHOR AND CRITIC

An uncompromising Marxist-influenced critic more widely appreciated in Europe than in his native country, he has written extensively on culture and society, as in *Ways of Seeing* (1972) and his novels, the late-modernist *G* (1972), the trilogy *Into Their Labours* (1991) which charts peasant life in France, and *Photocopies* (1996). He is also a poet and translator.

1 Nothing fortuitous happens in a child's world. There are no accidents. Everything is connected with everything else and everything can be explained by everything else ... For a young child everything that happens is a necessity.
*A Fortunate Man* (1967)

2 Is boredom anything less than the sense of one's faculties slowly dying?
ibid.

3 Nakedness reveals itself. Nudity is placed on display. . . . The nude is condemned to never being naked. Nudity is a form of dress.
*Ways of Seeing*, ch. 3 (1972)

4 The envied are like bureaucrats; the more impersonal they are, the greater the illusion (for themselves and for others) of their power.
ibid. ch. 7

5 A peasant becomes fond of his pig and is glad to salt away its pork. What is significant, and is so difficult for the urban stranger to understand, is that the two statements are connected by an *and* and not by a *but*.
*About Looking*, 'Why Look at Animals?' (1980)

6 The zoo cannot but disappoint. The public purpose of zoos is to offer visitors the opportunity of looking at animals. Yet nowhere in a zoo can a stranger encounter the look of an animal. At the most, the animal's gaze

flickers and passes on. They look sideways. They look blindly beyond.
ibid.

7 The camera relieves us of the burden of memory. It surveys us like God, and it surveys for us. Yet no other god has been so cynical, for the camera records in order to forget.
ibid. 'Uses of Photography'

8 One can say of language that it is potentially the only human home, the only dwelling place that cannot be hostile to man.
*And Our Faces, My Heart, Brief As Photos*, pt 2 (1984)

9 Emigration, forced or chosen, across national frontiers or from village to metropolis, is the quintessential experience of our time.
ibid.

10 Autobiography begins with a sense of being alone. It is an orphan form.
'Mother', first publ. In the *Threepenny Review* summer 1986, repr. in *Keeping a Rendezvous* (1992)

11 Every city has a sex and an age which have nothing to do with demography. Rome is feminine. So is Odessa. London is a teenager, an urchin, and, in this, hasn't changed since the time of Dickens. Paris, I believe, is a man in his twenties in love with an older woman.
'Imagine Paris', first publ. in *Harper's* January 1987, repr. in *Keeping a Rendezvous* (1992)

12 What makes shit such a universal joke is that it's an unmistakeable reminder of our duality, of our soiled nature and of our will to glory. It is the ultimate *lèse-majesté*.
'Muck and Its Entanglements', first publ. in *Harper's* May 1989, repr. in ibid. as 'A Load of Shit'

13 Compassion has no place in the natural order of the world which operates on the basis of necessity. Compassion opposes this order and is therefore best thought of as being in some way supernatural.
*Guardian* 19 December 1991

14 The first step towards building an alternative world has to be a refusal of the world-picture implanted in our minds and all the false promises used everywhere to justify and idealize the delinquent and insatiable need to sell. Another space is vitally necessary.
'Against the Great Defeat of the World', publ. in *Race and Class* October 98–March 1999

## Ingmar Bergman (b. 1918)
SWEDISH STAGE DIRECTOR AND FILM MAKER

A major director and winner of many international prizes, he has set the benchmark for the Swedish film. Often bleak in outlook and preoccupied with guilt, repression and loneliness, his films include *The Seventh Seal* (1956) and *The Virgin Spring* (1959), and the more optimisitic and autobiographical *Fanny and Alexander* (1982). He commented that 'to shoot a film is to organize a complete universe'.

1 Today the individual has become the highest form and the greatest bane of artistic creation. The smallest wound or pain of the ego is examined under the microscope as if it were of eternal importance. The artist considers his isolation, his subjectivity, his individualism almost holy. Thus we finally gather in one large pen, where we stand and bleat about our loneliness without listening to each other and without realizing that we are smothering each other to death.
Spoken introduction to *The Seventh Seal* (film, written and directed by Ingmar Bergman, 1956)

2 **My basic view of things is – not to have any basic view of things.**

Interview in *Bergman on Bergman*, 'Solna, 25 June 1968' (1970)

3 **Professionally, morals aren't too much of a problem. Over the years one has learned certain things by experience. They mount up. And gradually they crystallize into a pattern of behaviour which afterwards – to use a superior expression – one calls one's professional ethics.**

Interview in ibid. 'Rasunda, 3 July 1968'

4 **I hope I never get so old I get religious.**

*International Herald Tribune* 8 September 1989

## Ingrid Bergman (1915–82)

SWEDISH-BORN SCREEN ACTRESS

A hugely popular romantic star from 1939 when she was brought to the US by DAVID SELZNICK, she specialized in roles that mixed 'torment, indecision and incipient suffering', as described by critic David Thomson. She won an Oscar for *Gaslight* (1944) but was ostracized from Hollywood after her affair with the director Roberto Rossellini in 1949, to be forgiven in 1956 with a second Academy Award, for *Anastasia*, and to receive a third for *Murder on the Orient Express* (1974).

1 **Play it Sam. Play 'As Time Goes By'.**

Ilsa Lund (Ingrid Bergman), in *Casablanca* (film, screenplay by Julius Epstein, Philip Epstein and Howard Koch, 1942, from the unproduced play *Everybody Goes to Rick's* by Murray Burnett and Joan Alison; directed by Michael Curtiz). Ilsa makes the request to the piano player Sam (Dooley Wilson); later in the film, Rick Blaine (HUMPHREY BOGART) repeats the request: 'You played it for her, you can play it for me. If she can stand it, I can. Play it!' (usually misquoted 'Play it again Sam', the title of Woody Allen's 1972 movie). For the song, see HERMAN HUPFELD 1.

## Steven Berkoff (b. 1937)

BRITISH PLAYWRIGHT, ACTOR AND DIRECTOR

Having formed the London Theatre Group in 1968, he embarked on a series of adaptations of classic dramas, including works by Kafka and Edgar Allan Poe. Among his own politically radical, often brutal plays, in which he often acts, are *East* (1975) and *Greek* (1979). Of himself he once said: 'I often think of myself as a beautiful woman walking through a provincial village and being spat on by the locals.'

1 **so demure on the outside**
**such a whore within**
**fashion is so divine it makes dressing up a sin**

Helen, in *Decadence*, sc. 10 (1981)

2 **Wake up, you git, we need a war . . .**
**Establish once again our might and strength**
**Shake our old mane, out fly the moths**
**Oh God, I start to feel myself again**
**Now where is this damn Falkland Isle?**

Maggot Scratcher, in *Sink the Belgrano!* (1987)

3 **That just ain't cricket, is it dear?**
**Or they may say, and it will be true,**
**Britain does not rule the waves**
**She simply waives the bloody rules!**

Command, in ibid.

## Irving Berlin (1888–1989)

RUSSIAN-BORN US SONGWRITER

Originally named Israel Baline. He was a pivotal figure in US popular music, already established as a composer when 'Alexander's Ragtime Band' was a hit in 1911. This like many other of his songs was recorded by some of the most famous singers of the day. He received a presidential citation as composer of patriotic songs

in 1954. 'Irving Berlin has no place in American music,' Jerome Kern asserted, 'Irving Berlin *is* American music'.

1 **From the mountains to the prairies,**
**To the oceans white with foam,**
**God bless America,**
**My home sweet home!**

'God Bless America' (song, written 1917, recorded 1938). This unofficial national anthem originally written for (though not appearing in) the Broadway show *Yip Yip Yaphank* (1918) is said to have provoked Woody Guthrie to compose 'This Land Is Your Land'. See also WOODY GUTHRIE 1.

2 **The song is ended (but the melody lingers on).**

'The Song is Ended (But the Melody Lingers On)' (song) in *Will O' the Whispers* (stage musical, 1927). Sung by Jack 'Whispering' Smith in the show, the song was popularized by Ruth Etting, and re-recorded in 1948 by Nellie Lutcher.

3 **I'm puttin' on my top hat,**
**Tyin' up my white tie,**
**Brushin' off my tails.**

'Top Hat, White Tie and Tails' (song) in *Top Hat* (film, 1935). The song was performed by Fred Astaire.

4 **Heaven – I'm in Heaven –**
**And my heart beats so that I can hardly speak;**
**And I seem to find the happiness I seek**
**When we're out together dancing cheek to cheek.**

'Cheek to Cheek' (song) in ibid. Written for Ginger Rogers and Fred Astaire.

5 **There may be trouble ahead,**
**But while there's moonlight and music and love and**
**romance,**
**Let's face the music and dance.**

'Let's Face the Music and Dance' (song) in *Follow the Fleet* (film, 1936). The song was a hit for Fred Astaire.

6 **I'm dreaming of a white Christmas,**
**Just like the ones I used to know.**

'White Christmas' (song) in *Holiday Inn* (film, 1942). First recorded by BING CROSBY, the song was featured again in the film *White Christmas* (1954), and recorded by artists as diverse as FRANK SINATRA (1944), Mantovani (1952) and the Drifters (1954). Crosby's sales alone exceeded 25 million.

7 **There's no business like show business.**

'There's No Business Like Show Business' (song) in *Annie Get Your Gun* (musical show 1946, filmed 1949). Sung by Ethel Merman on Broadway and by Betty Hutton in the movie version, the title was borrowed for the 1954 movie in which MARILYN MONROE sang Berlin's 'Heat Wave'.

8 **Anything you can do, I can do better,**
**I can do anything better than you.**

'Anything You Can Do' (song) in ibid.

9 **The toughest thing about success is that you've got to keep on being a success. Talent is only a starting point in this business. You've got to keep on working that talent. Someday I'll reach for it and it won't be there.**

*Theatre Arts* February 1958

10 **Everybody ought to have a lower East Side in their life.**

*Vogue* 1 November 1962

## (Sir) Isaiah Berlin (1909–97)

LATVIAN-BORN BRITISH PHILOSOPHER

Regarded as one of the leading liberal thinkers of his generation, he was Professor of Social and Political Theory at Oxford (1957–67). Among his major works on political philosophy are *Karl Marx* (1939), *Historical Inevitability* (1954), a major critique of historical determinism and *The Age of Enlightenment* (1956). He published numerous essays and was a brilliant raconteur.

1 **Injustice, poverty, slavery, ignorance – these may be cured by reform or revolution. But men do not live only by fighting evils. They live by positive goals, individual and**

collective, a vast variety of them, seldom predictable, at times incompatible.

'Political Ideas in the Twentieth Century' (1950), repr. in *Four Essays on Liberty* (1969)

2 A great man need not be morally good, or upright, or kind, or sensitive, or delightful, or possess artistic or scientific talent. To call someone a great man is to claim that he has intentionally taken (or perhaps could have taken) a large step, one far beyond the normal capacities of men, in satisfying, or materially affecting, central human interests.

'Chaim Weizmann' (1958), repr. in *Personal Impressions* (1981)

3 It is only a very vulgar historical materialism that denies the power of ideas, and says that ideals are mere material interests in disguise. It may be that, without the pressure of social forces, political ideas are stillborn: what is certain is that these forces, unless they clothe themselves in ideas, remain blind and undirected.

'Two Concepts of Liberty' (1958), repr. in *Four Essays on Liberty* (1969)

4 One belief, more than any other, is responsible for the slaughter of individuals on the altars of the great historical ideals . . . the belief that somewhere, in the past or in the future, in divine revelation or in the mind of an individual thinker, in the pronouncements of history or science, or in the simple heart of an uncorrupted good man, there is a final solution.

ibid.

5 Scepticism, driven to extremes, defeats itself by becoming self-refuting.

*Four Essays on Liberty*, Introduction (1969)

## Georges Bernanos (1888–1948)

FRENCH AUTHOR

A Roman Catholic polemicist, he wrote in support of royalism and, in *A Diary of My Times* (1938), against Franco, while his preoccupation with the conflicting forces of good and evil is a theme of his novels *The Star of Satan* (1926) and *The Diary of a Country Priest* (1936, filmed 1951).

1 The wish to pray is a prayer in itself . . . God can ask no more than that of us.

*The Diary of a Country Priest*, ch. 4 (1936)

2 Faith is not a thing which one 'loses', we merely cease to shape our lives by it.

ibid.

3 Hell is not to love any more, madame. Not to love any more!

The priest, in ibid. ch. 5

4 No one ever discovers the depths of his own loneliness.

ibid. ch. 7

5 Civilization exists precisely so that there may be no masses but rather men alert enough never to constitute masses.

*The Last Essays of Georges Bernanos*, 'Why Freedom?' (1955)

## Carl Bernstein (b. 1944)

US JOURNALIST

Together with Bob Woodward he unmasked the Watergate cover-up which led to the downfall of President NIXON, as described in *All the President's Men* (1974, filmed 1976). In 1973 Bernstein and Woodward were awarded the Pulitzer Prize for public service. He was married to NORA EPHRON.

1 We are in the process of creating what deserves to be called the idiot culture. Not an idiot sub-culture, which every society has bubbling beneath the surface and which can provide harmless fun; but the culture itself. For the

first time, the weird and the stupid and the coarse are becoming our cultural norm, even our cultural ideal.

*Guardian* 3 June 1992

2 The failures of the press have contributed immensely to the emergence of a talk-show nation, in which public discourse is reduced to ranting and raving and posturing. We now have a mainstream press whose news agenda is increasingly influenced by this netherworld.

ibid.

## Leonard Bernstein (1918–90)

US COMPOSER AND CONDUCTOR

An accomplished composer in both the classical and modern idiom, he was also a popular and flamboyant conductor. His compositions include the symphony *The Age of Anxiety* (1949), *Chichester Psalms* (1965) and the musicals *On the Town* (1944) and *West Side Story* (1957).

1 Technique is communication: the two words are synonymous in conductors.

*The Times* 27 June 1989

## Yogi Berra (b. 1925)

US BASEBALL PLAYER

Real name Lawrence Peter Berra. He was named Most Valuable Player three times during his career as catcher with the New York Yankees and Mets (1946–65). He has held many world championship titles and is famous for his malapropisms.

1 It ain't over till it's over.

Attributed

## Chuck Berry (b. 1926)

US ROCK MUSICIAN

One of the first rock and roll stars to attract a large teenage following, he was a major influence on British and US rock bands of the 1960s. According to JOHN LENNON, 'if you tried to give rock 'n' roll another name, you might call it Chuck Berry'. With witty lyrics and trademark guitar riffs, his hits which included 'Johnny B. Goode' and 'Sweet Little Sixteen' (both 1958) were widely covered.

1 Roll over, Beethoven,
And tell Tchaikovsky the news.

'Roll Over, Beethoven' (song, 1956) on the album *Greatest Hits* (1965)

2 Hail, hail rock 'n' roll,
Deliver me from the days of old.

'School Days' (song, 1957) on ibid.

3 Go Johnny go!

'Johnny B. Goode' (song, 1958) on ibid. *Go Johnny Go* was the title of a rock and roll film in 1959, in which Berry appeared.

## John Berryman (1914–72)

US POET

A poet of the confessional style, he established his reputation with *Homage to Mistress Bradstreet* (1956) but is remembered chiefly for his *Dream Songs*, the 1964 volume of which won the Pulitzer Prize. An alcoholic, he committed suicide by jumping off a bridge into the Mississippi River.

1 We must travel in the direction of our fear.

'A Point of Age', publ. in *Poems* (1942)

2 Life, friends, is boring. We must not say so.
After all, the sky flashes, the great sea yearns,
we ourselves flash and yearn,
and moreover my mother told me as a boy
(repeatedly) 'Ever to confess you're bored
means you have no

Inner Resources.' I conclude now I have no inner resources, because I am heavy bored.

*77 Dream Songs*, no. 14 (1964)

3 The world is gradually becoming a place
Where I do not care to be any more.

*His Toy, His Dream, His Rest*, no. 149 (1968). The lines were incorporated into the final version of *The Dream Songs* (1969).

4 The artist is extremely lucky who is presented with the worst possible ordeal which will not actually kill him. At that point, he's in business.

Interview in the *Paris Review*, winter 1972, repr. in *Writers at Work* (fourth series, ed. George Plimpton, 1976)

## Bernardo Bertolucci (b. 1940)

ITALIAN FILM DIRECTOR

Having directed his first film aged 22, he went on to achieve success with *The Spider's Stratagem* (1970), *Last Tango in Paris* (1972), the epic *1900* (1976) and the sumptuously photographed *The Last Emperor* (1987).

1 If New York is the Big Apple, tonight Hollywood is the Big Nipple.

Said at Oscar presentation ceremony, quoted in the *Guardian* 13 April 1988. Bertolucci's film *The Last Emperor* notched up nine awards.

2 Socialism is finished. That's why I got into Buddhism . . . In fact I thought that, being a little orphan of Marx, here at least was another space where I could feel comfortable.

Quoted in the *Independent on Sunday* 1 May 1994. On his reasons for making the film *Little Buddha*.

## George Best (b. 1946)

NORTHERN IRISH FOOTBALLER

Arguably the finest British player since the Second World War, excelling in all positions, he played for Manchester United and was European Footballer of the Year (1968). Alcohol and fast-living meant that his footballing career was over by the time he was 25. He said, 'If I'd been born ugly, you'd never have heard of Pele.'

1 You just can't explain what it's like to score a great goal to someone who's never done it. I said years ago that if you'd given me the choice of going out and beating four men and smashing a goal in from thirty yards against Liverpool or going to bed with Miss World, it would have been a difficult choice. Luckily, I had both. It's just that you do one of those things in front of fifty thousand people.

Quoted in 'The Afterlife' by Paul Morley, first publ. 1991, repr. in *The Esquire Book of Sports Writing* (ed. Greg Williams, 1995)

## Mary McLeod Bethune (1875–1955)

US EDUCATOR

She was founder and President of the National Council of Negro Women (1935–49) and served as adviser on minority issues in the New Deal administration of President FRANKLIN D. ROOSEVELT.

1 The true worth of a race must be measured by the character of its womanhood.

Address to Chicago Women's Federation, 3 June 1933, publ. in *Black Women in White America*, 'A Century of Progress of Negro Women' (ed. Gerda Lerner, 1972)

## (Sir) John Betjeman (1906–84)

BRITISH POET

Quintessentially English, a champion of Victorian and Edwardian architecture, he was a self-deprecating and popular poet whose traditional verse forms mingled satire with nostalgia. His verse autobiography *Summoned by Bells* (1960) was an instant success,

and he was appointed Poet Laureate in 1972. His future mother-in-law Lady Chetwode said of him: 'We invite people like that to tea, but we don't marry them.'

1 Oh! Chintzy, chintzy cheeriness,
Half dead and half alive!

'Death in Leamington', publ. in *Mount Zion* (1931)

2 Broad of Church and broad of mind,
Broad before and broad behind,
A keen ecclesiologist,
A rather dirty Wykehamist.

'The Wykehamist', publ. in ibid. Opening lines.

3 Ghastly Good Taste, or a depressing story of the rise and fall of English architecture.

Title of book (1933)

4 He rose, and he put down *The Yellow Book*.
He staggered – and, terrible-eyed,
He brushed past the palms on the staircase
And was helped to a hansom outside.

'The Arrest of Oscar Wilde at the Cadogan Hotel', st. 9, publ. in *Continual Dew* (1937). Closing lines of poem.

5 Come, friendly bombs, and fall on Slough!
It isn't fit for humans now,
There isn't grass to graze a cow.
Swarm over, Death!

'Slough', st. 1, publ. in *Continental Dew* (1937). Betjeman's renowned antipathy towards modern architecture and town planning was particularly directed at the 'new towns' of the home counties.

6 Gracious Lord, oh bomb the Germans.
Spare their women for Thy Sake,
And if that is not too easy
We will pardon Thy Mistake.
But gracious Lord, whate'er shall be,
Don't let anyone bomb me.

'In Westminster Abbey', st. 2, publ. in *Old Lights for New Chancels* (1940)

7 Keep our Empire undismembered
Guide our Forces by Thy Hand,
Gallant blacks from far Jamaica,
Honduras and Togoland;
Protect them Lord in all their fights,
And, even more, protect the whites.

ibid. st. 3

8 Think of what our Nation stands for,
Books from Boots' and country lanes,
Free speech, free passes, class distinction,
Democracy and proper drains.

ibid. st. 4

9 For me, at any rate, England stands for the Church of England, eccentric incumbents, oil-lit churches, Women's Institutes, modest village inns, arguments about cow parsley on the altar, the noise of mowing machines on Saturday afternoons, local newspapers, local auctions, the poetry of Tennyson, Crabbe, Hardy and Matthew Arnold, local talent, local concerts, a visit to the cinema, branch-line trains, light railways, leaning on gates and looking across fields.

BBC broadcast 25 February 1943, first publ. in the *Listener* 11 March 1943 as 'Oh to be in England . . .', publ. in *Coming Home* as 'Coming Home' (1997)

10 Miss J. Hunter Dunn, Miss J. Hunter Dunn,
Furnish'd and burnish'd by Aldershot sun,
What strenuous singles we played after tea,
We in the tournament – you against me!

'A Subaltern's Love-song', st. 1, publ. in *New Bats in Old Belfries* (1945)

11 I have a Vision of the Future, chum.
The workers' flats in fields of soya beans

Tower up like silver pencils, score on score.

'The Planster's Vision', publ. in ibid.

12  And is it true? And is it true,
This most tremendous tale of all,
Seen in a stained-glass window's hue,
A Baby in an ox's stall?
The Maker of the stars and sea
Become a Child on earth for me?

'Christmas', st. 6, publ. in *A Few Late Chrysanthemums* (1954)

13  Phone for the fish-knives, Norman
As Cook is a little unnerved;
You kiddies have crumpled the serviettes
And I must have things daintily served.

'How to Get on in Society' (1954), publ. in ibid. Opening lines of poem.

14  Still they stand, the churches of England, their towers grey above billowy globes of elm trees, the red cross of St George flying over their battlements, the Duplex Envelope System employed for collections, schoolmistresses at the organ, incumbent in the chancel, scattered worshippers in the nave, Tortoise stove slowly consuming its ration as the familiar seventeenth-century phrases come echoing down arcades of ancient stone.

*English Parish Churches*, Introduction (1958)

15  The dread of beatings! Dread of being late!
And, greatest dread of all, the dread of games!

*Summoned by Bells*, ch. 7 (1960)

16  People's backyards are much more interesting than their front gardens, and houses that back on to railways are public benefactors.

Quoted in the *Observer* 20 March 1983

# Aneurin Bevan (1897–1960)

BRITISH POLITICIAN

Known as Nye Bevan. He served as Labour MP for Ebbw Vale 1929–60 and was spokesman for the South Wales miners. While Minister of Health (1945–51) he established the National Health Service (1948), later resigning in protest against proposed charges. A brilliant orator, though also a 'merchant of discourtesy' for WINSTON CHURCHILL, he inspired a 'Bevanite' faction of the party which opposed the reformist policies of CLEMENT ATTLEE, though he sided with HUGH GAITSKELL on the question of disarmament.

1  Freedom is the by-product of economic surplus.

Quoted in *Aneurin Bevan*, vol. 1, ch. 3 (1962) by Michael Foot. The remark was often reiterated by Bevan from the 1920s onwards.

2  The worst thing I can say about democracy is that it has tolerated the Right Honourable Gentleman [Neville Chamberlain] for four and a half years.

Speech to House of Commons 23 July 1929, publ. in *Hansard*. Bevan did not attempt to hide his poor opinion of CHAMBERLAIN. 'He has the lucidity which is the by-product of a fundamentally sterile mind,' he declared on another occasion. 'He does not have to struggle . . . with the crowded pulsations of a fecund imagination. On the contrary he is almost devoid of imagination.'

3  Fascism is not in itself a new order of society. It is the future refusing to be born.

Remark, July 1940, quoted in *Aneurin Bevan*, vol. 1, ch. 10 (1962) by Michael Foot.

4  His [Winston Churchill's] ear is so sensitively attuned to the bugle note of history that he is often deaf to the more raucous clamour of contemporary life. The seven-league tempo of his imagination hastens him on to the 'sunny uplands' of the future, but he is apt to forget that the slow steps of humanity must travel every inch of the weary road that leads there.

Remark made in late 1940, in ibid.

5  He [Clement Attlee] seems determined to make a trumpet sound like a tin whistle.

Remark in 1945, quoted in ibid. ch. 14. Referring to Attlee's playing a subordinate role to Conservative ANTHONY EDEN when the two were delegated to represent Britain at a UN conference in San Francisco. Attlee, according to Bevan, had 'consistently underplayed his position and opportunities. . . . He brings to the fierce struggle of politics the tepid enthusiasm of a lazy summer afternoon at a cricket match.'

6  This island is made mainly of coal and surrounded by fish. Only an organizing genius could produce a shortage of coal and fish at the same time.

Speech at Blackpool, 24 May 1945, quoted in the *Daily Herald* 25 May 1945. Bevan's speech was made on the day that WINSTON CHURCHILL announced the formation of a Conservative 'caretaker' government in the wake of VE Day and the dissolution of the wartime coalition. The Conservatives were to be ejected from office in the general election two months later, when Labour won a landslide victory.

7  No amount of cajolery, and no attempts at ethical or social seduction, can eradicate from my heart a deep burning hatred for the Tory Party . . . So far as I am concerned they are lower than vermin.

Speech at Manchester, 4 July 1948, quoted in *The Times* 5 July 1948. Bevan was referring to the social policies of the Conservative Party, which 'condemned millions of first-class people to semi-starvation'. His invective, which formed part of a speech to inaugurate the National Health Service, provoked outrage in the press and embarrassment within his own party.

8  He [Winston Churchill] is a man suffering from petrified adolescence.

Quoted in *Aneurin Bevan*, ch. 11 (1953) by Vincent Brome

9  We know what happens to people who stay in the middle of the road. They get run over.

Quoted in the *Observer* 6 December 1953

10  I know that the right kind of leader for the Labour Party is a kind of desiccated calculating machine.

Speech to Tribune Group at Labour Party Conference, 29 September 1954, quoted in *Aneurin Bevan*, vol. 2, ch. 11 (1973) by Michael Foot. The remark was taken to refer to HUGH GAITSKELL, though Bevan later denied this.

11  If we complain about the tune, there is no reason to attack the monkey when the organ grinder is present.

Speech to House of Commons, 16 May 1957, publ. in *Hansard*. Bevan was referring to Foreign Minister Selwyn Lloyd and Prime Minister HAROLD MACMILLAN, holding the latter accountable for the Suez fiasco the previous autumn. Though Macmillan, as Chancellor of the Exchequer, had no direct involvement in foreign affairs during the crisis, he had urged a tough response to Nasser's nationalization of the canal.

12  If you carry this resolution you will send Britain's Foreign Secretary naked into the conference chamber.

Speech at Labour Party Conference, Brighton, 3 October 1957, quoted in the *Daily Herald* 4 October 1957. As Shadow Foreign Secretary under Gaitskell's leadership of the party, Bevan spoke in opposition to a motion in favour of unilateral nuclear disarmament.

13  The Prime Minister [Harold Macmillan] has an absolute genius for putting flamboyant labels on empty luggage.

Queen's Speech debate in House of Commons, 3 November 1959, quoted in *Aneurin Bevan*, vol. 2, ch. 16 (1973) by Michael Foot

14  I read the newspapers avidly. It is my one form of continuous fiction.

*The Times* 29 March 1960

15  He is a man walking backwards with his face to the future.

Quoted in *The Fine Art of Political Wit*, ch. 9 (1964) by Leon Harris. Referring to Sir Walter Elliot, the Conservative Minister of Agriculture.

16  The purpose of getting power is to be able to give it away.

Quoted in *Aneurin Bevan*, vol. 2, ch. 1 (1973) by Michael Foot

17  You're not an M.P., you're a gastronomic pimp.

Quoted in ibid. ch. 6. Said to a colleague who complained of a heavy week of Rotarian lunches and Chamber of Commerce dinners.

## William Beveridge (1879–1963)

BRITISH ECONOMIST

Baron Beveridge. He was Director of the London School of Economics 1919–37 and Master of University College, Oxford (1937–45). In 1942 he produced the Beveridge Report, a scheme of comprehensive social insurance that was the blueprint for the British welfare state.

1 The object of government in peace and in war is not the glory of rulers or of races, but the happiness of the common man.
   *Social Insurance and Allied Services*, pt 7 (1942)

2 The adventure of full employment in a free society is not like the directed flight of an aircraft on a beam. It is a voyage among shifting and dangerous currents. All that can be done is to see that the craft is well found, and that the pilot has all the necessary controls, and the instruments to guide his use of them.
   *Full Employment in a Free Society*, pt 4 (1944)

3 Ignorance is an evil weed, which dictators may cultivate among their dupes, but which no democracy can afford among its citizens.
   ibid. pt 7

## Ernest Bevin (1881–1951)

BRITISH POLITICIAN

A veteran trades union campaigner, he held the post of General Secretary of the Transport and General Workers Union 1921–40, then became a Labour MP and served in Churchill's War Cabinet. As Foreign Secretary (1945–51) he was one of the architects of the Organization for European Economic Cooperation (1948) and NATO (1949). A.J.P. TAYLOR commented, 'He objected to ideas only when others had them.'

1 The most conservative man in the world is the British Trade Unionist when you want to change him.
   Speech to Trades Union Congress, Edinburgh, 8 September 1927, publ. in *Report of Proceedings of the Trades Union Congress* (1927)

2 My [foreign] policy is to be able to take a ticket at Victoria Station and go anywhere I damn well please.
   Quoted in the *Spectator* 20 April 1951

## Georges Bidault (1899–1983)

FRENCH RESISTANCE LEADER AND STATESMAN

He headed the National Council of Resistance in 1943 and the Mouvement Républicain Populaire, a Christian-Democratic Party. He served as prime minister in 1946, 1949–50, and in 1958 but opposed the Algerian policy pursued by DE GAULLE. Charged with treason, he was in exile 1962–8.

1 Freedom is when one hears the bell at 7 o'clock in the morning and knows it is the milkman and not the Gestapo.
   Quoted in the *Observer* 23 April 1950

2 The weak have one weapon: the errors of those who think they are strong.
   ibid. 15 July 1962

## Kathryn Bigelow (b. 1951)

US FILM-MAKER

She won acclaim as director of the contemporary horror film *Near Dark* (1987), followed by the thriller *Blue Steel* (1990), which is regarded as her best work. Later films include *Strange Days* (1995).

1 Films don't cause violence, people do. Violence defines

our existence. To shield oneself is more dangerous than trying to reflect it.
   Interview in the *Guardian* 23 December 1995

## Steve Biko (1946–77)

SOUTH AFRICAN ANTI-APARTHEID ACTIVIST

A symbol of resistance to apartheid, he became founder and leader of the Black Consciousness Movement in South Africa, and in 1972 President of the Black People's Convention. Banned from political activity in 1973 and frequently detained, he died in police custody. He was the subject of the film *Cry Freedom* (1987).

1 The claim by whites of monopoly on comfort and security has always been so exclusive that blacks see whites as the major obstacle in their progress towards peace, prosperity and a sane society. . . . At best therefore blacks see whiteness as a concept that warrants being despised, hated, destroyed and replaced by an aspiration with more human content in it. At worst blacks envy white society for the comfort it has usurped and at the centre of this envy is the wish – nay, the secret determination – in the innermost minds of most blacks who think like this, to kick whites off those comfortable garden chairs that one sees as he rides in a bus, out of town, and to claim them for themselves.
   'Fear – an Important Determinant in South African Politics', first publ. in 1971 in SASO newsletter, one of a series of articles entitled 'I Write What I Like' under the pseudonym of Frank Talk, repr. in *I Write What I Like* (ed. Aelred Stubbs, 1978). The words were repeated by the judge at Biko's trial in 1976.

2 Powerlessness breeds a race of beggars who smile at the enemy and swear at him in the sanctity of their toilets; who shout 'Baas' willingly during the day and call the white man a dog in their buses as they go home. Once again the concept of fear is at the heart of this two-faced behaviour on the part of the conquered blacks.
   ibid.

3 The white strategy so far has been to systematically break down the resistance of the blacks to the point where the latter would accept crumbs from the white table. This we have shown we reject unequivocally; and now the stage is therefore set for a very interesting turn of events.
   ibid. Closing words of article.

4 The philosophy of Black Consciousness therefore expresses group pride and the determination of the black to rise and attain the envisaged self. . . . At the heart of this kind of thinking is the realization by blacks that the most potent weapon in the hands of the oppressor is the mind of the oppressed.
   'Black Consciousness and the Quest for a True Humanity', first publ. in *Black Theology: the South African Voice* (ed. Basil Moore, 1973), repr. in ibid.

5 The power of a movement lies in the fact that it can indeed change the habits of people. This change is not the result of force but of dedication, of moral persuasion.
   Interview in July 1976, quoted in *Biko*, ch. 2 (1978) by Donald Woods

6 Whites must be made to realize that they are only human, not superior. Same with blacks. They must be made to realize that they are also human, not inferior.
   Quoted in the *Boston Globe* 26 October 1977

7 You are either alive and proud or you are dead, and when you are dead, you can't care anyway. And your method of death can itself be a politicizing thing. So you die in the riots. For a hell of a lot of them, in fact, there's really nothing to lose – almost literally, given the kind of situations they come from. So if you can overcome the

personal fear of death, which is a highly irrational thing, you know, then you're on the way.

Interview first publ. in *New Republic* 7 January 1978, repr. in *I Write What I Like*, 'On Death' (ed. Aelred Stubbs, 1978)

8 Listen, if you guys want to do this your way, you have got to handcuff me and bind my feet together, so that I can't respond. If you allow me to respond, I'm certainly going to respond. And I'm afraid you may have to kill me in the process even if it's not your intention.

To his gaolers, quoted in ibid. With these words Biko forecast the manner of his death at the hands of the South African police at Port Elizabeth Jail, 12 September 1977.

9 If you want to say something radical, you should dress conservative.

Advice given to the young BARBARA FOLLETT, quoted by her in the *Observer* 25 February 1996

## Laurence Binyon (1869–1943)
BRITISH POET

His collections include *Lyric Poems* (1894) and *Odes* (1901), though he is best remembered for his poem 'For the Fallen'. He was Professor of Poetry at Harvard (1933–4).

1 They shall grow not old, as we that are left grow old:
Age shall not weary them, nor the years condemn.
At the going down of the sun and in the morning
We will remember them.

'For the Fallen', first publ. in *The Times* 21 September 1914, repr. in *Collected Poems* (1931). The lines, which were set to music by Elgar, are inscribed on war memorials throughout Britain and the Commonwealth.

## William Norman Birkett (1883–1962)
BRITISH LAWYER

Baron Birkett of Ulveston. He established a reputation as counsel in murder trials and was prominent in the summing up of the Nuremberg Trials (1945–6). A Liberal MP (1923–4 and 1929–31), he was Lord Justice of Appeal 1950–57.

1 I do not object to people looking at their watches when I am speaking. But I strongly object when they start shaking them to make certain they are still going.

Quoted in the *Observer* 30 October 1960

## (Sir) John Birt (b. 1944)
BRITISH TELEVISION EXECUTIVE

He joined Granada television in 1968 and worked on *World in Action*, later to become Deputy Director of the BBC (1987) and Director-General (1993–99) during which time he instituted controversial reforms,

1 The BBC is the most successful cultural institution in the world, one of the great inventions of the twentieth century. Let it flower; let it blossom; let it flourish; let it pioneer; let it grow. It is not difficult to see why it became easier to bash the BBC than to revere it. But do not take the BBC for granted.

James MacTaggart Memorial Lecture, Edinburgh, 23 Aug. 1996, publ. in the *Guardian* 24 Aug. 1996

## (Sir) Harrison Birtwistle (b. 1934)
BRITISH COMPOSER

An avant-garde composer, he specializes in chamber music, much of his earlier work being written for the Pierrot Players (renamed Fires of London in 1970), which he co-founded in 1967 with Peter Maxwell Davies. Among his orchestral works are *Tragoedia* (1965) and his operas include *Punch and Judy* (1967) and *Gawain* (1991).

1 People basically only want very little from music, and I want a lot from it. It's capable of amazing journeys and meanings. And if you understand that, the problem with the kind of music I write is no problem at all.

Interview in the *Independent on Sunday* 7 April 1996

## Elizabeth Bishop (1911–79)
US POET

Having grown up in New England and Nova Scotia, she lived for sixteen years in Brazil, the subject of much of her poetry. She received the Pulitzer Prize in 1956 for her first two collections *North and South* (1946) and *Cold Spring* (1955). Her other writings, which include translations and autobiographical sketches, also reflect her itinerant life.

1 The armored cars of dreams, contrived to let us do
so many a dangerous thing.

'Sleeping Standing Up', st. 2, publ. in *Poems: North and South* (1946)

2 Topography displays no favorites; North's as near as West.
More delicate than the historians' are the map-makers' colors.

'The Map', publ. in ibid.

3 Should we have stayed at home and thought of here?
Where should we be today?
Is it right to be watching strangers in a play
in this strangest of theatres?

'Questions of Travel', st. 2, publ. in *Questions of Travel* (1965)

4 What childishness is it that while there's breath of life
in our bodies, we are determined to rush
to see the sun the other way around?

ibid.

5 The art of losing isn't hard to master;
so many things seem filled with the intent
to be lost that their loss is no disaster.

'One Art', publ. in *Geography III* (1976)

## Jacqueline Bisset (b. 1944)
BRITISH SCREEN ACTRESS

After a bit part in *The Knack* (1965) and a larger role in *Casino Royale* (1967), she moved to Hollywood in the late 1960s where she appeared in such major productions as *Airport* (1970), *The Sunday Woman* (1976) and *Dangerous Beauty* (1998).

1 Character contributes to beauty. It fortifies a woman as her youth fades. A mode of conduct, a standard of courage, discipline, fortitude and integrity can do a great deal to make a woman beautiful.

Quoted in the *Los Angeles Times* 16 May 1974

## Björk (b. 1965)
ICELANDIC SINGER

Her first solo album, *Debut*, was released after she left the Sugarcubes, in 1992, followed by *Post* in 1995. Crediting her gymnastic vocal technique and breath control to a study of karate, she maintains that pop music should reflect the different moods of the 'emotional roller coaster' of everyday life.

1 I tell women, 'Go and masturbate! Get loads of kinky books and masturbate every day! *They* do it from the age of nine!'

Remark in 1993, quoted in *NME* 4 February 1995

## Conrad Black (b. 1944)
CANADIAN NEWSPAPER PROPRIETOR

He acquired the *Daily Telegraph* newspaper group in 1985, becoming Chair in 1987.

1 My experience with journalists authorizes me to record

that a very large number of them are ignorant, lazy, opinionated, intellectually dishonest and inadequately supervised.

Testimony to a Canadian Senate Committee, quoted in the *Observer* 28 January 1996

## Shirley Temple Black (b. 1928)
US ACTRESS

The most successful child star of the 1930s, she starred in *Bright Eyes* (1934) in which she sang 'On the Good Ship Lollipop' and *Curly Top* (1935). After her screen career, she became involved in Republican politics, was White House Chief of Protocol (1976–7) and Ambassador to Czechoslovakia (1989–93).

1 I stopped believing in Santa Claus when I was six. Mother took me to see him in a department store and he asked for my autograph.

Quoted in *Halliwell's Who's Who in the Movies* (ed. John Walker, 1999)

## Tony Blair (b. 1953)
BRITISH POLITICIAN AND PRIME MINISTER

Elected leader of the Labour Party in 1994, he achieved a landslide victory in the 1997 general election, becoming the youngest prime minister to gain office since 1812. His rebranding of the party as New Labour has distanced it from traditional socialist concerns in favour of 'social market' values. For Michael Portillo, however, 'Tony Blair is to Mrs Thatcher what Bjorn Again is to Abba.' See also MICHAEL FOOT 3, SUN 9.

1 The art of leadership is saying no, not saying yes. It is very easy to say yes.

Quoted in the *Mail on Sunday* 2 October 1994

2 Any parent wants the best for their children. I am not going to make a choice for my child on the basis of what is the politically correct thing to do.

Quoted in the *Independent on Sunday* 1 January 1995. Blair provoked controversy by sending his children to a school outside the comprehensive system.

3 Ask me my three main priorities for Government, and I tell you: education, education and education.

Speech at Labour Party Conference, 1 October 1996, quoted in *The Times* 2 October 1996

4 People everywhere ... kept faith with Princess Diana. They liked her, they loved her, they regarded her as one of the people. She was the People's Princess, and that is how she will stay, how she will remain in our hearts and our memories forever.

Speech at Sedgefield, 31 Aug. 1997, quoted in *The Times* 1 September 1997. Blair had been informed of DIANA's death a few hours previously.

5 This is not a time for soundbites. We've left them at home. I feel the hand of history upon our shoulders.

Press conference in Belfast, BBC Radio 5 Live, 7 April 1998. The Prime Minister had arrived in Northern Ireland as the peace discussions appeared to be on the brink of collapse. Blair also used the phrase 'hand of history' on the occasion of the opening of the Northern Ireland Assembly at Stormont Castle, 2 December 1999, the day when the Republic of Ireland dropped its constitutional claim over Northern Ireland.

6 In these past few days, the irresistible force, the political will, has met the immovable object, the legacy of the past, and we have moved it.

Speech at Stormont, 10 April 1998, quoted in *The Times* 11 April 1998. Blair was celebrating Senator George Mitchell's announcement of the signing of the Good Friday Agreement after twenty-two months of negotiation.

## Raymond Blanc (b. 1949)
FRENCH CHEF AND RESTAURATEUR

In England since 1972, he began cooking in a Thames-side pub in 1975, progressing to a small restaurant, *Les Quat' Saisons*, in Oxford and opening the prestigious *Le Manoir aux Quat' Saisons* in 1984, quickly established as one of the top gastronomic destinations outside London. He also appears on television and has written *Cooking for Friends* (1991) and *Blanc Mange* (1994).

1 To me, when a mother puts food in a microwave for her children, it is an act of hate.

Quoted in the *Daily Telegraph* 21 October 1995

## Maurice Blanchot (b. 1907)
FRENCH LITERARY THEORIST AND AUTHOR

After wartime renunciation of Fascism, he became a man of letters, with prose that John Updike likened to 'a cascade of mystification bejewelled with melodramatic glances and gothic gewgaws'. His critical works include *The Space of Literature* (1955) and his fiction *Death Sentence* (1948) and *The Last Man* (1957).

1 To write is to make oneself the echo of what cannot cease speaking.

*The Space of Literature*, ch. 1, 'The Essential Solitude' (1955, transl. 1982)

## Alan Bleasdale (b. 1946)
BRITISH PLAYWRIGHT AND NOVELIST

He won a large audience for the TV series *The Boys from the Blackstuff* (1982) and *GBH* (1991), both set in his native Liverpool. Other work for TV includes *Melissa* (1997) and a popular adaptation of *Oliver Twist* (1999), while his stage works include *Are You Lonesome Tonight* (1985), a musical about Elvis Presley.

1 Gizza job, go on, gizzit!

Yosser Hughes, in *The Boys from the Blackstuff* (TV series, 1982). The catchphrase is usually quoted, 'gissa job!'

## Edward Blishen (1920–96)
BRITISH AUTHOR

For many years a teacher, he was the editor of anthologies and the author of reference works for children as well as of biography and novels, for example *Roaring Boys* (1955).

1 Life is amazing: and the teacher had better prepare himself to be a medium for that amazement.

*Donkey Work*, pt 2, ch. 5 (autobiography, 1983). Blishen rejected the idea that teaching is a discipline, rather 'half vocational, half an emptiness dressed up in garments borrowed from philosophy, psychology, literature'.

## Alexander Blok (1880–1921)
RUSSIAN POET

Considered the leading Russian Symbolist, he took the 1917 Revolution as inspiration for his masterpiece *The Twelve* (1918), though later became disillusioned with the Bolshevik régime. As TROTSKY commented, 'Certainly Blok was not one of us, but he came towards us. And that is what broke him.'

1 Ah, a bitter bitterness,
A sweet life we've won,
With a tattered overcoat
And an Austrian gun.

'The Twelve', sect. 3 (1918), repr. in *A Second Book of Russian Verse* (ed. C.M. Bowra, 1948). The poem describes the experiences of twelve guards during the October Revolution.

2 Like the dog, stands the bourgeois, hungry,
A silent question to the sky;
The old world, like a homeless mongrel,

With tail between its legs stands by.

ibid., sect. 9

3  On they march with sovereign tread,
   With a starving dog behind,
   With a blood-red flag ahead –
   In the storm where none can see,
   From the rifle bullets free,
   Gently walking on the snow,
   Where like pearls the snowflakes glow,
   Marches rose-crowned in the van
   Jesus Christ, the Son of Man.

ibid., sect. 12. Last lines of poem.

## Allan Bloom (1930–92)

US ACADEMIC AND AUTHOR

A Professor of Philosophy and Political Science whose writings have stoked debate about the state of America, he called himself 'the corrosive force that appeals to liberals'. His critique of the education system, *The Closing of the American Mind* (1987), caused most impact. *Giants and Dwarfs* (1990) and *Love and Friendship* (1991) are collections of essays.

1  Only Socrates knew, after a lifetime of unceasing labor, that he was ignorant. Now every high-school student knows that. How did it become so easy?

*The Closing of the American Mind*, Introduction (1987)

2  The spirit is at home, if not entirely satisfied, in America.

ibid. pt 2, 'Two Revolutions and Two States of Nature'

3  We are like ignorant shepherds living on a site where great civilizations once flourished. The shepherds play with the fragments that pop up to the surface, having no notion of the beautiful structures of which they were once a part.

ibid. 'Our Ignorance'

4  The most important function of the university in an age of reason is to protect reason from itself.

ibid. pt 3, 'From Socrates' *Apology* to Heidegger's *Rektoratsrede*'

## Harold Bloom (b. 1930)

US LITERARY CRITIC

Called the leading critic of our time, he has taught continuously at Yale University since 1955 while retaining his independence of the academic world, which he sees as dominated 'by fools, knaves, charlatans and bureaucrats'. He is a great popularizer of Shakespeare, but his best-known work is *The Anxiety of Influence* (1973). Later publications include *The Western Canon* (1994), a popular critical study.

1  The Anxiety of Influence.

Book title (1973). Bloom's most influential work used Freudian concepts to postulate an unconscious literary battle between generations of poets and authors.

2  People cannot stand the saddest truth I know about the very nature of reading and writing imaginative literature, which is that poetry does not teach us how to talk to other people: it teaches us how to talk to ourselves. What I'm desperately trying to do is to get students to talk to themselves as though they are indeed themselves, and not someone else.

Interview in the *Guardian* 6 March 1999

## David Blunkett (b. 1947)

BRITISH POLITICIAN

Elected MP for Sheffield, Brightside, in 1987, he became Secretary of State for Education and Employment in 1997. He has been blind since birth. A.N. WILSON described him as 'one of the most eloquent exponents of old-fashioned, unreconstituted old bossy-boots, Stafford Cripps-style Stalinism'.

1  Old Labour is the idea that you did things *to* people, New Labour is about enabling people to do things for themselves.

Quoted in the *Guardian* 18 July 1998

## Robert Bly (b. 1926)

US POET AND AUTHOR

Through his magazine *The Fifties* (later *The Sixties* and the *The Seventies*), he provided a vehicle for lesser known European and South American poets. The first book of his own poetry, *Silence in the Snowy Fields*, was published in 1962, *Morning Poems* in 1997.

1  Every modern male has, lying at the bottom of his psyche, a large, primitive being covered with hair down to his feet. Making contact with this Wild Man is the step the Eighties male or the Nineties male has yet to take. That bucketing-out process has yet to begin in our contemporary culture.

*Iron John*, ch. 1, 'Finding Iron John' (1990)

## Enid Blyton (1897–1968)

BRITISH CHILDREN'S WRITER

She achieved enormous popularity, publishing over 600 books featuring among others Noddy and Big Ears, the Famous Five and the Secret Seven.

1  Golliwogs are merely lovable black toys, not Negroes. Teddy bears are also toys, but if there happens to be a naughty one in my books for younger children, this does not mean that I hate bears.

Quoted in *The Enid Blyton Story* by Bob Mullan, ch. 5 (1987). Blyton's books were criticized from the 1960s for their stereotyping.

## Ivan F. Boesky (b. 1937)

US FINANCIER

The best known of Wall Street arbitrageurs, he was fined $100 million for insider dealing in 1986 and served a prison sentence.

1  Greed is all right, by the way . . . I think greed is healthy. You can be greedy and still feel good about yourself.

Commencement Address, School of Business Administration, University of California, Berkeley, 18 May 1986. Boesky's words were later picked up in Oliver Stone's film, *Wall Street* (1987), spoken by Gordon Gekko (played by Michael Douglas): 'Greed is good. Greed is right. Greed clarifies, cuts through, and captures. Greed has marked the upward surge of mankind.'

## Louise Bogan (1897–1970)

US POET AND CRITIC

Poetry editor for the *New Yorker* (1931–69), she published six volumes of her own verse, from *Body of This Death* (1923) to *The Blue Estuaries* (1968), as well as the highly regarded *Achievement in American Poetry 1900–1950* (1951).

1  Women have no wilderness in them,
   They are provident instead,
   Content in the tight hot cell of their hearts
   To eat dusty bread.

'Women', st. 1, publ. in *Body of this Death* (1923)

2  But childhood prolonged cannot remain a fairyland. It becomes a hell.

'Childhood's False Eden' (1940), repr. in *Selected Criticism: Poetry and Prose* (1955). Referring to KATHERINE MANSFIELD.

3  The intellectual is a middle-class product; if he is not born into the class he must soon insert himself into it,

in order to exist. He is the fine nervous flower of the bourgeoisie.

'Some Notes on Popular and Unpopular Art' (1943), repr. in ibid.

## Humphrey Bogart (1899–1957)
US SCREEN ACTOR

After an uneven stage career and myriad B-parts in movies, he rocketed to fame with the films *High Sierra* and *The Maltese Falcon* (both in 1941). Other successes which gave birth to the 'Bogie' cult included *Casablanca* (1942), *To Have and Have Not* (1944) and *The Big Sleep* (1946), the last two co-starring LAUREN BACALL, his fourth wife; *The African Queen* (1951) won him an Academy Award. The producer Stanley Kramer said of him: 'He was playing Bogart all the time, but he was really just a big bowl of sloppy mush.' See also INGRID BERGMAN 1, RAYMOND CHANDLER 1, DASHIELL HAMMETT 1.

1 Of all the gin joints in all the towns in all the world, she walks into mine.

Rick Blaine (Humphrey Bogart), in *Casablanca* (film, screenplay by Julius Epstein, Philip Epstein and Howard Koch, from the play *Everybody Goes to Rick's* by Murray Burnett and Joan Alison, directed by Michael Curtiz, 1942)

2 Here's looking at you, kid.

ibid. Toast spoken to Ilsa Lund (Ingrid Bergman)

3 I stick my neck out for nobody. I'm the only cause I'm interested in.

ibid. Bogart's words are echoed in another speech by him in John Huston's film *Key Largo* (1948), where he says, 'I fight nobody's battles but my own,' and also recall a similar statement by CLARK GABLE as Rhett Butler in *Gone With the Wind* (1939).

4 I'm no good at being noble, but it doesn't take much to see that the problems of three little people don't amount to a hill of beans in this crazy world. Someday you'll understand that.

ibid. Spoken in the final scenes of the film to Ilsa Lund (Ingrid Bergman), escaping from Casablanca with her husband.

5 Louis, I think this is the beginning of a beautiful friendship.

ibid. Spoken to Cpt. Louis Renault (Claude Rains) in the film's last words. In her 1980 autobiography, INGRID BERGMAN recounted the uncertainty over how the film was going to end, and even whether or not she was to get on the plane, until this closing scene was shot.

6 My, my. Such a lot of guns around town and so few brains.

Philip Marlowe (Humphrey Bogart), in *The Big Sleep* (film, screenplay by William Faulkner, Leigh Brackett and Jules Furthman adapted from Raymond Chandler's novel, directed by Howard Hawks, 1946)

7 You're not a star until they can spell your name in Karachi.

Quoted in *Star Billing* (1985) by David Brown. The showbiz saying has also been attributed to ROGER MOORE

8 Tennis, anyone?

Attributed sole line in first speaking part, but denied by Bogart. In contrast to his later cynical film roles, his early parts on stage were as romantic leads: as DAVID THOMSON commented, 'He was from the upper classes, and he usually played young men who asked girls for tennis.'

## Niels Bohr (1885–1962)
DANISH PHYSICIST

One of the foremost scientists of the twentieth century, he founded and directed the Institute of Theoretical Physics in Copenhagen 1920–62, produced a new model of atomic structure, and was a major contributor to the development of quantum physics. Although he had also assisted in the research for the atomic bomb, he later worked for control of nuclear weapons. He was awarded the Nobel Physics Prize in 1922.

1 An expert is a man who has made all the mistakes which can be made in a very narrow field.

Quoted in *The Harvest of a Quiet Eye* (1977) by Alan L. Mackay

## William Bolitho (1890–1930)
BRITISH AUTHOR

Full name William Bolitho Ryall. He was Paris correspondent for the *Manchester Guardian* and author of offbeat biographical studies in *Murder for Profit* (1926), a study of five mass murderers, and *Twelve against the Gods* (1929). He also wrote essays on international politics.

1 The shortest way out of Manchester is notoriously a bottle of Gordon's gin.

*Twelve against the Gods*, 'Cagliostro (and Seraphina)' (1930)

## Robert Bolt (1924–95)
BRITISH PLAYWRIGHT

He achieved major success with his play *A Man for All Seasons* (1960), and received an Academy Award for his screenplay when it was filmed (1967). He was also responsible for the screenplays of *Lawrence of Arabia* (1962), *Dr Zhivago* (1965) and *The Mission* (1986). He was married to the actress Sarah Miles.

1 Morality's *not* practical. Morality's a gesture. A complicated gesture learned from books.

Sir Thomas More, in *A Man for All Seasons*, act 2 (1960)

2 The nobility of England, my lord, would have snored through the Sermon on the Mount.

ibid.

3 The law is not a 'light' for you or any man to see by; the law is not an instrument of any kind. The law is a causeway upon which so long as he keeps to it a citizen may walk safely.

ibid.

## Edward Bond (b. 1934)
BRITISH PLAYWRIGHT

The brutal imagery of his early plays provoked controversy and bans on *Saved* (1965) and *Early Morning* (1968). The resulting public outcry helped to bring about the end of censorship for the English stage. Later works include *Bingo* (1974) and *War Plays* (1985).

1 I write about violence as naturally as Jane Austen wrote about manners. Violence shapes and obsesses our society, and if we do not stop being violent we have no future.

*Lear*, Preface (1972)

## Violet Bonham-Carter (1887–1969)
BRITISH POLITICIAN

Lady Asquith. The daughter of HERBERT ASQUITH, she was President of the Liberal Party 1944–5 and Governor of the BBC 1941–6. She published *Winston Churchill As I Knew Him* in 1965.

1 [He] has a brilliant mind until it is made up.

Quoted in *The Fine Art of Political Wit*, ch. 12 (1964) by Leon Harris. Referring to Labour politician Sir Stafford Cripps.

## Bono (b. 1960)
IRISH ROCK MUSICIAN

Original name Paul Hewson. He is leader of U2, which in the 1980s was called the world's biggest rock band, based on the sales of such albums as *War* (1983) and *The Joshua Tree* (1987). Bono, an evangelical Christian, was in the forefront of the Jubilee 2000 campaign to cancel Third World debt.

1 What a city, what a night, what a crowd, what a bomb, what a mistake, what a wanker you have for a President.

Acceptance speech at MTV Europe Music Awards in Paris, quoted in *Mojo*, January 1996. Referring to French nuclear testing in the Pacific.

2 These days, everyone wants John Lennon's sunglasses, accent and swagger, but no one is prepared to take their clothes off and stand naked like he did in his songs. Putting your head over the parapet means something completely different these days, but it's still a big part of what rock is all about for me. You have to use your celebrity, negotiate your position and be aware that celebrity can diminish a cause as much as illuminate it.

Interview in the *Guardian* 4 March 2000

## Murray Bookchin (b. 1921)

US ECOLOGIST

His books *Our Synthetic Environment* (1962) and *Crisis in Our Cities* (1965) were among the earliest warnings of the dangers to the environment. Opposed to the destructive elements in hierarchical societies, he argues that 'formless urban agglomerations' should be replaced by 'human-scaled ecotechnologies'.

1 Humanity has passed through a long history of one-sidedness and of a social condition that has always contained the potential of destruction, despite its creative achievements in technology. The great project of our time must be to open the other eye: to see all-sidedly and wholly, to heal and transcend the cleavage between humanity and nature that came with early wisdom.

*The Ecology of Freedom*, ch. 1 (1982)

## John Boorman (b. 1933)

BRITISH FILM-MAKER

His greatest successes over an uneven career include *Point Blank* (1967), *Deliverance* (1972), *Excalibur* (1981) and *Hope and Glory* (1987).

1 What is passion? It is surely the becoming of a person. Are we not, for most of our lives, marking time? Most of our being is at rest, unlived. In passion, the body and the spirit seek expression outside of self. Passion is all that is other from self. Sex is only interesting when it releases passion. The more extreme and the more expressed that passion is, the more unbearable does life seem without it. It reminds us that if passion dies or is denied, we are partly dead and that soon, come what may, we will be wholly so.

Journal entry, 16 May 1991, publ. in *Projections* (ed. John Boorman and Walter Donohue, 1992)

## Daniel J. Boorstin (b. 1914)

US HISTORIAN

Full name Daniel Joseph Boorstin. Professor of American History at Chicago University 1944–69, he is the author of *A History of the United States* (1980) and *The Americans* trilogy (1965, 1968 and 1973) among other works. *The Democratic Experience* (1973) won him the Pulitzer Prize in 1974. He was Librarian of Congress 1975–87.

1 We need not be theologians to see that we have shifted responsibility for making the world interesting from God to the newspaperman.

*The Image*, ch. 1 (1961)

2 The celebrity is a person who is known for his well-knownness.

ibid. ch. 2

3 We read advertisements . . . to discover and enlarge our

desires. We are always ready – even eager – to discover, from the announcement of a new product, what we have all along wanted without really knowing it.

ibid. ch. 5

4 The world of crime . . . is a last refuge of the authentic, uncorrupted, spontaneous event.

ibid. ch. 6

5 The most important American addition to the World Experience was the simple surprising fact of America. We have helped prepare mankind for all its later surprises.

Reith Lecture, October 1975, publ. in *The Exploring Spirit: America and the World Experience*, lecture 6 (1976)

## Jorge Luis Borges (1899–1986)

ARGENTINIAN AUTHOR

One of the foremost Latin American writers of the twentieth century, he is considered the progenitor of the 'magic realist' school. From 1923 he published poems and essays, and from 1941 collections of stories, notably *El Aleph* (1949) and *Dreamtigers* (1960). He lectured extensively for nearly forty years.

1 One concept corrupts and confuses the others. I am not speaking of the Evil whose limited sphere is ethics; I am speaking of the infinite.

*Avatars Of The Tortoise* (1939), repr. in *Other Inquisitions* (1960)

2 I thought that a man can be the enemy of other men, of the moments of other men, but not of a country: not of fireflies, words, gardens, streams of water, sunsets.

*Ficciones*, 'The Garden of Forking Paths' (1944, transl. 1962)

3 Like all writers, he [ Jaromir Hladik] measured the achievements of others by what they had accomplished, asking of them that they measure him by what he envisaged or planned.

ibid. 'The Secret Miracle'

4 Universal history is the history of a few metaphors.

'Pascal's Sphere', first publ. 1951, repr. in *Other Inquisitions* (1960)

5 Every writer 'creates' his own precursors. His work modifies our conception of the past, as it will modify the future.

'Kafka and his Precursors', first publ. 1951, repr. in ibid.

6 Literature is not exhaustible, for the sufficient and simple reason that a single book is not. A book is not an isolated entity: it is a narration, an axis of innumerable narrations. One literature differs from another, either before or after it, not so much because of the text as for the manner in which it is read.

'For Bernard Shaw', first publ. 1952, repr. in ibid.

7 To fall in love is to create a religion that has a fallible god.

'The Meeting in a Dream', first publ. 1952, repr. in ibid.

8 The truth is that we live out our lives putting off all that can be put off; perhaps we all know deep down that we are immortal and that sooner or later all men will do and know all things.

*Labyrinths*, 'Funes the Memorious' (1962)

9 I cannot walk through the suburbs in the solitude of the night without thinking that the night pleases us because it suppresses idle details, just as our memory does.

ibid. 'A New Refutation of Time'

10 Time is the substance from which I am made. Time is a river which carries me along, but I am the river; it is a tiger that devours me, but I am the tiger; it is a fire that consumes me, but I am the fire.

ibid.

11 The flattery of posterity is not worth much more than contemporary flattery, which is worth nothing.

*Dreamtigers*, 'Dead Men's Dialogue' (1964)

12 Each man is given, in dreams, a little personal eternity

which allows him to see the recent past and the near future.

'Nightmares', lecture in Buenos Aires 1976, publ. in *Seven Nights* (1980, transl. 1984)

13 **The Falklands thing was a fight between two bald men over a comb.**

*Time* 14 February 1983

14 **Life itself is a quotation.**

Quoted in *Cool Memories*, ch. 5 (1987) by Jean Baudrillard

## P.W. Botha (b. 1916)

SOUTH AFRICAN POLITICIAN AND PRIME MINISTER

Full name Pieter Willem Botha. He was Prime Minister 1978–84, and first State President (1984–9). Although committed to white supremacy, he initiated limited constitutional reforms and concessions to non-whites, but after a stroke was forced into resigning in favour of F.W. DE KLERK.

1 **There is only one element that can break the Afrikaner, and that is the Afrikaner himself. It is when the Afrikaner, like a baboon shot in the stomach, pulls out his own intestines. We must guard against that.**

Speech 26 April 1984, quoted in the *Independent on Sunday* 15 March 1992

2 **I'm not here to apologize.**

Statement in court, quoted in the *Daily Telegraph* 24 January 1998. Botha was answering charges of refusing to appear before the Truth and Reconciliation Commission.

## Ian Botham (b. 1955)

BRITISH CRICKETER

One of the world's greatest cricketing all rounders, he has played for Somerset, Worcester and Durham, was captain of England (1980–81) and was England's leading wicket taker by the end of his 102 tests (1977–92). Since his retirement from cricket he has raised funds for charities from numerous sponsored walks.

1 **When you're on the way up there are plenty of people climbing over each other to buy you drinks, but when things start going wrong, more often than not, you drink alone.**

*Botham: My Autobiography*, ch. 7 (1994)

2 **To be No. 1 in sport you have to have a narrow tunnel vision. Dedication. You want to call it selfishness, arrogance, whatever. It's dog eat dog. There are no prisoners taken; there's none expected.**

Interview in the *Guardian* 10 September 1994

## Pierre Boulez (b. 1925)

FRENCH COMPOSER AND CONDUCTOR

An advocate of the twentieth-century repertoire, he was Conductor of the New York Philharmonic Orchestra (1971–8) and the BBC Symphony Orchestra (1971–5). His reputation as a composer was established with *Le Marteau sans Maître* (1954), which like his other works explores serialism using electronic instruments.

1 **Revolutions are celebrated when they are no longer dangerous.**

*Guardian* 13 January 1989. Referring to the bicentenary celebrations of the French Revolution.

2 **Composing is a constant urge – it never stops. But it's organic, like a seed growing inside. Sometimes it has to wait, you must water it, trim it.**

Quoted in the *Daily Telegraph* 29 January 2000

## Paul Bourget (1852–1935)

FRENCH NOVELIST AND CRITIC

Such novels as *Le Disciple* (1889) are distinguished by their psychological insights. He became better known for his works of criticism, for example *Pages de doctrine et de critique* (1912).

1 **One must live the way one thinks or end up thinking the way one has lived.**

*Le Démon de Midi*, 'Conclusion' (1914)

## Boutros Boutros-Galli (b. 1922)

EGYPTIAN POLITICIAN AND DIPLOMAT

While Minister of State for Foreign Affairs (1977–91), he was a member of the diplomatic mission that resulted in the Camp David Agreement (1978). He was Secretary-General of the United Nations 1992–6, the first Arab and first African to hold the post.

1 **When I have tense relations with my wife, we speak Arabic. When we talk business, then we speak English. And when our relationship is better, then we talk French.**

Quoted in the *Mail on Sunday* 15 November 1998

## Elizabeth Bowen (1899–1973)

ANGLO-IRISH NOVELIST

She set her novels and short stories in the milieu she knew best, the country houses of the Anglo-Irish and the homes of London's upper classes. Her best-known works of fiction, which adeptly describe the emotional nuances of relationships, are *The Death of the Heart* (1938) and *The Heat of the Day* (1949).

1 **There is no end to the violations committed by children on children, quietly talking alone.**

*The House in Paris*, pt 1, ch. 2 (1935)

2 **Intimacies between women go backwards, beginning with revelations and ending up in small talk without loss of esteem.**

*The Death of the Heart*, pt 2, ch. 1 (1938)

3 **Only in a house where one has learnt to be lonely does one have this solicitude for *things*. One's relation to them, the daily seeing or touching, begins to become love, and to lay one open to pain.**

ibid. pt 2, ch. 2

4 **The heart may think it knows better: the senses know that absence blots people out. We really have no absent friends. The friend becomes a traitor by breaking, however unwillingly or sadly, out of our own zone: a hard judgment is passed on him, for all the pleas of the heart.**

ibid.

5 **Pity the selfishness of lovers: it is brief, a forlorn hope; it is impossible.**

ibid. ch. 4

6 **Nobody can be kinder than the narcissist while you react to life in his own terms.**

ibid. pt 3, ch. 3

7 **The charm, one might say the genius of memory, is that it is choosy, chancy, and temperamental: it rejects the edifying cathedral and indelibly photographs the small boy outside, chewing a hunk of melon in the dust.**

*Vogue* 15 September 1955

## David Bowie (b. 1947)

BRITISH ROCK MUSICIAN

Originally named David Jones. At the height of his success during the glam-rock era of the 1970s, he was known for his theatrical stage performances, flamboyant costumes and space-age lyrics. His biggest-selling albums included *Ziggy Stardust* (1972), *Heroes* (1977) and *Let's Dance* (1983), and he has also acted in the film *The Man*

*Who Fell to Earth* (1976) and on Broadway in *The Elephant Man* (1980).

1 Oh you pretty things
 Don't you know you're driving your
 Mamas and papas insane?
 Let me make it plain
 You gotta make way for Homo Superior.

 'Oh! You Pretty Things' (song) on the album *Hunky Dory* (1971)

2 I think that we have created a new kind of person in a way. We have created a child who will be so exposed to the media that he will be lost to his parents by the time he is twelve.

 Quoted in *Melody Maker* 22 January 1972

3 Yes, I believe very strongly in fascism. . . . People have always responded with greater efficiency under a regimental leadership. A liberal wastes time saying, 'Well, now, what ideas have you got?' Show them what to do, for God's sake. If you don't, nothing will get done. I can't stand people just hanging about.

 Interview in February 1976, repr. in *Bowie In His Own Words*, 'Politics' (ed. Miles, 1980). Bowie had earlier voiced similar opinions, in an interview in August 1975, though he later repudiated his remarks, which were merely 'glib, theatrical observations', calling himself 'apolitical'.

4 I
 I will be king
 and you
 you will be queen,
 though nothing will drive them away
 We can be heroes
 Just for one day.

 'Heroes' (song) on the album *Heroes* (1977)

5 Fashion – turn to the left
 Fashion – turn to the right.

 'Fashion' (song) on the album *Scary Monsters and Super Creeps* (1980)

# (Sir) Maurice Bowra (1898–1971)
BRITISH SCHOLAR

Professor of Poetry (1946–51) and Vice Chancellor at Oxford (1951–4), he wrote widely on classical literature and poetry, both ancient and modern. His books include *Greek Lyric Poetry* (1936), *From Virgil to Milton* (1945) and *Poetry and Politics, 1900–1960* (1966).

1 I'm a man more dined against than dining.

 Quoted in *Summoned by Bells*, ch. 9 (1960) John Betjeman. Alluding to Lear's words in *King Lear*: 'I am a man/More sinned against than sinning.'

# Boy George (b. 1961)
BRITISH SINGER

Original name George O'Dowd. With his glamorous looks, cross-dressing and openly gay image, he led his band Culture Club to a string of chart successes in the 1980s, before falling foul of drugs and over-exposure in the media. 'Most great pop careers are built on illusion,' he said, 'and I'm not very good at illusions.'

1 Sex has never been an obsession with me. It's just like eating a bag of crisps. Quite nice, but nothing marvellous.

 Quoted in the *Sun* 21 October 1982

2 If you have to be in a soap opera try not to get the worst role.

 Interview in *The Face* December 1984

3 In England, glamour's in the gutter, it's everywhere, anywhere you want to find it.

 Interview in *Smash Hits* 23 December 1982

# William Boyd (b. 1952)
BRITISH NOVELIST

Having spent his early years in Ghana, he often uses an African setting for his novels, among which are *A Good Man in Africa* (1981, filmed 1994) and *Brazzaville Beach* (1990). He also writes short stories and screenplays.

1 We all want to be happy, and we're all going to die . . . You might say those are the only two unchallengeably true facts that apply to every human being on this planet.

 Loomis Gage, in *Stars and Bars*, pt 2, ch. 6 (1984)

# Charles Boyer (1899–1978)
FRENCH ACTOR

After moving to Hollywood in 1929, he became known as the screen's 'great lover' playing romantic roles in *Mayerling* (1937) and *Algiers* (1938). He won a special Academy Award in 1943 for furthering Franco-American cultural relations.

1 Come with me to the Casbah.

 Attributed

# Malcolm Bradbury (b. 1932)
BRITISH AUTHOR

Closely involved since 1970 with the creative writing programme at the University of East Anglia, he has been one of the principal exponents of the satirical 'campus novel', as in *Eating People Is Wrong* (1959) and *The History Man* (1975). He has also written critical studies, short stories and plays for TV.

1 Reading someone else's newspaper is like sleeping with someone else's wife. Nothing seems to be precisely in the right place, and when you find what you are looking for, it is not clear then how to respond to it.

 Dr Jochum, in *Stepping Westward*, bk 1, ch. 1 (1965)

2 The English are polite by telling lies. The Americans are polite by telling the truth.

 Dr Bernard Froelich, in ibid. bk 2, ch. 5

3 A conventional good read is usually a bad read, a relaxing bath in what we know already. A true good read is surely an act of innovative creation in which we, the readers, become conspirators.

 *Sunday Times* 29 November 1987

# Ray Bradbury (b. 1920)
US SCIENCE FICTION AUTHOR

With his imaginative novels and short stories he took the genre of science fiction to a wider audience. His novels include *Fahrenheit 451* (1953, filmed 1966), and his short-story collection *The Martian Chronicles* (1950, filmed 1966, TV series 1980) is accounted a classic.

1 I don't try to describe the future. I try to prevent it.

 Quoted by ARTHUR C. CLARKE in the *Independent* 16 July 1992

# Omar Bradley (1893–1981)
US GENERAL

He commanded the US First Army at the Normandy invasion (1944) and was first Permanent Chairman of US Joint Chiefs of Staff 1949–53.

1 We have grasped the mystery of the atom and rejected the Sermon on the Mount . . . The world has achieved brilliance without wisdom, power without conscience. Ours is a world of nuclear giants and ethical infants.

 Armistice Day speech, 1948, publ. in *Collected Writings*, vol. 1 (1967)

2 The wrong war, at the wrong place, at the wrong time, and with the wrong enemy.

 Speech to Senate Committees on Armed Services and Foreign

Relations, 15 May 1951, publ. in *The Military Situation in the Far East*, 'Senate Hearings' (1951). Bradley was giving testimony before a Senate enquiry into General MACARTHUR's proposal to carry the Korean conflict into China; Bradley opposed the scheme, arguing that 'Red China is not the powerful nation seeking to dominate the world.'

3 I am convinced that the best service a retired general can perform is to turn in his tongue along with his suit, and to mothball his opinions.

Armed Forces Day address, quoted in *The New York Times* 17 May 1959

## Melvyn Bragg (b. 1939)

BRITISH BROADCASTER AND AUTHOR

A presenter of ITV's *The South Bank Show* and of discussion programmes on BBC Radio 4, he has also worked with Ken Russell on screenplays and documentaries and written over sixteen novels, often set in Cumbria, for example *The Hired Man* (1969) and *A Time to Dance* (1990).

1 There's nothing the British like better than a bloke who comes from nowhere, makes it, and then gets clobbered.

*Guardian* 23 September 1988. Referring to RICHARD BURTON, whose biography by Bragg, *Rich*, appeared that year.

## Marlon Brando (b. 1924)

US SCREEN ACTOR

A 'method' actor with a drawling voice, he caused a sensation for his steamy performance in *A Streetcar Named Desire* (1951), and won Oscars for *On the Waterfront* (1954) and *The Godfather* (1972), – though he refused the latter award in protest against Hollywood's stereotypical treatment of Native Americans. 'If any man can harness atomic energy Mr Brando is the man for the job,' wrote the critic Jympson Harman reviewing *A Streetcar Named Desire*, though BERTOLUCCI thought he was 'an angel as a man, a monster as an actor'. See also GEORGE GLASS 1.

1 What've ya got?

Johnny (Marlon Brando), on being asked what he is rebelling against, in *The Wild One* (film, screenplay by John Paxton from a story by Mick Rooney, directed by Laslo Benedek, 1953).

2 What do I get – a couple of bucks and a one-way ticket to Palookaville. It was you, Charley. You was my brother. You should've looked out for me. Instead of making me take them dives for the short-end money . . . You don't understand! I could've been a contender. I could've had class and been somebody. Real class. Instead of a bum, which is what I am. It was you, Charley.

Terry Mallon (Marlon Brando), in *On The Waterfront* (film, screenplay by Budd Schulberg, directed by Elia Kazan, 1954). The lines are addressed to Mallon's brother (Rod Steiger), whom he blamed for his failed boxing career. The screenplay was based on a series of Pulitzer Prize-winning articles called 'Crime on the Waterfront' by Malcolm Johnson, publ. in the *New York Sun* November–December 1948.

3 To grasp the full significance of life is the actor's duty, to interpret it is his problem, and to express it his dedication.

Said in 1960, quoted in *Marlon Brando*, ch. 1 (1974, rev. 1989) by David Shipman

4 Privacy is not something that I'm merely entitled to, it's an absolute prerequisite.

Quoted in ibid. ch. 11

5 Acting is the expression of a neurotic impulse. It's a bum's life . . . The principal benefit acting has afforded me is the money to pay for my psychoanalysis.

Quoted in *Marlon Brando: The Only Contender*, ch. 13 (1985) by Gary Carey

6 It is a simple fact that all of us use the techniques of acting to achieve whatever ends we seek. . . . Acting serves as the quintessential social lubricant and a device for protecting

our interests and gaining advantage in every aspect of life.

Quoted in *The Technique of Acting*, Introduction (1988) by Stella Adler

7 Mr Dean appears to be wearing my last year's wardrobe and using my last year's talent . . .

Quoted in *James Dean in his Own Words*, 'The Things They Said . . . About Jimmy' (ed. Mick St Michael, 1989). Referring to James Dean; an intense rivalry is said to have existed between the two actors.

8 I have the eyes of a dead pig.

*Screen International* 18 January 1991

9 I don't mind that I'm fat. You still get the same money.

*International Herald Tribune* 9 October 1989

## Wernher von Braun (1912–77)

GERMAN-BORN US ROCKET ENGINEER

After developing V-2 rockets for Germany in the Second World War he moved to the US to work on the project that launched the first American satellite, Explorer 1, in 1958. As Director of the Marshall Space Flight Center (1960–70), he developed the Saturn rocket used in the Apollo 8 moon landing in 1969.

1 Don't tell me that man doesn't belong out there [space]. Man belongs wherever he wants to go – and he'll do plenty well when he gets there.

*Time* 17 February 1958

## Richard Brautigan (1935–84)

US NOVELIST AND POET

Lacking conventional plot and character development, his original and bizarrely humorous novels *A Confederate General from Big Sur* (1965) and *Trout Fishing in America* (1967) established him as a cult figure of the late 1960s. He died from a self-inflicted gunshot wound.

1 If you get hung up on everybody else's hang-ups, then the whole world's going to be nothing more than one huge gallows.

*The Abortion: An Historical Romance 1966* (1970)

## Berke Breathed (b. 1957)

US CARTOONIST AND AUTHOR

Full name Guy Berkeley Breathed. He is regarded as one of America's most popular cartoonists with his long-running, nationwide strip 'Bloom County' (from 1980s). Collections of his cartoons include *Bloom County: Loose Tales* (1983) and *Bloom County Babylon* (1986).

1 I could draw *Bloom County* with my nose and pay my cleaning lady to write it, and I'd bet I wouldn't lose 10% of my papers over the next twenty years. Such is the nature of comic-strips. Once established, their half-life is usually more than nuclear waste.

*Time* 25 December 1989

## Bertolt Brecht (1898–1956)

GERMAN DRAMATIST AND POET

One of Germany's foremost dramatists and a committed Marxist, he collaborated with Kurt Weill to produce *The Threepenny Opera* in 1928. Most of his best work was composed during the fifteen years of his exile from Hitler's Germany (1933–48), including *Mother Courage* (1939) and *The Caucasian Chalk Circle* (1944). He received the Stalin Peace Prize in 1954. PETER HALL is quoted as saying, 'I don't regard Brecht as a man of iron-grey purpose and intellect, I think he is a theatrical whore of the first quality.'

1 Oh, the shark has pretty teeth, dear –
And he shows them pearly white –

Just a jackknife has Macheath, dear –
And he keeps it out of sight.

'The Ballad of Mack the Knife' in *The Threepenny Opera*, Prologue (1928)

2 A man who sees another man on the street corner with only a stump for an arm will be so shocked the first time he'll give him sixpence. But the second time it'll only be a threepenny bit. And if he sees him a third time, he'll have him cold-bloodedly handed over to the police.

Peachum, in ibid. act 1, sc. 1

3 Food first, then morality.

ibid. act 2, sc. 6, 'What Keeps Mankind Alive?'

4 For once you must try not to shirk the facts:
Mankind is kept alive by bestial acts.

ibid.

5 The law was made for one thing alone, for the exploitation of those who don't understand it, or are prevented by naked misery from obeying it.

Peachum, in ibid. act 3, sc. 7

6 What's breaking into a bank compared with founding a bank?

Mac, in ibid. sc. 9

7 You don't need to pray to God any more when there are storms in the sky, but you do have to be insured.

Pelagea Vlasova, in *The Mother*, sc. 10 (1932)

8 Don't be afraid of death so much as an inadequate life.

ibid.

9 Let nothing be called natural
In an age of bloody confusion,
Ordered disorder, planned caprice,
And dehumanized humanity, lest all things
Be held unalterable!

*The Exception and the Rule*, Prologue (1937)

10 Literary works cannot be taken over like factories, or literary forms of expression like industrial methods. Realist writing, of which history offers many widely varying examples, is likewise conditioned by the question of how, when and for what class it is made use of.

'The Popular and the Realistic', written 1938, first publ. 1958, repr. in *Brecht on Theatre* (ed. and transl. John Willett, 1964)

11 The world of knowledge takes a crazy turn
When teachers themselves are taught to learn.

*The Life of Galileo*, sc. 6 (1939, transl. Howard Brenton, 1980)

12 Unhappy the land that is in need of heroes.

Galileo, in ibid. sc. 13. Responding to Andrea's remark, 'Unhappy the land that has no heroes.'

13 Science knows only one commandment – contribute to science.

Andrea, in ibid. sc. 14

14 What they could do with round here is a good war. What else can you expect with peace running wild all over the place? You know what the trouble with peace is? No organization.

The Sergeant, in *Mother Courage and Her Children*, sc. 1 (1939)

15 War is like love, it always finds a way.

The Chaplain, in ibid. sc. 6

16 No one can be good for long if goodness is not in demand.

First God, in *The Good Woman of Setzuan*, sc. 1a (1941)

17 Mixing one's wines may be a mistake, but old and new wisdom mix admirably.

The Singer, in *The Caucasian Chalk Circle*, Prologue (1944)

18 Berlin, an etching by Churchill, after an idea by Hitler.

Journal entry, 27 October 1948, publ. in *Arbeitsjournal*, vol. 2 (1973)

19 We need a type of theatre which not only releases the feelings, insights and impulses possible within the particular historical field of human relations in which the action takes place, but employs and encourages those thoughts and feelings which help transform the field itself.

'A Short Organum for the Theatre', para. 35 (1949), repr. in *Brecht on Theatre* (ed. and transl. John Willett, 1964)

## Howard Brenton (b. 1942) and David Hare (b. 1947)
BRITISH PLAYWRIGHTS

Brenton is known for his provocative politicized plays such as *The Churchill Play* (1974) and *The Romans in Britain* (1980). As well as collaborating with David Hare on *Pravda* (1985), he co-wrote *Moscow Gold* (1990) with TARIQ ALI. See also DAVID HARE.

1 The press and politicians. A delicate relationship. Too close, and danger ensues. Too far apart and democracy itself cannot function without the essential exchange of information. Creative leaks, a discreet lunch, interchange in the Lobby, the art of the unattributable telephone call, late at night.

Quince, in *Pravda*, act 1, sc. 4 (1985)

## Jimmy Breslin (b. 1929)
US JOURNALIST AND AUTHOR

The voice of New York's Irish-American working class, he was an advocate of the 1970s New Journalism in which the writer became personally involved with his subject matter. He won the Pulitzer Prize for his collected newspaper columns in 1987. His other work includes fiction, including *World Without End, Amen* (1973), and biographies.

1 Rage is the only quality which has kept me, or anybody I have ever studied, writing columns for newspapers.

*The Times* 9 May 1990

## Robert Bresson (1907–99)
FRENCH FILM DIRECTOR

He gained international respect with the austere, introspective and intellectual films *The Ladies of the Bois de Boulogne* (1945), *Diary of a Country Priest* (1951) and *A Man Escaped* (1956). Before turning to film he studied painting, which, he said, 'taught me to make not beautiful images but necessary ones'.

1 My movie is born first in my head, dies on paper; is resuscitated by the living persons and real objects I use, which are killed on film but, placed in a certain order and projected onto a screen, come to life again like flowers in water.

*Notes on the Cinematographer*, '1950–1958: On Looks' (1975)

2 Model. Two mobile eyes in a mobile head, itself on a mobile body.

ibid. 'On Automatism'

3 The true is inimitable, the false untransformable.

ibid. 'The Real'

4 *When you do not know what you are doing* and what you are doing is the best – that is inspiration.

ibid.

5 Films can only be made by by-passing the will of those who appear in them, using not what they do, but what they are.

*The Times* 1 November 1990

## André Breton (1896–1966)
FRENCH SURREALIST WRITER

Having been a leader of the Dadaist group in 1916, he was later one of the founders of the Surrealist movement, publishing the

*Surrealist Manifesto* in 1924. *Magnetic Fields* (1920) was the first example of the Surrealist technique of automatic writing. His novel *Nadja* was published in 1928 and his collected poems in 1948.

1 Surrealism, n. Pure psychic automatism, by which it is intended to express, whether verbally or in writing, or in any other way, the real process of thought. Thought's dictation, free from any control by the reason, independent of any aesthetic or moral preoccupation.

*Manifesto of Surrealism* (1924)

2 It is living and ceasing to live that are imaginary solutions. Existence is elsewhere.

ibid. A reference to Rimbaud's famous line '*La vraie vie est absente*' (from his poem 'Délires'), usually translated 'Life is elsewhere.' See also V.S. PRITCHETT 5.

3 Perhaps I am doomed to retrace my steps under the illusion that I am exploring, doomed to try and learn what I should simply recognize, learning a mere fraction of what I have forgotten.

*Nadja* (1928)

4 It is impossible for me to envisage a picture as being other than a window, and . . . my first concern is then to know what it *looks out* on.

*Surrealism and Painting* (1928)

5 To speak of God, to think of God, is in every respect to show what one is made of . . . *I have always wagered against God* and I regard the little that *I have won* in this world as simply the outcome of this bet. However paltry may have been the stake (my life) I am conscious of having won to the full. Everything that is doddering, squint-eyed, vile, polluted and grotesque is summoned up for me in that one word: God!

Footnote in ibid.

6 The approval of the public is to be avoided like the plague. It is absolutely essential to keep the public from *entering* if one wishes to avoid confusion. I must add that the public must be kept panting in expectation at the gate by a system of challenges and provocations.

*Second Manifesto of Surrealism* (1930)

## Fanny Brice (1891–1951)

US ENTERTAINER

Original name Fanny Borach. A singing comedienne, she was a star of the *Ziegfeld Follies*, famous for her satiric sketches, the song '*My Man*', and for her 'Baby Snooks' character, which transferred to radio in 1938 and ran almost until her death.

1 Men always fall for frigid women because they put on the best show.

Quoted in *A Child of the Century*, bk 5, 'Don Juan in Hollywood' (1954) by Ben Hecht

## British Board of Film Censors

1 This film is so cryptic as to be almost meaningless. If there is a meaning, it is doubtless objectionable.

Statement refusing a certificate to the Surrealist film *The Seashell and the Clergyman* (*La Coquille et le clergyman*, film, 1928, screenplay by Antonin Artaud, directed by Germaine Dulac). This was the only one of ARTAUD's scenarios ever to be produced, and was ridiculed by him and other Surrealists at the première, possibly because he didn't feature in it or because it was introduced as his 'personal dream'.

## Vera Brittain (1896–1970)

BRITISH AUTHOR AND PACIFIST

Her experiences as a nurse in the First World War, recounted in her best known work, *Testament of Youth* (1933), helped to shape her life-long commitment to pacifism, which she interpreted from a feminist perspective. Her other works include fiction, poetry and a second volume of autobiography, *Testament of Experience* (1957). She was the mother of SHIRLEY WILLIAMS.

1 All that a pacifist can undertake – but it is a very great deal – is to refuse to kill, injure or otherwise cause suffering to another human creature, and untiringly to order his life by the rule of love though others may be captured by hate.

'What Can We Do In Wartime?', first publ. in *Forward* 9 September 1939, repr. in *Wartime Chronicle: Vera Brittain's Diary 1939–1945* (1989)

2 Politics are usually the executive expression of human immaturity.

*The Rebel Passion*, ch. 1 (1964)

3 I know one husband and wife who, whatever the official reasons given to the court for the break up of their marriage, were really divorced because the husband believed that nobody ought to read while he was talking and the wife that nobody ought to talk while she was reading.

Quoted in *Violets and Vinegar*, 'The Battle Done' (1980) by Jilly Cooper and Tom Hartman

## Benjamin Britten (1913–76)

BRITISH COMPOSER

Baron Britten of Aldeburgh. He wrote mainly for the voice, notably for Peter Pears as in *Peter Grimes* (1945). Other works include the orchestral *The Young Person's Guide to the Orchestra* (1946) and the operas *Billy Budd* (1951) and *A Midsummer Night's Dream* (1960). He founded the Aldeburgh Festival in 1948.

1 It is cruel, you know, that music should be so beautiful. It has the beauty of loneliness and of pain: of strength and freedom. The beauty of disappointment and never-satisfied love. The cruel beauty of nature, and everlasting beauty of monotony.

Letter, 29 June 1937, publ. in *Letters from a Life: Letters and Diaries of Benjamin Britten*, vol. 1, 'A Working Life' (1991). Britten wrote this whilst listening to the 'Abschied', the finale of Mahler's song cycle *Das Lied von der Erde*.

## Hermann Broch (1886–1951)

AUSTRIAN NOVELIST

He is known for his multidimensional and innovative novels, for example *The Sleepwalkers* (trilogy 1931–2), which charts the disintegration of nineteenth-century European society, and *The Death of Virgil* (1945), a study of Virgil's last hours. Imprisoned by the Nazis, he emigrated to America in 1940.

1 Those who live by the sea can hardly form a single thought of which the sea would not be part.

*The Spell*, Foreword (1976, transl. 1987)

2 No one's death comes to pass without making some impression, and those close to the deceased inherit part of the liberated soul and become richer in their humaneness.

ibid. ch. 2

3 While love ceaselessly strives toward that which lies at the hiddenmost centre, hatred only perceives the topmost surface and perceives it so exclusively that the devil of hatred, despite all his terror-inspiring cruelty, never is entirely free of ridicule and of a somewhat dilettantish aspect. One who hates is a man holding a magnifying-glass, and when he hates someone, he knows precisely that person's surface, from the soles of his feet all the way up to each hair on the hated head. Were one merely to seek information, one should inquire of the man who hates, but if one wishes to know what truly is, one better ask the one who loves.

ibid. ch. 9

4 The world has always gone through periods of madness so as to advance a bit on the road to reason.
The doctor, in ibid. ch. 11

## Fawn M. Brodie (1915–81)
US BIOGRAPHER

Her psychobiographies occasionally aroused controversy, as in the case of *No Man Knows My History* (1945), a biography of Joseph Smith, which caused her to be excommunicated from the Mormon church. Other works include *Thomas Jefferson: An Intimate History* (1974) and *Richard Nixon: The Shaping of His Character* (1981).

1 A man's memory is bound to be a distortion of his past in accordance with his present interests, and the most faithful autobiography is likely to mirror less what a man was than what he has become.
*No Man Knows My History*, ch. 19 (1945)

## Harold Brodkey (1930–96)
US AUTHOR

Real name Aaron Roy Weintraub. While staff writer on the *New Yorker* magazine for thirty years he worked on the autobiographical novel *The Runaway Soul*, which was finally published in 1991 to lukewarm response.

1 Athletes have studied how to leap and how to survive the leap some of the time and return to the ground. They don't always do it well. But they are our philosophers of actual moments and the body and soul in them, and of our manoeuvres in our emergencies and longings.
'Meditations on an Athlete', publ. in *Cape* July 1992

2 One may be tired of the world – tired of the prayer-makers, the poem-makers, whose rituals are distracting and human and pleasant but worse than irritating because they have no reality – while reality itself remains very dear. One wants glimpses of the real. God is an immensity, while this disease, this death, which is in me, this small tightly defined pedestrian event, is merely and perfectly real, without miracle – or instruction.
'Passage into Non-Existence', publ. in the *Independent on Sunday* 11 February 1996. The article was Brodkey's last piece of published writing before his death from AIDS.

## Joseph Brodsky (1940–1996)
RUSSIAN-BORN US POET AND CRITIC

Composed in both Russian and English, his poetry deals with loss and exile, influenced by his imprisonment and then banishment from the Soviet Union in 1972. His collections include *The End of a Beautiful Era* (1977) and *To Urania* (1984), and he has also published criticism. He was awarded the Nobel Prize for Literature in 1987.

1 The real history of consciousness starts with one's first lie.
'Less Than One', sect. 1, first publ. 1976, repr. in *Less Than One: Selected Essays* (1986)

2 Every individual ought to know at least one poet from cover to cover: if not as a guide through the world, then as a yardstick for the language.
'To Please a Shadow', sect. 5, first publ. 1983, repr. in ibid. Brodsky recommended W.H. AUDEN as qualified on both counts.

3 The delirium and horror of the East. The dusty catastrophe of Asia. Green only on the banner of the Prophet. Nothing grows here except mustaches.
*Less Than One: Selected Essays* (1986), 'Flight from Byzantium', sect. 9

4 Racism? But isn't it only a form of misanthropy? ... Snobbery? But it's only a form of despair.
ibid.

5 For aesthetics is the mother of ethics ... Were we to choose our leaders on the basis of their reading experience and not their political programs, there would be much less grief on earth. I believe – not empirically, alas, but only theoretically – that for someone who has read a lot of Dickens to shoot his like in the name of an idea is harder than for someone who has read no Dickens.
'Uncommon Visage', Nobel Prize acceptance speech, 1987, publ. in *On Grief and Reason* (1996)

6 After all, it is hard to master both life and work equally well. So if you are bound to fake one of them, it had better be life.
Interview in *Writers at Work* (eighth series, ed. George Plimpton, 1988)

7 There are worse crimes than burning books. One of them is not reading them.
Said at press conference on acceptance of US poet laureateship, Washington, DC, quoted in the *Independent on Sunday* 19 May 1991

## Jacob Bronowski (1908–74)
BRITISH SCIENTIST AND AUTHOR

A popularizer of science and the history of thought, he published *The Common Sense of Science* in 1951 and *The Western Intellectual Tradition* in 1960, but reached a far wider audience through his presentation of the television series *The Ascent of Man* in 1973.

1 Man masters nature not by force but by understanding. This is why science has succeeded where magic failed: because it has looked for no spell to cast over nature.
'The Creative Mind', lecture, 26 February 1953, given at the Massachusetts Institute of Technology, publ. in *Science and Human Values*, sect. 4 (1961)

2 Has there ever been a society which has died of dissent? Several have died of conformity in our lifetime.
'The Sense of Human Dignity', sect. 5, lecture given at the Massachusetts Institute of Technology, 19 March 1953, publ. in *Science and Human Values* (1961)

3 Science has nothing to be ashamed of even in the ruins of Nagasaki. The shame is theirs who appeal to other values than the human imaginative values which science has evolved.
ibid. sect. 11

4 No science is immune to the infection of politics and the corruption of power.
*Encounter* July 1971

5 That is the essence of science: ask an impertinent question, and you are on the way to a pertinent answer.
*The Ascent of Man*, ch. 4 (1973)

6 One aim of the physical sciences has been to give an exact picture of the material world. One achievement of physics in the twentieth century has been to prove that that aim is unattainable.
ibid. ch. 11

7 The University is a Mecca to which students come with something less than perfect faith. It is important that students bring a certain ragamuffin, barefoot irreverence to their studies; they are not here to worship what is known, but to question it.
ibid.

## Rupert Brooke (1887–1915)
BRITISH POET

The most dashing of the Georgian poets, he came to symbolize the golden youth sacrificed in the First World War after his death from blood poisoning en route to the Dardanelles. 'The Old Vicarage, Grantchester' and the 'war sonnets' published in *1914 and Other Poems* (1915) are his best known work. F.R. LEAVIS summarized his verse as 'rather like Keats's vulgarity with a Public School accent'.

1 The cool kindliness of sheets, that soon
   Smooth away trouble; and the rough male kiss
   Of blankets.
   'The Great Lover', publ. in *1914 and Other Poems* (1915)

2 One may not doubt that, somehow, good
   Shall come of water and of mud;
   And sure, the reverent eye must see
   A purpose in liquidity.
   'Heaven', publ. in ibid.

3 But somewhere, beyond Space and Time,
   Is wetter water, slimier slime!
   And there (they trust) there swimmeth One
   Who swam ere rivers were begun,
   Immense, of fishy form and mind,
   Squamous, omnipotent, and kind.
   ibid.

4 If I should die, think only this of me:
   That there's some corner of a foreign field
   That is for ever England.
   'The Soldier', first publ. in *New Numbers*, no. 4 (1914), repr. in *1914 and Other Poems* (1915). Brooke is buried on the island of Skyros, Greece.

5 Now, God be thanked Who has matched us with His hour,
   And caught our youth, and wakened us from sleeping,
   With hand made sure, clear eye, and sharpened power,
   To turn, as swimmers into cleanness leaping.
   'Peace', ibid.

6 And all the little emptiness of love!
   ibid.

## Anita Brookner (b. 1938)
BRITISH NOVELIST AND ART HISTORIAN

An expert on eighteenth-century painting, she is more widely known for her melancholy novels in which the main characters are women. The most successful, *Hôtel du Lac*, received the Booker Prize in 1984. Later novels include *A Friend from England* (1987) and *Visitors* (1997).

1 She was a handsome woman of forty-five and would remain so for many years.
   *Hôtel du Lac*, ch. 4 (1984)

2 You have no idea how promising the world begins to look once you have decided to have it all for yourself. And how much healthier your decisions are once they become entirely selfish.
   Mr Neville, in ibid. ch. 7

3 Good women always think it is their fault when someone else is being offensive. Bad women never take the blame for anything.
   ibid.

4 Writing novels preserves you in a state of innocence – a lot passes you by – simply because your attention is otherwise diverted.
   *Novelists in Interview* (ed. John Haffenden, 1985)

5 Time misspent in youth is sometimes all the freedom one ever has.
   Blanche Vernon, in *The Misalliance*, ch. 10 (1986)

6 It will be a pity if women in the more conventional mould are to be phased out, for there will never be anyone to go home to.
   Rachel, in *A Friend From England*, ch. 10 (1987)

7 What is interesting about self-analysis is that it leads nowhere – it is an art form in itself.
   Interview in *Writers at Work* (eighth series, ed. George Plimpton, 1988)

8 A complete woman is probably not a very admirable creature. She is manipulative, uses other people to get her own way, and works within whatever system she is in.
   ibid.

## Gwendolyn Brooks (b. 1917)
US POET

In 1950 she was the first black author to be awarded the Pulitzer Prize, which she won for her collection of poems, *Annie Allen* (1949). As with her first collection, *A Street in Bronzeville* (1945), this dealt principally with the lives of the urban black poor. The leaner, more energetic style of her later work, for example *In the Mecca* (1968), marked a change from her former sophisticated and intellectual tone.

1 Abortions will not let you forget.
   You remember the children you got that you did not get.
   'The Mother', publ. in *A Street in Bronzeville* (1945)

## Mel Brooks (b. 1926)
US FILM-MAKER AND ACTOR

An irreverent gag-writer and script-doctor turned director of his own screenplays, he excelled in brash bad taste. *The Producers* (1968) was followed by the spoofs *Blazing Saddles* (1974) and *Silent Movie* (1976), among others.

1 Springtime for Hitler and Germany,
   Winter for Poland and France.
   'Springtime for Hitler' in *The Producers* (film, written and directed by Mel Brooks, 1968). The song was the centrepiece of the musical of the same name staged by 'the producers' to guarantee a loss.

2 How could this happen? I was so careful. I picked the wrong play, the wrong director, the wrong cast. Where did I go right?
   Max Bialystock (Zero Mostel), in ibid.

3 Let's face it, sweetheart, without Jews, fags, and Gypsies, there is no theatre.
   Frederick Bronski (Mel Brooks), in *To Be or Not To Be* (film, screenplay by Thomas Meehan and Ronny Graham, directed by Alan Johnson, 1983)

## Heywood Broun (1888–1939)
US JOURNALIST AND NOVELIST

He is chiefly remembered for his columns 'It Seems to Me' in the *Tribune* and *World* in the 1920s and 'Shoot the Works' in the *New Republic* from 1935 until his death.

1 The tragedy of life is not that man loses, but that he almost wins.
   *Pieces of Hate, and Other Enthusiasms*, 'Sport for Art's Sake' (1922)

2 Just as every conviction begins as a whim so does every emancipator serve his apprenticeship as a crank. A fanatic is a great leader who is just entering the room.
   *New York World* 6 February 1928

3 A technical objection is the first refuge of a scoundrel.
   *New Republic* 15 December 1937

## Craig Brown (b. 1957)
BRITISH JOURNALIST

A specialist in parody and satire, he contributes to *Private Eye*, the *Daily Telegraph* and the *Independent*, for which he created the buffer-ish Wallace Arnold. His books include *The Private Eye Book of Craig Brown Parodies* (1995) and *The Little Book of Chaos* (1998).

1 Journalism could be described as turning one's enemies into money.
   *Daily Telegraph* 28 September 1990

2 The most common form of parody is, of course, self-

parody. It is a disease to which every columnist is prone, for it is always easier to reassemble the usual range of columnar emotions – outrage, pity, etc – than to feel them afresh.

*Spectator* 22 November 1999

## H. Rap Brown (b. 1943)

US RADICAL AND AUTHOR

Also known as Jamil Abdullah Al-Amin. A black activist, he was Chairman of the Student Nonviolent Coordinating Committee (SNCC) in Alabama and expressed his inflammatory views in *Die Nigger Die* (1969). While imprisoned for robbery in New York (1971–6), he converted to Islam and changed his name.

1 Violence is as American as cherry pie.
  Press conference at SNCC, Washington, DC, 27 July 1967, quoted in the *Evening Star* 27 July 1967

## James Brown (b. 1928)

US SOUL SINGER

The 'Godfather of Soul' grew up in rural poverty on a diet of gospel. His charismatic stage act was captured on the album *Live at the Apollo* (1962), which sold a million copies, unprecedented for an album by a black artist. Later hits include 'Papa's Got a Brand New Bag' (1965), 'Sex Machine' (1970) and 'Say It Loud, I'm Black and I'm Proud' (1968).

1 It's a man's world, but it wouldn't be nothing without a woman or a girl.
  'It's a Man's Man's Man's World' (song), on the album *It's a Man's Man's Man's World* (1966)

2 We're tired of beating our head against the wall
  And working for someone else
  We're people, we're like the birds and the bees
  But we'd rather die on our feet than keep living on our knees.
  . . .
  Say it loud! I'm black and I'm proud!
  'Say it Loud! I'm Black and I'm Proud!' (song, 1968, written with Alfred Ellis) on the album *Say it Loud! I'm Black and I'm Proud!* (1969)

## Lew Brown See BUDDY DE SYLVA and LEW BROWN.

## Lenny Bruce (1925–66)

US SATIRICAL COMEDIAN

One of the first comics to 'disturb rather than amuse', he built up a cult following on the stand-up circuit, establishing a reputation as the joker who told the truth. His biting routines were considered offensive and 'sick' by some, and he was imprisoned for obscenity in 1961 and banned from entering Britain in 1963.

1 A lot of people say to me, 'Why did you kill Christ?' 'I dunno . . . it was one of those parties, got out of hand, you know.' We killed him because he didn't want to become a doctor, that's why we killed him.
  *The Essential Lenny Bruce*, 'The Jews' (ed. John Cohen, 1967)

2 The reason I'm in this business, I assume all performers are – it's 'Look at me, Ma!' It's acceptance, you know – 'Look at me, Ma, look at me, Ma, look at me, Ma.' And if your mother watches, you'll show off till you're exhausted; but if your mother goes, *Ptshew!*
  ibid. 'Performing and the Art of Comedy'

3 The only honest art form is laughter, comedy. You can't fake it . . . try to fake three laughs in an hour – ha ha ha ha ha – they'll take you away, man. You can't.
  ibid.

4 All my humor is based upon destruction and despair.

If the whole world were tranquil, without disease and violence, I'd be standing on the breadline right in back of J. Edgar Hoover.
  ibid. The words also appear as the book's epigraph.

5 Satire is tragedy plus time. You give it enough time, the public, the reviewers will allow you to satirize it. Which is rather ridiculous, when you think about it.
  ibid.

6 The liberals can understand everything but people who don't understand them.
  ibid. 'Politics'

7 I'll die young but it's like kissing God.
  Quoted in *Playpower*, ch.4 (1970) by Richard Neville. On his drug addiction; Bruce died from a drugs overdose.

## Frank Bruno (b. 1961)

BRITISH BOXER

He became WBC World Heavyweight Champion in 1995 but was defeated by MIKE TYSON the following year, since when he has become a popular media figure.

1 Boxing is just show business with blood.
  *Guardian* 19 November 1991

2 Know what I mean, 'Arry?
  Often repeated remark to the sports commentator Harry Carpenter on TV interviews, from 1980s.

## Robert Brustein (b. 1927)

US STAGE DIRECTOR, AUTHOR AND CRITIC

During his period as Director of Yale Repertory Theater Company (1966–79), he was also Dean of Yale's school of drama, transforming it into a pre-eminent theatre school with the slogan 'We'll settle for nothing less than changing the whole face of the theater.' He was also Director of the American Repertory Theater, a leading drama critic, and author of *The Third Theater* (1969) and *Revolution as Theater* (1971).

1 Theatergoing is a communal act, moviegoing a solitary one.
  *Who Needs Theater?*, Introduction (1987)

2 The primary function of a theater is not to please itself, or even to please its audience. It is to serve talent.
  ibid. pt 3, 'The Humanist and the Artist'

## Bill Bryson (b. 1951)

US AUTHOR AND JOURNALIST

As well as his bestselling books on his travels in Europe and America, *The Lost Continent* (1989) and *Notes from a Small Island* (1995), he has published works on the English language, for example *Mother Tongue* (1990).

1 There are things you just can't do in life. You can't beat the phone company, you can't make a waiter see you until he's ready to see you, and you can't go home again.
  *The Lost Continent: Travels in Small Town America*, ch. 2 (1989)

2 The average Southerner has the speech patterns of someone slipping in and out of consciousness. I can change my shoes and socks faster than most people in Mississippi can speak a sentence.
  ibid. ch. 7

3 It is an interesting experience to become acquainted with a country through the eyes of the insane, and, if I may say so, a particularly useful grounding for life in Britain.
  *Notes from a Small Island*, ch. 5 (1995)

4 Why is it that women . . . find it so unsettling if you spend more than four minutes a day on the toilet?
  ibid. ch. 10

5 Here are instructions for being a pigeon: 1. Walk around aimlessly for a while, pecking at cigarette butts and other inappropriate items. 2. Take fright at someone walking along the platform and fly off to a girder. 3. Have a shit. 4. Repeat.

ibid.

## John Buchan (1875–1940)

BRITISH AUTHOR AND STATESMAN

Baron Tweedsmuir. MP for the Scottish Universities (1927–35) and Governor General of Canada (1935–40), he was also a prolific writer of fast-moving adventure stories, of which *The Thirty-Nine Steps* (1915, filmed 1935) is considered his best. 'I had some of my Gothic corners smoothed away,' he said, 'but . . . there remained a large spice of the Shorter Catechist in my make-up.'

1 Every man at the bottom of his heart believes that he is a born detective.

Leithen, in *The Power-House*, ch. 2 (1916)

2 An atheist is a man who has no invisible means of support.

Quoted in *On Being a Real Person*, ch. 10 (1943) by H.E. Fosdick

## Patrick Buchanan (b. 1938)

US JOURNALIST AND POLITICIAN

Host of the radio show *Buchanan & Co.*, he was speechwriter and senior adviser to President NIXON (1969–74) and an unsuccessful candidate for the Republican nomination for president in 1992 and 1996. An unapologetic 'America First' trade protectionist and pro-life conservative, he left the Republican Party in 1999 to join the Reform Party and make another bid for president in 2000.

1 Anti-Catholicism is the anti-semitism of the intellectual.

*Observer* 15 December 1991. Peter Viereck, in *Shame and Glory of the Intellectuals*, ch.3 (1953), had earlier written: 'Catholic-baiting is the anti-Semitism of the liberals.'

2 If America does not wish to end her days in the same nursing home as Britannia she had best end this geo-babble about new world orders. Our war, the Cold War, is over. It is time for America to come home.

ibid.

3 Listen, my friend, I've just come back from Mississippi and over there when you talk about the West Bank they think you mean Arkansas.

*Spectator* 13 March 1992

## Frank Buchman (1878–1961)

US EVANGELIST

He is principally known as the founder of the non-denominational Moral Rearmament Movement at Oxford in 1921, which after the Second World War became more politically oriented and opposed to Communism.

1 I thank heaven for a man like Adolf Hitler, who built a front line of defense against the anti-Christ of Communism.

Interview in the *New York World-Telegram* 25 Aug. 1936

2 There is enough in the world for everyone's need, but not enough for everyone's greed.

*Remaking the World* (1947)

## Art Buchwald (b. 1925)

US HUMORIST

Full name Arthur Buchwald. Known for his 'Art Buchwald' column, syndicated worldwide, he was hailed by DEAN ACHESON as 'the greatest satirist since Pope and Swift' and was celebrated for over twenty-five years as the 'court jester of Washington society'.

1 If you attack the establishment long enough and hard enough, they will make you a member of it.

*International Herald Tribune* 24 May 1989

## Pearl S. Buck (1892–1973)

US AUTHOR

Full name Pearl Sydenstricker Buck. She spent her early life in China, the setting for *The Good Earth* (1931), the first novel of a trilogy for which she was awarded the 1938 Nobel Prize for Literature. On returning to the US in 1932 she wrote of contemporary American life in *Dragon Seed* (1942) and other works, and also wrote biographies and short stories.

1 Race prejudice is not only a shadow over the colored – it is a shadow over all of us, and the shadow is darkest over those who feel it least and allow its evil effects to go on.

*What America Means to Me*, ch. 1 (1943)

## Gesualdo Bufalino (1920–96)

SICILIAN AUTHOR

'Discovered' by his fellow Sicilian author Leonardo Sciascia, he published his first book, *The Plague Sower* (1981), late in life, though it was written long before. Other titles followed in quick succession, and he won the prestigious Strega Prize for *Night's Lies* in 1988.

1 Don't forget that even our most obscene vices nearly always bear the seal of sullen greatness.

*Guardian* 21 May 1992. Speaking of the Sicilian character.

## Bill Buford (b. 1954)

US EDITOR AND AUTHOR

He was editor of *Granta* (1979–95) and subsequently literary and fiction editor of the *New Yorker*. Publications include *Among the Thugs* (1991), a study of football violence in England.

1 What principle governed the British sporting event? It appeared that, in exchange for a few pounds, you received one hour and forty-five minutes characterized by the greatest possible exposure to the worst possible weather, the greatest number of people in the smallest possible space and the greatest number of obstacles – unreliable transport, no parking, an intensely dangerous crush at the only exit, a repellent polio pond to pee into, last minute changes of the starting time – to keep you from ever attending a match again.

*Among the Thugs*, pt 1, 'A Station Outside Cardiff' (1991)

2 Violence is one of the most intensely lived experiences and, for those capable of giving themselves over to it, is one of the most intense pleasures.

ibid. pt 2, 'Dawes Road, Fulham'

3 The working class – a piece of language that serves to reinforce certain social customs and a way of talking that obscures the fact that the only thing hiding behind it is a highly mannered suburban society stripped of culture and sophistication and living only for its affectations: a bloated code of maleness, an exaggerated embarrassing patriotism, a violent nationalism, an array of bankrupt antisocial habits. This bored, empty, decadent generation consists of nothing more than what it appears to be. It is a lad culture without mystery, so deadened that it uses violence to wake itself up. It pricks itself so that it has feeling, burns its flesh so that it can smell.

ibid. pt 3, 'Düsseldorf'

## Charles Bukowski (1920–94)

GERMAN-BORN US AUTHOR AND POET

He gained a cult following for his poetry, short stories and novels, sardonic tales of survival in a down-and-out society. Published originally by underground presses or magazines, his works include *Flower, Fist and Bestial Wail* (1959) and *Notes of a Dirty Old Man* (1969). A film version of his stories appeared as *Tales of Ordinary Madness* in 1972.

1 A man does not get old because he nears death; a man gets old because he can no longer see the false from the good.

Letter written early 1962, publ. in *Screams from the Balcony: Selected Letters* (1993)

2 Show me a man who lives alone and has a perpetually clean kitchen, and 8 times out of 9 I'll show you a man with detestable spiritual qualities.

*Tales of Ordinary Madness*, 'Too Sensitive' (1967)

3 You begin saving the world by saving one man at a time; all else is grandiose romanticism or politics.

ibid.

4 Almost everybody is born a genius and buried an idiot.

*Notes of a Dirty Old Man* (1969)

5 If you want to know who your friends are, get yourself a jail sentence.

ibid.

6 Sexual intercourse is kicking death in the ass while singing.

ibid.

7 An intellectual is a man who says a simple thing in a difficult way; an artist is a man who says a difficult thing in a simple way.

ibid.

8 There's always somebody about to ruin your day, if not your life.

The narrator (Nicky Belane), in *Pulp*, ch. 28 (1994)

9 If I die, I hope to go with my head on that typewriter. It's my battlefield.

Interview in the *Los Angeles Times*, 1987, quoted in obituary in the *Los Angeles Times* 10 March 1994

## Basil Bunting (1900–1985)
BRITISH POET

Influenced by EZRA POUND and the Imagists, it was not until 1966 that he established his reputation with the lyrical *Briggflatts*, a semi-autobiographical poem which asserts the identity of his native Northumbria.

1 To appreciate present conditions
collate them with those of antiquity.

'Chomei at Toyama' (1932), publ. in *Collected Poems* (1968)

2 The mystic purchases a moment of exhilaration with a lifetime of confusion; and the exhilaration is incommunicable but the confusion is infectious and destructive. It is confusing and destructive to try and explain anything in terms of anything else, poetry in terms of psychology.

Letter to poet Louis Zukofsky, September 1932, quoted in *The Poetry of Basil Bunting*, ch. 2 (1991) by Victoria Forde

3 Can a moment of madness make up for
an age of consent?

'The Well of Lycopolis', written 1935, publ. in *Poems* (1950)

4 I hate Science. It denies a man's responsibility for his own deeds, abolishes the brotherhood that springs from God's fatherhood. It is a hectoring, dictating expertise, which makes the least lovable of the Church Fathers seem liberal by contrast. It is far easier for a Hitler or a Stalin to find a mock-scientific excuse for persecution than it was for Dominic to find a mock-Christian one.

Letter to the poet Louis Zukofsky, 1 January 1947, quoted in *The Poetry of Basil Bunting*, ch. 6 (1991) by Victoria Forde

5 Man's life so little worth,
do we fear to take or lose it?
No ill companion on a journey, Death

lays his purse on the table and opens the wine.

'The Spoils', first publ. in *Poetry* 1951, repr. in *Loquitur* (1965). Opening lines of poem.

6 But their determination to banish fools foundered ultimately in the installation of absolute idiots.

ibid. On the decline of government under the Turkish Seljuk dynasty.

7 Sooner or later we must absorb Islam if our own culture is not to die of anemia.

*Arabic and Persian Poems*, Foreword (1970) by Omar Pound

## Luis Buñuel (1900–1983)
SPANISH FILM-MAKER

He collaborated with SALVADOR DALI on his first films, *Un Chien andalou* (1928) and *L'Age d'or* (1930), both of which caused a sensation. His later films were more anti-Establishment in theme, and include *Los Olvidados* (1950), *Belle de jour* (1967) and *The Discreet Charm of the Bourgeoisie* (1972).

1 Work's a curse, Saturno. I say to hell with the work you have to do to earn a living! That kind of work does us no honour; all it does is fill up the bellies of the pigs who exploit us. But the work you do because you like to do it, because you've heard the call, you've got a vocation – that's ennobling! We should all be able to work like that. Look at me, Saturno – I don't work. And I don't care if they hang me, I *won't* work! Yet I'm alive! I may live badly, but at least I don't have to work to do it!

Don Lope (Fernando Rey), in *Tristana* (film, written and directed by Luis Buñuel, 1970). Buñuel's screenplay was derived from the novel of the same name by the Spanish novelist and dramatist Benito Pérez Galdós, but where Galdós criticized his character for laziness, Buñuel praised him.

2 You have to begin to lose your memory, if only in bits and pieces, to realize that memory is what makes our lives. Life without memory is no life at all, just as an intelligence without the possibility of expression is not really an intelligence. Our memory is our coherence, our reason, our feeling, even our action. Without it, we are nothing.

*My Last Breath*, ch. 1 (1983). 'I can only wait for the final amnesia,' Buñuel wrote, 'the one that can erase an entire life.'

3 The bar . . . is an exercise in solitude. Above all else, it must be quiet, dark, very comfortable – and, contrary to modern mores, no music of any kind, no matter how faint. In sum, there should be no more than a dozen tables, and a clientele that doesn't like to talk.

ibid. ch. 6

4 Tobacco and alcohol, delicious fathers of abiding friendships and fertile reveries.

ibid.

5 God and Country are an unbeatable team; they break all records for oppression and bloodshed.

ibid. ch. 14

6 A paranoiac . . . like a poet, is born, not made.

ibid. ch. 18

7 In the name of Hippocrates, doctors have invented the most exquisite form of torture ever known to man: survival.

ibid. ch. 21

## Julie Burchill (b. 1960)
BRITISH JOURNALIST AND AUTHOR

Starting in journalism working for the *New Musical Express*, she went on to co-found the *Modern Review*, and has also worked as a contentious columnist for the *Mail on Sunday*, the *Observer* and the *Guardian*. She has published numerous collections of articles as well as the novel *Ambition* (1989).

1 A woman who looks like a girl and thinks like a man is the best sort, the most enjoyable to be and the most pleasurable to have and to hold.
*Damaged Gods*, 'Born again Cows' (1986)

2 Feminism seeks to turn the biggest, bloodiest carnivore in the world – passion – into a right-on cud-chewing vegan. It can never work. Sex was never meant to be that way. Sex, on the whole, was meant to be short, nasty and brutish. If what you want is cuddling, you should buy a puppy.
'The Dead Zone', first publ. in 1988, repr. in *Sex and Sensibility* (1992)

3 It has been said that a pretty face is a passport. But it's not, it's a visa, and it runs out fast.
'Kiss and Sell', ibid.

4 A good part – and definitely the most fun part – of being a feminist is about frightening men.
*Time Out* 16 November 1989

5 Punk, far from being a peasants' revolt, was just another English spectacle, like the Royal Wedding: a chance for us to congratulate ourselves on our talent for tableaux . . . and to cock a snook at envious Americans.
*Modern Review* autumn 1991

6 She [Diana] showed the House of Windsor up for what it was: a dumb, numb dinosaur, lumbering along in a world of its own, gorged sick on arrogance and ignorance.
*Guardian* 2 September 1997

7 The Age of Diana has not ended but has rather just begun. Frozen forever at the height of her beauty, compassion and power by death, she will be the mourner at every royal wedding and the blushing bride at every Coronation.
*Diana*, Foreword (1998)

8 A wedding is a funeral which masquerades as a feast. And the greater the pageantry, the deeper the savagery.
ibid. ch. 1

9 A cynic should never marry an idealist. For the cynic, marriage represents the welcome end of romantic life, with all its agony and ecstasy. But for the idealist, it is only the beginning.
ibid. ch. 4

## Anthony Burgess (1917–93)
BRITISH AUTHOR AND CRITIC

Full name John Anthony Burgess Wilson. An inexhaustible writer with a wide-ranging intellect, he wrote novels, memoirs, biographies, reviews and libretti, though, to his own regret, he is chiefly known for *A Clockwork Orange* (1962, filmed 1971), a disturbing and violent vision of the future.

1 Bath twice a day to be really clean, once a day to be passably clean, once a week to avoid being a public menace.
*Inside Mr Enderby*, ch. 2, sect. 1 (1963). A 'grim apothegm' in a women's magazine.

2 Do they [disc jockeys] merit vitriol, even a drop of it? Yes, because they corrupt the young, persuading them that the mature world, which produced Beethoven and Schweitzer, sets an even higher value on the transient anodynes of youth than does youth itself . . . They are the Hollow Men. They are electronic lice.
*Punch* 20 September 1967

3 If you write fiction you are, in a sense, corrupted. There's a tremendous corruptibility for the fiction writer because you're dealing mainly with sex and violence. These remain

the basic themes, they're the basic themes of Shakespeare whether you like it or not.
Interview in *The Face* December 1984

4 [On the Vatican] All human life is here, but the Holy Ghost seems to be somewhere else.
Book review in the *Observer* 25 May 1986

5 I've always felt that English women had to be approached in a sisterly manner, rather than an erotic manner.
*The Times* 27 July 1988

6 The trouble began with Forster. After him it was considered ungentlemanly to write more than five or six novels.
*Guardian* 24 February 1989. Burgess himself wrote more than twenty novels.

7 We are supposed to be the children of Seth; but Seth is too much of an effete nonentity to deserve ancestral regard. No, we are the sons of Cain, and with violence can be associated the attacks on sound, stone, wood and metal that produced civilization.
Book review in the *Observer* 26 November 1989

8 In Europe we tend to see marital love as an eternity which encompasses hate and also indifference: when we promise to love we really mean that we promise to honour a contract. Americans, seeming to take marriage with not enough seriousness, are really taking love and sex with too much.
*You've Had Your Time*, ch. 2 (1990)

9 Novelists are perhaps the last people in the world to be entrusted with opinions. The nature of a novel is that it has no opinions, only the dialectic of contrary views, some of which, all of which, may be untenable and even silly. A novelist should not be too intelligent either, although . . . he may be permitted to be an intellectual.
ibid.

10 Violence among young people . . . is an aspect of their desire to create. They don't know how to use their energy creatively so they do the opposite and destroy.
*Independent* 31 January 1990

## Gelett Burgess (1866–1951)
US HUMORIST AND ILLUSTRATOR

His works include books on Goops (bad-mannered children), *Why Men Hate Women* (1927), and *Look Eleven Years Younger* (1937). He is credited with enlarging the English language with words such as 'blurb'.

1 Ah, yes, I wrote the 'Purple Cow' –
I'm sorry, now, I wrote it!
But I can tell you, anyhow,
I'll kill you if you quote it.
'Cinq Ans Après', publ. in *The Burgess Nonsense Book* (1914). Burgess penned the popular verse 'The Purple Cow' in 1895.

2 To appreciate nonsense requires a serious interest in life.
*The Romance of the Commonplace*, 'The Sense of Humor' (1916)

## George Burns (1896–1996)
US COMEDIAN

Original name Nathan Birnbaum. With his wife Gracie Allen he formed a highly succesful comedy double act as straight husband and scatty wife, performing from the 1920s to the 1950s in vaudeville, in films, on radio and on television. In later life he turned to acting and won an Oscar for his role in *The Sunshine Boys* (1975).

1 Too bad that all the people who know how to run the country are busy driving taxicabs and cutting hair.
*Life* December 1979

2 If it's a good script I'll do it. And if it's a bad script, and they pay me enough, I'll do it.

*International Herald Tribune* 9 November 1988

# Edgar Rice Burroughs (1875–1950)

US AUTHOR

His series of *Tarzan* books, the first of which appeared in 1914, led to films, radio programmes and comic strips. He was also the author of science fiction and other adventure stories.

1 Me Tarzan, you Jane.

Attributed to Tarzan. In Burroughs' book *Tarzan of the Apes* (1914), Tarzan's words are: 'I am Tarzan of the Apes. I want you. I am yours. You are mine' (ch. 18). In the movie, *Tarzan the Ape Man* (1932), Johnny Weissmuller, as Tarzan, never utters the words, 'Me Tarzan, you Jane.'

# William Burroughs (1914–97)

US AUTHOR

Associated with the Beats in the 1950s, he frankly depicted a heroin addict's life in *Junky* (1953) and *The Naked Lunch* (1959, filmed 1991). Other works such as *The Soft Machine* (1961) and *Cities of the Red Night* (1981) helped to establish his cult status, though *Time* magazine judged that his works 'added up to the world's pluperfect put-on'.

1 A junky runs on junk time. When his junk is cut off, the clock runs down and stops. All he can do is hang on and wait for non-junk time to start.

*Junky*, ch. 10 (1953)

2 1. Never give anything away for nothing.
2. Never give more than you have to give (always catch the buyer hungry and always make him wait).
3. Always take everything back if you possibly can.

The basic principles of dealing heroin, in *The Naked Lunch*, Introduction (1959)

3 Junk is the ideal product . . . the ultimate merchandise. No sales talk necessary. The client will crawl through a sewer and beg to buy.

*The Naked Lunch*, Introduction (1959)

4 America is not a young land: it is old and dirty and evil before the settlers, before the Indians. The evil is there waiting.

ibid. opening chapter (untitled)

5 A *functioning* police state needs no police.

Dr Benway, in ibid. 'Benway'

6 The exact objectives of Islam Inc. are obscure. Needless to say everyone involved has a different angle, and they all intend to cross each other up somewhere along the line.

ibid. 'Islam Inc. and the Parties of Interzone'

7 The face of 'evil' is always the face of total need.

'Deposition: Testimony Concerning a Sickness', publ. in *The Evergreen Review* January/February 1960, repr. as Introduction to *The Naked Lunch* (1962 edn)

8 I feel that any form of so called psychotherapy is strongly contraindicated for addicts . . . The question 'Why did you start using narcotics in the first place?' should never be asked. It is quite as irrelevant to treatment as it would be to ask a malarial patient why he went to a malarial area.

*The Soft Machine*, Appendix (1961, rev. 1966)

9 In my writing I am acting as a map maker, an explorer of psychic areas . . . a cosmonaut of inner space, and I see no point in exploring areas that have already been thoroughly surveyed.

Remark in 1964, quoted in *William Burroughs: The Algebra of Need*, pt 1, ch.1 (1977) by Eric Mottram

10 I think there are innumerable gods. What we on earth call God is a little tribal God who has made an awful mess. Certainly forces operating through human consciousness control events.

Interview in *Paris Review* fall 1965, repr. in *Writers at Work* (third series, ed. George Plimpton, 1967)

11 The people in power will not disappear voluntarily, giving flowers to the cops just isn't going to work. This thinking is fostered by the establishment; they like nothing better than love and nonviolence. The only way I like to see cops given flowers is in a flower pot from a high window.

*The Job: Interviews with Daniel Odier*, 'Prisoners of the Earth Come Out' (1969)

12 England has the most sordid literary scene I've ever seen. They all meet in the same pub. This guy's writing a foreword for this person. They all have to give radio programs, they *have* to do all this just in order to scrape by. They're all scratching each other's backs.

Taped conversation in New York, 1980, publ. in *With William Burroughs: A Report from the Bunker*, 'Burroughs in London' (1981) by Victor Bockris

13 I think that what we call love is a fraud perpetrated by the female sex, and that the point of sexual relations between men is nothing that we could call love, but rather what we might call *recognition*.

Quoted by Edmund White in 'This is Not a Mammal', first publ. in *Soho News* 18 February 1981, repr. in *The Burning Library* (1994)

14 Man is an artifact designed for space travel. He is not designed to remain in his present biologic state any more than a tadpole is designed to remain a tadpole.

*The Adding Machine*, 'Civilian Defense' (1985)

15 Kerouac opened a million coffee bars and sold a million pairs of Levis to both sexes. Woodstock rises from his pages.

ibid. 'Remembering Jack Kerouac' (1985)

16 In deep sadness there is no place for sentimentality.

*Queer*, ch. 8 (1985)

17 So cheat your landlord if you can and must, but do not try to shortchange the Muse. It cannot be done. You can't fake quality any more than you can fake a good meal.

*The Western Lands*, ch. 2 (1987)

18 Black magic operates most effectively in preconscious, marginal areas. Casual curses are the most effective.

ibid. ch. 3

# Richard Burton (1925–84)

BRITISH ACTOR

Originally Richard Walter Jenkins. He excelled at Shakespearian roles and was the narrator in the classic radio broadcast of DYLAN THOMAS's *Under Milk Wood* (1954) before taking up a career in Hollywood. He was twice married to Elizabeth Taylor with whom he co-starred in *Who's Afraid of Virginia Woolf?* (1966) and *The Taming of the Shrew* (1967).

1 Richard Burton is now my epitaph, my cross, my title, my image. I have achieved a kind of diabolical fame. It has nothing to do with my talents as an actor. That counts for little now. I am the diabolically famous Richard Burton.

Interview in 1963, quoted in *Elizabeth Taylor*, ch. 21 (1964) by Ruth Waterbury

2 When I played drunks I had to remain sober because I didn't know how to play them when I was drunk.

Quoted in *Halliwell's Who's Who in the Movies* (ed. John Walker, 1999)

## George Bush (b. 1924)

US REPUBLICAN POLITICIAN AND PRESIDENT

Director of the CIA 1976–7, he served as Republican Vice-President under RONALD REAGAN 1981–8, whom he succeeded as President 1989–93. His administration coincided with the fall of the Berlin Wall and the Gulf conflict in the wake of the 1990 Iraqi invasion of Kuwait. See also MICHAEL KINSLEY 1.

1 The vision thing.

Time 26 January 1987. Speaking of his long-term policies.

2 What's wrong with being a boring kind of guy?

Quoted in the Daily Telegraph 28 April 1988

3 I'm proud to be his partner. We've had triumphs, we've made mistakes, we've had sex.

Speech at College of Southern Idaho, 6 May 1988, quoted in the International Herald Tribune 13 May 1988. Bush's gaffe occurred in a speech extolling the Reagan/Bush partnership. He corrected himself: '... setbacks, we've had setbacks ...' Moments later he joked, 'I feel like the javelin competitor who won the toss and elected to receive.'

4 Let the others have the charisma. I've got the class.

Comment in California during presidential campaign, quoted in the Guardian 3 December 1988

5 The Congress will push me to raise taxes and I'll say no, and they'll push, and I'll say no, and they'll push me again. And I'll say to them: 'Read my lips: no new taxes.'

Acceptance speech for presidential nomination, Republican National Convention, New Orleans, 18 Aug. 1988, quoted in The New York Times 19 Aug. 1988. PEGGY NOONAN was mainly responsible for the speech, though the expression 'Read my lips' has been in general usage since at least the 1970s. Bush eventually raised taxes.

6 I want a kinder, gentler nation.

ibid. A similar form of words had been used by CHARLIE CHAPLIN at the end of The Great Dictator (1940), when he urged, 'More than cleverness, we need kindness and gentleness.'

7 I will keep America moving forward, always forward – for a better America, for an endless enduring dream and a thousand points of light.

ibid. The phrase 'a thousand points of light', written for Bush by speechwriter PEGGY NOONAN, was used on various occasions during the 1988 presidential campaign. The words are not original, echoing similar phrases by Charles Dickens and THOMAS WOLFE, among others. As president, Bush initiated a 'Points of Light' reform programme in June 1989.

8 We can see a new world coming into view. A world in which there is the very real prospect of a new world order.

Speech quoted in The New York Times 7 March 1991

## Vannevar Bush (1890–1974)

US ELECTRICAL ENGINEER AND PHYSICIST

A champion of the 'missionary' function of science, he built several of the earliest electronic analogue computers during the 1920s and 1930s, which paved the way for the development of digital computers. In 1941 he became Director of the Office of Scientific Research and Development (OSRD), which coordinated arms and scientific research during the Second World War. His Modern Arms and Free Men was published in 1949.

1 Science has a simple faith, which transcends utility. Nearly all men of science, all men of learning for that matter, and men of simple ways too, have it in some form and in some degree. It is the faith that it is the privilege of man to learn to understand, and that this is his mission. If we abandon that mission under stress we shall abandon it forever, for stress will not cease. Knowledge for the sake of understanding, not merely to prevail, that is the essence of our being. None can define its limits, or set its ultimate boundaries.

Science Is Not Enough, 'The Search for Understanding' (1967)

## Marilyn Butler (b. 1937)

BRITISH EDUCATOR AND AUTHOR

A professor of literature at Oxford and Exeter, she has written extensively on the Romantic period, including Jane Austen and the War of Ideas (1975) and Romantics, Rebels and Reactionaries (1981).

1 English literature is a kind of training in social ethics. ... English trains you to handle a body of information in a way that is conducive to action.

Guardian 3 March 1989

## A.S. Byatt (b. 1936)

BRITISH AUTHOR

Full name Antonia Susan Byatt. Art, literary and social history, and philosophy are woven into her novels, such as The Virgin in the Garden (1978) and Possession, which won the Booker Prize in 1990. She has also written on IRIS MURDOCH and eighteenth- and nineteenth-century poetry. She is the elder sister of MARGARET DRABBLE.

1 Pain hardens, and great pain hardens greatly, whatever the comforters say, and suffering does not ennoble, though it may occasionally lend a certain rigid dignity of manner to the suffering frame.

Quoted in the Daily Telegraph 21 July 1986

## David Byrne (b. 1952)

US ROCK MUSICIAN

Singer and main force behind Talking Heads, one of the most influential bands of the 1970s and 1980s, he has also composed film music and directed the film True Stories (1986). In 1980 he wrote the dance score The Catherine Wheel for Twyla Tharp.

1 Facts all come with points of view
Facts don't do what I want them to.

'Crosseyed and Painless' (song, written by David Byrne and Brian Eno) on the album Remain in Light (1980) by Talking Heads. The words were incorporated into 'Wordy Rappinghood', a hit for Tom Tom Club (an offshoot of Talking Heads) in 1981.

2 And you may find yourself behind the wheel of a large automobile
And you may find yourself in a beautiful house
With a beautiful wife
And you may ask yourself
Well, how did I get here?

'Once in a Lifetime' (song), on ibid.

3 To shake your rump is to be environmentally aware.

Sleeve notes to Byrne's compilation of Brazilian Samba music, O Samba: Brazil Classics 2 (1989)

## James Branch Cabell (1879–1958)
US NOVELIST AND ESSAYIST

He was highly regarded in his day for his romantic and satirical novels, set in the fantasy medieval world of Poictesme (pronounced *Pwahtem*). The most popular, *Jurgen* (1919), was considered by some pornographic.

1 **The optimist proclaims that we live in the best of all possible worlds; and the pessimist fears this is true.**
Coth of the Rocks, in *The Silver Stallion*, bk 4, ch. 26 (1926). The words recall those of Voltaire, 'All is for the best in the best of all possible worlds', from *Candide*, ch. 1 (1759).

## Irving Caesar (1895–1996)
US SONGWRITER

He was a Tin Pan Alley composer of more than 1,000 published songs, most famously 'Tea for Two' (1924), 'Crazy Rhythm' (1928) and 'Swanee' (1936). 'Sometimes I write lousy, but always fast,' he said. He was also responsible for the lyrics for the 1924 Broadway musical *No, No, Nanette*.

1 **Picture you upon my knee,**
**Just tea for two and two for tea.**
'Tea for Two' (song, 1925). Caesar claimed that he composed the song in less than five minutes (though also admitted it might have taken him as long as fifteen).

## John Cage (1912–92)
US COMPOSER

A pupil of Schoenberg (for whom he was 'not a composer, but an inventor – of genius'), he used new methods of notation, invented the 'prepared' piano and was a pioneer of aleatory (chance) music. *HPSCHD* (1969) used seven harpsichords and fifty-one tape recorders, *Roaratorio* (1979) incorporated words from *Finnegans Wake* by JAMES JOYCE, and *4′33″* (1952) was pure silence. He also wrote extensively about music.

1 **I have nothing to say**
**and I am saying    and that is**
**poetry.**
'Lecture on Nothing', publ. in *Silence* (1961)

2 **There is no such thing as silence.**
'Everything We Do Is Music', interview in the *Saturday Evening Post* 19 October 1968, repr. in *Conversing with Cage*, 'His Own Music (to 1970)' (ed. Richard Kostelanetz, 1988). Cage claimed his silent piece, *4′33″*, to be his personal favourite: 'It has three movements and in all of these movements there are no sounds. I wanted my work to be free of my own likes and dislikes, because I think music should be free of the feelings of the composer' (interview in *Soho Weekly News* 12 September 1974).

## James Cagney (1899–1986)
US SCREEN ACTOR

Shooting to fame as the feisty, dynamic gangster in the seminal film *The Public Enemy* (1931), he was in demand for the next thirty years, showing his versatility as Bottom in *A Midsummer Night's Dream* (1935) and drawing on his song-and-dance background for *Yankee Doodle Dandy* (1942), for which he won an Oscar. GRAHAM GREENE wrote: 'He can do nothing which is not worth watching.'

1 **You dirty, double-crossing rat.**
*Blonde Crazy* (film, 1931). The words were popularized and shortened to 'You dirty rat', which Cagney, in his autobiography *Cagney by Cagney* (1976), stridently denied ever having said.

## Sammy Cahn (1913–93)
US SONGWRITER

Original name Samuel Cohen. He collaborated with Jule Styne on films and Broadway musicals, including *Three Coins in the Fountain*

(1954), and later with Jimmy Van Heusen, for whom FRANK SINATRA won Oscars for recordings of 'All the Way' (1957), 'High Hopes' (1959), and 'Call Me Irresponsible' (1963).

1 Give me five minutes more,
   Only five minutes more,
   Let me stay,
   Let me stay in your arms.

   'Five Minutes More' (song, 1946, with music by Jule Styne). The song was recorded by FRANK SINATRA.

2 Love and marriage, love and marriage
   Go together like a horse and carriage
   Dad was told by mother
   You can't have one without the other.

   'Love and Marriage' (song, with music by Jimmy Van Heusen) from the TV musical *Our Town* (1955). The song was first aired by SINATRA, for whom it was a million-seller.

## James M. Cain (1892–1977)

US NOVELIST

Subscribing to the 'hard-boiled' school of American fiction, he is noted particularly for his early works, some of which – *The Postman Always Rings Twice* (1934, filmed 1946 and 1981) and *Mildred Pierce* (1941, filmed 1945) – became movie classics.

1 The postman always rings twice.

   *The Postman Always Rings Twice* (novel, 1934)

## (Sir) Michael Caine (b. 1933)

BRITISH STAGE AND SCREEN ACTOR

Originally named Maurice Micklewhite. A prolific performer, usually as a laid-back anti-hero, he is famous for his roles as the 'low-key James Bond' in *The Ipcress File* (1965), as a Cockney Lothario in *Alfie* (1966), a Liverpudlian academic in *Educating Rita* (1983) and an urbane adulterer in *Hannah and Her Sisters* (1986), for which he won an Oscar. He was awarded a second Oscar in 2000 for *Cider House Rules*. He is, he says, 'every bourgeois's nightmare – a Cockney with intelligence and a million dollars.'

1 Not many people know that.

   Catch-phrase and book title (1984). Caine's catch-phrase, which found its way into his films and was made the title of an 'Almanac of Amazing Information' compiled by him, is said to have been his comment when habitually offering information garnered from *The Guinness Book of Records*.

2 Be like a duck, my mother used to tell me. Remain calm on the surface and paddle like hell underneath.

   Interview in *Time Out* 16 September 1992

## Roberto Calasso (b. 1941)

ITALIAN AUTHOR

He writes dazzling and complex novels of ideas, specializing in turning ancient myths into modern literature, as in *The Marriage of Cadmus and Harmony* (1988), and *Ka* (1996).

1 To invite the gods ruins our relationship with them but sets history in motion. A life in which the gods are not invited is not worth living. It will be quieter, but there won't be any stories. And you could suppose that these dangerous invitations were in fact contrived by the gods themselves, because the gods get bored with men with no stories.

   *The Marriage of Cadmus and Harmony*, ch 12 (1988)

## Charles Calhoun See BILL HALEY.

## James Callaghan (b. 1912)

BRITISH POLITICIAN

Leonard James Callaghan, Baron Callaghan of Cardiff. Elected Labour MP in 1945, he held posts as Home and Foreign Secretary

before becoming Prime Minister (1976–9). His government was brought down by a vote of no confidence – the first in over fifty years – after a series of strikes had paralysed essential services. See ROY JENKINS 1.

1 I don't think other people in the world would share the view there is mounting chaos.

   Interview at London Airport, 10 January 1979, in the *Sun* 11 January 1979. Callaghan was returning from the Guadeloupe Summit conference after the Labour Party's policy of cooperation with the unions had been torn apart by a wave of strikes – the so-called 'winter of discontent' (see below). See *SUN* for its famous headline paraphrase: 'Crisis? What Crisis?'

2 I had known it was going to be a 'winter of discontent'.

   Quoted in the *Daily Telegraph* 9 February 1979. The New Year had seen a succession of labour disputes, with hospitals being picketed and refuse piled in the streets. Callaghan's failure to control the unions led directly to MARGARET THATCHER's election victory later that year, and to a subsequent raft of legislation designed to limit their power. The phrase is from the opening line of Shakespeare's *Richard III*, spoken by Gloucester.

## Italo Calvino (1923–85)

ITALIAN AUTHOR AND CRITIC

Early novels, including his first, *A Path to the Nest of Spiders* (1947), inspired by his experience among the anti-fascist partisans, are naturalistic, while later books, such as *Our Ancestors* (1960) and *If on a Winter's Night a Traveller* (1979) are 'magic realist' in style. 'He is far too intelligent to become really cerebral,' URSULA K. LE GUIN commented.

1 You only have to start saying of something: 'Ah, how beautiful! We must photograph it!' and you are already close to the view of the person who thinks that everything that is not photographed is lost, as if it had never existed, and that therefore in order really to live you must photograph as much as you can, and to photograph as much as you can you must either live in the most photographic way possible, or else consider photographable every moment of your life. The first course leads to stupidity; the second, to madness.

   *Difficult Loves*, 'The Adventure of a Photographer' (1970, transl. 1984)

2 It is not the voice that commands the story: it is the ear.

   Marco Polo, in *Invisible Cities* (1972)

3 The catalogue of forms is endless: until every shape has found its city, new cities will continue to be born. When the forms exhaust their variety and come apart, the end of cities begins.

   Narrator, in ibid. (1972)

4 The universe will express itself as long as somebody will be able to say 'I read, therefore it writes.'

   *If on a Winter's Night a Traveller*, pt 8, 'From the Diary of Silas Flannery' (1979)

5 Everything can change, but not the language that we carry inside us, like a world more exclusive and final than one's mother's womb.

   'By Way of an Autobiography', first publ. in *Grand Bazaar* September/October 1980, repr. in *The Literature Machine* (1987)

6 A classic is a book that has never finished saying what it has to say.

   One of a series of definitions of a 'classic', in 'Why Read the Classics?', first publ. in *L'Espresso* 28 June 1981, repr. in ibid.

## James Cameron (1911–85)

BRITISH JOURNALIST

He made his name as a freelance journalist, addressing issues of war and social justice with integrity and wit. He also wrote and presented TV shows such as *Men of Our Time* (1963).

1 Now, standing up unsteadily from the sea, was the famous Mushroom. . . . It climbed like a fungus; it looked like a towering mound of firm cream shot with veins and rivers of wandering red; it mounted tirelessly through the clouds as though it were made of denser, solider stuff, as no doubt it was. The only similes that came to mind were banal: a sundae, red ink in a pot of distemper. From behind me I heard a frenetic ticking of typewriters; very soon I found I was fumbling with my own. The reportage had begun. Many of us will never live it down.

*Point of Departure*, ch. 3 (1967). On the first atomic-bomb test on the Bikini atoll, summer 1946.

2 The *New York Times* is the best and the worst newspaper on earth, a daily monument to the sloppy and extravagant simplification of the overdone; the *Daily Mirror* is the worst and the best newspaper, a gymnastic in the dedicated technical expertise of the persuasive non-think. I have worked for them both, but I cannot yet determine which I like least.

ibid. ch. 4

3 Objectivity in some circumstances is both meaningless and impossible. I still do not see how a reporter attempting to define a situation involving some sort of ethical conflict can do it with sufficient demonstrable neutrality to fulfil some arbitrary concept of 'objectivity'. It never occurred to me, in such a situation, to be other than subjective, and as obviously so as I could manage to be. I may not always have been satisfactorily balanced; I always tended to argue that objectivity was of less importance than the truth, and that the reporter whose technique was informed by no opinion lacked a very serious dimension.

ibid.

4 The test of a good classical moralization is that it seems to have been written for oneself alone.

ibid. Discussing the saying, *Video meliora proboque; deteriora sequor* ('I see and approve the better things; I follow the worse').

5 Islam is the youngest of the major religions and it has the arrogance of youth.

Quoted by Moni Cameron ( James Cameron's wife) in letter in the *Guardian* 15 March 1989

6 Is not Christmas the only occasion when one gets drunk *for the children's sake*?

Quoted in the *Independent on Sunday* 20 December 1991

## James Cameron (b. 1954)
CANADIAN FILM DIRECTOR AND SCREENWRITER

Described as 'the high priest of Hollywood Bloat' and 'the movies' mad toymaker', he achieved his first major success with *The Terminator* (1984), followed by *Aliens* (1986) and the multi-award winning *Titanic* (1997).

1 The social battles of the video age are fought with images, not guns.

Commentary in *Strange Days* (film, 1995, screenplay by James Cameron and Jay Cocks, directed by Kathryn Bigelow)

2 Every paradigm on Earth is falling apart at the same time . . . every system, vision, constitution, revelation . . . is breaking down. Being toppled or abandoned . . . all at the same time! And you know what really scares me? There's no new ideas. Everything's been done. Rock music, punk music, rap music, techno, techno-Mex . . . long hair, short hair . . . no hair. Doesn't it feel like everything's been tried? Whaddya do that's new? Something new in art? Forget it. Somebody somewhere has done it.

Max Peltier, in ibid.

## Beatrix Campbell (b. 1947)
BRITISH JOURNALIST

A commentator on women's and social issues and columnist for periodicals including the *New Statesman* and *Feminist Review*, she is the author of *Wigan Pier Revisited* (1984) among other works.

1 Children's bodies aren't like automobiles with the assailant's fingerprints lingering on the wheel. The world of sexual abuse is quintessentially secret. It is the perfect crime.

*Unofficial Secrets*, ch. 2 (1988). In the book's Introduction, Campbell quotes a police source on the subject: 'Sexual abuse is like a corpse on a slab, saying nothing. You've got nothing to go on. It's a police officer's nightmare. You just want it to go away.'

2 These people [the Royal Family] like excitement. They have their ways of doing things – they've spent generations practising; and they have their ways of *having* things – called gratification. These people have got 'love' and 'hate' tattooed on their tiaras.

*Diana Princess of Wales*, pt 2, ch. 7 (1998)

3 The politics of seeing and being seen, are about power as well as pleasure, voyeurism and exhibitionism, censorship and surveillance, knowledge and ignorance, celebrity and harassment, espionage and jealousy.

ibid. pt 3, ch. 13

## Joseph Campbell (1904–87)
US WRITER ON MYTHOLOGY

He was concerned with mythological archetypes as in *The Hero With a Thousand Faces* (1949). His major work was a study of world mythology in four volumes, *The Masks of God*, (1959–67).

1 Religions, philosophies, arts, the social forms of primitive and historic man, prime discoveries in science and technology, the very dreams that blister sleep, boil up from the basic, magic ring of myth.

*The Hero With a Thousand Faces*, Prologue, sect. 1 (1949)

2 The myths of failure touch us with the tragedy of life, but those of success only with their own incredibility.

ibid. pt 1, ch. 3, sect. 2

## Mrs Patrick Campbell (1865–1940)
BRITISH ACTRESS

Born Beatrice Stella Tanner. A wide-ranging, passionate and intelligent actress, though, according to YEATS, possessing 'an ego like a raging tooth', she came to notice with her performance in *The Second Mrs Tanqueray* (1893). SHAW, with whom she formed a lasting friendship, created the part of Eliza Doolittle for her in *Pygmalion* (1914).

1 [Of Shaw] To be made to hold his tongue is the greatest insult you can offer him – though he might be ready with a poker to make you hold yours.

*My Life and Some Letters*, ch. 16 (1922)

2 The deep, deep peace of the double-bed after the hurly-burly of the chaise-longue.

Quoted in *While Rome Burns*, 'The First Mrs. Tanqueray' (1934) by ALEXANDER WOOLLCOTT. Discussing the benefits of her recent marriage. Woollcott remarked of Mrs Campbell: 'Her failure to be polite took on the proportions of a magnificent gesture.'

3 Does it *really* matter what these affectionate people do – so long as they don't do it in the streets *and frighten the horses*!

Quoted in *Mrs Patrick Campbell*, ch. 15 (1961) by Alan Dent. Referring to rumours of a homosexual liaison between two actors. The words are quoted in various forms, commonly 'I don't mind where people make love . . .' and 'My dear, I don't care what they do . . .'

# Albert Camus (1913–60)

FRENCH-ALGERIAN PHILOSOPHER AND AUTHOR

Throughout his works Camus deals with *l'homme révolté* (the misfit), as in the essay 'The Myth of Sisyphus' (1942) and his first novel *The Outsider* (1942), both of which explore the absurdity of the human situation. Later novels include *The Plague* (1947) and *The Fall* (1956). He received the Nobel Prize for Literature three years before his death in a car crash.

1 An intellectual is someone whose mind watches itself. I like this, because I am happy to be both halves, the watcher and the watched. 'Can they be brought together?' This is a practical question. We must get down to it. 'I despise intelligence' really means: 'I cannot bear my doubts.'
Journal entry, May 1936, publ. in *Carnets 1935–1942* (1962, transl. and ed. Philip Thody, 1963)

2 Culture: the cry of men in face of their destiny.
Entry in June 1937, in ibid.

3 There is but one truly serious philosophical problem and that is suicide. Judging whether life is or is not worth living amounts to answering the fundamental question of philosophy. All the rest – whether or not the world has three dimensions, whether the mind has nine or twelve categories – comes afterwards. These are games.
*The Myth of Sisyphus*, 'Absurdity and Suicide' (1942, transl. 1955). Opening sentences.

4 At any street corner the feeling of absurdity can strike any man in the face.
ibid. 'Absurd Walls'

5 The struggle itself towards the heights is enough to fill a man's heart. One must imagine Sisyphus happy.
ibid. 'The Myth of Sisyphus'. Closing words of book.

6 Mother died today. Or, maybe, yesterday; I can't be sure.
Meursault, in *The Outsider*, pt 1, ch. 1 (1942). Opening words of book.

7 If Christianity is pessimistic as to man, it is optimistic as to human destiny. Well, I can say that, pessimistic as to human destiny, I am optimistic as to man.
Address to monks of Latour-Maubourg, 1948, publ. in *Resistance, Rebellion and Death*, 'The Unbeliever and Christians' (1961)

8 Man is the only creature who refuses to be what he is.
*The Rebel*, Introduction (1951)

9 What is a rebel? A man who says no.
ibid. ch. 1. Opening sentence.

10 All modern revolutions have ended in a reinforcement of the power of the state.
ibid. ch. 3, 'State Terrorism and Irrational Terror'

11 Every revolutionary ends by becoming either an oppressor or a heretic.
ibid. 'Rebellion and Revolution'

12 In the midst of winter, I finally learned that there was in me an invincible summer.
*L'Été*, 'Return to Tipasa' (1954)

13 I sometimes think of what future historians will say of us. A single sentence will suffice for modern man: he fornicated and read the papers.
The narrator (Jean-Baptiste Clamence), in *The Fall* (1956)

14 You know what charm is: a way of getting the answer yes without having asked any clear question.
ibid.

15 Men are never convinced of your reasons, of your sincerity, of the seriousness of your sufferings, except by your death. So long as you are alive, your case is doubtful; you have a right only to their scepticism.
ibid.

16 Martyrs, *cher ami*, must choose between being forgotten, mocked, or made use of. As for being understood – never!
ibid.

17 I'll tell you a great big secret, *mon cher*. Don't wait for the Last Judgment. It takes place every day.
ibid.

18 Ah, *mon cher*, for anyone who is alone, without God and without a master, the weight of days is dreadful.
ibid.

19 I have always denounced terrorism. I must also denounce a terrorism which is exercised blindly, in the streets of Algiers for example, and which some day could strike my mother or my family. I believe in justice, but I shall defend my mother above justice.
Debate at the University of Stockholm, 1957, quoted in *Camus, A Biography*, ch. 45 (1979) by Herbert R. Lottman. Camus provoked much criticism with his remarks, taken as a betrayal of the struggle for Algerian independence.

20 We come into the world laden with the weight of an infinite necessity.
*Resistance, Rebellion and Death*, 'Reflections on the Guillotine' (1961)

21 The more I produce the less I am certain. On the road along which the artist walks, night falls ever more densely. Finally he dies blind.
Undated letter, quoted in *Camus: A Biography*, ch. 43 (1979) by Herbert R. Lottman

# Elias Canetti (1905–94)

BULGARIAN NOVELIST AND PHILOSOPHER

His first and only novel, *Die Blendung* (1936, translated as both *Auto da Fé* and *The Tower of Babel*), charts the destruction of a reclusive sinologist, while his greatest work, *Crowds and Power* (1960), focuses on his central preoccupation, the psychology of crowds. The first Bulgarian to receive the Nobel Prize for Literature (1981), he lived in England from 1938 but always wrote in German.

1 Justice begins with the recognition of the necessity of sharing. The oldest law is that which regulates it, and this is still the most important law today and, as such, has remained the basic concern of all movements which have at heart the community of human activities and of human existence in general.
*Crowds and Power*, 'Distribution and Increase' (1960)

2 Whether or not God is dead: it is impossible to keep silent about him who was there for so long.
*The Secret Heart Of The Clock: Notes, Aphorisms, Fragments 1973–1985*, '1973' (1991)

3 There is no doubt: the study of man is just beginning, at the same time that his end is in sight.
ibid. '1980'

# Eric Cantona (b. 1966)

FRENCH FOOTBALLER

A skilful forward and an idol for a generation of fans, he played for Manchester United (1993–7) and received the Player of the Year award in 1994. Both reflective and temperamental, he was made to perform community service in 1995 after kicking out at a fan who had insulted him. He has also embarked on an acting career.

1 When the seagulls follow the trawler, it is because they think sardines will be thrown into the sea.
Quoted in the *Independent* 1 April 1995, after he had won his appeal against a prison sentence for his conviction of assault on a hostile fan in January. 'Seagulls follow the trawler' was taken as the name of a sports discussion programme on BBC Radio 4 in 1999.

## Cao Yu (1910–96)

CHINESE DRAMATIST

Original name Wan Jiabao. China's foremost twentieth-century playwright, he studied Western literature, was influenced by Ibsen and G.B. SHAW, and took as his theme the corruption of society. His best known work *Thunderstorm* was produced in 1935.

1 Art for art's sake is a philosophy of the well-fed.
*Observer* 13 April 1980

## Karel Čapek (1890–1938)

CZECH WRITER

He is best remembered for the play *R.U.R. (Rossum's Universal Robots)* (1920), a cautionary tale of the dangers of mechanization, coining the word 'robot' (derived from the Czech word for forced labour). With his brother Josef, he wrote the comic satire *The Insect Play* (1921), a piece prophesying totalitarianism.

1 Man will never be enslaved by machinery if the man tending the machine be paid enough.
Quoted in obituary in the *News Chronicle* 27 December 1938

## Al Capone (1899–1947)

US GANGSTER

'Neapolitan by birth and Neanderthal by instinct', Alphonse Capone, *aka* Scarface, was America's most famous gangster. As crime czar of Chicago in the years of Prohibition, he allegedly earned $30 million a year through racketeering in brothels, gambling and bootlegging. Despite his hand in the St Valentine's Day massacre (1929), he escaped prosecution for murder but was eventually gaoled in 1931 for tax evasion.

1 My rackets are run on strictly American lines and they're going to stay that way.
Interview c. 1930, publ. in *Cockburn Sums Up*, 'Mr Capone, Philosopher' (1981) by Claud Cockburn

2 [Suburban Chicago . . . ] Virgin territory for whorehouses.
Quoted in *The Bootleggers*, ch. 16 (1961) by Kenneth Allsop

## Truman Capote (1924–84)

US AUTHOR

Original name Truman Streckfus Presons. A versatile writer, he is remembered for his lyrical first novel *Other Voices, Other Rooms* (1948), the light-hearted novella *Breakfast at Tiffany's* (1958, filmed 1961) and *In Cold Blood* (1966, filmed 1967), a tale of multiple murder, which he termed a non-fiction novel. GORE VIDAL said of him: 'He has made lying an art. A minor art.'

1 That isn't writing at all – it's typing.
Quoted in *New Republic* 9 February 1959. Remark in TV discussion, referring to the Beat novelists.

2 Venice is like eating an entire box of chocolate liqueurs at one go.
Quoted in the *Observer* 26 November 1961

3 Even an attorney of moderate talent can postpone doomsday year after year, for the system of appeals that pervades American jurisprudence amounts to a legalistic wheel of fortune, a game of chance, somewhat fixed in the favor of the criminal, that the participants play interminably.
*In Cold Blood*, ch. 4 (1966)

4 Failure is the condiment that gives success its flavor.
'Self-Portrait' (1972), repr. in *A Capote Reader* (1987)

5 Anyone who is consistently consistent has a head made of biscuit.
ibid.

6 When God hands you a gift, he also hands you a whip; and the whip is intended solely for self-flagellation.
*Music for Chameleons*, Preface (1980)

7 It's [Los Angeles] like a jumble of huts in a jungle somewhere. I don't understand how you can live there. It's really, completely dead. Walk along the street, there's nothing moving. I've lived in small Spanish fishing villages which were literally sunny all day long everyday of the week, but they weren't as boring as Los Angeles.
*Conversations With Truman Capote*, ch. 7 'Hollywood' (ed. Lawrence Grobel, 1985)

## Al Capp (1909–79)

US CARTOONIST

Original name Alfred Caplin. He introduced the comic strip, featuring the hillbilly character Li'l Abner and friends, to the *New York Mirror* in 1934. Its popularity ensured that it ran for more than forty years.

1 [Of abstract art] A product of the untalented, sold by the unprincipled to the utterly bewildered.
Quoted in the *National Observer* 1 July 1963

## Philip Caputo (b. 1941)

US AUTHOR AND JOURNALIST

He worked as a foreign correspondent for the *Chicago Tribune* (1969–72) and won a Pulitzer Prize in 1973 for his coverage of primary election fraud. The memoir *A Rumor of War* (1977) draws from his experiences as a soldier in Vietnam; *A Means of Escape* (1991) is an 'imaginative autobiography'.

1 Our mission was not to win terrain, or seize positions, but simply to kill: to kill Communists and to kill as many of them as possible. Stack 'em like cordwood. Victory was a high body-count, defeat a low kill-ratio, war a matter of arithmetic.
*A Rumor of War*, prologue (1977)

## (Sir) Neville Cardus (1889–1975)

BRITISH JOURNALIST AND CRITIC

He wrote mainly for the *Manchester Guardian*, which he joined in 1916 as music critic. He was soon responsible for the paper's cricket coverage as well, allowing him to draw frequent analogies between his twin passions.

1 It is far more than a game, this cricket. It somehow holds the mirror up to English nature. We are not hypocrites, but we try to make the best of things of contrary appeal.
*English Cricket* (1945)

2 It is because cricket does not always hurry along, a constant hurly burly, every player propelled here and there by the pace of continuous action, that there is time for character to reveal itself. We remember not the scores and the results in after years; it is the men who remain in our minds, in our imagination.
ibid.

3 Such reproductions may not interest the reader; but after all, this is my autobiography, not his; he is under no obligation to read further in it; he was under none to begin. . . . A modest or inhibited autobiography is written without entertainment to the writer and read with distrust by the reader.
*Autobiography*, pt 1 (1947)

## George Carey (b. 1935)

BRITISH ECCLESIASTIC, ARCHBISHOP OF CANTERBURY

Formerly a theology lecturer, he was appointed Bishop of Bath and Wells in 1987 and became primate of the Church of England in

1991. His liberal and modernising tendencies have attracted some criticism, not least for the introduction of women to the clergy and the institution of new forms of worship.

1 **People have described me as a 'management bishop' but I say to my critics 'Jesus was a management expert too.'**
Daily Telegraph 26 February 1991

2 **I believe with all my heart that the Church of Jesus Christ should be a Church of blurred edges.**
Independent 15 July 1992

## John Carey (b. 1934)
BRITISH AUTHOR AND CRITIC

Professor of English at Oxford since 1976 and principal book reviewer for the Sunday Times since 1977, he is the author of works on Milton, Thackeray, Donne and WILLIAM GOLDING, and of The Intellectuals and the Masses (1992), a cultural critique.

1 **A blank helpless sort of face, rather like a rose just before you drench it with DDT.**
Sunday Times 20 September 1981, repr. in Original Copy, pt 2, 'Keeping Up With the Coopers' (1987). Referring to photographs of society figure Lady DIANA COOPER.

2 **It follows that, if society wants to be civilized, it must establish conditions favourable to the preservation of the gifted few.**
The Intellectuals and the Masses, ch. 4 (1992)

## Peter Carey (b. 1943)
AUSTRALIAN AUTHOR

An innovative Australian writer, he successfully combines fantasy, comedy and history. His best-known novels are Bliss (1981, filmed 1985), set in the world of advertising in which Carey formerly worked, and the Booker Prize-winning Oscar and Lucinda (1988, filmed 1997).

1 **We're built, as a nation, on the grounds of a concentration camp. It's like saying 'OK, here's Auschwitz. Here's where we'll start our country.'**
Interview in City Limits 7 April 1988

## Robert Carlyle (b. 1956)
SCOTTISH ACTOR

First known for his TV role as the policeman Hamish Macbeth, he achieved box-office success in the films Trainspotting (1996), The Full Monty (1996) and Angela's Ashes (2000).

1 **[Of Scotland] Do you use the telephone, do you watch television, do you drive on the road with tyres? There's four things that have come out of this tiny, wee country. But it is also a country whose people are either capable of great or terrible things. A psychotic nation.**
Interview in The Times 17 January 1998

## Stokely Carmichael (1941–99)
US POLITICAL ACTIVIST

Trinidadian by birth, he was an outspoken activist in civil rights movements throughout the 1960s, though publicly broke with the Black Panthers in 1968. The following year he moved with his wife (the musician Miriam Makeba) to Guinea, where he was a supporter of Pan-Africanism, later changing his name to Kwame Touré.

1 **This is the 27th time I have been arrested – I ain't going to jail no more. I ain't going to jail no more. Every courthouse in Mississippi ought to be burned down to get rid of the dirt. We want Black Power!**
Speech from steps of courthouse in Greenwood, Mississippi, 17 June 1966, quoted in The New York Times 17 June 1966. The slogan

'Black Power' (uttered five times by Carmichael) was taken up by the gathered crowd, who were participating in the James Meredith March from Memphis to Jackson to promote black voting. Dr MARTIN LUTHER KING, also on the march, expressed his unease at the slogan and encouraged instead 'Freedom Now', though by the end of the march this had been eclipsed by Carmichael's more inflammatory call. Carmichael was responsible for popularizing the slogan, and published a book with that title in 1967 (see below).

2 **Those of us who advocate Black Power are quite clear in our own minds that a 'non-violent' approach to civil rights is an approach black people cannot afford and a luxury white people do not deserve.**
Black Power, ch. 2 (written with Charles Vernon Hamilton, 1967)

## Dale Carnegie (1888–1955)
US WRITER AND LECTURER

The distillation of his expertise on public speaking is published in How To Win Friends and Influence People (1936). Following on the success of this book, he set up numerous branches of the Dale Carnegie Institute for Effective Speaking and Human Relations.

1 **How to Win Friends and Influence People.**
Title of book (1936)

## E.H. Carr (1892–1982)
BRITISH AUTHOR AND ACADEMIC

Full name Edward Hallett Carr. He worked in the Foreign Office before becoming assistant editor of The Times (1941–6). His magnum opus was A History of Soviet Russia 1917–29 (14 vols., 1950–78). He was also the author of What Is History? (1961) and Fellow of Trinity College, Cambridge (1955–82).

1 **History begins when men begin to think of the passage of time in terms not of natural processes – the cycle of the seasons, the human life-span – but of a series of specific events in which men are consciously involved and which they can consciously influence.**
What Is History?, Lecture 6 (1961)

## Emily Carr (1871–1945)
CANADIAN ARTIST AND AUTHOR

She is known for her primitive-style paintings of Native Americans and forests of British Columbia. In 1940, after ill health forced her to give up painting, she concentrated on writing, her books including Klee Wyck (1941), stories of Indian life.

1 **It is not all bad, this getting old, ripening. After the fruit has got its growth it should juice up and mellow. God forbid I should live long enough to ferment and rot and fall to the ground in a squash.**
Journal entry, 12 December 1933, publ. in Hundreds and Thousands: The Journals of Emily Carr (1966). Written on the eve of her sixty-second birthday.

## J.L. Carr (1912–94)
BRITISH NOVELIST

Full name James Lloyd Carr. Originally a teacher, he turned to writing late in life, encapsulating English provincial life in such novels as The Harpole Report (1972) and, his most successful, A Month in the Country (1980), while his Dictionary of Extraordinary Cricketers (1977) has also become a minor classic.

1 **A school is not a factory. Its raison d'être is to provide opportunity for experience.**
The Harpole Report, ch. 6 (1972)

2 **You have not had thirty years' experience. . .You have had one year's experience 30 times.**
ibid. ch. 21

## Jim Carroll (b. 1951)
US AUTHOR

Jack Kerouac said: 'At thirteen years of age, Jim Carroll writes better prose than eighty-nine per cent of the novelists working today.' A heroin addict, he wrote autobiographically, gaining recognition for the poetry collection *Living at the Movies* (1973), and *The Basketball Diaries* (1980, filmed 1995), which he wrote between the ages of 12 and 15, and in which he explored the 'dark underbelly of the Sixties' counterculture'.

1 Junk is just another nine to five gig in the end, only the hours are a bit more inclined towards shadows.
*The Basketball Diaries*, 'Summer 66' (1980). On the life of a heroin addict.

## Johnny Carson (b. 1925)
US CHAT-SHOW HOST AND COMEDIAN

After presenting his own shows on television and hosting the game show *Who Do You Trust?* (1957–62), he took over *The Tonight Show*, hosting it for the next thirty years.

1 Heeeeere's Johnny!
Spoken by Ed McMahon introducing *The Tonight Show Starring Johnny Carson* (US TV variety show, 1962–92). The intro was often copied, and was famously – and manically – mimicked by JACK NICHOLSON's character (Jack Torrance) in *The Shining* (film, 1980).

## Rachel Carson (1907–64)
US MARINE BIOLOGIST AND AUTHOR

Through her books, notably *The Sea Around Us* (1951) and *Silent Spring* (1962), she increased public awareness of the dangers of environmental pollution, which in turn led to US legislation on the use of pesticides.

1 The sea lies all about us. . . . In its mysterious past it encompasses all the dim origins of life and receives in the end, after, it may be, many transmutations, the dead husks of that same life. For all at last returns to the sea – to Oceanus, the ocean river, like the ever-flowing stream of time, the beginning and the end.
*The Sea Around Us*, pt 3, ch.14 (1951)

2 Under the philosophy that now seems to guide our destinies, nothing must get in the way of the man with the spray gun.
*Silent Spring*, ch. 7 (1962)

3 The 'control of nature' is a phrase conceived in arrogance, born of the Neanderthal age of biology and the convenience of man.
ibid. ch. 17

## Angela Carter (1940–92)
BRITISH AUTHOR

Her considerable output of fiction, including *Nights at the Circus* (1984) and *Wise Children* (1991), combines eroticism, feminism and fantasy. An outspoken critic of contemporary society, she contributed to numerous newspapers and magazines and wrote the sceenplays for her stories *The Magic Toyshop* (1967, filmed 1986) and *The Company of Wolves* (1977, filmed 1984).

1 Midnight, and the clock strikes. It is Christmas Day, the werewolves' birthday, the door of the solstice still wide enough open to let them all slink through.
'The Company of Wolves', publ. in *Bananas* (ed. Emma Tennant, 1977)

2 Never stray from the path, never eat a windfall apple and never trust a man whose eyebrows meet in the middle.
ibid.

3 The victim style of the 1970s has a behavioural style to match. They never smile, these infants of the recession:

they sneer. Defiant untouchables, tattooed at the extremities and accessoried with offensive weapons, lips and fingernails stained black and blue and the skin round their eyes painted up like rococo window-frames.
'Ups and Downs for the Babes in Bondage', publ. in *New Society* 22 December 1977

4 We do not go to bed in single pairs; even if we choose not to refer to them, we still drag there with us the cultural impedimenta of our social class, our parents' lives, our bank balances, our sexual and emotional expectations, our whole biographies – all the bits and pieces of our unique existences.
*The Sadeian Woman*, 'Polemical Preface' (1979)

5 Pornographers are the enemies of women only because our contemporary ideology of pornography does not encompass the possibility of change, as if we were the slaves of history and not its makers. . . . Pornography is a satire on human pretensions.
ibid.

6 The bed is now as public as the dinner table and governed by the same rules of formal confrontation.
ibid. 'Speculative Finale'

7 If *Miss* means respectably unmarried, and *Mrs.* respectably married, then *Ms.* means nudge, nudge, wink, wink.
'The Language of Sisterhood', publ. in *The State of the Language* (ed. Christopher Ricks, 1980)

8 [Of D.H. Lawrence] If the Christ were content with humble toilers for disciples, that wasn't good enough for our Bert. He wanted dukes' half sisters and belted earls wiping his feet with their hair; grand apotheosis of the snob, to humiliate the objects of his own awe by making them venerate him.
*New Society* 3 June 1982

9 I think it's one of the scars in our culture that we have too high an opinion of ourselves. We align ourselves with the angels instead of the higher primates.
*Marxism Today* January 1985

10 I think the adjective 'post-modernist' really means 'mannerist'. Books about books is fun but frivolous.
*Novelists in Interview* (ed. John Haffenden, 1985)

11 Morality as regards woman has nothing to do with ethics; it means sexual morality and nothing but sexual morality. To be a wayward girl usually has something to do with pre-marital sex; to be a wicked woman has something to do with adultery. This means it is far easier for a woman to lead a blameless life than it is for a man; all she has to do is to avoid sexual intercourse like the plague.
*Wayward Girls and Wicked Women*, Introduction (ed. Angela Carter, 1986)

12 Just because we're sisters under the skin doesn't mean we've got much in common.
*Guardian* 25 October 1990

13 Comedy is tragedy that happens to *other* people.
*Wise Children*, ch. 4 (1991)

## Jimmy Carter (b. 1924)
US POLITICIAN AND PRESIDENT

Peanut farmer by trade, he was a progressive Democratic Governor of Georgia (1970–74), and while President (1977–81) was committed to international human rights. His successes included the Panama Canal treaty (1977), the Camp David Agreements (1978), and the restoration of full diplomatic relations with China (1979), though his failure to bring home the US hostages held in Iran contributed in large part to his defeat by RONALD REAGAN in the 1980 election. The trade union leader Lane Kirkland called Carter 'your typical smiling, brilliant, backstabbing, bullshitting southern nut-cutter'.

1 I've looked on a lot of women with lust. I've committed adultery in my heart many times. This is something God recognizes I will do – and I have done it – and God forgives me for it.

Interview in *Playboy* November 1976. In response to the widespread surprise that this remark caused at the height of the presidential campaign in which he stood against GERALD FORD, Carter's wife Rosalynn remarked simply, 'Jimmy talks too much . . .'

2 I thought a lot about our nation and what I should do as President. And Sunday night before last, I made a speech about two problems of our country – energy and malaise.

Speech at Bardstown, Kentucky, 31 July 1979, publ. in *Public Papers of the Presidents of the United States: Jimmy Carter, 1979*. The speech to which Carter referred, broadcast 15 July from the White House, did not include the word 'malaise', though Carter's identification of these two issues provoked much discussion.

3 I never really had any affinity for politics. I've always looked on politics as a means to an end. . . . It has never been a natural part of my life.

Interview in the *Guardian* 7 February 1998. In an interview with Carter's biographer, his vice-president WALTER MONDALE charged his former boss with having 'the coldest political nose of any politician'.

## Stephen Carter (b. 1954)
US LAWYER AND AUTHOR

An advocate of affirmative action for African Americans, he wrote widely on matters of race and on the role of religion in politics.

1 The new grammar of race is constructed in a way that George Orwell would have appreciated, because its rules make some ideas impossible to express – unless, of course, one wants to be called a racist.

*Reflections of an Affirmative Action Baby*, ch. 8 (1992)

## Sydney Carter (b. 1915)
BRITISH SONGWRITER
A teacher, he has written folk songs as well as popular hymns.

1 Dance then wherever you may be,
I am the Lord of the Dance, said he,
And I'll lead you all, wherever you may be
And I'll lead you all in the dance, said he.
'Lord of the Dance' (song), publ. in *Nine Carols or Ballads* (1967)

2 One more step along the world I go,
One more step along the world I go,
From the old things to the new
Keep me travelling along with You.
'One More Step Along the World I Go' (hymn, 1971)

## Martin Carthy (b. 1941)
ENGLISH FOLK SINGER AND MUSICIAN

He was prominent in the English folk revival of the 1960s, playing guitar with Steeleye Span and the Albion Band, and later wrote for PAUL SIMON and BOB DYLAN.

1 In the past, the English tried to impose a system wherever they went. They destroyed the nation's culture and one of the by-products of their systemization was that they destroyed their own folk culture.
Interview in the *Guardian* 29 December 1988

## (Dame) Barbara Cartland (1901–2000)
BRITISH NOVELIST

Hailed 'the queen of romantic fiction', she sold over 650 million copies of her 623 books, whose titles enabled her to claim the longest entry in *Who's Who*. She was famous for her pink chiffon and extravagant false eyelashes, and was portrayed by the wit

Arthur Marshall as 'a tireless purveyor of romance and now a gleaming telly-figure with a Niagara of jabber'.

1 The great majority of people in England and America are modest, decent and pure-minded and the amount of virgins in the world today is stupendous.
Interview in *Speaking Frankly* (1978) by Wendy Leigh. But on another occasion, Cartland was reported as saying: 'Only the English and the Americans are improper. East of Suez everyone wants a virgin.'

2 The right diet directs sexual energy into the parts that matter.
Quoted in the *Observer* 11 January 1981

3 France is the only place where you can make love in the afternoon without people hammering on your door.
Quoted in the *Guardian* 24 December 1984

## Raymond Carver (1939–88)
US POET AND SHORT-STORY WRITER

His stories, written in a simple, unadorned style that identified him with the 'dirty realism' school, usually depict the problems and failures of small-town blue-collar workers. He established his reputation with *Will You Please Be Quiet, Please?* (1976), followed by *Cathedral* (1984) and *Where I'm Calling From* (1988). JAY MCINERNEY said of him, 'The trout in Carver's streams were apt to be pollution-deformed mutants, the romance of drinking replaced by the dull grind of full-time alcoholism. Some commentators found his work depressing for these reasons. For many young writers, it was terribly liberating.'

1 Writers don't need tricks or gimmicks or even necessarily need to be the smartest fellows on the block. At the risk of appearing foolish, a writer sometimes needs to be able to just stand and gape at this or that thing – a sunset or an old shoe – in absolute and simple amazement.
'A Storyteller's Notebook', first publ. in *The New York Times Book Review* 15 February 1981, repr. as 'On Writing' in *Fires* (1985)

## Joyce Cary (1888–1957)
BRITISH AUTHOR

His experiences in Africa during the First World War furnished material for his early novels including *Mister Johnson* (1939), though he is best remembered for his later trilogies dealing with art and politics, and especially for *The Horse's Mouth* (1944), a picaresque portrait of a disreputable artist. V.S. PRITCHETT called him 'the chameleon among contemporary novelists'.

1 Sara could commit adultery at one end and weep for her sins at the other, and enjoy both operations at once.
The narrator (Gulley Jimson), in *The Horse's Mouth*, ch. 8 (1944)

2 The will is never free – it is always attached to an object, a purpose. It is simply the engine in the car – it can't steer.
Interview in *Writers at Work* (first series, ed. Malcolm Cowley, 1958)

## Pablo Casals (1876–1973)
SPANISH CELLIST, CONDUCTOR AND COMPOSER

Called by Rostropovich 'the greatest name in cello history', he is famous for his interpretations of Bach, especially the cello suites. He founded the Barcelona orchestra in 1919 and conducted it until 1936 when, in protest against the Franco regime, he moved to Prades in Catalan France. From 1956 until his death he lived in Puerto Rico.

1 I go back to Bach as a sick dog instinctively grubs at the roots and herbs that are its right medicine.
Quoted in the *Observer* 27 November 1921

2 [Of the cello] It is like a beautiful woman who has not

grown older, but younger with time, more slender, more supple, more graceful.

Quoted in *Time* 29 April 1957

## (Sir) Roger Casement (1864–1916)

COLONIAL ADMINISTRATOR AND IRISH NATIONALIST

An Ulster Protestant by birth, he gained his knighthood for denouncing cruelty and exploitation while acting as Consul in the Congo and Brazil. Back in Ireland, his efforts to enlist German support for the Easter Rising in 1916 resulted in his being hanged for high treason.

1 As I stand face to face with death, I feel just as if they were going to kill a boy. For I feel like a boy – and my hands are so free from blood and my heart always so compassionate and pitiful that I cannot comprehend that anyone wants to hang me.

Note found in Casement's condemned cell, Pentonville, London, August 1916, quoted in *The Lives of Roger Casement*, ch. 30 (1976) by B.L. Reid.

## William Casey (1913–87)

US LAWYER AND INTELLIGENCE CHIEF

As President Reagan's Director of the CIA from 1981 to 1987, he was responsible for intensifying the agency's anti-communist activities. His role in the Iran-Contra Affair was never resolved, as he died before testifying.

1 I pass the test that says a man who isn't a socialist at 20 has no heart, and a man who is a socialist at 40 has no head.

Quoted in obituary, *Washington Post* 7 May 1987. The saying has been attributed to French socialist politician and premier Aristide Briand.

## Johnny Cash (b. 1932)

US COUNTRY SINGER

Nicknamed 'The Man in Black', he was acknowledged as a top Country and Western recording artist in the late 1950s, becoming the youngest person ever chosen for the Country Music Hall of Fame. He has over 1,500 songs to his name, including 'I Walk The Line' (1956) and 'A Boy Named Sue' (1969).

1 I thank God for all the freedom we have in this country, I cherish it – even the right to burn the flag. But we also have the right to bear arms and if you burn my flag – *I'll shoot you!*

Quoted by Tony Parsons in the *Daily Telegraph* 10 April 1992. The speech is a routine preamble to Cash's hymn to the Stars and Stripes, 'Ragged Old Flag', usually to a standing ovation.

## Neal Cassady (1926–68)

US WRITER

An outlaw hero of the Beat Generation, he was mythologized as Dean Moriarty ('the holy con man with the shining mind') in JACK KEROUAC's *On the Road*. Fragments of autobiography and his correspondence with Kerouac and GINSBERG have been published in *The First Third and Other Writings* (1971), *As Ever* (1977), and *Grace Beats Karma* (1993).

1 Art is good when it springs from necessity. This kind of origin is the guarantee of its value; there is no other.

Letter to Jack Kerouac, 7–8 January 1948, quoted in *Memory Babe*, ch. 5, sect. 5 (1983) by Gerald Nicosia

2 Billboards, billboards, drink this, eat that, use all manner of things, EVERYONE, the best, the cheapest, the purest and most satisfying of all their available counterparts. Red lights flicker on every horizon, airplanes beware; cars flash

by, more lights. Workers repair the gas main. Signs, signs, lights, lights, streets, streets.

'Leaving LA by Train at Night, High . . .', written c. 1950, publ. in *The First Third and Other Writings* (1971)

## (Sir) Hugh Casson (b. 1910)

BRITISH ARCHITECT

After directing the architecture at the Festival of Britain (1948–51), he was Professor of Interior Design at the Royal College of Art (1953–75) and President of the Royal Academy (1976–84).

1 The British love permanence more than they love beauty.

Quoted in the *Observer* 14 June 1964

## Ted Castle (1907–79)

BRITISH JOURNALIST

Baron Castle of Islington. The husband of Labour politician Barbara Castle, he worked as Assistant Editor and Editor of *Picture Post* (1944–52) and was an alderman of the Greater London Council 1964–70.

1 In Place of Strife.

White Paper on industrial relations, 17 January 1969. The title was suggested to Employment Secretary Barbara Castle by her husband, as recalled in *The Barbara Castle Diaries*, 15 January 1969 (1984). It was probably inspired by ANEURIN BEVAN's book setting out his political credo, *In Place of Fear* (1952).

## Fidel Castro (b. 1926)

CUBAN REVOLUTIONARY AND PRESIDENT

Assuming premiership after ousting President Batista in 1959, he established a Communist regime and instituted a sweeping programme of reform. He saw off the US-backed Bay of Pigs invasion in 1961 and survived the Cuban Missile Crisis of 1962, but exchanged economic dependence on the US with reliance on the USSR, at a heavy cost to Cuba. He became President in 1976.

1 History will absolve me.

Last words of speech during trial, 16 October 1953, publ. in *The Penguin Book of Twentieth-Century Speeches* (ed. Brian MacArthur, 1999). Castro had led an unsuccessful assault on the Moncada barracks in July 1953. Sentenced to fifteen years' imprisonment, he was released within a year under an amnesty, returning from exile in 1956 and assuming power soon after. The words *La historia me absolverá* were the title of a revolutionary pamphlet published during the struggle.

2 I feel my belief in sacrifice and struggle getting stronger. I despise the kind of existence that clings to the miserly trifles of comfort and self-interest. I think that a man should not live beyond the age when he begins to deteriorate, when the flame that lighted the brightest moment of his life has weakened.

Letter written from a prison cell on the island of Pines, 19 December 1953, publ. in *Diary of the Cuban Revolution* (1980) by Carlos Franqui

3 I began revolution with 82 men. If I had [to] do it again, I do it with 10 or 15 and absolute faith. It does not matter how small you are if you have faith and plan of action.

*The New York Times* 22 April 1959

## Willa Cather (1876–1947)

US AUTHOR

Her novels and stories, none of which she allowed to appear in paperback, portray frontier life in Nebraska as she knew it in childhood, and the clash between the civilized and the natural environment. Of these *O Pioneers!* (1913) and *My Antonia* (1918) are judged her best achievements; *One of Ours* (1922) won the Pulitzer Prize. REBECCA WEST called her 'the most sensuous of writers'.

1 Artistic growth is, more than it is anything else, a refining

of the sense of truthfulness. The stupid believe that to be truthful is easy; only the artist, the great artist, knows how difficult it is.

*The Song of the Lark*, pt 6, ch. 11 (1915)

2 Winter lies too long in country towns; hangs on until it is stale and shabby, old and sullen.

*My Antonia*, bk 2, ch. 7 (1918)

3 Art, it seems to me, should simplify ... finding what conventions of form and what detail one can do without and yet preserve the spirit of the whole – so that all that one has suppressed and cut away is there to the reader's consciousness as much as if it were in type on the page.

'On the Art of Fiction' (written 1920), publ. in *On Writing* (1949)

4 When kindness has left people, even for a few moments, we become afraid of them as if their reason had left them. When it has left a place where we have always found it, it is like shipwreck; we drop from security into something malevolent and bottomless.

*My Mortal Enemy* (1926)

5 Oh, the Germans classify, but the French arrange!

Prologue to *Death Comes for the Archbishop* (1927)

6 That irregular and intimate quality of things made entirely by the human hand.

Describing Father Latour's study, in ibid. bk 1, ch. 3

7 Only solitary men know the full joys of friendship. Others have their family; but to a solitary and an exile his friends are everything.

Father Hector Saint-Cyr, in *Shadows on the Rock*, bk 3, ch. 5 (1931)

8 Religion and art spring from the same root and are close kin. Economics and art are strangers.

'Four Letters: Escapism', first publ. in *Commonweal* 17 April 1936, repr. in *On Writing* (1949)

## (Sir) Bernard Caulfield (b. 1914)

BRITISH LAWYER

He held the position of Judge of the High Court of Justice from 1968 until 1981.

1 Is Jeffrey Archer in need of cold, unloving, rubber-insulated sex? . . . Remember Mary Archer in the witness box. Your vision of her will probably never disappear. Has she elegance? Has she fragrance? Would she have – without the strain of this trial – a radiance?

Summary at libel case between JEFFREY ARCHER and the *News of the World* 23 July 1987, quoted in *The Times* 24 July 1987. Archer had been implicated in a scandal involving a call girl. Archer won the case and £500,000 damages, though it emerged during his bid to be Mayor of London in 1999 that he had asked a friend to commit perjury at the trial to protect his cover.

## Charles Causley (b. 1917)

BRITISH POET

His poetry reflects Cornwall, where he has lived and written for much of his life, often dealing with contemporary concerns in traditional form. He has written for both children and adults, including *A Field of Vision* (1988), and has edited poetry anthologies.

1 Timothy Winters comes to school
With eyes as wide as a football-pool,
Ears like bombs and teeth like splinters:
A blitz of a boy is Timothy Winters.

'Timothy Winters', publ. in *Union Street* (1957)

## Edith Cavell (1865–1915)

BRITISH NURSE

A heroine of the First World War, she was executed for assisting Allied soldiers to escape to the Netherlands from German-occupied Belgium.

1 Standing, as I do, in view of God and eternity, I realize that patriotism is not enough. I must have no hatred or bitterness towards anyone.

Quoted in *The Times* 23 October 1915. The words, often erroneously claimed to be Cavell's last, were spoken 11 October 1915, in conversation with her chaplain on the eve of her execution in Brussels.

## Paul Celan (1920–70)

GERMAN POET

Original name Paul Antschel. Though he never lived in Germany and emigrated to France in 1948, he was one of the foremost poets of post-Second World War German literature. His work is allusive, influenced by French Surrealism, and informed by his experience as a Jew in a forced-labour camp. He committed suicide.

1 Black milk of daybreak we drink you at night
we drink you at noon death is a master from Germany
we drink you at sundown and in the morning we drink
and we drink you
death is master from Germany his eyes are blue
he strikes you with leaden bullets his aim is true.

'Death Fugue', publ. in *Mohn und Gedächtnis* (1952, transl. Michael Hamburger as *Poppy and Memory*, 1988)

## Louis-Ferdinand Céline (1894–1961)

FRENCH AUTHOR

Original name Louis Ferdinand Destouches. A major innovator of twentieth-century French literature, his best-known novel, the autobiographical and misanthropic *Journey to the End of Night* (1932), aroused hostility, as did his vitriolic anti-Semitic pamphlets (1937–41). In 1944 he fled to Denmark where he was imprisoned, but, cleared of charges in 1951, he returned to Paris.

1 Love, Arthur, is a poodle's chance of attaining the infinite, and personally I have my pride.

The narrator (Ferdinand Bardamu), in *Journey to the End of the Night* (1932)

2 The North will at least preserve your flesh for you; Northerners are pale for good and all. There's very little difference between a dead Swede and a young man who's had a bad night. But the Colonial is full of maggots the day after he gets off the boat.

ibid.

3 To philosophize is only another way of being afraid and leads hardly anywhere but to cowardly make-believe.

ibid.

4 The whole business of your life overwhelms you when you live alone. One's stupefied by it. To get rid of it you try to daub some of it off on to people who come to see you, and they hate that. To be alone trains one for death.

ibid.

5 To hell with reality! I want to die in music, not in reason or in prose.

Letter, 30 June 1947, publ. in *Critical Essays on Louis-Ferdinand Céline* (ed. William K. Buckley, 1989)

6 Life is filigree work . . . What is written clearly is not worth much, it's the transparency that counts.

*Féerie pour une autre fois* (1952), quoted in *Céline*, ch. 8 (1975) by Patrick McCarthy

7 Experience is a dim lamp, which only lights the one who bears it.

Interview in *Writers at Work* (third series, ed. George Plimpton, 1967)

## Henry Chadwick (b. 1920)

BRITISH EDUCATOR AND HISTORIAN

A professor of divinity at Cambridge, he has published a series of books since 1953 on Christian thought and the early Christian Church, among them *Tradition and Exploration* (1994).

1 A Church which has lost its memory is in a sad state of senility.

*Daily Telegraph* 10 February 1988

## Marc Chagall (1889–1985)

FRENCH ARTIST

The rich colours and dream-like poetic images of Chagall, inspired partly by Russian folklore, made him a prominent avant-garde figure of the twentieth-century Paris school. After moving to America in 1941 he designed ballet sets and costumes, including for Stravinsky's *The Firebird* (1945), as well as murals and stained-glass windows.

1 When I am finishing a picture I hold some God-made object up to it – a rock, a flower, the branch of a tree or my hand – as a kind of final test. If the painting stands up beside a thing man cannot make, the painting is authentic. If there's a clash between the two, it is bad art.

*Saturday Evening Post* 2 December 1962

## Neville Chamberlain (1869–1940)

BRITISH POLITICIAN AND PRIME MINISTER

Prime minister 1937–40 of a coalition government, he was party to the Munich Agreement (1938) whereby the Sudetenland was ceded to Germany. In 1939, Hitler's invasion of the rest of Czechoslovakia caused a reversal of the appeasement policy. LLOYD GEORGE claimed that he viewed foreign policy 'through the wrong end of a municipal drainpipe'. See also ANEURIN BEVAN 2 and HUGH MACDIARMID 1.

1 How horrible, fantastic, incredible it is that we should be digging trenches and trying on gas masks here because of a quarrel in a faraway country between people of whom we know nothing.

BBC radio broadcast, 27 September 1938, quoted in *The Times* 28 September 1938. On Germany's annexation of the Sudetenland, Czechoslovakia, shortly before Chamberlain left for Munich to confer with Hitler, Mussolini and Daladier.

2 My good friends, this is the second time in our history that there has come back from Germany to Downing Street peace with honour. I believe it is peace for our time. We thank you from the bottom of our hearts. And now I recommend you to go home and sleep quietly in your beds.

Speech at Downing Street, 30 September 1938, publ. in *The Penguin Book of Twentieth-Century Speeches* (ed. Brian MacArthur, 1999). Chamberlain had returned the previous day from Munich, where it was agreed that the Sudetenland should be transferred to Germany while guaranteeing Czechoslovakia's remaining frontiers. Chamberlain's words are often misquoted 'peace in our time'.

3 This morning the British Ambassador in Berlin handed the German Government a final Note stating that, unless we heard from them by 11 o'clock that they were prepared at once to withdraw their troops from Poland, a state of war would exist between us. I have to tell you now that no such undertaking has been received, and that consequently this country is at war with Germany.

BBC radio broadcast 3 September 1939 on the declaration of war, publ. in ibid.

4 Whatever may be the reason, whether it was that Hitler thought he might get away with what he had got without fighting for it, or whether it was that after all the prep-

arations were not sufficiently complete – however, one thing is certain: he missed the bus.

Speech to Conservative and Unionist Associations, Central Hall, London, 4 April 1940, quoted in *The Times* 5 April 1940. Chamberlain referred to the postponement of Hitler's attack on the Western Front, the anxious period known as the 'Phoney War'. Five days later, German troops invaded Denmark and Norway, followed shortly after by the invasion of the Netherlands, Belgium, Luxembourg and France, and the start of the Battle of Britain.

## Raymond Chandler (1888–1959)

US CRIMEWRITER

Regarded as the 'pick of the hard-boiled mystery scribblers', he was largely responsible for elevating the pulp detective novel to a successful literary genre. *The Big Sleep* (1939), *Farewell My Lovely* (1940) and *The Long Goodbye* (1953), all featuring the cynical yet honourable detective Philip Marlowe, were subsequently made into films.

1 I don't mind if you don't like my manners. They're pretty bad. I grieve over them on the long winter evenings.

Philip Marlowe, in *The Big Sleep*, ch. 3 (1939). In the film version (1946), Marlowe, played by HUMPHREY BOGART, says, 'I don't mind if you don't like my manners. I don't like 'em myself . . .'

2 What did it matter where you lay once you were dead? In a dirty sump or in a marble tower on top of a high hill? You were dead, you were sleeping the big sleep, you were not bothered by things like that. Oil and water were the same as wind and air to you.

Philip Marlowe, in ibid. ch. 32

3 He looked about as inconspicuous as a tarantula on a slice of angel food.

Philip Marlowe describing Moose Malloy, in *Farewell, My Lovely*, ch. 1 (1940)

4 [Of Helen Grayle] It was a blonde. A blonde to make a bishop kick a hole in a stained-glass window.

Philip Marlowe, in ibid. ch. 13

5 [Of Helen Grayle] She gave me a smile I could feel in my hip pocket.

Philip Marlowe, in ibid. ch. 18

6 I needed a drink, I needed a lot of life insurance, I needed a vacation, I needed a home in the country. What I had was a coat, a hat and a gun.

Philip Marlowe, in ibid. ch. 34. The words have been parodied many times, memorably by CHARLES BUKOWSKI in *Pulp*, ch. 8 (1994), when the narrator, Nicky Belane, laments: 'I needed a vacation. I needed 5 women. I needed to get the wax out of my ears. My car needed an oil change. I'd failed to file my damned income tax. . . . I hadn't laughed in six years. I tended to worry when there was nothing to worry about. And when there was something to worry about, I got drunk.'

7 Down these mean streets a man must go who is not himself mean, who is neither tarnished nor afraid. . . . He is the hero, he is everything. He must be a complete man and a common man and yet an unusual man. He must be, to use a rather weathered phrase, a man of honor, by instinct, by inevitability, without thought of it, and certainly without saying it. He must be the best man in his world and a good enough man for any world.

'The Simple Art of Murder', first publ. in *Atlantic Monthly* December 1944, repr. in *Pearls Are a Nuisance* (1950). The opening words of this article – which defended detective fiction as a genre requiring 'writers with tough minds and a cool spirit of detachment' – inspired numerous pastiches, and the title of a collection of Chandler's writings, *Down These Mean Streets a Man Must Go* (1963) by Philip Durham. The phrase 'mean streets', however, had been in use since the nineteenth century to describe tough life in the city, and was borrowed by MARTIN SCORSESE as the title of his 1973 film about petty criminality in the Bronx.

8 The English may not always be the best writers in the world, but they are incomparably the best dull writers.
ibid.

9 If my books had been any worse, I should not have been invited to Hollywood, and . . . if they had been any better, I should not have come.
Letter to the *Atlantic Monthly*, 12 December 1945, repr. in *Raymond Chandler Speaking* (ed. Dorothy Gardiner and Kathrine S. Walker, 1962). Chandler's letter was responding to criticism of his article 'Writers in Hollywood'.

10 Would you convey my compliments to the purist who reads your proofs and tell him or her that I write in a sort of broken-down patois which is something like the way a Swiss waiter talks, and that when I split an infinitive, God damn it, I split it so it will stay split, and when I interrupt the velvety smoothness of my more or less literate syntax with a few sudden words of bar-room vernacular, that is done with the eyes wide open and the mind relaxed but attentive. The method may not be perfect, but it is all I have.
Letter to *Atlantic Monthly* editor Edward Weeks, 18 January 1948, publ. in ibid. The letter produced a comic sequel in which Chandler composed a poem to the proof-reader, a certain Margaret Mutch, titled 'Lines to a Lady with an Un-split Infinitive', in which she was made to reproach him: 'Though you went to Yale, your grammer is frail/she snarled as she jabbed his eye./Though you went to Princeton I never winced on/Such a horrible relative clause!'

11 I used to like this town. . . . Los Angeles was just a big dry sunny place with ugly homes and no style, but good-hearted and peaceful . . . Now . . . we've got the big money, the sharpshooters, the percentage workers, the fast dollar boys, the hoodlums out of New York and Chicago and Detroit – and Cleveland. We've got the flash restaurants and night clubs they run, and the hotels and apartment houses they own, and the grifters and con men and female bandits that live in them. The luxury trades, the pansy decorators, the Lesbian dress designers, the riff-raff of a big hardboiled city with no more personality than a paper cup.
Philip Marlowe, in *The Little Sister*, ch. 26 (1949)

12 I guess God made Boston on a wet Sunday.
Letter 21 March 1949, publ. in *The Selected Letters of Raymond Chandler* (ed. Frank MacShane, 1981). Chandler was referring to a novel by J.P. Marquand, *Point of No Return*, which he had just finished reading, in which the portrait of Boston reminded him of 'a steel engraving with no color at all'.

13 Alcohol is like love. The first kiss is magic, the second is intimate, the third is routine. After that you take the girl's clothes off.
Terry Lennox, in *The Long Goodbye*, ch. 4 (1954)

14 The kind of lawyer you hope the other fellow has.
ibid. ch. 17

15 You can always tell a detective on TV. He never takes his hat off.
Philip Marlowe, in *Playback*, ch. 14 (1958)

## Coco Chanel (1883–1971)
FRENCH *COUTURIÈRE*

Original name Gabrielle Bonheur Chanel. Described by PICASSO as 'the woman with the most sense in Europe' and by DALI 'the best dressed body and soul in the world', she ruled Parisian haute couture for almost sixty years with her elegant fashions.

1 Fashion is made to become unfashionable.
*Life* 19 Aug. 1957

2 Elegance does not consist in putting on a new dress.
Quoted in *Coco Chanel: Her Life, Her Secrets*, ch. 21 (1971) by Marcel Haedrich

3 Why am I so determined to put the shoulder where it

belongs? Women have very round shoulders that push forward slightly; this touches me and I say: 'One must not hide that!' Then someone tells you: 'The shoulder is on the back.' I've never seen women with shoulders on their backs.
ibid.

4 Fashion is architecture: it is a matter of proportions.
ibid.

5 Innovation! One cannot be forever innovating. I want to create classics.
ibid.

## (Sir) Charlie Chaplin (1889–1977)
BRITISH COMIC ACTOR AND FILM-MAKER

The best-known silent film star of all time, he combined pathos with clowning, making his brolly and bowler hat trademarks of the 'little fellow', as he styled himself. From 1919, when he formed United Artists together with Mary Pickford, Douglas Fairbanks and D.W. Griffith, he directed all his films, including *The Kid* (1921), *The Goldrush* (1925) and *Modern Times* (1936). 'Charlie Chaplin's genius was in comedy,' his second wife Lita Chaplin declared. 'He has no sense of humour, particularly about himself.'

1 All I need to make a comedy is a park, a policeman and a pretty girl.
*My Autobiography*, ch. 10 (1964)

2 The basic essential of a great actor is that he loves himself in acting.
ibid. ch. 16

3 The saddest thing I can imagine is to get used to luxury.
ibid. ch. 22

4 I remain just one thing, and one thing only – and that is a clown. It places me on a far higher plane than any politician.
Quoted in the *Observer* 17 June 1960

5 Life is a tragedy when seen in close-up, but a comedy in long-shot.
Quoted in obituary, *Guardian* 28 December 1977

6 I have no further use for America. I wouldn't go back there if Jesus Christ was President.
Quoted in *Halliwell's Who's Who in the Movies* (ed. John Walker, 1999)

## Arthur Chapman (1873–1935)
U.S JOURNALIST

He worked on a number of newspapers in Chicago, Denver and New York as editor and staff writer.

1 Out where the handclasp's a little stronger,
Out where the smile dwells a little longer,
That's where the West begins.
'Out Where the West Begins', st. 1, publ. in *Out Where the West Begins* (1917)

## Charles, Prince of Wales (b. 1948)

Invested Prince of Wales in 1969, he married Lady Diana Spencer (see Princess DIANA) in 1981, from whom he was divorced in 1996. With particular interests in architecture and organic farming, he is founder of the Prince's Trust charity. According to PAUL MC-CARTNEY, 'His heart is in the right place, but he is born into the wrong family.'

1 It looks as if we may be presented with a kind of vast municipal fire station . . . I would understand better this type of high-tech approach if you demolished the whole of Trafalgar Square, but what is proposed is like a monstrous

carbuncle on the face of a much loved and elegant friend.

Speech to Royal Institute of British Architects, Hampton Court, 30 May 1984, quoted in *The Times* 31 May 1984. Charles was referring to a proposed extension to London's National Gallery – a design which, in the ensuing furore, was rejected in favour of a more classical structure. Charles's words may have been inspired by a passage recently written by Princess Diana's step-mother, Raine Spencer, in *The Spencers on Spas* (1983): 'Alas, for our towns and cities. Monstrous carbuncles of concrete have erupted in gentle Georgian squares.' In January 2000, Charles called the Millennium Dome at Greenwich a 'monstrous blancmange'.

2 I rather feel that deep in the soul of mankind there is a reflection as on the surface of a mirror, of a mirror-calm lake, of the beauty and harmony of the universe. . . . So much depends, I think, on how each one of us is introduced to and made aware of that reflection within us.

Speech in Prince George (British Columbia), 4 May 1986, quoted in *The Prince of Wales: a Biography*, ch. 20 (1994) by Jonathan Dimbleby

3 I just come and talk to the plants, really – very important to talk to them, they respond I find.

Television interview 21 September 1986, quoted in the *Daily Telegraph* 22 December 1986. Charles's half-joking remark helped to establish his reputation as a new-age eccentric. Responding humorously to this, he was later quoted as saying, 'Only the other day I was inquiring of an entire bed of old-fashioned roses, forced to listen to my ramblings on the meaning of the universe as I sat cross-legged in the lotus position in front of them.' (*Daily Telegraph* 15 November 1988).

4 You have to give this much to the Luftwaffe: when it knocked down our buildings it did not replace them with anything more offensive than rubble. We did that.

Speech at Mansion House, London, 1 December 1987, quoted in *The Times* 2 December 1987

5 All the people I have in my office, they can't speak English properly. All the letters sent from my office I have to correct myself. And that is because English is taught so bloody badly.

Off-the-cuff remark to business executives, 29 June 1989, quoted in *The Prince of Wales: a Biography*, ch. 23 (1994) by Jonathan Dimbleby

6 Conservation must come before recreation.

*The Times* 5 July 1989

7 If English is spoken in heaven . . . God undoubtedly employs Cranmer as his speechwriter. The angels of the lesser ministries probably use the language of the New English Bible and the Alternative Service Book for internal memos.

Remark when judging a reading competition, quoted in *The Times* 20 December 1989

8 Perhaps we just have to accept it as God's will that the unorthodox individual is doomed to years of frustration, ridicule and failure in order to act his role in the scheme of things.

Quoted in the *Independent* 8 November 1998. Referring to an earlier speech made to the British Medical Association in 1984.

9 [On GM food] Are we going to allow the industrialization of Life itself, redesigning the natural world for the sake of convenience and embarking on an Orwellian future? And, if we do, will there eventually be a price to pay? Or should we be adopting a gentler, more considered approach, seeking always to work with the grain of Nature in making better, more sustainable use of what we have, for the long-term benefit of mankind as a whole?

*Daily Mail* 1 June 1999

10 We should show greater respect for the genius of nature's designs, rigorously tested and refined over millions of years. This means being careful to use science to understand how nature works, not to change what nature is, as we do when genetic manipulation seeks to transform a process of biological evolution into something altogether different.

Reith Lecture, broadcast 17 May 2000, BBC Radio 4. In an open letter to Charles publ. in the *Observer* 21 May 2000, RICHARD DAWKINS responded: 'If we want to sustain the planet into the future, the first thing we must do is stop taking advice from nature. Nature is a short-term Darwinian profiteer.'

11 In an age when it often seems that nothing can properly be regarded as important unless it can be described as 'modern', it is highly dangerous to talk about the lessons of the past. And are those lessons ever taught or understood adequately in an age when to pass on a body of acquired knowledge of this kind is often considered prejudicial to 'progress'?

ibid.

## Bruce Chatwin (1940–89)

BRITISH AUTHOR

Recuperation in Africa after a temporary blindness led him to an interest in nomads and the dispossessed, and to start writing books which combine fiction, travel and philosophy. These include *In Patagonia* (1977), *The Songlines* (1987) and the novella *Utz* (1988).

1 Music is a memory bank for finding one's way about the world.

Arkady, in *The Songlines*, ch. 21 (1987). Songlines are the invisible pathways that cover Australia, believed by Aborigines to mark ancestral and personal territory.

2 An object in a museum case must suffer the de-natured existence of an animal in the zoo. In any museum the object dies – of suffocation and the public gaze – whereas private ownership confers on the owner the right and the need to touch. As a young child will reach out to handle the thing it names, so the passionate collector, his eye in harmony with his hand, restores to the object the life-giving touch of its maker. The collector's enemy is the museum curator. Ideally, museums should be looted every fifty years, and their collections returned to circulation . . .

Kaspar Utz, in *Utz* (1988)

3 Wars, pogroms and revolutions offer excellent opportunities for the collector.

ibid.

4 There is no contradiction between the Theory of Evolution and belief in God and His Son on earth. If Christ were the perfect instinctual specimen – and we have every reason to believe He was – He must be the Son of God. By the same token, the First Man was also Christ.

*What Am I Doing Here*, pt 3, 'Kevin Volans' (1989). Chatwin listed this as one of the basic tenets aired in *The Songlines*.

## John Cheever (1912–82)

US AUTHOR

Called 'the Chekhov of the suburbs' for his portraits of middle-class life in New England, he was a regular contributor to the *New Yorker* from the age of 22. *The Stories of John Cheever* (1978) won him a Pulitzer Prize, while his best known novels are *The Wapshot Chronicle* (1957) and *The Wapshot Scandal* (1964).

1 When the beginnings of self-destruction enter the heart it seems no bigger than a grain of sand.

Journal entry, 1952, publ. in *John Cheever: The Journals*, 'The Late Forties and the Fifties' (ed. Robert Gottlieb, 1991)

2 I do not understand the capricious lewdness of the sleeping mind.

Journal entry, 1955, in ibid.

3 People named John and Mary never divorce. For better or for worser, in madness and in saneness, they seem bound together for eternity by their rudimentary nomenclature. They may loathe and despise one another, quarrel,

weep, and commit mayhem, but they are not free to divorce. Tom, Dick, and Harry can go to Reno on a whim, but nothing short of death can separate John and Mary.

Journal entry, 1966, in ibid. 'The Sixties'. Cheever's wife was named Mary.

4 Then it is dark; it is a night where kings in golden suits ride elephants over the mountains.

'The Country Husband', publ. in *The Stories of John Cheever* (1978)

5 My veins are filled, once a week with a Neapolitan carpet cleaner distilled from the Adriatic and I am as bald as an egg. However I still get around and am mean to cats.

Letter to Philip Roth discussing his treatment for cancer, 10 May 1982, publ. in *The Letters of John Cheever* (1989)

# Victor Mikhailovich Chernov (1873–1972)

RUSSIAN SOCIALIST REVOLUTIONARY AND WRITER

Founder of the Russian Social Revolutionary Party in 1902 and Minister of Agriculture in the provisional government of 1917, he opposed the Bolsheviks and lived the last part of his life in exile, in Paris until the outbreak of the Second World War, then in the US.

1 The savages set up gods to which they pray, and which they punish if one of their prayers is not answered . . . That is what is happening at this moment . . . Yesterday Kerensky; today Lenin and Trotsky; another tomorrow . . .

Speech at Peasants' Congress, Petrograd, 28 November 1917, quoted in *Ten Days that Shook the World*, ch. 12 (1926) by John Reed

# G.K. Chesterton (1874–1936)

BRITISH AUTHOR

An exuberant personality, he wrote poetry both in ballad and comic form, as well as social and literary criticism, much of it published in his own *G.K.'s Weekly*. The most famous of his fiction works are the stories of the priest-sleuth Father Brown (1911–35). After converting to Catholicism in 1922, he wrote on religious topics. 'Chesterton's resolute conviviality is about as genial as an *auto da fé* of teetotallers', GEORGE BERNARD SHAW once observed.

1 And Noah he often said to his wife when he sat down to dine,
'I don't care where the water goes if it doesn't get into the wine.'

'Wine and Water', publ. in *The Flying Inn*, ch. 5 (1914)

2 They haven't got no noses
The fallen sons of Eve;
Even the smell of roses
Is not what they supposes;
But more than mind discloses
And more than men believe.

'The Song of Quoodle', publ. in ibid. ch. 15

3 And goodness only knowses
The Noselessness of Man.

ibid.

4 Tea, although an Oriental,
Is a gentleman at least;
Cocoa is a cad and coward,
Cocoa is a vulgar beast.

'Song of Right and Wrong', publ. in ibid. ch. 18

5 The rolling English drunkard made the rolling English road.
A reeling road, a rolling road, that rambles round the shire.

'The Rolling English Road', publ. in ibid. ch. 21

6 But there is good news yet to hear and fine things to be seen

Before we go to Paradise by way of Kensal Green.

ibid. (closing lines of poem). London's Kensal Green Cemetery holds many of Britain's illustrious dead.

7 To be clever enough to get all that money, one must be stupid enough to want it.

Muscari, in *The Wisdom of Father Brown*, 'Paradise of Thieves' (1914)

8 Journalism largely consists in saying 'Lord Jones Dead' to people who never knew that Lord Jones was alive.

Mr Finn, in ibid. 'The Purple Wig'

9 Are they clinging to their crosses, F. E. Smith?

'Antichrist', publ. in *Poems* (1915). Referring to F.E. SMITH (Lord Birkenhead) pontificating on the Welsh Disestablishment Bill.

10 Strong gongs groaning as the guns boom far,
Don John of Austria is going to the war.

'Lepanto', publ. in ibid. Don John, brother of Philip II of Spain, commanded the combined Spanish, Venetian and Papal fleets which defeated the Turks at Lepanto in 1571.

11 They have given us into the hand of new unhappy lords,
Lords without anger and honour, who dare not carry their swords.
They fight by shuffling papers; they have bright dead alien eyes;
They look at our labour and laughter as a tired man looks at flies.

'The Secret People', publ. in ibid.

12 But we are the people of England; and we have not spoken yet.
Smile at us, pay us, pass us. But do not quite forget.

ibid. (closing lines of poem)

13 Your next-door neighbour . . . is not a man; he is an environment. He is the barking of a dog; he is the noise of a pianola; he is a dispute about a party wall; he is drains that are worse than yours, or roses that are better than yours.

*The Uses of Diversity*, 'The Irishman' (1920)

14 They died to save their country and they only saved the world.

'English Graves', publ. in *The Ballad of St Barbara* (1922)

15 It is as healthy to enjoy sentiment as to enjoy jam.

*Generally Speaking*, 'On Sentiment' (1928)

16 A puritan is a person who pours righteous indignation into the wrong things.

*The New York Times* 21 November 1930

17 Democracy means government by the uneducated, while aristocracy means government by the badly educated.

ibid. 1 February 1931

18 There is nothing the matter with Americans except their ideals. The real American is all right; it is the ideal American who is all wrong.

ibid.

19 The disadvantage of men not knowing the past is that they do not know the present. History is a hill or high point of vantage, from which alone men see the town in which they live or the age in which they are living.

*All I Survey*, 'On St George Revivified' (1933)

20 It isn't that they can't see the solution. It is that they can't see the problem.

*Scandal of Father Brown*, 'Point of a Pin' (1935)

21 Boyhood is a most complex and incomprehensible thing. Even when one has been through it, one does not understand what it was. A man can never quite understand a boy, even when he has been the boy.

*Autobiography*, ch. 3 (1936)

22 There is no better test of a man's ultimate chivalry and

integrity than how he behaves when he is wrong. . . . A stiff apology is a second insult.

*The Common Man*, 'The Real Dr Johnson' (1950)

23  Ten thousand women marched through the streets of London saying: 'We will not be dictated to,' and then went off to become stenographers.

Quoted in *G.K. Chesterton*, ch. 1 (1986) by M. Ffinch. Referring to eartly feminists.

24  Am in Market Harborough. Where ought I to be?

Attributed telegram to wife in London. In his *Autobiography*, ch. 16 (1936), Chesterton wrote: 'I cannot remember whether this story is true; but it is not unlikely, or, I think, unreasonable.'

## Maurice Chevalier (1888–1972)
FRENCH SINGER AND ACTOR

Distinguished by his straw hat, cane and syrupy voice, he first appeared in the Folies Bergères (1909–13), and later had a film career spanning three decades. AL JOLSON called him 'the greatest thing to come from France since Lafayette', and JEAN COCTEAU declared 'Paris has two monuments: the Eiffel tower and Maurice Chevalier.'

1  Thank heaven for little girls!
   For little girls get bigger every day.

'Thank Heaven for Little Girls' (song, written by ALAN JAY LERNER with music by Frederick Loewe) in *Gigi* (film, 1958)

2  Old age isn't so bad when you consider the alternative.

*The New York Times* 9 October, 1960. Remark on his seventy-second birthday.

## Chiang Kai-shek (1887–1975)
CHINESE STATESMAN AND PRESIDENT

He became commander-in-chief of the army of the Chinese Revolutionary National Party (Kuomintang) in 1925 and established himself as president (1928–38 and 1943–9). After the Communist takeover in 1949 he fled to Taiwan, where he remained as president until his death.

1  If one does not act, one cannot understand.

*China's Destiny*, ch. 6 (1943)

## Madame Chiang Kai-shek (b.1897)
CHINESE SOCIOLOGIST AND REFORMER

Also known as Soong Mei Ling, she was the wife of the former leader of China, and was involved throughout her life in children's aid and education organizations, as well as war relief.

1  There is no shadow of protection to be had by sheltering behind the slender stockades of visionary speculation, or by hiding behind the wagon-wheels of pacific theories.

Quoted in the *New York Herald Tribune* 21 March 1938

2  Every clique is a refuge for incompetence. It fosters corruption and disloyalty, it begets cowardice, and consequently is a burden upon and a drawback to the progress of the country. Its instincts and actions are those of the pack.

*China Shall Rise Again*, pt 1, ch. 8 (1941)

## Erskine Childers (1870–1922)
BRITISH-BORN IRISH WRITER AND NATIONALIST

The writer of the spy story *The Riddle of the Sands* (1903) was elected to the Irish Assembly as a Sinn Féin deputy in 1921. After the establishment of the Irish Free State, he fought in the Civil War but was captured and executed.

1  Come closer, boys. It will be easier for you.

To the firing squad at his execution, quoted in *The Zeal of the Convert*, ch. 26 (1976) by Burke Wilkinson. Childers was granted

an hour's postponement to see the sun rise and shook hands with each member of the firing squad before his execution 24 November 1922. The charge was 'outstandingly wicked activity'.

## Jacques Chirac (b. 1932)
FRENCH POLITICIAN AND PRESIDENT

Appointed Prime Minister in 1974, he resigned two years later after differences with Giscard d'Estaing, and re-established the Gaullist Party (RPR). He was Mayor of Paris in 1977–86, served a second term as Prime Minister (1986–8), and became President in 1995, soon facing international criticism for France's resumption of nuclear testing in the Pacific.

1  [Of Margaret Thatcher] I am not prepared to accept the economics of a housewife.

Quoted in the *Sunday Times* 27 December 1987. Chirac on another occasion explained his ideal of womanhood, 'the woman of the old days, who works hard, serves the men at their meals, never sits at table with them, and does not talk' (*Daily Telegraph* 7 February 1998).

## Noam Chomsky (b. 1928)
US LINGUIST AND POLITICAL ANALYST

From the mid-1950s he developed a revolutionary and influential theory of linguistics known as transformational-generative grammar, which he described in *Syntactic Structures* (1957) and revised in *Lectures on Government and Binding* (1981). He has been a strong critic of US foreign policy in numerous essays and the book *American Power and the New Mandarins* (1969).

1  Colorless green ideas sleep furiously.

*Syntactic Structures*, ch. 2 (1957). Example of a sentence which is 'grammatical' without being 'meaningful'. Chomsky gave the following example of a sentence lacking both meaning and correct grammatical structure: 'Furiously sleep ideas green colorless.'

2  The war [in Vietnam] is simply an obscenity, a depraved act by weak and miserable men, including all of us who have allowed it to go on and on with endless fury and destruction – all of us who would have remained silent had stability and order been secured. It is not pleasant to use such words, but candour permits no less.

*American Power and the New Mandarins*, Introduction (1969)

3  I have often thought that if a rational Fascist dictatorship were to exist, then it would choose the American system.

*Language and Responsibility*, pt 1, ch. 1 (with Mitsou Ronat, 1979)

4  There are many terrorist states in the world, but the United States is unusual in that it is *officially* committed to international terrorism, and on a scale that puts its rivals to shame.

*Necessary Illusions*, Appendix 5, " 'The Evil Scourge of Terrorism'" (1989)

5  The intellectual tradition is one of servility to power, and if I didn't betray it I'd be ashamed of myself.

Interview on *The Late Show*, BBC2, 25 November 1992. Responding to an accusation of betrayal by ARTHUR SCHLESINGER JR.

6  Science is a bit like the joke about the drunk who is looking under a lamppost for a key that he has lost on the other side of the street, because that's where the light is. It has no other choice.

Letter to Robert F. Barsky, 14 June 1993, quoted in *N.C.: A Life of Dissent*, epigraph to ch. 3 (1997) by Robert F. Barsky

## (Dame) Agatha Christie (1890–1976)
BRITISH MYSTERY WRITER

Her novels, which feature the egotistic Belgian detective Hercule Poirot and the ingenious Miss Marple, have sold more than 100,000,000 copies. Many have been filmed, notably *Murder on the Orient Express* (1934, filmed 1974) and *Death on the Nile* (1937, filmed 1978); her play *The Mousetrap* (1952) holds a world record for the longest continuous run at one theatre. She described herself as 'a sausage machine, a perfect sausage machine'.

1 **These little grey cells. It is 'up to them' – as you say over here.**
Hercule Poirot, in *The Mysterious Affair at Styles*, ch. 10 (1920). Christie's first detective novel introduced both Belgian sleuth Hercule Poirot and Poirot's famous reference to the efficacy of brain-power – the 'little grey cells' – to solve mysteries, a faith he drew attention to in almost every subsequent appearance.

2 **Every murderer is probably somebody's old friend. You cannot mix up sentiment and reason.**
Poirot, in ibid. ch. 11

3 **Crime is terribly revealing. Try and vary your methods as you will, your tastes, your habits, your attitude of mind, and your soul is revealed by your actions.**
Poirot, in *The ABC Murders*, ch. 17 (1936)

4 **There is nothing so dangerous for anyone who has something to hide as conversation! . . . A human being, Hastings, cannot resist the opportunity to reveal himself and express his personality which conversation gives him. Every time he will give himself away.**
ibid. ch. 31

5 **An archaeologist is the best husband any woman can have: the older she gets, the more interested he is in her.**
Attributed remark referring to her own second husband Sir Max Mallowan, quoted in news report 9 March 1954 (later denied by her)

## Ivan Chtcheglov (b. 1934)
FRENCH POLITICAL THEORIST

His reputation rests largely on his essay 'Formulary for a New Urbanism', a seminal work on architecture and urban life for the Situationist group Lettriste Internationale (1952–7). He wrote under the pseudonym Gilles Ivain.

1 **A mental disease has swept the planet: banalization . . . Presented with the alternative of love or a garbage disposal unit, young people of all countries have chosen the garbage disposal unit.**
'Formulary for a New Urbanism', publ. in *Internationale Situationiste* no. 1, June 1958, repr. in *Situationist International Anthology* (ed. Ken Knabb, 1981)

## Caryl Churchill (b. 1938)
BRITISH PLAYWRIGHT

Her greatest success is a satire on high finance, *Serious Money* (1986), written in rhyming couplets. Other plays include *Top Girls* (1982) and *The Skriker* (1994).

1 **Zac:**
**The IMF is not a charity.**
**It has to insist on absolute austerity.**
**Nigel:**
**Absolutely. It can't be namby pamby.**
**These countries must accept restricted diets.**
**The governments must explain, if there are food riots,**
**That paying the western banks is the priority.**
*Serious Money*, act 2 (1987)

2 **There's ugly greedy and sexy greedy, you dope.**
**At the moment you're ugly which is no hope.**
**If you stay ugly, god knows what your fate is.**
**But sexy greedy *is* the late eighties.**
Starr, in ibid.

## Frank E. Churchill (1901–42)
US COMPOSER

He joined WALT DISNEY studios in 1930 and composed for the *Silly Symphonies* in the 1930s, *Snow White and the Seven Dwarfs*

(1937), *Dumbo* (1941), for which he won an Oscar, and *Bambi* (1942). His early death was by suicide.

1 **Who's afraid of the big bad wolf?**
'Who's Afraid of the Big Bad Wolf?' (song, 1933, probably written in collaboration with Ann Ronell). See also EDWARD ALBEE 2.

## Jennie Jerome Churchill (1854–1921)
ANGLO-AMERICAN SOCIETY FIGURE

The mother of WINSTON CHURCHILL and a noted beauty, she assumed the role of society hostess partly to offset her unhappy marriage. She was also responsible for introducing women for the first time to the Conservative Party's Primrose League.

1 **Treat your friends as you do your pictures, and place them in their best light.**
*Small Talk on Big Subjects*, 'Friendship' (1916)

## (Sir) Winston Churchill (1874–1965)
BRITISH STATESMAN AND AUTHOR

One of the outstanding figures of the century, he was hailed by Henry 'Chips' Channon as the 'saviour of the civilized world' and credited with a 'hundred horse-power mind' by STANLEY BALDWIN. After an adventurous military career, his life was dominated by politics. Becoming Prime Minister in 1940, he led the wartime coalition government, lost the general election to CLEMENT ATTLEE in July 1945, but regained the premiership in 1951. Among his writings are *The Second World War* (1948–54) and *A History of the English-Speaking Peoples* (1956–8); he was awarded the Nobel Prize for Literature in 1953. See also ED MURROW 2.

1 **Business carried on as usual during alterations on the map of Europe.**
On the self-adopted 'motto' of the British people at the start of the First World War, in speech at Guildhall, London, 9 November 1914, publ. in *Complete Speeches*, vol. 3 (ed. Robert Rhodes James, 1974)

2 **Remember, we are confronted with a foe who would without the slightest scruple extirpate us, man, woman and child, by any method open to him if he had the opportunity. We are fighting a foe who would not hesitate one moment to obliterate every single soul in this great country this afternoon if it could be done by pressing a button. We are fighting a foe who would think as little of that as a gardener would think of smoking out a wasps' nest.**
Speech in Dundee, 5 June 1915, publ. in *The Speeches of Winston Churchill* (ed. David Cannadine, 1990). The speech was made shortly before Churchill's resignation from the Admiralty for his failed Dardanelles policy.

3 **Anyone can rat, but it takes a certain amount of ingenuity to re-rat.**
Remark in 1923, quoted in *Irrepressible Churchill* (1966) by Kay Halle. Churchill was referring to his own rejoining the Conservative Party, having earlier left it to join the Liberals.

4 **I decline utterly to be impartial as between the fire brigade and the fire.**
Speech to House of Commons, 7 July 1926, publ. in *Hansard*. Churchill was replying to complaints of bias while editing the *British Gazette* during the General Strike, when he referred to the strikers as 'the enemy'.

5 **It is a good thing for an uneducated man to read books of quotations. . . . The quotations, when engraved upon the memory, give you good thoughts. They also make you anxious to read the authors and look for more.**
*My Early Life*, ch. 9 (1930)

6 **The [First World] War was decided in the first twenty days of fighting, and all that happened afterwards consisted in battles which, however formidable and devastating, were**

but desperate and vain appeals against the decision of Fate.

*Liaison 1914*, Preface (1930) by E.L. Spears

7   I remember, when I was a child, being taken to the celebrated Barnum's circus, which contained an exhibition of freaks and monstrosities, but the exhibit on the programme which I most desired to see was the one described as 'The Boneless Wonder'. My parents judged that that spectacle would be too revolting and demoralizing for my youthful eyes, and I have waited 50 years to see the boneless wonder sitting on the Treasury Bench.

Referring to Labour Prime Minister Ramsay Macdonald, in speech to House of Commons, 28 January 1931, publ. in *Hansard*

8   It is alarming and also nauseating to see Mr Gandhi, a seditious Middle Temple lawyer, now posing as a fakir of a type well-known in the East, striding half-naked up the steps of the Viceregal Palace, while he is still organising and conducting a defiant campaign of civil disobedience, to parley on equal terms with the representative of the King Emperor.

Speech at Winchester House, Epping, 23 February 1931, publ. in *The Speeches of Winston Churchill* (ed. David Cannadine, 1990). Referring to Gandhi's release from prison in India to discuss political devolution with the Viceroy.

9   India is an abstraction ... India is no more a political personality than Europe. India is a geographical term. It is no more a united nation than the Equator.

Speech at Royal Albert Hall, 18 March 1931, quoted in *Maxims and Reflections* (ed. Colin Coote, 1947)

10  So they [Baldwin's Government] go on in strange paradox, decided only to be undecided, resolved to be irresolute, adamant for drift, solid for fluidity, all-powerful to be impotent.

Speech to House of Commons, 12 November 1936, publ. in *The Speeches of Winston Churchill* (ed. David Cannadine, 1990)

11  Dictators ride to and fro upon tigers which they dare not dismount. And the tigers are getting hungry.

Letter, 11 November 1937, publ. in *Step By Step* (1937). Churchill was quoting a 'Hindustani' proverb, though the *Concise Oxford Dictionary of Proverbs* (ed. John Simpson, 1982) cites this as Chinese.

12  All is over. Silent, mournful, abandoned, broken, Czechoslovakia recedes into darkness.. ... We have sustained a defeat without a war.

Speech to House of Commons, 5 October 1938, publ. in *The Speeches of Winston Churchill* (ed. David Cannadine, 1990). On the German annexation of the Sudetenland, in Czechoslovakia.

13  I cannot forecast to you the action of Russia. It is a riddle wrapped in a mystery inside an enigma.

Radio broadcast, 1 October 1939, publ. in *Winston S. Churchill: His Complete Speeches, 1897–1963*, vol. 6 (ed. Robert Rhodes James, 1974). Churchill added: 'But perhaps there is a key ... Russian national interest.'

14  I have nothing to offer but blood, toil, tears and sweat.

Churchill's maiden speech to House of Commons as Prime Minister, 13 May 1940, publ. in ibid.

15  You ask, What is our policy? I will say: It is to wage war, by sea, land, and air, with all our might and with all the strength that God can give us: to wage war against a monstrous tyranny, never surpassed in the dark, lamentable catalogue of human crime. That is our policy. You ask, What is our aim? I can answer in one word: Victory – victory at all costs, victory in spite of all terror; victory, however long and hard the road may be; for without victory there is no survival.

ibid.

16  We shall go on to the end, we shall fight in France, we shall fight on the seas and oceans, we shall fight with growing confidence and growing strength in the air, we shall defend our island, whatever the cost may be, we shall

fight on the beaches, we shall fight on the landing grounds, we shall fight in the fields and in the streets, we shall fight in the hills; we shall never surrender.

Speech to House of Commons, 4 June 1940, following the retreat from Dunkirk, publ. in ibid. 'And even if,' Churchill continued, in what appears to be a coded appeal to the US, 'which I do not for a moment believe, this island or a large part of it were subjugated and starving, then our Empire beyond the seas, armed and guarded by the British Fleet, would carry on the struggle, until in God's good time the new world, with all its power and might, steps forth to the rescue and the liberation of the old.'

17  Let us therefore brace ourselves to our duties, and so bear ourselves that if the British Empire and its Commonwealth last for a thousand years, men will still say, 'This was their finest hour.'

Speech to House of Commons, 18 June 1940, announcing the fall of France, and the start of the 'Battle of Britain', publ. in ibid. Two days later, a week after German troops had entered Paris, France concluded an armistice with Germany.

18  Never in the field of human conflict was so much owed by so many to so few.

Speech to House of Commons, 20 August 1940, publ. in ibid. Referring to the pilots who repulsed the German Luftwaffe during the Battle of Britain.

19  *Nous attendons l'invasion promise de longue date. Les poissons aussi.* (We are waiting for the long-promised invasion. So are the fishes.)

Radio broadcast to the French people, 21 October 1940, publ. in *Into Battle* (1941)

20  Here is the answer which I will give to President Roosevelt ... Give us the tools and we will finish the job.

Radio broadcast, 9 February 1941, publ. in ibid. The Lend Lease Bill, which allowed the president to sell, lend or lease material to countries whose defence was important to the USA, was then being debated by Congress; it was signed a month later.

21  The British nation is unique in this respect. They are the only people who like to be told how bad things are, who like to be told the worst.

Speech to House of Commons, 10 June 1941, publ. in *Hansard*

22  If Hitler invaded hell I would make at least a favourable reference to the devil in the House of Commons.

Comment to Churchill's private secretary, John Colville, 21 June 1941, regarding British support for Communist Russia, as recounted in *The Second World War*, vol. 3, 'The Grand Alliance', ch. 20 (1950)

23  All his usual formalities of perfidy were observed with scrupulous technique.

Of Hitler's invasion of Russia, in radio broadcast 21 June 1941

24  Do not let us speak of darker days; let us rather speak of sterner days. These are not dark days: these are great days – the greatest days our country has ever lived.

Speech at Harrow School, 29 October 1941, publ. in *Winston S. Churchill: His Complete Speeches, 1897–1963*, vol. 6 (ed. Robert Rhodes James, 1974)

25  When we consider the resources of the United States and the British Empire compared to those of Japan, when we remember those of China, which has so long and valiantly withstood invasion and when also we observe the Russian menace which hangs over Japan, it becomes still more difficult to reconcile Japanese action with prudence or even with sanity. What kind of a people do they think we are?

Speech to Joint Session of US Congress, 26 December 1941, publ. in ibid. Britain and the USA had declared war on Japan 8 December 1941, following the surprise attack on Pearl Harbor, Hawaii. Japanese forces rapidly advanced into US and British possessions in the Pacific and Asian mainland; Hong Kong surrendered on Christmas Day, 1941.

26  When I warned them [the French Government] that Britain would fight on alone whatever they did, their generals told their Prime Minister and his divided

Cabinet, 'In three weeks England will have her neck wrung like a chicken.' Some chicken! Some neck!

Speech to Canadian Parliament, Ottawa, 30 December 1941, publ. in ibid.

27 Now this is not the end. It is not even the beginning of the end. But it is, perhaps, the end of the beginnning.

Speech at Lord Mayor's Day Luncheon, Mansion House, 10 November 1942, publ. in *The End of the Beginning* (1943). Churchill was referring to the Eighth Army's victory against Rommel at El Alamein. See CHURCHILL 43.

28 We mean to hold our own. I have not become the King's First Minister in order to preside over the liquidation of the British Empire.

ibid.

29 The problems of victory are more agreeable than the problems of defeat, but they are no less difficult.

Speech to House of Commons, 11 November 1942, publ. in *Hansard*

30 We make this wide encircling movement in the Mediterranean, having for its primary object the recovery of the command of that vital sea, but also having for its object the exposure of the under-belly of the Axis, especially Italy, to heavy attack.

ibid. The words are the origin of the phrase 'the soft under-belly of the Axis'.

31 National compulsory insurance for all classes for all purposes from the cradle to the grave.

Radio broadcast, 21 March 1943, publ. in *Winston Churchill: His Complete Speeches 1897–1963*, vol. 7 (ed. Robert Rhodes James, 1974)

32 There is no finer investment for any community than putting milk into babies.

ibid.

33 The empires of the future are the empires of the mind.

Speech at Harvard, 6 September 1943, publ. in *Onwards to Victory* (1944)

34 We shape our buildings: thereafter they shape us.

Speech in London, 28 October 1943, on the rebuilding of the House of Commons after bomb damage, quoted in *Time* 12 September 1960

35 Neither the sure prevention of war, nor the continuous rise of world organization will be gained without what I have called the fraternal association of the English-speaking peoples. This means a special relationship between the British Commonwealth and Empire and the United States.

Speech at Westminster College, Fulton, Missouri, 5 March 1946, publ. in *Winston S. Churchill: His Complete Speeches, 1897–1963*, vol. 7 (ed. Robert Rhodes James, 1974).

36 A shadow has fallen upon the scenes so lately lighted by the Allied victory . . . From Stettin in the Baltic to Trieste in the Adriatic, an iron curtain has descended across the Continent.

ibid. The phrase 'iron curtain' was not original: Churchill had also used the phrase in early 1946 in a telegram to President TRUMAN, while the words had earlier been used by JOSEPH GOEBBELS in the Nazi propaganda weekly *Das Reich* 23 February 1945: 'Should the German people lay down their arms, the Soviets . . . would occupy all eastern and south-eastern Europe together with the greater part of the Reich. Over all this territory, which with the Soviet Union included, would be of enormous extent, an iron curtain (*ein eiserner Vorhang*) would at once descend.' The phrase had been used with reference to Communism from at least 1920, while the geographical area from Stettin to Trieste had already been defined by Friedrich Engels in an article for the *New York Daily Tribune* in 1853: 'It would appear that the natural frontier of Russia runs from Dantzic or perhaps Stettin to Trieste.'

37 No one pretends that democracy is perfect or all-wise. Indeed, it has been said that democracy is the worst form of Government except all those other forms that have been tried from time to time.

Speech to House of Commons, 11 November 1947, publ. in *Hansard*

38 The English never draw a line without blurring it.

ibid. 16 November 1948

39 Moral of the Work. In war: resolution. In defeat: defiance. In victory: magnanimity. In peace: goodwill.

Epigraph in each volume of *The Second World War* (1948–54). Churchill had conceived the formula shortly after the end of the First World War.

40 I felt as if I were walking with destiny, and that all my past life had been but a preparation for this hour and this trial. Eleven years in the political wilderness had freed me from ordinary Party antagonisms. My warnings over the last six years had been so numerous, so detailed, and were now so terribly vindicated, that no one could gainsay me. I could not be reproached either for making the war or with want of preparation for it. I thought I knew a good deal about it all, and I was sure I should not fail. Therefore, although impatient for the morning, I slept soundly and had no need for cheering dreams. Facts are better than dreams.

On assuming the office of prime minister in 1940, in *The Second World War*, vol. 1 'The Gathering Storm', bk 2, ch. 17 (1948)

41 Thus, then, on the night of the tenth of May, at the outset of this mighty battle, I acquired the chief power in the State, which henceforth I wielded in ever-growing measure for five years and three months of world war, at the end of which time, all our enemies having surrendered unconditionally or being about to do so, I was immediately dismissed by the British electorate from all further conduct of their affairs

ibid. Though re-elected prime minster in 1951, Churchill never forgot what he considered a slight by the electorate.

42 The candle in that great turnip has gone out.

Of Stanley Baldwin, as related by Patrick Leigh Fermor, quoted in journal entry 17 August 1950, publ. in *Diaries and Letters 1945–62* (1968) by Harold Nicolson

43 It may almost be said, 'Before Alamein we never had a victory. After Alamein we never had a defeat.'

*The Second World War*, vol. 4, ch. 33 (1951)

44 Without tradition, art is a flock of sheep without a shepherd. Without innovation, it is a corpse.

Address to the Royal Academy of Arts, quoted in *Time* 11 May 1954

45 Better to jaw-jaw than to war-war.

Remark at the White House, 26 June 1954, quoted in *The New York Times* 27 June 1954. The words were reported with slight variations in different newspapers, and also within the same edition of *The New York Times*.

46 He [Clement Attlee] is a modest little man who has a good deal to be modest about.

Quoted in the *Chicago Sunday Tribune Magazine of Books* 27 June 1954

47 A fanatic is one who can't change his mind and won't change the subject.

Quoted in *The New York Times* 5 July 1954

48 I am prepared to meet my Maker. Whether my Maker is prepared for the great ordeal of meeting me is another matter.

Remark, 30 November 1951, quoted in *Winston Churchill: His Wit and Wisdom*

49 I have never accepted what many people have kindly said – namely, that I inspired the nation. . .. It was the nation and the race dwelling all round the globe that had the lion's heart. I had the luck to be called upon to give the roar. I also hope that I sometimes suggested to the lion the right place to use his claws.

Speech at Westminster Hall, 30 November 1954, quoted in *The Times* 1 December 1954

50 This is the sort of English up with which I will not put.

Quoted in *The Complete Plain Words*, 'The Handling of Words' by

  Ernest Gowers (1954). Said to be a marginal comment by Churchill against a sentence that clumsily avoided ending with a preposition.

51 **Dead birds don't fall out of nests.**

Response to a colleague who told him his flies were open, quoted in *Letters*, vol. 2 (1957) by Lyttleton Hart-Davis

52 **[Of Viscount Montgomery] In defeat unbeatable: in victory unbearable.**

Quoted in *Ambrosia and Small Beer*, ch. 5 (1964) by Edward Marsh

53 **I have taken more out of alcohol than alcohol has taken out of me.**

Quoted in *By Quentin Reynolds*, ch. 11 (1964) by Quentin Reynolds

54 **The ability to foretell what is going to happen tomorrow, next week, next month, and next year. And to have the ability afterwards to explain why it didn't happen.**

Quoted in *The Churchill Wit* (1965) by Bill Adler. Describing the qualifications desirable in a prospective politician.

55 **A sheep in sheep's clothing.**

Said to refer to Clement Attlee, in *The Way the Wind Blows*, ch. 6 (1976) by Lord Home, though Churchill is later said to have claimed he had used the words to describe Labour Prime Minister Ramsay MacDonald. The phrase had also been used by the critic and essayist Sir Edmund Gosse of the 'woolly-bearded poet' Sturge Moore, quoted in *Under the Bridge* (1943) by F. Greenslet.

56 **An empty taxi arrived at 10 Downing Street, and when the door was opened Attlee got out.**

Attributed. In *Attlee*, ch. 16, sct. 2 (1982) by Kenneth Harris, it is said that Churchill's private secretary John Colville repeated this remark, which clearly discomfited Churchill, who, 'after an awful pause', replied: 'Mr Attlee is an honourable and gallant gentleman, and a faithful colleague who served his country well at the time of her greatest need. I should be obliged if you would make it clear whenever an occasion arises that I would never make such a remark about him, and that I strongly disapprove of anybody who does.' However, when Colville suggested that Attlee be invited to join his dining club, Churchill replied, 'I think not. He is an admirable character, but not a man with whom it is agreeable to dine.'

## Galeazzo Ciano (1903–44)

ITALIAN POLITICIAN

The Conte di Cortelazzo was son-in law of MUSSOLINI and a leading Fascist. As Minister of Foreign Affairs (1936–43), he openly opposed Italy's alliance with Germany after Hitler failed to consult Mussolini before invading Poland. He was later tried for treason by the pro-Mussolini faction and shot in the back.

1 **Victory has a hundred fathers but defeat is an orphan.**

Journal entry, 9 September 1942, publ. in *Diario 1939–1943* (1946). President KENNEDY is quoted as having made the same remark in the wake of the Bay of Pigs invasion in April 1961. The original Italian (*nessuno vuole riconoscere l'insuccesso*) is more accurately translated 'no one wants to recognize failure'.

## E.M. Cioran (1911–95)

ROMANIAN-BORN WRITER AND PHILOSOPHER

Full name Emil Mihai Cioran. The 'last of the moralists' lived in Paris from 1937 onwards, where, among the existentialists, situationists and nihilists, he found a congenial home for his ideas, which he regarded both as a continuation and as a negation of Nietzsche's philosophy.

1 **No human beings more dangerous than those who have suffered for a belief: the great persecutors are recruited from the martyrs not quite beheaded. Far from diminishing the appetite for power, suffering exasperates it.**

*A Short History of Decay*, ch. 1, 'Genealogy of Fanaticism' (1949)

2 **Reason is a whore, surviving by simulation, versatility, and shamelessness.**

*The Temptation to Exist*, 'Rages and Resignations: Luther' (1956)

3 **Much more than our other needs and endeavours, it is sexuality that puts us on an even footing with our kind:**

the more we practise it, the more we become like everyone else: it is in the performance of a reputedly bestial function that we prove our status as citizens: nothing is more *public* than the sexual act.

ibid. 'Rages and Resignations: Gogol'

4 **We derive our vitality from our store of madness.**

ibid. 'The Temptation to Exist'

5 **A civilization is destroyed only when its gods are destroyed.**

*The New Gods* (*Le Mauvais démiurge*), 'The New Gods' (1969)

6 **There is no means of *proving* it is preferable to be than not to be.**

ibid. 'Strangled Thoughts', sect. 1

7 **Alone, even doing nothing, you do not waste your time. You do, almost always, in company. No encounter with yourself can be altogether sterile: Something necessarily emerges, even if only the hope of some day meeting yourself again.**

ibid. sect. 2

8 **What we want is not freedom but its appearances. It is for these simulacra that man has always striven. And since freedom, as has been said, is no more than a *sensation*, what difference is there between being free and believing ourselves free?**

ibid. sect. 3

9 **We would not be interested in human beings if we did not have the hope of someday meeting someone worse off than ourselves.**

ibid.

10 **It is not worth the bother of killing yourself, since you always kill yourself *too late*.**

*The Trouble with Being Born*, ch. 2 (1973)

11 **Consciousness is much more than the thorn, it is the *dagger* in the flesh.**

ibid. ch. 3

12 **Progress is the injustice each generation commits with regard to its predecessors.**

ibid. ch. 8

13 **God: a disease we imagine we are cured of because no one dies of it nowadays.**

ibid. ch. 10

14 **One does not inhabit a country; one inhabits a language. That is our country, our fatherland – and no other.**

*Anathemas and Admirations*, 'On the Verge of Existence' (1986). This echoes a similar observation made by ALBERT CAMUS in his *Notebooks*: 'Yes, I have a fatherland: the French language.'

15 **The fact that life has no meaning is a reason to live – moreover, the only one.**

ibid. 'Fractures'

## Anthony Clare (b. 1942)

IRISH-BORN BRITISH PSYCHIATRIST

Having studied at University College, Dublin, and London University, he worked as a professor of psychiatry in those two cities. His high media profile is mainly due to his radio programmes, particularly *In The Psychiatrist's Chair*, a series of in-depth interviews with figures from public life, on BBC Radio 4 from 1982.

1 **Whatever is true about the nature of the unconscious itself, it might be said that since the time of Freud it has been shrinking. Less is buried there.**

*In The Psychiatrist's Chair*, Introduction (1984)

## Alan Clark (1928–99)

BRITISH POLITICIAN AND HISTORIAN

The son of KENNETH (LORD) CLARK was MP for Plymouth (1974–92) and Kensington and Chelsea (1997–9). Renowned for his womanizing and rakish ways, making him one of the more colourful personalities in the Conservative Party under MARGARET THATCHER, he reached his highest position in government as Minister of State for Defence (1989–92). He was also noted as a military historian (*Donkeys*, 1961, and *Aces High*, 1973) and an entertainingly candid diarist (*Diaries*, 1993).

1 Most of them [backbenchers in the House of Commons] are buffers, or demi-buffers, or *buffers-aspirant*. They amount to nothing.
Journal entry, 18 November 1986, publ. in *Diaries* (1993)

2 There are no true friends in politics. We are all sharks circling, and waiting, for traces of blood to appear in the water.
Journal entry, 30 November 1990, publ. in ibid. Clark was musing on the 'descending parabola' of his political career.

3 We all know the principal preoccupation of politicians is how they can do down their colleagues so that they can advance their own careers.
Interview with John Humphrys in *On the Ropes*, BBC Radio 4, 16 May 1995. Clark was explaining how his main regret from his political career was in not destabilizing his boss at the Ministry of Defence, Tom King.

4 Dear boy, I can hardly close the door.
On being asked if he had any skeletons in his cupboard, quoted in the *Observer* 27 December 1998

5 There is practically no figure whom the press would rather vilify than the wise virgin.
Quoted in the *Observer* 27 September 1998. On a newspaper claim that Margaret Thatcher used to hoard food.

## Eugenie Clark (b. 1922)

US MARINE BIOLOGIST AND AUTHOR

A pioneer in the artificial insemination of fish, she researched sea life chiefly in the South Seas. Among her books are *Lady with a Spear* (1953) and *The Lady and the Shark* (1969).

1 It seems as though women keep growing. Eventually they can have little or nothing in common with the men they chose long ago.
Quoted in *Ms.* August 1979

## Kenneth (Lord) Clark (1903–83)

BRITISH ART HISTORIAN

His career included stints as Director of the National Gallery (1934–45) and first Chairman of the Independent Television Authority (1954–7), though he was best known as a scholar and a communicator. As an expert on the Italian Renaissance, particularly Leonardo da Vinci, he wrote popular works on art and presented the TV series based on his book *Civilization* (1969).

1 People sometimes tell me that they prefer barbarism to civilization. I doubt if they have given it a long enough trial. Like the people of Alexandria, they are bored by civilization; but then all the evidence suggests that the boredom of barbarism is infinitely greater.
*Civilization*, ch.1 (1970)

2 Opera, next to Gothic architecture, is one of the strangest inventions of Western man. It could not have been foreseen by any logical process.
ibid. ch. 9

3 It is lack of confidence, more than anything else, that kills a civilization. We can destroy ourselves by cynicism and disillusion, just as effectively as by bombs. . . . The moral and intellectual failure of Marxism has left us with no alternative to heroic materialism, and that isn't enough. One may be optimistic, but one can't exactly be joyful at the prospect before us.
ibid. ch. 13. Last words of book.

## Ramsey Clark (b. 1927)

US LAWYER

As Attorney-General (1967–9) he prosecuted anti-Vietnam War protesters but took a more liberal stance after resuming private practice. More recently he was criticized for his support of SADDAM HUSSEIN.

1 A right is not what someone gives you; it's what no one can take from you.
*The New York Times* 2 October 1977

2 The measure of your quality as a public person, as a citizen, is the gap between what you do and what you say.
*International Herald Tribune* 18 June 1991

3 Oil and democracy don't mix. Oil has never enhanced democratic institutions or economic justice where it has been found.
*The Fire This Time*, ch. 6, 'The War and Human Rights' (1992)

## John Cooper Clarke (b. 1950)

BRITISH PUNK POET

Born and raised in Salford, he started reciting poetry in local folk clubs and began mixing his poems with musical backing in the 1970s. Live appearances with the Buzzcocks and other groups helped to establish his popularity among punk audiences, and inspired a new wave of poets and 'ranters'.

1 On a BSA with two bald tyres,
you drove a million miles.
You cut your hair with rusty pliers
and you suffer with the pillion piles.
You've got built-in obsolescence,
oh, you've got guts,
but you won't reach adolescence,
slow down psycle sluts!
'Psycle Sluts: Pt.1' on the album *Disguise in Love* (1978), publ. in *Ten Years in an Open Necked Shirt* (1983)

2 In a cybernetic fit of rage
She pissed off to another age
She lives in 1999
With her new boyfriend, a blob of slime.
Each time I see a translucent face
I remember the monster from outer space.
'i married a monster from outer space', ibid.

3 beans greens tangerines
and low cholesterol margarines
his limbs are loose his teeth are clean
he's a high-octane fresh-air fiend
you've got to admit he's keen
what can you do but be impressed
he's a health fanatic give it a rest.
'Health Fanatic', ibid.

4 people turn to poison quick
as lager turns to piss
sweethearts are physically sick
every time they kiss
it's a sociologist's paradise
each day repeats
uneasy cheesy greasy queasy beastly beezley street.
'Beezley Street' on the album *Snap Crackle and Bop* (1978), publ. in ibid.

5 roman catholic marxist leninist
happily married to an eloquent feminist.
'euro communist/gucci socialist', publ. in ibid. (1983)

## Jeremy Clarkson (b. 1960)

BRITISH JOURNALIST AND TV PRESENTER

A motoring guru known for his provocative banter, he contributes regularly to the *Sunday Times* and other newspapers and magazines including *Top Gear*, which he founded in 1993.

1 **The British motor industry is really owned by Nazis.**

Quoted in the *Daily Telegraph* 26 October 1998. The comment was made during an informal quiz show at the *Top Gear* stand at the National Motor Show. He also offended staff on the Hyundai stand by stating that South Koreans were 'too busy eating dogs to design a decent car'.

2 **To argue that a car is simply a means of conveyance is like arguing that Blenheim Palace is simply a house.**

Quoted in the *Guardian* 23 January 1999

## Julian Clary (b. 1959)

BRITISH COMEDIAN AND ENTERTAINER

A maestro of sexual innuendo and outrageous puns, he appeared with Fanny the Wonderdog in his stand-up camp comedy routine *The Joan Collins Fan Club* (1988) and in game shows such as *Trick or Treat* (1989) and *Sticky Moments* (1989–90).

1 **The English like eccentrics. They just don't like them living next door.**

*Daily Telegraph* 2 September 1992

## Eldridge Cleaver (1935–98)

US BLACK LEADER AND WRITER

After becoming a follower of MALCOLM X, he was Minister of Information for the Black Panthers and subsequently ran the party's headquarters in Algiers where he had fled after a shoot-out in 1968. He returned to New York in 1975, a born-again Christian.

1 **I, for one, do not think homosexuality is the latest advance over heterosexuality in the scale of human evolution. Homosexuality is a sickness, just as are baby-rape or wanting to become head of General Motors.**

*Soul on Ice*, pt 2, 'Notes on a Native Son' (1968)

2 **Americans think of themselves collectively as a huge rescue squad on twenty-four-hour call to any spot on the globe where dispute and conflict may erupt.**

ibid. 'Rallying Round the Flag'

3 **Every time I embrace a black woman I'm embracing slavery, and when I put my arms around a white woman, well, I'm hugging freedom. The white man forbade me to have the white woman on pain of death. . . . I will not be free until the day I can have a white woman in my bed.**

Lazarus, in ibid. 'The Allegory of the Black Eunuchs'

4 **It's been said that today, you're part of the solution or you're part of the problem. There is no more middle ground.**

'Stanford Speech', San Francisco, 1 October 1968, publ. in *Post Prison Writings and Speeches* (ed. Robert Scheer, 1969)

## John Cleese (b. 1939)

BRITISH COMIC ACTOR AND AUTHOR

Relying on his eccentric, often manic humour, he appeared in several comedy shows on TV in the 1960s before reaching an international audience with *Monty Python's Flying Circus* (1969–74). He subsequently co-wrote and starred in *Fawlty Towers* (1975, 1979) and the film *A Fish Called Wanda* (1988). Of his own short-comings, he once declared, 'Being bland, rather cruel and incompetent comes naturally to me.' See also MONTY PYTHON'S FLYING CIRCUS.

1 **Don't mention the war.**

Basil Fawlty, on the pending arrival of German guests, in *Fawlty Towers*, 'The Germans' (TV series co-written with Connie Booth, 1975), publ. in *The Complete Fawlty Towers* (1988)

2 **So Harry says, 'You don't like me any more. Why not?' And he says, 'Because you've got so terribly pretentious.' And Harry says, 'Pretentious? *Moi?*'**

Mr Johnson, chatting to Sybil, in ibid. 'The Psychiatrist' (1979)

3 **He's from Barcelona.**

Basil or Sybil apologizing for Manuel, in ibid. (various episodes). Manuel's most quoted remark is 'Qué?'

## Georges Clemenceau (1841–1929)

FRENCH STATESMAN

Known as 'The Tiger', he was elected to the Chamber of Deputies in 1876 and became outspoken leader of the extreme left. He held two terms as premier (1906–9, 1917–20), the latter of which gained him the title of 'Father of Victory', and presided at the peace talks in Versailles (1919), effecting German disarmament. He was an accomplished journalist and founded several papers including *L'Aurore* (1897).

1 **My home policy: I wage war; my foreign policy: I wage war. All the time I wage war! The Russians betray us, I continue to wage war. Rumania is forced to capitulate: I continue to wage war, and I will continue to the very end.**

Speech to Chamber of Deputies, 8 March 1918, publ. in *Discours de guerre* (1968). Clemenceau was about to confront the Ludendorff offensive of March–July 1918, which pushed deep into the Allied lines and was only halted when Foch's counter-offensive eventually drove the German army back behind its own border and led to the armistice.

2 **Yes, we have won the war, and not without difficulty. But now we must win the peace, and perhaps that will be harder.**

Remark to General J.H.H. Mordacq, 11 November 1918 (Armistice Day), quoted in *The Tiger*, ch.16 (1976). Clemenceau expressed the idea on different occasions; it has been quoted in a simplified form ('It is easier to make war than to make peace') from a speech at Verdun, 20 July 1919.

3 **America is the only nation in history which miraculously has gone directly from barbarism to degeneration without the usual interval of civilization.**

Attributed in the *Saturday Review of Literature* 1 December 1945

## Harlan Cleveland (b. 1918)

US GOVERNMENT OFFICIAL AND DIPLOMAT

He was Assistant Secretary for International Organization Affairs in Kennedy's first administration (1961–5) and Ambassador to NATO (1965–9). His publications include *The Obligations of Power* in 1966 and *NATO: The Transatlantic Bargain* in 1970.

1 **The revolution of rising expectations.**

'Reflections on the Revolution of Rising Expectations', speech at Colgate University, 1949, quoted in *The New Language of Politics* (1972) by William Safire. The title, which echoed that of Edmund Burke's essay 'Reflections on the Revolution in France' (1790), was recalled by Cleveland himself in a speech to the UN in 1954, 'The Evolution of Rising Responsibilities'.

## Jimmy Cliff (b. 1948)

JAMAICAN REGGAE SINGER

Original name James Chambers. The first reggae superstar, he had a worldwide hit with 'Wonderful World, Beautiful People' (1969) and starred in the film *The Harder They Come* (1972), for which he wrote and performed several of the soundtrack songs.

1 **O they tell me of a pie up in the sky**
**Waiting for me when I die**
**But between the day when you're born and when you die**
**They never seem to hear you when you cry**
**So as sure as the sun will shine**
**I'm going to get my share now, what's mine**
**And then the harder they come, the harder they fall**
**One and all.**

'The Harder They Come' (song, 1971), written and performed by Jimmy Cliff in *The Harder They Come* (film, 1972). Cliff starred in the film as Ivan, a small-time hood.

# Bill Clinton (b. 1946)

US POLITICIAN AND PRESIDENT

Democratic Governor of Arkansas (1979–81 and 1983–92), husband of HILLARY CLINTON, he was elected forty-second US president in 1993 and was re-elected in 1996. Though he played a significant role in the 1995 Bosnian settlement, his reputation was damaged irreparably by 'Zippergate', the Monica Lewinsky sex scandal, and he escaped impeachment by a whisker in 1998. See also HENRY KISSINGER 17.

1 When I was in England I experimented with marijuana a time or two, and I didn't like it. I didn't inhale.

Remark during TV debate with Jerry Brown, a rival candidate for the Democratic Party nomination, quoted in *The New York Times* 30 March 1992. Under close questioning to ascertain whether the two men had ever broken state, federal or international laws, Clinton admitted his misdemeanour while a Rhodes Scholar at Oxford University.

2 We need a new spirit of community, a sense that we are all in this this together, or the American Dream will continue to wither. Our destiny is bound up with the destiny of every other American.

Speech to supporters 4 November 1992, Little Rock, Arkansas, quoted in the *Guardian* 5 November 1992

3 Indeed I did have a relationship with Ms Lewinsky that was not appropriate. In fact it was wrong. It constituted a critical lapse in judgment and a personal failure on my part for which I am solely and completely responsible. . . . Even presidents have private lives.

Broadcast to the nation, 17 August 1998, publ. in the *Daily Telegraph* 19 August 1998. See also MONICA LEWINSKY 1.

4 It depends upon what the meaning of the word 'is' means. If 'is' means is, and never has been, that's one thing. If it means, there is none, that was a completely true statement.

Answer to grand jury, broadcast on CNN 21 September 1998. Clinton was attempting to justify his earlier statement, 'There is no sex of any kind, in any manner, shape or form, with Ms Lewinsky.'

5 The most difficult job in the world is not being President. It's being a parent.

Quoted in the *Observer* 25 October 1998

6 Just because we cannot do everything for everyone does not mean we should do nothing for anyone.

Speech broadcast on MSNBC 1 April 1999. On demands for US troops to be withdrawn from the Balkans. Three days later NATO members agreed to airlift up to 110,000 refugees out of the Kosovo region. NATO planes had begun bombing Serbian positions on 24 March.

# Hillary Clinton (b. 1947)

US LAWYER AND FIRST LADY

She has been twice named as one of America's top 100 lawyers, worked on the impeachment of President Nixon in 1984, and implemented school reforms. However, her proposal to reform national health care was blocked by Congress in 1994. In 2000 she moved from Washington to New York in order to run for the senate.

1 The great story here . . . is this vast right-wing conspiracy that has been conspiring against my husband since the day he announced for president.

*NBC Today*, 27 January 1998. On 'Zippergate' and the accusations of adultery and perjury made against BILL CLINTON.

# Brian Clough (b. 1935)

BRITISH FOOTBALLER AND MANAGER

Known as Ol' Big Head, caustic and non-conformist in style, he was 'the master motivator' of his day. As a player (1952–64) he scored more goals per game than any other post-War footballer and as manager of Nottingham Forest (1964–75) won the league

championship once, the League Cup four times and the European Cup twice.

1 I couldn't motivate a bee to sting you if it didn't have the equipment. I couldn't motivate a snake to bite you if it didn't have the teeth. You can only bring out of people what they are capable of giving. Two of the great myths circulating now are that Heinz's beans are the best and that I can get more out of men than they have inside them.

Quoted by Hugh McIlvanney in the *Observer* 15 November 1975, repr. in *McIlvanney on Football*, 'The Big Man and Other Giants' (1994)

# Harold Clurman (1901–80)

US STAGE DIRECTOR AND CRITIC

He co-founded and was Director of the experimental Group Theater (1931–40), and worked as a director in Hollywood and on Broadway. A respected drama critic, he contributed to the *Nation* from 1953 until his death, and published *Lies Like Truths* (1958) and *The Divine Pastime* (1974).

1 Unlike other people, our reviewers are powerful because they believe in nothing.

Quoted in *Who Needs Theatre?*, pt 1, 'The Vitality of Harold Clurman' (1987) by Robert Brustein

# Kurt Cobain (1967–94)

US ROCK MUSICIAN

Lead singer, guitarist and writer of Nirvana, the chief 'grunge' band of the 1990s, whose hits included the single 'Smells Like Teen Spirit' and the albums *Nevermind* (1991) and *In Utero* (1993). After drug problems he shot himself in his home in Seattle. See also BERNARD LEVIN 3.

1 I found it hard, it was hard to find,
Oh well, whatever, never mind.

'Smells Like Teen Spirit' (song) on the Nirvana album *Nevermind* (1991)

2 Teenage angst has paid off well,
Now I'm bored and old.

'Serve the Servants' (song) on the Nirvana album *In Utero* (1993)

3 Thank you all from the pit of my burning, nauseous stomach for your letters and concerns during the last years. I'm too much of an erratic, moody person, and I don't have the passion anymore.

Suicide note, publ. in *The Kurt Cobain Story*, ch. 1 (1994) by Dave Thompson. Parts of the note were read out by his wife Courtney Love at a memorial ceremony for the singer in Seattle, 10 April 1994. Cobain suffered intense pain and discomfort from habitual stomach cramps which resulted in fits of vomiting for which he'd been on regular medication. 'For five years during the time I had my stomach [pain],' he once said, 'I wanted to kill myself every day.'

# Eddie Cochran (1938–60)

US ROCK MUSICIAN

One of the giants of rock 'n' roll, he recorded the classics 'Summertime Blues' (1958), 'C'mon Everybody' (1959), on which he played all the instruments, and 'Three Steps to Heaven' (1960). He was killed in a car accident while on a British tour.

1 There ain't no cure for the summertime blues.

'Summertime Blues' (song, 1958, co-written with Cochran's manager, Jerry Capeheart) on the album *Swinging To My Baby* (1960)

# Alexander Cockburn (b. 1941)

ANGLO-IRISH JOURNALIST

Son of CLAUD COCKBURN and known as an acerbic political journalist, he has written widely for the US press, and published on such differing topics as the Amazonian rain forest, the Reagan era and, in *Idle Passion* (1975), chess.

1 **Be careful about Burma. Most people cannot remember whether it was Siam and has become Thailand, or whether it is now part of Malaysia and should be called Sri Lanka.**
'How to be a Foreign Correspondent', first publ. in *More* May 1976, repr. in *Corruptions of Empire*, pt 1 (1988)

2 **A childish soul not inoculated with compulsory prayer is a soul open to any religious infection.**
'Heatherdown', first publ. 1985, repr. in ibid.

3 **A 'just war' is hospitable to every self-deception on the part of those waging it, none more than the certainty of virtue, under whose shelter every abomination can be committed with a clear conscience.**
*New Statesman and Society* 8 February 1991

## Claud Cockburn (1904–1981)
BRITISH AUTHOR AND JOURNALIST

As a journalist he was acclaimed by MALCOLM MUGGERIDGE 'the most perfect specimen of the genus ever to exist'. He was correspondent for the *Daily Worker*, founded the left-wing newsletter *The Week* (1933) and became a freelance journalist in 1948.

1 **Small earthquake in Chile. Not many dead.**
Suggestion for a headline in *The Times* c. 1929, quoted in *In Time of Trouble*, ch. 10 (1956). As Cockburn (then working as a subeditor on the paper) explained, 'For further entertainment in the long evenings, someone had invented a game – a competition with a small prize for the winner – to see who could write the dullest headline. It had to be a genuine headline, that is to say one which was actually printed in the next morning's newspaper. I won it only once with a headline which announced: "Small Earthquake in Chile. Not many dead."' There is no trace of this headline ever being printed.

2 **What arouses the indignation of the honest satirist is not, unless the man is a prig, the fact that people in positions of power or influence behave idiotically, or even that they behave wickedly. It is that they conspire successfully to impose upon the public a picture of themselves as so very sagacious, honest and well-intentioned.**
*I, Claud*, 'The Worst Possible Taste' (1967)

## Jarvis Cocker (b. 1963)
BRITISH ROCK MUSICIAN

Dubbed by Ben Thompson the 'tower-block messiah' who 'dares to claim the middle ground between Alan Bennett and Barry White', he led his band Pulp to success in the 1990s with the albums *His 'n' Hers* (1994) and *Different Class* (1995). His lanky frame, fashionable attire and Michael Caine specs allied to his droll and catchy lyrics made him an icon for his times.

1 **You'll never live like common people,**
**you'll never do what common people do,**
**you'll never fail like common people,**
**you'll never watch your life slide out of view**
**and dance and drink and screw**
**because there's nothing else to do.**
'Common People' (song) on the album *Different Class* (1995) by Pulp

2 **Is this the way they say the future's meant to feel?**
**Or just 20,000 people standing in a field.**
**And I don't quite understand just what this feeling is.**
**But that's okay 'cos we're all sorted out for E's and wizz.**
'Sorted for E's and Wizz', ibid.

3 **The hangover is over**
**Men are over**
**Women are over**
**Cholesterol is over**
**Tapers are over**

**Irony is over**
**Bye bye bye bye.**
'The Day After the Revolution' (song) on the album *This is Hardcore* (1998) by Pulp

## Jean Cocteau (1889–1963)
FRENCH AUTHOR AND FILM-MAKER

Inspired by Diaghilev's phrase '*Étonne-moi*', he was in the forefront of most of the avant-garde movements of the first half of the twentieth century, associating with PICASSO, STRAVINSKY and the composers of Les Six. An artist of immense versatility, he was a poet, librettist, novelist, actor, film director, critic and painter.

1 **Art is science made clear.**
'Le Coq et l'Arlequin' (1918), later publ. in *Le Rappel à l'ordre* (1926), repr. in *Collected Works* vol. 9 (1950)

2 **Tact in audacity consists in knowing how far we may go too far.**
ibid.

3 **The worst tragedy for a poet is to be admired through being misunderstood.**
ibid.

4 **What the public criticizes in you, cultivate. It is you.**
ibid.

5 **If it has to choose who is to be crucified, the crowd will always save Barabbas.**
ibid. Barabbas was the thief and insurrectional leader reprieved at Christ's crucifixion, following the custom at Passover (*Matthew* 27).

6 **The Louvre is like the morgue; one goes there to identify one's friends.**
'Le Secret professionnel' (1922), later publ. in *Le Rappel à l'ordre* (1926), repr. in ibid.

7 **I am a lie who always speaks the truth.**
*Opéra*, 'Le Paquet rouge' (1925). Similarly, in his *Journals* (1956), Cocteau wrote, 'The matters I relate/Are true lies.'

8 **Living is a horizontal fall.**
*Opium* (1930)

9 **Everything one does in life, even love, occurs in an express train racing toward death. To smoke opium is to get out of the train while it is still moving. It is to concern oneself with something other than life or death.**
ibid. Cocteau experimented with opium in the 1920s, though he also wrote, 'It is not I who become addicted, it is my body.'

10 **Victor Hugo was a madman who believed himself to be Victor Hugo.**
ibid. Quoting himself from a previous occasion.

11 **Poetry is indispensable – if I only knew what for.**
Quoted in *The Necessity of Art*, ch. 1 (1959) by Ernst Fischer

12 **A film is a petrified fountain of thought.**
*Esquire* February 1961

## Dr F.D. Coggan (b. 1910)
BRITISH ECCLESIASTIC, ARCHBISHOP OF CANTERBURY

He was Bishop of Bradford (1956–61), Archbishop of York (1961–74) and Archbishop of Canterbury (1974–80). His theological works include *Sure Foundation* (1981) and *Servant Son* (1995).

1 **[The Church] can always be a gadfly in the conscience of those who make the economic order, and I think that is its main function.**
Interview on ITV, 11 June 1961

## George M. Cohan (1878–1942)
US SONGWRITER, PLAYWRIGHT AND PRODUCER

Steeped in vaudeville and theatre from an early age, he showed talent as an actor, singer, dancer, songwriter, playwright and screenwriter, and he can claim to have created the first American musical in *Little Johnny Jones* in 1903. The musical *Yankee Doodle Dandy* (1942), titled after one of his songs, was the story of his life, with JAMES CAGNEY in the lead role.

1 Over there, over there,
Send the word, send the word over there
That the Yanks are coming, the Yanks are coming,
The drums rum-tumming everywhere.
So prepare, say a prayer,
Send the word, send the word to beware.
We'll be over, we're coming over
And we won't come back till it's over, over there.

'Over There' (song, 1917). The song quickly became established as an upbeat patriotic classic: President WOODROW WILSON called it 'a genuine inspiration to all American manhood'.

## Leonard Cohen (b. 1934)
CANADIAN SINGER, POET AND NOVELIST

The 'Bard of the Bedsits' has published volumes of poetry since 1956, releasing the first of his many melancholic albums, *Songs of Leonard Cohen*, in 1967. His two most successful novels are *The Favourite Game* (1963) and *Beautiful Losers* (1966).

1 Let judges secretly despair of justice: their verdicts will be more acute. Let generals secretly despair of triumph; killing will be defamed. Let priests secretly despair of faith: their compassion will be true.
*The Spice-Box Of Earth*, 'Lines From My Grandfather's Journal' (1961)

2 Some say that no one ever leaves Montreal, for that city, like Canada itself, is designed to preserve the past, a past that happened somewhere else.
*The Favourite Game*, bk 2, ch. 19 (1963)

3 A woman watches her body uneasily, as though it were an unreliable ally in the battle for love.
ibid. bk 3, ch. 8

4 History is a needle
for putting men asleep
anointed with the poison
Of all they want to keep.
'On Hearing A Name Long Unspoken', st. 3, publ. in *Flowers For Hitler* (1964)

5 I am an old scholar, better-looking now than when I was young. That's what sitting on your ass does to your face.
*Beautiful Losers*, bk 1, 'The History of Them All' (1966)

6 To every people the land is given on condition. Perceived or not, there is a Covenant, beyond the constitution, beyond sovereign guarantee, beyond the nation's sweetest dreams of itself.
*Book of Mercy*, sect. 27 (1984)

7 The term clinical depression finds its way into too many conversations these days. One has a sense that a catastrophe has occurred in the psychic landscape.
*International Herald Tribune* 4 November 1988

8 I don't consider myself a pessimist at all. I think of a pessimist as someone who is waiting for it to rain. And I feel completely soaked to the skin.
Quoted in the *Independent on Sunday* 2 May 1993

9 I've always held the song in high regard because songs have got me through so many sinks of dishes and so many humiliating courting events.
Quoted in the *Observer* 27 September 1998

## Frank Moore Colby (1865–1925)
US EDITOR AND ESSAYIST

He wrote for encyclopaedias throughout his life, and edited the *New International Year Book* from 1898 until his death. He also contributed widely and wittily to magazines, including the *Bookman, New Republic* and *Vanity Fair. The Colby Essays* (1926) posthumously increased his popularity.

1 Men will confess to treason, murder, arson, false teeth, or a wig. How many of them will own up to a lack of humor?
*The Colby Essays*, vol. 1, 'Satire and Teeth' (1926)

2 Persecution was at least a sign of personal interest. Tolerance is composed of nine parts of apathy to one of brotherly love.
ibid. 'Trials of an Encyclopedist'

## Colette (1873–1954)
FRENCH AUTHOR

Born Sidonie Gabrielle Colette. Her series of Claudine novels (1900–1903) was written in collaboration with her first husband Gauthier-Villars under his pen name, Willy. She later established a reputation in her own right with tales of love, passion and animals such as *Chéri* (1920), *Gigi* (1945) and *La Chatte* (*The Cat*, 1953). In her old age, Cecil Beaton likened her to 'an old chinchilla marmoset sitting deep in a sofa'.

1 Among all the modernized aspects of the most luxurious of industries, the model, a vestige of voluptuous barbarianism, is like some plunder-laden prey. She is the object of unbridled regard, a living bait, the passive realization of an ideal. . . . No other female occupation contains such potent impulses to moral disintegration as this one, applying as it does the outward signs of riches to a poor and beautiful girl.
'Models', first publ. in *Vogue* (1925–7), repr. in *Journey for Myself* (1971)

2 Is suffering so very serious? I have come to doubt it. It may be quite childish, a sort of undignified pastime – I'm referring to the kind of suffering a man inflicts on a woman or a woman on a man. It's extremely painful. I agree that it's hardly bearable. But I very much fear that this sort of pain deserves no consideration at all. It's no more worthy of respect than old age or illness.
'Break of Day' (1928), repr. in *Earthly Paradise*, pt 4, 'The South of France' (ed. Robert Phelps, 1966)

3 It is wise to apply the oil of refined politeness to the mechanism of friendship.
*The Pure and the Impure*, ch. 9 (1933, transl. 1966)

4 But just as delicate fare does not stop you from craving for saveloys, so tried and exquisite friendship does not take away your taste for something new and dubious.
*Chambre d'hôtel*, 'The Rainy Moon' (1940)

5 Don't ever wear artistic jewelry; it wrecks a woman's reputation.
Aunt Alicia, in *Gigi* (1944). When asked (by Gilberte) 'What is an artistic jewel?' Aunt Alicia replies, 'It all depends. A mermaid in gold, with eyes of chrysoprase. An Egyptian scarab. A large engraved amethyst. A not very heavy bracelet said to have been chased by a master-hand. A lyre or star, mounted as a brooch. A studded tortoise. In a word, all of them frightful. Never wear baroque pearls, not even as hat-pins. Beware, above all things, of family jewels!'

6 A pretty little collection of weaknesses and a terror of spiders are our indispensable stock-in-trade with the men.
ibid.

## R.G. Collingwood (1889–1943)
BRITISH PHILOSOPHER

Professor of philosophy at Oxford (1934–41), he subscribed to the view that philosophy could only be understood within a historical framework. He was also an authority on Roman Britain.

1 Like other revolutionaries I can thank God for the reactionaries. They clarify the issue.
*An Autobiography*, ch. 6 (1939)

2 A man ceases to be a beginner in any given science and becomes a master in that science when he has learned that . . . he is going to be a beginner all his life.

*The New Leviathan*, pt 1, ch. 1, aph. 46 (1942)

## Joan Collins (b. 1933)
BRITISH ACTRESS

Debuting in 1951, she relaunched her career with starring roles in *The Stud* (1979) and *The Bitch* (1980), based on novels written by her sister Jackie Collins. She found greatest success as a powerful and glamorous schemer in the US TV soap opera *Dynasty* (1981–9). Her career, according to ERICA JONG, was 'a testimony to menopausal chic'.

1 I've never yet met a man who could look after me. I don't need a husband. What I need is a wife.

Quoted in the *Sunday Times* 27 December 1987

2 America should let Bill Clinton get back to doing his job, even if he will always be remembered among presidents for one with a penchant for bonking trailer-park trash.

Quoted in the *Observer* 13 September 1998

## Pauline Collins (b. 1940)
BRITISH ACTRESS

She is best known as a stage actress and for her appearances in the TV series *Upstairs, Downstairs* (1971–3), which also starred her husband John Alderton, and the film *Shirley Valentine* (1989).

1 You can't bring logic into this. We're talking about marriage. Marriage is like the Middle East. There's no solution.

Shirley (Pauline Collins), in *Shirley Valentine* (film, screenplay by Willy Russell based on his 1986 play, directed by Lewis Gilbert, 1989)

## John Coltrane (1926–67)
US JAZZ MUSICIAN

A brilliant and influential saxophonist, he formed a bridge between the bebop era of CHARLIE PARKER and the free-form movement of Ornette Coleman. Intense and emotional in style he experimented with 'changing the notes of a chord around to see how many ways I can play it'. Classic albums include *My Favorite Things* (1960) and *A Love Supreme* (1964).

1 All a musician can do is to get closer to the sources of nature, and so feel that he is in communion with the natural laws. Then he can feel he is interpreting them to the best of his ability.

Interview in *Jazz Journal* January 1962, repr. in *The John Coltrane Companion* (ed. Carl Woideck, 1998)

2 I think the main thing a musician would like to do is to give a picture to the listener of the many wonderful things he knows of and senses in the universe. That's what music is to me – it's just another way of saying this is a big, beautiful universe we live in, that's been given to us, and here's an example of just how magnificent and encompassing it is.

*Down Beat* 12 April 1962, repr. in ibid.

3 If the music doesn't say it, how can the words say it for the music?

Quoted in *Jazz is*, ch. 5 (1976) by Nat Hentoff

## Betty Comden (b. 1915) and
## Adolph Green (b. 1915)
US LIBRETTISTS, LYRICISTS AND SCREENWRITERS

During a fifty-year career this songwriting duo was associated with a string of Broadway hits, in some of which they also appeared. Among their collaborators were LEONARD BERNSTEIN, Jule Styne

and Gene Kelly; with the latter they made the films *On the Town* (1949), *Singin' in the Rain* (1952) and *It's Always Fair Weather* (1955).

1 New York, New York – a helluva town,
The Bronx is up but the Battery's down,
And people ride in a hole in the ground:
New York, New York – it's a helluva town.

'New York, New York' (song from the stage musical *On The Town*, 1944, filmed 1949). The song opens the story, which follows the adventures of a group of sailors on shore leave in New York.

2 The party's over, it's time to call it a day.

'The Party's Over' (song, with music by Jule Styne), in *The Bells are Ringing* (stage musical 1956, filmed 1960)

## Alex Comfort (1920–2000)
BRITISH SEXOLOGIST, AUTHOR AND POET

He was the author of *Sex and Society* (1963), *The Anxiety Makers* (1967) and *The Joy of Sex* (1972), his most famous work, dubbed the 'Kamasutra for the coffee table'. He himself observed, 'There's nothing new in the book. It's just reassurance, telling people it's OK.' Sexual themes also pervaded his novels, and his other works included poetry and a study of ageing.

1 The Joy of Sex.

Book title (1972)

2 There are two modes of sex, the duet and the solo, and a good concert alternates between them.

*The Joy of Sex*, Preface (1972, rev. 1991)

## Ivy Compton-Burnett (1884–1969)
BRITISH NOVELIST

Her stylized novels rely heavily on dialogue to portray the internal wranglings of upper-class Victorian or Edwardian families. Titles include *Pastors and Masters* (1925) and *Mother and Son* (1955). The novelist Brigid Brophy commented that her novels 'can no more be read for their narrative impetus or their development of character than those problems in which Harry is taller than Dick, who is shorter than Bill'.

1 Well, of course, people are only human. But it really does not seem much for them to be.

Dudley Gaveston, in *A Family and a Fortune*, ch. 2 (1939)

2 We must use words as they are used or stand aside from life.

Julius Hume, in *Mother and Son*, ch. 9 (1955)

3 There is danger in courage. Cowardice is a power for good. We hardly know what it prevents.

Angus, in *The Last and First*, ch. 6 (1971)

## Richard Condon (1915–96)
US NOVELIST, SCREENWRITER AND JOURNALIST

A Hollywood scriptwriter till the late 1950s, he devised a successful recipe of political thrillers and pulp prose mixed with a large dose of conspiracy paranoia. His most successful novels have almost all been filmed, including *The Manchurian Candidate* (1959, filmed 1962).

1 Television – the key to all minds and hearts because it permits the people to be entertained by their government, without ever having to participate in it.

*International Herald Tribune* 7 June 1990

## Billy Connolly (b. 1942)
SCOTTISH COMEDIAN

The 'Big Yin' quit his job as a welder on the Clyde shipyards in 1966 to go on stage with various musical groups, playing banjo and guitar, gradually concentrating more on his comedy act. He set out

– in his own words – 'to be a cross between Lenny Bruce and Robert the Bruce'. He has also made TV documentaries and appeared in films, notably as Queen Victoria's gamekeeper in *Mrs Brown* (1997).

1 **I would hate to have been born, lived and died and nobody noticed. It's proof you exist, that all the practising with your banjo in your bedroom paid off.**
On fame, in interview in 1984, quoted in *The Big Yin: The Life and Times of Billy Connolly*, ch. 10 (1994) by Jonathan Margolis

2 **[Of fellow Glaswegians] You're 'Connolly' all your life until you become famous, then you're 'that bastard Connolly'.**
Quoted in the *Observer* 9 June 1991

3 **I totally refuse to be part of it [political correctness] . . . those new comedy people who say no racism, no sexism, no that-ism, no this-ism. How dare you? Comedy's been here for thousands of years. How dare you start rewriting the rule book? There is no rule book. Funny is funny is funny.**
*South Bank Show*, ITV, 4 October 1992, quoted in *The Big Yin: The Life and Times of Billy Connolly*, ch. 10 (1994) by Jonathan Margolis

## Cyril Connolly (1903–74)
BRITISH CRITIC

A fastidious wit, he was noted mainly for his collections of essays, reflections and aphorisms in *Enemies of Promise* (1938) and *The Unquiet Grave* (written as 'Palinurus', 1944). He founded and edited the literary magazine *Horizon* (1939–50) and was a regular contributor to the *Sunday Times* (1951–74).

1 **Green leaves on a dead tree is our epitaph – green leaves, dear reader, on a dead tree.**
'The Journal of Cyril Connolly 1928–1937', publ. in *Journal and Memoir* by David Pryce-Jones (1983). Pryce-Jones chose these words for his book's epigraph.

2 **A best-seller is the golden touch of mediocre talent.**
ibid.

3 **Idleness [is] only a coarse name for my infinite capacity for living in the present.**
ibid.

4 **Destroy him as you will, the bourgeois always bounces up – execute him, expropriate him, starve him out *en masse*, and he reappears in your children.**
Quoted in the *Observer* 7 March 1937

5 **I shall christen this style the Mandarin, since it is beloved by literary pundits, by those who would make the written word as unlike as possible to the spoken one. It is the style of all those writers whose tendency is to make their language convey more than they mean or more than they feel, it is the style of most artists and all humbugs and one which is always menaced by a puritan opposition.**
*Enemies of Promise*, pt 1, ch. 2 (1938; rev. 1948). Connolly referred to a style of English prose popularized by authors such as Addison – who was 'responsible for many of the evils from which English prose has since suffered. He made prose artful and whimsical, he made it sonorous when sonority was not needed, affected when it did not require affectation . . .'

6 **Literature is the art of writing something that will be read twice; journalism what will be grasped at once.**
ibid. ch. 3

7 **As repressed sadists are supposed to become policemen or butchers so those with an irrational fear of life become publishers.**
ibid. pt 2, ch. 10

8 **Whom the gods wish to destroy they first call promising.**
ibid. ch. 13

9 **There is no more sombre enemy of good art than the pram in the hall.**
ibid. ch. 14

10 **All charming people have something to conceal, usually their total dependence on the appreciation of others.**
ibid. ch. 16

11 **Were I to deduce any system from my feelings on leaving Eton, it might be called *The Theory of Permanent Adolescence*. It is the theory that the experiences undergone by boys at the great public schools, their glories and disappointments, are so intense as to dominate their lives and to arrest their development. From these it results that the greater part of the ruling class remains adolescent, school-minded, self-conscious, cowardly, sentimental, and in the last analysis homosexual.**
ibid. pt 3, ch. 24

12 **Perfect fear casteth out love.**
Quoted in obituary notice in the *Observer* 1 December 1974, by Philip Toynbee, to whom Connolly made this remark during the Blitz. The reference is to the New Testament, 1 John 4:18, 'Perfect love casteth out fear.'

13 **The more books we read, the clearer it becomes that the true function of a writer is to produce a masterpiece and that no other task is of any consequence.**
*The Unquiet Grave*, pt 1 (1944, rev. 1951). Opening words of book.

14 **Slums may well be breeding-grounds of crime, but middle-class suburbs are incubators of apathy and delirium.**
ibid.

15 **No city should be too large for a man to walk out of in a morning.**
ibid.

16 **Civilization is an active deposit which is formed by the combustion of the Present with the Past. Neither in countries without a Present nor in those without a Past is it to be encountered.**
ibid. pt 2. Connolly continued: 'Proust in Venice, Matisse's birdcages overlooking the flower market at Nice, Gide on the seventeenth-century quais of Toulon, Lorca in Granada, Picasso by Saint-Germain-des-Prés: there lies civilization and for me it can exist only under those liberal regimes in which the Present is alive and therefore capable of assimilating the Past.'

17 **The goal of every culture is to decay through over-civilization; the factors of decadence – luxury, scepticism, weariness and superstition – are constant. The civilization of one epoch becomes the manure of the next.**
ibid.

18 **Imprisoned in every fat man a thin one is wildly signalling to be let out.**
ibid. The remark had been used earlier by fellow Old Etonian GEORGE ORWELL (see 7); for a later variant see KINGSLEY AMIS 4.

19 **The true index of a man's character is the health of his wife.**
ibid.

20 **We are all serving a life-sentence in the dungeon of self.**
ibid.

21 **Our memories are card indexes consulted and then returned in disorder by authorities whom we do not control.**
ibid. pt 3

22 **The boredom of Sunday afternoon, which drove de Quincey to drink laudanum, also gave birth to surrealism: hours propitious for making bombs.**
ibid.

23 **It is closing time in the gardens of the West and from now on an artist will be judged only by the resonance of his solitude or the quality of his despair.**
*Horizon* December 1949

## James Connolly (1870–1916)

IRISH SYNDICALIST AND REPUBLICAN LEADER

Having helped found the Irish Socialist Republican Party (1896) and, in New York (1902–10), the Industrial Workers of the World ('Wobblies'), he established the Irish Labour Party with James Larkin in 1912. He was shot by a British firing squad for his part in the Easter Rising of 1916.

1 Without the power of the Industrial Union behind it, Democracy can only enter the State as the victim enters the gullet of the Serpent.

*The Re-Conquest of Ireland*, ch. 9 (1915)

2 Ireland, as distinct from her people, is nothing to me; and the man who is bubbling over with love and enthusiasm for 'Ireland', and can yet pass unmoved through our streets and witness all the wrong and the suffering, the shame and the degradation wrought upon the people of Ireland – yea, wrought by Irishmen upon Irish men and women, without burning to end it, is, in my opinion, a fraud and a liar in his heart, no matter how he loves that combination of chemical elements he is pleased to call Ireland.

*Labour in Ireland*, Epigraph (1916)

## Jimmy Connors (b. 1952)

US TENNIS PLAYER

One of the first players to use a two-handed backhand, he established his position as one of the world's top players winning both Wimbledon (against Ken Rosewall) and the US Championship (against John McEnroe) in 1974. He won the US Open again in 1976, 1978 and 1982–3.

1 New Yorkers love it when you spill your guts out there [Flushing Meadow]. Spill your guts at Wimbledon and they make you stop and clean it up.

Quoted in the *Guardian* 24 December 1984

## Peter Conrad (b. 1948)

AUSTRALIAN AUTHOR AND CRITIC

He has written on opera, fiction and literary criticism and is also a reviewer and features writer for the *Observer*. *Feasting With Panthers or, The Importance of Being Famous* (1994) is a study on fame and achievement through his interviews with celebrities.

1 New York is more now than the sum of its people and buildings. It makes sense only as a mechanical intelligence, a transporter system for the daily absorbing and nightly redeploying of the human multitudes whose services it requires.

*The Art of the City*, ch. 13 (1984)

2 Losing faith in your own singularity is the start of wisdom, I suppose; also the first announcement of death.

*Down Under: Revisiting Tasmania*, pt 6, 'In the Family' (1988)

## Shirley Conran (b. 1932)

BRITISH DESIGNER AND JOURNALIST

The first woman editor of the *Observer Colour Magazine* (1964–9), she became a bestseller with her *Superwoman* series (1974–7, 1990), and her novels, including *Lace* (1982) and *Tiger Eyes* (1984).

1 Life is too short to stuff a mushroom.

*Superwoman*, Epigraph (1975)

2 I make no secret of the fact that I would rather lie on a sofa than sweep beneath it. But you have to be efficient if you're going to be lazy.

ibid. 'The Reason Why'

3 First things first, second things never.

Family motto, in ibid. 'How to be a Working Wife and Mother'

## (Sir) Terence Conran (b. 1931)

BRITISH BUSINESSMAN AND DESIGNER

A furniture designer by profession, he championed modern and affordable design through his Habitat Company (1971–88). He has written widely on interior design, following the principle that 'things that are intelligently designed improve the quality of life'. He was married to SHIRLEY CONRAN (1955–62), and was knighted in 1983.

1 Perhaps believing in good design is like believing in God, it makes you an optimist.

*Daily Telegraph* 12 June 1989

## Conservative Party manifesto, 1950

1 The Conservative Party by long tradition and settled belief is the party of Empire. We are proud of its past. We see it as the surest hope in our own day. We proclaim our abiding faith in its destiny.

'Britain Strong and Free', quoted by John Barnes in 'Ideology and Factions', publ. in *Conservative Century*, pt 2 (ed. Anthony Seldon and Stuart Ball, 1994)

## Peter Cook (1937–95)

BRITISH COMEDIAN

As a student at Cambridge he performed in *Beyond the Fringe* (1959–64), and later collaborated with Dudley Moore in the TV series *Not Only . . . But Also* (1965–71), inventing the forlorn figure A.L. Wisty. He was co-founder of and a regular contributor to the satirical magazine *Private Eye*. According to ALAN BENNETT, 'he proved that a life of self-indulgence, if led with a whole heart, may also bring a certain wisdom.'

1 I go to the theatre to be entertained. I don't want to see plays about rape, sodomy and drug addiction – I can get all that at home.

Cartoon caption in the *Observer* 8 July 1962. The quip also occurred in the revue *Beyond the Fringe*, and has been credited to ALAN BENNETT.

2 There's terrific merit in having no sense of humour, no sense of irony, practically no sense of anything at all. If you're born with these so-called defects you have a very good chance of getting to the top.

Quoted in *Beyond the Fringe . . . and Beyond*, pt 4 (1989) by Ronald Bergan

## Robin Cook (b. 1946)

BRITISH POLITICIAN

Original name Robert Cook. He became a Labour MP in 1974 and held the posts of Spokesman for Trade and Industry (1992–4) and Foreign Affairs (1994–7) in the shadow cabinet. He has been Chair of the Labour Party since 1996 and in 1997 was appointed Foreign Secretary.

1 It's better to send middle-aged men abroad to bore each other than send young men abroad to kill each other.

*Independent* 14 February 1998. Referring to UN negotiations with Saddam Hussein.

## Alistair Cooke (b. 1908)

BRITISH-BORN US BROADCASTER AND JOURNALIST

An urbane observer on current affairs in America, he has published several books, contributed to British newspapers and broadcast the weekly *Letter from America* on BBC radio since 1946.

1 If the fads of the young follow their usual practice and pass over into the settled habits of middle age, attributable to no country but to the period they were learned in, then in another quarter-century England indeed will be the

fifty-first state. For the most compelling social characteristic of the British people today is not the wide gamut of native qualities and habits, but the greater range of American habits, customs, and conventions they seem to have incorporated, without complaint, since the war.

'New Ways in English Life', publ. in *Manchester Guardian* 16 July 1959, repr. in *America Observed* (1988, selected by Ronald A. Wells)

2 Cocktail music he accepts as audible wallpaper.

'The Innocent American', in *Holiday* July 1962. The words are usually misquoted as 'Canned music is like audible wallpaper.'

3 All Presidents start out to run a crusade but after a couple of years they find they are running something less heroic and much more intractable: namely the presidency.

Radio broadcast, 1963, publ. in *Talk About America*, ch. 31 (1968)

4 Was Vietnam indeed a crusade or a vast miscalculation? Was it the wrong war in the wrong place, or the right war in the wrong place? What matters, or will come to matter to most people, I think, is not any new balance we can strike in the old argument; but the realization that America, which has never lost a war, is not invincible; and the very late discovery that an elephant can trumpet and shake the earth but not the self-possession of the ants who hold it.

*Letter from America*, BBC radio broadcast, 24 March 1968

# Sam Cooke (1931–64)

US SOUL MUSICIAN

His gospel-influenced vocal style and strong commercial appeal made him a major figure in soul music, inspiring endless covers of his songs 'You Send Me' (1957), 'Only Sixteen' (1959) and 'Bring it on Home to Me' (1963), among many others. He was shot dead in a motel room, apparently by a woman whose room he had mistakenly entered.

1 It's been a long time coming
But I know a change is gonna come.

'A Change is Gonna Come' (song) on the album *Ain't That Good News* (1964). The song was partly modelled on BOB DYLAN's 'Blowin' in the Wind' and assumed almost anthemic importance during the rise of the Black Consciousness movement. It was recorded by numerous artists including Prince Buster and, most famously, Otis Redding, who dedicated the song to Cooke in concert.

2 Don't know much about history
Don't know much biology.

'Wonderful World' (song, 1960). In *A Change is Gonna Come: Music, Race and the Soul of America* (1998) by Craig Werner, the author makes this comment on the lines: 'The cliché's worth a second thought. Because, if there are two things that a black man in pop music needed to encourage the white audience to forget, they were history and biology, at least the parts involving skin color and sexuality.'

# Calvin Coolidge (1872–1933)

US POLITICIAN AND PRESIDENT

As Republican president (1923–9) with the slogan 'Keep Cool with Coolidge', he was noted for non-interference in business, industry and foreign affairs and pursued policies aimed at reducing taxes and the national debt. Modest and frugal throughout his life, he was equally known for his dullness. H.L. MENCKEN summed him up, 'He had no ideas, but was not a nuisance.' See also DOROTHY PARKER 11.

1 There is no right to strike against the public safety by anybody, anywhere, any time.

Telegram to Samuel Gompers, President of American Federation of Labor, 14 September 1919, quoted in *Have Faith in Massachusetts* (1919). Coolidge, then Governor of Massachusetts, was referring to a strike by the Boston police.

2 Civilization and profits go hand in hand.

Speech in New York, 27 November 1920, quoted in *The New York Times* 28 November 1920

3 After all, the chief business of the American people is business.

Speech to the Society of American Newspaper Editors, Washington, DC, 17 January 1925, publ. in *Foundations of the Republic* (1926)

4 Well, they hired the money, didn't they?

Attributed comment in 1925 to US ambassador to France on a proposal to restructure European war debts, quoted in *The Wit and Wisdom of Calvin Coolidge* (ed. John H. McKee, 1933). Coolidge's biographer, Claud M. Fuess, failed to find any evidence that Coolidge spoke these words, though his wife observed, 'I don't know whether he said it, but it is just what he might have said.'

5 I do not choose to run for President in nineteen twenty-eight.

Statement to reporters, Rapid City, South Dakota, 2 Aug. 1927, quoted in *The New York Times* 3 Aug. 1927. The words are said to have been written out and handed to the assembled journalists, an extreme example of Coolidge's legendary taciturnity. One Washington hostess is supposed to have commented, 'every time he opens his mouth, a moth flies out.'

# Diana Cooper (1892–1986)

BRITISH ACTRESS, AUTHOR AND SOCIETY FIGURE

Married to the diplomat Duff Cooper, she made her name in the role of the Madonna in the play *The Miracle* (1923) by Max Reinhardt, which she toured extensively. She was an irrepressible communicator and inveterate letter writer; for Cecil Beaton, she was 'a card – a flamboyant eccentric – and a real professional extrovert in that the performance she gives is always of her best.' See also JOHN CAREY 1.

1 Age wins and one must learn to grow old ... I must learn to walk this long unlovely wintry way, looking for spectacles, shunning the cruel looking-glass, laughing at my clumsiness before others mistakenly condole, not expecting gallantry yet disappointed to receive none, apprehending every ache or shaft of pain, alive to blinding flashes of mortality, unarmed, totally vulnerable.

*Trumpets from the Steep*, ch. 8 (memoir, 1960)

# Gary Cooper (1901–61)

US SCREEN ACTOR

The embodiment of the strong, silent loner, he remained a Hollywood star for more than thirty years, a success he attributed to 'playing the part of Mr Average Joe American'. He appeared as the archetypal Western hero in *High Noon* (1952) and in film adaptations of Hemingway's books such as *For Whom the Bell Tolls* (1943).

1 In Westerns you were permitted to kiss your horse but never your girl.

'Well, It Was This Way', in the *Saturday Evening Post* 17 March 1958

# Jilly Cooper (b. 1937)

BRITISH WRITER AND JOURNALIST

A regular columnist for the *Sunday Times* (1969–82) and the *Daily Mail* (1982–7), she is author of *How to Stay Married* (1969) and a succession of steamy bestsellers including *Riders* (1978) and *Polo* (1991).

1 Nostalgia excuses everything, enabling people to click their tongues over the out-dated inequalities, yet guiltily enjoy the sense of hierarchy.

*Class*, Introduction (1980)

2 I've always felt reading romantic novels was a bit like eating a whole box of chocolates or going to bed with a

rotter. You can't stop because it's so nice, but afterwards you wish you hadn't.

Quoted in the *Sunday Correspondent* 24 December 1989

## Tommy Cooper (1922–84)
BRITISH COMEDIAN

With his trademark red fez, he was the comedian's comedian, but also enjoyed widepread popularity in variety and his own 1950s TV series *It's Magic*, in which he deliberately botched magic tricks. He died on stage during a live transmission of a TV show.

1 Just like that!

Catch-phrase and title of autobiography (1975)

## Wendy Cope (b. 1945)
BRITISH POET

After fifteen years as a primary-school teacher, she published her first volume of poems *Making Cocoa for Kingsley Amis* in 1986, following it with *Serious Concerns* (1992). A 'seriously funny' poet, she is known for her parodies and literary jokes.

1 I used to think all poets were Byronic.
They're mostly wicked as a ginless tonic
And wild as pension plans.

'Triolet', publ. in *Making Cocoa for Kingsley Amis* (1986)

2 The Thames runs, bones rattle, rats creep;
Tiresias fancies a peep –
A typist is laid,
A record is played –
Wei la la. After that it gets deep.

'Waste Land Limericks', publ. in ibid.

3 Bloody men are like bloody buses –
You wait for about a year
And as soon as one approaches your stop
Two or three others appear.

'Bloody Men', publ. in *Serious Concerns* (1992). The men/buses analogy had been current for some time: newspaper editor Wendy Henry was quoted in the *Observer* 30 January 1983: 'Men are like buses. If you miss one, there's always another round the corner. But don't get caught at the wrong stop.'

4 They say that men suffer,
As badly, as long.
I worry, I worry,
In case they are wrong.

'I Worry', publ. in ibid.

5 I think it's a question which particularly arises over women writers: whether it's better to have a happy life or a good supply of tragic plots.

*Independent* 9 March 1992

6 I'm aiming by the time I'm fifty to stop being an adolescent.

*Daily Telegraph* 9 December 1992

## Aaron Copland (1900–1990)
US COMPOSER

Original name Aaron Kaplan. Early pieces influenced by STRAVINSKY were a fusion of classical and jazz styles. Later works such as the ballet *Billy the Kid* (1938) and the Pulitzer Prize-winning *Appalachian Spring* (1944) drew on the American folk tradition. For BERNSTEIN he was 'the best we have'.

1 The whole problem can be stated quite simply by asking, 'Is there a meaning to music?' My answer to that would be, 'Yes'. And 'Can you state in so many words what the meaning is?' My answer to that would be, 'No.'

*What to Listen for in Music*, ch. 2 (1939)

2 At no point can you seize the musical experience and hold it. Unlike that moment in a film when a still shot suddenly immobilizes a complete scene, a single musical moment immobilized makes audible only one chord, which in itself is comparatively meaningless. This never-ending flow of music *forces* us to use our imaginations, for music is in a continual state of becoming.

*Music and Imagination: The Charles Eliot Norton Lectures 1951/2*, Introduction (1952)

3 Listening implies an inborn talent of some degree, which, again like any other talent, can be trained and developed. This talent has a certain 'purity' about it. We excercise it, so to speak, for ourselves alone; there is nothing to be gained from it in a material sense. Listening is its own reward; there are no prizes to be won, no contests of creative listening. But I hold that person fortunate who has the gift, for there are few pleasures in art greater than the secure sense that one can recognize beauty when one comes upon it.

ibid. pt 1, ch. 1

4 The greatest moments of the human spirit may be deduced from the greatest moments in music.

'Music as an Aspect of the Human Spirit', radio broadcast, 1954, publ. in *Musical Courier* 1 February 1955 and *Man's Right to Knowledge: Second Series* (1955)

## Francis Ford Coppola (b. 1939)
US FILM-MAKER

He won universal acclaim for the epic Mafia drama *The Godfather* (1972), which he co-wrote and directed, and its two sequels; the trilogy won a total of ten Academy Awards. Other films include *Apocalypse Now* (1979), a retelling of Conrad's *Heart of Darkness* transposed to the Vietnam War, and *The Cotton Club* (1984).

1 If anything in this life is certain, if history has taught us anything, it's that everyone can be killed.

Michael Corleone (Al Pacino), in *The Godfather Part II* (film, screenplay by Francis Ford Coppola and Mario Puzo, directed by Francis Ford Coppola, 1974)

2 Nothing else in the world smells like that . . . I love the smell of napalm in the morning . . . It smells like victory.

Colonel Kilgore (Robert Duvall), in *Apocalypse Now* (film, screenplay by John Milius and Francis Ford Coppola, produced and directed by Francis Ford Coppola, 1979). The film's title, credited to John Milius, was derived from a badge popular with hippies in the 1960s, 'Nirvana Now'.

3 I don't believe that talented people today have less gifts than their artistic ancestors. The *times* are exhausted – stories come from the structure of ideas, ethics, beliefs, actualities of the times. Our *times* are exhausted – not our artists.

Quoted in *Coppola*, ch. 8 (1989) by Peter Cowie

## Alan Coren (b. 1938)
BRITISH EDITOR AND HUMORIST

A professional wit, he was editor of *Punch* (1978–87), contributes regularly to newspapers, periodicals and radio programmes, and has published numerous books, among which are *The Bulletins of Idi Amin* (1974) and *A Bit on the Side* (1995).

1 Apart from cheese and tulips, the main product of the country is advocaat, a drink made from lawyers.

*The Sanity Inspector*, 'All You Need to Know about Europe' (1974)

2 The Act of God designation on all insurance policies: which means, roughly, that you cannot be insured for the accidents that are most likely to happen to you. If your ox kicks a hole in your neighbour's Maserati, however, indemnity is instantaneous.

*The Lady from Stalingrad Mansions*, 'A Short History of Insurance' (1977)

3 Having a high-profile magazine that loses lots of money,

being a vanity publisher if you like, is rather like having a trophy wife. It's nice to have her on your arm, but you can't do anything with her because you are too old and clapped out – and it's as expensive as running an Ivana Trump, I can tell you. Rich men do it because it gets them invited to the right dinner parties and to meet politicians, that sort of thing. It also means that when they are asked what they do they can say, 'I own the Spectator' rather than, 'I export pipe linings.'

Quoted in the *Observer* 11 February 1996

## F.M. Cornford (1874–1943)

BRITISH AUTHOR AND ACADEMIC

Full name Francis Macdonald Cornford. Professor of Ancient Philosophy at Cambridge University (1931–9), he was a leading Platonic scholar, and published mainly on the ancient Greeks, including *Before and After Socrates* (1932) and *Plato's Theory of Knowledge* (1935).

1 Propaganda is that branch of the art of lying which consists in nearly deceiving your friends without quite deceiving your enemies.

   Quoted in the *New Statesman* 15 September 1978

## Gregory Corso (b. 1930)

US POET

One of the Beat poets, he first came to attention in the late 1950s for his anarchic verse. His numerous collections include *Gasoline* (1958) and *Earth Egg* (1974). Critic KENNETH REXROTH said of him: 'At his worst he is an amusing literary curiosity; at his best, his poems are metaphysical hotfoots and poetic cannon cracks.'

1 I HATE OLD POETMEN!
   Especially old poetmen who retract
   who consult other old poetmen
   who speak their youth in whispers,
   saying: – I did those then
   but that was then
   that was then –

   'I Am 25', publ. in *Gasoline* (1958)

2 Must one keep home to keep Rome Rome? Surely then this England visit will spoil whatever dream I have of it.

   'How One Looks At It', publ. in *Long Live Man* (1962)

## Bill Cosby (b. 1937)

US COMEDIAN AND ACTOR

His role in the TV series *I Spy* (1965–8) was a landmark in the screen portrayal of African-Americans, winning him three Emmy Awards, while his congenial humour made *The Cosby Show* (1984–92) and *Cosby* (1996) consistently top of the TV ratings. He has also appeared in films and recorded over twenty albums.

1 No matter how calmly you try to referee, parenting will eventually produce bizarre behavior, and I'm not talking about the kids. *Their* behavior is always normal.

   *Fatherhood*, ch. 4 (1986)

## Elvis Costello (b. 1954)

BRITISH ROCK MUSICIAN

Original name Declan Patrick McManus. An individualistic lyricist and a powerful singer, he writes songs alternately vengeful and tender. He emerged in the punk era, co-wrote with PAUL MC-CARTNEY and collaborated with the classical Brodsky Quartet in the *Juliet Letters* (1992). His rock albums include *My Aim is True* (1977), *Punch the Clock* (1983) and *Spike* (1989).

1 Somebody said that someone got filled in
   For saying that people get killed in
   The result of their shipbuilding
   With all the will in the world
   Diving for dear life
   When we could be diving for pearls.

   'Shipbuilding' on the album *Punch the Clock* (1983). The song, which was inspired by the Falkland War, was first recorded by Robert Wyatt in 1982.

2 To me, getting it wrong is just another original idea. Ninety per cent of pop music is trying to copy something and getting it wrong.

   Quoted in the *Guardian* 19 September 1998

## Kevin Costner (b. 1955)

US ACTOR AND FILM-MAKER

Having gained critical acclaim for performances in *Bull Durham* (1988) and *Field of Dreams* (1989), he directed and starred in *Dances With Wolves* (1990), which won seven Oscars. This was followed by *Robin Hood: Prince of Thieves* (1991), *JFK* (1991) and *The Bodyguard* (1992).

1 Well, I believe in the soul, the cock, the pussy, the small of a woman's back, the hangin' curved ball, high fiber, good Scotch, that the novels of Susan Sontag are self-indulgent overrated crap. I believe Lee Harvey Oswald acted alone, I believe there ought to be a constitutional amendment outlawing astro-turf . . . I believe in the sweet spot, soft-core pornography, opening your presents Christmas morning rather than Christmas Eve, and I believe in long slow deep soft wet kisses that last three days.

   Crash Davis (Kevin Costner), in *Bull Durham* (film; written and directed by Ron Shelton, 1988)

## Billy Cotton (1899–1969)

BRITISH BANDLEADER

After an early career as a footballer, he formed his own band in 1924 which toured nationally from the 1930s. His *Billy Cotton Bandshow*, broadcast on radio and television (1949–68), became a national institution, a mixture of comedy and musical routines.

1 Wakey wakey!

   Standard show opener, from 1940s . The catch-phrase originated in a Sunday morning live radio show; in Cotton's words, 'The boys had been sitting up all night in third-class railway carriages. When we broke before the actual performance they just slumped where they were. I came into the studio only a few minutes before the red light was due to go on, and they were slouched around like a lot of tired giraffes. "Oi, come on," I said. "*Wakey Wakey!*" It worked, and everybody got so cheerful that the producer said that we could well start the actual show with it. And that was the beginning of Wakey Wakey.' (*I Did it My Way*, ch. 10, 1970)

## Douglas Coupland (b. 1961)

CANADIAN AUTHOR

His novel *Generation X* (1991) lent its name to the subculture of disaffected twenty-somethings whose lives it chronicled. Other works by this 'self-wrought oracle of our age' – *Microserfs* (1995), *Life After God* (short stories, 1994) and *Polaroids from the Dead* (1996), a collection of fiction and non-fiction pieces – describe the 'accelerated culture' of our times, in which 'even a place in time as recent as last week can now feel like it happened a decade ago'.

1 McJob: A low-pay, low-prestige, low-dignity, low-benefit, no-future job in the service sector.

   Marginal note in *Generation X*, 'The Sun is Your Enemy' (1991)

2 Consensus Terrorism: The process that decides in-office attitudes and behavior.

   Marginal note in ibid. 'I Am Not a Target Market'

3 Yuppies never gamble, they calculate. They have no aura: ever been to a yuppie party? It's like being in an empty

room: empty hologram people walking around peeking at themselves in mirrors and surreptitiously misting their tonsils with Bianca spray, just in case they have to kiss another ghost like themselves. There's just nothing *there*.
Dag, in ibid.

4 You really have to wonder why we even bother to get *up* in the morning. I mean, really: *Why work?* Simply to buy more *stuff*?
Dag, in ibid. 'Quit Your Job'

5 My friends are all either married, boring, and depressed; single, bored, and depressed; or moved out of town to avoid boredom and depression.
The narrator (Andy), in ibid. 'MTV Not Bullets'

6 You've had most of your important memories by the time you're thirty. After that, memory becomes water overflowing into an already full cup.
*Life After God*, 'My Hotel Year' (1994)

7 Sometimes I think the people to feel the saddest for are people who once knew what profoundness was, but who lost or became numb to the sensation of wonder – people who closed the door that leads us into the secret world – or who had the doors closed for them by time and neglect and decisions made in time of weakness
ibid.

8 When you're young, you always feel that life hasn't yet begun – that 'life' is always scheduled to begin next week, next month, next year, after the holidays – whenever. But then suddenly you're old and the scheduled life didn't arrive. You find yourself asking 'well then, exactly what was it I was having – that interlude – the scrambly madness – all that time I had before?'
ibid. 'Gettysburg'

9 There is something about a monolithic tech culture like Microsoft that makes humans seriously rethink fundamental aspects of the relationship between their brains and their bodies – their souls and their ambitions; things and thoughts.
*Microserfs*, 'Oop: Thursday–Later that week' (1995)

10 I've never met anyone who has entered the technological realm and not come out of it happier, enhanced and more fulfilled.
*Without Walls: J'Accuse – Technonerds* (television broadcast, Channel 4, 19 March 1996)

11 The New World isn't new anymore. The New World – the Americas – it's over. People don't have dominion over Nature. It's gone beyond that. Human beings and the world are now the same thing.
Jared, in *Girlfriend in a Coma*, ch. 34 (1998)

12 You'll soon be seeing us walking down your street, our backs held proud, our eyes dilated with truth and power. We might look like you, but you should know better. We'll draw our line in the sand and force the world to cross our line. Every cell in our body explodes with the truth. We *will* be kneeling in front of the Safeway, atop out-of-date textbooks whose pages we have chewed out. We'll be begging passers by to see the need to question and question and question and never stop questioning until the world stops spinning. We'll be adults who smash the tired, exhausted system. We'll crawl and chew and dig our way into a radical new world. We will change minds and souls from stone and plastic into linen and gold – that's what I believe. That's what I know.
Final words of ibid. ch. 36

# (Sir) Noël Coward (1899–1973)
BRITISH ACTOR, PLAYWRIGHT AND COMPOSER

Blessed, in his own words, with 'a talent to amuse', he was a sophisticated star of show business, versatile in all aspects of the theatre. He began acting at the age of twelve and wrote the classic comedy plays *Hay Fever* (1925), *Private Lives* (1930, filmed 1931) and *Blithe Spirit* (1941, filmed 1945), as well as numerous musicals and revues. He also appeared in films, and wrote and produced the patriotic *In Which We Serve* (1942) and *Brief Encounter* (1946).

1 Poor little rich girl,
You're a bewitched girl,
Better beware!
'Poor Little Rich Girl' (song) in *On With the Dance* (musical revue, 1925)

2 Very flat, Norfolk.
Amanda, in *Private Lives*, act 1 (1930)

3 Extraordinary how potent cheap music is.
ibid. Often quoted 'Strange how potent cheap music is', the version used in the 1930 recording of the play (spoken by Gertrude Lawrence)

4 Elyot: It doesn't suit women to be promiscuous.
Amanda: It doesn't suit men for women to be promiscuous.
ibid. act 2

5 Certain women should be struck regularly like gongs.
Elyot, in ibid. act 3

6 In Bengal to move at all
Is seldom, if ever, done,
But mad dogs and Englishmen
Go out in the midday sun.
'Mad Dogs and Englishmen' (song, 1930)

7 We give lovely parties that last through the night,
I dress as a woman and scream with delight,
We wake up at lunch time and find we're still tight.
What could be duller than that?
'Bright Young People' (song, 1930)

8 Let's drink to our sons who made part of the pattern and to our hearts that died with them. Let's drink to the spirit of gallantry and courage that made a strange Heaven out of unbelievable Hell, and let's drink to the hope that one day this country of ours, which we love so much, will find dignity and greatness and peace again.
Jane, toasting New Year's Eve with Robert, in *Cavalcade*, pt 3, sc. 1 (1932). Last speech of play.

9 Blues, nothing to win or to lose.
It's getting me down.
Blues, I've got those weary Twentieth Century Blues.
'Twentieth Century Blues' (song) in ibid. pt 3, sc. 2

10 Mad about the boy,
I know it's stupid to be mad about the boy,
I'm so ashamed of it
But must admit
The sleepless nights I've had about the boy.
On the Silver Screen
He melts my foolish heart in every single scene.
'Mad About the Boy' (song) in *Words and Music* (musical revue, 1932)

11 Don't put your daughter on the stage,
Mrs Worthington,
Don't put your daughter on the stage.
'Mrs Worthington' (song, 1935, with music by Cole Porter). Noël Coward sang the song in the original recording.

12 The stately Homes of England,
How beautiful they stand,
To prove the upper classes
Have still the upper hand.
'The Stately Homes of England' (song) in *Operette* (musical show, 1938). Parody of opening lines of Felicia Hemans's 1849 poem, 'The Homes of England': 'The stately homes of England,/How beautiful they stand!/Amidst their tall ancestral trees,/O'er all the pleasant land.' See also CRISP 9.

13 The good old imperialism was a bloody sight wiser and

healthier than all this woolly-headed, muddled, 'all men are equal' humanitarianism which has lost us so much pride and dignity and prestige in the modern world. The British Empire was a great and wonderful social, economic and even spiritual experiment, and all the parlour pinks and eager, ill-informed intellectuals cannot convince me to the contrary.

Journal entry, 3 February 1957, publ. in *The Noël Coward Diaries* (ed. Graham Payn and Sheridan Morley, 1982)

14 Please do not think that I criticize or cavil
At a genuine urge to roam,
But why oh why do the wrong people travel
When the right people stay back home?

'Why Do the Wrong People Travel?' (song) in *Sail Away* (musical show, 1962)

# Jim Crace (b. 1946)
BRITISH AUTHOR

Called by JOHN UPDIKE 'a writer of hallucinatory skill and considerable cruelty', he gained success with his first novel, *Continent* (1986), which was followed by *The Gift of Stones* (1988) and *Quarantine*, (1997).

1 Fame is something different from popularity. It is less demanding for a start and has more to do with talent than virtue. But not even much to do with talent.

*Continent*, 'Cross Country' (1986)

2 'The secret of the story-teller,' father said, 'is Never Smile. A straight mouth and a pair of honest eyes is all it takes to turn a stone to leaf.'

*The Gift of Stones*, ch. 14 (1988)

# Hart Crane (1899–1932)
US POET

Influenced by Rimbaud and T.S. ELIOT, he is remembered for his main work, the epic *The Bridge* (1930) which sought to knit American culture, past, present and future, through the symbol of Brooklyn Bridge. He committed suicide.

1 Cowslip and shad-blow, flaked like tethered foam
Around bared teeth of stallions, bloomed that spring
When first I read thy lines, rife as the loam
Of prairies, yet like breakers cliffward leaping!

'Cape Hatteras' in *The Bridge*, sect. 4 (1930)

2 yes, Walt,
Afoot again, and onward without halt, –
Not soon, nor suddenly, – no, never to let go
My hand
in yours,
Walt Whitman –
so –

Final lines of ibid.

3 And through that cordage, threading with its call
One arc synoptic of all tides below –
Their labyrinthine mouths of history
Pouring reply as though all ships at sea
Complighted in one vibrant breath made cry, –
'Make thy love sure – to weave whose song we ply!'

'Atlantis' in *The Bridge*, sect. 8 (1930)

4 We left the haven hanging in the night –
Sheened harbor lanterns backward fled the keel.
Pacific here at time's end, bearing corn. –
Eyes stammer through the pangs of dust and steel.

ibid.

# Edith Cresson (b. 1934)
FRENCH POLITICIAN AND PRIME MINISTER

She was appointed France's first woman prime minister under the presidency of François Mitterrand in 1991, though rising unemployment and loss of Socialist Party support led to her resignation within a year. Often outspoken, she has been called the 'fiery socialist equivalent of Margaret Thatcher', though her career crashed dramatically when, as a European Commissioner, she was at the centre of a financial scandal in 1999.

1 Life here is hellish for a woman in politics unless she is elderly and ugly.

Quoted in the *Guardian* 16 May 1991. On becoming Prime Minister.

2 Men are not in any sense irreplaceable, except in one's private life.

Quoted in the *International Herald Tribune* 20 May 1991

# Harry Crews (b. 1935)
US AUTHOR

A writer of unconventional tales that deal with ostensibly conventional people, he published his first novel *The Gospel Singers* in 1968, and an acclaimed autobiography *A Childhood* in 1995.

1 If you give someone a white shirt and a tie and a ring of keys you'll find out what kind of a son of a bitch he is. Give them to him in the morning and you'll know before noon.

Interview in *Dazed and Confused* April 1995

# Quentin Crisp (1908–99)
BRITISH AUTHOR AND RACONTEUR

Original name Dennis Pratt. With his gaudy make-up, diamante and tilted hat, he was one of Britain's greatest exponents of camp wit. His pithy, often scabrous observations were disseminated through one-man shows, but it was the success of his autobiography, *The Naked Civil Servant* (1968), which allowed him to move permanently to New York. He fulfilled his dream to be crowned Queen of England when he played the part of Elizabeth I in the film *Orlando* (1993). 'Had surgery existed in my youth,' he declared, 'I would have had the op and opened a knitting shop in Carlisle.' He died in Britain, on the eve of a tour.

1 In an expanding universe, time is on the side of the outcast. Those who once inhabited the suburbs of human contempt find that without changing their address they eventually live in the metropolis.

*The Naked Civil Servant*, ch. 1 (1968)

2 Keeping up with the Joneses was a full-time job with my mother and father. It was not until many years later when I lived alone that I realized how much cheaper it was to drag the Joneses down to my level.

ibid.

3 Masturbation is not only an expression of self-regard: it is also the natural emotional outlet of those who . . . have already accepted as inevitable the wide gulf between their real futures and the expectations of their fantasies.

ibid. ch. 2

4 Vice is its own reward. It is virtue which, if it is to be marketed with consumer appeal, must carry Green Shield stamps.

ibid. ch. 2

5 The poverty from which I have suffered could be diagnosed as 'Soho' poverty. It comes from having the airs and graces of a genius and no talent.

ibid. ch. 7

6 To know all is not to forgive all. It is to despise everybody.

ibid. ch. 11

7 There was no need to do any housework at all. After the first four years the dirt doesn't get any worse.

ibid. ch. 15

8 Life was a funny thing that happened to me on the way to the grave.

ibid. ch. 18

9 I became one of the stately homos of England.

ibid. ch. 24. Alluding to Noël Coward's song and Felicia Heman's poem. See also NOËL COWARD 12.

10 An autobiography is an obituary in serial form with the last instalment missing.

ibid. ch. 29

11 The very purpose of existence is to reconcile the glowing opinion we have of ourselves with the appalling things that other people think about us.

*How to Become a Virgin*, ch. 2 (1981)

12 It is explained that all relationships require a little give and take. This is untrue. Any partnership demands that we give and give and give and at the last, as we flop into our graves exhausted, we are told that we didn't give enough.

ibid. ch. 4

13 Wherever I am on this earth, I am and shall always be only a resident alien. People are never with me, they are always in my presence. I am never involved in conversation, I am always being interviewed.

ibid. 'The End'

14 Living *en famille* provides the strongest motives for rudeness combined with the maximum opportunity for displaying it.

*Manners from Heaven*, ch. 2 (1984)

15 Manners are love in a cool climate.

ibid. ch. 2

16 Euphemisms are not, as many young people think, useless verbiage for that which can and should be said bluntly; they are like secret agents on a delicate mission, they must airily pass by a stinking mess with barely so much as a nod of the head, make their point of constructive criticism and continue on in calm forbearance. Euphemisms are unpleasant truths wearing diplomatic cologne.

ibid. ch. 5

17 A gentleman doesn't pounce . . . he glides.

ibid. ch. 6

18 The formula for achieving a successful relationship is simple: you should treat all disasters as if they were trivialities but never treat a triviality as if it were a disaster.

ibid. ch. 7

19 Love is the extra effort we make in our dealings with those whom we do not like and once you understand that, you understand all. This idea that love overtakes you is nonsense. This is but a polite manifestation of sex. To love another you have to undertake some fragment of their destiny.

'Love Lies Bleeding', TV broadcast on Channel 4, 6 August 1991, publ. in *New Statesman and Society* 9 Aug. 1991

20 The time comes for everyone to do deliberately what he used to do by mistake. . . . If you are effeminate by nature, you have to find some way of telling the world that you know you are, otherwise they keep telling you.

Quoted in obituary in *The Times* 22 November 1999

## Julian Critchley (b. 1930)
BRITISH POLITICIAN

As Conservative MP for Aldershot (1970–97), he was never shy of venting his sceptical and often maverick political views, ensuring that he stayed an outsider in Westminster. His newspaper columns and numerous books – including *Palace of Varieties: an Insider's View of Westminster* (1989) and *A Bag of Boiled Sweets* (1994) – have kept him in the public eye.

1 The only safe pleasure for a parliamentarian is a bag of boiled sweets.

*Listener* 10 June 1982. The words 'a bag of boiled sweets' were taken as the title of Critchley's memoirs in 1994.

2 She [Margaret Thatcher] has demanded that the BBC 'set its house in order' and tends to believe the worst of the Foreign and Commonwealth Office. She cannot see an institution without hitting it with her handbag.

*The Times* 21 June 1982

3 In order to succeed in our party the backbencher must be as wise as a dove and as innocent as a serpent. He will, of course, have already recognized that what the party is presently suffering from is an addiction to an *idée en marche*, and he should promptly join the back of the column. Not to be a monetarist in today's party is to suffer from a severe handicap, it is the political equivalent of being young, black and unemployed.

*Westminster Blues*, ch. 12 (1985)

## Richmal Crompton (1890–1969)
BRITISH AUTHOR

Original name Richmal Crompton Lamburn. At first a Classics teacher, she made her name with the schoolboy character William Brown, who appeared in magazines from 1919, and in thirty-eight books, starting with *Just William* in 1922.

1 I'll thcream and thcream and thcream till I'm thick.

Violet Elizabeth Bott, in *Still William*, ch. 8 (1925). Violet, who demands that William 'play houth' with her, is renowned for her scream: in *William in Trouble* it would apparently 'have put a factory siren to shame' and was 'guaranteed to reduce anyone within ten yards of it to quite an expensive nervous breakdown'.

2 I like you better than *any* insect, Joan.

William, in ibid., ch. 14. William explains his intention to marry Joan, the girl next door, as long as he wasn't expected 'to talk a lot of soppy stuff'.

3 There's Conservatives an' they want to make things better by keepin' 'em jus' like what they are now. An' there's Lib'rals an' they want to make things better by alterin' them jus' a bit, but not so's anyone'd notice, an' there's communists an' they want to make things better by killin' everyone but themselves.

Henry, in *William the Bad*, ch. 3 (1930)

## David Cronenberg (b. 1943)
CANADIAN FILM-MAKER

An expert perpetrator of outlandish and experimental horror films, often on the subject of a biological disaster, he has achieved cult status with *The Dead Zone* (1983), *The Fly* (1986) and the controversial *Crash* (1996). Of himself, he has commented, 'I don't have a moral code. I'm a Canadian.'

1 Everybody's a mad scientist, and life is their lab. We're all trying to experiment to find a way to live, to solve problems, to fend off madness and chaos.

*Cronenberg On Cronenberg*, ch. 1 (ed. Chris Rodley, 1992)

2 I think of horror films as art, as films of confrontation. Films that make you confront aspects of your own life that are difficult to face. Just because you're making a horror film doesn't mean you can't make an artful film.

ibid. ch. 4

3 Censors tend to do what only psychotics do: they confuse reality with illusion.

ibid. ch. 5

## Bing Crosby (1903–77)

US SINGER AND ACTOR

Hugely popular throughout a career spanning fifty years, he was known for his rich, crooning voice and roles in light comedy. His version of the song 'White Christmas' (see IRVING BERLIN 6) (1942) sold over 30 million copies. With BOB HOPE and Dorothy Lamour, he starred in the *Road to . . .* comedy series; other films include *Going My Way* (1944), for which he won an Oscar, and *High Society* (1956).

> 1 **He was an average guy who could carry a tune.**
>
> Suggested epitaph for himself, in *Newsweek* 24 October 1977

## Tony Crosland (1918–77)

BRITISH POLITICIAN

Considered Labour's leading intellectual in his time, he became an MP in 1950 and was author of the influential analysis of his party's role *The Future of Socialism* (1956). He held five ministerial positions before his sudden death ten months after becoming Foreign Secretary.

> 1 **If it's the last thing I do, I'm going to destroy every fucking grammar school in England. And Wales. And Northern Ireland.**
>
> Quoted in *Tony Crosland*, ch. 16 (1982). Said to his wife *c.* 1965, when Crosland was secretary for education and science. 'The school system in Britain remains the most divisive, unjust, and wasteful of all aspects of social equality,' he wrote in *The Future of Socialism*.

## Amanda Cross See CAROLYN HEILBRUN.

## Richard Crossman (1907–74)

BRITISH POLITICIAN

Elected Labour MP for Coventry East in 1945, he held cabinet posts in the government of HAROLD WILSON. He is chiefly remembered for the detailed political diary which he kept from 1952 and which was published posthumously in four volumes, despite attempts at suppression. Bessie Braddock described him as 'a man of many opinions, most of them of short duration'.

> 1 **My Minister's room is like a padded cell, and in certain ways I am like a person who is suddenly certified a lunatic and put safely into this great, vast room, cut off from real life and surrounded by male and female trained nurses and attendants. When I am in a good mood they occasionally allow an ordinary human being to come and visit me; but they make sure that I behave right, and that the other person behaves right; and they know how to handle me. Of course, they don't behave *quite* like nurses because the Civil Service is profoundly deferential – 'Yes, Minister! No, Minister! If you wish it, Minister!'**
>
> Journal entry 22 October 1964, after his first week in the Cabinet as Minister of Housing, publ. in *The Crossman Diaries* (1979). Probably the source for the title of the TV series by ANTONY JAY and JONATHAN LYNN, *Yes Minister* (1980–82) and *Yes, Prime Minister* (1986–8), depicting a minister's relationship with the Civil Service.

## Kieran Crowley

US JOURNALIST

A *New York Post* reporter since 1978, he has specialized in the coverage of murders and has written the 'true crime' books *Sleep Little Dead* (1997) and *Burned Alive* (1999), as well as short fiction.

> 1 **I realize that to many ageing flower children it is heresy to say it, but the Woodstock festival was a catastrophe mitigated only by the camaraderie often seen at floods or train crashes.**
>
> Quoted in the *Daily Telegraph* 18 August 1989

## Dan Cruickshank (b. 1949)

BRITISH ARCHITECTURAL CRITIC

A specialist in Georgian architecture. he has worked as features editor of the *Architects' Journal* and published books including *Rape of Britain* (1975) and *Life in the Georgian City* (1989).

> 1 **In short, the building becomes a theatrical demonstration of its functional ideal. In this romanticism, High-Tech architecture is, of course, no different in spirit – if totally different in form – from all the romantic architecture of the past.**
>
> *Commerce and Culture*, ch. 4, 'Tradition' (ed. Stephen Bayley, 1989)

## Robert Crumb (b. 1943)

US CARTOONIST

One of the most influential comic-book artists in America, he was a product of the 1960s whose creations came to define a hippy subculture of political emancipation and sexual freedom. His *Zap* (from 1967) is regarded as the first underground comic book. A film of his life, *Crumb*, was made in 1996.

> 1 **Keep on truckin' . . . truckin' on down the line . . . hey, hey, hey**
>
> **I said keep on truckin' . . . truckin' my blues away.**
>
> Caption to cartoon first publ. in *Zap Comix* no. 1 (1967), repr. in *R. Crumb's Head Comix* (1968; rev. 1988). The cartoon showed various large-booted characters walking through the city. 'Keep on truckin'' became one of the key hippy slogans of the 1960s and 1970s, and was the subject of litigation proceedings over copyright ownership.
>
> 2 **When people are forced to deny their natural urges they get weird, twisted and mean.**
>
> Interview in *The Apex Treasury of Underground Comics* (ed. Susan Goodrick and Don Donahue, 1974)

## Billy Crystal (b. 1947)

US ACTOR

Originally a stand-up comedian, he came to public attention in the role of the first openly gay man in the US TV sitcom *Soap*. Later he established himself in films, such as *When Harry Met Sally* (1989), and on *Saturday Night Live* (1992). See also NORA EPHRON 3.

> 1 **Women need a reason to have sex. Men just need a place.**
>
> Mitch Robbins (Billy Crystal), in *City Slickers* (film, screenplay by Lowell Ganz and Babaloo Mandel, directed by Ron Underwood, 1991)

## Macaulay Culkin (b. 1980)

US ACTOR

The epitome of blond-headed cuteness, he made his stage debut at the age of four, and was the star of *Home Alone* (1990), becoming for a time one of the highest paid stars in Hollywood.

> 1 **Families suck! I wish they would all disappear.**
>
> Kevin (Macaulay Culkin), in *Home Alone* (film, screenplay by John Hughes, directed by Chris Columbus, 1990)

## E. E. Cummings (1894–1962)

US POET

Full name Edward Estlin Cummings. He won international acclaim with *The Enormous Room* (1922), an account of his wartime internment in France, but is now chiefly remembered for his poetry, either satirical or lyrical and set out in unorthodox typography.

> 1 **Humanity i love you because**
> **when you're hard up you pawn your**
> **intelligence to buy a drink**
>
> 'La Guerre no.2' in *XLI Poems* (1925)
>
> 2 **It is with roses and locomotives (not to mention acrobats**

Spring electricity Coney Island the 4th of July the eyes of mice and Niagara Falls) that my 'poems' are competing.

Foreword to *is 5* (1926)

3  next to of course god america i
love you land of the pilgrims and so forth oh
say can you see by the dawn's early my
country 'tis of centuries come and go
and are no more what of it we should worry
in every language even deafanddumb
thy sons acclaim your glorious name by gorry
by jing by gee by gosh by gum

'next to of course god america i' in ibid. (1926)

4  The tabloid newspaper actually means to the typical American of the era what the Bible is popularly supposed to have meant to the typical Pilgrim Father: *viz.* a very present help in times of trouble, plus a means of keeping out of trouble via harmless, since vicarious, indulgence in the pomps and vanities of this wicked world.

'The Tabloid Newspaper', publ. in *Vanity Fair* December 1926, repr. in *A Miscellany* (ed. George J. Firmage, 1958)

5  America makes prodigious mistakes, America has colossal faults, but one thing cannot be denied: America is always on the move. She may be going to Hell, of course, but at least she isn't standing still.

'Why I Like America', publ. in *Vanity Fair* May 1927, repr. in ibid.

6  a politician is an arse upon
which everyone has sat except a man.

*1 x 1*, 'No. 10' (1944)

7  pity this busy monster, manunkind,
not. Progress is a comfortable disease.

ibid. 'No. 14'

8  We doctors know
a hopeless case if – listen: there's a hell
of a good universe next door; let's go.

ibid. 'No. 14'

9  when man determined to destroy
himself he picked the was
of shall and finding only why
smashed it into because

ibid. 'No. 26'

10  anyone lived in a pretty how town
(with up so floating many bells down)
spring summer autumn winter
he sang his didn't he danced his did.

*50 Poems*, 'No. 29' (1949)

11  It takes three to make a child.

'Jottings', first publ. in *Wake* No. 10 (1951), repr. in *A Miscellany* (ed. George J. Firmage, 1958)

12  Knowledge is a polite word for dead but not buried imagination.

ibid.

13  for whatever we lose (like a you or a me)
it's always ourselves we find in the sea

'maggie and milly and molly and may', publ. in *95 Poems* (1958)

14  [Of New York City] The sensual mysticism of entire vertical being.

Quoted in the *Architectural Digest* September 1986

## William Thomas Cummings (1903–45)
US PRIEST

1  There are no atheists in the foxholes.

Sermon, Bataan (1942), quoted in *I Saw the Fall of the Philippines*, ch. 1 (1943) by Carlos P. Romulo. The peninsula saw ferocious fighting when it was heroically defended for three months by US and Filipino forces. Its capture by the Japanese in April 1942 was

followed by the notorious 'Bataan death march', in which thousands died.

## Mario Cuomo (b. 1932)
US POLITICIAN

A Democrat, he held office as Governor of New York (1983–94) and was regarded as a potential presidential nominee in 1984, 1988 and 1992.

1  You campaign in poetry. You govern in prose.

*New Republic* 8 April 1985

## Edwina Currie (b. 1946)
BRITISH POLITICIAN AND AUTHOR

She became Conservative MP for Derbyshire South in 1983, and while Minister for Women's Health (1986–8), her statement on salmonella in eggs caused a major food scandal. She lost her seat in 1997, since when she has built a successful career as a novelist and has a radio show on BBC Radio 5 Live.

1  Good Christian people who wouldn't dream of misbehaving will not catch Aids. My message to the businessmen of this country when they go abroad on business is that there is one thing above all they can take with them to stop them catching Aids – and that is the wife.

Speech at Runcorn, Cheshire, 12 February 1987, quoted in the *Guardian* 13 February 1987

2  Most of the egg production in this country sadly is now infected with salmonella.

TV interview, 3 March 1988. Currie's statement led to a national outcry and her resignation a fortnight later.

## Tim Curry (b. 1946)
BRITISH ACTOR

He came to prominence by recreating on celluloid his stage role in the hit rock musical *The Rocky Horror Picture Show* (1975), and has since appeared in films such as *Clue* (1986) and *The Hunt for Red October* (1990).

1  Give yourself to absolute pleasure.

Dr Frank N. Furter (Tim Curry), in *The Rocky Horror Picture Show* (film, screenplay by Jim Sharman and Richard O'Brien, based on Richard O'Brien's stage musical, directed by Jim Sharman, 1975)

## Richard Curtis (b. 1956)
BRITISH SCREENWRITER

An accomplished writer of comedy, he describes himself as a 'great campaigner for light-hearted cinema'. For TV he co-wrote the *Blackadder* (1984–9) and *Mr. Bean* (1989–95) series for Rowan Atkinson, and for the cinema had big hits with *Four Weddings and a Funeral* (1994) and *Notting Hill* (1999).

1  So basically you're saying marriage is just a way of getting out of an embarrassing pause in conversation.

Charles (Hugh Grant), in *Four Weddings and a Funeral* (film, screenplay by Richard Curtis, directed by Mike Newell, 1994). Gareth answers, 'Yup. The definitive ice-breaker.'

2  It's pretty easy. Just say 'I do' whenever anyone asks you a question.

Carrie (Andie MacDowell), in ibid.

## Lord Curzon (1859–1925)
BRITISH POLITICIAN

Described by LLOYD GEORGE as 'a supreme civil servant' and by MAX BEERBOHM as 'Britannia's butler', he was Viceroy of India 1898–1905, establishing the North West Frontier Province and the partition of Bengal. He resigned after a difference of opinion with Lord Kitchener in 1905, returned to politics in 1915 and was Foreign Secretary in the Conservative government (1919–24). A verse composed about him while he was at Oxford encapsulated one image of him: 'My name is George Nathaniel Curzon,/I am a most superior person,/My cheek is pink, my hair is sleek,/I dine at Blenheim twice a week.'

1 **Dear me, I never knew that the lower classes had such white skins.**

Attributed in *Superior Person*, ch. 12 (1969) by K. Rose. The words were supposedly said by Curzon (then touring the lines as a member of the War Cabinet during the First World War) when he saw troops bathing in beer kegs.

2 **Not even a public figure. A man of no experience. And of the utmost insignificance.**

Referring to Stanley Baldwin, quoted in *Curzon: the Last Phase*, ch. 12 (1934) by Harold Nicolson. Curzon is supposed to have made the remark on hearing that Baldwin had become Prime Minister in 1923, a post Curzon himself had long aspired to. A remark attributed to Baldwin when PM suggests his rival's rancour: 'I met Curzon in Downing Street, from whom I got the sort of greeting a corpse would give to an undertaker.'

### Edward Dahlberg (1900–1977)
US AUTHOR AND CRITIC

His travels as a hobo formed the basis for his first novels and his fictional autobiography *Because I was Flesh* (1964). In later life, he became something of a 'literary Jeremiah' attacking American materialism and modernism.

1 **The earnings of a poet could be reckoned by a metaphysician rather than a bookkeeper.**
*Alms for Oblivion*, 'For Sale' (1964)

2 **To write is a humiliation.**
*The Carnal Myth*, Introduction (1968)

### Daily Express

1 **It's that man again . . . !**
Headline in the *Daily Express* 2 May 1939, referring to HITLER. The acronym ITMA was the title of a weekly satire on BBC radio (1939–49) starring Tommy Handley

### Daily Mirror

1 **Whose finger do you want on the trigger?**
Headline in the *Daily Mirror* 21 September 1951. Warning against electing the Conservative Party into office in the coming general election.

### Dalai Lama (Tenzin Gyatso) (b. 1935)
SPIRITUAL AND TEMPORAL HEAD OF TIBET

He assumed his role as Dalai Lama in 1940 but he and his followers were forced to flee Tibet after the unsuccessful uprising against the occupying Chinese forces. He set up a government-in-exile in Dharamsala, India, and in 1989 was awarded the Nobel Prize for Peace in recognition of his nonviolent campaign to free his homeland.

1 **I have done nothing, really nothing for world peace. The only thing I do for peace is talk about it a great deal.**
Interview in the *Sunday Telegraph* 9 August 1998

### Richard J. Daley (1902–76)
US POLITICIAN

One of the last of the big city bosses, he was Democratic Mayor of Chicago from 1955 until his death, ruling through an efficient 'Daley Machine'. His control of his party in the city is thought to have ensured the return of JOHN KENNEDY in the presidential election of 1960.

1 **The policeman isn't there to create disorder; the policeman is there to preserve disorder.**
To the press, on the riots during the Democratic Convention in 1968, quoted in *Don't Make No Waves: Don't Back No Losers* (1975) by Milton N. Rakove. Daley was well known for his malapropisms. Others include: 'Ladies and gentlemen of the League of Women Voters' and 'It is amazing what they will be able to do once they get the atom harassed'.

### Salvador Dali (1904–89)
SPANISH PAINTER

After joining the Paris Surrealists in 1928, he became the most high-profile member of the group, to the extent that they later spurned him. His painting followed his 'paranoiac critical' method, featuring subconscious dream images juxtaposed with the Catalan landscape of his youth. 'The Persistence of Memory' (better known as 'Limp Watches', 1931) is probably his best known work. For ANDRÉ BRETON 'Dali is like a man who hesitates between talent and genius, or, as one might once have said, between vice and virtue.'

1 **Picasso is Spanish, I am too. Picasso is a genius. I am**

too. Picasso will be seventy-two and I about forty-eight. Picasso is known in every country of the world; so am I. Picasso is a Communist; I am not.

Lecture in Madrid, 12 October 1951, quoted in *Dali*, ch. 12 (1992) by Meredith Etherington Smith. Dali's lecture contained an apology to the Spanish Left who had branded him a coward and renegade during the Spanish Civil War, and he condemned Picasso's espousal of communism and his absence from Spain.

2 There is only one difference between a madman and me. I am not mad.

Journal entry May 1952, in *Diary of a Genius* (1966)

3 Don't bother about being modern. Unfortunately it is the one thing that, whatever you do, you cannot avoid.

Journal entry 15 July 1952, in ibid. (1966)

4 I seated ugliness on my knee, and almost immediately grew tired of it.

Entry 1 August 1953, in ibid. Dali's words echo those of Rimbaud: 'One evening I sat Beauty on my knees – And I found her bitter – And I reviled her' (*Une Saison en enfer*, 1874)

5 This grandiose tragedy that we call modern art.

*Dali by Dali*, 'The Futuristic Dali' (1970)

## Daniel Daly (1874–1937)

GUNNERY SERGEANT, US MARINES

1 Come on you sons of bitches! Do you want to live for ever?

Attributed, at Belleau Wood, 4 June 1918. A similar exhortation was said to have been made by Frederick the Great, 18 June 1757, when rallying his troops at Kolin, Bohemia.

## Mary Daly (b. 1928)

US writer and theologian

Influenced by feminism, her book *The Church and the Second Sex* (1968) was a critique on the male bias in the Roman Catholic church, while *Beyond God the Father* (1973) and *Pure Lust: Elemental Feminist Philosophy* (1984) presented a more radical feminist point of view.

1 If God is male, then male is God. The divine patriarch castrates women as long as he is allowed to live on in the human imagination.

*Beyond God the Father*, ch. 1 (1973)

## Serge Daney (1944–92)

FRENCH FILM CRITIC

Called one of France's greatest film critics, he wrote his first article for *Cahiers du Cinema* in 1964 and became its Editor 1973–81. During the 1980s he wrote a regular film column for *Libération*. He has also written on tennis and television.

1 In an age of synthetic images and synthetic emotions, the chances of an accidental encounter with reality are remote indeed.

'Falling out of Love', publ. in *Sight and Sound* July 1992

## Joe Darion (b. 1917)

US SONGWRITER

He was the lyricist for a number of Broadway musical shows in the 1960s, most successful of which was *Man of La Mancha* (1965, filmed 1972). Darion also wrote lyrics for the 1967 musical *Ilya Darling*, and the libretto for *The Trials of Galileo*, an opera-oratorio first broadcast on TV in 1967, later staged as *Galileo Galilei* (1975).

1 To dream the impossible dream,
To reach the unreachable star!

'The Impossible Dream' (song, 1965, music by Mitch Leigh). The song (as sung by Simon Gilbert) was dubbed onto the film *Man of La Mancha* (1972, adapted from the 1965 musical play by Darion

and Mitch Leigh) for PETER O'TOOLE to sing, in the role of Don Quixote.

## Linda Darnell (1921–65)

US SCREEN ACTRESS

Original name Monetta Eloisa Darnell. She was one of Hollywoood's most popular leading ladies of the 1940s, her exotic beauty decorating such films as *It Happened Tomorrow* (1944). JOAN COLLINS said of her: 'She was a firm believer in moving her facial muscles as little as possible.' She perished in a fire while watching a re-run of one of her old movies on TV.

1 I used to live in a sewer. Now I live in a swamp. I've come up in the world.

Edie Johnson (Linda Darnell), in *No Way Out* (film, screenplay by Lesser Samuels and Joseph L. Mankiewicz, directed by Joseph L. Mankiewicz, 1950).

## Charles Brace Darrow (1889–1967)

US INVENTOR

When Parker Bros rejected his game Monopoly in the early 1930s, he proceeded to produce it himself. As it proved popular Parker Bros reconsidered in 1935, since when over 200 million sets in twenty-six languages have been sold.

1 Go to jail. Go directly to jail. Do not pass go. Do not collect $200.

Instruction in Monopoly (1933). Monopoly was devised by Darrow c. 1931, adapted from the Landlord's Game invented by Joanna Pitman in 1904.

## Clarence Darrow (1857–1938)

US LAWYER AND WRITER

As a leading defence counsel he espoused freedom of expression and vociferously opposed capital punishment, Prohibition and segregation. Among the famous cases he defended was that of EUGENE DEBS who called the Pullman Strike (1894), and in 1925 the 'monkey trial' of John T. Scopes.

1 I do not pretend to know where many ignorant men are sure – that is all that agnosticism means.

Speech at Dayton, Tennessee, 13 July 1925, quoted in *The World's Most Famous Court Trial*, ch. 4 (1925). Darrow was defending John Thomas Scopes, on trial for teaching Darwinism. Scopes was found guilty, though the decision was later overturned by the State Supreme Court.

2 When I was a boy I was told that anybody could become President. I'm beginning to believe it.

Quoted in *Clarence Darrow for the Defence*, ch. 6 (1941) by Irving Stone

## Sir Francis Darwin (1848–1925)

BRITISH BOTANIST

Son of Charles Darwin, he is known for the publications on his father, *Life and Letters of Charles Darwin* (1887) and *More Letters of Charles Darwin* (1903), as well as his work on vegetable physiology.

1 In science the credit goes to the man who convinces the world, not to the man to whom the idea first occurs.

'Francis Galton', First Galton Lecture before the Eugenics Society, publ. in *Eugenics Review* April 1914

## René Daumal (1908–44)

FRENCH POET AND CRITIC

He was co-founder in 1928 of *Le Grand Jeu*, both a review and a quasi-mystical group which demanded, in Daumal's words, 'a revolution of reality returning to its source'. Though sharing many of the tenets of Surrealism, he broke with ANDRÉ BRETON and the Surrealists in 1930. His posthumous fame rests principally on his novels, *A Night of Serious Drinking* (1938) and *Mount Analogue* (1952). He died of TB, penniless and practically unknown.

1 **Each time dawn appears, the mystery is there in its entirety.**

'Poetry Black, Poetry White', first publ. in *Fontaine* March/April 1942, repr. in *The Powers of the Word* (ed./transl. Mark Polizzotti, 1991). *Chaque fois que l'aube paraît* was the title given to a posthumous anthology of Daumal's writings.

## Andrew Davies (b. 1936)
BRITISH SCREENWRITER

One of Britain's leading TV screenwriters, he has made skilful adaptations of *Circle of Friends* (1995), *Pride and Prejudice* (1995) and *Wives and Daughters* (1999).

1 **You might say that, my dear: I couldn't possibly comment.**

Francis Urquhart (Iain Richardson) to the journalist Mattie Storin (Susannah Harker), in *House of Cards* (TV series, 1992, written by Andrew Davies, based on the original novel by Michael Dobbs).

## Jack Davies (1913–94) and
## Ken Annakin (b. 1914)
BRITISH SCRIPTWRITER AND DIRECTOR

Davies was a comedy scriptwriter for Will Hay, Norman Wisdom and the 'Doctor' series of films. Annakin is better known as a director for such films as *Swiss Family Robinson* (1960) and *The Fast Lady* (1963).

1 **Those magnificent men in their flying machines, or How I flew from London to Paris in 25 hours and 11 minutes.**

Title of film (1965, directed by Ken Annakin). The film, from which an eponymous song was penned, was a comic account of the first London–Paris air race at the beginning of the twentieth century.

## Robertson Davies (1913–95)
CANADIAN NOVELIST AND JOURNALIST

Described as 'Jane Austen reworking Rabelais', he is known for his articles written under the pseudonym Samuel Marchbanks, and his tales of provincial university towns, small theatre companies and encounters with the 'world of wonders', as portrayed in the *Deptford Trilogy* (1970–75) and the *Cornish Trilogy* (1981–8).

1 **Nothing is so easy to fake as the inner vision.**

Saraceni, in *What's Bred in the Bone*, pt 4, 'What Would Not Out of the Flesh?' (1985)

2 **Canada is not really a place where you are encouraged to have large spiritual adventures.**

*The Enthusiasms of Robertson Davies*, 'The Table Talk of Robertson Davies' (1990)

3 **The world is burdened with young fogies. Old men with ossified minds are easily dealt with. But men who look young, act young and everlastingly harp on the fact that they are young, but who nevertheless think and act with a degree of caution that would be excessive in their grandfathers, are the curse of the world. Their very conservatism is secondhand, and they don't know what they are conserving.**

ibid.

## W. H. Davies (1871–1940)
BRITISH POET

Full name William Henry Davies. He emigrated to America in 1893, returning to England after the loss of a foot caused by 'jumping' a train. He lived as a tramp until he was over thirty, as described in his most successful work, *Autobiography of a Super-tramp* (1906), and he also published numerous collections of poetry.

1 **And hear the pleasant cuckoo, loud and long –**

**The simple bird that thinks two notes a song.**

'April's Charms', publ. in *Child Lovers* (1916)

2 **Girls scream,
Boys shout;
Dogs bark,
School's out.**

'School's Out', publ. in *The Poems of W.H. Davies* (1934)

## Angela Davis (b. 1944)
US PHILOSOPHER AND POLITICAL ACTIVIST

She combined an academic career with a commitment to black rights and the release of African-American political prisoners. She gained international publicity in 1970, when after a long trial she was acquitted of the charge of supplying guns for the murder of a judge. In 1980 she was the Communist vice-presidential candidate.

1 **No potential victim of the fascist terror should be without the knowledge that the greatest menace to racism and fascism is unity!**

*If They Come in the Morning . . .*, pt 2, 'Political Prisoners, Prisons and Black Liberation' (1971)

## Bette Davis (1908–89)
US SCREEN ACTRESS

Born Ruth Elizabeth Davis, she played strong, independent roles for more than five decades, memorably opposite Joan Crawford in *Whatever Happened to Baby Jane?* (1962). She won Oscars for *Dangerous* (1935) and *Jezebel* (1938), and was the first woman to receive the Life Achievement Award of the American Film Institute (1977). JACK L. WARNER remembered her as 'an explosive little broad with a straight left'.

1 **What a dump!**

Rosa Moline (Bette Davis) in *Beyond the Forest* (film, 1949, screenplay by Leonore Coffee based on a novel by Stuart Engstrand, directed by King Vidor). The line, which is spoken by Bette Davis about her small-town Wisconsin home that she dreams of escaping, was famously used in EDWARD ALBEE's *Who's Afraid of Virginia Woolf?* (1962). In the film version of this (1966), Martha (Elizabeth Taylor) mimics Bette Davis's voice. According to Davis, 'this is the only claim to fame that the film [*Beyond the Forest*] had or ever will have.'

2 **Oh, Jerry, don't let's ask for the moon – we have the stars.**

Charlotte Vale (Bette Davis), in *Now, Voyager* (film, screenplay by Casey Robinson based on the novel by Olive Higgins Prouty, directed by Irving Rapper, 1942). The movie's title is taken from Walt Whitman's *Leaves of Grass*.

3 **Fasten your seat belts. It's going to be a bumpy night.**

Margo Channing (Bette Davis), bracing for a rocky party, in *All About Eve* (film, written and directed by Joseph L. Mankiewicz, 1950)

4 **To look back is to relax one's vigil.**

*The Lonely Life*, ch. 1 (autobiography, 1962)

5 **I see – she's the original good time that was had by all.**

Attributed in *Parade* 15 February 1981, referring to a starlet

## Geena Davis (b. 1957)
US ACTRESS

Called 'a feminist spirit in the body of a goddess', she won an Oscar for her role in *The Accidental Tourist* (1988) and acclaim for the women's road movie *Thelma and Louise* (1991).

1 **[On sex] I finally understand what all the fuss is about now. It's just like a whole other ball game.**

Thelma (Geena Davis), in *Thelma and Louise* (film, screenplay by Callie Khouri, directed and co-produced by Ridley Scott, 1991)

## Miles Davis (1926–91)

US JAZZ MUSICIAN

Probably the most influential post-war jazz stylist and a superb trumpet player, he pioneered 'cool' jazz (with the album *Birth of the Cool*, 1949), modal improvisation (*Kind of Blue*, 1959), and jazz-rock fusion (*Bitches' Brew*, 1970). At the end of his career he experimented with rap rhythms.

1 I've come close to matching the feeling of that night in 1944 in music, when I first heard Diz and Bird, but I've never got there . . . I'm always looking for it, listening and feeling for it, though, trying to always feel it in and through the music I play everyday.

*Miles: The Autobiography*, Prologue (1989). Referring to Dizzy Gillespie and Charlie 'Bird' Parker.

2 A legend is an old man with a cane known for what he used to do. I'm still doing it.

*International Herald Tribune* 17 July 1991

## Sammy Davis Jr (1925–90)

US ENTERTAINER

Described by himself as a 'one-eyed Jewish Negro', he was an accomplished singer, tap dancer, musician, mime and comedian. After pursuing a successful night-club career, he starred in Broadway musicals such as *Mr. Wonderful* (1956), and also appeared in films including *Robin and the Seven Hoods* (1964), with fellow 'rat-pack' members FRANK SINATRA and Dean Martin, and *Sweet Charity* (1968).

1 Being a star has made it possible for me to get insulted in places where the average Negro could never hope to go and get insulted.

*Yes I Can*, pt 3, ch. 23 (1965)

## Richard Dawkins (b. 1941)

BRITISH BIOLOGIST AND AUTHOR

Described as 'our most radical Darwinian thinker', and known as a fervent atheist, he has become a successful popularizer of sociobiology and science, introducing the concepts of the 'selfish gene' and the 'meme' (the cultural counterpart of the gene). In 1995 he became the first Professor of Public Understanding of Science at Oxford. See also CHARLES, PRINCE OF WALES 10.

1 Much as we might wish to believe otherwise, universal love and the welfare of the species as a whole are concepts which simply do not make evolutionary sense.

*The Selfish Gene*, ch. 1 (1976)

2 They are in you and in me; they created us, body and mind; and their preservation is the ultimate rationale for our existence – they go by the name of genes, and we are their survival machines.

ibid. ch. 2

3 Natural selection, the blind, unconscious, automatic process which Darwin discovered, and which we now know is the explanation for the existence and apparently purposeful form of all life, has no purpose in mind. It has no mind and no mind's eye. It does not plan for the future. It has no vision, no foresight, no sight at all. If it can be said to play the role of the watchmaker in nature, it is the *blind* watchmaker.

*The Blind Watchmaker*, ch. 1 (1986)

4 However many ways there may be of being alive, it is certain that there are vastly more ways of being dead.

ibid.

5 The essence of life is statistical improbability on a colossal scale.

ibid. ch. 11

6 The universe we observe has precisely the properties we

should expect if there is, at bottom, no design, no purpose, no evil and no good, nothing but blind, pitiless indifference . . . DNA neither cares nor knows. DNA just is. And we dance to its music.

*River Out of Eden*, ch. 4 (1995)

7 We are going to die, and that makes us the lucky ones. Most people are never going to die because they are never going to be born.

*Unweaving the Rainbow*, ch. 1 (1998). Opening lines of book.

8 The spirit of wonder which led Blake to Christian mysticism, Keats to Arcadian myth and Yeats to Fenians and fairies, is the very same spirit that moves great scientists; a spirit which, if fed back to poets in scientific guise, might inspire still greater poetry.

ibid. ch. 2

## Christopher Dawson (1889–1970)

BRITISH HISTORIAN

An esteemed Catholic scholar, he published works on European history, culture and religion including *The Age of the Gods* (1928), *The Making of Europe* (1932) and *Religion and Culture* (1948).

1 As soon as men decide that all means are permitted to fight an evil, then their good becomes indistinguishable from the evil that they set out to destroy.

*The Judgement of the Nations* (1942)

## Lord Dawson of Penn (1864–1945)

BRITISH PHYSICIAN

Full name Bertrand Edward Dawson, Viscount Dawson of Penn. He was physician to King George V (1914–36), saving his life in 1928. He strongly believed in the promotion of the nation's health and in 1944 was a member of the committee to draw up a white paper for the inception of the National Health Service.

1 The King's life is moving peacefully towards its close.

Bulletin on the eve of the king's death, 20 January 1936, in *King George V*, ch. 1 (1983) by Kenneth Rose. The wording was supposedly drafted on a menu card at Buckingham Palace.

## Dorothy Day (1897–1980)

US WRITER AND REFORMER

A socialist, pacifist and Catholic convert, she co-founded the *Catholic Worker* in 1933 and established the Catholic Worker movement, which helped provide victims of the Depression with accommodation and work on community farms.

1 Tradition! We scarcely know the word anymore. We are afraid to be either proud of our ancestors or ashamed of them. We scorn nobility in name and in fact. We cling to a bourgeois mediocrity which would make it appear we are all Americans, made in the image and likeness of George Washington.

*The Long Loneliness*, pt 1 (1952)

2 The best thing to do with the best things in life is to give them up.

Quoted in *Time* 29 December 1975

## (Sir) Robin Day (1915–2000)

BRITISH JOURNALIST AND BROADCASTER

Known for his formidable interviewing techniques and his dotted bow-ties, he presented the BBC television programmes *Panorama* (1967–72) and *Question Time* (1979–89), and for radio *The World at One* (1979–87). He published . . . *But With Respect – Memorable Interviews* in 1993.

1 Television thrives on unreason, and unreason thrives on

television. It strikes at the emotions rather than the intellect.

*Financial Times* 8 November 1989

2 I am in the departure lounge of life; my only hope is that my plane will be delayed.

Speech at the Oxford Union, quoted in the *Daily Telegraph* 21 February 1998

## Cecil Day Lewis (1904–72)

BRITISH POET

In the 1930s his social poetry was influenced by the radical of ideas of W.H. AUDEN and his circle, but after the Second World War he became more of an Establishment figure, holding the post of Poet Laureate from 1968. He was professor of Poetry at Oxford (1951–6), wrote literary criticism, and, under the name of Nicholas Blake, detective fiction.

1 Desire is a witch
And runs against the clock.
It can unstitch
The decent hem
Where space tacks on to time;
It can unlock
Pandora's privacies.

*Transitional Poem*, pt 2 (1929)

2 With me, my lover makes
The clock assert its chime:
But when she goes, she takes
The mainspring out of time.

ibid. pt 3, sect. 27

3 Tempt me no more; for I
Have known the lightning's hour,
The poet's inward pride,
The certainty of power.

*The Magnetic Mountain*, sect. 24 (1933)

4 You that love England, who have an ear for her music,
The slow movement of clouds in benediction,
Clear arias of light thrilling over her uplands,
Over the chords of summer sustained peacefully.

ibid. sect. 32

5 We'd like to fight but we fear defeat,
We'd like to work but we're feeling too weak,
We'd like to be sick but we'd get the sack,
We'd like to behave, we'd like to believe,
We'd like to love, but we've lost the knack.

ibid. sect. 33

6 It is the logic of our times,
No subject for immortal verse –
That we who lived by honest dreams
Defend the bad against the worse.

'Where are the War Poets?', publ. in *Word Over All* (1943)

7 Hurry! We burn
For Rome so near us, for the Phoenix moment
When we have thrown off this traveller's trance,
And mother-naked and ageless-ancient
Wake in her warm nest of renaissance.

*An Italian Visit*, pt 2, 'Flight to Italy' (written 1948–9, publ. 1953)

8 I went to school with a glee of dolphins
Bowling their hoops round the brine tongued isles.

ibid. pt 5, 'Florence: Works of Art'

## Daniel Day Lewis (b. 1957)

BRITISH ACTOR

The son of CECIL DAY LEWIS, he gained critical acclaim for his role in *My Beautiful Laundrette* (1985) and won an Oscar for his portrayal of the handicapped writer Christy Brown in *My Left Foot* (1989).

1 Being at the centre of a film is a burden one takes on with innocence – the first time. Thereafter, you take it on with trepidation.

Interview in *City Limits* 7 April 1988

2 The thing about performance, even if it's only an illusion, is that it is a celebration of the fact that we do contain within ourselves infinite possibilities.

Interview in *Rolling Stone* 8 February 1990

## Simone de Beauvoir (1908–86)

FRENCH PHILOSOPHER AND AUTHOR

She is celebrated as a feminist and existentialist, and also known for her lifelong association with JEAN-PAUL SARTRE, with whom she founded the review *Les Temps modernes* (1945). Her most influential work, *The Second Sex* (1949), became a classic of feminism in the 1960s and even a 'sacred monster'. *The Mandarins* (1954) won her the Prix Goncourt.

1. It is not in giving life but in risking life that man is raised above the animal; that is why superiority has been accorded in humanity not to the sex that brings forth but to that which kills.

*The Second Sex*, bk 1, pt 2, ch. 1 (1949)

2 One is not born, but rather becomes, a woman.

ibid. bk 2, pt 4, ch. 1. The feminist critic ANDREA DWORKIN was perhaps alluding to De Beauvoir's famous statement when she wrote: 'Woman is not born: she is made. In the making, her humanity is destroyed. She becomes symbol of this, symbol of that: mother of the earth, slut of the universe; but she never becomes herself because it is forbidden for her to do so.' (*Pornography*, ch. 4, 1981)

3 To *make* oneself an object, to *make* oneself passive, is a very different thing from *being* a passive object.

ibid. bk 2, pt 4, ch. 3

4 Sex pleasure in woman . . . is a kind of magic spell; it demands complete abandon; if words or movements oppose the magic of caresses, the spell is broken.

ibid.

5 Between women love is contemplative; caresses are intended less to gain possession of the other than gradually to re-create the self through her; separateness is abolished, there is no struggle, no victory, no defeat; in exact reciprocity each is at once subject and object, sovereign and slave; duality become mutuality.

ibid. bk 2, pt 4, ch. 4

6 The curse which lies upon marriage is that too often the individuals are joined in their weakness rather than in their strength – each asking from the other instead of finding pleasure in giving. It is even more deceptive to dream of gaining through the child a plenitude, a warmth, a value, which one is unable to create for oneself; the child brings joy only to the woman who is capable of disinterestedly desiring the happiness of another, to one who without being wrapped up in self seeks to transcend her own existence.

ibid. bk 2, pt 5, ch.2

7 Since it is the Other within us who is old, it is natural that the revelation of our age should come to us from outside – from others. We do not accept it willingly.

*The Coming of Age*, pt 2, ch. 5 (1970)

8 It is old age, rather than death, that is to be contrasted with life. Old age is life's parody, whereas death transforms life into a destiny: in a way it preserves it by giving it the absolute dimension . . . Death does away with time.

*The Coming of Age*, Conclusion (1970)

## Louis de Bernières (b. 1951)
BRITISH NOVELIST

His stories are concerned with issues of freedom, power and ideology, as in his phenomenally successful *Captain Corelli's Mandolin* (1994). Among his other books are *The War of Don Emmanuel's Nether Parts* (1990) and *Señor Vivo and the Coca Lord* (1992).

1 A guilty man wishes only to be understood, because to be understood is to appear to be forgiven.
Carlo, in *Captain Corelli's Mandolin*, ch. 10 (1994)

2 It's a fact of life that the honour of a family derives from the conduct of its women. I don't know why this is, and possibly matters are different elsewhere. But we live here, and I note the fact scientifically in the same way that I observe that there is snow on Mt Aenos in January and that we have no rivers.
Dr Iannis, in ibid. ch. 47

3 Italians always act without thinking, it's the glory and the downfall of your civilization. A German plans a month in advance what his bowel movements will be at Easter, and the British plan everything in retrospect, so it always looks as though everything occurred as they intended. The French plan everything whilst appearing to be having a party, and the Spanish . . . well, God knows.
Dr Iannis to Captain Corelli, in ibid. ch. 49

4 Every Greek, man, woman, and child, has two Greeks inside. We even have technical terms for them. They are a part of us, as inevitable as the fact that we all write poetry and the fact that every one of us thinks that he knows everything that there is to know.
ibid. The two types, Iannis explained, corresponded to the 'Hellene' and the 'Romoi'.

5 God is an oppressor, He is incapable of human sympathy; behind a smiling face He hides an evil heart.
*The Book of Job*, Introduction (1998)

6 The real index of civilization is when people are kinder than they need be.
Robert, in 'The Turks Are So Wonderful With Children', publ. in the *Guardian* 1 January 2000

## Joost de Blank (1908–68)
SOUTH AFRICAN CHURCHMAN

Archbishop of Cape Town 1957–63.

1 Christ in this country would quite likely have been arrested under the Suppression of Communism Act.
Quoted in the *Observer* 27 October 1963

## Edward De Bono (b. 1933)
BRITISH PSYCHOLOGIST

His concept of 'lateral thinking', a creative approach to problem solving, devoid of preconceptions, was first propounded in *The Use of Lateral Thinking* (1967) and has since been widely used in business and management studies.

1 Some people are aware of another sort of thinking which . . . leads to those simple ideas that are obvious only after they have been thought of . . . the term 'lateral thinking' has been coined to describe this other sort of thinking; 'vertical thinking' is used to denote the conventional logical process.
*The Use of Lateral Thinking*, Foreword (1967)

2 Unhappiness is best defined as the difference between our talents and our expectations.
Quoted in the *Observer* 12 June 1977

3 Humour is by far the most significant activity of the human brain.
*Daily Mail* 29 January 1990

## Michel de Certeau (1925–86)
FRENCH AUTHOR AND CRITIC

Trained as a psychoanalytic theorist linked to the Freudian school of Paris, he was also an erudite historian, ethnologist, and former Jesuit priest. Holding academic posts in Paris and California, he became a respected postmodern cultural critic whose influential publications included *The Practice of Everyday Life* (1974) and *La Fable mystique* (1982).

1 The only freedom supposed to be left to the masses is that of grazing on the ration of simulacra the system distributes to each individual.
*The Practice of Everyday Life*, ch. 12 (1974)

## Malcolm de Chazal (1902–81)
FRENCH WRITER

From semi-isolation on Mauritius he wrote *Sens plastique* (1946), which described the sexual act as a mediator between birth and death and caused a sensation when published in Paris. His later works, such as *La Bible du mal* (1952), discuss mystical subjects.

1 The idealist walks on tiptoe, the materialist on his heels.
*Sens plastique*, vol. 2 (1946)

## Luciano De Crescenzo (b. 1928)
ITALIAN AUTHOR

His varied career has taken in spells as cartoonist, IBM executive, photographer and scriptwriter. His publications include *Thus Spake Bellavista* (1977), an account of Naples, and *History of Greek Philosophy: The Pre-Socratics* (1983).

1 A Neapolitan will tell you that he has never paid to watch a football match with as much pride as if he were telling you, for instance, that his ancestors fought in the Crusades. If, on the other hand, anyone in Naples finds himself having to pay for a ticket, it means he's a failure, he knows nobody and counts for nothing.
Antonio Caramanna, in *Thus Spake Bellavista*, ch. 6 (1977, transl. 1988)

## Lee De Forest (1873–1961)
US PHYSICIST AND INVENTOR

Known as the 'father of radio' and the 'grandfather of television', it was his invention of the Audion vacuum tube in 1906 that facilitated live radio broadcasting (1910), and subsequently contributed to the development of radio, telephone, radar, television and computers.

1 You have debased [my] child . . . You have made him a laughing-stock of intelligence . . . a stench in the nostrils of the gods of the ionosphere.
Speech to National Association of Broadcasters, quoted in obituary in *Time* 7 July 1961

## Charles De Gaulle (1890–1970)
FRENCH GENERAL AND PRESIDENT

After organizing the Free French movement from Britain during the Second World War, he led the provisional French government (1944–6) and was architect and first president of the Fifth Republic (1958–69). His domestic policy was guided by the extensive use of referenda, while abroad he oversaw the granting of independence to the African colonies and Algeria. He quelled the student riots of 1968 and was re-elected in the same year, to resign in 1969

1 Nothing strengthens authority so much as silence.

Quoted in *The Art of Living*, 'The Art of Leadership' (1940) by André Maurois

2 France has lost a battle. But France has not lost the war!

Speech in London, broadcast 18 June 1940, publ. in *Speeches of General de Gaulle* (1941). De Gaulle's famous words were not part of the official typescript for this speech, and not issued in written form until the following month.

3 Since they whose duty it was to wield the sword of France have let it fall shattered to the ground, I have taken up the broken blade.

Speech, 13 July 1940, publ. in *Discours et messages* (1942)

4 Now she is like everybody else. (*Maintenant elle est comme les autres.*)

Remark at the funeral of his handicapped daughter, Anne, 1948, quoted in *De Gaulle*, ch. 8 (1965) by Jean Lacouture. De Gaulle was devoted to his daughter, who had Down's Syndrome. 'Without Anne,' he explained, 'perhaps I should not have done all that I have done. She made me understand so many things. She gave me so much heart and spirit.'

5 I have understood you. (*Je vous ai compris.*)

Speech at Algiers, 4 June 1958, publ. in *Discours et messages*, vol. 3 (1970). De Gaulle was addressing French settlers, whose interests had shortly before been championed by General Raoul Salan after years of resistance to Algerian nationalists. De Gaulle was granted emergency powers to resolve the crisis.

6 Old France, weighed down with history, prostrated by wars and revolutions, endlessly vacillating from greatness to decline, but revived, century after century, by the genius of renewal!

*War Memoirs*, vol. 3, ch. 7 (1959)

7 In the tumult of men and events, solitude was my temptation; now it is my friend. What other satisfaction can be sought once you have confronted History?

ibid.

8 Politics are too serious a matter to be left to the politicians.

Quoted in *Attlee: A Prime Minister Remembers*, ch. 4 (1961). De Gaulle was responding to CLEMENT ATTLEE's remark that 'De Gaulle is a very good soldier and a very bad politician.'

9 How can anyone govern a nation that has two hundred and forty-six different kinds of cheese?

Quoted in *Newsweek* 1 October 1962. Speaking of France.

10 I respect only those who resist me; but I cannot tolerate them.

Quoted in *The New York Times Magazine* 12 May 1966

11 *Vive le Québec Libre!*
Long live Free Quebec!

Speech at Montreal, 24 July 1967, publ. in *Speeches of General de Gaulle* (1970). His rallying call aroused huge controversy, appearing to advocate the cause of Quebec separatists.

12 No country without an atom bomb could properly consider itself independent.

Quoted in *The New York Times* 12 May 1968

13 One does not arrest Voltaire.

Quoted in *Encounter* June 1975. Referring to the inflammatory Communist activities of JEAN-PAUL SARTRE during the 1960s.

14 We are not here to laugh.
(*On n'est pas là pour rigoler.*)

Said on frequent occasions, quoted in *Independent* 21 April 1990 on the centenary of De Gaulle's birth

## F.W. de Klerk (b. 1936)

SOUTH AFRICAN POLITICIAN AND PRESIDENT

Full name Frederik Willem de Klerk. Shortly after succeeding P.W. BOTHA as leader of the National Party, he became President (1989–94) and began the process of dismantling apartheid and negotiating a transition to majority rule. In 1990 he lifted the ban on the African National Congress (ANC) and released NELSON MANDELA, with whom in 1993 he received the Nobel Prize for Peace for establishing a non-racial democracy. He served as Vice-President in the Mandela administration (1994–6).

1 Today we have closed the book on apartheid.

Quoted in the *Independent* 19 March 1992. Referring to the results of the referendum endorsing his proposals for constitutional and political reform.

2 We have gone on our knees before God Almighty to pray for His forgiveness.

Apologising for apartheid, quoted in the *Observer* 25 August 1996. De Klerk's attitude contrasted starkly with Botha's (see P.W. BOTHA 2).

## Willem De Kooning (1904–97)

DUTCH-BORN US ARTIST

By the 1950s he was, with JACKSON POLLOCK, the leader of the Abstract Expressionist movement, centred in New York. A superb draughtsman, his work alternated between the abstract and figurative, usually with the female form in mind, as in the *Women* series (1950–53).

1 Whatever an artist's personal feelings are, as soon as an artist fills a certain area on the canvas or circumscribes it, he becomes historical. He acts from or upon other artists.

'A Desperate View', paper delivered to friends in New York 18 February 1949, first publ. in *William de Kooning* (1968) by Thomas B. Hess

2 The attitude that nature is chaotic and that the artist puts order into it is a very absurd point of view, I think. All that we can hope for is to put some order into ourselves.

'The Renaissance and Order', lecture in New York, 1950, publ. in *Collected Writings* (ed. George Scrivani, 1988)

3 If you pick up some paint with your brush and make somebody's nose with it, this is rather ridiculous when you think of it, theoretically or philosophically. It's really absurd to make an image, like a human image, with paint, today.

'Painting As Self Discovery', interview 30 December 1960, first publ. in *Location* Spring 1963 as 'Content Is A Glimpse . . .' quoted in *William de Kooning* (1988) by Diane Waldman

## Walter de la Mare (1873–1956)

BRITISH POET AND NOVELIST

He was placed by DYLAN THOMAS in a compartment marked 'Subtlety and Sensitivity. Perishable. With Care', and admired by AUDEN for the 'graceful architecture of his stanzas'. His lyrical writing reflects his preoccupation with fantasy and the imaginative world of childhood. He wrote for both children and adults, and edited a number of anthologies, including the highly rated *Come Hither* (1923). For RANDALL JARRELL, 'De la Mare's world is neither the best nor the worst but the most enchanted of all possible worlds.'

1 A face peered. All the grey night
In chaos of vacancy shone;
Nought but vast Sorrow was there –
The sweet cheat gone.

'The Ghost', publ. in *Motley and Other Poems* (1918)

2 Look thy last on all things lovely,
Every hour. Let no night
Seal thy sense in deadly slumber
Till to delight
Thou have paid thy utmost blessing;
Since that all things thou wouldst praise
Beauty took from those who loved them
In other days.

'Fare Well', publ. in ibid.

3 How shall I know that the end of things is coming?

The drummers will be drumming; the fiddlers at their
    thrumming;
Nuns at their beads; the mummers at their mumming;
Heaven's solemn Seraph stoopt weary o'er his summing;
The palsied fingers plucking, the way-worn feet
    numbing –
And the end of things coming.

'A Sign', publ. in *The Veil and Other Poems* (1921)

4 Hi! handsome hunting man
Fire your little gun.
Bang! Now the animal
Is dead and dumb and done.

'Hi!', publ. in *Poems for Children* (1930)

5 In the long drouth of life,
Its transient wilderness,
The mindless euthanasia of a kiss

Reveals that in
An instant's beat
Two souls in flesh confined
May yet in an immortal freedom meet.

'The Kiss', first publ. in *The Saturday Book* (1947), repr. in *Inward Companion: Poems* (1950)

## Lothar de Maizière (b. 1940)

GERMAN LAWYER AND POLITICIAN

Leader of the Christian Democratic Union (1989–90), he became the first democratically elected premier of East Germany in 1990 and as such negotiated the country's unification with West Germany. He resigned later in 1990 from the KOHL cabinet after allegations that he had been a member of the East German secret police.

1 The era of long parades past an official podium filled with cold faces is gone. Celebrating is now a right, not a duty.

Speech 1 May 1990, quoted in the *Independent* 5 May 1990. Referring to the fall of Communism, said while East German prime minister.

## Paul de Man (1919–83)

BELGIAN-BORN US LITERARY CRITIC

After emigrating to America following the Second World War, he taught at universities including Yale, where he became a leading advocate of deconstruction. His essays were published in *Blindness and Insight* (1971) and *Allegories of Reading* (1979).

1 Curiously enough, it seems to be only in describing a mode of language which does not mean what it says that one can actually say what one means.

'The Rhetoric of Temporality', sect. 2, first publ. in *Interpretation* (ed. Charles Singelton, 1969), repr. in *Blindness and Insight* (1971, rev. 1983)

2 The critical method which denies literary modernity would appear – and even, in certain respects, would be – the most modern of critical movements.

'Literary History and Literary Modernity', lecture September 1969, repr. in ibid.

3 Literature . . . is condemned (or privileged) to be forever the most rigorous and, consequently, the most reliable of terms in which man names and transforms himself.

*Allegories Of Reading*, pt 1, ch. 1, 'Semiology And Rhetoric' (1979)

4 Death is a displaced name for a linguistic predicament.

Quoted in *Signs of the Times*, ch. 4 (1991) by David Lehman. LEHMAN called this 'the ultimate statement of the deconstructive credo'.

## Agnes De Mille (1908–93)

US CHOREOGRAPHER AND DANCER

The niece of CECIL B. DE MILLE, she danced with the Ballet Rambert, and later choreographed musicals such as *Oklahoma!*

(1943) and *Carousel* (1945). She was known as an eloquent speaker, and published books on dance including *Martha* (1991), a biography of MARTHA GRAHAM.

1 Theater people are always pining and agonizing because they're afraid that they'll be forgotten. And in America they're quite right. They will be.

Quoted in *Life* 15 November 1963

## Cecil B. De Mille (1881–1959)

US FILM DIRECTOR-PRODUCER

Full name Cecil Blount De Mille (sometimes DeMille). Known as 'the foreman in a movie factory' and 'the director to end all directors', he started out by converting a Hollwood barn into a studio for his first film *The Squaw Man* (1913). He thereby started the industry on which he left his distinctive mark, particularly with his biblical and spectacular epics, for example *The Ten Commandments* (1923, remade 1956) and *The Greatest Show on Earth* (1952).

1 The really important question to ask about a motion picture is not 'What did it cost?', but 'What is it worth?' . . . Many, in all walks of life, testified to them this film [*The Ten Commandments*] had been not a moving picture, but an experience that moved their souls. That is what a picture can be worth and that is why some pictures are worth making, whatever they cost.

*The Autobiography of Cecil B. DeMille*, ch. 11, sect. 6 (ed. Donald Hayne, 1959). Commenting on the then astronomical cost of the film *The Ten Commandments* (1923 version) at $1.5 million; it grossed over $4 million. The cost of the 1956 version of De Mille's epic, which employed 25,000 extras, was $13.5 million.

2 What I have crossed out I didn't like. What I haven't crossed out I am dissatisfied with.

Note attached to rejected script, quoted in *Halliwell's Who's Who in the Movies* (ed. John Walker, 1999)

## Robert De Niro (b. 1943)

US ACTOR

Favouring tough, working-class roles, and closely associated with the director MARTIN SCORSESE, he has starred in *The Godfather, Part II* (1974), *Raging Bull* (1980), receiving Oscars for both, and *The Deerhunter* (1978). He made his directorial début in 1993 with *A Bronx Tale*.

1 They're all animals anyway. All the criminals come out at night. Whores, skunk pussies, buggers, queens, fairies, dopers, junkies, sick, venal. Someday a *real* rain will come and wash all this scum off the streets.

Voiceover by Travis Bickle (Robert De Niro), in *Taxi Driver* (film, screenplay by Paul Schrader, directed by Martin Scorsese, 1976)

2 Better to be a king for a night than a schmuck for a lifetime.

Rupert Pupkin (Robert De Niro), in *The King of Comedy* (film, screenplay by Paul Zimmerman, directed by Martin Scorsese, 1983)

## Buddy De Sylva (1895–1950) and Lew Brown (1893–1958)

US SONGWRITERS

De Sylva (born George Gard De Sylva) and Brown caught the spirit of the jazz age with such songs as 'Black Bottom' and 'The Birth of the Blues' (1926). With the composer Ray Henderson they wrote a series of revues and breezy Broadway musicals and set up their own publishing house. De Sylva later became a film producer, working with Shirley Temple, and was co-founder of Capitol records.

1 The moon belongs to everyone,
The best things in life are free,

'The Best Things in Life are Free' (song, 1927, with music by Ray Henderson)

## Peter De Vries (1910–93)
US AUTHOR

A regular contributor to the *New Yorker* from 1943, his antic humour underpinned by his Dutch Calvinist upbringing is displayed in such novels as *The Tunnel of Love* (1954) and *Slouching Towards Kalamazoo* (1983), depictions of the affluent American middle-classes.

1 Gluttony is an emotional escape, a sign something is eating us.

Crystal, in *Comfort Me With Apples*, ch. 15 (1956)

2 You can make a sordid thing sound like a brilliant drawing-room comedy. Probably a fear we have of facing up to the real issues. Could you say we were guilty of Noël Cowardice?

The narrator, in ibid.

3 It is the final proof of God's omnipotence that he need not exist in order to save us.

The Reverend Andrew Mackerel, in *The Mackerel Plaza*, ch. 1 (1958). This aphorism, De Vries added, 'seemed to his hearers so much better than anything Voltaire had said on the subject that he was given an immediate hike in pay and invited out to more dinners than he could possibly eat.'

4 Everybody hates me because I'm so universally liked.

The narrator, Joe Sandwich, in *The Vale of Laughter*, pt 1, ch. 1 (1967)

## Guy Debord (1931–94)
FRENCH PHILOSOPHER

A leading light of the Situationist movement, he dealt with the interplay of modernity, capitalism and everyday life. His main work is *The Society of the Spectacle* (1967). See also MARSHALL MCLUHAN 5

1 Boredom is always counter-revolutionary. Always.

'The Bad Old Days Will End', first publ. November 1963, repr. in *The Incomplete Works of the Situationist International* (ed. Christopher Gray, 1974)

2 In societies where modern conditions of production prevail, all of life presents itself as an immense accumulation of *spectacles*. Everything that was directly lived has moved away into a representation.

*The Society of the Spectacle*, ch. 1, sect. 1 (1967)

3 Young people everywhere have been allowed to choose between love and a garbage disposal unit. Everywhere they have chosen the garbage disposal unit.

*The Incomplete Works of the Situationist International*, 'Formula for a New City' (ed. Christopher Gray, 1974)

4 Quotations are useful in periods of ignorance or obscurantist beliefs.

*Panegyric*, pt 1 (first volume of autobiography, 1989)

## Eugene Debs (1855–1926)
US TRADE UNIONIST AND POLITICAL LEADER

In 1893 he became President of the newly established American Railway Union, then helped found the Socialist Party of America, standing as Socialist candidate for the US presidency five times between 1900 and 1920. Hearing him speak, said Art Young, was 'to listen to a hammer riveting a chamber in Hell for the oppressors of the poor'.

1 When great changes occur in history, when great principles are involved, as a rule the majority are wrong.

Speech 11 September 1918, Cleveland, Ohio, publ. in *Eugene V. Debs Speaks* (ed. Jean Y. Tussey, 1970). Debs was defending himself against charges of violating the 1917 Espionage Act, for which he was found guilty and sentenced to ten years in jail. He was pardoned by the incoming President Harding in 1921.

2 While there is a lower class, I am in it, while there is a criminal element, I am of it, and while there is a soul in prison, I am not free.

Speech from the dock at Cleveland, Ohio, 14 September 1918, publ. in *The Penguin Book of Twentieth-Century Speeches* (ed. Brian MacArthur, 1999)

## Midge Decter (b. 1927)
US AUTHOR, EDITOR AND SOCIAL CRITIC

She was Editor of *Harper's Magazine* (1968–71) and is author of, among other books, *The New Chastity* (1972), which takes issue with some of the core arguments of feminism.

1 Women's Liberation calls it enslavement but the real truth about the sexual revolution is that it has made of sex an almost chaotically limitless and therefore unmanageable realm in the life of women.

*The New Chastity and Other Arguments Against Women's Liberation*, ch. 2 (1972)

## Shelagh Delaney (b. 1939)
BRITISH PLAYWRIGHT

She is principally known for *A Taste of Honey* (1958, filmed 1961), which she began writing at the age of seventeen and earned her the title of 'Angry Young Woman'. Of her subsequent writing, her screenplays including *Dance with a Stranger* (1985) have won most praise.

1 Women never have young minds. They are born three thousand years old.

Jo's boyfriend, in *A Taste of Honey*, act 1, sc. 2 (1959)

## Don DeLillo (b. 1936)
US AUTHOR

A leading exponent of the 'postmodern novel', he writes oblique analyses of contemporary US society which focus on subcultures such as American football in *End Zone* (1972) and baseball in *Underworld* (1999). *Libra* (1988) and *Mao II* (1991) were more overtly political.

1 People stress the violence. That's the smallest part of it. Football is brutal only from a distance. In the middle of it there's a calm, a tranquility. The players accept pain. There's a sense of order even at the end of a running play with bodies strewn everywhere. When the systems interlock, there's a satisfaction to the game that can't be duplicated. There's a harmony.

Emmett Creed, in *End Zone*, ch. 28 (1972)

2 I've come to think of Europe as a hardcover book, America as the paperback version.

Owen Brademas, in *The Names*, ch. 1 (1982)

3 Don't you realize that as long as you have to sit down to pee, you'll never be a dominant force in the world? You'll never be a convincing technocrat or middle manager. Because people will know. She's in there *sitting down*.

James Axton to his wife Kathryn, in ibid. ch. 5 (1982)

4 Men with secrets tend to be drawn to each other, not because they want to share what they know but because they need the company of the like-minded, the fellow afflicted.

Walter Everett Jr, in *Libra*, pt 1, '17 April' (1988)

5 There's never a dearth of reasons to shoot at the President.

Larry Parmenter, in ibid. '26 April'

6 If we are on the outside, we assume a conspiracy is the perfect working of a scheme. Silent nameless men with unadorned hearts. A conspiracy is everything that ordinary life is not. It's the inside game, cold, sure, undistracted, forever closed off to us. We are the flawed ones, the innocents, trying to make some rough sense of the

daily jostle. Conspirators have a logic and a daring beyond our reach. All conspiracies are the same taut story of men who find coherence in some criminal act.

ibid. pt 2, 'In Dallas'

7 That's the thing about baseball . . . You do what they did before you. That's the connection you make. There's a whole long line. A man takes his kid to a game and thirty years later this is what they talk about when the poor old mutt's wasting away in the hospital.

Bill Waterson, in *Underworld,* 'Prologue, The Triumph of Death' (1997)

8 Prayer is a practical strategy, the gaining of temporal advantage in the capital markets of Sin and Remission.

Narrator, in ibid., pt 2, 'Elegy for Left Hand Alone, Mid-1980s–Early 1990s', ch. 8

9 If you know you're worth nothing, only a gamble with death can gratify your vanity.

ibid.

10 Corporations are great and appalling things. They take you and shape you in nearly nothing flat, twist and swivel you. And they do it without overt persuasion, they do it with smiles and nods, a collective inflection of the voice.

ibid. pt 3, 'The Cloud of Unknowing: Spring 1978', ch. 1

11 Sex is what you can get. For some people, most people, it's the most important thing they can get without being born rich or smart or stealing. This is what life can give you that's equal to others or better, even, that you don't have to go to college six years to get. And it's not religion and it's not science but you can explore it and learn things about yourself.

Donna, in ibid.

## Jack Dempsey (1895–1983)
US BOXER

Born William Harrison Dempsey and nicknamed 'the Manassa Mauler'. After working in copper mines, he took to boxing and became world heavyweight champion (1919–26). His 1921 title fight was the first to amass a million dollars from the gate. He retired in 1940 and became a successful restaurateur.

1 Honey, I just forgot to duck.

Quoted in *Dempsey,* ch. 24 (1977) by Jack and Barbara P. Dempsey. This celebrated remark made to his wife after losing a title fight in 1926 was repeated by RONALD REAGAN to NANCY REAGAN after John Hinckley III's assassination attempt on the president, 30 March 1981.

## Catherine Deneuve (b. 1943)
FRENCH ACTRESS

Born Cathérine Dorléac. Once called 'the most beautiful woman in the world', she is noted for her powerful dramatic presence in such films as *The Umbrellas of Cherbourg* (1964), *Repulsion* (1965) and Buñuel's *Belle de jour* (1967). In 1985 she was chosen as the model for Marianne, symbol of the French Republic.

1 Sexuality is such a part of life, but sexuality in movies – I have a hard time finding it.

Interview in *Première* April 1993

## Gérard Depardieu (b. 1948)
FRENCH ACTOR

An internationally acclaimed actor, he has appeared in over seventy films, including *Jean de Florette* (1986), *Cyrano de Bergerac* (1990), and *Le Tartuffe* (1984) in which he directed himself. The *New York Times* said of him: 'There appears to be nothing he cannot do well on the screen.'

1 I learnt to be in the light. The stage is like a cage of light.

People are no longer afraid of you – they are the ones out there in the dark, watching.

Quoted in *Depardieu,* ch. 3 (1991) by Marianne Gray. Describing how acting saved him from a life of crime.

2 At twenty you have many desires which hide the truth, but beyond forty there are only real and fragile truths – your abilities and your failings.

*Daily Mail* 4 March 1991

## John Derek (1926–98)
US ACTOR AND DIRECTOR

Born Derek Harris. A leading man in the 1940s and 1950s, he later turned to photography and directing films. He was married to Ursula Andress and later Bo Derek, whom he directed in *Tarzan the Ape Man* and *Fantasies* (both 1981).

1 Live fast, die young and have a good-looking corpse.

Nick Romano ( John Derek), in *Knock On Any Door* (film, screenplay by Daniel Taradash and John Monks Jr, based on Willard Motley's novel, directed by Nicholas Ray, 1949)

## Jacques Derrida (b. 1930)
ALGERIAN-BORN FRENCH LITERARY THEORIST

In the 1960s he introduced the theory of deconstruction into literary criticism, published in the paper 'Structure, Sign, and Play' (1966) and such books as *Speech and Writing* (1967). Always a controversial figure, he was awarded an honorary degree by Cambridge University in 1992 which was much disputed.

1 Writing in the common sense is the dead letter, it is the carrier of death. It exhausts life.

*Of Grammatology,* pt 1, ch. 1 (1967, rev. 1998)

2 There is nothing outside of the text.

ibid. pt 2, ch. 2

3 Were I not so frequently associated with this adventure of deconstruction, I would risk, with a smile, the following hypothesis: America *is* deconstruction . . . [The United States] is that historical space which today, in all its dimensions and through all its power plays, reveals itself as being undeniably the most sensitive, receptive, or responsive space of all to the themes and effects of deconstruction.

*Mémoirs: for Paul de Man* (1989). Written shortly after the death of the critic PAUL DE MAN in 1983.

## Helene Deutsch (1884–1982)
POLISH-BORN US PSYCHIATRIST

She was a pupil of SIGMUND FREUD, and developed her own exploration of feminine psychology, breaking new ground with her work on the female libido. Among her main works is *The Psychology of Women* (1944–5).

1 All observations point to the fact that the intellectual woman is masculinized; in her, warm, intuitive knowledge has yielded to cold unproductive thinking.

*The Psychology of Women,* vol. 1, ch. 8 (1944)

2 The embattled gates to equal rights indeed opened up for modern women, but I sometimes think to myself: 'That is not what I meant by freedom – it is only "social progress".'

*Confrontations With Myself,* ch. 1 (1973)

## Bernard DeVoto (1897–1955)
US HISTORIAN AND CRITIC

Winning acclaim for *Mark Twain's America* (1932), he continued his historical studies with a trilogy on the American West. He held the 'Easy Chair', a comment column on *Harper's Magazine* 1935–55.

1 You can no more keep a martini in the refrigerator than you can keep a kiss there. The proper union of gin and vermouth is a great and sudden glory; it is one of the happiest marriages on earth, and one of the shortest-lived.

*Harper's Magazine* December 1949

2 Sure the people are stupid: the human race is stupid. Sure Congress is an inefficient instrument of government. But the people are not stupid enough to abandon representative government for any other kind, including government by the guy who knows.

*The Easy Chair*, 'Sometimes They Vote Right Too' (1955)

## Lord Dewar (1864–1930)

BRITISH INDUSTRIALIST

Lord Dewar of Homestall, Sussex. He was Managing Director of Scotch Whisky Brands and one of the first whisky men to realize the potential of sports sponsorship. He published books of his epigrammatic humour, including *Dewarisms: Toasts and Maxims* (1906).

1 [There are] only two classes of pedestrians in these days of reckless motor traffic – the quick, and the dead.

Quoted in *Looking Back on Life*, ch. 28 (1933) by George Robey

## Diana, Princess of Wales (1961–97)

Born Lady Diana Frances Spencer, she married CHARLES, PRINCE OF WALES in 1991 and divorced in 1996. She was Honorary President of numerous charities and focused world attention on the issue of landmines. The subject of intense media coverage throughout her adult life – she became the most photographed woman in the world – her death in a car accident in August 1997 gave rise to unprecedented national mourning.

1 Everyone said I was the Marilyn Monroe of the 1980s and I was adoring every minute of it. Actually I've never sat down and said: 'Hooray how wonderful'. Never. The day I do we're in trouble.

Quoted in *Diana: Her True Story*, ch. 9 (1992) by Andrew Morton

2 I have it on very good authority that the quest for perfection our society demands can leave the individual gasping for breath at every turn. From early childhood, many have felt they were expected to be perfect but did not feel they had the right to express their true feelings to those around them – feelings of guilt, of self-revulsion and low personal esteem, creating in them a compulsion to *dissolve* like a *Disprin* and disappear.

Speech at International Eating Disorders conference in London, 27 April 1993, quoted in the *Guardian* 28 April 1993. Princess Diana suffered from bulimia.

3 I don't even know how to use a parking meter, let alone a phone box.

Quoted in the *Guardian* 22 August 1994. Said to Richard Kay, royal correspondent for the *Daily Mail*, on allegations that she had pestered art dealer Oliver Hoare with telephone calls.

4 When I see them [press photographers] around all the time, it is like being raped.

Quoted in the *Guardian* 6 April 1995

5 I'd like to be a queen of people's hearts, in people's hearts, but I don't see myself being Queen of this country.

Interview on *Panorama*, BBC1, 20 November 1995, publ. in *The Times* 21 November 1995

6 She won't go quietly, that's the problem. I'll fight to the end.

ibid. Speaking of herself.

7 There were three of us in this marriage.

ibid. Referring to Prince Charles's relationship with Camilla Parker-Bowles.

8 I touch people. I think everyone needs that. Placing a hand on a friend's face means making contact.

Interview in *Le Monde* 27 August 1997

## Leonardo DiCaprio (b. 1974)

US SCREEN ACTOR

After winning praise for roles in *What's Eating Gilbert Grape?* (1993) and *Romeo and Juliet* (1996), he became a global superstar for his part in *Titanic* (1997). In the words of director MARTIN SCORSESE, 'a wonderful actor in that tradition – Brando, Clift, Dean, to De Niro, Pacino, Hoffman to DiCaprio'.

1 I would not want to become an adult in every sense of the word. Who the hell does?

Quoted in the *Sunday Times* 16 January 2000

## Philip K. Dick (1928–82)

US SCIENCE FICTION WRITER

In his novels and short stories such as *Do Androids Dream of Electric Sheep?* (1968, filmed as *Blade Runner*, 1982), he explores standard science fiction ideas with a bizarre humour. His books dealing with mind-altering drugs generated a cult following in the 1960s.

1 Reality is that which, when you stop believing in it, doesn't go away.

Definition given in 1972, quoted by Dick in *I Hope I Shall Arrive Soon*, 'How to Build a Universe That Doesn't Fall Apart Two Days Later' (1986)

2 One of the most effective forms of industrial or military sabotage limits itself to damage that can never be thoroughly proven – or even proven at all – to be anything deliberate.

*A Scanner Darkly*, ch. 3 (1977)

3 Drug misuse is not a disease, it is a decision, like the decision to step out in front of a moving car. You would call that not a disease but an error of judgment.

ibid. Author's Note

4 We are not individuals. We are stations in a single Mind.

*Valis*, ch. 7 (1981)

5 Science fiction writers, I am sorry to say, really do not know anything. We can't talk about science, because our knowledge of it is limited and unofficial, and usually our fiction is dreadful.

*I Hope I Shall Arrive Soon*, 'How to Build a Universe That Doesn't Fall Apart Two Days Later' (1986)

6 The basic tool for the manipulation of reality is the manipulation of words. If you can control the meaning of words, you can control the people who must use the words.

ibid.

## Joan Didion (b. 1934)

US ESSAYIST

A laconic style pervades her essays and novels, which chronicle the transformation of American life in the 1960s. Some of her regular contributions to newspapers and periodicals are collected in *Slouching Towards Bethlehem* (1968) and *The White Room* (1979).

1 Most of our platitudes notwithstanding, self-deception remains the most difficult deception. The tricks that work on others count for nothing in that very well-lit back alley where one keeps assignations with oneself: no winning smiles will do here, no prettily drawn lists of good intentions.

'On Self-Respect', first publ. 1961, repr. in *Slouching Towards Bethlehem* (1968)

2 California is a place in which a boom mentality and a sense of Chekhovian loss meet in uneasy suspension; in

which the mind is troubled by some buried but ineradicable suspicion that things had better work here, because here, beneath that immense bleached sky, is where we run out of continent.

'Notes From a Native Daughter', first publ. 1965, repr. in ibid.

3 When we start deceiving ourselves into thinking not that we want something or need something, not that it is a pragmatic necessity for us to have it, but that it is a *moral imperative* that we have it, then is when we join the fashionable madmen, and then is when the thin whine of hysteria is heard in the land, and then is when we are in bad trouble.

'On Morality', first publ. 1965, repr. in ibid.

4 We are well advised to keep on nodding terms with the people we used to be, whether we find them attractive company or not. Otherwise they turn up unannounced and surprise us, come hammering on the mind's door at 4am of a bad night and demand to know who deserted them, who betrayed them, who is going to make amends. We forget all too soon the things we thought we could never forget.

'On Keeping a Notebook', first publ. 1966, repr. in ibid.

5 Writers are always selling somebody out.

Preface to *Slouching Towards Bethlehem* (1968)

6 [Of the Charles Manson murders] Many people I know in Los Angeles believe that the Sixties ended abruptly on August 9, 1969, ended at the exact moment when word of the murders on Cielo Drive traveled like brushfire through the community, and in a sense this is true. The tension broke that day. The paranoia was fulfilled.

'The White Album: A Chronicle of Survival in the Sixties', first publ. in *New West* 4 June 1979, repr. in *The White Album* (1979)

## Marlene Dietrich (1901–92)

GERMAN-BORN US ACTRESS AND ENTERTAINER

Originally Maria Magdalene Dietrich. One of the most glamorous and sensual of film stars, she starred in the German film *The Blue Angel* (1930), and thereafter, under the tutelage of its director Joseph von Sternberg, in Hollywood films such as *Blonde Venus* (1932). She performed for the Allied troops during the Second World War, and later became an international cabaret star. ERNEST HEMINGWAY said of her, 'If she had nothing but her voice, she could break your heart with it. But she also has that beautiful body and the timeless loveliness of her face'.

1 Falling in love again,
I never wanted to
What am I to do?
I can't help it.

'Falling in Love Again' (song, written by Fredrich Hollander and Sammy Lerner from German lyrics by Robert Liebmann) in the film *The Blue Angel* (1930)

2 It took more than one man to change my name to Shanghai Lily.

Shanghai Lily (Marlene Dietrich), in *Shanghai Express* (film, screenplay by Jules Furthman based on a story by Harry Hervey, directed by Josef von Sternberg, 1932)

3 A country without bordels is like a house without bathrooms.

*Marlene Dietrich's ABC*, 'Bordel' (1962)

4 There comes a time when suddenly you realize that laughter is something you remember and that *you* were the one laughing.

ibid. 'Laughter'

5 He [Ernest Hemingway] is gentle, as all real men are gentle; without tenderness, a man is uninteresting.

Quoted in *Papa Hemingway*, pt 1, ch. 1 (1955) by A.E. Hotchner.

HEMINGWAY, one of Dietrich's lovers, called her 'that damn Kraut', but also said she was 'the best who ever entered the ring'.

6 In Europe it doesn't matter if you're a man or a woman. We make love with anyone we find attractive.

Quoted in *Dietrich*, ch. 5 (1992) by Donald Spoto. Remark made to a woman fellow passenger, declining Marlene's advances. The actress was on a ship making her first voyage to America in 1930.

7 Most people who make movies are in real life a bitter disappointment. I, on the other hand, am so much better in real life.

Said to critic Sheridan Morley, quoted by him in the *Sunday Times* 24 May 1992

## Howard Dietz (1896–1983)

US SONGWRITER AND PUBLICIST

Director of advertising and publicity for Metro-Goldwyn-Mayer film studios (1919–57), he was responsible for devising its 'roaring lion' trademark and accompanying motto. He later teamed up with Arthur Schwartz and wrote Broadway musicals and revues, including the score for *The Band Wagon* (1931).

1 *Ars gratia artis.* (Art for art's sake.)

Motto of MGM studios, adopted in the 1930s. The phrase 'Art for art's sake' was not new: the French politician and philosopher Benjamin Constant (1767–1834) wrote, in his *Journal intime*: 'Art for art's sake, with no purpose, for any purpose perverts art. But art achieves a purpose which is not its own'.

## Annie Dillard (b. 1945)

US AUTHOR AND POET

She was Editor of *Harper's Magazine* (1973–85), and published *Pilgrim at Tinker Creek* (1974), which enjoyed an immediate success and has been compared to Thoreau's *Walden*.

1 I don't know what it is about fecundity that so appalls. I suppose it is the teeming evidence that birth and growth, which we value, are ubiquitous and blind, that life itself is so astonishingly cheap, that nature is as careless as it is bountiful, and that with extravagance goes a crushing waste that will one day include our own cheap lives.

Narrator, in *Pilgrim at Tinker Creek*, ch. 10 (1974)

## Joe DiMaggio (1914–99)

US BASEBALL PLAYER

Nicknamed 'Joltin' Joe' and 'The Yankee Clipper', he was the star player of the New York Yankees (1936–51) both as a batter and a fielder. He was briefly married to MARILYN MONROE in 1954.

1 A ball player's got to be kept hungry to become a big leaguer. That's why no boy from a rich family ever made the big leagues.

*The New York Times* 30 April 1961

## Isak Dinesen (1885–1962)

DANISH AUTHOR

Pen name of Baroness Karen Blixen, born Karen Christence Dinesen. On her marriage to her cousin in 1914 she moved to Kenya, remaining after her divorce in 1921 to manage their coffee plantation. She returned to Denmark in 1931 and wrote *Seven Gothic Tales* (1934) and her autobiography *Out of Africa* (1937, filmed 1985).

1 What is life, when you come to think upon it, but a most excellent, accurately set, infinitely complicated machine for turning fat playful puppies into old mangy blind dogs, and proud war horses into skinny nags, and succulent young boys, to whom the world holds great delight and terrors, into old weak men, with running eyes, who drink ground rhino-horn? What is man, when you come to

think upon him, but a minutely set, ingenious machine for turning, with infinite artfulness, the red wine of Shiraz into urine?

Mira, in *Seven Gothic Tales*, 'The Dreamers' (1934)

2  If I know a song of Africa – I thought – of the giraffe, and the African new moon lying on her back, of the ploughs in the fields, and the sweaty faces of the coffee-pickers, does Africa know a song for me?

*Out of Africa*, pt 1, ch. 4 (1937). The book's title derives from Pliny the Elder's *Historia Naturalis*: 'Africa always has something new to offer' (*Africa semper aliquid novi affert*).

3  The true aristocracy and the true proletariat of the world are both in understanding with tragedy. To them it is the fundamental principle of God, and the key, the minor key, to existence. They differ in this way from the bourgeoisie of all classes, who deny tragedy, who will not tolerate it, and to whom the word tragedy means in itself unpleasantness.

ibid. pt 5, ch. 1

# Christian Dior (1905–57)

FRENCH COUTURIER

He founded his own Paris house in 1945 and shocked the public with the extravagant designs of his New Look in 1947, which featured tight waists and long, full, pleated skirts. He later devised the 'H' and 'A' line, and discovered YVES SAINT LAURENT.

1  Women are most fascinating between the ages of thirty-five and forty, after they have won a few races and know how to pace themselves. Since few women ever pass forty, maximum fascination can continue indefinitely.

*Collier's Magazine* 10 June 1955

2  The maintenance of the tradition of fashion is in the nature of an act of faith. In a century which attempts to tear the heart out of every mystery, fashion guards its secret well, and is the best possible proof that there is still magic abroad.

*Dior By Dior*, pt 4, ch. 19 (1957)

# Thomas M. Disch (b. 1940)

US AUTHOR

Called by Walter Clemens 'the most formidably gifted unfamous American writer', he established the sceptical New Wave genre of science fiction. He also writes straight fiction, poetry, opera libretti and computer interactive fiction. Among his works is the novel *The House That Fear Built* (1976) and the poetry collection *ABCDEFG HIJKLM NOPQRSTUVWXYZ* (1981).

1  A predilection for genre fiction is symptomatic of a kind of arrested development.

Quoted in *The Face* March 1986

# Walt Disney (1901–66)

US ANIMATOR AND FILM-MAKER

Having created Mickey Mouse (for whom he provided the original voice) in 1927 and Donald Duck in 1936, he produced the first full-length colour cartoon film, *Snow White and the Seven Dwarfs* in 1937. As ALFRED HITCHCOCK remarked, 'Disney has the best casting. If he doesn't like an actor, he just tears him up.' His company also established a corpus of nature, adventure and family films.

1  I love Mickey Mouse more than any woman I've ever known.

Quoted in *Halliwell's Who's Who in the Movies* (ed. John Walker, 1999)

2  Dream, diversify – and never miss an angle.

Quoted in *The Disney Studio Story*, Introduction (1988) by Richard Holliss and Brian Sibley

# Mort Dixon (1892–1956)

US SONGWRITER

A leading lyricist of popular songs of the 1920s and 1930s, he collaborated with Ray Henderson, Harry Woods and ALLIE WRUBEL, among others, on such hits as 'That Old Gang of Mine' (1923), 'Bye Bye Blackbird' (1926) and 'You're My Everything' (1931).

1  Bye bye blackbird.

'Bye Bye Blackbird' (song, 1926, music by Ray Henderson)

2  I'm looking over a four leaf clover
That I overlooked before.

'I'm Looking Over a Four Leaf Clover' (song, 1927, with music by Harry Woods)

# Milovan Djilas (1911–95)

YUGOSLAV POLITICAL LEADER AND WRITER

A leading partisan in the Second World War and subsequently a minister in Tito's cabinet, he was made President of the Federal People's Assembly in 1953, but his outspoken criticism of the Communist Party caused him to lose his posts and leave the Party. He was at various times imprisoned for his political writings, which included the heretical *Conversations With Stalin* (1962).

1  The Party line is that there is no Party line.

Comment on reforms of Yugoslavian Communist Party, November 1951, quoted in *Disputed Barricade*, ch. 15 (1957) by Fitzroy Maclean

2  The terrible thing is that one cannot be a Communist and not let oneself in for the shameful act of recantation. One cannot be a Communist and preserve an iota of one's personal integrity.

*Encounter* December 1979

3  Normal life cannot sustain revolutionary attitudes for long.

*Guardian* 9 April 1990

# J. Frank Dobie (1888–1964)

US AUTHOR

Nicknamed Professor Pancho, he described himself as a 'historian of the longhorns, the mustangs, the coyote and other characters of the West' in such books as *Apache Gold* (1939) and *The Longhorns* (1941). His liberal views led to his dismissal from a university post in Texas in 1947.

1  The average PhD thesis is nothing but a transference of bones from one graveyard to another.

*A Texan in England*, ch. 1 (1945)

# E.L. Doctorow (b. 1931)

US NOVELIST

Full name Edgar Lawrence Doctorow. His books, taking the form of historical novels, westerns or science fiction, blend fact with invention. *Ragtime* (1975, filmed 1981) explores early twentieth-century America and *Billy Bathgate* (1989, filmed 1991) the Depression.

1  Tracks! Tracks! It seemed to the visionaries who wrote for the popular magazines that the future lay at the end of parallel rails. There were long-distance locomotive railroads and interurban electric railroads and street railways and elevated railroads, all laying their steel stripes on the land, criss-crossing like the texture of an indefatigable civilization.

*Ragtime*, pt 1, ch. 13 (1975)

2  There is no longer any such thing as fiction or nonfiction; there's only narrative.

*The New York Times Book Review* 27 January 1988

3  It's like driving a car at night. You never see further than

your headlights, but you can make the whole trip that way.

Interview in *Writers at Work* (eighth series, ed. George Plimpton, 1988). Discussing his writing technique.

4 Murders are exciting and lift people into a heart-beating awe as religion is supposed to do, after seeing one in the street young couples will go back to bed and make love, people will cross themselves and thank God for the gift of their stuporous lives, old folks will talk to each other over cups of hot water with lemon because murders are enlivened sermons to be analyzed and considered and relished, they speak to the timid of the dangers of rebellion, murders are perceived as momentary descents of God and so provide joy and hope and righteous satisfaction to parishioners, who will talk about them for years afterward to anyone who will listen.

*Billy Bathgate*, ch. 19 (1989)

5 Like art and politics, gangsterism is a very important avenue of assimilation into society.

*International Herald Tribune* 1 October 1990

6 Lullabies, school songs, anthems, battle hymns, work songs, chanteys, love songs, bawdy songs, laments, requiems. They're there in every age of life, for every occasion, in the sepulchral voices of the choir, in the stomp and shout of the whorehourse piano player. But all songs are songs of justification.

'Standards: How Great Songs Name Us', publ. in *Harper's* November 1991

## Ken Dodd (b. 1931)

BRITISH COMIC

A stand-up comedian, he has appeared in variety, pantomime, television and radio, usually armed with his tickling stick and finishing his act with a song, such as 'Happiness' (1964) or 'Tears' (1965).

1 The trouble with Freud is that he never played the Glasgow Empire Saturday night.

*The Laughter Makers*, television interview, quoted in *The Times* 7 August 1965

2 If I get a hard audience they are not going to get away until they laugh. Those seven laughs a minute – I've got to have them.

*Daily Telegraph* 20 September 1990

## Robert Doisneau (1912–94)

FRENCH PHOTOGRAPHER

Through his black-and-white photographs he immortalized post-Second World War Paris, capturing everyday life in spontaneous and humorous images in order to 'show the world as I would like it to be at all times'. He also worked as a fashion editor for *Vogue* and as a portraitist of Parisian artists and intellectuals.

1 A hundredth of a second here, a hundredth of a second there – even if you put them end to end, they still only add up to one, two, perhaps three seconds, snatched from eternity.

*Guardian* 4 April 1992

## J.P. Donleavy (b. 1926)

IRISH-AMERICAN AUTHOR

Full name James Patrick Donleavy. *The Ginger Man*, charting the progress of a comic anti-hero Dangerfield, was the first of a series of boozy and picaresque novels which ponder the meaning of life. He became an Irish citizen in 1967.

1 To marry the Irish is to look for poverty.

*The Ginger Man*, ch. 2 (1955)

2 But Jesus, when you don't have any money, the problem is food. When you have money, it's sex. When you have both, it's health, you worry about getting ruptured or something. If everything is simply jake then you're frightened of death.

O'Keefe, in ibid. ch. 5

3 When I die I want to decompose in a barrel of porter and have it served in all the pubs in Dublin.

Sebastian Dangerfield, in ibid. ch. 31

4 Writing is turning one's worst moments into money.

*Playboy* May 1979. He has expressed the same idea on different occasions.

## Terence Donovan (1936–96)

BRITISH PHOTOGRAPHER

He became a freelance photographer in 1959 and recorded the London of the Swinging Sixties through his black-and-white documentary-style images.

1 The magic of photography is metaphysical. What you see in the photograph isn't what you saw at the time. The real skill of photography is organized visual lying.

*Guardian* 19 November 1983

## Ariel Dorfman (b. 1942)

CHILEAN AUTHOR

Forced into exile by the 1973 military coup, Dorfman is known for his opposition to political oppression in Chile, which is reflected in his novels such as *My House is on Fire* (1990) and his plays, best known of which is *Death and the Maiden* (1991).

1 *Reader's Digest* is a tourist guidebook for the geography of ignorance.

*The Empire's Old Clothes*, ch.4 (1983)

2 The enemy is inside, and we find it hard to distinguish him from some of our innermost thoughts and nurturings.

ibid. 'Conclusion'

3 Compromise, an agreement, a negotiation. Everything in this country is done by consensus isn't it. Isn't that what this transition is all about? They let us have democracy, but they keep control of the economy and of the armed forces? The Commission can investigate the crimes but nobody is punished for them? There's freedom to say anything you want as long as you don't say everything you want?

Paulina, who was tortured under Pinochet's regime, in *Death and the Maiden*, act 2, sc. 1 (1991)

2 Margaret Thatcher is one of your great comedians. She says Pinochet brought democracy to Chile. That's like claiming she brought socialism to Britain.

Quoted in *The Times* 11 October 1999

## (Sir) Reginald Dorman-Smith (1899–1977)

BRITISH POLITICIAN

Conservative MP for Petersfield, Hampshire (1935–46), he served as Minister for Agriculture and Fisheries (1939–40) and Governor of Burma (1941–6).

1 Let 'Dig for Victory' be the motto of every one with a garden and of every able-bodied man and woman capable of digging an allotment in their spare time.

Radio broadcast, 3 October 1939, quoted in *The Times* 4 October 1939

## John Dos Passos (1896–1970)

US NOVELIST

Praised by critic EDMUND WILSON as 'perhaps the first really important writer to have succeeded in using colloquial American', he described the disillusionment of war and the decline of a materialist society in his novels, which include *Three Soldiers* (1921) and the trilogy *USA* (1930–36).

1 **The only man that gets anything out of capitalism is a crook, an' he gets to be a millionaire in short order . . .**
Tim O'Hara, in *42nd Parallel*, 'Mac' (first title in the *USA* trilogy, 1930)

2 **A revolutionist ought to be careful about the girls he went with, women took a classconscious workingman's mind off his aims, they were the main seduction of capitalist society.**
Nick Gigli, in *1919*, 'Ben Compton' (second title in the *USA* trilogy, 1932)

3 **People don't choose their careers; they are engulfed by them.**
*The New York Times* 25 October 1959

## Keith Douglas (1920–44)

BRITISH POET

One of the few British poets associated with the Second World War, he served as a tank commander in North Africa, and died in action in Normandy. Some of his poems were published during his time at Oxford, and *Selected Poems* appeared in 1943, but his account of the desert campaign, *Alamein to Zem Zem*, was published posthumously, in 1946.

1 **Remember me when I am dead**
**And simplify me when I'm dead.**
'Simplify me when I'm Dead', written 1941, publ. in *Collected Poems* (1966)

2 **Under the parabola of a ball,**
**a child turning into a man,**
**I looked into the air too long.**
**The ball fell in my hand, it sang**
**In the closed fist: *Open Open***
***Behold a gift designed to kill.***
'How to Kill', written in North Africa, 1943, publ. in ibid.

3 **The weightless mosquito touches**
**her tiny shadow on the stone,**
**and with how like, how infinite**
**a lightness, man and shadow meet.**
**They fuse. A shadow is a man**
**when the mosquito death approaches.**
ibid.

4 **For here the lover and killer are mingled**
**who had one body and one heart.**
**And death, who had the soldier singled**
**has done the lover mortal hurt.**
'*Vergissmeinnicht*', written at Homs (hospital) June/July 1943, publ. in ibid.

5 **If at times my eyes are lenses**
**through which the brain explores**
**constellations of feeling**
**my ears yielding like swinging doors**
**admit princes to the corridors**
**into the mind, do not envy me.**
**I have a beast on my back**
'Bête Noire', written early 1944 in England, publ. in ibid.

## Michael Douglas (b. 1944)

US SCREEN ACTOR

Son of Kirk Douglas, he co-produced *One Flew Over the Cuckoo's Nest* (1975) and produced and starred in *Romancing the Stone*

(1984). Other acting roles were more sinister, memorably so in *Wall Street*, for which he won an Oscar, and *Fatal Attraction* (both 1987).

1 **Lunch is for wimps.**
Gordon Gekko (Michael Douglas), in *Wall Street* (film, screenplay by Oliver Stone and Stanley Weiser, directed by Oliver Stone, 1987)

2 **Money isn't lost or made. It's just transformed from one perception to another.**
ibid.

3 **Everything's so repressive now – it's the No generation. You can't do anything, you can't eat anything, you have to abstain.**
Quoted in the *Independent on Sunday* 5 April 1992. Douglas was talking specifically about the making of the movie *Basic Instinct*.

4 ***I'm* the bad guy? . . . How did that happen? I did everything they told me to. Did you know I build missiles? I help to protect America. You should be rewarded for that.**
D-Fens (Michael Douglas), in *Falling Down* (film, screenplay by Ebbe Roe Smith, directed by Joel Schumacher, 1993)

## Norman Douglas (1868–1952)

BRITISH AUTHOR

His best-known novel, the symposium-like *South Wind* (1917) reflects the mix of his interests – art, ethics, food and religion – which are also found in his other works, including the travel books *Siren Land* (1911) and *Old Calabria* (1915). The writer Reginald Turner called him a mixture of 'Roman Emperor and Roman cab-driver'.

1 **You can tell the ideals of a nation by its advertisements.**
Don Francesco, in *South Wind*, ch. 7 (1917)

2 **Shall I give you my recipe for happiness? I find everything useful and nothing indispensable. I find everything wonderful and nothing miraculous. I reverence the body. I avoid first causes like the plague.**
Mr Keith, in ibid. ch. 18

3 **Many a man who thinks to found a home discovers that he has merely opened a tavern for his friends.**
Mr Keith, in ibid. ch. 24

4 **I wish the English still possessed a shred of the old sense of humour which Puritanism, and dyspepsia, and newspaper reading, and tea-drinking have nearly extinguished.**
ibid. ch. 32

5 **To find a friend one must close one eye. To keep him – two.**
*An Almanac* (1941)

## Coleman Dowell (1925–85)

US NOVELIST, PLAYWRIGHT AND LYRICIST

His novels dealing with sexual obsession and homosexuality include *One of the Children is Crying* (1968) and *White on Black on White* (1983). Among his plays is *Eve of the Green Grass* (1963). He committed suicide.

1 **Being is a fiction invented by those who suffer from becoming.**
Entry in Mrs October's journals, in *Mrs October Was Here*, pt 3, 'Tasmania, Now' (1973)

## (Sir) Arthur Conan Doyle (1859–1930)

BRITISH AUTHOR

Though he published other adventure stories as well as books on spiritualism, he is best known for his Sherlock Holmes stories, which established the genre of detective fiction and which critic EDMUND WILSON described as 'among the most amusing of fairytales and not among the least distinguished'.

1 The vocabulary of 'Bradshaw' is nervous and terse, but limited. The selection of words would hardly lend itself to the sending of general messages.

Sherlock Holmes, in *The Valley of Fear*, pt 1, ch. 1 (1915). Watson had suggested *Bradshaw*, the railway timetable, as containing the key to decipher a code; Holmes opted instead for *Whitaker's Almanack*.

2 Mediocrity knows nothing higher than itself, but talent instantly recognizes genius.

*The Valley of Fear*, pt 1, ch. 1 (1915)

3 But here, unless I am mistaken, is our client.

Sherlock Holmes, in *His Last Bow*, 'Wisteria Lodge', ch. 1 (1917)

4 [Of his brother, Mycroft] All other men are specialists, but his specialism is omniscience.

Sherlock Holmes, in ibid., 'The Bruce-Partington Plans'

5 Of all ruins that of a noble mind is the most deplorable.

ibid. 'The Dying Detective'. The words recall those of Scrope Davies (c. 1783–1852), who wrote, in a letter dated May 1835, 'Babylon in all its desolation is a sight not so awful as that of the human mind in ruins.'

6 Holmes: I followed you.
Watson: I saw none.
Holmes: That is what you may expect to see when I follow you.

ibid. 'Devil's Foot'

7 Good old Watson! You are the one fixed point in a changing age.

Sherlock Holmes, in ibid., 'His Last Bow'

8 Matilda Briggs . . . was a ship which is associated with the giant rat of Sumatra, a story for which the world is not yet prepared.

Sherlock Holmes, in *The Case-Book of Sherlock Holmes*, 'The Sussex Vampire' (1927)

## Roddy Doyle (b. 1958)
IRISH NOVELIST

A teacher who turned to writing plays and novels about the inner life of Dublin, he won praise with *The Commitments* (1987, filmed 1991), first of the Barrytown trilogy, and later won the Booker Prize with *Paddy Ha Ha Ha* (1993).

1 The Irish are the niggers of Europe, lads. An' Dubliners are the niggers of Ireland. . . . An' the northside Dubliners are the niggers o' Dublin. – Say it loud, I'm black an' I'm proud.

Jimmy Rabbitte, in *The Commitments* (1987) (see JAMES BROWN 2).

2 Soul is the politics o' the people. Our people. – Soul is the rhythm o' sex. . . . Soul is dynamic. It can't be caught. It can't be chained. They could chain the nigger slaves but they couldn't chain their soul.

ibid.

3 Being out of a job makes you passive. You spend a lot of time in bed, and you can't be angry while you're asleep.

Interview in the *Independent on Sunday* 14 April 1996. Referring to Jimmy in Doyle's 1990 novel, *The Snapper*.

## Margaret Drabble (b. 1939)
BRITISH NOVELIST

Her novels, including *The Radiant Way* (1987) and *The Gates of Ivory* (1991), explore the everyday experience and ideas of educated middle-class women. She has also written literary biographies, and is the wife of biographer Michael Holroyd and sister of the writer A.S. BYATT.

1 Human contact seemed to her [ Jane] so frail a thing that the hope that two people might want each other in the

same way, at the same time and with the possibility of doing something about it, seemed infinitely remote.

*The Waterfall* (1969)

2 Perhaps I could take a religion that denied free will, that placed God in his true place, arbitrary, carelessly kind, idly malicious, intermittently attentive, and himself subject as Zeus was, to necessity. Necessity is my God.

Jane, in ibid.

3 Faces, they have, those suburban people, faces and identity, despite their mortgages and their alarms: and there are few emotions more ignoble, more contemptible, than the terror that seizes such as myself when we drive, quickly, past their net curtained windows.

ibid. The protagonist, Jane, is visiting her parents-in-law in suburbia, which she does 'through social masochism, knowing that only by sinking could I avoid the deadly, human, incriminating impulse to rise.'

4 Affluence was, quite simply, a question of texture . . . The threadbare carpets of infancy, the coconut matting, the ill-laid linoleum, the utility furniture . . . had all spoken of a life too near the bones of subsistence, too little padded, too severely worn.

*The Needle's Eye*, pt 1 (1972)

5 England's not a bad country. It's just a mean, cold, ugly, divided, tired, clapped-out, post-imperial, post-industrial slag-heap covered in polystyrene hamburger cartons.

Alix, in *A Natural Curiosity* (1989)

6 You learn to put your emotional luggage where it will do some good, instead of using it to shit on other people, or blow up aeroplanes.

Quoted in the *Observer* 6 October 1991

## Nick Drake (1948–74)
BRITISH SINGER AND SONGWRITER

He recorded three albums before a premature death due to a (probably accidental) drugs overdose. His music was characterized by his wistful voice, nimble guitar work and often bleak lyrics.

1 Fame is but a fruit tree
So very unsound
It can never flourish
Till its stalk is in the ground.

'Fruit Tree' (song) on the album *Five Leaves Left* (1969)

## Marie Dressler (1869–1934)
CANADIAN-BORN US ACTRESS

Born Leila Marie Koerber, she started her career on the stage aged fourteen, later becoming a headliner in vaudeville. In her first film, *Tillie's Punctured Romance* (1914), she co-starred with CHARLIE CHAPLIN. She won an Oscar for her role in *Min and Bill* (1930).

1 By the time we hit fifty, we have learned our hardest lessons. We have found out that only a few things are really important. We have learned to take life seriously, but never ourselves.

*My Own Story*, ch. 17 (1934)

## Elizabeth Drew (1887–1965)
ANGLO-AMERICAN AUTHOR AND CRITIC

She wrote widely on literature including *The Modern Novel* (1926), *Discovering Drama* (1937) and *The Literature of Gossip* (1964).

1 The test of literature is, I suppose, whether we ourselves live more intensely for the reading of it.

*The Modern Novel*, 'Is There a "Feminine" Fiction?' (1926)

## (Sir) John Drummond (b. 1934)
BRITISH WRITER AND BROADCASTER

Involved with BBC Radio and TV since 1958, he has held the posts of Controller of Music (1985–92) and of Radio 3 (1987–92). He was Director of the Edinburgh International Festival (1978–83) and of the Proms (1985–95).

1 The arts are not just instantaneous pleasure – if you don't like it, the artist is wrong. I belong to the generation which says if you don't like it, you don't understand and you ought to find out.
*Guardian* 9 July 1992

## W.E.B. Du Bois (1868–1963)
US HISTORIAN AND CIVIL RIGHTS LEADER

Full name William Edward Burghardt Du Bois. In his writings he dealt with the history of African Americans, and in his politics he advocated equal rights and opposed all imperialism. He was a founder of the National Association for the Advancement of Colored People, joined the Communist Party aged 93, and died a Ghanaian citizen in Ghana.

1 Is a civilization naturally backward because it is different? Outside of cannibalism, which can be matched in this country, at least, by lynching, there is no vice and no degradation in native African customs which can begin to touch the horrors thrust upon them by white masters. Drunkenness, terrible diseases, immorality, all these things have been gifts of European civilization.
'Reconstruction and Africa', first publ. 1919, repr. in *The Seventh Son*, vol. 2 (1971)

2 If there is anybody in this land who thoroughly believes that the meek shall inherit the earth they have not often let their presence be known.
*The Gift of Black Folk*, ch. 9 (1924)

3 One thing alone I charge you. As you live, believe in life! Always human beings will live and progress to greater, broader and fuller life. The only possible death is to lose belief in this truth simply because the great end comes slowly, because time is long.
Last message, written 26 June 1957, and read at his funeral, 1963, publ. in *Journal of Negro History* April 1964

## Alexander Dubček (1921–92)
CZECHOSLOVAKIAN POLITICIAN

His policy of political liberalization whilst First Secretary of the Communist Party led to the invasion of Czechoslovakia in 1968 by Warsaw Pact forces. He was replaced by Husak a year later and deprived of Party membership in 1970. After Communism was abandoned in 1989, he was elected Chairman of the new Federal Assembly.

1 Socialism with a human face.
Dubček's words, repeated in various forms on different occasions, became a slogan of the 'Prague Spring' of 1968

## Al Dubin (1891–1945)
US SONGWRITER

Collaborating with the composer Harry Warren during the 1930s he wrote songs for twenty musicals, including the film *42nd Street* (1933). Among his successful songs are 'Keep Young and Beautiful' (1933) and 'Lullaby of Broadway' (1935).

1 Tiptoe through the tulips.
'Tiptoe through the Tulips' (song, 1929, with music by Joseph Burke)

## Jean Dubuffet (1901–85)
FRENCH SCULPTOR AND PAINTER

Regarded as the forerunner of late-twentieth-century art styles, he pioneered the concept of Art Brut (raw art), the antidote to museum art, derived from his studies of children and the mentally ill. He utilized all materials at hand, including scrap, to create his images.

1 Art is the most passionate orgy within man's grasp.
'Notes for the Well-Read' (1946), repr. in *Jean Dubuffet: Towards an Alternative Reality* (1987, ed. Marc Glimcher)

2 Art should always make people laugh a little and frighten them a little. Anything but bore them. Art has no right to be boring.
Rough draft for 'Popular Lecture in Painting' (1946), repr. in ibid.

3 It is not men who are great. It is man who is great. It is not wonderful to be exceptional. It is wonderful to be a man.
'Notes for the Well-Lettered', first publ. in *Prospectus* (1946), repr. in *Art in Theory* (ed. Charles Harrison and Paul Wood, 1992)

4 Caprice, independence and rebellion, which are opposed to the social order, are essential to the good health of an ethnic group. We shall measure the good health of this group by the number of its delinquents. Nothing is more immobilizing than the spirit of *deference*.
'Asphyxiating Culture' (1968), repr. in *Asphyxiating Culture and Other Writings* (1986)

## Marcel Duchamp (1887–1968)
FRENCH ARTIST

A precursor of conceptual art and leader of the Dadaists, his irreverence for conventional aesthetic values led him, in 1912, to devise his 'ready-mades', everyday objects that became works of art. He provoked scandal with the urinal he entered in an exhibition (1917) and his moustachioed *Mona Lisa* (1919). From 1915 he worked in America, becoming a US citizen in 1955.

1 I have forced myself to contradict myself in order to avoid conforming to my own taste.
Quoted in 'Marcel Duchamp: Anti-Artist' by Harriet and Sidney Janis, first publ. in *View* 21 March 1945, repr. in *Dada Painters and Poets* (1951) by Robert Motherwell

2 I am still a victim of chess. It has all the beauty of art – and much more. It cannot be commercialized. Chess is much purer than art in its social position.
*Time* 10 March 1952. Duchamp had given up painting in favour of chess in the 1920s. In an address to the New York State Chess Association 30 August 1952, he said: 'I have come to the personal conclusion that while all artists are not chess players, all chess players are artists.'

## Carol Ann Duffy (b. 1955)
BRITISH POET

Tackling a range of subjects in a humorous, often passionate style, she excels in her use of the monologue to articulate character types and moral dilemmas. Many championed her candidacy for the new poet laureateship in 1999. She has also written plays.

1 Some nights, although we are faithless, the truth
enters our hearts, that small familiar pain;
then a man will stand stock-still, hearing his youth
in the distant Latin chanting of a train.
'Prayer', publ. in *Mean Time* (1993)

2 Whatever 'in love' means,
true love is talented.
'September 1997', publ. in the *Guardian* 6 September 1997. Referring to the reply made by Prince CHARLES when asked, on his engagement to Princess DIANA, if he was in love: 'Yes, whatever that means'.

3 The dead are so talented.
The living walk by the edge of a vast lake
near the wise, drowned silence of the dead.
'Eurydice', publ. in *The World's Wife* (1999)

# Olympia Dukakis (b. 1931)
US ACTRESS

Principally a stage actress, she has also appeared in films including *Moonstruck* (1987), for which she won an Oscar, and the 1993 TV series *Tales from the City*.

1 The only thing that separates us from the animals is our ability to accessorize.
Clairee Belcher (Olympia Dukakis), in *Steel Magnolias* (film, screenplay by Robert Harling based on his own play, directed by Herbert Ross, 1989)

# John Foster Dulles (1888–1959)
US POLITICIAN AND LAWYER

Skilled in diplomacy, he advised upon the preparation of the United Nations charter in 1941 and negotiated the peace treaty with Japan in 1951. As a Republican and ardent anti-communist, he did much to strengthen the position of America and NATO during the Cold War, serving as Secretary of State (1953–9) under President EISENHOWER, who regarded him as 'one of the truly great men of our time'.

1 The ability to get to the verge without getting into the war is the necessary art. . . . If you try to run away from it, if you are scared to go to the brink, you are lost.
Quoted in *Life* 16 January 1956. The Democrat ADLAI STEVENSON characterized the Dulles–Eisenhower foreign policy as 'the power of positive brinking . . .'

# (Dame) Daphne Du Maurier (1907–89)
BRITISH NOVELIST

The granddaughter of George du Maurier, she wrote melodramatic romances set in a Cornish landscape such as *Jamaica Inn* (1936) and *Rebecca* (1938). She also published short stories and reminiscences about her family. 'I don't know another author who *imagines* so hard all the time,' commented a reader at Gollancz after perusing the manuscript of *Rebecca*.

1 Last night I dreamt I went to Manderley again.
*Rebecca*, ch. 1 (1938). Opening words.

2 It's people like me who have careers who really have bitched up the old relationship between men and women. Women ought to be soft and gentle and dependent. Disembodied spirits like myself are all *wrong*.
Letter to Ellen Doubleday, 2 September 1948, publ. in *Daphne Du Maurier*, ch. 14 (1993) by Margaret Forster

3 I think one has to choose, you know. Either to create after one's fashion, or be a woman and breed. The two don't go together and never will.
ibid. 22 February 1950, publ. in ibid. ch. 15

4 What makes people get the craving? . . . There never seems an answer. You might say loneliness. But to my mind, drinking and making love are the two most lonely pastimes on earth.
ibid. 8 August 1952, publ. in ibid. ch. 16. Reflecting on desire and lust.

# Isadora Duncan (1878–1927)
US DANCER

Born Dora Angela Duncan. A 'glorious bounding Minerva in the midst of a cautious corseted decade', she was a pioneer of modern dance, taking her inspiration from the flowing forms of classical Greek art to produce free, barefoot expression. She founded several

schools throughout Europe, and influenced Diaghilev in the development of the Ballets Russes. She died in a car accident.

1 The only dance masters I could have were Jean-Jacques Rousseau, Walt Whitman and Nietzsche.
*My Life*, ch. 8 (1927)

2 [Of Grand Duke Ferdinand of Hungary] Perhaps he was a bit different from other people, but what really sympathetic person is not a little mad?
ibid. ch. 11

3 Any intelligent woman who reads the marriage contract and then goes into it, deserves all the consequences.
ibid. ch. 19. Duncan herself was married (for one year) to the Russian poet Sergei Yesenin

4 The real American type can never be a ballet dancer. The legs are too long, the body too supple and the spirit too free for this school of affected grace and toe walking.
ibid. ch. 30

5 Farewell, my friends. I go to glory.
Quoted in *Isadora Duncan's End*, ch. 25 (1929) by Mary Desti. Duncan was accidentally strangled when her long scarf caught in the wheel of her car moments after uttering these words (*je vais à la gloire*), which have also been rendered as 'I see glory' (*je vois la gloire*).

# Ian Dunlop (b. 1940)
BRITISH ART CRITIC

1 The shock of the new.
Book title (1972). In full the title is *The Shock of the New: Seven Historic Exhibitions of Modern Art*.

# Douglas Dunn (b. 1942)
SCOTTISH POET

As a student and librarian at Hull, he fell under the influence of PHILIP LARKIN, especially in his early work which explores urban working-class culture. Later collections such as *Elegies* (1985), which mourns the death of his wife, and *Northlight* (1988) reflect wider themes.

1 Heavy rain everywhere washes up the bones of British.
Where did all that power come from, the wish
To be inert, but rich and strong, to have too much?
'A Poem in Praise of the British', publ. in *Terry Street* (1969)

2 Bored narcissists, for whom friendship is an ache,
Look for themselves in bus-queues and railway stations.
'Saturday Night Function', publ. in *The Happier Life* (1972)

3 Film is just a reflection
Of the matchless despair of the century.
There have been twenty centuries since charity began.
Indignation is day-to-day stuff;
It keeps us off the streets, it keeps us watching.
'I Am a Cameraman', publ. in *Love or Nothing* (1974)

4 Politics soften everything.
Truth is known only to its victims.
All else is photographs – a documentary
The starving and the playboys perish in.
Life disguises itself with professionalism.
ibid.

5 God so loved the world
He puked every time he looked at it,
With a few miraculous exceptions. He's gone now.
'The White Poet (Homage to Jules Laforgue)', publ. in ibid.

6 And I must mourn
Until Equator crawls to Capricorn
Or murder in the sun melts down
The Arctic and Antarctica.
'Reincarnations', publ. in *Elegies* (1985)

7 Ours was a gentle generation, pacific,
In love with music, art and restaurants,
And he with she, strolling among the canvases,
And she with him, at concerts, coats on laps.
Almost all of us were shy when we were young.
'December', publ. in ibid.

8 Snow is its own country, and it beckons
With its white finger crooked, and is calling
From the hush of its chilled bulk, its tons
And territories, its white ground falling.
'Snow Days', publ. in ibid.

9 Day by nomadic day
Our anniversaries go by,
Dates anchored in an inner sky,
To utmost ground, interior clay.
'Anniversaries', publ. in ibid.

## Finley Peter Dunne (1867–1936)
US JOURNALIST AND HUMORIST

Known as Mr Dooley, he presented from 1892 onwards a common-sense Irish-American slant on current events in newspaper sketches.

1 A man's idea in a card game is war – cruel, devastating and pitiless. A lady's idea of it is a combination of larceny, embezzlement and burglary.
*Mr Dooley on Making a Will*, 'On the Game of Cards' (1919)

2 The mission of a modern newspaper is to comfort the afflicted and afflict the comfortable.
Attributed

## J.W. Dunne (1875–1949)
BRITISH INVENTOR AND PHILOSOPHER

Full name John William Dunne. The designer of the first British military aeroplane (1906–7), he became increasingly interested in the impact of physics on philosophy and developed a theory which argued for the serial nature of time. His book *An Experiment with Time* (1927), which illustrated his theories through his own experiences of dreams and clairvoyance, was widely read and discussed, and was an influence on the 'time plays' of J.B. PRIESTLEY. His other publications include *The Serial Universe* (1934) and *Nothing Dies* (1940).

1 We have now arrived within introductory range of that very meek-spirited creature known to modern science as the '*Observer*'. It is a permanent obstacle in the path of our search for external reality that we can never entirely get rid of this individual.
*An Experiment with Time*, ch. 3 (1927, rev. 1939)

2 It is never entirely safe to laugh at the metaphysics of the 'man-in-the-street'. Basic ideas which have become enshrined in popular language cannot be wholly foolish or unwarranted.
ibid. ch. 17

## Will Durant (1885–1981)
US HISTORIAN

Gaining popularity with *The Story of Philosophy* (1926), he later collaborated with his wife Ariel to become a writer of popular philosophy and history. *The Story of Civilization* (eleven vols. 1935–75) won a Pulitzer Prize for its tenth volume, *Rousseau and Revolution* (1967).

1 Civilization is a stream with banks. The stream is some-times filled with blood from people killing, stealing, shouting and doing the things historians usually record, while on the banks, unnoticed, people build homes, make love, raise children, sing songs, write poetry and even whittle statues. The story of civilization is the story of what happened on the banks. Historians are pessimists because they ignore the banks for the river.
*Life* 18 October 1963

## Marguerite Duras (1914–96)
FRENCH AUTHOR AND FILM-MAKER

Born Marguerite Donnadieu in Vietnam, she was a successful novelist from the 1950s, but gained wider recognition for her screenplays, notably *Hiroshima, mon amour* (1959). She won the Prix Goncourt for her autobiographical novel *The Lover* (1984), which she also adapted for film in 1992.

1 Nowhere is one more alone than in Paris ... and yet surrounded by crowds. Nowhere is one more likely to incur greater ridicule. And no visit is more essential.
'Tourists in Paris', first publ. in *France-Observateur* (1957), repr. in *Outside: Selected Writings* (1984)

2 Journalism without a moral position is impossible. Every journalist is a moralist. It's absolutely unavoidable. A journalist is someone who looks at the world and the way it works, someone who takes a close look at things every day and reports what she sees, someone who represents the world, the event, for others. She cannot do her work without judging what she sees.
*Outside: Selected Writings*, Foreword (1984)

3 No other human being, no woman, no poem or music, book or painting can replace alcohol in its power to give man the illusion of real creation.
*Practicalities*, 'Alcohol' (1987)

4 I believe that always, or almost always, in all childhoods and in all the lives that follow them, the mother represents madness. Our mothers always remain the strangest, craziest people we've ever met.
ibid. 'House and Home'

5 You have to be very fond of men! Very, very fond. You have to be very fond of them to love them. Otherwise they're simply unbearable.
ibid. 'Men'

## Paul Durcan (b. 1944)
IRISH POET

Inventive and lyrical, his poetry disdains politics and portrays with compassion and surreal humour characters who are ostracized or victims of their circumstances. His collections include *O Westport in the Light of Asia Minor* (1975) and *Jesus, Break His Fall* (1980).

1 I have my troubles and I shall always have them
But I should rather live with you for ever
Than exchange my troubles for a changeless kingdom.
'The Difficulty That is Marriage', publ. in *Teresa's Bar* (1976)

2 At a ritual ceremony in a fairy ring fort
Near Bodenstown Graveyard, Co. Kildare
(Burial place of Theobald Wolfe Tone)
Margaret Thatcher joined the IRA
And the IRA joined Margaret Thatcher.
'Margaret Thatcher Joins IRA', publ. in *Sam's Cross* (1978)

3 Bring me back to the dark school – to the dark school of childhood:
To where tiny is tiny, and massive is massive.
'En Famille, 1979', publ. in *Jesus, Break His Fall* (1980)

## Leo Durocher (1906–91)
US BASEBALL COACH

Nicknamed Leo the Lip, he combined a brilliant baseball career with high living and gambling, though was also criticized for his aggressive approach to the game.

1 Take a look at them. All nice guys. They'll finish last. Nice guys. Finish last.

Remark about the New York Giants, 6 July 1946, quoted in *Nice Guys Finish Last*, pt 1 (1975)

# Lawrence Durrell (1914–91)
BRITISH AUTHOR

Elder brother to the zoologist Gerald Durrell, he was an expatriate for most of his life, using primarily Mediterranean settings for his fiction and poetry. He won acclaim for his *Alexandria Quartet* (1957–60), describing Bohemian life in pre-Second World War Egypt, and *Bitter Lemons* (1957), about Cyprus, where he settled in 1953.

1 Everyone loathes his own country and countrymen if he is any sort of artist.

Letter to Henry Miller, March 1948, publ. in *The Durrell–Miller Letters 1935–80* (1988)

2 Journeys, like artists, are born and not made. A thousand differing circumstances contribute to them, few of them willed or determined by the will – whatever we may think.

*Bitter Lemons*, 'Towards an Eastern Landfall' (1957). Opening words.

3 There are only three things to be done with a woman. You can love her, suffer for her, or turn her into literature.

Clea, in *Justine*, pt 1 (1957)

4 No one can go on being a rebel too long without turning into an autocrat.

Pursewarden writing to D.H. Lawrence, in *Balthazar*, pt 2, ch. 6 (1958)

5 Perhaps our only sickness is to desire a truth which we cannot bear rather than to rest content with the fictions we manufacture out of each other.

Justine, in *Clea*, ch. 1, sect. 3 (1960)

6 Music was invented to confirm human loneliness.

Clea, in ibid. ch. 1, sect. 4

7 Old age is an insult. It's like being smacked.

Interview in the *Sunday Times* 20 November 1988

8 The appalling thing is the degree of charity women are capable of. You see it all the time . . . love lavished on absolute fools. Love's a charity ward, you know.

Interview in the *Observer* 11 November 1990

# Ian Dury (1942–2000)
BRITISH ROCK MUSICIAN

Disabled through polio, he sang with Kilburn and the High Roads before reaching the charts with his band the Blockheads and the album *New Boots and Panties* (1977). He had hits with the singles 'Hit Me with Your Rhythm Stick' (1978) and 'Reasons to be Cheerful (Pt 3)' and later pursued an acting and writing career.

1 Sex and drugs and rock and roll.
   Is all my brain and body need
   Sex and drugs and rock and roll
   Is very good indeed.

'Sex and Drugs and Rock and Roll' (song, written with Chaz Jankel) on the album *Sex and Drugs and Rock and Roll* (1976) The song also appeared on a compilation of the same name in 1987.

2 I'm from Essex, in case you couldn't tell
   My given name is Dickie
   I come from Billericay
   And I'm doing . . . very well.

Intro to 'Billericay Dickie' (song, written with Nugent) on the album *New Boots and Panties* by Ian Dury and The Blockheads (1977)

3 I could be the catalyst that sparks the revolution
   I could be an inmate in a long term institution
   I could lean to wild extremes I could do or die

I could yawn and be withdrawn and watch them gallop by
What a waste.

'What a Waste' (song, 1978, written by the band) on the album *Sex and Drugs and Rock and Roll* (1987)

4 Hit me with your rhythm stick.

'Hit Me with Your Rhythm Stick' (song, 1978, written with Chaz Jankel), ibid.

5 There ain't half been some clever bastards.

'There Ain't Half Been Some Clever Bastards', ibid.

6 Reasons to be cheerful.

'Reasons to be Cheerful (Pt 3)' (song, 1979, written with Chaz Jankel) on the album *Do It Yourself* (1979) by Ian Dury and the Blockheads

7 I want to be straight, I want to be straight
   I'm sick and tired of taking drugs and staying up late.
   I want to confirm I want to conform
   I want to be be safe and I want to be snug and I want to be warm.

'I Want to be Straight' (song, written with Mickey Gallagher) on the album *Laughter* (1980)

8 Groups are an ecological miracle. In any group of six people you'll always find five bad apples.

Quoted in the *Daily Telegraph* 21 November 1998

# Eleonora Duse (1958–1924)
ITALIAN ACTRESS

A leading actress of the late nineteenth and early twentieth centuries rivalling SARAH BERNHARDT, she toured extensively and was mistress of the poet Gabriele D'Annunzio who wrote parts for her. She did not 'act' her parts, she said, but 'lived' them.

1 I did not use paint. I made myself up morally.

Quoted in *Le Gaulois* 27 July 1922

# Andrea Dworkin (b. 1946)
US FEMINIST CRITIC

Together with the lawyer CATHARINE MACKINNON, she has called for pornography to be outlawed, as argued in *Pornography: Men Possessing Women* (1980), among other works. In *Scapegoat: Jews, Israel and Women's Liberation* (2000) she turns her attention to women in Judaism. According to GLORIA STEINEM, 'In every century, there are a handful of writers who help the human race evolve. Andrea is one of them.'

1 Men who want to support women in our struggle for freedom and justice should understand that it is not terrifically important to us that they learn to cry; it is important to us that they stop the crimes of violence against us.

'The Rape Atrocity and the Boy Next Door', speech at State University of New York, 1 March 1975, publ. in *Our Blood*, ch. 4 (1976)

2 Only when manhood is dead – and it will perish when ravaged femininity no longer sustains it – only then will we know what it is to be free.

'The Root Cause', speech, 26 September 1975, Massachusetts Institute of Technology, publ. in *Our Blood*, ch. 9 (1976). Last words of book.

3 Seduction is often difficult to distinguish from rape. In seduction, the rapist bothers to buy a bottle of wine.

'Sexual Economics: The Terrible Truth', speech, 1976, publ. in *Letters from a War-Zone* (1987)

4 No woman needs intercourse; few women escape it.

*Right-Wing Women*, ch. 3 (1978)

5 Marriage as an institution developed from rape as a practice. Rape, originally defined as abduction, became marriage by capture. Marriage meant the taking was to extend

in time, to be not only use of but possession of, or ownership.
*Pornography*, ch. 1 (1981)

6 Money speaks, but it speaks with a male voice.
ibid.

7 Women, for centuries not having access to pornography and now unable to bear looking at the muck on the supermarket shelves, are astonished. Women do not believe that men believe what pornography says about women. But they do. From the worst to the best of them, they do.
ibid. ch. 5

## Bob Dylan (b. 1941)
US SINGER AND SONGWRITER

Original name Robert Zimmerman. One of the seminal influences on popular song in the 1960s, he started as a folk singer, his early songs 'Blowin' in the Wind' (1962) and 'The Times They Are A-Changin'' (1964) becoming anthems of the protest movement. His lyrics became more abstruse and later reflected his religious convictions. GEORGE HARRISON eulogized 'He makes William Shakespeare look like Billy Joel,' but he himself said 'They're just songs. Songs that are transparent so you can see every bit through them.'

1 The answer, my friend, is blowin' in the wind,
The answer is blowin' in the wind.
'Blowin' in the Wind' (song) on the album *The Freewheelin' Bob Dylan* (1963). On the sleeve notes to the record, Dylan wrote: 'The first way to answer the questions in the song is by asking them. But lots of people have to first find the wind.' One of Dylan's biographers, Bob Spitz, believed this might be the only one of his songs to be remembered a hundred years later. By the end of 1964 the song had been recorded by some sixty artists, and the lyric was quoted by Pope JOHN PAUL II during the Second Eucharist Congress in 1997.

2 I saw ten thousand talkers whose tongues were all
broken,
I saw guns and sharp swords in the hands of young
children,
And it's a hard, it's a hard, it's a hard, it's a hard,
It's a hard rain's a-gonna fall.
'A Hard Rain's A-Gonna Fall' (song) on the album *The Times They are a-Changin'* (1964).

3 Come mothers and fathers
Throughout the land
And don't criticize
What you can't understand
Your sons and your daughters
Are beyond your command
Your old road is rapidly agin'.
'The Times They are a-Changin'' (song) on ibid.

4 The line it is drawn
The curse it is cast
The slow one now
Will later be fast
As the present now
Will later be past
The order is
Rapidly fadin'.
And the first one now
Will later be last
For the times they are a-changin'.
ibid.

5 Flashing for the warriors whose strength is not to fight
Flashing for the refugees on the unarmed road of flight
An' for each an' ev'ry underdog soldier in the night
An' we gazed upon the chimes of freedom flashing.
'Chimes of Freedom' (song) on the album *Another Side of Bob Dylan* (1964)

6 Ah, but I was so much older then,
I'm younger than that now.
'My Back Pages' (song) on ibid.

7 You don't need a weather man
To know which way the wind blows.
'Subterranean Homesick Blues' (song) on the album *Bringing It All Back Home* (1965)

8 Don't follow leaders
And watch the parkin' meters.
ibid.

9 I ain't gonna work on Maggie's farm no more.
'Maggie's Farm' on ibid. 'Maggie's Farm' was later used as the name of a strip cartoon created by Steve Bell during MARGARET THATCHER's government.

10 In the dime stores and bus stations,
People talk of situations,
Read books, repeat quotations,
Draw conclusions on the wall.
'Love Minus Zero/No Limit' (song) on ibid.

11 She knows there's no success like failure
And that failure's no success at all.
ibid.

12 In ceremonies of the horsemen,
Even the pawn must hold a grudge.
ibid.

13 Hey! Mr Tambourine Man, play a song for me.
I'm not sleepy and there is no place I'm going to.
Hey! Mr Tambourine Man, play a song for me.
In the jingle jangle morning I'll come following you.
'Mr Tambourine Man' (song) on ibid.

14 At times I think there are no words
But these to tell what's true
And there are no truths outside the Gates of Eden.
'Gates of Eden' (song) on ibid.

15 He not busy being born
Is busy dying.
'It's Alright Ma (I'm Only Bleeding)' (song) on ibid. In a 'Communiqué' dated 1 May 1971, the anarchist Angry Brigade wrote: 'If you're not busy being born you're busy buying' (repr. in *The Angry Brigade 1967–84: Documents and Chronology*, 1985).

16 . . . Everything from toy guns that spark
To flesh-colored Christs that glow in the dark
It's easy to see without looking too far
That not much is really sacred.
ibid.

17 But even the President of the United States
Sometimes must have
To stand naked.
ibid.

18 Although the masters make the rules
For the wise men and the fools
I got nothing, Ma, to live up to.
ibid.

19 Money doesn't talk, it swears.
ibid.

20 The vagabond who's rapping at your door
Is standing in the clothes that you once wore.
Strike another match, go start anew
And it's all over now, Baby Blue.
'It's All Over Now, Baby Blue' (song) on ibid.

21 A song is anything that can walk by itself.
Sleeve notes on ibid.

22 You got a lotta nerve
To say you are my friend
When I was down

You just stood there grinning.

'Positively 4th Street' (song, 1965) on the album *Bob Dylan's Greatest Hits* (1967)

23  How does it feel
To be without a home
Like a complete unknown
Like a rolling stone?

'Like a Rolling Stone' (song) on the album *Highway 61 Revisited* (1965)

24  Something is happening here
But you don't know what it is
Do you, Mister Jones?

'Ballad of a Thin Man' (song) on ibid.

25  You know it balances on your head
Just like a mattress balances
On a bottle of wine
Your brand new leopard-skin pill-box hat.

'Leopard-Skin Pill-Box Hat' (song) on the album *Blonde on Blonde* (1966)

26  They'll stone you when you're riding in your car.
They'll stone you when you're playing your guitar.
Yes, but I would not feel so all alone,
Everybody must get stoned.

*Rainy Day Women 12 & 35* (song) on ibid.

27  To live outside the law, you must be honest.

'Absolutely Sweet Marie' (song) on ibid. A similar line appears in Don Siegel's film *The Line-Up* (1958).

28  She takes just like a woman, yes she does
She makes love just like a woman, yes she does
And she aches just like a woman
But she breaks just like a little girl.

'Just Like a Woman' (song) on ibid.

29  I see my light come shining
From the west unto the east
Any day now, any day now,
I shall be released.

'I Shall Be Released' (song, recorded 1967) on the album *The Basement Tapes* (by Bob Dylan and the Band, 1975)

30  You learn from a conglomeration of the incredible past –
whatever experience gotten in any way whatsoever.

*Tarantula*, 'Subterranean Homesick Blues & the Blond Waltz' (1970)

31  If I had wings and I could fly,
I know where I would go.
But right now I'll just sit here so contentedly
And watch the river flow.

'Watching the River Flow' (song, 1971) on the album *More Greatest Hits* (1972)

32  I like America, just as everybody else does. I love America, I gotta say that. But America will be judged.

On stage at Tempe, Arizona, 26 November 1979, quoted in *Wanted Man*, 'Saved: Bob Dylan's Conversion to Christianity' (ed. John Bauldie, 1990)

33  Democracy don't rule the world,
You'd better get that in your head;
This world is ruled by violence
But I guess that's better left unsaid.

'Union Sundown' (song) on the album *Infidels* (1983)

34  In writing songs I've learned as much from Cézanne as I have from Woody Guthrie.

Quoted in *Dylan: Behind the Shades*, ch. 25 (1991) by Clinton Heylin

35  People today are still living off the table scraps of the sixties. They are still being passed around – the music and the ideas.

*Guardian* 13 February 1992

# Freeman Dyson (b. 1923)
BRITISH-BORN US PHYSICIST AND AUTHOR

Professor of Physics at the Institute of Advanced Study, Princeton (1953–94), he is known for his research into quantum electrodynamics, and for his work on the nuclear test ban treaty. His publications on general scientific topics include *Disturbing the Universe* (1979).

1  If we had a reliable way to label our toys good and bad, it would be easy to regulate technology wisely. But we can rarely see far enough ahead to know which road leads to damnation. Whoever concerns himself with big technology, either to push it forward or to stop it, is gambling in human lives.

*Disturbing the Universe*, pt 1, ch. 1 (1979)

2  A good scientist is a person with original ideas. A good engineer is a person who makes a design that works with as few original ideas as possible. There are no prima donnas in engineering.

ibid. pt 1, ch. 10

Ear
119

## Terry Eagleton (b. 1943)

BRITISH CRITIC

He has written numerous books of literary criticism within a Marxist framework, including *Literary Theory: an Introduction* (1983) and *The Ideology of the Aesthetic* (1990). Since 1992 he has been Professor of English at Oxford.

1 Postmodernism is among other things a sick joke at the expense of . . . revolutionary avant-gardism.

'Capitalism, Modernism and Postmodernism', first publ. 1985, repr. in *Against The Grain*, ch. 9 (1986)

2 Chaucer was a class traitor
Shakespeare hated the mob
Donne sold out a bit later
Sidney was a nob.

'The Ballad of English Literature' (to the tune of 'Land of Hope and Glory'), publ. in ibid. ch. 14

3 Post-structuralism is among other things a kind of theoretical hangover from the failed uprising of '68 – a way of keeping the revolution warm at the level of language, blending the euphoric libertarianism of that moment with the stoical melancholia of its aftermath.

*Guardian* 27 October 1992

## Amelia Earhart (1897–1937)

US AVIATOR AND AUTHOR

A champion of women in aviation, she was in 1932 the first woman to fly solo across the Atlantic. She followed this with a solo flight from Hawaii to California in 1935, but lost her life in an attempt to fly around the world when her plane went down over the Pacific.

1 Courage is the price that Life exacts for granting peace,
The soul that knows it not, knows no release
From little things;
Knows not the livid loneliness of fear,
Nor mountain heights where bitter joy can hear
The sound of wings.

'Courage' (1927), publ. in *The Sound of Wings*, ch. 1 (biography, 1989) by Mary S. Lovell

## Gerald Early (b. 1952)

US AUTHOR

Professor of Modern Letters in St Louis, Missouri, he has written on themes of race, culture and identity in his essays, collected in *The Culture of Bruising* (1993) and *Tuxedo Junction* (1989).

1 Everyone in our culture wants to win a prize. Perhaps that is the grand lesson we have taken with us from kindergarten . . . everyone gets a ribbon, and praise becomes a meaningless narcotic to soothe egoistic distemper.

'Life With Daughters: Watching the Miss America Pageant', publ. in *Kenyon Review* autumn 1990, repr. in *The Culture of Bruising* (1993)

## Stephen T. Early (1889–1951)

US JOURNALIST AND GOVERNMENT OFFICIAL

One of America's top reporters, he was Press Secretary to President ROOSEVELT (1933–45), referred to by President TRUMAN as 'Roosevelt's secretary, friend and sagacious adviser', and until 1938 was involved in publicity for the New Deal.

1 I received a card the other day from Steve Early which said, 'Don't Worry Me – I am an 8 Ulcer Man on 4 Ulcer Pay.'

Quoted by Harry S. Truman in letter in 1949, publ. in *Mr President: Personal Diaries, Private Letters, Papers and Revealing Interviews of Harry S. Truman*, pt 5 (1952) by William Hillman

# Daniel Easterman (b. 1949)

IRISH AUTHOR

With a specialism in the Middle East, he has published academic books including *New Jerusalems: Reflections on Islam, Fundamentalism and the Rushdie Affair* (1993), and since 1980 also novels, such as *Day of Wrath* (1995) and *The Final Judgement* (1996). Under the pen name of Jonathan Aycliffe he writes ghost stories.

1 We ignore thriller writers at our peril. Their genre is the political condition. They massage our dreams and magnify our nightmares. If it is true that we always need enemies, then we will always need writers of fiction to encode our fears and fantasies.

*Million Magazine* September/October 1991

# Clint Eastwood (b. 1930)

US ACTOR AND FILM-MAKER

Having established himself as the lean loner in spaghetti Westerns such as *The Good, the Bad and the Ugly* (1966) and crime thrillers such as *Dirty Harry* (1971), he began directing his own films and received an Oscar for the revisionist Western *Unforgiven* (1992). He briefly held office as Mayor of Carmel-by-the-Sea, California (1986–8).

1 I know what you're thinking. Did he fire six shots or only five? Well, to tell you the truth, in all this excitement I've kinda lost track myself. But being this is a .44 Magnum, the most powerful handgun in the world, and would blow your head clean off – you've got to ask yourself one question: Do I feel lucky? Well, do ya, punk?

Harry Callahan (Clint Eastwood), in *Dirty Harry* (film, 1971, screenplay by Harry and Rita Fink and Dean Riesner, directed by Don Siegel). The words are addressed to a bank-robber, at whose head Harry has his gun aimed, following a foiled heist.

2 Everybody knows nobody ever stood in the street and let the heavy draw first. That's where I disagree with the [John] Wayne concept. I do all the stuff Wayne would never do. I play bigger-than-life characters but I'll shoot a guy in the back. I go by the expediency of the moment.

*Variety* 14 September 1976

3 Go ahead. Make my day.

Harry Callahan (Clint Eastwood), in *Sudden Impact* (film, 1983, screenplay by Joseph Stinson, produced and directed by Clint Eastwood). RONALD REAGAN, a self-confessed Eastwood fan, borrowed the words in 1985: 'I have only one thing to say to the tax increasers: "Go ahead and make my day."'

# Eazy-E (1963–95)

US RAPPER

Original name Eric Wright. A founding member of the controversial Californian group NWA (Niggaz With Attitude), he was one of the earliest exponents of 'gangsta rap' in the 1980s.

1 Fuck tha police coming straight out the underground
A young nigger got it bad cause I'm brown
And not the other color.

'Fuck tha Police' (song) on the album *Straight Outta Compton* (1989) by NWA. The inflammatory lyrics provoked outrage in the US, and calls for the recording to be withdrawn.

# Abba Eban (b. 1915)

ISRAELI POLITICIAN AND DIPLOMAT

Originally named Aubrey Solomon. After serving as Israeli representative in the UN, he was ambassador to the United States in Washington, DC (1950–59). He won a seat in the Knesset in 1959, and was Foreign Minister 1966–74, when his skills as orator and diplomat helped cement relations with America and the EU. He retired in 1988.

1 History teaches us that men and nations behave wisely once they have exhausted all other alternatives.

Speech in London, 16 December 1970, quoted in *The Times* 17 December 1970

2 It is our experience that political leaders do not always mean the opposite of what they say.

Quoted in the *Observer* 5 December 1971

# Umberto Eco (b. 1932)

ITALIAN SEMIOLOGIST AND NOVELIST

A high-profile European intellectual, long-time professor at Bologna University and pioneer in the science of signs, he has written extensively in his chosen and related fields, as in *A Theory of Semiotics* (1976). In 1980 he turned his hand to novel writing and produced the bestseller *The Name of the Rose*, a postmodern medieval murder mystery, followed in 1988 by *Foucault's Pendulum*.

1 There is a constant in the average American imagination and taste, for which the past must be preserved and celebrated in full-scale authentic copy; a philosophy of immortality as duplication. It dominates the relation with the self, with the past, not infrequently with the present, always with History and, even, with the European tradition.

'Travels in Hyperreality: The Fortresses Of Solitude' (1975), repr. in *Travels in Hyperreality* (1986)

2 Learning does not consist only of knowing what we must or we can do, but also of knowing what we could do and perhaps should not do.

Brother William, in *The Name of the Rose*, 'First Day: Compline' (1980)

3 Until then I had thought each book spoke of the things, human or divine, that lie outside books. Now I realized that not infrequently books speak of books: it is as if they spoke among themselves.

Narrator (Adso), in ibid. 'Fourth Day: Terce'

4 The good of a book lies in its being read. A book is made up of signs that speak of other signs, which in their turn speak of things. Without an eye to read them, a book contains signs that produce no concepts; therefore it is dumb.

Brother William, in ibid. 'Fifth Day: Vespers'

5 Perhaps the mission of those who love mankind is to make people laugh at the truth, *to make truth laugh*, because the only truth lies in learning to free ourselves from insane passion for the truth.

Brother William, in ibid. 'Seventh Day: Night'

6 I have never doubted the truth of signs, Adso; they are the only things man has with which to orient himself in the world.

Brother William, in ibid.

7 I would define the poetic effect as the capacity that a text displays for continuing to generate different readings, without ever being completely consumed.

*Reflections on the Name of the Rose*, 'Telling the Process' (1983)

8 The postmodern reply to the modern consists of recognizing that the past, since it cannot really be destroyed, because its destruction leads to silence, must be revisited: but with irony, not innocently. I think of the postmodern attitude as that of a man who loves a very cultivated woman and knows he cannot say to her, 'I love you madly', because he knows that she knows (and that she knows that he knows) that these words have already been written by Barbara Cartland. Still, there is a solution. He can say, 'As Barbara Cartland would put it, I love you madly.'

ibid. 'Postmodernism, Irony, the Enjoyable'

## (Sir) Arthur Stanley Eddington (1882–1944)
BRITISH ASTRONOMER AND PHYSICIST

Director of the Cambridge Observatories from 1914 and a pioneer in the field of astrophysics, he was the first to confirm EINSTEIN's theory of relativity, while observing the stars during the solar eclipse of 1919. His books helped to popularize science, especially *The Nature of the Physical World* (1928).

1 Let us draw an arrow arbitrarily. If as we follow the arrow we find more and more of the random element in the world, then the arrow is pointing towards the future; if the random element decreases the arrow points towards the past . . . I shall use the phrase 'time's arrow' to express this one-way property of time which has no analogue in space.

*The Nature of the Physical World* ch. 4 (1928). 'Time's Arrow' was the title MARTIN AMIS gave to his 1991 novel in which the sequence of time is reversed.

2 I ask you to look both ways. For the road to a knowledge of the stars leads through the atom; and important knowledge of the atom has been reached through the stars.

*Stars and Atoms*, 'Lecture 1' (1928)

3 It cannot be denied that for a society which has to create scarcity to save its members from starvation, to whom abundance spells disaster, and to whom unlimited energy means unlimited power for war and destruction, there is an ominous cloud in the distance though at present it be no bigger than a man's hand.

*New Pathways in Science*, ch. 8 (1935)

## Leon Edel (1907–97)
US BIOGRAPHER AND CRITIC

The foremost authority on HENRY JAMES, he published the definitive biography in five volumes (1953–72) and numerous editions of letters. He taught at New York University (1953–73) and was awarded the 1963 Pulitzer Prize and the National Book Award in recognition of his work on James.

1 The secret of biography resides in finding the link between talent and achievement. A biography seems irrelevant if it doesn't discover the overlap between what the individual did and the life that made this possible. Without discovering that, you have shapeless happenings and gossip.

Interview in *Writers at Work* (eighth series, ed. George Plimpton, 1988)

## (Sir) Anthony Eden (1897–1977)
BRITISH POLITICIAN AND PRIME MINISTER

First Earl of Avon. Elected a Conservative MP in 1923, he served as War Secretary under CHURCHILL, and as Foreign Secretary (1935–8, 1940–45, and 1951–5). As Prime Minister (1955–7) he was condemned for his conduct in the Suez crisis and resigned shortly afterwards. See also MALCOLM MUGGERIDGE 9.

1 Everyone is always in favour of general economy and particular expenditure.

Quoted in the *Observer* 17 June 1956

2 We are in an armed conflict; that is the phrase I have used. There has been no declaration of war.

Speech to House of Commons, 1 November 1956, publ. in *Hansard*. British and French planes had bombed Egyptian airfields on the preceding day, provoking protests in Britain and abroad. Eden justified the action: 'We best avoid wars by taking even physical action to stop small ones.'

3 It is either him [Colonel Nasser] or us, don't forget that.

Quoted in *We, the Nation*, ch. 14 (1995) by A.J. Davies

## Clarissa Eden (1920–85)
WIFE OF ANTHONY EDEN

Countess of Avon. Originally Clarissa Spencer Churchill, she was the niece of WINSTON CHURCHILL, and had a brief career in film production before marrying ANTHONY EDEN in 1952.

1 For the past few weeks I have really felt as if the Suez Canal was flowing through my drawing room.

Speech at Gateshead, 20 November 1956, quoted in the *Gateshead Post* 23 November 1956

## Jerry Edmonton (b. 1946)
CANADIAN ROCK MUSICIAN

Also known as Mars Bonfire, he was drummer with the rock band Steppenwolf in the 1960s and 1970s, and occasional composer of their lyrics.

1 Born to be wild.

'Born to be Wild' (song) on the album *Steppenwolf* (1968) by Steppenwolf. The song, which became a biker anthem, featured in Dennis Hopper's film *Easy Rider* (1969).

## Edward VIII (1894–1972)
KING OF GREAT BRITAIN AND NORTHERN IRELAND

Though succeeding to the throne in 1936, he was never crowned, abdicating after eleven months in order to marry Wallis Simpson, a twice-divorced American. After the Second World War, the couple spent the rest of their lives in Paris as Duke and Duchess of Windsor, ostracized by other members of the British royal family. Wallis once judged her husband a potential car salesman, who might be an 'admirable representative of Rolls Royce'.

1 These works brought all these people here. Something should be done to get them at work again.

Comment at the derelict Dowlais Iron and Steel Works in South Wales, 18 November 1936, quoted in the *Western Mail* 19 November 1936. 9,000 men had recently been laid off at the works. The remark is usually quoted 'Something must be done.'

2 I have found it impossible to carry the heavy burden of responsibility and to discharge my duties as King as I would wish to do without the help and support of the woman I love . . . I now quit altogether public affairs, and I lay down my burden.

Abdication speech, 11 December 1936, publ. in *The Times* 12 December 1936. WINSTON CHURCHILL is said to have had a hand in composing the speech, which was broadcast on radio.

3 The thing that impresses me most about America is the way parents obey their children.

Quoted in *Look* 5 March 1957

## Barbara Ehrenreich (b. 1941)
US AUTHOR AND COLUMNIST

She is best known for her outspoken but humorous newspaper columns, mainly on issues of health, sex and class and from a feminist angle. Among her books are *For Her Own Good* (1978) and *The Worst Years of Our Lives* (1991).

1 Exercise is the yuppie version of bulimia.

'Food Worship', first publ. 1985, repr. in *The Worst Years of Our Lives* (1991)

2 Like many other women, I could not understand why every man who changed a diaper has felt impelled, in recent years, to write a book about it.

'Wimps', first publ. in *The New York Times*, 1985, repr. in ibid.

3 Personally, I have nothing against work, particularly when performed, quietly and unobtrusively, by someone else. I just don't happen to think it's an appropriate subject for an 'ethic'.

'Goodbye To The Work Ethic', first publ. 1988, repr. in ibid.

4 **America is addicted to wars of distraction.**

*The Times* 22 April 1991

5 **When the Somalians were merely another hungry third world people, we sent them guns. Now that they are falling down dead from starvation, we send them troops. Some may see in this a tidy metaphor for the entire relationship between north and south. But it would make a whole lot more sense nutritionally – as well as providing infinitely more vivid viewing – if the Somalians could be persuaded to eat the troops.**

*Guardian* 9 January 1993

# John Ehrlichman (1925–99)
PRESIDENTIAL ASSISTANT TO RICHARD NIXON

As Chief Advisor on Domestic Policy under President NIXON and a key member of his inner circle, he attempted to seal the presidency from the encroaching investigations into the Watergate break-in, for which he and H.R. HALDEMAN were nicknamed the 'Berlin Wall'. He served an eighteen-month gaol term for conspiracy, perjury and obstruction of justice.

1 **I think we ought to let him hang there. Let him twist slowly, slowly in the wind.**

Telephone conversation with John Dean, March 1973, quoted in the *Washington Post* 27 July 1973. The words refer to Patrick Gray, a nominee for Director of the FBI from whom President NIXON had tacitly withdrawn his support.

2 **It'll play in Peoria.**

Attributed quip regarding the selling of political policy in 'middle America' (Peoria is in Illinois). Ehrlichman claimed to have originated the catch-phrase during Nixon's 1968 election campaign, though other sources suggest it was current much earlier, used in US variety shows in the 1930s.

# Albert Einstein (1879–1955)
GERMAN-BORN US THEORETICAL PHYSICIST

More responsible than anyone for changing our understanding of the universe in terms of space, time and gravitation, he was, in the words of C.P. Snow, 'the symbol of science, the master of the twentieth-century intellect . . . the spokesman for human hope'. His theory of relativity, which he had already conceived in embryonic form at the age of sixteen, was published in 1905, his general theory of relativity in 1915. He was awarded the Nobel Prize for Physics in 1921. In his later years he was an avowed pacifist, a 'grand old man' of peace. See also ROLAND BARTHES 4.

1 **By an application of the theory of relativity to the taste of readers, today in Germany I am called a German man of science, and in England I am represented as a Swiss Jew. If I come to be regarded as a *bête noire* the descriptions will be reversed, and I shall become a Swiss Jew for the Germans and a German man of science for the English!**

*The Times* 28 November 1919. Einstein expressed variations of this idea on different occasions.

2 **God is subtle, but he is not malicious.**

Quoted in *Einstein*, ch. 14 (1973) by R.W. Clark. The remark was made in April/May 1921, during Einstein's first visit to Princeton University, in response to the news that a 'nonzero aether drift' had been found at Mount Vernon observatory. The words were later carved above the fireplace of the Common Room of Fine Hall in Princeton's former Mathematical Institute; in 1946 Einstein gave a freer translation: 'God is slick, but he ain't mean.'

3 **Quantum mechanics is certainly imposing. But an inner voice tells me that it is not yet the real thing. The theory says a lot, but does not really bring us any closer to the secret of the 'old one'. I, at any rate, am convinced that *He* is not playing at dice.**

Letter to Max Born, 4 December 1926, publ. in *The Born–Einstein Letters* (ed. Max Born, 1971). The version usually remembered is 'God does not play dice [with the universe].' Nearly twenty years later, Einstein wrote to Born: 'You believe in the God who plays dice, and I in complete law and order in a world which objectively exists, and which I, in a wildly speculative way, am trying to capture . . . Even the great initial success of the quantum theory does not make me believe in the fundamental dice-game, although I am well aware that our younger colleagues interpret this as a consequence of senility. No doubt the day will come when we will see whose instinctive attitude was the correct one.' (7 September 1944)

4 **It has often been said, and certainly not without justification, that the man of science is a poor philosopher.**

'Physics and Reality', publ. in the *Franklin Institute Journal* March 1936, repr. in *Out of My Later Years*, ch. 12, sect. 1 (1950)

5 **The whole of science is nothing more than a refinement of everyday thinking.**

ibid.

6 **One may say 'the eternal mystery of the world is its comprehensibility.' . . . The fact that it is comprehensible is a miracle.**

ibid.

7 **Science without religion is lame, religion without science is blind.**

From a scientific paper at conference in New York City, September 1940, repr. in ibid. ch. 7, sect. 2, 'Science and Religion'

8 **We should take care not to make the intellect our god; it has, of course, powerful muscles, but no personality.**

From a broadcast for the United Jewish Appeal, 11 April 1943, publ. in ibid. ch. 50

9 **The unleashed power of the atom has changed everything save our modes of thinking and we thus drift toward unparalleled catastrophe.**

Telegram sent to prominent Americans, 24 May 1946, publ. in *The New York Times* 25 May 1946. Various versions of this statement exist, probably translations from the German which Einstein always preferred to use: see *Albert Einstein: A Documentary Biography*, ch. 8 (1956) by Carl Seelig, and *Albert Einstein: A Biography*, ch. 14 (1954) by Antonina Valentin.

10 **One has to divide one's time between politics and our equations. Equations are much more important to me, because politics is for the present, while . . . an equation is for eternity.**

Remark at Princeton, late 1940s, quoted in *Albert Einstein*, ch. 38 (1993) by Albrecht Fösling. Einstein was then involved with the Emergency Committee of Atomic Scientists (set up to inform the public about the atomic bomb and its effects), of which he became Chairman in May 1946.

11 **The most beautiful emotion we can experience is the mystical. It is the power of all true art and science. He to whom this emotion is a stranger, who can no longer wonder and stand rapt in awe, is as good as dead. To know that what is impenetrable to us really exists, manifesting itself as the highest wisdom and the most radiant beauty, which our dull faculties can comprehend only in their most primitive forms – this knowledge, this feeling, is at the centre of true religiousness. In this sense, and in this sense only, I belong to the rank of devoutly religious men.**

Quoted in *Einstein: His Life and Times*, ch. 12, sect. 5 (1947) by Philip Frank

12 **I cannot seriously believe in it [quantum theory] because the theory cannot be reconciled with the idea that physics should represent a reality in time and space, free from spooky actions at a distance.**

Letter to Max Born, 3 March 1947, publ. in *The Born–Einstein Letters* (ed. Max Born, 1971)

13 **When you are courting a nice girl an hour seems like a second. When you sit on a red-hot cinder a second seems like an hour. That's relativity.**

Quoted in the *News Chronicle* 14 March 1949

14 Perfection of means and confusion of goals seem – in my opinion – to characterize our age.

*Out of My Later Years*, ch. 14 (1950)

15 People like us, who believe in physics, know that the distinction between past, present and future is only a stubbornly persistent illusion.

Letter 21 March 1955, publ. in *Albert Einstein, Michele Besso: Correspondence 1903–1955*, no. 215 (1972)

16 A (Success) = X (Work) + Y (Play) + Z (Keep your mouth shut).

Quoted in *Albert Einstein: A Documentary Biography*, ch. 3 (1956) by Carl Seelig

17 As far as the laws of mathematics refer to reality, they are not certain; and as far as they are certain, they do not refer to reality.

Quoted by Fritjof Capra in *The Tao of Physics*, ch. 2 (1975)

# Dwight D. Eisenhower (1890–1969)

US GENERAL AND PRESIDENT

Supreme Commander of the Allied Forces in Western Europe leading the D-Day invasions in 1944, 'Ike' proved himself a skilful conciliator and communicator and was later given command over all NATO forces in Europe. Riding on a wave of popularity, he served two terms as Republican president (1953–61), during which he adopted a hard anti-communist line, though he succeeded in bringing the Korean war to an end. The journalist Murray Kempton called him 'the great tortoise upon whose back the world sat for eight years'. See also ADLAI STEVENSON 19.

1 Humility must always be the portion of any man who receives acclaim earned in the blood of his followers and the sacrifices of his friends.

Speech at Guildhall, London, 12 July 1945, publ. in *Eisenhower Speaks* (ed. Rudolph L. Treunfels, 1948)

2 Every gun that is made, every warship launched, every rocket fired, signifies, in the final sense, a theft from those who hunger and are not fed, those who are cold and are not clothed. The world in arms is not spending money alone. It is spending the sweat of its labourers, the genius of its scientists, the hopes of its children.

'The Chance for Peace', speech to the American Society of Newspaper Editors, Washington DC, 16 April 1953, publ. in *Public Papers of the Presidents of the United States* (1953)

3 Politics ought to be the part-time profession of every citizen who would protect the rights and privileges of free people and who would preserve what is good and fruitful in our national heritage.

Speech broadcast 28 January 1954, publ. in ibid. (1954)

4 You have a row of dominoes set up; you knock over the first one, and what will happen to the last one is that it will go over very quickly.

Press conference 7 April 1954, publ. in ibid. Referring to the situation in south-east Asia after the defeat of the French by the Viet-Minh.

5 In the councils of government, we must guard against the acquisition of unwarranted influence, whether sought or unsought, by the military-industrial complex. The potential for the disastrous rise of misplaced power exists and will persist. We must never let the weight of this combination endanger our liberties or democratic processes. We should take nothing for granted.

Farewell broadcast on radio and television 17 January 1961, quoted in *The New York Times* 18 January 1961

6 In preparing for battle I have always found that plans are useless, but planning is indispensable.

One of Eisenhower's favourite maxims, quoted by RICHARD NIXON in *Six Crises*, 'Khrushchev' (1962)

# T.S. Eliot (1888–1965)

ANGLO-AMERICAN POET AND CRITIC

Full name Thomas Stearns Eliot. Born in St Louis. He was one of the major poets of the twentieth century. By the time *The Waste Land* appeared (1922), he was regarded as the voice of a disillusioned post-First World War generation. His later verse plays and poetry, including *Murder in the Cathedral* (1936) and the *Four Quartets* (1936–42), reflect his conversion to Anglo-Catholicism. He was also an incisive critic, and he was awarded the Nobel Prize for Literature in 1948. See also TOM PAULIN 4.

1 Let us go then, you and I,
When the evening is spread out against the sky
Like a patient etherised upon a table

'The Love Song of J. Alfred Prufrock', publ. in *Prufrock and Other Observations* (1917). Opening lines of poem.

2 In the room the women come and go
Talking of Michelangelo.

ibid.

3 And indeed there will be time
To wonder, 'Do I dare?' and, 'Do I dare?'
Time to turn back and descend the stair,
With a bald spot in the middle of my hair . . .
Do I dare
Disturb the universe?

ibid.

4 I have measured out my life with coffee spoons

ibid.

5 No! I am not Prince Hamlet, nor was meant to be:
Am an attendant lord, one that will do
To swell a progress, start a scene or two,
Advise the prince

ibid.

6 I grow old . . . I grow old . . .
I shall wear the bottoms of my trousers rolled.

ibid.

7 Shall I part my hair behind? Do I dare to eat a peach?
I shall wear white flannel trousers, and walk upon the
     beach.
I have heard the mermaids singing, each to each.
I do not think that they will sing to me.

ibid.

8 It [tradition] cannot be inherited, and if you want it you must obtain it by great labour.

'Tradition and the Individual Talent', sect. 1, first publ. in *Egoist* September and December 1919, repr. in *Selected Prose of T.S. Eliot* (ed. Frank Kermode, 1975)

9 Art never improves, but . . . the material of art is never quite the same.

ibid.

10 The progress of an artist is a continual self-sacrifice, a continual extinction of personality.

ibid.

11 Poetry is not a turning loose of emotion, but an escape from emotion; it is not the expression of personality, but an escape from personality. But, of course, only those who have personality and emotions know what it means to want to escape from these things.

ibid.

12 Uncorseted, her friendly bust
Gives promise of pneumatic bliss.

'Whispers of Immortality', publ. in *Poems* (1919). Grishkin – the character described here – is thought to be a portrayal of Serafima Astafieva (1876–1934), a Russian dancer with the Diaghilev company who opened her own ballet school in London. EZRA POUND also referred to her in his *Pisan Cantos* 77 and 79 (1945).

13 Immature poets imitate; mature poets steal.

*The Sacred Wood*, 'Philip Massinger' (1920)

14 Here I am, an old man in a dry month,
Being read to by a boy, waiting for rain.

'Gerontion', publ. in *Ara Vos Prec* (1920). Opening lines of poem.

15 In the seventeenth century a dissociation of sensibility set in, from which we have never recovered; and this dissociation, as is natural, was due to the influence of the two most powerful poets of the century, Milton and Dryden.

'The Metaphysical Poets', first publ. in *The Times Literary Supplement* 20 October 1921, repr. in *Selected Prose of T.S. Eliot* (ed. Frank Kermode, 1975)

16 Poets in our civilization, as it exists at present, must be *difficult*.

ibid.

17 April is the cruellest month, breeding
Lilacs out of the dead land, mixing
Memory and desire, stirring
Dull roots with spring rain.

*The Waste Land*, pt 1, 'The Burial of the Dead' (1922). Opening lines of poem.

18 I will show you fear in a handful of dust.

ibid.

19 Unreal City,
Under the brown fog of a winter dawn

ibid. The lines are repeated in pt 3 of the poem, with 'noon' substituted for 'dawn'.

20 I had not thought death had undone so many.

ibid.

21 I Tiresias, though blind, throbbing between two lives,
Old man with wrinkled female breasts, can see
At the violet hour, the evening hour that strives
Homeward, and brings the sailor home from sea,
The typist home at teatime, clears her breakfast, lights
Her stove, and lays out food in tins.

ibid. pt 3, 'The Fire Sermon'

22 O City city, I can sometimes hear
Beside a public bar in Lower Thames Street,
The pleasant whining of a mandoline
And a clatter and a chatter from within
Where fishmen lounge at noon

ibid.

23 Who is the third who walks always beside you?
When I count, there are only you and I together
But when I look ahead up the white road
There is always another one walking beside you

ibid. pt 5, 'What the Thunder Said'

24 The awful daring of a moment's surrender
Which an age of prudence can never retract

ibid.

25 These fragments I have shored against my ruins

ibid.

26 Between the conception
And the creation
Between the emotion
And the response
Falls the Shadow

'The Hollow Men', sect. 5, publ. in *Poems 1909–1925* (1925)

27 *This is the way the world ends*
*This is the way the world ends*
*This is the way the world ends*
*Not with a bang but a whimper.*

ibid. Concluding lines of poem.

28 The dreamcrossed twilight between birth and dying

'Ash-Wednesday', pt 6 (1930), repr. in *Collected Poems 1909–1935* (1936)

29 So far as we are human, what we do must be either evil or good: so far as we do evil or good, we are human: and it is better, in a paradoxical way, to do evil than to do nothing: at least we exist.

'Baudelaire', first publ. as Introduction to *The Intimate Journals of Charles Baudelaire* (transl. Christopher Isherwood, 1930), repr. in *Selected Prose of T.S. Eliot* (ed. Frank Kermode, 1975)

30 Where is the Life we have lost in living?
Where is the wisdom we have lost in knowledge?
Where is the knowledge we have lost in information?

'Choruses from "The Rock" ', pt 1 (1934), repr. in *Collected Poems 1909–62* (1962)

31 And the wind shall say 'Here were decent godless people:
Their only monument the asphalt road
And a thousand lost golf balls.'

ibid. pt 3

32 And meanwhile we have gone on living,
Living and partly living,
Picking together the pieces,
Gathering faggots at nightfall,
Building a partial shelter,
For sleeping and eating and drinking and laughter.

The Chorus of Women of Canterbury, in *Murder in the Cathedral*, pt 1 (1935)

33 The last temptation is the greatest treason:
To do the right deed for the wrong reason.

Thomas, in ibid.

34 Time past and time future
What might have been and what has been
Point to one end, which is always present.

'Burnt Norton', pt 1 (1936), the first of *Four Quartets* (1943)

35 Footfalls echo in the memory
Down the passage which we did not take
Towards the door we never opened
Into the rose-garden.

ibid.

36 Human kind
Cannot bear very much reality.

ibid. The words also appeared in Eliot's *Murder in the Cathedral*, pt 2 (spoken by Thomas), and have been evoked or echoed by numerous other writers; for example GRAHAM GREENE in *Our Man in Havana* (1958), where Hasselbacher states, 'Reality in our century is not something to be faced', and in MARGARET DRABBLE's *Realms of Gold* (1975): 'The human mind can bear plenty of reality but not too much intermittent gloom.'

37 Where does one go from a world of insanity?
Somewhere on the other side of despair.

Harry, Lord Monchensey, in *The Family Reunion*, pt 2, sc. 2 (1939)

38 The Naming of Cats is a difficult matter,
It isn't just one of your holiday games;
You may think at first I'm as mad as a hatter
When I tell you, a cat must have THREE DIFFERENT NAMES.

'The Naming of Cats', publ. in *Old Possum's Book of Practical Cats* (1939)

39 Jellicle Cats come out tonight
Jellicle Cats come one come all:
The Jellicle Moon is shining bright –
Jellicles come to the Jellicle Ball

'The Song of the Jellicles', publ. in ibid.

40 Macavity's a Mystery Cat: he's called the Hidden Paw –
For he's the master criminal who can defy the Law.
He's the bafflement of Scotland Yard, the Flying Squad's despair:
For when they reach the scene of crime – *Macavity's not there!*

'Macavity: the Mystery Cat', publ. in ibid.

41 In my beginning is my end.

'East Coker', pt 1 (1940), the second of *Four Quartets* (1943). Opening line of poem. The motto of Mary Queen of Scots was 'In my end is my beginning.'

42 The dripping blood our only drink,
The bloody flesh our only food:
In spite of which we like to think
That we are sound, substantial flesh and blood –
Again, in spite of that, we call this Friday good.
*ibid.* pt 4

43 Each venture
Is a new beginning, a raid on the inarticulate
With shabby equipment always deteriorating
In the general mess of imprecision of feeling.
*ibid.* pt 5

44 The first condition of right thought is right sensation –
the first condition of understanding a foreign country is
to smell it.
*A Choice of Kipling's Verse*, Introduction (1941), repr. in *On Poetry
and Poets*, pt 2, 'Rudyard Kipling' (1957)

45 I do not know much about gods; but I think that the
river
Is a strong brown god – sullen, untamed and intractable
'The Dry Salvages', pt 1 (1941), the third of *Four Quartets* (1943).
Opening lines of poem.

46 War is not a life: it is a situation,
One which may neither be ignored nor accepted.
'A Note on War Poetry', first publ. in *London Calling* (1942) by
STORM JAMESON, repr. in *Collected Poems 1909–62* (1962)

47 It seems just possible that a poem might happen
To a very young man: but a poem is not poetry –
That is a life.
*ibid.*

48 And what the dead had no speech for, when living,
They can tell you, being dead: the communication
Of the dead is tongued with fire beyond the language of
the living.
'Little Gidding', pt 1 (1942), the fourth of *Four Quartets* (1943)

49 There are flood and drouth
Over the eyes and in the mouth,
Dead water and dead sand
Contending for the upper hand.
The parched eviscerate soil
Gapes at the vanity of toil,
Laughs without mirth.
This is the death of the earth.
*ibid.* pt 2

50 For last year's words belong to last year's language
And next year's words await another voice.
*ibid.*

51 A people without history
Is not redeemed from time, for history is a pattern
Of timeless moments.
*ibid.* pt 5

52 We shall not cease from exploration
And the end of all our exploring
Will be to arrive where we started
And know the place for the first time.
*ibid.*

53 Culture may even be described simply as that which makes
life worth living. ·
*Notes Towards a Definition of Culture*, ch. 1 (1948)

54 The term *culture* . . . includes all the characteristic activities and interests of a people: Derby Day, Henley Regatta,
Cowes, the twelfth of August, a cup final, the dog races,
the pin table, the dart board, Wensleydale cheese, boiled
cabbage cut into sections, beetroot in vinegar, nineteenth-
century Gothic churches and the music of Elgar.
*ibid.*

55 You will find that you survive humiliation.
And that's an experience of incalculable value.
Unidentified Guest (later identified as Sir Henry Harcourt-Reilly),
in *The Cocktail Party*, act 1, sc. 1 (1950)

56 Hell is oneself,
Hell is alone, the other figures in it
Merely projections. There is nothing to escape from
And nothing to escape to. One is always alone.
Edward, in ibid. act 1, sc. 3

57 The years between fifty and seventy are the hardest. You
are always being asked to do things, and yet you are not
decrepit enough to turn them down.
*Time* 23 October 1950

58 It's not wise to violate rules until you know how to observe
them.
Interview in *Writers at Work* (second series, ed. George Plimpton,
1963)

59 It [television] is a medium of entertainment which permits
millions of people to listen to the same joke at the same
time, and yet remain lonesome.
*New York Post* 22 September 1963

# Elizabeth II (b. 1926)
QUEEN OF GREAT BRITAIN AND NORTHERN IRELAND

Queen since 1952 and deeply committed to the concept of the
Commonwealth, she has always upheld the traditional, formal role
of the monarchy, at the expense of sometimes seeming out of touch.
Increasing press intrusions have forced a degree of modernization.

1 I declare before you all that my whole life, whether it be
long or short, shall be devoted to your service and the
service of our great Imperial family to which we all belong.
Speech to the Commonwealth, Cape Town, 21 April 1947, quoted
in *The Times* 22 April 1947

2 My husband and I . . .
Opening words of her first Christmas Message, 1953, New Zealand.
This introductory phrase became a regular feature of the Queen's
speeches, though the alternative 'Prince Philip and I . . .' was introduced in the 1960s when it was apparent that the familiar formula
was becoming a joke. On her 25th wedding anniversary, she
quipped, 'I think everybody really will concede that on this, of all
days, I should begin my speech with the words "My husband and
I".'

3 Like all the best families, we have our share of eccentricities, of impetuous and wayward youngsters and of
family disagreements.
Quoted in the *Daily Mail* 19 October 1989

4 It's all to do with the training: you can do a lot if you're
properly trained.
Television documentary BBC 1, 6 February 1992

5 1992 is not a year I shall look back on with undiluted
pleasure. In the words of one of my more sympathetic
correspondents, it has turned out to be an Annus Horribilis.
Speech at Guildhall, 24 November 1992, quoted in *The Times* 25
November 1992. In a speech commemorating her forty years on the
throne, the Queen's allusion to John Dryden's long poem 'Annus
Mirabilis' (1667) was lost on much of the nation, though the tabloid
press enjoyed it (see SUN 8). Dryden had described 1666 as a 'year
of marvels', whose events included the Great Fire of London. A fire
had gutted some of the State Apartments in Windsor Castle a few
days before the Queen's speech, while other personal disasters
included the separation of the Prince and Princess of Wales amid
sustained criticism against the royal family in the press.

6 Some things stay there, some things go out of the other
ear, and some things don't go in at all.
Quoted in the *Guardian* 20 April 1996. On her weekly meetings
with prime ministers.

## Elizabeth, Queen Mother (b. 1900)

WIFE OF KING GEORGE VI OF GREAT BRITAIN AND
NORTHERN IRELAND

She has been admired by the public since her travels abroad with her husband during the 1930s, an esteem which increased when she remained with him in London during the Blitz. After his death she undertook extensive public duties, in 1978 becoming Lord Warden of the Cinque Ports, the first woman to hold this office.

1 I'm glad we've been bombed. It makes me feel I can look the East End in the face.

Quoted in *King George VI*, pt 3, ch. 6 (1958) by John Wheeler-Bennett. Said to a policeman after the bombing of Buckingham Palace by German planes. The East End bore the brunt of the bombing in London during the Second World War. When it was suggested that the royal family be evacuated, the Queen is reported to have declared, 'The children will not leave unless I do. I shall not leave unless their father does, and the King will not leave the country in any circumstances whatever'.

## Duke Ellington (1899–1974)

US JAZZ MUSICIAN

Born Edward Kennedy Ellington. Described as a 'Harlem Dionysus', he was one of the outstanding jazz musicians of the century, writing numberless tunes for his own big band, including 'Creole Love Call' (1927) and 'Mood Indigo' (1930). He toured extensively, also composed suites, ballet and film scores, and was admired by Leopold Stokowski and IGOR STRAVINSKY. The novelist and poet Blaise Cendrars judged Ellington's music 'not only a new art form but a new reason for living'.

1 It don't mean a thing if it ain't got that swing.

'It Don't Mean a Thing if it Ain't Got that Swing' (song, 1932, written with Irving Mills). Ellington said that Bubber Miley, a member of the band in New Orleans during the late 1920s, was the first person he ever heard use the expression.

2 Playing 'bop' is like playing Scrabble with all the vowels missing.

*Look* 10 August 1954

## Alice Thomas Ellis (b. 1932)

BRITISH NOVELIST

Originally Anna Margaret Haycraft, she assumed her pseudonym for the publication of her novel *The Sin Eater* (1977) and is best known for *The Twenty-Seventh Kingdom* (1982). She has been a frequent contributor to the *Spectator* and the *Catholic Herald*, and since 1996 a columnist for the *Oldie*.

1 Death is the last enemy: once we've got past that I think everything will be alright.

'In the Psychiatrist's Chair', broadcast on BBC Radio 4, 19 August 1992

## Havelock Ellis (1859–1939)

BRITISH PSYCHOLOGIST

His major work, the seven-volume *Studies in the Psychology of Sex* (1897–1928), the first dispassionate and encyclopaedic treatment of the subject, was deemed scandalous, a 'filthy publication', and until 1935 was only legally available in the USA to doctors. He also published popular books on sex as well as essays on art and literature.

1 All civilization has from time to time become a thin crust over a volcano of revolution.

*Little Essays of Love and Virtue*, ch. 7 (1922)

2 It has always been difficult for Man to realize that his life is all an art. It has been more difficult to conceive it so than to act it so. For that is always how he has more or less acted it.

*The Dance Of Life*, ch. 1 (1923)

3 A man must not swallow more beliefs than he can digest.

ibid. ch. 5

4 The prevalence of suicide, without doubt, is a test of height in civilization; it means that the population is winding up its nervous and intellectual system to the utmost point of tension and that sometimes it snaps.

ibid. ch. 7

5 The sun, the moon and the stars would have disappeared long ago . . . had they happened to be within the reach of predatory human hands.

ibid.

## Ralph Ellison (1914–94)

US AUTHOR

His reputation rests on his first and only novel *The Invisible Man* (1953), the story of an idealistic young black intellectual's search for identity and his subsequent alienation, set in the slums of New York.

1 I am an invisible man. . . . I am a man of substance, of flesh and bone, fiber and liquids – and I might even be said to possess a mind. I am invisible, understand, simply because people refuse to see me.

The narrator, in *The Invisible Man*, Prologue (1952)

## Richard Ellmann (1918–87)

US BIOGRAPHER AND ESSAYIST

The outstanding biographer of his generation, he wrote on nineteenth- and twentieth-century English and Irish authors including Yeats, Joyce and Wilde. He was professor at Yale and then at Oxford 1970–84. ANTHONY BURGESS said that he 'brought American common sense and a European sensibility' to his work.

1 The imagination should queen it over the mind, with reason as her obsequious butler and memory as her underpaid maid-of-all-work.

'Wallace Stevens's Ice-Cream', first publ. in *Kenyon Review* (1957), repr. in *a long the riverrun*, pt 2 (1988)

2 If we must suffer, it is better to create the world in which we suffer, and this is what heroes do spontaneously, artists do consciously, and all men do in their degree.

'Yeats Without Analogue', lecture (1964), publ. in ibid. pt 1

3 Criticism prevents art from forgetting, prevents it from sinking into conformity.

'The Uses of Decadence: Wilde, Yeats, Joyce', lecture at Bennington, Vermont, 28 September 1983, repr. in ibid.

4 To delight in possession is to allow the conceivability of dispossession, to rely on constancy is impossible because it can only exist as a relation to inconstancy; what is absent calls attention to what is present.

ibid. pt 1, 'Becoming Exiles'

## Ben Elton (b. 1959)

BRITISH AUTHOR AND COMIC

A regular performer on the cabaret circuit and on television, he has co-written TV comedy series such as *The Young Ones* (1982, 1984) and *Blackadder* (1986–9) as well as plays and bestselling novels including *Stark* (1989) and *Popcorn* (1996, staged 1997).

1 The appropriation of radical thinking by lazy, self-obsessed hippies is a public relations disaster that could cost the earth.

*Stark*, 'Court, Hippies and Love at First Sight' (1989)

2 If only the strength of the love that people feel when it is reciprocated could be as intense and obsessive as the love we feel when it is not; then marriages would be truly made in heaven.

ibid. 'Private Investigations'

3 People aren't greedy any more, oh no. They're shop-aholics, victims of commercialism. Victims! People don't fail any more. They experience negative success. We are building a culture of gutless, spineless, self-righteous, whining cry-babies who have an excuse for everything and take responsibility for nothing.

Bruce Delamitri, in *Popcorn*, ch. 11 (1996)

4 You ain't no Pavlov, Bruce, and we ain't no dribbling dogs. There ain't nothing specific here. I am talking generally. I'm saying that you make killing cool.

Scout, to film-maker Bruce Delamitri, in ibid. ch. 36

5 If we're going to teach the kids to speak badly let's at least have people doing it who know the rules that are being broken.

Tom, Head of Youth, BBC Radio, in *Inconceivable* (1999). Sam's diary entry.

6 They never wear tights! It's amazing. In the middle of winter in Newcastle or Leeds you'll see them, making their way from bus station to club, groups of determined girls in tiny minidresses, naked but for a square inch or two of Lycra, bare arms folded against the howling wind, translucent white legs clicking along the sodden pavement in their impossibly precarious shoes. Never mind Scott of the Antarctic, these girls would have done it in half the time and got back before the chip shop closed.

Sam's diary entry, in ibid.

7 In our sad modern world female pop stars have to be very successful indeed before it is allowable for them to perform with their clothes on.

ibid.

## Paul Éluard (1895–1952)
FRENCH POET

Real name Eugène Grindal. His Surrealist poetry was influenced by his experiences as a soldier in the First World War and Resistance fighter during the Second World War. His collections include *Capital of Sorrow* (1926) and *Poetry and Truth* (1942).

1 Farewell sadness
Good-day sadness
You are inscribed in the lines of the ceiling.

'À Peine défigurée', publ. in *La Vie immédiate* (1932). *Bonjour tristesse* ('Good-day sadness') was the title given to FRANÇOISE SAGAN's first novel, an international bestseller in 1954.

## Dick Emery (1917–83)
BRITISH COMEDIAN

After success in the BBC radio series *Educating Archie* (1958), he showed his talent for characterization and drag sketches in *The Dick Emery Show* (1963–71). In 1982 he starred in the BBC comedy-thriller series *Emery*.

1 Ooh, you are awful . . . but I like you!

Catch-phrase from *The Dick Emery Show* (1963–71). Emery used the same words as the aging sex kitten Mandy in the 1950s radio show *Educating Archie*. 'You Are Awful' was a single by him, entering the top fifty in January 1973.

## Tracy Emin (b. 1963)
BRITISH ARTIST

An installation artist and 'bad girl' of British art, she uses a variety of media in her frequently confrontational, confessional and frank work. In 1995 she made *Everyone I Have Ever Slept With 1963–1995*, a work that became an icon of contemporary British art. *Sobasex* and *Every Part of Me is Bleeding* earned her a nomination for the Turner Prize in 1999.

1 You're not going to make it as an artist if you don't understand commerce and you work away in an attic for

twenty years, slagging off people like me, complaining about never being discovered.

Quoted in the *Daily Telegraph* 29 January 2000

## Brian Eno (b. 1948)
BRITISH MUSICIAN, PRODUCER AND ARTIST

Dressed in blue sequins and black boa, he was a pioneer synthesizer player with the band Roxy Music (1971–3). He later worked with DAVID BOWIE and Talking Heads (see DAVID BYRNE) as well as various avant-garde rock projects, and was a pioneer of ambient music with such albums as *Music for Airports* (1979).

1 An ambience is defined as an atmosphere, or a surrounding influence: a tint. . . . Ambient Music must be able to accommodate many levels of listening attention without enforcing one in particular; it must be as ignorable as it is interesting.

Sleevenotes to *Music for Airports* (1979). Eno called this album his first 'ambient' record, though the original concept was pioneered, he said, by Muzak Inc. in the 1950s.

2 What I find we're entering into now is not death of the author but diffusion of the author. Authorship gets spread through more and more people, you don't know who makes something now, where an idea comes from. I call this 'scenius' as opposed to genius. It's the intelligence of a whole situation, a whole network.

Interview in *i-D* October 1993

3 A culture is the sum of all the things about which humanity can choose to differ.

*A Year With Swollen Appendices*, 'Culture' (1996)

4 New technologies have the tendency to replace skills with judgement – it's not what you *can* do that counts, but what you *choose* to do, and this invites everyone to start crossing boundaries.

ibid. 'Sharing Music'

## Hans Magnus Enzensberger (b. 1929)
GERMAN POET AND CRITIC

The best known of the post-Brechtian German poets, he writes in a caustic and laconic style, often making use of the shock metaphor. His books include *Poems for People Who Don't Read Poems* (1968) and the narrative poem *The Sinking of the Titanic* (1978). He has also written on crime, culture and politics.

1 That one gets used to everything –
One gets used to that.
The usual name for it is
A learning process.

'The Force of Habit', publ. in *Gedichte 1955–70* (1971)

2 I am playing around
with the end, the end of the *Titanic*.
I've nothing better to do.
I have time, like a God.
I have nothing to lose.

*The Sinking of the Titanic*, 'Fourth Canto' (1978)

3 Even if they cannot name their own goal, people's self-directed activity expresses a practical critique of existing conditions.

'Swedish Autumn', first publ. 1982, repr. in *Europe, Europe* (1989)

4 Whenever anyone says that something or other is 'typically Italian', I want to jump up with impatience, overturn my chair, and run out of the room. Could anything be more barren than the study of 'national psychology', that moldy garbage heap of stereotypes, prejudices, and accepted ideas?

'Italian Extravagances', first publ. 1983, repr. in ibid.

5 The painter who dips his brush in the pot knows that his work is futile and that only one thing can be relied on:

really existing time, which takes hold of and conserves everything, even as it wears it down. History is a process of erosion. What we call socialism is only its viceroy.

'Hungarian Confusions', first publ. 1985, repr. in ibid.

6 Slowly
the scab peels off. A new tobacconist,
a new address. Pariahs, horribly relieved.
Shades growing paler. These are the documents.
This is the bunch of keys. This is the scar.

'The Divorce', publ. in *Gedichte 1950–85* (1986), repr. in *Selected Poems* (1994, transl. Michael Hamburger)

7 [Of Berlin] Pleasure and terror have given way to normality, and normality, wherever time is on its side, conquers everything.

*Europe, Europe*, 'Epilogue: The Seacoast of Bohemia' (1989)

8 Mediocrity in politics is not to be despised. Greatness is not needed.

*The Late Show* BBC2, 5 November 1990

## Nora Ephron (b. 1941)
US AUTHOR AND SCREENWRITER

Her forte is deft and witty treatments of sex, marriage and their traumas. Her writings include the screenplays for *When Harry Met Sally* (1989), *Sleepless in Seattle* (1993), which she also directed, and *Heartburn* (1986), adapted from her own 1983 novel that was itself based on the break-up of her marriage to Watergate journalist CARL BERNSTEIN.

1 I am continually fascinated at the difficulty intelligent people have in distinguishing what is controversial from what is merely offensive.

'Barney Collier's Book', publ. in *Esquire* January 1976

2 If pregnancy were a book they would cut the last two chapters.

Rachel Samstat (Meryl Streep), in *Heartburn* (film, 1986, screenplay by Nora Ephron adapted from her own novel, directed by Mike Nichols)

3 No man can be friends with a woman he finds attractive. He always wants to have sex with her. Sex is always out there. Friendship is ultimately doomed and that is the end of the story.

Harry Burns (Billy Crystal), in *When Harry Met Sally . . .* (film, 1989, screenplay by Nora Ephron, directed and co-produced by Rob Reiner)

4 I'll have what she's having.

Woman diner to waiter, having observed Sally Albright (Meg Ryan) acting an orgasm, in ibid.

5 Verbal ability is a highly overrated thing in a guy, and it's our pathetic need for it that gets us into so much trouble.

Becky (Rosie O'Donnell), in *Sleepless in Seattle* (film, 1993, screenplay by Jeff Ward, Nora Ephron and David S. Ward, directed by Nora Ephron)

## Susan Ertz (1894–1985)
BRITISH NOVELIST

Her novels, which largely deal with family relationships, include *Madame Claire* (1923), *Now We Set Out* (1935) and *Charmed Circle* (1956).

1 Millions long for immortality who do not know what to do with themselves on a rainy Sunday afternoon.

Mrs A., in *Anger in the Sky*, ch. 5 (1943)

## Linda Evangelista (b. 1965)
ITALIAN-CANADIAN MODEL

Along with Christy Turlington and Naomi Campbell, she was one of the three models for whom the term 'Supermodel' was coined in 1986, and she later became the *grande dame* of modelling.

1 We don't wake up for less than $10,000 a day.

Quoted in *Vogue* fall 1991, repr. in *Model*, '$10,000 A Day' (1995) by Michael Gross. She later commented, 'I feel that quote is going to be engraved on my tombstone. It was tongue-in-cheek, but it backfired. How many times do I have to apologise for a few careless words?'

2 Nobody is born with perfect eyebrows.

*Daily Telegraph* 13 August 1992

## (Dame) Edith Evans (1888–1976)
BRITISH ACTRESS

A versatile character actress, she made her name playing roles in Shakespeare and SHAW, though is most famous for her majestic Lady Bracknell in Wilde's *The Importance of Being Earnest*. She first appeared in film in *The Queen of Spades* (1948) and continued acting until her eighties. KENNETH TYNAN described her later acting style as 'tranquillized benevolence cascading from a great height, like royalty opening a bazaar'.

1 When a woman behaves like a man why doesn't she behave like a nice man?

Quoted in the *Observer* 30 September 1956

## Gavin Ewart (1916–95)
BRITISH POET

Although his first collection appeared in 1939, it was not until the 1970s that he devoted himself to writing full time, using a light verse style, often parodically. Among his collections are *The Pleasures of the Flesh* (1966) and *Penultimate Poems* (1989).

1 There are sorrows in herds that are too deep for words.

'How Tragedy Is Impossible', publ. in *Or Where a Young Penguin Lies Screaming* (1977)

2 Many an actor is funtastically handiclapped by the superphysical triviality of his profession.

'Pros' publ. in ibid.

3 The path of true love isn't smooth,
the ruffled feathers sex can soothe
ruffle again – for couples never
spend all their lives in bed together.

'24th March 1986', publ. in *Late Pickings* (1987)

4 If men's lives are worth giving, they're also worth
    saving.
Who let them start the bloody thing?
That's the question, there's the sting.

'The Falklands, 1982', publ. in *Selected Poems* (1996). Closing lines of poem.

## W.N. Ewer (1885–1976)
BRITISH JOURNALIST

Full name William Norman Ewer, nicknamed Trilby. Recruited as one of 'Lansbury's Lambs', he worked on the *Daily Herald* (1912–64), holding the post of Foreign Correspondent from 1919. He was also Overseas Service correspondent for the BBC.

1 I gave my life for freedom – this I know:
For those who bade me fight had told me so.

'Five Souls', publ. in *Five Souls and Other Verses* (1917)

## Clifton Fadiman (b. 1904)
US ESSAYIST

Calling himself an 'odd job man', he has written widely, including literary criticism and children's books such as *Wally the Wordworm* (1964).

1 [Of Gertrude Stein] I encountered the mama of dada again . . . and as usual withdrew worsted.
*Party of One* (1955)

2 A cheese may disappoint. It may be dull, it may be naive, it may be oversophisticated. Yet it remains cheese, milk's leap toward immortality.
*Any Number Can Play* (1957)

## Marianne Faithfull (b. 1946)
BRITISH SINGER

Daughter of an Austrian baroness, she was a wistful singer of the 1960s, actor in a number of plays and films and the much publicized girlfriend of MICK JAGGER. She resuscitated her musical career as a worldly *chanteuse* with the album *Broken English* (1979).

1 Maybe the most you can expect from a relationship that goes bad is to come out of it with a few good songs.
*Faithfull*, 'Colston Hall' (1994). Referring to her relationship with MICK JAGGER.

## Giovanni Falcone (1939–92)
ITALIAN JUDGE

His fearless investigations into organized crime in Sicily resulted in the conviction of over 300 members of the Mafia in 1987, and also in his murder.

1 One usually dies because one is alone, or because one has got into something over one's head. One often dies because one does not have the right alliances, because one is not given support. In Sicily the Mafia kills the servants of the State that the State has not been able to protect.
Closing words of *Men of Honour*, ch. 6 (1992). The car containing Falcone, his wife and three bodyguards was blown up 23 May 1992.

## Oriana Fallaci (b. 1930)
ITALIAN JOURNALIST AND AUTHOR

She has worked as a war correspondent but is most famous for her hard-nosed interviewing techniques, which she employed for various Italian and US press publications. Her books include *The Useless Sex* (1960), *Interview with History* (1976), and the novel *A Man* (1979).

1 We do not understand these Americans who, like adolescents, always speak of sex, and who, like adolescents, all of a sudden have discovered that sex is good not only for procreating children.
*The Egotists*, 'Hugh Hefner'(1963)

2 The bitter discovery that God does not exist has destroyed the concept of fate. But to deny fate is arrogance, to declare that we are the sole shapers of our existence is madness; if you deny fate, life becomes a series of missed opportunities, a regret for what never was and could have been, a remorse for what was not done and could have been done, and the present is wasted, twisted into another missed opportunity.
*A Man*, pt 2, ch. 1 (1971)

3 All banners, even the most noble, the most pure, are filthy with blood and shit. When you look at the glorious banners displayed in museums, in churches, venerated as relics to kneel before in the name of ideals, dreams, have no illusions: those brownish stains are not traces of rust,

they are dried blood, dried shit, and more often shit than blood.

ibid. pt 5, ch. 1

4 Death is a thief that never turns up by surprise . . . Death always announces itself by a kind of scent, impalpable perceptions, silent sounds.

ibid. pt 6, ch. 1

## Frantz Fanon (1925–61)

FRENCH WEST INDIAN PSYCHIATRIST, PHILOSOPHER AND POLITICAL ACTIVIST

His experiences during the Algerian revolution led him to write *The Wretched of the Earth* (1961), which, urging a 'collective catharsis', became a manifesto for liberation struggles against colonial powers. He died of leukaemia before seeing Algerian independence.

1 Fervour is the weapon of choice of the impotent.

*Black Skins White Masks*, Introduction (1952, transl. 1967)

2 However painful it may be for me to accept this conclusion, I am obliged to state it: for the black man there is only one destiny. And it is white.

ibid.

3 Colonialism is not a thinking machine, nor a body endowed with reasoning faculties. It is violence in its natural state, and it will only yield when confronted with greater violence.

*The Wretched of the Earth*, ch.1 (1961)

4 Nationalism, that magnificent song that made the people rise against their oppressors, stops short, falters and dies away on the day that independence is proclaimed.

ibid. ch. 3

## Eleanor Farjeon (1881–1965)

BRITISH CHILDREN'S AUTHOR

She wrote prolifically for children, for instance *Martin Pippin in the Apple Orchard* (1921) and, with her brother Herbert Farjeon, the educational *Kings and Queens* (1932).

1 Morning has broken
Like the first morning,
Blackbird has spoken
Like the first bird.

'A Morning Song (for the First Day of Spring)', publ. in *Children's Bells* (1957). The song was a hit for Cat Stevens in 1972.

## Farouk I (1920–65)

KING OF EGYPT

Increasingly absorbed in his hedonistic lifestyle, the last reigning king of Egypt (1936–52) was forced to abdicate in the coup d'état staged by General Neguib and Gamal Abdul Nasser in 1952. He went into exile and became a citizen of Monaco in 1959.

1 The whole world is in revolt. Soon there will be only five kings left – the King of England, the King of Spades, the King of Clubs, the King of Hearts and the King of Diamonds.

Remark in 1948, quoted in *Life* 10 April 1950. The words were addressed to John (later Lord) Boyd-Orr, first Director of the Food and Agriculture Organization, at a conference in Cairo, also quoted in Boyd-Orr's memoirs, *As I Recall*, ch. 21 (1966).

## The Fast Show

Television series on BBC 2 (1994–7) which consisted of short sketches written and produced by Paul Whitehouse and Charlie Higson, with contributions from actors including John Thomson, Simon Day, Arabella Weir, Caroline Aherne and Mark Williams.

1 Does my bum look big in this?

(Arabella Weir)

2 Ooh, suits you sir!

Paul Whitehouse and Mark Williams as tailors

3 Scorchio!

Weathergirl (Caroline Aherne)

4 This week, I 've been mostly eatin' . . .

'Jesse' (Paul Williams)

5 Very, very drunk.

'Rowley Birkin, QC' (Paul Whitehouse)

6 Which was nice.

'Patrick Nice' (Mark Williams)

## William Faulkner (1897–1962)

US NOVELIST

His novels, including *The Sound and the Fury* (1929) and *Absalom! Absalom!* (1936), are primarily narratives of 'the tragic fable of southern history' set in the fictional Mississippi county of Yoknatapawpha. He was awarded the Nobel Prize for Literature in 1949. 'Mr Faulkner', wrote CLIFTON FADIMAN, 'is interested in making your mind rather than your flesh creep'.

1 Poor man. Poor mankind.

Hightower, in *Light in August*, ch. 4 (1932). Referring to Joe Christmas, suspected of murder and liable to be lynched.

2 I believe that man will not merely endure: he will prevail. He is immortal, not because he alone among creatures has an inexhaustible voice, but because he has a soul, a spirit capable of compassion and sacrifice and endurance. The poet's, the writer's, duty is to write about these things.

Nobel Prize acceptance speech in Stockholm, 10 December 1950, publ. in *The Penguin Book of Twentieth-Century Speeches* (ed. Brian MacArthur, 1999)

3 Maybe the only thing worse than having to give gratitude constantly . . . is having to accept it.

Temple Drake, in *Requiem For a Nun*, act 2, sc. 1 (1951)

4 If a writer has to rob his mother, he will not hesitate; the 'Ode on a Grecian Urn' is worth any number of old ladies.

Interview in the *Paris Review* spring 1956, repr. in *Writers at Work* (first series, ed. Malcolm Cowley, 1958)

5 The best job that was ever offered to me was to become a landlord in a brothel. In my opinion it's the perfect milieu for an artist to work in.

ibid.

## Mohamed al-Fayed (b. 1933)

EGYPTIAN BUSINESSMAN

Extravagantly rich, he is based in London though has been repeatedly refused British nationality. Flagships of his business empire are the Ritz Hotel in Paris (acquired in 1979) and London's Harrods (1985). His son Dodi died along with Princess DIANA in 1997.

1 For me, he [Neil Hamilton] is nothing, he is not a human, he is someone who would sell his mother for money – no dignity, no honour, nothing.

Statement in libel trial, quoted in the *Guardian* 20 November 1999. Hamilton, who was suing al-Fayed, was accused of having taken advantage of the latter's generosity while a Conservative MP. 'He had discovered a golden goose,' declared the businessman. 'The eggs came in gold.'

## Jules Feiffer (b. 1929)

US CARTOONIST

He published his first cartoon collection *Sick, Sick, Sick* in 1958, and attracted a following in the 1960s with his satirical strip *Feiffer*.

1 I used to think I was poor. Then they told me I wasn't

poor, I was needy. Then they told me it was self-defeating to think of myself as needy, I was deprived. Then they told me deprived was a bad image, I was underprivileged. Then they told me underprivileged was overused, I was disadvantaged. I still don't have a dime. But I sure have a great vocabulary.

Cartoon caption, 1965, quoted in *Political Dictionary*, 'Disadvantaged' (1968, rev.1978) by William Safire

2 Much has been written about her [Lillian Hellman's] enemies. She picked them with care, and God knows they deserved her.

Graveside eulogy quoted in *Lilly: Reminiscences of Lillian Hellman*, pt 4, 'Kidding on the Square' (1988) by Peter Feibleman

## Elaine Feinstein (b. 1930)
BRITISH AUTHOR AND POET

Her disparate writings are concerned with the 'persistence of the past' and reflect her Russian background. Prominent works include *Badlands* (1986), a poetry collection, and *The Survivors* (1982) and *Dreamers* (1984), both novels, and she has also written radio plays, biographies and translations of Russian poetry.

1 She imagines herself clean as a fish,
   evasive, solitary, dumb. Her prayer:
   to make peace with her own monstrous nature.

'Patience', publ. in *Some Unease and Angels* (1977)

2 Poetry is
   powerless as grass.
   How then should it defend us?
   unless by strengthening
   our fierce and obstinate centres.

'Muse', publ. in *Badlands* (1986)

## Marty Feldman (1933–82)
BRITISH COMEDIAN

Known for his pop-eyed look ('like Dada on legs', as he put it) he began in television by writing comedy scripts before joining JOHN CLEESE and Tim Brooke-Taylor on *At Last the 1948 Show* in 1967. He went on to star in his own TV shows and later in the MEL BROOKS films *Young Frankenstein* (1973) and *Silent Movie* (1976).

1 I looked him up in the *Cattle-breeder's Guide* – he wasn't in there; I looked him up in the *Standard Book of British Birds* – he wasn't in there either; I finally found him in the Book of Revelations.

Sketch 17 March 1969, on *Marty* (TV show, BBC 2, 1968–9), publ. in *From Fringe to Flying Circus*, ch. 8 (1980) by Roger Wilmut. Referring to the creature (never revealed) in a large basket in a vet's waiting room. The sketch won the Silver Rose award at that year's Montreux Light Entertainment Festival.

2 Comedy, like sodomy, is an unnatural act.

*The Times* 9 June 1969

## Federico Fellini (1920–93)
ITALIAN FILM-MAKER

Among his idiosyncratic films, which he always scripted himself, *La Dolce Vita* (1960) was a *succès de scandale* for its cynical portrayal of Roman high life, while *8½* (1963) and *Amarcord* (1973) were autobiographical. Summing up his achievements, he stated, 'Although my father wanted me to become an engineer and my mother a bishop, I myself am quite content to have succeeded in becoming an adjective'.

1 Would you be able to give up everything, to start life all over again . . . to choose one thing, just one thing, and be faithful to it . . . to make it the thing that gives meaning to your life . . . something that contains everything else

. . . that becomes everything else just because of your boundless faith in it?

Guido Anselmi (Marcello Mastroianni), in *8½* (film, 1963, screenplay co-written by Fellini, Ennio Flaiano, Tullio Pinelli and Brunello Rondi, directed by Fellini)

2 It's better to destroy than to create when you're not creating those few things which are truly necessary.

Daumier, the critic ( Jean Rougeul) in ibid.

3 The movie business is macabre. Grotesque. It is a combination of a football game and a brothel.

*New Yorker*, 30 October 1965, repr. in *Fellini on Fellini*, 'Miscellany II', 'Like a puppet-master who falls in love with his puppets', sect. 21 (ed. Anna Keel and Christian Stritch, 1974)

4 Cinéma-vérité? I prefer 'cine-mendacity'. A lie is always more interesting than the truth. Lies are the soul of showmanship and I adore shows.

*L'Arc* 45 (1971), repr. in ibid. sect. 6

5 I have invented myself entirely: a childhood, a personality, longings, dreams and memories, all in order to enable me to tell them.

*Fellini on Fellini*, 'Miscellany I', 'I'm a liar, but an honest one', sect. 10 (ed. Anna Keel and Christian Strich, 1974)

6 Censorship is a way of admitting our own weakness and intellectual insufficiency.
   Censorship is always a political tool: certainly not an intellectual one. Criticism is an intellectual tool: it presupposes a knowledge of what one judges and opposes. Criticism does not destroy; it puts an object in its proper place among other objects.
   To censor is to destroy, or at least to oppose the process of reality.

ibid. 'Notes on Censorship'

7 What is an artist? A provincial who finds himself somewhere between a physical reality and a metaphysical one. . . . It's this in-between that I'm calling a province, this frontier country between the tangible world and the intangible one – which is really the realm of the artist.

Quoted by JOHN BERGER in 'Ev'ry Time We Goodbye' publ. in *Sight and Sound* June 1991, repr. in *Keeping a Rendezvous* (1992)

## James Fenton (b. 1949)
BRITISH POET AND CRITIC

His experience as a freelance journalist and foreign correspondent informs his poetry, which is strongly influenced by W.H. AUDEN. His poetry collections include *The Memory of War* (1982) and *Out of Danger* (1993), and his journalistic essays appear in *All the Wrong Places: Adrift in the Politics of Asia* (1988).

1 It is not what they built. It is what they knocked down.
   It is not the houses. It is the spaces between the houses.
   It is not the streets that exist. It is the streets that no
           longer exist.

'German Requiem' (1980), repr. in *The Memory of War* (1982)

2 He tells you, in the sombrest notes,
   If poets want to get their oats,
   The first step is to slit their throats.
   The way to divide
   The sheep of poetry from the goats
   Is suicide.

'Letter to John Fuller', publ. in *Children in Exile* (1983)

3 I didn't exist at Creation,
   I didn't exist at the Flood,
   And I won't be around for Salvation
   To sort out the sheep from the cud –
   Or whatever the phrase is. The fact is
   In soteriological terms
   I'm a crude existential malpractice

And you are a diet of worms.
'God, A Poem', publ. in ibid.

4 One does not become a guru by accident.
*The Times* 9 August 1984. Referring to playwright SAMUEL BECKETT.

5 Saigon was an addicted city, and we were the drug: the corruption of children, the mutilation of young men, the prostitution of women, the humiliation of the old, the division of the family, the division of the country – it had all been done in our name.
'The Fall of Saigon', first publ. in *Granta* no. 15, 1985, repr. in *All the Wrong Places* (1988)

6 Imitation, if it is not forgery, is a fine thing. It stems from a generous impulse, and a realistic sense of what can and cannot be done.
'Ars Poetica', no. 47, in the *Independent on Sunday* 16 December 1990

7 Tienanmen
Is broad and clean
And you can't tell
Where the dead have been
And you can't tell
When they'll come again
They'll come again
To Tienanmen
'Tienanmen', publ. in *Out of Danger* (1993). The poem is dated 15 June 1989, written in response to the savage suppression of protesters that had just taken place in Beijing's Tienanmen Square. Fenton later revealed that he wrote it to the tune of 'Strange Fruit' (see BILLIE HOLIDAY 1).

## Edna Ferber (1887–1968)
US AUTHOR

A prolific writer of short stories and novels vividly evoking America in the 1920s and 1930s, she won a Pulitzer Prize for *So Big* (1924) but is probably best known for *Show Boat* (1926), which became a hit on Broadway and on film.

1 Wasn't marriage, like life, unstimulating and unprofitable and somewhat empty when too well ordered and protected and guarded? Wasn't it finer, more splendid, more nourishing, when it was, like life itself, a mixture of the sordid and the magnificent; of mud and stars; of earth and flowers; of love and hate and laughter and tears and ugliness and beauty and hurt?
*Show Boat*, ch. 19 (1926, musical show 1927, filmed 1936 and 1951)

2 I am not belittling the brave pioneer men but the sunbonnet as well as the sombrero has helped to settle this glorious land of ours.
Sabra Cravat, in *Cimarron*, ch. 23 (1929, filmed 1931 and 1960)

3 It was part of the Texas ritual. We're rich as son-of-a-bitch stew but look how homely we are, just as plain-folksy as Grandpappy back in 1836. We know about champagne and caviar but we talk hog and hominy.
*Giant*, ch. 2 (1952, filmed 1956)

4 A woman can look both moral and exciting – if she also looks as if it was quite a struggle.
Quoted in *Reader's Digest* December 1954

5 Being an old maid is like death by drowning, a really delightful sensation after you cease to struggle.
Quoted in *The Algonquin Wits* (ed. Robert E. Drennan, 1968)

## Lawrence Ferlinghetti (b. 1919)
US POET AND PUBLISHER

Associated with the Beat movement in the 1950s, he co-founded the City Lights Bookstore in San Francisco which served both as gathering place and publishing house. He himself published over forty volumes of poetry, generally political and declamatory in style, including *An Eye on the World* (1967) and *When I Look at Pictures* (1990).

1 Constantly risking absurdity
          and death
whenever he performs
              above the heads
                of his audience
the poet like an acrobat
          climbs on rime
      to a high wire of his own making.
'A Coney Island of the Mind', sect. 15, publ. in *A Coney Island of the Mind* (1958)

2 I once started out
to walk around the world
but ended up in Brooklyn.
That Bridge was too much for me.
'Autobiography', publ. in ibid.

3 I see another war is coming
but I won't be there to fight it.
I have read the writing
on the outhouse wall.
I helped Kilroy write it.
ibid.

## Leslie Fiedler (b. 1917)
US CRITIC

His major work, *Love and Death in the American Novel* (1960), a 'sustained fouling of the American nest' according to poet and critic Donald Davie, presents writers as obsessed with death and incapable of portraying adult heterosexual relationships. He also wrote novels and short stories.

1 The 'text' is merely one of the contexts of a piece of literature, its lexical or verbal one, no more or less important than the sociological, psychological, historical, anthropological or generic.
*Love and Death in the American Novel*, Preface (1960)

2 To be an American (unlike being English or French or whatever) is precisely to *imagine* a destiny rather than to inherit one; since we have always been, insofar as we are Americans at all, inhabitants of myth rather than history.
'Cross the Border – Close the Gap', first publ. in *Playboy* December 1969, repr. in *Collected Essays* vol. 2 (1971)

## Sally Field (b. 1946)
US SCREEN ACTRESS

The daughter of a Hollywood starlet, she made her name in 1960s TV series such as *Gidget* and *The Flying Nun* and later starred in Hollywood movies, notably *Smokey and the Bandit* (1977), *Norma Rae* (1979) and *Steel Magnolias* (1989).

1 I happen to believe you make your own destiny. You have to do the best with what God gave you . . . Life is a box of chocolates, Forrest. You never know what you're goin' to get.
Mrs Gump (Sally Field), in *Forrest Gump* (film, 1994, screenplay by Eric Roth adapted from Winston Groom's novel, directed by Robert Zemeckis)

## Helen Fielding (b. 1958)
BRITISH AUTHOR

Creator of the 'Bridget Jones Diary' in the *Independent* in 1995, she successfully transferred the twenty-something heroine, obsessed with men and diets, to novel form with *Bridget Jones's Diary* (1996) and a sequel *The Edge of Reason* (1999). JILLY COOPER remarked of the author 'everyone is looking for love, but she made it hip and funny, rather than despairing'.

1 Being a woman is worse than being a farmer – there is so much harvesting and crop spraying to be done: legs to be waxed, underarms shaved, eyebrows plucked, feet pumiced, skin exfoliated and moisturized, spots cleansed, roots dyed, eyelashes tinted, nails filed, cellulite massaged, stomach muscles exercised. The whole performance is so highly tuned you only need to neglect it for a few days for the whole thing to go to seed . . . Is it any wonder girls have no confidence?

*Bridget Jones's Diary*, 'Tuesday 3 January' (1996)

2 You should have said 'I'm not married because I'm a *Singleton*, you smug, prematurely ageing, narrow-minded morons. And because there's more than one bloody way to live: one in four households are single, most of the royal family are single, the nation's young men have been proved by surveys to be *completely unmarriageable*, and as a result there's a whole generation of single girls like me with their own incomes and homes who have lots of fun and don't need to wash anyone else's socks. We'd be as happy as sandboys if people like you didn't conspire to make us feel stupid just because you're jealous.'

Shazzer, in ibid. 'Wednesday 1 February'. Bridget responds: 'Singletons! Hurrah for the Singletons!'

## Dorothy Fields (1904–74)
US SONGWRITER

A prolific lyricist, she often wrote in collaboration with Jerome Kern and Harold Arlen, producing such enduring songs as 'On the Sunny Side of the Street' (1930) and 'The Way You Look Tonight' (1936), for which she won an Oscar. She also wrote libretti for musicals, including *Annie Get Your Gun* (1946) for IRVING BERLIN and *Sweet Charity* (1966) for Cy Coleman.

1 Grab your coat, and get your hat,
Leave your worry on the doorstep,
Just direct your feet
To the sunny side of the street.

'On the Sunny Side of the Street' (song, co-written with Jimmy McHugh) in *The International Revue* (musical show, 1930)

2 You're calmer than the seals in the Arctic Ocean
At least they flap their fins to express emotion . . .

'A Fine Romance' (song, with music by Jerome Kern) in *Swing Time* (film, 1936)

3 So let me get right to the point.
I don't pop my cork for every guy I see.
Hey! big spender, spend a little time with me.

'Big Spender' (song, with music by Cy Coleman) in *Sweet Charity* (stage musical 1966, film 1969). The song was a hit for Shirley Bassey in 1967.

## W.C. Fields (1879–1946)
US ACTOR

Originally William Claude Dukinfield. 'I am free of all prejudices – I hate everybody equally,' declared this red-nosed, gravel-voiced, hard-drinking misogynist of a comedian. His early vaudeville career saw him perform at Buckingham Palace in 1901, and he later appeared in silent films such as *Sally of the Sawdust* (1925). He memorably played Micawber in *David Copperfield* (1934) and he wrote many of the numerous comedies he appeared in, including *My Little Chickadee* (with MAE WEST, 1940). See also LEO ROSTEN 1.

1 Here lies W.C. Fields. I would rather be living in Philadelphia.

Suggested epitaph, as told to *Vanity Fair* June 1925. Fields, who was born in Philadelphia, may have had in mind an anecdote about George Washington, who was reported to have uttered a similar sentiment regarding the choice of New York as federal capital in 1789. Fields's words (which were never actually used as his epitaph) are usually remembered, 'On the whole, I'd rather be in Phila-

delphia' the form in which RONALD REAGAN quoted them when recovering in hospital from an assassination attempt in 1981.

2 And remember, dearie, never give a sucker an even break.

Professor Eustace McGargle, in *Poppy* (film, 1936, screenplay by Waldemar Young and Virginia Van Upp from play by Dorothy Donnelly, directed by A. Edward Sutherland). Fields is earlier reported to have uttered these words on stage in the musical comedy *Poppy* (1923), though they do not appear in the libretto. 'Never give a sucker an even break' became Fields's catch-phrase, and the title of one of his last films, made in 1941 (called *What a Man* in Britain).

3 I was in love with a beautiful blonde once, she drove me to drink. 'Tis the one thing I'm indebted to her for.

The Great Man (W.C. Fields), in *Never Give a Sucker an Even Break* (film, 1941, screenplay by John T. Neville and Prescott Chaplin based on a story by W.C. Fields, directed by Edward F. Cline)

4 Hell, I never vote *for* anybody. I always vote *against*.

Quoted in *W.C. Fields: His Follies and Fortunes*, ch. 25 (1950) by Robert Lewis Taylor. Said to Gene Fowler who wrote two books about him.

5 If at first you don't succeed, try again. Then quit. No use being a damn fool about it.

Quoted in *Halliwell's Who's Who in the Movies* (ed. John Walker, 1999)

6 Fish fuck in it.

ibid. On why he never drank water.

## Eva Figes (b. 1932)
ANGLO-GERMAN AUTHOR AND TRANSLATOR

Having escaped with her family from Nazi Germany in 1939, she acquired British citizenship and went on to produce a diverse body of work that embraces fiction and feminist criticism. Her first novel, *Equinox* (1966), was followed by the highly praised *Winter's Journey* (1968) and *The Tree of Knowledge* (1990), written in a seventeenth-century prose style.

1 Providing for one's family as a good husband and father is a water-tight excuse for making money hand over fist. Greed may be a sin, exploitation of other people might, on the face of it, look rather nasty, but who can blame a man for 'doing the best' for his children?

'A View of My Own', publ. in *Nova* January 1973

2 If each man takes his conscience as his guide he is like to become a law unto himself, and conscience often tells us that which we would hear.

Mrs Deborah Clarke, in *The Tree of Knowledge*, ch. 4 (1990)

## Zlata Filipovič (b. 1980)
BOSNIAN DIARIST

Her diary written between September 1991 and October 1993 became a bestseller throughout Europe. Zlata and her parents left Sarajevo for France at the end of 1993.

1 Life goes on. The past is cruel, and that's exactly why we should forget it. The present is cruel too and I can't forget it. There's no joking with war. My present reality is the cellar, fear, shells, fire.

Journal entry, 13 May 1993, publ. in *Zlata's Diary* (1993)

2 The political situation? A STUPID MESS. The 'kids' are trying to come to some agreement again. They're drawing maps, colouring with their crayons, but I think they're crossing out human beings, childhood and everything that's nice and normal. They are really just like kids.

ibid. 21 August 1993

## Ernst Fischer (1899–1972)
AUSTRIAN EDITOR, POET AND CRITIC

Having joined the Communist Party in 1934 he spent the Second World War in Moscow as a journalist and broadcaster. Back in

Austria, he was elected to the National Assembly as Minister of Culture and Education but was expelled from the Party in 1969 for his criticism of the Soviet invasion of Czechoslovakia. *The Necessity of Art* (1959) and *Art Against Ideology* (1966) are regarded as his major works of 'Marxist aesthetics'.

1 As machines become more and more efficient and perfect, so it will become clear that *imperfection is the greatness of man.*

   *The Necessity of Art*, ch. 5 (1959)

2 Man, became man through work, who stepped out of the animal kingdom as transformer of the natural into the artificial, who became therefore the magician, man the creator of social reality, will always stay the great magician, will always be Prometheus bringing fire from heaven to earth, will always be Orpheus enthralling nature with his music. Not until humanity itself dies will art die.

   ibid.

3 To provoke dreams of terror in the slumber of prosperity has become the moral duty of literature.

   *Art Against Ideology*, ch. 1 (1966)

## Michael Fish (b. 1944)
BRITISH METEOROLOGIST

Britain's longest-serving TV weatherman (since 1974) joined the Meteorological Office in 1962 and the London Weather Centre in 1967.

1 A woman rang to say she heard there was a hurricane on the way. Well, don't worry, there isn't.

   Weather forecast on BBC TV, 15 October 1987. The 'Great Storm' which struck southern England that night claimed seventeen lives and caused approximately £300 million of damage. Winds gusted up to 110 mph, falling within the scale of hurricane force.

## Carrie Fisher (b. 1956)
US ACTRESS, AUTHOR AND SCREENWRITER

Daughter of Edde Fisher and Debbie Reynolds, she has had a varied career in Hollywood that has included appearances in the films *Star Wars* (as Princess Leia, 1977) and *The Blues Brothers* (1980) and work in television. The glitzy end of LA is is usually the milieu of her caustic and witty novels.

1 My extroversion is a way of managing my introversion.

   Dinah, in *Surrender the Pink*, ch. 3 (1990)

2 Who am I? I'm with him, that's who.

   ibid. ch. 7

3 Look at us we're chicks lost in the netherworld of our gender, absorbed in the world of potential purchase.

   ibid. ch. 9

## H.A.L. Fisher (1865–1940)
BRITISH HISTORIAN AND POLITICIAN

Full name Herbert Albert Laurens Fisher. He was Liberal MP for Hallam, Sheffield (1916–18), and the English Universities (1918–26). As President of the Board of Education, he introduced the 1918 Education Act, state scholarships to universities and the School Certificate. Among his published works are *Bonapartism* (1908) and *A History of Europe* (1935).

1 Men wiser and more learned than I have discerned in history a plot, a rhythm, a predetermined pattern. These harmonies are concealed from me. I can see only one emergency following upon another as wave follows upon wave, only one great fact with respect to which, since it is unique, there can be no generalizations, only one safe rule for the historian: that he should recognize in the development of human destinies the play of the contingent and the unforeseen.

   *A History of Europe*, Preface (1935)

2 Purity of race does not exist. Europe is a continent of energetic mongrels.

   ibid. ch. 1

3 Politics is the art of human happiness.

   ibid. ch. 31

## Lord Fisher (1841–1920)
BRITISH NAVAL COMMANDER

John Arbuthnot Fisher, First Baron of Kilverstone. Appointed First Sea Lord in 1904, he introduced the Dreadnought battleships and Invincible battle cruisers in preparation for the First World War, but resigned in 1915 in protest against the CHURCHILL-backed Dardanelles expedition.

1 Never contradict.
   Never explain.
   Never apologize.

   The 'secrets of a happy life', in letter to *The Times*, 5 September 1919

## M.F.K. Fisher (1908–92)
US CULINARY WRITER

Full name Mary Frances Kennedy Fisher. One of the most highly regarded of food writers, she drew on her experiences both in California and France to present food as a metaphor for life and love. Her books, autobiographical in style, include *The Gastronomical Me* (1943) and *An Alphabet for Gourmets* (1949). D'Erasmo said of her: 'She alone seems to have the silence, exile and cunning a writer would need to stalk people in their kitchens.'

1 Central heating, French rubber goods, and cookbooks are three amazing proofs of man's ingenuity in transforming necessity into art, and, of these, cookbooks are perhaps most lastingly delightful.

   *Serve It Forth,* 'The Curious Nose' (1937)

2 Once at least in the life of every human, whether he be brute or trembling daffodil, comes a moment of complete gastronomic satisfaction.

   ibid. 'The Pale Yellow Glove'

3 Sharing food with another human being is an intimate act that should not be indulged in lightly.

   *An Alphabet for Gourmets*, 'A is for Dining Alone' (1949)

4 The things men come to eat when they are alone are, I suppose, not much stranger than the men themselves.

   ibid. 'M is for Monastic'

5 Gastronomical perfection can be reached in these combinations: one person dining alone, usually upon a couch or a hillside; two people, of no matter what sex or age, dining in a good restaurant; six people, of no matter what sex or age, dining in a good home.

   ibid. 'From A–Z: The Perfect Dinner'

6 It was there [Dijon], I now understand, that I started to grow up, to study, to make love, to eat and drink, to be me and not what I was expected to be. It was there that I learned it is blessed to receive, as well as that every human being, no matter how base, is worthy of my respect and even my envy because he knows something that I may never be old or wise or kind or tender enough to know.

   *Long Ago in France*, Preface (1991)

## Robert Fisk (b. 1946)
BRITISH JOURNALIST AND AUTHOR

After covering events in Northern Ireland in the early 1970s, he achieved critical praise for his work as foreign correspondent in

Lebanon for *The Times* and *Independent*. His books include *Point of No Return* (1975) and *Pity The Nation* (1990) about Ulster and the Middle East respectively.

1 Journalism is about watching and witnessing history and recording it as honestly as we can . . . At best, journalists sit at the edge of history as vulcanologists might clamber to the lip of a smoking crater . . . to peer over . . . at what happens within.
*Pity The Nation*, Preface (1990)

2 It might be as well for the West to remember that history in the Middle East rarely rewards the just. It never favours the foreigner and it always takes its revenge upon those who see the region through their own eyes. Not once has a foreign military adventure in the Middle East achieved its end.
Quoted in the *Guardian* 14 August 1990

# F. Scott Fitzgerald (1896–1940)

US AUTHOR

Full name Francis Scott Fitzgerald. Spokesman of the 'Jazz Age' of the 1920s and considered the 'white hope of American letters' by H.L. MENCKEN, he evoked the hedonism and glitter of the period in his short stories and in his greatest novel, *The Great Gatsby* (1925). *Tender is the Night* (1934) was influenced by his wife ZELDA FITZGERALD's mental breakdown and his own descent into alcoholism and bankruptcy. He once admitted, 'Sometimes I don't know whether Zelda and I are real or whether we are characters in one of my novels.'

1 At eighteen our convictions are hills from which we look; at forty-five they are caves in which we hide.
*Bernice Bobs Her Hair*, sect. 2 (1920)

2 She had once been a Catholic, but discovering that priests were infinitely more attentive when she was in process of losing or regaining faith in Mother Church, she maintained an enchantingly wavering attitude.
Of Beatrice Blaine, in *This Side of Paradise*, bk 1, ch. 1 (1920)

3 My idea is always to reach my generation. The wise writer . . . writes for the youth of his own generation, the critics of the next, and the schoolmasters of ever afterward.
'Self-interview', publ. in the *New York Tribune* 7 May 1920, repr. in *Some Sort of Epic Grandeur*, ch. 16 (biography, 1981) by Matthew J. Bruccoli. The text was also used by Fitzgerald in 'The Author's Apology', a letter to the American Booksellers Convention, May 1920.

4 Everybody's youth is a dream, a form of chemical madness.
John, in *The Diamond as Big as the Ritz*, ch. 11 (1922). Kismine replies: 'How pleasant then to be insane!'

5 Personality is an unbroken series of successful gestures.
Narrator (Nick Carraway), in *The Great Gatsby*, ch. 1 (1925)

6 [Of Tom Buchanan] One of those men who reach such an acute limited excellence at twenty-one that everything afterward savors of anti-climax.
ibid.

7 Every one suspects himself of at least one of the cardinal virtues.
ibid. ch. 3

8 There are only the pursued, the pursuing, the busy, and the tired.
ibid. ch. 4

9 What'll we do with ourselves this afternoon? And the day after that, and the next thirty years?
Daisy Buchanan, in ibid. ch. 7

10 [Of Daisy Buchanan] Her voice is full of money.
Gatsby, in ibid. ch. 7. The narrator (Nick Carraway) adds, 'that was the inexhaustible charm that rose and fell in it, the jingle of it, the cymbals' song of it . . .'

11 They were careless people, Tom and Daisy – they smashed up things and creatures and then retreated back into their money or their vast carelessness, or whatever it was that kept them together, and let other people clean up the mess they had made.
ibid. ch. 9

12 For a transitory enchanted moment man must have held his breath in the presence of this continent, compelled into an aesthetic contemplation he neither understood nor desired, face to face for the last time in history with something commensurate to his capacity for wonder.
ibid. ch. 9

13 So we beat on, boats against the current, borne back ceaselessly into the past.
ibid. Closing words of book.

14 Let me tell you about the very rich. They are different from you and me. They possess and enjoy early, and it does something to them, makes them soft where we are hard, and cynical where we are trustful, in a way that, unless you were born rich, it is very difficult to understand. They think, deep in their hearts, that they are better than we are because we had to discover the compensations and refuges of life for ourselves. Even when they enter deep into our world or sink below us, they still think that they are better than we are. They are different.
*All the Sad Young Men*, 'The Rich Boy' (1926). The story's first sentence also occurs in Fitzgerald's notebooks (*The Crack-Up*, 'Notebook E', 1945) and was taken up by Hemingway in *The Snows of Kilimanjaro* (1936) (see ERNEST HEMINGWAY 16).

15 I hear you were seen running through Portugal in used B.V.D.'s, chewing ground glass and collecting material for a story about boule players; that you were publicity man for Lindbergh; that you have finished a novel a hundred thousand words long consisting entirely of the word 'balls' used in new groupings; that you have been naturalized a Spaniard, dress always in a wine-skin with 'zipper' vent and are engaged in bootlegging Spanish Fly between St. Sebastian and Biarritz where your agents sprinkle it on the floor of the Casino. I hope I have been misinformed but, alas!, it all has too true a ring.
Letter to Ernest Hemingway, December 1927, publ. in *The Letters of F. Scott Fitzgerald* (ed. Andrew Turnbull, 1963)

16 The early twenties when we drank wood alcohol and every day in every way grew better and better, and there was a first abortive shortening of the skirts, and girls all looked alike in sweater dresses, and people you didn't want to know said 'Yes, we have no bananas,' and it seemed only a question of a few years before the older people would step aside and let the world be run by those who saw things as they were – and it all seems rosy and romantic to us who were young then, because we will never feel quite so intensely about our surroundings any more.
'Echoes of the Jazz Age', first publ. in *Scribner's* November 1931. The passage also appeared in *The Crack-Up* (ed. Edmund Wilson, 1945). 'Though the Jazz Age continued,' Fitzgerald wrote, 'it became less and less an affair of youth. The sequel was like a children's party taken over by the elders.'

17 The hangover became a part of the day as well allowed-for as the Spanish siesta.
'My Lost City', first publ. in *Esquire* July 1932, repr. in *The Crack-Up* (ed. Edmund Wilson, 1945)

18 One writes of scars healed, a loose parallel to the pathology of the skin, but there is no such thing in the life of an individual. There are open wounds, shrunk sometimes to the size of a pin-prick but wounds still. The marks of suffering are more comparable to the loss of a finger, or the sight of an eye. We may not miss them, either, for one minute in a year, but if we should there is nothing to be done about it.
*Tender is the Night*, bk 2, ch. 11 (1934)

19 **The test of a first-rate intelligence is the ability to hold two opposed ideas in the mind at the same time, and still retain the ability to function.**
'The Crack-Up', article first publ. in *Esquire* February 1936, repr. in *The Crack-Up* (ed. Edmund Wilson, 1945). See also GEORGE ORWELL 47.

20 **In a real dark night of the soul it is always three o'clock in the morning, day after day.**
'Handle With Care', first publ. in *Esquire* March 1936, repr. in ibid. The article constituted the second part of Fitzgerald's *Crack-Up* series. *The Dark Night of the Soul* is the title of a poem and commentary by the sixteenth-century Spanish mystic San Juan de la Cruz (St John of the Cross).

21 **I am not a great man, but sometimes I think the impersonal and objective quality of my talent and the sacrifices of it, in pieces, to preserve its essential value has some sort of epic grandeur.**
Letter to his daughter Frances Scott Fitzgerald, spring 1940, publ. in ibid. The words 'some sort of epic grandeur' were used by Matthew J. Bruccoli as a title for his 1981 biography of Fitzgerald.

22 **There are no second acts in American lives.**
*The Last Tycoon*, 'Hollywood, ETC.' (ed. Edmund Wilson, 1941)

23 **Show me a hero and I will write you a tragedy.**
*The Crack-Up*, 'Notebook E' (ed. Edmund Wilson, 1945)

24 **No grand idea was ever born in a conference, but a lot of foolish ideas have died there.**
ibid.

25 **Men get to be a mixture of the charming mannerisms of the women they have known.**
ibid.

26 **Listen, little Elia: draw your chair up close to the edge of the precipice and I'll tell you a story.**
ibid.

27 **It is in the thirties that we want friends. In the forties we know they won't save us any more than love did.**
ibid. 'Notebook O'

28 **All good writing is *swimming under water* and holding your breath.**
Letter (undated) to his daughter Frances Scott Fitzgerald, publ. in ibid.

## Penelope Fitzgerald (1916–2000)
BRITISH AUTHOR

Her first publication was a biography of Edward Burne-Jones (1975), followed by one of her father, E.V.A. Knox, Editor of *Punch*, and his three eminent brothers (one of them the theologian RONALD KNOX), titled *The Knox Brothers* (1977). In 1977 she published her first novel, *The Golden Child*, followed by the Booker Prize-winner *Offshore* (1979) and *Human Voices* (1980), a satire of the BBC set in wartime.

1 **It's very good for an idea to be commonplace. The important thing is that a new idea should develop out of what is already there so that it soon becomes an old acquaintance. Old acquaintances aren't by any means always welcome, but at least one can't be mistaken as to who or what they are.**
Fred Fairly, in a lecture to his students at Cambridge, in *The Gate of Angels*, ch. 20 (1990)

## Robert Fitzgerald (1910–85)
US SCHOLAR AND TRANSLATOR

His translations of classical texts, including *Antigone* (1939), *The Odyssey* (1961) and *The Iliad* (1974), have become classics in their own right, acclaimed for their clarity. He also wrote poetry such as the collections *A Wreath for the Sea* (1943) and *Spring Shade* (1972).

1 **Is encouragement what the poet needs? Open question.**

Maybe he needs discouragement. In fact, quite a few of them need more discouragement, the most discouragement possible.
Interview in *Writers at Work* (eighth series, ed. George Plimpton, 1988)

## Zelda Fitzgerald (1900–1948)
US WRITER

Wife of F. SCOTT FITZGERALD, she wrote a series of sketches (1928–9) which were published in *College Humor*, and a novel *Save Me the Waltz*, which appeared in 1932. In 1930 she suffered the first of her mental breakdowns. She died in a hospital fire. 'I want to love first, and live incidentally,' she told her future husband in 1919.

1 **We grew up founding our dreams on the infinite promise of American advertising.**
Alabama Beggs, in *Save Me the Waltz*, ch. 4, sect. 3 (1932). She continued: 'I *still* believe that one can learn to play the piano by mail and that mud will give you a perfect complexion.'

2 **I wish I could write a beautiful book to break those hearts that are soon to cease to exist: a book of faith and small neat worlds and of people who live by the philosophies of popular songs.**
Letter to her psychiatrist, May 1934, quoted in *Zelda*, pt 3, ch. 17 (1970) by Nancy Milford

3 **Ernest, don't you think Al Jolson is greater than Jesus?**
Quoted by ERNEST HEMINGWAY in *A Moveable Feast*, ch. 18 (1964). Her remark anticipates John Lennon's famous claim (see JOHN LENNON 2).

## Bud Flanagan (1896–1968)
BRITISH SINGER AND COMEDIAN

Born Robert Winthrop. With his partner Chesney Allen he formed one of the most popular comedy duos of the 1930s and 1940s, whose numbers included 'Underneath the Arches' (1932), 'Umbrella Man' (1938) and 'Run, Rabbit, Run' (1939). In 1936 they joined the anarchic comedy team, the Crazy Gang.

1 **Underneath the Arches,**
**I dream my dreams away,**
**Underneath the Arches,**
**On cobble-stones I lay.**
'Underneath the Arches' (song, 1932, written with Chesney Allen). According to his autobiography, *My Crazy Life*, ch. 8 (1961), Flanagan conceived what was to be Flanagan and Allen's signature tune while backstage at the Derby Hippodrome in 1926. The 'Arches' were underneath London's Charing Cross station, a gathering-place for tramps. The song was renamed 'Underneath The Bridges' in America, where it was thought 'arches' might be misconstrued as 'feet'.

## Oliver Flanagan (1920–87)
IRISH POLITICIAN

He was a member of the Dáil Éireann (Irish parliament) 1947–87, joining Fine Gael in 1950 and rising to become Minister for Local Government 1975–6 and for Defence 1976–7. He was strongly opposed to changes in the contraception and divorce laws and a supporter of the pro-life amendment in the 1983 referendum.

1 **Let us hope and trust that there are sufficient proud and ignorant people left in this country to stand up to the intellectuals who are out to destroy faith and fatherland.**
Quoted in the *Irish Times* 10 April 1971

2 **There was no sex in Ireland until the BBC came.**
Quoted in *Ireland and the Irish: Portrait of a Changing Society*, ch. 6 (1994) by John Ardagh

## Michael Flanders (1922–75) and
## Donald Swann (1923–94)
BRITISH SONGWRITERS AND ENTERTAINERS

Flanders started his acting career at the Oxford Playhouse in 1941, later contracting the polio that confined him to a wheelchair. Swann contributed to revues from the 1940s and became a frequent broadcaster on musical topics. Between 1956 and 1967 their songwriting partnership produced such shows as *At the Drop of a Hat* (1956) and *At the Drop of Another Hat* (1963). Swann likened their collaboration to a 'cooking process', with the piano taking the place of the kitchen stove.

1 Mud, mud, glorious mud,
Nothing quite like it for cooling the blood!
So follow me, follow,
Down to the hollow
And there let us wallow
In glorious mud!
'The Hippopotamus' (song, written 1952), in *At the Drop of a Hat* (revue, 1956). The song was entirely written by Flanders who took the tune from 'Beer, Beer, Glorious Beer!', a familiar song of the time.

2 I'm a G-nu, I'm a G-nu,
The g-nicest work of g-nature at the zoo!
I'm a G-nu, how do you do?
You really ought to k-now w-ho's w-ho.
'The Gnu' (song) in ibid. According to Swann's autobiography *A Life In Song* (1991), the ditty derived from the frustrations of parking in central London: Kensington Borough Council had dug up the pavement outside Flanders' studio in order to facilitate wheel-chair access for him, but the path was often blocked by a car with the number plate letters GNU.

3 That monarch of the road,
Observer of the Highway Code,
That big six-wheeler
Scarlet-painted
London Transport
Diesel-engined
Ninety-seven horse power
Omnibus!
'A Transport of Delight' (song) in ibid.

4 Have Some Madeira, M'dear.
Title of song in ibid.

5 Eating people is wrong!
'The Reluctant Cannibal' (song), in ibid. The words also formed the title of a novel (1959) by MALCOLM BRADBURY.

6 Pee – Po – Belly – Bum – Drawers!
Let's write rude words all down our street,
Stick out our tongues at the people we meet,
Let's have an intellectual treat.
'P**, P*, B****, B**, D******' (song) in *Extiary* (1961)

## Ian Fleming (1908–64)
BRITISH AUTHOR

After a diverse career in journalism, finance and espionage, he achieved worldwide success with his spy thrillers featuring the suave agent 007, James Bond. From the first of these, *Casino Royale* (1952), he completed one a year, many being turned into successful films. He called his books 'straight pillow fantasies of the bang-bang, kiss-kiss variety'. See also ROSAMOND LEHMANN 1.

1 A medium Vodka dry Martini – with a slice of lemon peel. Shaken and not stirred, please. I would prefer Russian or Polish vodka.
James Bond, in *Dr. No*, ch. 14 (1958)

2 Some women respond to the whip, some to the kiss. Most of them like a mixture of both, but none of them answer

to the mind alone, to the intellectual demand, unless they are man dressed as woman.
From his notebooks, quoted in *The Life of Ian Fleming*, ch. 8, sect. 1 (1966) by John Pearson

## Peter Fleming (1907–71)
BRITISH TRAVEL WRITER

Described by Harold Nicolson as 'an astringent narrator of romantic and dangerous voyages', he established himself as one of the greatest exponents of the genre with his *Brazilian Adventure* (1933). *News from Tartary* (1936) chronicled his journeys in the Far East. He was the elder brother of IAN FLEMING.

1 Long Island represents the American's idea of what God would have done with Nature if he'd had the money.
Letter to his brother Rupert, 29 September 1929, quoted in *Peter Fleming*, ch. 4 (1974) by Rupert Hart-Davis

## Dario Fo (b. 1926)
ITALIAN PLAYWRIGHT

His theatre company formed in 1957 underwent years of censorship for its plays which, usually co-written and co-produced by his wife Franca Rame, blend satire and clowning with a strong left-wing slant. He scored an international success with *Accidental Death of an Anarchist* (1970), and was awarded the Nobel Prize for Literature in 1997.

1 Accidental Death of an Anarchist.
Title of play (1974, transl. 1991). The play, which was first performed in Italy in 1970 and in Britain in 1979, concerns the death of a suspect who fell, or was pushed, from the fourth-floor window of a police station during questioning. The title is adapted usually to suggest official corruption or suspicious circumstances.

2 Feletti: So scandal is an effective means of maintaining power and clearing the public's conscience.
Madman: Exactly. It is the catharsis that liberates tension . . . And you reporters are its worthy priesthood.
*Accidental Death of an Anarchist*, act 2

3 We're up to our necks in shit, it's true, and that's why we walk with our heads held high.
Madman, in ibid.

4 Can't Pay? Won't Pay!
Title of play (1974, transl. 1978). The original title of *Non si paga, non si paga* was the slogan used in the play by a group of housewives in a working-class suburb of Milan protesting against supermarket prices by stealing the goods. First translated as *We Can't Pay? We Won't Pay!*, the revised English title became *Can't Pay? Won't Pay!* for its 1981 London production and as such was adopted as a slogan by anti-Poll Tax protesters in the 1990s.

## Ferdinand Foch (1851–1929)
FRENCH GENERAL

He was Supreme Commander of the Allied Forces on the Western front in 1918 and dictated the terms of the armistice on 11 November. He achieved his lifelong ambition of restoring Alsace and Lorraine to France.

1 If defeat comes from moral causes, victory may come from moral causes also, and one may say: 'A battle won is a battle we will not acknowledge to be lost.'
Quoted in *Reputations*, 'Ferdinand Foch' (1928) by B.H. Liddell Hart. Foch's conclusion was reached from musing on his favourite aphorism by the French political philosopher Joseph de Maistre (1753–1821): 'A lost battle is a battle which one believes lost: in a material sense no battle can be lost.'

2 My centre is giving way, my right is in retreat; situation excellent. I shall attack.
Attributed, in ibid. Allegedly a message sent to General Joffre during the Battle of the Marne 8 September 1914, the words are probably apocryphal, reflecting the grim obstinacy with which Foch was

associated, indicated also by the repeated exhortation he made to his troops, even in the most hopeless conditions: *Attaquez!*. According to Liddell Hart, his reckless insistence during this battle resulted in the decimation of the companies under his command, and the eventual German withdrawal astonished the exhausted French troops. Other versions of the quote include: 'My right gives way, my centre yields, everything's fine – I shall attack.'

## J. Foley (1906–70)
BRITISH SONGWRITER

1 Old soldiers never die,
  They simply fade away.
'Old Soldiers Never Die' (song, 1920). The song may have originated in or prior to the First World War.

## Barbara Follett (b. 1942)
BRITISH LABOUR POLITICIAN

Called by the *Guardian* 'Labour's make-over matron', she was a member of the Labour Party's Steering Committee Women's Network from 1988 and a founder member of 'Emily's List' in the UK, which promoted women's candidacy for parliamentary office (1992). She was elected MP for Stevenage in 1997.

1 Lipstick is power.
Attributed in the *Observer* 25 February 1996. Follett repudiated her most quoted soundbite.

## Jane Fonda (b. 1937)
US SCREEN ACTRESS

Daughter of Henry Fonda and sister of Peter, she was cast in the 1960s as a 'sex kitten' but acquired a political and feminist voice which led her to oppose the Vietnam War. She confronted this issue in the film *Coming Home* (1973), for which she won an Oscar. She co-starred with her father in *On Golden Pond* (1981), and during the 1980s became known for her health and fitness books and videos.

1 I am not a do-gooder. I am a revolutionary. A revolutionary woman.
Statement in 1972, quoted in the *Los Angeles Weekly* 28 November 1980. Fonda is also quoted as declaring: 'To be a revolutionary you have to be a human being. You have to care about people who have no power.'

2 Today I'd be a dyed blonde, a numb and dumb pill-popping star, if I hadn't taken up a cause. I could very well be dead like Marilyn. Not through drugs but dead just the same.
*Daily Mail* 14 April 1980

3 A man has every season while a woman only has the right to spring. That disgusts me.
*Daily Mail* 13 September 1989

## Michael Foot (b. 1913)
BRITISH POLITICIAN

He was a political columnist and editor from the 1940s to the 1960s, Labour MP (1945–92) and Leader of the Labour Party (1980–83). Known for his oratorical skills and pacifist stance, lampooned as 'Worzel Gummidge' during the 1983 general election in which his party suffered a crushing defeat, he has also authored biographies of Byron, ANEURIN BEVAN and H.G. WELLS.

1 [Of Norman Tebbit] It is not necessary that every time he rises he should give his famous imitation of a semi-house-trained polecat.
Speech to House of Commons, 2 March 1978, publ. in *Hansard*

2 [Of John Major] It's quite a change to have a Prime Minister who hasn't got any political ideas at all.
Quoted in the *Observer* 24 February 1991

3 [Of Tony Blair] No rising hope on the political scene who offered his services to Labour when I happened to be its leader can be dismissed as an opportunist.
Quoted in the *Independent on Sunday* 19 February 1995

## Anna Ford (b. 1943)
BRITISH BROADCASTER

Having presented *Man Alive* and *Tomorrow's World* for the BBC (1976–8), she became an ITN newscaster and later a presenter with *TV-am* (1978–82). She has been a freelance broadcaster since 1989.

1 Let's face it, there are no plain women on television.
Quoted in the *Observer* 23 September 1979

2 The world men inhabit . . . is rather bleak. It is a world full of doubt and confusion, where vulnerability must be hidden, not shared; where competition, not co-operation, is the order of the day; where men sacrifice the possibility of knowing their own children and sharing in their up-bringing, for the sake of a job they may have chosen by chance, which may not suit them and which in many cases dominates their lives to the exclusion of much else.
*Men*, concluding chapter (1985)

## Gerald Ford (b. 1913)
US POLITICIAN AND PRESIDENT

He served as a Republican member of the US House of Representatives (1949–73), becoming President in the wake of the Watergate scandal in 1974. His pardon of RICHARD NIXON and the subsequent economic depression contributed to his defeat in the 1976 election. See also LYNDON JOHNSON 10.

1 I am a Ford, not a Lincoln.
Address on taking vice-presidential oath, 6 December 1973, quoted in *A Ford, Not a Lincoln*, ch. 2 (1975) by Richard Reeves. Ford explained: 'My addresses will never be as eloquent as Lincoln's. But I will do my best to equal his brevity and plain speaking.' Eight months later, Ford was sworn in as President. He told Congress: 'The truth is I am the people's man.' (12 August 1974)

2 Our long national nightmare is over. Our Constitution works; our great Republic is a government of laws and not of men. Here the people rule.
Speech on succeeding RICHARD NIXON as President, 9 August 1974, publ. in *Public Papers of the Presidents of the United States* (1974)

3 Truth is the glue that holds government together.
ibid. Ford used these words on various occasions.

4 There is no Soviet domination of Eastern Europe and there never will be under a Ford administration . . . The United States does not concede that those countries are under the domination of the Soviet Union.
TV debate with presidential contender JIMMY CARTER, 6 October 1976, publ. in *Great Debates* (1979) by S. Kraus. When asked to explain this statement, Ford admitted 'I was perhaps not as precise as I should have been'.

## Henry Ford (1863–1947)
US INDUSTRIALIST

The pioneer of mass production, called the 'demi-god of the machine age', he started the Ford Motor Company in 1903, and by 1909 had produced the famous Model T, of which 15 million were sold in the next nineteen years.

1 History is more or less bunk. It's tradition. We don't want tradition. We want to live in the present and the only history that is worth a tinker's damn is the history we make today.
Interview in the *Chicago Tribune* 25 May 1916. Ford had to defend his views of history during an eight-day cross-examination in the course of a libel suit he had initiated against the *Tribune*, after an editorial had described him as an 'anarchist' and 'ignorant idealist'.

2 **Luck and destiny are the excuses of the world's failures.**

Quoted in the *Observer* 16 March 1930

## Lena Guilbert Ford (1870–1916)

US POET

She became famous for her song 'Till the Boys Come Home!' (1914), which she wrote in England and was a great success during the First World War. She was killed during a German Zeppelin raid on London.

1 Keep the home fires burning,
  While your hearts are yearning,
  Though your lads are far away
  They dream of home.
  There's a silver lining
  Through the dark cloud shining;
  Turn the dark cloud inside out,
  Till the boys come home.

'Till the Boys Come Home!' (song, 1914). Music by IVOR NOVELLO, who is credited with the song's famous first line.

## Richard Ford (b. 1944)

US AUTHOR

Regarded as one of America's best fiction writers, he is known for the novels *The Sportswriter* (1986) and the Pulitzer Prize-winner *Independence Day* (1995, filmed 1996), and the short story collection *Rock Springs* (1987).

1 **Married life requires shared mystery even when all the facts are known.**

*The Sportswriter*, ch. 5 (1986)

2 **Construed ... as turf, home just seems a provisional claim, a designation you make upon a place, not one it makes on you. A certain set of buildings, a glimpsed, smudged window-view across a schoolyard, a musty aroma sniffed behind a garage when you were a child, all of which come crowding in upon your latter-day senses – those are pungent things and vivid, even consoling.**

'An Urge for Going', publ. in *Harper's* February 1992. 'But to me', Ford added, 'they are also inert and nostalgic and unlikely to connect you to the real, to that essence art can sometimes achieve, which is permanence.'

## George Foreman (b. 1948)

US BOXER

He took the world heavyweight title from Joe Frazier in 1973, losing it in the following year to MUHAMMAD ALI in what was dubbed the 'Rumble in the Jungle' in Zaire. He retired from boxing in 1977 to become an evangelist, but regained the heavyweight title in 1994 at the age of 45, the oldest world heavyweight champion ever. He retired again the following year.

1 **I want to keep fighting because it is the only thing that keeps me out of the hamburger joints. If I don't fight, I'll eat this planet.**

*The Times* 17 January 1990

## Howell Forgy (1908–83)

US NAVAL CHAPLAIN

1 **Praise the Lord and pass the ammunition!**

Quoted in *The New York Times* 1 November 1942, said during the Japanese attack on Pearl Harbor, 7 December 1941. The words have also been attributed to William Maguire, and were used as the title of a Frank Loesser song in 1942.

## George Formby (1904–61)

BRITISH ENTERTAINER AND ACTOR

Portraying himself as a gormless working-class Lancashire lad, he

accompanied himself on the ukelele on jaunty songs teeming with double entendres. He transferred his music hall routine to a string of successful films in the 1930s and 1940s, and during the Second World War was Britain's highest paid entertainer.

1 **With my little ukelele in my hand.**

'With my Little Ukelele In My Hand' (song, 1933, with music by Jack Cottrell). Formby's record company Decca withdrew the first issue of the recording after protests at the song, particularly the last verse, which tells of the birth of a baby: 'My heart did jump with joy/I could see he was a boy/For he had a ukelele in his hand'.

2 **If you could see what I can see**
  **When I'm cleaning windows!**

'When I'm Cleaning Windows' (song, 1937, written by Fred E. Cliffe with music by Harry Clifford) sung by Formby in *Keep Your Seats, Please* (film, 1937). The record was marked NTBB ('Not to be broadcast') by the BBC, whose controller, Lord Reith, labelled it a 'disgusting little ditty'. Particular offence was caused by the lines 'Ladies' nighties I have spied/I've often seen what goes inside/When I'm cleaning windows!'

3 **I'm leaning on a lamp-post at the corner of the street,**
  **In case a certain little lady comes by.**

'Leaning on a Lamp-Post' (song, written by NOEL GAY) in the film *Feather Your Nest* (1937). The song was revived in 1966 by Herman's Hermits.

4 **With my little stick of Blackpool rock.**
  **Along the Promenade I stroll**
  **It may be sticky but I never complain**
  **It's nice to have a nibble at it now and again.**

'With My Little Stick of Blackpool Rock' (song, 1937, written by Fred E. Cliffe with music by Harry Clifford)

5 **Auntie Maggie's Remedy**
  **It's guaranteed never to fail**
  **Now that's the stuff that will do the trick**
  **It's sold at every chemist for one and a kick**

'Auntie Maggie's Remedy' (song, written by George Formby with music by Eddie Latta) in the film *Turned Out Nice Again!* (1941)

## E.M. Forster (1879–1970)

BRITISH NOVELIST AND ESSAYIST

Full name Edward Morgan Forster. His fiction largely concerns the 'muddle' engendered by the English upper classes, especially when abroad. His novels *A Room with a View* (1908), *Howards End* (1910) and *A Passage to India* (1924) have been filmed. KATHERINE MANSFIELD denigrated his writing as only 'warming the teapot', while VIRGINIA WOOLF called him 'limp and damp and milder than the breath of a cow'. See also ANTHONY BURGESS 6.

1 **It is not that the Englishman can't feel – it is that he is afraid to feel. He has been taught at his public school that feeling is bad form. He must not express great joy or sorrow, or even open his mouth too wide when he talks – his pipe might fall out if he did.**

'Notes on the English Character', first publ. 1920, repr. in *Abinger Harvest* (1936)

2 **The Germans are called brutal, the Spanish cruel, the Americans superficial, and so on; but we are perfide Albion, the island of hypocrites, the people who have built up an Empire with a Bible in one hand, a pistol in the other, and financial concessions in both pockets. Is the charge true? I think it is.**

ibid. Forster defined English hypocrisy as 'unconscious deceit' and 'muddle-headedness'.

3 **Ideas are fatal to caste.**

*A Passage to India*, pt 1, ch. 7 (1924)

4 **The so called white races are really pinko-grey.**

Mr Fielding, in ibid. This 'silly aside' caused scandal at Fielding's Anglo-Indian club, Forster explained, for Fielding 'did not realize that "white" has no more to do with a colour than "God Save the King" with a god, and that it is the height of impropriety to consider what it does connote'.

5 Nothing in India is identifiable, the mere asking of a question causes it to disappear or to emerge in something else.

ibid. pt 1, ch. 8

6 Hope, politeness, the blowing of a nose, the squeak of a boot, all produce 'boum'.

ibid. pt 2, ch. 14. This sound of the echo in the Marabar caves, 'entirely devoid of distinction', seemed to murmur to Mrs Moore, 'Pathos, piety, courage – they exist, but are identical, and so is filth. Everything exists, nothing has value.'

7 The final test for a novel will be our affection for it, as it is the test of our friends, and of anything else which we cannot define.

Aspects of the Novel, 'Introductory' (1927)

8 Yes – oh dear yes – the novel tells a story.

ibid. ch. 2. Closing words of chapter.

9 Curiosity is one of the lowest of the human faculties. You will have noticed in daily life that when people are inquisitive they nearly always have bad memories and are usually stupid at bottom.

ibid. ch. 5 'The Plot'

10 Logic! Good gracious! What rubbish! How can I tell what I think till I see what I say?

ibid. Riposte of 'that old lady in the anecdote who was accused by her nieces of being illogical'. Almost the same words also appeared in The Art of Thought (1926) by the political scientist Graham Wallas, this time ascribed to a 'little girl' who had been told to be sure of her meaning before she spoke.

11 Ulysses . . . is a dogged attempt to cover the universe with mud, an inverted Victorianism, an attempt to make crossness and dirt succeed where sweetness and light failed, a simplification of the human character in the interests of Hell.

ibid. ch. 6 'Fantasy'. Forster also called Ulysses 'perhaps the most interesting literary experiment of our day'.

12 One always tends to overpraise a long book, because one has got through it.

Abinger Harvest, 'T.E. Lawrence' (1936)

13 Lord I disbelieve – help thou my unbelief.

'What I Believe', written 1939, publ. in Two Cheers for Democracy (1951). A reference to Mark 9:24, 'Lord, I believe, help thou mine unbelief'.

14 My law-givers are Erasmus and Montaigne, not Moses and St Paul.

ibid.

15 I hate the idea of causes, and if I had to choose between betraying my country and betraying my friend, I hope I should have the guts to betray my country.

ibid.

16 Two cheers for Democracy: one because it admits variety and two because it permits criticism.

ibid. Forster thought two cheers were 'quite enough'; three he reserved for 'Love the Beloved Republic' (from Swinburne's poem, 'Hertha'). KINGSLEY AMIS commented: 'Two cheers were probably as many as Forster could manage in favour of anything, from democracy to stamp-collecting . . . The Forsters of this world go on as if they would prefer to be spared the vulgarities entailed in running a decent society, one which deserves four cheers for its citizens and others too'.

17 The more highly public life is organized the lower does its morality sink.

ibid.

18 Tolerance is a very dull virtue. It is boring. Unlike love, it has always had a bad press. It is negative. It merely means putting up with people, being able to stand things.

'Tolerance', written 1941, publ. in ibid. The essay looked ahead to the post-War world, and the necessity to accept former enemies. 'I don't . . . regard tolerance as a great eternally established divine principle,' Forster wrote. 'It is just a makeshift, suitable for an overcrowded and overheated planet.'

19 The only books that influence us are those for which we are ready, and which have gone a little farther down our particular path than we have yet got ourselves.

'A Book that Influenced Me', written 1941, publ. in ibid.

20 The humanist has four leading characteristics – curiosity, a free mind, belief in good taste, and belief in the human race.

'Gide and George', written 1943, publ. in ibid.

21 Creative writers are always greater than the causes that they represent.

ibid.

22 Art for art's sake? I should think so, and more so than ever at the present time. It is the one orderly product which our middling race has produced. It is the cry of a thousand sentinels, the echo from a thousand labyrinths, it is the lighthouse which cannot be hidden . . . it is the best evidence we can have of our dignity.

Address to PEN Club Congress, quoted in Monitor (ed. Huw Weldon, 1962)

# Bruce Forsyth (b. 1928)
BRITISH ENTERTAINER

Original name Bruce Forsyth-Johnson. Having trained as a dancer he made his TV début in Music Hall (1954), became a national celebrity as compère on Sunday Night at the London Palladium (1958–60), hosted and performed one-man cabaret routines on ATV's Bruce Forsyth Show throughout the 1960s, and compèred the BBC's popular The Generation Game (1971–8, 1990–94).

1 Nice to see you, to see you nice.

Catch-phrase from the Bruce Forsyth Show (1960s)

2 Didn't he do well!

Catch-phrase from the Generation Game (1970s onward)

# Michel Foucault (1926–84)
FRENCH ESSAYIST AND PHILOSOPHER

Influenced both by Nietzsche and by structuralist philosophy, he was concerned with the 'principles of exclusion' by which society operates, with particular reference to the sick, the insane and the criminal. His major works include Madness and Civilization (1961) and The Order of Things (1966).

1 Freedom of conscience entails more dangers than authority and despotism.

Madness and Civilization, ch. 7 (1961)

2 Marxism exists in nineteenth-century thought as a fish exists in water; that is, it ceases to breathe anywhere else.

The Order of Things, ch. 7 (1966)

3 As the archeology of our thought easily shows, man is an invention of recent date. And one perhaps nearing its end.

ibid. ch. 10

4 Sexuality is a part of our behaviour. It's part of our world freedom. Sexuality is something that we ourselves create. It is our own creation, and much more than the discovery of a secret side of our desire. We have to understand that with our desires go new forms of relationships, new forms of love, new forms of creation. Sex is not a fatality; it's a possibility for creative life. It's not enough to affirm that we are gay but we must also create a gay life.

'Sex, Power and the Politics of Identity', interview October 1982, first publ. in Advocate 7 August 1984, repr. in Michel Foucault (1989) by Didier Eribon

5 Modernity is the attitude that makes it possible to grasp the 'heroic' aspect of the present moment.

The Foucault Reader, 'What Is Enlightenment?', pt 2 (ed. Paul Rabinow, 1984)

## H.W. Fowler (1859–1933)

BRITISH LEXICOGRAPHER

Full name Henry Watson Fowler. With his brother Frank he compiled the first *Concise Oxford Dictionary* (1911), but he is most associated with his *Modern English Usage* (1926), which became an essential household reference work.

1 A writer expresses himself in words that have been used before because they give his meaning better than he can give it himself, or because they are beautiful or witty, or because he expects them to touch a chord of association in his reader, or because he wishes to show that he is learned or well read. Quotations due to the last motive are invariably ill advised; the discerning reader detects it & is contemptuous; the undiscerning is perhaps impressed, but even then is at the same time repelled, pretentious quotations being the surest road to tedium.

   *A Dictionary of Modern English Usage*, 'Quotation' (1926). Referring to 'literary or decorative quotation'.

2 The English-speaking world may be divided into (1) those who neither know nor care what a split infinitive is; (2) those who do not know, but care very much; (3) those who know & condemn; (4) those who know & approve; & (5) those who know & distinguish.

   ibid. 'Split Infinitive'. Fowler defined the first category as 'the vast majority . . . a happy folk, to be envied by most of the minority classes'.

## (Sir) Norman Fowler (b. 1938)

BRITISH POLITICIAN

Elected an MP in 1970, he rose to be Minister of Employment (1987–90), special adviser to MARGARET THATCHER during the 1992 election, and Chairman of the Conservative Party (1992–4).

1 I have a young family and for the next few years I should like to devote more time to them.

   Resignation letter to the Prime Minister, publ. in the *Guardian* 4 January 1990. Margaret Thatcher's reply was: 'I am naturally very sorry to see you go, but understand your reasons for doing so, particularly your wish to be able to spend more time with your family'. The expression 'spend more time with his family' immediately became a euphemism for getting sacked, though there was no official indication that Fowler had been dismissed

## John Fowles (b. 1926)

BRITISH NOVELIST

Influenced by Greek philosophy and French existentialism, his novels explore abstract psychological themes, as in *The Collector* (1963, filmed 1965), with which he made his name, and *The Magus* (1966, rev. 1977). His pastiche of a Victorian romance, *The French Lieutenant's Woman* (1969), was filmed in 1981 with a screenplay by HAROLD PINTER.

1 Duty largely consists of pretending that the trivial is critical.

   *The Magus*, ch. 18 (1965)

2 There is only one good definition of God: the freedom that allows other freedoms to exist.

   *The French Lieutenant's Woman*, ch. 13 (1969)

3 You do not even think of your own past as quite real; you dress it up, you gild it or blacken it, censor it, tinker with it . . . fictionalize it, in a word, and put it away on a shelf – your book, your romanced autobiography. We are all in flight from the real reality. That is the basic definition of Homo sapiens.

   ibid.

4 And so are we all novelists, that is, we have a habit of writing fictional futures for ourselves, although perhaps today we incline more to put ourselves into a film. We

screen in our minds hypotheses about how we might behave, about what might happen to us. And these novelistic or cinematic hypotheses often have very much more effect on how we actually do behave, when the real future becomes the present, than we generally allow.

   ibid. ch.45

5 Serious modern fiction has only one subject: the difficulty of writing serious modern fiction.

   Miles Green, in *Mantissa* (1982)

6 There are only two races on this planet – the intelligent and the stupid.

   *Daily Telegraph* 15 August 1991

## Edward Fox (b. 1934)

BRITISH ACTOR

Leading man of the 1970s and 1980s in restrained English style, he has appeared in the films *The Day of the Jackal* (1973) and *The Dresser* (1983), and for TV in *Edward and Mrs Simpson* (1978).

1 Being a gentleman is the number one priority, the chief question integral to our national life.

   *Daily Telegraph* 14 February 1992

## Janet Frame (b. 1924)

NEW ZEALAND NOVELIST AND POET

Considered one of New Zealand's greatest writers, her early life was overshadowed by the death of two of her sisters. Misdiagnosed as a schizophrenic, she spent the years 1947–54 in mental hospitals. Her novels include *Scented Gardens for the Blind* (1963), and her three volumes of autobiography were made into the film *An Angel at My Table* (1990).

1 Every morning I woke in dread, waiting for the day nurse to go on her rounds and announce from the list of names in her hand whether or not I was for shock treatment, the new and fashionable means of quieting people and of making them realize that orders are to be obeyed and floors are to be polished without anyone protesting and faces are made to be fixed into smiles and weeping is a crime.

   *Faces in the Water*, ch. 1 (1961). Referring to her life in a psychiatric institution.

2 For your own good is a persuasive argument that will eventually make a man agree to his own destruction.

   ibid. ch. 4

3 It would be nice to travel if you knew where you were going and where you would live at the end or do we ever know, do we ever live where we live, we're always in other places, lost, like sheep.

   *You Are Now Entering the Human Heart*, 'The Day of the Sheep' (1983)

4 Writing a novel is not merely going on a shopping expedition across the border to an unreal land: it is hours and years spent in the factories, the streets, the cathedrals of the imagination.

   *The Envoy from Mirror City*, ch. 20 (first volume of autobiography, 1985)

## Anatole France (1844–1924)

FRENCH AUTHOR

Roused into politics by the Dreyfus case (1896), he inveighed against Church and State in such works as *The Gods Are Thirsty* (1912) and *The Angels' Revolt* (1914), a satire on Christian theology. He was awarded the Nobel Prize for Literature in 1921.

1 You think you are dying for your country; you die for the industrialists.

   *L'Humanité* 18 July 1922

## Anne Frank (1929–45)

GERMAN JEWISH REFUGEE AND DIARIST

Her diary, a moving testimony of the years (1942–4) when she and her family were in hiding in Nazi-occupied Amsterdam, was published in 1947 by her father, the only member of the family to survive. It has since been translated into over fifty languages.

1 One must apply one's reason to everything here, learning to obey, to shut up, to help, to be good, to give in, and I don't know what else. I'm afraid I shall use up all my brains too quickly, and I haven't got so very many. Then I shall not have any left for when the war is over.

Journal entry 22 December 1942, publ. in *The Diary of a Young Girl*, (1947)

2 They mustn't know my despair, I can't let them see the wounds which they have caused, I couldn't bear their sympathy and their kind-hearted jokes, it would only make me want to scream all the more. If I talk, everyone thinks I'm showing off; when I'm silent they think I'm ridiculous; rude if I answer, sly if I get a good idea, lazy if I'm tired, selfish if I eat a mouthful more than I should, stupid, cowardly, crafty, etc. etc.

Journal entry 30 January 1943, in ibid.

3 I want to go on living even after my death! And therefore I am grateful to God for giving me this gift, this possibility of developing myself and of writing, of expressing all that is in me.

Journal entry 4 April 1944, in ibid.

4 I don't believe that the big men, the politicians and the capitalists alone are guilty of the war. Oh, no, the little man is just as keen, otherwise the people of the world would have risen in revolt long ago! There is an urge and rage in people to destroy, to kill, to murder, and until all mankind, without exception, undergoes a great change, wars will be waged, everything that has been built up, cultivated and grown, will be destroyed and disfigured, after which mankind will have to begin all over again.

Journal entry 3 May 1944, in ibid.

5 I have often been downcast, but never in despair; I regard our hiding as a dangerous adventure, romantic and interesting at the same time. In my diary I treat all the privations as amusing. I have made up my mind now to lead a different life from other girls and, later on, different from ordinary housewives. My start has been so very full of interest, and that is the sole reason why I have to laugh at the humorous side of the most dangerous moments.
ibid.

6 Is discord going to show itself while we are still fighting, is the Jew once again worth less than another? Oh, it is sad, very sad, that once more, for the umpteenth time, the old truth is confirmed: 'What *one* Christian does is his own responsibility, what *one* Jew does is thrown back at all Jews.'

Journal entry 22 May 1944, in ibid. Referring to anti-Semitism in Holland.

7 It's really a wonder that I haven't dropped all my ideals because they seem so absurd and impossible to carry out. Yet, I keep them, because in spite of everything I still believe that people are really good at heart. I simply can't build up my hopes on a foundation consisting of confusion, misery, and death. I see the world gradually being turned into a wilderness, I hear the ever-approaching thunder, which will destroy us too, I can feel the sufferings of millions and yet, if I look up into the heavens, I think that it will all come right, that this cruelty too will end, and that peace and tranquillity will return again.

Journal entry 15 July 1944, in ibid. Less than three weeks after writing this entry, on 4 August 1944, Anne along with the other occupants of the secret annexe in which they had been hiding were arrested by the Nazis and sent to concentration camps in Germany.

## Hans Frank (1900–1946)

GERMAN NAZI POLITICIAN

Nazi Germany's leading lawyer, he was appointed in 1939 Governor-General of Poland, where he established concentration camps and ran a repressive régime of brutality and extermination. He was tried at Nuremberg and hanged.

1 Our Constitution is the will of the Führer.

*Völkischer Beobachter* 20 May 1936, quoted in *Hitler: A Study in Tyranny*, ch. 7, sect. 6 (1952, rev. 1962) by Alan Bullock

2 There is no independence of law against National Socialism. Say to yourselves at every decision which you make: 'How would the Führer decide in my place?' In every decision ask yourselves: 'Is this decision compatible with the National Socialist conscience of the German people?' Then you will have a firm iron foundation which, allied with the unity of the National Socialist People's State and with your recognition of the eternal nature of the will of Adolf Hitler, will endow your own sphere of decision with the authority of the Third Reich, and this for all time.

Speech to jurists in 1936, quoted in *The Rise and Fall of the Third Reich*, ch. 8 'Justice in the Third Reich' (1959) by William L. Shirer. Frank was at the time Commissioner of Justice and President of the German Law Academy.

## Felix Frankfurter (1882–1965)

US ACADEMIC AND JUDGE

He taught at Harvard Law School (1914–39), and was a co-founder of the American Civil Liberties Union in 1920. As Associate Justice of the US Supreme Court (1939–62), he advocated judicial self-restraint.

1 The words of the Constitution . . . are so unrestricted by their intrinsic meaning or by their history or by tradition or by prior decisions that they leave the individual Justice free, if indeed they do not compel him, to gather meaning not from reading the Constitution but from reading life.

'The Supreme Court', quoted in *Parliamentary Affairs* vol. 3, no.1, winter 1949

2 Judicial judgment must take deep account . . . of the day before yesterday in order that yesterday may not paralyze today.

Quoted in the *National Observer* 1 March 1965

## Aretha Franklin (b. 1942)

US SOUL SINGER

Raised in Detroit, where she sang gospel songs in the church of her father, C.L. Franklin, the most celebrated gospel preacher of the 1950s, she came to be known as 'Lady Soul' for her impassioned singing on a series of hits in the 1960s. She later returned to her gospel roots though still revered as a diva of soul, much in demand for duets with younger stars, giving her more chart success in the 1980s.

1 R-E-S-P-E-C-T
Find out what it means to me.

'Respect' (song, written by Otis Redding), on the album *I Never Loved a Man the Way I Loved You* (1967). The song was a hit for Otis Redding in 1965.

## Michael Franti

US RAPPER

A six-foot-six ex-baseball player, he is a singer of articulate and cutting lyrics with a voice compared to GIL SCOTT HERON. He was formerly a member of Disposable Heroes of Hiphoprisy (1990–93), a band on the 'liberal' wing of 1990s rap.

1 TV is the place
Where the pursuit of happiness has become the pursuit
   of trivia
Where toothpaste and cars have become sex objects
Where imagination is sucked out of children
by a cathode ray nipple.
TV is the only wet nurse that would create a cripple.
Television, the drug of the nation,
Breeding ignorance and feeding radiation.
'Television, The Drug of the Nation' (song) on the album *Hypocrisy is the Greatest Luxury* (1992) by Disposable Heroes of Hiphoprisy

2 If ever I would stop thinking about music and politics
I would tell you that music is the expression of emotion
and that politics is merely the decoy of perception
'Music and Politics' (song) on ibid.

## Michael Frayn (b. 1933)
BRITISH PLAYWRIGHT, NOVELIST AND JOURNALIST

A satirical wit pervades his columns for the *Manchester Guardian* and the *Observer* and his many successful comedies for the stage, for example *Noises Off* (1982). He has also written novels, screenplays and translations of Tolstoy and Chekhov.

1 It's not excellence which leads to celebrity, but celebrity which leads to excellence. One makes one's reputation, and one's reputation enables one to achieve the conditions in which one can do good work.
John Dyson, in *Towards the End of the Morning*, ch. 4 (1967)

2 Happily married couples stood not face to face, absorbed in each other, but back to back looking outwards upon the world.
Bob Bell (musing to himself), in ibid. ch. 8

3 So I want to tell you how important it is to make things. That's how man lives, by making. To be is to make. To make food, to make drink, to make shelter – yes, but also to make thought. Because to think is to make.
Horvath, in *Make or Break*, act 1 (1980)

4 That's what it's all about. Doors and sardines. Getting on – getting off. Getting the sardines on – getting the sardines off. That's farce. That's the theatre. That's life.
Lloyd (the director), in *Noises Off*, act 1 (1982)

## Jonathan Freedland (b. 1967)
British journalist

Columnist and leader writer for the *Guardian*, he was Washington correspondent until 1997. He has also worked for the *Washington Post* and as a presenter on Radio 5 Live, and is author of *Bringing Home the Revolution* (1998), a comparison of US and British political and social institutions.

1 We simultaneously disdain and covet American culture, condemning it as junk food, even as we reach for another helping – a kind of binge-and-puke social bulimia.
*Bringing Home the Revolution*, Introduction (1998)

## Max Freedman See BILL HALEY 1.

## Matt Frei (b. 1963)
BRITISH JOURNALIST

A correspondent for the BBC in Hong Kong and Rome, he has also been a regular contributor to the *Spectator*, the *London Review of Books*, the *Wall Street Journal* and *The Times*. His first book was *Italy: The Unfinished Revolution* (1995).

1 [Of German reunification] It's like the Beatles coming together again – let's hope they don't go on a world tour.
*Listener* 21 June 1990

## Marilyn French (b. 1929)
US AUTHOR

She is best known for her first novel *The Women's Room* (1977), one of the first books to tackle radical feminist issues in easily accessible fiction. Other novels include *The Bleeding Heart* (1981) and she has also published literary criticism and essays which depict a patriarchal US society.

1 I hate discussions of feminism that end up with who does the dishes, she said. So do I. But at the end, there are always the damned dishes.
Isolde, in *The Women's Room*, ch. 1, sect. 21 (1977)

2 Whatever they may be in public life, whatever their relations with men, in their relations with women, all men are rapists and that's all they are. They rape us with their eyes, their laws, their codes.
Valerie, in ibid. ch. 5, sect. 19

## Sigmund Freud (1856–1939)
AUSTRIAN PSYCHIATRIST

He was a pioneer of the study of the unconscious mind and developed the basic techniques of psychoanalysis through free association and the analysis of dreams. His theory of infantile sexuality and the proposition that dreams and neuroses have their basis in repressed sexuality were expounded in *The Interpretation of Dreams* (1899), *Totem and Taboo* (1913) and *The Ego and the Id* (1923), among other works. See also W.H. AUDEN 15; R.D. LAING 1.

1 A strong egoism is a protection against disease, but in the last resort we must begin to love in order that we may not fall ill, and must fall ill if, in consequence of frustration, we cannot love.
'On Narcissism: An Introduction' (1914), repr. in *Complete Works, Standard Edition*, vol. 14 (ed. James Strachey and Anna Freud, 1954)

2 We believe that civilization has been created under the pressure of the exigencies of life at the cost of satisfaction of the instincts.
*Introductory Lectures on Psychoanalysis*, lecture 1 (1915), repr. in ibid. vol. 15 (1963)

3 The analytic psychotherapist thus has a threefold battle to wage – in his own mind against the forces which seek to drag him down from the analytic level; outside the analysis, against opponents who dispute the importance he attaches to the sexual instinctual forces and hinder him from making use of them in his scientific technique; and inside the analysis, against his patients, who at first behave like opponents but later on reveal the overvaluation of sexual life which dominates them, and who try to make him captive to their socially untamed passion.
'Observations on Transference-Love', first publ. 1915, repr. in ibid. vol. 12 (1958)

4 If a man has been his mother's undisputed darling he retains throughout life the triumphant feeling, the confidence in success, which not seldom brings actual success along with it.
'A Childhood Recollection from Dichtung und Wahrheit', first publ. 1917, repr. in ibid. vol. 17 (1955)

5 The ego is not master in its own house.
'A Difficulty in the Path of Psycho-Analysis', first publ. 1917, repr. in ibid. Freud's conclusion was reached in the light of his conviction that sexual instincts could not be wholly tamed, and that mental processes were unconscious and could 'only reach the ego and come under its control through incomplete and untrustworthy perceptions'.

6 I have found little that is 'good' about human beings on the whole. In my experience most of them are trash, no

matter whether they publicly subscribe to this or that ethical doctrine or to none at all. That is something that you cannot say aloud, or perhaps even think.

*Letter, 9 October 1918, publ. in Psycho-Analysis and Faith: The Letters of Sigmund Freud and Oscar Pfister (1963)*

7 Incidentally, why was it that none of all the pious ever discovered psycho-analysis? Why did it have to wait for a completely godless Jew?

*ibid.*

8 We know less about the sexual life of little girls than of boys. But we need not feel ashamed of this distinction; after all, the sexual life of adult women is a 'dark continent' for psychology.

*The Question of Lay Analysis, pt 4 (1926). The phrase 'dark continent' was written in English.*

9 A civilization which leaves so large a number of its participants unsatisfied and drives them into revolt neither has nor deserves the prospect of a lasting existence.

*The Future of an Illusion, ch. 2 (1927)*

10 Devout believers are safeguarded in a high degree against the risk of certain neurotic illnesses; their acceptance of the universal neurosis spares them the task of constructing a personal one.

*ibid. ch. 8*

11 It is always possible to bind together a considerable number of people in love, so long as there are other people left over to receive the manifestations of their aggression.

*Civilization and its Discontents ch. 5 (1930)*

12 Civilization is a process in the service of Eros, whose purpose is to combine single human individuals, and after that families, then races, peoples and nations, into one great unity, the unity of mankind. Why this has to happen, we do not know; the work of Eros is precisely this.

*ibid. ch. 6*

13 The only bodily organ which is really regarded as inferior is the atrophied penis, a girl's clitoris.

*New Introductory Lectures on Psychoanalysis, Lecture 31, 'The Dissection of the Psychical Personality' (1933). Freud was refuting the claims of 'Individual Psychologists' that the 'inferiority complex' can be traced back to self-perceived organic defects.*

14 Where *id* was, there *ego* shall be.

*ibid. The intention of psychoanalysis, Freud explained, is 'to strengthen the ego, to make it more independent of the super-ego, to widen its field of perception and enlarge its organization, so that it can appropriate fresh portions of the id . . . It is a work of culture,' he added in the closing words of the lecture, 'not unlike the draining of the Zuider Zee.'*

15 I do not think our successes can compete with those of Lourdes. There are so many more people who believe in the miracles of the Blessed Virgin than in the existence of the unconscious.

*ibid. Lecture 34, 'Explanations, Applications and Orientations'*

16 What progress we are making. In the Middle Ages they would have burned me. Now they are content with burning my books.

*Remark in 1933, quoted in Sigmund Freud: Life and Work, vol. 3, pt 1, ch. 4 (1957) by Ernest Jones. Referring to the public burning of his books in Berlin.*

17 A certain degree of neurosis is of inestimable value as a drive, especially to a psychologist.

*Quoted in Fragments of an Analysis with Freud, ch. 3, '22 January 1935' (1954) by Joseph Wortis*

18 Homosexuality is assuredly no advantage, but it is nothing to be ashamed of, no vice, no degradation; it cannot be classified as an illness; we consider it to be a variation of the sexual function, produced by a certain arrest of sexual development. Many highly respectable individuals of ancient and modern times have been homosexuals, several

of the greatest men among them (Plato, Michelangelo, Leonardo da Vinci, etc.). It is a great injustice to persecute homosexuality as a crime – and a cruelty, too. If you do not believe me, read the books of Havelock Ellis.

*Letter to a woman requesting treatment for her son, 9 April 1935, publ. in The Letters of Sigmund Freud (1961)*

19 Every normal person, in fact, is only normal on the average. His ego approximates to that of the psychotic in some part or other and to a greater or lesser extent.

*'Analysis Terminable and Interminable', sect. 5 (1937), repr. in Complete Works, Standard Edition, vol. 23 (ed. James Strachey and Anna Freud, 1964)*

20 The great question that has never been answered, and which I have not yet been able to answer, despite my thirty years of research into the feminine soul, is 'What does a woman want?' [*Was will das Weib?*]

*Quoted in Sigmund Freud: Life and Work, vol. 2, pt 3, ch. 16 (1955) by Ernest Jones. Freud's views on women are summarized in Peter Gay's biography, Freud: A Life of Our Time, pt 10 (1988).*

21 Yes, America is gigantic, but a gigantic mistake.

*Quoted in Memories of a Psycho-analyst, ch. 9 (1959) by Ernest Jones. 'America is the most grandiose experiment the world has seen,' Freud said on another occasion, 'but, I am afraid, it is not going to be a success.' (Freud: the Man and his Cause, pt 3, ch. 12, 1980, by Ronald W. Clark)*

# Nancy Friday (b. 1937)
US AUTHOR

A chronicler of sexual fantasies, which she defines as 'the triumph of love over rage', she has published *My Secret Garden* (1973), a study of female sexuality, *Men in Love* (1980) and *Women on Top* (1991) as well as contributing to *Cosmopolitan* and *Playboy* magazines.

1 Women are learning that nobody gives you an orgasm, nobody makes you sexual, except yourself.

*Men in Love, ch. 1 (1980)*

2 I find that my years of research have confirmed something even the most uninstructed woman takes as given: Inside every adult male is a denied little boy. He loved his father, but was taught to show that love only through mindless imitation of his father's mindless imitation of *his* father's Victorian authoritarianism. He loved his mother, but feared her power.

*ibid. ch. 22*

3 I have always believed that our erotic daydreams are the true X-rays of our sexual souls . . . An analyst collects his patients' dreams like gold coins. We should value our erotic reveries no less seriously, because they are the complex expressions of what we consciously desire and unconsciously fear. To know them is to know ourselves better.

*Women on Top, pt 1, 'Report from the Erotic Interior' (1991)*

4 Sex is antithetical to material greed. By definition greed is an insatiable appetite which . . . requires constant feeding . . . Rigidity, the vigilant, ever-acquiring eye – these are greed's henchmen, the enemy of sex which cries out for openness, ease, surrender. For the mating game to even begin, the animal must abandon at least momentarily the search for nuts and berries to pick up the erotic scent. In the very simplest of terms, there is no time for sex in a materially greedy world.

*ibid.*

5 Early twentieth-century man lived in a dizzying, swivel-headed attitude toward women's sexuality. He needed to see woman as chaste, passive, spiritual, she who was so close to heaven she could save his very soul after a murderous day of competition in the new industrial

society. This was known as 'the cult of the household nun'.

ibid. pt 2, 'A Little History'

6 The meaning of what it is to be a woman has never been more open-ended and therefore more filled with anxiety. We want to be independent/we want to be taken care of. We want men to treat us as sexual equals/we want men to sweep us away into sexual oblivion. We seduce men/we expect them to know, without being told, what it is we want done to our bodies. Men do their best, some better than others, but all work in the dark.

ibid. pt 2, 'What is a Real Woman?'

## Betty Friedan (b. 1921)
US WRITER

Her book, *The Feminist Mystique* (1963) was a seminal influence in the women's movement in Britain and the US. She was a founder of the National Organization for Women (NOW) (1966) and called the first International Feminist Congress in 1973, though has repudiated some aspects of contemporary feminism. *The Fountain of Age* (1993) explores old age.

1 The problem that has no name stirring in the minds of so many American women today is not a matter of loss of femininity or too much education, or the demands of domesticity. It is far more important than anyone recognizes. It is the key to these other new and old problems which have been torturing women and their husbands and children, and puzzling their doctors and educators for years. It may well be the key to our future as a nation and a culture. We can no longer ignore that voice within women that says: 'I want something more than my husband and my children and my home'.

*The Feminine Mystique*, ch. 1 (1963)

2 Instead of fulfilling the promise of infinite orgiastic bliss, sex in the America of the feminine mystique is becoming a strangely joyless national compulsion, if not a contemptuous mockery.

ibid. ch. 11

3 The feminine mystique has succeeded in burying millions of American women alive.

ibid. ch. 13

4 It is easier to live through someone else than to become complete yourself.

ibid. ch. 14

5 The women's movement has for years been the scapegoat for the rage of threatened, insecure housewives who can no longer count on husbands for lifelong support.

*The Second Stage*, ch. 1 (1981)

6 Make policy, not coffee.

ibid. The slogan was adopted during the National Organization for Women's Political Caucus in 1971.

## Milton Friedman (b. 1912)
US ECONOMIST

A convinced monetarist, he was adviser to President REAGAN (1981–9) and the inspiration for the economic policies of the Conservative government under MARGARET THATCHER (1979–90). He won the Nobel Prize for Economics in 1976.

1 History suggests that capitalism is a necessary condition for political freedom. Clearly it is not a sufficient condition.

*Capitalism and Freedom*, ch. 1 (1962)

2 We are all Keynesians now.

Quoted in *Time* 31 December 1965. In a letter to the magazine's editor, 4 February 1966, Friedman protested that the quote was taken out of context, since he had added 'in another [sense], nobody is any longer a Keynesian'.

3 People are out of work. Interest rates go up. Money gets tight. It's unpleasant. Only later do the good effects of an end to rising prices show up. The problem is getting through the painful cure without wanting another drink. The greatest difficulty in curtailing inflation is that, after a while, people begin to think they'd rather have the sickness than the cure.

*Playboy* February 1973, repr. as Introduction to *There's No Such Thing as a Free Lunch* (1975)

4 Perfect competition is a theoretical concept like the Euclidean line, which has no width and no depth. Just as we've never seen that line there has never been truly free enterprise.

ibid.

5 What kind of society isn't structured on greed?

ibid.

## Brian Friel (b. 1929)
IRISH PLAYWRIGHT AND AUTHOR

The best known of contemporary Irish dramatists, he gained recognition with *Philadelphia, Here I Come!* (1964). His other plays, including *Translations* (1980) and *Dancing at Lughnasa* (1990), deal with the relationship of people to the land and its customs. He has also written short stories.

1 People with a culture of poverty suffer much less from repression than we of the middle class suffer and indeed, if I may make the suggestion with due qualification, they often have a hell of a lot more fun than we have.

Dodds, in *The Freedom of the City*, act 1 (1974)

2 It is not the literal past, the 'facts' of history, that shape us, but images of the past embodied in language . . . We must never cease renewing those images; because once we do, we fossilize.

Hugh, in *Translations*, act 3 (1981)

3 The Troubles [in Northern Ireland] are a pigmentation in our lives here, a constant irritation that detracts from real life. But life has to do with something else as well, and it's the other things which are the more permanent and real.

Interview in *Vanity Fair* October 1991

## Max Frisch (1911–91)
SWISS NOVELIST AND PLAYWRIGHT

He adopted an Expressionist style in his examinations of the moral dilemmas of the mid twentieth century, as in the novels *Stiller* (1954) and *Homo Faber* (1957), and the plays *Andorra* (1961) and *The Fire Raisers* (1962).

1 It's precisely the disappointing stories, which have no proper ending and therefore no proper meaning, that sound true to life.

Stiller, in *I'm Not Stiller*, 'First Notebook' (1954)

2 Technology . . . the knack of so arranging the world that we don't have to experience it.

Hanna, in *Homo Faber*, 'Second Stop' (1957)

## Erich Fromm (1900–1980)
GERMAN-BORN US PSYCHOLOGIST

Bringing a neo-Freudian perspective to issues of alienation and materialism in the post-Second World War era, he wrote books which blend psychoanalysis with sociology and philosophy and also show the influences of Marx and existentialism. His principal works are *Escape from Freedom* (1941), *The Sane Society* (1955), and *The Art of Loving* (1956).

1 Man is the only animal for whom his own existence is a problem which he has to solve.
*Man For Himself*, ch. 3 (1947)

2 Man's main task in life is to give *birth* to himself, to become what he potentially is. The most important product of his effort is his own personality.
ibid. ch. 4

3 To die is poignantly bitter, but the idea of having to die without having lived is unbearable.
ibid.

4 Reason is man's instrument for arriving at the truth, intelligence is man's instrument for manipulating the world more successfully; the former is essentially human, the latter belongs to the animal part of man.
*The Sane Society*, ch. 3 (1955)

5 By alienation is meant a mode of experience in which the person experiences himself as an alien. He has become, one might say, estranged from himself. He does not experience himself as the center of his world, as the creator of his own acts – but his acts and their consequences have become his masters, whom he obeys, or whom he may even worship. The alienated person is out of touch with himself as he is out of touch with any other person.
ibid. ch. 5, 'Alienation'

6 In the nineteenth century the problem was that *God is dead*; in the twentieth century the problem is that *man is dead*. In the nineteenth century inhumanity meant cruelty; in the twentieth century it means schizoid self-alienation. The danger of the past was that men became slaves. The danger of the future is that men may become robots.
ibid. ch. 9. Fromm was echoing a speech made by ADLAI STEVENSON at Columbia University in 1954: 'We are not in danger of becoming slaves any more, but of becoming robots.'

7 Just as modern mass production requires the standardization of commodities, so the social process requires standardization of man, and this standardization is called equality.
*The Art of Loving*, ch. 2 (1956)

# (Sir) David Frost (b. 1939)

BRITISH BROADCASTER

'David Frost has risen without trace,' Kitty Muggeridge famously told her husband, MALCOLM MUGGERIDGE, in the mid-1960s. He has been a doyen of television since his appearances on the satirical show *That was the Week That Was* (1962–3) and subsequently established himself as an incisive interviewer on British and American TV. He co-founded London Weekend Television and in 1983 co-founded and presented *TV-am*.

1 Vote Labour and you build castles in the air. Vote Conservative and you can live in them.
*That was the Week That Was*, BBC TV, 31 December 1962

2 Hello, good evening, and welcome.
*The Frost Report* (TV show, 1966–7). The words were used to open each show in this and subsequent Frost series.

# Robert Frost (1874–1963)

US POET

His poetry, lyrical and traditional in form and inspired by rural New England in subject matter, preserves an inner tension and ambiguity. Collections such as *New Hampshire* (1923) won him a wide readership and a total of four Pulitzer prizes, so that in later life he came to be regarded as the unofficial US poet laureate. The critic YVOR WINTERS described him as a 'poet of the minor theme, the casual approach, and the discreetly eccentric attitude'.

1 Something there is that doesn't love a wall, And wants it down.
'Mending Wall', publ. in *North of Boston* (1914)

2 My apple trees will never get across And eat the cones under his pines, I tell him. He only says, 'Good fences make good neighbors'.
ibid.

3 And nothing to look backward to with pride, And nothing to look forward to with hope.
'The Death of the Hired Man', publ. in ibid.

4 Home is the place where, when you have to go there, They have to take you in.
Husband, in ibid. Wife replies: 'I should have called it/Something you somehow haven't to deserve.'

5 Most of the change we think we see in life Is due to truths being in and out of favor.
'The Black Cottage', publ. in ibid.

6 The best way out is always through.
'A Servant to Servants', publ. in ibid.

7 Pressed into service means pressed out of shape.
'The Self-Seeker', publ. in ibid.

8 I shall be telling this with a sigh
Somewhere ages and ages hence:
Two roads diverged in a wood, and I –
I took the one less traveled by,
And that has made all the difference.
'The Road Not Taken', publ. in *Mountain Interval* (1916)

9 One could do worse than be a swinger of birches.
'Birches', publ. in ibid.

10 A poem . . . begins as a lump in the throat, a sense of wrong, a homesickness, a lovesickness . . . It finds the thought and the thought finds the words.
Letter to the poet and anthologist Louis Untermeyer, 1 January 1916, publ. in *The Letters of Robert Frost to Louis Untermeyer* (1963)

11 I met a Californian who would
Talk California – a state so blessed
He said, in climate, none had ever died there
A natural death, and Vigilance Committees
Had had to organize to stock the graveyards
And vindicate the state's humanity.
'New Hampshire', publ. in *New Hampshire* (1923)

12 No wonder poets sometimes have to *seem*
So much more business-like than business men.
Their wares are so much harder to get rid of.
ibid.

13 Some say the world will end in fire,
Some say in ice.
From what I've tasted of desire
I hold with those who favor fire.
But if it had to perish twice,
I think I know enough of hate
To say that for destruction ice
Is also great
And would suffice.
'Fire and Ice', publ. in ibid.

14 The woods are lovely, dark and deep.
But I have promises to keep,
And miles to go before I sleep,
And miles to go before I sleep.
'Stopping by Woods on a Snowy Evening', publ. in ibid. The lines were found on a scrap of paper on the desk of Indian Prime Minister JAWAHARLAL NEHRU when he died – presumed to be the last words he read – and they were regularly quoted by JOHN F. KENNEDY to wind up speeches during his 1960 presidential campaign.

15 Tree at my window, window tree,
My sash is lowered when night comes on;
But let there never be curtain drawn
Between you and me.

'Tree at My Window', publ. in *West-Running Brook* (1928)

16 I have been one acquainted with the night.

'Acquainted with the Night', publ. in ibid.

17 Writing free verse is like playing tennis with the net down.

Address to Milton Academy, Massachusetts, 17 May 1935, publ. in *Interviews with Robert Frost* (1966) by Edward Latham

18 They cannot scare me with their empty spaces
Between stars – on stars where no human race is.
I have it in me so much nearer home
To scare myself with my own desert places.

'Desert Places', publ. in *A Further Range* (1936)

19 Two such as you with such a master speed
Cannot be parted nor be swept away
From one another once you are agreed
That life is only life forevermore
Together wing to wing and oar to oar.

'The Master Speed', publ. in ibid. The verse was inscribed on the gravestone of Frost and his wife Elinor in 1963.

20 No memory of having starred
Atones for later disregard,
Or keeps the end from being hard.

'Provide, Provide', publ. in ibid.

21 I never dared be radical when young
For fear it would make me conservative when old.

'Precaution', publ. in ibid.

22 No tears in the writer, no tears in the reader.

'The Figure a Poem Makes', preface to *Collected Poems* (1939)

23 The land was ours before we were the land's.
She was our land more than a hundred years
Before we were her people.

'The Gift Outright', publ. in *The Witness Tree* (1942). Frost recited this poem at the inauguration of President KENNEDY, 20 January 1961.

24 Happiness makes up in height what it lacks in length.

Poem title in ibid.

25 And were an epitaph to be my story
I'd have a short one ready for my own.
I would have written of me on my stone:
I had a lover's quarrel with the world.

'The Lesson for Today', publ. in ibid.

26 We dance round in a ring and suppose,
But the Secret sits in the middle and knows.

'The Secret Sits', publ. in ibid.

27 Poetry is a way of taking life by the throat.

Quoted in *Robert Frost: the Trial by Existence*, ch. 18 (1960) by Elizabeth S. Sergeant

28 Forgive, O Lord, my little jokes on Thee
And I'll forgive Thy great big one on me.

'Cluster of Faith', publ. in *In the Clearing* (1962)

29 You don't have to deserve your mother's love. You have to deserve your father's. He's more particular … The father is always a Republican towards his son, and his mother's always a Democrat.

Interview in *Writers at Work* (second series, ed. George Plimpton, 1963)

30 Thinking isn't agreeing or disagreeing. That's voting.

ibid.

31 Always fall in with what you're asked to accept. Take what is given, and make it over your way. My aim in life has always been to hold my own with whatever's going. Not against: with.

*Vogue* 14 March 1963

32 Poetry is what is lost in translation.

Quoted in *Robert Frost: a Backward Look*, ch. 1 (1964) by Louis Untermeyer. In similar vein, Samuel Taylor Coleridge wrote, in *Biographia Literaria* (1817): 'In poetry, in which every line, every phrase, may pass the ordeal of deliberation and deliberate choice, it is possible, and barely possible, to attain that *ultimatum* which I have ventured to propose as the infallible test of a blameless style; namely: its *untranslatableness* in words of the same language without injury to the meaning.'

# Christopher Fry (b. 1907)
### BRITISH PLAYWRIGHT

Born Christopher Fry Harris. Described by John Mason Brown as 'a fellow who has wandered from one Elizabethan Age into another', he specializes in free-verse dramas that combine comedy and an underlying mysticism, such as *The Lady's Not for Burning* (1948) and *Venus Observed* (1950). He also made successful translations of ANOUILH and GIRAUDOUX and wrote the commentary for the 1953 film of the Coronation.

1 It is the individual man
In his individual freedom who can mature
With his warm spirit the unripe world.

Moses, in *The Firstborn*, act 1, sc. 1 (1946)

2 I travel light; as light,
That is, as a man can travel who will
Still carry his body around because
Of its sentimental value.

Thomas, in *The Lady's Not for Burning*, act 1 (1949). The play's title was famously adapted: see MARGARET THATCHER 10.

3 What after all
Is a halo? It's only one more thing to keep clean.

ibid.

4 Religion
Has made an honest woman of the supernatural,
And we won't have it kicking over the traces again.

Tappercoom, in ibid. act 2

5 The moon is nothing
But a circumambulating aphrodisiac
Divinely subsidized to provoke the world
Into a rising birth-rate.

Thomas Mendip, in ibid. act 3

6 Poetry is the language in which man explores his own amazement … says heaven and earth in one word … speaks of himself and his predicament as though for the first time. It has the virtue of being able to say twice as much as prose in half the time, and the drawback, if you do not give it your full attention, of seeming to say half as much in twice the time.

*Time* 3 April 1950

7 Comedy is an escape, not from truth but from despair; a narrow escape into faith.

*Time* 20 November 1950

8 Coffee in England is just toasted milk.

*New York Post* 29 November 1962

# Roger Fry (1866–1934)
### BRITISH CRITIC AND PAINTER

A member of the Bloomsbury group, he was a champion of Cézanne and organized the first London exhibition of Post-Impressionists in 1910. He wrote widely on art and aesthetics arguing the precedence of form over content, and set up the Omega Workshops (1913–19) for the benefit of young artists. BRIAN SEWELL called him 'the father of foolish criticism'.

1 Art is significant deformity.

Quoted in *Roger Fry*, ch. 8 (1940) by Virginia Woolf

## Stephen Fry (b. 1957)

BRITISH ACTOR AND AUTHOR

Television appearances in the comedy series *Blackadder* (1986 and 1989), *A Bit of Fry & Laurie* (1989–94) and *Jeeves and Wooster* (1991–3) were followed by the lead part in the film *Wilde* (1997). His writings include *The Hippopotamus* (1994) and *Moab is My Washpot* (1997). On the subject of his popularity, he once judged himself 'placed somewhere between Alan Bennett and the Queen Mother, a sort of public kitten'.

1 We are more afraid of being pretentious than of being dishonest.

Quoted in the *Guardian* 31 December 1994

2 There is no logical explanation for despair. You can no more reason yourself into cheerfulness than you can reason yourself an extra six inches in height. You can only be better prepared.

Speech to launch the Samaritans' annual report, 17 May 1996, quoted in the *Guardian* 18 May 1996

## Northrop Frye (1912–91)

CANADIAN LITERARY CRITIC

He established his reputation as one of the leading literary theorists of his generation with *Fearful Symmetry* (1947) and *Anatomy of Criticism* (1957), which stress the recurrence of literary archetypes and attempt to classify symbols and genres. *The Great Code* (1982) examines the symbolism of the Bible.

1 It is clear that all verbal structures with meaning are verbal imitations of that elusive psychological and physiological process known as thought, a process stumbling through emotional entanglements, sudden irrational convictions, involuntary gleams of insight, rationalized prejudices, and blocks of panic and inertia, finally to reach a completely incommunicable intuition.

*Anatomy of Criticism*, 'Formal Phase: Symbol as Image' (1957)

2 Popular art is normally decried as vulgar by the cultivated people of its time; then it loses favor with its original audience as a new generation grows up; then it begins to merge into the softer lighting of 'quaint', and cultivated people become interested in it, and finally it begins to take on the archaic dignity of the primitive.

ibid. 'Mythical Phase: Symbol as Archetype'

## Carlos Fuentes (b. 1928)

MEXICAN AUTHOR AND CRITIC

He had already embarked on a career as a diplomat when he won recognition for his first collection of short stories, *The Masked Days* (1954). Since then he has written prolifically, including numerous works of fiction both realistic and fantastic in style; *Terra Nostra* (1975), embodying his ideas on Latin America's Spanish heritage, and *The New Hispano-American Novel* (1969), an influential work of literary criticism.

1 What the United States does best is to understand itself. What it does worst is understand others.

*Time* 16 June 1986

2 By its very nature, the novel indicates that we are becoming. There is no final solution. There is no last word.

*Guardian* 24 February 1989

3 If the Soviet Union can give up the Brezhnev Doctrine for the Sinatra Doctrine, the United States can give up the James Monroe Doctrine for the Marilyn Monroe Doctrine: Let's all go to bed wearing the perfume we like best.

Quoted in *The Times* 23 February 1990

4 I don't think any good book is based on factual experience. Bad books are about things the writer already knew before he wrote them.

*International Herald Tribune* 5 November 1991

## Francis Fukuyama (b. 1952)

US HISTORIAN

His main work, *The End of History and the Last Man* (1992), asserts that liberal democracy will win over all other forms of government and was commonly cited as a description of the state of the world following the end of the Cold War.

1 What we may be witnessing is not just the end of the Cold War but the end of history as such: that is, the end point of man's ideological evolution and the universalization of Western liberal democracy.

*Independent* 20 September 1989

2 While it is often the enemy of democracy, nationalism has also been democracy's handmaiden, from the time of the French Revolution.

*Independent* 3 March 1992

## J. William Fulbright (1905–95)

US POLITICIAN

Full name James William Fulbright. Elected as a Democrat to Congress in 1942 and to the Senate in 1944, he established a system of exchange programmes for teachers and students between the US and other countries (1946). He opposed McCarthyism and the Vietnam War. Among his writings are *The Arrogance of Power* (1967).

1 In the long course of history, having people who understand your thought is much greater security than another submarine.

*The New York Times* 26 June 1986. Speaking of the Fulbright scholarship programme.

## R. Buckminster Fuller (1895–1983)

US ENGINEER AND POET

Full name Richard Buckminster Fuller. His career as a designer and inventor was largely dedicated to deriving maximum benefits from the minimum of expenditure and energy, to which end he developed the Dymaxion (a contraction of dynamic, maximum and ion) House in 1927, and after 1945 the geodesic dome. He also authored many books and became Professor of Poetry at Harvard in 1962.

1 Here is God's purpose –
for God, to me, it seems,
is a verb
not a noun,
proper or improper.

Untitled poem, written 1940, publ. in *No More Secondhand God* (1963)

2 Either war is obsolete or men are.

*New Yorker* 8 January 1966

3 Dare to be naïve.

*Synergetics*, 'Moral of the Work' (1975)

## Paul Fussell (b. 1924)

US HISTORIAN

Called a 'thinking man's John Wayne' for his vigorous prose, he has written on both world wars, as in *The Boy Scout Handbook and Other Observations* (1982), as well as on the American class system, in *Class: A Guide through the American Status System* (1983).

1 **The worst thing about war was the sitting around and wondering what you were doing morally.**

*The Times* 28 November 1991

## Rose Fyleman (1877–1957)

BRITISH CHILDREN'S AUTHOR

A formidable character who had little time for children, she nevertheless devoted a career to writing for them. Her first collection of verse 'Fairies and Chimneys' (1918) proved her most popular.

1 **There are fairies at the bottom of our garden!**

'The Fairies', publ. in *Punch* 23 May 1917, repr. in *Fairies and Chimneys* (1918)

## Jostein Gaarder (b. 1952)
NORWEGIAN PHILOSOPHER AND AUTHOR

He was a teacher of philosophy in school for eleven years. *Sophie's World* (1991) was the first of his books to be published in English, followed by *The Solitaire Mystery* (1996) and *Through a Glass Darkly* (1998).

1 A lot of people experience the world with the same incredulity as when a magician pulls a rabbit out of a hat . . . We know that the world is not all sleight of hand and deception because we are in it, we are part of it. Actually we *are* the white rabbit being pulled out of the hat. The only difference between us and the white rabbit is that the rabbit does not realize it is taking part in a magic trick.
*Sophie's World*, 'The Top Hat' (1991)

## Clark Gable (1901–60)
US SCREEN ACTOR

Having previously laboured as an oil-driller and lumberjack, he worked his way up to become 'the King of Hollywood' by the time he played Fletcher Christian in *Mutiny on the Bounty* (1935). His most famous roles were in *Gone with the Wind* (1939) and his last film, *The Misfits* (1961). His off-screen life was never as glamorous as his film roles, as his third wife, actress Carole Lombard, once commented: 'Listen, he's no Clark Gable at home!'

1 Frankly, my dear, I don't give a damn!
Rhett Butler (Clark Gable), in *Gone with the Wind* (film, 1939, screenplay by Sidney Howard based on the 1936 novel by MAR-GARET MITCHELL, directed by Victor Fleming and others). The final words of Rhett's farewell to Scarlett O'Hara (Vivien Leigh), in answer to her lament, 'Where shall I go? What shall I do?' Because of the wish not to offend the censors, the words were spoken with the emphasis on 'give' to soften the impact of the oath following. Producer DAVID O. SELZNICK was nevertheless fined $5000. For the author's version see MARGARET MITCHELL 8.

## Zsa Zsa Gabor (b. 1919)
HUNGARIAN-BORN US ACTRESS

Although her acting career took her no further than B-films and sitcoms, she was 'famous for being famous', a denizen of gossip columns for her wealth and numerous marriages and affairs. Her liaison with Rafael Trujillo, the corrupt dictator of the Dominican Republic, provoked the comment, 'the most expensive courtesan since Madame de Pompadour'. She published guides on men.

1 I never hated a man enough to give him diamonds back.
Quoted in the *Observer* 25 August 1957

2 A man in love is incomplete until he has married – then he's finished.
Quoted in *Newsweek* 28 March 1960

3 Husbands are like fires. They go out when unattended.
ibid.

## Serge Gainsbourg (1928–91)
FRENCH SINGER, SONGWRITER AND FILM-MAKER

Original name Lucien Ginzburg. Prominent in the French chanson tradition, he wrote for Johnny Hallyday, Juliette Greco and Petula Clark, among other singers, also recording many of his own songs and composing film scores. Notorious for his provocative statements and lifestyle, he 'acted out the country's post-war vices', according to his biographer: 'alcoholism, nicotine, exhibitionism, incest, sex-mania and self-love.'

1 *Je t'aime . . . moi non plus.*
'Je t'aime . . . moi non plus' (song with Jane Birkin, 1969). The Gainsbourg/Birkin duet was formally condemned by the Vatican and banned by many radio stations, even in its instrumental version, but it still reached no. 2 in the British charts in July 1969 and no. 1 on its reissue in October 1969. The song was originally recorded in

December 1967 by BRIGITTE BARDOT, then romantically involved with Gainsbourg, after she had asked him to write for her 'the most beautiful love song that you could imagine, dedicated to me'. However, when news of the erotic recording with its groaning and heavy breathing leaked out to the press, Bardot begged Gainsbourg to withdraw the record, which was consequently not released until 1986 in aid of an animal charity. Gainsbourg directed a film titled *Je t'aime . . . moi non plus*, giving Gérard Depardieu one of his first film roles in 1976.

2 Ugliness is superior to beauty, because ugliness lasts.

Quoted in *GQ* January 2000. Described as having 'the face of a squashed frog', Gainsbourg refused to have mirrors in his home.

## Hugh Gaitskell (1906–63)
BRITISH POLITICIAN

Elected a Labour MP in 1945, he became Leader of the Opposition in 1955, opposing EDEN's policy over Suez and in 1960 his own party's vote for unilateral disarmament. TONY BENN called him a 'divisive leader' with 'a real civil servant's mind, very little imagination and hardly any understanding of how people worked'. See also ANEURIN BEVAN 10.

1 I have never had a great many baths and I can assure those that have them as a habit that it does not make a great difference to their health if they have fewer . . . As for appearance, most of that is underneath and nobody sees it.

Speech at Hastings, 1947, quoted in *The Fine Art of Political Wit*, ch. 8 (1964) by Leon Harris. Gaitskell, who was then Minister for Fuel and Power, was proposing an economy drive; his remark elicited the rejoinder by WINSTON CHURCHILL in the House of Commons: 'When Ministers of the Crown speak like this . . . the Prime Minister and his friends have no need to wonder why they are getting increasingly into bad odour.'

2 There are some of us, Mr Chairman, who will fight and fight and fight again to save the Party we love.

Speech at Labour Party Conference, Scarborough, 5 October 1961, publ. in *The Penguin Book of Twentieth-Century Speeches* (ed. Brian MacArthur, 1999). The plea referred to calls to reject the Party's defence policy in favour of unilateral nuclear disarmament, which Gaitskell believed would tear the Party asunder. The vote resulted in a defeat of the official policy, although this was overturned at the following year's Conference.

3 It [Britain's membership of the EEC] does mean . . . the end of Britain as an independent European state . . . It means the end of a thousand years of history. You may say, 'Let it end', but, my goodness, it is a decision that needs a little care and thought.

Speech at Labour Party Conference, Brighton, 3 October 1962, publ. in ibid. MACMILLAN's Conservative government had initiated negotiations for joining the European Community, although DE GAULLE's declared intention in 1963 to veto any application by Britain made the issue a less pressing concern.

## J.K. Galbraith (b. 1908)
US ECONOMIST

Full name John Kenneth Galbraith. A Keynesian economist who was adviser to Presidents Kennedy and Johnson, he advocates government spending but deplores consumerism. His books, particularly *The Affluent Society* (1958) and *The Age of Uncertainty* (1977), had a popular appeal.

1 In the usual (though certainly not in every) public decision on economic policy, the choice is between courses that are almost equally good or equally bad. It is the narrowest decisions that are most ardently debated. If the world is lucky enough to enjoy peace, it may even one day make the discovery, to the horror of doctrinaire free-enterprisers and doctrinaire planners alike, that what is called capitalism and what is called socialism are both capable of working quite well.

'The American Economy: Its Substance and Myth', first publ. in

*Years of the Modern* (ed. J.W. Chase, 1949), repr. in *The Galbraith Reader* (1979).

2 Wealth is not without its advantages and the case to the contrary, although it has often been made, has never proved widely persuasive.

*The Affluent Society*, ch. 1, sect. 1 (1958). Opening words.

3 Consumer wants can have bizarre, frivolous, or even immoral origins, and an admirable case can still be made for a society that seeks to satisfy them. But the case cannot stand if it is the process of satisfying wants that creates the wants.

ibid. ch. 11, sect. 2

4 It is a far, far better thing to have a firm anchor in nonsense than to put out on the troubled seas of thought.

ibid. ch. 11, sect. 4. Of the resistance of conventional wisdom to the 'economics of affluence'.

5 In a community where public services have failed to keep abreast of private consumption things are very different. Here, in an atmosphere of private opulence and public squalor, the private goods have full sway.

ibid. ch. 18, sect. 2

6 Meetings are a great trap. Soon you find yourself trying to get agreement and then the people who disagree come to think they have a right to be persuaded. Thus they acquire power; thus meetings become a source of opposition and trouble. However, they are indispensable when you don't want to do anything.

Journal entry, 22 April 1961, in *Ambassador's Journal*, ch. 5 (1969). The journal was written while Galbraith was serving as US Ambassador to India 1961–3.

7 Politics is not the art of the possible. It consists in choosing between the disastrous and the unpalatable.

Letter to President KENNEDY, 2 March 1962, publ. in ibid. ch. 15 (1969). Galbraith was referring to Bismarck's celebrated saying, *Die Politik ist die Lehre von Möglichen* ('Politics is the art of the possible').

8 By all but the pathologically romantic, it is now recognized that this is not the age of the small man.

*The New Industrial State*, ch. 3 (1967)

9 There are few ironclad rules of diplomacy but to one there is no exception. When an official reports that talks were useful, it can safely be concluded that nothing was accomplished.

'The American Ambassador', publ. in the *Foreign Service Journal* June 1969

10 All successful revolutions are the kicking in of a rotten door. The violence of revolutions is the violence of men who charge into a vacuum.

*The Age of Uncertainty*, ch. 3 (1977)

11 All of the great leaders have had one characteristic in common: it was the willingness to confront unequivocally the major anxiety of their people in their time. This, and not much else, is the essence of leadership.

ibid. ch. 12

12 In any great organization it is far, far safer to be wrong with the majority than to be right alone.

*Guardian* 28 July 1989

13 There's a certain part of the contented majority who love anybody who is worth a billion dollars.

*Guardian* 23 May 1992. Referring to millionaire presidential candidate H. ROSS PEROT.

14 The Third Way is a purely political concept. The increase in numbers and power of the middle-income groups means that governments choose to meet their needs first. The Third Way is a justification of that necessity.

Interview with ROY HATTERSLEY in the *Guardian* 17 October 1998

## Noel Gallagher (b. 1967)

BRITISH ROCK MUSICIAN

Leader and main songwriter of Oasis (from 1983), he has guided the group to huge success and constant press attention, largely fuelled by the band's 'mad for it' attitude. Hit albums by Oasis include *Definitely Maybe* (1994), which went platinum, and *(What's the Story) Morning Glory?* (1995).

1 What people have got to understand is that we are lads. We have burgled houses and nicked car stereos, and we like girls and we swear and we go to the football and take the piss.

Interview in *Melody Maker* 30 March 1996. The confession prompted an investigation by Greater Manchester police and a defence by the mother of Noel and Liam Gallagher: 'As far as I know they were never involved in any crime. They were just normal boys . . . Really, they are very thoughtful and kind and all they think about are their family and friends.'

2 Drugs is like getting up and having a cup of tea in the morning.

Radio interview 28 January 1997, quoted in the *Daily Telegraph* 31 January 1997

3 I would hope we mean more to people than putting money in a church basket and saying ten Hail Marys on a Sunday. Has God played Knebworth recently?

Interview in the *New Musical Express* 12 July 1997

4 We were supposed to be the ones who turned up at the awards ceremony poking fun at the Establishment and getting pissed and getting on everyone's nerves. As it panned out we became the Establishment, and I didn't particularly like that.

Interview in *GQ* February 2000

## Paul Gallico (1897–1976)

US NOVELIST

He turned to fiction after working as a sports columnist and editor at the *New York Daily News* and settling in England in 1936. Of his forty-odd books, best known is *The Snow Goose* (1941), set in the Lincolnshire Fens. *The Poseidon Adventure* (1969) was made into one of the first big-budget disaster movies (1972).

1 No one can be as calculatedly rude as the British, which amazes Americans, who do not understand studied insult and can only offer abuse as a substitute.

*The New York Times* 14 January 1962

## José Antonio Viera Gallo (b. 1943)

CHILEAN POLITICIAN

A member of Allende's government, he was Under-Secretary of Justice (1970–72).

1 Socialism can only arrive by bicycle.

Quoted in *Energy and Equity*, Foreword (1974) by Ivan Illich

## Indira Gandhi (1917–84)

INDIAN POLITICIAN

Daughter of India's first prime minister, JAWAHARLAL NEHRU, she was leader of the Congress Party (1966–77) and Prime Minister (1966–77, 1980–84). She was assassinated by members of her Sikh bodyguard after the storming of the Golden Temple at Amritsar. 'My father was a statesman, I'm a political woman,' she is quoted. 'My father was a saint. I'm not.'

1 I myself, in my heart, say that people should have all the children they want. But it's a mistaken idea, like many of our ideas that go back thousands of years, and it must be rooted out . . . But how can you change . . . an age-old habit? The only way is to plan births by one means or another. And the sterilization of men is one method of birth control. The surest, most radical method.

Interview in February 1972, publ. in *Interview With History*, ch. 7 (1976) by Oriana Fallaci

2 There exists no politician in India daring enough to attempt to explain to the masses that cows can be eaten.

Quoted by Oriana Fallaci in 'Indira's Coup', publ. in the *New York Review of Books* 18 September 1975

3 Even if I died in the service of the nation, I would be proud of it. Every drop of my blood . . . will contribute to the growth of this nation and make it strong and dynamic.

Speech in Delhi, 30 October 1984. Said on the eve of her assassination.

## Mahatma Gandhi (1869–1948)

INDIAN POLITICAL AND SPIRITUAL LEADER

Full name Mohandas Karamchand Gandhi. After striving for civil rights in South Africa, he transformed the Indian National Congress (1925–34) into a vehicle for nationalism and was hailed as India's supreme leader and the driving force behind independence (1947). To this end he pursued a course of non-violent civil disobedience, fasts and passive resistance, for which he came to be regarded popularly as a saint. He was assassinated by a Hindu fanatic. EINSTEIN made the judgement: 'In our time of utter moral decadence he was the only statesman to stand for a higher human relationship in the political sphere.' See also JAWAHARLAL NEHRU 3.

1 I claim that in losing the spinning wheel we lost our left lung. We are, therefore, suffering from galloping consumption. The restoration of the wheel arrests the progress of the fell disease.

*Young India* 13 October 1921

2 A policy is a temporary creed liable to be changed, but while it holds good it has got to be pursued with apostolic zeal.

Letter to the general secretary of the Congress Party, India, 8 March 1922, publ. in *Gandhi's Letters on Indian Affairs*, 'To Co-workers' (1923)

3 Non-violence is the first article of my faith. It is the last article of my faith.

Speech in defence trial, Ahmedabad, 18 March 1922, publ. in *Young India* 23 March 1922, repr. in *The Penguin Book of Twentieth-Century Speeches* (ed. Brian MacArthur, 1999). Gandhi was charged with sedition for three articles published in his newspaper *Young India*. Pleading guilty and demanding of the judge 'the highest penalty that can be inflicted upon me for what in law is a deliberate crime and what appears to me to be the highest duty of a citizen', he was sentenced to six years' imprisonment but was released after two years on grounds of ill health.

4 I have nothing new to teach the world. Truth and Non-violence are as old as the hills. All I have done is to try experiments in both on as vast a scale as I could.

*Harijan* 28 March 1936

5 An unjust law is itself a species of violence. Arrest for its breach is more so.

*Non-Violence in Peace and War*, vol. 2, ch. 150 (1949)

6 Reporter: 'Mr Gandhi, what do you think of Western civilization?'
Gandhi: 'I think it would be a very good idea.'

Attributed. There is no evidence of any exchange having taken place, although E.F. Schumacher (in *Good Work*, ch. 2, 1979) mentions seeing a film of Gandhi disembarking at Southampton, England, in 1930, in which Gandhi is asked his opinion on *modern* civilization and gives the answer as above.

## Greta Garbo (1905–90)

SWEDISH-BORN US SCREEN ACTRESS

Originally Greta Lovisa Gustafsson. 'The only one who has ever been really mysterious,' according to Joan Crawford, she successfully transferred her compelling and enigmatic screen presence from silent films to the talkies in 1930. She was acclaimed for her starring roles in *Mata Hari* (1931), *Anna Karenina* (1935) and *Camille* (1937) but retired in 1941. Her famous reclusiveness enhanced her image as 'the Swedish Sphinx'. See KENNETH TYNAN 1.

1 I want to be alone.

Grusinskaya (Greta Garbo), in *Grand Hotel* (film, 1932, screenplay by William A. Drake based on *Menschen im Hotel*, the German play and novel by Vicki Baum, directed by Edmund Goulding). The phrase was associated with Garbo, although she claims never to have said it word for word: 'I only said I want to be *left* alone.' However, the screenplay shows her to speak the words three times to the Baron ( John Barrymore), and she expressed the same sentiment in the film *The Single Standard* (1929): 'I am walking alone because I want to be alone.'

2 Tomorrow I got to work with a lot of people who are dead. It's so sad. I'm an onlooker. I've passed being active in life. It's not a question of time and age – but it's just what you are yourself. One doesn't do the things one doesn't want to do.

Remark, February 1932, quoted in *Self-Portrait with Friends: The Selected Diaries of Cecil Beaton*, ch. 4 (ed. Richard Buckle, 1979)

3 What a waste of the best years of my life – always alone – it was so stupid not being able to partake more. Now I'm just a gipsy, living a life apart, but I know my ways and I must not see people.

Remark, 4 March 1948, ibid. ch. 16

## Jerry Garcia (1942–95)

US ROCK MUSICIAN

Full name Jerome John Garcia. He was a founder member of the Grateful Dead (1966), a San Francisco acid-rock band famed for its four- to five-hour sets and dedicated following of 'Deadheads'. Albums include *Workingman's Dead* (1970), *Europe 72* (1972) and *Built to Last* (1989), and he also recorded solo albums. Nicknamed Captain Trips, he had increasing drugs and alcohol problems during the 1980s, and these culminated in a fatal overdose.

1 Nobody stopped thinking about those psychedelic experiences. Once you've been to some of those places, you think, 'How can I get back there again but make it a little easier on myself?'

Interview in *Rolling Stone*, 30 November 1989

2 What we do is as American as lynch mobs. America has always been a complex place.

ibid. Speaking of the Grateful Dead.

3 We're like bad architecture or an old whore. If you stick around long enough, eventually you get respectable.

Quoted in *Captain Trips*, ch. 9 (1994) by Sandy Troy. Speaking of the Grateful Dead.

## Federico García Lorca (1898–1936)

SPANISH POET AND PLAYWRIGHT

Spain's best known poet and dramatist of the twentieth century drew from the folk and flamenco traditions of Andalusia in his poems such as *Gypsy Ballads* (1928) and his trilogy of plays, *Blood Wedding* (1933), *Yerma* (1934) and *The House of Bernarda Alba* (1936). The recurring theme of violent death in his work anticipated his own assassination by Nationalist partisans during the Spanish Civil War.

1 Green oh how I love you green.
  Green wind. Green boughs.

'Sleepwalking Ballad', publ. in *Gypsy Ballads* (written 1924–7, publ. 1928, transl. 1995). Opening lines.

2 They ride the roads
  with souls of patent leather.
  Hunched and nocturnal,
  they command, where they appear,

the silence of dark rubber
and fears of fine sand.

'Ballad of the Spanish Civil Guard', publ. in ibid.

3 To see you naked is to recall the earth.

'Qasida of the Recumbent Woman, publ. in *The Divan of the Tamarit* (written 1931–4, publ. 1940, transl. 1990)

4 The two elements the traveller first captures in the big city are extrahuman architecture and furious rhythm. Geometry and anguish.

'A Poet in New York', lecture in Madrid, March 1932, publ. in *Poet in New York* (1940, transl. 1988). 'At first glance, the rhythm may be confused with gaiety,' Lorca continued, 'but when you look more closely at the mechanism of social life and the painful slavery of both men and machines, you see that it is nothing but a kind of typical, empty anguish that makes even crime and gangs forgivable means of escape.'

5 The only things that the United States has given to the world are skyscrapers, jazz, and cocktails. That is all. And in Cuba, in *our* America, they make much better cocktails.

Interview 1933, publ. in *Obras Completas*, vol. 3 (1986)

6 I'm hurt, hurt and humiliated beyond endurance, seeing the wheat ripening, the fountains never ceasing to give water, the sheep bearing hundreds of lambs, the she-dogs, until it seems the whole country rises to show me its tender sleeping young while I feel two hammer-blows here instead of the mouth of my child.

Yerma, in *Yerma*, act 2, sc. 2 (1934)

7 At five in the afternoon.
  It was exactly five in the afternoon.
  A boy brought the white sheet
  *at five in the afternoon.*

'The Goring and the Death', publ. in *Lament for Ignacio Sánchez Mejías* (1935, transl. 1995). The poem describes the death of a bullfighter.

## Gabriel García Márquez (b. 1928)

COLOMBIAN AUTHOR

His most famous novel, *One Hundred Years of Solitude* (1967), written while in exile after his left-wing views had run up against the Colombian government, was one of the earliest works to be labelled 'magic realist'. Later books include *Love in the Time of Cholera* (1985) and *Strange Pilgrims* (1992). He was awarded the Nobel Prize for Literature in 1982.

1 They felt that they had been the victims of some new and showy gypsy business and they decided not to return to the movies, considering that they already had too many troubles of their own to weep over the acted-out misfortunes of imaginary beings.

*One Hundred Years of Solitude* (1967). Referring to the people of Macondo, who have learned from the mayor's proclamation that the movies are not real and that 'the cinema was a machine of illusion and did not merit the emotional outbursts of the audience'.

2 The only difference today between Liberals and Conservatives is that the Liberals go to mass at five o'clock and the Conservatives at eight.

Colonel Aureliano Buendía, in ibid.

3 The world must be all fucked up when men travel first class and literature goes as freight.

The Catalan bookstore owner in Macondo, in ibid.

4 Necessity has the face of a dog.

Mina, in *In Evil Hour* (1968)

5 No, not rich. I am a poor man with money, which is not the same thing.

Uncle Leo XII, in *Love in the Time of Cholera* (1985)

6 The problem with marriage is that it ends every night

after making love, and it must be rebuilt every morning before breakfast.

Dr Urbino, in ibid.

## John Garfield (1913–52)
US ACTOR

Original name Julius Garfinkle. After acting with New York's Group Theatre, he moved to films in 1938 to play roles that often reflected his own experiences on the wrong side of the tracks. He formed his own production company in the late 1940s but was blacklisted shortly after for failing to name friends as communists.

1 With my brains and your looks, we could go places.

Frank Chambers ( John Garfield), in *The Postman Always Rings Twice* (film, 1946, screenplay by Harry Ruskin and Niven Busch adapted from James M. Cain's novel, directed by Tay Garnett)

2 I wasn't strong enough to resist corruption, but I was strong enough to fight for a piece of it.

Joe Morse ( John Garfield), in *Force of Evil* (film, 1948, screenplay by Abraham Polonsky and Ira Wolfert adapted from Ira Wolfert's novel, directed by Abraham Polonsky)

## Alex Garland (b. 1970)
BRITISH NOVELIST

Dubbed 'the new Graham Greene' by J.G. BALLARD, he published his first book, *The Beach*, a backpacker's rites of passage tale, in 1996. It quickly became a cult bestseller and was filmed in 2000. It was followed by *The Tesseract* (1998), a psychological thriller set in the Philippines.

1 I had ambiguous feelings about the differences between tourists and travellers – the problem being that the more I travelled, the smaller the differences became. But the one difference I could still latch on to was that tourists went on holidays while travellers did something else. They *travelled.*

Richard, in *The Beach*, 'Getting There: Talk' (1996)

## Judy Garland (1922–69)
US SCREEN ACTRESS AND SINGER

Original name Frances Gumm. Known for the fragile intensity of her voice, she was the cheerful, innocent child star of *The Wizard of Oz* (1939), and, under the direction of her husband Vincente Minnelli, the lead in *Meet Me in St Louis* (1944). She was later caught in a spiral of depression and drugs but returned to the screen with *A Star Is Born* (1954).

1 Somewhere over the rainbow
Way up high,
There's a land that I heard of
Once in a lullaby.

'Over the Rainbow' (song, written by Yip Harburg with music by Harold Arlen) sung as Dorothy in *The Wizard of Oz* (film, 1939). The song was re-recorded by Garland on the album *The London Sessions* (1960), by which time, according to her biographer, 'the song no longer belonged to Dorothy; it belonged, forever, to Judy Garland'. Other artists to have recorded it include FRANK SINATRA, Ella Fitzgerald, WILLIE NELSON and ARETHA FRANKLIN.

2 Toto, I've a feeling we're not in Kansas anymore . . . Now I know we're not in Kansas.

Dorothy, in *The Wizard of Oz* (film, 1939, screenplay by Noel Langley, Florence Ryerson and Edgar Allan Wolfe from book by L. Frank Baum, directed by Victor Fleming). The words, uttered on arriving in the Land of Oz and addressed to Dorothy's dog, do not appear in L. Frank Baum's original book, *The Wonderful Wizard of Oz* (1900).

3 I was born at the age of twelve on a Metro-Goldwyn-Mayer lot.

Quoted in the *Observer* 18 February 1951

## John Garner (1868–1967)
US POLITICIAN

A Democratic leader in the House of Representatives, he was chosen as Speaker in 1931 and served as Vice-President (1933–41) under FRANKLIN ROOSEVELT. Although responsible for steering New Deal legislation through Congress, he opposed Roosevelt's renomination in 1940.

1 The vice-presidency isn't worth a pitcher of warm piss. It doesn't amount to a hill of beans.

Quoted in *Cactus Jack*, ch. 11 (1978) by O.C. Fisher. The words are commonly misquoted '. . . pitcher of warm spit'. In 1963 Garner declared: 'Worst damnfool mistake I ever made was letting myself be elected Vice President of the United States. Should have stuck . . . as Speaker of the House . . . Gave up the second most important job in Government for eight long years as Roosevelt's spare tire.'

## Marcus Garvey (1887–1940)
JAMAICAN CIVIL RIGHTS CAMPAIGNER

Calling himself a 'black Napoleon', he founded the Universal Negro Improvement Association in 1914 and from New York led the first American black nationalist movement, which rejected integration and favoured resettlement in Liberia. However, his vision was not realized, and he died in obscurity, although he was to be an important influence on the Rastafarian movement.

1 Look for me in the whirlwind or the storm, look for me all around you, for, with God's grace, I shall come and bring with me countless millions of Black slaves who have died in America and the West Indies and the millions in Africa to aid you in the fight for Liberty, Freedom and Life.

'First Message to the Negroes of the World from Atlanta Prison' 10 February 1925, publ. in *The Philosophy and Opinions of Marcus Garvey*, vol. 2 (ed. Amy Jacques Garvey, 1923, rev. 1986)

2 No race has the last word on culture and on civilization. You do not know what the black man is capable of; you do not know what he is thinking and therefore you do not know what the oppressed and suppressed Negro, by virtue of his condition and circumstance, may give to the world as a surprise.

Speech at Royal Albert Hall, London, 6 June 1928, publ. in *Marcus Garvey and the Vision of Africa*, pt 5 (ed. John Henrik Clarke, 1974)

3 Day by day we hear the cry of AFRICA FOR THE AFRICANS. This cry has become a positive, determined one. It is a cry that is raised simultaneously the world over because of the universal oppression that affects the Negro.

Quoted in *The Philosophy and Opinions of Marcus Garvey*, vol. 1, ch. 1 (ed. Amy Jacques Garvey, 1923, rev. 1986)

## Bill Gates (b. 1955)
US SOFTWARE ENGINEER AND ENTREPRENEUR

Ninety per cent of the world's computers are provided with software from his Seattle-based company Microsoft, which he co-founded in 1975. By the age of 35 he had become one of the richest men in the world, but in 2000 he relinquished his position as Chairman in order to spend more time on software research.

1 One thing is clear: We don't have the option of turning away from the future. No one gets to vote on whether technology is going to change our lives.

*The Road Ahead*, ch. 1 (1995, rev. 1996)

2 Success is a lousy teacher. It seduces smart people into thinking they can't lose.

ibid. ch. 3

3 People often overestimate what will happen in the next two years and underestimate what will happen in ten.

ibid. 'Afterword'

## Jean-Paul Gaultier (b. 1952)

FRENCH FASHION DESIGNER

He launched his own collection in 1976 and his perfume in 1993. He has designed for ballet and films, was responsible for MADONNA's pointed bra in 1990 and has co-presented *Eurotrash* on British TV.

1 Men also have to be seductive – and with men it is more difficult because it's not in their education.

Interview in the *Observer* 29 November 1998

## Noel Gay (1898–1954)

BRITISH COMPOSER

Original name Richard Moxon Armitage. A musical prodigy and classically trained at the Royal College of Music, he began writing popular compositions under his pseudonym in 1927. His greatest successes were the stage musical *Me and My Girl* (1937), the longest running show of the 1930s, and his novelty songs, such as 'Run Rabbit Run' (1939) and 'Leaning on a Lamp-post' (1937). See also GEORGE FORMBY 3.

1 The sun has got its hat on
Hip hip hip hooray
The sun has got its hat on
And it's coming out to play.

'The Sun Has Got Its Hat On' (song, 1932, with lyrics by Ralph Butler). The song was sung by Jack Hulbert in 1932 and was a hit for Jonathan King in 1971.

2 Any time you're Lambeth way,
Any evening any day,
You'll find us all
Doin' the Lambeth walk.

'The Lambeth Walk' (song, with lyrics by Arthur Rose, music by Noel Gay and Douglas Furber) in *Me and My Girl* (stage musical, 1937). Sung by Lupino Lane as Bill Snibson on stage, the song was popularized by Russ Morgan and his Orchestra. Lane also starred in the 1939 film version of the show, titled *The Lambeth Walk*.

3 Run, rabbit, run, rabbit, run, run, run.
Run, rabbit, run, rabbit, run, run, run.
Bang, bang, bang, bang, goes the farmer's gun,
Run, rabbit, run, rabbit, run, run, run.

'Run Rabbit Run!' (song, with lyrics by Ralph Butler) in *The Little Dog Laughed* (musical show, 1939). The song was performed by BUD FLANAGAN, who starred alongside the Crazy Gang and the Hoffman Sisters. The song and show were a smash hit during the 'phoney war' (1939–40).

## Gloria Gaynor (b. 1949)

US SOUL SINGER

With her powerful voice backed by disco rhythms, the 'Queen of Soul' had hits during the 1970s but lost favour with the advent of electronic dance music. In 1982 she became a born-again Christian.

1 I never can say goodbye.

'Never Can Say Goodbye' (song, written by Clifton Davis) on the album *Never Can Say Goodbye* (1974). The song had been a hit for Isaac Hayes and the Jackson Five, both in 1971. It reached no. 1 for Gaynor, helping to ignite the disco boom.

2 As long as I know how to love, I know I'll stay alive,
I've got all my life to live, I've got so much love to give,
I will survive! I will survive!

'I Will Survive' (song, written by Dino Fekaris and Freddie Perren) on the album *Love Tracks* (1979). The top-selling disco hit became an enduring feminist and gay anthem and is said to be the most requested karaoke song.

## (Sir) Eric Geddes (1875–1937)

BRITISH POLITICIAN

He was elected Conservative MP for Cambridge in 1917 and while Minister of Transport (1919–21) oversaw the amalgamation of the

railways. As chairman of the 'Geddes Axe' committee, he was responsible for drastic cuts in the economy and for devising ways of increasing revenue.

1 The Germans, if this Government is returned, are going to pay every penny; they are going to be squeezed as a lemon is squeezed – until the pips squeak. My only doubt is not whether we can squeeze hard enough, but whether there is enough juice.

Speech at Cambridge, 10 December 1918, quoted in the *Cambridge Daily News* 11 December 1918. On German war reparations following the First World War.

## (Sir) Bob Geldof (b. 1954)

IRISH ROCK SINGER

He was lead singer of the Boomtown Rats (1975–86). In 1984 he raised £8 million for African famine relief through the Band Aid record 'Do They Know It's Christmas' and a year later a further £48 million through Live Aid charity concerts. In 1999 he was also prominent in the Jubilee 2000 campaign to cancel Third World debt.

1 Most people get into bands for three very simple rock and roll reasons: to get laid, to get fame, and to get rich.

*Melody Maker* 27 August 1977

2 I don't like Mondays.

'I Don't Like Mondays' (song) on the album *The Fine Art of Surfacing* (1979) by the Boomtown Rats. The lyrics were inspired by the story of schoolgirl Brenda Spencer, who went on a shooting spree in San Diego, California, in January 1979, giving these words as the reason. Spencer's parents attempted to have the record banned, and many US radio stations refused to play it.

3 Feed the world
Let them know it's Christmas time again.

'Do They Know It's Christmas?' (song, 1984, co-written with Midge Ure). The record became the biggest selling British single of all time.

4 Irish Americans are about as Irish as black Americans are African.

Quoted in the *Observer* 22 June 1986

## Henry Geldzahler (b. 1935)

BELGIAN-BORN US CURATOR AND ART CRITIC

A critic of contemporary art, he has written on ANDY WARHOL and DAVID HOCKNEY and was the first curator of the department of twentieth-century art at the Metropolitan Museum of Art, New York (1967–78).

1 The history of modern art is also the history of the progressive loss of art's audience. Art has increasingly become the concern of the artist and the bafflement of the public.

'The Art Audience and the Critic', first publ. in the *Hudson Review* spring 1965, repr. in *The New Art: A Critical Anthology* (ed. Gregory Battcock, 1966, rev. 1973)

2 The thing that's extraordinary is that no art remains shocking for more than ten or twelve years. There is no shocking art that doesn't reduce itself to triviality or beauty.

*Looking at Pictures* (1990)

## Martha Gellhorn (1908–98)

US JOURNALIST AND AUTHOR

She made her name in war reportage from the Spanish Civil War, the Second World War, Vietnam and Central America, as collected in *The Face of War* (1959, rev. 1967, 1986 and 1993). Her fiction includes *The Trouble I've Seen* (1936), short stories describing the effects of the Depression, and the novel *The Wine of Astonishment* (1948). She was married to ERNEST HEMINGWAY (1940–45), and lived in Mexico, Kenya and Wales.

1 Serious, careful, honest journalism is essential, not because it is a guiding light but because it is a form of honorable behavior, involving the reporter and the reader.
*The Face of War*, Introduction (1959)

2 It is in our ancient tradition to murder each other; but only we, in the present, should pay the price of our abominable stupidity. Nothing that concerns us, in our brief moment of history, gives us the right to stop time, to blot out the future, to end the continuing miracles and glories and tragedies and wretchedness of the human race.
ibid.

3 After a lifetime of war-watching, I see war as an endemic human disease, and governments are the carriers.
*The Face of War*, Introduction (1959, rev. 1986)

4 America has made no reparation to the Vietnamese, nothing. We are the richest people in the world and they are among the poorest. We savaged them, though they had never hurt us, and we cannot find it in our hearts, our honor, to give them help – because the government of Vietnam is Communist. And perhaps because they won.
ibid. 'The War in Vietnam – Vietnam Again, 1986'. Gellhorn went on to say: 'After all this time I still cannot think calmly about that war. It was the only war I reported on the wrong side.'

## Jean Genet (1910–86)
FRENCH PLAYWRIGHT AND NOVELIST

Dealing chiefly with the alienated and marginalized underworld of Paris, his novels, beginning with *Our Lady of the Flowers* (1943), and plays, such as *The Maids* (1947), explore the nature of good and evil. He spent much of his early life in reformatories and prison and was pardoned in 1948 following a petition by a group of intellectuals including JEAN-PAUL SARTRE, whose book *Saint Genet* (1952) further enhanced his reputation.

1 To achieve harmony in bad taste is the height of elegance.
*The Thief's Journal* (1949, transl. 1965)

2 Excluded by my birth and tastes from the social order, I was not aware of its diversity . . . Nothing in the world was irrelevant: the stars on a general's sleeve, the stock-market quotations, the olive harvest, the style of the judiciary, the wheat exchange, flower-beds . . . Nothing. This order, fearful and feared, whose details were all inter-related, had a meaning: my exile.
ibid.

3 What we need is hatred. From it our ideas are born.
Bobo, in *The Blacks* (1958)

4 Are you there, Africa with the bulging chest and oblong thigh? Sulking Africa, wrought of iron, in the fire, Africa of the millions of royal slaves, deported Africa, drifting continent, are you there? Slowly you vanish, you withdraw into the past, into the tales of castaways, colonial museums, the works of scholars.
Felicity, in ibid.

5 Crimes of which a people is ashamed constitute its real history. The same is true of man.
Notes for *The Screens* (1961, transl. 1973)

6 Anyone who hasn't experienced the ecstasy of betrayal knows nothing about ecstasy at all.
*Prisoner of Love*, pt 1 (1986)

## George V (1865–1936)
KING OF GREAT BRITAIN AND IRELAND

Before succeeding to the throne in 1910 'he did nothing at all but kill animals and stick in stamps,' according to his biographer HAROLD NICOLSON. As king, he was guided by constitutional duty, and he established the monarchy as a symbol of national unity. He was instrumental in the formation of the national government of 1931 and instigated the tradition of the Christmas Day broadcasts in 1932. 'I march with the times' was his watchword.

1 How is the Empire?
Attributed last words, as reported to the nation 21 January 1936 – the day after the King's death – in a broadcast tribute by Prime Minister STANLEY BALDWIN. Other accounts deny this was the King's last utterance, although a memorandum of Lord Wigram, the King's Private Secretary, was made at 11 a.m., 20 January: 'He murmured something about the Empire, and I replied that "All is well, Sir, with the Empire"' (quoted in *Dawson of Penn*, 1950, by Francis Watson). The time of his death was given as 11.55 p.m.

2 Bugger Bognor.
Attributed deathbed remark, in *King George V*, ch. 9 (1983) by Kenneth Rose. The King apparently uttered the words on being assured by a courtier that he would soon be in Bognor. However, according to the King's Librarian, Owen Morshead, the exclamation was made much earlier, in 1929, in response to a suggestion that the town should be named Bognor Regis in commemoration of George V's convalescence there following a serious illness.

## George VI (1895–1952)
KING OF GREAT BRITAIN AND NORTHERN IRELAND

He succeeded to the throne following the abdication of his brother EDWARD VIII in 1936. During the Second World War he won popularity by remaining in London throughout the Blitz and by his many broadcasts. In 1947 he substituted the title Head of the Commonwealth for Emperor of India.

1 It is not the walls that make the city, but the people who live within them. The walls of London may be battered, but the spirit of the Londoner stands resolute and undismayed.
Radio broadcast to the Empire, 23 September 1940, during the German bomber offensive

2 Abroad is bloody.
Attributed, in *A Certain World*, 'Royalty' (1970) by W.H. AUDEN. See also NANCY MITFORD.

## Gladys George (c. 1898–1954)
US ACTRESS

Having begun her stage career at the age of three, she starred in vaudeville and on Broadway and toured in popular farces in the 1920s and 1930s. She had greater success in Hollywood, appearing in the films *Valiant is the World for Carrie* (1936), *The Roaring Twenties* (1939) and *The Maltese Falcon* (1941).

1 He used to be a big shot.
Panama Smith (Gladys George), in *The Roaring Twenties* (film, 1939, screenplay by Jerry Wald, Richard Macaulay and Robert Rossen based on a story by MARK HELLINGER, directed by Raoul Walsh). These last words of the movie refer to the character played by JAMES CAGNEY, who has been fatally wounded.

## Ira Gershwin (1896–1983)
US LYRICIST

Originally Israel Gershvin. The elder brother of George Gershwin, he wrote the sophisticated lyrics to most of his brother's songs for more than twenty successful Broadway musicals. In 1937, after George's death, he worked with Jerome Kern, Kurt Weill and Harold Arlen.

1 I got rhythm,
I got music,
I got my man
Who could ask for anything more?
'I Got Rhythm' (song, with music by George Gershwin) in *Girl Crazy* (stage musical 1930, film 1932 and 1943). Originally sung by Ethel Merman, the number was performed in the 1943 film version by JUDY GARLAND, and by Gene Kelly in the movie *An American in Paris* (1951).

2 Summertime and the living is easy,
  Fish are jumping, and the cotton is high.

  'Summertime' (song, co-written with Du Bose Heyward with music
  by George Gershwin) in *Porgy and Bess* (stage musical 1935, film
  1959). The lyrics from this opener for *Porgy and Bess*, like those of
  other songs from the show, were based on an original poem in the
  novel *Porgy* (1926) by Du Bose Heyward. It was a hit for BILLIE
  HOLIDAY in 1936.

3 It ain't necessarily so,
  The things that you're liable
  To read in the Bible,
  It ain't necessarily so.

  'It Ain't Necessarily So', ibid. The song was recorded by BING
  CROSBY in 1938, among others, and sung by SAMMY DAVIS JR in
  the film adaptation.

4 A foggy day in London Town
  Had me low and had me down.
  I viewed the morning with alarm,
  The British Museum had lost its charm.

  'A Foggy Day' (song, with music by George Gershwin) in *A Damsel
  in Distress* (film, 1937). The number is performed in the film by
  Fred Astaire.

5 Holding hands at midnight
  'Neath a starry sky,
  Nice work if you can get it,
  And you can get it if you try.

  'Nice Work If You Can Get It', ibid.

6 You like potato and I like po-tah-to,
  You like tomato and I like to-mah-to;
  Potato, po-tah-to, tomato, to-mah-to –
  Let's call the whole thing off!

  'Let's Call the Whole Thing Off' (song, with music by George
  Gershwin) in *Shall We Dance* (film, 1937). Sung by Fred Astaire and
  Ginger Rogers.

## J. Paul Getty (1892–1976)
US OIL MILLIONAIRE AND ARTS PATRON

Full name Jean Paul Getty. The oil business made him one of the
world's richest men, with a personal wealth estimated at over $1
billion in 1968, although he was also notoriously stingy. He exhibited parts of his extensive art collection in the museum founded
by and named after him in California in 1953.

1 If you can actually count your money, then you are not
  really a rich man.

  Quoted in the *Observer* 3 November 1957

## Stella Gibbons (1902–89)
BRITISH AUTHOR

She worked for much of her life as a journalist and wrote numerous
novels and short stories but is best known for her parody on rural
life, *Cold Comfort Farm* (1933).

1 Something nasty in the woodshed.

  *Cold Comfort Farm*, ch. 8 and *passim* (1932). This recurring motif
  of some unspecific secret and shameful act witnessed in the past
  was used in the novel as an ironic symbol of corrupting knowledge.

## Kahlil Gibran (1883–1931)
SYRIAN-BORN US POET AND NOVELIST

From Beirut he moved to Boston in 1895 where he met Mary
Haskell, who was to be his life-long benefactor, and published his
first literary essays. His writings both in Arabic and English combine romanticism with mysticism, influenced by the Bible, Sufism
and William Blake. His most enduring work, *The Prophet* (1923),
has sold more than 20 million copies.

1 Love gives naught but itself and takes naught but from
  itself.

Love possesses not nor would it be possessed;
For love is sufficient unto love.

*The Prophet*, 'On Love' (1923)

2 You may give them your love but not your thoughts.
  For they have their own thoughts.
  You may house their bodies but not their souls,
  For their souls dwell in the house of tomorrow, which
      you cannot visit, not even in your dreams.

  ibid. 'On Children'

3 Life is indeed darkness save when there is urge,
  And all urge is blind save when there is knowledge,
  And all knowledge is vain save when there is work,
  And all work is empty save when there is love.

  ibid. 'On Work'

4 The lust for comfort, that stealthy thing that enters the
  house a guest, and then becomes a host, and then a master.

  ibid. 'On Houses'

5 Beauty is eternity gazing at itself in a mirror.

  ibid. 'On Beauty'

6 Verily the kindness that gazes upon itself in a mirror
      turns to stone,
  And a good deed that calls itself by tender names
      becomes the parent to a curse.

  ibid. 'The Farewell'

7 A little knowledge that *acts* is worth infinitely more than
  much knowledge that is idle.

  *The Voice of the Master*, pt 2, ch. 8 (1960)

8 When we turn to one another for counsel we reduce the
  number of our enemies.

  ibid. pt 2, ch. 10

## William Gibson (b. 1948)
US SCIENCE FICTION AUTHOR

His acclaimed first novel *Neuromancer* (1984) helped to establish
the genre of 'cyberpunk' and popularized the notion of computer
cyberspace. The 'high-tech lowlifes' of this and other novels also
feature in his short stories collected in *Burning Chrome* (1986). He
describes his writing technique as 'making a ball out of rubber
bands'.

1 I think that the computer as some sort of discrete object
  that one owns and is very, very aware of . . . will become
  a very quaint and antique concept.

  Interview in *Rapid Eye 3* (ed. Simon Dwyer, 1995). Gibson predicted
  computers becoming 'small and transparent and finally invisible'.

2 The old futures have a way of hanging around . . . I think
  now that everyone sort of knows that the real future is
  going to be cluttered with all the same junk we have today,
  except it will be old and beat up and there will be more of
  it.

  Interview in *Sight and Sound* July 1995

## André Gide (1869–1951)
FRENCH AUTHOR

With the declared intention of 'disturbing' his readers, he founded
his reputation on his novels, spare in style, such as *The Immoralist*
(1902) and *Strait is the Gate* (1909). He also published literary and
social criticism and helped found the *La Nouvelle Revue française*
(1908). He was awarded the Nobel Prize for Literature in 1947. The
author Peter Quennell called him 'an elderly fallen angel travelling
incognito'.

1 The most decisive actions of our life – I mean those that
  are most likely to decide the whole course of our future –
  are, more often than not, unconsidered.

  Hildebrant, in *The Counterfeiters*, pt 3, ch. 16 (1925)

2 Old hands soil, it seems, whatever they caress, but they

too have their beauty when they are joined in prayer. Young hands were made for caresses and the sheathing of love. It is a pity to make them join too soon.

Journal entry, 21 January 1929, publ. in *Journals 1889–1949* (ed. Justin O'Brien, 1951)

3 The sole art that suits me is that which, rising from unrest, tends toward serenity.

ibid. 23 November 1940

## Gilbert (of Gilbert and George) See GILBERT PROESCH.

## George Gilder (b. 1939)
US EDITOR, SPEECHWRITER AND AUTHOR

Conservative in outlook, he was speechwriter for Rockefeller (1964), NIXON (1968) and Dole (1976) and was labelled 'the nation's leading male chauvinist-pig author' by *Time* magazine in 1974. His anti-feminist *Sexual Suicide* was published in 1973 and his 'theology' for capitalism, *Wealth and Poverty*, in 1981.

1 Sexuality, family unity, kinship, masculine solidarity, maternity, motivation, nurturing, all the rituals of personal identity and development, all the bonds of community, seem 'sexist', 'superstitious', 'mystical', 'inefficient', 'discriminatory'. And, of course, they are – and they are also indispensable to a civilized society.

*Sexual Suicide*, Introduction (1973)

2 Unlike femininity, relaxed masculinity is at bottom empty, a limp nullity. While the female body is full of internal potentiality, the male is internally barren ... Manhood at the most basic level can be validated and expressed only in action.

ibid. pt 1, ch. 1

## Terry Gilkyson (1916–99)
US SONGWRITER AND ACTOR

Full name Hamilton Gilkyson III. Although he acted in several films in the 1950s, he became better known as songwriter for such films as *Swiss Family Robinson* (1960) and *The Jungle Book* (1967). He also wrote and composed for TV.

1 The bare necessities, the simple bare necessities
Forget about your worries and your strife.

'Bare Necessities' (song) in *The Jungle Book* (film, 1967). Sung by Phil Harris as Baloo and Bruce Reitherman as Mowgli.

## Eric Gill (1882–1940)
BRITISH SCULPTOR, ENGRAVER, WRITER AND TYPOGRAPHER

A Catholic whose sexual practices provoked calls for his work to be withdrawn, he carved the sculptures *Stations of the Cross* in Westminster Cathedral (1914–18) and *Prospero and Ariel* (1930) on the BBC's Broadcasting House. He illustrated for the Golden Cockerell Press, wrote numerous books on crafts and devised typefaces, including the first sanserif type, Gill Sans.

1 That state is a state of Slavery in which a man does what he likes to do in his spare time and in his working time that which is required of him. This state can only exist when what a man likes to do is to please himself.

'Slavery and Freedom', first publ. 1918, repr. in *Art-Nonsense and Other Essays* (1929). Opening paragraph.

2 Art is skill, that is the first meaning of the word.

*Art*, ch. 1 (1934). Yet in his essay, 'Art and Love' (1927), Gill pointed out: 'As no one would think it an adequate definition of Man to say that he is a two-legged mammal, so no one should be satisfied with the definition of Art that it is simply skill, or that it is skill in the imitation of nature.'

3 Man cannot live on the human plane, he must be either above or below it.

*Autobiography*, 'Conclusion' (1940)

4 Culture is a sham if it is only a sort of Gothic front put on an iron building – like Tower Bridge – or a classical front put on a steel frame – like the *Daily Telegraph* building in Fleet Street. Culture, if it is to be a real thing and a holy thing, must be the product of what we actually do for a living – not something added, like sugar on a pill.

*Essays*, 'Education for What?' (1948)

5 Catholics are necessarily at war with this age. That we are not more conscious of the fact, that we so often endeavour to make an impossible peace with it – that is the tragedy. You cannot serve God and Mammon.

ibid. 'Idiocy or Ill-Will?'

6 Man does not live by bread alone, but by science he attempts to do so. Hence the deadliness of all that is purely scientific.

ibid. 'Art'

## Penelope Gilliatt (1932–93)
BRITISH NOVELIST

As well as novels, including *A State of Change* (1967) and *The Cutting Edge* (1978), she wrote short stories, the screenplay for *Sunday, Bloody Sunday* (1971) and critical writing on the cinema and theatre.

1 Boston is one of the few American cities that regrets the past ... Boston's like England. Up to its ears in yellowing photographs.

*A State of Change*, pt 1, ch. 7 (1967)

2 Why is it that beautiful women never seem to have any curiosity? Is it because they know they're classical? With classical things the Lord finished the job. Ordinary ugly people know they're deficient and they go on looking for the pieces.

ibid. pt 2, ch. 8

3 I don't know why revolutions have to be successful to be taken seriously. The ones that don't ride to power and change a regime go into a sort of intellectual doghouse and they're thought to have a moral flow. It might be just a failure of craftiness, or not having the right maniac on the scene, or something else not particularly despicable.

Kakia, in ibid.

4 Russians have always been hugely concerned with ethics and hardly at all with conduct.

Don, in ibid. The remark follows the observation by Christabel: 'Russia does at least try to conduct its life so as to make the good things available to everyone.'

## Gary Gilmore (1941–77)
US CONVICT

Convicted for the murder of two students, he was the first person to be executed in the USA since 1967, a sentence that he requested in preference to life imprisonment. The execution by firing squad took place in Utah State Penitentiary.

1 Your Honor, I don't want to take up a lot of your time with my words. I believe I was given a fair trial and I think the sentence is proper and I am willing to accept it like a man. I don't wish to appeal ... I desire to be executed on schedule, and I just wish to accept that with the grace and dignity of a man.

Speech to the Supreme Court, 9 November 1976, quoted in *The Executioner's Song*, bk 2, pt 1, ch. 1, sect. 7 (1979) by Norman Mailer. Gilmore's last words to the firing squad were 'Let's do it!'

## (Sir) Ian Gilmour (b. 1926)
BRITISH POLITICIAN

A Conservative MP, he was a cabinet minister in the HEATH and THATCHER governments until 1981, holding posts in Defence in government and in opposition. His views of the Thatcher era are expressed in *Dancing with Dogma* (1992).

1 Conservatives do not worship democracy. For them majority rule is a device . . . And if it is leading to an end that is undesirable or inconsistent with itself, then there is a theoretical case for ending it.
*Inside Right*, pt 3, ch. 5 (1977)

## Newt Gingrich (b. 1943)
US POLITICIAN

A powerful and confrontational spokesman for the Republican Party and a convinced Reaganite, he was elected Speaker of the House of Representatives in 1994, when he sought to reduce the size and influence of federal powers in order to implement an 'opportunity society'. In 1997 he was fined $300,000 for misleading the House.

1 In every election in American history both parties have their clichés. The party that has the clichés that ring true wins.
*International Herald Tribune* 1 August 1988

## Allen Ginsberg (b. 1926)
US POET

Known as the 'spiritual godfather' of the counterculture in the 1960s and 1970s, his *Howl and Other Poems* (1956) was claimed by the Beat generation as its poetic manifesto. He coined the phrase 'flower power', experimented with drugs and later campaigned for civil rights and gay liberation.

1 Fortunately art is a community effort – a small but select community living in a spiritualized world endeavoring to interpret the wars and the solitudes of the flesh.
Journal entry, 11 July 1954, publ. in *Journals: Early Fifties Early Sixties*, 'Mexico and Return to US' (ed. Gordon Ball, 1977)

2 I saw the best minds of my generation destroyed by madness, starving hysterical naked,
dragging themselves through the negro streets at dawn looking for an angry fix,
angelheaded hipsters burning for the ancient heavenly connection to the starry dynamo in the machinery of night,
who poverty and tatters and hollow-eyed and high sat up smoking in the supernatural darkness of cold-water flats floating across the tops of cities contemplating jazz.
'Howl', publ. in *Howl and Other Poems* (1956). Opening lines.

3 What thoughts I have of you tonight, Walt Whitman, for I walked down the sidestreets under the trees with a headache self-conscious looking at the full moon.
In my hungry fatigue, and shopping for images, I went into the neon fruit supermarket, dreaming of your enumerations!
'A Supermarket in California', publ. in ibid. Opening lines.

4 A perfect beauty of a sunflower! a perfect excellent lovely sunflower existence! a sweet natural eye to the new hip moon,
woke up alive and excited grasping in the sunset shadow sunrise golden monthly breeze.
'Sunflower Sutra', publ. in ibid.

5 America I'm putting my queer shoulder to the wheel.
'America', publ. in ibid. Last line.

6 Downtown Manhattan, clear winter noon, and I've been up all night, talking, talking, reading the Kaddish aloud, listening to Ray Charles blues shout blind on the phonograph.
'Kaddish', sect. 1, publ. in *Kaddish and Other Poems* (1960)

7 This is the end, the redemption from Wilderness, way for the Wonderer, House sought for All, black handkerchief washed clean by weeping – page beyond Psalm – Last change of mine and Naomi – to God's perfect Darkness – Death, stay thy phantoms!
ibid.

8 Democracy! Bah! When I hear that word I reach for my feather Boa!
'Subliminal' written in journal, October 1960, publ. in *Journals: Early Fifties Early Sixties*, 'New York City' (ed. Gordon Ball, 1977)

9 No monster vibration, no snake universe hallucinations. Many tiny jeweled violet flowers along the path of a living brook that looked like Blake's illustration for a canal in grassy Eden: huge Pacific watery shore, Orlovsky dancing naked like Shiva long-haired before giant green waves, titanic cliffs that Wordsworth mentioned in his own Sublime, great yellow sun veiled with mist hanging over the planet's oceanic horizon. No harm.
Letter, 2 June 1966, publ. in *Paris Review* summer 1966. On an LSD experience in Big Sur, California.

10 What if someone gave a war and Nobody came?
Life would ring the bells of Ecstasy and Forever be Itself again.
'Graffiti 12th Cubicle Men's Room Syracuse Airport', publ. in *The Fall of America* (1972). The words of the first line were current during the anti-war protests of the 1960s and were adapted as the title of a 1970 film, *Suppose They Gave a War and Nobody Came?*, starring Brian Keith and Tony Curtis. The original inspiration was probably a poem by CARL SANDBURG.

11 Nobody saves America by sniffing cocaine
Jiggling yr knees blankeyed in the rain
When it snows in yr nose you catch cold in yr brain.
Lines publ. in *Ginsberg: A Biography*, ch. 16 (1989) by Barry Miles

12 Poetry is not an expression of the party line. It's that time of night, lying in bed, thinking what you really think, making the private world public, that's what the poet does.
Quoted in ibid. ch. 17

## Natalia Ginzburg (1916–91)
ITALIAN NOVELIST

One of the best known of Italian post-war writers, she writes with 'an ear tuned in to the subtlest frequencies of domestic life', in the words of Annapaola Concogni, in a cool, simple style, which has been compared to Chekhov's. Her novels include *The Dry Heart* (1947), *Family Sayings* (1963) and *The Manzoni Family* (1987).

1 You aren't ill: it is just that you are made of second-rate materials.
Alberto to his wife Miranda, in *Family Sayings* (1963, rev. 1984)

## Nikki Giovanni (b. 1943)
US POET

Originally named Yolande Giovanni. Called the 'Princess of Black Poetry', she was prominent in the black literary movement of the late 1960s, as popular for her recordings and reading and speaking engagements as for her poetry and essays. Among her poetry collections are *Black Feeling, Black Talk* (1968) and *Cotton Candy on a Rainy Day* (1978).

1 it's a sex object if you're pretty
and no love
or love and no sex if you're fat
'Woman Poem', publ. in *Black Judgment* (1969)

2 **There're two people in the world that are not likeable: a master and a slave.**

*A Dialogue* (with JAMES BALDWIN, 1973). The book is a transcription of a discussion between Giovanni and Baldwin in London, 4 November 1971.

3 **I think one of the nicest things that we created as a generation was just the fact that we could say, Hey, I don't like white people.**

ibid.

## George Gipp See RONALD REAGAN.

## Jean Giraudoux (1882–1944)
FRENCH AUTHOR AND DIPLOMAT

He combined a thirty-year career in the diplomatic service (1910–40) with a writing vocation. Many of his novels and plays, which include *Judith* (1931) and *Tiger at the Gates* (1935), are retellings of biblical stories and Greek myths.

1 **I tell you, sir, the only safeguard of order and discipline in the modern world is a standardized worker with interchangeable parts. That would solve the entire problem of management.**

The President, in *The Madwoman of Chaillot*, act 1 (1945)

## Maurice Girodias (1919–90)
FRENCH PUBLISHER

The Olympia Press, which he founded in Paris in 1953, was responsible for the publication of works by GENET, BECKETT, HENRY MILLER and WILLIAM BURROUGHS and was the first to publish NABOKOV's *Lolita*.

1 **Conservatism, colonialism, racism, and religious intolerance are part of the make-up of the French bourgeois, who is just as bigoted, brainlessly selfish, and frightened as his counterparts in the other countries ... France is now entirely dominated, owned, manipulated, exploited, milked, policed, by *les bourgeois* for *les bourgeois*.**

*The Olympia Reader*, Introduction (ed. Maurice Girodias, 1965)

## Edna Gladney
US PHILANTHROPIST

A 'distinguished lady in Texas' (although born in Wisconsin), she made a career of rescuing illegitimate children and raising them in her private orphanage in Texas. She was instrumental in passing a law that eliminates from public record whether orphans are born illegitimately.

1 **There are no illegitimate children, there are only illegitimate parents.**

Quoted in *Kiss Hollywood Goodbye*, ch. 18 by ANITA LOOS. MGM paid Gladney a large sum for this widely quoted line, which was to form the basis of the 1941 film *Blossoms in the Dust*, starring Greer Garson (screenplay by Loos, directed and produced by Mervyn LeRoy). It is not clear if Gladney originated the words, however. The lawyer Léon Yankwich was supposed to have made a similar remark in June 1928, during a hearing at the State District Court, Southern District of California, and he was quoting the journalist O.O. McIntyre. In 1971 the words were ascribed to BERNADETTE MCALISKEY.

## Ellen Glasgow (1874–1945)
US NOVELIST

Her unsentimental novels, for example *Barren Ground* (1925) and *The Sheltered Life* (1932), describe the social divisions and hypocrisies of Virginia and the plight of women in the American South. According to CARL VAN DOREN: 'Southern romance is dead. Ellen Glasgow has murdered it.' She was awarded the Pulitzer Prize for *In This Our Life* (1941).

1 **Women like to sit down with trouble as if it were knitting.**

Jenny Blair, in *The Sheltered Life*, pt 3, sect. 3 (1932)

2 **I have observed with wonder so many intellectual and literary fashions that I have come at last to rely positively upon one conviction alone. No idea is so antiquated that it was not once modern. No idea is so modern that it will not some day be antiquated ... To seize the flying thought before it escapes us is our only touch with reality.**

'Empy American Novels', address to the Modern Language Association (1936), repr. in *The New York Times* 1 January 1937

3 **No matter how vital experience might be while you lived it, no sooner was it ended and dead than it became as lifeless as the piles of dry dust in a school history book.**

*In This Our Life*, pt 3, ch. 9 (1941)

## George Glass (1910–84)
US FILM EXECUTIVE

Sometimes known as Georges Glass, he worked extensively as a film producer in Europe and Hollywood in a career spanning more than thirty years.

1 **An actor is a kind of guy who if you ain't talking about him ain't listening.**

Quoted in *Brando*, ch. 8 (1973) by Bob Thomas. The quote is frequently ascribed to MARLON BRANDO, who may have heard it from Glass. The actor Michael Wilding is similarly quoted as saying, 'You can pick out actors by the glazed look that comes into their eyes when the conversation wanders away from themselves.'

## Misha Glenny (b. 1958)
BRITISH JOURNALIST, WRITER AND BROADCASTER

An expert on Central and Eastern Europe, he reported for the *Guardian* before joining the BBC as a foreign correspondent (1989–93). Among his publications are *The Rebirth of History* (1990) and *The Fall of Yugoslavia* (1992).

1 **After the end of the Cold War, some governments have tended to forget Eastern Europe, allowing the new democracies to stew in the gelatinous leftovers of communism. But the peoples of the new democracies will not forget the West – Europe has become the most unstable continent in the world.**

*The Rebirth of History*, ch. 9 (1990, rev. 1993)

## Frederic Glezer (b. 1937)
US LITERACY LOBBYIST AND LIBRARIAN

1 **[On watching TV] A three- to four- to five-hour experience with nothingness.**

Quoted in *Newsweek* 1 December 1986

## Jean-Luc Godard (b. 1930)
FRENCH FILM-MAKER AND AUTHOR

His first feature film *À bout de souffle* (*Breathless*, 1959) established him as a leader of the *nouvelle vague* movement in cinema. In subsequent films he made use of free improvisation and anti-narration, adopting an increasingly political and didactic stance after 1968, as in *Wind from the East* (1969).

1 **The cinema is not a craft. It is an art. It does not mean team-work. One is always alone; on the set as before the blank page.**

'Bergmanorama', first publ. in *Cahiers du Cinéma* July 1958, repr. in *Godard on Godard* (ed. Tom Milne, 1972)

2  I don't know if I'm free because I'm unhappy or unhappy because I'm free.

Patricia Franchini (Jean Seberg), in *Breathless* (film, 1959, written and directed by Jean-Luc Godard)

3  Photography is truth . . . and the cinema is the truth twenty-four times a second.

Bruno Forestier (Michel Subor), in *Le Petit Soldat* (film, 1960, written and directed by Jean-Luc Godard)

4  When I hear the word culture, I take out my chequebook.

Jeremy Prokosh (Jack Palance), a film producer, in *Le Mépris* (film, 1963, adapted by Jean-Luc Godard from *A Ghost at Noon* by Alberto Moravia, directed by Jean-Luc Godard). See also HERMANN GOERING 2.

5  More and more I see the human predicament as a dialogue between lovers.

Natasha von Braun (Anna Karina), in *Alphaville* (film, 1965, written and directed by Jean-Luc Godard)

6  Give us this day our television, and an automobile, but deliver us from freedom.

Madeleine (Chantal Goya), in *Masculin-féminin* (film, 1966, adapted by Jean-Luc Godard from two short stories by Guy de Maupassant, directed by Jean-Luc Godard)

7  To me style is just the outside of content, and content the inside of style, like the outside and the inside of the human body – both go together, they can't be separated.

Quoted in *Godard*, Introduction (1967) by Richard Roud

8  All you need for a movie is a gun and a girl.

Journal entry, 16 May 1991, quoted in *Projections* (ed. John Boorman and Walter Donohue, 1992)

## Alfred Godley (1856–1925)
BRITISH SCHOLAR

A classical scholar who was deemed 'an almost perfect writer of elegant Latin', he wrote humorous and satirical prose and verse as well as publishing on classical authors. He was Public Orator for Oxford University (1910–25).

1  What is this that roareth thus?
Can it be a Motor Bus?
Yes, the smell and hideous hum
Indicat Motorem Bum . . .
Domine, defende nos
Contra hos Motores Bos!

'The Motor Bus' in letter, 10 January 1914, publ. in *Reliquiae*, vol. 1 (1926)

## Joseph Goebbels (1897–1945)
GERMAN NAZI LEADER

As HITLER's Minister of Propaganda in 1933, he had a gift for demagoguery and in 1943 was given extended powers to run the country while Hitler was in charge of the war. After the German defeat he killed his six children, and, with his wife, committed suicide.

1  We enter parliament in order to supply ourselves, in the arsenal of democracy, with its own weapons . . . If democracy is so stupid as to give us free tickets and salaries for this bear's work, that is its affair . . . We do not come as friends, nor even as neutrals. We come as enemies. As the wolf bursts into the flock, so we come.

*Der Angriff* 30 April 1928

2  We can do without butter, but, despite all our love of peace, not without arms. One cannot shoot with butter, but with guns.

Speech in Berlin, 17 January 1936, quoted in *Allgemeine Zeitung* 18 January 1936. The origin of the 'guns or butter' quote is unverifiable. In the summer of 1936, in a radio broadcast on the Four Year Plan, HERMANN GOERING announced: 'Guns will make us powerful; butter will only make us fat.'

## Hermann Goering (1893–1946)
GERMAN NAZI LEADER

Having joined the Nazi government when Hitler assumed power (1933), he was responsible for founding the Gestapo, establishing concentration camps and building up the Luftwaffe. In 1940 he became Marshal of the Reich but fell from grace in 1943 and was dismissed in 1945. He committed suicide after being sentenced at the Nuremberg trials.

1  I herewith commission you to carry out all preparations with regard to . . . a total solution of the Jewish question in those territories of Europe which are under German influence . . . I furthermore charge you to submit to me as soon as possible a draft showing the . . . measures already taken for the execution of the intended final solution of the Jewish question.

Military directive to Reinhard Heydrich, 31 July 1941, quoted in *The Rise and Fall of the Third Reich*, ch. 27 (1960) by William L. Shirer. According to Shirer, the German word *Endlösung* was erroneously rendered 'desired solution' at Goering's trial at Nuremberg, thus allowing the judge to accept Goering's insistence that he had never used the terms 'total' or 'final solution'; 'the first time I learned of these terrible exterminations was right here at Nuremberg,' Goering declared. Heydrich, Deputy Chief of the Gestapo, has also been associated with the phrase.

2  Whenever I hear the word culture, I reach for my revolver.

Attributed. Whether or not Goering ever uttered these words, the only recorded reference to them is in the play *Schlageter* (1933) by Hanns Johst (1890–1978), Nazi playwright and President of the Reich Chamber of Literature. The line is spoken by a stormtrooper in act 1, sc. 1: 'When I hear the word culture, I cock my Browning.' Many variations have been coined (see ALLEN GINSBERG 8; JEAN-LUC GODARD 4).

## Isaac Goldberg (1887–1938)
US CRITIC

The literary editor of *American Freeman* (1923–32), he was special lecturer on Hispano-American literature at Harvard 1933–4, and instrumental in introducing the modern literature of Latin America to English-speaking readers. He also published biographies of W.S. Gilbert (1913) and George Gershwin (1931) and translated Italian and Yiddish plays.

1  Diplomacy is to do and say
The nastiest things in the nicest way.

*The Reflex* October 1927

## Whoopi Goldberg (b. 1955)
US SCREEN ACTRESS AND COMEDIENNE

Original name Caryn Johnson. Formerly a stand-up comedienne, she made her screen debut in *The Color Purple* (1985) and won an Oscar for her part in *Ghost* (1990). She is usually cast in clownish roles, as in *Sister Act* (1992).

1  I'm not an African. The Africans know I'm not an African. I'm an American. This is my country. My people helped to build it and we've been here for centuries. Just call me black if you want to call me anything.

Interview in the *Daily Telegraph* 20 April 1998. On the label 'African-American'.

## (Sir) William Golding (1911–93)
BRITISH AUTHOR

He achieved success with his first novel, *Lord of the Flies* (1954), whose themes of human fallibility and the potential of evil recurred in such later works as *The Spire* (1964) and the Booker Prize-winning *Rites of Passage* (1980). He was awarded the Nobel Prize for Literature in 1983.

1 Sleep is when all the unsorted stuff comes flying out as from a dustbin upset in a high wind.

*Pincher Martin*, ch. 6 (1956)

2 Marx, Darwin and Freud are the three most crashing bores of the Western world. The simplistic popularization of their ideas has thrust our world into a mental strait-jacket from which we can only escape by the most anarchic violence.

'Belief and Creativity' lecture given in Hamburg, Germany, April 1980, repr. in *A Moving Target* (1982)

3 It may be – I hope it is – redemption to guess and perhaps perceive that the universe, the hell which we see for all its beauty, vastness, majesty, is only part of a whole which is quite unimaginable.

ibid.

4 The writer probably knows what he meant when he wrote a book, but he should immediately forget what he meant when he's written it.

*Novelists in Interview* (ed. John Haffenden, 1985)

5 Childhood is a disease – a sickness that you grow out of.

Quoted in the *Guardian* 22 June 1990. Golding worked for many years as a school-teacher.

## Albert Goldman (1927–94)

US AUTHOR AND CRITIC

A critic of music and pop culture, called by *Newsweek* 'half scholarly intellectual and half funky pop rock schlock freak', he wrote icono-clastic biographies of Lenny Bruce (1974), Elvis Presley (1981) and John Lennon (1988) in addition to numerous articles for *Life*, *The New York Times* and *New York* magazine.

1 Commercial to the core, Elvis was the kind of singer dear to the heart of the music business. For him to sing a song was to sell a song. His G clef was a dollar sign.

*Elvis*, ch. 14 (1981)

## Emma Goldman (1869–1940)

LITHUANIAN-BORN US ANARCHIST

She emigrated to America in 1885 and became part of the anarchist movement in New York. Imprisoned for inciting unemployed workers to riot in 1893 and for opposing conscription during the First World War, she was deported to Russia in 1919 and spent most of the rest of her life in France. Among her writings are *My Disillusionment in Russia* (1923) and *Living My Life* (1931).

1 The individual whose vision encompasses the whole world often feels nowhere so hedged in and out of touch with his surroundings as in his native land.

'The Individual, Society and the State', first publ. c. 1940, repr. in *Red Emma Speaks*, pt 1 (ed. Alix Kates Shulman, 1972)

## William Goldman (b. 1931)

US SCREENWRITER AND NOVELIST

Regarded as one of the most successful screenwriters of the day, he won Academy Awards for *Butch Cassidy and the Sundance Kid* (1970) and *All the President's Men* (1983). He has also adapted his own novels for the screen, including *Marathon Man* (1975, filmed 1976) and *The Princess Bride* (1974, filmed 1987).

1 As far as the filmmaking process is concerned, stars are essentially worthless – and absolutely essential.

*Adventures in the Screen Trade*, ch. 1 (1983)

2 Studio executives are intelligent, brutally overworked men and women who share one thing in common with baseball managers: They wake up every morning of the world with the knowledge that sooner or later they're going to get fired.

ibid.

3 Whoever invented the meeting must have had Hollywood in mind. I think they should consider giving Oscars for meetings: Best Meeting of the Year, Best Supporting Meeting, Best Meeting Based on Material from Another Meeting.

ibid. ch. 2

## (Sir) James Goldsmith (1933–97)

ANGLO-FRENCH BUSINESSMAN

One of the wealthiest men in Britain, he built up a considerable business empire, openly maintained separate families in Britain and France and was regularly pilloried in *Private Eye* for his flamboyant lifestyle. He was elected a French European MP (1995–7) and financed and led the Referendum Party in the British general election of 1997.

1 In my lifetime there has never been a moment when the establishment has been right. The slaves of this world are those who wish to belong to its ranks.

Quoted in the *Observer* 20 July 1997

## Barry Goldwater (1909–98)

US POLITICIAN

As a Republican, he represented Arizona in the Senate (1953–64, 1969–87) and held an extreme anticommunist stance. Defeated as presidential candidate in the 1964 election, he chaired the Armed Services Commission in 1969 and later became a 'symbol of high-minded conservative Republicanism'.

1 I would remind you that extremism in the defense of liberty is no vice! And let me remind you also that moder-ation in the pursuit of justice is no virtue!

Speech accepting presidential nomination at Republican National Convention, San Francisco, 16 July 1964, quoted in *The New York Times* 17 July 1964. Goldwater later attributed these words to Cicero. LYNDON B. JOHNSON, as Democratic nominee for the presidency, replied in a speech in New York, 31 October 1964: 'Extremism in the pursuit of the Presidency is an unpardonable vice. Moderation in the affairs of the nation is the highest virtue.' Johnson won a sweeping victory against Goldwater in the presidential election three days later.

## Samuel Goldwyn (1882–1974)

POLISH-BORN US FILM PRODUCER

Originally named Samuel Goldfish. Arriving alone in England at the age of eleven, he migrated to America two years later, where he swiftly rose from impoverished glovemaker to heading one of Hollywood's mightiest film studios. He was famed for his mala-propisms. He was uncreative himself, but had the knack of assembling creative teams, including William Wyler, who directed such films as *Wuthering Heights* (1939) and *The Best Years of Our Lives* (1946) for Samuel Goldwyn Productions.

1 Gentlemen, include me out!

Attributed in *The Goldwyn Touch*, ch. 10 (1986) by Michael Freedland. The remark is supposed to have been made in October 1933, on resigning from the Motion Picture Producers and Distribu-tors of America over a labour dispute, but Goldwyn himself denied ever having used the words, claiming instead to have said: 'Gentlemen, I'm withdrawing from the association.'

2 That is the kind of ad I like. Facts, facts, facts.

Quoted in *Goldwyn: the Man Behind the Myth*, ch. 16 (1976) by Arthur Marx. Goldwyn was referring to an advertisement for the film *We Live Again* (1934), which described it: 'The greatest motion picture in all history, by the world's most outstanding writer. The directorial genius of Mamoulian, the beauty of Anna Sten and the producing genius of Goldwyn have combined to make the greatest entertainment in the world.' The movie flopped.

3 **A verbal contract isn't worth the paper it is written on.**

Attributed in *The Great Goldwyn*, ch. 1 (1937) by Alva Johnston. In *They Never Said It* (1989) by Paul F. Boller Jr and John George, Goldwyn's actual words are reported as, 'His verbal contract is worth more than the paper it's written on,' referring to movie executive Joseph M. Schenck, who was regarded as completely trustworthy. This popular version is probably one of the many 'Goldwynisms' cooked up by his own staff.

4 **That's the way with these directors, they're always biting the hand that lays the golden egg.**

ibid.

5 **I had a monumental idea this morning, but I didn't like it.**

ibid.

6 **[Too caustic?] To hell with the cost. If it's a good picture, we'll make it.**

To a director who was asked his opinion of a script, quoted in ibid.

7 **God makes stars. I just produce them.**

Quoted in the *Daily Express* 16 May 1939

8 **Any man who goes to a psychiatrist should have his head examined.**

Quoted in *Moguls*, ch. 3 (1969) by Norman Zierold

9 **I don't think anybody should write his autobiography until after he's dead.**

Quoted in *Goldwyn: the Man Behind the Myth*, Prologue (1976) by Arthur Marx

10 **Pictures are for entertainment, messages should be delivered by Western Union.**

Quoted in ibid. ch. 15

11 **I read part of it all the way through.**

Quoted in ibid. ch. 27

# (Sir) E.H. Gombrich (b. 1909)

AUSTRIAN-BORN BRITISH ART CRITIC AND HISTORIAN

Full name Ernst Hans Joseph Gombrich. He emigrated to England in 1936, to work at the Warburg Institute, University of London, winning recognition for his popular works *The Story of Art* (1950) and *Art and Illusion* (1960).

1 **There really is no such thing as Art. There are only artists.**
*The Story of Art*, Introduction (1950). Opening words.

2 **For that strange precinct we call 'art' is like a hall of mirrors or a whispering gallery. Each form conjures up a thousand memories and after-images. No sooner is an image presented as art than, by this very act, a new frame of reference is created which it cannot escape.**
'Aspects of Form: A Symposium on Form in Nature and Art' (ed. L.L. Whyte, 1951), repr. as 'Meditations on a Hobby Horse' in *Meditations on a Hobby Horse and Other Essays on the Theory of Art* (1963)

# F. Gonzalez-Crussi (b. 1936)

MEXICAN PROFESSOR OF PATHOLOGY AND AUTHOR

'Attempting to join science and the humanities,' as he himself has said, he produced collections of pithy and humorous essays drawn from his experience as a practising pathologist. Among these are *Notes of an Anatomist* (1985) and *Three Forms of Sudden Death and Other Reflections on the Grandeur and Misery of the Body* (1986).

1 **Ceremony and ritual spring from our heart of hearts: those who govern us know it well, for they would sooner deny us bread than dare alter the observance of tradition.**
*Notes of an Anatomist*, 'On Embalming' (1985)

# Linda Goodman (b. 1929)

US ASTROLOGER

Born Mary Alice Kemery. Her books *Sun Signs* (1968) and *Love Signs* (1978), which incorporated popular psychology, were best-sellers, and she has also published poetry. Claiming to be 400 years old, she founded a religion called Manni.

1 **The stars which shone over Babylon and the stable in Bethlehem still shine as brightly over the Empire State Building and your front yard today. They perform their cycles with the same mathematical precision, and they will continue to affect each thing on earth, including man, as long as the earth exists.**
*Linda Goodman's Sun Signs*, Afterword (1968)

# Lord Goodman (1913–95)

BRITISH LAWYER AND PUBLIC FIGURE

Arnold Goodman. Chairman of the Arts Council of Great Britain and British Lion Films (1965–72) and director of the Royal Opera House (1972–83), he was adviser to three prime ministers and the only person to have been both granted a peerage by a Labour prime minister (HAROLD WILSON) and made a Companion of Honour by a Conservative one (EDWARD HEATH).

1 **That is one of the great advantages of the arts: they are a consolation for loneliness.**
Interview in *Singular Encounters*, 'Lord Goodman' (1990) by Naim Attallah

# Paul Goodman (1911–72)

US AUTHOR, POET AND CRITIC

His fiction, poetry, literary criticism and social commentaries championed the cause of the individual against organizations. GEORGE STEINER said that in the 1960s he was 'about the only American voice that young English pacifists and nuclear disarmers find convincing'. Among his works is *The Individual and Culture* (1969).

1 **When the Devil quotes Scriptures, it's not, really, to deceive, but simply that the masses are so ignorant of theology that somebody has to teach them the elementary texts before he can seduce them.**
*Five Years*, 'Spring and Summer 1956', sect. 6 (1966)

2 **When a village ceases to be a community, it becomes oppressive in its narrow conformity. So one becomes an individual and migrates to the city. There, finding others likeminded, one re-establishes a village community. Nowadays only New Yorkers are yokels.**
ibid. 'Winter and Spring 1956–1957', sect. 8

# Mikhail Gorbachev (b. 1931)

RUSSIAN POLITICAL LEADER

General Secretary of the Soviet Communist Party (1985–91) and President of the USSR (1990–91), he introduced *perestroika*, a restructuring of the Soviet political and economic system, and *glasnost*, a new openness and political freedom, which speeded up the break-up of the Soviet Union in 1991. He was also instrumental in ending the Cold War, for which he received the Nobel Peace Prize in 1990. See also MARGARET THATCHER 17.

1 **The essence of perestroika lies in the fact that *it unites socialism with democracy* ... We want more socialism and, therefore, more democracy.**
*Perestroika*, pt 1, ch. 1 (1987)

2 **I am a Communist, a convinced Communist! For some that may be a fantasy. But to me it is my main goal.**
Speech at Second National Congress of People's Deputies, Moscow, December 1989, quoted in *The New York Times* 26 December 1989. A week earlier, however, *Newsweek* had quoted Gorbachev as confiding to MARGARET THATCHER: 'I don't even know if I'm a Communist any more.' Both pronouncements are discussed in *Gorbachev*, pt 6, 'Sakharov's Warning' (1991) by GAIL SHEEHY.

3 I believe, as Lenin said, that this revolutionary chaos may yet crystallize into new forms of life.

Quoted in *The Times* 18 May 1990, in reference to the secession of the Baltic republics and other regional disputes

4 The market came with the dawn of civilization and it is not an invention of capitalism . . . If it leads to improving the well-being of the people there is no contradiction with socialism.

Quoted in the *Guardian* 21 June 1990

5 My life's work has been accomplished. I did all that I could.

Quoted in the *Observer* 15 December 1991. On being ousted as Soviet President.

## Nadine Gordimer (b. 1923)
SOUTH AFRICAN AUTHOR

Apartheid and its destructive effects, both on the privileged and the oppressed, are the main themes of her short stories and novels. Her works include the autobiographical *The Lying Days* (1953), the Booker Prize-winning *The Conservationist* (1974) and *A Burger's Daughter* (1979), which was banned in South Africa. She was awarded the Nobel Prize for Literature in 1991.

1 The country of the tourist pamphlet always is another country, an embarrassing abstraction of the desirable that, thank God, does not exist on this planet, where there are always ants and bad smells and empty Coca-Cola bottles to keep the grubby finger-print of reality upon the beautiful.

*A World of Strangers*, ch. 1 (1958)

2 If you live in Europe . . . things change . . . but continuity never seems to break. You don't have to throw the past away.

Madame Bagnelli, in *Burger's Daughter*, pt 2 (1979)

3 If people would forget about utopia! When rationalism destroyed heaven and decided to set it up here on earth, that most terrible of all goals entered human ambition. It was clear there'd be no end to what people would be made to suffer for it.

Bernard, in ibid.

4 Responsibility is what awaits outside the Eden of Creativity.

'The Essential Gesture', lecture at University of Michigan, 12 October 1984, first publ. in *The Tanner Lectures on Human Values* (ed. Sterling M. McMurrin, 1985), repr. in *The Essential Gesture* (ed. Stephen Clingman, 1988)

5 There is no moral authority like that of sacrifice.

ibid.

6 Censorship is never over for those who have experienced it. It is a brand on the imagination that affects the individual who has suffered it, forever.

'Censorship and its Aftermath', address at the International Writer's Day conference, London, June 1990, publ. in *Index on Censorship* August 1990

## Mack Gordon (1904–59)
POLISH-BORN US SONGWRITER

Original name Morris Gittler. He sang in minstrel shows and vaudeville before teaming up with Harry Revel to create songs for Hollywood films in the 1930s. With the prolific composer Harry Warren, he also produced some of America's most memorable songs of the 1940s, such as 'Chattanooga Choo Choo' (1941) and 'Kalamazoo' (1942), both hits for Glen Miller.

1 Pardon me boy,
  Is that the Chattanooga Choo-choo?
  Track twenty-nine,
  Boy you can give me a shine.

'Chattanooga Choo-choo' (song, written 1934 with music by Harry

Warren) in *Sun Valley Serenade* (musical show and film, 1941). Sung by Dorothy Dandridge in the film, the number was recorded by Glenn Miller and his Orchestra, for whom it sold a million and became the first record to be awarded a gold disc.

## Teresa Gorman (b. 1931)
BRITISH POLITICIAN

A right-wing libertarian and businesswoman, she was elected Conservative MP in 1987 and has been outspoken on women's issues and against Britain's membership of the EU. In 1994 she lost the party whip after rebelling on payments to the EU budget but has remained steadfast in her opposition to Europe since having the whip restored.

1 The Conservative Establishment has always treated women as nannies, grannies and fannies.

Quoted in the *Guardian* 27 December 1998

## Stuart Gorrell (1902–63)
US SONGWRITER

A schoolfriend of Hoagy Carmichael, he was later an editor at the *Miami Herald*.

1 Georgia, Georgia, no peace I find,
  Just an old sweet song keeps Georgia on my mind.

'Georgia on my Mind' (song, 1930, with music by Hoagy Carmichael). The song was first sung by Hoagy Carmichael, was a hit for Mildred Bailey (1932), Ray Charles (1960) and WILLIE NELSON (1978) and has been adopted as the state song of Georgia.

## Stephen Jay Gould (b. 1941)
US PALAEONTOLOGIST AND AUTHOR

He proposes the theory of 'punctuated equilibrium' – evolution in stops and starts – and opposes biological determinism. A highly regarded popularizer of science, his award-winning books include *Hens' Teeth and Horses' Toes* (1983), *Wonderful Life* (1989) and *Eight Little Piggies* (1993).

1 *Homo sapiens* . . . a tiny twig on an improbable branch of a contingent limb on a fortunate tree.

*Wonderful Life: The Burgess Shale and the Nature of History*, ch. 4 'Walcott's Vision and the Nature of History' (1990)

2 Science is an integral part of culture. It's not this foreign thing, done by an arcane priesthood. It's one of the glories of the human intellectual tradition.

*Independent* 24 January 1990

3 We think that we are reading nature by applying rules of logic and laws of matter to our observations. But we are often telling stories–in the good sense, but stories nonetheless.

*Bully for Brontosaurus*, ch. 5 (1991)

4 Knowledge and wonder are the dyad of our worthy lives as intellectual beings.

ibid. ch. 35

5 Progress in knowledge is not a tower to heaven built of bricks from the bottom up, but a product of impasse and breakthrough, yielding a bizarre and circuitous structure that ultimately rises nonetheless.

*Eight Little Piggies*, pt 3, essay 9 (1993)

6 The real tragedy of human existence is not that we are nasty by nature, but that a cruel structural asymmetry grants to rare events of meanness such power to shape our history.

ibid. pt 5, essay 19

7 People in the past, in religious civilizations, had a real, profound terror of apocalyptic catastrophe. What frightens us in our secular age is the computer breakdown

that'll occur if computers interpret the oo of the year 2000 as a return to 1900.

'Time Scales and the Year 2000', Introduction to *Conversations about the End of Time* (ed. Catherine David, Frédéric Lenoir and Jean-Philippe de Tonnac, 1999)

## Philip Gourevitch (b. 1961)
US JOURNALIST AND AUTHOR

A staff writer at the *New Yorker*, he reported on the Rwanda massacres of 1994, about which he published his award-winning account, *We wish to inform you that tomorrow we will be killed with our families* (1998).

1 Genocide, after all, is an exercise in community building. A vigorous totalitarian order requires that the people be invested in the leaders' scheme, and while genocide may be the most perverse and ambitious means to this end, it is also the most comprehensive.

*We wish to inform you that tomorrow we will be killed with our families*, pt 1, ch.7 (1998)

2 Rwanda had presented the world with the most unambiguous case of genocide since Hitler's war against the Jews, and the world sent blankets, beans, and bandages to camps controlled by the killers, apparently hoping that everybody would behave nicely in the future.

ibid. ch.11

## (Sir) Lew Grade (1906–98)
UKRAINE-BORN BRITISH FILM AND TV ENTREPRENEUR

Baron Grade of Elstree, born Louis Winogradsky. Once a champion tap-dancer, he was a dominant figure in show business for more than forty years, as a theatrical agent from 1943, managing director of ATV (1962–76) and film producer.

1 All my shows are great. Some of them are bad. But they are all great.

Quoted in the *Observer* 14 September 1975

2 It would have been cheaper to lower the Atlantic.

Attributed comment on his film *Raise the Titanic* (1980), which took only $7 million at the box office after costing $40 million to make

## Michael Grade (b. 1943)
BRITISH BROADCASTING EXECUTIVE

Nephew of LEW GRADE, he was the BBC's youngest ever Controller in 1984. He was then made Director of Programmes and head of Channel 4 (1988–97) and was on the board of the New Millennium Experience (from 1997).

1 The BBC keeps us all honest.

Quoted in the *Independent on Sunday* 19 February 1995

## Graffiti

1 Kilroy was here.

Second World War, left by US servicemen, particularly Air Transport Command. The words may have originated with a shipyard inspector in Massachusetts, who left his name on goods he had passed.

2 Imagination has seized power.

(*L'imagination prend le pouvoir.*)

Paris, 1968, quoted in *Paris '68*, ch. 2 (1988) by Marc Rohan

3 One non-revolutionary weekend is infinitely more bloody than a month of permanent revolution.

School of Oriental Languages, London, 1968, publ. in *Leaving the 20th Century: The Incomplete Work of the Situationist International* (ed./transl. Christopher Gray, 1974)

4 Clapton is God.

London, late 1960s. Referring to guitarist Eric Clapton. 'I never ever

saw that written anywhere or heard people say it after gigs,' Clapton later stated in an interview. 'I would think that it had just got out of proportion . . . I completely ignored it, really.'

5 A woman needs a man like a fish needs a bicycle.

1970s. Also attributed to GLORIA STEINEM.

6 God made us Catholics but the armalite made us equal.

Belfast, 1970s

7 It doesn't matter who you vote for, the government always gets in.

London, 1970s

8 *Liberté! Fraternité! Sexualité!*

Paris Métro, 1980s

9 If voting changed anything, they'd abolish it.

1980s. The words were taken as the title of a book by KEN LIVINGSTONE in 1987.

10 They came, they saw, they did a little shopping.

Berlin wall, following the influx of thousands of East Berliners into West Berlin after the lifting of travel restrictions; reported in *Newsweek* 4 December 1989

11 Workers of the world forgive me.

On the bust of Karl Marx in Bucharest, reported in *The Times* 4 May 1990

12 Dead twat.

On the statue of WINSTON CHURCHILL in Parliament Square, London, daubed by 'anti-capitalist' rioters, 1 May 2000

## Harry Graham (1874–1936)
BRITISH AUTHOR AND RHYMESTER

1 Weep not for little Leonie,
Abducted by a French Marquis!
Though loss of honour was a wrench,
Just think how it's improved her French.

'Compensation', publ. in *More Ruthless Rhymes for Heartless Homes* (1930)

## Martha Graham (1894–1991)
US DANCER AND CHOREOGRAPHER

Providing the first real alternative to classical ballet, she started the Martha Graham School of Contemporary Dance in 1927, became America's leading exponent of Expressionist dance and influenced a generation of choreographers. Among her most famous works are *Appalachian Spring* (1944) and *Clytemnestra* (1958).

1 Nothing is more revealing than movement.

'The American Dance', publ. in *Modern Dance* (ed. Virginia Stewart, 1935)

2 We look at the dance to impart the sensation of living in an affirmation of life, to energize the spectator into keener awareness of the vigor, the mystery, the humor, the variety, and the wonder of life. This is the function of the American dance.

ibid.

3 There is a supreme lucidity, which is the precisely calculated awareness which is called madness.

*The Notebooks of Martha Graham*, 'The Trysting Tent' (1973)

4 No artist is ahead of his time. He *is* his time; it is just that others are behind the times.

Quoted in the *Observer* 8 July 1979

## Philip L. Graham (1915–63)
US NEWSPAPER PUBLISHER

He took control of the *Washington Post* in 1946, turning it into a leading newspaper of the day. Known as a talented fixer, he suffered from manic depression and committed suicide.

1 **News is the first rough draft of history.**

Attributed. The aphorism has also been ascribed to *Washington Post* editor Ben C. Bradlee, but Bradlee himself, in an interview in *Vanity Fair* September 1991, credited it to Phil Graham, formerly his boss at the *Post*.

## Gloria Grahame (1924–81)
US ACTRESS

Original name Gloria Hallward. A blonde leading lady, she found her niche in film noir playing morally ambiguous women. She played opposite FRANK SINATRA and HUMPHREY BOGART, and her films include *In a Lonely Place* (1950) and *The Bad and the Beautiful* (1952), for which she won an Oscar.

1 **I was born when you kissed me. I died when you left me. I lived a few weeks while you loved me.**

Laurel Gray (Gloria Grahame), quoting the unfinished script of screenwriter Dixon Steele (Humphrey Bogart) at the end of *In a Lonely Place* (film, 1950, screenplay by Andrew Solt adapted from novel by Dorothy B. Hughes, directed by Nicholas Ray)

2 **I've been rich and I've been poor. Believe me, rich is better.**

Debby Marsh (Gloria Grahame), in *The Big Heat* (film, 1953, screenplay by Sidney Boehm from novel by William P. McGivern, directed by Fritz Lang). The words may have been inspired by a quote associated with US singer SOPHIE TUCKER.

3 **We're all sisters under the mink.**

ibid.

## Percy Grainger (1882–1961)
AUSTRALIAN-BORN US COMPOSER AND PIANIST

He settled in America in 1914 and after collecting folk tunes in England and Europe contributed to a folk revival with pieces such as *Shepherd's Hey* (1911) and *Molly on the Shore* (1914). He was one of the first composers to write for electronic instruments and also devised a synthesizer.

1 **Salvation Army Booth objected to the devil having all the good tunes. I object to jazz and vaudeville having all the best instruments.**

*Spoon River*, Preface (1939). The quotation referred to is usually associated with the clergyman Rowland Hill (1744–1833), who 'did not see any reason why the devil should have all the good tunes'.

## Antonio Gramsci (1891–1937)
ITALIAN POLITICAL THEORIST

Born and raised in Sardinia, he established the Italian Communist Party in 1921, became its leader in 1924 but was arrested when Mussolini banned the party in 1926. He spent the rest of his life in prison, where he wrote thirty notebooks published posthumously as *Letters from Prison* (1947).

1 **I would like you to understand completely, also emotionally, that I'm a political detainee and will be a political prisoner, that I have nothing now or in the future to be ashamed of in this situation. That, at bottom, I myself have in a certain sense asked for this detention and this sentence, because I've always refused to change my opinion, for which I would be willing to give my life and not just remain in prison. That therefore I can only be tranquil and content with myself.**

Letter to his mother, 10 May 1928, publ. in: *Letters from Prison* (1947, transl. 1993)

2 **I'm a pessimist because of intelligence, but an optimist because of will.**

Letter, 19 December 1929, publ. in ibid.

3 **If you think about it seriously, all the questions about the** soul and the immortality of the soul and paradise and hell are at bottom only a way of seeing this very simple fact: that every action of ours is passed on to others according to its value, of good or evil, it passes from father to son, from one generation to the next, in a perpetual movement.

Letter to his mother, 15 June 1931, publ. in ibid.

4 **I turn and turn in my cell like a fly that doesn't know where to die.**

Letter, 20 July 1931, publ. in ibid.

## Grandmaster Flash (b. 1958)
US RAP MUSICIAN

Original name Joseph Saddler. Top DJ of the 1970s and one of the pioneers of hip-hop, he worked with the rap and break-dancing team, the Furious Five. His single 'Freedom' (1980) earned a gold disc and was followed by 'Grandmaster Flash on the Wheels of Steel' (1981) and the crossover hit 'The Message' (1982).

1 **It's like a jungle sometimes,**
**It makes me wonder**
**How I keep from going under.**

'The Message' (song, written by Sylvia Robinson and Duke Bootee, 1982) on the album *Greatest Messages* (1984) by Grandmaster Flash and the Furious Five

## Bernie Grant (1944–2000)
BRITISH POLITICIAN

Called by JEREMY PAXMAN 'the most colourful of Britain's post-war black MPs' and by DOUGLAS HURD 'the high priest of race conflict', he was the first black council leader in Britain (Haringey), leading the Labour majority 1985–7. He was also founder and Chairman of the All Party Group on Race and Community (1995–7).

1 **The police were to blame for what happened on Sunday night and what they got was a bloody good hiding.**

Press statement outside Tottenham Town Hall, 8 October 1985, quoted in *The Times* 9 October 1985. Grant was speaking in the wake of the Broadwater Farm riots in north London, during which PC Keith Blakelock was murdered.

## Cary Grant (1904–86)
BRITISH-BORN US ACTOR

Original name Archibald Leach. For over three decades he was a debonair leading man who played both light comedic roles opposite MARLENE DIETRICH, MAE WEST and, in *Bringing Up Baby* (1938), KATHARINE HEPBURN, and parts in HITCHCOCK thrillers, including *Suspicion* (1941), *Notorious* (1946), *To Catch a Thief* (1955) and *North by Northwest* (1959). He received a Special Academy Award in 1970.

1 **Old Cary Grant fine. How you?**

Attributed telegram, quoted in *Cary Grant* (1983) by R. Schickel. The words are supposed to be in response to a cable sent by a journalist to Grant's press agent: 'How old Cary Grant?'

## Günter Grass (b. 1927)
GERMAN AUTHOR

Germany's leading living novelist, often cast in the role of the 'conscience of his generation', he caused controversy with his first novel *The Tin Drum* (1959) for its depiction of the Nazis. His subsequent novels challenge the *status quo* and reading of past events. He was also speechwriter for Willy Brandt when Brandt was Mayor of West Berlin.

1 **Even bad books are books and therefore sacred.**

The narrator (Oskar Matzerath), in *The Tin Drum*, bk 1, 'Rasputin and the Alphabet' (1959)

2 Art is uncompromising and life is full of compromises.
Quoted by ARTHUR MILLER, in *Paris Review* summer 1966

3 Melancholy has ceased to be an individual phenomenon, an exception. It has become the class privilege of the wage earner, a mass state of mind that finds its cause wherever life is governed by production quotas.
*From the Diary of a Snail*, 'On Stasis in Progress' (1972)

4 If work and leisure are soon to be subordinated to this one utopian principle – absolute busyness – then utopia and melancholy will come to coincide: an age without conflict will dawn, perpetually busy – and without consciousness.
ibid.

5 We already have the statistics for the future: the growth percentages of pollution, overpopulation, desertification. The future is already in place.
Interview in *New Statesman and Society* 22 June 1990

6 Art is so wonderfully irrational, exuberantly pointless, but necessary all the same. Pointless and yet necessary, that's hard for a puritan to understand.
ibid.

7 Believing: it means believing in our own lies. And I can say that I am grateful that I got this lesson very early.
*Omnibus*, television broadcast on BBC1, 3 November 1992

## Robert Graves (1895–1985)
BRITISH POET AND AUTHOR

Although his diverse output included autobiography (*Goodbye to All That*, 1929), historical novels (*I, Claudius* and *Claudius the God*, both 1934), studies of mythology (*The Greek Myths*, 1955) and literary criticism, he regarded himself primarily as a poet and was Professor of Poetry at Oxford (1961–6). His last volume of *Collected Poems* was published in 1975. JOHN CAREY said of him: 'He had a mind like an alchemist's laboratory; everything that got into it came out new, weird and gleaming.'

1 Children are dumb to say how hot the day is,
How hot the scent is of the summer rose,
How dreadful the black wastes of evening sky,
How dreadful the tall soldiers drumming by.
'The Cool Web', publ. in *Poems* (1927)

2 There's a cool web of language winds us in,
Retreat from too much joy or too much fear.
ibid.

3 Goodbye to all that.
Title of autobiography (1929)

4 Down, wanton, down! Have you no shame
That at the whisper of Love's name,
Or Beauty's, presto! up you raise
Your angry head and stand at gaze?
'Down, Wanton, Down!', publ. in *Poems 1930–1933* (1933)

5 To evoke posterity
Is to weep on your own grave,
Ventriloquizing for the unborn.
'To Evoke Posterity', publ. in *Collected Poems* (1938)

6 To be a poet is a condition rather than a profession.
'The Cost of Letters', reply to questionnaire in *Horizon* September 1946

7 The reason why the hairs stand on end, the eyes water, the throat is constricted, the skin crawls and a shiver runs down the spine when one writes or reads a true poem is that a true poem is necessarily an invocation of the White Goddess, or Muse, the Mother of All Living, the ancient power of fright and lust – the female spider or the queen bee whose embrace is death.
*The White Goddess*, ch. 1 (1948)

8 Counting the beats,
Counting the slow heart beats,
The bleeding to death of time in slow heart beats,
Wakeful they lie.
'Counting the Beats', publ. in *Poems and Satires* (1951)

9 Why have such scores of lovely girls
Married impossible men?
Simple sacrifice may be ruled out,
And missionary endeavour, nine times out of ten.
'A Slice of Wedding Cake', publ. in *Steps* (1958)

10 Love, the sole Goddess fit for swearing by,
Concedes us graciously the little lie:
The white lie, the half lie, the lie corrective
Without which love's exchange might prove defective,
Confirming hazardous relationships
By kindly *maquillage* of Truth's pale lips.
'Friday Night', publ. in *5 Pens in Hand* (1958)

11 A difficult achievement for true lovers
Is to lie mute, without embrace or kiss,
Without a rustle or a smothered sigh,
Basking each in the other's glory.
'The Starred Coverlet', publ. in *More Poems* (1961)

12 Nine-tenths of English poetic literature is the result either of vulgar careerism or of a poet trying to keep his hand in. Most poets are dead by their late twenties.
Quoted in the *Observer* 11 November 1962

13 If there's no money in poetry, neither is there poetry in money.
Speech at London School of Economics, 6 December 1963, publ. in *Mammon and the Black Goddess*, 'Mammon' (1965)

14 Perfect reliance on the impossible
By strict avoidance of all such conjecture
As underlies the so-called possible:
That is true love's adventure.
'To Put It Simply', publ. in *Poems 1968–70* (1970)

15 Are not all centuries, like men,
Born hopeful too and gay,
And good for seventy years, but then
Hope slowly seeps away?
'The Imminent Seventies', publ. in ibid.

16 Poets are guardians
Of a shadowy island
With granges and forest
Warmed by the Moon
'The Title of Poet', publ. in *Poems 1970–1972* (1972)

## Alasdair Gray (b. 1934)
SCOTTISH NOVELIST

Previously a scriptwriter for TV and radio, from the 1980s he wrote novels dealing with contemporary Scotland, including *Lanark* (1981) and *The Fall of Kelvin Walker* (1985). Anthony Burgess called him 'the best novelist since Sir Walter Scott'.

1 Glasgow, the sort of industrial city where most people live nowadays but nobody imagines living.
The Oracle, in *Lanark*, bk 3, ch. 11 (1981)

2 Everyone sees life through their job. To the doctor the world is a hospital, to the broker it is a stock exchange, to the lawyer a vast criminal court, to the soldier a barracks and area of manoeuvre, to the farmer soil and bad weather, to truck-drivers a road system, to dustmen a midden, to prostitutes a brothel, to mothers an inescapable nursery, to children a school, to film stars a looking-glass, to undertakers a morgue, and to myself a security installation powered by the sun and only crackable by death.
*1982, Janine*, ch. 4 (1984)

3 Outside babyhood hardly anyone feels healthy for long,

but viewed in health and without prejudice the universe is an orchard of strange lovely bodies: fruit, stars and people freely grown for us by God (if we're religious) or by the universe itself, if we ain't.

Dad, in *Something Leather*, ch. 11 (1990)

## John Gray (b. 1951)

US PSYCHOTHERAPIST AND AUTHOR

He specializes in gender differences and the promotion of understanding between the sexes. His books include *Men Are From Mars, Women Are From Venus* (1992) and *What Your Mother Didn't Tell You and Your Father Didn't Know* (1994).

1 Men mistakenly expect women to think, communicate, and react the way men do; women mistakenly expect men to feel, communicate and respond the way women do. We have forgotten that men and women are supposed to be different. As a result our relationships are filled with unnecessary friction and conflict. Clearly recognizing and respecting these differences dramatically reduces confusion when dealing with the opposite sex. When you remember that men are from Mars and women are from Venus, everything can be explained.

*Men Are from Mars, Women Are from Venus*, ch. 1 (1992)

2 One of the big challenges for men is correctly to interpret and support a woman when she is talking about her feelings. The biggest challenge for women is correctly to interpret and support a man when he isn't talking.

ibid. ch. 5, 'When Martians Don't Talk'

## Simon Gray (b. 1936)

BRITISH PLAYWRIGHT

His wry and comedic plays, which take as their milieu the worlds of academia and publishing, include *Wise Child* (1967), *Melon* (1987) and *Cell Mates* (1995). He has also written for television.

1 Everybody in Los Angeles lives miles away, not from anywhere, because there isn't actually an anywhere to live away from, but from each other.

*How's That for Telling 'Em, Fat Lady?*, ch. 2 (1988)

2 Faith is . . . is a matter of believing what's impossible to believe. Do you, um, see? Otherwise it's not faith. It's certainty.

Ronnie, in *Hidden Laughter*, act 1, sc. 1 (1990)

3 People should worry about each other. Because worry is just love in its worst form. But it's still love.

Louise, in ibid. act 1, sc. 2

4 I'm fanatical about sport: there seems to me something almost religious about the fact that human beings can organize play, the spirit of play.

Interview in the *Independent on Sunday* 19 February 1995

## Hannah Green (b. 1932)

US NOVELIST

Original name Joanne Greenberg. She is mainly known for her autobiographical novel *I Never Promised You a Rose Garden* (1964), the story of a fight against schizophrenia. Other works, which treat a range of subjects in a straightforward narrative style, include *In This Sign* (1968) and the short stories *High Crimes and Misdemeanors* (1979).

1 I never promised you a rose garden.

Title of novel (1964, filmed 1977). A song with this title written by Joe South was the only hit for country singer Lynn Anderson in 1971.

## Henry Green (1905–73)

BRITISH NOVELIST

Original name Henry Vincent Yorke. Pursuing a literary career alongside his work as an engineer, he wrote impressionistic novels that relied on dialogue rather than plot, for example *Living* (1929), an insight into life on the factory floor, and *Loving* (1943).

1 Prose is not to be read aloud but to oneself at night, and it is not quick as poetry, but rather a gathering web of insinuations which go further than names however shared can ever go. Prose should be a long intimacy between strangers with no direct appeal to what both may have known. It should slowly appeal to feelings unexpressed, it should in the end draw tears out of the stone.

*Pack My Bag: a Self Portrait* (1940)

## Jonathon Green (b. 1948)

BRITISH ANTHOLOGIST AND LEXICOGRAPHER

In the 1960s and 1970s he wrote for *Rolling Stone*, *IT* and *Oz*. As a lexicographer of slang and jargon, he broadcasts regularly on language topics and is the author of many dictionaries, including the *Dictionary of Slang* (1998).

1 Today, as those who were young then, or just becoming adults, are passing into middle age, the 60s seem the most inescapable of all those nostalgia-girt decades. Whether hymned by ageing hippies, still wreathed in rosy fantasies, or vilified by contemporary politicians, desperately hunting an easy scapegoat for over-complex ills, the image remains: something happened.

*Days in the Life*, Introduction (1988)

2 Slang is the counter-language. A jackanapes lexicon of the dispossessed. The language of the rebel, the outlaw, the despised, the marginal, the young. Above all it is the language of the city.

*Dictionary of Slang*, Introduction (1998)

3 Women? Let's get real: we called them chicks. What they did was 'chick work', which tended to be secretarial in its myriad forms . . . Whatever their own agenda, girls were there for sex, joint-rolling and throwing together the all too mandatory slop.

*Sunday Times* 7 November 1999. Referring to women in the 1960s.

## Peter Greenaway (b. 1942)

BRITISH FILM-MAKER

His films, which are often accompanied by the music of Michael Nyman, are characterized by an intellectual obliqueness that has frequently alienated critics and led to accusations of elitism and pretension. His first major success, *The Draughtsman's Contract* (1982), was followed by, among others, *A Zed and Two Noughts* (1985), *Prospero's Books* (1991) and *The Pillow-Book* (1996).

1 The Cook, The Thief, His Wife and Her Lover

Title of film (written and directed by Peter Greenaway, 1989)

2 We don't need books to make films. It's the last thing we want – it turns cinema into the bastard art of illustration.

Quoted in the *Independent on Sunday* 10 July 1994

## Graham Greene (1904–91)

BRITISH AUTHOR

He wrote stories, plays, biographies and film criticism but is best known for his so-called Catholic novels such as *Brighton Rock* (1938) and *The Heart of the Matter* (1948), which deal with issues of failure, faith and justice, often hedged with seediness or corruption. EVELYN WAUGH advised him not to give up writing about God as it would be like 'P.G. Wodehouse dropping Jeeves halfway through the Wooster series'. See also T.S. ELIOT 36.

1 There is always one moment in childhood when the door opens and lets the future in.

*The Power and the Glory*, pt 1, ch. 1 (1940)

2 Behind the complicated details of the world stand the simplicities: God is good, the grown-up man or woman knows the answer to every question, there is such a thing as truth, and justice is as measured and faultless as a clock. Our heroes are simple: they are brave, they tell the truth, they are good swordsmen and they are never in the long run really defeated. That is why no later books satisfy us like those which were read to us in childhood – for those promised a world of great simplicity of which we knew the rules, but the later books are complicated and contradictory with experience; they are formed out of our own disappointing memories.

*The Ministry of Fear*, bk 1, ch. 7, sect. 1 (1943)

3 Surely we choose our death as much as we choose our job. It grows out of our acts and our evasions, out of our fears and out of our moments of courage.

'The Lost Childhood' (1947) repr. in *The Lost Childhood and Other Essays* (1951)

4 A child, after all, knows most of the game – it is only an attitude to it that he lacks.

ibid.

5 Against the beautiful and the clever and the successful, one can wage a pitiless war, but not against the unattractive: then the millstone weighs on the breast.

*The Heart of the Matter*, bk 1, pt 1, ch. 2, sect. 2 (1948)

6 People talk about the courage of condemned men walking to the place of execution: sometimes it needs as much courage to walk with any kind of bearing towards another person's habitual misery.

ibid. bk 1, pt 1, ch. 2, sect. 3

7 The truth has never been of any real value to any human being – it is a symbol for mathematicians and philosophers to pursue. In human relations kindness and lies are worth a thousand truths.

Scobie, in ibid. bk 1, pt 1, ch. 2, sect. 4

8 Despair is the price one pays for setting oneself an impossible aim. It is, one is told, the unforgivable sin, but it is a sin the corrupt or evil man never practises. He always has hope. He never reaches the freezing-point of knowing absolute failure.

ibid. bk 1, pt 1, ch. 2, sect. 4

9 He [Harris] felt the loyalty we feel to unhappiness – the sense that that is where we really belong.

ibid. bk 2, pt 2, ch. 1, sect. 1

10 His [Major Scobie's] hilarity was like a scream from a crevasse.

ibid. bk 3, pt 1, ch. 1, sect. 1

11 Death's at the bottom of everything, Martins. Leave death to the professionals.

Major Calloway (Trevor Howard), in *The Third Man* (film, 1950, screenplay by Graham Greene, directed by Carol Reed). *The Third Man* was first written as a preliminary draft for the film's screenplay, and later published as a novella (in which these lines do not appear).

12 The world doesn't make any heroes anymore.

ibid.

13 Innocence always calls mutely for protection when we would be so much wiser to guard ourselves against it: innocence is like a dumb leper who has lost his bell, wandering the world, meaning no harm.

*The Quiet American*, pt 1, ch. 3, sect. 3 (1955). Later in the book, the narrator describes Pyle – the idealistic 'quiet American' of the title – in similar terms: 'What's the good? He'll always be innocent, you can't blame the innocent, they are always guiltless. All you can do is control them or eliminate them. Innocence is a kind of insanity' (pt 3, ch. 2, sect. 1).

14 Those who marry God can become domesticated too – it's just as hum-drum a marriage as all the others. The word 'Love' means a formal touch of the lips as in the ceremony of the Mass, and '*Ave Maria*' like 'dearest' is a phrase to open a letter.

*A Burnt-Out Case*, pt 1, ch. 1, sect. 2 (1961)

15 Cynicism is cheap – you can buy it at any Monoprix store – it's built into all poor-quality goods.

*The Comedians*, pt 1, ch. 1, sect. 3 (1966)

16 However great a man's fear of life, suicide remains the courageous act, the clear-headed act of a mathematician. The suicide has judged by the laws of chance – so many odds against one that to live will be more miserable than to die. His sense of mathematics is greater than his sense of survival.

Dr Magiot, in ibid. ch. 4, sect. 1

17 We mustn't complain too much of being comedians – it's an honourable profession. If only we could be good ones the world might gain at least a sense of style. We have failed – that's all. We are bad comedians, we aren't bad men.

The ambassador, in ibid. ch. 5, sect. 2

18 If you have abandoned one faith, do not abandon all faith. There is always an alternative to the faith we lose. Or is it the same faith under another mask?

Dr Magiot, in ibid. pt 3, ch. 4, sect. 4

19 Communism, my friend, is more than Marxism, just as Catholicism ... is more than the Roman Curia. There is a *mystique* as well as a *politique* ... Catholics and Communists have committed great crimes, but at least they have not stood aside, like an established society, and been indifferent. I would rather have blood on my hands than water like Pilate.

Dr Magiot, in ibid. pt 3, ch. 4, sect. 4

20 God ... created a number of possibilities in case some of his prototypes failed – that is the meaning of evolution.

Mr Visconti, in *Travels with My Aunt*, pt 2, ch. 7 (1969)

21 Morality comes with the sad wisdom of age, when the sense of curiosity has withered.

*A Sort of Life*, ch. 7, sect. 1 (1971)

22 A petty reason perhaps why novelists more and more try to keep a distance from journalists is that novelists are trying to write the truth and journalists are trying to write fiction.

Letter to 'Atticus' (Stephen Pile) in the *Sunday Times*, 18 January 1981, repr. in *Yours, Etc: Letters to the Press, 1945–1989* (1989)

23 Success is more dangerous than failure, the ripples break over a wider coastline.

Quoted in the *Independent* 4 April 1991. Recalled at Greene's death by critic Miriam Allot.

# Germaine Greer (b. 1939)
AUSTRALIAN FEMINIST WRITER

Her book *The Female Eunuch* (1970) was a seminal influence on a generation of women, although it was also criticized for placing too much emphasis on sexual liberation. Subsequent books include *Sex and Destiny* (1984), dealing with the politics of fertility, and *The Change* (1991), which treats the menopause. She appears as a cultural commentator on TV and is Professor of English and Comparative Literature at Warwick University.

1 If you think you are emancipated, you might consider the idea of tasting your menstrual blood – if it makes you sick, you've a long way to go, baby.

*The Female Eunuch*, 'The Wicked Womb' (1970)

2 Freud is the father of psychoanalysis. It had no mother.
ibid. 'The Psychological Sell'

3 Even crushed against his brother in the Tube the average Englishman pretends desperately that he is alone.
ibid. 'Womanpower'

4 Every time a woman makes herself laugh at her husband's often-told jokes she betrays him. The man who looks at his woman and says 'What would I do without you?' is already destroyed.
ibid. 'Egotism'

5 Love, love, love – all the wretched cant of it, masking egotism, lust, masochism, fantasy under a mythology of sentimental postures, a welter of self-induced miseries and joys, blinding and masking the essential personalities in the frozen gestures of courtship, in the kissing and the dating and the desire, the compliments and the quarrels which vivify its barrenness.
ibid. 'Obsession'

6 Women have very little idea of how much men hate them.
ibid. 'Loathing and Disgust'

7 Women's liberation, if it abolishes the patriarchal family, will abolish a necessary substructure of the authoritarian state, and once that withers away Marx will have come true willy-nilly, so let's get on with it.
ibid. 'Revolution'

8 The surest guide to the correctness of the path that women take is *joy in the struggle*. Revolution is the festival of the oppressed.
ibid. 'Revolution'

9 The tragedy of machismo is that a man is never quite man enough.
'My Mailer Problem', first publ. in *Esquire* September 1971, repr. in *The Madwoman's Underclothes* (1986)

10 [On Australia] Where else in the world is a generous man defined as one who would give you his arsehole and shit through his ribs?
'The New Maharajahs', first publ. in the *Sunday Times* 16 January 1972, repr. in ibid.

11 The compelled mother loves her child as the caged bird sings. The song does not justify the cage nor the love the enforcement.
'Abortion', first publ. in the *Sunday Times* 21 May 1972, repr. in ibid.

12 We in the West do not refrain from childbirth because we are concerned about the population explosion or because we feel we cannot afford children, but because we do not like children.
*Sex and Destiny*, ch. 1 (1984)

13 The most threatened group in human societies as in animal societies is the unmated male: the unmated male is more likely to wind up in prison or in an asylum or dead than his mated counterpart. He is less likely to be promoted at work and he is considered a poor credit risk.
ibid. ch. 2

14 The only perfect love to be found on earth is not sexual love, which is riddled with hostility and insecurity, but the wordless commitment of families, which takes as its model mother-love.
*The Madwoman's Underclothes*, Introduction (1986). Greer goes on: 'This is not to say that fathers have no place, for father-love, with its driving for self-improvement and discipline, is also essential to survival, but that uncorrected father-love, father-love as it were practised by both parents, is a way to annihilation.'

15 Human beings have an inalienable right to invent themselves; when that right is pre-empted it is called brainwashing.
*The Times* 1 February 1986

16 English culture is basically homosexual in the sense that the men only really care about other men.
*Daily Mail* 18 April 1988

17 Libraries are reservoirs of strength, grace and wit, reminders of order, calm and continuity, lakes of mental energy, neither warm nor cold, light nor dark. The pleasure they give is steady, unorgastic, reliable, deep and long-lasting. In any library in the world, I am at home, unselfconscious, still and absorbed.
*Daddy, We Hardly Knew You*, 'Still in Melbourne, January 1987' (1989)

18 Orgasmism is a Western neurosis, but I say once you've had one, you've had them all.
Interview in *A Little Light Friction*, 'Germaine Greer' (1989) by Val Hennessy

19 An enema under the influence of Ecstasy would probably feel much like this.
*Independent on Sunday* 3 June 1990. Referring to D.H. LAWRENCE's description of the female orgasm in *Lady Chatterley's Lover*.

20 The misery of the middle-aged woman is a grey and hopeless thing, born of having nothing to live for, of disappointment and resentment at having been gypped by consumer society, and surviving merely to be the butt of its unthinking scorn.
*The Change: Women, Ageing and the Menopause*, Introduction (1991)

21 The climacteric marks the end of apologizing. The chrysalis of conditioning has once for all to break and the female woman finally to emerge.
ibid. ch. 17

# Hubert Gregg (b. 1914)
BRITISH SONGWRITER AND ENTERTAINER

A versatile actor, radio performer, playwright, songwriter and presenter, he composed the music and lyrics for numerous revues, including *Strike a Note* (1943). The best known of his many songs are 'Maybe It's Because I'm a Londoner' (1947) and 'I'm Going to Get Lit Up When the Lights Go Up in London' (1944). He has also presented the BBC radio show 'Thanks For the Memory' since 1972.

1 Maybe it's because I'm a Londoner
That I love London so,
Maybe it's because I'm a Londoner –
That I think of her – Wherever I go.
I get a funny feeling inside of me –
Just walking up and down, –
Maybe it's because I'm a Londoner
That I love London Town.
'Maybe It's Because I'm a Londoner' (song, 1947). The song was recorded by BILLY COTTON and his band in 1949.

# Dick Gregory (b. 1932)
US COMEDIAN AND CIVIL RIGHTS ACTIVIST

He was the first black comedian to achieve success among white audiences, using satire to score his points. In the 1960s he became involved with the civil rights movement and Black Power, abandoning his comedy routines as 'they take time away from serving humanity'. His beliefs are presented in *The Shadow That Scares Me* (1968).

1 Civil Rights: What black folks are given in the US on the installment plan, as in civil-rights bills. Not to be confused with *human rights*, which are the dignity, stature, humanity, respect, and freedom belonging to all people by right of their birth.
*Dick Gregory's Political Primer* (1972). See also MALCOLM X 6.

## Joyce Grenfell (1910–79)
BRITISH ACTRESS AND WRITER

The daughter of one of the American Langhorne sisters (one of whom was NANCY ASTOR), she appeared in revue until the early 1950s and subsequently presented her own one-woman shows, most famously *Joyce Grenfell Requests the Pleasure* (from 1954). Her songs and comic monologues lightly mocked old-fashioned middle-class values.

1 George – don't do that.
  Catch-phrase in various sketches in the 1950s and the title of the collection, *George – Don't Do That* (1977)

2 Stately as a galleon, I sail across the floor,
  Doing the military two-step, as in the days of yore.
  'Stately as a Galleon' (song), publ. in *Stately as a Galleon* (1978)

3 Progress everywhere today does seem to come so *very* heavily disguised as Chaos.
  'English Lit.', publ. in ibid.

## Clifford Grey (1887–1941)
BRITISH SONGWRITER

Original name Percival Davis. A prolific lyricist and librettist for the London and New York stages, he provided songs for a string of musical comedies and revues, including 'The Bing Boys Are Here' (1916) and 'Mr Cinders' (1929).

1 If you were the only girl in the world
  And I were the only boy.
  'If You Were the Only Girl in the World' (song, with music by Nat Ayer) in the musical show *The Bing Boys Are Here* (1916). The song was first performed by George Roby and Violet Lorraine, introduced in America by Rudy Vallee in the film *The Vagabond Lover* (1929), and sung by Gordon McCrae and Doris Day in the film *By the Light of the Silvery Moon* (1953).

## Joel Grey (b. 1932)
US SINGER AND ACTOR

Original name Joe Katz, he created the role of the MC in the stage show *Cabaret* (1966), winning an Academy Award for the same part in the film version (1972). He also starred in *George M!*, a musical biography of GEORGE M. COHAN, which was his last success on Broadway. See also LIZA MINNELLI 1.

1 Meine Damen und Herren, Mesdames et Messieurs,
  Ladies und Gentlemen – comment ça va?
  Do you feel good? . . . I am your host . . .
  Wilkommen! Bienvenue! Welcome!
  Im Cabaret! Au Cabaret! To Cabaret!
  'Wilkommen' (song, written by Fred Ebb and John Kander), sung by the Master of Ceremonies ( Joel Grey) in *Cabaret* (musical play by Joe Masterhoff, 1966, filmed 1972)

## Lord Grey (1862–1933)
BRITISH STATESMAN

Sir Edward Grey, First Viscount of Falloden. As Foreign Secretary (1905–16) he was responsible for the Russian entente of 1907 and sided with France in the Agadir incident in 1911.

1 The lamps are going out all over Europe; we shall not see them lit again in our lifetime.
  Said in London, 3 August 1914, quoted in *Twenty-Five Years*, vol. 2, ch. 18 (1925). The words were spoken on the eve of Britain's declaration of war against Germany.

## D.W. Griffith (1874–1948)
US PRODUCER-DIRECTOR

Full name David Wark Griffith. He was responsible for many of

the conventions of present-day cinematic technique, experimenting with flash-backs, fade-outs and moving cameras. His masterpiece, *The Birth of a Nation* (1915), was described by President WOODROW WILSON as 'like writing history with lightning'. He co-founded United Artists in 1919, but his career declined with the Depression, and he released his last film, *The Struggle*, in 1931.

1 We do not fear censorship for we have no wish to offend with improprieties or obscenities, but we do demand, as a right, the liberty to show the dark side of wrong, that we may illuminate the bright side of virtue – the same liberty that is conceded to the art of the written word, that art to which we owe the Bible and the works of Shakespeare.
  'A Plea for the Art of the Motion Picture' released as Prologue to *The Birth of a Nation* (film, 1915)

## Melanie Griffith (b. 1957)
US ACTRESS

Daughter of the actress Tippi Hedren, she was described by critic Joe Queenan as 'the instantly recognizable Griffith Girl: a trashy babe in black underpants and matching garter belt with a squeaky voice, a butt that is not to be trifled with, and a heart as wide as Asia.' Among her films are *Working Girl* (1988), *Pacific Heights* (1990) and *Lolita* (1997).

1 I have a head for business and a bod for sin. Is there anything wrong with that?
  Tess McGill (Melanie Griffith), in *Working Girl* (film, 1988, screenplay by Kevin Wade, directed by Mike Nichols)

## Mervyn Griffith-Jones (1909–79)
BRITISH LAWYER

He was one of the British Prosecuting Counsel at the Nuremberg trials (1945–6) and a member of the standing committee on Criminal Law Revision (1958).

1 Would you approve of your young sons, young daughters – because girls can read as well as boys – reading this book? Is it a book that you would have lying around in your own house? Is it a book that you would even wish your wife or your servants to read?
  Opening address to jury during the prosecution of Penguin Books Ltd, 20 October 1961, publ. in *The Trial of Lady Chatterley* (ed. C.H. Rolph, 1961). Griffith-Jones was senior prosecuting counsel in the case brought against Penguin for publishing an unexpurgated edition of D.H. Lawrence's *Lady Chatterley's Lover*. Rolph noted the 'visible – and risible – effect on the jury' of these remarks, and surmised that this 'may well have been the first nail in the prosecution's coffin'.

## John Grigg (b. 1924)
BRITISH AUTHOR AND JOURNALIST

Lord Altrincham. He was a columnist for the *Guardian* and *The Times*, wrote on twentieth-century social history, including studies of NANCY ASTOR and LLOYD GEORGE, and authored vol. 6 of the *History of the Times* (1993).

1 Autobiography is now as common as adultery and hardly less reprehensible.
  *Sunday Times* 28 February 1962

## Georg Groddeck (1866–1934)
GERMAN PSYCHOANALYST

Regarded as one of the founding fathers of psychosomatic medicine, he opened the sanatorium Marienhöhe in 1900 and ran it until his death. His books which included psycholanalytical studies and fiction were burnt by the Nazis.

1 One must not forget that recovery is brought about not

by the physician, but by the sick man himself. He heals himself, by his own power, exactly as he walks by means of his own power, or eats, or thinks, breathes or sleeps.

*The Book of the It*, 'Letter 32' (1923)

## Matt Groening (b. 1954)

US CARTOONIST

Having acquired a minor cult following for his weekly comic strip *Life in Hell* in the *Los Angeles Reader* in 1980, he created *The Simpsons* in 1987 as a filler between skits on *The Tracy Ullman Show* for the Fox TV network. The family, consisting of the slob Homer, the beehived Marge and their offspring Bart, Lisa and the infant Maggie, were given a thirteen-episode series of half-hour slots, which premiered in January 1990. First receiving mixed reviews, the show soon became one of the hottest marketing properties of the decade.

1 **Eat my shorts!**

Bart Simpson, in *The Simpsons* (TV cartoon, from 1987)

2 **D'oh!**

Homer Simpson's habitual expression of exasperation, in ibid.

## Andrei Andreyevich Gromyko (1909–89)

SOVIET STATESMAN AND DIPLOMAT

He was Soviet Ambassador to America from 1943, taking part in the 'big three' conferences of Teheran, Yalta and Potsdam, and as United Nations representative (1946–9) he exercised his right of veto no fewer than twenty-five times. While Foreign Minister (1957–85) during the Cold War he maintained his dour and humourless demeanour. He was President of the USSR (1985–8).

1 **Greece is a sort of American vassal; the Netherlands is the country of American bases that grow like tulip bulbs; Cuba is the main sugar plantation of the American monopolies; Turkey is prepared to kow-tow before any United States pro-consul and Canada is the boring second fiddle in the American symphony.**

*New York Herald Tribune* 30 June 1953

## Walter Gropius (1883–1969)

GERMAN ARCHITECT

An early pioneer of the International Style, he was a co-founder and Director of the Bauhaus School of Design (1919–28) and Professor of Architecture at Harvard (1938–52). By using modern techniques and materials (glass, metals and textiles), he aimed to bridge 'the gap between the rigid mentality of the businessman and technologist and the imagination of the creative artist'.

1 **Architects, painters, and sculptors must recognize anew and learn to grasp the composite character of a building both as an entity and in its separate parts. Only then will their work be imbued with the architectonic spirit which it has lost as 'salon art' . . . Together let us desire, conceive, and create the new structure of the future, which will embrace architecture and sculpture and painting in one unity and which will one day rise toward heaven from the hands of a million workers like the crystal symbol of a new faith.**

'The Bauhaus Proclamation April 1919', repr. in *The Bauhaus*, ch. 2 (1962) by Hans Wingler

## George Grosz (1893–1959)

GERMAN ARTIST

A member of the Berlin Dadaists in the post-First World War period, he produced vitriolic satirical drawings criticizing German social mores, government, militarism and Nazism, work that has been described as the 'most definitive catalogue of man's depravity

in all history'. In 1932 he fled Berlin and in 1938 became a naturalized US citizen.

1 **The bourgeoisie and the petty bourgeoisie have armed themselves against the rising proletariat with, among other things, 'culture'. It's an old ploy of the bourgeoisie. They keep a standing 'art' to defend their collapsing culture.**

'The Art Scab' (written with John Heartfield), first publ. in *Der Gegner*, vol. 1, nos. 10–12, 1920, repr. in *Art Is In Danger* (transl. 1987)

2 **The cult of individuality and personality, which promotes painters and poets only to promote itself, is really a business. The greater the 'genius' of the personage, the greater the profit.**

'Instead of a Biography', first publ. in *Der Gegner*, vol. 2. no. 3, 1920, repr. in ibid.

## John Guare (b. 1938)

US PLAYWRIGHT

Describing himself in one of his own plays as 'the world's oldest living promising young playwright', he wrote black comedies about modern America, such as *The House of Blue Leaves* (1972) and *Bosoms of Neglect* (1979), as well as historical plays.

1 **Avoiding humiliation is the core of tragedy and comedy.**

*Independent* 17 October 1988

2 **We live in a world where amnesia is the most wished-for state. When did history become a bad word?**

*International Herald Tribune* 13 June 1990

3 **Show business offers more solid promises than Catholicism.**

*Independent* 25 April 1992

## Bob Guccione (b. 1930)

US PUBLISHER

Chiefly identified with the magazine *Penthouse*, which he founded in 1965, he is the publisher of a range of magazines, including *Omni* and the *Saturday Review*. He also produced the film *Caligula* in 1979.

1 **You have to penetrate a woman's defenses. Getting into her head is a prerequisite to getting into her body.**

Interview in *Speaking Frankly* (1978) by Wendy Leigh

2 **If I were asked for a one line answer to the question 'What makes a woman good in bed?' I would say, 'A man who is good in bed.'**

ibid.

## Philip Guedalla (1889–1944)

BRITISH AUTHOR

A writer with a taste for the epigram, he believed that historical works should be entertaining as well as conscientious. His books include *Palmerston* (1926), *The Hundred Days* (1934) and *The Hundred Years* (1936), which anticipated the centenary of Queen Victoria's accession.

1 **History repeats itself. Historians repeat each other.**

*Supers and Supermen*, 'Some Historians' (1920)

2 **The work of Henry James has always seemed divisible by a simple dynastic arrangement into three reigns: James I, James II, and the Old Pretender.**

ibid. 'Some Critics'

3 **Any stigma, as the old saying is, will serve to beat a dogma.**

*Masters and Men*, 'Ministers of State' (1923)

4 **Biography is a very definite region bounded on the north**

by history, on the south by fiction, on the east by obituary, and on the west by tedium.

Quoted in the *Observer* 3 March 1929

## 'Che' Guevara (1928–67)

ARGENTINIAN REVOLUTIONARY LEADER

Full name Ernesto Guevara de la Serna. The most iconized figure of the twentieth century was second in command to FIDEL CASTRO during the Cuban revolution of 1959, subsequently holding government posts under him. Leaving Cuba in 1965, he became a guerrilla leader in South America and was captured and executed in Bolivia.

1 When asked whether or not we are Marxists, our position is the same as that of a physicist or a biologist who is asked if he is a 'Newtonian', or if he is a 'Pasteurian'.

   'We Are Practical Revolutionaries', publ. in *Verde Olivo* 8 October 1960, repr. in *Venceremos!: The Speeches and Writings of Ernesto Che Guevara* (ed. John Gerassi, 1968)

2 Many will call me an adventurer, and I am, but of a different kind – one who risks his skin in order to prove his convictions.

   Letter, 1965, publ. in ibid. From his last letter to his parents before leaving Cuba to set up guerrilla forces in Bolivia.

3 Let me say, with the risk of appearing ridiculous, that the true revolutionary is guided by strong feelings of love. It is impossible to think of an authentic revolutionary without this quality.

   'Socialism and Man in Cuba', open letter to the editor of a Uruguayan newspaper *La Marcha*, 1967, publ. in *Che Guevara on Revolution* (ed. Jay Mallin, 1969)

## Hervé Guibert (1955–91)

FRENCH AUTHOR AND PHOTOGRAPHER

A photo critic for *Le Monde* and editor and photographer for *L'Autre Journal*, he also wrote novels, for example *Les Aveugles* (1985). A collection of his photographs, *Ghost Image*, was published in 1996, after his death from AIDS.

1 AIDS was . . . an illness in stages, a very long flight of steps that led assuredly to death, but whose every step represented a unique apprenticeship. It was a disease that gave death time to live and its victims time to die, time to discover time, and in the end to discover life.

   *To the Friend Who Did Not Save My Life*, ch. 61 (1991)

## Texas Guinan (1884–1933)

US ACTRESS

Original name Mary Louise Cecilia Guinan. With the catch-phrase 'Hello, sucker!' she was a celebrated nightclub hostess of speakeasies in the 1920s and as such the subject of repeated raids by Prohibition agents trying to enforce unpopular liquor laws. She was remembered for introducing the greatest dance team at the time, George Raft and his brother Dick at her 300 Club.

1 Fifty million Frenchmen can't be wrong.

   Catch-phrase in the 1920s. This was already a popular saying among US soldiers during the First World War and possibly dates from earlier. It was the title of a song recorded by SOPHIE TUCKER in 1927, of COLE PORTER's first Broadway hit (1929) and of a 1931 film.

## Nubar Gulbenkian (1896–1972)

BRITISH OIL TYCOON AND SOCIALITE

Son of Calouste Gulbenkian, who established the Gulbenkian Foundation, he worked for his father and was Commercial Attaché to the Iranian Embassy (1926–51 and 1956–65).

1 The best number for a dinner party is two – myself and a dam' good head waiter.

   *Daily Telegraph* 14 January 1965

## Thom Gunn (b. 1929)

BRITISH POET

Initially regarded as a Movement poet, his style became freer on his move to California in 1954. He has written on his homosexuality in *The Passage of Joy* (1982) and the AIDS epidemic in *The Man with Night Sweats* (1992).

1 I prod, you react. Thus to and fro
   We turn, to see ourselves perform the same
   Comical acts inside the tragic game.
   'Carnal Knowledge', publ. in *Fighting Terms* (1954)

2 No plausible nostalgia, no brown shame,
   I had when treating with my enemies.
   And always when a living impulse came
   I acted, and my action made me wise.
   *And I regretted nothing.*
   'Incident on a Journey', publ. in ibid.

3 On motorcycles, up the road, they come:
   Small, black, as flies hanging in heat, the Boys,
   Until the distance throws them forth, their hum
   Bulges to thunder held by calf and thigh.
   In goggles, donned impersonality,
   In gleaming jackets trophied with the dust,
   They strap in doubt – by hiding it, robust –
   And almost hear a meaning in their noise.
   'On the Move', publ. in *The Sense of Movement* (1957)

4 Distorting hackneyed words in hackneyed songs
   He turns revolt into a style, prolongs
   The impulse to a habit of the time.
   'Elvis Presley', publ. in ibid. The poem gave GEORGE MELLY the title for his study of the pop arts in Britain, *Revolt into Style* (1970).

5 My thoughts are crowded with death
   and it draws so oddly on the sexual
   that I am confused
   confused to be attracted
   by, in effect, my own annihilation.
   'In Time of Plague', publ. in *The Man With Night Sweats* (1992)

## John Gunther (1901–70)

US JOURNALIST AND AUTHOR

He became known for his series of analyses of countries that began with the bestselling *Inside Europe* (1936), social studies that combine first-hand insights with documentary material.

1 Ours is the only country deliberately founded on a good idea.

   *Inside USA*, Foreword (1947)

## George Gurdjieff (c. 1877–1949)

GREEK-ARMENIAN RELIGIOUS TEACHER AND MYSTIC

Original name George S. Georgiades. He founded the first of his Institutes for the Harmonious Development of Man in Moscow (1912), where he propounded a system of raising consciousness called the Fourth Way, which involved group movement, manual work and a minimum of sleep.

1 A man can only attain knowledge with the help of those who possess it. This must be understood from the very beginning. *One must learn from him who knows.*

   Quoted in *In Search of the Miraculous*, ch. 2 (1949) by P.D. Ouspensky

2 A considerable percentage of the people we meet on the street are people who are empty inside, that is, they are actually *already dead*. It is fortunate for us that we do not see and do not know it. If we knew what a number of people are actually dead and what a number of these dead people govern our lives, we should go mad with horror.

   Quoted in ibid., ch. 8

3 **A man may be born, but in order to be born he must first die, and in order to die he must first awake.**

Quoted in ibid. ch. 11. Gurdjieff continued: 'If a man dies without having been awakened he cannot be born. If a man is born without having died he may become an "immortal thing". Thus the fact that he has not "died" prevents a man from being "born"; the fact of his not having awakened prevents him from "dying"; and should he be born without having died he is prevented from "being".'

4 **A man will renounce any pleasures you like but he will not give up his suffering.**

Quoted in ibid. ch. 13

5 **Every ceremony or rite has a value if it is performed without alteration. A ceremony is a book in which a great deal is written. Anyone who understands can read it. One rite often contains more than a hundred books.**

Quoted in ibid. ch. 15

6 **A 'sin' is something which is not necessary.**

Quoted in ibid. ch. 17

## Ivor Gurney (1890–1937)
BRITISH POET AND COMPOSER

After being gassed in the First World War, he published two volumes of poetry from hospital: *Severn and Somme* (1917) and *War's Embers* (1919). He spent the years from 1922 until his death in a mental hospital, leaving poems that reflected a love of his native Gloucestershire, as well as some 300 songs.

1 **There are strange hells within the minds war made**
**Not so often, not so humiliatingly afraid**
**As one would have expected – the racket and fear guns**
**made.**

'Strange Hells' (1919–22), publ. in *Collected Poems* (1982)

2 **Fierce indignation is best understood by those**
**Who have time or no fear, or a hope in its real good.**
**One loses it with a filed soul or in sentimental mood.**

'Sonnet – September 1922', publ. in ibid.

3 **And more than he,**
**I paid the prices of life**
**Standing where Rome immortal heard October's strife,**
**A war poet whose right of honour cuts falsehood like a**
**knife.**

'Poem for End' (1922–5), publ. in ibid.

4 **Only, who thought of England as two thousand years**
**Must keep of today's life the proper anger and fears:**
**England that was paid for by building and ploughing**
**and tears.**

ibid.

## Arlo Guthrie (b. 1947)
US SINGER AND SONGWRITER

Son of WOODY GUTHRIE, he became known as the 'new crown prince of folk music' after the song 'Alice's Restaurant' (1967), from which a film was made (1969). He was active in festivals and protest marches in the 1960s and 1970s and later converted to Catholicism. In 1992 he purchased the Old Trinity House in Housatonic, Massachusetts, where he wrote 'Alice' and where the movie was filmed, converting it into a 'community centre'. 'I'm just your average small town monk with a church, have been for years,' he said.

1 **You can get anything you want at Alice's Restaurant.**

'Alice's Restaurant Massacree' (song), on the album *Alice's Restaurant* (1967)

2 **Coming into Los Angeles, bringing in a couple of keys,**
**Don't touch my bags, if you please, Mister Customs**
**Man.**

'Coming into Los Angeles' (song) on the album *Running Down the Road* (1969)

## Woody Guthrie (1912–67)
US SINGER AND SONGWRITER

Full name Woodrow Wilson Guthrie. He travelled the road during the Depression, gathering many of the 'Dust Bowl ballads' that he would later perform on radio and composing his own. His support for left-wing causes prevented him from gaining greater recognition, but there was a revival of interest in his music in the 1960s. His autobiography, *Bound For Glory* (1943), was turned into a biopic in 1976.

1 **This land is your land, this land is my land,**
**From California to the New York Island.**
**From the redwood forest to the Gulf Stream waters**
**This land was made for you and me.**

'This Land Is Your Land' (song, 1956). The song is said to have been written in response to Irving Berlin's patriotic hymn, 'God Bless America' (see IRVING BERLIN 1). In *Tarantula* (1970) BOB DYLAN wrote: 'This land is your land and this land is my land – sure, but the world is run by those that never listen to music anyway.'

## J.S. Habgood (b. 1927)

BRITISH ECCLESIASTIC

Archbishop of York 1983–95, he was unashamedly liberal in his stance. Among his published works are *Church and Nation in a Secular Age* (1983) and *Confessions of a Conservative Liberal* (1988).

1 [Of extreme feminists] **Movements born in hatred very quickly take on the characteristics of the thing they oppose.**
   Quoted in the *Observer* 4 May 1986

2 **All knowledge is ambiguous.**
   *Observer* 14 April 1991

## Jean Hagen (1924–77)

US ACTRESS

Original name Jean Verhagen. She was a comedy actress, known for her screen roles, as in *Adam's Rib* (1949), and as the 'silent star with the ghastly voice' in *Singin' in the Rain* (1952).

1 **If we bring a little joy into your humdrum lives, it makes us feel our work ain't been in vain for nothin'.**
   Lina Lamont ( Jean Hagen), in *Singin' in the Rain* (film musical, 1952, screenplay by Betty Comden and Adolph Green, directed by Gene Kelly and Stanley Donen)

2 **Talent is an amalgam of high sensitivity; easy vulnerability; high sensory equipment (seeing, hearing, touching, smelling, tasting – *intensely*); a vivid imagination as well as a grip on reality; the desire to communicate one's own experience and sensations, to make one's self heard and seen.**
   *Respect for Acting*, pt 1, ch. 1 (1973)

## Merle Haggard (b. 1937)

US COUNTRY MUSICIAN

As a prisoner in San Quentin he joined the prison band after seeing JOHNNY CASH perform there in 1958. He pursued a recording career after his release, notching up more than twenty-five country hits, mostly dealing with hard drinking, hard living and blue-collar issues. He reached a wider audience with such numbers as 'The Fighting Side of Me' (1970) and 'If We Make It Through December' (1974).

1 **I'm proud to be an Okie from Muskogee**
   **A place where even squares can have a ball.**
   'Okie From Muskogee' (song, 1969, written by Merle Haggard and Phil Ochs). Although a tongue-in-cheek homage to provincial American values, this song and its follow-up, 'The Fighting Side of Me' (1970), won Haggard a new right-wing audience and a reputation for being President NIXON's favourite country singer.

## William Hague (b. 1961)

BRITISH POLITICIAN

With an early interest in politics, memorably addressing the Conservative Party Conference when he was sixteen years old, he became an MP in 1989 and leader of the opposition in 1997. The right-wing Tory MP John Redwood, demoted from the shadow cabinet in 1999, disparagingly referred to his 'unredeemable trainspotting vacuity overlaid by the gloss of management theory'.

1 [Of 'the British way'] **Not just sleepy villages, polite manners, friendly vicars, and the novels of Scott and Austen . . . but also the ambitious, the bold, the brassy, the vigorous, the exciting, the leading world nation that we are and can be.**
   Speech to Centre for Policy Studies, quoted in the *Daily Telegraph* 19 January 1999

2 **If all we had needed to govern the country was someone**

who repeated everything we'd said before, we could have bought a parrot.

Speech at Conservative Party Conference in Blackpool, 7 October 1999, quoted in the *Guardian* 8 October 1999

## Peter Hain (b. 1950)
BRITISH POLITICAL ACTIVIST AND POLITICIAN

After his family were forced to leave South Africa and came to Britain in 1966, he fought against apartheid as leader of the Young Liberals, raising media coverage in a campaign that was targeted particularly against sports events. He was elected Labour MP for Neath in 1991 and became Minister of Foreign Affairs in 1999.

1 A sporting system is the by-product of society and its political system, and it is just boyhood dreaming to suppose you can ever take politics out of sport.

*Observer* 2 May 1971

## J.B.S. Haldane (1892–1964)
BRITISH SCIENTIST

Full name John Burdon Sanderson Haldane. Researching population genetics and the mathematics of natural selection, he worked first at University College, London (1937–57), and then at Orissa, India, where he emigrated in 1957. His popular works include *Possible Worlds* (1927) and *Science in Everyday Life* (1939).

1 Until politics are a branch of science we shall do well to regard political and social reforms as experiments rather than short-cuts to the millennium.

*Possible Worlds and Other Essays*, 'Science and Politics' (1927)

2 While I do not suggest that humanity will ever be able to dispense with its martyrs, I cannot avoid the suspicion that with a little more thought and a little less belief their number may be substantially reduced.

ibid. 'The Duty of Doubt'

3 The wise man regulates his conduct by the theories both of religion and science. But he regards these theories not as statements of ultimate fact but as art-forms.

ibid. 'Science and Theology as Art-Forms'. Closing words of essay.

4 My own suspicion is that the Universe is not only queerer than we suppose, but queerer than we *can* suppose.

ibid. 'Possible Worlds'

5 In fact, words are well adapted for description and the arousing of emotion, but for many kinds of precise thought other symbols are much better.

*The Inequality of Man*, 'God-Makers' (1932)

6 A fairly bright boy is far more intelligent and far better company than the average adult.

Quoted in *The New York Times* 13 June 1948

7 I wish I had the voice of Homer
To sing of rectal carcinoma.

'Cancer's a Funny Thing', publ. in *New Statesman* 21 February 1964. Opening lines of a poem describing Haldane's colostomy. 'The main functions of my rhyme,' Haldane wrote, 'were to induce cancer patients to be operated on early and to be cheerful about it.'

8 I'd lay down my life for two brothers or eight cousins.

Attributed in *New Scientist* 8 August 1974

## H.R. Haldeman (1926–93)
US WHITE HOUSE OFFICIAL

Full name Harry Robbins Haldeman. He was White House Chief of Staff during President NIXON's administration (1969–73), earning the nickname 'the Iron Chancellor'. His involvement in the Watergate cover-up resulted in conviction for perjury, conspiracy and obstruction of justice, for which he was given an eighteenth-month prison sentence.

1 Once the toothpaste is out of the tube, it is awfully hard to get it back in.

Remark to John Dean, 8 April 1973, publ. in *Hearings Before the Select Committee on Presidential Campaign Activities of U.S. Senate: Watergate and Related Activities*, vol. 4 (1973). Referring to the exposure of the White House's involvement in the bugging of the Watergate building.

## Nancy Hale (b. 1908)
US WRITER AND EDITOR

In 1935 she became *The New York Times*'s first woman reporter. She published short stories, memoirs and novels, of which *The Prodigal Women* (1942), a study of motherhood and identity, was a bestseller.

1 The best work of artists in any age is the work of innocence liberated by technical knowledge.

*Mary Cassatt: A Biography of the Great American Painter*, pt 2, ch. 7 (1975)

## Alex Haley (1921–92)
US AUTHOR

His work depicts the struggles of African-Americans. The *Autobiography of Malcolm X* (1965) has become a classic of black American literature, but he is best known for *Roots: The Saga of an American Family* (1976), documenting the history of seven generations. In 1977 it was turned into an immensely popular TV series and won a Pulitzer Prize the following year.

1 It is rightly said that when a griot dies, it is as if a library has burned to the ground. The griots symbolize how all human ancestry goes back to some place, and some time, where there was no writing. Then, the memories and the mouths of ancient elders was the only way that early histories of mankind got passed along . . . for all of us today to know who we are.

*Roots*, 'Acknowledgements' (1976). Referring to the transmitters of oral history in West African villages.

## Bill Haley (1925–81)
US ROCK MUSICIAN

Responsible more than anyone for popularizing rock 'n' roll, Haley initially performed cowboy songs and western swing, but his composition 'Crazy Man Crazy' (1953) by Bill Haley and His Comets was the first record considered 'rock and roll' to enter Billboard's pop chart. However, it was 'Rock Around the Clock' (1954) that catapulted him to global fame, and his follow-ups 'Shake, Rattle and Roll' (1954), 'Mambo Rock' (1955) and 'See You Later Alligator' (1956) also sold well. After 1956 he was eclipsed by younger, more rebellious rock stars.

1 One-two-three o'clock, four o'clock rock!
Five-six-seven o'clock, eight o'clock rock!
Nine-ten-eleven o'clock, twelve o'clock rock!
We're gonna rock around the clock tonight!

'Rock Around the Clock' (song, 1954, written by Max Freedman and 'Jimmy De Knight', pseudonym of Haley's publisher James Myers) by Bill Haley and His Comets. The song was a minor hit in 1952 for Sunny Dae but became the biggest hit of the rock 'n' roll era for Haley when his recording was adopted as the title music to the film *Blackboard Jungle* (1955), selling more than 25 million copies. The 1956 film *Rock Around the Clock* featured this and Haley's other hits and caused riots in cinemas when the song was played.

2 Shake, rattle and roll.

Title of song (1954, written by Charles Calhoun). Originally a hit for 'blues-shouter' Big Joe Turner, it was the first hit for Bill Haley and His Comets.

3 See you later, alligator,
After 'while, crocodile;
Can't you see you're in my way, now,

**Don't you know you cramp my style?**
'See You Later Alligator' (song, 1956, written by Charles Calhoun). The record was Haley's last US top-ten hit.

## Gus Hall (b. 1910)
US POLITICAL ACTIVIST

A communist since his youth, he was imprisoned for subversive activities (1951–7) and became General Secretary of the Communist Party of the USA in 1959. Among his many books are *Karl Marx* (1983) and *Fighting Racism* (1985). He was candidate for the US presidency four times.

1 *Perestroika* basically is creating material incentives for the individual. Some of the comrades deny that, but I can't see it any other way. In that sense human nature kinda goes backwards. It's a step backwards. You have to realize the people weren't quite ready for a socialist production system.
Interview in the *Independent* 19 May 1990

## Jerry Hall (b. 1956)
US MODEL AND ACTRESS

The ex-wife of Mick Jagger, she has been a contributing editor to the *Tatler* and a judge for the Whitbread Book Awards in 1999, as well as modelling fashions. Her acting career includes roles in the films *Urban Cowboy* (1980) and *Batman* (1989).

1 My mother said it was simple to keep a man, you must be a maid in the living room, a cook in the kitchen and a whore in the bedroom. I said I'd hire the other two and take care of the bedroom bit.
Quoted in the *Observer* 6 October 1985

## (Sir) Peter Hall (b. 1930)
BRITISH THEATRE, OPERA AND FILM DIRECTOR

He was responsible for establishing the Royal Shakespeare Company as a permanent company, was a key player in the formation of the National Theatre, has directed opera and films and was appointed Artistic Director of Glyndebourne in 1984. 'We caused a revolution in the speaking of Shakespeare's verse,' he said of his work at the RSC, 'and, at the gate of heaven, if I was asked to justify myself, I would say that is the best thing I've done in my life.'

1 Theatres have to be run on obsession.
Quoted in the *Observer* 10 August 1986

2 The English hate the arts because they are so good at them. It's the great paradox.
Quoted in the *Observer* 7 September 1997

## Radclyffe Hall (1883–1943)
BRITISH NOVELIST

Full name Marguerite Radclyffe Hall. She is best remembered for her novel *The Well of Loneliness* (1928), banned in Britain for many years because of its open treatment of lesbianism. It was republished in 1949.

1 You're neither unnatural, nor abominable, nor mad; you're as much a part of what people call nature as anyone else; only you're unexplained as yet – you've not got your niche in creation.
*The Well of Loneliness*, bk 2, ch. 20, sect. 3 (1928). These are the words that 'Puddle' (the tutor, Miss Puddleton) resolves to say to the book's lesbian heroine, Stephen Gordon. The book was temporarily suspended in the USA and, after a notorious trial, was banned in Britain, where the editor of the *Sunday Express* wrote that he 'would sooner give a healthy boy or girl a dose of prussic acid than a copy of it'.

2 I am one of those whom God marked on the forehead.

Like Cain, I am marked and blemished. If you come to me . . . the world will abhor you, will persecute you, will call you unclean. Our love may be faithful even unto death and beyond – yet the world will call it unclean.
Stephen, in ibid. ch. 37, sect. 3

## Margaret Halsey (b. 1910)
US AUTHOR

She called herself both a 'humorist and a moral positivist', writing on topics ranging from racism and neglect of children to the foibles of the English. Her works include *With Malice Toward Some* (1938) and *The Folks at Home* (1952).

1 The boneless quality of English conversation, which, so far as I have heard it, is all form and no content. Listening to Britons dining out is like watching people play first-class tennis with imaginary balls.
*With Malice Toward Some*, pt 1, 'June 12' (1938)

2 Humility is not my forte, and whenever I dwell for any length of time on my own shortcomings, they gradually begin to seem mild, harmless, rather engaging little things, not at all like the staring defects in other people's characters.
ibid. pt 1, 'June 15'

3 Englishwomen's shoes look as if they had been made by someone who had often heard shoes described, but had never seen any.
ibid. pt 2

## Edith Hamilton (1867–1963)
US CLASSICAL SCHOLAR AND TRANSLATOR

She was Bryn Mawr Fellow in Latin (1894–5) and headmistress of Bryn Mawr preparatory school in Baltimore (1896–1922). Devoted to classical studies, she published *The Greek Way* (1930), *The Roman Way* (1932) and translations of classical myths in *Mythology* (1942).

1 The anthropologists are busy, indeed, and ready to transport us back into the savage forest where all human things . . . have their beginnings; but the seed never explains the flower.
*The Greek Way*, ch. 1 (1930)

2 There are few efforts more conducive to humility than that of the translator trying to communicate an incommunicable beauty. Yet, unless we do try, something unique and never surpassed will cease to exist except in the libraries of a few inquisitive book lovers.
*Three Greek Plays*, Introduction (1937)

## Richard Hamilton (b. 1922)
BRITISH ARTIST

He was a pioneer of Pop art in Britain, introducing the genre with the collage 'Just What Is It That Makes Today's Homes So Different, So Appealing?' (1956), exhibited at Tübingen in Germany. His ideas are articulately expressed in his *Collected Words 1953–82*.

1 If the artist is not to lose much of his ancient purpose he may have to plunder the popular arts to recover the imagery which is his rightful inheritance.
'For the Finest Art Try – POP', first publ. in *Gazette* no. 1, 1961, repr. in *Collected Words 1953–1982* (1982)

2 Any interior is a set of anachronisms, a museum with the lingering residues of decorative styles that an inhabited space collects. Banal or beautiful, exquisite or sordid, each says a lot about its owner and something about humanity in general.
'Interiors', publ. in *Vanguard* September 1978, repr. in ibid.

# James Hamilton-Paterson (b. 1941)

BRITISH AUTHOR

He won plaudits for his first novel *Gerontius* (1989) and for *The Ghosts of Manila* (1994). As well as poetry and short story collections, he has published explorations of the sea that are both scientific and literary, notably *Seven Tenths: The Sea and its Thresholds* (1992).

1 To name something is to take control of it. It could be argued that the Old Testament story of Genesis was less a matter of creation than of naming, of God taking control of chaos.

*Seven-Tenths: The Sea and its Thresholds*, ch. 1, sect. 2 (1992)

2 There is a psychological accuracy in this insistence that a proper life cannot be lived without pilgrimage, a journey, a great excursion and abandoning of towns, village, hearth. Only in this way is the unsuspected majesty of the world revealed.

ibid. ch. 7, sect. 2

# Dag Hammarskjöld (1905–61)

SWEDISH STATESMAN

Describing himself as the 'curator of the secrets of 82 nations', he was Secretary-General of the United Nations (1953–61), during which time he opposed Britain over the Suez crisis (1956) and initiated peace moves in the Middle East (1957–8). He was posthumously awarded the Nobel Peace Prize in 1961 after his death in a plane crash in Zambia, where he was attempting to mediate in the Congo crisis.

1 We are not permitted to choose the frame of our destiny. But what we put into it is ours.

Note written 1950, publ. in *Markings*, 'Night is Drawing Nigh' (1964)

2 The U.N. is not just a product of do-gooders. It is harshly real. The day will come when men will see the U.N. and what it means clearly. Everything will be all right – you know when? When people, just people, stop thinking of the United Nations as a weird Picasso abstraction, and see it as a drawing they made themselves.

*Time* magazine 27 June 1955

3 In our era, the road to holiness necessarily passes through the world of action.

Note written 1955, publ. in *Markings*, 'Night is Drawing Nigh' (1964)

4 Your body must become familiar with its death – in all its possible forms and degrees – as a self-evident, imminent, and emotionally neutral step on the way towards the goal you have found worthy of your life.

Note written 1957, publ. in ibid.

5 I don't know Who – or what – put the question, I don't know when it was put. I don't even remember answering. But at some moment I did answer *Yes* to Someone – or Something – and from that hour I was certain that existence is meaningful and that, therefore, my life, in self-surrender, had a goal.

Note written Whit Sunday 1961, publ. in ibid.

# Oscar Hammerstein II (1895–1960)

US SONGWRITER

He collaborated with the composers Sigmund Romberg and Jerome Kern in, for instance, *Show Boat* (1927), but mainly with Richard Rodgers with whom he formed a sixteen-year partnership. Together they produced some of the best known American musicals, such as *Oklahoma!* (1943) and *South Pacific* (1949), both of which won Pulitzer Prizes.

1 Ol' man river, dat ol' man river,
He must know sumpin', but don't say nothin'

He just keeps rollin',
He keeps on rollin' along.

'Ol' Man River' (song, with music by Jerome Kern) in the stage musical *Show Boat* (1927, filmed 1936 and 1951)

2 The last time I saw Paris
Her heart was warm and gay,
I heard the laughter of her heart in every street café.

'The Last Time I Saw Paris' (song, with music by Jerome Kern) in the film *Lady Be Good* (1941). Hammerstein's last major collaboration with Jerome Kern was inspired by news of the German occupation of Paris and won an Oscar. The movie bears no relation to the stage musical of the same name, scored by GEORGE GERSHWIN in 1924.

3 Oh, what a beautiful mornin',
Oh, what a beautiful day!
I got a beautiful feelin'
Ev'rything's goin' my way.

'Oh, What a Beautiful Mornin'' (song, with music by Richard Rodgers) in *Oklahoma!* (stage musical 1943, film 1955)

4 The corn is as high as an elephant's eye,
And it looks like it's climbin' clear up to the sky.

ibid.

5 June is bustin' out all over.

'June is Bustin' Out All Over' (song, with music by Richard Rodgers) in *Carousel* (stage musical 1945, film 1956)

6 You'll never walk alone.

'You'll Never Walk Alone', ibid. Recorded at various times by JUDY GARLAND, FRANK SINATRA and Gerry and the Pacemakers, the song has been adopted by crowds at British football matches, chiefly associated with Liverpool FC.

7 Some enchanted evening,
You may see a stranger,
You may see a stranger,
Across a crowded room.

'Some Enchanted Evening' (song, with music by Richard Rodgers) in *South Pacific* (stage musical, 1949, film, 1958)

8 I'm gonna wash that man right out of my hair.

'I'm Gonna Wash That Man Right Out of My Hair', ibid.

9 The hills are alive with the sound of music.

'The Sound of Music' (song, with music by Richard Rodgers) in *The Sound of Music* (stage musical, 1959, film, 1965)

10 Climb every mountain, ford every stream
Follow every rainbow, till you find your dream!

'Climb Every Mountain', ibid.

# Dashiell Hammett (1894–1961)

US CRIME WRITER

Formerly a Pinkerton detective agent, he was responsible for introducing the 'hard-boiled' school of crime fiction. Many of his successful books are better known as films, for example *The Maltese Falcon* (1930, filmed 1941) and *The Thin Man* (1932, filmed 1934). He lived with LILLIAN HELLMAN in the later part of his life, and together they were persecuted for their left-wing views during the McCarthy era.

1 When a man's partner is killed he's supposed to do something about it. It doesn't make any difference what you thought of him. He was your partner, and you're supposed to do something about it.

Sam Spade, in *The Maltese Falcon*, 'If They Hang You' (1930). The words are spoken thus by HUMPHREY BOGART in the movie *The Maltese Falcon*, scripted and directed by JOHN HUSTON (1941).

# Katharine Hamnett (b. 1947)

BRITISH FASHION DESIGNER

Her designs are noted for their loose lines and use of natural fabrics and are executed by her own company, which she established in 1979. Known for her support of CND, she famously wore a T-shirt with the slogan '58% don't want Pershing' for an audience with MARGARET THATCHER in 1984. In 1998 she joined the Conservative Party because of her opposition to EMU and Labour's policy on China.

1 The origins of clothing are not practical. They are mystical and erotic. The primitive man in the wolf-pelt was not keeping dry; he was saying: 'Look what I killed. Aren't I the best?'

*Independent on Sunday* 10 March 1991

## Christopher Hampton (b. 1946)
BRITISH PLAYWRIGHT

He was the first resident playwright at London's Royal Court Theatre, where most of his plays have been produced. Highly regarded for his *Tales from Hollywood* (1982), he scored his greatest success with *Les Liaisons Dangereuses* (1985, filmed 1998), an adaptation of the novel by Pierre Choderlos de Laclos. Earlier works include *The Philanthropist* (1970) and *Treats* (1976).

1 I have always thought of sophistication as rather a feeble substitute for decadence.

Braham, in *The Philanthropist*, sc. 3 (1970)

2 Masturbation is the thinking man's television.

ibid.

3 A great number of the disappointments and mishaps of the troubled world are the direct result of literature and the allied arts. It is our belief that no human being who devotes his life and energy to the manufacture of fantasies can be anything but fundamentally inadequate.

Celia, in ibid. sc. 5

4 I always divide people into two groups. Those who live by what they know to be a lie, and those who live by what they believe, falsely, to be the truth.

Don, in ibid.

5 If I had to give a definition of capitalism I would say: the process whereby American girls turn into American women.

Carlos, in *Savages*, sc. 16 (1974)

6 Asking a working writer what he thinks about critics is like asking a lamp-post what it feels about dogs.

*Sunday Times* 16 October 1977

## Han Suyin (b. 1917)
CHINESE-BORN BRITISH AUTHOR

Born Elizabeth Chow, changed name to Elizabeth Comber and wrote as Han Suyin. In 1939 she settled in England, where she trained as a doctor and wrote numerous works of fiction and history. Her autobiographical novel *A Many-Splendored Thing* (1952) was filmed as *Love is A Many-Splendored Thing* (1955), and she later wrote *China*, an autobiography in six volumes, the first of which, *The Crippled Tree*, was published in 1965

1 Exploitation and oppression is not a matter of *race*. It is the system, the apparatus of world-wide brigandage called imperialism, which made the Powers behave the way they did. I have no illusions on this score, nor do I believe that any Asian nation or African nation, in the same state of dominance, and with the same system of colonial profit-amassing and plunder, would have behaved otherwise.

*The Crippled Tree*, pt 1, ch. 9 (1965)

## Tony Hancock (1924–68)
BRITISH COMEDIAN

He was renowned as the pompous and lugubrious misfit with a sardonic wit in *Hancock's Half-Hour*, first on radio (1954–9), then on television (1956–61). His later declining popularity combined with chronic alcoholism contributed to his suicide. J.B. PRIESTLEY

described him as 'a comedian with a touch of genius who had no enemy except himself'.

1 It's red hot, mate. I hate to think of this sort of book getting in the wrong hands. As soon as I've finished this, I shall recommend they ban it.

'The Missing Page', broadcast 26 February 1960, in *Hancock's Half-Hour* (BBC TV series written by Ray Galton and Alan Simpson, 1956–61)

2 I don't mind giving them a reasonable amount, but a pint . . . why that's very nearly an armful.

'The Blood Donor', broadcast 23 June 1961, in ibid.

3 The secret of my work is a knowledge of what constitutes living in general, I think. You take the weaknesses of your own character and of other people's characters and you exploit them. You show yourself up, and you show them up.

Interview with John Freeman on *Face to Face* (BBC TV), quoted in *Hancock's Half-Hour*, a book of scripts, epigraph (1974) by Ray Galton and Alan Simpson

## Peter Handke (b. 1942)
AUSTRIAN NOVELIST, PLAYWRIGHT AND DIRECTOR

An abrasive writer who spurns the German literary canon, he set the tone of much of his later writing with his first play, *Insulting the Audience* (1966), an example of anti-theatre writing that alternately abuses and praises the audience. His story *The Goalie's Anxiety at the Penalty Kick* (1970) was filmed by WIM WENDERS in 1972, initiating a collaboration that included *Wings of Desire* (1989), for which Handke wrote the screenplay. He also wrote and directed the film *The Left-Handed Woman* (1977), adapted from his own novel.

1 Fiction, inventing an event as a vehicle for my information about the world, is no longer necessary, it is just a hindrance. Progress in literature in general seems to me to consist of a gradual removal of unnecessary fictions. More and more vehicles fall away, the story becomes unnecessary. It is more to do with the imparting of experiences, verbal and non-verbal, and it is no longer necessary to invent a story for that.

*I Am an Inhabitant of an Ivory Tower* (1967)

2 If a nation loses its storytellers, it loses its childhood.

*Independent* 9 June 1988

3 If Thomas Mann counts as the greatest German writer of this century, writing makes no sense at all. Anyone who follows him is already lost as far as I'm concerned.

Quoted in the *Guardian* 13 August 1994

## Terry Hands (b. 1941)
BRITISH THEATRE AND OPERA DIRECTOR

He co-founded the Everyman Theatre in Liverpool, then with TREVOR NUNN became joint Artistic Director of the Royal Shakespeare Company (1978–86) and later Chief Executive (1986–91).

1 We may pretend that we're basically moral people who make mistakes, but the whole of history proves otherwise.

*The Times* 11 August 1992

## Tom Hanks (b. 1956)
US SCREEN ACTOR

A versatile mainstream actor, he came to attention in *Splash* (1984), achieved international success with *Big* (1988) and won Academy Awards for his lead roles in *Philadelphia* (1993) and *Forrest Gump* (1994).

1 The prejudice surrounding AIDS exacts a social death which precedes the actual physical one.

Andrew Beckett (Tom Hanks), in *Philadelphia* (film, 1993,

screenplay by Ron Nyswaner, directed by Jonathan Demme). Hanks is reading a Supreme Court ruling from a previous case.

2 **Stupid is as stupid does.**

Forrest Gump (Tom Hanks) quoting his mother, in *Forrest Gump* (film, 1994, screenplay by Eric Roth based on a novel by Winston Groom, directed by Robert Zemeckis). Forrest Gump habitually repeats his mother's *bons mots*. See also SALLY FIELD 1.

3 **What I do for a living is go to work and pretend I'm somebody else . . . Acting is what I do and, unfortunately I can't do much of anything else. It's this or nothing. I can *pretend* to build automobiles.**

Quoted in *Tom Hanks*, ch. 11 (1995) by Roy Trakin

4 **I do think that a sense of humor gets you much farther in the movies than it does in real life. There was a long period of time where I swear to God being funny just didn't get you laid no matter how funny you were.**

ibid. ch. 15

## William Hanna (b. 1910) and
## Joseph Barbera (b. 1911)
US ANIMATORS

They were the creators of *Tom and Jerry*, hailed as 'the cinema's purest representation of pure energy', for MGM (1937–57) and went on to found their own company, producing semi-animated cartoons such as *Yogi Bear*, *Huckleberry Hound* and *The Flintstones*.

1 **Yabba dabba do!**

Fred Flintstone, in *The Flintstones* (TV cartoon, 1960–66, produced by Hanna and Barbera). Fred Flintstone (voiced by Alan Reed) and Barney Rubble were modelled on Jackie Gleason and Art Carney in the TV sitcom, *The Honeymooners* (1955–71).

## Brian Hanrahan (b. 1949)
BRITISH JOURNALIST

He was BBC Far East correspondent (1983–5), Moscow correspondent (1986–9) and has been a diplomatic correspondent since 1989.

1 **I'm not allowed to say how many planes joined the raid, but I counted them all out, and I counted them all back.**

BBC news report, 1 May 1982, publ. in *'I Counted Them All Out and I Counted Them All Back'*, 'Air Battles' (1982, with Robert Fox). The broadcast from the Falkland Islands described the safe return of British Harriers to HMS *Hermes* after their first attack on the landing strip of Port Stanley.

## Otto Harbach (1873–1963)
US SONGWRITER

A prolific lyricist and librettist, he collaborated with Sigmund Romberg, Jerome Kern and George Gershwin, but failed to achieve fame in his own right. His hits include the musical *No, No, Nanette* (1925) and the song 'Smoke Gets in Your Eyes' (1932).

1 **When a lovely flame dies**
**Smoke gets in your eyes.**

'Smoke Gets in your Eyes' (song, with music by Jerome Kern) in *Roberta* (musical show 1933, film 1935)

## Yip Harburg (1898–1981)
US SONGWRITER

Born Isidore Hochberg, changed to Edgar Y. Harburg. Probably the least celebrated of the great songwriters, he wrote socially conscious and idealistic songs and was also active in civil rights movements. 'Brother, Can You Spare a Dime?' (1932) captured the mood of the Depression, while he conceived his songs for *The Wizard of Oz* (1939) as escapist fantasies. See also JUDY GARLAND 1.

1 **Once I built a railroad,**
**Now it's done,**

**Brother, can you spare a dime?**

'Brother, Can You Spare a Dime?' (song, with music by Jay Gorney), in *Americana* (musical show, 1932). The line has been often rendered, 'Buddy, can you spare a dime?' Asked to re-word the song for *The New York Times* some fifty years later, Harburg came up with: 'Once had depression/But with a dime/A guy wasn't out of luck./Now we've got inflation, drugs and crime./Brother can you spare a buck?'

2 **Say, it's only a paper moon,**
**Sailing over a cardboard sea.**

'It's Only a Paper Moon' (song, written with Billy Rose, music by Harold Arlen) in *The Great Magoo* (stage musical, 1932)

3 **We got no Mussolini, got no Mosley,**
**We got Popeye and Gipsy Rose Lee.**

'God's Country' (song) in *Hooray for What?* (stage musical, 1937). The song also featured in the Busby Berkeley movie *Babes in Arms* (1939), and was covered by FRANK SINATRA and Vic Damone.

4 **Follow the yellow brick road.**

'We're Off to See the Wizard' (song, with music by Harold Arlen), in *The Wizard of Oz* (film, 1939)

5 **We're off to see the Wizard**
**The wonderful Wizard of Oz.**

ibid.

6 **I could while away the hours**
**Conversin' with the flowers,**
**Consultin' with the rain;**
**With the thoughts I'd be thinkin'**
**I could be another Lincoln**
**If I only had a brain . . .**

The Scarecrow (Ray Bolger), singing 'If I Only Had a Brain' (song, with music by Harold Arlen), in ibid.

7 **Wanna cry, wanna croon.**
**Wanna laugh like a loon.**
**It's that Old Devil Moon in your eyes.**

'Old Devil Moon' (song, with music by Burton Lane), in *Finian's Rainbow* (stage musical 1947, filmed 1968)

## Gilbert Harding (1907–60)
BRITISH BROADCASTER

He became quiz master for the BBC radio programme *Round Britain Quiz* in 1947 and also appeared on the radio quiz *Twenty Questions* and TV's *What's my Line?* He was notorious for his rudeness and his anti-Establishment stance, as he himself commented: 'I am full of the milk of human kindness, damn it. My trouble is that it gets clotted so easily.'

1 **If, sir, I possessed . . . the power of conveying unlimited sexual attraction through the potency of my voice, I would not be reduced to accepting a miserable pittance from the BBC for interviewing a faded female in a damp basement.**

Recalled by Wynford Vaughan Thomas, in *Gilbert Harding By His Friends*, 'Gilbert and Outside Broadcasts' (ed. Stephen Grenfell, 1961). Response to a request by MAE WEST's manager to sound more 'sexy' when interviewing the actress.

## Warren G. Harding (1865–1923)
US PRESIDENT

Full name Warren Gamaliel Harding. As Republican President (1921–3), he opposed US membership of the League of Nations and convened the 1922 Washington conference that limited the naval strength of world powers. Politically naïve, he was unaware of the corruption among his cabinet (the Teapot Dome Scandal), the imminent exposure of which probably precipitated his death. H.L. MENCKEN called him 'a tin horn politician with the manner of a rural corn doctor and the mien of a ham actor', while WOODROW WILSON criticized him for his 'bungalow mind'.

1 **America's present need is not heroics, but healing; not nostrums, but normalcy; not revolution, but restoration.**

Speech in Boston, 14 May 1920, quoted in *Rededicating America*, ch.

17 (1920) by Frederick E. Schortemeier. 'Back to normalcy' was Harding's campaign slogan in that year.

## Elizabeth Hardwick (b. 1916)
US CRITIC AND AUTHOR

Known mainly for her brilliant literary and social criticism in the *New York Review of Books*, which she helped to found in 1963, she also wrote novels dealing with the fragility of human relationships. She was married (1949–72) to ROBERT LOWELL.

1 This is the unspoken contract of a wife and her works. In the long run wives are to be paid in a peculiar coin – consideration for their feelings. And it usually turns out this is an enormous, unthinkable inflation few men will remit, or if they will, only with a sense of being over-charged.
*Seduction and Betrayal: Women and Literature*, 'Amateurs' (1974)

2 The fifties – they seem to have taken place on a sunny afternoon that asked nothing of you except a drifting belief in the moment and its power to satisfy.
*Bartleby in Manhattan and Other Essays*, 'Domestic Manners' (1983)

## Oliver Hardy (1892–1957)
US COMEDIAN

Original name Norvell Hardy. He was the overbearing and rotund member of the comedy duo Laurel and Hardy, formed in 1926. The partnership resulted in more than 200 films, and successfully made the transition from the silent era to the talkies.

1 Here's another nice mess you've gotten me into.
Ollie in *The Laurel-Hardy Murder Case* (film, 1930). This is the earliest use of the famous catch-phrase that featured in various Laurel and Hardy films, always uttered by Oliver Hardy to Stan Laurel, although Laurel (1890–1965) is credited with most of the scriptwork and directed many of the films. The words are generally misquoted as 'another fine mess', which was the title of a Laurel and Hardy short released in 1930, but have not been traced to any dialogue in this form.

## Thomas Hardy (1840–1928)
BRITISH NOVELIST AND POET

His novels set in 'Wessex' (his native Dorset and around) are mainly tragedies played out against a harsh natural world. The controversial *Tess of the d'Urbevilles* (1891) branded him an atheist, and after the publication of *Jude the Obscure* in 1896 he confined himself to writing poetry. D.H. LAWRENCE remarked: 'What a commonplace genius he has, or a genius for the commonplace, I don't know which.'

1 Yonder a maid and her wight
Come whispering by:
War's annals will cloud into night
Ere their story die.
'In Time of "The Breaking of Nations" ', written 1915, publ. in *Moments of Vision* (1917)

2 My opinion is that a poet should express the emotion of all the ages and the thought of his own.
Remark 1918, quoted in *The Later Years of Thomas Hardy*, ch. 15 (1930) by Florence Emily Hardy

3 The value of old age depends upon the person who reaches it. To some men of early performance it is useless. To others, who are late to develop, it just enables them to finish the job.
'Birthday Notes' written 1920, quoted in ibid.

4 After two thousand years of mass
We've got as far as poison-gas.
'Christmas: 1924', publ. in *Winter Words* (1928)

5 Well, World, you have kept faith with me,
Kept faith with me;

Upon the whole you have proved to be
Much as you said you were.
'He Never Expected Much', publ. in *Winter Words* (1928). The poem is subtitled 'A Consideration on My Eighty-Sixth Birthday'.

## David Hare (b. 1947)
BRITISH PLAYWRIGHT

Co-founder of the Joint Stock Theatre Company in 1974 and resident playwright at the Royal Court Theatre (1969–71), he is the author of fiercely satirical plays. *Pravda* (written with Howard Brenton, 1985) comments on Fleet Street, while his 1990s trilogy addresses different areas of the establishment: the Church of England in *Racing Demon* (1990), the legal system in *Murmuring Judges* (1991) and politicians in *The Absence of War* (1994). See also HOWARD BRENTON AND DAVID HARE.

1 The theatre is the best way of showing the gap between what is said and what is seen to be done, and that is why, ragged and gap-toothed as it is, it has still a far healthier potential than some poorer, abandoned arts.
'The Playwright as Historian', publ. in the *Sunday Times* 26 November 1978

2 How the right wing always appropriate good manners. Yes? They always have that. Form and decorum. A permanent excuse for not addressing themselves to what people actually say, because they can always turn their heads away if a sentence is not correctly formulated.
Stephen, in *A Map of the World*, act 1 (1982)

3 This feeling, finally, that we may change things – this is at the centre of everything we are. Lose that . . . lose that, lose everything.
Mehta, in ibid. act 2

4 England's funny. You only get the point of it eight days a year. The sun comes out and you remember. You think oh, yes, all this . . . all this around us – *that's* what it's for.
Anne Rice, in *Strapless*, pt 5 (1989)

5 Like everything in England, it turns out to be a matter of class. You just listen. Educated clerics don't like evangelicals, because evangelicals drink sweet sherry and keep budgerigars and have ducks in formations on their walls. Yes, and they also have the distressingly downmarket habit of trying to get people emotionally involved.
Tony, in *Racing Demon*, act 2, sc. 1 (1990)

6 Policing's largely the fine art of getting through biros.
Sandra, in *Murmuring Judges*, act 1, sc. 5 (1991)

7 [Of the theatre] I love its volatility. Its special beauty seems to me to come from the fact that at seven-thirty you have no idea how you will be feeling at ten-fifteen. And at ten-fifteen you will look back, as across an ocean, to the almost unrecognizable stranger who arrived at seven-thirty.
*Writing Left-Handed*, ch. 3 (1991)

8 Writers always sound insufferably smug when they sit back and assert that their job is only to raise questions and not to answer them. But, in good part, it is true. And once you become committed to one particular answer, your freedom to ask new questions is seriously impaired.
ibid.

9 Acting is a judgment of character.
Said to critic Michael Billington, quoted by him in the *Guardian* 2 October 1993

## W.F. Hargreaves (1846–1919)
BRITISH SONGWRITER

1 I'm Burlington Bertie
I rise at ten thirty and saunter along like a toff,
I walk down the Strand with my gloves on my hand,

Then I walk down again with them off.

'Burlington Bertie from Bow' (song, 1915). The song was first performed by Ella Shields, male impersonator and Hargreaves's wife. Among the artists who covered it are ELSA LANCHESTER and JULIE ANDREWS (as Gertrude Lawrence in the 1968 film *Star!*).

## Tom Harkin (b. 1939)
US SENATOR

He was elected Senator in 1984 and was a Democratic candidate for the presidency in 1992. He co-authored *Five Minutes to Midnight: Why the Nuclear Threat is Growing Faster Than Ever* (1990).

1 The Gulf War was like teenage sex. We got in too soon and out too soon.

Quoted in the *Independent on Sunday* 29 September 1991

## Lord Harlech (1918–85)
BRITISH DIPLOMAT AND BUSINESSMAN

Born William David Ormsby Gore. He became Conservative MP for Oswestry in 1950 and served as British Ambassador in Washington (1961–5), when he was close to President KENNEDY. On his return to Britain he won the franchise for Harlech television (1967).

1 Britain will be honoured by historians more for the way she disposed of an empire than for the way in which she acquired it.

*The New York Times* 28 October 1962

## Jean Harlow (1911–37)
US ACTRESS

Real name Harlean Carpenter. Nicknamed the 'Blonde Bombshell', she became the first sex symbol of the talkies, playing opposite Clark Gable and Spencer Tracy. Her comedy films include *Platinum Blonde* (1931) and *Bombshell* (1933). GRAHAM GREENE wrote of her: 'Her technique was the gangster's technique – she toted a breast like a man totes a gun.' See also MARGOT ASQUITH 3.

1 Would you be shocked if I put on something more comfortable?

Helen ( Jean Harlow), in *Hell's Angels* (film, 1930, screenplay by H. Behn, H. Estabrook and J.M. March based on a story by Marshall Neilan and Joseph Moncure March, produced and co-directed by Howard Hughes, J. Whale, M. Nielan and L. Reed). The line is usually misquoted: 'Excuse me while I slip into something more comfortable.' Harlow, aged just eighteen, acted the part of an English girl who, clad in a backless velvet evening gown with beaded straps, addresses the question to Ben Lyons (Monty Rutledge).

## Michael Harrington (1928–89)
US SOCIAL SCIENTIST AND AUTHOR

A passionate champion of the poor and dispossessed, he is principally known for his study of poverty *The Other America* (1962). He was a member of the Catholic Worker Movement from the 1950s.

1 That the poor are invisible is one of the most important things about them. They are not simply neglected and forgotten as in the old rhetoric of reform; what is much worse, they are not seen.

*The Other America*, ch. 1, sect. 1 (1962)

2 To be a Negro is to participate in a culture of poverty and fear that goes far deeper than any law for or against discrimination . . . After the racist statutes are all struck down, after legal equality has been achieved in the schools and in the courts, there remains the profound institutionalized and abiding wrong that white America has worked on the Negro for so long.

ibid. ch. 4

3 Our affluent society contains those of talent and insight who are driven to prefer poverty, to choose it, rather than

to submit to the desolation of an empty abundance. It is a strange part of the other America that one finds in the intellectual slums.

ibid. ch. 5, sect. 1

4 Life [in the slums] is lived in common, but not in community.

ibid. ch. 7, sect. 4

5 If there is technological advance without social advance, there is, almost automatically, an increase in human misery, in impoverishment.

ibid. Appendix, sect. 1

## Frank Harris (1856–1931)
IRISH JOURNALIST AND AUTHOR

Original name James Thomas Harris. He was a successful editor in London and New York but is chiefly remembered for his scandalous autobiography *My Life and Loves* (five volumes, 1922–8). He also wrote biographies of Oscar Wilde, and GEORGE BERNARD SHAW, who described him as a 'man of splendid visions, unreasonable expectations, fierce appetites'.

1 All that is amiable and sweet and good in life, all that ennobles and chastens, I have won from women.

*My Life and Loves*, vol. 2, Foreword (1925)

2 There is a subtle compensation in everything, and the cheapening of books, the vulgarization of knowledge, has a great deal to answer for. We have forgotten how to use books, and they revenge themselves on us.

ibid. vol. 3, ch. 1 (1926)

3 Stupidity and malevolence are the twin rulers of human destiny and there is no hope for the future save in the soul of man, and even there high purpose is fitful and often dwarfed by animal necessities.

ibid. vol. 5, ch. 1 (1928)

## Martyn Harris (b. 1952)
BRITISH JOURNALIST AND AUTHOR

He was a feature writer for *New Society* 1979–82 and subsequently on the *Daily Telegraph*. His novels include *Do It Again* (1989).

1 Pull out a Monte Cristo at a dinner party and the political liberal turns into the nicotine fascist.

*Daily Telegraph* 20 January 1989

## Richard Harris (b. 1932)
IRISH STAGE AND SCREEN ACTOR

He made his name in the West End of London in J.P. DONLEAVY's *The Ginger Man* (1959) and his screen debut with *Alive and Kicking* (1958). His off-stage antics often mirrored the unruly, dissolute roles he played, as in *This Sporting Life* (film, 1963).

1 [On his drinking] I often sit back and think 'I wish I'd done that' and find out later that I already have.

Quoted in the *Sun* 19 May 1988

## Robert Harris (b. 1957)
BRITISH JOURNALIST AND AUTHOR

He was Political Editor for the *Observer* in 1987 and subsequently columnist for the *Sunday Times*. His *Selling Hitler* (1986) was an account of the forging of HITLER's diaries, but his greatest successes have been his fictional reworkings of history, *Fatherland* (1992) and *Archangel* (1998).

1 We believe in God, we believe in Germany which He created in His world, and in the Führer, Adolf Hitler, whom He has sent us.

SS cadets, in *Fatherland*, pt 2, ch. 3 (1992)

2 There can now be no doubt that it is Stalin rather than Hitler who is the most alarming figure of the twentieth century. I say this – I say this not merely because Stalin killed more people than Hitler – though clearly he did – and not even because Stalin was more of a psychopath than Hitler – although clearly he was. I say it because Stalin was not a one-off like Hitler, an eruption from nowhere. Stalin stands in a historical tradition of rule by terror which existed before him, which he refined, and which could exist again. His, not Hitler's, is the spectre that should worry us.
Kelso, in *Archangel*, ch. 11 (1998)

3 In Russia, the past carries razors and a pair of handcuffs.
Suvorin, in ibid.

4 The great western myth . . . That just because a place has a McDonalds and MTV and takes American Express it's exactly the same as everywhere else – it doesn't have a past any more, it's Year Zero.
Kelso, in ibid. ch. 16

5 History is too important to be left to the historians.
Quoted in the *Observer* 25 October 1998

## Rolf Harris (b. 1930)
AUSTRALIAN TELEVISION PRESENTER

With a fast-talking, fast-drawing style, Harris began working for the BBC in 1954 as a presenter of children's shows. The *Rolf Harris Show* ran 1967–71, and since 1997 he has presented *Animal Hospital*. His hit records include 'Sun Arise' (1962 and 1997), 'Two Little Boys' (1969 and 1970) and 'Stairway to Heaven' (1993).

1 Tie me kangaroo down, sport.
'Tie Me Kangaroo Down, Sport' (song, 1960) on the album *Sun Arise* (1963)

## Sydney Harris (b. 1917)
US JOURNALIST

Known for his witty aphorisms, he wrote the column 'Strictly Personal', which was syndicated to about 200 newspapers in North America. His books include *Pieces of Eight* (1982).

1 People who think they're generous to a fault usually think that's their only fault.
*On the Contrary*, ch. 7 (1962)

2 A cynic is not merely one who reads bitter lessons from the past; he is one who is prematurely disappointed in the future.
ibid.

## Barbara Grizzuti Harrison (b. 1934)
US AUTHOR AND PUBLICIST

She has written travel books and extensively on cults. Her second book, *Visions of Glory* (1978), was an exploration of Jehovah's Witnesses, with whom she was involved for eleven years.

1 Fantasies are more than substitutes for unpleasant reality; they are also dress rehearsals, plans. All acts performed in the world begin in the imagination.
'Talking Dirty', publ. in *Ms* October 1973

2 Kindness and intelligence don't always deliver us from the pitfalls and traps: there are always failures of love, of will, of imagination. There is no way to take the danger out of human relationships.
'Secrets Women Tell Each Other', publ. in *McCall's* August 1975

## George Harrison (b. 1943)
BRITISH ROCK MUSICIAN

Lead guitarist with the Beatles, he became involved in Indian mysticism, particularly the Hare Krishna movement. He was the first ex-Beatle to secure a chart-topping LP (*All Things Must Pass*) and single ('My Sweet Lord'), both in 1970, and later founded a successful film production company, *HandMade Films* (1978).

1 This place [the Apple office in London's Savile Row] has become a haven for drop-outs. The trouble is, some of our best friends are drop-outs.
Quoted in *Shout! The True Story of the Beatles*, pt 4, 'May 1969' (1981) by Philip Norman

## Jane Harrison (1850–1928)
BRITISH CLASSICAL SCHOLAR AND WRITER

She is known for her writings on classical art, religion and literature, among which are *Prolegomena to the Study of Greek Religion* (1903).

1 To be womanly is one thing, and one only; it is to be sensitive to man, to be highly endowed with the sex instinct; to be manly is to be sensitive to woman.
*Alpha and Omega*, 'Homo Sum' (1915)

2 Marriage, for a woman at least, hampers the two things that made life to me glorious – friendship and learning.
*Reminiscences of a Student's Life*, 'Conclusion' (1925)

## Paul Harrison (b. 1936)
US PLAYWRIGHT AND DIRECTOR

He is known for bringing together African tradition and modern American thought in his work, which includes a book of critical essays, *The Drama of Nomo* (1972), and the plays *Dr Jazz* (1975) and *Abercrombie Apocalypse* (1982).

1 The poor tread lightest on the earth. The higher our income, the more resources we control and the more havoc we wreak.
*Guardian* 1 May 1992

## Tony Harrison (b. 1937)
BRITISH POET, PLAYWRIGHT AND TRANSLATOR

A classicist from a working-class background, he caused controversy with his poem *v.* (1985), which dealt with the desecration of his parents' grave, and later with 'The Blasphemers' Banquet' (1989). His plays include *Phaedra Britannica* (1975), and he has also made translations and adaptations for the theatre.

1 A language near extinction best preserves
the deepest grammar of our nothingness.
'Art and Extinction', no. 6, publ. in *Continuous: School of Eloquence* (1981)

2 Every poem is a momentary defeat of pessimism.
Interview in *Poetry Review* January 1984

3 The ones we choose to love become our anchor
when the hawser of the blood-tie's hacked, or frays.
*v.* (1985)

4 Its blasphemy enabled man
to break free from the Bible and Koran
with their life-denying fundamentalists
and hell fire such fanatics love to fan.
'The Blasphemers' Banquet' (BBC1, 31 July 1989), televised poem first publ. in *Tony Harrison: Bloodaxe Critical Anthologies 1* (ed. Neil Astley, 1991). Referring to *The Satanic Verses*, by SALMAN RUSHDIE.

5 The Prospero of poisons, the Faustus of the front,
bringing mental magic to modern armament.
*Square Rounds*, pt 2 (1992). The speaker is intended to be the German chemist Fritz Haber, Nobel prizewinner and 'father' of chemical warfare.

## Lorenz Hart (1895–1943)
US SONGWRITER

His twenty-five-year collaboration with the composer Richard Rodgers resulted in twenty-six Broadway musicals distinguished by their lyrical sophistication, of which *Pal Joey* (1940) is generally regarded their masterwork. His unreliability was exacerbated by the alcoholism that led Rodgers to call him 'a partner, a best friend – and a source of permanent irritation'.

1 We'll have Manhattan,
The Bronx and Staten
Island too.

'Manhattan' (song, with music by Richard Rodgers), in *Garrick Gaieties* (revue, 1925). The show was Rodgers and Hart's first Broadway success as a songwriting team, and the song was also a hit, successfully recorded by Paul Whiteman and Ben Selvin.

2 When love congeals
It soon reveals
The faint aroma of performing seals,
The double crossing of a pair of heels.
I wish I were in love again!

'I Wish I Were in Love Again' (song, with music by Richard Rodgers), in *Babes in Arms* (stage show 1937, filmed 1939). The song was a hit for SOPHIE TUCKER and Peggy Lee.

3 I get too hungry for dinner at eight.
I like the theatre, but never come late.
I never bother with people I hate.
That's why the lady is a tramp.

'The Lady is a Tramp' (song, with music by Richard Rodgers), in ibid.

4 I'm wild again
Beguiled again
A simpering, whimpering child again,
Bewitched, bothered and bewildered am I.

'Bewitched, Bothered and Bewildered' (song, with music by Richard Rodgers), in *Pal Joey* (stage show 1940, filmed 1957)

## L.P. Hartley (1895–1972)
BRITISH AUTHOR

Full name Leslie Poles Hartley. His novels, which include *Eustace and Hilda* (1947) and *The Go-Between* (1953, filmed 1971), typically portray psychological relationships among the middle classes, often with a sinister or macabre slant.

1 The past is a foreign country; they do things differently there.

*The Go-Between*, Prologue (1953). Opening sentence.

## Ihab Hassan (b. 1925)
EGYPTIAN-BORN US CRITIC

In his own words his preoccupations are 'avant-garde moments, the postmodern phenomenon, travel as quest, vision and transgression, the collision and interanimation of cultures, especially Oriental and Occidental'. His books include *Radical Innocence: The Contemporary American Novel* (1961) and *Out of Egypt: Fragments of an Autobiography* (1986)

1 The (post) structuralist temper requires too great a depersonalization of the writing/speaking subject. Writing becomes plagiarism; speaking becomes quoting. Meanwhile, we do write, we do speak.

'The Re-Vision of Literature', publ. in *New Literary History* autumn 1976, repr. in *The Right Promethean Fire* (1980)

## Max Hastings (b. 1945)
BRITISH JOURNALIST AND EDITOR

As a freelance journalist he covered world-wide conflicts, such as the South Atlantic (1982). He has made documentaries for television and was Editor of the *Daily Telegraph* (1986–95) and since 1996 has been Editor of the *Evening Standard*.

1 If you can't get a job as a pianist in a brothel you become a royal reporter.

*Daily Express* 9 June 1992

## Roy Hattersley (b. 1932)
BRITISH POLITICIAN

Baron Hattersley of Sparkbrook. Elected a Labour MP in 1964, he held ministerial office in the CALLAGHAN government and became Shadow Chancellor and Deputy Leader of the Labour Party (1983–92). A regular contributor to the press and TV debates, he has also published popular novels and memoirs. He described his role as 'the great bystander, the shadowy figure', although PHILIP LARKIN called him 'that great bloated unsmiling accuser'.

1 Morality and expediency coincide more than the cynics allow.

*Guardian* 30 September 1988

2 In my opinion, any man who can afford to buy a newspaper should not be allowed to own one.

Quoted in *Maxwell, the Outsider*, ch. 13 (1988) by Tom Bower

3 In politics, being ridiculous is more damaging than being extreme.

*Evening Standard* 9 May 1989. Hattersley himself was cruelly lampooned in the television puppet satire, *Spitting Image*.

4 The proposition that Muslims are welcome in Britain if, and only if, they stop behaving like Muslims is a doctrine which is incompatible with the principles that guide a free society.

*Independent* 21 July 1989

5 There is no doubt that, as works of art, books that lack canine interest are incomplete.

Quoted in the *Sunday Times Review* 27 September 1998. On the publication of Hattersley's book, written in the persona of Buster, his dog.

## Charles Haughey (b. 1925)
IRISH STATESMAN

He was elected a Fianna Fáil MP in 1957 and dismissed from Jack Lynch's government in 1970 for allegedly importing guns for the IRA, although subsequently acquitted. Prime Minister 1979–81, 1982 and 1987–92, he finally resigned over a phone-tapping scandal.

1 Ireland is where strange tales begin and happy endings are possible.

*Daily Telegraph* 14 July 1988

## Václav Havel (b. 1936)
CZECH PLAYWRIGHT AND PRESIDENT

His dissidence, expressed through such plays as *The Garden Party* (1963) and *Largo Desolato* (1985), and his support for Charter 77 resulted in two terms of imprisonment (1979–83 and 1989). He was elected President of Czechoslovakia following the Velvet Revolution of 1989 but resigned in protest over the break-up of the federation in 1992, assuming presidency of the independent Czech Republic the following year.

1 True enough, the country is calm. Calm as a morgue or a grave, would you not say?

'Letter to Dr Gustáv Husák' (8 April 1975), publ. in *Living in Truth*, pt 1 (1986)

2 You do not become a 'dissident' just because you decide one day to take up this most unusual career. You are thrown into it by your personal sense of responsibility, combined with a complex set of external circumstances. You are cast out of the existing structures and placed in a position of conflict with them. It begins as an attempt to do your work well, and ends with being branded an enemy of society.

'The Power of the Powerless', sect. 14 (1978), repr. in *Living in Truth*, pt 1 (1986)

3 There are times when we must sink to the bottom of our

misery to understand truth, just as we must descend to the bottom of a well to see the stars in broad daylight.

ibid. sect. 16

4 I think theatre should always be somewhat suspect.

*Disturbing the Peace*, ch. 2 (1986)

5 The truth is not simply what you think it is; it is also the circumstances in which it is said, and to whom, why, and how it is said.

ibid.

6 [The] attempt to devote oneself to literature alone is a most deceptive thing, and ... often, paradoxically, it is literature that suffers for it.

ibid. ch. 3

7 None of us knows all the potentialities that slumber in the spirit of the population, or all the ways in which that population can surprise us when there is the right interplay of events.

ibid.

8 There's always something suspect about an intellectual on the winning side.

ibid. ch. 5

9 Hope is definitely not the same thing as optimism. It is not the conviction that something will turn out well, but the certainty that something makes sense, regardless of how it turns out.

ibid.

10 The exercise of power is determined by thousands of interactions between the world of the powerful and that of the powerless, all the more so because these worlds are never divided by a sharp line: everyone has a small part of himself in both.

ibid.

11 The cliché organizes life; it expropriates people's identity; it becomes ruler, defence lawyer, judge, and the law.

ibid.

12 I really do inhabit a system in which words are capable of shaking the entire structure of government, where words can prove mightier than ten military divisions.

Speech in Germany, October 1989, accepting a peace prize, quoted in the *Independent* 9 December 1989

13 People have passed through a very dark tunnel at the end of which there was a light of freedom. Unexpectedly they passed through the prison gates and found themselves in a square. They are now free and they don't know where to go.

Address to Institute of Contemporary Arts, London, quoted in the *Independent* 24 March 1990

14 If you want to see your plays performed the way you wrote them, become President.

ibid.

15 We are finding out that what looked like a neglected house a year ago is in fact a ruin.

On the state of Czechoslovakia and other ex-Soviet Bloc countries, in the *Daily Telegraph* 3 January 1991

## Jacquetta Hawkes (1910–96)
BRITISH ARCHAEOLOGIST AND WRITER

Before taking up writing she carried out excavations in Britain, France and Palestine (1931–40) and became Secretary to the UK Commission for UNESCO (1943–9). Her books, such as *Early Britain* (1945) and *The Shell Guide to British Archaeology* (1986), contributed much to the popularization of archaeology. With her husband, J.B. PRIESTLEY, she wrote *Journey Down the Rainbow* (1955).

1 The only inequalities that matter begin in the mind. It is

not income levels but differences in mental equipment that keep people apart, breed feelings of inferiority.

*New Statesman* January 1957

## Stephen Hawking (b. 1942)
BRITISH THEORETICAL PHYSICIST

His work in quantum mechanics, black holes and the big bang theory of the universe was partially elucidated in his surprise bestseller *A Brief History of Time* (1988). Severely disabled by a neuromotor disease since the 1960s, he is confined to a wheelchair and communicates through a computer.

1 If we find the answer to that, it would be the ultimate triumph of human reason – for then we would know the mind of God.

*A Brief History of Time*, ch. 11 (1988). Closing words of book, referring to the question 'why it is that we and the universe exist'.

2 Have we been visited by aliens? ... I don't believe we have. I think that any such visit would be obvious and probably unpleasant. What would be the point of aliens revealing themselves only to a few cranks?

*Radio Times* 17 February 1996

## Screamin' Jay Hawkins (b. 1929)
US ROCK SINGER

Original name Jalacy Hawkins. A boxer turned rhythm and blues performer, he was famed for his voodoo stage act, which involved skulls, a flaming coffin and outlandish garb. His signature tune, 'I Put a Spell on You' (1956), has been widely covered. He had a cameo role in Jim Jarmusch's film *Mystery Train* (1989).

1 I put a spell on you, because you're mine
You'd better stop the things you're doing
Ha! Haa! Haa! – What's up! – I ain't lyin'!
Yeaaaaahhhh! I can't stand it, oh no,
Your runnin' around,
I can't stand no – I can't stand you putting me down.

'I Put a Spell on You' (song, 1956, co-written with Herb Slotkin). Some radio stations refused to play the song on the grounds that it was 'cannibalistic'. Nina Simone, who covered the song in 1965, called it a song that 'no one could ignore'.

## Ian Hay (1876–1952)
BRITISH PLAYWRIGHT AND NOVELIST

Real name John Hay Beith. His light and humorous novels portray eccentric characters. His first, *Pip* (1907), was a bestseller, although *The First Hundred Thousand* (1915) is the most famous. He adapted several of his own books into plays, notably *Tilly of Bloomsbury* (1918), from his novel *Happy-Go-Lucky* (1913).

1 War is hell and all that, but it has a good deal to recommend it. It wipes out all the small nuisances of peace-time.

Wagstaffe, in *The First Hundred Thousand*, ch. 10 (1915). Among the 'small nuisances' Wagstaffe listed suffragettes, futurism, the tango, party politics and golf-maniacs.

## Colin Haycraft (1929–94)
BRITISH PUBLISHER

Before assuming chairmanship of Duckworth and Co. in 1971, he was a Director of Weidenfeld & Nicolson and Managing Director of the World University Library.

1 A publisher is a specialized form of bank or building society, catering for customers who cannot cope with life and are therefore forced to write about it.

Letter to the *Sunday Times* 11 February 1990. 'Hype,' added Haycraft, 'springs eternal in every publisher's breast.'

## Sterling Hayden (1916–86)

US SCREEN ACTOR

Real name John Hamilton. Billed as 'the Beautiful Blond Viking God', he numbered *The Asphalt Jungle* (1950) and *The Killing* (1956) among the most successful films in an uneven career. In 1951 he confessed to past membership of the Communist Party before the House Committee on Un-American Activities and testified against others in Hollywood, to his later regret. 'I started at the top and worked my way down,' was his summary of his achievements.

1 I know you like a book, ya little tramp. You'd sell out you're own mother for a piece of fudge . . . You've got a great big dollar there where most women have a heart.

Johnny Clay (Sterling Hayden) speaking to Sherry Peatty (Marie Windsor), in *The Killing* (film, 1956, screenplay by Stanley Kubrick and Jim Thompson adapted from *The Clean Break* by Lionel White, directed by Stanley Kubrick)

2 I can no longer sit back and allow Communist infiltration, Communist indoctrination, Communist subversion and the international Communist conspiracy to sap and impurify all of our precious bodily fluids.

General D. Ripper (Sterling Hayden), in *Dr. Strangelove: Or How I Learned To Stop Worrying And Love The Bomb* (film, 1963, screenplay by Stanley Kubrick, Terry Southern and Peter George based on Peter George's novel *Red Alert*, produced and directed by Stanley Kubrick)

## Friedrich August von Hayek (1899–1992)

AUSTRIAN-BORN BRITISH ECONOMIST

Called the 'father of monetarism', he was a strong critic of Keynesian theory and directly opposed to government intervention in a free market. He was Professor of Economic Science at London (1931–50), became a British citizen in 1938 and in 1974 shared the Nobel Prize for Economics.

1 Planning and competition can be combined only by planning for competition, but not by planning against competition.

*The Road to Serfdom*, ch. 3 (1944)

2 The system of private property is the most important guarantee of freedom, not only for those who own property, but scarcely less for those who do not.

ibid. ch. 8

3 There are no better terms available to describe [the] difference between the approach of the natural and the social sciences than to call the former 'objective' and the latter 'subjective' . . . While for the natural scientist the contrast between objective facts and subjective opinions is a simple one, the distinction cannot as readily be applied to the object of the social sciences. The reason for this is that the object, the 'facts' of the social sciences are also opinions – not opinions of the student of the social phenomena, of course, but opinions of those whose actions produce the object of the social scientist.

*The Counter-Revolution of Science*, pt 1, ch. 3 (1952)

## Denis Healey (b. 1917)

BRITISH POLITICIAN

Baron Healey of Riddlesden. Elected a Labour MP in 1952, he went on to become Minister for Defence in the WILSON government (1964–70), when he was responsible for the reduction in British forces east of Suez. He was Chancellor of the Exchequer (1974–9) and Deputy Leader (1980–83).

1 Their [the Conservative Party's] Europeanism is nothing but imperialism with an inferiority complex.

Quoted in the *Observer* 7 October 1962

2 His speech was rather like being savaged by a dead sheep.

Speech to House of Commons, 14 June 1978, publ. in *Hansard*.

Referring to a criticism of Healey's Budget proposals by Shadow Chancellor GEOFFREY HOWE. According to Healey's memoirs (*The Time of My Life*, pt 3, ch. 21, 1989), this off-the-cuff remark was inspired by WINSTON CHURCHILL's comment that an attack by Labour politician CLEMENT ATTLEE was 'like being savaged by a pet lamb'. In 1983, after being congratulated by Healey on his appointment as Foreign Secretary, Howe commented that it was 'like being nuzzled by an old ram'. Healey's rejoinder: 'It would be the end of a beautiful friendship if he accused me of necrophilia.'

3 Mrs Thatcher has added the diplomacy of Alf Garnett to the economics of Arthur Daley.

Quoted in the *Observer* 31 December 1989

4 I sometimes think that the critical difference between a democracy and a dictatorship is that in a dictatorship there are only two people out of every hundred who take a personal interest in politics; in a democracy there are three.

*The Time of My Life*, pt 2, ch. 7 (1989)

## Seamus Heaney (b. 1939)

IRISH POET

Regarded as the greatest Irish poet since YEATS, his poetry expresses a close relationship with landscape, as in *Death of a Naturalist* (1966), and also addresses the political situation in Ireland. He became Professor of Poetry at Oxford in 1989 and was awarded the Nobel Prize for Literature in 1995. GAVIN EWART saluted him in a poem: 'He's very popular among his mates,/I think I'm Auden, he thinks he's Yeats.'

1 Between my finger and my thumb
The squat pen rests.
I'll dig with it.

'Digging', publ. in *Death of a Naturalist* (1966). Closing words of poem.

2 We have no prairies
To slice a big sun at evening –
Everywhere the eye concedes to
Encroaching horizon,
Is wooed into the cyclops' eye
Of a tarn.

'Bogland', publ. in *Door into the Dark* (1969)

3 The ground itself is kind, black butter

Melting and opening underfoot,
Missing its last definition
By millions of years.

ibid.

4 Who would connive
in civilized outrage
yet understand the exact
and tribal, intimate revenge.

'Punishment', publ. in *North*, pt 1 (1975)

5 The famous
Northern reticence, the tight gag of place
And times: yes, yes. Of the 'wee six' I sing
Where to be saved you only must save face
And whatever you say, you say nothing.

'Whatever You Say Say Nothing', publ. in ibid. pt 2

6 Elderberry? It is shires dreaming wine.

'Glanmore Sonnets', publ. in *Field Work* (1979)

7 Don't be surprised
If I demur, for, be advised
My passport's green.
No glass of ours was ever raised
To toast The Queen.

'An Open Letter to Blake and Andrew' (1983). The poem is addressed to BLAKE MORRISON and ANDREW MOTION, editors of *The Penguin Book of Contemporary British Poetry* (1982), who included him in the anthology.

8 Everywhere being nowhere,
who can prove
one place more than another?
'Birthplace', publ. in *Station Island*, pt 1 (1984)

9 We are earthworms of the earth, and all that
has gone through us is what will be our trace.
'Station Island', publ. in ibid. pt 2

10 Passive
Suffering makes the world go round.
Peace on earth, men of good will, all that
Holds good as long as the balance holds,
The scales ride steady and the angels' strain
Prolongs itself at an unearthly pitch.
'Weighing In', publ. in *Spirit Level* (1996)

11 Generations of gifted northern poets have let the linguistic
cat out of the sectarian bag, setting it free in the great
street carnival of 'protholics and catestants'.
Quoted in the *Observer* 12 April 1998

# (Sir) Edward Heath (b. 1916)
BRITISH STATESMAN

A keen sailor and accomplished musician, he entered Parliament
as a Conservative MP in 1950 and as Prime Minister (1970–74)
took Britain into the Common Market, which he afterwards considered his greatest achievement. Brought down by striking miners,
he was replaced by MARGARET THATCHER and became increasingly critical of her and other 'Eurosceptics'. JONATHAN AITKEN
called him 'a peddler of dreams from Broadstairs-les-deux-Eglises'.

1 When the people said 'the miners won a great victory' or
'the Government lost that one', what did they mean? In
the country we live in, there could not be any 'we' or
'they'. There was only 'us' – all of us. If the Government
is defeated then the country is defeated.
Spoken after the settlement of the miners' strike, February 1972,
quoted in *Edward Heath*, pt 4, ch. 21 (1993) by John Campbell p. 420

2 The unpleasant and unacceptable face of capitalism.
Speech to House of Commons, 15 May 1973, publ. in *Hansard*.
Referring to the 'Lonrho affair', in which Duncan Sandys, a non-
executive director of the company and Conservative MP, was paid
£130,000 compensation via an offshore account during a period of
deep recession. The resulting enquiry led to legislation requiring
companies to disclose payments and MPs to register their private
interests.

3 We [the Conservative Party] are the trades union for the
pensioners and for children; we are the union for the
disabled and the sick; we are the union for those who live
in slums or for those who want to buy homes. We are the
union for the unemployed and the low paid. We are the
union for those in poverty and for the hard pressed . . .
We are the union for the nation as a whole.
Election campaign speech, Manchester, 20 February 1974, quoted
in *The Times* 21 February 1974

4 Better a three-day week than a no-day week.
Quoted in the *Observer* 28 July 1974. Heath had announced at the
end of 1973 that industry would work to a three-day week during
the energy crisis.

5 I have no interest in sailing round the world. Not that
there is any lack of requests for me to do so.
*Observer* 19 June 1977. Heath, a skilled ocean-racing yachtsman,
captained the British team to victory with his boat *Morning Cloud*
in the Sydney–Hobart race (1969) and in the Admiral's Cup (1971).

6 Either you agree with everything and you just become a
lackey, in which case you will be described as loyal and
'dry', or you have contrary views and express them,
without in any way indulging in personalities, in which
case you are disloyal and 'wet' and ought to be chucked
out. I object to the whole level of political discussion at
the moment, that there must never be a U-turn, that

people are 'wet' or 'dry' and so on. This is childish. Why
cannot we discuss the merits of these things, instead of
trying to encapsulate them in words like 'wet' or 'dry' or
'U-turn'?
Quoted in *The Times* 4 July 1981. Commenting on MARGARET
THATCHER's insistence on monetarist policies at the expense of
high unemployment and inflation. In September 1981 Thatcher
sacked three more 'wets' – Christopher Soames, Mark Carlisle and
IAN GILMOUR – in favour of NIGEL LAWSON, CECIL PARKINSON
and NORMAN TEBBIT.

7 We cannot live permanently by taking in each other's
washing.
An often-repeated remark during the 1980s, quoted in *Edward
Heath*, pt 6, ch. 36 (1993) by John Campbell. Heath was concerned
at the loss of Britain's manufacturing capacity, scorning the idea of
a service economy.

# Ben Hecht (1894–1964)
US JOURNALIST, AUTHOR AND SCREENWRITER

He lost his job as journalist on the *Chicago Daily News* after
publication of his novel *Fantazius Mallare* (1922) because of its
'obscenity'. A writer of (and uncredited collaborator in) numerous
screenplays, among them *The Scoundrel* (1935) and *Notorious*
(1946), he once commented: 'Writing a good movie brings a writer
about as much fame as steering a bicycle.'

1 Movies are one of the bad habits that corrupted our
century. Of their many sins, I offer as the worst their effect
on the intellectual side of the nation. It is chiefly from
that viewpoint I write of them – as an eruption of trash
that has lamed the American mind and retarded Americans from becoming a cultured people.
*A Child of the Century*, bk 5 'What the Movies Are' (1954). Hecht
continued: 'They have slapped into the American mind more
human misinformation in one evening than the Dark Ages could
muster in a decade.'

2 I discovered early in my movie work that a movie is never
any better than the stupidest man connected with it. There
are times when this distinction may be given to the writer
or director. Most often it belongs to the producer.
ibid. bk 5 'Illustrations by Doré (Gustave)'. Hecht saw the producer's chief task as 'the job of turning good writers into movie
hacks. These sinister fellows were always my bosses.'

# Eric Heffer (1922–91)
BRITISH POLITICIAN

A traditional socialist, he was elected Labour MP for Walton,
Liverpool in 1964 and served as a junior minister under HAROLD
WILSON (1974–5) and as a member of MICHAEL FOOT's shadow
cabinet in 1981.

1 Jesus Christ was not a conservative. That's a racing certainty.
*Observer* 20 February 1983

# Hugh Hefner (b. 1926)
US PUBLISHER

In 1953 he was founder of *Playboy* magazine, whose glossy soft-porn
content made him conspicuously wealthy. The concept was extended to *Playboy* clubs, complete with bunnygirl hostesses, in the
face of increasing criticism by feminist groups in the 1970s.

1 Much of what *Playboy* is really all about is the projection
of the adolescent fantasies I have never really lost. The
boy has been father to the man.
Quoted in *Hefner*, ch. 11 (1974) by Frank Brady

# Martin Heidegger (1889–1976)
GERMAN PHILOSOPHER

His standing largely rests on his incomplete work *Being and Time* (1927), an analysis of being and the individual's relationship to death. Although rejecting the label 'existentialist', he was nevertheless a key influence on the work of SARTRE. His Nazi sympathies damaged his reputation.

1 Man acts as though *he* were the shaper and master of language, while in fact *language* remains the master of man.
'Building Dwelling Thinking', lecture, 5 August 1951, publ. in *Poetry, Language, Thought* (1971)

2 The German language 'speaks Being', while all the others merely 'speak of Being'.
Quoted in Prologue to *An Appetite for Poetry: Essays in Literary Interpretation* (1989) by Frank Kermode

# Muhammad Heikal (b. 1923)
EGYPTIAN JOURNALIST

He gained fame as Editor-in-chief (1957–74) of *Al-Ahram*, the Cairo newspaper called *The New York Times* of the Arab world for its standards of objectivity.

1 We [the Arabs] have proved we are not modern. We have proved we are not religious in the real sense of the word. We have proved that we cannot afford democracy.
*Independent* 11 March 1992. On the conduct of Arab governments in the wake of the Gulf War.

# Carolyn Heilbrun (b. 1926)
US AUTHOR AND ACADEMIC

A committed feminist, she examines women's roles through analysing literary texts. Her books, such as *Reinventing Womanhood* (1979) and *Writing a Woman's Life* (1989), emphasize the importance of assertiveness and achievement for women's fulfilment. Writing as Amanda Cross, her cerebral detective novels satirize literary-academic milieux.

1 In former days, everyone found the assumption of innocence so easy; today we find fatally easy the assumption of guilt.
Kate Fansler, in *Poetic Justice* ch. 2 (written as Amanda Cross, 1970)

2 Women are liberated the moment they stop caring what other women think of them.
Emilia Airhart, in ibid. ch. 7

3 We cannot guess the outcome of our actions . . . Which is why our actions must always be acceptable in themselves, and not as strategies.
Professor Frederick Clemance, in ibid. ch. 11. He adds: 'Kant put it differently and better.'

4 The married are those who have taken the terrible risk of intimacy and, having taken it, know life without intimacy to be impossible.
'Marriage is the Message', publ. in *Ms* August 1974

# Cynthia Heimel (b. 1947)
US COLUMNIST

An outspoken, humorous and feisty columnist, she voices opinions on subjects ranging from the sex war and the vagaries of politics to dogs. She has also published collections of essays including *Get Your Tongue Out of My Mouth, I'm Kissing You Good-bye* (1993).

1 The '60s, contrary to popular belief, are not dead . . . And deep in the heart of every forty-year-old accountant is the secret knowledge that he was there, then. He may not admit it, he may not want to do anything about it, but he still gets a twinge of fury when he hears 'Day Tripper' in Muzak, and a hidden part of his brain sings, 'What a drag it is to get old' at three in the morning while he's trying to get some sleep. He knows what's been lost.
'Highway 1967 Revisited', first publ. in *Playboy* 1987, repr. in *If You Can't Live Without Me, Why Aren't You Dead Yet?*, 'The Writer's Life' (1991)

# Piet Hein (b. 1905)
DANISH INVENTOR AND POET

He is known for the grook (*gruk* in Danish), a short aphoristic form that he created during the Nazi occupation and that expresses serious concerns through humour. He has translated many into English.

1 The human spirit sublimates
the impulses it thwarts:
a healthy sex life mitigates
the lust for other sports.
'Hint and Suggestion', publ. in *Grooks* (1966)

2 They're busy making bigger roads,
and better roads and more,
so that people can discover
even faster than before
that everything is everywhere alike.
'Road Sense', publ. in ibid.

3 The road to wisdom? – Well, it's plain
and simple to express:
Err
and err
and err again
but less
and less
and less.
'The Road to Wisdom', publ. in ibid.

# Joseph Heller (1923–99)
US NOVELIST

Drawing on his experience in the Second World War, he produced his bestselling novel *Catch 22* (1961), a satire on war and bureaucracy. Other works include the more experimental *Something Happened* (1974) and *God Knows* (1984).

1 Death to all modifiers.
Yossarian, in *Catch-22*, ch. 1 (1961)

2 He [Yossarian] had decided to live for ever or die in the attempt.
*Catch-22*, ch. 3 (1961)

3 He [Colonel Cargill] was a self-made man who owed his lack of success to nobody.
ibid.

4 There's a rule saying I have to ground anyone who's crazy . . . There's a catch. Catch-22. Anyone who wants to get out of combat duty isn't really crazy.
Doc Daneeka, in ibid. ch. 5. The narrator explains: 'Orr was crazy and could be grounded. All he had to do was ask; and as soon as he did, he would no longer be crazy and would have to fly more missions.'

5 Some men are born mediocre, some men achieve mediocrity, and some men have mediocrity thrust upon them. With Major Major it had been all three.
ibid. ch. 9. The words evoke Shakespeare: 'Some are born great, some achieve greatness, and some have greatness thrust upon 'em' (Malvolio, quoting Maria's letter in *Twelfth Night* act 2, sc. 5).

6 Frankly, I'd like to see the government get out of war altogether and leave the whole field to private industry.
Milo Minderbinder, in ibid. ch. 24

7 I think that maybe in every company today there is always at least one person who is going crazy slowly.

Narrator (Bob Slocum), in *Something Happened*, 'The office in which I work' (1974)

8 It's a wise person, I guess, who knows he's dumb, and an honest person who knows he's a liar. And it's a dumb person, I guess, who's convinced he is wise.

ibid.

## Mark Hellinger (1903–47)
US JOURNALIST, SCRIPTWRITER AND PRODUCER

Producer of more than twenty films and writer of films such as *Strictly Confidential* (1934), *Comet Over Broadway* (1938) and *Riding High* (1950), he was also a hugely popular newspaper writer and was considered the first Broadway columnist.

1 Every murder turns on a bright hot light, and a lot of people . . . have to walk out of the shadows.

Narrator, in *The Naked City* (film, 1948, screenplay by Albert Maltz and Malvin Wald, directed by Jules Dassin). Hellinger's last production was narrated by himself.

2 There are eight million stories in the naked city. This has been one of them.

Afterword in ibid. Hellinger's sign-off was used at the end of each episode of the TV series of the same name (1958–62).

## Lillian Hellman (1905–84)
US PLAYWRIGHT

A left-wing activist who was regarded as the foremost woman playwright of her generation, she dealt with political and social issues in her plays, such as lesbianism in *The Children's Hour* (1934) and industrialism in *The Little Foxes* (1939). She lived for thirty-one years with DASHIELL HAMMETT until his death in 1966. See also JULES FEIFFER 2, MARY MCCARTHY 12.

1 Cynicism is an unpleasant way of saying the truth.

Ben, in *The Little Foxes*, act 1 (1939)

2 It's an indulgence to sit in a room and discuss your beliefs as if they were a juicy piece of gossip.

Sara Müller, in *Watch on the Rhine*, act 2 (1941)

3 I cannot and will not cut my conscience to fit this year's fashions.

Letter to John S. Wood, Chairman of the House Committee on Un-American Activities, 19 May 1952, quoted in *Nation* 31 May 1952. The letter contained Hellman's refusal to testify against colleagues accused of communist affiliations.

4 People change and forget to tell each other. Too bad – causes so many mistakes.

Anna, in *Toys in the Attic*, act 3 (1960)

5 They're fancy talkers about themselves, writers. If I had to give young writers advice, I would say don't listen to writers talking about writing or themselves.

*The New York Times* 21 February 1960

6 Intellectuals can tell themselves anything, sell themselves any bill of goods, which is why they were so often patsies for the ruling classes in nineteenth-century France and England, or twentieth-century Russia and America.

Journal entry, 30 April 1967, publ. in Hellman's memoir, *An Unfinished Woman*, ch. 13 (1969)

7 It is a mark of many famous people that they cannot part with their brightest hour: what worked once must always work.

*Pentimento*, 'Theatre' (1973). Referring to TALLULAH BANKHEAD, who 'had been the nineteen-twenties' most daring girl, but what had been dashing, even brave, had become by 1939 shrill and tiring'.

8 Every time she [Elizabeth Taylor] gets laid she gets married. Nobody told her you can do it and stay single.

Quoted in *Lilly: Reminiscences of Lillian Hellman*, pt 4 (1988) by Peter Feibleman

## Leona Helmsley (b. 1920)
US BUSINESSWOMAN

Dubbed 'the Queen of Mean' by the tabloids, she was sentenced in 1992 to four years in prison, 750 hours of community service and $7.1 million in fines for tax evasion. In 1998 she was left a second fortune by her husband.

1 We don't pay taxes. Only the little people pay taxes.

Quoted in *The New York Times* 12 July 1989. The words were reported by Helmsley's former housekeeper during her employer's trial for tax evasion.

## Ernest Hemingway (1899–1961)
US AUTHOR

Themes of honour and virility recur in his novels and short stories, which tell of war, bullfighting, big-game hunting and fishing. He served as war correspondent in the Spanish Civil War and the Second World War and was awarded the Nobel Prize for Literature in 1954. Major works include *A Farewell to Arms* (1929), *For Whom the Bell Tolls* (1940) and *The Old Man and the Sea* (1952), for which he won a Pulitzer Prize. He took his own life with a shotgun. Describing his profoundly influential prose style, Ford Madox Ford said: 'Hemingway's words strike you, each one, as if they were pebbles fetched fresh from a brook.' See also MARLENE DIETRICH 5, MIKE TYSON 2.

1 Switzerland is a small, steep country, much more up and down than sideways, and is all stuck over with large brown hotels built on the cuckoo clock style of architecture.

Quoted in *Toronto Star Weekly* 4 March 1922

2 The age demanded that we dance
And jammed us into iron pants.
And in the end the age was handed
The sort of shit that it demanded.

'The Age Demanded', publ. in *Der Querschnitt* February 1925, repr. in *Sylvia Beach and the Lost Generation*, ch. 9 (1983) by Noel Riley Fitch

3 God knows people who are paid to have attitudes toward things, professional critics, make me sick; camp following eunuchs of literature. They won't even whore. They're all virtuous and sterile. And how well meaning and high minded. But they're all camp followers.

Letter to Sherwood Anderson, 23 May 1925, publ. in *Selected Letters* (ed. Carlos Baker, 1981)

4 You're an expatriate. You've lost touch with the soil. You get precious. Fake European standards have ruined you. You drink yourself to death. You become obsessed by sex. You spend all your time talking, not working. You are an expatriate, see? You hang around cafés.

Bill Gorton to Jake Barnes, in *The Sun Also Rises*, bk 2, ch. 12 (1926, filmed 1957). Jake replies: 'It sounds like a swell life.'

5 In the fall the war was always there but we did not go to it any more.

*Men Without Women*, 'In Another Country' (1927). F. SCOTT FITZGERALD regarded this sentence as 'one of the most beautiful prose sentences I've ever read'.

6 I was always embarrassed by the words sacred, glorious and sacrifice and the expression in vain. We had heard them, sometimes standing in the rain almost out of earshot, so that only the shouted words came through, and had read them, on proclamations that were slapped up by billposters over other proclamations, now for a long time, and I had seen nothing sacred, and the things that were glorious had no glory and the sacrifices were like the stockyards at Chicago if nothing was done with the meat except to bury it.

Frederic Henry, in *A Farewell to Arms*, ch. 27 (1929, filmed 1932 and 1957)

7 Grace under pressure.

Definition of 'guts', in interview by DOROTHY PARKER in the *New*

*Yorker* 30 November 1929. The formula was invoked by JOHN F. KENNEDY at the start of his collection of essays, *Profiles of Courage* (1956), possibly originating in the Latin motto, *Fortiter in re, suaviter in modo* ('strong in deed, gentle in manner').

8 Our nada who art in nada, nada be thy name thy kingdom nada thy will be nada in nada as it is in nada. Give us this nada our daily nada and nada us our nada as we nada our nadas and nada us not into nada but deliver us from nada; pues nada. Hail nothing full of nothing, nothing is with thee.

The older waiter, in 'A Clean, Well-Lighted Place', publ. in *Winner Take Nothing* (1933)

9 About morals, I know only that what is moral is what you feel good after and what is immoral is what you feel bad after.

*Death in the Afternoon*, ch. 1 (1932)

10 All our words from loose using have lost their edge.

ibid. ch. 7

11 Bullfighting is the only art in which the artist is in danger of death and in which the degree of brilliance in the performance is left to the fighter's honor.

ibid. ch. 9

12 Madame, all stories, if continued far enough, end in death, and he is no true-story teller who would keep that from you.

ibid. ch. 11

13 A serious writer is not to be confounded with a solemn writer. A serious writer may be a hawk or a buzzard or even a popinjay, but a solemn writer is always a bloody owl.

ibid. ch. 16

14 All good books are alike in that they are truer than if they had really happened and after you are finished reading one you will feel that all that happened to you and afterwards it all belongs to you; the good and the bad, the ecstasy, the remorse, and sorrow, the people and the places and how the weather was.

'Old Newsman Writes: A Letter from Cuba', first publ. in *Esquire* December 1934, repr. in *By-Line Ernest Hemingway* (ed. William White, 1967)

15 All modern American literature comes from one book by Mark Twain called *Huckleberry Finn* . . . American writing comes from that. There was nothing before. There has been nothing as good since.

*The Green Hills of Africa*, ch. 1 (1935)

16 The rich were dull and they drank too much or they played too much backgammon. They were dull and they were repetitious. He remembered poor Julian and his romantic awe of them and how he had started a story once that began, 'The very rich are different from you and me.' And how someone had said to Julian, 'Yes, they have more money.'

'The Snows of Kilimanjaro', first publ. in *Esquire* August 1936, repr. in *The Fifth Column and the First Forty-Nine Stories* (1938). In its original publication, 'Julian' was named as F. Scott Fitzgerald, who in 1926 had opened a story: 'Let me tell you about the very rich. They are different from you and me.' See also F. SCOTT FITZGERALD 14.

17 But did thee feel the earth move?

Robert Jordan speaking to Maria, in *For Whom the Bell Tolls*, ch. 13 (1940, filmed 1943). During their lovemaking, Jordan had 'felt the earth move out and away from under them'. The words do not appear in the film version.

18 He [his father] was just a coward and that was the worst luck any man could have.

Robert Jordan, in ibid. ch. 30

19 The world is a fine place and worth fighting for.

Robert Jordan, in ibid. ch. 43

20 Cowardice, as distinguished from panic, is almost always simply a lack of ability to suspend the functioning of the imagination.

*Men at War*, Introduction (1942)

21 All my life I've looked at words as though I were seeing them for the first time.

Letter, 9 April 1945, publ. in *Selected Letters* (ed. Carlos Baker, 1981)

22 It wasn't by accident that the Gettysburg address was so short. The laws of prose writing are as immutable as those of flight, of mathematics, of physics.

Letter, 23 July 1945, publ. in ibid. Hemingway was discussing the difficulties of sustaining an epic at a high pitch.

23 Scott [Scott Fitzgerald] took LITERATURE so solemnly. He never understood that it was just writing as well as you can and finishing what you start.

Letter to Arthur Mizener, 12 May 1950, publ. in ibid. Mizener wrote a biography of SCOTT FITZGERALD and edited his essays and short stories.

24 I started out very quiet and I beat Mr Turgenev. Then I trained hard and I beat Mr de Maupassant. I've fought two draws with Mr Stendhal, and I think I had an edge in the last one. But nobody's going to get me in any ring with Mr Tolstoy unless I'm crazy or I keep getting better.

*New Yorker* 13 May 1950

25 Writing and travel broaden your ass if not your mind and I like to write standing up.

Letter, 9 July 1950, publ. in *Selected Letters* (ed. Carlos Baker, 1981)

26 Man is not made for defeat. A man can be destroyed but not defeated.

*The Old Man and the Sea* (1952). Quoted as the last words in A.E. Hotchner's biography, *Papa Hemingway* (1966).

27 There isn't any symbolism. The sea is the sea. The old man is an old man. The boy is a boy and the fish is a fish. The shark are all sharks no better and no worse. All the symbolism that people say is shit. What goes beyond is what you see beyond when you know.

Letter to the critic Bernard Berenson, 13 September 1952, publ. in *Selected Letters* (ed. Carlos Baker, 1981). Referring to Hemingway's novella *The Old Man and the Sea*.

28 Actually if a writer needs a dictionary he should not write. He should have read the dictionary at least three times from beginning to end and then have loaned it to someone who needs it. There are only certain words which are valid and similies (bring me my dictionary) are like defective ammunition (the lowest thing I can think of at this time).

Letter to Bernard Berenson, 20 March 1953, publ. in ibid. Hemingway's spelling, as manifested in his letters, was deeply flawed. See also 37 below.

29 Writing, at its best, is a lonely life. Organizations for writers palliate the writer's loneliness, but I doubt if they improve his writing. He grows in public stature as he sheds his loneliness and often his work deteriorates. For he does his work alone and if he is a good enough writer he must face eternity, or the lack of it, each day.

Address recorded for the Nobel Prize Committee, accepting the Nobel Prize for Literature, 10 December 1954, publ. in *Hemingway: the Writer as Artist*, ch. 13 (1963) by Carlos Baker

30 How simple the writing of literature would be if it were only necessary to write in another way what has been well written. It is because we have had such great writers in the past that a writer is driven far out past where he can go, out to where no one can help him.

ibid.

31 The most essential gift for a good writer is a built-in, shock-proof, shit detector. This is the writer's radar and all great writers have had it.

Interview in the *Paris Review* spring 1958, repr. in *Writers at Work* (second series, ed. George Plimpton, 1963)

32 We are all apprentices in a craft where no one ever becomes a master.

*New York Journal-American* 11 July 1961

33 All things truly wicked start from an innocence.

*A Moveable Feast*, ch. 17 (1964)

34 Never confuse movement with action.

Quoted by MARLENE DIETRICH in *Papa Hemingway*, pt 1, ch. 1 (1966) by A.E. Hotchner. 'In those five words,' Dietrich commented, 'he gave me a whole philosophy.'

35 You write a book like that that you're fond of over the years, then you see that happen to it, it's like pissing in your father's beer.

After seeing DAVID O. SELZNICK's remake of *A Farewell to Arms* (1957), quoted in ibid.

36 If you are lucky enough to have lived in Paris as a young man, then wherever you go for the rest of your life it stays with you, for Paris is a moveable feast.

Quoted in ibid. pt 1, ch. 3. The words 'a moveable feast' were used – on Hotchner's recommendation – as the title of Hemingway's posthumously published Paris memoirs. This paragraph appears as the book's epigraph.

37 Poor Faulkner. Does he really think big emotions come from big words? He thinks I don't know the ten-dollar words. I know them all right. But there are older and simpler and better words, and those are the ones I use.

Quoted in ibid. pt 1, ch. 4. Hemingway's rebuke was made after being informed (by Hotchner) that WILLIAM FAULKNER considered Hemingway 'had no courage' and 'had never been known to use a word that might send the reader to the dictionary'. For Hemingway, Faulkner was 'Old Corndrinking Mellifluous'.

38 To be a successful father . . . there's one absolute rule: when you have a kid, don't look at it for the first two years.

Quoted in ibid. pt 2, ch. 5

## Jimi Hendrix (1942–70)

US ROCK MUSICIAN

Full name James Marshall Hendrix. Half-Cherokee Indian from his mother's side, he was the most influential rock guitarist of the 1960s, legendary for his virtuoso technique and flamboyant style. He transferred from New York to London in 1966, when he quickly established himself and had hits with 'Hey Joe', 'Purple Haze' (both 1967) and 'All Along the Watchtower' (1968), among others. His early death was the result of drugs abuse.

1 Hey Joe,
  Where're you going with that gun in your hand?

'Hey Joe' (song, 1966, written by Billy Roberts) on the album *Smash Hits* (1968). The song was a US hit for LA garage band the Leaves in 1966, although it had earlier been performed by David Crosby with the Byrds.

2 Purple haze all in my brain,
  Lately things don't seem the same,
  Actin' funny, but I don't know why,
  'Scuse me while I kiss the sky.

'Purple Haze' (song, 1967) on ibid.

3 I believe everybody should have a room where they get rid of all their . . . releases, where they can do all their releases. So my room was a stage.

Interview 12 September 1970, publ. in *Radio 1's Classic Interviews* (ed. Jeff Simpson, 1992). The interview, which has never been fully broadcast, took place two days before Hendrix was found dead in his London hotel room.

4 I'd like to take part in a change of reality.

ibid. In answer to the question, 'Do you want to change the world?'

5 Blues is easy to play, but hard to feel.

Quoted in *Crosstown Traffic*, ch. 6 (1989) by Charles Shaar Murray

## Arthur W.D. Henley

1 Nobody loves a fairy when she's forty.

'Nobody Loves a Fairy When She's Forty' (song, 1934, written by Arthur le Clerq). The song was recorded by Tessie O'Shea.

## Katharine Hepburn (b. 1909)

US ACTRESS

An untypical Hollywood star for her independence of spirit and feisty manner, she had a famous though highly private relationship with Spencer Tracy that lasted for twenty-seven years, during which they appeared together in nine films. Her other films include *The Philadelphia Story* (1940), *The African Queen* (1951) and *On Golden Pond* (1981), for all of which she won Oscar awards or nominations. She also appeared in stage musicals and on television. HUMPHREY BOGART remarked: 'She doesn't give a damn how she looks. I don't think she tries to be a character. I think she is one.' See also DOROTHY PARKER 13.

1 The average Hollywood film star's ambition is to be admired by an American, courted by an Italian, married to an Englishman and have a French boyfriend.

*New York Journal-American* 22 February 1954

2 Only the really plain people know about love – the very fascinating ones try so hard to create an impression that they very soon exhaust their talents.

*Look* 18 February 1958

3 To keep your character intact you cannot stoop to filthy acts. It makes it easier to stoop the next time.

Quoted in the *Los Angeles Times* 24 November 1974

## (Sir) A.P. Herbert (1890–1971)

BRITISH AUTHOR AND POLITICIAN

Full name Alan Patrick Herbert. A brilliant comic librettist, he was the author of *La Vie Parisienne* (1929) and *Bless the Bride* (1947). His novels include *The Secret Battle* (1919), which led to an improvement in court martial procedure, and *Holy Deadlock* (1934), which showed up the iniquities of the divorce laws. He also wrote for *Punch*, and was an Independent MP for Oxford (1935–50).

1 People must not do things for fun. We are not here for fun. There is no reference to fun in any act of Parliament.

Lord Light, in *Uncommon Law*, 'Is it a Free Country?' (1935)

2 The critical period in matrimony is breakfast-time.

ibid. 'Is Marriage Lawful?'

3 The Englishman never enjoys himself except for a noble purpose.

Mr Justice Plush, in ibid. 'Is Fox-Hunting Fun?'

4 An Act of God was defined as '*something which no reasonable man could have expected*'.

Mr David, in ibid. 'Act of God'

## Oliver Herford (1863–1935)

US POET AND ILLUSTRATOR

Called by William Dean Howells the 'Charles Lamb of his day', he contributed illustrations, caricatures, verses and essays to numerous periodicals from the 1890s to the 1930s, including the *Ladies Home Journal* and *Harper's Magazine*. *A Little Book of Bores* (1906) and *Confessions of a Caricaturist* (1917) are among his collections.

1 [He] has a whim of iron.

*Excuse It Please*, 'Impossible Pudding' (1929). Referring to King Barumph in the story, although the remark had earlier been attributed to Herford about his wife.

## Michael Herr (b. 1940)

US JOURNALIST

He covered the Vietnam War for *Esquire* in 1967, later describing his impressions in *Dispatches* (1977). He was script consultant to COPPOLA's *Apocalypse Now* (1979) and wrote the screenplay for *Full Metal Jacket* (1987).

1 We came to fear something more complicated than death, an annihilation less final but more complete, and we got out. Because . . . we all knew that if you stayed too long you became one of those poor bastards who had to have a war on all the time, and where was that?

*Dispatches*, 'Colleagues', sect. 3 (1977)

2 Vietnam was what we had instead of happy childhoods.

ibid.

3 All the wrong people remember Vietnam. I think all the people who remember it should forget it, and all the people who forgot it should remember it.

*Observer* 15 January 1989

## Édouard Herriot (1872–1957)

FRENCH STATESMAN

A radical Socialist politician, he was Prime Minister 1924–5, 1926 and 1932. While President of the Chamber of Deputies, he opposed the Vichy government, was arrested and became a prisoner of the Nazis. He was later President of the National Assembly (1947–54).

1 When it's a question of peace one must talk to the Devil himself.

*Quoted in the* Observer *21 September 1953*

## John Hersey (1914–93)

US NOVELIST AND JOURNALIST

He is known for his documentary fiction of the Second World War, including *A Bell for Adano* (1944), which won the Pulitzer Prize, and *Hiroshima* (1946), the first eye-witness account of the nuclear explosion.

1 What has kept the world safe from the bomb since 1945 has not been deterrence, in the sense of fear of specific weapons, so much as it's been memory. The memory of what happened at Hiroshima.

*Interview in* Writers at Work *(eighth series, ed. George Plimpton, 1988)*

## Werner Herzog (b. 1942)

GERMAN FILM-MAKER

Original name Werner Stipetic. A leading member of the New Cinema in Germany, he is recognized for his metaphysical films in which landscape plays a prominent role, such as *Aguirre: the Wrath of God* (1973), *Heart of Glass* (1976) and *Where the Green Ants Dream* (1984).

1 You should look straight at a film; that's the only way to see one. Film is not the art of scholars but of illiterates.

*Interview in* The New York Times *11 September 1977*

2 For such an advanced civilization as ours to be without images that are adequate to it is as serious a defect as being without memory.

ibid.

## Michael Heseltine (b. 1933)

BRITISH POLITICIAN

Elected a Conservative MP in 1966, he was Secretary of State for the Environment (1979–83) and Defence Secretary (1983–6), resigning over the take-over of Westland helicopters. Nicknamed 'Tarzan' for his outdoors image, he unsuccessfully stood for the

Party leadership following MARGARET THATCHER's resignation (1990) and served as Deputy Prime Minister under JOHN MAJOR (1995–7), retiring from politics in 2000.

1 There you have it! The final proof. Labour's brand new, shining, modernists' economic dream. But it's not Brown's – it's Balls'!

*Remark at the Conservative Party Conference, Bournemouth, 12 October 1994, quoted in the* Daily Telegraph *13 October 1994. Heseltine was referring to Gordon Brown's recent speech on Labour's economic policy, specifically: 'Our new economic approach is rooted in ideas which stress the importance of macroeconomics, neo-classical endogenous growth theory and the symbiotic relationships between growth and investment in people and infrastructure.' This was said by Heseltine to have been written by a '27-year-old choral-singing researcher named Ed Balls'.*

## Hermann Hesse (1877–1962)

GERMAN NOVELIST AND POET

Imbued with the influences of German romanticism, Eastern religion and Jungian psychoanalysis, his works include *Siddhartha* (1922), *Steppenwolf* (1927) and *The Glass Bead Game* (1943). He won the Nobel Prize for Literature in 1946 and acquired a cult following after his death.

1 What constitutes a real, live human being is more of a mystery than ever these days, and men – each one of whom is a valuable, unique experiment on the part of nature – are shot down wholesale.

*Narrator (Sinclair), in* Demian, *Prologue (1919)*

2 In each individual the spirit is made flesh, in each one the whole of creation suffers, in each one a Saviour is crucified.

ibid.

3 I am fond of music I think because it is so amoral. Everything else is moral and I am after something that isn't. I have always found moralizing intolerable.

*ibid. ch. 5*

4 One never reaches home, but wherever friendly paths intersect the whole world looks like home for a time.

*Frau Eva, in ibid. ch. 7*

5 Every age, every culture, every custom and tradition has its own character, its own weakness and its own strength, its beauties and cruelties; it accepts certain sufferings as matters of course, puts up patiently with certain evils. Human life is reduced to real suffering, to hell, only when two ages, two cultures and religions overlap.

*Steppenwolf, Preface (1927)*

6 What I always hated and detested and cursed above all things was this contentment, this healthiness and comfort, this carefully preserved optimism of the middle classes, this fat and prosperous brood of mediocrity.

*ibid. 'For Madmen Only'*

7 The bourgeois treasures nothing more highly than the self . . . And so at the cost of intensity he achieves his own preservation and security. His harvest is a quiet mind which he prefers to being possessed by God, as he prefers comfort to pleasure, convenience to liberty, and a pleasant temperature to that deathly inner consuming fire.

*ibid. 'Treatise on the Steppenwolf '*

8 To study history means submitting to chaos and nevertheless retaining faith in order and meaning. It is a very serious task, young man, and possibly a tragic one.

*Father Jacobus, in* The Glass Bead Game, *ch. 4 (1943, transl. 1960)*

9 The call of death is a call of love. Death can be sweet if we answer it in the affirmative, if we accept it as one of the great eternal forms of life and transformation.

*Letter, 1950, publ. in* Hermann Hesse: A Pictorial Biography, *'Montagnola' (ed. Volker Michels, 1973)*

## Lord Hewart (1870–1943)

BRITISH JUDGE

Gordon Hewart, first Viscount Hewart. He was Liberal MP for Leicester (1913–22), Attorney-General (1919–22) and Lord Chief Justice (1922–40). He was judged a brilliant advocate but less effective as a judge.

1 Justice should not only be done, but should manifestly and undoubtedly be seen to be done.

Remark in 'Rex v. Surrey Justices', 9 November 1923, publ. in *King's Bench Reports*, vol. 1 (1924). Ruling on the quashing of a conviction on technical grounds.

## Robert Hewison (b. 1943)

BRITISH CULTURAL HISTORIAN

He is theatre critic and commentator on the arts for the *Sunday Times*, and Professor of Literary and Cultural Studies at Lancaster. His books include *Ruskin in Venice* (1978) and *The Heritage Industry* (1987).

1 Individually, museums are fine institutions, dedicated to the high values of preservation, education and truth; collectively, their growth in numbers points to the imaginative death of this country.

*The Heritage Industry*, Introduction (1987)

2 If the only new thing we have to offer is an improved version of the past, then today can only be inferior to yesterday. Hypnotized by images of the past, we risk losing all capacity for creative change.

ibid.

3 Postmodernism is modernism with the optimism taken out.

ibid. ch. 6

4 The turn of the century raises expectations. The end of a millennium promises apocalypse and revelation. But at the close of the twentieth century the golden age seems behind us, not ahead. The end game of the 1990s promises neither nirvana nor armageddon, but entropy.

*Future Tense*, ch. 1 (1990)

## Du Bose Heyward See IRA GERSHWIN 2, 3.

## George V. Higgins (1939–99)

US NOVELIST

Full name George Vincent Higgins. His first-hand experiences as journalist and attorney contributed to the success of his literary thrillers, which often have Boston as a backdrop. These include *The Friends of Eddie Coyle* (1972) and *Outlaws* (1987).

1 Data is what distinguishes the dilettante from the artist.

*Guardian* 17 June 1988

2 Politics is a choice of enemas. You're gonna get it up the ass, no matter what you do.

Ed Cobb, in *Victories*, ch. 7 (1991)

## Benny Hill (1925–92)

BRITISH COMEDIAN

Original name Alfred Hawthorne. He was considered the last of the visual comics and wrote scripts and music as well as playing most of the characters in *The Benny Hill Show* on television (1957–66). Although he excelled in a saucy British humour, his sketches were popular world-wide.

1 That's what show business is – sincere insincerity.

Quoted in the *Observer* 12 June 1977

## Christopher Hill (b. 1912)

BRITISH HISTORIAN

A Marxist historian, he has written widely on the period of the Civil War, including *The English Revolution, 1640* (1940). Among his other books are *Reformation to Industrial Revolution* (1967) and *Milton and the English Revolution* (1978). He was Master of Balliol College, Oxford (1965–78).

1 Only very slowly and late have men come to realize that unless freedom is universal it is only extended privilege.

*The Century of Revolution*, ch. 20 (1961)

2 History has to be rewritten in every generation, because although the past does not change the present does; each generation asks new questions of the past, and finds new areas of sympathy as it re-lives different aspects of the experiences of its predecessors.

*The World Turned Upside Down*, Introduction (1972)

## Damon Hill (b. 1960)

BRITISH RACING DRIVER

Son of Formula One driver Graham Hill and winner of more than twenty Grands Prix, he took first place for the Williams team in the 1996 world championship. He retired from Formula One racing in 1999.

1 Winning is everything. The only ones who remember when you come second are your wife and your dog.

Quoted in the *Sunday Times* 18 December 1994

## Sidney Hillman (1887–1946)

LITHUANIAN-BORN US TRADE UNIONIST

Original name Simcha Hillman. He emigrated to the US in 1907, became President of the Amalgamated Clothing Workers of America in 1914, a position he kept until his death, and pioneered such reforms as the forty-hour week. He was Vice-president of the World Federation of Trade Unions (1945–6).

1 Politics is the science of how who gets what, when and why.

*Political Primer for all Americans* (1944)

## Heinrich Himmler (1900–1945)

GERMAN NAZI LEADER

He was made head of the SS in 1929 and of the Gestapo in 1936 and was responsible for directing the extermination of the Jews. During the Second World War he became HITLER's second-in-command, and after his capture in 1945 he committed suicide.

1 My honour is my loyalty.
(*Meine Ehre heisst Treue.*)

Formulated as the watchword of the SS Nazi élite, translated by HANNAH ARENDT in *The Origins of Totalitarianism*, ch. 10 (1951). The US Government Printing Office's *Nazi Conspiracy and Aggression* (1946–8), vol. 5 gives an alternative translation: 'My honour signifies faithfulness.'

2 Whether nations live in prosperity or starve to death like cattle interests me only in so far as we need them as slaves to our *Kultur*; otherwise it is of no interest to me. Whether 10,000 Russian females fall down from exhaustion while digging an antitank ditch interests me only in so far as the antitank ditch for Germany is finished.

Address to SS officers at Posen, 4 October 1943, quoted in *The Rise and Fall of the Third Reich*, ch. 27 (1959) by William L. Shirer

## Beatrice Hinkle (1874–1953)

US PSYCHIATRIST

In 1899 she was the first woman to be City Physician of San Francisco. She was also the first American practitioner of JUNG's analytical psychology, and through her translation of Jung's work *On the Psychology of the Unconscious* (1916) played a key role in diffusing his theories. Her book *The Re-creating of the Individual* (1923) established her as a pioneering feminist critic of FREUD.

1 Fundamentally the male artist approximates more to the psychology of woman, who, biologically speaking, is a purely creative being and whose personality has been as mysterious and unfathomable to the man as the artist has been to the average person.

*The Re-creating of the Individual*, 'The Psychology of the Artist' (1923)

## Hirohito (1901–89)
EMPEROR OF JAPAN

Ostensibly against Japanese expansionism in 1931–40, he urged a peaceful solution in the Second World War but was too late to prevent the dropping of the atom bombs on Hiroshima and Nagasaki. After the end of the war he renounced his divinity.

1 We have resolved to endure the unendurable and suffer what is unsufferable.

Statement 15 August 1945, quoted by A.J.P. TAYLOR in the *Listener* 9 September 1976. The declaration was made following the dropping of the atomic bomb on Hiroshima and was the first time a Japanese emperor had made a direct address to his people.

## Damien Hirst (b. 1965)
BRITISH ARTIST

His often provocative installations and most famously his pickled animals raise questions of life and mortality, while precipitating both debate over the role of art and demonstrations by animal activists. He was awarded the Turner Prize in 1995 with *Mother and Child Divided*.

1 I sometimes feel that I have nothing to say and I want to communicate this.

*Independent* 21 July 1992

2 I think the idea is more important than the object. The object can look after itself. It will probably last long after I'm dead. I'm more frightened of being stabbed myself. You can always get another shark.

Interview by WILL SELF in *Modern Painters* summer 1994, repr. in *Junk Mail* (1995) by Will Self. Hirst was referring to one of his installations of a shark preserved in formaldehyde. Coincidentally, the day after this interview, one of his new exhibits at the Serpentine Gallery, also a preserved animal, was vandalized.

3 As an artist you have to reinvent yourself everyday. Which I think is what you do anyway as a person, which is why people fall out, split up, get together . . . It's like a turning over.

Interview in *The Idler* July/August 1995

4 I think there's a handful of eye people and billions of ear people. Some people go look at it and think it's great, so they buy it, and all these other people hear that they've bought it so they buy it too.

Interview in *Big Issue* 1–7 September 1997

5 I've got two ways of looking at this. I am either a genius – hummmm, fantastic – or the art world is incapable of dealing with the kind of art that is going on today. My answer is the art world is fucked. I'm not a genius.

Quoted in the *Observer* 14 September 1997

## Ian Hislop (b. 1960)
BRITISH JOURNALIST AND BROADCASTER

He was a television scriptwriter for *Spitting Image* (1984–9), became editor of *Private Eye* in 1989 and since 1991 has captained a team on the BBC quiz show *Have I Got News For You*. He has also written plays for television.

1 It's the gap between how they *think* they are coming over and how they *actually* come over. In their case, it's the *gulf* between their self-perception and the reality. The job of a satirist is to point it out.

Interview in the *Guardian* 27 April 1996. Referring to what makes JAMES GOLDSMITH, JEFFREY ARCHER and DIANA, PRINCESS OF WALES natural subjects for satire.

## (Sir) Alfred Hitchcock (1899–1980)
BRITISH FILM-MAKER

Based in Hollywood from the 1940s, he was a master of the suspense thriller, noted for his novel camera techniques and audience manipulation. His films, in which he usually made cameo walk-ons, include *The Thirty Nine Steps* (1935), *Rear Window* (1954), *Psycho* (1960) and *The Birds* (1963). 'His reputation has suffered from the fact that he has given audiences more pleasure than is permissible in serious cinema,' was critic Andrew Sarris's tribute.

1 Actors are cattle.

Quoted in the *Saturday Evening Post* 22 May 1943. The remark caused Carole Lombard, his star of the time, to lead a herd of oxen on to the set. He later told the press, 'I didn't say actors are cattle. What I said was, actors should be *treated* like cattle.'

2 Drama is life with the dull bits cut out.

Quoted in the *Observer* 10 July 1960. Speaking to FRANÇOIS TRUFFAUT in 1962, Hitchcock explained: 'Making a film means, first of all, to tell a story. That story can be an improbable one, but it should never be banal. It must be dramatic and human. What is drama, after all, but life with the dull bits cut out?'

3 Some films are slices of life. Mine are slices of cake.

Interview August 1962, publ. in *Hitchcock*, ch. 4 (1966, rev. 1984) by François Truffaut. The quote re-surfaced (more coherently) as 'For me, the cinema is not a slice of life, but a piece of cake,' quoted in the *Sunday Times* 6 March 1977.

4 Dialogue should simply be a sound among other sounds, just something that comes out of the mouths of people whose eyes tell the story in visual terms.

ibid. ch. 11

5 I find commercials fascinating. They are so exquisitely vulgar and so delightfully tasteless that they must be irresistible to everyone save the few who aren't enchanted by discussions of nasal passages and digestive tracts.

Screen Producers Guild dinner, 7 March 1965, publ. in *Hitchcock on Hitchcock*, 'After-Dinner Speech' (ed. Sidney Gottlieb, 1995). The television commercial, Hitchcock added, 'is the only instance where Man has invented a torture and then provided the victim with a means of escape'.

6 The invention of television can be compared to the introduction of indoor plumbing. Fundamentally it brought no change in the public's habits. It simply eliminated the necessity of leaving the house.

ibid.

7 One of television's greatest contributions is that it brought murder back into the home where it belongs.

Quoted in the *Observer* 19 December 1965

8 Blondes are the best victims. They're like virgin snow which shows up the bloody footprints.

*Sunday Times* 1 September 1973

9 In the old days villains had moustaches and kicked the dog. Audiences are smarter today. They don't want their villain to be thrown at them with green limelight on his face. They want an ordinary human being with failings.

Quoted in *Filmgoer's Companion* (ed. Leslie Halliwell, 1984)

10 I'm not against the police; I'm just afraid of them.

Quoted in *New Society* 10 May 1984

11 There is no terror in a bang, only in the anticipation of it.

Quoted in *Halliwell's Who's Who in the Movies* (ed. John Walker, 1999)

# Adolf Hitler (1889–1945)

GERMAN DICTATOR

By 1921 he had assumed leadership of the National Socialist German Workers' Party (Nazi Party) and after a failed attempt at overthrowing the government wrote his political manifesto, *Mein Kampf*, from prison (1925). Made Chancellor in 1933, he initiated the expansionist policy that led to the Second World War. Within Germany he pursued a fanatical anti-Semitic policy and was responsible for the deaths of millions of Jews, Slavs, Romanies and homosexuals. He committed suicide. See also HENRY MILLER 9, EZRA POUND 23.

1 If today I stand here as a revolutionary, it is as a revolutionary against the Revolution.

Speech 26 February 1924, quoted in *Hitler, a Study in Tyranny*, ch. 2, sect. 7 (1952, rev. 1962) by Alan Bullock. Hitler's statement was made while he was on trial for his part in the unsuccessful *putsch* against the Republican government in Munich, Germany, which had itself overthrown the Bavarian monarchy in 1918.

2 The broad masses of a population are more amenable to the appeal of rhetoric than to any other force.

*Mein Kampf*, vol. 1, ch. 3 (1925)

3 All great movements are popular movements. They are the volcanic eruptions of human passions and emotions, stirred into activity by the ruthless Goddess of Distress or by the torch of the spoken word cast into the midst of the people.

ibid.

4 The art of leadership ... consists in consolidating the attention of the people against a single adversary and taking care that nothing will split up that attention ... The leader of genius must have the ability to make different opponents appear as if they belonged to one category.

ibid.

5 Mankind has grown strong in eternal struggles and it will only perish through eternal peace.

ibid. ch. 4

6 As soon as by one's own propaganda even a glimpse of right on the other side is admitted, the cause for doubting one's own right is laid.

ibid. ch. 6

7 The great mass of people ... will more easily fall victim to a big lie than to a small one.

ibid. ch. 10

8 Germany will either be a world power or will not be at all.

ibid. vol. 2, ch. 14

9 Struggle is the father of all things ... It is not by the principles of humanity that man lives or is able to preserve himself above the animal world, but solely by means of the most brutal struggle.

Speech at Kulmbach, 5 February 1928, quoted in *Hitler, a Study in Tyranny*, ch. 1, sect. 3 (1952, rev. 1962) by Alan Bullock

10 When an opponent declares, 'I will not come over to your side,' I calmly say, 'Your child belongs to us already ... What are you? You will pass on. Your descendants, however, now stand in the new camp. In a short time they will know nothing else but this new community.'

Speech 6 November 1933, quoted in *The Rise and Fall of the Third Reich*, ch. 8, 'Education in the Third Reich' (1959) by William L. Shirer

11 If it rests with Germany war will not come again. This country has a more profound impression than any other of the evil that war causes ... In our belief Germany's present-day problems cannot be settled by war.

Interview in the *Daily Mail* 6 August 1934

12 Whoever lights the torch of war in Europe can wish for nothing but chaos. We, however, live in the firm conviction that in our time will be fulfilled, not the decline, but the renaissance of the West. That Germany may make an imperishable contribution to this great work is our proud hope and our unshakeable belief.

Speech to Reichstag, Berlin, 21 May 1935, quoted in *Hitler, a Study in Tyranny*, ch. 6, sect. 4 (1952, rev. 1962) by Alan Bullock

13 I go the way that Providence dictates with the assurance of a sleepwalker.

Speech in Munich, 15 March 1936, quoted in ibid. ch. 7, sect. 1. On Germany's reoccupation of the Rhineland.

14 I am convinced that 1941 will be the crucial year of a great New Order in Europe. The world shall open up for everyone. Privileges for individuals, the tyranny of certain nations and their financial rulers shall fall. And, last of all, this year will help to provide the foundations of a real understanding among peoples, and with it the certainty of conciliation among nations ... Those nations who are still opposed to us will some day recognize the greater enemy within. They will join us in a combined front, a front against Jewish exploitation and racial degeneration.

Speech at Berlin Sportpalast, 30 January 1941, quoted in ibid. ch. 11, sect. 4. Closing words of speech.

15 The heaviest blow that ever struck humanity was the coming of Christianity. Bolshevism is Christianity's illegitimate child. Both are inventions of the Jew.

Remarks 11–12 June 1941, recorded by Martin Bormann, publ. in *Hitler's Table Talk* (1953). At a later date (10 October 1941), Hitler is reported: 'Christianity is a rebellion against natural law, a protest against nature. Taken to its logical extreme, Christianity would mean the systematic cultivation of the human failure.'

16 After fifteen years of work I have achieved, as a common German soldier and merely with my fanatical will-power, the unity of the German nation, and have freed it from the death sentence of Versailles.

Proclamation 21 December 1941, addressing troops after taking over as Commander-in-Chief of the army

17 I don't see much future for the Americans ... Everything about the behaviour of American society reveals that it's half Judaized, and the other half negrified. How can one expect a State like that to hold together?

Remarks 7 January 1942, recorded by Martin Bormann, publ. in *Hitler's Table Talk* (1953)

18 Churchill is the very type of a corrupt journalist. There's not a worse prostitute in politics. He himself has written that it's unimaginable what can be done in war with the help of lies. He's an utterly amoral repulsive creature. I'm convinced that he has his place of refuge ready beyond the Atlantic. He obviously won't seek sanctuary in Canada. In Canada he'd be beaten up. He'll go to his friends the Yankees. As soon as this damnable winter is over, we'll remedy all that.

ibid. 18 February 1942

19 Is Paris burning?
(*Brennt Paris?*)

Attributed inquiry by telephone to General Alfred Jodl, 25 August 1944, in Rastenburg, Germany. Hitler had ordered Paris to be destroyed rather than allow it to fall into Allied hands. The words were taken as the title of a book by Larry Collins and Dominique Lapierre (1965) and of a film with an all-star cast and screenplay contributions by Gore Vidal and Francis Ford Coppola (1966). In June 1940 Hitler is reported to have said to the architect ALBERT SPEER: 'In the past I have often wondered whether we would not have to destroy Paris. But when we are finished in Berlin, Paris will only be a shadow. So why should we destroy it?'

# Edward Hoagland (b. 1932)

US NOVELIST AND ESSAYIST

He has said, 'in all my books witnessing things is what counts', and it is for his observations on wild animals and nature that he is best known. After writing novels, such as *The Peacock's Tail* (1965), he turned to life-affirming non-fiction, including *The Courage of Turtles* (1971) and *African Calliope* (1979), and has contributed widely to periodicals.

1 Animals used to provide a lowlife way to kill and get away with it, as they do still, but, more intriguingly, for some people they are an aperture through which wounds drain. The scapegoat of olden times, driven off for the bystanders' sins, has become a tender thing, a running injury. There, running away . . . is me: hurt it and you are hurting me.

'Lament the Red Wolf', first publ. in *Sports Illustrated* 14 January 1974, repr. in *Heart's Desire* (1988)

2 In order to really enjoy a dog, one doesn't merely try to train him to be semihuman. The point of it is to open oneself to the possibility of becoming partly a dog.

'Dogs and the Tug of Life', first publ. in *Harper's Magazine* February 1975, repr. in ibid. (1988)

3 There is a time of life somewhere between the sullen fugues of adolescence and the retrenchments of middle age when human nature becomes so absolutely absorbing one wants to be in the city constantly, even at the height of summer.

'City Walking', first publ. in *The New York Times Book Review* 1 June 1975, repr. in ibid.

4 Men often compete with one another until the day they die; comradeship consists of rubbing shoulders jocularly with a competitor.

'Heaven and Nature', first publ. in *Harper's Magazine* March 1988, repr. in ibid.

5 The question of whether it's God's green earth is not at centre stage, except in the sense that if so, one is reminded with some regularity that He may be dying.

*Guardian* 20 January 1990

6 Like a kick in the butt, the force of events wakes slumberous talents.

*Guardian* 11 August 1990

## Russell Hoban (b. 1925)

US AUTHOR AND ILLUSTRATOR

He is known for the novels *Turtle Diary* (1975, filmed 1985, with screenplay by HAROLD PINTER) and *Riddley Walker* (1980), written in a new post-apocalyptic language, and as a writer of children's books, notably the classic *The Mouse and His Child* (1969).

1 If the past cannot teach the present and the father cannot teach the son, then history need not have bothered to go on, and the world has wasted a great deal of time.

Jachin-Boaz, in *The Lion of Boaz-Jachin and Jachin-Boaz*, ch. 1 (1973)

2 After all, when you come right down to it, how many people speak the same language even when they speak the same language?

Boaz-Jachin, in ibid. ch. 27

3 Sometimes there's nothing but Sundays for weeks on end. Why can't they move Sunday to the middle of the week so you could put it in the OUT tray on your desk?

'The tightly furled man', in ibid. ch. 32. 'Forgive us our Sundays,' he added, 'as we forgive those who Sunday against us.'

4 Me, what's that after all? An arbitrary limitation of being bounded by the people before and after and on either side. Where they leave off, I begin, and vice versa.

William G, in *Turtle Diary*, ch. 11 (1975)

5 Sometimes I think that the biggest difference between men and women is that more men need to seek out some terrible lurking thing in existence and hurl themselves upon it . . . Women know where it lives but they can let it alone.

Neaera, in ibid. ch. 18

6 Nothing to be done really about animals. Anything you do looks foolish. The answer isn't in us. It's almost as if we're put here on earth to show how silly they aren't.

George Fairbairn, in ibid. ch. 42

7 Language is an archaeological vehicle . . . the language we speak is a whole palimpsest of human effort and history.

*Novelists in Interview* (ed. John Haffenden 1985)

## E.J. Hobsbawm (b. 1917)

BRITISH HISTORIAN

Full name Eric John Hobsbawm. A leading European expert on the history of the working classes, he is author of *The Age of Revolution 1789–1848* (1962), *The Age of Capital 1848–75* (1975) and *Politics for a Rational Left* (1989). He has also written on jazz. A.J.P. TAYLOR commented, 'He has taken to heart Lenin's dictum "patiently explain".'

1 War has been the most convenient pseudo-solution for the problems of twentieth-century capitalism. It provides the incentives to modernization and technological revolution which the market and the pursuit of profit do only fitfully and by accident, it makes the unthinkable (such as votes for women and the abolition of unemployment) not merely thinkable but practicable . . . What is equally important, it can re-create communities of men and give a temporary sense to their lives by uniting them against foreigners and outsiders. This is an achievement beyond the power of the private enterprise economy . . . when left to itself.

*Observer* 26 May 1968

2 There is not much that even the most socially responsible scientists can do as individuals, or even as a group, about the social consequences of their activities.

*New York Review of Books* 19 November 1970

3 It seems that American patriotism measures itself against an outcast group. The right Americans are the right Americans because they're not like the wrong Americans, who are not really Americans.

*Marxism Today* January 1988

4 Xenophobia looks like becoming the mass ideology of the 20th-century *fin-de-siècle*. What holds humanity together today is the denial of what the human race has in common.

Lecture to the American Anthropological Association, publ. in *Anthropology Today* February 1992

5 Nations without a past are contradictions in terms. What makes a nation *is* the past, what justifies one nation against others is the past, and historians are the people who produce it.

ibid.

## David Hockney (b. 1937)

BRITISH ARTIST

Associated with the Pop Art movement in his early days, he developed a figurative style as in 'Mr and Mrs Clark and Percy' (1971). Since the mid-1960s he has lived in California, where he was inspired to use intense colours, most famously in his swimming pool series. He is also a printmaker and photographer and has designed for the opera. ROBERT HUGHES called him the 'Cole Porter of contemporary art'.

1 Television is becoming a collage – there are so many channels that you move through them making a collage yourself. In that sense, everyone sees something a bit different.

*Hockney On Photography*, 'New York: November 1985' (ed. Wendy Brown, 1988)

2 Art has to move you and design does not, unless it's a good design for a bus.

Press conference, Tate Gallery, 25 October 1988, London, quoted in the *Guardian* 26 October 1988

3 We live in an age where the artist is forgotten. He is a researcher. I see myself that way.

Quoted in the *Observer* 9 June 1991

4 Tobacco may kill you but it's slow and it's rather a pleasure. People smoke for their mental health don't they? It's part of their total health, I'd say.

Interview in the *Guardian* 25 March 1995. On taking up smoking after a period of abstinence.

5 Seeing is the function of memory.

Quoted in the *Observer* 30 May 1999

## Glenn Hoddle (b. 1957)
BRITISH FOOTBALL MANAGER AND PLAYER

He played for Tottenham Hotspur, Swindon Town and Chelsea before becoming England's manager (1996–9), when his reliance on the healer Eileen Drewery aroused controversy. In 2000 he was appointed manager of Southampton. He was described by *Zit* magazine as a 'tame, cultured ball wizard who thought "tackle" was something you put in your fishing bag'.

1 You and I have been physically given two hands and two legs and half decent brains. Some people have not been born like that for a reason. The karma is working from another lifetime. I have nothing to hide about that. It is not only people with disabilities. What you sow, you have to reap.

*The Times* 30 January 1999. This comment caused him to lose his position as England's manager, although he defended himself: 'What disabled people must know is that they will always have my overwhelming support, care, consideration and dedication.' The blind Labour minister DAVID BLUNKETT quipped in reply: 'If Hoddle is right, I must have been a failed football coach in a previous incarnation.'

## Ralph Hodgson (1871–1962)
BRITISH POET

Associated with the Georgian poets, he addressed the themes of England, nature and cruelty to animals in his work, which included the verse collections *The Last Blackbird* (1907), *Eve* (1913) and *Poems* (1917).

1 'Twould ring the bells of Heaven
The wildest peal for years,
If Parson lost his senses
And people came to theirs,
And he and they together
Knelt down with angry prayers
For tamed and shabby tigers
And dancing dogs and bears,
And wretched, blind, pit ponies,
And little hunted hares.

'Bells of Heaven', publ. in *Poems* (1917)

2 Time, you old gypsy man,
Will you not stay,
Put up your caravan
Just for one day?

'Time, You Old Gypsy Man', publ. in ibid.

## Peter Høeg (b. 1957)
DANISH AUTHOR

A dancer, actor, fencer and mountaineer before becoming a writer, he established himself as one of Denmark's foremost writers with *The History of Danish Dreams* (1988) and achieved international recognition with the wistful *Miss Smilla's Feeling for Snow* (1992) and *The Woman and the Ape* (1996).

1 Reading snow is like listening to music. To describe what you've read is to try to explain music in writing.

Smilla, in *Miss Smilla's Feeling for Snow*, 'The City' pt 1, ch. 7 (1992)

2 Deep inside I know that trying to fathom things out leads to blindness, that the desire to understand has a built-in brutality that erases what you seek to comprehend. Only experience is sensitive.

Smilla, in ibid. 'The City' pt 3, ch. 6

3 Time is no law of nature. It is a plan. When you look at it with awareness, or start to touch it, then it starts to disintegrate.

Katarina, in *Borderliners*, pt 1, ch. 14 (1993)

4 Contrary to what adults believe the joy of children at play comes not from having no knowledge of Death – every living creature has that. It comes from their divining what the grown-ups have lost sight of; that even though Death makes a fierce opponent, it is not invincible.

*The Woman and the Ape*, pt 3, ch. 1 (1996)

## Eric Hoffer (1902–83)
US PHILOSOPHER

An admirer of Montaigne, a self-educated scholar and working-class philosopher, he held a part-time job as a dockworker while producing collections of essays and aphorisms, for example *The Passionate State of Mind* (1955) and *Reflections on the Human Condition* (1972).

1 More! is as effective a revolutionary slogan as was ever invented by doctrinaires of discontent. The American, who cannot learn to want what he has, is a permanent revolutionary.

*The Passionate State of Mind*, aph. 22 (1955)

2 Youth itself is a talent – a perishable talent.

ibid. aph. 32

3 When people are free to do as they please, they usually imitate each other.

ibid. aph. 33. Hoffer added: 'A society which gives unlimited freedom to the individual, more often than not attains a disconcerting sameness. On the other hand, where communal discipline is strict but not ruthless . . . originality is likely to thrive.'

4 Facts are counterrevolutionary.

ibid. aph. 73

5 To have a grievance is to have a purpose in life.

ibid. aph. 166. Hoffer added: 'It not infrequently happens that those who hunger for hope give their allegiance to him who offers them a grievance.'

6 The basic test of freedom is perhaps less in what we are free to do than in what we are free not to do. It is the freedom to refrain, withdraw and abstain which makes a totalitarian regime impossible.

ibid. aph. 176

7 To know a person's religion we need not listen to his profession of faith but must find his brand of intolerance.

ibid. aph. 215

8 Our greatest pretenses are built up not to hide the evil and the ugly in us, but our emptiness. The hardest thing to hide is something that is not there.

ibid. aph. 217

9 To spell out the obvious is often to call it in question.

ibid. aph. 220

10 We do not really feel grateful toward those who make our dreams come true; they ruin our dreams.

ibid. aph. 232

11 The beginning of thought is in disagreement – not only with others but also with ourselves.
ibid. aph. 266

12 A great man's greatest good luck is to die at the right time.
ibid. aph. 276

13 The individual who has to justify his existence by his own efforts is in eternal bondage to himself.
*The Ordeal of Change*, ch. 5 (1964)

14 Our passionate preoccupation with the sky, the stars, and a God somewhere in outer space is a homing impulse. We are drawn back to where we came from.
*The New York Times* 21 July 1969. Commenting on the first manned moon-landing.

15 Absolute faith corrupts as absolutely as absolute power.
*Reflections on the Human Condition*, aph. 13 (1972)

16 Capitalism is at its liberating best in a noncapitalist environment. The crypto-businessman is the true revolutionary in a Communist country.
ibid. aph. 73

17 An empty head is not really empty; it is stuffed with rubbish. Hence the difficulty of forcing anything into an empty head.
ibid. aph. 88

18 People who bite the hand that feeds them usually lick the boot that kicks them.
ibid. aph. 141

19 It is a sign of creeping inner death when we can no longer praise the living.
ibid. aph. 147

20 The end comes when we no longer talk with ourselves. It is the end of genuine thinking and the beginning of the final loneliness.
ibid. aph. 150

21 Unpredictability, too, can become monotonous.
ibid. aph. 224

## Abbie Hoffman (1935–89)

US POLITICAL ACTIVIST

Full name Abbott Hoffman. A left-wing activist, he was founder (1968) of the Yippies ( Youth International Party), an organization dedicated to protesting against Vietnam and the American political system. His exploits, for instance his courtroom antics as a defendant in the Chicago Seven trial (1969), gained much media attention. He committed suicide.

1 The first duty of a revolutionary is to get away with it.
Attributed, 1970

2 Avoid all needle drugs. The only dope worth shooting is Richard Nixon.
*Steal This Book* (1971)

3 Sacred cows make the best hamburgers.
Attributed

## Al Hoffman (1902–60) and
## Dick Manning (b. 1912)

US COMPOSERS AND SONGWRITERS

Hoffman composed romantic ballads in the 1930s and novelty songs in the 1940s and 1950s. He wrote for JUDY GARLAND, and the 1954 hit for Max Bygraves, 'Gilly-Gilly Ossenfeffer Katzen Ellen Bogen By The Sea'. Manning, born Samuel Medoff, was a composer as well as a songwriter and was best known for novelty songs.

1 Takes two to tango.
'Takes Two to Tango' (song, 1952). Originally sung by Pearl Bailey, it was later recorded by LOUIS ARMSTRONG, Hermione Gingold and GILBERT HARDING.

## Dustin Hoffman (b. 1937)

US ACTOR

He received accolades for his antiheroic screen roles in *The Graduate* (1967) and *Midnight Cowboy* (1969), going on to win an Academy Award in *Rain Man* (1988). He provoked the comment from screenwriter Larry Gelbart: 'Never argue with a man who is shorter than his Oscar.'

1 Mrs Robinson, you're trying to seduce me. Aren't you?
Ben Braddock (Dustin Hoffman), in *The Graduate* (film, 1967, screenplay by Calder Willingham and Buck Henry based on the novel by Charles Webb, directed by Mike Nichols)

2 One thing about being successful is that I stopped being afraid of dying. Once you're a star you're dead already. You're embalmed.
Quoted in *Filmgoer's Companion* (ed. Leslie Halliwell, 1984)

3 They [the Beatles] sort of Europeanized us all. Before them, our society hadn't been the Great Society as much as it had been the Revlon Society.
Interview in the *Observer* 19 February 1989

4 I envy people who can just look at a sunset. I wonder how you can shoot it. There is nothing more grotesque to me than a vacation.
ibid.

5 If you have this enormous talent, it's got you by the balls, it's a *demon*. You can't be a family man and a husband and a caring person and *be* that animal. Dickens wasn't that nice a guy.
*Empire* August 1992

## Max Hoffman (1869–1927)

GERMAN GENERAL

An officer in the Prussian army from 1899, he was official German military observer in Manchuria on the Japanese side 1904–5 and became a general in 1917.

1 Ludendorff: The English soldiers fight like lions.
Hoffman: True. But don't we know that they are lions led by donkeys.
Attributed in *The Donkeys*, epigraph (1961) by ALAN CLARK, a history of the British military command during the First World War. The saying is also attributed to Napoleon.

## Gerard Hoffnung (1925–59)

BRITISH HUMORIST AND MUSICIAN

He first published his cartoons in the *Evening Post* (1947), later drawing for *Punch* and other periodicals. In the mid-1950s he instigated the Hoffnung Music Festivals at the Festival Hall. They were animated in the television series *Tales from Hoffnung* in 1965.

1 Have you tried the famous echo in the Reading Room of the British Museum?
Speech to Oxford Union, 4 December 1958. Suggested advice to tourists.

## Quintin Hogg (b. 1907)

BRITISH POLITICIAN

Baron Hailsham of St Marylebone. He became a Conservative MP in 1938, held various posts in the cabinet and was Chairman of the Conservative Party (1957–9). In 1963 he renounced his title and re-entered the House of Commons in order to bid (unsuccessfully) for the Party leadership, after which he served two terms as Lord Chancellor (1970–74 and 1979–87). Judge Pickles called him a 'quixotic dictator'. See also REGINALD PAGET 1.

1 Being Conservative is only another way of being British.
Remark in 1967, quoted by John Barnes in 'Ideology and Factions',

publ. in *Conservative Century*, pt 2 (ed. Anthony Seldon and Stuart Ball, 1994)

## Richard Hoggart (b. 1918)
BRITISH CRITIC

He has helped to broaden literary studies to encompass education, communications and working-class culture, and has held a number of official positions in the arts and at UNESCO (1971–5). Publications include *Auden* (1951), *The Uses of Literacy* (1957) and *An Idea and Its Servants* (1978).

1 My argument is ... that we are moving towards the creation of a mass culture; that the remnants of what was at least in parts an urban culture 'of the people' are being destroyed; and that the new mass culture is in some important ways less healthy than the often crude culture it is replacing.
*The Uses of Literacy*, ch. 1, sect. B (1957)

2 Compared even with the pub around the corner, this is all a peculiarly thin and pallid form of dissipation, a sort of spiritual dry-rot amid the odour of boiled milk.
ibid. ch. 8, sect. A. Referring to northern milk-bars.

3 Almost all of us at some time settle for trash, even though we may know better.
*Independent on Sunday* 19 February 1995

## Simon Hoggart (b. 1946)
BRITISH JOURNALIST

He worked for the *Observer* as US correspondent, columnist and political editor (1985–93) and since 1993 has been parliamentary reporter for the *Guardian*. His books include *House of Ill Fame* (1985) and *America: A User's Guide* (1990). He has been chairman of BBC radio's *News Quiz* from 1996.

1 The formal Washington dinner party has all the spontaneity of a Japanese imperial funeral.
*Observer* 31 December 1989

2 Disney World has acquired by now something of the air of a national shrine. American parents who don't take their children there sense obscurely that they have failed in some fundamental way, like Muslims who never made it to Mecca.
*America: A User's Guide*, ch. 9 (1990)

3 Reagan was a flesh and blood version of any other mute national emblem, say the Statue of Liberty. Everyone knows what she represents, but no one would dream of asking her opinion.
ibid. ch. 11

## Billie Holiday (1915–59)
US BLUES SINGER

Originally named Eleanora Fagan and known as 'Lady Day'. Initially promoted by eminent talent scout John Hammond in 1933, she had an uneven career but was capable of sublime performances distinguished by her intense, emotional delivery and idiosyncratic phrasing. Her later years were blighted by drug addiction. The actress JEANNE MOREAU commented: 'She could express more emotion in one chorus than most actresses can in three acts.' See also STUDS TERKEL 1.

1 Southern trees bear a strange fruit
  Blood on the leaf and blood at the root
  Black bodies swingin' in the southern breeze
  Strange fruit hangin' in the poplar trees.
'Strange Fruit' (song, 1939). The song originated as an anti-lynching poem written by Lewis Allan, and was set to music by Danny Mendelson and pianist Sonny White.

2 Mama may have, papa may have,
  But God bless the child that's got his own!
'God Bless the Child' (song, 1941, written with Arthur Herzog Jr)

3 I can't stand to sing the same song the same way two nights in succession, let alone two years or ten years. If you can, then it ain't music, it's close-order drill or exercise or yodeling or something, not music.
*Lady Sings the Blues*, ch. 4 (written with William Dufty, 1956, rev. 1975)

4 You can be up to your boobies in white satin, with gardenias in your hair and no sugar cane for miles, but you can still be working on a plantation.
ibid. ch. 11

5 In this country, don't forget, a habit is no damn private hell. There's no solitary confinement outside of jail. A habit is hell for those you love. And in this country it's the worst kind of hell for those who love you.
ibid. ch. 24. Referring to her addiction to drugs. Holiday spent nearly a year in jail for narcotics offences in the year following her first solo concert in New York, 1946.

## Jack Holland (b. 1947)
IRISH JOURNALIST AND AUTHOR

His political articles and analyses have appeared widely in British, Irish and American periodicals; his books on the history of Northern Ireland include *Too Long A Sacrifice: Life and Death in Northern Ireland Since 1969* (1981).

1 The tragedy of Northern Ireland is that it is now a society in which the dead console the living.
*The New York Times Magazine* 15 July 1979

## Andrew Holleran (b. 1943)
US JOURNALIST AND AUTHOR

His openly autobiographical work explores gay concerns, as in his collection of essays, *Ground Zero* (1980), focusing on the effect of AIDS and changes in the gay community.

1 They [club regulars] seldom looked happy. They passed one another without a word in the elevator, like silent shades in hell, hell-bent on their next look from a handsome stranger. Their next rush from a popper. The next song that turned their bones to jelly and left them all on the dance floor with heads back, eyes nearly closed, in the ecstasy of saints receiving the stigmata.
*Dancer from the Dance*, ch. 2 (1978)

## R.J. Hollingdale (b. 1930)
BRITISH AUTHOR, CRITIC AND TRANSLATOR

Full name Reginald John Hollingdale. Specializing in German writers and philosophers, he has written on and translated Nietzsche, Schopenhauer and Goethe and also published the book *Western Philosophy* (1980).

1 I admit that the generation which produced Stalin, Auschwitz and Hiroshima will take some beating; but the radical and universal consciousness of the death of God is still ahead of us; perhaps we shall have to colonize the stars before it is finally borne in upon us that God is not out there.
*Thomas Mann: A Critical Study*, ch. 8 (1971)

## Ian Holm (b. 1932)
BRITISH STAGE AND SCREEN ACTOR

Original name Ian Holm Cuthbert. A leading actor with the Royal Shakespeare Company in the 1960s, he later suffered a twenty-year period of stage fright until his performance of King Lear in 1997.

His films include *Chariots of Fire* (1989) and *The Sweet Hereafter* (1997).

1 You still don't know what you're dealing with, do you? . . . Perfect organism. Its structural perfection is matched only by its hostility. I admire its purity, a survivor; unclouded by conscience, remorse or delusions of morality.
Ash (Ian Holm), in *Alien* (film, 1979, screenplay by Dan O'Bannon, directed by Ridley Scott)

## John H. Holmes (1879–1964)
US UNITARIAN MINISTER

Known as a 'crusading cleric' and an avowed pacifist, he founded the Community Church in New York City in 1919, advocating that the church should take on 'the new task of redeeming the social order'. To that end he helped found the National Association for the Advancement of Colored People (NAACP) in 1909 and was Chairman of the American Civil Liberties Union (ACLU) (1939–49).

1 This, now, is the judgement of our scientific age – the third reaction of man upon the universe! This universe is not hostile, nor yet is it friendly. It is simply indifferent.
*The Sensible Man's View of Religion*, ch. 4 (1932)

## Larry Holmes (b. 1949)
US BOXER

Known as the 'Easton Assassin', he was World Heavyweight Champion (1978–85), winning forty-eight out of his fifty-one contests.

1 All fighters are prostitutes and all promoters are pimps.
Quoted in the *Guardian* 24 December 1984

## Richard Holmes (b. 1945)
BRITISH BIOGRAPHER

He has specialized in nineteenth-century writers, and his work includes *Shelley: The Pursuit* (1974), *Footsteps: Adventures of a Romantic Biographer* (1985) and two biographies of Coleridge (1989 and 1998). His approach to biography is as a storyteller who has emotional and imaginative contact with his subject.

1 A biography is like a handshake down the years, that can become an arm-wrestle.
Remark at Waterstone's Debate, 16 October 1990, quoted in the *Sunday Times* 21 October 1990

## Oliver Wendell Holmes Jr (1841–1935)
US JUDGE

Nicknamed 'The Great Dissenter', he was Supreme Court Justice (1902–32) when he established a reputation for the elegance of his writings and judgements on common law and equity. Only 'clear and present danger' was the basis for limiting free speech, he believed. 'One of my old formulas is to be an enthusiast in the front part of your heart and ironical at the back,' he stated.

1 The most stringent protection of free speech would not protect a man in falsely shouting fire in a theatre and causing a panic.
Supreme Court opinion in *Schenk v. United States, Baer v. United States* (1919)

2 Oh, to be seventy again!
Attributed remark at ninety, after seeing a beautiful young woman

## Robert Holmes à Court (1937–90)
SOUTH-AFRICAN-BORN AUSTRALIAN BUSINESSMAN

Until the stock market crash in 1987, he was the richest person in Australia. His Bell Group held 30 per cent of Broken Hill Proprietary, Australia's largest company.

1 It's a well-known proposition that you know who's going to win negotiation: it's he who pauses the longest.
*Sydney Morning Herald* 24 May 1986

## Miroslav Holub (1923–98)
CZECH BIOLOGIST AND POET

'I have a single goal but two ways to reach it,' he explained of his own dual career as a doctor specializing in immunology and as a poet. Although forbidden from publishing in his home country 1968–82, he became well known abroad for such verse collections as *Where the Blood Flows* (1963) and *On the Contrary* (1982).

1 Here in the Lord's bosom rests
The tongues of beggars,
The lungs of generals,
The eyes of informers,
The skins of martyrs
In the absolute
Of the microscope's lenses.
'Pathology', publ. in *Day Duty* (1958)

2 The word is the first small step
to freedom
from oneself.
'Brief Reflection on the Word Pain', publ. in *On the Contrary* (1982)

3 Evolution is nothing but
a long string of false steps;
and it may happen that a severed head
will sing.
'The Minotaur's Thoughts on Poetry', publ. in ibid.

4 In laughter we stretch the mouth from ear to ear,
or at least in that direction,
we bare our teeth and in that way reveal
long-past stages in evolution
when laughter still was an expression of
triumph over a slain neighbour.
'Brief Reflection on Laughter', publ. in ibid.

5 Humankind can generally be divided into hunters and people who cope with the consequences.
'Shedding Life', essay first publ. in *Science 86*, repr. in *The Dimension of the Present Moment and Other Essays* (1990)

6 Life is about trying without winning. That is why humanity developed the instinct for sport.
Remark at the Cheltenham Festival of Literature, October 1995, quoted in the *Daily Telegraph* 21 October 1995

## (Sir) Alec Douglas-Home (1903–95)
BRITISH STATESMAN

Baron Home of the Hirsel. Elected Conservative MP in 1931, he was Foreign Secretary (1960–63) and became Prime Minister in 1963 following MACMILLAN's resignation. He lost the 1964 general election to WILSON, but was Foreign Secretary again under HEATH (1970–74).

1 There are two problems in my life. The political ones are insoluble and the economic ones are incomprehensible.
Quoted in *The New York Times* 9 January 1964

## John Lee Hooker (b. 1917)
US BLUES MUSICIAN

Singer, songwriter and guitarist, he featured a percussive guitar style, which could be heard on his first record 'Boogie Chillen' (1948). 'Dimples' (1956) and 'Boom Boom' (1962) became perennial juke box hits, and he made a triumphant comeback with his most commercially successful album *The Healer* (1989).

1 It's never hard to sing the blues. Everyone in the world

has the blues ... poor people have the blues because they're poor and hungry. Rich people can't sleep at night because they're trying to hold on to their money and everything they have.

*Detroit Free Press* 8 September 1991

## Herbert Hoover (1874–1964)

US PRESIDENT

Called 'the Great Engineer' for the public works projects initiated by him (such as the Hoover Dam), he served as Republican President (1929–33), but his opposition to government intervention in the aftermath of the Slump of 1929 and his repeated assertion that 'prosperity cannot be restored by raids upon the public treasury' caused him to lose popularity. His mobilization of humanitarian relief during and after the Second World War helped to restore him to favour.

1 **The American system of rugged individualism.**

Speech in Madison Square Garden, New York City, 22 October 1928, quoted in *New Day*, 'New York City: Restored under Republican Direction' (1928). Hoover was contrasting American values with 'a European philosophy of diametrically opposed doctrines – doctrines of paternalism and state socialism.'

2 **The slogan of progress is changing from the full dinner pail to the full garage.**

ibid. 'New York City: Higher Standards of Living'

3 **Older men declare war. But it is youth that must fight and die. And it is youth who must inherit the tribulation, the sorrow and the triumphs that are the aftermath of war.**

Speech at Republican National Convention, Chicago, 27 June 1944, publ. in *Official Report of the Proceedings of the 23rd Republican National Convention* (1944)

## J. Edgar Hoover (1895–1972)

US DIRECTOR OF THE FBI

Full name John Edgar Hoover. Director of the FBI from 1924 until his death, he opposed communism, the Kennedy administration and the civil rights movement, in particular MARTIN LUTHER KING. In the words of *Time* magazine, 'he fashioned his career as an improbable bureaucratic morality play peopled by bad guys and G-men'.

1 **Truth-telling, I have found, is the key to responsible citizenship. The thousands of criminals I have seen in forty years of law enforcement have had one thing in common: every single one was a liar.**

*Family Weekly* 14 July 1963

## Arthur Hopcraft (b. 1932)

BRITISH AUTHOR

He was a reporter on the *Guardian* and a sportswriter for the *Observer* (1964–73) and has written *The Football Man: People and Passions in Soccer* (1968), *The Great Apple Raid* (1970) and numerous television plays (1971–89).

1 **The point about football in Britain is that it is not just a sport people take to, like cricket or tennis or running long distances. It is inherent in the people. It is built into the urban psyche, as much a common experience to our children as are uncles and school. It is not a phenomenon; it is an everyday matter. There is more eccentricity in deliberately disregarding it than in devoting a life to it. It has more significance in the national character than theatre has.**

*The Football Man*, Introduction (1968)

## Bob Hope (b. 1903)

US COMEDIAN

Original name Leslie Thomas Hope. Wisecracking repartee was his forte, as featured in the *Road to ...* series of films, which he made with BING CROSBY and Dorothy Lamour. He was a dedicated entertainer to the troops during the Second World War and the conflicts in Korea and Vietnam, and received five special Academy Awards.

1 **I get goose pimples. Even my goose pimples have goose pimples.**

Wallie Campbell (Bob Hope), in *The Cat and The Canary* (film, 1939, screenplay by Walter DeLeon and Lynn Starling based on play by John Willard, directed by Elliott Nugent)

2 **How did you get into that dress – with a spray gun?**

Hot Lips Barton (Bob Hope), in *Road to Rio* (film, 1947, screenplay by Edmund Beloin and Jack Rose, directed by Norman McLeod). The question is directed to Lucia Maria De Andrade (Dorothy Lamour).

3 **If you watch a game, it's fun. If you play it, it's recreation. If you work at it, it's golf.**

Quoted in *Reader's Digest* October 1958

4 **I don't generally feel anything until noon, then it's time for my nap.**

*International Herald Tribune* 3 August 1990

## Christopher Hope (b. 1944)

SOUTH AFRICAN AUTHOR

'A master of robustly inventive satire', according to PENELOPE LIVELY, he writes on his native South Africa, which he left in 1976. His books include *The Hottentot Room* (1986), *White Boy Running* (1988) and *Serenity House* (1992). He has also published poetry and children's fiction.

1 **Nothing an interested foreigner may have to say about the Soviet Union today can compare with the scorn and fury of those who inhabit the ruin of a dream.**

*Sunday Times* 15 April 1990

## Dennis Hopper (b. 1935)

US ACTOR AND FILM-MAKER

He first appeared in *Rebel Without a Cause* (1955) and made his mark with the archetypal road movie *Easy Rider* (1969) in which he starred and directed. His roles in later films are usually as villainous psychopaths, as in *Blue Velvet* (1986) and *Speed* (1994).

1 **Well let's face it, what right have you to a life, unless you devote it to dispelling the confines that our parents worked so hard to achieve ... although don't forget that we're all parents now.**

Interview in *Blitz* May 1983

2 **Once we get out of the 80s, the 90s are going to make the 60s seem like the 50s.**

The fugitive (Dennis Hopper), in *Flashback* (film, 1990, screenplay by David Loughery, directed by Franco Amurri)

3 **Sure I remember the Seventies. There was a lot of drawn blinds and dark rooms.**

Interview in *The Face* May 1993

## Nick Hornby (b. 1957)

BRITISH AUTHOR

His partly autobiographical fiction is hugely popular for its humour and earthiness. His subject matter in his three first novels *Fever Pitch* (1992, filmed 1996), *High Fidelity* (1995) and *About a Boy* (1998) is masculinity, expressed through obsessions for football, music and relationships.

1 The natural state of the football fan is bitter disappointment, no matter what the score.

*Fever Pitch*, '1968–1975: Home Début' (1992)

2 I used to believe, although I don't now, that growing and growing up are analogous, that both are inevitable and uncontrollable processes. Now it seems to me that growing up is governed by the will, that one can *choose* to become an adult, but only at given moments.

ibid. '1976–1986: A Fourth Division Town'. Hornby continues, 'These moments come along fairly infrequently – during crises in relationships, for example, or when one has been given the chance to start afresh somewhere – and one can ignore them or seize them.'

3 I am not saying that the anally retentive woman does not exist, but she is vastly outnumbered by her masculine equivalent; and while there are women with obsessions, they are usually, I think, obsessive about people, or the focus for their obsession changes frequently.

ibid. '1976–1986: Boys and Girls'

4 Radio football is football reduced to its lowest common denominator. Shorn of the game's aesthetic pleasures, or the comfort of a crowd that feels the same way as you, or the sense of security that you get when you see that your defenders and goalkeeper are more or less where they should be, all that is left is naked fear.

ibid. '1976–1986: Filling a Hole'

5 There must be many fathers around the country who have experienced the cruellest, most crushing rejection of all: their children have ended up supporting the wrong team.

ibid. '1976–1986: My Brother'

6 Even though there is no question that sex is a nicer activity than watching football (no nil–nil draws, no offside trap, no cup upsets, *and* you're warm), in the normal run of things, the feelings it engenders are simply not as intense as those brought about by a once-in-a-lifetime last-minute Championship winner.

ibid. '1986–1992: The Greatest Moment Ever'

7 Be tolerant of those who describe a sporting moment as their best ever. We do not lack imagination, nor have we had sad and barren lives; it is just that real life is paler, duller, and contains less potential for unexpected delirium.

ibid.

8 One moment you're ticking along, cleaning the toilet bowl and expressing your feelings and doing all the other things that a modern chap is supposed to do; the next, you're manipulating and sulking and double-dealing and fibbing with the best of them. I can't work it out.

*High Fidelity*, ch. 5 (1995)

9 Sex is about the only grown-up thing I know how to do; it's weird, then, that it's the only thing which can make me feel like a ten-year-old.

ibid. ch. 10

10 You can never do the right thing by someone if you've stopped sleeping with them. You can't see a way back, or through, or round, however hard you try.

ibid. ch. 25

11 Women get it wrong when they complain about media images of women. Men understand that not everyone has Bardot's breasts, or Jamie Lee Curtis's neck, or Felicity Kendall's bottom, and we don't mind at all. Obviously we'd take Kim Bassinger over Hattie Jacques, just as women would take Keanu Reeves over Bernard Manning, but it's not the body that's important, it's the level of abasement.

ibid. ch. 27

## Marilyn Horne (b. 1934)
US OPERA SINGER

A mezzo-soprano singer, she made her debut in *The Bartered Bride* (1954) in Los Angeles and her Metropolitan Opera debut in 1970. She was acclaimed for her roles in *Wozzeck* and *Carmen* and worked to revive the lesser known operas of Handel and Rossini.

1 You have to know exactly what you want out of your career. If you want to be a star, you don't bother with other things.

Quoted in *Divas: Impressions of Six Opera Superstars* (1959) by Winthrop Sargeant

## Karen Horney (1885–1952)
US PSYCHIATRIST

She was critical of orthodox Freudian theory and argued for a more holistic approach, especially in relation to feminine psychosexuality. She founded the Association for the Advancement of Psychoanalysis and published *Our Inner Conflicts* (1945) and *Neurosis and Human Growth* (1950).

1 Is not the tremendous strength in men of the impulse to creative work in every field precisely due to their feeling of playing a relatively small part in the creation of living beings, which constantly impels them to an overcompensation in achievement?

*Feminine Psychology*, 'The Flight from Womanhood' (1926)

## Janette Turner Hospital (b. 1942)
AUSTRALIAN AUTHOR

Her novels *The Ivory Swing* (1982) and *Borderline* (1985) cross cultural and national boundaries, as she herself has in her writing career having lived in Australia, Europe and North America. Her short story collections include *Dislocations* (1986) and she has also published detective fiction under the pseudonym Alex Juniper.

1 We inherit plots . . . There are only two or three in the world, five or six at most. We ride them like treadmills.

*Independent* 7 April 1990

## A.E. Housman (1859–1936)
BRITISH POET AND CLASSICAL SCHOLAR

Full name Alfred Edward Housman. His poetical reputation grew from a single volume of verse, *A Shropshire Lad* (1896), after which he wrote little verse though continued to write and lecture on poetry. Despite his mediocre academic record at Oxford, he became Professor of Latin at London and Cambridge.

1 Experience has taught me, when I am shaving of a morning, to keep watch over my thoughts, because, if a line of poetry strays into my memory, my skin bristles so that the razor ceases to act.

'The Name and Nature of Poetry', lecture at Senate House, Cambridge, 9 May 1933, publ. 1933, repr. in *A.E. Housman: Selected Prose* (ed. John Carter, 1961). The seat of this sensation, Housman explained, 'is the pit of the stomach'. The lecture was his first public utterance on the subject of poetry.

2 In every American there is an air of incorrigible innocence, which seems to conceal a diabolical cunning.

Quoted in *Voices: A Memoir*, 'The Sneeze' (1983) by Frederic Prokosch. Said to Prokosch, an author and poet whose volume *The Asiatics* had been recently published to critical acclaim. Housman had asked of Prokosch, 'Is your air of simplicity just a part of your cunning, or is your cunning just an aspect of your inner simplicity?'

3 Indeed – very good. I shall – have to repeat – that – on the Golden Floor.

Last words, as reported in letter to Richard Perceval Graves, 12 May 1976, quoted in *A.E. Housman, The Scholar Poet*, ch. 12 (1979) by

Richard Perceval Graves. The words were spoken to Housman's doctor, who had just recounted the response of an actor when asked what members of his profession did in their spare time: 'Well, I suppose you could say we spend half our time lying on the sands looking at the stars, and the other half lying on the Stars looking at the sands!'

## Libby Houston (b. 1941)
BRITISH POET AND BOTANIST

Inspired by the Beat poets, she began writing poetry in the 1960s. Her verse, including the collections *At the Mercy* (1981), *Necessity* (1988) and *Cover of Darkness* (1999), combines a naturalist's eye with sharp metaphysical humour.

1 The base emotions Plato banned
  have left a radio-active and not radiant land.
  'Judging Lear', publ. in *At the Mercy* (1981)

2 When your dreams tire, they go underground
  and out of kindness that's where they stay.
  'Gold', publ. in *Necessity* (1988)

## Geoffrey Howe (b. 1926)
BRITISH POLITICIAN

Baron Howe of Aberavon. As Conservative Chancellor of the Exchequer in the first THATCHER government (1979–83), he reduced inflation at the cost of higher unemployment. He became Foreign Secretary in 1983, and in 1989 Deputy Prime Minister and Leader of the House of Commons. He resigned in 1990, making a public statement of his disagreements with the Prime Minister. Journalist Peter Freedman described him as having 'all the dash and panache of the Hush Puppies which are his favourite footwear'.

1 It is rather like sending your opening batsmen to the crease only for them to find the moment that the first balls are bowled that their bats have been broken before the game by the team captain.
  Resignation speech as Deputy Prime Minister to House of Commons, 13 November 1990, publ. in *Conflict of Loyalty*, Appendix 2 (1994). The speech refers to the difficulties he faced as Foreign Secretary as the result of by MARGARET THATCHER's anti-European stance.

## Frankie Howerd (1922–92)
BRITISH COMEDIAN

Original name Francis Alex Howard. A stand-up comedian from the 1940s, he appeared in revues in the 1950s, and in STEPHEN SONDHEIM's stage musical *A Funny Thing Happened on the Way to the Forum* (1963). However, he is best known for his part as the slave Lurcio in the TV series *Up Pompeii* (1969–71, filmed 1971), in which he was master of the suggestive innuendo. His films include *Carry on Doctor* (1968) and *Up the Chastity Belt* (1972).

1 I was amazed.
  Catch-phrase from 1940s. Other phrases associated with Howerd include 'Mock ye not!' and 'Nay, nay, and thrice nay!', adapted to 'Woe, woe, and thrice woe' as spoken by the soothsayer on the TV show, *Up Pompeii*.

## (Sir) Fred Hoyle (b. 1915)
BRITISH ASTRONOMER

He founded the Institute of Theoretical Astronomy in Cambridge, where he was also Professor of Astronomy (1958–72). Maintaining that life originated in bacteria and viruses in space, he has written science fiction and the popular science books *The Nature of the Universe* (1952) and *Frontiers of Astronomy* (1955).

1 Space isn't remote at all. It's only an hour's drive away if your car could go straight upwards.
  *Observer* 9 September 1979

## Kin Hubbard (1868–1930)
US HUMORIST AND JOURNALIST

Full name Frank McKinney Hubbard. Working at the *Indianapolis Sun* from 1899 until his death, he became well known for caricatures of political figures but achieved national fame for his character Abe Martin, who first appeared in 1904 and by 1910 was syndicated to about 200 cities.

1 Classic music is th' kind that we keep thinkin'll turn into a tune.
  *Comments of Abe Martin and His Neighbors* (1923)

2 Nobuddy ever fergits where he buried a hatchet.
  *Indianapolis News* 4 January 1925, repr. in *Abe Martin's Broadcast* (1930)

3 When a fellow says, it hain't the money but the principle o' the thing, it's th' money.
  *Hoss Sense and Nonsense* (1926)

4 Th' only way t' entertain some folks is t' listen t' 'em.
  *Abe Martin's Wisecracks* (ed. E.V. Lucas, 1930)

5 All th' world loves a good loser.
  ibid.

6 Makin' a long stay short is a great aid t' popularity.
  ibid.

## Ruth Hubbard (b. 1924)
US BIOLOGIST

Her work, such as *Biological Woman – The Convenient Myth* (1983) and *The Politics of Women's Biology* (1990), explores science from an accessible feminist perspective.

1 Every theory is a self-fulfilling prophecy that orders experience into the framework it provides.
  'Have Only Men Evolved?', publ. in *Women Look at Biology Looking At Women* (ed. Ruth Hubbard, Mary Sue Henifin and Barbara Fried, 1979)

## Richard Huelsenbeck (1892–1974)
GERMAN POET AND PSYCHOANALYST

With HUGO BALL he was the co-founder of Dadaism in 1916 and brought the movement to Berlin. He settled in New York in 1936, from which time he worked as a psychoanalyst.

1 I am firmly convinced that all art will become dadaistic in the course of time, because from Dada proceeds the perpetual urge for its renovation.
  'Dada Lives', publ. in *Transition* no. 25 Autumn 1936, transl. in *The Dada Painters and Poets: An Anthology* (ed. Robert Motherwell, 1951)

## Arianna Huffington (b. 1950)
GREEK AUTHOR

Former name Arianna Stassinopoulos. A provocative and intellectual writer, her work covers biography, for example *Picasso: Creator and Destroyer* (1988), as well as studies on the women's movement, *The Female Woman* (1973), and spirituality, *The Other Revolution* (1979).

1 Our current obsession with creativity is the result of our continued striving for immortality in an era when most people no longer believe in an after-life.
  *The Female Woman*, 'The Working Woman' (1973)

2 Not only is it harder to be a man, it is also harder to become one.
  ibid. 'The Male Man' (1973)

3 Liberation is an evershifting horizon, a total ideology that can never fulfil its promises ... It has the therapeutic quality of providing emotionally charged rituals of solidarity in hatred – it is the amphetamine of its believers.

ibid. 'The Liberated Woman? ... and Her Liberators' (1973)

## Langston Hughes (1902–67)
US POET AND AUTHOR

Known as the 'poet laureate of Harlem', he was a major influence in the development of black literature in America. His poems, incorporating black idiom and rhythms of jazz and blues, were published in collections such as *The Weary Blues* (1926) and his humorous sketches, 'Simple Stories', appeared in the 1950s in books, comic strips and on the stage.

1 I got the Weary Blues
And I can't be satisfied.

'The Weary Blues', written 1922, publ. in *The Weary Blues* (1926). In his autobiography Hughes claimed that these lines originated in 'the first blues verse I'd ever heard'.

2 I, too, sing America.
I am the darker brother.
They send me to eat in the kitchen when company
comes.
But I laugh,
And eat well,
And grow strong.

'I, Too', first publ. in *Survey Graphic* March 1925, repr. in *Selected Poems* (1954)

3 Jazz to me is one of the inherent expressions of Negro life in America: the eternal tom-tom beating in the Negro soul – the tom-tom of revolt against weariness in a white world, a world of subway trains, and work, work, work; the tom-tom of joy and laughter, and pain swallowed in a smile.

'The Negro Artist and the Racial Mountain', publ. in *Nation* 23 June 1926

4 I swear to the Lord
I still can't see
Why Democracy means
Everybody but me.

'The Black Man Speaks', publ. in *Jim Crow's Last Stand* (1943)

5 But softly
As the tune comes from his throat
Trouble
Mellows to a golden note.

'Trumpet Player', publ. in *Fields of Wonder* (1947)

6 Good morning, daddy!
Ain't you heard
The boogie-woogie rumble
Of a dream deferred?

'Dream Boogie', publ. in *Montage of a Dream Deferred* (1951)

7 What happens to a dream deferred?
Does it dry up
like a raisin in the sun?
Or fester like a sore –
And then run?
Does it stink like rotten meat?
Or crust and sugar over –
like a syrupy sweet?

Maybe it just sags
like a heavy load.

*Or does it explode?*

'Harlem', publ. in ibid.

8 It's powerful ... that one drop of Negro blood – because just *one* drop of black blood makes a man coloured. *One* drop – you are a Negro! ... Black is powerful.

*Simple Takes a Wife* (1953)

## Richard Hughes (1900–76)
BRITISH NOVELIST AND PLAYWRIGHT

He travelled widely, wrote the first radio drama *Danger* (1924) for the BBC, but is best known for his study of childhood *A High Wind in Jamaica* (1929).

1 The yachtsman leaves no tracks. A thousand keels may plough a strait, but they leave it virgin. Except for desert and the snows, there is hardly an inch of land on the round earth where man has not left his mark again and again; but most of the surface of the ocean is to-day as if Man had not been created.

*The Saturday Book*, 'Sailing' (1946)

## Robert Hughes (b. 1938)
AUSTRALIAN AUTHOR AND CRITIC

Senior art critic for *Time* magazine since 1970, his wide-ranging books include essays on art in *The Shock of the New* (1980), a history of convict transports to Australia, *The Fatal Shore* (1987), and *Culture of Complaint* (1993) a discussion of political correctness in America.

1 Would Australians have done anything differently if their country had not been settled as the jail of infinite space? Certainly they would. They would have remembered more of their own history.

*The Fatal Shore*, ch. 17 (1987)

2 The contest between education and TV – between argument and conviction by spectacle – has been won by television.

*Culture of Complaint*, ch. 1 (1993)

3 The self is now the sacred cow of American culture, self-esteem is sacrosanct.

ibid.

## Ted Hughes (1930–98)
BRITISH POET

'Among the grey-suited modern poets ... he stood out like the bloodstained survivor of a Greek tragedy' was critic JOHN CAREY's appreciation of this poet, whose work is characterized by its muscularity and raw animal and nature imagery. Early collections include *The Hawk in the Rain* (1957) and *Lupercal* (1960) and later works *Tales from Ovid* (1997), and *Birthday Letters* (1998), which chronicles the story of his marriage to SYLVIA PLATH. He was Poet Laureate from 1984 and also wrote for children.

1 I saw the horses:
Huge in the dense grey – ten together –
Megalith-still. They breathed, making no move,
With draped manes and tilted hind-hooves,
Making no sound.
I passed: not one snorted or jerked its head.
Grey silent fragments
Of a grey silent world.

'The Horses', publ. in *The Hawk in the Rain* (1957)

2 This house has been far out at sea all night,
The woods crashing through darkness, the booming
hills,
Winds stampeding the fields under the window
Floundering black astride and blinding wet.

'Wind', publ. in ibid.

3 Russia and America circle each other;
Threats nudge an act that were without doubt

A melting of the mould in the mother,
Stones melting about the root.
'A Woman Unconscious', publ. in *Lupercal* (1960)

4 The future's no calamitous change
But a malingering of now,
Histories, towns, faces that no
Malice or accident much derange.
'A Woman Unconscious', publ. in ibid.

5 Daylong this tomcat lies stretched flat
As an old rough mat, no mouth and no eyes,
Continual wars and wives are what
Have tattered his ears and battered his head.
'Esther's Tomcat', publ. in ibid.

6 My feet are locked upon the rough bark.
It took the whole of Creation
To produce my foot, my each feather:
Now I hold Creation in my foot.
'Hawk Roosting', publ. in ibid.

7 Pike, three inches long, perfect
Pike in all parts, green tigering the gold.
'Pike', publ. in ibid.

8 The sea cries with its meaningless voice
Treating alike its dead and its living,
Probably bored with the appearance of heaven
After so many millions of nights without sleep,
Without purpose, without self-deception.
'Pibroch', publ. in *Wodwo*, pt 3 (1967)

9 Any form of violence, any vehement form of activity,
invokes the bigger energy, the elemental power circuit of
the universe.
Interview in 1971, quoted in the *Sunday Times* 1 November 1998

10 The flame-red moon, the harvest moon,
Rolls along the hills, gently bouncing,
A vast balloon,
Till it takes off, and sinks upward
To lie in the bottom of the sky, like a gold doubloon.
'The Harvest Moon', publ. in *Season Songs* (1976)

11 Death invented the phone it looks like the altar of death
Do not worship the telephone
It drags its worshippers into actual graves
With a variety of devices, through a variety of disguised
voices
'Do Not Pick Up the Telephone', publ. in *Earth Numb* (1979)

12 The river is a god

Knee-deep among the reeds, watching men,
Or hung by the heels down at the door of a dam

It is a god, and inviolable.
And will wash itself of all deaths.
'River', publ. in *The River* (1983)

13 You were never
More than a step from Paradise.
You had instant access, your analyst told you,
To the core of your Inferno –
The pit of your hairy flower.
'Child's Park', publ. in *Birthday Letters* (1998). Addressed to SYLVIA
PLATH, the poems were written over a period of twenty-five years
after her suicide in 1963.

## (Sir) Richard Hull (1907–89)
BRITISH GENERAL

He was appointed Chief of Staff, Middle East Land Forces (1953–
4) and supervised the evacuation from Suez. In 1957 he oversaw
the abolition of national service and from 1965–7 was Chief of
Defence Staff.

1 Conscription may have been good for the country, but it
damn near killed the army.
Quoted in *Anatomy of Britain Today*, ch. 19 (1965) by Anthony
Sampson

## Basil Hume (1923–99)
BRITISH ECCLESIASTIC

A Roman Catholic Benedictine monk and Abbot of Ampleforth
(1963–76), he was the first monk to occupy the office of Archbishop
of Westminster (1976–99). His books include *Searching for God*
(1977) and *Towards a Civilization of Love* (1988). Widely respected
for his modesty and piety, he was called 'my cardinal' by QUEEN
ELIZABETH II.

1 Moral choices do not depend on personal preference and
private decision but on right reason and, I would add,
divine order.
*The Times* 16 March 1990

2 If people pray, their consciousnesses become more sensitive. It is very difficult to be a praying person and then go
and be beastly to your neighbour.
Quoted in *The Times* 11 April 1998

## Hubert H. Humphrey (1911–78)
US POLITICIAN AND VICE-PRESIDENT

He gained a reputation as a liberal politician and was an eloquent
speaker, but as Vice-President under LYNDON JOHNSON from 1964
alienated many by his support for continuing the Vietnam War.
He won the Democratic presidential nomination in 1968, but
narrowly lost to NIXON.

1 There are not enough jails, not enough policemen, not
enough courts to enforce a law not supported by the
people.
Speech at Williamsburg, 1 May 1965, quoted in *The New York Times*
2 May 1965

2 The right to be heard does not automatically include the
right to be taken seriously.
Speech to National Student Association at Madison, 23 August 1965,
quoted in *The New York Times* 24 August 1965

3 Here we are, just as we ought to be, here we are, the
people, here we are in a spirit of dedication, here we are
the way politics ought to be in America, the politics of
happiness, the politics of purpose and the politics of joy.
Speech in Washington, D.C., 27 April 1968, quoted in *The New
York Times* 28 April 1968. 'The Politics of Joy' was Humphrey's
presidential campaign slogan in 1968.

## Barry Humphries (b. 1934)
AUSTRALIAN ENTERTAINER

He created the Barry Mackenzie comic strip in *Private Eye* (1964–73),
but is most famous for his satirical creations of Sir Les Patterson and
the housewife superstar Dame Edna Everage. He has also appeared in
one-man stage shows, for example *A Nice Night's Entertainment* (1962).

1 Oh, I was down by Manly Pier
Drinking tubes of ice-cold beer
With a bucket full of prawns upon me knee.
But when I'd swallowed the last prawn
I had a Technicolor yawn
And I chundered in the old Pacific sea.
'Chunder Down Under' (1964), publ. in *A Nice Night's Entertain-
ment* (1981). In the glossary in *Bazza Pulls It Off* (1972) Humphries
defines the word 'chunder', which he claims to have popularized,
as 'to enjoy oneself in reverse'.

2 Feminist: a woman, usually ill-favoured . . . in whom the
film-making instinct has displaced the maternal.
*A Nice Night's Entertainment*, Glossary (1981)

3 My work is really addressed to a provincial English audience, and whether we like it or not, and whatever American affectations we may entertain here in Australia, we are really provincial English society. Our humour touches the same nerve.

*Age* 19 February 1983

4 The only people really keeping the spirit of irony alive in Australia are taxi-drivers and homosexuals.

*Australian Women's Weekly* February 1983

## Robert Hunter (b. 1938)

US ROCK LYRICIST

He was the non-performing songwriter for the band the Grateful Dead, and also recorded solo albums, for example *Tiger Rose* (1975) and *Jack O'Roses* (1980). *Down in the Groove* (1987) was co-written with BOB DYLAN.

1 What a long strange trip it's been.

'Truckin'' (song) on the album *American Beauty* (1971) by the Grateful Dead. This best known of the Grateful Dead's lyrics ('WALSTIB' to dedicated fans) has been adopted on badges and posters and as the title of books and articles evoking the 1960s. A retrospective Grateful Dead album of 1977 also had this as the title.

## Herman Hupfeld (1894–1951)

US SONGWRITER

Although he did not write full scores, he contributed songs for stage shows and films of the 1920s and 30s. He is best remembered for 'As Time Goes By' (1931), but was also responsible for 'Sing Something Simple' (1930) and 'Let's Put Out the Lights and Go To Sleep' (1932).

1 You must remember this, a kiss is still a kiss,
   A sigh is just a sigh;
   The fundamental things apply,
   As time goes by.

'As Time Goes By' (song), in *Everybody's Welcome* (show, 1931). The song was picked up and featured in the movie, *Casablanca* (1943), sung by Dooley Wilson as Sam, although the extent of Wilson's active involvement has been questioned. In *Everybody's Welcome* the song was sung by Frances Williams. See also INGRID BERGMAN 1.

## Douglas Hurd (b. 1930)

BRITISH POLITICIAN

Baron Hurd of Westwell. Elected Conservative MP in 1974, he became Home Secretary in 1985 and Foreign Secretary (1989–95). He was an unsuccessful candidate in the contest for leadership following MARGARET THATCHER's resignation in 1990. He writes political thrillers as a hobby.

1 [On aid to Russia] It is not helpful to help a friend by putting coins in his pockets when he has got holes in his pockets.

Quoted in the *Observer* 9 June 1991

## Zora Neale Hurston (1903–60)

US AUTHOR AND ANTHROPOLOGIST

A leading figure of the Harlem Renaissance, she influenced generations of black women writers with her novel *Their Eyes Were Watching God* (1937) and her collections of African-American folk tales *Mules and Men* (1935) and *Tell My Horse* (1938). In later years her conservative ideas alienated her from her contemporaries. See also YOKO ONO 2.

1 But I am not tragically colored. There is no great sorrow dammed up in my soul, nor lurking behind my eyes. I do not mind at all. I do not belong to the sobbing school of negrohood who hold that nature somehow has given them a lowdown dirty deal . . . No, I do not weep at the world – I am too busy sharpening my oyster knife.

'How It Feels to be Colored Me', essay first publ. 1928, repr. in *I Love Myself When I Am Laughing* (1979)

2 Ships at a distance have every man's wish on board.

*Their Eyes Were Watching God*, ch. 1 (1937)

## Saddam Hussein (b. 1937)

IRAQI PRESIDENT

As President and head of the armed forces of Iraq from 1979, he waged war with Iran (1980–88) and suppressed the Kurdish rebels who sought independence. In 1990 his invasion of Kuwait led to the Gulf War and his defeat by Arab and Western forces (1991). NORMAN SCHWARZKOPF said of him: 'He is neither a strategist, nor is he schooled in the operational art, nor is he a tactician, nor is he a general, nor is he a soldier. Other than that, he is a great military man.'

1 The great, the jewel and the mother of battles has begun.

Speech at the start of the Gulf War, 6 January 1991, quoted in the *Independent* 19 January 1991

## John Huston (1906–87)

US FILM-MAKER AND ACTOR

An unpredictable director, his forte was adventure films and film noir. He made his debut with *The Maltese Falcon* (1941) and won an Oscar for *The Treasure of the Sierra Madre* (1948). In later life he also acted, as in *The Cardinal* (1963) and *Chinatown* (1974).

1 After all, crime is only a lefthanded form of human endeavor.

Emmerich (Louis Calhern), in *The Asphalt Jungle* (film, 1950, written and directed by John Huston from novel by W.R. Burnett)

2 Talk to them [actors] about things they don't know. Try to give them an inferiority complex. If the actress is beautiful, screw her. If she isn't, present her with a valuable painting she will not understand. If they insist on being boring, kick their asses or twist their noses. And that's about all there is to it.

Quoted in *Things I Did . . . and Things I Think I Did* (1984) by Jean Negulesco. Advice to a young director on how to handle actors.

3 Hollywood has always been a cage . . . a cage to catch our dreams.

Quoted in the *Sunday Times* 27 December 1987

## Lauren Hutton (b. 1943)

US ACTRESS AND MODEL

Original name Mary Hutton. Formerly a Playboy Bunny, she became one of America's highest paid models in the 1960s, and also acted in films, for example *A Wedding* (1978) and *American Gigolo* (1979).

1 Models are the physical mirror of femininity. They *should* come in all sizes, shapes, and ages, and now they do. If my two careers mean anything, it's that.

Quoted in *Model*, pt 2 (1995) by Michael Gross

## Will Hutton (b. 1950)

BRITISH JOURNALIST AND AUTHOR

An influential thinker on government and society, he was Editor-in-chief of the *Observer* (1998–9) and has written *The Revolution That Never Was; An Assessment of Keynesian Economics* (1986) and *The State We're In* (1995), both addressing the economic, social and political degeneration of Britain.

1 There needs to be fear and greed in the system in order to make it tick.

*The State We're In*, ch. 7 (1995)

2 Private schools, in short, are one of the most important economic and social institutions in these islands. Everybody knows it, but to say so is taboo.

*Observer* 6 September 1998. He also commented, 'The drift to private schools is becoming a stampede. We are building one of the most unequal and nastiest societies on earth – and nobody is protesting.'

## Aldous Huxley (1894–1963)
BRITISH AUTHOR

His early works of the 1920s were brilliant satires of upper-class and intellectual life; but he produced his best work in the 1930s, including the dystopic *Brave New World* (1932). His novel *Island* (1962) presented an alternative utopian model of society. *The Doors of Perception* (1954) recorded his experiments with psychotropic drugs in California, where he lived from 1937.

1 I can sympathize with people's pains, but not with their pleasures. There is something curiously boring about somebody else's happiness.

*Limbo*, 'Cynthia' (1920)

2 Beauty for some provides escape,
Who gain a happiness in eyeing
The gorgeous buttocks of the ape
Or Autumn sunsets exquisitely dying.

'Ninth Philosopher's Song', in *Leda* (1920)

3 Most of one's life is one prolonged effort to prevent oneself thinking.

Mr Topes, in *Mortal Coils*, 'Green Tunnels' (1922)

4 There are few who would not rather be taken in adultery than in provincialism.

Mr Boldero, in *Antic Hay*, ch. 10 (1923)

5 I have discovered the most exciting, the most arduous literary form of all, the most difficult to master, the most pregnant in curious possibilities. I mean the advertisement ... It is far easier to write ten passably effective Sonnets, good enough to take in the not too inquiring critic, than one effective advertisement that will take in a few thousand of the uncritical buying public.

*On the Margin*, 'Advertisement' (1923)

6 I'm afraid of losing my obscurity. Genuineness only thrives in the dark. Like celery.

Miss Thriplow, in *Those Barren Leaves*, pt 1 ch. 1 (1925)

7 If it were not for the intellectual snobs who pay – in solid cash – the tribute which philistinism owes to culture, the arts would perish with their starving practitioners. Let us thank heaven for hypocrisy.

*Jesting Pilate*, pt 1 (1926)

8 [Of Los Angeles] Thought is barred in this City of Dreadful Joy and conversation is unknown.

ibid. pt 4

9 Those who believe that they are exclusively in the right are generally those who achieve something.

*Proper Studies*, 'A Note on Dogma: Varieties of Human Type' (1927)

10 It takes two to make a murder. There are born victims, born to have their throats cut, as the cut-throats are born to be hanged.

Maurice Spandrell, in *Point Counter Point*, ch. 12 (1928)

11 A bad book is as much of a labour to write as a good one; it comes as sincerely from the author's soul.

*Point Counter Point*, ch. 13 (1928)

12 Consistency is contrary to nature, contrary to life. The only completely consistent people are the dead.

*Do What You Will*, 'Wordsworth in the Tropics' (1929)

13 Single-mindedness is all very well in cows or baboons; in an animal claiming to belong to the same species as Shakespeare it is simply disgraceful.

ibid. 'Pascal' sect. 24

14 Experience is not a matter of having actually swum the Hellespont, or danced with the dervishes, or slept in a doss-house. It is a matter of sensibility and intuition, of seeing and hearing the significant things, of paying attention at the right moments, of understanding and co-ordinating. Experience is not what happens to a man; it is what a man does with what happens to him.

*Texts and Pretexts*, Introduction (1932)

15 Official dignity tends to increase in inverse ratio to the importance of the country in which the office is held.

*Beyond the Mexique Bay*, 'Puerto Barrios' (1934)

16 People will insist on treating the *mons Veneris* as though it were Mount Everest. Too silly!

Mary Amberly, in *Eyeless in Gaza*, ch. 30 (1936)

17 So long as men worship the Caesars and Napoleons, Caesars and Napoleons will duly rise and make them miserable.

*Ends and Means*, ch. 8 (1937)

18 There's only one corner of the universe you can be certain of improving, and that's your own self.

Carlo Malpighi (quoting Bruno Rontini), in *Time Must Have a Stop*, ch. 7 (1944)

19 If we could sniff or swallow something that would, for five or six hours each day, abolish our solitude as individuals, atone us with our fellows in a glowing exaltation of affection and make life in all its aspects seem not only worth living, but divinely beautiful and significant, and if this heavenly, world-transfiguring drug were of such a kind that we could wake up next morning with a clear head and an undamaged constitution – then, it seems to me, all our problems (and not merely the one small problem of discovering a novel pleasure) would be wholly solved and earth would become paradise.

*Music at Night and Other Essays*, 'Wanted, a New Pleasure' (1949). Huxley's earlier writings revealed a different attitude: 'I prefer being sober to even the rosiest and most agreeable intoxications,' he wrote in his Introduction to *Texts and Pretexts* (1932). 'The peyotl-trances of Swinburne, for example, have always left me perfectly *compos mentis*; I do not catch the infection.'

20 Speed, it seems to me, provides the one genuinely modern pleasure.

ibid. 'Wanted, a New Pleasure'

21 Man is an intelligence, not served by, but in servitude to his organs.

*Themes and Variations*, 'Variations on a Philosopher' (1950)

22 A priest's life is not supposed to be well-rounded; it is supposed to be one-pointed – a compass, not a weathercock.

*The Devils of Loudun*, ch. 1 (1952)

23 Pure Spirit, one hundred degrees proof – that's a drink that only the most hardened contemplation-guzzlers indulge in. Bodhisattvas dilute their Nirvana with equal parts of love and work.

Susila, in *Island*, ch. 15 (1962)

24 It's with bad sentiments that one makes good novels.

Letter, 10 July 1962, quoted in *Aldous Huxley: the Critical Heritage* (ed. Donald Watt, 1975). Huxley believed this to be the explanation for why his novel *Island* – published that year and greatly criticized – was 'so inadequate'.

25 Idealism is the noble toga that political gentlemen drape over their will to power.

Quoted in the *New York Herald Tribune* 25 November 1963

## Elspeth Huxley (1907–97)

BRITISH AUTHOR

She wrote widely on her native land Kenya, as in her best known novel, *The Flame Trees of Thika* (1959).

1 Only man is not content to leave things as they are but must always be changing them, and when he has done so, is seldom satisfied with the result.

*The Mottled Lizard*, ch. 4 (1962). The book is the second volume of her autobiography.

## (Sir) Julian Huxley (1887–1975)

BRITISH BIOLOGIST

The brother of ALDOUS HUXLEY, he was the first director of UNESCO (1946–8), helped found the World Wildlife Fund (now called World Wildlife Fund for Nature) and wrote popular science books including *Essays of a Biologist* (1923).

1 God can no longer be considered controller of the universe in any but a Pickwickian sense. Operationally, God is beginning to resemble not a ruler but the last fading smile of a cosmic Cheshire cat.

*Religion without Revelation*, ch. 3 (1957 edn)

## Dolores Ibárruri (1895–1989)

SPANISH POLITICIAN AND JOURNALIST

Known as *La Pasionaria* (The Passion Flower). She was an emotional orator and the Republic's most effective propagandist during the Spanish Civil War. Elected as a communist Deputy to the Cortes in 1936, she left Spain for the USSR after Franco's victory, returning to be re-elected to the Cortes at the age of eighty-one. She always dressed in black.

1 *No pasarán!*
   (They shall not pass!)

   Radio broadcast from Paris 18 July 1936, quoted in *The Spanish Civil War*, bk 2, ch. 16 (1961, rev. 1965) by Hugh Thomas. This rallying call for the women of Spain to defend the Republic became a slogan in the ensuing civil war. Previous attributions for the words include Marshal Pétain (1856–1951) during the defence of Verdun in 1916: *Ils ne passeront pas*.

2 It is better to die on your feet than to live on your knees!

   Radio broadcast from Paris 3 September 1936, quoted in ibid. In her autobiography (1966), Ibárruri stated that she had first used the words in a previous broadcast in Spain, 18 July, when she had also uttered *No pasarán!* (see above). Like that slogan, this also became a slogan in the ensuing civil war and also has an earlier attribution: to Mexican revolutionary Emiliano Zapata (c. 1877–1919).

## Ice Cube (b. 1969)

US RAP MUSICIAN

Born O'Shea Jackson. He was a founder member of the LA rap group Niggaz With Attitude (NWA), whose solo releases, for example *AmeriKKKa's Most Wanted* (1990) and *Death Certificate* (1991), were if anything more confrontational than NWA's recordings and were attacked for the violence, homophobia and sexism of the lyrics. He has also developed an acting career, starring in *Boyz 'n the Hood* (1991), whose title was taken from the debut single by NWA written by him (1986), in the comedy cult classic *Friday* (1995) and in its sequel *Next Friday* (2000).

1 Up early in the morning, dressed in black
   Don't ask why 'cuz I'm down in a suit and tie
   They killed a homie that I went to school with (damn)
   I tell you, life ain't shit to fool with.

   'Dead Homiez' (song) on album *AmeriKKKa's Most Wanted* (1990). Opening lines.

2 If I'm more of an influence to your son as a rapper than you are as a father . . . you got to look at yourself as a parent.

   Interview in *Rolling Stone* 4 October 1994

## Ice-T (b. 1958)

US RAP MUSICIAN

Original name Tracey Marrow. One of the West Coast's most outspoken 'gangsta' rappers, he took his name from Blaxploitation author Iceberg Slim. 'The Coldest Rapper', released in 1983, made him LA's first hip-hop artist, and 'Cop Killer' on the album *Body Count* (1992) caused a furore and was later withdrawn.

1 You're just a toy punk to mess with that junk
   You want some real dope, come look in my trunk
   The dope I'm sellin' is life, a hundred percent legit
   So get real, fool, and try some real hit.

   'I'm your Pusher' (song, written by Ice-T and Afrika Islam) on the album *Power* (1988)

2 You better think it out
   We should be able to say anything
   Our lungs were meant to shout.
   Say what you feel, yell out what's real
   Even though it may not bring mass appeal
   Your opinion is yours, mine is mine
   If you don't like what I'm sayin' fine.

   'Freedom of Speech' (song, written by Ice-T and Afrika Islam) on the album *The Iceberg/Freedom of Speech . . . Just Watch What You Say* (1990)

3 I started off rapping for people just like myself, people who were in awe of wealth and flash. It was a conversation between me and them. But now most of those who buy my records are listening in on others' conversation. They are the aural equivalent of voyeurs, thrilled at this crazy world that has nothing to do with their experience.

*Observer* 27 October 1991

4 Crime is an equal-opportunity employer. It never discriminates. Anybody can enter the field. You don't need a college education. You don't need a G.E.D. You don't have to be any special color. You don't need white people to like you. You're self-employed. As a result, criminals are very independent people.

*The Ice Opinion*, ch. 3 (written with Heidi Sigmund, 1994)

5 Passion makes the world go round. Love just makes it a safer place.

ibid. ch. 4

## Harold L. Ickes (1874–1952)

US POLITICIAN

Full name Harold LeClair Ickes. A Republican turned Democrat, he was a lifelong supporter of President ROOSEVELT and was his 'hatchet man' during presidential campaigns. As head of the Public Works Administration, he implemented New Deal projects (1933–9). He resigned in 1946, after serving under TRUMAN, and joined the staff of *New Republic* in 1949.

1 I am against government by crony.

Speech February 1946, on resigning from his post as Secretary of the Interior, referring to President TRUMAN's award of government positions to old friends.

2 The trouble with Senator Long is that he is suffering from halitosis of the intellect. That's presuming Emperor Long has an intellect.

Quoted in *The Politics of Upheaval*, pt 2, ch. 14, sect. 5 (1960) by Arthur M. Schlesinger Jr. The remarks were a riposte to Long's suggestion that Ickes could go 'slap damn to hell', during an altercation over Roosevelt's New Deal, which Senator Huey Long, nicknamed 'Emperor of Louisiana', strongly opposed.

## Michael Ignatieff (b. 1947)

CANADIAN AUTHOR AND CRITIC

He describes himself as an 'academic who went over the monastery wall' but is more commonly known as the 'thinking woman's crumpet'. Among his books are the family memoir *The Russian Album* (1987), the novel *Scar Tissue* (1993) and a biography of ISAIAH BERLIN. He was host of the BBC *The Late Show* (1989) and editorial columnist for the *Observer* (1990–93).

1 Most of us no longer watch television; we graze, zapping back and forth between channels whenever our boredom threshold is triggered. No one does any one thing at a time. A new culture has taken shape which caters for people with the attention span of a flea.

*Three-Minute Culture*, BBC 2, 15 January 1989

## Ivan Illich (b. 1926)

AUSTRIAN-BORN US PHILOSOPHER AND AUTHOR

His works, such as *Deschooling Society* (1971) and *Towards a History of Need* (1978), are critiques of economic policy, particularly in respect of the Third World. His belief that technology, institutions and a philosophy of materialism have engendered there a new form of dependency has received widespread acceptance.

1 The compulsion to do good is an innate American trait. Only North Americans seem to believe that they always should, may, and actually can choose somebody with

whom to share their blessings. Ultimately this attitude leads to bombing people into the acceptance of gifts.

*Celebration of Awareness*, Preface to ch. 2 (1969)

2 There is no greater distance than that between a man in prayer and God.

ibid. ch. 4

3 School divides life into two segments, which are increasingly of comparable length. As much as anything else, schooling implies custodial care for persons who are declared undesirable elsewhere by the simple fact that a school has been built to serve them.

ibid. ch. 8

4 My friends, it is your task to surprise yourselves, and us, with the education you succeed in inventing for your children. Our hope of salvation lies in our being surprised by the Other. Let us learn always to receive further surprises.

ibid. ch. 9

5 Man must choose whether to be rich in things or in the freedom to use them.

*Deschooling Society*, ch. 4 (1971)

## Gary Indiana

US AUTHOR

After *Scar Tissue* (1987), a collection of fictional commentaries on contemporary culture, he turned to novel writing with such works as *Horse Crazy* (1989) and *Rent Boy* (1994). His *Three Month Fever* (1999) on Andrew Cucanan, the killer of Gianni Versace, gave him wider mainstream recognition.

1 Affection is the mortal illness of lonely people.

*Horse Crazy*, ch. 1 (1989)

2 [On AIDS] We listen to the hum and throb of the hospital and watch the soundless river shatter light into thousands of white drops. It isn't fair. We used to say: How can we live like this? And now the question really is: How can we die like this?

ibid. ch. 5

## William Ralph Inge (1860–1954)

BRITISH PHILOSOPHER AND ECCLESIASTIC

As Dean of St Paul's, London (1911–34), he was known as the 'Gloomy Dean' on account of his pessimistic sermons and newspaper articles. Among his popular works are *Outspoken Essays* (1919 and 1922). Other works include *Christian Mysticism* (1899) and studies of Plotinus, on whom he was an expert.

1 It takes in reality only one to make a quarrel. It is useless for the sheep to pass resolutions in favour of vegetarianism, while the wolf remains of a different opinion.

'Patriotism', first publ. 1915, repr. in *Outspoken Essays* (first series, 1919)

2 Public opinion, a vulgar, impertinent, anonymous tyrant who deliberately makes life unpleasant for anyone who is not content to be the average man.

'Our Present Discontents' in ibid.

3 A man may build himself a throne of bayonets, but he cannot sit on it.

Lecture given at St Andrews, Scotland, 1918, repr. in *The Philosophy of Plotinus*, vol. 2, Lecture 22 (1923). The words were quoted by BORIS YELTSIN from a tank during the failed military coup in Russia, August 1991.

4 Every institution not only carries within it the seeds of its own dissolution, but prepares the way for its most hated rival.

'The Victorian Age', Rede Lecture, Cambridge University, 1922, publ. in ibid.

5 Literature flourishes best when it is half a trade and half an art.

ibid.

6 Events in the past may be roughly divided into those which probably never happened and those which do not matter. This is what makes the trade of historian so attractive.

*Assessments and Anticipations*, 'Prognostications' (1929)

7 I think middle-age is the best time, if we can escape the fatty degeneration of the conscience which often sets in at about fifty.

Quoted in the *Observer* 8 June 1930

8 Worry is interest paid on trouble before it falls due.

*Observer* 14 February 1932

# (Sir) Bernard Ingham (b. 1932)

BRITISH GOVERNMENT PRESS OFFICER

After working as a left-wing journalist in his native Yorkshire and on the *Guardian*, he was Chief Information Officer under TONY BENN (1975–8) and subsequently Chief Press Secretary to MARGARET THATCHER (1979–90). Gruff and forthright, he was detested by his enemies (called a 'truculent, arrogant bully' by Tam Dalyell) and regarded with only qualified approval by members of the Conservative Party (John Biffen called him 'the sewer rather than the sewage'), but he was highly esteemed by Thatcher, to whom he was devotedly loyal.

1 What greatly concerns me and many other Socialists is that there are thousands of highly moral, upright and indeed religious people who are nevertheless Tory to the bone. They are quite frankly enigmas to simple souls like me.

Column as 'Albion' in the *Leeds Weekly Citizen* 11 June 1965, quoted in *Good and Faithful Servant*, Preface (1990) by Robert Harris. When asked in 1990 about his earlier vitriol vis-à-vis the Conservative Party, he answered: 'I don't think I loathed it. I just didn't like what it represented. It stood for privilege and I think Mrs Thatcher has changed all that.'

2 I . . . have never regarded the Official Secrets Act as a constraint on my operations. Indeed, I regard myself as licensed to break that law as and when I judge necessary; and I suppose it is necessary to break it every other minute of every working day.

Speech to IBA, 1981, quoted in ibid. ch. 8. 'I'm the man who is licensed to leak,' he told a gathering in 1990.

3 I sometimes compare press officers to riflemen on the Somme – mowing down wave upon wave of distortion, taking out rank upon rank of supposition, deduction and gossip.

Address at Press Gallery luncheon, quoted in the *Independent* 8 February 1990

# Richard Ingrams (b. 1937)

BRITISH JOURNALIST AND EDITOR

In 1962 he co-founded the satirical magazine *Private Eye* of which he was Editor (1963–86). He subsequently founded and edited the *Oldie* (from 1992), a magazine for 'good sense and quality writing', which he saw as an antidote to 'yoof' culture.

1 Publish and be sued.

Personal motto, as suggested on *Quote . . . Unquote*, BBC Radio 4, 4 May 1977. The words echo those attributed to the Duke of Wellington, 'Publish and be damned!', said to have been the Duke's response in 1842 to an attempt to blackmail him over the publication of letters to his mistress Harriet Wilson.

2 If your lawyers tell you that you have a very good case, you should settle immediately.

Quoted in *Maxwell: The Outsider*, ch. 14 (1988, rev. 1991) by Tom Bower. On losing a libel action taken out by ROBERT MAXWELL against *Private Eye*, November 1985, concerning allegations in July 1985 that Maxwell had paid for Labour Party leader NEIL KINNOCK's travel expenses in the hope of a peerage. Ingrams blamed the jury for his losing the case, who 'while good and true [are] immensely thick'.

3 It's important for people not to hold a high opinion of politicians, and one of the strengths of the British is that they don't on the whole. Even Mrs Thatcher, the most successful politician of our time, who has done more than anyone, is not liked very much in her own country, and that's a good attitude. The danger begins when people start admiring politicians.

Interview in *Singular Encounters* (1990) by Naim Attallah

# Eugène Ionesco (1912–94)

ROMANIAN-BORN FRENCH PLAYWRIGHT

Regarding humour as his 'outlet, release and salvation', he was a prominent figure of the Theatre of the Absurd. His early one-act plays, such as *The Bald Prima Donna* (1950), deal with self-estrangement and the failure of communication, while later full-length plays feature the semi-autobiographical character Bérenger.

1 Yoghurt is very good for the stomach, the lumber regions and apotheosis.

Mr Smith, in *The Bald Prima Donna* (1950)

2 Life is an abnormal business.

Jean, in *The Rhinoceros*, act 1 (1959)

3 An avant-garde man is like an enemy inside a city he is bent on destroying, against which he rebels; for like any system of government, an established form of expression is also a form of oppression.

'A Talk about the Avant-Garde' lecture, Helsinki, June 1959, publ. in *Notes and Counter Notes* (1962)

4 Banality is a symptom of non-communication. Men hide behind their clichés.

'Further Notes, 1960', publ. in ibid.

5 All history is nothing but a succession of 'crises' – of rupture, repudiation and resistance . . . When there is no 'crisis', there is stagnation, petrification and death.

'Have I Written Anti-Theatre?' publ. in ibid.

6 Since the death instinct exists in the heart of everything that lives, since we suffer from trying to repress it, since everything that lives longs for rest, let us unfasten the ties that bind us to life, let us cultivate our death wish, let us develop it, water it like a plant, let it grow unhindered. Suffering and fear are born from the repression of the death wish.

*Fragments of a Journal* (1967)

7 Beauty is a precious trace that eternity causes to appear to us and that it takes away from us. A manifestation of eternity, and a sign of death as well.

*Present Past – Past Present*, ch. 5 (1968)

8 The light of memory, or rather the light that memory lends to things, is the palest light of all . . . Just as dreams do, memory makes me profoundly aware of the unreality, the evanescence of the world, a fleeting image in the moving water.

ibid.

9 Boredom! I've got used to that. You get used to it, or rather, you don't get used to it, but you get used to not getting used to it.

Jean, in *Journeys Among The Dead* (1981)

10 Shakespeare was the great one before us. His place was between God and despair.

*International Herald Tribune* 17 June 1988

## (Sir) Muhammad Iqbal (1873–1938)

INDIAN POET AND PHILOSOPHER

His writings, classical in style and intended for recitation, were formative on the movement that led to the creation of the separate Muslim state of Pakistan. His best known work is *Secrets of the Self* (1915), for which he was criticized for superimposing Nietzschean ideas onto Islam.

1 Thou didst create the night, but I made the lamp.
Thou didst create clay, but I made the cup.
Thou didst create the deserts, mountains and forests,
I produced the orchards, gardens and groves.
It is I who made the glass out of stone,
And it is I who turn a poison into an antidote.
*Quoted in* The Clear Light of Day, *ch. 2 (1980) by Anita Desai*

## Clifford Irving (b. 1930)

US AUTHOR AND HOAXER

He is best known for his fake 'autobiography' of Howard Hughes, which he revealed before publication (1972) as an elaborate hoax and for which he was sentenced to two and a half years' imprisonment and fined $10,000; his book *Hoax* (1981) tells the story. Among his other works are *Fake!* (1968), the story of a Hungarian art forger, and books written under the pen name John Luckless.

1 A criminal trial is like a Russian novel: it starts with exasperating slowness as the characters are introduced to a jury, then there are complications in the form of minor witnesses, the protagonist finally appears and contradictions arise to produce drama, and finally as both jury and spectators grow weary and confused the pace quickens, reaching its climax in passionate final argument.
*Sunday Times 14 August 1988*

## John Irving (b. 1942)

US AUTHOR

He is known for his surreal yet plausible black comedies, often with a homicidal thread. They include *The World According to Garp* (1978, filmed 1982), *The Cider House Rules* (1985, filmed 2000) and *A Prayer for Owen Meany* (1989).

1 Sigmund Freud was a novelist with a scientific background. He just didn't know he was a novelist. All those damn psychiatrists after him, they didn't know he was a novelist either.
*Interview in* Writers at Work *(eighth series, ed. George Plimpton, 1988)*

2 It [baseball] is a game with a lot of waiting in it; it is a game with increasingly heightened anticipation of increasingly limited results.
*A Prayer for Owen Meany, ch. 1 (1989)*

## Christopher Isherwood (1904–86)

BRITISH-BORN US NOVELIST

His life as a teacher in Germany (1929–33) inspired the sketches of social disintegration in *Mr Norris Changes Trains* (1935) and *Goodbye to Berlin* (1939). The latter was later to form the basis for John Van Druten's play *I am a Camera* (1951) and Bob Fosse's musical film *Cabaret* (1966). He emigrated to the USA in 1946 with W.H. AUDEN, with whom he collaborated on three verse plays.

1 I am a camera with its shutter open, quite passive, recording, not thinking.
*Goodbye to Berlin, 'A Berlin Diary (Autumn 1930)' (1939)*

2 California is a tragic country – like Palestine, like every Promised Land.
*'Los Angeles', first publ. in* Horizon, *1947, repr. in* Exhumations *(1966)*

## Kazuo Ishiguro (b. 1954)

JAPANESE-BORN BRITISH NOVELIST

Set in Japan or Britain, Ishiguro's novels are a melancholy revisiting of the past. The best known are *An Artist of the Floating World* (1986) and *The Remains of the Day* (1989, filmed 1993).

1 By the very nature of a witticism, one is given very little time to assess its various possible repercussions before one is called to give voice to it, and one gravely risks uttering all manner of unsuitable things if one has not first acquired the necessary skill and experience.
*Mr Stevens, in* The Remains of the Day, *'Day Three – Morning. Taunton, Somerset' (1989)*

2 I can't even say I made my own mistakes. Really – one has to ask oneself – what dignity is there in that?
*Mr Stevens, in ibid. 'Day Six – Evening. Weymouth'*

## Eddie Izzard (b. 1962)

BRITISH COMEDIAN

A debonair cross-dresser, who calls himself a 'male tomboy', he has largely shunned television, preferring to deliver his quizzical and original observations through his one-man shows and videos. 'The only reason I've got where I am today is because of saying "Errrrr . . ." and wearing make-up,' he once said.

1 How to survive boarding school. Do not express emotion, do not feel emotion, do not have emotion. If someone hits you, hit them back; if someone argues with you, argue back – never give an inch, never look vulnerable and you will survive.
*Interview in the* Observer *5 October 1997. Izzard was sent to boarding school at the age of six when his mother was dying of cancer. He says he cried for a year.*

2 Women have this vast variety of lingerie, stockings and tights and different patterns, and shoes, with different-sized heels, in red and black, and skirts – short, long, with slits – push-the-boob things . . . there's so much around in women's things that is erotic. While men have: shirt shirt shirt jumper shirt jumper jacket jumper shirt jacket trousers trousers shirt trousers flat shoes.
*Interview in* The Times *10 December 1999*

## George Jackson (1941–71)

US BLACK ACTIVIST AND AUTHOR

Sentenced in 1960 for armed robbery, he undertook a programme of self-education and became a convinced communist and black activist as a prisoner in St Quentin and Soledad. While still under sentence he was accused with three others (together known as the Soledad Brothers) of the murder of a guard and was later killed in controversial circumstances. *Soledad Brother* (1970) was written from prison.

1 If we are to be men again we must stop working for nothing, competing against each other for the little they allow us to possess, stop selling our women or allowing them to be used and handled against their will, stop letting our children be educated by the barbarian, using their language, dress, and customs, and most assuredly stop turning our cheeks.

Letter to his father from Soledad Prison, 30 March 1965, publ. in *Soledad Brother* (1970)

2 Non-violent theory is practicable in civilized lands among civilized people, the Asians and Africans, but a look at European history shows that anything of great value that ever changed hands was taken by force of arms.

Letter to his mother from Soledad Prison, March 1967, publ. in ibid.

3 Every time I hear the word 'law' I visualize gangs of militiamen or Pinkertons busting strikes, pigs wearing sheets and caps that fit over their pointed heads. I see a white oak and a barefoot black hanging, or snake-eyes peeping down the lenses of telescopic rifles, or conspiracy trials.

*Blood in my Eye*, 'Classes at War' (1972)

## Glenda Jackson (b. 1936)

BRITISH ACTRESS AND POLITICIAN

Before entering parliament as Labour MP for Hampstead and Highgate (1992), she pursued a career on stage, notably in *Hedda Gabler* (1975) and as a film actress, winning Oscars for her roles in *Women in Love* (1969) and *A Touch of Class* (1974). Her former husband, Roy Hodge, said of her: 'If she went into politics she'd be prime minister.'

1 Acting is not about dressing up. Acting is about stripping bare. The whole essence of learning lines is to forget them so you can make them sound like you thought of them that instant.

*Sunday Telegraph* 26 July 1992

## Holbrook Jackson (1874–1948)

BRITISH AUTHOR AND CRITIC

He published works on literary figures and on William Morris in whom he had a lifelong interest, including *On Art and Socialism* (1947). As a passionate bibliophile, he wrote *Anatomy of Bibliomania* (two volumes, 1930 and 1931) and *Bookman's Holiday* (1945).

1 Pedantry is the dotage of knowledge.

*Anatomy of Bibliomania*, vol. 1, pt 7, 'A Cure for Pedantry' (1930)

## Jesse Jackson (b. 1941)

US CLERGYMAN AND CIVIL RIGHTS LEADER

A persuasive Baptist preacher and black civil rights activist, he worked with MARTIN LUTHER KING, and in 1984 and 1988 he contested the Democratic Party's presidential nominations, the first Afro-American to bid for the office. In 1990 he was elected as 'statehood senator' for Washington.

1 I hear that melting-pot stuff a lot, and all I can say is that we haven't melted.

*Playboy* November 1969

2 **When we're unemployed, we're called lazy; when the whites are unemployed, it's called a depression.**
Interview in *The Americans*, 'When Whites Are Unemployed, It's Called a Depression' (1970) by David Frost

3 **Racism as a form of skin worship, and as a sickness and a pathological anxiety for America, is so great, until the poor whites – rather than fighting for jobs or education – fight to remain pink and fight to remain white. And therefore they cannot see an alliance with people that they feel to be inherently inferior.**
Interview in ibid.

4 **The burden of being black is that you have to be superior just to be equal. But the glory of it is that, once you achieve, you have achieved, indeed.**
*Christian Science Monitor* 26 September 1979

5 **I am not a perfect servant. I am a public servant doing my best against the odds. As I develop and serve, be patient. God is not finished with me yet.**
Speech at Democratic National Convention, San Francisco, 16 July 1984, quoted in the *New Left Review*, vol. 149, 1985

6 **Our flag is red, white, and blue, but our nation is a rainbow – red, yellow, brown, black and white, we are *all* precious in God's sight!**
Speech at Democratic National Convention, San Francisco, 17 July 1984, quoted in *Jesse: The Life and Pilgrimage of Jesse Jackson*, ch. 15 (1996) by Marshall Frady. Jackson – who also compared America to a quilt: 'many pieces, many colors, many sizes, all woven and held together by a common thread' – named his political organization the 'National Rainbow Coalition'.

7 **My constituency is the desperate, the damned, the disinherited, the disrespected and the despised.**
Speech at Democratic National Convention, San Francisco, 17 July 1984, quoted in *Jesse Jackson*, ch. 8 (1991) by Robert Jakoubek

8 **Great things happen in small places. Jesus was born in Bethlehem. Jesse Jackson was born in Greenville.**
*Daily Mail* 9 March 1988

9 **A cheque or credit card, a Gucci bag strap, anything of value will do. Give as you live.**
Quoted in the *Daily Telegraph* 6 April 1988. Comments while fund-raising in Aspen, Colorado.

10 **We've removed the ceiling above our dreams. There are no more impossible dreams.**
*Independent* 9 June 1988

11 **If you wake up in the morning and think you're white, you're bound to meet someone before five o'clock who will let you know you are just another nigger.**
*Sun* 20 September 1989

## Mahalia Jackson (1911–72)
US GOSPEL SINGER

The 'Queen of the Gospel Song' was already a popular recording star by the 1940s. In 1947 'Move On Up a Little Higher' became the first gospel record to sell a million copies. From 1955 she was active in the civil rights movement, and she sang at the funeral of MARTIN LUTHER KING.

1 **It's easy to be independent when you've got money. But to be independent when you haven't got a thing – that's the Lord's test.**
*Movin' On Up*, ch. 1 (1966, written with Evan McLoud Wylie)

2 **This musical thing has been here since America been here. This is trial and tribulation music.**
Quoted in *Time* magazine 28 June 1968

## Michael Jackson (b. 1958)
US SINGER AND DANCER

The youngest member of the soul pop family group the Jackson Five, he began a solo career in 1971. Under the direction of musical producer QUINCY JONES, he had an impressive run of hits, including the album *Thriller* (1982), which sold a world record 40 million copies, helped by state-of-the-art videos featuring his deft dancing technique. His reclusive lifestyle and extensive skin-toning and plastic surgery have generated much press interest, as did his brief marriage to ELVIS PRESLEY's daughter in 1994. His reputation suffered when allegations of child abuse were made in 1993.

1 **I love *E.T.* 'cos it reminds me of me. Someone from another world coming down and you becoming friends with them and this person is, like, 800 years old and he's filling you with all kinds of wisdom and he can teach you how to fly. That whole fantasy thing which I think is great. I mean, who don't wanna fly?**
Interview in *Smash Hits* 20 January 1983. Jackson collaborated with *E.T.* director Steven Spielberg on the 'E.T. Storybook' album and also narrated it.

2 **Well they say the sky's the limit
And to me that's really true
But my friend you have seen nothing
Just wait 'til I get through . . .
Because I'm bad, I'm bad.**
'Bad' on the album *Bad* (1987)

3 **I'm not going to spend
My life being a color
Don't tell me you agree with me
When I saw you kicking dirt in my eye
But, if you're thinkin' about my baby
It don't matter if you're black or white.**
'Black or White' on the album *Dangerous* (1991)

## Bianca Jagger (b. 1944)
NICARAGUAN MODEL AND HUMAN RIGHTS ACTIVIST

Called the world's best dressed human rights campaigner, she was MICK JAGGER's first wife and has since dedicated herself to good causes. She also acted in the film *The Cannonball Run* (1980).

1 **My marriage ended on my wedding day.**
Quoted in *The Life and Good Times of the Rolling Stones* (1989) by Philip Norman. Referring to her wedding to Mick Jagger in St Tropez in 1971. The chaotic event had attracted a mob of reporters and photographers, eliciting the comment from him: 'I am not in a goldfish bowl and I am not the king of France.'

## Mick Jagger (b. 1943)
BRITISH ROCK MUSICIAN

The once rebellious lead singer with the Rolling Stones, he has taken on a number of acting roles, notably in *Ned Kelly* and *Performance* (both 1970), and released solo albums, although has always returned to the band of which he once remarked: 'I don't think of the Rolling Stones as an institution, more a mental home.' See also GEORGE MELLY 3.

1 **The only performance that makes it, that really makes it, is the one that ends in madness.**
Turner (Mick Jagger), in *Performance*, (film, 1970, screenplay by Donald Cammell, directed by Donald Cammell and Nicolas Roeg)

2 **People have this obsession. They want you to be like you were in 1969. They want you to, because otherwise their youth goes with you . . . It's very selfish, but it's understandable.**
Quoted in the *Observer* 10 January 1993

## Mick Jagger (b. 1943) and
## Keith Richards (b. 1943)
BRITISH ROCK MUSICIANS

The Jagger–Richards partnership produced nearly all of the Rolling Stones' original material and also provided the essential chemistry of the band, in which Richards' distinct guitar style was well matched by Jagger's prancing energy. Their r-'n'-b-driven songs expressed the anger and sexuality of the 1960s, for example the hit singles 'The Last Time' and '(I Can't Get No) Satisfaction' (both 1965) and the albums *Beggar's Banquet* (1968) and *Let It Bleed* (1969).

1 **I can't get no satisfaction.**
'(I Can't Get No) Satisfaction' (song, 1965) on the album *Big Hits (High Tide and Green Grass)* (1966) by the Rolling Stones

2 **Get off of my cloud**
'Get Off Of My Cloud' (song, 1965) on ibid.

3 **She goes running for the shelter**
**Of a mother's little helper,**
**And it helps her on her way,**
**Gets her through her busy day.**
'Mother's Little Helper' (song) on the album *Aftermath* (1966) by the Rolling Stones

4 **I shouted out, 'Who killed the Kennedy's?'**
**When after all, it was you and me.**
'Sympathy for the Devil' (song) on the album *Beggars' Banquet* (1969) by the Rolling Stones. The song, whose lyrics were inspired by Jagger's reading of Mikhail Bulgakov's *The Master and Margarita*, was the subject of a film by JEAN-LUC GODARD, *Sympathy for the Devil* (1969).

5 **But what can a poor boy do**
**Except to sing for a rock 'n' roll band,**
**'Cause in sleepy London town**
**There's just no place for a street fighting man!**
'Street Fighting Man' (song) on ibid.

6 **You can't always get what you want**
**But if you try sometimes**
**You just might find**
**You get what you need.**
'You Can't Always Get What You Want' (song) on the album *Let It Bleed* (1970) by the Rolling Stones

7 **I know it's only rock 'n' roll but I like it.**
'It's Only Rock 'n' Roll' (song) on the album *It's Only Rock 'n' Roll* (1974) by the Rolling Stones

## Tom Jaine (b. 1943)
BRITISH COOKERY WRITER

He was editor of the *Good Food Guide* (1989–93) and since 1993 has been the proprietor of Prospect Books. He contributes to the *Sunday Telegraph* and has published a number of cookery books, including *Fish Times Thirty: Recipes from a Dartmouth Restaurant* (1980) and *Making Bread at Home: 50 Recipes from Around the World* (1995).

1 **If cooking becomes an art form rather than a means of providing a reasonable diet, then something is clearly wrong.**
*Daily Telegraph* 19 October 1989

## Lord Jakobovits (1921–99)
BRITISH RABBI

Full name Emmanuel Jakobovits. He was Chief Rabbi of the Commonwealth (1967–91) and instrumental in mending rifts in the Jewish community in Britain. He published *Journal of a Rabbi* (1966) and *If Only My People . . . Zionism in My Life* (1985).

1 **Silence, indifference and inaction were Hitler's principal allies.**
*Independent* 5 December 1989. Referring to the prosecution of war criminals.

2 **We must pursue the peace efforts as if there were no terrorism, and fight the terrorists as if there were no peace efforts.**
Letter to *The Times* 5 March 1996, following a spate of bomb attacks by Hamas in Tel Aviv and Jerusalem

## Clive James (b. 1939)
AUSTRALIAN AUTHOR, CRITIC AND BROADCASTER

He has published several volumes of criticism, mock-epic verse and autobiography, although, he says, 'everything I write is auto-biographical'. His long-running TV shows give opportunities for his showmanship and wise-cracking wit. For AUBERON WAUGH his appeal lies in his 'robust, knockabout talent, not to mention an amiable eccentricity of judgement'.

1 **Prejudices are useless. Call Los Angeles any dirty name you like – Six Suburbs in Search of a City, Paradise with a Lobotomy, anything – but the fact remains that you are already living in it before you get there.**
'Postcard from Los Angeles 1', first publ. in the *Observer* 16 June 1979, repr. in *Flying Visits* (1984)

2 **All television ever did was shrink the demand for ordinary movies. The demand for extraordinary movies increased. If any one thing is wrong with the movie industry today, it is the unrelenting effort to astonish.**
ibid.

3 **As a work of art it has the same status as a long conversation between two not very bright drunks.**
'A Blizzard of Tiny Kisses', first publ. in the *London Review of Books*, 1980, repr. in *From the Land of Shadows* (1982). Referring to *Princess Daisy* by Judith Krantz, which fetched what was then a record advance of $3,208,875 when the rights were sold at auction in New York.

4 **A sceptic finds *Dallas* absurd. A cynic thinks the public doesn't.**
*Glued to the Box*, Introduction (1983). Referring to the US soap opera that captured a world-wide market (1978–91).

5 **Anyone afraid of what he thinks television does to the world is probably just afraid of the world.**
ibid.

## C.L.R. James (1901–89)
TRINIDADIAN JOURNALIST AND AUTHOR

Full name Cyril Lionel Robert James. He came to England in 1933 to work as cricket correspondent on the *Manchester Guardian*, although it was during his time in the USA (1938–53) that he evolved his essentially Marxist political ideas. He is best known for *Beyond the Boundary* (1963), a blend of sport and politics. As the critic Alastair Niven asked: 'Was there ever a less polemical or more persuasive radical?'

1 **Cricket is first and foremost a dramatic spectacle. It belongs with the theatre, ballet, opera and the dance.**
*Beyond a Boundary*, pt 6, ch. 16 (1963)

## Henry James (1843–1916)
US AUTHOR

An American transplanted to Europe, he returned frequently to the theme of the old and new worlds and the collision between them. His major works include *The Portrait of a Lady* (1881), *The Ambassadors* (1903) and the psychological ghost story *The Turn of the Screw* (1898). WILLIAM FAULKNER called him 'the nicest old lady I ever met', while for VIRGINIA WOOLF he was 'that courtly, worldly, sentimental old gentleman [who] can still make us afraid of the dark'. See also NEWS OF THE WORLD 1.

1 **However British you may be, I am more British still.**
Quoted in *Henry James at Home*, ch. 7, sect. 5 (1969) by H. Montgomery Hyde. The remark addressed to two English friends in August 1914 was reported in a letter written to *The Times* 4 March 1916 by the poet and critic Edmund Gosse. James had lived in England since 1876 and took British citizenship in 1915 as a gesture of support for Britain's war effort.

2 **It is art that *makes* life, makes interest, makes importance**

... and I know of no substitute whatever for the force and beauty of its process.

Letter to H.G. WELLS, 10 July 1915, publ. in *Henry James Letters*, vol. 4 (ed. Leon Edel, 1984). Wells replied (13 July): 'I don't clearly understand your concluding phrases . . . I can only read sense into it by assuming that you are using "art" for every conscious human activity. I use the word for a research and attainment that is technical and special.'

3 Happy you poets who can be present and *so* present by a simple flicker of your genius, and not, like the clumsier race, have to lay a train and pile up faggots that may not after prove in the least combustible!

Letter to W.B. YEATS, 25 August 1915, in private collection. This observation was later incorporated into Yeats's poem, 'In Memory of Major Robert Gregory'.

4 So here it is at last, the distinguished thing!

Quoted in *A Backward Glance*, ch. 14 (1934) by Edith Wharton. The words are often claimed to be James's last words but were actually said to have been spoken by him 2 December 1915, when he suffered a stroke at the beginning of his last illness. The anecdote was recounted to Wharton by James's friend Lady Prothero and was described by his biographer LEON EDEL as 'a beautiful bit of apocrypha'.

5 Tell the boys to follow, to be faithful, to take me seriously.

Last words, quoted in *Henry James at Home*, ch. 7, sect. 4 (1969) by H. Montgomery Hyde. James is said to have uttered the words in one of his last conscious moments when his mind was dwelling on his work. He died on 28 February 1916.

## P.D. James (b. 1920)
BRITISH AUTHOR

Phyllis Dorothy White, Baroness James of Holland Park. Often described as the 'Queen of Crime', her experience as a nurse and as a civil servant in the police and criminal departments of the Home Office provided useful background for her chilling detective novels, such as *Death of an Expert Witness* (1977) and *A Taste for Death* (1986). She is possessed of a 'keen, cunning mind and a positively bloody imagination', according to Peter Gorner of the *Chicago Tribune*.

1 What the detective story is about is not murder but the restoration of order.

Interview in *The Face* December 1986

2 Great literature cannot grow from a neglected or impoverished soil. Only if we actually tend or care will it transpire that every hundred years or so we might get a *Middlemarch*.

*Daily Telegraph* 14 April 1988

3 A man who lives with nature is used to violence and is companionable with death. There is more violence in an English hedgerow than in the meanest streets of a great city.

Jonah the tramp, in *Devices and Desires*, ch. 40 (1989)

4 Creativity doesn't flourish in an atmosphere of despotism, coercion and fear.

Quoted in the *Sunday Times* 7 March 1999. Commenting on management practices in the BBC under JOHN BIRT.

## Selma James (b. 1930)
US AUTHOR AND POLITICAL ACTIVIST

A writer on feminist issues, she is the author of *A Woman's Place* (1972) and *Sex, Race and Class* (1976).

1 We have needed to define ourselves by reclaiming the words that define us. They have used language as weapons. When we open ourselves to what they say and how they say it, our narrow prejudices evaporate and we are nourished and armed.

*The Ladies and the Mammies: Jane Austen and Jean Rhys*, ch. 1 (1983)

## Storm Jameson (1891–1986)
BRITISH NOVELIST

She made her name with two trilogies describing the lives of a family of Yorkshire shipbuilders between the wars, *The Triumph of Time* (1927–31) and *The Mirror in Darkness* (1934–6). She also published poetry, criticism and seven volumes of autobiography.

1 Mere human beings can't afford to be fanatical about anything . . . Not even about justice or loyalty. The fanatic for justice ends by murdering a million helpless people to clear a space for his law-courts. If we are to survive on this planet, there must be compromises.

Vancura, in *A Cup of Tea for Mr Thorgill*, ch. 28 (1957)

## Kathleen Jamie (b. 1962)
BRITISH POET

In addition to her poetry, which is characterized by its strong Scottish flavour, she has written travel books about Asia. Her collections include *Black Spiders* (1982) and *The Way We Live* (1987).

1 Pass the tambourine, let me bash out the praises
to the Lord God of movement, to Absolute
non-friction, flight, and the scary side:
death by avalanche, birth by failed contraception.

'The Way We Live', publ. in *The Way We Live* (1987)

## Elizabeth Janeway (1913–93)
US AUTHOR

A major spokeswoman for the women's movement, she is perceived as a balanced and sometimes ironic commentator on shifting gender roles. Her books include *Men's World – Woman's Place* (1971) and *Between Myth and Morning* (1974).

1 As long as mixed grills and combination salads are popular, anthologies will undoubtedly continue in favor.

*The Writer's Book*, ch. 32 (ed. Helen Hull, 1950)

2 I am not sure how many 'sins' I would recognize in the world. Some would surely be defused by changed circumstances. But I can imagine none that is more irredeemably sinful than the betrayal, the exploitation, of the young by those who should care for them.

'Incest: A Rational Look at the Oldest Taboo', publ. in *Ms.* November 1981

## Tama Janowitz (b. 1957)
US AUTHOR

She is known for her postmodernist and humorous fiction, which portrays the inner life of New York City. She is, in the words of Thomas de Pietro of the *Hudson Review*, a 'literary Cyndi Lauper, a connoisseur of kitsch'. She wrote her first novel, *American Dad*, in 1981 and adapted her volume of connected short stories, *Slaves of New York* (1986), as the screenplay for the film of the same name (1989).

1 I was like a social worker for lepers. My clients had a chunk of their body they wanted to give away; for a price I was there to receive it. Crimes, sins, nightmares, hunks of hair: it was surprising how many of them had something to dispose of. The more I charged, the easier it was for them to breathe freely once more.

*Slaves of New York*, 'Modern Saint 271' (1986)

2 Long after the bomb falls and you and your good deeds are gone, cockroaches will still be here, prowling the streets like armored cars.

ibid.

3 With publicity comes humiliation.

*International Herald Tribune* 8 September 1992

## Derek Jarman (1942–94)

BRITISH FILM-MAKER, ARTIST AND AUTHOR

A restlessly experimental spirit informs his work, as evident in his first film, *Sebastiane* (1976), which had Latin dialogue, and in one of his last, *Blue* (1993), which featured an unchanging blue screen. DAVID THOMSON called him a 'prisoner' of the constraints imposed upon him '. . . whose relentless eye turns his bars into vines, barber poles, and beribboned serpents'.

1 Now is the time of departure. The last streamer that ties us to what is known, parts. We drift into a sea of storms.

Narrator in *Jubilee* (film, 1977, written and directed by Derek Jarman)

2 Understand that sexuality is as wide as the sea. Understand that your morality is not law. Understand that we are you. Understand that if we decide to have sex whether safe, safer, or unsafe, it is our decision and you have no rights in our lovemaking.

*At Your Own Risk: A Saint's Testament*, '1940's' (1992)

3 All men are homosexual, some turn straight. It must be very odd to be a straight man because your sexuality is hopelessly defensive. It's like an ideal of racial purity.

ibid.

4 An orgasm joins you to the past. Its timelessness becomes the brotherhood; the brethren are lovers; they extend the 'family'. I share that sexuality. It was then, is now and will be in the future.

ibid. '1950's'

5 The modern queer was invented by Tennessee Williams. Brando in blue jeans, sneakers, white T-shirt and leather jacket. When you saw that, you knew they were available.

ibid. '1960's'

6 I wouldn't wish the eighties on anyone, it was the time when all that was rotten bubbled to the surface. If you were not at the receiving end of this mayhem you could be unaware of it. It was possible to live through the decade preoccupied by the mortgage and the pence you saved on your income tax. It was also possible for those of us who saw what was happening to turn our eyes in a different direction; but what, in another decade, had been a trip to the clap clinic was now a trip to the mortuary.

ibid. '1980's'

7 [On being HIV positive] I'm not afraid of death but I am afraid of dying. Pain can be alleviated by morphine but the pain of social ostracism cannot be taken away.

ibid.

8 Paradise haunts gardens, and some gardens are paradises. Mine is one of them. Others are like bad children – spoilt by their parents, over-watered and covered with noxious chemicals.

*Derek Jarman's Garden* (text by Derek Jarman, photographs by Howard Sooley, 1995). Jarman created his own garden at Prospect Cottage, on an inhospitable stretch of shingle on the Kent coast, within sight of the nuclear power station at Dungeness. He incorporated driftwood, shells and sculptures made from stones and other flotsam found on the beach.

## Randall Jarrell (1914–65)

US POET AND CRITIC

His often harrowing poetry was written, according to *Time* magazine, in 'plain American, which dogs and cats can read', while ROBERT LOWELL called him 'almost brutally serious about literature'. Verse collections include *The Woman at the Washington Zoo* (1960) and *The Lost World* (1965). He was also known as a mordant and erudite critic and editor. He died in a car accident.

1 Six miles from earth, loosed from its dream of life,
   I woke to black flak and the nightmare fighters.

When I died they washed me out of the turret with a hose.

'The Death of the Ball Turret Gunner' (1945), repr. in *Selected Poems* (1955)

2 When you begin to read a poem you are entering a foreign country whose laws and language and life are a kind of translation of your own; but to accept it because its stews taste exactly like your old mother's hash, or to reject it because the owl-headed goddess of wisdom in its temple is fatter than the Statue of Liberty, is an equal mark of that want of imagination, that inaccessibility to experience, of which each of us who dies a natural death will die.

*Poetry and the Age*, 'The Obscurity of the Poet' (1953)

3 The work of art is as done as it will ever get, and all the critics in the world can't make its crust a bit browner; they may help *us*, the indigent readers, but they haven't done a thing to it. Around the throne of God, where all the angels read perfectly, there are no critics – there is no need for them.

ibid. 'The Age of Criticism'

4 His [President Robbins's] voice not only took you into his confidence, it laid a fire for you and put your slippers by it and then went into the other room to get into something more comfortable.

*Pictures from an Institution*, pt 1, ch. 10 (1954)

5 Old faces are forbidding or beautiful for what is expressed in them; in a face that is young enough almost everything but the youth is hidden, so that it is beautiful both for what is there and what cannot yet be there.

ibid. pt 4, ch. 4

6 It is better to entertain an idea than to take it home to live with you for the rest of your life.

ibid. ch. 9

7 Europeans and Americans are like men and women: they understand each other worse, and it matters less, than either of them suppose.

ibid.

## Antony Jay (b. 1930)

BRITISH AUTHOR AND JOURNALIST

After working as a director and producer for the BBC (1955–64), he became a freelance writer and published *Management and Machiavelli* (1967) and *Corporation Man* (1971). He later co-scripted with JONATHAN LYNN the BBC television series satirizing high politics, *Yes Minister* (1980–82) and *Yes, Prime Minister* (1986–8).

1 You gave the world the guillotine
   But still we don't know why the heck
   You have to drop it on our neck.
   We're glad of what we did to you,
   At Agincourt and Waterloo.
   And now the Franco-Prussian War
   Is something we are strongly for.
   So damn your food and damn your wines,
   Your twisted loaves and twisting vines,
   Your *table d'hôte*, your *à la carte*,
   Your land, your history, your art.
   From now on you can keep the lot.
   Take every single thing you've got,
   Your land, your wealth, your men, your dames,
   Your dream of independent power,
   And dear old Konrad Adenauer,
   And stick them up your Eiffel Tower.

*Time* magazine 8 February 1963. Referring to France's rejection of Britain's entry into the Common Market.

## Douglas Jay (1907–96)

BRITISH POLITICIAN

Baron Jay of Battersea. Labour MP 1945–83, he was financial secretary to the Cabinet 1950–51 and president of the Board of Trade 1964–7. He was dismissed from the WILSON Cabinet because of his opposition to British entry into the EEC.

1 In the case of nutrition and health, just as in the case of education, the gentleman in Whitehall really does know better what is good for people than the people know themselves.
   *The Socialist Case*, ch. 30 (1937)

## (Sir) James Jeans (1877–1946)

BRITISH ASTROPHYSICIST AND MATHEMATICIAN

His work in the field of physics focused on the theory of gases and energy radiation, and in the field of astronomy on giant and dwarf stars and spiral nebulae. *The Dynamical Theory of Gases* (1904) became a standard technical text, and *The Universe Around Us* (1929) and *Through Space and Time* (1934) did much to popularize astronomy.

1 From the intrinsic evidence of his creation, the Great Architect of the Universe now begins to appear as a pure mathematician.
   *The Mysterious Universe*, ch. 5 (1930)

## (Sir) Geoffrey Jellicoe (1900–96)

BRITISH ARCHITECT AND HISTORIAN

His writings, notably *Landscape of Man* (1975), were influential on the development of landscapes and gardens. His designs, such as the Kennedy Memorial at Runnymede (1965), and gardens at Sutton Place, Sussex (1980–84), often incorporate water and sculpture.

1 Architecture is to make us know and remember who we are.
   *International Herald Tribune* 6 November 1989

## David Jenkins (b. 1925)

BRITISH ECCLESIASTIC

He was Professor of Theology at Leeds (1979–84) before becoming Bishop of Durham (1984–94), in which capacity he caused controversy over his interpretation of the virgin birth and the resurrection. His beliefs are to be found in, among other works, *The Contradiction of Christianity* (1976) and *God, Politics and the Future* (1988).

1 I wouldn't put it past God to arrange a virgin birth if He wanted, but I very much doubt if He would.
   *Church Times* 4 May 1984

2 No statement about God is simply, literally true. God is far more than can be measured, described, defined in ordinary language, or pinned down to any particular happening.
   *Guardian* 24 December 1984

3 As I get older I seem to believe less and less and yet to believe what I do believe more and more.
   *Daily Telegraph* 2 November 1988

## Roy Jenkins (b. 1920)

BRITISH POLITICIAN

Baron Jenkins of Hillhead. He was elected a Labour MP in 1948 and served as Home Secretary (1965–7 and 1974–6) and Chancellor of the Exchequer (1967–70). He stepped down as a Labour MP to take up the post of President of the European Commission (1977–81). He was the first leader of the Social Democratic Party in 1981 but lost his seat in the 1987 election, whereupon he was appointed Chancellor of Oxford University.

1 [Of James Callaghan] There is nobody in politics I can remember and no case I can think of in history where a man combined such a powerful political personality with so little intelligence.
   Quoted in *The Crossman Diaries*, 5 September 1969 (1979). Remark to Richard Crossman, who demurred: 'I think Jim Callaghan is a wonderful political personality, easily the most accomplished politician in the Labour Party.'

2 The politics of the left and centre of this country are frozen in an out-of-date mould which is bad for the political and economic health of Britain and increasingly inhibiting for those who live within the mould. Can it be broken?
   Speech to Parliamentary Press Gallery, 9 June 1980, quoted in *The Times* 10 June 1980. Jenkins co-founded the Social Democratic Party in 1981, which was said to have 'broken the mould of British politics'.

## Elizabeth Jennings (b. 1926)

BRITISH POET

Writing in traditional verse form, she explores personal themes of suffering and isolation, influenced by her faith as a Roman Catholic and by a period of mental illness in the 1960s and consequent suicide attempt. *The Mind Has Mountains* (1966) reflects this time, while later collections include *Moments of Grace* (1979) and *Tributes* (1989).

1 But every season is a kind
   Of rich nostalgia. We give names –
   Autumn and summer, winter, spring –
   As though to unfasten from the mind
   Our moods and give them outward forms.
   We want the certain, solid thing.
   'Song at the Beginning of Autumn', publ. in *A Way of Looking* (1955)

2 We will the tragedy upon
   Ourselves. There is more suffering
   In watching jealousy or grief
   Move to completion in a life
   Not ours, than in the offering
   To have the entire burden on
   Our hearts and feel the pain within.
   'The Nature of Tragedy', publ. in ibid.

3 Do they know they're old,
   These two who are my father and my mother
   Whose fire from which I came, has now grown cold?
   'One Flesh', publ. in *The Mind Has Mountains* (1966)

4 I have come into the hour of a white healing.
   Grief's surgery is over and I wear
   The scar of my remorse and of my feeling.
   'Into the Hour', publ. in *Moments of Grace* (1979)

5 Never to possess,
   Therefore never lose, –
   This is a creed of fire,
   The burning of excess,
   The cold ash of loss,
   Continual desire.
   'Ways', publ. in *Extending the Territory* (1985)

6 Imagination greets the baleful tide
   And seeks a ceremony in its coming.
   Desire for vision is incorrigibly
   Demanding. We are the citizens, not seers,
   Asking our little governments to bring
   Order and shape to guide a way to sing.
   'Imagination', publ. in ibid.

## Jiang Qing (1914–91)

CHINESE PARTY OFFICIAL

Third wife of the Chinese Communist Party leader MAO ZEDONG from 1939, she played a ruthless and prominent role in the Cultural

Revolution (1966–9). On Mao's death in 1976, she was the leading member of the 'Gang of Four', which was foiled in its bid for power, was arrested for treason and in 1981 received a death sentence, commuted to life imprisonment. In 1991 the Chinese government reported that she had committed suicide.

1 There cannot be peaceful coexistence in the ideological realm. Peaceful coexistence corrupts.

Said in April 1967, quoted in *Mao and China: From Revolution to Revolution*, ch. 15 (1972) by Stanley Karnow

## C.E.M. Joad (1891–1953)

BRITISH PHILOSOPHER AND AUTHOR

Full name Cyril Edwin Mitchinson Joad. Author of more than forty books, he made the subject of philosophy accessible to the general reader, as in *Guide to Philosophy* (1936), often incorporating his own controversial views.

1 It all depends what you mean by . . .

Typical intervention when answering questions on 'The Brains Trust', BBC radio (1941–8)

2 A good soul like a good body should be as unobtrusive as possible; in so far as it functions properly, it should not be noticed for good or for ill.

*The Book of Joad*, ch. 2, 'Food and Women' (1932)

3 Conscience was the barmaid of the Victorian soul. Recognizing that human beings were fallible and that their failings, though regrettable, must be humoured, conscience would permit, rather ungraciously perhaps, the indulgence of a number of carefully selected desires.

ibid. ch. 11, 'Morals and My Lack of Them'

## (Sir) Elton John (b. 1947)

BRITISH ROCK MUSICIAN

Original name Reginald Kenneth Dwight. A regular chart-topper in the 1970s and 1980s, he has relied on a flamboyant, often outrageous, stage presence to accompany his piano-based songs, most of which are written in collaboration with lyricist Bernie Taupin. Bestselling albums include the double *Goodbye Yellow Brick Road* (1973). He became Chairman of Watford Football Club in 1976 and Honorary President in 1990. 'If you mention the queen to most Aussie kids,' KATHY LETTE remarked, 'they think you mean Elton John.'

1 And it seems to me you lived your life
  Like a candle in the wind.

'Candle in the Wind' (song, with lyrics by Bernie Taupin), on the album *Goodbye Yellow Brick Road* (1973). The song, which was about MARILYN MONROE, was re-released in 1997 with new words addressed to the 'Princess of Wales' (see 4 below). 'Candle in the Wind' was the title of a 1941 play by Maxwell Anderson.

2 Saturday night's alright for fighting.

'Saturday Night's Alright for Fighting' (song, with lyrics by Bernie Taupin), on ibid.

3 I cannot bear successful people who are miserable.

Quoted in the *Sydney Morning Herald* 4 January 1986

4 Goodbye English rose,
  May you ever grow in our hearts

'Candle in the Wind '97' (song, 1997, with lyrics by Bernie Taupin). The song was re-written to mark the death of Princess DIANA and played by Elton John at her funeral in Westminster Abbey.

## Pope John XXIII (1881–1963)

ITALIAN ECCLESIASTIC

Angelo Giuseppe Roncalli. Elected Pope in 1958 on the twelfth ballot, he was responsible for convening the Second Vatican Council in 1962 by which he intended to update and reform the Church, with the ultimate aim of Christian unity, but he died after the first session. The Council was continued by Pope Paul VI.

1 In order to imbue civilization with sound principles and enliven it with the spirit of the gospel, it is not enough to be illumined with the gift of faith and enkindled with the desire of forwarding a good cause. For this end it is necessary to take an active part in the various organizations and influence them from within. And since our present age is one of outstanding scientific and technical progress and excellence, one will not be able to enter these organizations and work effectively from within unless he is scientifically competent, technically capable and skilled in the practice of his own profession.

Encyclical 10 April 1963: *Pacem in Terris*, pt 5

2 Learn how to be a policeman, because that cannot be improvised. As regards being pope, you will see later. Anybody can be pope; the proof of this is that I have become one.

Letter to a young boy, publ. in *The Wit and Wisdom of Good Pope John* (ed. Henri Fesquet, 1963)

## Pope John Paul II (b. 1920)

POLISH ECCLESIASTIC

Karol Jozef Wojtyla. The first non-Italian to be elected Pope (1978) since 1522, he has travelled extensively, defending the Church in communist countries and speaking out against married priests, birth control, abortion, genetic manipulation, euthanasia and capital punishment. In March 2000 he made a public apology for the historic sins of the Catholic church.

1 As the family goes, so goes the nation and so goes the whole world in which we live.

Quoted in the *Observer* 7 December 1986

2 The question confronting the Church today is not any longer whether the man in the street can grasp a religious message, but how to employ the communications media so as to let him have the full impact of the Gospel message.

*International Herald Tribune* 8 May 1989

3 The cemetery of the victims of human cruelty in our century is extended to include yet another vast cemetery, that of the unborn.

Quoted in the *Observer* 9 June 1991

4 It would be simplistic to say that Divine Providence caused the fall of communism. In a certain sense communism as a system fell by itself. It fell as a consequence of its own mistakes and abuses. *It proved to be a medicine more dangerous than the disease itself.* It did not bring about true social reform, yet it did become a powerful threat and challenge to the entire world. But *it fell by itself, because of its own inherent weakness.*

*Crossing the Threshold of Hope*, 'Was God at Work in the Fall of Communism?' (1994)

5 [Of abortion] *It is not possible to speak of the right to choose when a clear moral evil is involved*, when what is at stake is the commandment *Do not kill!*

ibid. 'The Defense of Every Life'

## Gerald W. Johnson (1890–1980)

US AUTHOR

Full name Gerald White Johnson. Called 'the best editorial writer in the South and a highly civilized man' by H.L. MENCKEN, he was an authority on American history and government. His prolific writing career spanned six decades and included *American Heroes and Hero-Worship* (1943) as well as books for young people.

1 Heroes are created by popular demand, sometimes out of the scantiest materials, or none at all.

*American Heroes and Hero-Worship*, ch. 1 (1943)

# James Weldon Johnson (1871–1938)

US AUTHOR AND DIPLOMAT

He was consul in Venezuela and Nicaragua (1906–12) and prominent in the National Association for the Advancement of Colored People (1916–30). His novel *The Autobiography of an Ex-Colored Man* (1912), volumes of his own poetry, such as *God's Trombones* (1927), and his anthologies of black poetry contributed to the Harlem Renaissance of the 1920s.

1 And God stepped out on space,
And He looked around and said,
'I'm lonely –
I'll make me a world.'

'The Creation' st. 1, written and first publ. 1918, repr. in *God's Trombones: Seven Negro Sermons in Verse* (1927)

2 Young man –
Young man –
Your arm's too short to box with God.

'The Prodigal Son', publ. in ibid.

3 It is from the blues that all that may be called American music derives its most distinctive character.

*Black Manhattan*, ch. 11 (1930)

# Lady Bird Johnson (b. 1912)

US FIRST LADY

Full name Claudia Alta Taylor Johnson. Anthony Howard described her as being, 'despite her folksy style, a clever, formidable businesswoman'. She owned and operated KTBC radio and TV station in Austin, Texas, served on numerous boards and was active in the political campaigns of her husband, LYNDON B. JOHNSON. Her memoir *A White House Diary* was published in 1970.

1 It all began so beautifully. After a drizzle in the morning, the sun came out bright and clear. We were driving into Dallas. In the lead car were President and Mrs Kennedy ...

First entry, 22 November 1963, in *A White House Diary* (1970)

2 The first lady is, and always has been, an unpaid public servant elected by one person, her husband.

Journal entry 14 March 1968, publ. in ibid.

# Linton Kwesi Johnson (b. 1952)

ANGLO-JAMAICAN POET AND SINGER

During the 1970s he was the voice of dub poetry. Among his collections, written in Jamaican patois, are *Voices of the Living and the Dead* (1974) and *Dread Beat 'n' Blood* (1975, album 1978). He was also involved in the local politics of Brixton.

1 Brothers and sisters rocking,
a dread beat pulsing fire, burning.

'Dread Beat 'n' Blood' (poem, 1975), set to music and released on the album *Dread, Beat 'n' Blood* (1978) by Poet and the Roots

2 Inglan is a bitch
There's no escapin' it.

'Inglan is a Bitch' on the album *Bass Culture* (1980)

# Lyndon B. Johnson (1908–73)

US DEMOCRATIC POLITICIAN AND PRESIDENT

Full name Lyndon Baines Johnson. A Texan Democrat and an earthily persuasive political operator, he became thirty-sixth President (1963–9) following the assassination of President KENNEDY. His greatest achievements were in the field of civil rights, notably the Civil Rights Act (1964) and the Voting Rights Act (1965), and he was called by RALPH ELLISON 'the greatest American president for the poor and for the Negroes', but his escalation of the Vietnam

War lost him his popularity. See also BARRY GOLDWATER 1, POLITICAL SLOGANS 9

1 Son, in politics you've got to learn that overnight chicken shit can turn to chicken salad.

Quoted in *Richard Nixon: The Shaping of his Character*, ch. 25 (1983) by FAWN BRODIE. Johnson, who had previously referred to RICHARD NIXON as 'chicken shit', was replying to a reporter who had questioned him on his embracing Nixon on the latter's return from a vice-presidential tour of South America in May 1958, during which he had been mobbed by an angry crowd in Caracas. WALTER LIPPMANN called the tour 'a diplomatic Pearl Harbor' and the *Boston Globe* said it was 'one of the most ineptly handled episodes in this country's foreign relations'.

2 The world has narrowed to a neighborhood before it has broadened to a brotherhood.

Speech in New York City, 17 December 1963, publ. in *Public Papers of the Presidents of the United States, Lyndon B. Johnson: 1963–64*

3 This administration today, here and now, declares unconditional war on poverty in America.

State of the Union address to Congress, 8 January 1964, publ. in ibid.

4 I don't believe in labels. I want to do the best I can. I want to be progressive without getting both feet off the ground at the same time. I want to be prudent without having my mind closed to anything that is new or different. I have often said that I was proud that I was a free man first and an American second, and a public servant third and a Democrat fourth, in that order, and I guess as a Democrat, if I had to place a label on myself, I would want to be a progressive who is prudent.

TV and radio interview, 15 March 1964, publ. in ibid.

5 The Great Society is a place where every child can find knowledge to enrich his mind and to enlarge his talents ... It is a place where the city of man serves not only the needs of the body and the demands of commerce but the desire for beauty and the hunger for community ... It is a place where men are more concerned with the quality of their goals than the quantity of their goods.

Speech in Ann Arbor, Michigan, 22 May 1964, publ. in ibid. The slogan, 'Great Society', had been current for several years, possibly originating as the title of a book by economist Graham Wallas in 1914. As suggested by Richard N. Goodwin, Secretary General of the International Peace Corps Secretariat and occasional speechwriter, it became closely associated with Johnson's presidency, featuring in his acceptance speech at the Democratic Party National Convention, August 1964 (see Hugh Sidey's *A Very Personal Presidency*, 1968).

6 [Of the Vietnam War] This is not a jungle war, but a struggle for freedom on every front of human activity.

Television broadcast 4 August 1964

7 We are not about to send American boys 9 or 10,000 miles away from home to do what Asian boys ought to be doing for themselves.

Speech at Akron University, Ohio, 21 October 1964, publ. in *Public Papers of the Presidents of the United States, Lyndon B. Johnson: 1963–64*

8 I don't want loyalty. I want *loyalty*. I want him to kiss my ass in Macy's window at high noon and tell me it smells like roses. I want his pecker in my pocket.

Quoted in *The Best and the Brightest*, ch. 20 (1972) by David Halberstam. Referring to a prospective assistant.

9 Better to have him [J. EDGAR HOOVER] inside the tent pissing out, than outside pissing in.

ibid.

10 Jerry Ford is so dumb he can't fart and chew gum at the same time.

Quoted in *A Ford, Not a Lincoln*, ch. 1. by Richard Reeves (1975). Reeves asserts that Johnson's put-down was 'cleaned up' by 'the late President's aides and history'.

## Pamela Hansford Johnson (1912–81)

BRITISH AUTHOR AND CRITIC

She published psychological novels concerning people under stress, such as the *Too Dear for My Possessing* trilogy (1940–48), but also wrote in a lighter vein, as in *The Unspeakable Skipton* (1959). According to ANTHONY BURGESS: 'Some of her books are characterized by a sort of grave levity, others by a sort of light gravity.' She was married to the writer C.P. SNOW.

1 There are few things more disturbing than to find, in somebody we detest, a moral quality which seems to us demonstrably superior to anything we ourselves possess. It augurs not merely an unfairness on the part of creation, but a lack of artistic judgement . . . Sainthood is acceptable only in saints.

*Night and Silence, Who is Here? – An American Comedy*, ch. 23 (1963)

## Paul Johnson (b. 1928)

BRITISH JOURNALIST

He was Editor of the *New Statesman* in the 1960s but later retreated from his socialist position. His books, which combine an historical with a socially critical approach, include *A History of Christianity* (1976), *Enemies of Society* (1977) and *A History of the Jews* (1987).

1 While the music is performed, the cameras linger savagely over the faces of the audience. What a bottomless chasm of vacuity they reveal! Those who flock round the Beatles, who scream themselves into hysteria, whose vacant faces flicker over the TV screen, are the least fortunate of their generation, the dull, the idle, the failures . . .

'The Menace of Beatlism', publ. in *New Statesman* 28 February 1964

2 The most socially subversive institution of our time is the one-parent family.

Quoted in the *Sunday Correspondent* 24 December 1989

## Philip Johnson (b. 1906)

US ARCHITECT

He coined the term 'International Style' in 1932, and, following the theories of MIES VAN DER ROHE, embraced postmodernism. He was Director of Architecture and Design at the Museum of Modern Art 1932–54, and was responsible for the Seagram Building (with Mies van der Rohe, 1945) and the AT&T building (1978–84), both in New York. He published *Architecture 1949–65* in 1966.

1 The automobile is the greatest catastrophe in the entire history of City architecture.

'The Town and the Automobile, or the Pride of Elm Street' (1955), repr. in *Writings* (1979)

2 Architecture is the art of how to waste space.

*The New York Times* 27 December 1964

3 All architects want to live beyond their deaths.

Quoted in the *Observer* 27 December 1987

## R.W. Johnson (b. 1916)

US JOURNALIST AND NEWSPAPER EXECUTIVE

1 Any solution to a problem changes the problem.

*Washingtonian* November 1979

## Al Jolson (1886–1950)

RUSSIAN-BORN US SINGER AND ENTERTAINER

Original name Asa Yoelson. Calling himself 'The World's Greatest Entertainer', he wooed vaudeville audiences of the 1920s as a blackface comedian and singer of sentimental songs, such as 'Mammy', 'Sonny Boy' and 'Swanee'. In 1927 he starred in the first talking picture, *The Jazz Singer*. GEORGE BURNS stated that it was easy to make him happy: 'You just had to cheer him for breakfast,

applaud wildly for lunch, and give him a standing ovation for dinner.'

1 California here I come.

'California Here I Come' (song, co-written by Jolson, BUDDY DE SYLVA and Joseph Mayer) from the stage musical *Bombo* (1921)

2 Wait a minute, wait a minute, you ain't heard nothing yet. Wait a minute I tell you. You ain't heard nothing yet. Do you want to hear 'Toot, Toot, Tootsie'?

Jakie Rabinowitz (Al Jolson), in *The Jazz Singer* (film, 1927, screenplay by Alfred A. Cohen, directed by Louis Silver). These were Al Jolson's first spoken words in the first talking picture. The screenplay was based on *The Day of Atonement*, a story written and adapted for the stage by Samson Raphaelson and supposedly based on Al Jolson's own life. 'You ain't heard nothing yet' had been Jolson's slogan since 1906 and was the title of a song recorded by him in 1919, written by BUDDY DE SYLVA and GUS KAHN (Kahn also co-wrote 'Toot, Toot, Tootsie').

## Beverly Jones (b. 1927)

US FEMINIST WRITER

1 Romance, like the rabbit at the dog track, is the elusive, fake, and never attained reward which, for the benefit and amusement of our masters, keeps us running and thinking in safe circles.

*The Florida Paper on Women's Liberation*, 'The Dynamics of Marriage and Motherhood' (1970)

## Chuck Jones (b. 1912)

US ANIMATOR AND CARTOON DIRECTOR

Original name Charles Jones. Particularly adept at slapstick routines, he worked for Warner Bros from 1933, creating the characters Road Runner and Wile E. Coyote and directing Bugs Bunny and Daffy Duck cartoons.

1 Beep! Beep!

The Road Runner, in *Looney Tunes/Merrie Melodies* (Warner Brothers cartoon, 1949–66). This only line of dialogue between the Road Runner at full sprint and Wile E. Coyote was voiced by Mel Blanc. The characters were created by Chuck Jones (who directed most of the episodes) and Michael Maltese and first introduced in a Warner Brothers' *Looney Tunes* cartoon called *Fast and Furry-Ous* (1949).

## Quincy Jones (b. 1933)

US MUSICIAN, ARRANGER AND PRODUCER

One of the music industry's most enduringly successful figures, he has worked in jazz, pop and rock and composed scores for more than forty films. He produced three of MICHAEL JACKSON's biggest selling albums (1980–87), and in 1985 he organized and produced the all-star charity recording 'We Are the World' for famine relief in Africa.

1 [On the blues] When you get your ass kicked that hard, it makes you go to the innermost depths of what you are all about as a human being. Now, maybe most people have not been kicked that hard, but it's still in everybody, and this music rings a bell that you can hear throughout the fucking world.

Quoted in *Rolling Stone* 1 July 1976

## Steve Jones (b. 1944)

BRITISH GENETICIST

Called the 'Charles Darwin of the television era', he is Professor of Genetics at London University and a noted popularizer of science. His publications include *The Language of Genes* (1993), *In the Blood* (1996) and *Almost Like a Whale* (1999).

1 Evolution is to the social sciences as statues are to birds: a

convenient platform upon which to deposit badly digested ideas.

*Almost Like a Whale: The Origin of the Species Updated*, 'An Historical Sketch of the Progress of Opinion on the Origin of Species' (1999). Jones had earlier used the aphorism in another context: 'Evolution is to allegory as statues are to birdshit: a convenient platform upon which to deposit badly digested ideas' (quoted in the *Guardian* 31 July 1997).

2 Evolution is, for most of the time, a race to stay in the same place.

ibid. ch. 6

3 When we no longer look at an organic being as a savage looks at a ship, as at something wholly beyond his comprehension; when we regard every production of nature as one which has had a history; when we contemplate every complex structure and instinct as the summing up of many contrivances, each useful to the possessor, nearly in the same way as when we look at any great mechanical invention as the summing up of the labour, the experience, the reason, and even the blunders of numerous workmen; when we thus view each organic being, how far more interesting, I speak from experience, will the study of natural history become!

ibid. ch. 14

4 Gravity is the universal glue that makes the cosmos stick together.

Quoted in the *Daily Telegraph* 6 January 1999

# Erica Jong (b. 1942)
US AUTHOR AND POET

Her first volume of poetry, *Fruits and Vegetables* (1971), won her a reputation as a feminist writer, although she is best known for her first novel *Fear of Flying* (1973) and its sequel *How to Save Your Own Life* (1977), which wittily chronicled the sexual adventures of Isadora Wing.

1 Perhaps all artists were, in a sense, housewives: tenders of the earth household.

'The Artist as Housewife: the Housewife as Artist', publ. in *The First Ms. Reader* (ed. Francine Klagsbrun, 1972)

2 Solitude is un-American ... There is simply no dignified way for a woman to live alone. Oh, she can get along financially perhaps (though not nearly as well as a man), but emotionally she is never left in peace. Her friends, her family, her fellow workers never let her forget that her husbandlessness, her childlessness – her *selfishness*, in short – is a reproach to the American way of life.

The narrator (Isadora Wing), in *Fear of Flying*, ch. 1 (1973)

3 The zipless fuck is absolutely pure. It is free of ulterior motives. There is no power game. The man is not 'taking' and the woman is not 'giving'. No one is attempting to cuckold a husband or humiliate a wife. No one is trying to prove anything or get anything out of anyone. The zipless fuck is the purest thing there is. And it is rarer than the unicorn. And I have never had one.

ibid. Jong explained, 'Zipless ... because the incident has all the swift compression of a dream and is seemingly free of all remorse and guilt.'

4 Men have always detested women's gossip because they suspect the truth: their measurements are being taken and compared ... Men can mock it, but they can't prevent it. Gossip is the opiate of the oppressed.

ibid. ch. 6

5 There is nothing fiercer than a failed artist. The energy remains, but, having no outlet, it implodes in a great black fart of rage which smokes up all the inner windows of the soul. Horrible as successful artists often are, there is nothing crueler or more vain than a failed artist.

ibid. ch. 9

6 Men and women, women and men. It will never work.

ibid. ch. 16

7 Back in the days when men were hunters and chestbeaters and women spent their whole lives worrying about pregnancy or dying in childbirth, they often had to be taken against their will. Men complained that women were cold, unresponsive, frigid ... They wanted their women wanton. They wanted their women wild. Now women were finally learning to be wanton and wild – and what happened? The men wilted.

ibid.

8 Each month
the blood sheets down
like good red rain.

'Gardener', publ. in *Half Lives* (1973)

9 Jealousy is all the fun you *think* they had ...

*How To Save Your Own Life*, epigraph to 'Bennett tells all in Woodstock ...' (1977)

10 Advice is what we ask for when we already know the answer but wish we didn't.

ibid. epigraph to 'A day in the life ...'

11 In a bad marriage, friends are the invisible glue. If we have enough friends, we may go on for years, intending to leave, talking about leaving – instead of actually getting up and leaving.

ibid. 'A day in the life ...'

12 Isn't that the problem? That women have been swindled for centuries into substituting adornment for love, fashion (as it were) for passion? ... All the cosmetics names seemed obscenely obvious to me in their promises of sexual bliss. They were all firming or uplifting or invigorating. They made you *tingle*. Or *glow*. Or feel *young*. They were prepared with hormones or placentas or royal jelly. All the juice and joy missing in the lives of these women were to be supplied by the contents of jars and bottles. No wonder they would spend twenty dollars for an ounce of face makeup or thirty for a half-ounce of hormone cream. What price bliss? What price sexual ecstasy?

ibid.

13 There is a rhythm to the ending of a marriage just like the rhythm of a courtship – only backward. You try to start again but get into blaming over and over. Finally you are both worn out, exhausted, hopeless. Then lawyers are called in to pick clean the corpses. The death has occurred much earlier.

ibid. 'There is a rhythm to the ending ...'

14 Where is Hollywood located? Chiefly between the ears. In that part of the American brain lately vacated by God.

ibid. epigraph to 'Hello to Hollywood ...'

15 Every country gets the circus it deserves. Spain gets bullfights. Italy gets the Catholic Church. America gets Hollywood.

ibid. epigraph to 'Take the Red-Eye ...'

16 Oh Doris Lessing, my dear – your Anna is *wrong* about orgasms. They are no proof of love – any more than that other Anna's fall under the wheels of that Russian train was a proof of love. It's all female shenanigans, cultural *mishegoss*, conditioning, brainwashing, male mythologizing. What does a woman want? She wants what she has been told she ought to want. Anna Wulf wants orgasm, Anna Karenina, death. Orgasm is no proof of anything. Orgasm is proof of orgasm. Someday every woman will have orgasms – like every family has color TV – and we can all get on with the real business of life.

ibid. 'The street where I lived ...'

17 Do you want me to tell you something really subversive? Love *is* everything it's cracked up to be. That's why people

are so cynical about it . . . It really *is* worth fighting for, being brave for, risking everything for. And the trouble is, if you don't risk anything, you risk even *more*.

Hans, in ibid. 'Intuition, extuition . . .'

## Janis Joplin (1943–70)
US ROCK SINGER

An impassioned blues-style singer – 'I'd rather not sing than sing quiet' – she performed with the band Big Brother and the Holding Company before going solo in 1968. Her career, however, was cut short by her addiction to alcohol and drugs, and her biggest hit, 'Me and Bobby McGee', was released posthumously on the album *Pearl* in 1971. 'On stage I make love to 25,000 people,' she declared, 'then I go home alone.'

1 Fourteen heart attacks and he [former President Eisenhower] had to die in my week. In MY week.

Quoted in *New Musical Express* 12 April 1969. EISENHOWER's death prevented Joplin's photograph appearing on the cover of *Newsweek*.

2 Oh, Lord, won't you buy me a Mercedes Benz?
My friends all drive Porsches,
I must make amends.

'Mercedes Benz' (song) on the album *Pearl* (1971)

3 It's not what isn't, it's what you wish *was* that makes unhappiness . . . I think I think too much. That's why I drink.

Quoted in *Rock 'N' Roll Babylon*, ch. 3 by Gary Herman (1982)

## June Jordan (b. 1936)
US POET AND CIVIL RIGHTS ACTIVIST

She campaigned for the inclusion of black studies on university curricula and, together with architect R. BUCKMINSTER FULLER, created a plan for the architectural redesign of Harlem. Her poetry collections, such as *Things That I Do in the Dark* (1977) and *Passion* (1980), and her essays *Moving Towards Home* (1989) address the issues of feminism, racism and minority struggles.

1 There is a man who exists as one of the most popular *objects* of leadership, legislation, and quasi-literature in the history of all men . . . This man, that object of attention, attack, and vast activity, cannot make himself be heard, let alone to be understood. *He has never been listened to* . . . That man is Black and alive in white America where the media of communication do not allow the delivery of his own voice, his own desires, his own rage.

'On Listening: A Good Way to Hear', publ. in the *Nation* 1967, repr. in *Moving Towards Home: Political Essays* (1989)

2 Body and soul, Black America reveals the extreme questions of contemporary life, questions of freedom and identity: *How can I be who I am?*

'Black Studies: Bringing Back The Person', first publ. in *The Evergreen Review* October 1969, repr. in ibid.

3 As a poet and writer, I deeply love and I deeply hate words. I love the infinite evidence and change and requirements and possibilities of language; every human use of words that is joyful, or honest or new, because experience is new . . . But as a Black poet and writer, I hate words that cancel my name and my history and the freedom of my future: I hate the words that condemn and refuse the language of my people in America.

'White English/Black English: The Politics of Translation', first publ. 1972, repr. in ibid.

4 Our children will not survive our habits of thinking, our failures of the spirit, our wreck of the universe into which we bring new life as blithely as we do. Mostly, our children will resemble our own misery and spite and anger, because we give them no choice about it. In the name of mother-

hood and fatherhood and education and good manners, we threaten and suffocate and bind and ensnare and bribe and trick children into wholesale emulation of our ways.

'Old Stories: New Lives', keynote address to Child Welfare League of America, 1978, publ. in ibid.

5 We are the wrong people of
the wrong skin on the wrong continent and what
in the hell is everybody being reasonable about

'Poem about My Rights', publ. in *Passion* (1980)

6 In America, you can segregate the people, but the problems will travel. From slavery to equal rights, from state suppression of dissent to crime, drugs and unemployment, I can't think of a supposedly Black issue that hasn't wasted the original Black target group and then spread like measles to outlying white experience.

'Problems of Language in a Democratic State', first publ. 1982, repr. in *Moving Towards Home: Political Essays* (1989)

7 [Of the US presidential elections] 'Mos anytime you see whitemen spose to fight each other an' you not white, well you know you got trouble, because they blah-blah loud about Democrat or Republican an' they huffin' an' puff about democracy someplace else but relentless, see, the deal come down evil on somebody don' have no shirt an' tie, somebody don' live in no whiteman house no whiteman country.

'White Tuesday', written November 1984, publ. in ibid.

## Michael Joseph (1897–1958)
BRITISH PUBLISHER

He founded Michael Joseph Ltd in 1935, publishing C.S. Forester and H.E. BATES, among others. He wrote on the art of writing and on cats, such as *Cat's Company* (1930).

1 Authors are easy enough to get on with – if you are fond of children.

Quoted in the *Observer* 29 May 1949

## Marcel Jouhandeau (1888–1979)
FRENCH AUTHOR

Almost entirely autobiographical, his novels usually portray inhabitants of Chaminadour, a fictionalized version of his native town, and include *La Jeunesse de Théophile* (1921), *Le Parricide imaginaire* (1930) and *Marcel et Élise* (1953).

1 To really know someone is to have loved and hated him in turn.

*Défense de l'enfer*, 'Erotologie' (1935)

## James Joyce (1882–1941)
IRISH AUTHOR

A key figure in twentieth-century literature, he revolutionized the novel with his use of experimental language and 'stream of consciousness' technique. His major works, mostly written in self-imposed exile from Ireland, are *Dubliners* (1914), *A Portrait of the Artist as a Young Man* (1916), *Ulysses* (1922, but banned in Britain and the USA until 1936) and *Finnegans Wake* (1939). He shocked many of his contemporaries (see, for example, E.M. FORSTER 11, D.H. LAWRENCE 18, VIRGINIA WOOLF 8), but for SAMUEL BECKETT 'his writing is not about something. It is the thing itself.'

1 Love (understood as the desire of good for another) is in fact so unnatural a phenomenon that it can scarcely repeat itself, the soul being unable to become virgin again and not having energy enough to cast itself out again into the ocean of another's soul.

Notes to the play *Exiles* (written 1914–15, publ. 1952)

2 What did that mean, to kiss? You put your face up like that to say goodnight and then his mother put her face down. That was to kiss. His mother put her lips on his cheek; her lips were soft and they wetted his cheek; and they made a tiny little noise: kiss. Why did people do that with their two faces?

Stephen Dedalus, in *A Portrait of the Artist as a Young Man*, ch. 1 (1916)

3 When the soul of a man is born in this country there are nets flung at it to hold it back from flight. You talk to me of nationality, language, religion. I shall try to fly by those nets.

Stephen Dedalus, in ibid. ch. 5. Speaking to the young patriot Davin.

4 Do you know what Ireland is? Ireland is the old sow that eats her farrow.

ibid.

5 Pity is the feeling which arrests the mind in the presence of whatsoever is grave and constant in human sufferings and unites it with the human sufferer. Terror is the feeling which arrests the mind in the presence of whatsoever is grave and constant in human sufferings and unites it with the secret cause.

ibid.

6 To speak of these things and to try to understand their nature and, having understood it, to try slowly and humbly and constantly to express, to press out again, from the gross earth or what it brings forth, from sound and shape and colour which are the prison gates of our soul, an image of the beauty we have come to understand – that is art.

ibid.

7 Art is the human disposition of sensible or intelligible matter for an aesthetic end.

ibid. The definition appeared earlier in Joyce's 'Paris Notebook' dated 28 March 1903.

8 The artist, like the God of the creation, remains within or behind or beyond or above his handiwork, invisible, refined out of existence, indifferent, paring his fingernails.

ibid.

9 Whatever else is unsure in this stinking dunghill of a world a mother's love is not.

Cranly, in ibid.

10 I will tell you what I will do and what I will not do. I will not serve that in which I no longer believe, whether it call itself my home, my fatherland, or my church: and I will try to express myself in some mode of life or art as freely as I can and as wholly as I can, using for my defence the only arms I allow myself to use – silence, exile and cunning.

Stephen Dedalus, in ibid.

11 Welcome, O life! I go to encounter for the millionth time the reality of experience and to forge in the smithy of my soul the uncreated conscience of my race . . . Old father, old artificer, stand me now and ever in good stead.

ibid. Said by Stephen departing from Ireland, in the closing lines of the book. 'Old artificer' is a reference to Daedalus, the mythical craftsman, whose flight from Crete ended in the drowning of his son. Joyce's own experience on fleeing Ireland was largely of debt and penury.

12 While you have a thing it can be taken from you . . . but when you give it, you have given it. No robber can take it from you. It is yours then for ever when you have given it. It will be yours always. That is to give.

Richard Rowan, in *Exiles*, act 1 (1918)

13 You forget that the kingdom of heaven suffers violence: and the kingdom of heaven is like a woman.

Robert Hand, in ibid. act 2

14 Writing in English is the most ingenious torture ever devised for sins committed in previous lives. The English reading public explains the reason why.

Letter, 5 September 1918, publ. in *Selected Letters of James Joyce* (ed. Richard Ellmann, 1975)

15 The snotgreen sea. The scrotumtightening sea.

Buck Mulligan, in *Ulysses*, ch. 1 ('Telemachus') (1922)

16 It is a symbol of Irish art. The cracked lookingglass of a servant.

Stephen Dedalus, in ibid. Referring to Buck Mulligan's purloined mirror.

17 I fear those big words which make us so unhappy.

Stephen Dedalus, in ibid. ch. 2 ('Nestor')

18 History is a nightmare from which I am trying to awake.

ibid.

19 A man of genius makes no mistakes. His errors are volitional and are the portals of discovery.

Stephen Dedalus, in ibid. ch. 9 ('Scylla and Charybdis')

20 A nation is the same people living in the same place.

Leopold Bloom, in ibid. ch. 12 ('Cyclops')

21 Greater love than this, he said, no man hath that a man lay down his wife for his friend. Go thou and do likewise. Thus, or words to that effect, said Zarathustra, sometime regius professor of French letters to the university of Oxtail nor breathed there ever that man to whom mankind was more beholden.

Stephen Dedalus, in ibid. ch. 14 ('Oxen of the Sun'). 'Greater love . . .' parodies John 15:13. Joyce's passage refers to 'those delicate poets' Francis Beaumont and John Fletcher, who 'had but the one doxy between them'.

22 British Beatitudes! . . . Beer, beef, business, bibles, bull-dogs, battleships, buggery and bishops.

ibid.

23 frseeeeeeeefronnnng train somewhere whistling the strength those engines have in them like big giants and the water rolling all over and out of them all sides like the end of Loves old sweeeetsonnnng the poor men that have to be out all the night from their wives and families in those roasting engines

Molly Bloom's soliloquy, in ibid. ch. 18 ('Penelope')

24 He kissed me under the Moorish wall and I thought well as well him as another and then I asked him with my eyes to ask again yes and then he asked me would I yes to say yes my mountain flower and first I put my arms around him yes and drew him down to me so he could feel my breasts all perfume yes and his heart was going like mad and yes I said yes I will Yes.

ibid. Closing words of book.

25 riverrun, past Eve and Adam's, from swerve of shore to bend of bay, brings us by a commodious vicus of recirculation back to Howth Castle and Environs.

*Finnegans Wake*, pt 1, ch. 1 (1939). Opening words of book. The book's closing words ('A way a lone a last a loved a long the') form the first part of this sentence which provided a title for a volume of essays by RICHARD ELLMANN, Joyce's biographer: *a long the riverrun* (1988).

26 That ideal reader suffering from an ideal insomnia.

ibid. ch. 5

27 You have become of twosome twiminds forenenst gods, hidden and discovered, nay, condemned fool, anarch, egoarch, hiresiarch, you have reared your disunited kingdom on the vacuum of your own most intensely doubtful soul.

ibid. ch. 7. Part of Shaun's diatribe against his wastrel brother Shem, whose loose counterpart in real life was Stanislaus Joyce (James's younger brother) berating James.

28 O, you were excruciated, in honour bound to the cross of your own cruelfiction!

ibid.

29 Oft in the smelly night will they wallow for a clutch of the famished hand, I say, them bearded jezabelles you hired to rob you, while on your sodden straw impolitely you encored (Airish and nawboggaleesh!) those hornmade ivory dreams you reved of the Ruth you called your companionate, a beauty from the bible, of the flushpots of Euston and the hanging garments of Marylebone.

ibid.

30 All moanday, tearsday, wailsday, thumpsday, frightday, shatterday till the fear of the Law.

ibid. pt 2, ch. 2

31 Three quarks for Muster Mark!

ibid. ch. 4. This seabirds' chorus song is the origin of 'quark', the name given to the hypothetical particle postulated by the physicists Murray Gell-Mann and George Zweig in 1963.

32 I should tell you that honestly, on my honour of a Near-wicked, I always think in a wordsworth's of that primed favourite continental poet, Daunty, Gouty and Shop-keeper, A.G., whom the generality admoyers in this that is and that this is to come.

Humphrey Chimpden Earwicker, making an incoherent speech in his defence, in ibid. pt 3, ch. 3

33 [On 'the stream of consciousness'] When I heard the word 'stream' uttered with such a revolting primness, what I think of is urine and not the contemporary novel. And besides, it isn't new, it is far from the *dernier cri*. Shakespeare used it continually, much too much in my opinion, and there's *Tristram Shandy*, not to mention the *Agamemnon* . . .

Quoted in *Voices: A Memoir*, 'At Sylvia's' (1983) by Frederic Prokosch. Joyce was replying to the assertion by the young author and poet Prokosch that Molly Bloom's final monologue in *Ulysses* exemplified this form. 'Molly Bloom was a down-to-earth lady,' Joyce said. 'She would never have indulged in anything so refined as a stream of consciousness.'

## William Joyce (1906–46)
BRITISH FASCIST

'Lord Haw-Haw', as he was nicknamed, was expelled from OSWALD MOSLEY's Fascist Party in 1937 and founded his own British National-ist Socialist League. Having fled to Germany before the onset of the Second World War, he broadcast propaganda against Britain throughout the war and was hanged for treason after his capture in 1945.

1 Germany calling! Germany calling!

Opening words of propaganda broadcasts, from Hamburg during the Second World War, September 1939–April 1945

## Mike Judge (b. 1963)
ECUADOR-BORN US ANIMATOR AND FILM-MAKER

He is best known for the animated TV series *Beavis and Butt-head* (1992–7) and *King of the Hill* (1997). The film *Beavis and Butt-head Do America* appeared in 1996.

1 I like stuff that's cool, I don't like stuff that sucks.

Butt-head, in *Beavis and Butt-head* (cartoon created and voiced by Mike Judge, written by Sam Johnson and Chris Marcil, shown on MTV from September 1992)

## Walid Jumblatt (b. 1949)
LEBANESE POLITICIAN

He has been leader of the Druze and Progressive Socialist Party since 1977 and was Minister of Public Works (1989–92).

1 Here, even the law of the jungle has broken down.

Quoted in the *Sunday Times* 29 December 1985

## Carl Jung (1875–1961)
SWISS PSYCHIATRIST

He was a collaborator with FREUD from 1907 and President of the International Psychoanalytic Association 1911–14, but his work *The Psychology of the Unconscious* (1912) instigated a rift with Freud over the relevance of sexuality in psychological problems. Jung developed his own theories of 'analytical psychology', placing emphasis on the 'collective unconscious' and 'individuation'. *Psychological Types* (1921) introduced the concept of introversion and extroversion.

1 So often among so-called 'primitives' one comes across spiritual personalities who immediately inspire respect, as though they were the fully matured products of an undisturbed fate.

'Marriage as a Psychological Relationship' (1925), repr. in *Collected Works*, vol. 17 (ed. William McGuire, 1954)

2 Nothing is more repulsive than a furtively prurient spirituality; it is just as unsavoury as gross sensuality.

ibid.

3 The wine of youth does not always clear with advancing years; sometimes it grows turbid.

*The Stages of Life* (1930), repr. in ibid. vol. 8 (1960)

4 The psychiatrist knows only too well how each of us becomes the helpless but not pitiable victim of his own sentiments. Sentimentality is the superstructure erected upon brutality.

*Ulysses: A Monologue* (1932), repr. in ibid. vol. 15 (1966)

5 If there is anything that we wish to change in the child, we should first examine it and see whether it is not something that could better be changed in ourselves.

*The Development of Personality* (1934), repr. in ibid. vol. 17 (1954)

6 Personality is the supreme realization of the innate idiosyncrasy of a living being. It is an act of high courage flung in the face of life, the absolute affirmation of all that constitutes the individual, the most successful adaptation to the universal conditions of existence coupled with the greatest possible freedom for self-determination.

ibid.

7 Instead of being at the mercy of wild beasts, earthquakes, landslides, and inundations, modern man is battered by the elemental forces of his own psyche. This is the World Power that vastly exceeds all other powers on earth. The Age of Enlightenment, which stripped nature and human institutions of gods, overlooked the God of Terror who dwells in the human soul.

ibid.

8 From the middle of life onward, only he remains vitally alive who is ready to *die with life*.

*The Soul and Death* (1934), repr. in ibid. vol. 8 (1960)

9 I cannot love anyone if I hate myself. That is the reason why we feel so extremely uncomfortable in the presence of people who are noted for their special virtuousness, for they radiate an atmosphere of the torture they inflict on themselves. That is not a virtue but a vice.

Basel seminar (1934), multigraphed for private circulation by the Psychology Club, Zurich, repr. in ibid. vol. 18 (1977)

10 Neurosis is always a substitute for legitimate suffering.

*Psychology and Religion* (1938), repr. in ibid. vol. 11 (1958)

11 Our blight is ideologies – they are the long-expected Antichrist!

'Psychological Commentary on "The Tibetan Book of the Great Liberation"' (1939, rev. 1954), repr. in ibid.

12 Yoga in Mayfair or Fifth Avenue, or in any other place which is on the telephone, is a spiritual fake.

ibid.

13 Masses are always breeding grounds of psychic epidemics.

*Concerning Rebirth* (1940), repr. in ibid. vol. 9, pt 1 (1959)

14 An inflated consciousness is always egocentric and conscious of nothing but its own existence. It is incapable of learning from the past, incapable of understanding contemporary events, and incapable of drawing right conclusions about the future. It is hypnotized by itself and therefore cannot be argued with. It inevitably dooms itself to calamities that must strike it dead.

*Psychology and Alchemy*, Epilogue (1944) repr. in ibid. vol. 12 (1968)

15 It is a fact that cannot be denied: the wickedness of others becomes our own wickedness because it kindles something evil in our own hearts.

*After the Catastrophe* (1945), repr. in ibid. vol. 10 (1964)

16 The wise man who is not heeded is counted a fool, and the fool who proclaims the general folly first and loudest passes for a prophet and Führer, and sometimes it is luckily the other way round as well, or else mankind would long since have perished of stupidity.

*Mysterium Coniunctionis* (1955–6), repr. in ibid. vol. 14 (1963)

17 Resistance to the organized mass can be effected only by the man who is as well organized in his individuality as the mass itself.

*The Undiscovered Self*, ch. 4 (1957)

18 Because the European does not know his own unconscious, he does not understand the East and projects into it everything he fears and despises in himself.

Foreword to *Beelden uit het onbewuste* (1957) by R.J. Van Helsdingen, repr. in *The Collected Works*, vol. 18 (ed. William McGuire, 1977)

19 In all chaos there is a cosmos, in all disorder a secret order.

'Archetypes of the Collective Unconscious' (1935, rev. 1954), repr. in ibid. vol. 9, pt 1 (1959)

20 The word 'belief' is a difficult thing for me. I don't *believe*. I must have a reason for a certain hypothesis. Either I *know* a thing, and then I know it – I don't need to believe it.

Interview in 1959, publ. in *Face to Face* (1964) by Hugh Burnett. Jung's statement helps to explain the answer he gave when asked if he believed in God: 'I do not believe ... I know.' (quoted by LAURENS VAN DER POST in *Jung and the Story of Our Time*, 1976).

21 The images of the unconscious place a great responsibility upon a man. Failure to understand them, or a shirking of ethical responsibility, deprives him of his wholeness and imposes a painful fragmentariness on his life.

*Memories, Dreams, Reflections*, ch. 6 (1962)

22 A man who has not passed through the inferno of his passions has never overcome them.

ibid. ch. 9, sect. 4

23 As far as we can discern, the sole purpose of human existence is to kindle a light in the darkness of mere being.

ibid. ch. 11

24 Every form of addiction is bad, no matter whether the narcotic be alcohol or morphine or idealism.

ibid. ch. 12

25 Life is – or has – meaning and meaninglessness. I cherish the anxious hope that meaning will preponderate and win the battle.

ibid. 'Retrospect'

26 I am incapable of determining ultimate worth or worthlessness; I have no judgement about myself and my life. There is nothing I am quite sure about. I have no definite convictions – not about anything really. I only know that I was born and exist, and it seems to me that I have been carried along.

ibid.

## Theodore Kaczynski (b. 1942)
US TERRORIST

Known as 'Unabomber' and called the 'Luddite King' by the media, he killed three people and injured twenty-nine others in his campaign of random bombings inspired by his hatred of technology. In 1995 he persuaded the national press to publish his lengthy manifesto *The Industrial Society and its Future*, written from his hiding-place near Lincoln, Montana, where he had lived as a hermit since leaving his position as maths professor at the University of California in 1979. Following a tip-off by his brother, he was tracked down in 1996 and sentenced to life imprisonment.

1 The Industrial Revolution and its consequences have been a disaster for the human race. They have greatly increased the life-expectancy of those of us who live in 'advanced' countries, but they have destabilized society, have made life unfulfilling, have subjected human beings to indignities, have led to widespread psychological suffering (in the Third World to physical suffering as well) and have inflicted severe damage on the natural world. The continued development of technology will worsen the situation.

*The Industrial Society and Its Future*, 'Introduction, 1', publ. in the *Washington Post* 19 September 1995

2 The positive ideal that we propose is Nature. That is, WILD nature; those aspects of the functioning of the Earth and its living things that are independent of human management and free of human interference and control. And with wild nature we include human nature.

ibid. 'Strategy', sect. 183

3 The only points on which we absolutely insist are that the single overriding goal must be the elimination of modern technology, and that no other goal can be allowed to compete with this one.

ibid. sect. 206

## Pauline Kael (b. 1919)
US FILM CRITIC

'The sanest, saltiest, most resourceful and least attitudinizing movie critic in the USA,' according to writer and producer Richard Schickel, she reviewed for the *New Yorker* 1968–91. Her articles have appeared in *Kiss Kiss Bang Bang* (1968) and *Nights at the Movies* (1982).

1 The United States has now achieved what critics of socialism have always posited as the end result of a socialist state: a prosperous, empty, uninspiring uniformity. (If we do not have exactly what Marx meant by a classless society, we do have something so close to it that the term is certainly no longer an alluring goal.)

'The Glamour of Delinquency', first publ. 1955, repr. in *I Lost it at the Movies* (1965)

2 The first prerogative of an artist in any medium is to make a fool of himself.

'Is There a Cure for Film Criticism?' first publ. 1962, repr. in ibid.

3 Regrettably, one of the surest signs of the Philistine is his reverence for the superior tastes of those who put him down.

'Zeitgeist and Poltergeist', first publ. 1964, repr. in ibid.

4 It seems likely that many of the young who don't wait for others to call them artists, but simply announce that they are, don't have the patience to make art.

'Movie Brutalists', first publ. 1966, repr. in *Kiss Kiss Bang Bang* (1968)

5 The words 'Kiss Kiss Bang Bang', which I saw on an Italian movie poster, are perhaps the briefest statement imaginable of the basic appeal of movies. This appeal is what attracts us, and ultimately what makes us despair

when we begin to understand how seldom movies are more than this.

*Kiss Kiss Bang Bang*, 'A Note on the Title' (1968)

6 Watching old movies is like spending an evening with those people next door. They bore us, and we wouldn't go out of our way to see them; we drop in on them because they're so close. If it took some effort to see old movies, we might try to find out which were the good ones, and if people saw only the good ones maybe they would still respect old movies. As it is, people sit and watch movies that audiences walked out on thirty years ago. Like Lot's wife, we are tempted to take another look, attracted not by evil but by something that seems much more shameful – our own innocence.

ibid. 'Movies on Television'

7 Irresponsibility is part of the pleasure of all art, it is the part the schools cannot recognize.

'Trash, Art, and the Movies', first publ. 1968, repr. in *Going Steady* (1970)

8 In the arts, the critic is the only independent source of information. The rest is advertising.

Quoted in *Newsweek* 24 December 1973

9 Robert Redford . . . has turned almost alarmingly blond – he's gone past platinum, he must be into plutonium; his hair is coordinated with his teeth.

*Reeling*, pt 2, 'The Sting' (1976)

## Franz Kafka (1883–1924)

CZECH AUTHOR

His vision of the world, the original 'Kafkaesque' nightmare, is that of man overwhelmed by incomprehensible labyrinths of totalitarian bureaucracy. His short stories and essays such as *The Metamorphosis* (1915) were published during his lifetime, but his novels, *The Trial* (1925), *The Castle* (1926) and *America* (1927), appeared posthumously, despite his orders that they should be destroyed. All were written in German. He died of tuberculosis shortly after moving to Berlin.

1 As Gregor Samsa awoke one morning from uneasy dreams he found himself transformed in his bed into a gigantic insect.

*The Metamorphosis*, ch. 1 (1915, transl. 1933). Opening sentence.

2 All human errors are impatience, a premature breaking off of methodical procedure, an apparent fencing-in of what is apparently at issue.

*The Collected Aphorisms*, no. 2 (October 1917–February 1918), publ. in *Shorter Works*, vol. 1 (ed. and transl. Malcolm Pasley, 1973)

3 A first sign of the beginning of understanding is the wish to die.

ibid. no. 13

4 In theory there is a possibility of perfect happiness: To believe in the indestructible element within one, and not to strive towards it.

ibid. no. 68

5 A belief is like a guillotine, just as heavy, just as light.

ibid. no. 87

6 It is not necessary that you leave the house. Remain at your table and listen. Do not even listen, only wait. Do not even wait, be wholly still and alone. The world will present itself to you for its unmasking, it can do no other, in ecstasy it will writhe at your feet.

ibid. no. 109

7 My guiding principle is this: Guilt is never to be doubted.

Officer, in *In the Penal Settlement* (1920, transl. 1933), repr. in *Metamorphosis and Other Stories* (1961)

8 Life's splendour forever lies in wait about each one of us in all its fullness, but veiled from view, deep down, invis-

ible, far off. It *is* there, though, not hostile, not reluctant, not deaf. If you summon it by the right word, by its right name, it will come.

Journal entry, 18 October 1921, publ. in *The Diaries of Franz Kafka: 1910–23* (ed. Max Brod, 1948 and 1949)

9 Anyone who cannot come to terms with his life while he is alive needs one hand to ward off a little his despair over his fate . . . but with his other hand he can note down what he sees among the ruins.

Journal entry, 19 October 1921, publ. in ibid.

10 If there is a transmigration of souls then I am not yet on the bottom rung. My life is a hesitation before birth.

Journal entry, 24 January 1922, publ. in ibid.

11 Someone must have been telling lies about Joseph K., for without having done anything wrong he was arrested one fine morning.

*The Trial*, ch. 1 (1925, transl. 1935). Opening words.

12 You may object that it is not a trial at all; you are quite right, for it is only a trial if I recognize it as such.

Joseph K., in ibid. ch. 2

13 It's often safer to be in chains than to be free.

The Advocate, in ibid. ch. 8. An allusion to Rousseau's famous dictum, 'Man is born free, and everywhere he is in chains' (from *The Social Contract*, 1762).

14 Human nature, essentially changeable, unstable as the dust, can endure no restraint; if it binds itself it soon begins to tear madly at its bonds, until it rends everything asunder, the wall, the bonds and its very self.

*The Great Wall of China* (1931, transl. 1949), repr. in *Metamorphosis and Other Stories* (1961)

15 Try with all your might to comprehend the decrees of the high command, but only up to a certain point; then avoid further meditation.

ibid. A 'very wise maxim' regarding the rationale behind the construction of the Great Wall of China.

## Gus Kahn (1886–1941)

US SONGWRITER

A Tin Pan Alley writer, he wrote for films and Broadway shows, most successfully in collaboration with Walter Donaldson, and provided AL JOLSON with a number of hit songs. Other compositions include 'Yes, Sir, That's My Baby' (1925) and 'My Baby Just Cares for Me' (1930).

1 All God's chillun got rhythm.

'All God's Chillun Got Rhythm' (song, with music by Bronislaw Kaper and Walter Jurmann) in the Marx brothers' film, *A Day at the Races* (1937). The number was sung by Ivie Andersen in the film, and subsequently recorded by Benny Bergan and his Orchestra, Judy Garland and June Christy.

## Kaixi Wuer

CHINESE STUDENT LEADER

Prominent during the student demonstrations in Tiananmen Square (1989), he headed the Autonomous Student Association and was famous for a televised confrontation with Premier Li Peng. He escaped to France after the demonstrations were crushed.

1 A black sun has appeared in the sky of my motherland.

Quoted in the *Independent* 29 June 1989. On the massacre in Tiananmen Square, Beijing, 3 June.

## Ryszard Kapuściński (b. 1932)

POLISH JOURNALIST

His work, which focuses on Poland and the revolutions and civil wars of the Third World, includes *The Emperor* (1978), a portrait of Haile Selassie, and writings on Africa and Kyrghistan.

1 When is a crisis reached? When questions arise that can't be answered.

'A Warsaw Diary', publ. in *Granta* no. 15 (1985)

2 Our salvation is in striving to achieve what we know we'll never achieve.

ibid.

3 We follow the mystics. They know where they are going. They, too, go astray, but when they go astray they do so in a way that is mystical, dark, and mysterious.

ibid.

4 Do not be misled by the fact that you are at liberty and relatively free; that for the moment you are not under lock and key: you have simply been granted a reprieve.

ibid.

5 In Poland a man must be one thing: white or black, here or there, with us or against us – clearly, openly, without hesitations . . . We lack the liberal, democratic tradition rich in all its gradations. We have instead the tradition of struggle: the extreme situation, the final gesture.

ibid.

6 First you destroy those who create values. Then you destroy those who know what the values are, and who also know that those destroyed before were in fact the creators of values. But real barbarism begins when no one can any longer judge or know that what he does is barbaric.

ibid.

7 [On journalists] Our job is like a baker's work – his rolls are tasty as long as they're fresh; after two days they're stale; after a week, they're covered with mould and fit only to be thrown out.

*The Soccer War*, 'The Plan of the Never-Written Book', sect. 33 (1990)

8 Although a system may cease to exist in the legal sense or as a structure of power, its values (or anti-values), its philosophy, its teachings remain in us. They rule our thinking, our conduct, our attitude to others. The situation is a demonic paradox: we have toppled the system but we still carry its genes.

*Independent on Sunday* 1 September 1991

9 The so-called new Russian man is characterized mainly by his complete exhaustion. You may find yourself wondering if he has the strength to enjoy his new-found freedom. He is like a long-distance runner who, on reaching the finishing line, is incapable even of raising his hands in a gesture of victory.

ibid. 27 October 1991

## Yousuf Karsh (b. 1908)

ARMENIAN-BORN CANADIAN PHOTOGRAPHER

Famous for his studies of world personalities, he first caught attention for his portrait of WINSTON CHURCHILL (1941), reputedly the most reproduced photograph of all time. ROY STRONG said of his subjects that 'Karsh supplies the halo'.

1 If there is a single quality that is shared by all great men, it is vanity. But I mean by 'vanity' only that they appreciate their own worth. Without this kind of vanity they would not be great. And with vanity alone, of course, a man is nothing.

*Cosmopolitan* December 1955

## Gary Kasparov (b. 1963)

AZERBAIJANI CHESS PLAYER

Born Harry Weinstein. At twenty-two he was the youngest person to win a world chess championship (1985). In 1993, he led the breakaway Professional Chess Association in forming a rival cham-

pionship, which he won, and in 1996 he outwitted the most advanced chess-playing computer, Deep Blue, although he lost to it in the following year.

1 When your house is on fire, you can't be bothered with the neighbours. Or, as we say in chess, if your king is under attack you don't worry about losing a pawn on the queen's side.

Interview in the *Observer* 3 December 1989. Referring to Mikhail Gorbachev's attitude to changes in Eastern Europe.

## George S. Kaufman (1889–1961)

US PLAYWRIGHT AND DIRECTOR

Full name George Simon Kaufman. He was a theatrical lion of New York in the 1920s and 1930s and author of many Broadway hits, which he often directed. Many of his greatest successes were collaborations, for example with EDNA FERBER in *Dinner at Eight* (1932, filmed 1933), Morrie Ryskind in *Strike Up the Band* (1930, Pulitzer Prize 1931) and Moss Hart in *You Can't Take It with You* (1936, filmed 1938, Pulitzer Prize).

1 Satire is what closes Saturday night.

Quoted in *George S. Kaufman and his Friends*, ch. 6 (1974) by Scott Meredith

## Gerald Kaufman (b. 1930)

BRITISH POLITICIAN

Elected Labour MP for Manchester in 1970, he was political press adviser to HAROLD WILSON before becoming Under-Secretary of State in the Department of Industry (1975–9) and then Shadow Foreign Secretary (1987–92). He has also worked for the *Daily Mirror*, the *New Statesman* and *The Times* and as film critic for the *Listener*.

1 The longest suicide note in history

Quoted in *The Time of My Life*, ch. 23 (1989) by DENIS HEALEY. Referring to the Labour Party's manifesto for the 1983 general election, 'New Hope For Britain'. 'The scale of our defeat was devastating,' Healey wrote of the results of the subsequent election.

## Kenneth Kaunda (b. 1924)

ZAMBIAN POLITICIAN AND PRESIDENT

Imprisoned (1958–60) for his involvement in the Zambian African National Congress, he later led Zambia to independence, becoming its first President (1964–91). He rallied other southern African nations in opposition to the white minority governments of South Africa and Rhodesia, against which he imposed sanctions. He survived several coups in the 1980s, but lost the 1991 election to Frederick Chiluba.

1 When [the Englishman] wants a new market for his adulterated Manchester goods, he sends a missionary to teach the Natives the Gospel of Peace. The Natives kill the missionary, he flies to arms in defence of Christianity, fights for it, conquers for it, and takes the market as a reward from heaven.

Letter to missionaries, March 1952, publ. in *Zambia Shall Be Free*, ch. 16 (1962)

2 The moment you have protected an individual you have protected society.

Quoted in the *Observer* 6 May 1962

3 Some people draw a comforting distinction between 'force' and 'violence' . . . I refuse to cloud the issue by such word-play . . . The power which establishes a state is violence; the power which maintains it is violence; the power which eventually overthrows it is violence . . . Call an elephant a rabbit only if it gives you comfort to feel that you are about to be trampled to death by a rabbit.

Quoted in *Kaunda on Violence*, pt 1 (1980)

4 The drama [in South Africa] can only be brought to its

climax in one of two ways – through the selective brutality of terrorism or the impartial horrors of war.

Quoted in ibid. pt 2

## Patrick Kavanagh (1904–67)

IRISH POET AND AUTHOR

Initially labelled a 'peasant poet' after the publication of his first collection, *Ploughman and Other Poems* (1936), he achieved wider recognition for the new realism of 'The Great Hunger' (1942), an epic poem of the Irish famine. The later work *Come Dance with Kitty* (1960) addressed everyday issues.

1 Clay is the word and clay is the flesh
  Where the potato-gatherers like mechanized scarecrows move
  Along the side-fall of the hill – Maguire and his men.

  'The Great Hunger' (1942), repr. in *Soul for Sale* (1947)

2 A sweeping statement is the only statement worth listening to. The critic without faith gives balanced opinions, usually about second-rate writers.

  *Collected Pruse*, 'Signposts' (1967)

3 Malice is only another name for mediocrity.

  ibid.

## Nikos Kazantzakis (1883–1957)

GREEK AUTHOR

The most controversial figure of twentieth-century Greek literature, he is best known for *Zorba the Greek* (1946, filmed 1964) and *The Last Temptation of Christ* (1959, filmed 1988). His 'principal anguish', he once said, was 'the incessant, merciless battle between the spirit and the flesh'.

1 Life is trouble. Death, no. To live – do you know what that means? To undo your belt and look for trouble.

  Zorba, in *Zorba the Greek*, ch. 8 (1946)

## Jonathan Keates (b. 1946)

BRITISH AUTHOR AND CRITIC

He has written biographies of Stendhal, Handel and Purcell and also books on Italy, for example *Italian Journeys* (1991).

1 In classical antiquity he [Prince Charles] would have been blinded and castrated, dressed as a woman and kept in a temple, his pronouncements delivered to the people by a special college of priests.

  *Observer* 7 January 1990

## Diane Keaton (b. 1946)

US SCREEN ACTRESS

Originally named Diane Hall. She played opposite WOODY ALLEN, with whom she was romantically involved, in such films as *Annie Hall* (1977) for which she won an Oscar. Other films include *The Godfather* (1972, 1974, 1990) and *Marvin's Room* (1997). The critic John Simon compared her acting style to a 'nervous breakdown in slow motion'.

1 Well, la-de-da!

  Annie, in *Annie Hall*, (film, 1977, screenplay by Woody Allen and Marshall Brickman, directed by Woody Allen)

## Barrie Keeffe (b. 1945)

BRITISH PLAYWRIGHT

A prolific writer for the theatre, film, TV and radio, he is known for his punchy and humorous portrayals of the iniquities of the British class system and of London's East End where he grew up. His plays include the trilogy *Gimme Shelter* (1977) and *Wild Justice* (1992).

1 I write plays for people who wouldn't be seen dead in the theatre.

  *Evening Standard* 8 June 1989

## Brian Keenan (b. 1950)

IRISH TEACHER AND HOSTAGE IN LEBANON

Kidnapped while a lecturer at the American University in Beirut, he spent four and a half years (1986–90) held captive by a fundamentalist Shi'ite group, as recounted in *An Evil Cradling* (1992).

1 Hostage is a crucifying aloneness. It is a silent, screaming slide into the bowels of ultimate despair. Hostage is a man hanging by his fingernails over the edge of chaos, feeling his fingers slowly straightening. Hostage is the humiliating stripping away of every sense and fibre of body and mind and spirit that make us what we are. Hostage is a mutant creation filled with fear, self-loathing, guilt and death-wishing. But he is a man, a rare, unique and beautiful creation of which these things are no part.

  News conference in Dublin, 30 August 1990, quoted in the *Independent* 31 August 1990. Following his release from captivity in Lebanon.

## Garrison Keillor (b. 1942)

US BROADCASTER AND AUTHOR

Original name Gary Keillor. He hosted a live, weekly radio show, 'A Prairie Home Companion', (1974–87) and delivered a popular monologue on Lake Wobegon, a fictional Midwestern town based on his memories of semi-rural Minnesota. His wry and laconic tales are published in *Lake Wobegon Days* (1985) and *We Are Still Married* (1989).

1 It has been a quiet week in Lake Wobegon.

  Opening to each broadcast of *A Prairie Home Companion* (radio show, 1974–87)

2 Lake Wobegon . . . where all the women are strong, all the men are good-looking, and all the children are above average.

  *A Prairie Home Companion* (radio show, 1974–87)

3 Nothing you do for children is ever wasted. They seem not to notice us, hovering, averting our eyes, and they seldom offer thanks, but what we do for them is never wasted.

  *Leaving Home*, 'Easter' (1987)

4 A lovely thing about Christmas is that it's compulsory, like a thunderstorm, and we all go through it together.

  ibid. 'Exiles'

5 Humor, a good sense of it, is to Americans what manhood is to Spaniards and we will go to great lengths to prove it. Experiments with laboratory rats have shown that, if one psychologist in the room laughs at something a rat does, all of the other psychologists in the room will laugh equally. Nobody wants to be left holding the joke.

  *We Are Still Married*, Introduction (1989)

6 Even in a time of elephantine vanity and greed, one never has to look far to see the campfires of gentle people.

  ibid. 'The Meaning of Life'

7 A good newspaper is never nearly good enough but a lousy newspaper is a joy forever.

  'That Old "Picayune-Moon" ', publ. in *Harper's Magazine* September 1990

## Penelope Keith (b. 1939)

BRITISH ACTRESS

Most famous for her parts in the TV sitcoms *The Good Life* (1976–8) and *To the Manor Born* (1979–81), she made her stage debut in 1959 and has since played numerous parts on stage, in film and on television.

1 Shyness is just egotism out of its depth.
*Daily Mail* 27 June 1988

## Hans Keller (1919–85)
AUSTRIAN-BORN BRITISH MUSICOLOGIST

Having arrived in Britain in 1938, he worked as a music journalist and wrote criticism, joining the BBC in 1959.

1 I never was an opera fan – about twenty-five musically supreme masterpieces in this curious medium apart.
*Criticism*, Preface (ed. Julian Hogg, 1987)

## Helen Keller (1880–1968)
US AUTHOR AND LECTURER

Profoundly blind and deaf since an infant, she was educated by her lifelong companion Anne Sullivan and gained a degree in 1904. Most of her life was spent campaigning for women's suffrage, pacifism and socialism as well as raising funds for the deaf and blind. Her story is told in *The Story of My Life* (1902) and dramatized in the Pulitzer Prize-winning *The Miracle Worker* (1959, filmed 1962).

1 Science may have found a cure for most evils; but it has found no remedy for the worst of them all – the apathy of human beings.
*My Religion*, pt 1, ch. 6 (1927)

## Petra Kelly (1947–92)
GERMAN POLITICIAN

Originally Petra Lehmann. She co-founded Die Grünen (Green Party) in 1979, which entered the Bundestag in 1983 with twenty-eight seats. After the loss of all its seats in the 1990 election, she became disenchanted with the provincialism of the Party's views, which clashed with her ideal of seeing a world-wide ecological movement. She died in an apparent joint suicide pact with her lover, an ex-general.

1 We, the generation that faces the next century, can add the . . . solemn injunction 'If we don't do the impossible, we shall be faced with the unthinkable'.
Quoted in *Vanity Fair* January 1993

## Penny Kemp (b. 1951) and
## Derek Wall (b. 1965)
BRITISH ECOLOGISTS

Penny Kemp was co-chair of the Green Party 1988–9 and has written for press and periodicals as well as contributing to *The Sanitary Protection Scandal* (1989) and co-writing *A Green Manifesto for the 1990s* (with Derek Wall, 1990). Derek Wall has been active in Green politics since 1979 and was one of three European Speakers for the UK's Green Party. His publications include *Getting There – Towards a Green Society* (1990).

1 How to be green? Many people have asked us this important question. It's really very simple and requires no expert knowledge or complex skills. Here's the answer. Consume less. Share more. Enjoy life.
*A Green Manifesto for the 1990s*, Dedication (1990)

## Sally Kempton (b. 1943)
US AUTHOR

The daughter of the *Newsday* columnist Murray Kempton and an acerbic essayist, she abandoned New York journalism in 1974 to follow the guru Muktananda and became a swami in 1982 with the spiritual name of Durgananda.

1 I became a feminist as an alternative to becoming a masochist.
'Cutting Loose', publ. in *Esquire* July 1970

2 Women are natural guerrillas. Scheming, we nestle into the enemy's bed, avoiding open warfare, watching the options, playing the odds.
ibid.

## Thomas Keneally (b. 1935)
AUSTRALIAN NOVELIST

Before becoming a writer he studied for the Catholic priesthood but was not ordained. His 'faction' novels chart critical moments in history, as in *The Chant of Jimmie Blacksmith* (1972) and *Confederates* (1979). His Holocaust tale, *Schindler's Ark* (1982), won the Booker Prize and was filmed as *Schindler's List* (1993). He is a leading figure in the Australian Republican Movement.

1 We have found that it *is* possible for Australians to have literary ideas about the place, that Australia is not outside the universe. In short Australia – which used to have one unifying rite, cricket – has now become pluralist. I cannot but predict it will be a disaster for Australian cricket.
*Summer Days*, 'The Cyclical Supremacy of Australia in World Cricket' (1981)

2 In a way Australia is like Catholicism. The company is sometimes questionable and the landscape is grotesque. But you always come back.
*Woman's Day* 4 July 1983

## Florynce R. Kennedy (b. 1916)
US LAWYER AND CIVIL RIGHTS ACTIVIST

Full name Florynce Rae Kennedy. She has been an outspoken champion of African-Americans, women, the poor, homosexuals and prostitutes. In 1966 she founded the Media Workshop against media racism and in the 1970s promoted women's right to abortion. Her New York practice included Billie Holiday and Charlie Parker's estate.

1 Niggerization is the result of oppression – and it doesn't just apply to the black people. Old people, poor people, and students can also get niggerized.
Quoted by GLORIA STEINEM, in 'The Verbal Karate of Florynce R. Kennedy, Esq.', publ. in *Ms.* March 1973

2 If men could get pregnant, abortion would be a sacrament.
ibid.

3 There are very few jobs that actually require a penis or vagina. All other jobs should be open to everybody.
Quoted by John Brady, in 'Freelancer with No Time to Write', publ. in *Writer's Digest* February 1974

## G.A. Studdert Kennedy (1883–1929)
BRITISH POET

Full name (Rev.) Geoffrey Anketell Studdert Kennedy. He was awarded the Military Cross for his service as chaplain in the First World War and later became chaplain to GEORGE V. Under the pseudonym 'Woodbine Willie' he published *Rough Rhymes of a Padre* (1918), and among his other works are *The Hardest Part* (1918) and *Food for the Fed-Up* (1921).

1 Waste of Blood, and waste of Tears,
Waste of youth's most precious years,
Waste of ways the saints have trod,
Waste of Glory, waste of God,
War!
'Waste', publ. in *More Rough Rhymes of a Padre* (1918)

## Jacqueline Kennedy (1929–94)

US FIRST LADY

Later named Jacqueline Kennedy Onassis. Admired for her elegance and style, she married JOHN F. KENNEDY in 1953 and as First Lady promoted arts, history and conservation issues. She lost much of the nation's sympathy after her husband's death by her marriage to shipping magnate Aristotle Onassis in 1968. After Onassis's death she pursued a career in publishing.

1 If you bungle raising your children, I don't think whatever else you do well matters very much.

Quoted in *Kennedy*, pt 4, ch. 15 (1965) by Theodore C. Sorenson

## Jimmy Kennedy (1902–84)

BRITISH SONGWRITER

Before teaming up with Michael Carr (see below), Kennedy had hits with 'The Teddy Bears' Picnic' (1932) and with 'The Isle of Capri' (1934) sung by Gracie Fields. With George Grosz (Hugh Williamson) he wrote 'Red Sails in the Sunset' (1935) and was successful in America in 1940 with 'My Prayer' and 'South of the Border'.

1 If you go down in the woods today
You're sure of a big surprise
If you go down in the woods today
You'd better go in disguise
For every Bear that ever there was
Will gather there for certain because,
Today's the day the Teddy Bears have their Picnic.

'Teddy Bears' Picnic' (song, 1932). The words, set to a 1904 tune by John W. Bratton, were supposed to be about Theodore Roosevelt taking time off from his presidential campaigning to go bear-hunting. The song was recorded by Henry Hall in 1933, quickly becoming a children's classic.

2 In out in out shake it all about,
You do the Hokey Cokey
And you turn around,
That's what it's all about.

'Hokey Cokey' (song, 1942). The 'Cockney' lyrics were set to a traditional tune.

## Jimmy Kennedy (1902–84) and
## Michael Carr (1904–68)

BRITISH SONGWRITERS

Their string of hits began in 1935 and ranged from cowboy songs to show tunes. Carr, born Maurice Cohen, had an early success with 'Ole Faithful' (1934), a fake cowboy song, and from the 1950s concentrated on instrumental music, composing 'Man of Mystery' (1960) and 'Kon-Tiki' (1961) for the Shadows.

1 We're going to hang out our washing on the Siegfried Line.

'We're Going to Hang out Our Washing on the Siegfried Line' (song, 1939). This 'Tipperary' of the Second World War was the last of a string of hits enjoyed by the Kennedy/Carr partnership. The Siegfried Line was Germany's main belt of militarization on its western frontier in 1939.

## John F. Kennedy (1917–63)

US DEMOCRATIC POLITICIAN AND PRESIDENT

Full name John Fitzgerald Kennedy. A Democrat, he was, in 1960, the first Roman Catholic and youngest man to become President. Immensely popular for his wit, charm, youth and good looks, he is remembered for his firmness in the Cuban missile crisis (1962), in which he induced the Soviet Union to withdraw its missiles, and for the 1963 Nuclear Test Ban Treaty. He was assassinated while driving through Dallas. Said to combine the best qualities of ELVIS PRESLEY and FRANKLIN D. ROOSEVELT by one senator, he called himself 'an idealist without illusions'.

1 I just received the following wire from my generous Daddy – 'Dear Jack, Don't buy a single vote more than is necessary. I'll be damned if I'm going to pay for a landslide'.

Speech at Gridiron Dinner, Washington, D.C., 15 March 1958, quoted in *The Wit of President Kennedy*, 'The Family' (1964) by Bill Adler

2 We stand today on the edge of a new frontier – the frontier of the 1960s – a frontier of unknown opportunities and perils – a frontier of unfulfilled hopes and threats . . . The New Frontier of which I speak is not a set of promises – it is a set of challenges.

Acceptance speech at the Democratic Convention, Los Angeles, 15 July 1960, publ. in *The Penguin Book of Twentieth-Century Speeches* (ed. Brian MacArthur, 1999). Theodore C. Sorensen in his biography *Kennedy* (1965) took credit for drafting this speech.

3 Do you realize the responsibility I carry? I'm the only person between Nixon and the White House.

Teasing remark to a liberal supporter during the 1960 election campaign. quoted in *Kennedy*, pt 2, ch. 7 (1965) by Theodore C. Sorensen. In the event, NIXON won 49.6 per cent of the total vote, giving Kennedy the narrowest victory in a presidential election since 1888.

4 Our growing softness, our increasing lack of physical fitness, is a menace to our security.

'The Soft America' (1960), repr. in *Sport and Society: an Anthology* (ed. John T. Talamini and Charles H. Page, 1973)

5 To those people in the huts and villages across the globe struggling to break the bonds of mass misery, we pledge our best efforts to help them help themselves, for whatever period is required – not because the communists may be doing it, not because we seek their votes, but because it is right. If a free society cannot help the many who are poor, it cannot save the few who are rich.

Inaugural address, Washington, D.C., 20 January 1961, publ. in *The Penguin Book of Twentieth-Century Speeches* (ed. Brian MacArthur, 1999)

6 We dare not tempt them with weakness. For only when our arms are sufficient beyond doubt can we be certain beyond doubt that they will never be employed.

ibid.

7 Let us never negotiate out of fear. But let us never fear to negotiate.

ibid.

8 All this [reform programme] will not be finished in the first 100 days. Nor will it be finished in the first 1,000 days, nor in the life of this Administration, nor even perhaps in our lifetime on this planet. But let us begin.

ibid. Kennedy's administration lasted a little over 1,000 days.

9 And so, my fellow Americans, ask not what your country can do for you – ask what you can do for your country. My fellow citizens of the world, ask not what America will do for you, but what together we can do for the freedom of man.

ibid. Kennedy had previously expressed the same idea in a televised campaign address 20 September 1960. Among the many antecedents that have been cited, Oliver Wendell Holmes Sr stated in his Memorial Day Address (1884): 'It is now the moment . . . to recall what our country has done for each of us, and to ask ourselves what we can do for our country in return.'

10 I do not think it altogether inappropriate to introduce myself to this audience. I am the man who accompanied Jacqueline Kennedy to Paris, and I have enjoyed it.

Speech at SHAPE Headquarters, Paris, 2 June 1961, publ. in *Public Papers of the Presidents of the United States: 1961*. Referring to the massive publicity generated by the Kennedys' visit to Paris – focused particularly on JACKIE KENNEDY.

11 Conformity is the jailer of freedom and the enemy of growth.

Address to the UN General Assembly, 25 September 1961, publ. in ibid.

12 Washington is a city of Southern efficiency and Northern charm.

Remark in November 1961, quoted in *Portrait of a President* (1962) by William Manchester

13 We must use time as a tool, not as a couch.

Quoted in the *Observer* 10 December 1961

14 We test and then they test and we have to test again. And you build up until somebody uses them.

Remark in 1961, quoted in *A Thousand Days*, ch. 17 (1965) by ARTHUR M. SCHLESINGER JR

15 Those who make peaceful revolution impossible will make violent revolution inevitable.

Speech at the White House, 13 March 1962, publ. in *Public Papers of the Presidents of the United States: 1962*. Addressing diplomats who represented Latin American republics.

16 There is always inequity in life. Some men are killed in a war and some men are wounded, and some men never leave the country . . . Life is unfair.

Press conference 21 March 1962, quoted in *A Thousand Days*, ch. 4 (1965) by Arthur M. Schlesinger Jr

17 I think this is the most extraordinary collection of talent, of human knowledge, that has ever been gathered together at the White House – with the possible exception of when Thomas Jefferson dined alone.

Remark at a dinner for Nobel prize-winners, 29 April 1962, Washington, D.C., publ. in *Public Papers of the Presidents of the United States: 1962*

18 Most of us are conditioned for many years to have a political viewpoint – Republican or Democratic, liberal, conservative, or moderate. The fact of the matter is that most of the problems . . . that we now face are technical problems, are administrative problems. They are very sophisticated judgments, which do not lend themselves to the great sort of passionate movements which have stirred this country so often in the past. [They] deal with questions which are now beyond the comprehension of most men.

Press conference, May 1962, quoted in 'Policy-Planning for the Establishment' by David Eakins, publ. in *A New History of Leviathan* (ed. Ronald Radosh and Murray Rothbard, 1972)

19 If we cannot end now our differences, at least we can help make the world safe for diversity.

Commencement address, American University, Washington, D.C., 10 June 1963, publ. in *Public Papers of the Presidents of the United States: 1963*. Referring to Soviet-American relations.

20 No one has been barred on account of his race from fighting or dying for America – there are no 'white' or 'colored' signs on the foxholes or graveyards of battle.

Message to Congress, 19 June 1963, quoted in *The New York Times* 20 June 1963. Referring to the proposed civil rights bill.

21 All free men, wherever they may live, are citizens of Berlin. And therefore, as a free man, I take pride in the words 'Ich bin ein Berliner'.

Speech in West Berlin, 26 June 1963, publ. in *The Penguin Book of Twentieth-Century Speeches* (ed. Brian MacArthur, 1999). Kennedy's words recalled Cicero, *Civis Romanus sum* ('I am a Roman citizen'), from *In Verrem*, speech 5. Kennedy should more correctly have said *Ich bin Berliner*; *ein Berliner* suggests a type of doughnut.

22 The United States has to move very fast to even stand still.

Quoted in the *Observer* 21 July 1963

23 I never know when I press these whether I am going to blow up Massachusetts or start the project.

Speech at Salt Lake City, September 1963, quoted in *The Wit of President Kennedy*, 'The Presidency' (ed. Bill Adler, 1964). Kennedy was supposed to pull a switch to activate generators in the Colorado River basin, 150 miles distant.

24 When power leads man towards arrogance, poetry reminds him of his limitations. When power narrows the area of man's concern, poetry reminds him of the richness and diversity of existence. When power corrupts, poetry cleanses.

Speech at Amherst College, 26 October 1963, quoted in *The New York Times* 27 October 1963. The occasion of Kennedy's last major public address was the dedication of the Robert Frost Library at the college. Previously, in a speech at Harvard, 14 June 1956, Kennedy said: 'If more politicians knew poetry, and more poets knew politics, I am convinced the world would be a little better place to live.'

25 In free society art is not a weapon . . . Artists are not engineers of the soul.

Speech at Amherst College, 26 October 1963, quoted in *The New York Times* 27 October 1963. The phrase 'Engineers of human souls' had been previously used by JOSEF STALIN and Maxim Gorky in the 1930s.

26 It was involuntary. They sank my boat.

Quoted in *A Thousand Days*, ch. 4 (1965) by ARTHUR M. SCHLESINGER JR. Answer to small boy who asked how he became a war hero.

27 I suppose if you had to choose just one quality to have that would be it: vitality.

Quoted in ibid. ch. 25

28 There is a terrific disadvantage in not having the abrasive quality of the press applied to you daily . . . Even though we never like it, and even though we wish they didn't write it, and even though we disapprove, there isn't any doubt that we could not do the job at all in a free society without a very, very active press.

Quoted in *Kennedy*, pt 3, ch. 12 (1965) by Theodore C. Sorensen. With reference to KHRUSHCHEV's control of the Soviet press.

29 Domestic policy can only defeat us; foreign policy can kill us.

Quoted in *The Imperial Presidency*, ch. 11, sect. 7 (1973) by ARTHUR M. SCHLESINGER JR

30 You never know what's hit you. A gunshot is the perfect way.

Quoted in *The Kennedys*, pt 3, ch. 3 (1984) by Peter Collier and David Horowitz. Remark when asked how he would choose to die.

31 Forgive your enemies, but never forget their names.

Attributed. The quote has also been ascribed to ROBERT KENNEDY.

## Joseph P. Kennedy (1888–1969)

US TYCOON AND DIPLOMAT

Full name Joseph Patrick Kennedy. A self-made millionaire by the age of thirty, he was Ambassador to Britain (1937–40) and subsequently concentrated on grooming his children JOHN KENNEDY, ROBERT KENNEDY and Edward for political careers. His eldest son, Joseph, was killed in action in the Second World War.

1 When the going gets tough, the tough get going.

Quoted in *Honey Fitz* (1962), ch. 20, by J.H. Cutler. The quotation has also been ascribed to US football coach Knute Rockne (1888–1931)

## Nigel Kennedy (b. 1956)

BRITISH VIOLINIST

Having studied under Yehudi Menuhin, he made his debut as a concert soloist in 1977 and was later credited with helping to create a classical renaissance in Britain, selling millions of copies of his recordings of Vivaldi and Beethoven. His punk-ish appearance and commercial instincts (he re-branded himself 'Kennedy' in 1999) have drawn criticism in the classical world, leading John Drummond, former head of Radio 3 and Proms director, to call him the 'Liberace of the 1990s'.

1 When I get those really intense moments it doesn't feel like it's the violin that's giving them to me, it's like I'm in touch with some realm of consciousness which is much bigger than I am . . . It's the music which takes over.

Interview in the *Guardian* 1 March 1997

## Robert F. Kennedy (1925–68)

US POLITICIAN AND LAWYER

Full name Robert Francis Kennedy. The third son of JOSEPH P. KENNEDY, he was presidential campaign manager for his brother JOHN F. KENNEDY and as Attorney-General (1961–4) promoted the Civil Rights Act of 1964. He became senator for New York in 1955 but was assassinated in California during his campaign for presidential nomination. The journalist Murray Kempton called him 'the highest ranking withdrawn adolescent since Alexander Hamilton in 1794'.

1 Every society gets the kind of criminal it deserves. What is equally true is that every community gets the kind of law enforcement it insists on.

The Pursuit of Justice, pt 3, 'Eradicating Free Enterprise in Organized Crime' (1964)

2 What is objectionable, what is dangerous, about extremists is not that they are extreme, but that they are intolerant. The evil is not what they say about their cause, but what they say about their opponents.

ibid. pt 3, 'Extremism, Left and Right'

3 The free way of life proposes ends, but it does not prescribe means.

ibid. pt 5, 'Berlin East and West'

4 One-fifth of the people are against everything all the time.

Speech at University of Pennsylvania, 6 May 1964, quoted in the Philadelphia Inquirer 7 May 1964

## Elizabeth Kenny (1886–1952)

AUSTRALIAN NURSE

She began nursing in the Australian Outback and pioneered the technique of using muscle therapy rather than splints and immobilization to treat poliomyelitis. She subsequently established clinics in Britain, America and Australia. Her autobiography, And They Shall Walk, was published in 1943.

1 The record of one's life must needs prove more interesting to him who writes it than to him who reads what has been written.

And They Shall Walk, Foreword (1943, written with Martha Ostenso)

## Corita Kent (b. 1918)

US ARTIST

A member of the Sisters of the Immaculate Heart of Mary, she expressed her basic tenet of 'learning to love one another' in her painting. Her combinations of brightly coloured images and text were considered threatening by some members of the Church, however, who described her as a 'guerrilla with a paint brush', and she was eventually pressurized into leaving the sisterhood.

1 Women's liberation is the liberation of the feminine in the man and the masculine in the woman.

Quoted in the Los Angeles Times 11 July 1974

## Alvin Kernan (b. 1923)

US ACADEMIC

He has written widely on satire and English literature, and on Shakespeare and Ben Jonson in particular. His works include The Plot of Satire (1965) and The Death of Literature (1990).

1 In the electronic age, books, words and reading are not likely to remain sufficiently authoritative and central to knowledge to justify literature.

International Herald Tribune 12 December 1990

## Jack Kerouac (1922–69)

US AUTHOR

Original name Jean Louis Kerouac. He published his first novel, The Town and the City, in 1950, but it was not until On the Road

(1957) that he became established as the voice of the Beat generation. Later titles, which include The Dharma Bums (1958) and Doctor Sax (1959), failed to have the same impact. 'My work comprises one vast book like Proust's Remembrance of Things Past,' he once said, 'except that my remembrances are written on the run instead of afterwards in a sickbed.'

1 I must change my life, now, I have reached 21 and I am indeed earnest about all things. This does not mean I will cease my debauching.

Undated letter, 1943, publ. in Selected Letters 1940–1956 (ed. Ann Charters, 1995)

2 All of life is a foreign country.

Letter, 24 June 1949, publ. in The Beat Vision: A Primary Sourcebook (ed. Arthur and Kit Knight, 1987)

3 The requirements for prose and verse are the same, i.e. blow – What a man most wishes to hide, revise, and unsay, is precisely what Literature is waiting and bleeding for. Every doctor knows, every Prophet knows the convulsion of truth.

Letter to Malcolm Cowley, 11 September 1955, publ. in Selected Letters 1940–1956 (ed. Ann Charters, 1995). The critic Malcolm Cowley was then an editorial adviser for Viking Press, which he later persuaded to publish On the Road.

4 But then they danced down the street like dingledodies, and I shambled after as I've been doing all my life after people who interest me, because the only people for me are the mad ones, the ones who are mad to live, mad to talk, mad to be saved, desirous of everything at the same time, the ones who never yawn or say a commonplace thing, but burn, burn, burn, like fabulous yellow roman candles exploding like spiders across the stars and in the middle you see the blue centerlight pop and everybody goes 'Awww!'

Narrator (Sal Paradise), in On the Road, pt 1, ch. 1 (1957)

5 [On arriving in San Francisco] We wandered around, carrying our bundles of rags in the narrow romantic streets. Everybody looked like a broken-down movie extra, a withered starlet; disenchanted stunt-men, midget auto-racers, poignant California characters with their end-of-the-continent sadness, handsome, decadent, Casanova-ish men, puffy-eyed motel blondes, hustlers, pimps, whores, masseurs, bellhops – a lemon lot, and how's a man going to make a living with a gang like that?

ibid. pt 2, ch. 9

6 [Of Dean Moriarty] Standing in front of everybody, ragged and broken and idiotic, right under the lightbulbs, his bony mad face covered with sweat and throbbing veins, saying, 'Yes, yes, yes,' as though tremendous revelations were pouring into him all the time now, and I am convinced they were, and the others suspected as much and were frightened. He was BEAT – the root, the soul of Beatific.

ibid. pt 3, ch. 3. The character of Moriarty was modelled on that of NEAL CASSADY.

7 Do you know there's a road that goes down to Mexico and all the way to Panama? – and maybe all the way to the bottom of South America where the Indians are seven feet tall and eat cocaine on the mountainside? Yes! You and I, Sal, we'd dig the whole world with a car like this because, man, the road must eventually lead to the whole world. Ain't nowhere else it can go – right?

Dean Moriarty, in ibid. pt 3, ch. 9

8 John Clellon Holmes . . . and I were sitting around trying to think up the meaning of the Lost Generation and the subsequent Existentialism and I said, 'You know, this is really a beat generation' and he leapt up and said 'That's it, that's right!'

Interview in Playboy June 1959, explaining the origin of the label 'Beat Generation'. On another occasion, Kerouac ascribed the expression's origin to Herbert Huncke, a Times Square hustler he'd met a decade earlier, and the words also appeared in Holmes's novel *Go* (1952), originally titled *The Beat Generation* and publ. as *The Beat Boys* in Britain (1959).

9 **It is not my fault that certain so-called bohemian elements have found in my writings something to hang their peculiar beatnik theories on.**
*New York Journal-American* 8 December 1960

## Jean Kerr (b. 1923)
US AUTHOR AND PLAYWRIGHT

In her own words, she wrote 'realistic comedy' set in an affluent suburbia peopled by literate characters facing minor dilemmas. Among her essay collections is *Please Don't Eat the Daisies* (1957) and her plays include *Mary, Mary* (1961). She was married to WALTER KERR, with whom she sometimes collaborated. ELIZA-BETH JANEWAY praised her 'wonderful ear and eye for those moments of lunacy'.

1 **As someone pointed out recently, if you can keep your head when all about you are losing theirs, it's just possible you haven't grasped the situation.**
*Please Don't Eat the Daisies*, Introduction (1957)

2 **I'm tired of all this nonsense about beauty being only skin-deep. That's deep enough. What do you want – an adorable pancreas?**
*The Snake Has All the Lines*, 'Mirror, Mirror on the Wall' (1958)

3 **Even though a number of people have tried, no one has yet found a way to drink for a living.**
Sydney, in *Poor Richard*, act 1 (1963)

4 **Hope is the feeling you have that the feeling you have isn't permanent.**
Felicia, in *Finishing Touches*, act 3 (1973)

## Walter Kerr (1913–96)
US CRITIC

Drama critic for more than thirty years (with the *New York Herald Tribune*, 1951–66, and *The New York Times*, 1966–83) he was highly respected for his reviews for which he won a Pulitzer Prize in 1978. It was his credo that good theatre equated with popular theatre, and he was described by the critic KENNETH TYNAN as 'vaulting over the barrier we erect between "serious" and "light" criticism'.

1 **Me no Leica.**
Attributed review of *I am a Camera* (1951), John Van Druten's dramatization of 'Sally Bowles' from *Goodbye to Berlin* by CHRIS-TOPHER ISHERWOOD, quoted in *No Turn Unstoned*, ch. 5 (1982) by Diana Rigg

## Gerald Kersh (1911–68)
BRITISH AUTHOR AND JOURNALIST

A bestselling writer of crime fiction, he gained fame with his third book, *Harry Fabian: Night and the City* (1938). He was also known for his series of short stories featuring Karmesin. As Piers England, he was an influential propagandist for the *People* during the Second World War.

1 **Now, you mummy's darlings, get a rift on them boots. Definitely shine 'em, my little curly-headed lambs, for in our mob, war or no war, you die with clean boots on.**
*They Die With Their Boots Clean*, Prologue (1941)

2 **I can't believe in the God of my Fathers. If there is one Mind which understands all things, it will comprehend me in my unbelief. I don't know whose hand hung Hesperus in the sky, and fixed the Dog Star, and scattered the shining dust of Heaven, and fired the sun, and froze the darkness between the lonely worlds that spin in space.**
Old Silence, in ibid. pt 3, 'The Tempering'

## Ken Kesey (b. 1935)
US AUTHOR

His experience as an aide in a mental hospital formed the basis for his bestselling satirical novel *One Flew Over the Cuckoo's Nest* (1962), which netted six Oscars when filmed in 1975. After the limited success of *Sometimes a Great Notion* (1964) he gave up writing and became leader of the 'Merry Pranksters', an itinerant hippie group whose exploits were recorded in TOM WOLFE's *The Electric Kool-Aid Acid Test* (1968).

1 **I've watched her ['the Big Nurse', Miss Ratched] get more and more skilful over the years. Practice has steadied and strengthened her until now she wields a sure power that extends in all directions on hairlike wires too small for anybody's eye but mine; I see her sit in the center of this web of wires like a watchful robot, tend her network with mechanical insect skill, know every second which wires run where and just what current to send up to get the results she wants.**
Narrator (Chief Bromden), in *One Flew Over the Cuckoo's Nest*, pt 1 (1962). The book's title derives from a children's folk rhyme: 'One flew east, one flew west,/One flew over the cuckoo's nest.'

2 **I'd rather be a lightning rod than a seismograph.**
Quoted in *The Electric Kool-Aid Acid Test*, ch. 1 (1968) by TOM WOLFE

3 **You're either on the bus or off the bus. If you're on the bus, and you get left behind, then you'll find it again. If you're off the bus in the first place – then it won't make a damn.**
Quoted in ibid. ch. 6

## Ellen Key (1849–1926)
SWEDISH AUTHOR AND FEMINIST

Known as the 'Pallas of Sweden', she wrote on feminism, child welfare, sex and marriage, advocating that mothers should stay in the home while women without children should be active in politics and peace issues. Her most famous book is *The Century of the Child* (1900).

1 **Art, that great undogmatized church.**
*The Renaissance of Motherhood* pt 2, ch. 1 (1914)

## John Maynard Keynes (1883–1946)
BRITISH ECONOMIST

Baron Keynes of Tilton. Regarding himself as 'a voice crying in the wilderness' who 'had, therefore, to cry loudly', he was one of the most influential economists of the twentieth century and a pioneer in the field of macroeconomics. His major works, *A Treatise on Money* (1930) and *The General Theory of Employment, Interest and Money* (1936), favoured increased government spending as a cure for rising unemployment. He advised the Treasury during both world wars and influenced ROOSEVELT to set up the New Deal.

1 **The disruptive powers of excessive national fecundity may have played a greater part in bursting the bonds of convention than either the power of ideas or the errors of autocracy.**
*The Economic Consequences of Peace* (1919) repr. in *Collected Writings*, vol. 2 (1971)

2 **Lenin was right. There is no subtler, no surer means of overturning the existing basis of society than to debauch the currency. The process engages all the forces of economic law on the side of destruction, and does it in a manner which not one man in a million is able to diagnose.**
ibid. ch. 6. Keynes repeated this assertion in *Essays in Persuasion*, ch. 2 (1931): 'The best way to destroy the capitalist system is to debauch the currency. By a continuing process of inflation governments can confiscate, secretly and unobserved, an important part of the wealth of their citizens.' The words attributed to Lenin have never been found in his writings.

3 *Long run* is a misleading guide to current affairs. *In the long run* we are all dead.

A Tract on Monetary Reform, ch. 3 (1923)

4 The Labour Party . . . is a class party, and the class is not my class . . . The *class* war will find me on the side of the educated *bourgeoisie*.

Am I a Liberal? (1925) repr. in Collected Writings, vol. 9 (1972)

5 A study of the history of opinion is a necessary preliminary to the emancipation of the mind. I do not know which makes a man more conservative – to know nothing but the present, or nothing but the past.

The End of Laissez-Faire, ch. 1 (1926)

6 Marxian Socialism must always remain a portent to the historians of Opinion – how a doctrine so illogical and so dull can have exercised so powerful and enduring an influence over the minds of men, and, through them, the events of history.

ibid. ch. 3

7 I think that Capitalism, wisely managed, can probably be made more efficient for attaining economic ends than any alternative system yet in sight, but that in itself it is in many ways extremely objectionable.

ibid. ch. 5

8 Most men love money and security more, and creation and construction less, as they get older.

Essays in Persuasion, ch. 5, 'The Future' (1931)

9 For at least another hundred years we must pretend to ourselves and to every one that fair is foul and foul is fair; for foul is useful and fair is not. Avarice and usury and precaution must be our gods for a little longer still.

ibid. Keynes argued that the 'detestable . . . love of money' and other vices of greed must continue until the economy has grown enough to satisfy human wants and provide the potential for removing poverty.

10 If economists could manage to get themselves thought of as humble, competent people on a level with dentists, that would be splendid.

ibid.

11 Nothing mattered except states of mind, chiefly our own.

Essays in Biography, ch. 39 (1933). Referring to the 'Apostles' group at Cambridge University.

12 The decadent international but individualistic capitalism in the hands of which we found ourselves after the war is not a success. It is not intelligent. It is not beautiful. It is not just. It is not virtuous. And it doesn't deliver the goods.

National Self-Sufficiency, sect. 3 (1933), repr. in Collected Writings, vol. 11 (1982)

13 Words ought to be a little wild for they are the assault of thoughts on the unthinking.

New Statesman and Nation 15 July 1933

14 The difficulty lies, not in the new ideas, but in escaping from the old ones, which ramify, for those brought up as most of us have been, into every corner of our minds.

The General Theory of Employment, Interest and Money, Preface (1936)

15 The social object of skilled investment should be to defeat the dark forces of time and ignorance which envelope our future.

ibid. bk 4, ch. 12, sect. 5

16 It is better that a man should tyrannize over his bank balance than over his fellow-citizens and whilst the former is sometimes denounced as being but a means to the latter, sometimes at least it is an alternative.

ibid. ch. 24, 'Concluding Notes'

17 The ideas of economists and political philosophers, both when they are right and when they are wrong, are more

powerful than is commonly understood. Indeed the world is ruled by little else. Practical men, who believe themselves to be quite exempt from any intellectual influence, are usually the slaves of some defunct economist.

ibid.

18 It is ideas, not vested interests, which are dangerous for good or evil.

ibid. ch. 24

19 The day is not far off when the economic problem will take the back seat where it belongs, and the arena of the heart and the head will be occupied or reoccupied, by our real problems – the problems of life and of human relations, of creation and behaviour and religion.

First Annual Report of the Arts Council (1945–6)

## Imran Khan (b. 1952)
PAKISTANI CRICKETER

He played eighty-eight test matches for Pakistan, forty-eight as captain, and led his country to victory in the 1992 World Cup. In the same year he retired and took up politics, leading the Movement for Justice Party which, though polling 5 per cent of the vote, failed to win a seat in the 1997 election.

1 [Of cricket] There is no essential discrepancy between the game's time-honoured virtues and the world we live in. It is a matter of creatively adapting the form in order to preserve the content. So far much valuable time has been wasted on quibbling over what 'isn't cricket', and not much has been devoted to what cricket should become.

All Round View, ch. 13 (1988)

## Ayatollah Ruhollah Khomeini (1900–89)
IRANIAN RELIGIOUS AND POLITICAL LEADER

Original name Ruhollah Musawi. After the revolution that expelled Shah Pahlavi in 1979, he established a fundamentalist Islamic republic and was named Iran's political and religious leader for life. He was hostile to both superpowers, suppressed internal opposition and supported the prolongation of the Iran–Iraq War (1980–88).

1 I would like to inform all the intrepid Muslims in the world that the author of the book entitled *The Satanic Verses*, which has been compiled, printed and published in opposition to Islam, the prophet and the Qur'an, as well as those publishers who were aware of its contents, have been declared *madhur el dam* [those whose blood must be shed]. I call on all zealous Muslims to execute them quickly, wherever they find them, so that no one will dare to insult Islam again. Whoever is killed in this path will be regarded as a martyr.

Fatwa, or legal ruling, issued 14 February 1989, quoted in A Satanic Affair, ch. 5 (1990) by Malise Ruthven

## Nikita Khrushchev (1894–1971)
SOVIET POLITICIAN AND PREMIER

During his term as First Secretary of the Communist Party (1953–64) he broke with Stalinist policies and laid the basis for liberalizing Soviet communism and for the independence of European communist parties. He was Premier from 1958–64, but the Sino–Soviet split, Cuban missile crisis (1962) and mismanagement of agriculture helped to bring about his replacement by Brezhnev and Kosygin.

1 If anyone believes that our smiles involve abandonment of the teaching of Marx, Engels and Lenin he deceives himself. Those who wait for that must wait until a shrimp learns to whistle.

Speech in Moscow, 17 September 1955, quoted in The New York Times 18 September 1955

2 Comrades! We must abolish the cult of the individual decisively, once and for all.

Speech to the secret session of the Twentieth Congress of the Soviet Communist Party, 25 February 1956, quoted in the *Manchester Guardian* 11 June 1956. Khrushchev used the occasion to identify STALIN as the chief exponent of the cult of the individual (also translated 'cult of the personality') by 'the glorification of his own person'.

3 Everyone can err, but Stalin considered that he never erred, that he was always right. He never acknowledged to anyone that he made any mistake, large or small, despite the fact that he made not a few mistakes in the matter of theory and in his practical activity.

Speech to the Twentieth Congress of the Soviet Communist Party, February 1956, quoted in *Stalin*, pt 2, ch. 6 (ed. T.H. Rigby, 1966)

4 It doesn't depend on you whether or not we exist. If you don't like us, don't accept our invitations and don't invite us to come to see you. Whether you like it or not, history is on our side. We will bury you.

Speech to Western diplomats at the Kremlin, 18 November 1956, quoted in *The Times* 19 November 1956. Khrushchev later explained this remark as an idiomatic expression to mean 'we will outlive you' (i.e. communism will triumph). On another occasion, 24 August 1963, addressing a group of Westerners in Split, Yugoslavia, he referred to his controversial statement: 'Of course we will not bury you with a shovel. Your own working class will bury you.'

5 If one cannot catch a bird of paradise, better take a wet hen.

Quoted in *Time* magazine 6 January 1958

6 When you are skinning your customers you should leave some skin on to grow again so that you can skin them again.

Quoted in the *Observer* 28 May 1961. Advice to British businessmen.

7 They talk about who won and who lost. Human reason won. Mankind won.

Quoted in the *Observer* 11 November 1962. Referring to the Cuban missile crisis.

8 Politicians are the same all over: they promise to build a bridge even where there is no river.

Quoted in the *New York Herald-Tribune* 22 August 1963. Khrushchev used the same figure of speech at a press conference, Glen Cove, New York, October 1960.

9 He who cannot eat horsemeat need not do so. Let him eat pork. But he who cannot eat pork, let him eat horsemeat. It's simply a question of taste.

*New York World-Telegram and Sun* 25 August 1964

10 If you live among wolves you have to act like a wolf.

Quoted in the *Observer* 20 September 1964

11 If we were to promise people nothing better than only revolution, they would scratch their heads and say: 'Is it not better to have good goulash?'

Quoted in the *Observer* 27 December 1964

## Jean Kierans (b. 1930)
FORMER GIRLFRIEND OF JOHN MAJOR

Thirteen years older than MAJOR, a divorcee friend of his mother's, she became his lover in 1963. Major moved in with her in 1967 and ended the relationship in 1970 when he married. News of the affair broke in *Esquire* magazine in 1995.

1 It makes me laugh now when I hear him called a grey man. That's just a cover. It's a mask.

Quoted in the *Independent on Sunday* 19 February 1995

## Krzysztof Kieślowski (1941–96)
POLISH FILM-MAKER

After making short TV documentaries, he established himself as an innovative director with a series of films on the Ten Command-

ments, including the Oscar-winning *A Short Film about Killing* (1988). *Three Colours: Blue, White, Red* (1983–4) and *The Double Life of Veronique* (1991) furthered his reputation as a master stylist. He summed up his work: 'I simply wanted to show that life was complicated.'

1 I'm frightened of all those people who show you the way, who know. Because really . . . nobody really knows, with a few exceptions. Unfortunately, the actions of these people usually end in tragedy – like the Second World War or Stalinism or something. I'm convinced that Stalin and Hitler knew exactly what they were to do. They knew very well. But that's how it is. That's fanaticism. That's knowing. That's the feeling of absolutely knowing. And the next minute, it's army boots. It always ends up like that.

*Kieślowski on Kieślowski*, ch. 1 (1993)

2 [On Americans] I think they're just as unhappy as we are, except that we still talk about it sometimes. . .they only say that everything's fine, that it's fantastic . . . If I had to be confronted for a whole year with people saying that everything's fantastic then I simply couldn't stand it.

ibid. ch. 4

3 Our mouths are full of such words as freedom, but what does it really mean? Does it not perhaps mean being totally alone, living in a total vacuum?

Quoted in appreciation in the *Guardian* 14 March 1996

## Dorothy Kilgallen (1913–65)
US COLUMNIST AND TELEVISION PERSONALITY

She is best known for her contributions to newspapers and magazines and her appearances on the television programme *What's My Line?* and the radio programme *Breakfast with Dorothy and Dick*. She wrote *Girl around the World* (1937) among other writings.

1 Doorman – a genius who can open the door of your car with one hand, help you in with the other, and still have one left for the tip.

Quoted in *Violets and Vinegar*, 'Come Away, Poverty's Catching' (ed. Jilly Cooper and Tom Hartman, 1980)

## B.B. King (b. 1925)
US BLUES MUSICIAN

Original name Riley B. King, known as B.B. (Blues Boy). Distinguished by a powerful voice and the sparse riffs played on his guitar 'Lucille', he has been a major figure in blues for more than forty years. His major albums include *Live at the Regal* (1965) and *Indianola Mississippi Seeds* (1970).

1 The blues was like that problem child that you may have had in the family. You was a little bit ashamed to let anybody see him, but you loved him. You just didn't know how other people would take it.

Interview in the *Sunday Times* 4 November 1984

## Don King (b. 1931)
US BOXING PROMOTER

From a criminal background, he became boxing's most successful promoter, numbering among his clients MUHAMMAD ALI, Sugar Ray Leonard and MIKE TYSON. In the words of boxer LARRY HOLMES: 'He doesn't care about black or white. He just cares about green.'

1 I'm one of the world's great survivors. I'll always survive because I've got the right combination of wit, grit and bullshit.

Quoted in the *Sunday Times* 18 December 1994

2 I dare to be great. The man without imagination stands

unhurt and hath no wings. This is my credo, this is my forte.

Interview in the *Independent on Sunday* 10 March 1996

# Florence King (b. 1936)

US AUTHOR

Calling herself a woman who 'rips the teats off sacred cows', she has written *Southern Ladies and Gentlemen* (1975), a guide to Southern types, *When Sisterhood Was in Flower* (1978), on feminism, and *Reflections in a Jaundiced Eye* (1989), which targets self-help. Her other books include thirty-seven erotic novels.

1 He travels fastest who travels alone, and that goes double for she. Real feminism is spinsterhood.

*Reflections in a Jaundiced Eye*, 'Spinsterhood is Powerful' (1989). Referring to Kipling, 'He travels the fastest who travels alone' (from 'The Winners' in *The Story of the Gadsbys*, 1890).

2 For men who want to flee Family Man America and never come back, there is a guaranteed solution: homosexuality is the new French Foreign Legion.

ibid. 'From Captain Marvel to Captain Valium'

3 We want a president who is as much like an American tourist as possible. Someone with the same goofy grin, the same innocent intentions, the same naive trust; a president with no conception of foreign policy and no discernible connection to the U.S. government, whose Nice Guyism will narrow the gap between the U.S. and us until nobody can tell the difference.

ibid. 'Nice Guyism'

4 The witty woman is a tragic figure in American life. Wit destroys eroticism and eroticism destroys wit, so women must choose between taking lovers and taking no prisoners.

ibid. 'The State of the Funny Bone'

# Martin Luther King Jr (1929–68)

US CLERGYMAN AND CIVIL RIGHTS LEADER

An inspiring orator, he led the civil rights and integration movement of the 1950s and 1960s, and was instrumental in the bus boycott in Montgomery, Alabama (1955), and the march of 200,000 demonstrators on Washington, D.C. (1963). His non-violent policy of passive resistance, conditioned by his Baptist upbringing, won him the Nobel Peace Prize in 1964, although he was criticized by black militants. His assassination in Memphis caused national mourning.

1 It is my hope that as the Negro plunges deeper into the quest for freedom and justice he will plunge even deeper into the philosophy of non-violence. The Negro all over the South must come to the point that he can say to his white brother: 'We will match your capacity to inflict suffering with our capacity to endure suffering. We will meet your physical force with soul force. We will not hate you, but we will not obey your evil laws. We will soon wear you down by pure capacity to suffer.'

Letter, 28 October 1957

2 I want to be the white man's brother, not his brother-in-law.

*New York Journal-American* 10 September 1962

3 It may be true that the law cannot make a man love me, but it can keep him from lynching me, and I think that's pretty important.

Quoted in the *Wall Street Journal* 13 November 1962

4 Nothing in all the world is more dangerous than sincere ignorance and conscientious stupidity.

*Strength to Love*, ch. 4, sect. 3 (1963)

5 The means by which we live have outdistanced the ends for which we live. Our scientific power has outrun our spiritual power. We have guided missiles and misguided men.

ibid. ch. 7

6 We have genuflected before the god of science only to find that it has given us the atomic bomb, producing fears and anxieties that science can never mitigate.

ibid. ch. 13

7 Freedom is never voluntarily given by the oppressor; it must be demanded by the oppressed.

'Letter from Birmingham Jail', open letter to clergymen, 16 April 1963, first publ. in *Atlantic Monthly* August 1963, repr. in *Why We Can't Wait* (1963)

8 I submit that an individual who breaks a law that conscience tells him is unjust, and who willingly accepts the penalty of imprisonment in order to arouse the conscience of the community over its injustice, is in reality expressing the highest respect for law.

ibid.

9 I have almost reached the regrettable conclusion that the Negro's great stumbling block in his stride toward freedom is not the White Citizen's Counciler or the Ku Klux Klanner, but the white moderate.

ibid.

10 Shallow understanding from people of good will is more frustrating than absolute misunderstanding from people of ill will.

ibid.

11 Law and order exist for the purpose of establishing justice, and . . . when they fail in this purpose they become the dangerously structured dams that block the flow of social progress.

ibid.

12 We who engage in non-violent direct action are not the creators of tension. We merely bring to the surface the hidden tension that is already alive.

ibid.

13 We will have to repent in this generation not merely for the hateful words and actions of the bad people but for the appalling silence of the good people.

ibid.

14 The question is not whether we will be extremist but what kind of extremist we will be.

ibid.

15 There can be no deep disappointment where there is not deep love.

ibid. Speaking of the church, which 'we have blemished and scarred . . . through social neglect and through fear of being nonconformists'.

16 Abused and scorned though we may be, our destiny is tied up with America's destiny. Before the pilgrims landed at Plymouth, we were here. Before the pen of Jefferson etched the majestic words of the Declaration of Independence across the pages of history, we were here. For more than two centuries our forebears labored in this country without wages; they made cotton king; they built the homes of their masters while suffering gross injustice and shameful humiliation – and yet out of a bottomless vitality they continued to thrive and develop. If the inexpressible cruelties of slavery could not stop us, the opposition we now face will surely fail.

ibid. The first sentence of this extract recalls a speech by abolitionist Frederick Douglass, in Boston, 12 February 1862: 'The destiny of the colored American . . . is the destiny of America.'

17 If a man hasn't discovered something that he will die for, he isn't fit to live.

Speech in Detroit, 23 June 1963, quoted in *The Days of Martin Luther King*, ch. 4 (1971) by James Bishop

18 No, no, we are not satisfied, and we will not be satisfied until justice rolls down like waters and righteousness like a mighty stream.

'I Have a Dream', speech, at civil rights march, Washington, D.C., 28 August 1963, publ. in *A Testament of Hope: Essential Writings* (ed. James Melvin Washington, 1986). King was quoting the Old Testament, Amos 5:24.

19 I have a dream that one day on the red hills of Georgia the sons of former slaves and the sons of former slave owners will be able to sit down together at the table of brotherhood. I have a dream that one day even the state of Mississippi, a desert state sweltering with the heat of injustice and oppression, will be transformed into an oasis of freedom and justice. I have a dream that my four little children will one day live in a nation where they will not be judged by the color of their skin but by the content of their character. I have a dream today.

ibid.

20 A riot is at bottom the language of the unheard.

*Where Do We Go From Here?* ch. 4 (1967)

21 It doesn't matter with me now. Because I've been to the mountaintop. And I don't mind. Like anybody, I would like to live a long life. Longevity has its place. But I'm not concerned about that now. I just want to do God's will. And He's allowed me to go up to the mountain. And I've looked over, and I've seen the Promised Land . . . Mine eyes have seen the glory of the coming of the Lord.

'I See the Promised Land', speech in Memphis, 3 April 1968, publ. in *A Testament of Hope: Essential Writings* (ed. James Melvin Washington, 1986). The last words are from Julia Ward Howe's 'Battle Hymn of the Republic'. The speech was made on the day preceding King's assassination.

22 Free at last, Free at last
Thank God Almighty
I'm free at last

Epitaph on King's tomb, in South View Cemetery, Atlanta, Georgia. The words are from the spiritual with which he often closed his speeches.

# Stephen King (b. 1947)

US AUTHOR

His prolific output of horror fiction, for example *Carrie* (1974, filmed 1976), *Salem's Lot* (1975, filmed 1979) and *The Shining* (1977, filmed 1980), has made his name synonymous with the genre.

1 Talent is cheaper than table salt. What separates the talented individual from the successful one is a lot of hard work.

Quoted in the *Independent on Sunday* 10 March 1996

# Miles Kington (b. 1941)

BRITISH HUMORIST

A frequent broadcaster and contributor to periodicals, he was literary editor of *Punch* (1967–80). He is also a double-bass player with the parlour group Instant Sunshine. His books include *Let's Parler Franglais* (1982).

1 Most English conversation is not conversation at all, but the exchange of little ritual expressions which only work if you know the exact context.

*Independent* 6 December 1989

# Neil Kinnock (b. 1942)

BRITISH LABOUR POLITICIAN

A Welsh firebrand in the mould of ANEURIN BEVAN, he succeeded MICHAEL FOOT as leader of the Labour Party (1983–92) and resigned after Labour's defeat in the 1992 general election. He became a European Commissioner in 1994. MICHAEL HESELTINE called him 'the self-appointed king of the gutter'. See also SUN 6.

1 If Margaret Thatcher wins – I warn you not to be ordinary. I warn you not to be young. I warn you not to fall ill. I warn you not to get old.

Speech at Bridgend, 7 June 1983, publ. in *The Penguin Book of Twentieth-Century Speeches* (ed. Brian MacArthur, 1999). The eve-of-election speech made a strong impact, contributing to Kinnock's election as Labour leader four months later.

2 [On nuclear disarmament] I would die for my country, but I could never let my country die for me.

Speech to Labour Party Conference, 30 September 1986, quoted in the *Guardian* 1 October 1986

3 The enemy of idealism is zealotry.

Quoted in the *Observer* 27 December 1987

# Michael Kinsley (b. 1951)

US JOURNALIST

He has been Editor of the *New Republic* and *Harper's Magazine*, and Managing Editor of the *Washington Monthly*. For many years he wrote the 'TRB from Washington' column in the *New Republic*, and he also contributes to the *Wall Street Journal* and *Time* magazine.

1 [On George Bush] He's nice enough not to want to be associated with a nasty remark but not nice enough not to make it. Lacking the courage of one's nastiness does not make one nice.

*Time* magazine 16 July 1990

2 A gaffe is when a politician tells the truth.

*Guardian* 14 January 1992

# Rudyard Kipling (1865–1936)

BRITISH AUTHOR AND POET

He worked as a journalist in India (1882–9), where he set his *Plain Tales from the Hills* (1888), the earliest of his stories dealing with the India of the Raj. *The Jungle Book* (1894) and *Just So Stories* (1902) were written for children, and his popular poetry reflected the concerns of the common man. He was awarded the Nobel Prize for Literature in 1907. T.S. ELIOT referred to him as a 'laureate without laurels'.

1 Power without responsibility – the prerogative of the harlot throughout the ages.

Quoted in *The Kipling Journal* December 1971, repr. in *Kipling: Interviews and Recollections* (ed. Harold Orel, 1983). The remark had been quoted at a dinner by Arthur Windham Baldwin, son of STANLEY BALDWIN, having been apparently made originally c. 1917 in reply to Max Aitken (Lord Beaverbrook), who had said to Kipling, regarding his recent acquisition of the *Daily Express*: 'What I want is power. Kiss 'em one day and kick 'em the next.' The words were borrowed (with Kipling's permission) by his cousin Stanley Baldwin in a speech, 17 March 1931, attacking press barons Lord Beaverbrook and Lord Rothermere, whose newspapers he described as 'engines of propaganda'.

2 If any question why we died,
Tell them, because our fathers lied.

'Common Form', publ. in *The Years Between* (1919)

3 Words are, of course, the most powerful drug used by mankind.

Speech 14 February 1923, quoted in *The Times* 15 February 1923

4 For the female of the species is more deadly than the male.

'The Female of the Species', publ. in *Rudyard Kipling's Verse* (1927)

5 A people always ends by resembling its shadow.

Quoted in *The Art of Writing*, 'The Writer's Craft', sect. 2 (1960) by André Maurois. Said c. 1930 to the author and critic ANDRÉ MAUROIS, on the subject of the transformation of Germany.

## Jeane Kirkpatrick (b. 1926)
US PUBLIC OFFICIAL AND DIPLOMAT

She joined the REAGAN cabinet as Ambassador to the United Nations (1981–5), when she became known for her forthright promotion of US interests. Her writings include *Political Women* (1974) and *Dismantling the Parties* (1978).

1 Vietnam presumably taught us that the United States could not serve as the world's policeman; it should also have taught us the dangers of trying to be the world's midwife to democracy when the birth is scheduled to take place under conditions of guerrilla war.

'Dictatorship and Double Standards', publ. in *Commentary* November 1979

## Henry Kissinger (b. 1923)
GERMAN-BORN US POLITICIAN AND DIPLOMAT

Considered the second most powerful member of the NIXON administration, he served as National Security Adviser (1968–73) during which time he improved both Sino and Soviet relations, and as Secretary of State (1973–7), when his 'shuttle diplomacy' was crucial in Arab–Israeli peace negotiations. For his efforts in resolving the Vietnam War he was jointly awarded the Nobel Peace Prize (1973). TOM LEHRER commented: 'Satire died the day they gave Henry Kissinger the Nobel Peace Prize. There were no jokes left after that.'

1 [On the Vietnam War] The conventional army loses if it does not win. The guerrilla wins if he does not lose.

*Foreign Affairs* January 1969

2 There can't be a crisis next week. My schedule is already full.

*The New York Times Magazine* 1 June 1969

3 Intelligence is not all that important in the exercise of power, and often actually doesn't help ... A fellow who does my job doesn't need to be too intelligent.

Interview, publ. in *Interview with History* (1970) by ORIANA FALLACI

4 [Explaining his popularity] I've always acted alone. Americans like that enormously. Americans like the cowboy who leads the wagon train by riding ahead alone on his horse, the cowboy who rides all alone into the town, the village, with his horse and nothing else. Maybe even without a pistol, since he doesn't shoot. He acts, that's all, by being in the right place at the right time.

ibid.

5 We are all the President's men.

Said in 1970, after the invasion of Cambodia, quoted in the *Sunday Times* 4 May 1975. Kissinger's statement inspired the title of the book by *Washington Post* reporters CARL BERNSTEIN and Bob Woodward, *All the President's Men* (1974, filmed 1976), describing their investigation into the Watergate break-in.

6 Power is the great aphrodisiac.

Quoted in *The New York Times* 19 January 1971

7 Even a paranoid can have enemies.

Quoted in *Time* magazine 24 January 1977

8 Some of the critics viewed Vietnam as a morality play in which the wicked must be punished before the final curtain and where any attempt to salvage self-respect from the outcome compounded the wrong. I viewed it as a genuine tragedy. No one had a monopoly on anguish.

*The White House Years*, ch. 8 (1979)

9 We cannot always assure the future of our friends; we have a better chance of assuring our future if we remember who our friends are.

ibid. ch. 29. Referring to the changing US policy towards the Shah of Iran.

10 The superpowers often behave like two heavily-armed blind men feeling their way around a room, each believing himself in mortal peril from the other, whom he assumes to have perfect vision.

Quoted in the *Observer* 30 September 1979

11 Most foreign policies that history has marked highly, in whatever country, have been originated by leaders who were opposed by experts ... It is, after all, the responsibility of the expert to operate the familiar and that of the leader to transcend it.

*Years of Upheaval*, ch. 10, 'The Foreign Service' (1982)

12 [On the downfall of RICHARD NIXON] To have striven so hard, to have molded a public personality out of so amorphous an identity, to have sustained that superhuman effort only to end with every weakness disclosed and every error compounding the downfall – that was a fate of biblical proportions. Evidently the Deity would not tolerate the presumption that all can be manipulated; an object lesson of the limits of human presumption was necessary.

ibid. ch. 25, 'The End of the Road'

13 Blessed are the people whose leaders can look destiny in the eye without flinching but also without attempting to play God.

ibid.

14 Moderation is a virtue only in those who are thought to have an alternative.

Quoted in the *Observer* 24 January 1982

15 I am being frank about myself in this book. I tell of my first mistake on page 850.

Quoted in the *Observer* 2 January 1983. Referring to the second volume of his memoirs, *Years of Upheaval*.

16 The American foreign policy trauma of the sixties and seventies was caused by applying valid principles to unsuitable conditions.

*Guardian* 16 December 1992. Arguing against a role for the USA as 'world policeman'.

17 Mr Clinton does not have the strength of character to be a war criminal.

*Independent* 16 January 1999

## Carolyn Kizer (b. 1925)
US POET

Her poems, which the poet D.J. Enright has called 'thick with catastrophes and fortitude', use often grotesque imagery to explore feminist themes, sometimes showing an Eastern influence. Her collection *Yin* (1984) received a Pulitzer Prize; others include *The Ungrateful Garden* (1961) and *Midnight Was My City* (1971).

1 Our masks, always in peril of smearing or cracking,
In need of continuous check in the mirror or silverware,
Keep us in thrall to ourselves, concerned with our
	surfaces.

'Pro Femina', publ. in *Knock Upon Silence* (1965)

## Paul Klee (1879–1940)
SWISS ARTIST

One of the most influential and prolific artists of the twentieth century, he joined the Expressionist group *Der Blaue Reiter* (1911–12) and taught at the Bauhaus (1920–31). His freely expressive, inventive and colourful paintings, such as 'Twittering Machine' (1922), suggest a childlike innocence, although the critic Cyril

Asquith deemed them to resemble 'not pictures, but a sample book of patterns of linoleum'.

1 Colour possesses me. I don't have to pursue it. It will possess me always, I know it. That is the meaning of this happy hour: Colour and I are one. I am a painter.
Journal entry, written in Tunisia, 16 April 1914, publ. in *The Diaries of Paul Klee 1898–1918*, no. 926 (1957, transl. 1965)

2 One eye sees, the other feels.
Journal entry 1914, publ. in ibid. no. 937

3 The more horrible this world ... the more abstract our art, whereas a happy world brings forth an art of the here and now.
Journal entry 1915, publ. in ibid. no. 951

4 Everything vanishes around me, and works are born as if out of the void. Ripe, graphic fruits fall off. My hand has become the obedient instrument of a remote will.
Journal entry January/February 1918, publ. in ibid. no. 1104

5 Art does not reproduce the visible; rather, it makes visible.
'Creative Credo', sect. 1, written 1918, publ. 1920, repr. in *The Inward Vision* (1957)

6 The creative impulse suddenly springs to life, like a flame, passes through the hand onto the canvas, where it spreads farther until, like the spark that closes an electric circuit, it returns to the source: the eye and the mind.
ibid. sect. 4

7 [On the role of the artist] Standing at his appointed place, the trunk of the tree, he does nothing other than gather and pass on what comes to him from the depths. He neither serves nor rules – he transmits. His position is humble. And the beauty at the crown is not his own. He is merely a channel.
*On Modern Art* (1924)

8 An active line on a walk, moving freely without a goal. A walk for a walk's sake.
*Pedagogical Sketchbook*, ch. 1 (1925). On his hieroglyphic drawing style.

# Joseph Klein

US AUTHOR

A journalist for three decades, including as Washington correspondent for the *New Yorker* and Senior Editor at *Newsweek*, he published *Woody Guthrie: A Life* (1980) and *Paybacks: Five Marines After Vietnam* (1984) before his anonymously published bestseller *Primary Colors* (1996), which he followed with *The Running Mate* (2000).

1 It was interesting how even mediocre politicians reflexively found their way to the elemental rules of the game – in this case: Never attack an opponent when he is in the process of killing himself.
*Primary Colors*, ch. 4 (1996)

2 [Of politicians] We tell them what they want to hear – and when we tell them something they *don't* want to hear, it's usually because we've calculated that's what they really want. We live an eternity of false smiles – and why? Because it's the price you pay to lead.
Jack Stanton, in ibid. ch. 9

# Richard Klein (b. 1941)

US AUTHOR

An academic at Johns Hopkins and Cornell universities in the USA and Director of Cornell University in Paris (1986–7), he has written on food and wine. His books include *Cigarettes Are Sublime* (1993) and *Eat Fat* (1996).

1 It is their uselessness that ensures the aesthetic appeal of cigarettes – the sublimely, darkly beautiful pleasure that cigarettes bring to the lives of smokers. It is a pleasure that is democratic, popular, and universal; it is a form of beauty that the world of high as well as popular culture has for more than a century recognized and explicitly celebrated, in prose and poetry, in images both still and moving.
*Cigarettes Are Sublime*, Introduction (1993)

2 Fat is beautiful, sexy, and strong. Politicians cultivate it, singers require it, gourmets appreciate it, and lovers play with it. *Fat* is a fabulous three-letter word.
*Eat Fat*, 'A Preface in Conclusion' (1996)

# Mark Knopfler (b. 1949)

BRITISH ROCK MUSICIAN

Lead singer, guitarist and songwriter with Dire Straits, one of the most successful bands of the 1980s, he came to notice for his fluid guitar style on 'Sultans of Swing', a single off the band's eponymous debut album (1978). They scored world-wide success with 1985's *Brothers in Arms*, but in 1990 Knopfler reverted to a lower key format with a new band, the Notting Hillbillies.

1 That ain't working, that's the way you do it
Get your money for nothing and chicks for free.
'Money For Nothing' (song, co-written with STING), on the album *Brothers in Arms* (1985)

2 My idea of heaven is a place where the Tyne meets the Delta, where folk music meets the blues.
Interview in *Mojo* April 1996

# Ronald Knox (1888–1957)

BRITISH SCHOLAR AND PRIEST

Anglican chaplain to Trinity College, Oxford University (1912–17), he converted to Roman Catholicism and became Catholic chaplain to the university (1926–39). He wrote an authorized translation of the Bible (1945–9), apologetics and detective novels, including *Still Dead* (1934) and *Let Dons Delight* (1939).

1 There was once a man who said, 'God
Must think it exceedingly odd
If he finds that this tree
Continues to be
When there's no one about in the Quad.'
Publ. in *The Complete Limerick Book* (1924) by Langford Reed. Knox's limerick was anonymously answered: 'Dear Sir, Your astonishment's odd:/I am always about in the Quad./And that's why the tree/Will continue to be,/Since observed by/Yours faithfully,/God.'

2 Only man has dignity; only man, therefore, can be funny.
*Essays In Satire*, Introduction (1928)

3 It is stupid of modern civilization to have given up believing in the devil, when he is the only explanation of it.
*Let Dons Delight*, ch. 8 (1939)

4 [On babies] A loud noise at one end and no sense of responsibility at the other.
Quoted by C. Blackmore in 1976 Reith lecture. RONALD REAGAN amended Knox's definition during his campaign for the governorship of California in 1965, describing government as 'an alimentary canal with a big appetite at one end and no responsibility at the other'.

# Ted Koehler (1894–1973)

US SONGWRITER

He wrote for such films as *Love Affair* (1939) and *My Wild Irish Rose* (1947), and in collaboration with Harold Arlen, Burton Lane and other composers had such hits as 'I Love a Parade' (1931) and 'Stormy Weather' (1933). In the 1930s and 1940s he produced floor shows for the Cotton Club and Broadway.

1 Don't know why
There's no sun up in the sky,

Stormy weather
Since my man and I ain't together
It keeps raining all the time.

'Stormy Weather' (song, 1933, music by Harold Arlen). Originally sung by Ethel Walters in *Cotton Club Review* (musical show, 1933), the song was later performed by Lena Horne in the film *Stormy Weather* (1943) and by Connee Boswell in the film *Swing Parade* (1946).

# Arthur Koestler (1905–83)

HUNGARIAN-BORN BRITISH AUTHOR

A journalist and one-time member of the Communist Party, he escaped to England in 1940 where he published his best known novel, *Darkness at Noon*, a fictional account of the Stalinist purges. He also wrote on the history of science, politics and parapsychology. A member of the Voluntary Euthanasia Society, he ended his life in a joint suicide pact with his wife.

1 The ultimate truth is penultimately always a falsehood. He who will be proved right in the end appears to be wrong and harmful before it.

Extract from Rubashov's diary, in *Darkness at Noon*, 'The Second Hearing' (1940)

2 Politics can be relatively fair in the breathing spaces of history; at its critical turning points there is no other rule possible than the old one, that the end justifies the means.

Extract from Rubashov's diary, in ibid.

3 [On the teaching of the Party] The definition of the individual was: a multitude of one million divided by one million.

ibid. 'The Grammatical Fiction'

4 Space-ships and time machines are no escape from the human condition. Let Othello subject Desdemona to a lie-detector test; his jealousy will still blind him to the evidence. Let Oedipus triumph over gravity; he won't triumph over his fate.

'The Boredom of Fantasy', first publ. 1953, repr. in *The Trail of the Dinosaur*, pt 2 (1955)

5 One question that people always ask at home is never asked here: 'What happened to Communism in Russia?' Everybody yawns when a visitor brings it up, because the answer is so obvious to every Russian. The answer is that there never was Communism in Russia; there were only Communists.

'The Shadow of a Tree', first publ. 1953, repr. in ibid. Koestler went on: 'The régime did not want Communists; it wanted robots. It will take at least a generation to change them back into humans again.'

6 If conquerors be regarded as the engine-drivers of History, then the conquerors of thought are perhaps the pointsmen who, less conspicuous to the traveller's eye, determine the direction of the journey.

*The Sleepwalkers*, pt 1, ch. 2, sect. 4 (1959)

7 Nobody before the Pythagoreans had thought that mathematical relations held the secret of the universe. Twenty-five centuries later, Europe is still blessed and cursed with their heritage. To non-European civilizations, the idea that numbers are the key to both wisdom and power, seems never to have occurred.

ibid.

8 True creativity often starts where language ends.

*The Act of Creation*, bk 1, pt 2, ch. 7 (1964)

9 The moment of truth, the sudden emergence of a new insight, is an act of intuition. Such intuitions give the appearance of miraculous flashes, or short-circuits of reasoning. In fact they may be likened to an immersed chain, of which only the beginning and the end are visible above the surface of consciousness. The diver vanishes at one end of the chain and comes up at the other end, guided by invisible links.

ibid. ch. 8

10 God seems to have left the receiver off the hook, and time is running out.

*The Ghost in the Machine*, ch. 18 (1967)

11 [On the first manned moon-landing] Prometheus is reaching out for the stars with an empty grin on his face.

*The New York Times* 21 July 1969

12 The most persistent sound which reverberates through man's history is the beating of war drums.

*Janus: A Summing Up*, 'Prologue: The New Calendar', sect. 1 (1978)

# Helmut Kohl (b. 1930)

GERMAN POLITICIAN

The longest serving post-war German leader, he became Chairman of the Christian Democratic Party from 1973 and was Chancellor of West Germany (1982–90), and presided over the reunification of East and West Germany to become Chancellor of a united Germany (1990–98). After his electoral defeat by Gerhard Schroeder, his reputation was damaged by his refusal to reveal the source of party donations.

1 Everybody should know that Germany will not go it alone: there will be no restless Reich.

*International Herald Tribune* 3 October 1990

2 I doubt that the evil spirits of the past, under which we in Europe have already suffered more than enough this century, have been banished for ever.

*Independent* 28 October 1992

# Barbara Kolb (b. 1939)

US COMPOSER

Her music has been called a fusion of Debussy with jazz. Her best known piece is *Soundings* (1971–2), and later works, such as *Umbrian Colors* (1986) and *Millefoglie* (1987), take their inspiration from the visual arts.

1 Composing a piece of music is very feminine. It is sensitive, emotional, contemplative. By comparison, doing housework is positively masculine.

Quoted in *Time* magazine 10 November 1975

# Käthe Kollwitz (1867–1945)

GERMAN ARTIST

Her bold and powerful lithographs, such as *Death* (1934–6), etchings, for instance *The Peasants' War* series (1902–1908), and woodcuts focus on victims of poverty, inhumanity and war and were a vehicle for her radical and pacifist sympathies. She has been described as the last great German Expressionist, although her antecedents were nineteenth-century.

1 Where do all the women who have watched so carefully over the lives of their beloved ones get the heroism to send them to face the cannon?

Journal entry, 27 August 1914, publ. in *Diaries and Letters* (ed. Hans Kollwitz, 1955)

2 Bisexuality is almost a necessary factor in artistic production; at any rate, the tinge of masculinity within me helped me in my work.

Journal entry, 1942, publ. in ibid.

# George Konrád (b. 1933)

HUNGARIAN AUTHOR

His first novel, *The Case Worker* (1969), which drew on his experience as a social worker, was followed by *The City Builder* (1977), a series of dreams, reminiscences and invective. Believing that his duty as a writer was to remain in Hungary, he was briefly imprisoned in 1974 for subversive agitation.

1 Many people feel empty, a world that seemed so strong just collapsed. Forty years have been wasted on stupid strife for the sake of an unsuccessful experiment. The values gathered together have vanished, the strategies for survival have become ridiculous. And so forty years of our lives have become a story, a bad anecdote. But it may be possible to remember these adventures with a kind of irony.

*Sunday Correspondent* 15 April 1990. Referring to the collapse of Soviet power in Eastern Europe.

2 You take a number of small steps which you believe are right, thinking maybe tomorrow somebody will treat this as a dangerous provocation. And then you wait. If there is no reaction, you take another step: courage is only an accumulation of small steps.

ibid. On surviving as a writer in communist Hungary.

## Lawrence Korb (b. 1939)

US POLITICIAN

He has written on national security policy in such books as *The Price of Preparedness* (1977) and *The Fall and the Rise of the Pentagon* (1979).

1 If Kuwait grew carrots we wouldn't give a damn.

*International Herald Tribune* 21 August 1990. On the motives for 'Operation Desert Storm' against Iraq.

## Wladyslaw Kozdra (1920–86)

POLISH COMMUNIST PARTY OFFICIAL

1 The trumpets of the Beatles are not the trumpets of Jericho which will cause the walls of socialism to come tumbling down.

Speech at Eighth Plenary Session of the Central Committee of the Polish Communist Party, 16–17 May 1967, quoted in *Rock Around the Bloc*, ch. 6 (1990) by Timothy Ryback

## Larry Kramer (b. 1935)

US PLAYWRIGHT AND NOVELIST

In 1969 he produced and scripted Ken Russell's film *Women in Love*, but he became better known for his writings on the gay scene in New York. His play *The Normal Heart* (1985) was an angry indictment of the growth of, and responses to, AIDS.

1 We're all going to go crazy, living this epidemic every minute, while the rest of the world goes on out there, all around us, as if nothing is happening, going on with their own lives and not knowing what it's like, what we're going through. We're living through war, but where they're living it's peacetime, and we're all in the same country.

Ned, in *The Normal Heart*, act 2, sc. 11 (1985)

2 The only way we'll have real pride is when we demand recognition of a culture that isn't just sexual. It's all there – all through history we've been there; but we have to claim it, and identify who was in it, and articulate what's in our minds and hearts and all our creative contributions to this earth. And until we do that, and until we organize ourselves block by neighborhood by city by state into a united visible community that fights back, we're doomed.

Ned, in ibid. act 2, sc. 13

## Karl Kraus (1874–1936)

AUSTRIAN SATIRIST

One of Austria's greatest satirists, he edited his own satirical journal, *Die Fackel* (1899–1936), waging a one-man war against all forms of

corruption. He was particularly scathing about the liberal press and the bourgeoirie, which he also attacked in his poetry and plays.

1 In these great times which I knew when they were this small; which will become small again, provided they have time left for it; and which, because in the realm of organic growth, no such transformation is possible, we had better call fat times and, truly hard times as well; in these times in which things are happening that could not be imagined and in which what can no longer be *imagined* must *happen*, for if one could imagine it, it would not happen; in these serious times which have died laughing at the thought that they might become serious; which, surprised by their own tragedy, are reaching for diversion and, catching themselves redhanded, are groping for words; in these loud times which boom with the horrible symphony of actions which produce reports and of reports which cause actions: in these times you should not expect any words of my own from me – none but these words which barely manage to prevent silence from being misinterpreted.

'In These Great Times', speech in Vienna, 19 November 1914, first publ. in *Die Fackel* December 1914, repr. in *In These Great Times: A Karl Kraus Reader* (ed. Harry Zohn, 1976)

2 Culture is the tacit agreement to let the means of subsistence disappear behind the purpose of existence. Civilization is the subordination of the latter to the former.

ibid.

3 If one reads a newspaper only for information, one does not learn the truth, not even the truth about the paper. The truth is that the newspaper is not a statement of contents but the contents themselves; and more than that, it is an instigator.

ibid.

4 [On war correspondents] The heroes of obtrusiveness, people with whom no soldier would lie down in the trenches, though he has to submit to being interviewed by them, break into recently abandoned royal castles so that they can report, 'We got there first!' It would be far less shameful to be paid for committing atrocities than for fabricating them . . . If the reporter has killed our imagination with his truth, he threatens our life with his lies.

ibid.

5 The esthete stands in the same relation to beauty as the pornographer stands to love, and the politician stands to life.

*Die Fackel* 5 October 1915, repr. in *Anti-Freud: Karl Kraus's Criticism of Psychoanalysis and Psychiatry* ch. 8 (1976) by Thomas Szasz

6 News reports stand up as people, and people wither into editorials. Clichés walk around on two legs while men are having theirs shot off.

Grumbler, in Prologue (1917) to *The Last Days of Mankind* (1919), repr. in *In These Great Times: A Karl Kraus Reader* (ed. Harry Zohn, 1976)

7 My unconscious knows more about the consciousness of the psychologist than his consciousness knows about my unconscious.

*Die Fackel* 18 January 1917, repr. in *Anti-Freud: Karl Kraus's Criticism of Psychoanalysis and Psychiatry*, ch. 6 (1976) by Thomas Szasz

8 War: first, one hopes to win; then one expects the enemy to lose; then, one is satisfied that he too is suffering; in the end, one is surprised that everyone has lost.

*Die Fackel* 9 October 1917, repr. in ibid. ch. 8

## Jiddu Krishnamurti (1895–1986)

INDIAN MYSTIC

Hailed as a 'world teacher' and messiah by the Theosophical Society's President Annie Besant in 1925, he renounced any grandiose claims and began a career advocating spiritual freedom without the need of organized religion. He set up the Krishnamurti Foundation for the dissemination of these ideas.

1 I maintain that Truth is a pathless land, and you cannot approach it by any path whatsoever, by any religion, by any sect.

Speech in Holland, 3 August 1929, quoted in *Krishnamurti*, ch. 2 (1931) by Lilly Heber

## Kris Kristofferson (b. 1936)
US SINGER, SONGWRITER AND ACTOR

Encouraged by JOHNNY CASH to devote himself full-time to song-writing, he made his name with two songs, 'Me and Bobby McGhee' (1969) and 'Help Me Make It Through the Night' (1971), going on to record a number of country albums. His acting career began with the film *Cisco Pike* (1971), and he also starred in *Pat Garrett and Billy the Kid* (1973) and *A Star Is Born* (1975). He was married to singer Rita Coolidge for six years.

1 Freedom's just another word for nothing left to lose.

'Me and Bobby McGhee' (song, 1969, written with Fred Foster). The song, first recorded by Roger Miller in 1969, was a posthumous hit for JANIS JOPLIN in 1971 and the title track of a Kristofferson album later that year.

## Arthur Kroker (b. 1945),
## Marilouise Kroker and
## David Cook (b. 1946)
CANADIAN SOCIOLOGISTS

Arthur and Marilouise Kroker have edited studies of *fin-de-millennium* theory, culture and politics such as *Body Invaders* (1988) and *Hysterical Male* (1991). Together they wrote *The Postmodern Scene* (1986) and, with David Cook, an academic at the University of Toronto, *Panic Encyclopedia* (1989).

1 The future of America may or may not bring forth a black President, a woman President, a Jewish President, but it most certainly always will have a suburban President. A President whose senses have been defined by the suburbs, where lakes and public baths mutate into back yards and freeways, where walking means driving, where talking means telephoning, where watching means TV, and where living means real, imitation life.

*Panic Encyclopedia*, 'Panic Suburbs' (1989)

## Louis Kronenberger (1904–80)
US CRITIC, EDITOR AND AUTHOR

He is best known for his biographies of the Duchess of Marlborough (1958) and of Oscar Wilde (1976) and has also written sophisticated novels such as *A Month of Sundays* (1961) and essays on English and American history and culture, for example *The Thread of Laughter* (1952).

1 The trouble with our age is that it is all signpost and no destination.

*Company Manners*, 'The Spirit of the Age' (1954)

## Joseph Wood Krutch (1893–1970)
US AUTHOR AND CRITIC

'Maybe the most I can claim,' he wrote, 'is that I know more about botany than any other New York critic, and more about the theatre than any other botanist.' He published critical studies and biographies while drama critic for *The Nation* (1924–52), then moved to Arizona where he also wrote on natural history. His essays are collected in *The Modern Temper* (1929) and *The Measure of Man* (1954).

1 Cats seem to go on the principle that it never does any harm to ask for what you want.

*Twelve Seasons*, February (1949)

2 The most serious charge which can be brought against New England is not Puritanism but February.

ibid.

## Elisabeth Kübler-Ross (b. 1926)
SWISS-BORN US PSYCHIATRIST

She was instrumental in highlighting the psychological needs of terminally ill patients and the duty to make death a dignified experience. Her ideas are expressed in *On Death and Dying* (1969) and *Death: The Final Stage* (1974).

1 Guilt is perhaps the most painful companion of death.

*On Death and Dying*, ch. 9 (1969)

## Stanley Kubrick (1928–99)
US FILM-MAKER

Famed for his meticulous procedures and ambitious technique, he showed his skill in a wide range of genres from science fiction (*2001: A Space Odyssey*, 1968) to youth violence (*A Clockwork Orange*, 1971) and horror (*The Shining*, 1979). He spent the last part of his life as a semi-recluse in England. See also STERLING HAYDEN 1, 2, GEORGE C. SCOTT 1.

1 The great nations have always acted like gangsters, and the small nations like prostitutes.

*Guardian* 5 June 1963

2 Confront a man in his office with a nuclear alarm, and you have a documentary. If the news reaches him in his living room, you have a drama. If it catches him in the lavatory, the result is comedy.

Quoted in *Stanley Kubrick Directs* (1972) by Alexander Walker. Discussing comic method in his film *Dr. Strangelove* (1964).

3 Ghost stories appeal to our craving for immortality. If you can be afraid of a ghost, then you have to believe that a ghost may exist. And if a ghost exists then oblivion might not be the end.

*Newsweek* 26 May 1980. Referring to his film *The Shining*.

4 Somebody has said that man is the missing link between primitive apes and civilized human beings. You might say that the idea is inherent in *2001*. We are semi-civilized, capable of cooperation and affection, but needing some sort of transfiguration into a higher form of life.

Quoted in *Stanley Kubrick: A Film Odyssey* (1975) by Gene D. Phillips.

## Milan Kundera (b. 1929)
CZECH-BORN FRENCH AUTHOR AND CRITIC

The writer EDMUND WHITE summed him up 'currently the favored spokesman for the uneasy conscience of the French intellectual'. He moved to France in 1975 after being banned in his home country. His novels blend fact with fiction, philosophy and politics and include *The Joke* (1967) and *The Unbearable Lightness of Being* (1984, filmed 1988).

1 Optimism is the opium of the people.

*The Joke*, pt 3, ch. 3 (1967, transl.1982). The line, written by Ludvik on a postcard, was used by the Party as incriminating evidence against him, though it was only meant as 'a joke'.

2 No great movement designed to change the world can bear to be laughed at or belittled. Mockery is a rust that corrodes all it touches.

Kostka, in ibid. pt 6, ch. 18

3 The struggle of man against power is the struggle of memory against forgetting.

Mirek, in *The Book of Laughter and Forgetting*, pt 1, sect. 2 (1978)

4 The reason we write books is that our kids don't give a damn. We turn to an anonymous world because our wife stops up her ears when we talk to her.

ibid. pt 4, sect. 9

5 There is nothing heavier than compassion. Not even one's own pain weighs so heavy as the pain one feels with someone, for someone, a pain intensified by the imagination and prolonged by a hundred echoes.

*The Unbearable Lightness of Being*, pt 1 ch. 15 (1984)

6 Her [Sabina's] drama was a drama not of heaviness but of lightness. What fell to her lot was not the burden but the unbearable lightness of being.

ibid. pt 3, ch. 10

7 No matter how much we scorn it, kitsch is an integral part of the human condition.

ibid. pt 6, ch. 12

8 Mankind's true moral test, its fundamental test (which lies deeply buried from view), consists of its attitude towards those who are at its mercy: animals.

ibid. pt 7 ch. 2

9 A novel that does not uncover a hitherto unknown segment of existence is immoral. Knowledge is the novel's only morality.

*The New York Review of Books* 19 July 1984

10 For a novelist, a given historic situation is an *anthropologic laboratory* in which he explores his basic question: *What is human existence?*

Postscript to 1986 edn of *Life Is Elsewhere* (first publ. 1973)

11 The light that radiates from the great novels time can never dim, for human existence is perpetually being forgotten by man and thus the novelists' discoveries, however old they may be, will never cease to astonish.

*Guardian* 3 June 1988

12 Without the meditative background that is criticism, works become isolated gestures, ahistorical accidents, soon forgotten.

'On Criticism, Aesthetics, and Europe', publ. in *Review of Contemporary Fiction* summer 1989

13 The serial number of a human specimen is the face, that accidental and unrepeatable combination of features. It reflects neither character nor soul, nor what we call the self. The face is only the serial number of a specimen.

*Immortality*, pt 1 ch. 3 (1991)

14 Hate traps us by binding us too tightly to our adversary.

ibid. ch. 5

15 Listening to a news broadcast is like smoking a cigarette and crushing the butt in the ashtray.

Paul, in ibid. pt 3, 'The Brilliant Ally of His Own Gravediggers'

16 War and culture, those are the two poles of Europe, her heaven and hell, her glory and shame, and they cannot be separated from one another. When one comes to an end, the other will end also and one cannot end without the other. The fact that no war has broken out in Europe for fifty years is connected in some mysterious way with the fact that for fifty years no new Picasso has appeared either.

ibid.

17 *I think, therefore I am* is the statement of an intellectual who underrates toothaches.

ibid. pt 4, ch. 11. Referring to the famous formula by Descartes.

18 All great novels, all true novels, are bisexual.

*The Times* 16 May 1991

## Akira Kurosawa (1910–98)

JAPANESE FILM-MAKER

He introduced Japanese cinema to the West with *Rashomon* (1950) and his samurai epics such as *The Seven Samurai* (1954) were the inspiration for Hollywood and spaghetti westerns. Known for his painstaking approach, he also made historical and literary adaptations, for example *Ran* (1985), based on *King Lear*.

1 We have survived again.

The samurai Kanbei to Shichiroji, after they have battled to save a village from a bandit attack, in *The Seven Samurai*, (film, 1954, screenplay by Shinobu Hashimoto, Hideo Oguni and Akira Kurosawa, directed by Akira Kurosawa)

2 [On his scientific ignorance] I am incapable of operating an ordinary still camera or even putting fluid in a cigarette lighter. My son tells me that when I use the telephone it's as if a chimpanzee were trying to place a call.

*Something Like an Autobiography*, 'The Goblin's Nose' (1982)

## Labour Party Constitution

1 To secure for the workers by hand or by brain the full fruits of their industry, and the most equitable distribution thereof that may be possible, upon the basis of the common ownership of the means of production, distribution, and exchange.

Clause 4, drafted in 1918 by SIDNEY WEBB and Arthur Henderson and revised in 1926. There were regular attempts to drop this commitment to nationalization, including by HUGH GAITSKELL after Labour's defeat in 1959, and ROY HATTERSLEY in 1993; it was finally rescinded by New Labour in 1995

## Christian Lacroix (b. 1951)
FRENCH FASHION DESIGNER

After working for Jean Patou from 1981, he opened his own couture and ready-to-wear business in 1987. He is known for his ornate creations, including the puffball skirt, low necklines and use of ethnic fabrics.

1 So much contemporary art and design is a parody, a joke, and full of allusions to the past. It's like that because it is the end of an era, like the end of the nineteenth century. Not such a comfortable period to live in. Everything must be a kind of caricature to register, everything must be larger than life.

Quoted in the *Sunday Times* October 1987, repr. in *Sultans of Style*, 'Christian Lacroix' (1990) by Georgina Howell

2 Haute Couture should be fun, foolish and almost unwearable.

Quoted in the *Observer* 27 December 1987

3 For me, elegance is not to pass unnoticed but to get to the very soul of what one is.

*International Herald Tribune* 21 January 1992

## Suzanne LaFollette (1893–1983)
US EDITOR AND AUTHOR

A journalist for forty years, she was a committed libertarian and feminist, advocating economic freedom for both sexes in such works as *Concerning Women* (1926). She became an ardent anticommunist during and after the Second World War and in 1955 founded, with William F. Buckley, the *National Review*, of which she remained Managing Editor until 1959. 'I haven't moved,' she commented. 'The world has moved to the left of me.'

1 There is nothing more innately human than the tendency to transmute what has become customary into what has been divinely ordained.

*Concerning Women*, 'The Beginnings of Emancipation' (1926)

2 Most people, no doubt, when they espouse human rights, make their own mental reservations about the proper application of the word 'human'.

ibid.

3 Laws are felt only when the individual comes into conflict with them.

ibid.

## Karl Lagerfeld (b. 1938)
GERMAN-BORN FRENCH FASHION DESIGNER

Design director for Chanel, he showed his first collection under his own label in 1984.

1 Only the minute and the future are interesting in fashion – it exists to be destroyed. If everybody did everything with respect, you'd go nowhere.

Quoted in *Vanity Fair* February 1992

## John Lahr (b. 1941)
US LITERARY AND DRAMA CRITIC

The son of vaudeville, Broadway and Hollywood actor Bert Lahr (the 'Cowardly Lion' in *The Wizard of Oz*), he made his own name with his shrewd biography of playwright JOE ORTON, *Prick Up Your Ears* (1978, filmed 1987). He is also known as a contributor to periodicals and writes the theatre column for *Village Voice*.

1 Society drives people crazy with lust and calls it advertising.
*Guardian* 2 August 1989

## R.D. Laing (1927–89)
BRITISH PSYCHIATRIST

Full name Ronald David Laing. Influenced by existentialism, he was the originator of the anti-psychiatry movement and made extensive studies of schizophrenia, believing it to spring from tensions within the nuclear family and to be unresponsive to conventional treatments. His ideas are expressed in his first book, *The Divided Self* (1959), and later in *The Politics of the Family* (1971).

1 Freud was a hero. He descended to the 'Underworld' and met there stark terrors. He carried with him his theory as a Medusa's head which turned these terrors to stone.
*The Divided Self*, pt 1, ch. 1 (1959)

2 Schizophrenia cannot be understood without understanding despair.
ibid. ch. 2

3 True guilt is guilt at the obligation one owes to oneself to be oneself. False guilt is guilt felt at not being what other people feel one ought to be or assume that one is.
*The Self and Others*, ch. 10 (1961)

4 We are all murderers and prostitutes – no matter to what culture, society, class, nation one belongs, no matter how normal, moral, or mature, one takes oneself to be.
*The Politics of Experience*, Introduction (1967)

5 Alienation as our present destiny is achieved only by outrageous violence perpetrated by human beings on human beings.
ibid.

6 From the moment of birth, when the stone-age baby confronts the twentieth-century mother, the baby is subjected to these forces of violence, called love, as its mother and father have been, and their parents and their parents before them. These forces are mainly concerned with destroying most of its potentialities. This enterprise is on the whole successful.
ibid. ch. 3

7 The brotherhood of man is evoked by particular men according to their circumstances. But it seldom extends to all men. In the name of our freedom and our brotherhood we are prepared to blow up the other half of mankind and to be blown up in our turn.
ibid. ch. 4

8 There is no such 'condition' as 'schizophrenia', but the label is a social fact and the social fact a *political event*.
ibid. ch. 5

9 The experience and behaviour that gets labelled schizophrenic is a special strategy that a person invents in order to live in an unliveable situation.
ibid.

10 Madness need not be all breakdown. It may also be breakthrough. It is potential liberation and renewal as well as enslavement and existential death.
ibid. ch. 6

## Constant Lambert (1905–51)
BRITISH COMPOSER

During his time as Musical Director of Sadler's Wells (1930–47) he was a major figure in establishing British ballet. He is best known for his jazz concert piece *Rio Grande* (1929), written for voices and orchestra.

1 To put it vulgarly, the whole trouble with a folk song is that once you have played it through there is nothing much you can do except play it over again and play it rather louder.
*Music Ho!*, ch. 3 (1934)

## George Lamming (b. 1927)
BARBADIAN AUTHOR

He was born and brought up in Carrington's Village, Barbados, the inspiration for his fictional village in his first novel, *In the Castle of My Skin* (1953), an account of emergence from a colonial ideology amid social and political unrest. Other works include the novels *Season of Adventure* (1960) and *Natives of My Person* (1972) and his essays, *The Pleasures of Exile* (1960).

1 No black boy wanted to be white, but it was also true that no black boy liked the idea of being black . . . When you asked Boy Blue why he was so black he would answer 'Just as I wus goin' to born the light went out'. The light had gone out for many of us.
Narrator (G), in *In the Castle of My Skin*, ch. 6 (1953)

## Norman Lamont (b. 1942)
BRITISH POLITICIAN

Baron Lamont of Lerwick. He was elected Conservative MP in 1972 and supported JOHN MAJOR's successful leadership campaign in 1990. Appointed Chancellor of the Exchequer, he drew much criticism when in 1992 he was forced to withdraw from the European Exchange Rate Mechanism and devalue the pound, despite previous assurances to the contrary. He later became a trenchant critic of Major's policies.

1 The green shoots of economic spring are appearing once again.
Speech at Conservative Party Conference, Blackpool, 9 October 1991, quoted in *The Times* 10 October 1991. The phrase is usually remembered as 'green shoots of economic recovery'.

2 We give the impression of being in office but not in power.
Resignation statement to House of Commons, 9 June 1993, publ. in *The Times* 10 June 1993. Lamont had been replaced as Chancellor of the Exchequer in a Cabinet reshuffle two weeks earlier.

## Giuseppe Tomasi di Lampedusa (1896–1957)
SICILIAN AUTHOR

In the last years of his life he wrote his only novel, *The Leopard* (1958, filmed 1963), the nostalgic but cynical tale of an aristocratic family in Sicily in the aftermath of Italy's unification, now regarded as a classic of modern Italian literature.

1 If we want everything to remain as it is, it will be necessary for everything to change.
Prince Tancredi, in *The Leopard*, ch. 1 (1958)

## Burt Lancaster (1913–94)
US SCREEN ACTOR

Full name Burton Stephen Lancaster. Adept in both tough-guy roles and parts requiring emotional sensitivity, he became established as a star from his first film, *The Killers* (1946). Subsequent films include *Elmer Gantry* (1960, Academy Award), *The Birdman of Alcatraz* (1962) and *The Leopard* (1963). 'Most people seem to think I'm the kind of guy who shaves with a blowtorch,' he once said. 'Actually I'm bookish and worrisome.'

1 **My right hand hasn't seen my left hand in thirty years.**

J.J. Hunsecker (Burt Lancaster), in *Sweet Smell of Success* (film, 1957, screenplay by Clifford Odets and Ernest Lehman, adapted from short story by Ernest Lehman, directed by Alexander Mackendrick)

## Elsa Lanchester (1902–86)
BRITISH-BORN US ACTRESS

Original name Elizabeth Sullivan. She performed on the stage and in film before moving to Hollywood in 1940. Among her films are *The Bride of Frankenstein* (1935) and *Witness for the Prosecution* (1957). She was married to the actor Charles Laughton.

1 **She looked as though butter wouldn't melt in her mouth – or anywhere else.**

Attributed. Referring to actress Maureen O'Hara.

## Martin Landau (b. 1931)
US SCREEN ACTOR

Formerly a cartoonist with the New York *Daily News*, he trained as an actor and found roles in television, including in *Mission Impossible* (1966–8), and as hoods in a variety of Hollywood films, including HITCHCOCK's *North by Northwest* (1959). In 1994 he memorably portrayed Bela Lugosi in Tim Burton's *Ed Wood*.

1 **Captains go down with their ships, not businessmen.**

Abe Karatz (Martin Landau), in *Tucker – the Man and His Dream* (film, 1988, screenplay by Arnold Schulman, directed by Francis Ford Coppola)

## Ann Landers (b. 1918)
US COLUMNIST

Original name Esther Pauline Lederer. She was a long-running agony aunt for the *Chicago Sun-Times*, trusted for her direct, 'sensible shoes' advice. Her precepts were published in *The Ann Landers Encyclopedia: Improve Your Life Emotionally, Medically, Sexually, Spiritually* (1978), among other titles.

1 **All married couples should learn the art of battle as they should learn the art of making love. Good battle is objective and honest – never vicious or cruel. Good battle is healthy and constructive, and brings to a marriage the principle of equal partnership.**

*Ann Landers Says Truth Is Stranger . . .*, ch. 11 (1968)

2 **At every party there are two kinds of people – those who want to go home and those who don't. The trouble is, they are usually married to each other.**

*International Herald Tribune* 19 June 1991

## Baron Lane (b. 1918)
BRITISH JUDGE

Baron Geoffrey Lane of St Ippollitts. He was made a QC in 1962 and served as Lord Justice of Appeal (1974–9) and Lord Chief Justice of England (1980–92).

1 **Loss of freedom seldom happens overnight. Oppression doesn't stand on the doorstep with toothbrush moustache and swastika armband – it creeps up insidiously . . . step by step, and all of a sudden the unfortunate citizen realizes that it is gone.**

Quoted in the *Independent* 3 February 1990. Referring to proposed legal reforms.

## Helmut Lang (b. 1956)
AUSTRIAN FASHION DESIGNER

Associated with an urban minimalist style, he designs clothes that are 'cool for grownups'. In 1998–9 he was the first designer to show

his collection on the internet, and in 1999 he joined forces with Prada.

1 **Fashion designers must give a social reflection of the things which are going on. Fashion is a kind of communication. It's a language without words. Fashion is about attitude, not hemlines.**

Interview in *i-D* December 1993

## Julia Lang (b. 1921)
BRITISH BROADCASTER

1 **Are you sitting comfortably? Then I'll begin.**

Introductory words to *Listen with Mother* (daily children's stories on BBC radio, 1950–82). She also used the words '. . . Then we'll begin'.

## Dorothea Lange (1895–1979)
US PHOTOGRAPHER

Her photographs of the homeless of San Francisco led to a commission in 1935 to document the migrant workers of the Depression, with the aim of bringing their plight to public attention. In collaboration with her husband, the economist Paul Taylor, she published a collection of these photographs, *An American Exodus: A Record of Human Erosion* (1939).

1 **The camera is an instrument that teaches people how to see without a camera.**

Quoted in the *Los Angeles Times* 13 August 1978

## Halvard Lange (1902–70)
NORWEGIAN HISTORIAN AND POLITICIAN

A Labour politician, he was Foreign Minister of Norway (1946–65) and as a founding father of NATO was responsible for Norway's entry into that organization.

1 **We do not regard Englishmen as foreigners. We look on them only as rather mad Norwegians.**

Quoted in the *Observer* 9 March 1957

## Susanne K. Langer (1895–1985)
US PHILOSOPHER

Full name Susan Knauth Langer. Influenced by the German philosopher Ernst Cassirer, she wrote on linguistic analysis and aesthetics, as in *Feeling and Form* (1953) and *Mind: An Essay on Human Feeling* (three volumes, 1967–82).

1 **Art is the objectification of feeling, and the subjectification of nature.**

*Mind, An Essay on Human Feeling*, vol. 1, pt 2, ch. 4 (1967)

## Lewis H. Lapham (b. 1935)
US ESSAYIST AND EDITOR

Full name Lewis Henry Lapham. Calling himself a 'novelist manqué and a historian manqué', he was made Editor of *Harper's Magazine* in 1975 and has commentated extensively on money, power and materialism in the USA, as in *Money and Class in America* (1988) and *The Agony of Mammon* (1999).

1 **Under the rules of a society that cannot distinguish between profit and profiteering, between money defined as necessity and money defined as luxury, murder is occasionally obligatory and always permissible.**

*Money and Class in America*, ch. 4 (1988)

2 **To the United States the Third World often takes the form of a black woman who has been made pregnant in a moment of passion and who shows up one day in the reception room on the forty-ninth floor threatening to**

make a scene. The lawyers pay the woman off, sometimes uniformed guards accompany her to the elevators.

ibid. ch. 5, sect. 1

3 I never can pass by the Metropolitan Museum of Art in New York without thinking of it not as a gallery of living portraits but as a cemetery of tax-deductible wealth.

ibid. ch. 9

4 The more prosperous and settled a nation, the more readily it tends to think of war as a regrettable accident; to nations less fortunate the chance of war presents itself as a possible bountiful friend.

*Harper's Magazine* March 1991

5 Thirty years ago it was 'the conservative establishment' that was at fault, a conspiracy largely composed of university professors, bureaucrats, and TV executives who couldn't play guitar and trembled at the sound of Dylan's harmonica. Now it is 'the liberal establishment' that is at fault, a conspiracy largely composed of university professors, bureaucrats, and TV executives who tremble before the wisdom of Arianna Huffington.

ibid. March 1996

## Frances Moore Lappé (b. 1944)
US ECOLOGIST AND AUTHOR

Her arguments for greater and more equitable control over food production and distribution to prevent world hunger are expressed in *Diet for a Small Planet* (1971) and *Food First: Beyond the Myth of Scarcity* (1977).

1 The act of putting into your mouth what the earth has grown is perhaps your most direct interaction with the earth.

*Diet For A Small Planet*, pt 1 (1971)

## Philip Larkin (1922–85)
BRITISH POET

A librarian all his life (at Hull from 1955), he achieved status as unofficial poet laureate as a melancholy, colloquial and stoic voice, preoccupied with transience and death at the cost of being, as he put it, a 'gloomy old sod'. The letters and writings published after his death also revealed intolerance and racism. His major poems are published in *The Less Deceived* (1955), *The Whitsun Weddings* (1964) and *High Windows* (1974). JOHN CAREY has commented: 'His attitude to most accredited sources of pleasure would make Scrooge seem unduly frolicsome.'

1 Poetry = heightened talking. Novel = heightened story. Painting = a heightened seeing.

Letter to J.B. Sutton, 23 May 1941, publ. in *Selected Letters of Philip Larkin 1940–1985* (ed. Anthony Thwaite, 1992)

2 I have just farted with the sound of an iron ruler twanging in a desk-lid and the smell of a west wind over a decaying patch of red cabbages.

ibid. 31 December 1941

3 I search myself for illusions like a monkey looking for fleas.

ibid. 13 July 1949

4 Most people, I'm convinced, don't think about life at all. They grab what they think they want and the subsequent consequences keep them busy in an endless chain till they're carried out feet first.

ibid. 30 October 1949

5 I am beginning to think of the creative imagination as a fruit machine on which victories are rare and separated by much vain expense, and represent a rare alignment of mental and spiritual qualities that normally are quite at odds.

Letter to Alan Pringle, 26 February 1950, publ. in ibid.

6 I have no ideas about poetry at all. For me, a poem is the crossroads of my thoughts, my feelings, my imaginings, my wishes, and my verbal sense: normally these run parallel; often two or more cross; but only when all cross at one point do you get a poem.

Letter to J.B. Sutton, 10 July 1951, publ. in ibid.

7 What are days for?
Days are where we live.
They come, they wake us
Time and time over.

'Days', written August 1953, publ. in *The Whitsun Weddings* (1964)

8 A serious house on serious earth it is,
In whose blent air all our compulsions meet,
Are recognized, and robed as destinies.

'Church Going', publ. in *The Less Deceived* (1955)

9 Why should I let the toad *work*
Squat on my life?
Can't I use my wit as a pitchfork
And drive the brute off?

'Toads', publ. in ibid.

10 Home is so sad. It stays as it was left,
Shaped to the comfort of the last to go
As if to win them back.

'Home is so Sad', written 1958, publ. in *The Whitsun Weddings* (1964)

11 The only way of getting shut of your family is to put your neck into the noose of another one. Such is nature's abhorrence of a vacuum.

Letter to Judy Egerton, 25 May 1958, publ. in *Selected Letters of Philip Larkin 1940–1985* (ed. Anthony Thwaite, 1992)

12 Life doesn't wait to be asked: it comes grinning in, sits down uninvited and helps itself to bread and cheese, and comments uninhibitedly on the decorations.

ibid.

13 Above all, though, children are linked to adults by the simple fact that they are in process of turning into them. For this they may be forgiven much. Children are bound to be inferior to adults, or there is no incentive to grow up.

'The Savage Seventh', essay, publ. in the *Spectator* 10 October 1959, repr. in *Required Writing* (1983)

14 Selflessness is like waiting in a hospital
In a badly-fitting suit on a cold wet morning.
Selfishness is like listening to good jazz
With drinks for further orders and a huge fire.

'None of the books have time', written 1960, publ. in *Collected Poems* (1988)

15 A poem is usually a highly professional artificial thing, a verbal device designed to reproduce a thought or emotion indefinitely: it shd have no dead parts, and every word should be completely unchangeable and unmoveable.

Letter to Pamela Kitson, 12 March 1965, publ. in *Selected Letters* (ed. Anthony Thwaite, 1992)

16 Marriage, well. I think of it as a marvellous thing for other people, like going to the stake.

ibid. Larkin had earlier written, in a letter dated 30 July 1950: 'There is no hell like marriage. The hell of loneliness, while still hell, is not so bad as the hell of marriage. And all for what, eh, you tell me that? . . . To put forward all one's self-control and resilience *just to go on living with someone* – by God!'

17 The trees are coming into leaf
Like something almost being said.

'The Trees', written 1967, publ. in *High Windows* (1974)

18 Sexual intercourse began
In nineteen sixty-three
(Which was rather late for me) –
Between the end of the *Chatterley* ban

And the Beatles' first LP.

'Annus Mirabilis', written 1967, publ. in ibid.

19 The hardness and the brightness and the plain
Far-reaching singleness of that wide stare

Is a reminder of the strength and pain
Of being young; that it can't come again,
But is for others undiminished somewhere.

'Sad Steps', written 1968, publ. in ibid.

20 They fuck you up, your mum and dad.
They may not mean to, but they do.
They fill you with the faults they had
And add some extra, just for you.

'This Be The Verse', written 1971, publ. in ibid. In a letter, 6 June 1982, Larkin complained of the notoriety of this poem, which 'will clearly be my "Lake Isle of Innisfree". I fully expect to hear it recited by a thousand Girl Guides before I die.'

21 Man hands on misery to man.
It deepens like a coastal shelf.
Get out as early as you can,
And don't have any kids yourself.

ibid

22 Quarterly, is it, money reproaches me:
'Why do you let me lie here wastefully?
I am all you never had of goods and sex.
You could get them still by writing a few cheques.'

'Money', publ. in ibid.

23 Perhaps being old is having lighted rooms
Inside your head, and people in them, acting.
People you know, yet can't quite name.

'The Old Fools', publ. in ibid.

24 Deprivation is for me what daffodils were for Wordsworth.

Interview in the *Observer* 1979, repr. in *Required Writing* (1983)

25 I see life more as an affair of solitude diversified by company than an affair of company diversified by solitude.

ibid.

26 One of the sadder things, I think,
Is how our birthdays slowly sink:
Presents and parties disappear,
The cards grow fewer year by year,
Till, when one reaches sixty-five,
How many care we're still alive?

'Dear CHARLES, My Muse, asleep or dead', written for the poet CHARLES CAUSLEY (1982), publ. in *Collected Poems* (1988)

27 The diatonic scale is what you use if you want to write a national anthem, or a love song, or a lullaby. The chromatic scale is what you use to give the effect of drinking a quinine martini and having an enema at the same time.

Interview in the *Paris Review* 1982, repr. in *Required Writing* (1983)

## Christopher Lasch (1932–94)

US HISTORIAN

*The Culture of Narcissism* (1977) is the best known of his powerful indictments of modern America as a consumer-oriented society, for which he proposed the remedy of a return to community values and the work ethic. Other books include *The Minimal Self* (1984).

1 A society that has made 'nostalgia' a marketable commodity on the cultural exchange quickly repudiates the suggestion that life in the past was in any important way better than life today.

*The Culture of Narcissism*, Preface (1977)

2 Today Americans are overcome not by the sense of endless possibility but by the banality of the social order they have erected against it.

ibid. ch. 1, 'The Therapeutic Sensibility'

3 Every age develops its own peculiar forms of pathology, which express in exaggerated form its underlying character structure.

ibid. ch. 2, 'Social Influences on Narcissism'

4 The job of the press is to encourage debate, not to supply the public with information.

'Journalism, Publicity, and the Lost Art of Political Argument', first publ. in the *Gannett Center Journal* Spring 1990, repr. in *Harper's Magazine* September 1990. According to Lasch: 'Information, usually seen as the precondition of debate, is better understood as its by-product.'

## Stan Laurel see OLIVER HARDY 1.

## Ralph Lauren (b. 1939)

US FASHION DESIGNER

Original name Ralph Lipschitz. His Polo range of menswear and linked women's and children's wear as well as home furnishings, evoke old money and country house elegance. STEPHEN BAYLEY remarked: 'His shops suggest that if you acquire style, you acquire meaning as well.'

1 People ask how can a Jewish kid from the Bronx do preppy clothes? Does it have to do with class and money? It has to do with dreams.

*International Herald Tribune* 7 April 1992

## James Laver (1899–1975)

BRITISH ART CRITIC AND AUTHOR

A keeper at London's Victoria and Albert Museum (1922–59), he wrote on art criticism, as in *French Painting and the 19th Century* (1937), but is chiefly known for his works on the history of fashion, such as *Taste and Fashion* (1937).

1

| The same costume will be | |
| --- | --- |
| Indecent | 10 years before its time |
| Shameless | 5 years before its time |
| *Outré* (daring) | 1 year before its time |
| Smart | |
| Dowdy | 1 year after its time |
| Hideous | 10 years after its time |
| Ridiculous | 20 years after its time |
| Amusing | 30 years after its time |
| Quaint | 50 years after its time |
| Charming | 70 years after its time |
| Romantic | 100 years after its time |
| Beautiful | 150 years after its time |

*Taste and Fashion*, ch. 18 (1937)

2 The erogenous zone is always shifting, and it is the business of fashion to pursue it, without ever catching it up.

Quoted in *New Society* 2 February 1984

## Denis Law (b. 1940)

BRITISH FOOTBALLER

Known as 'the King' to his fans, he was a consistent goal scorer, with lightning reflexes and a fiery temperament. After signing to Manchester City in 1960, he played for Manchester United (1962–73) before returning to City. He retired after the World Cup Finals in 1974.

1 The one thing that has never changed in the history of the game is the shape of the ball.

Quoted in the *Sunday Times* 18 December 1994

# D.H. Lawrence (1885–1930)

BRITISH AUTHOR

Although acclaimed for his novel *Sons and Lovers* (1913), he was forced abroad by hostile reaction to subsequent work such as *The Rainbow* (1915) and after 1919 lived principally in Italy and Mexico. He is remembered for the treatments of sexual relationships in *Women in Love* (1921) and *Lady Chatterley's Lover* (publ. in Italy in 1928, in Britain in 1960) and also for his collections of poetry, such as *Birds, Beasts and Flowers* (1923). He liked to write when he was feeling spiteful, he admitted, as it was like 'having a good sneeze'. See also ANGELA CARTER 8, GERMAINE GREER 19.

1 Primarily I am a passionately religious man, and my novels must be written from the depth of my religious experience.

Letter to writer and critic Edward Garnett, 22 April 1914, publ. in *The Letters of D.H. Lawrence*, vol. 2 (ed. George J. Zytaruk and James T. Boulton, 1981). 'I shall always be a priest of love,' Lawrence had earlier written (letter, 25 December 1912).

2 The source of all life and knowledge is in man and woman, and the source of all living is in the interchange and the meeting and mingling of these two: man-life and woman-life, man-knowledge and woman-knowledge, man-being and woman-being.

Letter, 2 June 1914, publ. in ibid.

3 I can only see death and more death, till we are black and swollen with death.

ibid. 2 June 1915

4 You must drop all your democracy. You must not believe in 'the people'. One class is no better than another. It must be a case of Wisdom, or Truth. Let the working classes *be* working classes. That is the truth. There must be an aristocracy of people who have wisdom, and there must be a Ruler: a Kaiser: no Presidents and democracies.

Letter to BERTRAND RUSSELL, c. 14 July 1915, publ. in ibid. 'The more I see of democracy the more I dislike it,' wrote Lawrence seven years later, while in Australia. 'It just brings everything down to the mere vulgar level of wages and prices, electric light and water closets, and nothing else' (letter, 13 June 1922).

5 The deadly Hydra now is the hydra of Equality. Liberty, Equality and Fraternity is the three-fanged serpent.

Letter to BERTRAND RUSSELL, 16 July 1915, publ. in ibid.

6 Not I, not I, but the wind that blows through me! A fine wind is blowing the new direction of Time.

'Song of a Man who has Come Through', publ. in *Look! We Have Come Through!* (1917)

7 Comes over one an absolute necessity to move. And what is more, to move in some particular direction. A double necessity then: to get on the move, and to know whither.

*Sea and Sardinia*, ch. 1 (1923). Opening words of book.

8 How beautiful maleness is, if it finds its right expression.

ibid. ch. 3

9 Never trust the artist. Trust the tale. The proper function of a critic is to save the tale from the artist who created it.

*Studies in Classic American Literature*, ch. 1 (1923)

10 Be still when you have nothing to say; when genuine passion moves you, say what you've got to say, and say it hot.

ibid. ch. 2

11 A snake came to my water-trough
On a hot, hot day, and I in pyjamas for the heat,
To drink there.

'Snake', publ. in *Birds, Beasts and Flowers* (1923). Opening lines of poem.

12 I can't bear art that you can walk round and admire. A book should be either a bandit or a rebel or a man in the crowd.

Letter, 22 January 1925, publ. in *The Letters of D.H. Lawrence*, vol. 5 (ed. James T. Boulton, 1987)

13 To the Puritan, all things are impure, as somebody says.

*Etruscan Places*, ch. 1 (written 1927, publ. 1932). Probably referring to St Paul's words in Titus 1:15: 'Unto the pure all things are pure.'

14 Museums, museums, museums, object-lessons rigged out to illustrate the unsound theories of archaeologists, crazy attempts to co-ordinate and get into a fixed order that which has no fixed order and will not be co-ordinated! It is sickening! Why must all experience be systematized?

ibid. ch. 6. Bemoaning the removal of excavated Etruscan tombs to the archaeological museum in Florence. 'A museum is not a first-hand contact,' continued Lawrence, 'it is an illustrated lecture. And what one wants is the actual vital touch.'

15 Ours is essentially a tragic age, so we refuse to take it tragically.

*Lady Chatterley's Lover*, ch. 1 (1928). Opening words of book.

16 John Thomas says good-night to lady Jane, a little droop-ingly, but with a hopeful heart.

ibid. Closing words of letter from Mellors to Connie Chatterley and last words of book. An expurgated version of the book that first appeared in 1932 was published in 1972 with the title *John Thomas and Lady Jane*.

17 My God, what a clumsy *olla putrida* James Joyce is! Nothing but old fags and cabbage-stumps of quotations from the Bible and the rest, stewed in the juice of delib-erate, journalistic dirty-mindedness.

Letter to Maria and ALDOUS HUXLEY, 15 August 1928, publ. in *The Letters of D.H. Lawrence*, vol. 6 (ed. James T. Boulton, Margaret H. Boulton and Gerald M. Lacy, 1991). *Olla putrida* is Latin for 'putrid pot' or incongruous mixture.

18 The upshot was, my paintings must burn
that English artists might finally learn.

'Innocent England', publ. in *Collected Poems*, vol. 2 (1964). Poem written on the suppression of an exhibition of his paintings in London, 1928, on grounds of obscenity.

19 How beastly the bourgeois is
especially the male of the species
– presentable, eminently presentable.

'How Beastly the Bourgeois Is', publ. in *Pansies* (1929)

20 I never saw a wild thing
Sorry for itself.
A small bird will drop frozen dead
From a bough
Without ever having felt sorry for itself.

'Self-Pity', publ. in ibid.

21 When I read Shakespeare I am struck with wonder
That such trivial people should muse and thunder
In such lovely language.

'When I Read Shakespeare', publ. in ibid.

22 If a woman hasn't got a tiny streak of a harlot in her, she's a dry stick as a rule.

*Pornography and Obscenity* (1930) repr. in *Phoenix: The Posthumous Papers of D.H. Lawrence*, pt 3 (ed. E McDonald, 1936)

23 Pornography is the attempt to insult sex, to do dirt on it.

ibid. Lawrence admitted, however, that the definition of por-nography varied according to the individual: 'What is pornography to one man is the laughter of genius to another.'

24 The one thing that it seems impossible to escape from, once the habit is formed, is masturbation. It goes on and on, on into old age, in spite of marriage or love affairs or anything else. And it always carries this secret feeling of futility and humiliation, futility and humiliation. And this is, perhaps, the deepest and most dangerous cancer of our civilization. Instead of being a comparatively pure and harmless vice, masturbation is certainly the most dangerous sexual vice that a society can be afflicted with, in the long run. Comparatively pure it may be – purity being what it is. But harmless!!!

ibid.

25 And if tonight my soul may find her peace
in sleep, and sink in good oblivion,
and in the morning wake like a new-opened flower
then I have been dipped again in God, and new-created.

'Shadows', publ. in *Last Poems* (1932)

## T.E. Lawrence (1888–1935)

BRITISH SOLDIER AND SCHOLAR

Full name Thomas Edward Lawrence and known as Lawrence of Arabia. Famous for leading a successful Arab revolt against the Turks in the First World War, he recorded his exploits in *The Seven Pillars of Wisdom* (1926). He changed his name to John Hume Ross in order to enter the RAF anonymously in 1922, and to T.E. Shaw in 1923 when he transferred to the Royal Tank Corps. He was killed in a motorcycle accident.

1 Often I wish I had known at the beginning the weary lag that any sudden reputation brings. I should have refrained from doing even the little that I did; and now I would be left alone and able to live as I chose. To have news value is to have a tin can tied to one's tail.

Letter, 1 April 1935, publ. in *The Letters of T.E. Lawrence* (ed. Malcolm Brown, 1988). Written a few weeks before his death.

## Nigel Lawson (b. 1932)

BRITISH POLITICIAN

Baron Lawson of Blaby. Before entering politics as a Conservative MP in 1974, he was a financial journalist, and Editor of the *Spectator* (1966–70). He was made Chancellor of the Exchequer in 1983, resigning in 1989 over criticism of his advocacy of lower interest rates and full British membership of the European monetary system.

1 To govern is to choose. To appear to be unable to choose is to appear to be unable to govern.

*Daily Mail* 26 March 1991

## Nigella Lawson (b. 1960)

BRITISH JOURNALIST AND BROADCASTER

A social commentator in newspapers, including *The Times*, she has also written *How To Eat* (1998) and *How To Be a Domestic Goddess* (2000). She is the daughter of NIGEL LAWSON and is married to the journalist John Diamond.

1 Pregnancy is the ultimate display of potency, just as potency, in another sense, is said to be the ultimate aphrodisiac. No wonder, then, that a private sexual act should be interpreted as the greatest public come on. Perhaps it's good to see that, even in politics, life insistently asserts itself.

*Observer* 21 November 1999. Commenting on the announcement of the pregnancy of Cherie Blair, wife of TONY BLAIR.

## Irving Layton (b. 1912)

CANADIAN POET

Original name Israel Lazarovitch. He is known as an outspoken and flamboyant character and for his verse, which includes both satirical digs against the bourgeoisie and explicitly erotic love poetry. Among his collections are *Here and Now* (1945), *A Red Carpet for the Sun* (1959) and *The Swinging Flesh* (1961).

1 If poetry is like an orgasm, an academic can be likened to someone who studies the passion-stains on the bedsheets.

*The Whole Bloody Bird*, 'Obs II' (1969)

2 In Pierre Elliot Trudeau, Canada has at last produced a political leader worthy of assassination.

ibid.

3 Conscience: self-esteem with a halo.

ibid. 'Aphs'

4 When you argue with your inferiors, you convince them of only one thing: they are as clever as you.

ibid.

5 Idealist: a cynic in the making.

ibid.

6 My neighbour
doesn't want to be loved
as much as
he wants to be envied.

ibid.

7 An aphorism
should be
like a burr:
sting,
stick,
and leave
a little soreness
afterwards.

ibid.

## John Le Carré (b. 1931)

BRITISH AUTHOR

Pen name of David John Moore Cornwell. He was a member of the Foreign Service (1960–64) before becoming a full-time writer of spy thrillers, complex explorations of the seedy side of espionage, which feature the self-effacing agent George Smiley. Works include *The Spy Who Came in from the Cold* (1963, filmed 1965), *Tinker, Tailor, Soldier, Spy* (1974) and *The Russia House* (1989, filmed 1991).

1 What do you think spies are: priests, saints and martyrs? They're a squalid procession of vain fools, traitors too, yes; pansies, sadists and drunkards, people who play cowboys and Indians to brighten their rotten lives.

Leamas, in *The Spy Who Came in from the Cold*, ch. 25 (1963)

2 It's easy to forget what intelligence consists of: luck and speculation. Here and there a windfall, here and there a scoop.

Leclerc, in *The Looking-Glass War*, pt 2, ch. 9 (1965)

3 A committee is an animal with four back legs.

Smiley (quoting Karla), in *Tinker, Tailor, Soldier, Spy*, pt 3, ch. 34 (1974)

4 For decades to come the spy world will continue to be the collective couch where the subconscious of each nation is confessed.

Quoted in the *Observer* 19 November 1989

5 It was *man* who ended the Cold War in case you didn't notice. It wasn't weaponry, or technology, or armies or campaigns. It was just *man*. Not even Western man either, as it happened, but our sworn enemy in the East, who went into the streets, faced the bullets and the batons and said: we've had enough. It was *their* emperor, not ours, who had the nerve to mount the rostrum and declare he had no clothes. And the ideologies trailed after these impossible events like condemned prisoners, as ideologies do when they've had their day . . . One day, history may tell us who really won.

Smiley, in *The Secret Pilgrim*, ch. 12 (1990)

6 You ask can we ever trust the Bear? . . . I will give you several answers at once. The first is no, we can never trust the Bear. For one reason, the Bear doesn't trust himself. The Bear is threatened and the Bear is frightened and the Bear is falling apart. The Bear is disgusted with his past, sick of his present and scared stiff of his future. He often was. The Bear is broke, lazy, volatile, incompetent, slip-

pery, dangerously proud, dangerously armed, sometimes brilliant, often ignorant. Without his claws, he'd be just another chaotic member of the Third World ... The second answer is yes, we can trust the Bear completely. The Bear has never been so trustworthy. The Bear is begging to be part of us, to submerge his problems in us, to have his own bank account with us, to shop in our High Street and be accepted as a dignified member of our forest as well as his ... The Bear needs us so desperately that we may safely trust him to need us.

Smiley, in ibid. ch. 12

7 I don't think it is given to any of us to be impertinent to great religions with impunity.

*International Herald Tribune* 23 May 1989. Referring to SALMAN RUSHDIE and his book *The Satanic Verses*, which was deemed to be offensive to Islam.

## Le Corbusier (1887–1965)

SWISS-BORN FRENCH ARCHITECT

Pseudonym of Charles-Édouard Jeanneret. One of the most influential of twentieth-century architects, he was a pioneer of the International Style, characterized by the use of steel and reinforced concrete, open-plan interiors and geometric forms. His theories are set out in *Towards a New Architecture* (1923) and *Le Modulor* (1948). His plans for multi-storey villas using the Modulor system were realized in the (now demolished) Unité d'habitation, Marseilles (1952)

1 A house is a machine for living in.
(*Une maison est une machine-à-habiter.*)
*Towards a New Architecture*, ch. 1, 'Eyes Which Do Not See: Airplanes' (1923, transl. 1946)

2 Our own epoch is determining, day by day, its own style. Our eyes, unhappily, are unable yet to discern it.
ibid. ch. 1, 'Eyes Which Do Not See'

3 A hundred times have I thought New York is a catastrophe ... it is a beautiful catastrophe.
Quoted in the *New York Herald Tribune* 6 August 1961

## Ursula Le Guin (b. 1929)

US AUTHOR

Her science fiction and fantasy novels propose alternative political and social versions of contemporary systems on earth, as in *The Left Hand of Darkness* (1969) and *The Dispossessed* (1974). For children she has written the allegorical 'Earthsea' trilogy (1968, 1971, 1972) and the overtly feminist *Tehanu* (1990).

1 When action grows unprofitable, gather information; when information grows unprofitable, sleep.
'Ekumenical' saying, in *The Left Hand of Darkness*, ch. 3 (1969)

2 It is a terrible thing, this kindness that human beings do not lose. Terrible, because when we are finally naked in the dark and cold, it is all we have. We who are so rich, so full of strength, we end up with that small change. We have nothing else to give.
Narrator (Estraven), in ibid. ch. 13

3 In so far as one denies what is, one is possessed by what is not, the compulsions, the fantasies, the terrors that flock to fill the void.
*The Lathe of Heaven*, ch. 10 (1971)

4 Let the athletes die young and laurel-crowned. Let the soldiers earn the Purple Hearts. Let women die old, white-crowned, with human hearts.
'The Space Crone', first publ. in *The Co-Evolution Quarterly* summer 1976, repr. in *Dancing at the Edge of the World* (1989)

5 The children of the revolution are always ungrateful, and the revolution must be grateful that it is so.
'Reciprocity of Prose and Poetry', address in Washington, D.C., 1983, publ. in *Dancing at the Edge of the World* (1989)

6 If science fiction is the mythology of modern technology, then its myth is tragic.
'The Carrier Bag Theory of Fiction', written 1986, first publ. in *Women of Vision* (ed. Denise M. Du Pont, 1988), repr. in ibid.

7 We are volcanoes. When we women offer our experience as our truth, as human truth, all the maps change. There are new mountains.
Bryn Mawr Commencement Address, 1986, publ. in ibid.

8 If you want your writing to be taken seriously, don't marry and have kids, and above all, don't die. But if you have to die, commit suicide. They approve of that.
'Prospects for Women in Writing', speech in Portland, Maine, September 1986, publ. in ibid.

9 My imagination makes me human and makes me a fool; it gives me all the world and exiles me from it.
'Winged: the Creatures on my Mind', publ. in *Harper's Magazine* August 1990

## Jean-Marie Le Pen (b. 1928)

FRENCH NATIONALIST POLITICIAN

A noted populist of extreme right-wing views, he formed the French National Front in 1972, which, with its policies in favour of capital punishment and the repatriation of immigrants, gained around 12 per cent of the national vote in the elections to the Assembly in 1986. He was elected to the European Parliament in 1984 and made unsuccessful bids for the presidency in 1988 and 1995.

1 [Of the Holocaust] I have not made a study of it, but believe that it is a minor point in the history of the war.
Quoted in the *Sunday Times* 27 December 1987

## Eda J. Le Shan (b. 1922)

US ACADEMIC AND AUTHOR

Her published work includes books of self-help and social commentary, including *How to Survive Parenthood* (1965), *Raising your Child without a Script* (1970) and *Learning to Say Goodbye* (1976).

1 In all our efforts to provide 'advantages' we have actually produced the busiest, most competitive, highly pressured and over-organized generation of youngsters in our history – and possibly the unhappiest. We seem hell-bent on eliminating much of childhood.
*The Conspiracy Against Childhood*, ch. 1 (1967)

## Bernard Leach (1887–1979)

BRITISH POTTER

For more than fifty years he was a leading figure of twentieth-century ceramics, aiming to combine functionality with beauty at an affordable price. After a period of study in Japan, he established his pottery in St Ives, Cornwall.

1 Do not pursue skills, technique will follow the idea. The idea will find technique, it is included in the real gift.
*The Potter's Challenge*, ch. 1 (1976)

2 The pot is the man: his virtues and his vices are shown therein – no disguise is possible.
ibid. ch. 4

## Stephen Leacock (1869–1944)

BRITISH-BORN CANADIAN HUMORIST AND ECONOMIST

J.B. PRIESTLEY said that he made a living 'by what he did in his spare time for fun', which was writing his humorous and satirical pieces, such as *Literary Lapses* (1910) and *Frenzied Fiction* (1917). He also published works on economics.

1 Advertising may be described as the science of arresting

the human intelligence long enough to get money from it.

*The Garden of Folly*, 'The Perfect Salesman' (1924)

2 Writing is simple: you just jot down amusing ideas as they occur to you. The jotting presents no problem; it is the occurring that is difficult.

Quoted by ROBERTSON DAVIES in *The Penguin Stephen Leacock*, Introduction (1981)

## Timothy Leary (1920–96)
US PSYCHOLOGIST

Known as the 'guru of psychedelic utopias', and called by RICHARD NIXON 'the most dangerous man in America', he was at the forefront of the debate over LSD. He was several times imprisoned for his proselytizing zeal on behalf of psychotropic drugs and in later life was an advocate of new technology and designed computer software. His last wish was to have his remains launched into space.

1 My advice to people today is as follows: If you take the game of life seriously, if you take your nervous system seriously, if you take your sense organs seriously, if you take the energy process seriously, you must turn on, tune in, and drop out.

Lecture, 1966, publ. in *The Politics of Ecstasy*, ch. 21 (1968). Thirty years later Leary suggested a variation of this slogan, 'Tune in, turn on, boot up', quoted in interview in the *Guardian* 2 December 1995.

2 I declare that the Beatles are mutants. Prototypes of evolutionary agents sent by God with a mysterious power to create a new species – a young race of laughing freemen . . . They are the wisest, holiest, most effective avatars the human race has ever produced.

Quoted in *Shout! The True Story of the Beatles*, pt 4, 'August 1967' (1981) by Philip Norman

3 I declare that World War III is now being waged by short-haired robots whose deliberate aim is to destroy the complex web of free wild life by the imposition of mechanical order.

*Manifesto* (1970) repr. in *Counterculture and Revolution* (ed. David Horowitz, Michael P. Lerner and Craig Pykes, 1972). Leary's *Manifesto* was written after escaping from prison and fleeing to Algeria.

4 Science is all metaphor.

Interview 24 September 1980, publ. in *Contemporary Authors*, vol. 107 (1983)

5 In the information age, you don't teach philosophy as they did after feudalism. You perform it. If Aristotle were alive today he'd have a talk show.

*Evening Standard* 8 February 1989

6 How you die is the most important thing you ever do. It's the exit, the final scene of the glorious epic of your life. It's the third act and, you know, everything builds up to the third act.

Interview in the *Guardian* 2 December 1995. Leary, who had been diagnosed as suffering with cancer in January 1995, intended to expire live on the internet, although this was not in the end carried out.

## William Least Heat-Moon (b. 1939)
US AUTHOR

Original name William Trogdon. Of mixed Native American blood, as a writer he has been compared with Mark Twain and Henry Thoreau. His books chronicle those parts of America 'where time and men and deeds connect': *Blue Highways* (1983), which charts his journey around the perimeter of the country by back roads, *PrairyErth* (1991), which focuses on Chase County, Kansas, and *River Horse* (1999), which describes a voyage by waterways from New York to Astoria.

1 Beware thoughts that come in the night. They aren't

turned properly; they come in askew, free of sense and restriction, deriving from the most remote of sources.

*Blue Highways: A Journey into America*, pt 1, ch. 1 (1983). Opening words.

2 To say nothing is out here is incorrect; to say the desert is stingy with everything except space and light, stone and earth is closer to the truth.

ibid. pt 4, ch. 8

3 Whoever the last true cowboy in America turns out to be, he's likely to be an Indian.

ibid. pt 5, ch. 2

## F.R. Leavis (1895–1978)
BRITISH LITERARY CRITIC

Full name Frank Raymond Leavis. He stressed high standards in English literature and criticism, attacked mass culture and championed George Eliot, JAMES JOYCE and D.H. LAWRENCE. With his wife, Q.D. Leavis, he founded and edited the quarterly *Scrutiny* (1932–53) and published, among others works, *The Great Tradition* (1948) and *The Common Pursuit* (1952).

1 [On Georgian poetry] The opposition to the Georgians was already at the time in question ( just after the war) Sitwellism. But the Sitwells belong to the history of publicity rather than of poetry.

*New Bearings in English Poetry*, ch. 2 (1932)

2 One of the supreme debts one great writer can owe another is the realization of unlikeness.

*The Great Tradition*, ch. 1 (1948)

3 I have, then, given my hostages. What I think and judge I have stated as responsibly and clearly as I can. Jane Austen, George Eliot, Henry James, Conrad, and D.H. Lawrence: the great tradition of the English novel is *there*.

ibid.

## Fran Lebowitz (b. 1951)
US JOURNALIST

EDMUND WHITE described her as 'for the eternal verities of sleep, civilized conversation and cigarette smoking'. Her satirical essays, tart and light-hearted in style, appear in the collections *Metropolitan Life* (1978) and *Social Studies* (1981).

1 All God's children are not beautiful. Most of God's children are, in fact, barely presentable.

*Metropolitan Life*, 'Manners' (1978)

2 There is no such thing as inner peace. There is only nervousness or death. Any attempt to prove otherwise constitutes unacceptable behavior.

ibid.

3 If you are of the opinion that the contemplation of suicide is sufficient evidence of a poetic nature, do not forget that actions speak louder than words.

ibid. 'Letters'

4 Being a woman is of special interest only to aspiring male transsexuals. To actual women it is merely a good excuse not to play football.

ibid.

5 Original thought is like original sin: both happened before you were born to people you could not have possibly met.

*Social Studies*, 'People' (1981)

6 The opposite of talking isn't listening. The opposite of talking is waiting.

ibid.

7 Do not, on a rainy day, ask your child what he feels like doing, because I assure you that what he feels like doing, you won't feel like watching.

ibid. 'Parental Guidance'

8 Remember that as a teenager you are at the last stage in your life when you will be happy to hear that the phone is for you.
ibid. 'Tips for Teens'

9 Stand firm in your refusal to remain conscious during algebra. In real life, I assure you, there is no such thing as algebra.
ibid.

10 To put it rather bluntly, I am not the type who wants to go back to the land; I am the type who wants to go back to the hotel.
ibid. 'Things'

11 If you are a dog and your owner suggests that you wear a sweater . . . suggest that he wear a tail.
ibid. 'Pointers for Pets'

## Huddie 'Leadbelly' Ledbetter (1889–1949)
US FOLK AND BLUES MUSICIAN

Of black and Cherokee Indian origins, he worked as a cotton-picker and labourer in Louisiana before receiving a thirty-year gaol sentence for murder in 1917. Pardoned in 1925, supposedly for his musical abilities, he served three more sentences, during one of which he was discovered by the father-and-son archivists John and Alan Lomax, who recorded him for a Library of Congress project and later launched him on the New York folk scene.

1 Look a here people, listen to me,
Don't try to find no home in Washington DC
Lord, it's a bourgeois town, it's a bourgeois town.
'Bourgeois Blues' (song, c. 1933, written with Alan Lomax) on the album *Easy Rider* (1962). The song was recorded in Louisiana State Prison by musicologist Alan Lomax, who helped to obtain Leadbelly's release in 1934.

2 Let the Midnight Special
Shine her light on me.
'Midnight Special' (song, traditional), recorded 1940, publ. in *Our Singing Country* (1941) by John A. and Alan Lomax. The song, which was already known as a southern prison song when Leadbelly recorded it, refers to a train running past the prison, whose headlight falling on an inmate was supposed to mean that he would go free.

## Gypsy Rose Lee (1914–70)
US STRIPTEASE ARTISTE

Originally named Rose Louise Hovick. Admired by artists and intellectuals, she was the most famous stripper of the 1930s and appeared in the *Ziegfeld Follies* (1936). She also published mystery novels, and her autobiography (1957) was adapted for the stage musical *Gypsy* (1959, filmed 1962). 'Royalties are all very well,' she once said, 'but shaking the beads brings in the money quicker.'

1 God is love, but get it in writing.
Attributed

## Harper Lee (b. 1926)
US AUTHOR

A descendant of Robert E. Lee, she won the Pulitzer Prize for her first and only novel *To Kill a Mockingbird* (1960, filmed 1962), a tale of racial injustice in the American south narrated by a six-year-old girl.

1 Until I feared I would lose it, I never loved to read. One does not love breathing.
Scout, in *To Kill a Mockingbird*, pt 1, ch. 2 (1960)

2 The one thing that doesn't abide by majority rule is a person's conscience.
Atticus Finch, in ibid. ch. 11

3 Folks don't like to have somebody around knowin' more than they do. It aggravates 'em. You're not gonna change any of them by talkin' right, they've got to want to learn themselves, and when they don't want to learn there's nothing you can do but keep your mouth shut or talk their language.
Calpurnia, in ibid. pt 2, ch. 12

4 I'm no idealist to believe firmly in the integrity of our courts and in the jury system – that is no ideal to me, it is a living, working reality. Gentlemen, a court is no better than each man of you sitting before me on this jury. A court is only as sound as its jury, and a jury is only as sound as the men who make it up.
Speech to the jury by Atticus Finch, in ibid. ch. 20

5 As you grow older, you'll see white men cheat black men every day of your life, but let me tell you something and don't you forget it – whenever a white man does that to a black man, no matter who he is, how rich he is, or how fine a family he comes from, that white man is trash.
Atticus Finch to his son Jem, in ibid. ch. 23

## Spike Lee (b. 1956)
US FILM-MAKER

Originally Shelton Jackson Lee. He has aroused controversy for his depictions of racial tensions in the inner city, such as *She's Gotta Have It* (1986) and *Do the Right Thing* (1989), while *Malcolm X* (1992) drew criticism for its alleged bias. On the burden of being a black film-maker, he remarked: 'There are so few black films that when you do one it has to represent every black person in the world.'

1 This [racism] is something that white America is going to have to work out themselves. If they decide they want to stop it, curtail it, or to do the right thing . . . then it will be done, but not until then.
Interview in *Roger Ebert's Home Movie Companion* (1990)

2 If we became students of Malcolm X, we would not have young black men out there killing each other like they're killing each other now. Young black men would not be impregnating young black women at the rate going on now. We'd not have the drugs we have now, or the alcoholism.
Interview in *i-D* January 1993. Lee's lengthy biopic, *Malcolm X* (1992), was described as 'a movie about the need for religion, or moral steadfastness'.

## Tommy Lee (b. 1962)
US ROCK MUSICIAN

Born Thomas Lee Bass. From 1981 he was drummer with the LA heavy metal band Mötley Crüe, whose mission statement was 'sex, drugs, pizza and more sex' and whose stage act included chainsawing mannequins and setting their trousers on fire. He achieved further fame for his showbiz relationship with wife Pamela Anderson.

1 You rip! Boom! Boom! Boom! Let's get together.
Chat-up line to *Bay Watch* star Pamela Anderson, whom he married five days later, quoted in *FHM* March 1996

## Henri Lefebvre (1901–91)
FRENCH PHILOSOPHER

He was artistic director of the French radio broadcasting company Radiodiffusion Français (1944–9) and also wrote widely on philosophy, notably on Marx, as in *The Sociology of Marx* (1966). Other publications include *Le Somme et le rest* (1959).

1 The most remarkable aspect of the transition we are living through is not so much the passage from want to affluence as the passage from labour to leisure . . . Leisure contains the future, it is the new horizon.
*Everyday Life in the Modern World* (1962) ch. 1, 'What Should the

New Society be Called?' Lefebvre continued, 'The prospect then is one of unremitting labour to bequeath to future generations a chance of founding a society of leisure that will overcome the demands and compulsions of productive labour so that time may be devoted to creative activities or simply to pleasure and happiness.'

## David Lehman (b. 1948)
US POET, EDITOR AND CRITIC

He was book critic for *Newsweek* and has published the poetry collections *Some Nerve* (1973) and *Day One* (1979), as well as a study of crime fiction, *The Perfect Murder* (1989).

1 Words can have no single fixed meaning. Like wayward electrons, they can spin away from their initial orbit and enter a wider magnetic field. No one owns them or has a proprietary right to dictate how they will be used.
*Signs of the Times*, ch. 1 (1991)

2 There is an air of last things, a brooding sense of impending annihilation, about so much deconstructive activity, in so many of its guises; it is not merely postmodernist but preapocalyptic.
ibid.

3 Obscurantism is the academic theorist's revenge on society for having consigned him or her to relative obscurity – a way of proclaiming one's superiority in the face of one's diminished influence.
ibid. ch. 3

## Rosamond Lehmann (1903–90)
BRITISH AUTHOR

Her fiction is characterized by sensitive portrayals of young women undergoing the 'torment of loving', and includes *An Invitation to the Waltz* (1932) and its sequel *The Weather in the Streets* (1936). Among her other works is her autobiography *The Swan in the Evening* (1967).

1 The trouble with Ian [Fleming] is that he gets off with women because he can't get on with them.
Quoted in *The Life of Ian Fleming*, ch. 8, sect. 1 (1966) by John Pearson. The novelist Ian Fleming was famed for his voracious and cynical sexual appetite (see IAN FLEMING 2). Lehmann's description is said to be borrowed from ELIZABETH BOWEN (untraced).

## Tom Lehrer (b. 1928)
US HUMORIST

He is known for the songs that he wrote and performed throughout the 1950s and 1960s, accompanying himself on the piano. Sharply satirical in content, they exhibited black humour ('Poisoning Pigeons in the Park') and parodied and quoted other songs ('I Hold Your Hand in Mine, Dear').

1 Even though the prospect sickens,
Brother, here we go again.
On Christmas Day you can't get sore,
Your fellow man you must adore,
There's time to cheat him all the more
The other three hundred and sixty-four.
'A Christmas Carol' (song) on the album *An Evening Wasted with Tom Lehrer* (1959)

2 How I ache for the touch of your lips, dear,
But much more for the feel of your whips, dear,
You can raise welts,
Like nobody else,
As we dance to the Masochism Tango!
'The Masochism Tango' (song) on ibid.

3 Life is like a sewer. What you get out of it depends on what you put into it.
Preamble to 'We Will All Go Together When We Go' (song) on ibid.

## Jerry Leiber and
## Mike Stoller See ELVIS PRESLEY 1.

## Fred W. Leigh (1870–1924)
BRITISH SONGWRITER

He joined the publishing firm Francis Day and Hunter c. 1900 and became literary editor there, a post he held until his death. He wrote songs associated with Marie Lloyd, among others, for example 'Don't Dilly-Dally on the Way' (1919, written with Charles Collins).

1 I always hold in having it if you fancy it,
If you fancy it that's understood!
And suppose it makes you fat? I don't worry over that,
'Cos a little of what you fancy does you good!
'A Little of What You Fancy Does You Good' (song, 1915, written with George Arthurs)

2 Why am I always the bridesmaid,
Never the blushing bride?
'Why Am I Always the Bridesmaid?' (song, 1917, written with Charles Collins and Lily Morris)

3 My old man said, 'Follow the van,
Don't dilly-dally on the way!'
'Don't Dilly-Dally on the Way' (song, 1919, written with Charles Collins). The song, which was also known as 'My Old Man Says "Follow the Van"' and 'The Cock-linnet Song', was popularized by Marie Lloyd.

## Mike Leigh (b. 1943)
BRITISH FILM-MAKER

His plays, which are closely observed satires of everyday life, are written from improvisations at rehearsal stage. His work for television includes *Abigail's Party* (1977) and for film *High Hopes* (1989), *Life is Sweet* (1991) and *Secrets and Lies* (1996).

1 Thanks for the mammaries.
Johnny (David Thewlis), with his hand inside Sophie's top, in *Naked* (film, 1993, written and directed by Mike Leigh)

2 Was I bored? No, I wasn't fuckin' bored. I'm never bored. That's the trouble with everybody – you're all so bored. You've 'ad nature explained to you and you're bored with it. You've 'ad the living body explained to you and you're bored with it. You've 'ad the universe explained to you and you're bored with it. So now you just want cheap thrills and like plenty of 'em, and it dun't matter 'ow tawdry or vacuous they are as long as it's new, as long as it's new, as long as it flashes and fuckin' bleeps in forty fuckin' different colours. Well, whatever else you can say about me, I'm not fuckin' bored!
Johnny (David Thewlis) to Louise, in ibid.

3 I don't 'ave a future. Nobody 'as a future. The party's over. Take a look around you, man. It's all breakin' up.
Johnny (David Thewlis), in ibid.

4 Morals are a matter of taste.
Interview in *Naked and Other Screenplays* (1995)

## Michel Leiris (1901–90)
FRENCH ANTHROPOLOGIST AND AUTHOR

After an association with the Surrealists (1925–9) he joined the Dakar-Djibouti expedition of 1931–3. On his return he worked as an anthropologist and also published several confessional autobiographies, including *Manhood* (1939), and anthropological essays, such as *Phantom Africa* (1934).

1 Dream is not a revelation. If a dream affords the dreamer some light on himself, it is not the person with closed eyes who makes the discovery but the person with open eyes

lucid enough to fit thoughts together. Dream – a scintillating mirage surrounded by shadows – is essentially *poetry*.

Quoted by Roger Shattuck in *Nights as Day, Days as Night*, Introduction (1961)

## Prue Leith (b. 1940)

BRITISH CHEF, CATERER AND WRITER

Regarded as the 'doyenne of British cookery', she founded a restaurant, Leith's, in 1969 and Leith's School of Food and Wine in 1975. A writer and broadcaster on cookery for thirty years, she published her first novel, *Leaving Patrick*, in 1999.

1 When you get to fifty-two food becomes more important than sex.

*Guardian* 11 November 1992

## Curtis E. LeMay (1906–90)

US AIR FORCE GENERAL

Full name Curtis Emerson LeMay. He commanded the B29 bombers that dropped the atom bombs on Japan in 1945 and subsequently became the first head of America's Strategic Air Command, the USAF's elite nuclear bomber strike force (1948–57), and Air Force Chief of Staff (1961–5). He was said to be the inspiration for the gung-ho General Jack D. Ripper in Kubrick's film *Dr. Strangelove* (1963) (see STERLING HAYDEN 2).

1 My solution to the problem would be to tell them [the North Vietnamese] they've got to draw in their horns and stop aggression or we're going to bomb them back into the Stone Age.

Quoted in *Mission with LeMay* (1965). The words inspired the ironic slogan 'Bombs Away with Curt LeMay!'

## Jack Lemmon (b. 1925)

US ACTOR

Often cast in comedy films, such as *Some Like It Hot* (1959), the start of a seven-film collaboration with BILLY WILDER, he also won acclaim for *Save the Tiger* (1973) and *Missing* (1982). His association with Walter Matthau produced, among other films, *The Odd Couple* (1968).

1 Look at that! Look how she moves! That's just like jell-O on springs. She must have some sort of built-in motor or something, huh? I tell you it's a whole different sex.

Jerry/Daphne (Jack Lemmon) in *Some Like It Hot* (film, 1959, screenplay by Billy Wilder and I.A.L. Diamond, directed and produced by Billy Wilder). Said to Joe/Josephine (Tony Curtis) on the station platform, the first time they set eyes on Sugar Kane (MARILYN MONROE).

## Vladimir Ilyich Lenin (1870–1924)

RUSSIAN REVOLUTIONARY LEADER

Original name Vladimir Ilyich Ulyanov. Both glorified as a great revolutionary and vilified for his ruthlessness, he was the leading figure in the Bolshevik revolution of 1917 and became the first head of a Soviet government. The Marxist-Leninist policies that he established came to be the basis of communist ideology everywhere.

1 Imperialism is capitalism at that stage of development at which the dominance of monopolies and finance capitalism is established; in which the export of capital has acquired pronounced importance; in which the division of the world among the international trusts has begun, in which the division of all territories of the globe among the biggest capitalist powers has been completed.

*Imperialism, the Highest Stage of Capitalism*, ch. 7 (1916). The formulation has elsewhere been translated: 'Imperialism is the monopoly stage of capitalism.'

2 Capitalists are no more capable of self-sacrifice than a man is capable of lifting himself up by his own bootstraps.

*Letters From Afar*, ch. 4 (1917)

3 While the State exists there can be no freedom; when there is freedom there will be no State.

*The State and Revolution*, ch. 5, sect. 4 (1919)

4 When one makes a Revolution, one cannot mark time; one must always go forward – or go back. He who now talks about the 'freedom of the press' goes backward, and halts our headlong course towards Socialism.

Speech at Smolny, 17 November 1917, quoted in *Ten Days That Shook the World*, ch. 11 (1926) by JOHN REED

5 If Socialism can only be realized when the intellectual development of all the people permits it, then we shall not see Socialism for at least five hundred years.

Speech at Peasants' Congress, Petrograd, 27 November 1917, quoted in ibid. ch. 12

6 Politics begin where the masses are, not where there are thousands, but where there are millions, that is where serious politics begin.

Report to Seventh Congress of the Russian Communist Party, 7 March 1918, publ. in *Selected Works*, vol. 7 (1937)

7 All our lives we fought against exalting the individual, against the elevation of the single person, and long ago we were over and done with the business of a hero, and here it comes up again: the glorification of one personality. This is not good at all. I am just like everybody else.

Remark after being shot in 1918, quoted in *Not By Politics Alone*, ch. 2 (1973) by Tamara Deutsche

8 You cannot make a revolution in white gloves.

Lenin to Kropotkin in May 1919, quoted in ibid.

9 [Of George Bernard Shaw] A good man fallen among Fabians.

Quoted in *Six Weeks in Russia in 1919*, 'Notes of a Conversation with Lenin' (1919) by Arthur Ransome. Remark made to Arthur Ransome.

10 You all know that even when women have full rights, they still remain fatally downtrodden because all housework is left to them. In most cases housework is the most unproductive, the most barbarous and the most arduous work a woman can do. It is exceptionally petty and does not include anything that would in any way promote the development of the woman.

'The Tasks of the Working Women's Movement in the Soviet Republic', first publ. 1919, repr. in *Collected Works*, vol. 30 (1965)

11 Communism is Soviet power plus the electrification of the whole country.

Report on the Work of the Council of People's Commissars, 22 December 1920, repr. in *Collected Works*, vol. 31 (1966). The words were used as a slogan to promote the plans of the State Committee for the Electrification of Russia.

12 It is true that liberty is precious – so precious that it must be rationed.

Attributed in *Soviet Communism: A New Civilization?* (1936) by Beatrice and SIDNEY WEBB

## John Lennon (1940–80)

BRITISH ROCK MUSICIAN

After separating from the Beatles in 1970 he pursued a solo career in tandem with his wife, the conceptual artist YOKO ONO. His initially angry songs, such as 'Working Class Hero' (1970), became mellower at the end of the decade with such songs as 'Watching the Wheels' (1980). His most successful albums were *Imagine* (1971) and *Double Fantasy* (1980). He was shot to death by a fan outside his apartment in New York. See also BONO 2, JOHN LENNON AND PAUL MCCARTNEY, YOKO ONO 2.

1 Will people in the cheaper seats clap your hands? All the rest of you, if you'll just rattle your jewellery.

To the audience at Royal Command Performance, London, 4 November 1963, quoted in *Shout! The True Story of the Beatles*, pt 2, 'November 1963' (1981) by Philip Norman. Lennon, here announcing the band's final number of their performance, 'Twist and Shout', had earlier warned manager Brian Epstein that he was going to ad lib if the audience proved responsive: 'I'll just tell 'em to rattle their fuckin' jewellery.'

2 Christianity will go. It will vanish and shrink. I needn't argue with that; I'm right and I will be proved right. We're more popular than Jesus now; I don't know which will go first – rock and roll or Christianity.

Interview in the *Evening Standard* 4 March 1966. 'Jesus was all right,' Lennon explained, 'but his disciples were thick and ordinary. It's them twisting it that ruins it for me.' His remarks provoked an angry reaction, especially in the USA, causing Lennon to explain himself at a press conference in Chicago, 11 August 1966: 'I'm not saying that we're better or greater, or comparing us with Jesus Christ as a person, or God as a thing, or whatever it is. I just said what I said, and it was wrong, or it was taken wrong. And now it's all this.' His words recall a similar comment by Zelda Fitzgerald (see ZELDA FITZGERALD 3).

3 Christ, you know it ain't easy,
You know how hard it can be,
The way things are going
They're going to crucify me.

'The Ballad of John and Yoko' (song, 1969) on the album *Hey Jude* (1970) by the Beatles. The song, which was banned by some radio stations for what they perceived as blasphemy, is also credited to PAUL MCCARTNEY, who played piano, bass and drums on the record.

4 All we are saying is give peace a chance.

'Give Peace a Chance' (song) on the album *Live Peace in Toronto* (1969) by the Plastic Ono Band. The song (credited also to PAUL MCCARTNEY), was originally recorded during the eight-day bed-in by Lennon and YOKO ONO in an Amsterdam hotel in May 1969, with participation by ALLEN GINSBERG and TIMOTHY LEARY, among others. It became an anthem for anti-Vietnam War and other peace protesters.

5 The Blue Meanies, or whatever they are, still preach violence all the time in every newspaper, every TV show and every magazine. The least Yoko and I can do is hog the headlines and make people laugh. We're quite willing to be the world's clowns if it will do any good. For reasons known only to themselves, people print what I say. And I say 'peace'.

Quoted in *Shout! The True Story of the Beatles*, pt 4, 'May 1969' (1981) by Philip Norman. On the peace campaign waged by Lennon and YOKO ONO.

6 Lots of people who complained about us receiving the MBE received theirs for heroism in the war – for killing people. We received ours for entertaining other people. I'd say we deserve ours more.

Quoted in *Beatles Illustrated Lyrics*, vol. 1 (ed. Alan Aldridge, 1969)

7 A working class hero is something to be
If you want to be a hero then just follow me.

'Working Class Hero' (song) on the album *John Lennon/Plastic Ono Band* (1970) by John Lennon and the Plastic Ono Band

8 God is a concept by which we measure our pain.

'God' (song) on ibid.

9 You have to be a bastard to make it, and that's a fact. And the Beatles are the biggest bastards on earth.

Interview in *Lennon Remembers* (ed. Jann Wenner, 1970)

10 Imagine there's no heaven,
It's easy if you try,
No hell below us,
Above us only sky,
Imagine all the people
Living for today.

'Imagine' (song) on the album *Imagine* (1971)

11 One has to completely humiliate oneself to be what the Beatles were, and that's what I resent. I didn't know, I didn't foresee. It happened bit by bit, gradually, until this complete craziness is surrounding you, and you're doing exactly what you don't want to do with people you can't stand – the people you hated when you were ten.

Interview in *Rolling Stone* 7 January 1971

12 We were all on this ship in the sixties, our generation, a ship going to discover the New World. And the Beatles were in the crow's nest of that ship.

Interview for French TV, March 1974, publ. in *Imagine* (ed. Andrew Solt and Sam Egan, 1988)

13 New York is what Paris was in the twenties . . . the centre of the art world. And we want to be in the centre. It's the greatest place on earth . . . I've got a lot of friends here and I even brought my own cash.

*The Tomorrow Show*, NBC-TV, April 1975, publ. in ibid. Lennon was given his long-awaited green card (residency permit) in the USA the following year.

14 Life is what happens to you while you're busy making other plans.

'Beautiful Boy' (song) on the album *Starting Over* (1980). The line has also been attributed to Betty Talmadge (divorced wife of Senator Herman Talmadge) and Thomas La Mance (unknown).

15 My defences were so great. The cocky rock and roll hero who knows all the answers was actually a terrified guy who didn't know how to cry. Simple.

Interview in *Playboy* September 1980

16 I've had the boyhood thing of being Elvis. Now I want to be with my best friend, and my best friend's my wife. Who could ask for anything more?

Interview for KFRC RKO Radio (San Francisco), 8 December 1980, the day of Lennon's murder, publ. in *Imagine* (ed. Andrew Solt and Sam Egan, 1988)

17 My role in society, or any artist or poet's role, is to try and express what we all feel. Not to tell people how to feel. Not as a preacher, not as a leader, but as a reflection of us all.

ibid.

18 It's amazing how low you go to get high.

*Skywriting by Word of Mouth*, 'The Art of Deception is in the Eye of the Beholder' (ed. Yoko Ono, 1986)

19 An outlaw by profession, an inlaw by marriage. His tail lights were deteriorating, but his collection of porcelain remained a constant companion.

ibid. 'Spare Me the Agony of Your Birth Control'

# John Lennon (1940–80) and
# Paul McCartney (b. 1942)
BRITISH ROCK MUSICIANS

Hailed by the critic William Mann as the most important songwriters since Schubert, they co-wrote most of the songs performed by the Beatles, Lennon's mordant wit and surreal humour a foil for McCartney's melodies and whimsicality. See also PAUL MCCARTNEY.

1 She loves you, yeh, yeh, yeh,

'She Loves You' (song, 1963) on the album *A Collection of Beatles Oldies (But Goldies)* (1966) by the Beatles. The song was the group's all-time top-selling UK single.

2 It's been a hard day's night,
And I've been working like a dog.

'A Hard Day's Night' (song) on the album *A Hard Day's Night* (1964) by the Beatles. The phrase 'hard day's night' originated with RINGO STARR's comment on a heavy filming schedule shooting the film that was later given this title. It was called a typical 'Ringoism' by John Lennon, who also used the words in his book, *In His Own Write* (1964).

3 I don't care too much for money,
For money can't buy me love.
'Can't Buy Me Love' (song) on ibid.

4 She's got a ticket to ride, but she don't care.
'Ticket to Ride' (song) on the album *Help!* (1965) by the Beatles

5 Yesterday, all my troubles seemed so far away,
Now it looks as though they're here to stay,
Oh I believe in yesterday.
'Yesterday' (song) on ibid. The song, wholly written by McCartney
and originally titled 'Scrambled Eggs' ('. . . Oh my baby how I love
your legs'), was to hold the record as the most covered song in
history.

6 He's a real nowhere man
Sitting in his nowhere land
Making all his nowhere plans for nobody.
'Nowhere Man' (song) on the album *Rubber Soul* (1966) by the
Beatles

7 Waits at the window,
Wearing the face that she keeps in a jar by the door.
Who is it for?
'Eleanor Rigby' (song) on the album *Revolver* (1966) by the Beatles.
For novelist A.S. BYATT the lyric has 'the minimalist perfection of
a Beckett story'.

8 We all live in a yellow submarine.
'Yellow Submarine' (song) on ibid.

9 The Magical Mystery Tour
Is coming to take you away.
'Magical Mystery Tour' (song) on TV film and album *Magical
Mystery Tour* (1967) by the Beatles

10 What do you see when you turn out the light?
I can't tell you but I know it's mine.
Oh, I get by with a little help from my friends.
'With a Little Help from my Friends' (song) on the album *Sgt.
Pepper's Lonely Hearts Club Band* (1967) by the Beatles

11 I've got to admit it's getting better.
'Getting Better' (song) on ibid.

12 Will you still need me,
Will you still feed me,
When I'm sixty-four?
'When I'm Sixty-four' (song) on ibid.

13 I heard the news today, oh boy.
Four thousand holes in Blackburn Lancashire.
And though the holes were rather small,
They had to count them all.
'A Day in the Life' (song) on ibid.

14 I'd love to turn you on.
ibid.

15 All you need is love.
'All You Need is Love' (song, 1967) on the album *Yellow Submarine*
(1969) by the Beatles. The song was written specially for 'Our
World', the first world-wide satellite TV broadcast, 25 July 1967, in
which it was performed and transmitted live to 400 million viewers.
The words were used as the title of both a book and TV documentary
by Tony Palmer charting the history of popular music (1976).

16 When I hold you in my arms
And I feel my finger on your trigger
I know no one can do me no harm
Because happiness is a warm gun.
'Happiness is a Warm Gun' (song), on *The Beatles* (1968). The
title was inspired by an advertising slogan for the National Rifle
Association in the USA.

17 And in the end, the love you take
Is equal to the love you make.
'The End' (song), on the album *Abbey Road* (1970) by the Beatles.
Lennon once called these the best lines McCartney had ever written.

## Annie Lennox (b. 1954)
BRITISH SINGER

Born Griselda Anne Lennox. One of the two members of the
Eurythmics (the other was guitarist Dave Stewart), she contributed
androgynous looks and a powerful voice to make this one of the
most successful bands of the 1980s. Her first solo album *Diva* (1992)
was an international bestseller.

1 Sisters are doing it for themselves,
Standing on their own two feet,
Ringing on their own bells.
'Sisters Are Doing It For Themselves' (song, written by Dave
Stewart) on the album *Be Yourself Tonight* (1985) by the Eurythmics.
Sung as a duet with soul diva ARETHA FRANKLIN.

2 There are two kinds of artists left: those who endorse
Pepsi and those who simply won't.
*Guardian* 30 November 1990

## (Sir) Graham Leonard (b. 1921)
BRITISH ECCLESIASTIC

Known for his Anglo-Catholic sympathies, he argued against the
proposed unification of Anglicans and Methodists in the 1970s,
and as Anglican Bishop of London (1981–91) he opposed the
ordination of women to the priesthood. He was received into the
Roman Catholic Church in 1994.

1 The purpose of population is not ultimately peopling
earth. It is to fill heaven.
Speech to Church of England Synod, 10 February 1983, quoted in
the *Observer* 13 February 1983

## Alan Jay Lerner (1918–86)
US SONGWRITER

From 1942 until 1962 he worked in collaboration with the composer
Frederick Loewe to produce immensely successful Broadway musicals such as *Paint Your Wagon* (1951, filmed 1969), *My Fair Lady*
(1956, filmed 1964) and the film *Gigi* (1958), which won an Academy
Award. See also MAURICE CHEVALIER 1.

1 Wouldn't it be lovely . . .
'Wouldn't it be Lovely?' (song) in *My Fair Lady* (stage show 1956,
film 1964). Sung by Eliza Doolittle.

2 The rain in Spain stays mainly in the plain.
'The Rain in Spain' (song) in ibid. The words are a phonetic exercise
devised by Henry Higgins for Eliza Doolittle.

3 I could have danced all night.
'I Could Have Danced All Night' (song) in ibid.

4 I'm getting married in the morning,
Ding! dong! the bells are gonna chime.
Pull out the stopper;
Let's have a whopper;
But get me to the church on time!
'Get Me to the Church on Time' (song) in ibid.

5 Ask every person if he's heard the story,
And tell it strong and clear if he has not,
That once there was a fleeting wisp of glory
Called Camelot . . .
Don't let it be forgot
That once there was a spot
For one brief shining moment that was known
As Camelot.
'Camelot' (song), in *Camelot* (stage musical 1960, film 1967). The
song was named by JACKIE KENNEDY in an interview shortly
after JOHN F. KENNEDY's assassination as having had particular
significance for her husband's presidency: 'Camelot had suddenly
become the symbol of those thousand days when people the world
over saw a bright new light of hope shining from the White House.
For myself, I have never been able to see a performance of *Camelot*
again.' Official Kennedy biographer William Manchester called his
book *One Brief Shining Moment* (1983).

## Max Lerner (1902–92)

US AUTHOR AND COLUMNIST

A highly respected social and political commentator, he wrote the books *It Is Later Than You Think* (1938), *Ideas for the Ice Age* (1941) and *The Unfinished Country* (1959). He stressed the importance of family values in *The Child and Parent in American Civilization* (1958).

1 A President is best judged by the enemies he makes when he has really hit his stride.

'The Education of Harry Truman', first publ. in the *New York Star* 9 January 1949, repr. in *The Unfinished Country* pt 4 (1959)

2 There is a hate layer of opinion and emotion in America. There will be other McCarthys to come who will be hailed as its heroes.

'McCarthyism: The Smell of Decay', first publ. in the *New York Post* 5 April 1950, repr. in ibid. pt 4. The article saw the first coining of the word 'McCarthyism', as Lerner affirmed in a later column, 3 February 1954: 'For my own part I doubt seriously whether the word will outlast the political power of the man from whom it derives.'

3 Having a thirteen-year-old in the family is like having a general-admission ticket to the movies, radio and TV. You get to understand that the glittering new arts of our civilization are directed to the teen-agers, and by their suffrage they stand or fall.

'Teen-ager', first publ. in the *New York Post* 4 June 1952, repr. in ibid. pt 1

4 The real sadness of fifty is not that you change so much but that you change so little.

'Fifty first', publ. in the *New York Post* 18 December 1952, repr. in ibid. pt 1

5 The crime of book purging is that it involves a rejection of the word. For the word is never absolute truth, but only man's frail and human effort to approach the truth. To reject the word is to reject the human search.

'The Vigilantes and the Chain of Fear', first publ. in the *New York Post* 24 June 1953, repr. in ibid. pt 4. Referring to the McCarthy book burnings.

6 I am neither an optimist nor pessimist, but a possibilist.

Entry in *Who's Who in America* (1992)

## Doris Lessing (b. 1919)

BRITISH NOVELIST

Brought up in Rhodesia, she moved to London in 1949 where she published her first novel *The Grass is Singing* (1950), a study of interracial relationships in Africa. She followed it with *Martha Quest* (1952), the first in a series of five semi-autobiographical novels. *The Golden Notebook* (1962) has come to be considered as a classic of feminist literature.

1 When old settlers say 'One has to understand the country,' what they mean is, 'You have to get used to our ideas about the native.' They are saying, in effect, 'Learn our ideas, or otherwise get out; we don't want you.'

*The Grass is Singing*, ch. 1 (1950)

2 It is terrible to destroy a person's picture of himself in the interests of truth or some other abstraction.

ibid. ch. 2

3 If a fish is the movement of water embodied, given shape, then cat is a diagram and pattern of subtle air.

*Particularly Cats*, ch. 2 (1967)

4 What is charm then? The free giving of a grace, the spending of something given by nature in her role of spendthrift ... something extra, superfluous, unnecessary, essentially a power thrown away.

ibid. ch. 9

5 This world is run by people who know how to do things. They know how things work. They are *equipped*. Up there,

there's a layer of people who run everything. But we – we're just peasants. We don't understand what's going on, and we can't do anything.

Dorothy, in *The Good Terrorist* (1985)

6 Space or science fiction has become a dialect for our time.

*Guardian* 7 November 1988

7 The great secret that all old people share is that you really haven't changed in seventy or eighty years. Your body changes, but you don't change at all. And that, of course, causes great confusion.

*Sunday Times* 10 May 1992

8 Political correctness is the natural continuum from the party line. What we are seeing once again is a self-appointed group of vigilantes imposing their views on others. It is a heritage of communism, but they don't seem to see this.

ibid.

## Kathy Lette (b.1958)

AUSTRALIAN NOVELIST

Her books *Girls' Night Out* (1988), *Foetal Attraction* (1993) and *Mad Cows* (1996, filmed 1999) are rapid-fire, wisecracking portraits of independent women confronting issues of love, sex, babies and men. 'I like a female character who's got a bit of armpit stubble and occasionally goes for gold in the hypocrisy olympics,' she stated.

1 I didn't 'fall' pregnant! I was bloody well pushed.

Madeline Wolfe, in *Foetal Attraction*, pt 1, 'First Stage' (1993)

2 I speak as your native guide to the mysterious tribe called the English. Dress code is everything. You can be a card-carrying Nazi, you can pay gigolos to eat gnocchi out of your navel and you won't be pilloried – as long as you never, ever wear linen with tweed.

Gillian Cassells, in ibid. pt 1, 'A New Taste Sensation'

3 What a woman needs is to marry a rich old boy, the sort of human handbag you can put down by the door at parties and pick up on the way home for the cab fare. With a complementary toy boy on the side.

ibid.

4 All this male angst over size. It's *attitude* women are interested in. Women like a penis which says, 'G'day! God, am I glad to see *you*.'

Maddy, in *Mad Cows*, ch. 10 (1996)

## Oscar Levant (1906–72)

US PIANIST AND COMPOSER

Hypochondriacal, witty, neurotic and eccentric, he was a respected interpreter of Gershwin and wrote film scores for Hollywood in the 1920s and 1930s. He also appeared as himself in such films as *Rhapsody in Blue* (1945) and *An American in Paris* (1951). 'In some moments I was difficult, in odd moments impossible, in rare moments loathsome, but at my best unapproachably great,' was his judgement on himself.

1 Epigram: a wisecrack that played Carnegie Hall.

*Coronet Magazine* September 1958

2 Strip away the phony tinsel of Hollywood and you find the real tinsel underneath.

*Inquisition in Eden* (1965)

## Leslie Lever (1905–77)

BRITISH SOLICITOR AND POLITICIAN

Baron Lever of Ardwick. He was senior partner in Leslie Lever and Co., Lord Mayor of Manchester (1957–8) and Labour MP for the Ardwick division of Manchester (1950–70).

1 Generosity is a part of my character, and I therefore hasten to assure this Government that I will never make an allegation of dishonesty against it wherever a simple explanation of stupidity will suffice.

*Speech to House of Commons, quoted in The Fine Art of Political Wit, ch. 12 (1964) by Leon Harris*

## Denise Levertov (b. 1923)

US POET

After emigrating to America in 1948, she came under the influence of WILLIAM CARLOS WILLIAMS and the Black Mountain poets in the 1950s and was active in anti-Vietnam War protests in the 1960s. Her collections include *With Eyes at the Back of Our Heads* (1959), *Relearning the Alphabet* (1970) and *Footprints* (1972). The poet KENNETH REXROTH described her as 'classically independent' and compared her work to 'the more melancholy songs of Brahms'.

1 Two by two in the ark of
the ache of it.

*'The Ache of Marriage', publ. in O Taste and See (1964)*

2 If woman is inconstant,
good, I am faithful to

ebb and flow, I fall
in season and now

is a time of ripening.

*'Stepping Westward', publ. in The Sorrow Dance (1967)*

## Carlo Levi (1902–75)

ITALIAN WRITER AND PAINTER

His first and most successful novel, *Christ Stopped at Eboli* (1945, filmed 1979), was a compassionate and painterly description of the Italian south based on his experience of internment during the Second World War as a consequence of his anti-fascist activities. His other works include *Of Fear and Freedom* (1947) and *The Linden Tree* (1959).

1 Christ never came this far, nor did time, nor the individual soul, nor hope, nor the relation of cause to effect, nor reason nor history.

*Christ Stopped at Eboli, ch. 1 (1945). Referring to Basilicata, in southern Italy. The book was the first to publicize the true plight of the Italian south.*

2 We always find tedious places, languid and dark places, in books, in the best books. And especially in paintings, which are mythical landscapes of the soul, no matter what subject they represent, and cannot be without intricate pathless woods, without swamps, without this idle and nocturnal tedium.

*The Watch, ch. 3, sect. 2 (1950)*

3 Here in Italy every tree, every stone in the street has a history, something's happened, perhaps a thousand years ago, but there's always someone who remembers it or has heard about it and can tell you about it. Over there a tree is a tree, a stone is a stone, and a man is nothing but a man. They are honest and simple but you might feel that something is missing.

*ibid. ch. 9, sect. 2*

## Primo Levi (1919–87)

ITALIAN CHEMIST AND AUTHOR

His survival of the concentration camp at Auschwitz was a constant theme in his books and formed the basis for his autobiographical trilogy beginning with *If This Is a Man* (1947). His scientific background was evident in most of his works, for example, *The Periodic Table* (1975). He committed suicide.

1 Consider whether this is a man,
Who labours in the mud
Who knows no peace
Who fights for a crust of bread
Who dies at a yes or a no.

*'Shemà', written 1946, publ. in Shemà: Collected Poems of Primo Levi (1976)*

2 Sooner or later in life everyone discovers that perfect happiness is unrealizable, but there are few who pause to consider the antithesis: that perfect unhappiness is equally unattainable. The obstacles preventing the realization of both these extreme states are of the same nature: they derive from our human condition which is opposed to everything infinite.

*If This Is a Man, ch. 1 (1947)*

3 But consider what value, what meaning is enclosed even in the smallest of our daily habits, in the hundred possessions which even the poorest beggar owns: a handkerchief, an old letter, the photo of a cherished person. These things are part of us, almost like limbs of our body; nor is it conceivable that we can be deprived of them in our world, for we immediately find others to substitute the old ones, other objects which are ours in their personification and evocation of our memories.

*ibid. ch. 2*

4 For me chemistry represented an indefinite cloud of future potentialities which enveloped my life to come in black volutes torn by fiery flashes, like those which had hidden Mount Sinai. Like Moses, from that cloud I expected my law, the principle of order in me, around me, and in the world . . . I would watch the buds swell in spring, the mica glint in the granite, my own hands, and I would say to myself: 'I will understand this, too, I will understand everything.'

*The Periodic Table, 'Hydrogen' (1975)*

5 In order for the wheel to turn, for life to be lived, impurities are needed, and the impurities of impurities in the soil, too, as is known, if it is to be fertile. Dissension, diversity, the grain of salt and mustard are needed: Fascism does not want them, forbids them, and that's why you're not a Fascist; it wants everybody to be the same, and you are not. But immaculate virtue does not exist either, or if it exists it is detestable.

*ibid. 'Zinc'*

6 Every man is the enemy
of every other,
With everyone split by an inner border,
The right hand enemy of the left.
On your feet, old men, enemies of yourselves:
Our war is never over.

*'Partisan', written 1981, publ. in Collected Poems (1988)*

7 The future of humanity is uncertain, even in the most prosperous countries, and the quality of life deteriorates; and yet I believe that what is being discovered about the infinitely large and infinitely small is sufficient to absolve this end of the century and millennium. What a very few are acquiring in knowledge of the physical world will perhaps cause this period not to be judged as a pure return of barbarism.

*Other People's Trades, 'News from the Sky' (1985)*

8 To be considered stupid and to be told so is more painful than being called gluttonous, mendacious, violent, lascivious, lazy, cowardly: every weakness, every vice, has found its defenders, its rhetoric, its ennoblement and exaltation, but stupidity hasn't.

*ibid. 'The Irritable Chess-players'*

9 The bond between a man and his profession is similar to that which ties him to his country; it is just as complex,

often ambivalent, and in general it is understood completely only when it is broken: by exile or emigration in the case of one's country, by retirement in the case of a trade or profession.

ibid. 'Ex-Chemist'

10 Anyone who has obeyed nature by transmitting a piece of gossip experiences the explosive relief that accompanies the satisfying of a primary need.

'About Gossip', first publ. in *La Stampa* 24 June 1986, repr. in *The Mirror Maker* (1989)

11 The aims of life are the best defence against death.

*The Drowned and the Saved*, ch. 6 (1988)

## Bernard Levin (b. 1928)

BRITISH JOURNALIST AND CRITIC

He has written political commentary and criticism for numerous newspapers and magazines and has also been a radio scriptwriter and broadcaster. Among his books are *The Pendulum Years* (1970) and *The Way We Live Now* (1984).

1 In every age of transition men are never so firmly bound to one way of life as when they are about to abandon it, so that fanaticism and intolerance reach their most intense forms just before tolerance and mutual acceptance come to be the natural order of things.

*The Pendulum Years*, ch. 4 (1970). Referring to John Profumo, 'the last victim of the old, unpermissive standards'.

2 Between them, then, Walrus and Carpenter, they divided up the Sixties.

ibid. ch. 12. Referring to HAROLD MACMILLAN and HAROLD WILSON.

3 For those even more ignorant than I was, I should say that the team [the rock group Nirvana] is guitar-led, though unfortunately not by Segovia. I expected a great deal of raucous noise, and got it, but listening carefully, I realized that this stuff is not just shouting, and is even up to making a musical point. Yet I knew that it would fail the crucial test; I do not believe that I would or could continue to listen to such music, and the reason is surely obvious: it is ultimately without roots.

Quoted in the *Guardian* 31 December 1994. On the suicide of Nirvana's KURT COBAIN, of whom Levin wrote: 'Why should not ten million youths find their idol in a foul-mouthed, brutish, violent singer-guitarist, drugged to the eyebrows and hating himself and his way of life?'

## Emmanuel Levinas (1905–95)

FRENCH PHILOSOPHER

Influenced by MARTIN HEIDEGGER and regarded as one of the foremost exponents of the work of Husserl, he was in turn an influence on SARTRE and DERRIDA. His philosophy of ethics is explained in *Existence and Existents* (1947), *Totality and Infinity* (1961) and *Otherwise Than Being, or Beyond Essence* (1974), and he also wrote Talmudic commentaries.

1 If the 1945 victory demonstrates that in history, vice is ultimately punished and virtue recognized, we do not wish once more to bear the brunt of this demonstration.

'The Diary of Leon Brunschvicg', first publ. 1949, repr. in *Difficult Freedom*, pt 1 (1990)

2 The faith that moves mountains and conceives of a world without slaves immediately transports itself to utopia, separating the reign of God from the reign of Caesar. This reassures Caesar.

'Place and Utopia', first publ. 1950, repr. in ibid. pt 3

3 Evil is not a mystical principle that can be effaced by a ritual, it is an offence perpetrated on man by man. No one, not even God, can substitute himself for the victim.

'A Religion for Adults', first publ. 1957, repr. in ibid. pt 1

4 Monotheism has not only a horror of idols, but a nose for false prophecy. A special patience – Judaism – is required to refuse all premature messianic claims.

'Judaism and the Present', first publ. 1969, repr. in ibid. pt 5

## Joseph E. Levine (1905–87)

US FILM PRODUCER AND EXECUTIVE

Describing himself as a wheeler dealer, he achieved success through his innovative use of intensive advertising and saturation booking and by importing European films such as *Divorce Italian Style* (1961) and *8½* (1963). He also produced his own films, including *The Carpetbaggers* (1963).

1 You can fool all the people all the time if the advertising is right and the budget is big enough.

Quoted in *Halliwell's Who's Who in the Movies* (ed. John Walker, 1999)

## Claude Lévi-Strauss (b. 1908)

FRENCH ANTHROPOLOGIST

He was a major innovator in the study of anthropology, formulating through his studies of myth, kinship and religion the principles of structuralism. His theories are set down in the four-volume *Mythologies* (1964–71). He defined his position as one of 'serene pessimism'.

1 Being human signifies, for each one of us, belonging to a class, a society, a country, a continent and a civilization.

*Tristes Tropiques*, ch. 38 (1955)

2 The world began without man, and it will end without him.

ibid. ch. 40

3 Language is a form of human reason, which has its internal logic of which man knows nothing.

*The Savage Mind*, ch. 9 (1962)

4 The scientific mind does not so much provide *the right answers as ask the right questions.*

*The Raw and the Cooked*, 'Overture' (1964)

5 I therefore claim to show, not how men think in myths, but how myths operate in men's minds without their being aware of the fact.

ibid.

6 Since music is a language with some meaning at least for the immense majority of mankind, although only a tiny minority of people are capable of formulating a meaning in it, and since it is the only language with the contradictory attributes of being at once intelligible and untranslatable, the musical creator is a being comparable to the gods, and music itself the supreme mystery of the science of man, a mystery that all the various disciplines come up against and which holds the key to their progress.

ibid.

7 Journeys, those magic caskets full of dreamlike promises, will never again yield up their treasures untarnished . . . The first thing we see as we travel around the world is our own filth, thrown into the face of mankind.

Quoted in the *Independent on Sunday* 4 August 1991

## Bernard-Henri Lévy (b. 1948)

FRENCH PHILOSOPHER

A 'New Philosopher', he came to the forefront of radical French thought in the mid-1970s. His *Barbarism with a Human Face* (1977) was a denunciation of Marxism and *Testament of God* (1979) was a treatise on 'aesthetic spirituality'.

1 The only successful revolution of this century is totalitarianism.

*Time* magazine 12 September 1977

2 I think enthusiasm is one of the worst temptations for an intellectual. It is almost a rule that when intellectuals enthuse, they are wrong.

*International Herald Tribune* 21 January 1991

3 Between the barbarity of capitalism, which censures itself much of the time, and the barbarity of socialism, which does not, I guess I would choose capitalism.

Quoted in the *Independent on Sunday* 31 March 1991

## Monica Lewinsky (b. 1973)

US FORMER WHITE HOUSE AIDE

She was catapulted to fame over her sexual relationship with President CLINTON, begun in 1995. After Clinton was cleared of charges of perjury and obstruction, she told her story in *Monica's Story* (1999) by Andrew Morton and in numerous public interviews.

1 I would just like to say that no one ever asked me to lie, and I was never promised a job for my silence. And I am sorry, I'm really sorry for everything that's happened. And I hate Linda Tripp.

Concluding her evidence to the Grand Jury, quoted in the *Daily Telegraph* 23 September 1998. Linda Tripp was a colleague at the White House who taped Lewinsky's confidences regarding her affair with President CLINTON.

## C.S. Lewis (1898–1963)

BRITISH AUTHOR

Full name Clive Staples Lewis. He published more than forty works of Christian apologetics, the best known of which is the satirical *Screwtape Letters* (1942). Christian allegory also runs through his classic series for children *The Chronicles of Narnia* (1950–56) and his works of science fiction.

1 There are two equal and opposite errors into which our race can fall about the devils. One is to disbelieve in their existence. The other is to believe, and to feel an excessive and unhealthy interest in them. They themselves are equally pleased by both errors and hail a materialist or a magician with the same delight.

*The Screwtape Letters*, Preface (1942)

2 The safest road to Hell is the gradual one – the gentle slope, soft underfoot, without sudden turnings, without milestones, without signposts.

Screwtape, in ibid. 'Letter 12'

3 Much of the modern resistance to chastity comes from men's belief that they 'own' their bodies – those vast and perilous estates, pulsating with the energy that made the worlds, in which they find themselves without their consent and from which they are ejected at the pleasure of Another!

ibid. 'Letter 21'

4 Courage is not simply *one* of the virtues but the form of every virtue at the testing point, which means at the point of highest reality.

Quoted in *The Unquiet Grave*, pt 3 (1944, rev. 1951) by CYRIL CONNOLLY

5 I remember summing up what I took to be our destiny, in conversation with my best friend at Chartres, by the formula, 'Term, holidays, term, holidays, till we leave school, and then work, work, work till we die.'

*Surprised by Joy*, ch. 4 (1955)

6 Literary experience heals the wound, without undermining the privilege, of individuality. There are mass emotions which heal the wound; but they destroy the privilege . . . Like a night sky in the Greek poem, I see

with a myriad eyes, but it is still I who see. Here, as in worship, in love, in moral action, and in knowing, I transcend myself; and am never more myself than when I do.

*An Experiment in Criticism* (1961). Last words of book.

7 No one ever told me that grief felt so like fear.

*A Grief Observed*, pt 1 (1961). Opening words of book of mourning for Lewis's dead wife, Joy Davidman. Their affair and marriage, her death from cancer and his bereavement were recounted in *Shadowlands*, a play (1979), TV film (1985) and big-screen film (1993).

8 It is hard to have patience with people who say 'There is no death' or 'Death doesn't matter.' There is death. And whatever is matters. And whatever happens has consequences, and it and they are irrevocable and irreversible. You might as well say that birth doesn't matter.

ibid.

9 Talk to me about the truth of religion and I'll listen gladly. Talk to me about the duty of religion and I'll listen submissively. But don't come talking to me about the consolations of religion or I shall suspect that you don't understand.

ibid. pt 2

10 There is, hidden or flaunted, a sword between the sexes till an entire marriage reconciles them.

ibid. pt 3

11 If, as I can't help suspecting, the dead also feel the pains of separation (and this may be one of their purgatorial sufferings), then for both lovers, and for all pairs of lovers without exception, bereavement is a universal and integral part of our experience of love.

ibid.

12 Can a mortal ask questions which God finds unanswerable? Quite easily, I should think. All nonsense questions are unanswerable.

ibid. pt 4

## Jerry Lee Lewis (b. 1935)

US ROCK MUSICIAN

Rowdy, raucous and rebellious, he was the personification of 1950s rock and roll. His piano-pounding caught the public imagination with his classics 'Whole Lotta Shakin' Going On' and 'Great Balls of Fire' (both 1957), although his career was shadowed by the obloquy aroused by his marriage in 1958 to his fourteen-year-old cousin.

1 You shake my nerves and you rattle my brain.
Too much love drives a man insane.
You broke my will, but what a thrill.
Goodness gracious, great balls of fire!

'Great Balls of Fire' (song, 1957, written by Jack Hammer and Otis Blackwell) on the album *The Golden Hits of Jerry Lee Lewis* (1964). *Great Balls of Fire!* was the title of a 1989 film based on his life.

2 If the Lord made anything better than a woman, he kept it for himself.

Quoted in *Early Rockers*, ch. 9 (1982) by Howard Elson. Lewis has been married six times.

3 I'm not putting Elvis down, but he was a shitass, a yellow belly, and I hated the fucker.

Said in 1988, quoted in *New Musical Express* 4 February 1995

## Sinclair Lewis (1885–1951)

US NOVELIST

He caused a sensation with his first novel *Main Street* (1920), an exposé of small-town life in the Midwest, and continued in the same satirical vein with *Babbitt* (1922), which centres on real-estate dealing, *Arrowsmith* (1925) describing medical science, and *Elmer*

*Gantry* (1927) evangelical religion. In 1930 he was the first American to be awarded the Nobel Prize for Literature.

1 In other countries, art and literature are left to a lot of shabby bums living in attics and feeding on booze and spaghetti, but in America the successful writer or picture-painter is indistinguishable from any other decent businessman.

George Follansbee Babbitt, in *Babbitt*, ch. 14, sect. 3 (1922). Addressing the Zenith Real Estate Board.

2 Damn the great executives, the men of measured merriment, damn the men with careful smiles, damn the men that run the shops, oh, damn their measured merriment.

Martin Arrowsmith, in *Arrowsmith*, ch. 25 (1925)

3 Our American professors like their literature clear and cold and pure and very dead.

Speech to Swedish Academy in Stockholm, 12 December 1930, on accepting the Nobel Prize for Literature, quoted in *Literature 1901–1967* (1969) by H. Frenz

## (Percy) Wyndham Lewis (1882–1957)
BRITISH AUTHOR AND PAINTER

He was a leader of the Vorticist school of abstract painting and served as a bombardier and war artist in the First World War, recounted in *Blasting and Bombardiering* (1937). He is best known for the satires *The Apes of God* (1930) and *The Childermass* (1928), first volume of *The Human Age* (completed 1955–6). His reputation suffered on account of his pro-Fascist sympathies, later recanted. 'I do not think I had ever seen a nastier-looking man,' remarked ERNEST HEMINGWAY. 'Under the black hat, when I had first seen them, the eyes had been those of an unsuccessful rapist.'

1 If you do not regard feminism with an uplifting sense of the gloriousness of woman's industrial destiny, or in the way, in short, that it is prescribed, by the rules of the political publicist, that you should, that will be interpreted by your opponents as an attack on *woman*.

*The Art of Being Ruled*, 'The Family and Feminism', sect. 6 (1926)

2 Almost anything that can be praised or advocated has been put to some disgusting use. There is no principle, however immaculate, that has not had its compromising manipulator.

ibid. sect. 8

3 The ideas of a time are like the clothes of a season: they are as arbitrary, as much imposed by some superior will which is seldom explicit. They are utilitarian and political, the instruments of smooth-running government.

ibid. 'Beyond Action and Reaction', sect. 3

4 *We are the first men of a Future that has not materialized. We belong to a 'great age' that has not 'come off'. We moved too quickly for the world. We set too sharp a pace.*

*Blasting and Bombardiering*, pt 5, 'The Period of "Ulysses", "Blast", "The Waste Land" ' (1937)

5 I feel most at home in the United States, not because it is intrinsically a more interesting country, but because no one really belongs there any more than I do. We are all there together in its wholly excellent vacuum.

*America and Cosmic Man*, 'The Case Against Roots' (1948)

## Liberace (1919–87)
US ENTERTAINER

Original name Wladziu Valentino Liberace. With his rhinestones, candelabra, gold lamé and coiffed hair, he pursued a long career playing romantic arrangements of popular classics. His own show ran from 1952 to 1957, and in 1985 he broke all box office records at Radio City Music Hall, New York. Cassandra of the *Daily Mail* called him 'a superb piece of calculating candyfloss'.

1 When the reviews are bad I tell my staff that they can join me as I cry all the way to the bank.

*Liberace: An Autobiography*, ch. 2. (1973). The catch-phrase 'I cried all the way to the bank' was used in Liberace's stage act from the 1950s.

## R.M. Lindner (1914–56)
US NOVELIST

Full name Robert Mitchell Lindner. Among his books are *Rebel Without a Cause: the Hypnoanalysis of a Criminal Psychopath* (1944), *Stone Walls and Men* (1946), *Prescription for Rebellion* (1952) and *Must You Conform?* (1956).

1 Rebel Without a Cause.

Title of book (1944, filmed 1955). The phrase is most associated with the film's star, James Dean, touted in the publicity as 'the bad boy from a good family'.

## Maureen Lipman (b. 1946)
BRITISH ACTRESS

Well known as a comedy actress, she has appeared on stage, notably in the one-woman show *Re: Joyce* (1988) about JOYCE GRENFELL, and has also made numerous television appearances, including as Beattie ('You Got an Ology?') in British Telecom commercials. A columnist for women's magazines, she has also published humorous books.

1 Men are . . . a mystery. After all, they spit, they punch, they scream, they rant, they kick each other when they're down and think nothing of putting their hands down their shorts and fiddling about. Of course, if they did it in the street they'd be arrested – but if they do it on a pitch they're worth £7 million!

*You Can Read Me Like a Book* ch. 6 (1995)

## Walter Lippmann (1889–1974)
US JOURNALIST

He was chief editorial writer for the *New York World* until 1931 but made his name through his daily columns syndicated through the *New York Herald Tribune*. He won the Pulitzer Prize for international reporting (1962). Among his books are *The Good Society* (1937) and *The Public Philosophy* (1955). He said that he considered the newspaper column 'the laboratory or clinic in which I test the philosophy and keep it from becoming too abstract'.

1 The great social adventure of America is no longer the conquest of the wilderness but the absorption of fifty different peoples.

*A Preface to Politics* ch. 6 (1914)

2 The best servants of the people, like the best valets, must whisper unpleasant truths in the master's ear. It is the court fool, not the foolish courtier, whom the king can least afford to lose.

ibid.

3 In making the great experiment of governing people by consent rather than by coercion, it is not sufficient that the party in power should have a majority. It is just as necessary that the party in power should never outrage the minority.

'The Indispensable Opposition', publ. in *Atlantic Monthly* (1939), repr. in *The Essential Lippman*, pt 6, sect. 2 (ed. Clinton Rossiter and James Lare, 1982)

4 The final test of a leader is that he leaves behind him in other men the conviction and the will to carry on.

'Roosevelt Is Gone', first publ. in the *New York Herald Tribune* 14 April 1945, repr. in ibid. pt 10, sect. 5. 'The genius of a good leader,' Lippmann added, 'is to leave behind him a situation which common sense, without the grace of genius, can deal with successfully.'

5 When distant and unfamiliar and complex things are

communicated to great masses of people, the truth suffers a considerable and often a radical distortion. The complex is made over into the simple, the hypothetical into the dogmatic, and the relative into an absolute.

*The Public Philosophy* ch. 2, sect. 3 (1955)

6 Successful democratic politicians are insecure and intimidated men. They advance politically only as they placate, appease, bribe, seduce, bamboozle, or otherwise manage to manipulate the demanding and threatening elements in their constituencies.

ibid. sect. 4

## Little Richard (b. 1932)
US ROCK MUSICIAN

Original name Richard Penniman. Raised a Seventh-Day Adventist in Georgia, he had one of the most powerful voices in rock 'n' roll, coupled with an outrageously camp stage presence. A run of hit singles, including 'Tutti-Frutti' (1955), 'Long Tall Sally' (1956) and 'Good Golly Miss Molly' (1958), ended when he turned to religion. His subsequent career alternated between the church and occasional come-backs, although he never matched his former success.

1 Awop-bop-a-loo-mop alop-bam-boom!

'Tutti-Frutti' (song, 1955, written with J. Lubin and Dorothy La Bostrie) on the album *Here's Little Richard* (1957)

2 The girl can't help it.

Song title (1956, written by BOBBY TROUPE) on ibid. The title was also used for what has been called the best rock 'n' roll film ever (1956), in which Little Richard made an explosive cameo performance.

3 They shoulda called me Little Cocaine, I was sniffing so much of the stuff! My nose got big enough to back a diesel truck in, unload it, and drive it right out again.

Quoted in *The Life and Times of Little Richard*, pt 4 (1984) by Charles White

## Joan Littlewood (b. 1914)
BRITISH STAGE DIRECTOR

She set up the Theatre Workshop in Manchester 1945, moving to Stratford East, London, in 1953, where she was acclaimed for her experimental techniques involving improvisation and audience participation. Her most successful productions were *Fings Ain't Wot They Used T'Be* (1959) and *Oh, What a Lovely War!* (1963).

1 Oh, what a lovely war!

Song and title of stage show (1963, filmed 1969, written with Charles Chilton and Gerry Raffles)

## Liu Shao-Ch'i (1898–1969)
CHINESE LEADER

He was elected to China's politburo in 1934, wrote *How to be a Good Communist* in 1939 and in 1959 rose to become Chairman of the People's Republic of China. His recovery programme, initiated after the failure of the Great Leap Forward, was seen as a return to capitalism, and he was denounced during the Cultural Revolution and in 1967 stripped of his post.

1 There is no such thing as a perfect leader either in the past or present, in China or elsewhere. If there is one, he is only pretending, like a pig inserting scallions into its nose in an effort to look like an elephant.

Said 13 July 1947, quoted in *Mao and China: From Revolution to Revolution*, ch. 4 (1972) by Stanley Karnow

## Penelope Lively (b. 1933)
BRITISH NOVELIST

A vivid sense of the past and of place ('I write with a very strong sense of topography') pervades her writing, both in her work for

children and in her adult fiction. Notable are her children's books *The Ghost of Thomas Kempe* (1973) and the memoir *Oleander, Jacaranda* (1994), in which she recalls her childhood in Egypt, and the adult novels *Moon Tiger* (1987) and *Cleopatra's Sister* (1993), set in North Africa.

1 Wars are fought by children. Conceived by their mad demonic elders, and fought by boys.

*Moon Tiger*, ch. 8 (1987)

2 I believe that the experience of childhood is irretrievable. All that remains, for any of us, is a headful of brilliant frozen moments, already dangerously distorted by the wisdoms of maturity.

*Oleander, Jacaranda*, Preface (1994)

## Ken Livingstone (b. 1945)
BRITISH POLITICIAN

Comfortable with controversy, he implemented left-wing policies while serving as leader of the Greater London Council (1981–6) until the council was dismantled by the Conservative government. He was elected Labour MP for Brent East, London in 1987 and was expelled from the Labour Party when he ran as an independent candidate for the London mayoral election in 2000, which he won.

1 [On journalism] What a squalid and irresponsible little profession it is ... Nothing prepares you for how bad Fleet Street really is until it craps on you from a great height.

Quoted in *City Limits* 1 May 1986

2 The problem is that many MPs never see the London that exists beyond the wine bars and brothels of Westminster.

*The Times* 19 February 1987

3 Anybody who enjoys being in the House of Commons probably needs psychiatric care.

*Evening Standard* 26 February 1988

4 Politics is a marathon not a sprint.

*New Statesman* 10 October 1997

5 You can judge politicians by how they treat refugees; they do to them what they would like to do to everyone else if they could get away with it.

Quoted in the *Independent on Sunday* 13 June 1999

## David Lloyd George (1863–1945)
BRITISH POLITICIAN AND PRIME MINISTER

First Earl of Dwyfor. He was elected Liberal MP for Caernarfon Boroughs in 1890. A pioneer of social reform, he introduced old age pensions and national insurance while Chancellor of the Exchequer (1908–15). As head of a coalition government (1916–22), he secured a unified Allied command in the First World War and was later described by HITLER as 'the man who won the war'. JOHN MAYNARD KEYNES referred to him as 'this extraordinary figure of our time, this syren, this goat-footed bard, this half-human visitor to our age from the hag-ridden magic and enchanted woods of Celtic antiquity'. See also MARGOT ASQUITH 2.

1 We have been living in a sheltered valley for generations. We have been too comfortable and too indulgent – many, perhaps, too selfish – and the stern hand of fate has scourged us to an elevation where we can see the great everlasting things that matter for a nation – the great peaks we had forgotten, of Honour, Duty, Patriotism, and, clad in glittering white, the great pinnacle of Sacrifice pointing like a rugged finger to Heaven.

Speech at Queen's Hall, London, 21 September 1914, publ. in *The Penguin Book of Twentieth-Century Speeches* (ed. Brian MacArthur, 1999)

2 At eleven o'clock this morning came to an end the cruellest and most terrible war that has ever scourged mankind. I

hope we may say that thus, this fateful morning, came to an end all wars.

Speech to House of Commons, London, 11 November 1918, publ. in *Hansard*. The speech was made on the day that the armistice was signed between the allied powers and Germany. *The War That Will End War* was the title of a novel by H.G. WELLS (1914).

3 What is our task? To make Britain a fit country for heroes to live in.

Speech at Wolverhampton, England, 24 November 1918, publ. in *The Penguin Book of Twentieth-Century Speeches* (ed. Brian Mac-Arthur, 1999). The words were frequently recalled in the years of low wages and unemployment that followed.

4 The finest eloquence is that which gets things done and the worst is that which delays them.

Speech at Paris Peace Conference, 18 January 1919, quoted in *The Times* 20 January 1919

## (Sir) Robert Lockhart (1886–1970)

BRITISH AUTHOR, DIPLOMAT AND JOURNALIST

In 1918, while serving as the unofficial British representative to the Bolshevik government, he was accused of conspiring in a plot to kill LENIN but escaped a death sentence when he was exchanged for a Russian prisoner. He wrote for the *Evening Standard* and served as Deputy Under-secretary to the Foreign Office during the Second World War. His books include *Memoirs of a British Agent* (1932) and *My Europe* (1952).

1 As a cure for the cold, take your toddy to bed, put one bowler hat at the foot, and drink until you see two.

Quoted in the *Independent* 25 November 1989

## David Lodge (b. 1935)

BRITISH NOVELIST AND CRITIC

Using both realism and parody, he treats Roman Catholicism in *The British Museum Is Falling Down* (1965) and *How Far Can You Go?* (1980), academia in *Changing Places* (1975) and the conflicting worlds of education and industry in *Nice Work* (1988, televised 1989). His literary criticism includes *The Novelist at the Crossroads* (1971) and *Working with Structuralism* (1981).

1 Literature is mostly about having sex and not much about having children. Life is the other way round.

Adam Appleby, in *The British Museum Is Falling Down*, ch. 4 (1965)

2 As to our universities . . . they are élitist where they should be egalitarian and egalitarian where they should be élitist.

Charles, in *Nice Work*, pt 5, ch. 4 (1988)

## Henry Cabot Lodge Jr (1902–85)

US SENATOR AND UN DELEGATE

He won a Republican seat in the Senate in 1936, losing it in 1952 to JOHN F. KENNEDY. He subsequently served as Ambassador to the United Nations until 1960 and Ambassador to Vietnam (1963–4 and 1965–7), and was chief US negotiator at the Vietnam peace talks in 1969.

1 [Of the UN] This organization is created to prevent you from going to hell. It isn't created to take you to heaven.

*The New York Times* 28 January 1954

## Haniel Long (1888–1956)

US AUTHOR, POET AND PUBLISHER

Among his poetical works are *Atlantides* (1933) and *The Grist Mill* (1945). His novels include *Interlinear to Cabeza de Vaca* (1936) and *Malinche* (1939).

1 And who is any of us, that without starvation he can go through the kingdoms of starvation?

*Interlinear to Cabeza de Vaca* (1936)

2 Our deeds disguise us. People need endless time to try on

their deeds, until each knows the proper deeds for him to do. But every day, every hour, rushes by. There is no time.

*Malinche* (1939)

3 Has a man any fault a woman cannot weave with and try to change into something better, if the god her man prays to is a mother holding a baby?

ibid.

## Anita Loos (1888–1981)

US NOVELIST AND SCREENWRITER

In six decades she wrote 150 screenplays and scenarios as well as Broadway plays and memoirs, although her name is chiefly associated with the novel *Gentlemen Prefer Blondes* (1925, filmed 1928 and 1953), a witty portrait of the Roaring Twenties. Always cavalier about her success, she would only say: 'I did it for the money.'

1 I really think that American gentlemen are the best after all, because kissing your hand may make you feel very very good but a diamond and a sapphire bracelet lasts forever.

*Gentlemen Prefer Blondes*, 'Paris is Divine' (1925). Lorelei Lee's journal entry 27 April.

2 Pleasure that isn't paid for is as insipid as everything else that's free.

*Kiss Hollywood Good-by*, ch. 2 (1974)

3 Show business is the best possible therapy for remorse.

ibid. ch. 13

4 That our popular art forms have become so obsessed with sex has turned the U.S.A. into a nation of hobbledehoys; as if grown people don't have more vital concerns, such as taxes, inflation, dirty politics, earning a living, getting an education, or keeping out of jail.

ibid. ch. 21

5 If we have to tell Hollywood good-by, it may be with one of those tender, old-fashioned, seven-second kisses exchanged between two people of the *opposite* sex, with all their clothes on.

ibid. ch. 21. Last lines of book.

## Sophia Loren (b. 1934)

ITALIAN ACTRESS

Original name Sofia Scicolone. A teenage beauty queen and model before taking up acting, she was promoted by her husband Carlo Ponti and became internationally renowned. She often played opposite Marcello Mastroianni and her many films include *Two Women* (1961), for which she won an Oscar, and *The Millionairess* (1961). The actor Alan Ladd compared working with her to 'being bombed by watermelons'.

1 Sex appeal is fifty percent what you've got and fifty percent what people think you've got.

Quoted in *Halliwell's Who's Who in the Movies* (ed. John Walker, 1999)

## Konrad Lorenz (1903–89)

AUSTRIAN ETHOLOGIST

Known as the father of ethology, he contributed to the knowledge of behavioural patterns in animals, particularly in birds, and in 1935 recorded the phenomenon of imprinting. His books include *Man Meets Dog* (1950) and *On Aggression* (1963). He shared the Nobel Prize for Physiology and Medicine in 1973.

1 It is a good morning exercise for a research scientist to discard a pet hypothesis every day before breakfast. It keeps him young.

*On Aggression*, ch. 2 (1963)

2 Historians will have to face the fact that natural selection

determined the evolution of cultures in the same manner as it did that of species.

ibid. ch. 13

## Joe Louis (1914–81)
US BOXER

Original name Joseph Louis Borrow and nicknamed the 'Brown Bomber'. Winning sixty-seven out of seventy professional fights, he was World Heavyweight Champion between 1937 and 1949, defending his title a record twenty-five times.

1 He can run. But he can't hide.

Quoted in *Louis: My Life Story* (1947). The threat was addressed to Billy Conn, his opponent in a World Championship match, 19 June 1946, which Louis won.

## (Sir) Bernard Lovell (b. 1913)
BRITISH ASTRONOMER

A pioneer in the study of radio astronomy, he founded Jodrell Bank Experimental Station (now Nuffield Radio Astronomy Laboratories) near Manchester and was its Director from 1951–81. Among his books are *Radio Astronomy* (1951) and *Voice of the Universe* (1987).

1 The pursuit of the good and evil are now linked in astronomy as in almost all science . . . The fate of human civilization will depend on whether the rockets of the future carry the astronomer's telescope or a hydrogen bomb.

'Fourth Reith Lecture', publ. in *The Individual and the Universe* (1959)

## James Lovell (b. 1928)
US ASTRONAUT

He was crew member of the Gemini 7 (1965), Gemini 12 (1966) and Apollo 8 (1968) space missions, and as commander of the unsuccessful Apollo 13 moon mission (1970) safely returned the spacecraft to earth. He was Deputy Director of the Johnson Space Center in Houston, Texas (1971–3).

1 Houston, we've had a problem.

On Apollo 13 space mission, 14 April 1970, quoted in *The Times* 15 April 1970. Following an explosion in the service module, which led to the abandonment of the moon landing, although the crew was able to return safely to earth three days later. The words have also been ascribed to another crew member, John Swigert.

## Amy Lowell (1874–1925)
US POET

After her first collection, *A Dome of Many-Colored Glass* (1912), she met EZRA POUND, who said of her: 'When I get through with that girl she'll think she was born in free verse.' She became the leader of the Imagist movement in America, writing what she called 'polyphonic prose' and 'unrhymed cadence'. Her works include *Sword Blade and Poppy Seeds* (1914) and *What's O'Clock* (1925), for which she was posthumously awarded the Pulitzer Prize.

1 All books are either dreams or swords,
You can cut, or you can drug, with words.

'Sword Blades and Poppy Seed', publ. in *Sword Blades and Poppy Seed* (1914)

2 For the man who should loose me is dead,
Fighting with the Duke in Flanders,
In a pattern called a war.
Christ! What are patterns for?

'Patterns', publ. in *Men, Women and Ghosts* (1916)

3 Moon!
Moon!
I am prone before you.

Pity me,
And drench me in loneliness.

'On a Certain Critic', publ. in *Pictures of a Floating World* (1919)

4 A man must be sacrificed now and again
To provide for the next generation of men.

'A Critical Fable' (1922)

## Robert Lowell (1917–77)
US POET

His early collections, such as the Pulitzer Prize-winning *Lord Weary's Castle* (1946), reflected his conversion to Roman Catholicism in conflict with his Boston ancestry. *Life Studies* (1959), which dealt with such episodes from his personal life as mental illness, marital discord and alcoholism, indicated a new style both confessional and ironic, which characterized his later collections, including *Imitations* (1961), *For the Union Dead* (1964) and *The Old Glory* (1965).

1 I saw the spiders marching through the air,
Swimming from tree to tree that mildewed day
In latter August when the hay
Came creaking to the barn.

'Mr Edwards and the Spider', written 1946, publ. in *Poems 1938–1949* (1950)

2 This is death.
To die and know it. This is the Black Widow, death.

ibid.

3 These are the tranquilized *Fifties*,
and I am forty. Ought I to regret my seedtime?

'Memories of West Street and Lepke', publ. in *Life Studies* (1959)

4 I was a fire-breathing Catholic C.O.,
and made my manic statement,
telling off the state and president, and then
sat waiting sentence in the bull pen
beside a Negro boy with curlicues
of marijuana in his hair.

ibid. Lowell was an ardent convert to Roman Catholicism in the 1940s.

5 At forty-five,
What next, what next?
I meet my father,
my age, still alive.

'Middle Age', publ. in *For The Union Dead* (1964)

6 Their monument sticks like a fishbone
in the city's throat.

'For The Union Dead', publ. in ibid.

7 The Aquarium is gone. Everywhere,
giant finned cars nose forward like fish;
a savage servility
slides by on grease.

ibid.

8 If we see light at the end of the tunnel,
It's the light of the oncoming train.

'Since 1939', publ. in *Day by Day* (1977)

9 Folly comes from something –
the present, yes,
we are in it,
it's the infection
of things gone.

'We Took Our Paradise', publ. in ibid.

## Malcolm Lowry (1909–57)
BRITISH NOVELIST

His best known novel, *Under the Volcano* (1947), which describes the last day of an alcoholic British consul in Mexico, drew on his own experience as a nomadic alcoholic. He lived mainly in British

Columbia, returning to Britain in 1954. He died of barbiturate poisoning.

1 What I have absolutely no sympathy with is the legislator, the man who seeks, for his own profit, to exploit the weaknesses of those who are unable to help themselves and then to fasten some moral superscription upon it. This I loathe so much that I cannot conceivably explain how much it is.

Letter, 1937, publ. in *Selected Letters of Malcolm Lowry* (1967). Lowry was fulminating against his persecution by 'spies and dogs' in Oaxaca, Mexico, where he was drinking heavily while writing *Under the Volcano*.

2 How alike are the groans of love to those of the dying.

Narrator, in *Under the Volcano*, ch. 12 (1947)

## E.V. Lucas (1868–1938)

BRITISH JOURNALIST AND ESSAYIST

Full name Edward Verrall Lucas. He was a prolific writer of novels, travel books and essays in the style of Charles Lamb, on whom he was an authority. His essay collections include *Adventures and Misgivings* (1938).

1 I have noticed that the people who are late are often so much jollier than the people who have to wait for them.

*365 Days and One More*, 'October 3' (1926). 'I am a believer in punctuality,' Lucas wrote in 1932, 'though it makes me very lonely.'

2 There can be no defence like elaborate courtesy.

*Reading, Writing and Remembering*, ch. 8 (1932)

## George Lucas (b. 1944)

US FILM-MAKER

Although reminding STEVEN SPIELBERG of 'Walt Disney's version of a mad scientist', he has become one of the most commercially successful film-makers of today, and in 2000 topped the Forbes 'rich list'. He co-wrote and directed *American Graffiti* (1973) and wrote and directed *Star Wars* (1977), also contributing to the latter's various sequels.

1 Star Wars.

Title of film (written and directed by George Lucas, 1977). The film won seven Academy Awards and was the highest grossing film at the time. In 1983 President REAGAN announced the Strategic Defense Initiative, a missile defence system based in space, which was immediately nicknamed the Star Wars defence.

2 May the Force be with you!

Ben 'Obi-wan' Kenobi (Alec Guinness), in ibid.

3 The Empire Strikes Back.

Title of film (1980, screenplay by Leigh Brackett and Laurence Kasdan from original story by George Lucas, directed by Irvin Kershner)

## Clare Boothe Luce (1903–87)

US DIPLOMAT AND AUTHOR

Also known as Clare Boothe, she was Managing Editor of *Vanity Fair* (1930–34) and the author of the Broadway hits *The Women* (1936, filmed 1939) and *Kiss the Boys Goodbye* (1938, filmed 1941). She subsequently embarked on a political career and was elected to the House of Representatives as a Republican in 1942. She was US Ambassador to Italy (1953–7).

1 Lying increases the creative faculties, expands the ego, lessens the friction of social contacts ... It is only in lies, wholeheartedly and bravely told, that human nature attains through words and speech the forbearance, the nobility, the romance, the idealism, that – being what it is – it falls so short of in fact and in deed.

*Vanity Fair* October 1930

2 A man has only one escape from his old self: to see a different self – in the mirror of some woman's eyes.

Mrs Morehead, in *The Women* act 1, sc. 3 (1936). Directed by George Cukor, the film version achieved some notoriety with a cast of 135 women and no men.

3 You know, that's the only good thing about divorce; you get to sleep with your mother.

Little Mary, in ibid. act 2, sc. 4

4 Much of what Mr Wallace calls his global thinking is, no matter how you slice it, still 'globaloney'. Mr Wallace's warp of sense and his woof of nonsense is very tricky cloth out of which to cut the pattern of a post-war world.

Speech to Congress, 9 February 1943, publ. in *Congressional Record*, vol. 89. Referring to Vice-president Henry Wallace's views on foreign policy, in Boothe Luce's maiden speech in the House, when she first coined the term *globaloney*.

5 To put a woman on the ticket would challenge the loyalty of women everywhere to their sex, because it would be made to seem that the defeat of the ticket meant the defeat for a hundred years of women's chance to be truly equal with men in politics.

Quoted in the *New York World-Telegram* 28 June 1948

6 Communism is the opiate of the intellectuals [with] no cure except as a guillotine might be called a cure for dandruff.

*Newsweek* 24 January 1955

7 But if God had wanted us to think just with our wombs, why did He give us a brain?

Nora, in *Slam the Door Softly* (1970)

## John Lukacs (b. 1924)

HUNGARIAN-BORN US HISTORIAN

Known as a 'philosopher historian', he has published *Decline and Rise of Europe* (1965), *1945: Year Zero* (1978) and *Outgrowing Democracy: A History of the United States in the Twentieth Century* (1984).

1 All the isms are wasms – except one, the most powerful ism of this century, indeed, of the entire democratic age, which is nationalism.

'The Stirrings of History', publ. in *Harper's Magazine* August 1990

## Alison Lurie (b. 1926)

US AUTHOR

EDMUND WHITE has compared Lurie's work to that of HENRY JAMES, seeing in it 'long unbroken threads, seamless progressions of effects'. Her novels, such as *Foreign Affairs* (1984), which won a Pulitzer Prize, recount the lives of the sophisticated and academic upper middle class. She later turned to non-fictional commentary.

1 Conspicuous consumption in dress still survives in two locations: the private lives of the urban rich and the public lives of the urban poor.

*The Language of Clothes*, Preface (1981, rev. 1992)

## Witold Lutoslawski (1913–94)

POLISH COMPOSER AND CONDUCTOR

A prolific and well-travelled composer and a conductor of his own pieces, he is best known for his orchestral work. The twelve-tone work *Funeral Music* (1958) for string orchestra marked a turning point in his style from such traditional pieces as *Symphonic Variations* (1938) and *Variations on a Theme of Paganini* for two pianos (1941) to compositions that contained aleatory and improvisational forms, as in *Venetian Games* (1961).

1 One can create a masterpiece by using any means of expression, no matter how absurd, just as one can make

a beautiful gesture lying at the edge, or even the bottom, of a precipice.

*Conversations with Witold Lutoslawski*, ch. 9 (ed. Tadeusz Kaczynski, 1972, transl. 1984)

2 The collection of antiques which is a symphony orchestra belongs more properly to the past. A modern composer is forced to translate into the language of these old instruments what his imagination proposes to him in a form which has nothing in common with them.

ibid. ch. 13

3 People whose sensibility is destroyed by music in trains, airports, lifts, cannot concentrate on a Beethoven quartet.

*Independent on Sunday* 13 January 1991

## Rosa Luxemburg (1870–1919)
POLISH-BORN GERMAN REVOLUTIONARY

Known as 'Red Rosa' and idolized by many on the left, she was a brilliant speaker and incisive political writer. She co-founded what would later be the Polish Communist Party before moving to Germany in 1898. Here in 1916 she set up, with Karl Liebknecht, the Spartacus League, an organization that developed into the German Communist Party. She was murdered by army officers after organizing an abortive uprising in Berlin.

1 Freedom is always and exclusively freedom for the one who thinks differently.

Prison notes 1918, publ. in *The Russian Revolution*, ch. 6 (1922, transl. 1961)

2 Without general elections, without unrestricted freedom of press and assembly, without a free struggle of opinion, life dies out in every public institution, becomes a mere semblance of life, in which only the bureaucracy remains as the active element. Public life gradually falls asleep, a few dozen party leaders of inexhaustible energy and boundless experience direct and rule . . . Such conditions must inevitably cause a brutalization of public life: attempted assassinations, shootings of hostages, etc.

ibid.

## Gavin Lyall (b. 1932)
BRITISH JOURNALIST AND NOVELIST

At first writing adventure thrillers, he turned to tales of espionage, such as *The Secret Servant* (1980) and *The Crocus List* (1985). He has also written on the history of military aviation.

1 Opinionated writing is always the most difficult . . . simply because it involves retaining in the cold morning-after crystal of the printed word the burning flow of molten feeling.

Introduction to *Roundabout* (1962) by Katharine Whitehorn

## John Lydon (b. 1957)
BRITISH ROCK MUSICIAN

As Johnny Rotten, he joined the seminal punk band the Sex Pistols in 1975 as singer and leering *agent provocateur*. The band's three-year career produced such vitriolic anthems as 'Anarchy in the UK' (1976) and 'God Save the Queen' (1977) and inspired a generation of punk rockers. Weary of his role ('My reputation is a media creation,' he insisted), he formed Public Image Limited, with which he performed and recorded post-punk industrial music.

1 I am an Anti-Christ
I am an anarchist
Don't know what I want but I know where to get it
I wanna destroy passers-by
Because I wanna be anarchy!

'Anarchy in the U.K.' (song, 1976, written by Johnny Rotten, Steve Jones, Glen Matlock and Paul Cook) on the album *Never Mind the Bollocks* (1977) by the Sex Pistols

2 There's no love at all . . . You can't love anything. Love is what you feel for a dog or a pussy cat. It doesn't apply to humans, and if it does it just shows how low you are.

Interview, 19 November 1976, publ. in *1988: The New Wave Punk Rock Explosion*, 'The Sex Pistols' (1977) by Caroline Coon

3 When there's no future
How can there be sin
We're the flowers in the dustbin
We're the poison in your human machine
We're the future
Your future
God Save the Queen.

'God Save the Queen/No Future' (song, written by Johnny Rotten, Steve Jones, Glen Matlock and Paul Cook) on the album *Never Mind the Bollocks* (1977) by the Sex Pistols. Despite a broadcasting ban on the song, which was released to coincide with the twenty-fifth anniversary celebrations of Queen Elizabeth II's accession, it reached no. 2 in the British charts.

4 We're pretty . . . pretty vacant
And we don't care.

'Pretty Vacant' (song, written by Johnny Rotten, Steve Jones, Glen Matlock and Paul Cook) on ibid.

5 I'm not here for your amusement. You're here for mine.

To audience in Memphis, Tennessee, 1978, quoted in *Sex Pistols File* (ed. Ray Stevenson, 1984)

6 No one in this band is a musician. We all hate the term. We're something close to factory workers. Machinists. Skilled operators.

Quoted in *Rock 'N' Roll Babylon*, ch. 4 (1982) by Gary Herman

7 Punks in their silly leather jackets are a cliché. I have never liked the term and have never discussed it. I just got on with it and got out of it when it became a competition.

*Observer* 4 May 1986

8 Sex is two minutes of squelching.

Quoted in *Vox* March 1994

## David Lynch (b. 1946)
US FILM-MAKER

His first film, *Eraserhead* (1977), established him as a film-maker of dark and bizarre originality. *Elephant Man* (1980), the surrealistic thriller *Blue Velvet* (1986) and *Wild at Heart* (1990) followed this success, but he is probably known best for the cult TV series *Twin Peaks* (1989–91).

1 When you sleep, you don't control your dream. I like to dive into a dream world that I've made, a world I chose and that I have complete control over.

*La Revue du Cinéma* February 1987, quoted in *David Lynch*, ch. 5 (1992) by Michel Chion

2 Damned fine cup of coffee!

Agent Dale Cooper (Kyle MacLachlan), in *Twin Peaks* (TV series, 1989–91, written and created by David Lynch and Mark Frost). 'Damned fine cheese cake!' and 'Damned fine pie!' are other frequent remarks associated with Agent Cooper.

3 This whole world is wild at heart and weird on top.

Lula (Laura Dern), in *Wild at Heart* (film, 1990, written by David Lynch adapted from Barry Gifford's novel, directed by David Lynch)

## Robert Lynd (1879–1949)
ANGLO-IRISH ESSAYIST AND JOURNALIST

He was a leading campaigner for the reprieve of ROGER CASEMENT, became Literary Editor of the *Daily News* (later the *News Chronicle*, 1913–47) and published numerous volumes of essays he wrote for the *New Statesman* (1913–45) as 'YY', as well as many books on literature and Ireland.

1 There are some people who want to throw their arms round you simply because it is Christmas; there are other

people who want to strangle you simply because it is Christmas.

*The Book of This and That*, 'On Christmas' (1915)

## Russell Lynes (1910–91)
US EDITOR AND CRITIC

Most of his journalistic career was devoted to *Harper's Magazine*, of which he became Assistant Editor in 1944. His writings include *Highbrow, Lowbrow, Middlebrow* (1949), *Snobs* (1950) and *The Tastemakers* (1954), all critiques on social pretension in America.

1 It is always well to accept your own shortcomings with candor but to regard those of your friends with polite incredulity.

'The Art of Accepting', publ. in *Vogue* 1 September 1952

2 The art of acceptance is the art of making someone who has just done you a small favor wish that he might have done you a greater one.

*Reader's Digest* December 1954

3 A lady is nothing very specific. One man's lady is another man's woman; sometimes, one man's lady is another man's wife. Definitions overlap but they almost never coincide.

'Is There a Lady in the House?', publ. in *Look* 22 July 1958

## Jonathan Lynn (b. 1943)
BRITISH FILM-MAKER

A former actor turned comedy screenwriter and director, he co-scripted with ANTONY JAY the BBC television series *Yes Minister* (1980–82 and 1986–8) (see RICHARD CROSSMAN 1) and has written and directed the films *Clue* (1985) and *Nuns on the Run* (1990).

1 Husbands should be like kleenex: soft, strong, and disposable.

Mrs White (Madeline Kahn), in *Clue* (film, 1985, written and directed by Jonathan Lynn)

## Loretta Lynn (b. 1935)
US SINGER

She established herself as a leading country singer of the 1960s and 1970s with such albums as *Blue Kentucky Girl* (1965) and *Woman of the World* (1969). Through her songs, which she wrote herself, she spoke for working-class women trapped by early marriages and pregnancies. Her autobiography, *Coal Miner's Daughter* (1976), became a bestseller and was made into a film in 1980.

1 A woman's two cents worth is worth two cents in the music business.

Quoted in the *Los Angeles Times* 26 May 1974

## (Dame) Vera Lynn (b. 1917)
BRITISH SINGER

During the Second World War she become Britain's most popular singing star, catching the mood of the moment with her optimistic 'We'll Meet Again' (1941) and patriotic 'White Cliffs of Dover' (1941). Known as the 'Forces' Sweetheart', she broadcast her own radio series *Sincerely Yours* (1941–7) and in 1952 she was the first British artist to top both the British and American charts with 'Auf Widerseh'n'.

1 We'll meet again
Don't know where, don't know when,
But I know we'll meet again
Some sunny day.

'We'll Meet Again' (song, 1939, written by ROSS PARKER and HUGH CHARLES)

## Jean-François Lyotard (1924–98)
FRENCH PHILOSOPHER

He abandoned his position as a Marxist in the 1950s and 1960s to become a leading theorist of postmodernism. In his book *The Postmodern Condition* (1979) he argued against truth as perceived in 'grand narratives' (all political, religious, historical and scientific theories) in favour of the 'small narratives', which involve the local and personal and concentrate on the individual.

1 Knowledge in the form of an informational commodity indispensable to productive power is already, and will continue to be, a major – perhaps *the* major – stake in the world-wide competition for power. It is conceivable that the nation-states will one day fight for control of information, just as they battled in the past for control over territory, and afterwards for control over access to and exploitation of raw materials and cheap labour.

*The Postmodern Condition: A Report on Knowledge*, Introduction (1979, rev. 1986)

2 Eclecticism is the degree zero of contemporary general culture: one listens to reggae, watches a western, eats McDonald's food for lunch and local cuisine for dinner, wears Paris perfume in Tokyo and 'retro' clothes in Hong Kong; knowledge is a matter for TV games. It is easy to find a public for eclectic works.

'Answering the Question: What is Postmodernism?', first publ. in *Critique* April 1982, repr. in ibid.

3 A work can become modern only if it is first postmodern. Postmodernism thus understood is not modernism at its end but in the nascent state, and this state is constant.

ibid.

## Bernadette McAliskey (b. 1947)

NORTHERN IRISH POLITICIAN

Original name Bernadette Devlin. In 1969 she became the youngest MP in the House of Commons since William Pitt the Younger when she won the Mid-Ulster seat for the Independent Unity Party. Confrontational in style, she was arrested in 1970 during the Bogside riots in Belfast and sentenced to nine months in prison. She co-founded the Irish Republican Socialist Party in 1975.

> 1 **To gain that which is worth having, it may be necessary to lose everything else.**
>
> *The Price of my Soul*, Preface (1969)

## Douglas MacArthur (1880–1964)

US GENERAL

As Supreme Commander of the South West Pacific Area in the Second World War, he accepted the Japanese surrender and administered post-war Japan (1945–50). He led UN forces during the first nine months of the Korean War (1950–51) but was dismissed when he advocated extending the war against China. Recognized as a brilliant strategist, he was also considered arrogant, leading EISENHOWER to remark: 'I studied dramatics under him for twelve years.'

> 1 **I came through and I shall return.**
>
> Statement in Adelaide, Australia, 20 March 1942, quoted in *The New York Times* 21 March 1942. The pledge was made on disembarking from the Philippines, which he had been ordered to evacuate following an unsuccessful defence of the Bataan peninsula. MacArthur subsequently pursued a brilliant 'leap-frogging' strategy, which enabled him to return to the Philippines in October 1944. His men celebrated his victory with the song: 'By the grace of God and a few Marines/MacArthur returned to the Philippines.'

> 2 **Like the old soldier of the ballad, I now close my military career and just fade away, an old soldier who tried to do his duty as God gave him the light to see that duty. Goodbye.**
>
> Speech to Congress, 19 April 1951, publ. in *Congressional Record*, vol. 97. Referring to his dismissal as commander of UN forces in Korea for dissenting with the Truman administration's conduct of the war. TRUMAN called the speech 'nothing but a bunch of damn bullshit' (in Merle Miller's *Plain Speaking: Conversations with Harry S. Truman*, ch. 25, 1973). The 'ballad' referred to by MacArthur was a barrack-room ditty, which originated as a British army song in the First World War.

## (Dame) Rose Macaulay (1881–1958)

BRITISH NOVELIST AND ESSAYIST

She was a writer of humorous and urbane novels, often concerned with the choices of flesh or spirit, the civilized or the barbaric. Titles include *They Were Defeated* (1932), *The World My Wilderness* (1950) and *The Towers of Trebizond* (1956), and she also published travel books and journalism.

> 1 **Sleeping in a bed – it is, apparently, of immense importance. Against those who sleep, from choice or necessity, elsewhere society feels righteously hostile. It is not done. It is disorderly, anarchical.**
>
> *A Casual Commentary*, 'Beds and 'Omes' (1925)

> 2 **Cranks live by theory, not by pure desire. They want votes, peace, nuts, liberty, and spinning-looms not because they love these things, as a child loves jam, but because they think they ought to have them. That is one element which makes the crank.**
>
> ibid. 'Cranks'

> 3 **As to the family, I have never understood how that fits in with the other ideals – or, indeed, why it should be an ideal at all. A group of closely related persons living under one roof; it is a convenience, often a necessity, sometimes**

a pleasure, sometimes the reverse; but who first exalted it as admirable, an almost religious ideal?

*The World My Wilderness*, ch. 20 (1950)

# Eugene J. McCarthy (b. 1916)
US SENATOR AND AUTHOR

Full name Eugene Joseph McCarthy. He entered the House of Representatives as a Democrat in 1949 and challenged President JOHNSON for the presidential nomination in 1968 on a platform of opposition to the Vietnam War. Although Johnson stood down, he failed to gain the nomination, left the Senate in 1970 and turned to writing.

1 The only thing that saves us from the bureaucracy is inefficiency. An efficient bureaucracy is the greatest threat to liberty.

*Time* magazine 12 February 1979

# Joseph McCarthy (1908–57)
US POLITICIAN

Elected a Republican senator in 1946, he created controversy in 1950 with unproven allegations of infiltration of the State Department by communists. The ensuing investigations, which were portrayed by many as a 'McCarthyite witch-hunt', led to blacklisting, damaged reputations and loss of jobs and were brought to an end in 1954 when McCarthy was officially censured by the Senate for unbecoming conduct. For journalist Richard Rovere he was 'this Typhoid Mary of conformity', while HARRY S. TRUMAN called him simply 'a pathological character assassin'.

1 McCarthyism is Americanism with its sleeves rolled.

Speech in Wisconsin, 1952, quoted in *Senator Joe McCarthy*, ch. 1 (1973) by Richard Rovere

# Mary McCarthy (1912–89)
US AUTHOR AND CRITIC

She was a critic for the *Partisan Review*, among other publications, and the writer of satirical novels such as *The Groves of Academe* (1952) and *A Charmed Life* (1955). Her most famous work is *The Group* (1963, filmed 1966), a story of eight Vassar graduates. She was married (1938–46) to the critic Edmund Wilson.

1 When an American heiress wants to buy a man, she at once crosses the Atlantic. The only really materialistic people I have ever met have been Europeans.

'America the Beautiful: the Humanist in the Bathtub', first publ. in *Commentary* September 1947, repr. in *On the Contrary* (1961)

2 The American character looks always as if it had just had a rather bad haircut, which gives it, in our eyes at any rate, a greater humanity than the European, which even among its beggars has an all too professional air.

ibid.

3 The happy ending is our national belief.

ibid.

4 The immense popularity of American movies abroad demonstrates that Europe is the unfinished negative of which America is the proof.

ibid.

5 In verity . . . we are the poor. This humanity we would claim for ourselves is the legacy, not only of the Enlightenment, but of the thousands and thousands of European peasants and poor townspeople who came here bringing their humanity and their sufferings with them. It is the absence of a stable upper class that is responsible for much of the vulgarity of the American scene. Should we blush before the visitor for this deficiency?

ibid.

6 Liberty, as it is conceived by current opinion, has nothing

inherent about it; it is a sort of gift or trust bestowed on the individual by the state pending *good behavior*.

'The Contagion of Ideas' speech, 1952, publ. in ibid.

7 Every age has a keyhole to which its eye is pasted.

'My Confession', first publ. 1953, repr. in ibid.

8 There are no new truths, but only truths that have not been recognized by those who have perceived them without noticing. A truth is something that everybody can be shown to know and to have known, as people say, all along.

'The Vita Activa', first publ. in the *New Yorker* 18 October 1958, repr. in ibid.

9 The labor of keeping house is labor in its most naked state, for labor is toil that never finishes, toil that has to be begun again the moment it is completed, toil that is destroyed and consumed by the life process.

ibid.

10 In violence we forget who we are.

*On the Contrary*, pt 3, 'Characters in Fiction' (1961)

11 I suppose everyone continues to be interested in the quest for the self, but what you feel when you're older, I think, is that . . . you really must *make* the self. It is absolutely useless to look for it, you won't find it, but it's possible in some sense to make it. I don't mean in the sense of making a mask, a Yeatsian mask. But you finally begin in some sense to make and choose the self you want.

Interview in *Writers at Work* (second series, ed. George Plimpton, 1963)

12 Every word she [Lillian Hellman] writes is a lie, including 'and' and 'the'.

Interview on *Dick Cavett Show*, January 1980, quoted in *The New York Times* 16 February 1980. McCarthy was quoting herself referring to LILLIAN HELLMAN in the 1930s. McCarthy's remark resulted in a row and prolonged law suit, which probably contributed to the wasting illness that eventually killed her; see Carol Brightman, *Writing Dangerously: Mary McCarthy and Her World* (1993).

# (Sir) Paul McCartney (b. 1942)
BRITISH ROCK MUSICIAN

Labelled as the gentler, more melodic half of the LENNON–MCCARTNEY partnership, he was bass-guitarist with the Beatles and charged with instigating the band's break-up. His subsequent hits, some recorded with Wings, the band he formed with his wife Linda, made him one of the world's richest musicians, and he has also made and scored a film, *Give My Regards to Broad Street* (1984), co-written (with Colin Davis) the classical 'Liverpool Oratorio' (1991), and co-founded the Liverpool Institute of Performing Arts (1996).

1 I really wish people who look with anger at the weirdos, at the happenings and psychedelic freakouts, would instead of looking with anger look with nothing. If they could be unbiased about it, they'd realize that what these people are talking about is something they'd really like for themselves: personal freedom.

Interview on Granada TV, 1967, quoted in *It Was Twenty Years Ago Today*, ch. 5 (1987) BY DEREK TAYLOR

2 I didn't leave The Beatles. The Beatles have left The Beatles but no one wants to be the one to say the party's over.

Said in 1970, quoted in *The Beatles . . . After the Break-up*, 'You Say Goodbye and I Say Hello . . .' (1991) by David Bennaham

3 What's wrong with sentimental? Sentimental means you *love*, you *care*, you *like* stuff. The thing is, we're *frightened* to be sentimental.

Interview in *Smash Hits* 24 November 1983

4 It's like if you've been an astronaut and you've been to the moon, what do you do with the rest of your life?

Said in 1990, quoted in *The Beatles . . . After the Break-up*, 'I Am the Walrus' (1991) by David Bennaham

5 Ballads and babies. That's what happened to me.

*Time* magazine 8 June 1992. On his fiftieth birthday.

6 It looked so callous in print. You can't take the print back and say, 'Look, let me just rub that print in shit and pee over it and then cry over it for three years, then you'll see what I meant when I said that word'.

Quoted in *Paul McCartney: Many Years From Now*, ch. 14 (1997) by Barry Miles. Referring to his response to reporters asking him to comment on JOHN LENNON's death, 'It's a drag'. He added, 'What I meant was "Fuck off! Don't invade my privacy".'

7 [On starting off in a band] You say you're trying to 'make it', but at that time you just mean 'do well', to get this music thing to feel good so you enjoy it and other people enjoy it, so you'll get asked back.

Quoted in ibid. 'Afterword'

8 I'm a smoke screen expert . . . I lie all the time. It is the price of fame.

Quoted in the *Observer* 26 April 1998

9 She [Linda McCartney] did actually often play the electric piano with more than one finger – they just weren't looking then.

Quoted in the *Observer* 18 October 1998. On critics who claimed Linda played keyboards with only one finger.

## Ewan MacColl (1915–89)

BRITISH FOLK SINGER AND SONGWRITER

Original name James Miller. Together with JOAN LITTLEWOOD he formed the influential Theatre Workshop in 1945 and was a leading figure in the folk revival of the 1950s and 1960s. With his wife Peggy Seeger he devised an innovatory series of *Radio Ballads*, a combination of interviews, narration and songs broadcast by the BBC (1958–65). Among his best known songs are 'Dirty Old Town' (1950) and 'The First Time Ever I Saw Your Face' (1958).

1 I found my love by the gasworks crofts
Dreamed a dream by the old canal
Kissed my girl by the factory wall
Dirty old town, dirty old town.

'Dirty Old Town' (song, 1950). MacColl wrote the song in order to facilitate a scene change in his play *Landscape with Chimneys*. It was recorded by the Spinners and revived by Shane MacGowan's band the Pogues in 1985.

2 Dylan is to me the perfect symbol of the anti-artist in our society. He is against everything – the last resort of someone who doesn't really want to change the world . . . Dylan's songs accept the world as it is.

Interview in *Melody Maker* September 1965, quoted in *No Direction Home*, ch. 8 by Robert Shelton (biography of BOB DYLAN, 1989)

## Frank McCourt

US AUTHOR

Of Irish parentage, he worked as a teacher and lecturer in New York for thirty years before his first book *Angela's Ashes* became an international bestseller (1996, filmed 1999). This bleak memoir of his Irish childhood 'does for the town of Limerick what the young Joyce did for Dublin', according to *The New York Times*, and was followed by its sequel *'Tis* in 1999.

1 When I look back on my childhood I wonder how I survived at all. It was, of course, a miserable childhood: the happy childhood is hardly worth your while. Worse than the ordinary miserable childhood is the miserable Irish childhood, and worse yet is the miserable Irish Catholic childhood.

*Angela's Ashes*, ch. 1 (1996)

## Carson McCullers (1917–67)

US AUTHOR

Described as 'Southern Gothic' in style, her novels focus on the misfits and outcasts of society. She came to recognition with her first novel, *The Heart Is a Lonely Hunter* (1940), and her novella *The Ballad of the Sad Café* (1951) was dramatized by EDWARD ALBEE in 1963. 'Spiritual isolation is the basis of most of my themes,' she once commented. From the age of twenty-nine she was confined to a wheelchair.

1 All men are lonely. But sometimes it seems to me that we Americans are the loneliest of all. Our hunger for foreign places and new ways has been with us almost like a national disease. Our literature is stamped with a quality of longing and unrest, and our writers have been great wanderers.

'Look Homeward, Americans', first publ. in *Vogue* 1 December 1940, repr. in *The Mortgaged Heart* (ed. Margarita G. Smith, 1972)

2 There's nothing that makes you so aware of the improvisation of human existence as a song unfinished. Or an old address book.

Ferris, in 'The Sojourner', publ. in *The Ballad of the Sad Café* (1951)

## Hugh MacDiarmid (1892–1978)

SCOTTISH POET AND CRITIC

Original name Christopher Murray Grieve. With his deliberate use of Scots dialect and colloquialisms, he established himself in the 1920s as the leading figure of the 'Scottish Renaissance'. His views on Scotland, present and future, are represented in his major work, *A Drunk Man Looks at the Thistle* (1926). An ardent Marxist, he was co-founder of the Scottish Nationalist Party in 1928.

1 [Of Neville Chamberlain]
There is no such excuse for this Brummagen
'peace-maker',
This ig-Nobel prizewinner,
This ersatz-Christian,
This 'J'aime Berlin'!
Never were accessories to crime more cold-blooded;
The callous and irresponsible betrayal
Of the Czech Republic has brought not peace
But a new and sharper sword . . .

'When the Gangs Came to London: On the Recent Thanksgiving for "Peace" ', first publ. in *The Times Literary Supplement* 17 March 2000. The recently unearthed poem was sent to Catherine Carswell, 17 October 1938 (dedicated to her and Karel Čapek). The last lines echo Matthew 10:34: 'Think not that I came to send peace on the earth: I came not to send peace, but a sword.'

2 Auden, MacNeice, Day Lewis, I have read them all,
Hoping against hope to hear the authentic call.
. . .
And I know the explanation I must pass is this
– You cannot light a match on a crumbling wall.

'British Leftish Poetry, 1930–1940', from poem sequence *Impavidi Progrediamur* (c. 1940–60), publ. in *Collected Poems* (1962)

3 Man does not cease to interest me
When he ceases to be miserable.
Quite the contrary!
That it is important to aid him
In the beginning goes without saying,
Like a plant it is essential
To water at first,
But this is in order to get it to flower
And I *am* concerned with the blossom.

'Reflections in a Slum', from ibid. Concluding lines of poem.

## Country Joe McDonald (b. 1942)

US SINGER AND SONGWRITER

Performing politically inspired songs from c. 1960, he formed Country Joe and the Fish in 1965, a band combining protest with psychedelic rock. He pursued a solo career during the 1970s and became increasingly involved in ecological issues.

> 1 And it's one, two, three what are we fightin' for?
> Don't ask me I don't give a damn, next stop is Vietnam!
> And it's five, six, seven, open up the pearly gates,
> There ain't no time to wonder why,
> *Whoopee!* – we're all going to die.
>
> 'I-Feel-Like-I'm-Fixin'-to-Die-Rag' (song, 1965) on the album *I-Feel-Like-I'm-Fixin'-to-Die-Rag* (1968) by Country Joe and the Fish. The song became a feature of the anti-war rallies and festivals at which Country Joe appeared.

## (Sir) Trevor McDonald (b. 1939)

TRINIDAD-BORN BRITISH JOURNALIST AND BROADCASTER

A dedicated cricket enthusiast who has written biographies of the cricketers Clive Lloyd (1985) and Viv Richards (1987), he became the most familiar black face on television as newscaster for ITN's *News at Ten* (1990–99).

> 1 Men of my age live in a state of continual desperation.
> *Today* 8 December 1989
>
> 2 I am a West Indian peasant who has drifted into this business and who has survived. If I knew the secret, I would bottle it and sell it.
> Quoted in the *Independent* 20 April 1996

## Ian McEwan (b. 1948)

BRITISH AUTHOR

His early work, beginning with the stories *First Love, Last Rites* (1975), is characterized by a preoccupation with the erotic and macabre. Novels include *The Child in Time* (1987), *Black Dogs* (1992) and *Amsterdam*, winner of the 1998 Booker Prize.

> 1 One has to have the courage of one's pessimism.
> Interview in the *Guardian* 26 May 1983
>
> 2 By concentrating on what is good in people, by appealing to their idealism and their sense of justice, and by asking them to put their faith in the future, socialists put themselves at a severe disadvantage.
> Interview in *City Limits* 27 May 1983
>
> 3 For children, childhood is timeless. It's always the present. Everything is in the present tense. Of course they have memories. Of course, time shifts a little for them and Christmas comes round in the end. But they don't *feel* it. Today is what they feel, and when they say 'When I grow up . . .' there's always an edge of disbelief – how could they ever be other than what they are?
> Charles Darke, in *The Child in Time*, ch. 2 (1987)
>
> 4 A disruptive minority of humankind regarded journeys, even short ones, as the occasion for pleasant encounters. There were people ready to inflict intimacies on strangers. Such travellers were to be avoided if you belonged to the majority for whom a journey was the occasion for silence, reflection, daydream. The requirements were simple: an unobstructed view of a changing landscape, however dull, and freedom from the breath of other passengers, their body warmth, sandwiches and limbs.
> Narrator, in ibid. ch. 3
>
> 5 [On novel-writing] You enter a state of controlled passivity, you relax your grip and accept that even if your declared intention is to justify the ways of God to man, you might end up interesting your readers rather more in Satan.
> *A Move Abroad*, Preface (1989)
>
> 7 It is not the first duty of the novelist to provide blueprints for insurrection, or uplifting tales of successful resistance

for the benefit of the opposition. The naming of what is there is what is important.
> ibid.
>
> 8 It is photography itself that creates the illusion of innocence. Its ironies of frozen narrative lend to its subjects an apparent unawareness that they will change or die. It is the future they are innocent of. Fifty years on we look at them with the godly knowledge of how they turned out after all – who they married, the date of their death – with no thought for who will one day be holding the photographs of us.
> Jeremy in *Black Dogs*, pt 1 (1992)
>
> 9 This is our mammalian conflict – what to give to the others, and what to keep for yourself. Treading that line, keeping the others in check, and being kept in check by them, is what we call morality.
> *Enduring Love*, ch. 1 (1997)
>
> 10 Mostly, we are good when it makes sense. A good society is one that makes sense of being good.
> ibid.

## John McGinley

US SCREEN ACTOR

After his debut in *Sweet Liberty* (1986) he has appeared in several of OLIVER STONE's films such as *Wall Street* (1987) and *Nixon* (1995). Other films include *Seven* (1995) and *The Rock* (1996).

> 1 You're a real blue flame special, aren't you son? Young, dumb and full of come, I know. What I don't know is how you got assigned here. Guess we must have ourselves an asshole shortage, huh?
> Ben Harp (John McGinley), in *Point Break* (film, screenplay by Pete Iliff, directed by Kathryn Bigelow, 1991). McGinley is grilling FBI agent Keanu Reeves, newly posted to an LA police department.

## Phyllis McGinley (1905–78)

US POET AND AUTHOR

A wry essayist and deftly humorous versifier, she was praised by W.H. AUDEN among others. Her poetry collections include *A Pocketful of Wry* (1940) and *Times Three* (1960), for which she was awarded the Pulitzer Prize.

> 1 Gossip isn't scandal and it's not merely malicious. It's chatter about the human race by lovers of the same. Gossip is the tool of the poet, the shop-talk of the scientist, and the consolation of the housewife, wit, tycoon and intellectual. It begins in the nursery and ends when speech is past.
> 'A New Year and No Resolutions', publ. in *Woman's Home Companion* January 1957
>
> 2 Our bodies are shaped to bear children, and our lives are a working out of the processes of creation. All our ambitions and intelligence are beside that great elemental point.
> *The Province of the Heart*, 'The Honor of Being a Woman' (1959)
>
> 3 Say what you will, making marriage work is a woman's business. The institution was invented to do her homage; it was contrived for her protection. Unless she accepts it as such – as a beautiful, bountiful, but quite unequal association – the going will be hard indeed.
> ibid.
>
> 4 Frigidity is largely nonsense. It is this generation's catchword, one only vaguely understood and constantly misused. Frigid women are few. There is a host of diffident and slow-ripening ones.
> ibid.
>
> 5 Women are the fulfilled sex. Through our children we are

able to produce our own immortality, so we lack that divine restlessness which sends men charging off in pursuit of fortune or fame or an imagined Utopia. That is why we number so few geniuses among us. The wholesome oyster wears no pearl, the healthy whale no ambergris, and as long as we can keep on adding to the race, we harbor a sort of health within ourselves.

ibid. 'Some of My Best Friends . . .'

6 A Mother's hardest to forgive.
Life is the fruit she longs to hand you,
Ripe on a plate. And while you live,
Relentlessly she understands you.
'The Adversary', publ. in *A Certain Age* (1960)

7 The knowingness of little girls
Is hidden underneath their curls.
'What Every Woman Knows', publ. in *Times Three* (1960)

8 For little boys are rancorous
When robbed of any myth,
And spiteful and cantankerous
To all their kin and kith.
But little girls can draw conclusions
And profit from their lost illusions.
ibid.

## Patrick McGoohan (b. 1928)
US-BORN BRITISH ACTOR

He appeared in the films *The Dam Busters* (1954), *Ice Station Zebra* (1968) and *Escape from Alcatraz* (1979) but is best known for his TV personae as secret agent John Drake in *Danger Man* (1960–67) and as Number Six in the cult series *The Prisoner* (1967–8).

1 I am not a number – I am a free man!
Number Six (Patrick McGoohan), in preamble to each episode of *The Prisoner* (TV series, 1967–8, created by Patrick McGoohan, George Markstein and David Tomblin). Number Six (who is never named) states during one episode: 'I will not be pushed stamped, filed, indexed, briefed, debriefed, or numbered. My life is my own.'

2 But what is the greatest evil? If you are going to epitomize evil, what is it? Is it the bomb? The greatest evil that one has to fight constantly, every minute of the day until one dies, is the worse part of oneself.
Quoted in *The Prisoner and Danger Man*, 'I Am Not a Number, I Am a Free Man' (1989) by Dave Rogers

## Roger McGough (b. 1937)
BRITISH POET

With BRIAN PATTEN and Adrian Henri, he was one of the 'Liverpool Poets', Pop art in style and committed to public performance. His off-beat, punning humour is shown in such collections as *The Mersey Sound* (1967), *Gig* (1973) and *Waving at Trains* (1982). He has also written for children and was a member of the novelty group Scaffold (1962–73).

1 Let me die a youngman's death
Not a free from sin tiptoe in
Candle wax and waning death
Not a curtains drawn by angels borne
'What a nice way to go' death
'Let Me Die a Youngman's Death', publ. in *The Mersey Sound* (1967)

2 Teach me, o Lord, to be permissive
the 'sixties way to save the soul
three leers for sexual freedom
let the good times rock'nroll.
'My little plastic mac', publ. in *Watchwords* (1969)

3 May your poems run away from home
and live between the lines.
May they break and enter, assault and batter,

And loiter in the mind with intent.
'the most unforgettable character I've ever met gives advice to the young poet', publ. in *Gig* (1973)

## George McGovern (b. 1922)
US POLITICIAN

A radical reforming Democrat, he was elected to the House of Representatives in 1956 and directed the Food for Peace Program under President KENNEDY in the early 1960s, serving as Senator 1963–81. He was a leading opponent of the war in Vietnam, and as Democratic presidential candidate was heavily defeated by NIXON in 1972.

1 You know, sometimes, when they say you're ahead of your time, it's just a polite way of saying you have a real bad sense of timing.
*Guardian* 14 March 1990

## (Sir) Ian MacGregor (1912–98)
BRITISH INDUSTRIALIST

After years spent in the USA, he returned to Britain to be Chairman of the British Steel Corporation in the early 1980s. As Chairman of the National Coal Board (1983–6) he instigated a programme of drastic cut-backs, which were heavily opposed by trade unions and led to the miners' strike of 1984–5.

1 [Of the miners' strike] People are now discovering the price of insubordination and insurrection. And boy, are we going to make it stick!
Quoted in the *Sunday Telegraph* 10 March 1985

## Thomas McGuane (b. 1939)
US NOVELIST

Known for the black humour targeted at what he terms the 'snivelization' of America, his novels feature anti-heroes grappling with the conditions of contemporary society, as in *The Sporting Club* (1969) and *Nobody's Angel* (1979). A collection of his sports writing is published in *An Outside Chance* (1980).

1 America is like one of those old-fashioned six-cylinder truck engines that can be missing two sparkplugs and have a broken flywheel and a crankshaft that's 5000 millimetres off fitting properly, and two bad ball-bearings, and still runs. We're in that kind of situation. We can have substantial parts of the population committing suicide, and still run and look fairly good.
*Sunday Correspondent* 1 April 1990

## Roger McGuinn (b. 1942)
US ROCK MUSICIAN

Born Jim McGuinn. He was founder member of the folk-rock West Coast group the Byrds in 1964, whose first hit was BOB DYLAN's 'Mr Tambourine Man' (1965). The Byrds' album *Sweetheart of the Rodeo* (1968) set the pattern for country rock, although McGuinn's solo career was undistinguished.

1 Eight miles high,
And when you touch down
You'll find that
It's stranger than known.
'Eight Miles High' (song, written by Roger McGuinn, Gene Clark and David Crosby) on the album *Fifth Dimension* (1966) by the Byrds. The song was one of the first to be banned for its drugs allusions.

## Barry McGuire (b. 1937)
US SINGER AND SONGWRITER

The lead vocalist with The New Christy Minstrels, he had an international solo hit with the protest song 'Eve of Destruction'

(1965). As part of the Los Angeles rock scene he was name-dropped in The Mamas and the Papas song 'Creeque Alley' (1967), but never matched his earlier success and later became a religious singer as a born-again Christian.

1 And you tell me
Over and over again my friend
That you don't believe we're on the eve of destruction.
'Eve of Destruction' (song, written by P.F. Sloan) on the album *Eve of Destruction* (1965). The song was countered soon afterwards by the conservative 'Dawn of Correction' by the Spokesmen (1965).

## William McIlvanney (b. 1936)
BRITISH NOVELIST

Many of his novels reflect the tough working-class culture of his childhood in Scotland, and he has also published a series of thrillers featuring the Glasgow detective Jack Laidlaw, including *Laidlaw* (1977) and *Strange Loyalties* (1991).

1 Who thinks the law has anything to do with justice? It's what we have because we can't have justice.
Laidlaw, in *Laidlaw*, ch. 35 (1977)

## Jay McInerney (b. 1955)
US AUTHOR

His first novel, *Bright Lights, Big City* (1984, filmed 1988), in which the narrator speaks in the second person and present tense throughout, gained him popularity and a reputation for a preppy debauchery. Successive novels included *Ransom* (1985), *The Story of My Life* (1988) and *Brightness Falls* (1992).

1 Don't ask a writer what he's working on. It's like asking someone with cancer about the progress of his disease.
Jeff, in *Brightness Falls*, ch. 1 (1992)

2 A party is like a marriage . . . making itself up while seeming to follow precedent, running on steel rails into uncharted wilderness while the promises shiver and wobble on the armrests like crystal stemware.
Corrine, in ibid.

3 I think men talk to women so they can sleep with them and women sleep with men so they can talk to them.
Jeff, in ibid. ch. 8

4 The new puritanism. Sloth, gluttony, recreational drugs were out. Narcissism, blind ambition and greed by contrast were free of side- or after-effects, at least in this life, and who was counting on the other anymore?
Narrator, in ibid. ch. 10

5 I think writing does come out of a deep well of loneliness and a desire to fill some kind of gap. No one in his right mind would sit down to write a book if he were a well-adjusted, happy man.
Interview in the *Independent on Sunday* 19 April 1992

## Colin MacInnes (1914–76)
BRITISH AUTHOR AND CRITIC

According to GEORGE MELLY, 'the first adult to recognize the significance of pop', he is best known for his 'London' trilogy, *City of Spades* (1957), a portrait of the city's West Indian community, *Absolute Beginners* (1959, filmed 1986) on teenagers and jazz, and *Mr Love and Justice* (1960), a tale of underworld vice.

1 In England, pop art and fine art stand resolutely back to back.
'Pop Songs and Teenagers', first publ. in *Twentieth Century* February 1958, repr. in *England, Half English* (1961)

2 Today, age is needy and, as its powers decline, so does its income; but full-blooded youth has wealth as well as vigour. In this decade, we witness the second Children's

Crusade, armed with strength and beauty, against all 'squares', all adult nay-sayers.
ibid.

3 Yes, I tell you, it had a real savage splendour in the days when we found that no one couldn't sit on our faces any more because we'd loot to spend at last, and our world was to be our world, the one we wanted and not standing on the doorstep of somebody else's waiting for honey, perhaps.
The narrator, in *Absolute Beginners*, 'in June' (1959)

4 As for the boys and girls, the dear young absolute beginners, I sometimes feel that if they only *knew* this fact, this very simple fact, namely how powerful they really are, then they could rise up overnight and enslave the old tax-payers, the whole damn lot of them – toupets and falsies and rejuvenators and all – even though they number millions and sit in the seats of strength.
ibid. The narrator adds: 'Youth has power, a kind of divine power straight from mother nature.'

5 The great thing about the jazz world, and all the kids that enter into it, is that no one, not a soul, cares what your class is, or what your race is, or what your income, or if you're a boy, or girl, or bent, or versatile, or what you are – so long as you dig the scene and can behave yourself, and have left all that crap behind you, too, when you come in the jazz club door.
ibid.

## Alasdair MacIntyre (b. 1929)
BRITISH PHILOSOPHER

His writings underline the role of eighteenth- and nineteenth-century Scottish philosophy and the influence of Greek schools of thought. Titles include *After Virtue* (1981), *Whose Justice? Which Rationality?* (1986) and *Three Versions of Moral Enquiry* (1989).

1 A striking feature of moral and political argument in the modern world is the extent to which it is innovators, radicals, and revolutionaries who revive old doctrines, while their conservative and reactionary opponents are the inventors of new ones.
*A Short History of Ethics*, ch. 17 (1966)

## (Sir) Ian McKellen (b. 1939)
BRITISH ACTOR

Recognized as one of the leading Shakespearian actors of his generation, he established his reputation with roles including Richard II (1968) and Macbeth (1976). His films include *Scandal* (1989) and *Richard III* (1996). He is an active voice for gay rights and a member of the Stonewall lobbying group.

1 Constant conditioning in my youth and social pressure in every department of my life all failed to convert me to heterosexuality.
*The Times* 5 December 1991

## Kelvin MacKenzie (b. 1946)
BRITISH JOURNALIST

Known as a Murdoch man, he was Editor of the SUN newspaper in 1981–94, reinforcing the paper's populist appeal and taking its circulation to more than 4.5 million. He went from the *Sun* to head BSkyB but left shortly after and became Managing Director of Mirror Group Newspapers in 1998.

1 If they [editors of the 'quality press'] have a popular thought they have to go into a darkened room and lie down until it passes.
*Independent* 19 September 1989

## Catharine A. MacKinnon (b. 1946)

US LAWYER AND FEMINIST CRITIC

Since her first book *Sexual Harassment of Working Women: A Case of Sex Discrimination* (1979), she has fought for women's legal and social equality. In 1983 she campaigned (unsuccessfully) with the feminist ANDREA DWORKIN to have pornography legally recognized as a violation of human rights. Among her other publications are *Feminism Unmodified* (1987) and *Only Words* (1993).

1 Politically, I call it rape whenever a woman has sex and feels violated.
*Feminism Unmodified* (1987)

2 If pornography is part of your sexuality, then you have no right to your sexuality.
Quoted in the *San Francisco Examiner* 29 November 1992

3 In a society in which equality is a fact, not merely a word, words of racial or sexual assault and humiliation will be nonsense syllables.
*Only Words*, ch. 3 (1993)

## Shirley MacLaine (b. 1934)

US ACTRESS

Born Shirley MacLean Beaty, sister of WARREN BEATTY. A comedy actress with impish appeal, she made her screen debut with HITCHCOCK's *The Trouble with Harry* (1955) and went on to appear in *The Apartment* (1960) and *Sweet Charity* (1968). She won an Oscar for her performance in *Terms of Endearment* (1983).

1 I do not see plays because I can nap at home for free, and I don't see movies because they're trash and they've got nothing but naked people in 'em, and I don't read books because if they're any good they're going to make them into mini-series.
Ouiser Boudreaux (Shirley MacLaine), in *Steel Magnolias* (film, 1989, screenplay by Robert Harling, adapted from his play, directed by Herbert Ross)

## Malcolm McLaren (b. 1946)

BRITISH ROCK IMPRESARIO

The Chelsea boutique he opened in 1971 with VIVIENNE WESTWOOD sold the bondage designs that characterized the punk era. He managed punk bands the New York Dolls (1974–5), the Sex Pistols (1976–8) and Bow Wow Wow (1980–84) and later recorded his own albums. The *Sunday Telegraph*'s James Delingpole wrote: 'No one can compete with McLaren when he is ranting like a highly-strung washer-woman about his favourite subject – himself.'

1 Our culture has become something that is completely and utterly in love with its parent. It's become a notion of boredom that is bought and sold, where nothing will happen except that people will become more and more terrified of tomorrow, because the new continues to look old, and the old will always look cute.
'Punk and History' transcript of discussion in New York City, 24 September 1988, publ. in *Discourses: Conversations in Postmodern Art and Culture* (ed. Russell Ferguson *et al.*, 1990)

2 Rock and roll doesn't necessarily mean a band. It doesn't mean a singer, and it doesn't mean a lyric, really . . . It's that question of trying to be immortal.
ibid.

3 This is the end of an era in pop music. It's the end of ideology. Everything is branded. It began with the compilation album – 'music to drive to', 'music to eat to' – thus denying each artist their own ideological spirit. Pop is now given away with a few Esso coupons at your local garage.
Quoted in the *Observer* 20 September 1998

## Mignon McLaughlin (b. c. 1915)

US AUTHOR AND EDITOR

A contributor to magazines and periodicals, she wrote *The Neurotic's Notebook* (1963) and a follow-up in 1966.

1 Every society honors its live conformists and its dead troublemakers.
*The Neurotic's Notebook* (1963)

2 It's innocence when it charms us, ignorance when it doesn't.
ibid.

3 For the happiest life, days should be rigorously planned, nights left open to chance.
*Atlantic Monthly* July 1965

## Don McLean (b. 1945)

US SINGER AND SONGWRITER

After being appointed 'Hudson River Troubadour' by the New York State Council on the Arts, he toured schools and small communities around the eastern United States 1968–70. His song 'American Pie' became an unexpected radio hit in 1971, as did 'Vincent' (about Vincent van Gogh) the same year. Later recordings veered increasingly towards country music.

1 And the three men I admire the most,
The Father, Son and Holy Ghost,
They caught the last train for the coast
The day the music died.
'American Pie' (song) on the album *American Pie* (1971). On the death of Buddy Holly, the Big Bopper and Richie Valens in a plane crash, 2 February 1959. The song charted again on its re-release in 1991 and was a hit for MADONNA in 2000.

## Archibald MacLeish (1892–1982)

US POET AND POLITICIAN

After publishing collections of short verse, such as *Streets in the Moon* (1926), and the narrative poem *Conquistador* (1932, Pulitzer Prize), he turned to writing political verse plays, including *The Fall of the City* (1937) and *Air Raid* (1938). He had a parallel career as an academic and public official, serving as Librarian of Congress (1939–44) and Assistant Secretary of State (1944–5), and contributing to the draft of UNESCO's constitution.

1 A poem should not mean
But be.
'Ars Poetica', publ. in *Streets in the Moon* (1926)

2 America is promises to
Take!
America is promises to
Us
To take them
Brutally
With love but
Take them.
'America Was Promises', publ. in *America Was Promises* (1939)

3 The dissenter is every human being at those moments of his life when he resigns momentarily from the herd and thinks for himself.
'In Praise of Dissent', publ. in *The New York Times* 16 December 1956

4 To see the earth as we now see it, small and beautiful in that eternal silence where it floats, is to see ourselves as riders on the earth together, brothers on that bright loveliness in the unending night – brothers who *see* now they are truly brothers.
'Riders on Earth Together, Brothers in Eternal Cold', first publ. in *The New York Times* 25 December 1968, repr. in *Riders on Earth* (1978) as 'Bubble of Blue Air'. Referring to the first pictures of the earth from the moon.

5 Poets . . . are literal-minded men who will squeeze a word till it hurts.

'Apologia', first publ. in *Harvard Law Review* June 1972, repr. in ibid. as 'Art and Law'

6 We are as great as our belief in human liberty – no greater. And our belief in human liberty is only ours when it is larger than ourselves.

'Now Let Us Address the Main Question: Bicentennial of What?', publ. in *The New York Times* 3 July 1976, repr. in ibid. as 'The Ghost of Thomas Jefferson'

## Micheál MacLiammóir (1899–1978)
IRISH ACTOR

Original name Alfred Willmore. A successful child actor in London, he returned to Ireland where he changed his name and was one of the founders of Dublin's Gate Theatre (1928). He also painted and wrote and as an actor had success with his one-man shows in the 1960s, notably *The Importance of Being Oscar* (1960).

1 We are born at the rise of the curtain and we die with its fall, and every night in the presence of our patrons we write our new creation, and every night it is blotted out forever; and of what use is it to say to audience or to critic, 'Ah, but you should have seen me last Tuesday'?

'Hamlet in Elsinore', publ. in *The Bell* October 1952. Referring to acting in the theatre.

2 He [Orson Welles] knew that he was precisely what he himself would have chosen to be had God consulted him on the subject of his birth; he fully appreciated and approved what had been bestowed, and realized that he couldn't have done the job better himself, in fact he would not have changed a single item.

*All For Hecuba*, ch. 4, 'Changes' (autobiography, 1947). Impressions on first meeting ORSON WELLES. MacLiammóir's most celebrated film role was playing Iago in Welles's *Othello* (1952).

## Marshall McLuhan (1911–80)
CANADIAN COMMUNICATIONS THEORIST

He wrote in a light epigrammatic style on the effects of mass media on contemporary society, concluding that 'all media work us over completely'. His theories are expounded in *The Gutenberg Galaxy* (1962) and *Understanding Media* (1964).

1 Today the tyrant rules not by club or fist, but, disguised as a market researcher, he shepherds his flocks in the ways of utility and comfort.

*The Mechanical Bride*, Preface (1951)

2 Today it is not the classroom nor the classics which are the repositories of models of eloquence, but the ad agencies.

ibid. 'Plain Talk'

3 For tribal man space was the uncontrollable mystery. For technological man it is time that occupies the same role.

ibid. 'Magic that Changes Mood'

4 It is the weak and confused who worship the pseudosimplicities of brutal directness.

ibid. 'The Tough as Narcissus'

5 The new electronic interdependence recreates the world in the image of a global village.

*The Gutenberg Galaxy*, 'Chapter Gloss' (1962). GUY DEBORD commented on this famous phrase: 'The Sage of Toronto . . . spent several decades marvelling at the numerous freedoms created by a "global village" instantly and effortlessly accessible to all. Villages, unlike towns, have always been ruled by conformism, isolation, petty surveillance, boredom and repetitive malicious gossip about the same families. Which is a precise enough description of the global spectacle's present vulgarity.'

6 A point of view can be a dangerous luxury when substituted for insight and understanding.

ibid. 'Typographic Man Can Express but is Helpless to Read the Configuration of Print Technology'

7 If the nineteenth century was the age of the editorial chair, ours is the century of the psychiatrist's couch.

*Understanding Media*, Introduction (1964)

8 The mark of our time is its revulsion against imposed patterns.

ibid.

9 The medium is the message. This is merely to say that the personal and social consequences of any medium – that is, of any extension of ourselves – result from the new scale that is introduced into our affairs by each extension of ourselves, or by any new technology.

ibid. ch. 1

10 The name of a man is a numbing blow from which he never recovers.

ibid. ch. 2

11 Money: The poor man's credit card.

ibid. title of ch. 14

12 Where the whole man is involved there is no work. Work begins with the division of labor.

ibid. ch. 14

13 The car has become the carapace, the protective and aggressive shell, of urban and suburban man.

ibid. ch. 22

14 Ideally, advertising aims at the goal of a programmed harmony among all human impulses and aspirations and endeavors. Using handicraft methods, it stretches out toward the ultimate electronic goal of a collective consciousness.

ibid. ch. 23

15 The more the data banks record about each one of us, the less we exist.

*Playboy* March 1969

16 Diaper backward spells repaid. Think about it.

Remark at American Booksellers Association luncheon, Washington, D.C., June 1969, quoted in the Vancouver *Sun* 7 June 1969

17 Politics will eventually be replaced by imagery. The politician will be only too happy to abdicate in favor of his image, because the image will be much more powerful than he could ever be.

*Maclean's* June 1971

18 Television brought the brutality of war into the comfort of the living room. Vietnam was lost in the living rooms of America – not on the battlefields of Vietnam.

Quoted in the *Montreal Gazette* 16 May 1975

19 Advertising is the greatest art form of the twentieth century.

*Advertising Age* 3 September 1976

## Kristen McMenamy (b. 1965)
US MODEL

1 The fashion industry has taught me insanity.

Interview in *i-D* June 1993

## Harold Macmillan (1894–1986)
BRITISH POLITICIAN AND PRIME MINISTER

Lord Stockton. The nickname 'Supermac' pinned on him by the cartoonist Vicky reflected the popular appeal of this Tory intellectual and aristocrat. During his premiership (1957–63) Britain experienced full employment and relative prosperity, although he failed to negotiate British entry into the EEC. He was famously imperturbable, once declaring: 'It is the duty of Her Majesty's Government neither to flap nor to falter.' See also ANEURIN BEVAN 11, 13.

1 Forever poised between a cliché and an indiscretion.
*Newsweek* 30 April 1956. On the role of a foreign secretary.

2 Let us be frank about it: most of our people have never had it so good.
Speech, 20 July 1957, Bedford, quoted in *The Times* 22 July 1957. The slogan was already current in the USA at the end of the Second World War.

3 I thought the best thing to do was to settle up these little local difficulties, and then turn to the wider vision of the Commonwealth.
Statement at London airport, 7 January 1958, quoted in *The Times* 8 January 1958. The remark, made when Macmillan was preparing to leave on a Commonwealth tour, referred to the resignation of the Chancellor of the Exchequer, Peter Thorneycroft, and treasury ministers ENOCH POWELL and Nigel Birch in protest against public spending increases. His words furthered Macmillan's reputation for 'unflappability'.

4 At home you always have to be a politician. When you're abroad you almost feel yourself a statesman.
Speech in Melbourne, 17 February 1958, quoted in *Look* 15 April 1958. Remark made during the first visit to Australia by a British prime minister.

5 We have seen the awakening of national consciousness in peoples who have for centuries lived in dependence upon some other power ... The wind of change is blowing through the continent, and, whether we like it or not, this growth of national consciousness is a political fact.
Speech to South African Parliament, Cape Town, 3 February 1960, publ. in *The Penguin Book of Twentieth-Century Speeches* (ed. Brian MacArthur, 1999)

6 As usual the Liberals offer a mixture of sound and original ideas. Unfortunately none of the sound ideas is original and none of the original ideas is sound.
Speech in London, 7 March 1961, quoted in *The Times* 8 March 1961

7 Power? It's like a dead sea fruit. When you achieve it, there's nothing there.
Quoted in *The New Anatomy of Britain*, ch. 37 (1971) by Anthony Sampson

8 If you don't believe in God, all you have to believe in is decency ... Decency is very good. Better decent than indecent. But I don't think it's enough.
Said to William F. Buckley Jr on *Firing Line*, New York, 20 November 1980, quoted in *Macmillan*, vol. 2, ch. 19 (1989) by Alistair Horne

9 Memorial services are the cocktail parties of the geriatric set.
Quoted in ibid. ch. 20

## Larry McMurtry (b. 1936)
US SCREENWRITER, NOVELIST AND ESSAYIST

Using his home state of Texas as backdrop to his novels, he helped to establish western fiction as a serious literary genre with such works as *Horseman, Pass By* (1961, filmed as *Hud*, 1963). He adapted his own nostalgic tale *The Last Picture Show* (1966) for the film version (1971), and *Terms of Endearment* (1975) is also better known as a film (1983). *Lonesome Dove* (1986) was awarded a Pulitzer Prize.

1 Self-parody is the first portent of age.
Danny Deck, in *Some Can Whistle*, pt 1, ch. 14 (1989)

2 True maturity is only reached when a man realizes he has become a father figure to his girlfriends' boyfriends – and he accepts it.
ibid. ch. 12

3 The lives of happy people are dense with their own doings – crowded, active, thick ... But the sorrowing are nomads,

on a plain with few landmarks and no boundaries; sorrow's horizons are vague and its demands are few.
ibid. pt 4, ch. 9

## Louis MacNeice (1907–63)
IRISH POET

Associated with the left-wing poets of the 1930s, he combined lyricism and colloquial speech patterns in such collections as *Autumn Journal* (1938) and *Solstices* (1961). He also worked as a producer for the BBC and wrote many innovative radio documentaries and dramas, including *The Dark Tower* (1947).

1 World is crazier and more of it than we think,
Incorrigibly plural. I peel and portion
A tangerine and spit the pips and feel
The drunkenness of things being various.
'Snow', publ. in *Poems* (1935)

2 The sunlight on the garden
Hardens and grows cold,
We cannot cage the minute
Within its net of gold,
When all is told
We cannot beg for pardon.
'Sunlight on the Garden', publ. in *Earth Compels* (1938)

3 It's no go the merrygoround, it's no go the rickshaw,
All we want is a limousine and a ticket for the peepshow.
'Bagpipe Music', publ. in ibid.

4 It's no go the Government grants, it's no go the elections,
Sit on your arse for fifty years and hang your hat on a pension.
ibid.

5 Some on commission, some for the love of learning,
Some because they have nothing better to do
Or because they hope these walls of books will deaden
The drumming of the demon in their ears.
'The British Museum Reading Room', publ. in *Plant and Phantom* (1941)

## Madonna (b. 1959)
US SINGER AND ACTRESS

Full name Madonna Louise Ciccone. Moving from Detroit to New York in 1978, she established herself as a dancer and actress before making the first of many dance-oriented albums in 1983. Projecting herself as an icon of female independence and sexuality, she has also starred in a number of films, for example *Evita* (1996), and published a book of erotic photographs of herself, *Sex* (1992). 'They used to say that I was a slut, a pig, an easy lay, a sex bomb, Minnie Mouse or even Marlene Dietrich's daughter,' she once said, 'but I'd rather say that I'm just a hyperactive adult.'

1 You know that we are living in a material world
And I am a material girl.
'I Am a Material Girl' (song, written by Peter Brown and Robert Rans) on the album *Like a Virgin* (1984)

2 Express yourself
So you can respect yourself
'Express Yourself' (song, written by Madonna and Stephen Bray) on the album *Like a Prayer* (1989)

3 Catholicism is not a soothing religion. It's a painful religion. We're all gluttons for punishment.
Interview in *Rolling Stone* 23 March 1989

4 To me, the whole process of being a brushstroke in someone else's painting is a little difficult.
Interview in *Vanity Fair* April 1991

5 Everyone probably thinks that I'm a raving nympho-

maniac, that I have an *insatiable* sexual appetite, when the truth is I'd rather read a book.

*Q Magazine* June 1991

6 I always thought of losing my virginity as a career move.

Quoted in *Madonna Unauthorized*, Epilogue (1991) by Christopher Andersen

## John Gillespie Magee (1922–41)

US-BORN PILOT WITH ROYAL CANADIAN AIR FORCE

He died while on a bombing mission over Germany, leaving as a legacy the poem 'High Flight', made famous when quoted by RONALD REAGAN following the *Challenger* space shuttle disaster in 1986.

1 Oh! I have slipped the surly bonds of earth,
And danced the skies on laughter-silvered wings;

'High Flight' written 1941, publ. in *More Poems from the Forces* (ed. K. Rhys, 1943). Opening lines of sonnet.

2 And while with silent lifting mind I've trod
The high, untrespassed sanctity of space,
Put out my hand and touched the face of God.

ibid. Last lines of sonnet.

## Anna Magnani (1908–73)

EGYPTIAN-BORN ITALIAN ACTRESS

Brought up in the slums, she earned a living as a singer and occasional actress before her big break in Roberto Rossellini's film *Rome, Open City* (1945). She received an Academy Award for her first Hollywood role in *The Rose Tattoo* (1955). For Jean Renoir, she was 'the complete animal – an animal created for the stage and screen'.

1 Great passions, my dear, don't exist: they're liars' fantasies. What do exist are little loves that may last for a short or a longer while.

Quoted in *The Egotists*, 'Anna Magnani' (1963) by Oriana Fallaci

## Magnus Magnusson (b. 1929)

BRITISH WRITER AND BROADCASTER

A former assistant editor of *The Scotsman*, he is known for his popular television documentaries on archaeology, such as *Chronicle* (1966–80), and for chairing the inquisitorial quiz programme *Mastermind* (1972–97). His writings include *Introducing Archaeology* (1972), *BC, the Archaeology of the Bible Lands* (1977), and *Vikings! Magnus on the Move* (1980).

1 I've started, so I'll finish.

*Mastermind* quiz series (BBC, 1972–97). Magnusson's words after the final show were: 'I've started, now I've finished.'

## René Magritte (1898–1967)

BELGIAN SURREALIST PAINTER

A leading practitioner and theorist of Surrealism, he joined the Paris Surrealists in 1927. His style remained consistent throughout his career, and he is probably best known for his images of figures in bowler hats, as in the painting *Threatened Assassin* (1927). His work was influential on Pop art in the 1960s.

1 To be a surrealist . . . means barring from your mind all remembrance of what you have seen, and being always on the lookout for what has never been.

*Time* magazine 21 April 1947

2 The mind loves the unknown. It loves images whose meaning is unknown, since the meaning of the mind itself is unknown.

Quoted in *Magritte*, ch. 1 (1970) by Suzi Gablik

3 The present reeks of mediocrity and the atom bomb.

Quoted in ibid. ch. 5. 'I don't want to belong to my own time, or for that matter, to any other,' Magritte added.

## Naguib Mahfouz (b. 1911)

EGYPTIAN NOVELIST

He established his reputation with his epic of family and social history, *Cairo Trilogy* (1956–7), and *Miramar* (1967), though *Children of Gebelawi* (1959), an allegory of the science/faith dichotomy, was banned in Egypt. In 1988 he was the first Egyptian to be awarded the Nobel Prize for Literature.

1 Inwardly art is a means of expurgation, outwardly a means of battle, incumbent on men born and reared in sin and determined to rebel against it. Nothing else matters.

*Wedding Song*, 'Abas Karam Younis' (1981)

## Norman Mailer (b. 1923)

US AUTHOR

Prolific and often prolix as a writer, he won immediate fame with *The Naked and the Dead* (1948), a war novel that was primarily a critique of American society. His 'new journalism' also attracted critical acclaim, for example *Armies of the Night* (1968), on the 1967 protest march on the Pentagon, and *Executioner's Song* (1979), a study of GARY GILMORE, both of which gained Pulitzer Prizes. GORE VIDAL demurred: 'He is now what he wanted to be: the patron saint of bad journalism.'

1 For jazz is orgasm, it is the music of orgasm, good orgasm and bad, and so it spoke across a nation, it had the communication of art even where it was watered, perverted, corrupted, and almost killed, it spoke in no matter what laundered popular way of instantaneous existential states to which some whites could respond, it was indeed a communication by art because it said, 'I feel this, and now you do too'.

'The White Negro' sect. 2, first publ. in *Dissent*, summer 1957, repr. in *Advertisements for Myself* (1959)

2 Hip is the sophistication of the wise primitive in a giant jungle.

ibid. sect. 3

3 The final purpose of art is to intensify, even, if necessary, to exacerbate, the moral consciousness of people.

'Hip, Hell, and the Navigator', first publ. in the *Western Review* winter 1959, repr. in *Conversations with Norman Mailer* (ed. J. Michael Lennon, 1988)

4 Each day a few more lies eat into the seed with which we are born, little institutional lies from the print of newspapers, the shock waves of television, and the sentimental cheats of the movie screen.

*Advertisements for Myself*, 'First Advertisement for Myself' (1959)

5 There is probably no sensitive heterosexual alive who is not preoccupied with his latent homosexuality.

ibid. 'The Homosexual Villain'

6 The White Protestant's ultimate sympathy must be with science, factology, and committee rather than with sex, birth, heat, flesh, creation, the sweet and the funky; they must vote, manipulate, control, and direct, these Protestants who are the center of power in our land, they must go for what they believe is reason when it is only the Square logic of the past.

ibid. 'Advertisement for "Games and Ends"'

7 Masculinity is not something given to you, but something you gain. And you gain it by winning small battles with honor.

'Petty Notes on Some Sex in America', first publ. 1961–2, repr. in *Cannibals and Christians* (1966). 'Because there is very little honor left in American life,' Mailer continued, 'there is a certain built-in tendency to destroy masculinity in American men.'

8 A modern democracy is a tyranny whose borders are undefined; one discovers how far one can go only by traveling in a straight line until one is stopped.
*The Presidential Papers*, Preface (1963)

9 Ultimately a hero is a man who would argue with the gods, and so awakens devils to contest his vision. The more a man can achieve, the more he may be certain that the devil will inhabit a part of his creation.
ibid.

10 Writing books is the closest men ever come to child-bearing.
'Mr Mailer Interviews Himself', first publ. in *The New York Times Book Review* 17 September 1965, repr. in *Conversations with Norman Mailer* (ed. J. Michael Lennon, 1988)

11 Sentimentality is the emotional promiscuity of those who have no sentiment.
*Cannibals and Christians*, 'My Hope for America' (1966)

12 New York is one of the capitals of the world and Los Angeles is a constellation of plastic, San Francisco is a lady, Boston has become Urban Renewal, Philadelphia and Baltimore and Washington blink like dull diamonds in the smog of Eastern Megalopolis, and New Orleans is unremarkable past the French Quarter. Detroit is a one-trade town, Pittsburgh has lost its golden triangle, St Louis has become the golden arch of the corporation, and nights in Kansas City close early. The oil depletion allowance makes Houston and Dallas naught but checkerboards for this sort of game. But Chicago is a great American city. Perhaps it is the last of the great American cities.
*Miami and the Siege of Chicago*, 'The Siege of Chicago' (1969). Opening paragraph.

13 The horror of the Twentieth Century was the size of each new event, and the paucity of its reverberation.
*A Fire on the Moon*, pt 1, ch. 1 (1970)

14 So we think of Marilyn who was every man's love affair with America. Marilyn Monroe who was blonde and beautiful and had a sweet little rinky-dink of a voice and all the cleanliness of all the clean American backyards.
*Marilyn*, ch. 1 (1973)

15 There is nothing safe about sex. There never will be.
*International Herald Tribune* 24 January 1992

## John Major (b. 1943)
BRITISH POLITICIAN AND PRIME MINISTER

Taking over from MARGARET THATCHER as Conservative Prime Minister in 1990, he won the 1992 general election but faced increasing criticism over the economy and European policy. Although he launched the Northern Irish peace initiative and abolished the unpopular 'poll tax', he was seen as 'grey' and ineffectual by many and in 1997 suffered the greatest ever Tory election defeat, losing to TONY BLAIR. He announced his retirement from parliament in 2000. See also MICHAEL FOOT 2.

1 The first requirement of politics is not intellect or stamina but patience. Politics is a very long run game and the tortoise will usually beat the hare.
*Daily Express* 25 July 1989

2 The harsh truth is that if the policy isn't hurting, it isn't working. I know there is a difficult period ahead but the important thing is that we cannot and must not fudge the determination to stop inflation in its tracks.
Speech at Northampton, 27 October 1989, quoted in *The Times* 28 October 1989. This was Major's first speech as Chancellor of the Exchequer after the resignation of NIGEL LAWSON.

3 The politician who never made a mistake never made a decision.
Interview on 'The World This Weekend', BBC Radio 4, 25 November 1990

4 I want to see us build a country that is at ease with itself, a country that is confident, and a country that is prepared and willing to make the changes necessary to provide a better quality of life for all our citizens. I don't promise you that it will be easy, and I don't promise you that it will be quick, but I believe it is an immensely worthwhile job. Now, if you will forgive me, because it will be neither easy nor quick, I will go into Number 10 straight away and make a start right now.
Speech outside No. 10 Downing Street, 28 November 1990, quoted in *John Major*, ch. 1 (1991) by Nesta Wyn Ellis. Major had won the Conservative Party leadership election, thus becoming Prime Minister.

5 A consensus politician is someone who does something that he doesn't believe is right because it keeps people quiet when he does it.
*Daily Mail* 4 January 1991

6 Only in Britain could it be thought a defect to be 'too clever by half'. The probability is that too many people are too stupid by three-quarters.
Quoted in the *Observer* 7 July 1991

7 Society needs to condemn a little more and understand a little less.
Interview in *Mail on Sunday* 21 February 1993. On the killing of James Bulger.

8 Fifty years on from now, Britain will still be the country of long shadows on county grounds, warm beer, invincible green suburbs, dog lovers and – as George Orwell said – old maids bicycling to Holy Communion through the morning mist.
Speech to Conservative Group for Europe, Intercontinental Hotel, London, 22 April 1993, quoted in the *Daily Telegraph* 23 April 1993

9 It is time to get back to basics: to self-discipline and respect for the law, to consideration for others, to accepting responsibility for yourself and your family, and not shuffling it off on the state.
Speech to Conservative Party Conference, Blackpool, 8 October 1993, quoted in *The Times* 9 October 1993

## Janet Malcolm (b. 1934)
US JOURNALIST, ESSAYIST AND CRITIC

Among other works, she has written on photography in *Diana and Nikon: Essays on the Aesthetic of Photography* (1980) and on the methods and motives of psychoanalysts in *Psychoanalysis: the Impossible Profession* (1981).

1 Every journalist who is not too stupid or too full of himself to notice what is going on knows that what he does is morally indefensible. He is a kind of confidence man, preying on people's vanity, ignorance, or loneliness, gaining their trust and betraying them without remorse.
*The Journalist and the Murderer*, pt 1 (1990). Opening paragraph of book, which discusses the case of journalist Joe McGinniss, who won the trust of an alleged murderer, then wrote a bestseller, *Fatal Vision* (1984), proclaiming his guilt.

2 Fidelity to the subject's thought and to his characteristic way of expressing himself is the sine qua non of journalistic quotation.
ibid. Malcolm, who had been accused in a legal dispute of fabricating quotations, argued in her book that capturing the gist of a statement is primary, while accurate quotation is impossible. 'When we talk with somebody, we are not aware of the language we are speaking,' she wrote. 'Our ear takes it in as English, and only if we see it transcribed verbatim do we realize that it is a kind of foreign tongue.'

## Malcolm X (1925–65)
US BLACK CIVIL RIGHTS ACTIVIST

Original name Malcolm Little. He converted to Islam and joined the Black Muslims (Nation of Islam) while in prison for burglary

(1946–53). On his release he attracted a following through his advocacy of black separatism, self-assertion and self-defence. He modified this stance on founding the Organization of Afro-American Unity in 1964, causing a rift with Black Muslims which ended with his assassination. He was the subject of a biopic directed by SPIKE LEE in 1992.

1 If you're born in America with a black skin, you're born in prison, and the masses of black people in America today are beginning to regard our plight or predicament in this society as one of a prison inmate.

Interview in June 1963, publ. in *Malcolm X: The Man and His Times*, pt 3, 'Malcolm X Talks with Kenneth B. Clark' (ed. John Henrik Clarke, 1969)

2 There is nothing in our book, the Koran, that teaches us to suffer peacefully. Our religion teaches us to be intelligent. Be peaceful, be courteous, obey the law, respect everyone; but if someone puts his hand on you, send him to the cemetery. That's a good religion.

'Message to the Grass Roots', speech in Detroit, November 1963, publ. in *Malcolm X Speaks*, ch. 1 (1965). On Malcolm X's adherence to the Islamic faith, ALICE WALKER commented: 'If Malcolm X had been a black woman, his last message to the world would have been entirely different. The brotherhood of Moslem men – all colors – may exist there, but part of the glue that holds them together is the thorough suppression of women.'

3 It's just like when you've got some coffee that's too black, which means it's too strong. What do you do? You integrate it with cream, you make it weak. But if you pour too much cream in it, you won't even know you ever had coffee. It used to be hot, it becomes cool. It used to be strong, it becomes weak. It used to wake you up, now it puts you to sleep.

ibid.

4 Sitting at the table doesn't make you a diner, unless you eat some of what's on that plate. Being here in America doesn't make you an American. Being born here in America doesn't make you an American.

'The Ballot or the Bullet', speech in Cleveland, Ohio, 3 April 1964, publ. in ibid. ch. 3

5 We have formed an organization known as the Organization of Afro-American Unity . . . To fight whoever gets in our way, to bring about the complete independence of people of African descent here in the Western hemisphere, and first here in the United States, and bring about the freedom of these people by any means necessary. That's our motto. We want freedom by any means necessary. We want justice by any means necessary. We want equality by any means necessary.

Speech at OAAU Founding Rally, Audubon Ballroom, New York, 28 June 1964, publ. in *Malcolm X: By Any Means Necessary* (ed. George Breitman, 1970). The words 'by any means necessary' became a rallying call among radical movements in the 1960s.

6 The common goal of 22 million Afro-Americans is respect as *human beings*, the God-given right to be a *human being*. Our common goal is to obtain the *human rights* that America has been denying us. We can never get civil rights in America until our *human rights* are first restored. We will never be recognized as citizens there until we are first recognized as *humans*.

'Racism: the Cancer that is Destroying America', publ. in *Egyptian Gazette* 25 August 1964. See also DICK GREGORY 1.

7 I believe in the brotherhood of man, all men, but I don't believe in brotherhood with anybody who doesn't want brotherhood with me. I believe in treating people right, but I'm not going to waste my time trying to treat somebody right who doesn't know how to return the treatment.

Speech in New York, 12 December 1964, publ. in *Malcolm X: The Man and His Times*, pt 5, 'Communication and Reality' (ed. John Henrik Clarke, 1969)

8 You can't separate peace from freedom because no one can be at peace unless he has his freedom.

'Prospects for Freedom in 1965', speech in New York, 7 January 1965, publ. in *Malcolm X Speaks*, ch. 12 (1965)

# John Malkovich (b. 1953)

US ACTOR

He was co-founder of the Steppenwolf Theatre Company in Chicago in 1976, making his cinematic debut in *Places in the Heart* (1984). His roles range from psychotic to romantic, and in 1999 he played himself in *Being John Malkovich*.

1 [On acting in the theatre] It's not a field, I think, for people who need to have success every day: if you can't live with a nightly sort of disaster, you should get out. I wouldn't describe myself as lacking in confidence, but I would just say that . . . the ghosts you chase you never catch.

Interview in the *Independent on Sunday* 5 April 1992

2 Where women are concerned, the rule is never to go out with anyone better dressed than you.

ibid.

# George Leigh Mallory (1886–1924)

BRITISH MOUNTAINEER

He lost his life during his third attempt to climb Everest after previous ventures in 1921 and 1922. He also pursued an academic career, and was Assistant Master of Charterhouse College, Cambridge (1910–15).

1 Because it's there.

Interview in *The New York Times* 18 March 1923. On being asked why he wanted to climb Mount Everest.

# David Malouf (b. 1934)

AUSTRALIAN NOVELIST AND POET

His fiction, which has been praised for its vivid, sensuous and cosmopolitan qualities, frequently takes on historical themes, as in *An Imaginary Life* (1978), a novel about Ovid, and his epic *The Great World* (1990). He has also written librettos, such as *Baa Baa Black Sheep* (1993, with Michael Berkeley).

1 All safe as houses, fire
   kennelled in a matchbox,
   the water of drowned valleys
   dammed behind taps.
   Barring accidents, or malice –
   nothing's disaster-proof.

'On Refusing an All-risk Insurance Policy', publ. in *Bicycle and Other Poems* (1970)

# André Malraux (1901–76)

FRENCH STATESMAN AND MAN OF LETTERS

Both intellectual and man of action, he fought with the Republicans in the Spanish Civil War, with Chinese nationalists in Indochina and in the French Resistance during the Second World War. His novels are highly influenced by his war-time experiences and include *Man's Fate* (1933) and *Man's Hope* (1937, filmed 1938). In peace time he held a number of cabinet positions in the Gaullist administration (1945–69).

1 There are not fifty ways of fighting, there's only one, and that's to win. Neither revolution nor war consists in doing what one pleases.

*Man's Hope*, pt 2, sect. 2, ch. 12 (1937)

2 All art is a revolt against man's fate.

*The Voices of Silence*, pt 4, ch. 7 (1951)

3 Remote from ourselves in dream and in time, India be-

longs to the Ancient Orient of our soul . . . What is Zeus, compared with Shiva? The only god of antiquity whose language is worthy of India is the god without temples – Fate.

*Anti-Memoirs*, 'The Temptation of the West' sect. 1 (1967)

4 The attempt to force human beings to despise themselves. That is what I call hell.

ibid. 'The Human Condition', sect. 2. Referring to the concentration camps in Nazi Germany.

## David Mamet (b. 1947)

US PLAYWRIGHT

A prolific author of plays, screenplays and essays, he drew praise for *Sexual Perversity in Chicago* (1974) and his breakthrough play, *American Buffalo* (1975), dramatic depictions of masculine, intensely competitive worlds. His 1992 play about sexual harassment *Oleanna* (filmed 1994) provoked accusations of misogyny. His screenplays include *The Postman Always Rings Twice* (1981). He won the Pulitzer Prize for *Glengarry Glen Ross* (1984).

1 We respond to a drama to that extent to which it corresponds to our dreamlife.

*Writing in Restaurants*, 'A National Dream-Life' (1986)

2 The product of the artist has become less important than the *fact* of the artist. We wish to absorb this person. We wish to devour someone who has experienced the tragic. In our society this person is much more important than anything he might create.

ibid. 'Exuvial Magic: an Essay Concerning Fashion'

3 The poker player learns that sometimes both science and common sense are wrong; that the bumblebee *can* fly; that, perhaps, one should never trust an expert; that there are more things in heaven and earth than are dreamt of by those with an academic bent.

ibid. 'Things I Have Learned Playing Poker on the Hill'

4 The art of the theater is action. It is the study of commitment. The word is an act. To *say* the word in such a way as to make it heard and understood by all in the theater is a commitment – it is the highest art to see a human being out on a stage speaking to a thousand of his or her peers saying, 'These words which I am speaking are the *truth* – they are not an approximation of any kind. They are the God's truth, and I support them with my life,' which is what the actor does on stage. Without this commitment, acting becomes prostitution and writing becomes advertising.

ibid. 'Against Amplification'

5 Life in the movie business is like the beginning of a new love affair: it's full of surprises and you're constantly getting fucked.

Charlie Fox, in *Speed-the-Plow*, sc. 1 (1988)

6 A good film script should be able to do completely without dialogue.

*Independent* 11 November 1988

7 I can envision no device more capable of spreading ignorance and illiteracy than the computer. It is, I think, like the atom bomb, a naturally evolved engine of destruction, a sign, like the Tower of Babel, that civilization has run its course.

*Jafsie and John Henry*, 'Why Don't You Write With a Computer?' (2000)

## Nelson Mandela (b. 1918)

SOUTH AFRICAN POLITICAL LEADER

The international symbol of the anti-apartheid movement, he spent the years 1964–90 in prison for his role in the banned African National Congress. On his release he was elected President of the

ANC, and then South Africa's first black president (1994–9). He received the Nobel Peace Prize in 1993 and published his autobiography, *Long Walk to Freedom*, in 1994.

1 For my own part I have made my choice. I will not leave South Africa, nor will I surrender. Only through hardship, sacrifice and militant action can freedom be won. The struggle is my life. I will continue fighting for freedom until the end of my days.

Press statement, 26 June 1961, published by ANC in London, repr. in *The Struggle Is My Life*, pt 2 'The Struggle Is My Life' (1978)

2 Whatever he himself may say in his defence, the white man's moral standards in this country must be judged by the extent to which he has condemned the vast majority of its inhabitants to serfdom and inferiority.

Defence statement at trial in Pretoria, 15 October–7 November 1962, publ. in ibid. 'Black Man in a White Court'

3 The whole life of any thinking African in this country drives him continuously to a conflict between his conscience on the one hand and the law on the other.

Address to court after closure of prosecution case, in ibid.

4 Only free men can negotiate. Prisoners cannot enter into contracts.

Statement from prison, 10 February 1985, quoted in *Higher than Hope*, ch. 30 (1988) by Fatima Meer. Refusing the terms set for his release by South African president P.W. BOTHA. The statement was read by Zindzi Mandela, Nelson's daughter, at a United Democratic Front rally at the Jabulani Stadium, Soweto.

5 The prison . . . operates to break the human spirit, to exploit human weakness, undermine human strength, destroy initiative, individuality, negate intelligence and process an amorphous, robot-like mass. The great challenge is how to resist, how not to adjust, to keep intact the knowledge of the society outside and to live by its rules, for that is the only way to maintain the human and the social within you.

Quoted in ibid. ch. 25

6 [On solitary confinement] There is nothing more terrifying than to be alone with sheer time. Then the ghosts come crowding in. They can be very sinister, very mischievous, raising a thousand doubts in your mind about the people outside, their loyalty. Was your sacrifice worth the trouble? What would your life have been like if you hadn't got involved?

ibid.

7 To be father of a nation is a great honour, but to be the father of a family is a greater joy.

*Long Walk to Freedom* ch. 109 (1994)

## Winnie Mandela (b. 1934)

SOUTH AFRICAN POLITICAL LEADER

Full name Nomzano Zaniewe Winifred Mandela. During the imprisonment of her husband, NELSON MANDELA, she campaigned for his release and for the African National Congress. Despite a conviction for kidnapping in 1991, she was appointed Minister for Arts, Culture, Science and Technology in May 1994 but was dismissed in 1995, although remaining a powerful force within the ANC. She separated from her husband in 1992 and divorced in 1996.

1 Together, hand in hand, with that stick of matches, with our necklace, we shall liberate this country.

Speech in black townships, quoted in the *Guardian* 15 April 1986

## Osip Mandelstam (1891–1938)

RUSSIAN POET

Considered one of the major poets of the twentieth century, he was associated with the Acmeist movement and published the collections *Kamen* (*Stone*, 1913) and *Tristia* (*Sad Things*, 1922). He was harshly criticized by the Bolsheviks for the indifference to contemporary themes in his work and in 1934 was arrested and exiled for a poem denouncing STALIN. He died *en route* to a forced labour camp.

1 I have studied the science of good-byes,
the bare-headed laments of night.
'Tristia' st. 1, publ. in *Tristia* (1922), repr. in *Selected Poems* (1973)

2 O indigence at the root of our lives,
how poor is the language of happiness!
Everything's happened before and will happen again,
but still the moment of each meeting is sweet.
ibid. st. 3

3 In poetry, war is always being waged. It is only in periods of social imbecility that there is peace or a peace treaty is concluded. Like generals, the bearers of word roots take up arms against each other. Word roots battle in the darkness, depleting each other's food supplies and the juices of the earth.
'Vulgata: Some Notes on Poetry', essay, first publ. 1923, repr. in *The Complete Critical Prose and Letters* (ed. Jane Gary Harris *et al.*, 1979)

4 To read Pasternak's verse is to clear your throat, to fortify your breathing, to fill your lungs; surely such poetry could provide a cure for tuberculosis. No poetry is more healthful at the present moment! It is like *koumiss* after evaporated milk.
'Boris Pasternak', essay, first publ. 1923, repr. in ibid. as 'Some Notes on Poetry'

5 No matter how you stars want to shine,
First apply on the dotted line,
We're sure to renew your permission
For shining or writing or extinction.
Untitled poem, written October 1930, publ. in *Osip Mandelstam: 50 poems* (1977)

6 Poetry, you put storms to good use.
'To the German Language', written August 1932, publ. in *Selected Poems* (1973)

7 [Of Stalin]
But whenever there's a snatch of talk
it turns to the Kremlin mountaineer,
the ten thick worms his fingers,
his words like measures of weight,
the huge laughing cockroaches on his top lip
the glitter of his boot-rims.
'The Stalin Epigram', written 1933, publ. in *Selected Poems* (1973). The private circulation of the poem led to Mandelstam's first arrest in 1934.

8 A quotation is not an excerpt. A quotation is a cicada. Its natural state is that of unceasing sound. Having once seized hold of the air, it will not let it go.
'Conversation About Dante' sect. 2, written 1933–4, publ. in *The Complete Critical Prose and Letters* (ed. Jane Gary Harris *et al.*, 1979)

## Christopher Manes (b. 1957)
US ECOLOGIST

He is prominent among environmental activists for his book *Green Rage* (1990) and for the video documentary *Earth First! The Politics of Radical Environmentalism* (1988). 'My work,' he explains, 'aims at deflating the pretension that humanity has the right or the duty or even the wisdom to dominate and control nature.'

1 Such is the scope of the environmental crisis that it makes us question our entire history on Earth, back to the origins of civilization. People in the future may very well look back and wonder how the last generations could have gotten caught up in such minor distractions as two world wars, space flight, and the nuclear arms race.
*Green Rage*, ch. 2 (1990)

2 [Of the ecology movement] It entered the seventies as a vague critic of our society and exited as an institution, wrapped in the consumerism and political ambitions it once condemned. In their drive to win credibility with the government agencies and corporations ... the new professional environmentalists seemed to have wandered into the ambiguous world of George Orwell's *Animal Farm*, where it was increasingly difficult to tell the farmers from the pigs.
ibid. ch. 3

## Michael Manley (1924–97)
JAMAICAN POLITICIAN AND PRIME MINISTER

The son of Norman Manley, Jamaica's Prime Minister 1959–62, he succeeded his father as President of the People's National Party (1969) and served as Prime Minister 1972–80 and 1989–92. During his terms he championed Third World interests, was one of the founders of the Caribbean Community and Common Market in 1973 and introduced a free education system.

1 You know people exaggerate that all is wild in Jamaica. I think that sometimes people fire a shot to try to make you nervous. They are not trying to hurt you.
*Daily Telegraph* 8 February 1989

## Golo Mann (b. 1909)
GERMAN HISTORIAN

Diverging from the literary careers of his father THOMAS MANN and his brother KLAUS MANN, he established a reputation as a historian and is known chiefly for his *History of Germany Since 1789* (1968) and for a major biography, *Wallenstein: His Life Narrated* (1971).

1 Closest to the truth are those who deal lightly with it because they know it is inexhaustible.
Quoted in *Thomas Mann and His Family*, 'Golo Mann: The Liberation of an Unloved One' (1987) by Marcel Reich-Ranicki. Writing of satirist Heinrich Heine.

2 Man is always more than he can know of himself; consequently, his accomplishments, time and again, will come as a surprise to him.
ibid. An insight gleaned from philosopher Karl Jaspers.

## Klaus Mann (1906–49)
GERMAN AUTHOR

Like other family members, THOMAS MANN and GOLO MANN, he was a refugee from pre-war Nazi Germany and settled in America, serving in the US Army during the Second World War as a journalist. He later founded the literary magazine *Decision* in New York, his autobiography, *The Turning Point*, appeared in 1942, and his *Pathetic Symphony*, about Tchaikovsky, in 1948.

1 [Of his homosexuality] One cannot serve this Eros without becoming a stranger in society as it is today; one cannot commit oneself to this form of love without incurring a mortal wound.
Quoted in *Thomas Mann and His Family*, 'Klaus Mann' (1987) by Marcel Reich-Ranicki

## Thomas Mann (1875–1955)
GERMAN AUTHOR AND CRITIC

He is celebrated as the author of *Buddenbrooks* (1901) and *The Magic Mountain* (1924), for which he won the Nobel Prize for Literature, and of novellas such as *Tonio Kröger* (1902) and *Death in Venice* (1913, filmed 1971). Much of his work examines the role and responsibilities of the artist in society. A supporter of the Weimar Republic, he fled Nazi Germany and in 1940 became an American citizen. See also PETER HANDKE 3.

1 A man lives not only his personal life, as an individual,

but also, consciously or unconsciously, the life of his epoch and his contemporaries.

*The Magic Mountain*, ch. 2, 'At Tienappels' ' (1924)

2 There is something suspicious about music, gentlemen. I insist that she is, by her nature, equivocal. I shall not be going too far in saying at once that she is politically suspect.

Herr Settembrini, in ibid. ch. 4, 'Politically Suspect'

3 Time has no divisions to mark its passage, there is never a thunderstorm or blare of trumpets to announce the beginning of a new month or year. Even when a new century begins it is only we mortals who ring bells and fire off pistols.

ibid. ch. 5, 'Whims of Mercurius'

4 Opinions cannot survive if one has no chance to fight for them.

ibid. ch. 6, 'Of the City of God'

5 A man's dying is more the survivors' affair than his own.

ibid. 'A Soldier, And Brave'

6 We, when we sow the seeds of doubt deeper than the most up-to-date and modish free-thought has ever dreamed of doing, we well know what we are about. Only out of radical skepsis, out of moral chaos, can the Absolute spring, the anointed Terror of which the time has need.

Leo Naphta, in ibid. ch. 7, 'Hysterica Passio'

7 An art whose medium is language will always show a high degree of critical creativeness, for speech is itself a critique of life: it names, it characterizes, it passes judgment, in that it creates.

'Lessing speech', Prussian Academy of Art, Berlin, 22 January 1929, first publ. 1930, repr. in *Essays of Three Decades* (1942)

8 Unhappy German nation, how do you like the Messianic rôle allotted to you, not by God, nor by destiny, but by a handful of perverted and bloody-minded men?

'This War', first publ. 1939, repr. in *Order of the Day* (1942)

9 The Freudian theory is one of the most important foundation stones for an edifice to be built by future generations, the dwelling of a freer and wiser humanity.

*The New York Times* 21 June 1939

10 It is a strange fact that freedom and equality, the two basic ideas of democracy, are to some extent contradictory. Logically considered, freedom and equality are mutually exclusive, just as society and the individual are mutually exclusive.

'The War and the Future', speech 1940, publ. in *Order of the Day* (1942)

11 What we call National-Socialism is the poisonous perversion of ideas which have a long history in German intellectual life.

ibid.

12 I have always been an admirer, I regard the gift of admiration as indispensable if one is to amount to something; I don't know where I would be without it.

Letter, 1950, quoted in *Thomas Mann and His Family*, 'Thomas Mann – The Birth of Criticism' (1987) by Marcel Reich-Ranicki

13 Every reasonable human being should be a moderate Socialist.

*The New York Times* 18 June 1950, quoted in *Thomas Mann: A Critical Study*, ch. 2 (1971) by R.J. Hollingdale

# Dick Manning See AL HOFFMAN AND DICK MANNING.

# Katherine Mansfield (1888–1923)
NEW ZEALAND-BORN BRITISH AUTHOR

She spent much of her life in Europe, at school in England and as an aspiring writer in France. Her stories, collected in *Bliss* (1919)

and *The Garden Party* (1920) among other titles, are noted for their sympathetic psychological realism though they did not meet with the approval of VIRGINIA WOOLF, who remarked: 'Her mind is a very thin soil, laid an inch or two upon very barren rock.' She also wrote poetry, posthumously edited and published by her husband JOHN MIDDLETON MURRY. She died of tuberculosis. See also LOUISE BOGAN 2.

1 To work – to work! It is such infinite delight to know that we still have the best things to do.

Letter to BERTRAND RUSSELL, 7 December 1916, publ. in *Collected Letters*, vol. 1 (ed. Vincent O'Sullivan and Margaret Scott, 1984)

2 It's a terrible thing to be alone – yes it is – it is – but don't lower your mask until you have another mask prepared beneath – as terrible as you like – but a *mask*.

Letter to JOHN MIDDLETON MURRY, July 1917, publ. in ibid. Referring to Murry's writing, which she found 'indecent' for his tendency to 'abase' himself, during a period when he was most influenced by the style of D.H. LAWRENCE.

3 I'm a writer first and a woman after.

ibid. 3 December 1920

4 Everything in life that we really accept undergoes a change. So suffering must become Love. That is the mystery.

Journal entry 19 December 1920, publ. in *The Journal of Katherine Mansfield* (1927)

# Mao Zedong (1893–1976)
CHINESE LEADER

One of the founders of the Chinese Communist Party in 1921, he became its leader from 1935 until his death, and following the war of liberation (1937–49) China's President. His 'Thoughts' became doctrine for the mass of Chinese and fashionable among western radicals in the 1960s. His reputation as theorist and voice of Third World revolution is overshadowed by the oppression under his rule, notably during the Cultural Revolution (1966–9).

1 A revolution is not a dinner party, or writing an essay, or painting a picture, or doing embroidery; it cannot be so refined, so leisurely and gentle, so temperate, kind, courteous, restrained and magnanimous. A revolution is an insurrection, an act of violence by which one class overthrows another.

Report March 1927, publ. in *Selected Works*, vol. 1 (1954)

2 Politics is war without bloodshed while war is politics with bloodshed.

'On Protracted War' (May 1938), publ. in ibid. vol. 2 (1961)

3 Weapons are an important factor in war, but not the decisive factor; it is people, not things, that are decisive. The contest of strength is not only a contest of military and economic power, but also a contest of human power and morale. Military and economic power is necessarily wielded by people.

ibid.

4 Our attitude towards ourselves should be 'to be insatiable in learning' and towards others 'to be tireless in teaching'.

'The Role of the Chinese Communist Party in the National War' (October 1938), publ. in ibid.

5 Every Communist must grasp the truth, 'Political power grows out of the barrel of a gun'.

'Problems of War and Strategy', speech, 6 November 1938, publ. in ibid. JEAN GENET observed: 'Power may be at the end of a gun, but sometimes it's also at the end of the shadow or the image of a gun.'

6 War can only be abolished through war, and in order to get rid of the gun it is necessary to take up the gun.

ibid.

7 So long as a person who has made mistakes does not hide his sickness for fear of treatment or persist in his mistakes until he is beyond cure, so long as he honestly and sin-

cerely wishes to be cured and to mend his ways, we should welcome him and cure his sickness so that he can become a good comrade. We can never succeed if we just let ourselves go and lash out at him. In treating an ideological or a political malady, one must never be rough and rash but must adopt the approach of 'curing the sickness to save the patient', which is the only correct and effective method.

'Rectify the Party's Style of Work' (1 February 1942), publ. in ibid. vol. 3 (1961)

8 There is in fact no such thing as art for art's sake, art that stands above classes, art that is detached from or independent of politics. Proletarian literature and art are part of the whole proletarian revolutionary cause.

'Talks at the Yenan Forum on Literature and Art' (May 1942), publ. in ibid.

9 Take the ideas of the masses (scattered and unsystematic ideas) and concentrate them (through study turn them into concentrated and systematic ideas), then go to the masses and propagate and explain these ideas until the masses embrace them as their own, hold fast to them and translate them into action, and test the correctness of these ideas in such action. Then once again concentrate ideas from the masses and once again go to the masses so that the ideas are persevered in and carried through. And so on, over and over again in an endless spiral, with the ideas becoming more correct, more vital and richer each time. Such is the Marxist theory of knowledge.

'Some Questions Concerning Methods of Leadership' (1 June 1943), publ. in ibid.

10 An army without culture is a dull-witted army, and a dull-witted army cannot defeat the enemy.

'The United Front in Cultural Work' (30 October 1944), publ. in ibid.

11 The people, and the people alone, are the motive force in the making of world history.

'On Coalition Government' (24 April 1945), publ. in ibid.

12 All reactionaries are paper tigers. In appearance, the reactionaries are terrifying, but in reality they are not so powerful. From a long-term point of view, it is not the reactionaries but the people who are really powerful.

'Talk with the American correspondent Anne Louise Strong', August 1946, publ. in ibid., vol. 4 (1961). Mao returned to this theme in a later speech in Moscow, 18 November 1957: 'Was not Hitler a paper tiger? Was Hitler not overthrown? . . . US imperialism has not yet been overthrown and it has the atomic bomb. I believe it also will be overthrown. It, too, is a paper tiger.'

13 Classes struggle, some classes triumph, others are eliminated. Such is history; such is the history of civilization for thousands of years.

Said in August 1949, quoted in *Mao and China: From Revolution to Revolution* (1972) by Stanley Karnow

14 Communism is not love. Communism is a hammer which we use to crush the enemy.

Quoted in *Time* magazine 18 December 1950

15 Letting a hundred flowers blossom and a hundred schools of thought contend is the policy for promoting the progress of the arts and the sciences and a flourishing socialist culture in our land.

Speech in Beijing, 27 February 1957, quoted in *Quotations from Chairman Mao Tse-Tung*, ch. 32 (1966)

16 Apart from their other characteristics, the outstanding thing about China's 600 million people is that they are 'poor and blank.' This may seem a bad thing, but in reality it is a good thing. Poverty gives rise to the desire for change, the desire for action and the desire for revolution. On a blank sheet of paper free from any mark, the freshest and most beautiful characters can be written, the freshest and most beautiful pictures can be painted.

'Introducing a Co-operative' (15 April 1958) quoted in ibid. ch. 3

## Diego Maradona (b. 1960)
ARGENTINIAN FOOTBALLER

Celebrated internationally as a brilliant and controversial striker, he became the world's most expensive footballer on joining Barcelona for £5 million in 1982. He played a key role in Argentina's victory in the 1986 World Cup, but his career was marred by cocaine use.

1 The goal was scored a little bit by the hand of God, a little by the head of Maradona.

Quoted in the *Observer* 29 June 1986. Referring to the goal bounced off his fist that ousted England from the Mexico World Cup finals.

## Marcel Marceau (b. 1923)
FRENCH MIME ARTIST

Internationally recognized for his mastery of mime, he extended the possibilities of the art in such works as the mime-drama *Don Juan* (1964) and the ballet *Candide* (1971). In 1978 he became Director of the École de Mimodrame Marcel Marceau.

1 Do not the most moving moments of our lives find us all without words?

*Reader's Digest* June 1958

2 I have spent more than half a lifetime trying to express the tragic moment.

*Guardian* 11 August 1988

## Paul Marcinkus (b. 1922)
US ECCLESIASTIC

He was Director of the Institute of Religious Works, or Vatican bank, which was damaged by the spectacular failure of the Banco Ambrosiano in 1982. The Holy See resisted all attempts by magistrates investigating the crash to force the now-retired Marcinkus to submit to Italian justice.

1 You can't run the Church on Hail Marys.

Quoted in the *Observer* 25 May 1986

## Imelda Marcos (b. 1929)
FILIPINO FIRST LADY

Nicknamed the 'Iron Butterfly', the wife of Ferdinand Marcos, President of the Philippines (1965–86), she was publicly disgraced by revelations of nepotism, embezzlement of state funds and a prodigiously large collection of shoes. Forced into exile in 1986, she returned to Manila in 1991 and was elected to the Philippines House of Representatives in 1995.

1 I get so tired listening to one million dollars here, one million dollars there, it's so petty.

Quoted in *The Times* 22 June 1990. Marcos was complaining of the numerous witnesses called to testify to her financial profligacy during her trial on charges of embezzlement in New York.

## Greil Marcus (b. 1945)
US ROCK JOURNALIST

A contributor of articles and reviews to *The New York Times*, *Village Voice* and *Rolling Stone*, where he was Associate Editor (1969–70) and Book Editor (1975–80), he is best known for the acclaimed classic *Mystery Train: Images of America in Rock 'n' Roll Music* (1975).

1 We make the oldest stories new when we succeed, and we are trapped by the old stories when we fail.

*Mystery Train*, Prologue (1975)

2 It may be that the most interesting American struggle is the struggle to set oneself free from the limits one is born to, and then to learn something of the value of those limits.
*ibid.* 'Robert Johnson, 1938'

3 No failure in America, whether of love or money, is ever simple; it is always a kind of betrayal, of a mass of shadowy, shared hopes.
*ibid.*

4 Rock 'n' roll is a combination of good ideas dried up by fads, terrible junk, hideous failings in taste and judgment, gullibility and manipulation, moments of unbelievable clarity and invention, pleasure, fun, vulgarity, excess, novelty and utter enervation.
*ibid.* 'Randy Newman: Pop'

5 We fight our way through the massed and leveled collective safe taste of the Top 40, just looking for a little something we can call our own. But when we find it and jam the radio to hear it again it isn't just ours – it is a link to thousands of others who are sharing it with us. As a matter of a single song this might mean very little; as culture, as a way of life, you can't beat it.
*ibid.*

6 It is a sure sign that a culture has reached a dead end when it is no longer intrigued by its myths.
*ibid.* 'Elvis: Presliad: Fanfare'

7 Punk to me was a form of free speech. It was a moment when suddenly all kinds of strange voices that no reasonable person could ever have expected to hear in public were being heard all over the place.
'Punk and History', transcript of a discussion, 24 September 1988, New York, publ. in *Discourses: Conversations in Postmodern Art and Culture* (ed. Russell Ferguson *et al.*, 1990)

## Herbert Marcuse (1898–1979)
GERMAN-BORN US POLITICAL PHILOSOPHER

A refugee from Nazi Germany in 1934, he adopted US citizenship in 1940 and held academic and government posts. In the 1960s he was a major influence on young intellectuals with his blend of psychoanalytic theory and libertarian left-wing thought, in works such as *Eros and Civilization* (1955) and *One-Dimensional Man* (1964).

1 If the worker and his boss enjoy the same television program and visit the same resort places, if the typist is as attractively made up as the daughter of her employer, if the Negro owns a Cadillac, if they all read the same newspaper, then this assimilation indicates not the disappearance of classes, but the extent to which the needs and satisfactions that serve the preservation of the Establishment are shared by the underlying population.
*One-Dimensional Man*, ch. 1 (1964)

2 The web of domination has become the web of Reason itself, and this society is fatally entangled in it.
*ibid.* ch. 5

3 Self-determination, the autonomy of the individual, asserts itself in the right to race his automobile, to handle his power tools, to buy a gun, to communicate to mass audiences his opinion, no matter how ignorant, how aggressive, it may be.
*An Essay on Liberation*, ch. 1 (1969)

## Jacques Maritain (1882–1973)
FRENCH PHILOSOPHER

He was one of the most influential Catholic theologians of the twentieth century and a leading neo-Thomist philosopher, known by such works as *The Degrees of Knowledge* (1932) and *Scholasticism*

*in Politics* (1940). His liberal and left-wing interpretation of Roman Catholic doctrine drew controversy.

1 I don't see America as a mainland, but as a sea, a big ocean. Sometimes a storm arises, a formidable current develops, and it seems it will engulf everything. Wait a moment, another current will appear and bring the first one to naught.
*Reflections on America*, ch. 4 (1948)

## (Dame) Alicia Markova (b. 1910)
BRITISH BALLERINA

Born Lilian Alicia Marks. She joined Diaghilev's Ballets Russes in 1924 and was prima ballerina of the Vic-Wells (now the Royal Ballet) 1933–5. With her partner Anton Dolin she toured extensively, notably in *Giselle*, and in 1950 she founded the Festival Ballet Company.

1 Glorious bouquets and storms of applause ... are the trimmings which every artist naturally enjoys. But to *move* an audience in such a role, to hear in the applause that unmistakable note which breaks through good theatre manners and comes from the heart, is to feel that you have won through to life itself. Such pleasure does not vanish with the fall of the curtain, but becomes part of one's own life.
*Giselle and I*, ch. 18 (1960)

## Bob Marley (1945–81)
JAMAICAN REGGAE MUSICIAN

Son of an army captain from Liverpool, raised in poverty in Kingston, Jamaica, he made his first record in 1961 but it was not until the albums *Catch a Fire* (1972) and *Natty Dread* (1975), recorded with the Wailers, that he achieved international recognition and became the first reggae superstar. His songs drew heavily on his Rastafarian beliefs.

1 Get up, stand up,
   Stand up for your rights.
   Get up, stand up,
   Don't give up the fight.
'Get Up, Stand Up' (song, written with PETER TOSH) on the album *Burnin'* (1973) by the Wailers

2 Them belly full but we 'ungry
   A hungry mob is a angry mob.
'Them Belly Full' (song, written by Legon Cogil and Carlton Barrett) on the album *Natty Dread* (1975) by Bob Marley and the Wailers

3 Until the philosophy which holds one race superior and another inferior is finally and permanently discredited and abandoned, everywhere is war ... and until there are no longer first-class and second-class citizens of any nation, until the colour of a man's skin is of no more significance than the colour of his eyes, me seh war. And until the basic human rights are equally guaranteed to all without regard to race, there is war. And until that day, the dream of lasting peace, world citizenship, rule of international morality, will remain but a fleeting illusion to be pursued, but never attained ... now everywhere is war.
'War' (song) on the album *Rastaman Vibration* (1976) by Bob Marley and the Wailers. The words of the song are based on a speech given to the United Nations by the Ethiopian Emperor Haile Selassie in 1968.

4 The real reggae must come from Jamaica, because other people could not play it all the while, anyway – it would go against the whole life. Reggae has t'be inside you ... Reggae music is simple, all the while ... Cannot be taught, that's a fact.
Interview in *Melody Maker* 12 June 1976, repr. in *Melody Maker: Classic Rock Interviews* (ed. Allan Jones, 1994)

5 Emancipate yourselves from mental slavery.
None but ourselves can free our minds.

'Redemption Song' (song) on the album *Uprising* (1980) by Bob Marley and the Wailers

## Don Marquis (1878–1937)
US HUMORIST AND JOURNALIST

Known for his poems, essays and humorous writings, he was the creator in 1927 of archy and mehitabel, a cat and literary-minded cockroach which debate life's serious questions in light verse.

1 A fierce unrest seethes at the core
Of all existing things:
It was the eager wish to soar
That gave the gods their wings.

'Unrest', publ. in *Dreams and Dust* (1915)

2 my youth i shall never forget
but there s nothing i really regret
wotthehell wotthehell
there s a dance in the old dame yet
toujours gai toujours gai

'the song of mehitabel', publ. in *archy and mehitabel* (1927)

3 persian pussy from over the sea
demure and lazy and smug and fat
none of your ribbons and bells for me
ours is the zest of the alley cat

'mehitabel s extensive past', publ. in ibid.

4 procrastination is the
art of keeping
up with yesterday

'certain maxims of archy', publ. in ibid.

5 every cloud
has its silver
lining but it is
sometimes a little
difficult to get it to
the mint

ibid.

6 an optimist is a guy
who has never had
much experience

ibid.

7 did you ever
notice that when
a politician
does get an idea
he usually
gets it all wrong

'mehitabel again', publ. in *archys life of mehitabel* (1933)

8 now and then
there is a person born
who is so unlucky
that he runs into accidents
which started out to happen
to somebody else

'archy says', publ. in ibid.

9 Bores bore each other too; but it never seems to teach them anything.

Quoted in *A Little Book of Aphorisms* (1947) by Frederic B. Wilcox

10 The art of newspaper paragraphing is to stroke a platitude until it purrs like an epigram.

ibid. ADLAI STEVENSON borrowed this idea when he quipped, 'The Republicans stroke platitudes until they purr like epigrams' (quoted in Leon Harris, *The Fine Art of Political Wit*, ch. 1, 1964).

11 Middle age is the time when a man is always thinking that in a week or two he will feel as good as ever.

ibid.

12 A demagogue is a person with whom we disagree as to which gang should mismanage the country.

ibid.

13 I get up in the morning with an idea for a three-volume novel and by nightfall it's a paragraph in my column.

Quoted in *O Rare Don Marquis*, ch. 6 (1962) by E. Anthony

14 Writing a book of poetry is like dropping a rose petal down the Grand Canyon and waiting for the echo.

ibid. This aphorism emerged as the distillation of what had been a long piece on the futility of writing poetry for Don Marquis's 'Sun Dial' column, which he rejected on the grounds of it being too much a plaint, publishing instead this one sentence.

15 Poetry is what Milton saw when he went blind.

ibid. ch. 11. 'That line would have pleased Milton himself,' observed the poet Louis Untermeyer.

16 By the time a bartender knows what drink a man will have before he orders, there is little else about him worth knowing.

ibid. FRANKLIN P. ADAMS cited this aphorism to illustrate Marquis's gift for 'telling a whole story in a sentence'.

## Anthony Marriott (b. 1931) and Alistair Foot
BRITISH PLAYWRIGHTS

They collaborated on a number of plays, starting with *Uproar in the House* (1967), and are best known for *No Sex Please – We're British* (1971), a long-running West End farce.

1 No sex please – we're British.

Title of play (1971)

## Wynton Marsalis (b. 1961)
US JAZZ MUSICIAN

Equally at home with the classical and jazz repertoires, he emerged in the 1980s with a jazz trumpet style akin to that of the young MILES DAVIS. He has toured with Art Blakey's Jazz Messengers, recorded with Herbie Hancock, and made his own albums that include *Think of One* (1983) and *Soul Gestures in Southern Blue* (1991). In 1997 he was awarded the Pulitzer Prize for music.

1 Jazz is music that really deals with what it means to be an American. The irony is when they wrote the Declaration of Independence and the United States Constitution, they didn't even think of a Black man. Yet Louis Armstrong, the grandson of a slave, is the one more than anybody else [who] could translate into music that feeling of what it is to be an American.

'We Must Preserve Our Jazz Heritage', publ. in *Ebony* February 1986

## Thomas R. Marshall (1854–1925)
US POLITICIAN

A Democratic Governor of Indiana (1909–13), he served two terms as Vice-president under WOODROW WILSON (1913–17 and 1917–21).

1 What this country needs is a really good 5-cent cigar.

Quoted in the *New York Tribune* 4 January 1920

## Steve Martin (b. 1945)
US COMEDIAN AND COMIC ACTOR

Starting out as a stand-up comic, he made his film debut in *The Absent Minded Waiter* (1977) and went on to demonstrate his comedic agility in such films as *All of Me* (1984) and *Dirty Rotten Scoundrels* (1988). He also wrote, produced and starred in *Roxanne* (1987) and *LA Story* (1991).

1 All dames are alike. They reach down your throat so they

can grab your heart, they pull it out, they throw it on the floor and they step on it with their high heels. They spit on it. They shove it in the oven and they cook the shit out of it. Then they slice it into little pieces, slam it on a hunk of toast and serve it to you. And they expect you to say: thanks honey, it's delicious!

Rigby Reardon (Steve Martin), in *Dead Men Don't Wear Plaid* (film, 1982, screenplay by George Gipe, Carl Reiner and Steve Martin, directed by Carl Reiner)

2 I believe entertainment can aspire to be art, and can become art, but if you set out to make art you're an idiot.

*Today* 17 May 1989

## Strother Martin (1920–80)

US SCREEN ACTOR

A champion diver who worked as a swimming instructor in Hollywood, he picked up character roles, often as villains, in numerous films in the 1950s. He later played parts in westerns, as in *True Grit* and *Butch Cassidy and the Sundance Kid* (both 1969).

1 What we've got here is a failure to communicate.

Camp commandant (Strother Martin), in *Cool Hand Luke* (film, 1967, screenplay and original novel by Donn Pearce, directed by Stuart Rosenberg). The words appeared as a publicity slogan for the movie.

## Groucho Marx (1895–1977)

US COMIC ACTOR

Original name Julius Marx. Called the 'Oscar Wilde of the wisecrack' by critic Philip French, he was one of the four Marx Brothers who started in vaudeville, moved on to Broadway in the early 1920s and made their first film, *The Cocoanuts*, in 1929. Most successful of the thirteen madcap films they made together are *Animal Crackers* (1930), *Monkey Business* (1931), *Duck Soup* (1933) and *A Night at the Opera* (1935). Groucho's chief contributions were his cigar, moustache, a sloping walk and a constant stream of pungent asides by way of commentary to the action. After the Second World War he became a TV star as quizmaster on the weekly 'You Bet Your Life' series (1947–62). Humorist S.J. PERELMAN summed him up: 'The man was a major comedian, which is to say that he had the compassion of an icicle, the effrontery of a carnival shill and the generosity of a pawnbroker.'

1 I hope all your teeth have cavities, and don't forget; abscess makes the heart grow fonder.

Hammer (Groucho Marx), in *The Cocoanuts* (film, 1929, screenplay by Morrie Ryskind from the play by GEORGE KAUFMAN and IRVING BERLIN, directed by Robert Florey and Joseph Santley)

2 One morning I shot an elephant in my pajamas. How he got into my pajamas I'll never know.

Captain Jeffrey Spaulding (Groucho Marx), in *Animal Crackers* (film, 1930, screenplay by Morrie Ryskind based on a musical by Morrie Ryskind and GEORGE KAUFMAN, directed by Victor Heerman)

3 That's what I always say. Love flies out the door when money comes innuendo.

Groucho as himself, in *Monkey Business* (film, 1931, screenplay by Arthur Sheekman based on a story by S.J. PERELMAN, W.B. Johnstone and Roland Pertwee; directed by Norman McLeod)

4 Oh, why can't we break away from all this, just you and I, and lodge with my fleas in the hills? I mean, flee to my lodge in the hills.

ibid.

5 Oh, I realize it's a penny here and a penny there, but look at me: I've worked myself up from nothing to a state of extreme poverty.

ibid.

6 Remember, you're fighting for this woman's honor, which is probably more than she ever did.

Rufus T. Firefly (Groucho Marx), in *Duck Soup* (film, 1933,

screenplay by Bert Kalmar, Arthur Sheekman, Nat Perrin and Harry Ruby, directed by Leo McCarey). Referring to Mrs Teasdale (Margaret Dumont).

7 Either he's dead or my watch has stopped.

Dr Hackenbush (Groucho Marx), in *A Day at the Races* (film, 1937, screenplay by Robert Pirosh, George Seaton and George Oppenheimer, directed by Sam Wood)

8 Emily, I've a little confession to make. I really am a horse doctor. But marry me, and I'll never look at another horse.

ibid. Proposing to Mrs Upjohn (Margaret Dumont).

9 The trouble with writing a book about yourself is that you can't fool around. If you write about someone else, you can stretch the truth from here to Finland. If you write about yourself the slightest deviation makes you realize instantly that there may be honor among thieves, but *you* are just a dirty liar.

*Groucho and Me*, ch. 1 (1959). Opening sentence of book.

10 Although it is generally known, I think it's about time to announce that I was born at a very early age.

ibid.

11 From the moment I picked your book up until I laid it down I was convulsed with laughter. Someday I intend reading it.

Quoted in *Life* 9 February 1962. Referring to *Dawn Ginsbergh's Revenge* by S.J. PERELMAN.

12 Please accept my resignation. I don't care to belong to any club that will have me as a member.

Quoted in *The Groucho Letters*, Introduction (1967). WOODY ALLEN paraphrases the quote in the opening scene of *Annie Hall* (1977), where he attributes it to SIGMUND FREUD and remarks: 'That's the key joke of my adult life in terms of my relationship with women.'

13 I never forget a face, but in your case I'll be glad to make an exception.

Quoted in *People I Have Loved, Known or Admired*, 'Groucho', sect. 2 (1970) by Leo Rosten

14 I find television very educational. Every time someone switches it on I go into another room and read a good book.

Quoted in *Halliwell's Filmgoer's Companion* (1984)

15 I've been around so long I can remember Doris Day before she was a virgin.

Attributed in *Halliwell's Who's Who in the Movies* (ed. John Walker, 1999)

## Harpo Marx (1888–1964)

US COMIC ACTOR

Full name Adolph Marx. The silent brother of the Marx Brothers, he took his stage name from the harp he played. His humour depended on eloquent miming and his props: a red wig and an oversized coat that held a collection of bric-a-brac, including a taxi horn, which he sounded at inappropriate moments.

1 Join the Army and See the Navy.

Sign paraded by Brownie (Harpo Marx) in *Duck Soup* (film, 1933, screenplay by Bert Kalmar, Arthur Sheekman, Nat Perrin and Harry Ruby, directed by Leo McCarey)

## Hugh Masakela (b. 1939)

SOUTH AFRICAN JAZZ TRUMPETER

He left South Africa in 1960 to study in London and later in New York, during which time he introduced Western audiences to township jazz. *Trumpet Africa* (1962) dates from this period. During the 1970s and 1980s he performed in Africa, but did not return to South Africa until 1990. He was married to the singer Miriam Makeba.

1 The Afro-American experience is the only real culture

that America has. Basically, every American tries to walk, talk, dress and behave like African Americans.

*International Herald Tribune* 17 May 1990

## Jackie Mason (b. 1931)

US COMIC

Original name Jacob Moshe Maza. He studied to become a rabbi before becoming a stand-up comedian, soon making his mark by his Jewish humour delivered at a roller-coaster pace in a Brooklyn accent. His one-man shows include *The World According to Me!* (New York, 1986), and he has also made films, including *The Jerk* (1979) and *Caddyshack 2* (1988).

1 [Of England] This is the only country in the world where the food is more dangerous than sex.

*Daily Telegraph* 17 February 1989

2 If an Englishman gets run down by a truck he apologizes to the truck.

*Independent* 20 September 1990

## Allan Massie (b. 1938)

BRITISH AUTHOR

A novelist and journalist of Scottish background, he draws on historical themes, often from classical Rome. Among his works are *Change and Decay in All Around I See* (1978), *These Enchanted Woods* and *Caesar* (both 1993).

1 Do you know what a soldier is, young man? He's the chap who makes it possible for civilized folk to despise war.

Colonel Fernie, in *A Question of Loyalties*, pt 2 ch. 1 (1989)

2 Blunders are an inescapable feature of war, because choice in military affairs lies generally between the bad and the worse.

Marshal Pétain, in ibid. pt 3, ch. 11

## Brian Masters (b. 1939)

BRITISH AUTHOR

He earned critical plaudits for *Now Barabbas Was a Rotter* (1978), a biography of Marie Corelli, and for his eighteenth-century study, *Georgiana, Duchess of Devonshire* (1981).

1 Evil is something you recognize immediately you see it: it works through charm.

*Daily Telegraph* 31 May 1991

## Harry Mathews (b. 1930)

US NOVELIST

Also a poet and translator, he is best known for his fiction, notably his witty cult classics *The Conversions* (1962), *Tlooth* (1966) and *The Sinking of the Odradek* (1975).

1 Translation is the paradigm, the exemplar of all writing . . . It is translation that demonstrates most vividly the yearning for transformation that underlies every act involving speech, that supremely human gift.

*Country Cooking and Other Stories*, 'The Dialect of the Tribe' (1980)

2 Syntax and vocabulary are overwhelming constraints – the rules that run us. Language is using *us* to talk – we think we're using the language, but language is doing the thinking, we're its slavish agents.

Interview in *City Limits* 26 May 1988

## Henri Matisse (1869–1954)

FRENCH ARTIST

Considered one of the most important artists of the twentieth century, he was a leading influence in the Fauvist school, his paintings of traditional subjects characterized by sinuous lines and flamboyant, bright colour, as in *Portrait of Madame Matisse* (1905) and *The Dance* (1910). 'What I dream of,' he wrote, 'is an art of balance, of purity and serenity devoid of troubling and depressing sub-matter.' Later work includes the stained glass for the Chapelle du Rosaire at Vence (1948–51).

1 You study, you learn, but you guard the original naiveté. It has to be within you, as desire for drink is within the drunkard or love is within the drunkard or love is within the lover.

Quoted in *Time* magazine 26 June 1950

2 There is nothing more difficult for a truly creative painter than to paint a rose, because before he can do so he has first to forget all the roses that were ever painted.

Comment recalled in obituaries, 5 November 1954

## W. Somerset Maugham (1874–1965)

BRITISH AUTHOR

Full name William Somerset Maugham. An immensely prolific novelist and essayist, he earned popular fame for such works as *Of Human Bondage* (1915), *The Moon and Sixpence* (1919), *Cakes and Ale* (1930) and *The Razor's Edge* (1944). He is also renowned as a writer of short stories.

1 Like all weak men he laid an exaggerated stress on not changing one's mind.

*Of Human Bondage*, ch. 39 (1915). Referring to the Vicar of Blackstable.

2 Money is like a sixth sense without which you cannot make a complete use of the other five.

Monsieur Foinet, in ibid. ch. 51

3 Impropriety is the soul of wit.

*The Moon and Sixpence*, ch. 4 (1919)

4 It is not true that suffering ennobles the character; happiness does that sometimes, but suffering, for the most part, makes men petty and vindictive.

ibid. ch. 17. Nearly twenty years later Maugham used almost identical words to describe the suffering he witnessed as a medical student, in *The Summing Up*, ch. 19 (1938).

5 Hypocrisy is the most difficult and nerve-racking vice that any man can pursue; it needs an unceasing vigilance and a rare detachment of spirit. It cannot, like adultery or gluttony, be practised at spare moments; it is a whole-time job.

*Cakes and Ale*, ch. 1 (1930)

6 The Americans . . . have invented so wide a range of pithy and hackneyed phrases that they can carry on an amusing and animated conversation without giving a moment's reflection to what they are saying and so leave their minds free to consider the more important matters of big business and fornication.

ibid. ch. 2

7 The ideal has many names, and beauty is but one of them.

ibid. ch. 11

8 From the earliest times the old have rubbed it into the young that they are wiser than they, and before the young had discovered what nonsense this was they were old too, and it profited them to carry on the imposture.

Ashenden, in ibid. ch. 11

9 Poor Henry [Henry James], he's spending eternity wandering round and round a stately park and the fence is just too high for him to peep over and they're having tea just too far away for him to hear what the countess is saying.

Edward Driffield, in ibid. HENRY JAMES, he said, 'had turned his back on one of the great events of the world's history, the rise of the United States, in order to report tittle-tattle at tea parties in English country houses'. In a notebook entry in 1937, Maugham wrote of James: 'He did not live, he observed life from a window, and too often was inclined to content himself with no more than what his friends told him they saw when *they* looked out of a window.'

10 The common idea that success spoils people by making them vain, egotistic, and self-complacent is erroneous; on the contrary, it makes them, for the most part, humble, tolerant, and kind. Failure makes people cruel and bitter.

ibid. ch. 48

11 There is no explanation for evil. It must be looked upon as a necessary part of the order of the universe. To ignore it is childish, to bewail it senseless.

ibid. ch. 73

12 Sentimentality is only sentiment that rubs you up the wrong way.

Entry 1941 in *A Writer's Notebook* (1949)

13 I made up my mind long ago that life was too short to do anything for myself that I could pay others to do for me.

ibid.

14 I am told that today rather more than 60 per cent of the men who go to university go on a Government grant. This is a new class that has entered upon the scene. It is the white-collar proletariat . . . They do not go to university to acquire culture but to get a job, and when they have got one, scamp it. They have no manners and are woefully unable to deal with any social predicament. Their idea of a celebration is to go to a public house and drink six beers. They are mean, malicious and envious . . . They are scum.

*Sunday Times* 25 December 1955. Referring to the generation of 'Angry Young Men' as portrayed in KINGSLEY AMIS's 1954 novel *Lucky Jim*. These people, Maugham continued, 'will in due course leave the university. Some will doubtless sink back, perhaps with relief, into the modest social class from which they emerged; some will take to drink, some to crime and go to prison . . . A few will go into Parliament, become Cabinet Ministers and rule the country. I look upon myself as fortunate that I shall not live to see it.'

15 The crown of literature is poetry. It is its end and aim. It is the sublimest activity of the human mind. It is the achievement of beauty and delicacy. The writer of prose can only step aside when the poet passes.

*Saturday Review* 20 July 1957

16 What has influenced my life more than any other single thing has been my stammer. Had I not stammered I would probably . . . have gone to Cambridge as my brothers did, perhaps have become a don and every now and then published a dreary book about French literature.

*Newsweek* 23 May 1960

## Armistead Maupin (b. 1944)
US JOURNALIST AND AUTHOR

He wrote for various newspapers, including the *San Francisco Chronicle* (1976–7), before publishing the six-novel sequence *Tales of the City* (1978–90), primarily a sympathetic portrait of gay life in San Francisco.

1 Too much of a good thing is wonderful.

*More Tales of the City*, 'The Road to Ruin' (1980). Motto inscribed on a brass plaque outside the Pinus club.

2 Mona's Law. That's what she calls it. She says you can have a hot job, a hot lover and a hot apartment, but you can't have all three at the same time.

Michael, in ibid. 'Mona's Law'

3 I think a lot of gay people who are not dealing with their homosexuality get into right-wing politics.

*Guardian* 22 April 1988

## François Mauriac (1885–1970)
FRENCH AUTHOR

Describing his aim as a writer to attempt 'to make the Catholic universe of evil palpable, tangible, odorous', he wrote novels which explore the conflicts of good and evil, sin and redemption, including *Flesh and Blood* (1920), *The Knot of Vipers* (1932) and *La Pharisienne* (1941). He won the Nobel Prize for Literature in 1952.

1 I love Germany so dearly that I hope there will always be two of them.

Quoted in *Newsweek* 20 November 1989

## André Maurois (1885–1967)
FRENCH AUTHOR AND CRITIC

Born Emile Salomon Wilhelm Herzog. A prominent man of letters for fifty years, he became internationally known for his novels *The Thought Reading Machine* (1938) and *Woman Without Love* (1945), and for fictionalized biographies such as *Ariel* (1923), a life of Shelley, and *The Quest for Proust* (1949). He also wrote histories and critical and philosophical essays.

1 Self-pity comes so naturally to all of us, that the most solid happiness can be shaken by the compassion of a fool.

*Ariel*, ch. 16 (1923)

2 A successful marriage is an edifice that must be rebuilt every day.

*The Art of Living*, 'The Art of Marriage' (1940)

3 Growing old is no more than a bad habit which a busy man has no time to form.

ibid. 'The Art of Growing Old'. 'The true evil,' Maurois wrote, 'is not the weakening of the body, but the indifference of the soul.'

4 The difficult part in an argument is not to defend one's opinion, but rather to know it.

Quoted in *A Little Book of Aphorisms* (1947) by Frederic B. Wilcox

5 Style [is] the hallmark of a temperament stamped on the material in hand.

*The Art of Writing*, 'The Writer's Craft', sect. 2 (1960)

6 A great biography should, like the close of a great drama, leave behind it a feeling of serenity. We collect into a small bunch the flowers, the few flowers, which brought sweetness into a life, and present it as an offering to an accomplished destiny.

ibid. 'The Writer's Craft', sect. 5

## Robert Maxwell (1923–91)
CZECH-BORN BRITISH PUBLISHER

Original name Jan Ludvik Hoch. As a self-made communications tycoon, he had business interests extending from continental Europe to Israel and China and acted as adviser to government and industry, leading him once to claim to have 'indispensably contributed to saving eastern Europe'. In Britain he was Chairman of the Mirror Group from 1984, from which, following his mysterious death at sea, it emerged that he had siphoned money from employee pension funds to offset the losses of his private firms.

1 It's the editors who interfere in the publisher's prerogative, not the other way round.

Said in July 1985, quoted in *Maxwell: The Outsider*, ch. 13 (1988, rev. 1991) by Tom Bower. Referring to his relations with Mirror Group Newspapers.

2 Ordinary people may not understand the meaning of democracy but they've a passionate regard for fair play.

Quoted in *Maxwell*, ch. 1 (1988) by Joe Haines

3 When I fire someone it is like a thunderclap. My primary duty is to hire and fire editors. I treat them like a Field Marshal.

*Independent* 13 May 1990

4 When I pass a belt, I can't resist hitting below it.

*International Herald Tribune* 18 March 1991

## Vladimir Mayakovsky (1893–1930)
RUSSIAN POET AND DRAMATIST

A founder of the Russian Futurist movement, his early work, such as the declamatory *A Cloud in Trousers* (1915), was calculated to shock the bourgeoisie by its depoetized language. He embraced the Bolshevik cause during the Russian Revolution with the popular 'Ode to Revolution' (1918) and 'Left March' (1919), and with his play *150,000,000* (1920). He played a prominent public role throughout the 1920s but later found himself increasingly criticized and took his own life. In 1935 STALIN declared that 'indifference to his memory and works is a crime'.

1 Or if you prefer
   as the sky changes tone
   I'll be absolutely tender
   not a man but a cloud in trousers.
   'The Cloud in Trousers' (1915), repr. in *Russian Poetry: the Modern Period* (ed. John Glad and Daniel Weissbort, 1978)

2 No gray hair in my soul
   no doddering tenderness,
   I rock the world with the thunder of my voice,
   strolling, looking good –
   twenty-two.
   ibid.

3 The bull of the days is skewballed.
   The cart of the years is slow.
   Our god is speed. The heart is our drum.
   'Our March' st. 2 and 6, written 1917, publ. in *The Heritage of Russian Verse* (ed. and transl. Dimitri Obolensky, 1962)

4 My verse
   has brought me
   no roubles to spare:
   no craftsmen have made
   mahogany chairs for my house.
   'At the top of my voice', written 1929–30, repr. in *Twentieth-Century Russian Poetry* (ed. Albert C. Todd and Max Hayward, 1993)

5 Comrade life,
   let us
   march faster,
   March
   faster through what's left
   of the five-year plan.
   ibid.

6 The ship of love has foundered on life's reef. You and I are even. And why should we list our mutual grievances, our hurts, our griefs? See how the world has grown.
   Unfinished poem in letter written 12 April 1930, publ. in ibid. Mayakovsky's last poem was found in his papers after his suicide.

## Curtis Mayfield (b. 1942)
US SINGER AND SONGWRITER

After eleven years leading the gospel-influenced soul group the Impressions, he launched a solo career in 1970 and had hits with 'Move On Up' (1970) and *Superfly* (1972), the soundtrack to the film of the same name. In 1990 he was paralysed from the neck down as a result of an accident on stage.

1 People get ready
   There's a train a-coming
   You don't need no baggage
   You just get on board
   All you need is faith to hear the diesels humming
   Don't need no ticket you just thank the Lord.
   'People Get Ready' (song, 1964) by the Impressions

## Margaret Mead (1901–78)
US ANTHROPOLOGIST

Described by JACOB BRONOWSKI as 'splendidly sensible', she popularized anthropology through her studies of the people of Samoa and New Guinea, notably with the classic *Coming of Age in Samoa* (1928). She was outspoken on matters of women's rights, sexual morality, drug abuse, birth control and the environment.

1 As the traveler who has once been from home is wiser than he who has never left his own doorstep, so a knowledge of one other culture should sharpen our ability to scrutinize more steadily, to appreciate more lovingly, our own.
   *Coming of Age in Samoa*, Introduction (1928)

2 A society which is clamoring for choice, which is filled with many articulate groups, each urging its own brand of salvation, its own variety of economic philosophy, will give each new generation no peace until all have chosen or gone under, unable to bear the conditions of choice. The stress is in our civilization.
   ibid. ch. 14

3 Coming to terms with the rhythms of women's lives means coming to terms with life itself, accepting the imperatives of the body rather than the imperatives of an artificial, man-made, perhaps transcendentally beautiful civilization. Emphasis on the male work-rhythm is an emphasis on infinite possibilities; emphasis on the female rhythms is an emphasis on a defined pattern, on limitation.
   *Male and Female*, ch. 8 (1949)

4 The suffering of either sex – of the male who is unable, because of the way in which he was reared, to take the strong initiating or patriarchal role that is still demanded of him, or of the female who has been given too much freedom of movement as a child to stay placidly within the house as an adult – this suffering, this discrepancy, this sense of failure in an enjoined role, is the point of leverage for social change.
   ibid. ch. 15

5 Each home has been reduced to the bare essentials – to barer essentials than most primitive people would consider possible. Only one woman's hands to feed the baby, answer the telephone, turn off the gas under the pot that is boiling over, soothe the older child who has broken a toy, and open both doors at once. She is a nutritionist, a child psychologist, an engineer, a production manager, an expert buyer, all in one. Her husband sees her as free to plan her own time, and envies her; she sees him as having regular hours and envies him.
   ibid. ch. 16

6 I was brought up to believe that the only thing worth doing was to add to the sum of accurate information in the world.
   *The New York Times* 9 August 1964

7 It is an open question whether any behavior based on fear of eternal punishment can be regarded as ethical or should be regarded as merely cowardly.
   Quoted in *Redbook* February 1971

8 The mind is not sex-typed.
   *Blackberry Winter*, ch. 5 (1972)

9 The city as a center where, any day in any year, there may be a fresh encounter with a new talent, a keen mind or a gifted specialist – this is essential to the life of a country. To play this role in our lives a city must have a soul – a university, a great art or music school, a cathedral or a great mosque or temple, a great laboratory or scientific center, as well as the libraries and museums and galleries that bring past and present together. A city must be a

place where groups of women and men are seeking and developing the highest things they know.

Quoted in *Redbook* August 1978

## (Sir) Peter Medawar (1915–87)
BRITISH IMMUNOLOGIST

In 1960 he shared a Nobel Prize for his studies, which contributed to successful human organ transplants. Director of the Institute for Medical Research (1962–75), he published general essays on science, as in *The Art of the Soluble* (1967) and *The Limits of Science* (1985).

1 If politics is the art of the possible, research is surely the art of the soluble. Both are immensely practical-minded affairs.

'The Act of Creation', first publ. in the *New Statesman* 19 June 1964, repr. in *The Art of the Soluble* (1967)

2 Considered in its entirety, psychoanalysis won't do. It's an end product, moreover, like a dinosaur or a zeppelin; no better theory can ever be erected on its ruins, which will remain for ever one of the saddest and strangest of all landmarks in the history of twentieth-century thought.

*The Hope of Progress*, 'Further Comments on Psychoanalysis' (1972)

3 Today the world changes so quickly that in growing up we take leave not just of youth but of the world we were young in . . . Fear and resentment of what is new is really a lament for the memories of our childhood.

*Pluto's Republic*, 'On "The Effecting of All Things Possible"' (1982)

## Golda Meir (1898–1978)
UKRAINIAN-BORN ISRAELI POLITICIAN AND PRIME MINISTER

Originally named Goldie Myerson. After emigrating to the USA in 1906, she moved to Palestine in 1921 where she was prominent in the Labour Movement. She held various government posts following the creation of the state of Israel and was elected Prime Minister in 1966, resigning in 1974 in the wake of the Arab–Israeli war of 1973.

1 There was no such thing as a Palestinian people . . . it is not as though there was a Palestinian people and we came and threw them out and took their country away from them. They did not exist.

*Sunday Times* 15 June 1969

2 We have always said that in our war with the Arabs we had a secret weapon – no alternative.

*Life* 3 October 1969

3 [On the future of Israel] To be or not to be is not a question of compromise. Either you be or you don't be.

Quoted in *The New York Times* 12 December 1974

4 Pessimism is a luxury that a Jew can never allow himself.

Quoted in the *Observer* 29 December 1974

## David Mellor (b. 1949)
BRITISH POLITICIAN

Elected Conservative MP for Putney in 1979, he was Minister for the Arts (1990) and Chief Secretary to the Treasury (1990–92). Revelations about an extra-marital affair forced him to resign from his position as Secretary of State for National Heritage in 1992, since when he has turned to football journalism on BBC Radio 5, and he was voted Radio Personality of the Year in 1995.

1 The popular press is drinking in the last chance saloon.

Interview on Channel 4, 21 December 1989, quoted in *The Times* 22 December 1989. The comment was sparked by intrusive press coverage of the recent Hillsborough disaster. 'What is of interest to the public is not always in the public interest,' he added.

2 The tabloids are like animals, with their own behavioural

patterns. There's no point in complaining about them, any more than complaining that lions might eat you.

*Independent* 3 November 1992

3 Lawyers are like rhinoceroses: thick-skinned, short-sighted, and always ready to charge.

*Question Time*, BBC1, 3 December 1992

## George Melly (b. 1926)
BRITISH JAZZ MUSICIAN, CRITIC AND AUTHOR

Known as 'Goodtime George' and dressed in velour stetson and double-breasted suit, he was a bluesy jazz-singer with his band the Feetwarmers before and while contributing television and film reviews for *Punch*, the *New Statesman*, *New Society* and the *Observer*. His writings include *I Flook* (1962), the autobiography *Owning Up* (1965) and *Revolt into Style* (1970).

1 The mistake which most critics make is to persist in trying to evaluate pop culture as if it were something else: the equivalent of insisting on considering a bicycle as if it were a horse.

*Revolt into Style*, Introduction (1970)

2 The pop manner has become respectable, pop matter is suspect. In the mass media too the revolt has turned into a style.

ibid. 'Film, TV, Radio, Theatre: All My Hating'. The phrase 'revolt into style' is borrowed from a poem by THOM GUNN 4.

3 Surely nothing could be that funny.

Quoted in the *Independent on Sunday* 1 January 1995. On being told by MICK JAGGER that his wrinkles were laughter lines.

4 Who wants to be 98? Someone who's 97.

Quoted by ANTHONY CLARE in *In the Psychiatrist's Chair*, Radio 4, 24 October 1999

## H.L. Mencken (1880–1956)
US JOURNALIST

Full name Henry Louis Mencken. Known as 'the sage of Baltimore' for his lifelong association with the *Baltimore Sun*, he was, with GEORGE JEAN NATHAN, co-editor of *Smart Set* (1914–23) and co-founder and Editor of the *American Mercury* (1924–33). He used his columns as a vehicle to attack what he called the 'booboise' and lambast all aspects of society. His writings are collected in six volumes of *Prejudices* (1919–27). WALTER LIPPMANN called him 'the most powerful personal influence on this whole generation of educated people'.

1 Democracy is the theory that the common people know what they want, and deserve to get it good and hard.

*Little Book in C Major* (1916)

2 Conscience is the inner voice which warns us that someone may be looking.

ibid.

3 Time is a great legalizer, even in the field of morals.

*A Book of Prefaces*, ch. 4, sect. 6 (1917)

4 Philadelphia has always been one of the most Pecksniffian of American cities, and thus probably leads the world.

*The American Language*, note (1919). Referring to the replacement of 'a virgin' by 'a young girl' in the city's public ledger describing characters in a play in 1916. 'Pecksniffian', meaning hypocritically benevolent, alludes to Seth Pecksniff in Dickens's *Martin Chuzzlewit* (1843).

5 The public, with its mob yearning to be instructed, edified and pulled by the nose, demands certainties; it must be told definitely and a bit raucously that this is true and that is false. But there *are* no certainties.

*Prejudices*, ch. 3 (first series, 1919)

6 All successful newspapers are ceaselessly querulous and bellicose. They never defend anyone or anything if they

can help it; if the job is forced upon them, they tackle it by denouncing someone or something else.

ibid. ch. 13

7 Every man sees in his relatives, and especially in his cousins, a series of grotesque caricatures of himself.

*Smart Set* August 1919, repr. in *Prejudices*, 'The Relative' (third series, 1922)

8 Puritanism: The haunting fear that someone, somewhere, may be happy.

*A Book of Burlesques*, 'Sententiae' (1920)

9 An idealist is one who, on noticing that a rose smells better than a cabbage, concludes that it will also make better soup.

ibid.

10 Adultery is the application of democracy to love.

ibid.

11 It is the dull man who is always sure, and the sure man who is always dull.

*Prejudices*, ch. 1 (second series, 1920)

12 To sum up:
1. The cosmos is a gigantic fly-wheel making 10,000 revolutions a minute.
2. Man is a sick fly taking a dizzy ride on it.
3. Religion is the theory that the wheel was designed and set spinning to give him the ride.

*Smart Set* December 1920, repr. in *A Mencken Chrestomathy*, pt 1, 'Coda' (1949)

13 Injustice is relatively easy to bear; what stings is justice.

*Prejudices*, ch. 3 (third series, 1922)

14 Faith may be defined briefly as an illogical belief in the occurrence of the improbable . . . A man full of faith is simply one who has lost (or never had) the capacity for clear and realistic thought. He is not a mere ass: he is actually ill.

ibid. ch. 14

15 No one in this world, so far as I know . . . has ever lost money by underestimating the intelligence of the great masses of the plain people.

*Chicago Tribune* 19 September 1926

16 It [New York] is the place where all the aspirations of the Western World meet to form one vast master aspiration, as powerful as the suction of a steam dredge. It is the icing on the pie called Christian civilization.

*Prejudices*, ch. 9 (sixth series, 1927)

17 If Los Angeles is not the one authentic rectum of civilization, then I am no anatomist. Any time you want to go out again and burn it down, count me in.

Letter to F. SCOTT FITZGERALD and ZELDA FITZGERALD, 15 March 1927, on their return from working in Hollywood, quoted in *Invented Lives* (1984) by James R. Mellon

18 When women kiss it always reminds one of prize-fighters shaking hands.

*A Mencken Chrestomathy*, ch. 30 (1949)

19 Whenever you hear a man speak of his love for his country, it is a sign that he expects to be paid for it.

ibid. 'Sententiae: The Mind of Men'

20 Self-repect – The secure feeling that no one, as yet, is suspicious.

ibid.

21 Whenever a husband and wife begin to discuss their marriage they are giving evidence at a coroner's inquest.

ibid. 'Sententiae: Masculum et Feminam Creavit Eos'

22 No matter how happily a woman may be married, it always pleases her to discover that there is a nice man who wishes that she were not.

ibid.

23 Husbands never become good; they merely become proficient.

ibid.

24 Archbishop – A Christian ecclesiastic of a rank superior to that attained by Christ.

ibid. 'Sententiae: Arcana Coelestia'

25 Theology – An effort to explain the unknowable by putting it into terms of the not worth knowing.

ibid.

26 A society made up of individuals who were all capable of original thought would probably be unendurable.

*Minority Report: H.L. Mencken's Notebooks*, no. 13 (1956)

27 It is now quite lawful for a Catholic woman to avoid pregnancy by a resort to mathematics, though she is still forbidden to resort to physics and chemistry.

ibid. no. 62

28 There are people who read too much: bibliobibuli. I know some who are constantly drunk on books, as other men are drunk on whiskey or religion. They wander through this most diverting and stimulating of worlds in a haze, seeing nothing and hearing nothing.

ibid. no. 71

29 The chief contribution of Protestantism to human thought is its massive proof that God is a bore.

ibid. no. 309

## Carlos Menem (b. 1935)

ARGENTINIAN POLITICIAN AND PRESIDENT

In 1989 he became the first Peronist President of Argentina since the overthrow of Juan Perón in 1973. By his introduction of free-market policies, he succeeded in stabilizing the economy and reducing inflation.

1 The conflict should never have happened, we deeply regret it.

*Sun* 23 October 1998. Contrary to the *Sun*'s headline, 'Argentina says: We're sorry for the Falklands', Menem denied making an apology. 'Saying sorry is something completely different,' he was reported in the *Guardian* 24 October 1998. 'That is not the way I expressed it.' Some detected the hand of TONY BLAIR's press secretary, Alastair Campbell, in the article. Menem was due to make a state visit to Britain the following week.

## (Sir) Robert Menzies (1894–1978)

AUSTRALIAN POLITICIAN AND PRIME MINISTER

Leader of the Australian Liberal Party, he was elected Prime Minister in 1939, resigned in 1941 but served again in 1949–66, making him Australia's longest serving prime minister. His policies encouraged industrial growth and immigration from Europe, and supported the USA in the Vietnam War.

1 Men of genius are not to be analysed by commonplace rules. The rest of us who have been or are leaders, more commonplace in our quality, will do well to remember two things. One is *never to forget posterity when devising a policy*. The other is *never to think of posterity when making a speech*.

*The Measure of the Years*, ch. 1 (1970)

## Johnny Mercer (1909–76)

US SONGWRITER

A highly prolific lyricist and winner of four Oscars, he collaborated with Jerome Kern on such songs as 'I'm Old-Fashioned' (1942) and with Harold Arlen on 'Blues in the Night' (1941) and the musicals *St Louis Woman* (1946) and *Saratoga* (1959). He also recorded his own compositions, such as 'Baby It's Cold Outside' (1949), and founded Capitol Records in 1942, signing Nat 'King' Cole.

1 **That old black magic.**

Title of song (with music by Harold Arlen) in *Star Spangled Rhythm* (film, 1943). First sung by Johnny Johnston, the song was later identified with singer Billy Daniels.

2 **You've got to ac-cent-tchu-ate the positive**
**Elim-my-nate the negative**
**Latch on to the affirmative**
**Don't mess with Mister In-between.**

'Ac-cent-tchu-ate the Positive' (song, with music by Harold Arlen) in the musical film *Here Comes the Waves* (1944). The song was recorded by Mercer himself.

## Maurice Merleau-Ponty (1908–61)
FRENCH PHILOSOPHER

Regarded as one of the most prominent post-Second World War European philosophers, he was influenced by Husserl and noted for his contributions to phenomenology, as in *The Phenomenology of Perception* (1945). With SARTRE and DE BEAUVOIR he founded *Les Temps modernes* and, until disillusioned by the Korean War, was a fellow-traveller in the Communist Party.

1 **The world is . . . the natural setting of, and field for, all my thoughts and all my explicit perceptions. Truth does not 'inhabit' only 'the inner man,' or more accurately, there is no inner man, man is in the world, and only in the world does he know himself.**

*Phenomenology of Perception*, Preface (1945)

## Thomas Merton (1915–68)
US AUTHOR AND MONK

A trappist monk from 1941, he was also a highly productive writer of poetry, religious works and essays. His autobiographical *The Seven Storey Mountain* (1948) became an international bestseller and later works on Zen Buddhism revealed his interest in Oriental mysticism.

1 **Death is someone you see very clearly with eyes in the center of your heart: eyes that see not by reacting to light, but by reacting to a kind of a chill from within the marrow of your own life.**

*The Seven Storey Mountain*, pt 1, ch. 3 (1948)

2 **The logic of worldly success rests on a fallacy: the strange error that our perfection depends on the thoughts and opinions and applause of other men! A weird life it is, indeed, to be living always in somebody else's imagination, as if that were the only place in which one could at last become real!**

ibid. pt 3, ch. 2

## Oliver Messiaen (1908–92)
FRENCH COMPOSER AND ORGANIST

His music, much of it written for organ, is mystical in character, reflecting his deep Roman Catholic faith, and often makes use of transcriptions of birdsong. Among his major works are *La Nativité du Seigneur* (1935) for organ, *Quartet for the End of Time* (1941) and the *Turangalîla* symphony (1948) in ten movements. He was organist at La Trinité, Paris, for more than forty years.

1 **My faith is the grand drama of my life. I'm a believer, so I sing words of God to those who have no faith. I give bird songs to those who dwell in cities and have never heard them, make rhythms for those who know only military marches or jazz, and paint colours for those who see none.**

*Independent* 9 December 1988

## George Michael (b. 1963)
BRITISH SINGER AND SONGWRITER

Original name Giorgos Kyriacou Panayiotou. As a member of Wham! (with Andrew Ridgeley), he scored a UK and US no. 1 with

'Wake Me Up Before You Go Go' (1984), and his 'Faith' (1987) was a big solo hit. He came out as a gay following his arrest in a public toilet in Los Angeles in 1998, an event he parodied in the video accompanying his song, 'Outside'.

1 **If you don't want people to think you're gay, you don't grow a moustache that makes you look like you've failed a Village People audition.**

*Daily Telegraph* 7 November 1998

## James A. Michener (1907–97)
US NOVELIST

Full name James Albert Michener. The sweeping narrative of his lengthy, fact-filled novels, such as *Hawaii* (1959), *Chesapeake* (1978) and *Poland* (1983), led *Newsweek* to describe him as 'the literary world's Cecil B. DeMille'. His first novel, *Tales of the South Pacific* (1947), won the Pulitzer Prize and was the basis of the stage musical *South Pacific* in 1949 (filmed 1958).

1 **I was brought up in the great tradition of the late nineteenth century: that a writer never complains, never explains and never disdains.**

Quoted in the *Observer* 26 November 1989

## Ludwig Mies van der Rohe (1886–1969)
GERMAN-BORN US ARCHITECT

Originally Ludwig Mies. He was Director of the Bauhaus (1929–33) after Walter Gropius, before moving to America. Following his principles of 'skin and bones' construction, he was the leading figure of the International Style, and pioneer of the glass and steel skyscraper.

1 **Less is more.**

*New York Herald Tribune* 28 June 1959. Among the many rejoinders to this, FRANK LLOYD WRIGHT wrote, 'Less is only more where more is no good' (*The Future of Architecture*, 1953).

## George Mikes (1912–87)
HUNGARIAN-BORN BRITISH HUMORIST

Described by *The Times Literary Supplement* as 'the man with the heavy accent in the corner taking notes', he came to Britain in 1938 and recorded his observations on his adopted country in a series of satirical books including *How to be an Alien* (1946) and *As Others See You* (1961).

1 **On the Continent people have good food; in England people have good table manners.**

*How to be an Alien: A Handbook for Beginners and More Advanced Pupils*, ch. 1, sect. 1 (1946)

2 **Continental people have sex lives; the English have hot-water bottles.**

ibid. sect. 6. Thirty years later, Mikes referred to this notorious dictum: 'Things *have* progressed. Not on the continent, where people still have sex lives; but they have progressed here because the English now have electric blankets' (*How to be Decadent*, 1977).

3 **An Englishman, even if he is alone, forms an orderly queue of one.**

ibid. sect. 14. Mikes expanded on this in *How to be Decadent* (1977): 'In shops the English stand in queues; in government offices they sit in queues; in churches they kneel in queues; at sale times, they lie in queues all night.'

4 **Whatever else an Italian may lack, he has an Ego. Sometimes two. It is nice to think that even the poorest Italian may possess two Egos while even the richest Englishman, as a rule, has none.**

*Italy for Beginners*, 'Tourists and Natives: Two Redeeming Sins' (1956)

# Edna St Vincent Millay (1892–1950)

US POET

The foremost American woman poet of the 1920s and a skilful sonneteer, she epitomized the free spirit of the jazz age in such volumes as *A Few Figs from Thistles* (1920) and *The Harp Weaver and Other Poems* (1923, Pulitzer Prize). Her traditional style and sentimental approach fell from favour, but she has been reappraised for her early feminist principles by MAYA ANGELOU and others.

1 God, I can push the grass apart
  And lay my finger on Thy heart.
  'Renascence', publ. in *Renascence and Other Poems* (1917)

2 The soul can split the sky in two,
  And let the face of God shine through.
  ibid.

3 My candle burns at both ends;
  It will not last the night;
  But ah, my foes, and oh, my friends –
  It gives a lovely light.
  'First Fig', publ. in *A Few Figs from Thistles* (1920)

4 Safe upon the solid rock the ugly houses stand:
  Come and see my shining palaces built upon the sand!
  'Second Fig', publ. in ibid.

5 Death devours all lovely things;
  Lesbia with her sparrow
  Shares the darkness – presently
  Every bed is narrow.
  'Passer Mortuus Est', publ. in *Second April* (1921)

6 After all, my erstwhile dear,
  My no longer cherished,
  Need we say it was not love,
  Now that love is perished?
  ibid.

7 I know I am but summer to your heart,
  And not the full four seasons of the year.
  'I Know I Am But Summer to Your Heart', publ. in *The Harp Weaver and Other Poems* (1923)

8 Euclid alone
  Has looked on Beauty bare. Fortunate they
  Who, though once only and then but far away,
  Have heard her massive sandal set on stone.
  'Euclid Alone Has Looked on Beauty Bare', publ. in ibid.

9 Childhood is the kingdom where nobody dies.
  Nobody that matters, that is.
  'Childhood is the Kingdom Where Nobody Dies', publ. in *Wine from These Grapes* (1934)

10 Set the foot down with distrust on the crust of the world
   – it is thin.
   'The Underground System', publ. in *Huntsman, What Quarry?* (1939)

# Alice Duer Miller (1874–1942)

US NOVELIST AND POET

Her short stories and novellas were collected in *Summer Holiday* (1941), while her most famous poem is *The White Cliffs* (1940). She was also active in the women's suffrage movement.

1 They make other nations seem pale and flighty,
  But they do think England is God almighty,
  And you must remind them now and then
  That other countries breed other men.
  *The White Cliffs* (1940). Part of a long narrative poem extolling Britain's resistance during the Second World War.

2 I am American bred,
  I have seen much to hate here – much to forgive,
  But in a world where England is finished and dead,
  I do not wish to live.
  ibid.

# Arthur Miller (b. 1915)

US PLAYWRIGHT

He established himself in the first rank of post-war dramatists with his plays *Death of a Salesman* (1949, Pulitzer Prize) and *The Crucible* (1953). The first of these concerned conflicts within the nuclear family, also the subject matter of *All My Sons* (1947) and *After the Fall* (1964), while the latter took the Salem witch trials of 1692 as an allegory for 1950s McCarthyism, of which Miller had personal experience. His marriage (1956–61) to MARILYN MONROE was the inspiration for his screenplay for *The Misfits* (1960), in which she starred.

1 He's liked, but he's not well liked.
  Biff, in *Death of a Salesman*, act 1 (1949). Referring to Bernard, his schoolfriend.

2 A small man can be just as exhausted as a great man.
  Linda, in ibid. Referring to her husband Willy Loman.

3 I don't say he's a great man. Willy Loman never made a lot of money. His name was never in the paper. He's not the finest character that ever lived. But he's a human being, and a terrible thing is happening to him. So attention must be paid.
  ibid.

4 For a salesman, there is no rock bottom to the life. He don't put a bolt to a nut, he don't tell you the law or give you medicine. He's a man way out there in the blue, riding on a smile and a shoeshine. And when they start not smiling back – that's an earthquake. And then you get yourself a couple of spots on your hat, and you're finished. Nobody dast blame this man. A salesman is got to dream, boy. It comes with the territory.
  Charley, in ibid. 'Requiem'

5 By whatever means it is accomplished, the prime business of a play is to arouse the passions of its audience so that by the route of passion may be opened up new relationships between a man and men, and between men and Man.
  *Collected Plays*, Introduction, sect. 7 (1958)

6 A good newspaper, I suppose, is a nation talking to itself.
  Quoted in the *Observer* 26 November 1961

7 A suicide kills two people, Maggie. That's what it's for.
  Quentin, in *After the Fall*, act 2 (1964)

8 A playwright . . . is . . . the litmus paper of the arts. He's got to be, because if he isn't working on the same wave length as the audience, no one would know what in hell he was talking about. He is a kind of psychic journalist, even when he's great.
  Interview in the *Paris Review* summer 1966

9 The concentration camp is the final expression of human separateness and its ultimate consequence. It is organized abandonment.
  ibid. Miller regarded this concept as underpinning his 1964 play *After the Fall*, which included a concentration camp in its staging.

10 In the theater, while you recognized that you were looking at a house, it was a house in quotation marks. On screen, the quotation marks tend to be blotted out by the camera.
   *The New York Times* 15 September 1985. On a television production of *Death of a Salesman*.

11 Without alienation, there can be no politics.
   Interview in *Marxism Today* January 1988

12 I'm the end of the line; absurd and appalling as it may seem, serious New York theatre has died in my lifetime.
   *The Times* 11 January 1989

13 I love her too, but our neuroses just don't match.
   Lyman, in *The Ride Down Mount Morgan*, act 1 (1991). Discussing his wife.

14 Maybe all one can do is hope to end up with the right regrets.

Tom, in ibid.

# Henry Miller (1891–1980)

US AUTHOR

While in Paris (1930–39) he wrote the books for which he is best known, *Tropic of Cancer* (1934), *Black Spring* (1936) and *Tropic of Capricorn* (1938). Autobiographical in tone and overtly sexual, they were banned in Britain and America until the 1960s, when they became bestsellers. Of his word-rich writing style, author Gerald Brenan commented: 'Miller is not really a writer but a non-stop talker to whom someone has given a typewriter.' See also KATE MILLETT 5.

1 It is true I swim in a perpetual sea of sex but the actual excursions are fairly limited.

Letter, 1 February 1932, publ. in *Letters to Anaïs Nin*, pt 1 (1965)

2 This is not a book. This is libel, slander, defamation of character. This is not a book, in the ordinary sense of the word. No, this is a prolonged insult, a gob of spit in the face of Art, a kick in the pants to God, Man, Destiny, Time, Love, Beauty . . . what you will. I am going to sing for you, a little off key perhaps, but I will sing.

*Tropic of Cancer* (1934). See EZRA POUND 19.

3 An artist is always alone – if he *is* an artist. No, what the artist needs is *loneliness*.

ibid.

4 Every man with a bellyful of the classics is an enemy to the human race.

ibid.

5 What is not in the open street is false, derived, that is to say, *literature*.

*Black Spring*, 'The Fourteenth Ward' (1936)

6 Confusion is a word we have invented for an order which is not understood.

*Tropic of Capricorn*, 'On the Ovarian Trolley: An Interlude' (1939)

7 What does it matter how one comes by the truth so long as one pounces upon it and lives by it?

*Tropic of Capricorn* (1939)

8 What holds the world together, as I have learned from bitter experience, is sexual intercourse.

ibid.

9 Hitler is no worse, nay better, in my opinion, than the other lugs. He makes the German mistake of being tactless, that's all.

Letter to LAWRENCE DURRELL, March 1939, publ. in *The Durrell–Miller Letters 1935–80* (1988). Written shortly after the Nazis had marched into Czechoslovakia.

10 Why are we so full of restraint? Why do we not give in all directions? Is it fear of losing ourselves? Until we do lose ourselves there is no hope of finding ourselves.

*The World of Sex* (1940)

11 Moralities, ethics, laws, customs, beliefs, doctrines – these are of trifling import. All that matters is that the miraculous become the norm.

ibid.

12 The aim of life is to live, and to live means to be aware, joyously, drunkenly, serenely, divinely aware.

*The Wisdom of the Heart*, 'Creative Death' (1941)

13 In expanding the field of knowledge, we but increase the horizon of ignorance.

ibid. 'The Wisdom of the Heart'

14 The American ideal is youth – handsome, empty youth.

ibid. 'Raimu'. In America, Miller explained, 'youth means simply athleticism, disrespect, gangsterism, or sickly idealism expressing itself through thinly disguised and badly digested social science theories acted out by idiots who are desperadoes at heart'.

15 Life, as it is called, is for most of us one long postponement.

ibid. 'The Enormous Womb'

16 I have never been able to look upon America as young and vital but rather as prematurely old, as a fruit which rotted before it had a chance to ripen.

*The Air-Conditioned Nightmare*, 'Dr Souchon: Surgeon-Painter' (1945)

17 Music is a beautiful opiate, if you don't take it too seriously.

ibid. 'With Edgar Varèse in the Gobi Desert'

18 Sex is one of the nine reasons for reincarnation. The other eight are unimportant.

*Sexus*, ch. 21 (1949)

19 I didn't have to think up so much as a comma or a semicolon; it was all given, straight from the celestial recording room. Weary, I would beg for a break, an intermission, time enough, let's say, to go to the toilet or take a breath of fresh air on the balcony. Nothing doing!

*Big Sur and the Oranges of Hieronymous Bosch*, pt 2, 'A Fortune in Francs' (1957). On the composition of *Tropic of Capricorn*. Miller went on: 'How could I possibly imagine then that some few years later a judicial triumvirate, eager to prove me a sinner, would accuse me of having written such passages "for gain"?'

20 Obscenity is a cleansing process, whereas pornography only adds to the murk.

Interview in the *Paris Review* summer 1961, repr. in *Writers at Work* (second series, ed. George Plimpton, 1963). Miller is quoted as saying: 'I am for obscenity and against pornography.'

21 Whenever a taboo is broken, something good happens, something vitalizing . . . Taboos after all are only hangovers, the product of diseased minds, you might say, of fearsome people who hadn't the courage to live and who under the guise of morality and religion have imposed these things upon us.

ibid.

22 One becomes aware in France, after having lived in America, that sex pervades the air. It's there all around you, like a fluid.

ibid.

# Jonathan Miller (b. 1934)

BRITISH DOCTOR, HUMORIST AND DIRECTOR

Dubbed 'renaissance man' for his combined career in medical research and the arts, he came to notice in the *Beyond the Fringe* revues (1961–4), then as an innovative director of Shakespeare and opera (particularly for English National Opera). For BBC television he directed *Alice in Wonderland* (1966) and wrote and presented *The Body in Question* (1977).

1 I wasn't driven into medicine by a social conscience but by rampant curiosity.

Quoted in the *Observer* 5 February 1983

2 Jokes have little to do with spontaneous humour. The teller has the same relationship to them that he or she might have to Hertz Rent-a-Car. A joke is a hired object, with many previous users, and very often its ashtrays are filled with other people's cigarettes, and its gears are worn and slipping, because other people have driven this joke very badly before you got behind the wheel.

'Among Chickens', publ. in *Granta* no. 23, spring 1988

3 What makes literature interesting is that it does not survive its translation. The characters in a novel are made out of the sentences. That's what their substance is.

*Sunday Times* 12 February 1989

4 Attitudes to museums have changed. If it had Marilyn

Monroe's knickers or Laurence Olivier's jockstrap they would flock to it.

*Daily Telegraph* 7 June 1989. On the low attendances at his recently opened Theatre Museum.

5 Errors of taste are very often the outward sign of a deep fault of sensibility.

*Guardian* 21 May 1992

6 There are no élitist people there are only élitist ideas.

Interview in the *Guardian* 12 September 1998

## Roger Miller (1936–92)

US COUNTRY SINGER AND SONGWRITER

Based in Nashville, he had some success as a songwriter for Ray Price and Andy Williams before his self-penned songs 'Dang Me' (1964) and 'King of the Road' (1965) become million-sellers, notching up eight Grammy awards between them. The folksy 'England Swings' (1965) and 'Little Green Apples' (1968) were also hits on both sides of the Atlantic, although he never had another one after 1970.

1 I'm a man of means by no means
  King of the road.

'King of the Road' (song) on the album *The Return of Roger Miller* (1965)

2 England swings like a pendulum do
  Bobbies on bicycles two by two
  Westminster Abbey, the tower of Big Ben,
  The rosy red cheeks of the little children.

'England Swings' (song) on the album *Golden Hits* (1965)

## Kate Millett (b. 1934)

US FEMINIST AUTHOR

Her first book, the bestselling *Sexual Politics* (1970), was an indictment of the patriarchal value systems inherent in politics and literature that she held responsible for the suppression of women in society. She was active in US civil rights movements in the 1970s, and in 1979 campaigned for women's rights in Iran.

1 However muted its present appearance may be, sexual dominion obtains nevertheless as perhaps the most pervasive ideology of our culture and provides its most fundamental concept of power.

*Sexual Politics*, ch. 2 (1970)

2 Because of our social circumstances, male and female are really two cultures and their life experiences are utterly different.

ibid. ch. 2, sect. 2

3 The concept of romantic love affords a means of emotional manipulation which the male is free to exploit, since love is the only circumstance in which the female is (ideologically) pardoned for sexual activity.

ibid. sect. 4

4 Perhaps nothing is so depressing an index of the inhumanity of the male-supremacist mentality as the fact that the more genial human traits are assigned to the underclass: affection, response to sympathy, kindness, cheerfulness.

ibid. ch. 4. Referring to a table of character traits assignable to male and female roles.

5 [Henry] Miller does have something highly important to tell us; his virulent sexism is beyond question an honest contribution to social and psychological understanding which we can hardly afford to ignore. But to confuse this neurotic hostility, this frank abuse, with sanity, is pitiable. To confuse it with freedom were vicious, were it not so very sad.

ibid. ch. 6

6 To be a rebel is not to be a revolutionary. It is more often but a way of spinning one's wheels deeper in the sand.

ibid. ch. 8, sect. 2

## Spike Milligan (b. 1918)

BRITISH COMEDIAN AND HUMOROUS WRITER

Born Terence Alan Milligan. Hailed by RICHARD INGRAMS as 'one of the few really original comic geniuses of our time', he co-scripted and performed in *The Goon Show* for BBC radio (1951–60), which JOHN LENNON called 'a conspiracy against reality, a coup d'état of the mind'. He made regular stage and television appearances in the 1960s and 1970s, and has written many humorous books of verse, fiction and autobiography, including *Puckoon* (1963) and *Adolf Hitler, My Part in His Downfall* (1971).

1 Ying tong iddle I po.

Ned Seagoon (Harry Secombe), in *The Goon Show* (BBC radio comedy series, 1951–60, co-written by Spike Milligan), publ. in *The Goon Show Scripts* (ed. Spike Milligan, 1972). The words were set to music and released as 'The Ying Tong Song' in 1956.

2 I'm a hero wid coward's legs, I'm a hero from the waist up.

*Puckoon*, ch. 2 (1963)

3 Money couldn't buy friends, but you got a better class of enemy.

Mrs Doonan, in ibid. ch. 6

4 Her protruding breasts were pressed flat between his body and hers. He had felt them, he had fondled them, he lifted them, he pressed them, he weighed them, he valued them, he counted them, he massaged them, he stood back from them, he pulled them, he sat on them and picking up a banjo he played them.

ibid. ch. 10

5 Contraceptives should be used on every conceivable occasion.

Camden Theatre, London, 30 April 1972, publ. in *The Last Goon Show of Them All* (1972)

## C. Wright Mills (1916–62)

US SOCIOLOGIST

Full name Charles Wright Mills. Influenced by Marx and MAX WEBER in his critique of the American establishment, he contributed to the popular understanding of sociology with such books as *White Collar* (1951) and *The Power Elite* (1956).

1 Commercial jazz, soap opera, pulp fiction, comic strips, the movies set the images, mannerisms, standards, and aims of the urban masses. In one way or another, everyone is equal before these cultural machines; like technology itself, the mass media are nearly universal in their incidence and appeal. They are a kind of common denominator, a kind of scheme for pre-scheduled, mass emotions.

*White Collar*, ch. 15, sect. 3 (1951)

2 By the power elite, we refer to those political, economic, and military circles which as an intricate set of overlapping cliques share decisions having at least national consequences. In so far as national events are decided, the power elite are those who decide them.

*The Power Elite*, ch. 1 (1956)

3 The life-fate of the modern individual depends not only upon the family into which he was born or which he enters by marriage, but increasingly upon the corporation in which he spends the most alert hours of his best years.

ibid.

4 Power is not of a man. Wealth does not center in the person of the wealthy. Celebrity is not inherent in any

personality. To be celebrated, to be wealthy, to have power requires access to major institutions.

ibid.

5 In the world of the celebrity, the hierarchy of publicity has replaced the hierarchy of descent and even of great wealth.

Quoted in *Talking to Myself*, bk 4, ch. 1 (1977) by STUDS TERKEL

## A.A. Milne (1882–1958)

BRITISH AUTHOR

Full name Alan Alexander Milne. Although well known during the 1920s as a writer for *Punch* and of light comedies, he is now remembered for his classic children's stories and poems written for his son, Christopher Robin, and the play *Toad of Toad Hall* (1929), based on Kenneth Grahame's *The Wind in the Willows*.

1 James James
Said to his Mother,
'Mother,' he said, said he;
'You must never go down to the end of the town, if you
    don't go down with me.'

'Disobedience', publ. in *When We Were Very Young* (1924)

2 Nobody,
My darling
Could call me
A fussy man –
BUT
*I do like a little bit of butter to my bread!*

'The King's Breakfast', publ. in ibid.

3 A bear, however hard he tries,
Grows tubby without exercise.

'Teddy Bear', publ. in ibid.

4 How sweet to be a Cloud
Floating in the Blue!

Winnie-the-Pooh, in *Winnie-the-Pooh*, ch. 1 (1926)

5 I am a Bear of Very Little Brain, and long words Bother me.

ibid. ch. 4

6 Pathetic. That's what it is. Pathetic.

Eeyore, in ibid. ch. 6

7 Now then, Pooh, time for a little something.

Piglet, in ibid.

8 My spelling is Wobbly. It's good spelling but it Wobbles, and the letters get in the wrong places.

Winnie-the-Pooh, in ibid.

## Czeslaw Milosz (b. 1911)

LITHUANIAN-BORN POLISH POET

During the 1930s he established himself as Poland's leading avant-garde poet but subsequently spent thirty-five years in exile in France and America. His essays, collected in *The Captive Mind* (1953), denounced the Polish intellectual acquiescence to communism, and his poetry includes *Bells in Winter* (1978). In 1980 he was awarded the Nobel Prize for Literature.

1 Grow your tree of falsehood from a small grain of truth.
Do not follow those who lie in contempt of reality.

Let your lie be even more logical than the truth itself,
So the weary travellers may find repose.

'Child of Europe' sect. 4, publ. in *Selected Poems* (1973)

## Liza Minnelli (b. 1946)

US ACTRESS

The daughter of JUDY GARLAND and director Vincente Minnelli, she inherited her mother's powerful and vibrant singing voice and

experienced similar marriage and drug problems. Her greatest success came with the musical *Cabaret* (1972), for which she won an Academy Award. Later films include *New York, New York* (1977) and *Arthur* (1981).

1 Money makes the world go round
the world go round
the world go round,
Money makes the world go round
That clinking clanking sound!

'Money' (song, written by Fred Ebb and John Kander) in *Cabaret* (musical play, 1966 by Joe Masterhoff, filmed 1972). The words are sung by Sally Bowles (Liza Minnelli) and the Master of Ceremonies (JOEL GREY)

2 In Hollywood now when people die they don't say, 'Did he leave a will?' but 'Did he leave a diary?'

Interview in the *Observer* 13 August 1989

## Helen Mirren (b. 1945)

BRITISH ACTRESS

Admired for her cool sexuality, she has acted on stage with the Royal Shakespeare Company, in the films *Cal* (1984) *The Cook, the Thief, His Wife and Her Lover* (1989) and *The Madness of King George* (1994), and on television as detective Jane Tennison in Lynda La Plante's series *Prime Suspect* (1991–3 and 1996).

1 The part never calls for it [nudity]. And I've never ever used that excuse. The box office calls for it.

Quoted in the *Guardian* 31 December 1994

## Yukio Mishima (1925–70)

JAPANESE AUTHOR

Original name Kimitake Hiraoke. A leading Japanese novelist, he also published poetry and versions of Noh and Kabuki plays. *Confessions of a Mask* (1949) deals with his attempts to disguise his homosexuality, and *The Sea of Fertility* tetralogy (1972–4) evokes, in his own words, 'the old beautiful tradition of Japan, which is disappearing very quickly day by day'. Increasingly obsessed with death and sacrifice, he committed a ritual Samurai suicide, *seppuku*.

1 The sound of the rain is like the voices of tens of thousands of monks reading sutras . . . No-one's words can compete with this mercilessly powerful rain. The only thing that can compete with the sound of this rain, that can smash this deathlike wall of sound, is the shout of a man who refuses to stoop to this chatter, the shout of a simple spirit that knows no words.

*Thirst for Love*, ch. 4 (*Ai No Kawaki*, 1950, transl. 1969)

2 From the moment that a man no longer responds in the slightest to the motives that regulate the material world, that world appears to be at complete repose.

*Death in Midsummer and Other Stories*, 'The Priest of Shiga Temple and His Love' (1966)

3 Literary art takes its materials from life, but although life is thus the mother of literature, it is also her bitter enemy; although life is inherent in the author himself, it is also the eternal antithesis of art.

*Mishima on Hagakure*, 'Hagakure and I' (1977)

4 Ours is an age in which everything is based on the premise that it is best to live as long as possible. The average life span has become the longest in history, and a monotonous plan for humanity unrolls before us.

ibid. 'Hagakure is Alive Today'

5 Youth possesses the impulse to resist and the impulse to surrender, in equal measure. One might re-define these as the impulse to be free and the impulse to die. The manifestation of these impulses, no matter how political the form it assumes, is like an electric current that results from a difference in electrical charge – in other

words, from the fundamental contradictions of human existence.

ibid.

6 If we value so highly the dignity of life, how can we not also value the dignity of death? No death may be called futile.

ibid. 'How to Read *Hagakure*'

## Mistinguett (1874–1956)

FRENCH DANCER AND SINGER

Original name Jeanne Marie Bourgeois. An immensely popular and vivacious music hall artiste until her seventies, she displayed her highly insured legs and elaborate spangly costumes at the Folies Bergère, with her partner MAURICE CHEVALIER, and at the Moulin Rouge.

1 A kiss can be a comma, a question mark or an exclamation point. That's basic spelling that every woman ought to know.

*Theatre Arts* December 1955

## Adrian Mitchell (b. 1932)

BRITISH POET AND AUTHOR

One of the pioneers of the Underground Poetry of the 1960s, he upholds individual freedom and social responsibility in his verse, and attacks government hypocrisy and the arms race. He describes himself thus: 'My brain socialist/My heart anarchist/My eyes pacifist/My blood revolutionary.' Among his collections are *Out Loud* (1966) and *On the Beach at Cambridge* (1986).

1 Most people ignore most poetry
                because
most poetry ignores most people.

*Poems*, Epigraph (1964)

2 Retire, retire into a fungus basement
Where nothing moves except the draught
And the light and dark grey figures
Doubling their money on the screen;
Where the cabbages taste like the mummy's hand
And the meat tastes of feet;
Where there is nothing to say except:
'Remember?' or 'Your turn to dust the cat'.

'Old Age Report', publ. in *Ride the Nightmare* (1971)

## Elma Mitchell (b. 1919)

BRITISH POET

Full name Elizabeth Manuel Mitchell. Formerly a librarian, she has published the collections *The Poor Man in the Flesh* (1976), *The Human Cage* (1979) and *Furnished Room* (1983).

1 Women reminded him of lilies and roses.
Me they remind rather of blood and soap,
Armed with a warm rag, assaulting noses,
Ears, neck, mouth and all the secret places.

'Thoughts after Ruskin', publ. in *The Poor Man in the Flesh* (1976)

## Joni Mitchell (b. 1943)

CANADIAN-BORN US SINGER, SONGWRITER

Original name Roberta Joan Anderson. She set the pattern for musical introspection in the late 1960s and 1970s with her folk-based albums such as the impassioned *Blue* (1971). Later recordings, for example *The Hissing of Summer Lawns* (1975) and *Mingus* (1979), mixed jazz and rock.

1 I've looked at life from both sides now
From up and down, and still somehow
It's life illusions I recall

I really don't know life at all.

'Both Sides Now' (song) on the album *Clouds* (1969). The song was covered by Judy Collins in 1970.

2 We are stardust,
We are golden,
And we got to get ourselves
Back to the garden.

'Woodstock' (song, 1969) on the album *Ladies of the Canyon* (1970). The song was a hit for Matthews Southern Comfort.

3 They paved paradise
And put up a parking lot
With a pink hotel,
A boutique, and a swinging hot spot.

'Big Yellow Taxi' (song) on ibid.

4 All the people at this party, they've got a lot of style,
They've got stamps of many countries, they've got
            passport smiles.
Some are friendly, some are cutting, some are watchin' it
            from the wings,
Some are standin' in the center givin' to get something.

'People's Parties' (song) on the album *Court and Spark* (1974)

5 There are things to confess that enrich the world, and things that need not be said.

*Independent* 13 May 1988

6 I'm not a pitiable creature. It's just that I suffer very eloquently.

Interview in the *Observer* 18 October 1998

## Juliet Mitchell (b. 1940)

NEW ZEALAND-BORN BRITISH AUTHOR

An editor with *New Left Review*, she wrote her early books, such as *Women's Estate* (1971), from a Marxist feminist perspective. *Psychoanalysis and Feminism* (1974) evaluated the place of Freudian theory in feminist thought.

1 A fixed image of the future is in the worst sense ahistorical.

'Women – The Longest Revolution', publ. in *New Left Review* November–December 1966

2 'Leaders' are rarely ousted by anyone other than would-be leaders. In not wishing to act like 'men', there is no need for us to act like 'women'. The rise of the oppressed should not be a glorification of oppressed characteristics.

*Women's Estate*, ch. 10 (1971)

## Margaret Mitchell (1900–49)

US NOVELIST

Over a period of ten years she wrote her first and only novel *Gone with the Wind* (1936), which won a Pulitzer Prize and was made into one of the most successful films of all time (1939). She confessed to not understanding the enormous popularity of the book, maintaining that it was 'basically just a simple yarn of fairly simple people'.

1 Land is the only thing in the world that amounts to anything, for 'tis the only thing in this world that lasts . . .'Tis the only thing worth working for, worth fighting for – worth dying for.

Gerald O'Hara, in *Gone with the Wind*, vol. 1, pt 1, ch. 2 (1936)

2 I'm tired of everlastingly being unnatural and never doing anything I want to do. I'm tired of acting like I don't eat more than a bird, and walking when I want to run and saying I feel faint after a waltz, when I could dance for two days and never get tired. I'm tired of saying, 'How wonderful you are!' to fool men who haven't got one-half the sense I've got, and I'm tired of pretending I don't know anything, so men can tell me things and feel important while they're doing it.

Scarlett O'Hara, in ibid. ch. 5

3 Until you've lost your reputation, you never realize what a burden it was or what freedom really is.

ibid.

4 What most people don't seem to realize is that there is just as much money to be made out of the wreckage of a civilization as from the upbuilding of one.

Rhett Butler, in ibid. pt 2, ch. 9

5 Fighting is like champagne. It goes to the heads of cowards as quickly as of heroes. Any fool can be brave on a battlefield when it's be brave or else be killed.

Ashley Wilkes, in ibid. vol. 2, pt 4, ch. 31

6 Southerners can never resist a losing cause.

Rhett Butler, in ibid. ch. 34

7 Death and taxes and childbirth! There's never any convenient time for any of them!

Scarlett O'Hara, in ibid. ch. 38

8 I was never one to patiently pick up broken fragments and glue them together again and tell myself that the mended whole was as good as new. What is broken is broken – and I'd rather remember it as it was at its best than mend it and see the broken places as long as I lived . . . I wish I could care what you do or where you go, but I can't. My dear, I don't give a damn.

Rhett Butler, in ibid. pt 5, ch. 63. See CLARK GABLE 1 for the film version of this speech.

9 After all, tomorrow is another day.

Scarlett O'Hara, in ibid. Closing words of book and film.

## Warren Mitchell (b. 1926)
BRITISH ACTOR

Original name Warren Misell. He is best known as the foul-mouthed Alf Garnett in the BBC television comedy series *Till Death Us Do Part* (1966–78). He has performed frequently on stage, including as Willy Loman in *Death of a Salesman* (1979).

1 Comedy comes from conflict, from hatred.

*The Times* 31 December 1990

## Robert Mitchum (1917–97)
US ACTOR

A boxer and labourer before working as an extra in Hollywood, he played tough guys for more than thirty years in such films as *Night of the Hunter* (1955), *The Sundowners* (1960) and *Farewell My Lovely* (1975). Always self-deprecating of his talents, he says he survived because 'I work cheap and don't take up much time'.

1 You know something – you're a pretty nice guy, for a girl.

Frank Jessup (Robert Mitchum), in *Angel Face* (film, 1953, screenplay by Frank Nugent and Oscar Millard, directed and produced by Otto Preminger)

## Nancy Mitford (1904–73)
BRITISH AUTHOR

The eldest of the six aristocratic Mitford sisters, she wrote the autobiographical novels *The Pursuit of Love* (1945) and *Love in a Cold Climate* (1949). Her sister Jessica said she had the 'aspect of an elegant pirate's moll', while the writer Anne Fremantle regarded her as 'the nearest our blurred, woolly and sadisto-sentimental age has gotten to the sane simplicity of Jane Austen'.

1 Uncle Matthew's four years in France and Italy between 1914 and 1918 had given him no great opinion of foreigners. 'Frogs,' he would say, 'are slightly better than Huns or Wops, but abroad is unutterably bloody and foreigners are fiends.'

*The Pursuit of Love*, ch. 15 (1945)

2 Ancestry has never counted much in England. The English

lord knows himself to be such a very genuine article that, when looking for a wife, he can rise above such baubles as seize quartiers. Kind hearts, in his view, are more than coronets, and large tracts of town property more than Norman blood.

'The English Aristocracy', first publ. in *Encounter*, repr. in *Noblesse Oblige* (1956).

## Issey Miyake (b. 1938)
JAPANESE FASHION DESIGNER

He has shown his collections in New York since 1971 and in Paris since 1973. His loose-fitting fashions blend East with West and emphasize a layered and textured look.

1 Design is not for philosophy – it's for life.

*International Herald Tribune* 23 March 1992

## Wilson Mizner (1876–1933)
US DRAMATIST AND WIT

Before becoming a playwright, he hustled for a medicine show, was a professional cardsharp, managed a celebrity prize fighter and was one of the first prospectors in the Klondike gold rush His most successful plays were co-written, including *The Only Law* (1909, with G. Bronson Howard), *The Deep Purple* (1910, with Paul Armstrong) and *The Greyhound* (1912, also with Armstrong).

1 Be nice to people on your way up because you'll meet them on your way down.

Quoted in *The Legendary Mizners*, ch. 4 (1953) by Alva Johnson. Also attributed to the comic Jimmy Durante.

2 A trip through a sewer in a glass-bottomed boat.

ibid. Mizner's description of Hollywood was reworked by Mayor James J. Walker: 'A reformer is a guy who rides through a sewer in a glass-bottomed boat' (speech as mayor of New York, 1928).

3 If you steal from one author, it's plagiarism; if you steal from many, it's research.

ibid.

4 Working for Warner Brothers is like fucking a porcupine: it's a hundred pricks against one.

Quoted in *Bring on the Empty Horses*, 'Degrees of Friendliness' (1975) by David Niven

## Walter Mondale (b. 1928)
US POLITICIAN AND VICE-PRESIDENT

A Democratic Senator 1964–76, he was JIMMY CARTER's Vice-president (1977–81). He won the Democratic presidential nomination in 1984 but was heavily defeated by RONALD REAGAN. He was appointed US Ambassador to Japan in 1993.

1 Where's the beef?

Campaign slogan for 1984 Democratic presidential nomination. Originally an advertising slogan for Wendy's Hamburgers, the words were taken up by Mondale's campaign team after a televised debate on 11 March 1984, in which the candidate told rival Gary Hart, 'When I hear your new ideas I'm reminded of that ad, *Where's the beef?*'

2 Political image is like mixing cement. When it's wet, you can move it around and shape it, but at some point it hardens and there's almost nothing you can do to reshape it.

Quoted in the *Independent on Sunday* 12 May 1991

## Marilyn Monroe (1926–62)
US SCREEN ACTRESS

Original name Norma Jean Mortenson or Baker. Described by LAURENCE OLIVIER (with whom she acted) as a 'professional amateur' and by the actress Cybill Shepherd as having curves 'in places where other women don't even have places', she was the supreme 1950s sex icon, but remained insecure and died from a drugs overdose. She was the archetypal 'dumb blonde' in the comedies *Gentlemen Prefer Blondes* (1953), *Bus Stop* (1956) and *Some Like It Hot* (1959). See also NORMAN MAILER 14, BILLY WILDER 5.

1 **Does this boat go to Europe, France?**
   Lorelei Lee (Marilyn Monroe), in *Gentlemen Prefer Blondes* (film, 1953, screenplay by Charles Lederer based on novel by Anita Loos, directed by Howard Hawkes). The words do not appear in the 1925 novel by ANITA LOOS.

2 **Diamonds are a girl's best friend.**
   'Diamonds Are a Girl's Best Friend' (song, written by Leo Robin with music by Jule Styne) in ibid. The song first appeared in the 1949 stage show of *Gentlemen Prefer Blondes*

3 **I don't care how rich he is – as long as he has a yacht, his own private railroad car, and his own toothpaste.**
   Sugar Kane (Marilyn Monroe), in *Some Like It Hot* (film, 1959, screenplay by Billy Wilder and I.A.L. Diamond, produced and directed by Billy Wilder)

4 **I always get the fuzzy end of the lollipop.**
   ibid.

5 **Unfortunately, I am involved in a freedom ride protesting the loss of the minority rights belonging to the few remaining earthbound stars. All we demanded was our right to twinkle.**
   Telegram, to Mr and Mrs Robert Kennedy, turning down a party invitation, 13 June 1962, shown on *Marilyn: Something's Got to Give*, Channel 4, 2 August 1992

6 **Fame will go by and, so long, I've had you, fame. If it goes by, I've always known it was fickle. So at least it's something I experienced, but that's not where I live.**
   *Life* 3 August 1962. Conclusion of taped conversation, published on the day that Monroe died.

7 **My work is the only ground I've ever had to stand on . . . To put it bluntly I seem to have a whole superstructure with no foundation.**
   Quoted in *Marilyn*, ch. 7 (1973) by NORMAN MAILER

8 **Hollywood's a place where they'll pay you a thousand dollars for a kiss, and fifty cents for your soul. I know, because I turned down the first offer often enough and held out for the fifty cents.**
   Quoted in *Marilyn Monroe In Her Own Words*, 'Acting' (1990)

9 **Husbands are chiefly good as lovers when they are betraying their wives.**
   ibid. 'Weddings and Divorces'

10 **I always felt I was a nobody, and the only way for me to be somebody was to be – well, somebody else. Which is probably why I wanted to act.**
   Quoted in *Marilyn Monroe: the Biography*, ch. 15 (1993) by Donald Spoto

## C.E. Montague (1867–1928)
BRITISH AUTHOR AND JOURNALIST

Full name Charles Edward Montague. A journalist with the *Manchester Guardian* from 1898, he dyed his hair in order to appear young enough to enlist in the army in the First World War but was invalided home. Among his numerous books are *Disenchantment* (1922), which recounts his army experiences, and the novel *Rough Justice* (1926).

1 **There is no limit to what a man can do so long as he does not care a straw who gets the credit for it.**
   *Disenchantment*, ch. 15, sect. 3 (1922)

2 **A lie will easily get you out of a scrape, and yet, strangely and beautifully, rapture possesses you when you have taken the scrape and left out the lie.**
   ibid. sect. 4

3 **War hath no fury like a non-combatant.**
   ibid. ch. 16

## Eugenio Montale (1896–1981)
ITALIAN POET

Director of the Italian Scientific-Literary Cabinet 1929–38, he was literary and music editor of the Milan newspaper *Corriere della Sera* from 1947. His poems focus on the 'pain of living' in a style that mixes scientific terminology with colloquialisms and dialect. Among his collections are *Cuttlefish Bones* (1925), *Le Occasioni* (1939) and *Satura* (1962). He was awarded the Nobel Prize for Literature in 1975.

1 **To make one, too many lives are needed.**
   'Summer', publ. in *Le Occasioni* (1939), repr. in *Selected Poems* (1964). This last line of the poem was remembered by ITALO CALVINO in a newspaper tribute to Montale after the poet's death.

2 **All religions of the only God
   are one: just the cooks and the cooking vary.**
   'The Death of God', publ. in *Satura* (1962), repr. in *New Poems* (1976). Opening words of poem.

3 **Words
   are everyone's property and in vain
   do they hide in dictionaries,
   for there's always a rogue
   who digs up the rarest
   and most stinking truffles.**
   'Words', ibid.

4 **The new man is born too old to tolerate the new world. The present conditions of life have not yet erased the traces of the past. We run too fast, but we still do not move enough . . . He looks but he does not contemplate, he sees but he does not think.**
   *Poet In Our Time* (1972)

5 **Youth is the vilest of all illusions.**
   'Sorapis, 40 Years Ago', publ. in *Diario del '71 e del '72* (1973), repr. in *New Poems* (1976)

6 **Tear up your pages, throw them in a sewer,
   take no degree in anything,
   and you will be able to say that you were
   perhaps alive for a moment or an instant.**
   'The Decline of Values', ibid.

## Maria Montessori (1870–1952)
ITALIAN EDUCATIONIST

She gave her name to a system of education for children aged from three to six, which lays the emphasis on freedom of expression, self-direction and the right to develop at one's own pace. She travelled and lectured widely and was the first woman in Italy to gain a medical degree (1894).

1 **If education is always to be conceived along the same antiquated lines of a mere transmission of knowledge, there is little to be hoped from it in the bettering of man's future. For what is the use of transmitting knowledge if the individual's total development lags behind?**
   *The Absorbent Mind*, ch. 1 (1949)

2 **If help and salvation are to come, they can only come from the children, for the children are the makers of men.**
   ibid.

3 **There is . . . in every child a painstaking teacher, so skilful that he obtains identical results in all children in all parts of the world. The only language men ever speak perfectly is the one they learn in babyhood, when no one can teach them anything!**
   ibid.

4 We teachers can only help the work going on, as servants wait upon a master.

ibid.

## Viscount Montgomery (1887–1976)

BRITISH SOLDIER

Bernard Montgomery, First Viscount Montgomery of Alamein. As commander of the Eighth Army, he defeated Rommel at the battle of El Alamein (1942) and played a key role in the invasion of Sicily and Italy the following year. Promoted to Field Marshal in 1944, he commanded the allied forces in the Normandy invasion. His books include *A History of Warfare* (1968). See also WINSTON CHURCHILL 52.

1 Rule 1, on page 1 of the book of war, is: 'Do not march on Moscow'. Various people have tried it, Napoleon and Hitler, and it is no good . . . Rule 2 of war . . . is: 'Do not go fighting with your land armies in China'. It is a vast country, with no clearly defined objectives, and an army fighting there would be engulfed by what is known as the Ming Bing, the people's insurgents.

Speech to House of Lords, 30 May 1962, publ. in *Hansard* (Lords).

2 Far from helping these unnatural [homosexual] practices along, surely our task is to build a bulwark which will defy evil influences which are seeking to undermine the very foundations of our national character – defy them; do not help them. I have heard some say . . . that such practices are allowed in France and in other NATO countries. We are not French, and we are not other nationals. We are British, thank God!

ibid. 26 May 1965. Debating Sexual Offences Bill.

## Monty Python's Flying Circus

The surreal BBC TV comedy series (1969–74) was written and performed by Graham Chapman (1941–89), JOHN CLEESE (b. 1939), Terry Gilliam (b. 1940), Eric Idle (b. 1943), Terry Jones (b. 1942) and MICHAEL PALIN (b. 1943). It was successfully exported to the USA and spawned the films *Monty Python and the Holy Grail* (1975), *Life of Brian* (1979) and *The Meaning of Life* (1983)

1 And now for something completely different.

John Cleese, as newsreader. The words became a catch-phrase used by various characters as a link between sketches in different episodes.

2 Nudge, nudge, wink, wink, say no more, know what I mean . . .

Eric Idle, in first series, episode 3, first broadcast 19 October 1969

3 This parrot is no more! It has ceased to be! It's expired and gone to meet its maker! This is a late parrot! It's a stiff! . . . THIS IS AN EX-PARROT!

John Cleese, in ibid. episode 8, first broadcast 7 December 1969

4 I'm a lumberjack
And I'm OK,
I sleep all night
And I work all day.

I cut down trees, I skip and jump,
I like to press wild flowers.
I put on women's clothing
And hang around in bars.

'The Lumberjack Song' in ibid. episode 9, first broadcast 14 December 1969

5 Nobody expects the Spanish Inquisition!

Michael Palin, in second series, episode 2, first broadcast 22 September 1970

6 When you're chewing on life's gristle
Don't grumble, give a whistle
And this'll help turn things out for the best . . .

And . . . always look on the bright side of life.

Mr Frisbee III (Eric Idle), in *Monty Python's Life of Brian* (film, 1979, written by John Cleese, Graham Chapman, Terry Gilliam, Eric Idle, Terry Jones and Michael Palin, directed by Terry Jones, 1979). Sung while being crucified, in film's closing sequence.

## Brian Moore (1921–99)

IRISH-BORN CANADIAN NOVELIST

Misfits, Catholicism and sectarian conflict are recurrent themes in his work, in which women are frequently protagonists. His novels include *The Lonely Passion of Judith Hearne* (1955, filmed 1987), *I Am Mary Dunne* (1968) and *The Great Victorian Collection* (1975).

1 There comes a point in many people's lives when they can no longer play the role they have chosen for themselves. When that happens, we are like actors finding that someone has changed the play.

*Sunday Times* 15 April 1990. 'What I write about,' Moore added, 'is the mess that follows.'

2 The world's made up of individuals who don't want to be heroes.

ibid.

3 Research is usually a policeman stopping a novel from progressing.

ibid.

## Clayton Moore (1914–99)

US SCREEN ACTOR

Originally named Jack Carlton Moore. He entered show business as a trapeze artist in Chicago in 1934, then moved to Hollywood where he played small roles as both heroes and villains throughout the 1940s. In 1949 he was assigned the role of the Lone Ranger in the transfer of the radio hit to television and continued in the part until the series ended in 1957.

1 Hi-yo, Silver, away!

The Lone Ranger (Clayton Moore), in *The Lone Ranger* (TV series, 1949–57, created by Fran Striker and George Trendle). Heard at the beginning of each episode of the show, which ran for sixteen years on radio before making its TV debut with Moore as the Masked Man on his 'fiery horse with the speed of light'.

## Marianne Moore (1887–1972)

US POET

T.S. ELIOT praised the 'swift dissolving image' of her verse, which is characterized by its individual metrical style and her sharp observation and wit. 'Miss Moore's forms have the lacy, mathematical extravagance of snowflakes,' commented RANDALL JARRELL. Her publications include *Observations* (1924) and *Collected Poems* (1951), which won the Pulitzer Prize.

1 nor till the poets among us can be
'literalists of
the imagination' – above
insolence and triviality and can present

for inspection, 'imaginary gardens with real toads in
them,' shall we have

it.

'Poetry', first publ. in *Others* July 1919, repr. in *Selected Poems* (1935)

2 with its baby rivers and little towns, each with its abbey
or its cathedral,
with voices – one voice perhaps, echoing through the
transept
– the
criterion of suitability and convenience.

'England', first publ. in *Dial* April 1920, repr. in ibid.

3 My father used to say,
'Superior people never make long visits,
have to be shown Longfellow's grave

or the glass flowers at Harvard.'

'Silence', first publ. in *Dial* October 1924, repr. in ibid.

4 The deepest feeling always shows itself in silence; not in silence, but restraint.

ibid.

5 Poetry, that is to say the poetic, is a primal necessity.

'Comment', first publ. in *Dial* August 1926, repr. in *Complete Prose* (1987)

6 When one cannot appraise out of one's own experience, the temptation to blunder is minimized, but even when one can, appraisal seems chiefly useful as appraisal of the appraiser.

'Comment', first publ. in *Dial* October 1928, repr. in ibid.

7 The catnip that art is, or *ignis fatuus*, or drop on the cactus, does seem worth the martyrdom of pursuit.

Letter to WILLIAM CARLOS WILLIAMS, 26 January 1934, publ. in *The Selected Letters of Marianne Moore*, 'The Poet in Brooklyn: 1930–1934' (ed. Bonnie Costello, 1998)

8 O to be a dragon
a symbol of the power of Heaven – of silkworm size or immense; at times invisible.
Felicitous phenomenon!

'O To Be a Dragon', publ. in *O To Be a Dragon* (1959)

9 Camels are snobbish
and sheep, unintelligent;
water buffaloes, neurasthenic –
even murderous.
Reindeer seem over-serious.

'The Arctic Ox (Or Goat)', publ. in ibid.

10 A writer is unfair to himself when he is unable to be hard on himself.

Interview in *Writers at Work* (second series, ed. George Plimpton, 1963)

11 I see no reason for calling my work poetry except that there is no other category in which to put it.

Quoted in the *New York Mirror* 31 May 1959. On accepting the National Book Award for poetry.

## Roger Moore (b. 1927)

BRITISH SCREEN ACTOR

Previously a model for knitted cardigans, he appeared as a suave action man in the television series *The Saint* (1962–9) and *The Persuaders* (1971–2). He took over the role of agent 007 in seven James Bond films (1973–85), among them *The Man with the Golden Gun* (1974) and *For Your Eyes Only* (1981).

1 [Of his acting range] Left eyebrow raised, right eyebrow raised.

Quoted in *Star Billing*, 'Seven Comments on the Art of Acting' (1985) by David Brown

## Alberto Moravia (1907–90)

ITALIAN AUTHOR

Original name Alberto Pincherle. He made his mark with *The Time of Indifference* (1929, filmed 1964), a portrayal of middle-class decadence. This theme, along with those of alienation and loveless sexuality, permeates his other works, for example in *The Woman of Rome* (1947, filmed 1954) and *The Empty Canvas* (1960).

1 Although not all men possess the same intellectual capacity and the same knowledge, they all, even the most wretched, have their own moral world in its entirety.

*The Woman of Rome*, Preface (1947)

## Jeanne Moreau (b. 1928)

FRENCH ACTRESS

Her sensual beauty and formidable acting skills were utilized by directors of the French *Nouvelle Vague*, as in Louis Malle's *Les Amants* (1958), ROGER VADIM's *Les Liaisons dangereuses* (1959) and TRUFFAUT's *Jules et Jim* (1961). She also directed *Lumière* (1975) and *L'Adolescente* (1978).

1 Acting deals with very delicate emotions. It is not putting up a mask. Each time an actor acts he does not hide; he exposes himself.

*The New York Times* 30 June 1976

## Robin Morgan (b. 1941)

US FEMINIST AUTHOR AND POET

As a chronicler of the women's movement in the USA, she edited the seminal collection of essays *Sisterhood is Powerful* (1970), followed by a wider ranging collection from different countries, *The Anatomy of Freedom* (1982).

1 It isn't until you begin to fight in your own cause that you (a) become really committed to winning, and (b) become a genuine ally of other people struggling for their freedom.

*Sisterhood is Powerful*, Introduction (1970)

2 There's something contagious about demanding freedom.

ibid.

3 Don't accept rides from strange men, and remember that all men are as strange as hell.

'Letter to a Sister Underground', publ. in ibid.

## Christopher Morley (1890–1957)

US NOVELIST, JOURNALIST AND POET

He is best known for his novel *Kitty Foyle* (1939) and also published poetry and essay collections. As editor he promoted the works of Joseph Conrad, and he also influenced American reading habits in his role as a judge for the Book-of-the-Month Club (1926–54).

1 Life is a foreign language: all men mispronounce it.

*Thunder on the Left*, ch. 14 (1925)

2 Dancing is a wonderful training for girls, it's the first way you learn to guess what a man is going to do before he does it.

*Kitty Foyle*, ch. 11 (1939)

## Robert Morley (1908–92)

BRITISH ACTOR AND HUMORIST

He remained a committed stage actor while also pursuing a screen career from 1938, appearing in the films *Oscar Wilde* (1960) and *Too Many Chefs* (1978), among others. His humorous observations and anecdotes are collected in *A Musing Morley* (1974) and *The Pleasures of Ages* (1988). 'It is a great help for a man to be in love with himself,' he once observed. 'For an actor it is absolutely essential.'

1 The British tourist is always happy abroad as long as the natives are waiters.

Quoted in the *Observer* 20 April 1958

2 The French are a logical people, which is one reason the English dislike them so intensely. The other is that they own France, a country which we have always judged to be much too good for them.

*A Musing Morley*, 'France and the French' (1974)

## Desmond Morris (b. 1928)

BRITISH ZOOLOGIST

He was presenter of television's *Zoo Time* in the late 1950s and keeper of mammals for the Zoological Society (1959–67) before his bestsellers *The Naked Ape* (1967) and *The Human Zoo* (1969) made him a household name. Interested particularly in the animal elements of human behaviour, he went on to produce books on football culture and babies and presented *The Animals Roadshow* on TV in the 1980s.

1 We never stop investigating. We are never satisfied that we know enough to get by. Every question we answer leads on to another question. This has become the greatest survival trick of our species.
*The Naked Ape*, ch. 4 (1967)

2 We are, to put it mildly, in a mess, and there is a strong chance that we shall have exterminated ourselves by the end of the century. Our only consolation will have to be that, as a species, we have had an exciting term of office.
ibid. ch. 5

3 The city is not a concrete jungle, it is a human zoo.
*The Human Zoo*, Introduction (1969)

## Philip Morris cigarettes

1 There is no 'safe' cigarette. These are and have been the messages of public health authorities world-wide. Smokers and potential smokers should rely on these messages in making all smoking-related decisions.
Posted on the Philip Morris website, 13 October 1999, quoted in the *Independent* 14 October 1999. First public admission by the Philip Morris company that smoking is not harmless.

## Blake Morrison (b. 1950)
BRITISH POET AND CRITIC

He is known for his poem collections including *The Ballad of the Yorkshire Ripper* (1987), his study of fatherhood in *And When Did You Last See Your Father?* (1993) and his reflections on the James Bulger murder, *As If* (1997).

1 The selective memory isn't selective enough.
*Independent on Sunday* 16 June 1991

2 Every age has its own story, or rewrites the same story; every Age too.
*As If*, ch. 1 (1997)

3 [On the James Bulger case] Some deaths are emblematic, tipping the scales, and little James's death – green fruit shaken from the bough, an ear of grain sown back in the earth – seemed like the murder of hope: the unthinkable thought of, the undoable done. If child-killings are the worst killings, then a child child-killing must be worse than worst, a new superlative in horror.
ibid.

4 By sparing the rod we've bred a generation of hoodlums. Cherub-faced muggers. Rapists who don't have pubic hair yet. Pre-pubescents with glittering knives. What's childhood coming to? Keep your kids well back. Childhood's not a place for children.
ibid. ch. 2. On popular reactions to the Bulger case.

5 A child in my lap, being read to, and I find myself erect.
ibid. ch. 10

6 Without art, confessionalism is masturbation.
*Too True*, Introduction (1998)

7 Certainly, porn has its uses: like a pet dog, it can console the lonely; like oysters, it can sharpen a lover's appetite; like cocoa, it can get the restless off to sleep.
ibid. 'The Trouble With Porn' sect. 3

## Jim Morrison (1943–71)
US ROCK MUSICIAN

Calling himself the Lizard King and contributing a theatrical blend of eroticism and barely repressed violence to 1960s psychedelia, he was the singer and main inspiration of the Doors, a Los Angeles rock group formed in 1966. Influenced by French Romantic poetry, he became increasingly erratic and in thrall to drugs, and died in mysterious circumstances in Paris.

1 Come on baby light my fire.
'Light My Fire' (song, written by the Doors) on the album *The Doors* (1967) by the Doors

2 This is the end,
Beautiful friend.
This is the end,
My only friend, the end.
It hurts to set you free
But you'll never follow me.
'The End' (song, written by the Doors), on ibid. The song was featured in FRANCIS FORD COPPOLA's film *Apocalypse Now* (1979).

3 Father?
'Yes, son?'
'I want to kill you.'
'Mother, I want to . . .'
ibid.

4 We want the world and we want it now!
'When the Music's Over' (song, written by the Doors) on the album *Strange Days* (1967) by the Doors

5 I am the Lizard King
I can do anything.
'The Celebration of the Lizard' (poem and song) on the album *Waiting For the Sun* (1968) by the Doors

6 They got the guns but we got the numbers.
'Five to One' (song, by the Doors) on ibid.

7 I'm interested in anything about revolt, disorder, chaos, especially activity that appears to have no meaning. It seems to me to be the road toward freedom.
Quoted in *Time* magazine 24 January 1968

8 The Lords appease us with images. They give us books, concerts, galleries, shows, cinemas. Especially the cinemas. Through art they confuse us and blind us to our enslavement. Art adorns our prison walls, keeps us silent and diverted and indifferent.
'The Lords: Notes on Vision' (1969), repr. in *The Lords and the New Creatures* (1970)

9 The most loving parents and relatives commit murder with smiles on their faces. They force us to destroy the person we really are: a subtle kind of murder.
Quoted in *In Their Own Words: The Doors*, ch. 1 (1988) by Andrew Doe and John Tobler

## Toni Morrison (b. 1931)
US NOVELIST AND EDITOR

Full name Chloe Anthony Morrison. Her novels use the history and culture of African-Americans as the basis for explorations of emotions and relationships, and include *Tar Baby* (1981), *Beloved* (1987, Pulitzer Prize) and *Jazz* (1992). In 1993 she was the first African-American to win the Nobel Prize for Literature.

1 [Of Sula] Like any artist with no art form, she became dangerous.
*Sula* (1973)

2 Grab this land! Take it, hold it, my brothers, make it, my brothers, shake it, squeeze it, turn it, twist it, beat it, kick it, kiss it, whip it, stomp it, dig it, plow it, seed it, reap it, rent it, buy it, sell it, own it, build it, multiply it, and pass it on – can you hear me? Pass it on!
Macon Dead, in *Song of Solomon*, pt. 1, ch. 10 (1977)

3 At some point in life the world's beauty becomes enough. You don't need to photograph, paint or even remember it. It is enough.
*Tar Baby*, ch. 8 (1981)

4 An innocent man is a sin before God. Inhuman and therefore untrustworthy. No man should live without absorbing the sins of his kind, the foul air of his innocence,

even if it did wilt rows of angel trumpets and cause them to fall from their vines.

ibid.

5 Of course I'm a black writer . . . I'm not *just* a black writer, but categories like black writer, woman writer and Latin American writer aren't marginal anymore. We have to acknowledge that the thing we call 'literature' is more pluralistic now, just as society ought to be. The melting pot never worked. We ought to be able to accept on equal terms everybody from the Hasidim to Walter Lippmann, from the Rastafarians to Ralph Bunche.

Quoted in *Newsweek* 30 March 1981

6 How soon country people forget. When they fall in love with a city it is forever, and it is like forever. As though there never was a time when they didn't love it. The minute they arrive at the train station or get off the ferry and glimpse the wide streets and the wasteful lamps lighting them, they know they are born for it. There, in a city, they are not so much new as themselves: their stronger, riskier selves.

*Jazz*, ch. 2 (1991)

7 In this country American means white. Everybody else has to hyphenate.

*Guardian* 29 January 1992

## Van Morrison (b. 1945)
IRISH ROCK MUSICIAN

Original name George Ivan Morrison. Belfast-born and an institution in rock music, he formed the rhythm and blues band Them in 1963, which had hits with his compositions 'Here Comes the Night' and 'Gloria' (both 1965). Opinion polls regularly place his first two solo albums, *Astral Weeks* (1968) and *Moondance* (1970), among the best albums ever made.

1 Music is spiritual. The music business is not.

*The Times* 6 July 1990

## Morrissey (b. 1959)
BRITISH ROCK MUSICIAN

Full name Stephen Patrick Morrissey. Described by *Melody Maker* as 'the Peregrine Worsthorne of pop', he was singer with the Smiths, a Manchester band whose success rested on the marriage of Morrissey's fey romanticism and guitarist Johnny Marr's musicianship. Since the band's split in 1987, he has pursued a solo career, recording *Viva Hate!* in 1988.

1 I was happy in the haze of a drunken hour
   But heaven knows I'm miserable now.

'Heaven Knows I'm Miserable Now' (song, 1984, written with Johnny Marr) on the album *Hatful of Hollow* by the Smiths (1985)

2 Hang the deejay.

'Panic' (song, 1986, written with Johnny Marr) on the album *The World Won't Listen* (1987)

3 I always thought being famous was the only thing worth doing in human life, and anything else was just perfunctory. I thought anonymity was easy: it was easy to be a simple, nodding individual who got on the bus. I wasn't terribly impressed by obscurity.

Interview in *Melody Maker* 12 March 1988, repr. in *Classic Rock Interviews*, 'Viva Hate' (ed. Allan Jones, 1994)

4 I believe that everything went downhill from the moment McDonald's was given a licence to invade England . . . To me, it was like the outbreak of war and I couldn't understand why English troops weren't retaliating.

Quoted in the *Guardian* 26 February 1994

## John Mortimer (b. 1923)
BRITISH BARRISTER AND NOVELIST

He is best known for his novels featuring the amiable and eccentric lawyer Rumpole, adapted for television as *Rumpole of the Bailey* (1978–80). The light-hearted style of his novels, such as *Paradise Postponed* (1985) and *Summer's Lease* (1988), cushions his biting satire of the English upper-middle class. He has also written plays, including *A Voyage Round My Father* (1970, televised 1982), screenplays and translations.

1 The shelf life of the modern hardback writer is somewhere between the milk and the yoghurt.

Quoted in the *Sunday Times* 27 December 1987

2 When you get to my age life seems little more than one long march to and from the lavatory.

Haverford Downs, in *Summer's Lease*, pt 2, ch. 3 (1988)

3 The worst fault of the working classes is telling their children they're not going to succeed, saying: 'There is life, but it's not for you.'

*Daily Mail* 31 May 1988

4 The freedom to make a fortune on the Stock Exchange has been made to sound more alluring than freedom of speech.

Quoted in the *Independent* 29 October 1988

5 Farce is tragedy played at a thousand revolutions per minute.

*The Times* 9 September 1992

6 At Harrow, you could have any boy for a box of Cadbury's milk chocolate.

Quoted in the *Sunday Times* 27 September 1998. Referring to his schooldays at Harrow.

7 Champagne socialist.

Attributed description of himself

## (Sir) Claus Moser (b. 1922)
GERMAN-BORN BRITISH ACADEMIC

A public figure in the arts and academic worlds, he has been Chairman of the Royal Opera House (1974–87) and Warden of Wadham College (1984–93).

1 Education costs money, but then so does ignorance.

*Daily Telegraph* 21 August 1990

2 For hundreds of years Britain has been brilliant at educating an élite: the problem is the other eighty per cent.

BBC Radio 4 16 November 1990

## (Sir) Oswald Mosley (1896–1980)
BRITISH FASCIST LEADER

He was successively a Conservative, Independent and Labour MP (1918–31) before founding in 1932 the British Union of Fascists, known as Blackshirts. Modelling himself on HITLER and instigating anti-Semitic violence in London's East End, he was interned (1940–43) during the Second World War, and in 1948 he founded the right-wing Union Movement. His second wife was Diana Mitford.

1 I have always felt a clear choice existed between two states of mind, the writing of history and the making of history. He who is interested in the latter should only be detained by the former just long enough to absorb its lessons.

*My Life*, ch. 3 (1968)

2 Great men of action . . . never mind on occasion being ridiculous; in a sense it is part of their job, and at times they all are. A prophet or an achiever must never mind an occasional absurdity, it is an occupational risk.

ibid. ch. 12

3 When the bystanders see an elephant coming down the street, it is idle to tell them it is a pleasant Sunday after-

noon outing organized by the Young Men's Christian Association. We were a distinctive movement of intense national patriotism, but in the age of fascism it was clearly jejune and possibly dishonest to deny that we were fascist.

ibid. ch. 16

4 Ideas in a void have never appealed to me; action must follow thought or political life is meaningless.

ibid. ch. 17

5 I am not, and never have been, a man of the right. My position was on the left and is now in the centre of politics.

Letter to *The Times* 26 April 1968

## Robert Motherwell (1915–91)
US ARTIST

In the 1940s he was a key member of the New York Abstract Expressionists, producing massive painted images and collages which retained figurative and narrative elements. His main works include *Elegies to the Spanish Republic* (1949–76), a series of more than 100 paintings on the theme of the Spanish Civil War. He also wrote on the theory of modern art.

1 The public history of modern art is the story of conventional people not knowing what they are dealing with.

*The Dada Painters and Poets: An Anthology*, Preface (ed. Robert Motherwell, 1951)

## Andrew Motion (b. 1952)
BRITISH POET AND BIOGRAPHER

His reflective, highly personal verse, published in *Secret Narratives* (1983) and *Love in a Life* (1991) among other collections, shows the influence of Keats, EDWARD THOMAS and PHILIP LARKIN, all of whom have been subjects of critical studies and biographies by him. He was created Poet Laureate in 1999.

1 I admit that I also yearn to leave my mark on society, and not see machines or people trample it foolishly.

On the one hand it's only shit; on the other, shit's shit, and what we desire in the world is less, not more, of it.

'It is an Offence', publ. in *Love in a Life* (1991)

2 For a million years one life simply turns into the next –
The spider hangs between driftwood and sea holly,
the sparrow hawk balances exactly over a shrew,
the hare sits bolt upright and urgent, all ears:
there is no reason why any of this should change.

'Salt Water', publ. in *Salt Water* (1997)

3 Beside the river, swerving under ground,
your future tracked you, snapping at your heels:
Diana, breathless, hunted by your own quick hounds.

'Mythology', publ. in *The Times* 6 Sept. 1997, repr. in *News That Stays News* (ed. Simon Rae, 1999)

4 The fact of the matter is that it is a difficult time in our history for white, straight, middle-aged, middle-class males.

Quoted in *Daily Telegraph* 20 May 1999. Said on his appointment as poet laureate.

## Louis Mountbatten (1900–79)
BRITISH NAVAL COMMANDER AND STATESMAN

First Earl Mountbatten of Burma. The great-grandson of Queen Victoria, he became Chief of Combined Operations Command (1941–3) and Supreme Commander in South-East Asia. In 1945 he received the Japanese surrender, and as the last Viceroy of India he oversaw the granting of independence to India. He was assassinated by an IRA bomb while aboard his yacht in Ireland.

1 If the Third World War is fought with nuclear weapons, the fourth will be fought with bows and arrows.

*Maclean's* 17 November 1975

## Malcolm Muggeridge (1903–90)
BRITISH JOURNALIST AND BROADCASTER

Throughout his journalistic career, working for the *Manchester Guardian*, the *Evening Standard* and the *Daily Telegraph* and as Editor of *Punch* (1953–7), he remained a tireless iconoclast. His views became increasingly informed by his Christian beliefs, earning him the nickname 'Saint Mug', and in 1982 he embraced Roman Catholicism. KENNETH TYNAN compared him to a 'garden gnome expelled from Eden . . . come to rest as a gargoyle brooding over a derelict cathedral'.

1 Good taste and humour are a contradiction in terms, like a chaste whore.

*Time* magazine 14 September 1953. Defending his editorship of *Punch*.

2 There's nothing in this world more instinctively abhorrent to me than finding myself in agreement with my fellow-humans.

*Any Questions?* BBC radio broadcast, 29 April 1955, publ. in *Muggeridge Through the Microphone*, 'Mini-Mania' (1967)

3 This horror of pain is a rather low instinct and . . . if I think of human beings I've known and of my own life, such as it is, I can't recall any case of pain which didn't, on the whole, enrich life.

*Meeting Point*, BBC1 television broadcast, 11 August 1963, publ. in ibid. 'The Problem of Pain'

4 There is something ridiculous and even quite indecent in an individual *claiming* to be happy. Still more a people or a nation making such a claim . . . This lamentable phrase 'the pursuit of happiness' is responsible for a good part of the ills and miseries of the modern world.

*Woman's Hour*, BBC radio broadcast, 5 October 1965, publ. in ibid. 'Happiness'

5 Sex is the mysticism of materialism and the only possible religion in a materialistic society.

Television broadcast, BBC1, 21 October 1965, quoted in ibid. 'The American Way of Sex'

6 The orgasm has replaced the Cross as the focus of longing and the image of fulfilment.

*Tread Softly For You Tread on My Jokes*, 'Down with Sex' (1966)

7 Television was not invented to make human beings vacuous, but is an emanation of their vacuity.

ibid. 'I Like Dwight'

8 The genius of Man in our time has gone into jet-propulsion, atom-splitting, penicillin-curing, etc. There is none over for works of imagination; of spiritual insight or mystical enlightenment. I asked for bread and was given a tranquillizer. It is important to recognize that in our time man has not written one word, thought one thought, put two notes or two bricks together, splashed colour on to canvas or concrete into space, in a manner which will be of any conceivable *imaginative* interest to posterity.

ibid.

9 [Of ANTHONY EDEN] As has been truly said in his days as an active politician, he was not only a bore; he bored for England.

ibid. 'Boring for England'

10 One of the peculiar sins of the twentieth century which we've developed to a very high level is the sin of credulity. It has been said that when human beings stop believing in God they believe in nothing. The truth is much worse: they believe in anything.

*Woman's Hour*, BBC radio broadcast, 23 March 1966, publ. in

*Muggeridge Through the Microphone*, 'An Eighth Deadly Sin' (1967)

11 The trouble with kingdoms of heaven on earth is that they're liable to come to pass, and then their fraudulence is apparent for all to see. We need a kingdom of heaven in Heaven, if only because it can't be realized.

*Jesus Rediscovered*, 'Me and Myself' (1979)

12 Civilization – a heap of rubble scavenged by scrawny English Lit vultures.

Quoted in *New Society* 6 October 1983

## Edwin Muir (1887–1959)
BRITISH POET

Brought up on the island of Orkney, he later lived in Prague where he produced translations of Kafka with his wife, the novelist Willa Anderson. His poem collections, including *The Voyage* (1946) and *The Labyrinth* (1949), combine myth and dreams.

1 Late in the summer the strange horses came.
We heard a distant tapping on the road,
A deepening drumming; it stopped, went on again
And at the corner changed to hollow thunder.
We saw the heads
Like a wild wave charging and were afraid.

'The Horses', publ. in *One Foot in Eden* (1956)

## Frank Muir (1920–98)
BRITISH HUMORIST

With DENIS NORDEN, he formed a highly successful comedy-writing team (1947–64), responsible for such series as *Take It From Here* (1947–58) and *Whack-O!* (1958–60). He was also a regular radio and television performer, appearing on *My Word* and *Call My Bluff* (1965–88).

1 Wit is a weapon. Jokes are a masculine way of inflicting superiority. But humour is the pursuit of a gentle grin, usually in solitude.

*Daily Mail* 26 April 1990

2 [Of Joan Bakewell] The thinking man's crumpet.

Attributed

## Arthur Mullard (1910–95)
BRITISH COMIC ACTOR AND BOXER

A boxer, rag and bone merchant and bouncer before getting work in films as an extra and stunt man, he became a popular character actor as a burly Cockney in comic roles. He appeared on television in the 1961 sitcom *The Arthur Askey Show* and also in numerous films, including *Oliver Twist* (1948), *Chitty Chitty Bang Bang* (1968) and *On the Buses* (1971).

1 Boxing got me started on philosophy. You bash them, they bash you and you think, what's it all for?

Quoted in the *Independent on Sunday* 17 December 1995

## Lewis Mumford (1895–1990)
US SOCIAL PHILOSOPHER

In his works *Technics and Civilization* (1934) and *Myth and Machine* (1967, 1970) he analysed the impact of technology on society, though he was best known for his studies on urbanism, as in *The Culture of Cities* (1938) and *The City in History* (1961).

1 Every generation revolts against its fathers and makes friends with its grandfathers.

*The Brown Decades*, ch. 1 (1931)

2 The clock, not the steam-engine, is the key-machine of the modern industrial age.

*Technics and Civilization*, ch. 1, sect. 2 (1934)

3 War is the supreme drama of a completely mechanized society.

ibid. ch. 6, sect. 11

4 Today, the notion of progress in a single line without goal or limit seems perhaps the most parochial notion of a very parochial century.

ibid. ch. 8, sect. 12

5 However far modern science and technics have fallen short of their inherent possibilities, they have taught mankind at least one lesson: Nothing is impossible.

ibid. sect. 13

6 The city is a fact in nature, like a cave, a run of mackerel or an ant-heap. But it is also a conscious work of art, and it holds within its communal framework many simpler and more personal forms of art. Mind *takes form* in the city; and in turn, urban forms condition mind.

*The Culture of Cities*, Introduction (1938)

7 By his very success in inventing labor-saving devices, modern man has manufactured an abyss of boredom that only the privileged classes in earlier civilizations have ever fathomed.

*The Conduct of Life*, 'The Challenge of Renewal' (1951)

8 Every new baby is a blind desperate vote for survival: people who find themselves unable to register an effective political protest against extermination do so by a biological act.

*The City in History*, ch. 18 (1961)

## (Dame) Iris Murdoch (1919–99)
BRITISH NOVELIST AND PHILOSOPHER

A fellow in philosophy at Oxford (1948–63), she wove the plots of her novels around the complex lives of characters in search of love and freedom. Her fiction includes *The Bell* (1958), *The Sea, the Sea* (1978) and *The Green Knight* (1993), and she also published studies on Plato and SARTRE. She was married to the author John Bayley.

1 In almost every marriage there is a selfish and an unselfish partner. A pattern is set up and soon becomes inflexible, of one person always making the demands and one person always giving way.

Martin Lynch-Gibbon, in *A Severed Head*, ch. 2 (1961)

2 One doesn't have to get anywhere in a marriage. It's not a public conveyance.

ibid. ch. 3

3 You cannot have both truth and what you call civilization.

Honor Klein, in ibid. ch. 9

4 Falling out of love is chiefly a matter of *forgetting* how charming someone is.

Anderson Palmer, in ibid. ch. 24

5 I think being a woman is like being Irish . . . Everyone says you're important and nice, but you take second place all the same.

Frances Bellman, in *The Red and the Green*, ch. 2 (1965). Iris Murdoch was born in Dublin of Anglo-Irish parents.

6 Being good is just a matter of temperament in the end.

Kate Gray, in *The Nice and the Good*, ch. 14 (1968)

7 Happiness is a matter of one's most ordinary everyday mode of consciousness being busy and lively and unconcerned with self. To be damned is for one's ordinary everyday mode of consciousness to be unremitting agonizing preoccupation with self.

Willy Kost, in ibid. ch. 22

8 No love is entirely without worth, even when the frivolous calls to the frivolous and the base to the base.

Narrator, in ibid. ch. 39

9 Writing is like getting married. One should never commit oneself until one is amazed at one's luck.

*The Black Prince*, 'Bradley Pearson's Foreword' (1972). The narrator is here discussing his own literary output: three short books in forty years.

10 A good man often appears *gauche* simply because he does not take advantage of the myriad mean little chances of making himself look stylish. Preferring truth to form, he is not constantly at work upon the façade of his appearance.

Bradley Pearson, in ibid. pt 1

11 Bereavement is a darkness impenetrable to the imagination of the unbereaved.

Montague Small, in *The Sacred and Profane Love Machine* (1974)

12 The priesthood is a marriage. People often start by falling in love, and they go on for years without realizing that that love must change into some other love which is so unlike it that it can hardly be recognized as love at all.

Brendan Craddock, in *Henry and Cato*, pt 2 'The Great Teacher' (1976)

13 Human affairs are not serious, but they have to be taken seriously.

ibid.

14 Art is the final cunning of the human soul which would rather do anything than face the gods.

Plato, in *Acastos: Two Platonic Dialogues*, 'Art and Eros: A Dialogue about Art' (first performed on stage 1980, publ. 1986)

15 In philosophy if you aren't moving at a snail's pace you aren't moving at all.

Socrates, in ibid. 'Above the Gods: A Dialogue about Religion'

16 Possibly, more people kill themselves and others out of hurt vanity than out of envy, jealousy, malice or desire for revenge.

*The Philosopher's Pupil*, 'The Events in Our Town' (1983)

17 He [Whit Meynell] was a sociologist; he had got into an intellectual muddle early on in life and never managed to get out.

ibid.

18 As for truth – well, it's like brown – it's not in the spectrum . . . Truth is *sui generis*.

Rozanov, in ibid.

19 All art is a struggle to be, in a particular sort of way, virtuous.

*Novelists in Interview* (ed. John Haffenden, 1985)

20 Philosophy! Empty thinking by ignorant conceited men who think they can digest without eating!

Levquist, in *The Book and the Brotherhood*, pt 1, 'Midsummer' (1987)

21 Perhaps misguided moral passion is better than confused indifference.

Jenkin Riderhood, in ibid. pt 2, 'Midwinter'

22 We shall be better prepared for the future if we see how terrible, how *doomed* the present is.

David Crimond, in ibid.

23 But fantasy *kills* imagination, pornography is death to art.

Alfred Ludens, in *The Message to the Planet*, pt 1 (1989)

24 I daresay anything can be made holy by being sincerely worshipped.

Maisie Tether, in ibid. pt 5

25 Perhaps when distant people on other planets pick up some wave-length of ours all they hear is a continuous scream.

Alfred Ludens, in ibid. pt 6

26 A bad review is even less important than whether it is raining in Patagonia.

*The Times* 6 July 1989

# Rupert Murdoch (b. 1931)

AUSTRALIAN-BORN US MEDIA TYCOON

His newspaper empire in Britain ranges from the *News of the World* and the *Sun*, into which he introduced the 'page three girl', to *The Times*. He moved into the American market in 1976 and acquired the *New York Post* and Twentieth-Century Fox film studios. In the view of SIMON HOGGART: 'He believes that people crave rubbish and that he has the right to grow rich providing it.'

1 William Shakespeare wrote for the masses. If he were alive today, he'd probably be the chief scriptwriter on *All in the Family* or *Dallas*.

Quoted in the *Sunday Express* 30 December 1984

2 Much of what passes for quality on British television is no more than a reflection of the narrow élite which controls it and has always thought that its tastes were synonymous with quality.

Address to the Edinburgh Television Festival, 25 August 1989, quoted in the *Guardian* 1 January 1990

3 Modernization is Americanization. It is the American way of organizing society that is prevailing in the world.

'The Wriston Lecture', Manhattan Institute, New York, 9 November 1989, quoted in *Rupert Murdoch: Ringmaster of the Information Circus*, ch. 14 (1992) by William Shawcross

# Bill Murray (b. 1950)

US SCREEN ACTOR

Since coming to notice on TV's *Saturday Night Live*, he has appeared in the films *Ghostbuster* (1984), *Little Shop of Horrors* (1986) and *Groundhog Day* (1993).

1 We're Americans with a capital A. Do you know what that means? That means that our forefathers were kicked out of every decent country in the world. We are the wretched refuse. We're underdogs. We're mutts . . . We're all very, very different. But there is one thing we all have in common: we were all stupid enough to enlist in the army.

John Winger (Bill Murray), in *Stripes* (film, 1981, screenplay by Len Blum, Dan Goldberg and Harold Ramis, directed and co-produced by Ivan Reirman)

# Les Murray (b. 1938)

AUSTRALIAN POET

His rural upbringing gave him a close acquaintance with the Australian landscape which he celebrates in his verse. His collections, which have made him one of his country's leading literary figures, include *The Vernacular Republic: Poems 1961–1981* (1982) and *Translations from the Natural World* (1992).

1 Axe-fall, echo and silence. It will be centuries
before many men are truly at home in this country,
and yet, there have always been some, in each
        generation,
there have always been some who could live in the
        presence of silence.

'Noonday Axeman', publ. in *The Ilex Tree* (1965)

2 Men must have legends, else they will die of strangeness.

ibid.

3 Nothing's said till it's dreamed out in words
and nothing's true that figures in words only.

'Poetry and Religion', publ. in *The Daylight Moon* (1987)

4 Then, strung out and spotty, you wriggle and sigh
and kiss all the fellows and make them all die.

'Midnight Lake', publ. in *Dog Fox Field* (1991). Final couplet of poem.

5 Australians are like most who won't read this poem
or any, since literature turned on them
and bodiless jargons without reverie
scorn their loves as illusion and biology,

compared with bloody History, the opposite of home.

'A Brief History', publ. in *Subhuman Redneck Poems* (1996). Last stanza of poem.

6 Sex is a Nazi. The students all knew
this at your school. To it, everyone's subhuman
for parts of their lives. Some are all their lives.
You'll be one of those if these things worry you.

'Rock Music', publ. in ibid.

7 For the truth, we are silent. For the flattering dream,
in massed farting reassurance, we spasm and scream.

ibid. Last stanza of poem.

# Ed Murrow (1908–65)

US NEWSCASTER

An esteemed figure in the development of American broadcasting, he reported on wartime Britain for CBS and produced and presented the current affairs programmes *See It Now* (1951–8) and *Person to Person* (1953–60). His exposé of JOSEPH MCCARTHY in 1954 contributed to the latter's downfall.

1 [Of Joseph McCarthy] No one can terrorize a whole nation, unless we are all his accomplices.

'See It Now', CBS television broadcast, 7 March 1954

2 He [Winston Churchill] mobilized the English language and sent it into battle to steady his fellow countrymen and hearten those Europeans upon whom the long dark night of tyranny had descended.

TV broadcast to mark CHURCHILL's eightieth birthday, 30 November 1954, publ. in *In Search of Light* (1967)

# John Middleton Murry (1889–1957)

BRITISH CRITIC AND EDITOR

He wrote numerous essays and criticism and was founder and editor of the *Adelphi* (1923–48). Married to KATHERINE MANSFIELD, he edited her poems, stories and correspondence and published her biography in 1933. Later he became a prominent pacifist and radical Christian, editing *Peace News* (1940–46).

1 If the Nazis have really been guilty of the unspeakable crimes circumstantially imputed to them, then – let us make no mistake – pacifism is faced with a situation with which it cannot cope. The conventional pacifist conception of a reasonable or generous peace is irrelevant to this reality.

*Peace News* 22 September 1944

# Benito Mussolini (1883–1945)

ITALIAN DICTATOR

Formerly a socialist, he helped found the Italian fascist movement in 1919, became Prime Minister in 1922 and by 1925 had established himself as dictator, or 'Duce'. He annexed Abyssinia (1936) and entered the Second World War on HITLER's side, but after defeats in Africa and the invasion of Sicily he was overthrown and killed attempting to flee the country. For ERNEST HEMINGWAY, 'There is something wrong, even histrionically, with a man who wears white spats with a black shirt.' See also EZRA POUND 18.

1 I could have transformed this grey hall into an armed camp of Blackshirts, a bivouac for corpses. I could have nailed up the doors of Parliament.

Speech 16 November 1922, quoted in *Benito Mussolini*, pt 1, ch. 4 (1962, rev. 1965 and 1975) by Christopher Hibbert. First speech to the Italian Chamber of Deputies after becoming Prime Minister.

2 Fascism, the more it considers and observes the future and the development of humanity, quite apart from political considerations of the moment, believes neither in the possibility nor the utility of perpetual peace.

'The Political and Social Doctrine of Fascism', publ. in *Enciclopedia Italiana* (1932)

3 War alone brings up to their highest tension all human energies and imposes the stamp of nobility upon the peoples who have the courage to make it.

ibid.

4 It is humiliating to remain with our hands folded while others write history. It matters little who wins. To make a people great it is necessary to send them to battle even if you have to kick them in the pants. That is what I shall do.

Quoted in journal entry by Galeazzo Ciano, 11 April 1940, publ. in *Diary 1939–1943* (1946) by Galeazzo Ciano. Said to Count Ciano, Mussolini's son-in-law and Minister for Foreign Affairs. Italy entered the Second World War on 10 June 1940.

# Mike Myers (b. 1964)

CANADIAN COMIC ACTOR AND SCREENWRITER

Coming to notice on NBC's *Saturday Night Live* (1989–94), he adapted his 'Wayne's World' sketch into two successful films *Wayne's World* (1992) and *Wayne's World 2* (1993). He subsequently starred as the spoof spy Austin Powers in *Austin Powers: International Man of Mystery* (1997) and *Austin Powers: The Spy Who Shagged Me* (1999).

1 No way dude.

Wayne Campbell (Mike Myers), in *Wayne's World* (film, 1992, screenplay by Mike Myers, Bonnie Turner and Terry Turner, directed by Penelope Spheeris). The oft-repeated line was featured regularly on 'Saturday Night Live'.

2 Garth, marriage is punishment for shoplifting, in some countries.

ibid.

3 Shall we shag now, or shall we shag later?

Austin Powers, in *Austin Powers: International Man of Mystery* (film, 1997, screenplay by Mike Myers, directed by Jay Roach)

## Vladimir Nabokov (1899–1977)

RUSSIAN-BORN US NOVELIST AND POET

He began to write in English on his move to America in 1940 and gained instant notoriety for *Lolita* (1955, filmed 1962 and 1997), the story of a middle-aged intellectual's infatuation for a twelve-year-old girl. Other novels that display his wit and erudition include *The Real Life of Sebastian Knight* (1941) and *Pnin* (1957). He was also a keen lepidopterist, a theme of *Pale Fire* (1962). 'He writes prose the only way it should be written,' JOHN UPDIKE commented, ' – that is ecstatically.'

1 There are aphorisms that, like airplanes, stay up only while they are in motion.

Koncheyev, in *The Gift*, ch. 1 (1937, transl. 1963)

2 Lolita, light of my life, fire of my loins. My sin, my soul. Lo-lee-ta: the tip of the tongue taking a trip of three steps down the palate to tap, at three, on the teeth. Lo. Lee. Ta.

Humbert Humbert (narrator), in *Lolita*, pt 1, ch. 1 (1955). Opening lines of book.

3 You can always count on a murderer for a fancy prose style.

ibid.

4 My very photogenic mother died in a freak accident (picnic, lightning) when I was three, and, save for a pocket of warmth in the darkest past, nothing of her subsists within the hollows and dells of memory.

ibid. ch. 2

5 Between the age limits of nine and fourteen there occur maidens who, to certain bewitched travelers, twice or many times older than they, reveal their true nature which is not human, but nymphic (that is, demoniac); and these chosen creatures I propose to designate as 'nymphets'.

ibid. ch. 5. This passage was cut in the 1962 film directed by STANLEY KUBRICK.

6 [Describing an embryo] The tiny madman in his padded cell.

ibid. ch. 11

7 The cradle rocks above an abyss, and common sense tells us that our existence is but a brief crack of light between two eternities of darkness.

*Speak, Memory*, ch. 1, sect. 1 (1955, rev. 1966). Opening words of Nabokov's autobiography.

8 Imagination, the supreme delight of the immortal and the immature, should be limited. In order to enjoy life, we should not enjoy it too much.

ibid.

9 Let me say at once that I reject completely the vulgar, shabby, fundamentally medieval world of Freud, with its crankish quest for sexual symbols (something like searching for Baconian acrostics in Shakespeare's works) and its bitter little embryos spying, from their natural nooks, upon the love life of their parents.

ibid.

10 Treading the soil of the moon, palpating its pebbles, tasting the panic and splendor of the event, feeling in the pit of one's stomach the separation from terra . . . these form the most romantic sensation an explorer has ever known . . . this is the only thing I can say about the matter. The utilitarian results do not interest me.

*The New York Times* 21 July 1969. Referring to the first manned moon-landing.

11 A novelist is, like all mortals, more fully at home on the surface of the present than in the ooze of the past.

*Strong Opinions*, ch. 20 (1973)

12 Style and Structure are the essence of a book; great ideas are hogwash.

Interview in *Writers at Work* (fourth series, ed. George Plimpton, 1976)

## Ralph Nader (b. 1934)

US CONSUMER RIGHTS AND GREEN ACTIVIST

Called the 'scourge of corporate morality', he was the leader of many consumer campaigns and pressure groups including 'Nader's Raiders'. His book *Unsafe at Any Speed* (1965) contributed to safer car design regulations and in 1980 he became head of the Public Citizen Foundation. 'I am in favor of lawyers without clients,' he said, 'lawyers should represent systems of justice.'

1 For almost seventy years the life insurance industry has been a smug sacred cow feeding the public a steady line of sacred bull.

Testimony to US Senate subcommittee, quoted in *The New York Times* 19 May 1974

## (Sir) V.S. Naipaul (b. 1932)

TRINIDAD-BORN BRITISH AUTHOR

Full name Vidiadhar Surajprasad Naipaul. Describing himself as 'content to be a colonial, without a past, without ancestors', he takes alienation and the experience of 'universal wanderers' as his primary subject matter. He portrayed life in the Caribbean in his early novel *A House for Mr Biswas* (1961), and described his impressions of Islamic states in Asia in *Among the Believers* (1981) and of American evangelical Christianity in *A Turn in the South* (1989).

1 I'm the kind of writer that people think other people are reading.

*Radio Times* 24–30 March 1979

2 To read a newspaper for the first time is like coming into a film that has been on for an hour. Newspapers are like serials. To understand them you have to take knowledge to them; the knowledge that serves best is the knowledge provided by the newspaper itself.

*The Enigma of Arrival* (1987), 'The Journey'. On reading *The New York Times* for the first time.

## Ogden Nash (1902–71)

US POET

A frequent contributor to the *New Yorker*, he caused both scandal and amusement with his puns and parodies, clever rhymes and free verse, lines of which vary from one word or extend the length of a paragraph. His collections include *Free Wheeling* (1931), *I'm a Stranger Here Myself* (1938), and *Everyone But Thee and Me* (1962). CLIFTON FADIMAN judged that Nash suffered from two disadvantages: 'he is a humorist, and he is easy to understand.'

1 Candy
Is dandy
But Liquor
Is quicker.

'Reflections on Ice-Breaking', publ. in *Hard Lines* (1931)

2 The cow is of the bovine ilk;
One end is moo, the other, milk.

'The Cow', publ. in *Free Wheeling* (1931)

3 No matter how deep and dark your pit, how dank your shroud,
Their heads are heroically unbloody and unbowed.

'Look For the Silver Lining', publ. in *Happy Days* (1933). On 'The cheery souls who drop around after every catastrophe and think they are taking the curse off/By telling you about somebody who is even worse off'.

4 I don't mind their having a lot of money, and I don't care how they employ it,
But I do think that they damn well ought to admit they enjoy it.

'The Terrible People', publ. in ibid.

5 Man is a victim of dope

In the incurable form of hope.

'Good-by, Old Year, You Oaf or Why Don't They Pay the Bonus?', publ. in *The Primrose Path* (1935)

6 Every New Year is the direct descendant, isn't it, of a long line of proven criminals?

ibid.

7 Here is a pen and here is a pencil,
Here's a typewriter, here's a stencil,
Here is a list of today's appointments,
And all the flies in all the ointments,
The daily woes that a man endures –
Take them, George, they're yours!

'Let George Do It, If You Can Find Him', publ. in ibid.

8 If you are really Master of your Fate,
It shouldn't make any difference to you whether Cleopatra or the Bearded Lady is your mate.

'The Anatomy of Happiness', publ. in *I'm a Stranger Here Myself* (1938)

9 The most exciting happiness is the happiness generated by forces beyond your control.

ibid.

10 I think remorse ought to stop biting the consciences that feed it.

'A Clean Conscience Never Relaxes', publ. in ibid.

11 Every Englishman is convinced of one thing, viz.:
That to be an Englishman is to belong to the most exclusive club there is.

'England Expects', publ. in ibid.

12 How easy for those who do not bulge
To not overindulge!

'A Necessary Dirge', publ. in ibid.

13 Whether elected or appointed
He considers himself the Lord's anointed,
And indeed the ointment lingers on him
So thick you can't get your fingers on him.

'The Politician', publ. in ibid.

14 I do not like to get the news, because there has never been an era when so many things were going so right for so many of the wrong persons.

'Everybody Tells Me Everything', publ. in *The Face is Familiar* (1940)

15 And one of his partners asked 'Has he vertigo?' and the other glanced out and down and said 'Oh no, only about ten feet more.'

'Mr Artesian's Conscientiousness', publ. in ibid.

16 I have a bone to pick with Fate.
Come here and tell me, girlie,
Do you think my mind is maturing late,
Or simply rotted early?

'Lines on Facing Forty', publ. in *Good Intentions* (1942)

17 The further through life I drift
The more obvious it becomes that I am lacking in thrift.

'A Penny Saved is Impossible from Good Intentions', publ. in ibid.

18 You scour the Bowery, ransack the Bronx,
Through funeral parlors and honky-tonks.
From river to river you comb the town
For a place to lay your family down.

'Nature Abhors a Vacancy', publ. in *Versus* (1949)

19 Indoors or out, no one relaxes
In March, that month of wind and taxes,
The wind will presently disappear,
The taxes last us all the year.

'Thar She Blows', publ. in ibid.

20 Your hair may be brushed, but your mind's untidy,
You've had about seven hours' sleep since Friday,
No wonder you feel that lost sensation;

You're sunk from a riot of relaxation.

'We'll All Feel Better By Wednesday', publ. in ibid.

21 **A door is what a dog is perpetually on the wrong side of.**

'A Dog's Best Friend is his Illiteracy', publ. in *The Private Dining Room* (1953)

22 **Good wine needs no bush,**
**And perhaps products that people really want need no**
**hard-sell or soft-sell TV push.**
**Why not?**
**Look at pot.**

'Most Doctors Recommend or Yours For Fast Fast Fast Relief ', publ. in *The Old Dog Barks Backwards* (1972)

## Paul Nash (1889–1946)
BRITISH ARTIST

He was the official war artist of both world wars and remembered above all for the Cubist-influenced 'The Menin Road' (1918), and 'Totes Meer' ('Dead Sea', 1940–41).

1 **I am no longer an artist, interested and curious. I am a**
**messenger who will bring back word from the men who**
**are fighting to those who want the war to go on for ever.**
**Feeble, inarticulate, will be my message, but it will have a**
**bitter truth, and may it burn their lousy souls.**

Letter to his wife, 13 November 1917, publ. in *Outline: An Autobiography and Other Writings* (1949)

## Taslima Nasreen (b. 1962)
BANGLADESHI AUTHOR

Dubbed 'the female Salman Rushdie', she came to international notice when her novel *Shame* (1993), an account of the persecution of Muslim women, led to death threats from Islamic fundamentalists and forced her into exile. Her novel *My Childhood Days* was banned by the Bangladeshi government in 1999.

1 **Our religion doesn't give women any human dignity.**
**Women are considered slaves . . . I write against the re-**
**ligion because if women want to live like human beings,**
**they will have to live outside the religion and Islamic law.**

*The Times* 22 June 1994

## George Jean Nathan (1882–1958)
US EDITOR AND CRITIC

Said to be the highest paid drama critic ever, he co-edited the magazine *Smart Set* with H.L. MENCKEN and in 1924 founded with Mencken the *American Mercury*, to which he contributed (1924–30 and 1940–51). He also wrote plays and edited the annual *Theatre Book of the Year* (1943–51). GEORGE BERNARD SHAW wrote to him: 'I . . . rank you as Intelligent Reader and Playgoer Number One.'

1 **The aim of great drama is not to make men happy with**
**themselves as they are, but with themselves as they might,**
**yet alas cannot, be.**

*The Critic and the Drama*, ch. 2, sect. 1 (1922)

2 **In the words of a friend of mine, I drink to make other**
**people interesting.**

*The Autobiography of an Attitude*, 'On Alcohol' (1925). The joke is usually ascribed to Nathan himself.

3 **To speak of morals in art is to speak of legislature in sex.**
**Art is the sex of the imagination.**

*American Mercury* July 1926, repr. in *The World of George Jean Nathan* (ed. Charles S. Angoff, 1998)

4 **All criticism, after all, is a criticism of the critic himself**
**before it is one of the criticized.**

*Art of the Night*, 'Advice to a Young Critic', no. 18 (1928)

5 **The test of a real comedian is whether you laugh at him**
**before he opens his mouth.**

*American Mercury* September 1929, repr. in *The World of George Jean Nathan* (ed. Charles S. Angoff, 1998)

6 **All really great drama is a form of scandal.**

ibid.

## Terry Nation (1930–97)
BRITISH SCREENWRITER

He began as a stand-up comedian but made his reputation as the creator of science fiction adventures on TV, notably the BBC series *Doctor Who* (1963–89). He was also the originator of the series *Survivors* (1975–7) and *Blake's Seven* (1978–81).

1 **We are the daleks! Exterminate! Exterminate!**

The Daleks, in *Doctor Who* (BBC television serial, 1963–89)

## Yitzhak Navon (b. 1921)
ISRAELI POLITICIAN AND PRESIDENT

Having served as a Deputy in the Knesset (1965–78), he spent five years as Israeli President and after 1984 was Deputy Prime Minister and Minister of Education and Culture in the national unity government. He is also known for his writings and television programmes on the Sephardi communities in Spain and in Jerusalem.

1 **It's not that I don't have opinions, rather that I'm paid**
**not to think aloud.**

Quoted in the *Observer* 16 January 1983

## Martina Navratilova (b. 1956)
CZECH-BORN US TENNIS PLAYER

The dominant woman player of the 1980s, she won a record nine Wimbledon singles titles. She retired from competitive singles tennis in 1994 and has been outspoken on a number of issues, including gay and animal rights and the status of women in tennis.

1 **I'm not just involved in tennis but committed. Do you**
**know the difference between involvement and commit-**
**ment? Think of ham and eggs. The chicken is involved.**
**The pig is committed.**

Quoted in the *International Herald Tribune* 3 September 1982

2 **I came to live in a country I love; some people label me a**
**defector. I have loved men and women in my life; I've**
**been labelled 'the bisexual defector' in print. Want to**
**know another secret? I'm even ambidextrous. I don't like**
**labels. Just call me Martina.**

*Martina Navratilova – Being Myself*, ch. 1 (1985)

3 **The moment of victory is much too short to live for that**
**and nothing else.**

*Guardian* 21 June 1989

## Jawaharlal Nehru (1889–1964)
INDIAN POLITICIAN AND PRIME MINISTER

Known as 'Pandit' ('Teacher') Nehru. Leader of the socialist wing of the Indian National Congress, he spent a total of eighteen years in prison, although he was still able to play a prominent part in achieving Indian independence in 1947. As the country's first prime minister, a position he held until his death, he pursued a policy of non-alignment and reached a settlement with Pakistan over Kashmir. He was the father of INDIRA GANDHI.

1 **The British Government in India is like a tooth that is**
**decaying but is still strongly embedded. It is painful, but**
**it cannot be easily pulled out.**

*Towards Freedom* (1935)

2 At the stroke of the midnight hour, while the world sleeps, India will awake to life and freedom.

Speech to Indian Assembly, 14 August 1947, quoted in *Freedom at Midnight*, Preface (1975) by Larry Collins and Dominique LaPierre. Spoken on the eve of independence.

3 [Following Gandhi's assassination] The light has gone out of our lives and there is darkness everywhere and I do not quite know what to tell you and how to say it. Our beloved leader, Bapu as we call him, the father of the nation, is no more.

Broadcast on All-India Radio, 30 January 1948, quoted in *The Life of Mahatma Gandhi*, ch. 1 (1951) by Louis Fischer. GANDHI was assassinated by a Hindu separatist, an event that provoked nation-wide rioting.

4 I shall be the last Englishman to rule in India.

Quoted in *A Life in Our Times*, ch. 26 (1981) by J.K. Galbraith. Nehru spent the years 1905–12 in England: at Harrow School and Trinity College, Cambridge, and at the Inner Temple, London, where he qualified as a barrister.

## Andrew Neil (b. 1949)

BRITISH JOURNALIST AND EDITOR

Appointed Editor of the *Sunday Times* by RUPERT MURDOCH in 1983, he modernized the paper and gave it a marked Thatcherite political stance. He has been a freelance writer, since 1996 Editor-in-chief and since 1999 Publisher of Press Holdings. He has appeared regularly on television.

1 Our establishment has presided over economic decline and bequeathed a culture of mediocrity. Why join a bunch of losers?

*Evening Standard* 26 May 1993

## Paula Nelson (b. 1945)

US BUSINESS EXECUTIVE

An author of financial self-help books, she has published *The Joy of Money* (1975), a guide to women's financial freedom, and *Paula Nelson's Guide to Getting Rich* (1986).

1 Americans want action for their money. They are fascinated by its self-reproducing qualities if it's put to work . . . Gold-hoarding goes against the American grain; it fits in better with European pessimism than with America's traditional optimism.

*The Joy of Money*, ch. 15 (1975)

## Richard Nelson (b. 1950)

US PLAYWRIGHT

The clash of personal beliefs with political ideologies is the theme of many of his plays, which include *Conjuring an Event* (performed 1976), *Jungle Coup* (1978) and *Principia Scriptoriae* (1986). He has also translated and adapted works.

1 If you take away ideology, you are left with a case by case ethics which in practice ends up as me first, me only, and in rampant greed.

*Independent* 12 July 1989

## Willie Nelson (b. 1933)

US SINGER AND SONGWRITER

Already successful as a songwriter in Nashville, he cut his first LP in 1962, though had greater success with his records in the 1970s, notably *Red Headed Stranger* (1975), by which time he was a famous exponent of the alternative 'outlaw' style of country music. He has also acted in films, including *Honeysuckle Rose* (1980).

1 I'm a country songwriter and we write cry-in-your-beer songs. That's what we do. Something that you can slow dance to.

Interview in the *Independent* 11 May 1996

## Howard Nemerov (1920–91)

US POET, NOVELIST AND CRITIC

His poetry, which takes in nature and philosophical issues, has been likened to that of ROBERT FROST. He has also written novels, such as *The Melodramatist* (1949), and works of criticism. JOYCE CAROL OATES called him unclassifiable, being a 'romantic, realist, comedian, satirist, relentless and indefatigable brooder upon the most ancient mysteries'. His *Collected Poems* (1977) won the Pulitzer Prize, and he was US Poet Laureate in 1988–90.

1 And I speak to you now with the land's voice,
It is the cold wild land that says to you
A knowledge glimmers in the sleep of things:
The old hills hunch before the north wind blows.

'A Spell before Winter', publ. in *Collected Poems* (1977)

2 The only way out is the way through, just as you cannot escape from death except by dying. Being unable to write, you must examine in writing this being unable, which becomes for the present – henceforth? – the subject to which you are condemned.

*Journal of the Fictive Life*, 'Reflexions of the Novelist Felix Ledger', sect. B (1965)

3 Obvious enough that generalities work to protect the mind from the great outdoors; is it possible that this was in fact their first purpose?

ibid. sect. C

4 I've never read a political poem that's accomplished anything. Poetry makes things happen, but rarely what the poet wants.

*International Herald Tribune* 14 October 1988. See also W.H. AUDEN 17.

## Pablo Neruda (1904–73)

CHILEAN POET AND DIPLOMAT

Born Ricardo Eliezer Neftalí Reyes, he took his pseudonym from the nineteenth-century Czech poet Jan Neruda. He was well known for his *Twenty Love Poems and a Song of Despair* (1924) before serving as a diplomat and Senator (1927–48). His major work, the epic *General Song* (1950), was a wide-ranging hymn to Latin America. GARCIA LORCA called him 'a poet closer to death than to philosophy, closer to pain than to insight, closer to blood than to ink'. He was awarded the Nobel Prize for Literature in 1971.

1 If you should ask me where I've been all this time
I have to say 'Things happen'.

'There is No Forgetting: Sonata' (1935), repr. in *Selected Poems* (ed. Nathaniel Tarn, 1970). Opening lines of poem.

2 The dark of a day gone by
Grown fat on our grieving blood.

ibid.

3 Night, snow, and sand make up the form
of my thin country,
all silence lies in its long line,
all foam flows from its marine beard,
all coal covers it with mysterious kisses.
Gold burns in its fingers like an ember
and silver illuminates like a green moon
its thickened shadow of a sullen planet.

'Discoverers of Chile' (1950), repr. in ibid.

4 Many of the creative spirits of our time do not realize that what seems to them to be the deepest expression of their being is often deadly poison injected into them by their

most implacable enemies. Dying capitalism is filling the cup of human creation.

'Our Duty Toward Life', publ. in *Let the Rail Splitter Awake and Other Poems* (1950)

5  No one can claim the name of Pedro,
nobody is Rosa or Maria,
all of us are dust or sand,
all of us are rain under rain.
They have spoken to me of Venezuelas,
of Chiles and Paraguays;
I have no idea what they are saying.
I know only the skin of the earth
and I know it has no name.

'Too Many Names' (1958), repr. in *Selected Poems* (ed. Nathaniel Tarn, 1970)

6  The word
was born in the blood,
grew in the dark body, beating,
And flew through the lips and the mouth.

'The Word' (1962), repr. in ibid. Opening lines of poem.

7  And it was at that age . . . Poetry arrived
in search of me. I don't know, I don't know where
it came from, from winter or a river.
I don't know how or when,
no, they were not voices, they were not
words, nor silence,
but from the street I was summoned,
from the branches of night,
abruptly from the others,
among violent fires
or returning alone,
there I was without a face
and it touched me.

'Poetry' (1964), repr. in ibid. The words appeared at the end of *Il Postino*, the 1994 film by Michael Radford that related Neruda's exile on an Italian island.

8  As for me, I am – or think I am – hard-nosed, small-eyed, sparse of hair, swollen in the abdomen, long-legged, broad-footed, yellow-complexioned, generous in love, impossible at figures, confused by words, tender-handed, slow-walking, pure-hearted, fond of stars and tides and swells, an admirer of beetles, a walker of sands, institutionally dull, perpetually Chilean, friend to my friends, silent to my enemies, meddlesome among birds, bad-mannered at home, timid in gatherings, daring in solitude, repentant without reason . . . persistently in disorder, brave out of necessity, a coward without guilt, lazy by vocation, loveable to women, congenitally active, a poet by curse, and a first-rate fool.

'Panorama' publ. in *Defectos escogidos* (1973), quoted in *Neruda: An Intimate Biography*, pt 8, sect. 182 (1985) by Volodia Teitelboim

9  I can live only in my own country. I cannot live without having my feet and my hands on it and my ear against it, without feeling the movement of its waters and its shadows, without feeling my roots reach down into its soil for maternal nourishment.

*Memoirs*, ch. 8 (1974). Referring to his work and travels abroad in 1940–43.

10  Using language like clothes or the skin on your body, with its sleeves, its patches, its transpirations, and its blood and sweat stains, that's what shows a writer's mettle. This is style.

ibid. ch. 11

11  Latin America is very fond of the word 'hope'. We like to be called the 'continent of hope'. Candidates for deputy, senator, president, call themselves 'candidates of hope'. This hope is really something like a promise of heaven, an IOU whose payment is always being put off. It is put

off until the next legislative campaign, until next year, until the next century.

ibid.

12  The human crowd has been the lesson of my life. I can come to it with the born timidity of the poet, with the fear of the timid, but once I am in its midst, I feel transfigured. I am part of the essential majority, I am one more leaf on the great human tree.

ibid.

## Rabbi Julia Neuberger (b. 1950)
BRITISH RABBI, WRITER AND BROADCASTER

The first female rabbi in Britain, and respected for her liberal views, she is associated with the hospice movement and in 1993 became Chancellor of the University of Ulster, only the second non-royal woman to hold such a post in the UK.

1  We don't like children much. We tend to fear our young.

Quoted in the *Daily Telegraph* 21 October 1995

## Richard Neville (b. 1941)
AUSTRALIAN JOURNALIST

He co-founded *Oz* in 1963 and after moving to England in 1966 started the English counterpart. In 1971 he was charged with publishing a magazine likely 'to corrupt public morals' and spent fifteen months in prison. Since 1979 he has been a journalist and broadcaster in Australia.

1  Is marijuana addictive? Yes, in the sense that most of the really pleasant things in life are worth endlessly repeating.

*Playpower*, 'Johnny Pot Wears Gold Sandals and a Black Derby Hat' (1971)

## Andrea Newman (b. 1938)
BRITISH AUTHOR

Her novels, which describe the cut and thrust of personal relationships, include *A Bouquet of Barbed Wire* (1969, televised 1976), *A Gift of Poison* (1991) and *A Share of the World* (1992).

1  I love the male body, it's better designed than the male mind.

*Today* 30 September 1988

## Barnett Newman (1905–70)
US ARTIST

Originally Baruch Newman. In 1948 he was one of the founders of the 'Subject of the Artist' school in New York. In the same year he painted 'Onement I', the first of his 'zip paintings' in which a single stripe bisects a solid field of colour. He is also known for the 'Stations of the Cross' series, exhibited in 1966.

1  The human in language is literature, not communication. Man's first cry was a song. Man's first address to a neighbor was a cry of power and solemn weakness, not a request for a drink of water.

'The First Man Was an Artist', publ. in *Tiger's Eye* October 1947, repr. in *Art in Theory*, pt 5A (ed. Charles Harrison and Paul Wood, 1992)

## News of the World

1  All human life is there.

Slogan from the 1950s. The words were possibly derived from HENRY JAMES, 'Cats and monkeys, monkeys and cats – all human life is there!', in his short story 'The Madonna of the Future' (1873).

## Ngo Dinh Diem (1901–63)

VIETNAMESE POLITICIAN

He became Prime Minister in 1954 under Emperor Bao Dai, whom he ousted in 1955, establishing himself as President of the newly declared Republic of Vietnam (South Vietnam). His nepotism, promotion of fellow Roman Catholics and suppression of communists led to the withdrawal of US support and an eventual military coup in which he was assassinated.

1 Follow me if I advance! Kill me if I retreat! Revenge me if I die!

On becoming President of Vietnam in 1954, reported in *Time* magazine 8 November 1963. The same exhortation had been used by MUSSOLINI to his officers after an attempt on his life.

## Jack Nicholson (b. 1937)

US SCREEN ACTOR

Known for his roguish parts, he rose to fame as the wired lawyer in *Easy Rider* (1969) and has since appeared in numerous films, including *One Flew Over the Cuckoo's Nest* (1975) and *Terms of Endearment* (1983), for which he won Academy Awards.

1 I mean, it's real hard to be free when you're bought and sold in the market-place.

George Hanson ( Jack Nicholson), in *Easy Rider* (film, 1969, written by DENNIS HOPPER, Peter Fonda and Terry Southern, directed by Dennis Hopper)

2 All work and no play makes Jack a dull boy.

Jack Torrance ( Jack Nicholson), in *The Shining* (film, 1980, screenplay by Stanley Kubrick and Diane Johnson, produced and directed by Stanley Kubrick). The proverb typed by Nicholson covers the pages of the manuscript he is supposed to be working on.

3 Americans don't like sexual movies – they like sexy movies.

*Rolling Stone* March 1984

4 Our generation are the new old. I remember what someone of 60 looked like when I was a kid. They didn't look like me.

Quoted in the *Daily Telegraph* 21 February 1998

5 There's so much darn porn, I never get out of the house.

Quoted in the *Sunday Times* 7 March 1999. On why he is giving up using the Internet.

## Jack Nicklaus (b. 1940)

US GOLFER

Nicknamed the 'Golden Bear', he has won eighteen professional major titles (1962–86), which constitutes a world record. He has also designed and built golf courses.

1 The older you get the stronger the wind gets – and it's always in your face.

Quoted in the *International Herald Tribune* 28 February 1990. Said on his fiftieth birthday.

## (Sir) Harold Nicolson (1886–1968)

BRITISH DIPLOMAT AND AUTHOR

He held a variety of diplomatic posts until 1929, when he took up a journalist career. His publications include biographies of LORD CURZON (1934) and GEORGE V (1952) as well as books on politics, although he is best remembered for his *Diaries and Letters 1930–62* (1968). He was the husband of VITA SACKVILLE-WEST.

1 We shall have to walk and live a Woolworth life hereafter.

Journal entry 4 June 1941, publ. in *Diaries and Letters 1939–45* (ed. Nigel Nicolson, 1967). On post-Second World War Britain.

2 God how I loathe these communists! My hatred for Mussolini was just a passing dislike, my fear of Hitler but a momentary apprehension, compared to my deep and burning detestation of the Marxists.

Letter to his wife, VITA SACKVILLE-WEST, 25 September 1947, publ. in *Diaries and Letters 1945–62* (ed. Nigel Nicolson, 1968)

## Reinhold Niebuhr (1892–1971)

US THEOLOGIAN AND HISTORIAN

He was a Lutheran pastor before becoming an influential teacher at the Union Theological Seminary, New York (1928–60). Adopting the principles of Christian Realism, he worked to obtain social justice from within the Socialist and subsequently Democratic parties. Among his many works are *Moral Man and the Immoral Society* (1932) and *The Nature and Destiny of Man* (two volumes, 1941–3).

1 A wise architect observed that you could break the laws of architectural art provided you had mastered them first. That would apply to religion as well as to art. Ignorance of the past does not guarantee freedom from its imperfections.

Entry 1928 in *Leaves from the Notebook of a Tamed Cynic* (1930)

2 Life is a battle between faith and reason in which each feeds upon the other, drawing sustenance from it and destroying it.

ibid.

3 Man's capacity for justice makes democracy possible, but man's inclination to injustice makes democracy necessary.

*The Children of Light and the Children of Darkness*, Foreword (1944)

4 O God, give us serenity to accept what cannot be changed, courage to change what should be changed, and wisdom to distinguish the one from the other.

'Serenity Prayer', attributed to Niebuhr in *Courage to Change* (1961) by June Bingham. The prayer, which exists in varying forms, has been used by Alcoholics Anonymous since the 1940s. Niebuhr said: 'It may have been spooking around for years, even centuries, but I don't think so. I honestly do believe that I wrote it myself.' However, claims have been made of previous versions from both fourteenth-century England and eighteenth-century Germany.

## Martin Niemöller (1892–1984)

GERMAN PROTESTANT PASTOR AND THEOLOGIAN

A submarine commander in the First World War, he was ordained a Protestant pastor in 1924 and became an outspoken critic of the Nazis for which he spent time in concentration camps (1937–45). In 1945 he was responsible for the Evangelical Church's 'Stuttgart Confession of Guilt' for not opposing Hitler more forcefully. He served as President of the World Council of Churches in 1961–8.

1 When Hitler attacked the Jews . . . I was not a Jew, therefore, I was not concerned. And when Hitler attacked the Catholics, I was not a Catholic, and therefore, I was not concerned. And when Hitler attacked the unions and the industrialists, I was not a member of the unions and I was not concerned. Then, Hitler attacked me and the Protestant church – and there was nobody left to be concerned.

Attributed. The original passage has never been traced.

## Anaïs Nin (1903–77)

FRENCH-BORN US NOVELIST AND DIARIST

She was known principally for her journals (seven volumes, 1966–80), a chronicle of avant-garde society in Paris and New York as well as a penetrating and frank self-exploration. Her fiction, which reflects her interest in dreams and psychoanalysis, includes the short stories *Under a Glass Bell* (1948) and the novels *House of Incest* (1936) and *Collages* (1964).

1 Woman does not forget she needs the fecundator, she

does not forget that everything that is born of her is planted in her.

Journal entry August 1937, publ. in *The Diary of Anaïs Nin*, vol. 2 (1967)

2 Electric flesh-arrows . . . traversing the body. A rainbow of color strikes the eyelids. A foam of music falls over the ears. It is the gong of the orgasm.

ibid. October 1937

3 The violence and obscenity are left unadulterated, as manifestation of the mystery and pain which ever accompanies the act of creation.

Preface to *Tropic of Cancer* (1934) by HENRY MILLER

4 I stopped loving my father a long time ago. What remained was the slavery to a pattern.

*Under a Glass Bell*, 'Birth' (1948)

5 I never liked the language of Henry Miller. I don't think pornography has added to our sensual life.

Quoted in *The Times* 1 June 1970. Nin had a ten-year relationship with Miller in France and America.

# Richard Nixon (1913–92)

US POLITICIAN AND PRESIDENT

As Republican President (1969–74) he oversaw US withdrawal from Vietnam and the resumption of diplomatic relations with China. In 1974 he became the first and only US president to resign, to save himself from impeachment in the wake of the Watergate scandal. He was given a full pardon by GERALD FORD in the same year. See also ADLAI STEVENSON 9, HUNTER S. THOMPSON 1.

1 Once you get into this great stream of history you can't get out. You can drown. Or you can be pulled ashore by the tide. But it is awfully hard to get out when you are in the middle of the stream – if it is intended that you stay there.

Quoted in *Richard Nixon: A Political and Personal Portrait*, ch. 10 (1959) by Earl Mazo. On revoking his decision to retire in 1954.

2 The one thing sure about politics is that what goes up comes down and what goes down often comes up.

Quoted in ibid. ch. 17

3 A public man must never forget that he loses his usefulness when he as an individual, rather than his policy, becomes the issue.

*Life* 8 June 1959. The remark appeared in a tribute to JOHN FOSTER DULLES on his death. Dulles, Nixon asserted, recognized this 'fundamental truth'.

4 The more you stay in this kind of job, the more you realize that a public figure, a major public figure, is a lonely man.

Interview when Vice-president, quoted in *Nixon and Rockefeller: A Double Portrait*, 'A Talk with Nixon' (1960) by Stewart Alsop

5 The easiest period in a crisis situation is actually the battle itself. The most difficult is the period of indecision – whether to fight or run away. And the most dangerous period is the aftermath. It is then, with all his resources spent and his guard down, that an individual must watch out for dulled reactions and faulty judgment.

*Six Crises*, Introduction (1962). 'Crisis can indeed be an agony,' Nixon observed. 'But it is the exquisite agony which a man might not want to experience again – yet would not for the world have missed.'

6 As I leave you I want you to know – just think how much you're going to be missing. You won't have Nixon to kick around any more because, gentlemen, this is my last press conference.

Press conference, 5 November 1962, quoted in *The New York Times* 8 November 1962, following defeat in the California gubernatorial election

7 The Cold War isn't thawing; it is burning with a deadly heat. Communism isn't sleeping; it is, as always, plotting, scheming, working, fighting.

'Cuba, Castro and John F. Kennedy', publ. in *Reader's Digest* November 1964

8 Let us begin by committing ourselves to the truth, to see it like it is and tell it like it is, to find the truth, to speak the truth and to live the truth.

Speech accepting the Republican presidential nomination, 8 August 1968, Miami, quoted in *The New York Times* 9 August 1968

9 This is the greatest week in the history of the world since the Creation, because as a result of what happened in this week, the world is bigger, infinitely.

Remarks on USS *Hornet*, 24 July 1969, welcoming back the crew of Apollo 11 four days after the first moon-landing, quoted in *Nixon: The Triumph of a Politician*, vol. 2, ch. 13 (1989) by Stephen Ambrose. A few days later, Ambrose relates, the evangelist Billy Graham mentioned three greater days: Christ's birth, Christ's death and Christ's resurrection. Nixon's scribbled response was: 'tell Billy RN referred to a *week* not *a day*.'

10 Let us understand: North Vietnam cannot defeat or humiliate the United States. Only Americans can do that.

Television address, 3 November 1969, quoted in ibid. ch. 14. In his *Memoirs*, Nixon commented: 'Very few speeches actually influence the course of history. The November 3 speech was one of them.'

11 Expletive deleted.

Taped transcripts of conversations September 1972–April 1973, publ. in *The Presidential Transcripts* (1974). The tapes, which were played for the judicial committee of the House of Representatives 30 April 1974, were edited transcripts of meetings between Nixon and his advisers in the Oval Office over a period of seven months. Public reaction seemed more shocked by the sleazy language used by the President and his inner circle than by the revelations of Nixon appearing to condone corrupt practices. The first recorded meeting took place between Nixon, H.R. HALDEMAN and John Dean on 15 September 1972, when Nixon, referring to a bug that Dean had found in a telephone at the Watergate Building, declared: '[expletive deleted] do they really want to believe that we planted that?'

12 [On Watergate] There can be no whitewash at the White House.

Television address, 30 April 1973, quoted in *The New York Times* 1 May 1973. In July 1972 agents of Nixon's re-election committee were arrested in the Democratic Party headquarters after an attempt to tap telephones there, of which Nixon denied all knowledge.

13 I welcome this kind of examination because people have got to know whether or not their President is a crook. Well, I'm not a crook.

Press conference, 17 November 1973, publ. in *The New York Times* 18 November 1973

14 Defeat doesn't finish a man – quit does. A man is not finished when he's defeated. He's finished when he quits.

Note written with reference to Edward Kennedy and the Chappaquiddick Bridge incident, July 1969, quoted in *Before the Fall*, pt 3, ch. 4 (1975) by WILLIAM SAFIRE

15 When the President does it, that means that it is not illegal.

TV interview with DAVID FROST, 20 May 1977, publ. in *I Gave Them a Sword*, ch. 8 (1978) by David Frost

16 Castro couldn't even go to the bathroom unless the Soviet Union put the nickel in the toilet.

Remark to interviewer September 1980, quoted in *Exile: The Unquiet Oblivion of Richard M. Nixon*, ch. 17 (1984) by Robert Sam Anson

17 No event in American history is more misunderstood than the Vietnam War. It was misreported then, and it is misremembered now.

'No More Vietnams', publ. in *The New York Times* 28 March 1985

18 Finishing second in the Olympics gets you silver. Finishing second in politics gets you oblivion.

Quoted in the *Sunday Times* 13 November 1988. On the defeat of Michael Dukakis by GEORGE BUSH in the presidential election.

19 I played by the rules of politics as I found them.
*The Times* 26 March 1990

## Kwame Nkrumah (1909–72)

GHANAIAN PRESIDENT

Called the 'Gandhi of Africa', he was the leader of the Gold Coast's struggle for independence, becoming Prime Minister of Ghana (1957–60), as it was renamed. As President (1960–66) he established an authoritarian regime, with one-party rule by the Convention People's Party, and aligned himself with the Soviet bloc. He was overthrown by a coup but was granted status as co-head of state in Guinea, where he remained in exile.

1 The best way of learning to be an independent sovereign state is to be an independent sovereign state.
Speech to Legislative Assembly, Accra, 18 May 1956, quoted in *Axioms of Kwame Nkrumah* (1967)

2 Revolutions are brought about by men, by men who think as men of action and act as men of thought.
*Consciencism*, ch. 2 (1964)

3 It is far easier for the proverbial camel to pass through the needle's eye, hump and all, than for an erstwhile colonial administration to give sound and honest counsel of a *political* nature to its liberated territory.
ibid. ch. 4

## (Sir) Sidney Nolan (1917–92)

AUSTRALIAN ARTIST

He is noted for his paintings of the Australian outback, most famously the 'Ned Kelly' series (1946), although he also painted subjects taken from his extensive travels and from the world of mythology, as in the 'Leda and the Swan' series.

1 When the critics come around it's always too late.
Quoted in the *Daily Telegraph* 15 September 1992

## Peggy Noonan (b. 1950)

US AUTHOR AND PRESIDENTIAL SPEECHWRITER

As a special assistant and speechwriter to RONALD REAGAN and GEORGE BUSH, she was valued for her memorable turns of phrase, often incorporating literary references in her speeches. 'A political speech is a soliloquy,' she said, 'a moment of prepared self-revelation that has no equal.' She published her memoirs in *What I Saw at the Revolution* (1990). See also GEORGE BUSH 7.

1 You don't have to be old in America to say of a world you lived in, That world is gone.
*What I Saw at the Revolution*, ch. 1 (1990)

2 A speech is poetry: cadence, rhythm, imagery, sweep! A speech reminds us that words, like children, have the power to make dance the dullest beanbag of a heart.
ibid. ch. 5

3 The battle for the mind of Ronald Reagan was like the trench warfare of World War I: Never have so many fought so hard for such barren terrain.
ibid. ch. 14

4 What did I learn in my time in government?
   If you join government, calmly make your contribution and move on. Don't go along to get along; do your best and when you have to – and you will – leave, and be something else.
   Don't fall in love with politicians, they're all a disappointment. They can't help it, they just are.
   Beware the politically obsessed. They are often bright and interesting, but they have something missing in their natures; there is a hole, an empty place, and they use politics to fill it up. It leaves them somehow misshapen.
ibid. 'Another Epilogue'

## Denis Norden (b. 1922)

BRITISH HUMORIST

With his long-standing partner FRANK MUIR he wrote extensively for BBC radio, for example *Take It From Here* (1947–58) and *Bedtime with Braden* (1950–54). He also appeared on radio and TV quiz shows and presented LWT's *It'll Be Alright on the Night* (1977–97).

1 It's a funny kind of month, October. For the really keen cricket fan it's when you discover that your wife left you in May.
*She* October 1977

## Edward Norman (b. 1938)

BRITISH ECCLESIASTIC AND ACADEMIC

He was Dean of Peterhouse, Cambridge (1971–88), and Canon Residentiary (from 1995) and Chancellor (since 1999) at York Minster. His publications include *Church and Society in Modern England* (1976) and *Entering the Darkness: Christianity and its Modern Substitutes* (1991).

1 Many are called but few are chosen. There are sayings of Christ which suggest that the Church he came to establish will always be a minority affair.
*The Times* 20 February 1992

## Philip Norman (b. 1943)

BRITISH AUTHOR AND JOURNALIST

Joining the *Sunday Times* in 1965, he built a reputation for his 'Atticus' column and as an interviewer. He is also known for his rock biographies of the Beatles (*Shout*, 1981), the Rolling Stones (*Symphony for the Devil*, 1984) and Elton John (*Elton*, 1991), among other subjects.

1 [Of KEITH RICHARDS] That the public can grow accustomed to any face is proved by the increasing prevalence of Keith's ruined physiognomy on TV documentaries and chat shows, as familiar and homely a horror as Grandpa in *The Munsters*.
*The Life and Good Times of the Rolling Stones*, Introduction (1989). Richards, Norman wrote, 'is as endearing a personality as ever lurked within the aspect of Count Dracula on a bad morning. Who, looking into that grave-hollowed face, would ever suspect quick wit, authentic humour or the boozy, affectionate voice of some old-time theatrical actor-manager?'

## Oliver North (b. 1943)

US MARINE OFFICER

He was appointed by RONALD REAGAN to the staff of the National Security Council in 1981 as Deputy Director for Political Military Affairs. Allegations relating to his part in the Iran-Contra affair, whereby funds from arms sales to Iran were transferred to Contra guerrillas in Nicaragua, caused his resignation in 1986. He successfully appealed against his conviction, and in 1991 all charges were dropped.

1 I'm trusting in the Lord and a good lawyer.
Quoted in the *Observer* 7 December 1986. On investigations into the Iran-Contra scandal.

## Ivor Novello (1893–1951)

WELSH ACTOR, COMPOSER AND PLAYWRIGHT

Original name David Ivor Davies. His song 'Keep the Home Fires Burning' (see LENA GUILBERT FORD 1) became one of the most popular songs of the First World War. During the 1920s and 1930s he combined careers as actor-manager and composer, and later acquired matinée idol status in such romantic musical shows as *Crest of a Wave* (1937) and *Perchance to Dream* (1945).

1 There's something Vichy about the French.

Quoted by Edward Marsh in letter, March 1941, publ. in *Ambrosia and Small Beer*, ch. 4 (ed. Christopher Hassall, 1964)

## Trevor Nunn (b. 1940)

BRITISH STAGE DIRECTOR

Artistic Director of the Royal Shakespeare Theatre Company (1968–87), he was responsible for two new theatres in Stratford, the Other Place (1974) and the Swan (1986). He has directed *Cats* (1981) and *Les Misérables* (1985), and in 1997 he was appointed Director of the Royal National Theatre.

1 Soundbite and slogan, strapline and headline: at every turn we meet hyperbole. The soaring inflation of the English language is more urgently in need of control than the economic variety.

*Independent* 6 June 1998

## Jeff Nuttall (b. 1933)

BRITISH POET, PAINTER AND MUSICIAN

Speaking of his contribution to the sex and drugs ethos of the 1960s, he said that it was to 'fertilize this very scorched earth for those yet to come'. His book *Bomb Culture* (1968) was one of the key works of that decade. He also wrote fiction, plays and poems, toured his own performance group and was a lecturer in fine arts.

1 [On post-1945 youth culture] Not one of us, no solitary one, had any serious political preoccupation or any belief in the changeability of society and events. No single solitary one amongst us had the slightest spark of hope or gave a damn about a thing except the crackling certainty of Now.

*Bomb Culture*, 'Pop', sect. 2 (1968)

2 What is missed by the mystics . . . is that there is a purpose, and a *divine* purpose, to the human alienation from the cosmos. The recognition, definition of Being, in wonderment and ecstasy can only be carried out by a conscious entity alienated from the eternal totality. You can't dig It if you *are* It. No man beholds his own face.

ibid. 'The Underground', sect. 4

## Julius Nyerere (b. 1922)

TANZANIAN PRESIDENT

From 1954 he organized the Tanganyika African National Union, becoming President of independent Tanganyika in 1962 and first President of Tanzania in 1964. His efforts to establish an African socialism failed, particularly in the aftermath of the war with Idi Amin's Uganda (1978–9), and he retired in 1985. 'The Prime Minister is like the great banyan tree,' remarked the politician Kanoji Patel. 'Thousands shelter beneath it, but nothing grows.'

1 When we were at school we were taught to sing the songs of the Europeans. How many of us were taught the songs of the Wanyamwezi or of the Wahehe? Many of us have learnt to dance the rumba, or the cha cha, to rock and roll and to twist and even to dance the waltz and foxtrot. But how many of us can dance, or have even heard of the gombe sugu, the mangala, nyang'umumi, kiduo, or lele mama?

*Tanzania National Assembly Official Reports* (1962), quoted in *African All-Stars*, pt 1 (1987) by Chris Stapleton and Chris May

2 Our mistake was in the assumption that freedom – real freedom – would necessarily and with little trouble follow liberation from alien rule . . . Our countries are effectively being governed by people who have only the most marginal interest in our affairs.

Quoted by CHRISTOPHER HILL in the *Guardian Weekly* 6 May 1984

## Ann Oakley (b. 1944)
BRITISH SOCIOLOGIST AND AUTHOR

Her non-fiction work focuses on the roles of housewives and mothers, as in *The Sociology of Housework* (1974) and *Becoming a Mother* (1979), while her best-known novel, *The Men's Room* (1988, televised 1991), is a steamy tale of academic adultery.

1 Clearly, society has a tremendous stake in insisting on a woman's natural fitness for the career of mother: the alternatives are all too expensive.
   *Woman's Work: The Housewife, Past and Present*, ch. 8 (1974)

2 Housework is work directly opposed to the possibility of human self-actualization.
   ibid. ch. 9

3 If love . . . means that one person absorbs the other, then no real relationship exists any more. Love evaporates; there is nothing left to love. The integrity of self is gone.
   *Taking It Like a Woman*, 'Love: Irresolution' (1984)

4 Families are nothing other than the idolatry of duty.
   ibid. 'The War Between Love and the Family II'

5 There are always women who will take men on their own terms. If I were a man I wouldn't bother to change while there are women like that around.
   Quoted in the *Observer* 27 October 1991

## Joyce Carol Oates (b. 1938)
US AUTHOR

Using a range of genres from Gothic horror fiction to social commentary, she exposes the violence and decay in American life in her depiction of 'the moral and social conditions of my generation'. Her novels include *Them* (1969), *Son of the Morning* (1978) and *A Bloodsmoor Romance* (1982). Later works include *On Boxing* (1987) and *Blonde* (2000), a work of fiction based on the life of MARILYN MONROE.

1 The worst cynicism: a belief in luck.
   *Do What You Will*, pt 2 ch. 15 (1970)

2 Nothing is accidental in the universe – this is one of my Laws of Physics – except the entire universe itself, which is Pure Accident, pure divinity.
   ibid. 'The Summing Up: Meredith Dawe'

3 It is not her body that he wants but it is only through her body that he can take possession of another human being, so he must labor upon her body, he must enter her body, to make his claim.
   *Unholy Loves*, 'In the Founders' Room' (1979)

4 Our enemy is by tradition our savior, in preventing us from superficiality.
   Quoting an aphorism, in 'Master Race', publ. in *Partisan Review 50th Anniversary Edition* (ed. William Phillips, 1985)

5 The television screen, so unlike the movie screen, sharply reduced human beings, revealed them as small, trivial, flat, in two banal dimensions, drained of color. Wasn't there something reassuring about it! – that human beings were in fact merely images of a kind registered in one another's eyes and brains, phenomena composed of microscopic flickering dots like atoms. They *were* atoms – nothing more. A quick switch of the dial and they disappeared and who could lament the loss?
   *You Must Remember This*, pt 1, ch. 13 (1987)

6 When you're 50 you start thinking about things you haven't thought about before. I used to think getting old was about vanity – but actually it's about losing people you love. Getting wrinkles is trivial.
   Interview in the *Guardian* 18 August 1989

## Conor Cruise O'Brien (b. 1917)

IRISH HISTORIAN, DIPLOMAT AND CRITIC

Once described by the *New Statesman* as 'a modern version of that nineteenth-century radical phenomenon, the Only White Man the Natives Trust', he published a powerful eyewitness account of the Congo crisis, *To Katanga and Back* (1962), and wrote about the death of Patrice Lumumba in his play *Murderous Angels* (1968). Elected to the Irish parliament in 1969, he was Minister for Communications in 1973 but lost his seat in 1977 after making forthright denunciations of IRA terrorism. He has been Editor-in-chief of London's *Observer* and is a regular commentator on international affairs.

1 Irishness is not primarily a question of birth or blood or language; it is the condition of being involved in the Irish situation, and usually of being mauled by it.

'Irishness', publ. in the *New Statesman* 17 January 1959, written as Donat O'Donnell

2 The United Nations cannot do anything, and never could; it is not an animate entity or agent. It is a place, a stage, a forum and a shrine . . . a place to which powerful people can repair when they are fearful about the course on which their own rhetoric seems to be propelling them.

*New Republic* 4 November 1985

3 Nothing does more to activate Christian divisions than talk about Christian unity.

*The Times* 3 October 1989

## Edna O'Brien (b. 1932)

IRISH AUTHOR

The typical O'Brien heroine seeks to escape a repressive upbringing but ends disillusioned, often as a result of failed relationships. Her novels, some of which were originally banned in Ireland for their treatment of sex, include *The Country Girls* (1960), *The Lonely Girl* (1962, filmed as *The Girl With Green Eyes*, 1963, scripted by her) and *A Pagan Place* (1970).

1 I am committing suicide through lack of intelligence, and through not knowing, not learning to know, how to live.

The narrator, Martha, in 'The Love Object', first publ. in the *New Yorker* (1963), repr. in *The Love Object* (1968)

2 After the rich, the most obnoxious people in the world are those who serve the rich.

Ellen, in *August Is a Wicked Month*, ch. 8 (1965)

3 Countries are either mothers or fathers, and engender the emotional bristle secretly reserved for either sire.

*Mother Ireland*, ch. 1 (1976)

4 Irish? In truth I would not want to be anything else. It is a state of mind as well as an actual country. It is being at odds with other nationalities, having a quite different philosophy about pleasure, about punishment, about life, and about death. At least it does not leave one pusillanimous.

ibid. ch. 7

5 Oh shadows of love, inebriations of love, foretastes of love, trickles of love, but never yet the one true love.

Narrator (Mary Hooligan), in *Night* (1972)

6 In every question and every remark tossed back and forth between lovers who have not played out the last fugue, there is one question and it is this: 'Is there someone new?'

*Lantern Slides*, 'Long Distance' (1990)

## Flann O'Brien (1911–66)

IRISH AUTHOR

Pseudonym of Brian O'Nolan. Influenced by JAMES JOYCE and encouraged by GRAHAM GREENE, he published the experimental *At Swim-Two-Birds* (1939) and *The Poor Mouth* (1941), the latter

originally written in Gaelic. His last novel, *The Third Policeman*, was published posthumously in 1967. As Myles na Gopaleen, he wrote a lively column for the *Irish Times* from 1940 until his death.

1 When money's tight and is hard to get
And your horse has also ran,
When all you have is a heap of debt –
A PINT OF PLAIN IS YOUR ONLY MAN.

*At Swim-Two-Birds*, ch. 1 (1939)

2 The gross and net result of it is that people who spent most of their natural lives riding iron bicycles over the rocky roadsteads of this parish get their personalities mixed up with the personalities of their bicycle as a result of the interchanging of the atoms of each of them and you would be surprised at the number of people in these parts who nearly are half people and half bicycles.

Sergeant, in *The Third Policeman*, ch. 6 (written 1940, publ. 1967)

## Sean O'Casey (1880–1964)

IRISH PLAYWRIGHT

Original name John Casey. Although his play-writing career spanned decades, it is for his early realist works documenting Ireland's troubled modern history that he is best remembered, notably *The Shadow of a Gunman* (1923), *Juno and the Paycock* (1924) and *The Plough and the Stars* (1926). *The Silver Tassie* (1929) was the first of his works to be rejected by Dublin's Abbey Theatre, provoking his move to England where he spent the rest of his life.

1 You cannot put a rope around the neck of an idea; you cannot put an idea up against a barrack-square wall and riddle it with bullets; you cannot confine it in the strongest prison cell that your slaves could ever build.

*The Story of Thomas Ashe*, ch. 4 (1917)

2 Th' whole worl's in a state o' chassis!

Jack Boyle, in *Juno and the Paycock*, act 1 and *passim* (1924). Also the last words of play.

3 As far as I can see, the Polis as Polis, in this city, is Null an' Void!

Mrs Madigan, in ibid. act 3. Referring to Dublin during the Irish Civil War in 1922.

4 There's no reason to bring religion into it. I think we ought to have as great a regard for religion as we can, so as to keep it out of as many things as possible.

Fluther Good, in *The Plough and the Stars*, act 1 (1926)

5 It's my rule never to lose me temper till it would be dethrimental to keep it.

ibid.

6 Work! Labour, the *aspergas me* of life; the one great sacrament of humanity from which all other things flow – security, leisure, joy, art, literature, even divinity itself.

*Rose and Crown*, 'In New York Now' (fifth volume of autobiography, 1952)

7 Wealth often takes away chances from men as well as poverty. There is none to tell the rich to go on striving, for a rich man makes the law that hallows and hollows his own life.

ibid. 'Pennsylvanian Visit'

8 Jesus, Buddha, Mahommed, great as each may be, their highest comfort given to the sorrowful is a cordial introduction into another's woe. Sorrow's the great community in which all men born of woman are members at one time or another.

ibid. 'Wild Life in New Amsterdam'

9 What time has been wasted during man's destiny in the struggle to decide what man's next world will be like! The keener the effort to find out, the less he knew about the present one he lived in.

*Sunset and Evening Star*, 'Shaw's Corner' (sixth volume of autobiography, 1954)

10 The flame from the angel's sword in the garden of Eden has been catalysted into the atom bomb; God's thunderbolt became blunted, so man's dunderbolt has become the steel star of destruction.

ibid. 'And Evening Star'

11 Here, with whitened hair, desires failing, strength ebbing out of him, with the sun gone down and with only the serenity and the calm warning of the evening star left to him, he drank to Life, to all it had been, to what it was, to what it would be. Hurrah!

ibid. Final paragraph of book.

12 Laughter is wine for the soul – laughter soft, or loud and deep, tinged through with seriousness . . . the hilarious declaration made by man that life is worth living.

*Green Crows*, 'Saturday Night' (1956)

13 Here we have bishops, priests, and deacons, a Censorship Board, vigilant librarians, confraternities and sodalities, Duce Maria, Legions of Mary, Knights of this Christian order and Knights of that one, all surrounding the sinner's free will in an embattled circle.

Letter to the *Irish Times* 8 June 1957

14 [Of JOHN F. KENNEDY's assassination] What a terrible thing has happened to us all! To you there, to us here, to all everywhere. Peace who was becoming bright-eyed, now sits in the shadow of death; her handsome champion has been killed as he walked by her very side. Her gallant boy is dead. What a cruel, foul, and most unnatural murder!

Letter to Mrs Rose Russell (leader of New York City Teachers Union), publ. in *The New York Times* 27 November 1963

## Flannery O'Connor (1925–64)
US AUTHOR

Raised a devout Roman Catholic in the predominantly Protestant fundamentalist South, she took as her main theme the nature of evil. Her 'Southern Gothic' novels and short stories, often peopled by the marginalized and the violent, include *Wise Blood* (1952) and *A Good Man is Hard to Find* (1955). Suffering from the disease lupus, she was an invalid from the age of twenty-five.

1 I preach there are all kinds of truth, your truth and somebody else's. But behind all of them there is only one truth and that is that there's no truth.

The preacher Hazel Motes, in *Wise Blood*, ch. 10 (1952)

2 Manners are of such great consequence to the novelist that any kind will do. Bad manners are better than no manners at all, and because we are losing our customary manners, we are probably overly conscious of them; this seems to be a condition that produces writers.

'The Fiction Writer and His Country', publ. in *The Living Novel: A Symposium* (ed. Granville Hicks, 1957)

3 I have found that anything that comes out of the South is going to be called grotesque by the Northern reader, unless it *is* grotesque, in which case it is going to be called realistic.

'Some Aspects of The Grotesque in Southern Fiction', lecture in Macon, Georgia, autumn 1960, first publ. 1965, repr. in *Mystery and Manners* (ed. Sally and Robert Fitzgerald, 1972)

4 While the South is hardly Christ-centered, it is most certainly Christ-haunted.

ibid.

5 Being a Georgia author is a rather specious dignity, on the same order as, for the pig, being a Talmadge ham.

'The Regional Writer', first publ. 1963, repr. in ibid.

6 It seems that the fiction writer has a revolting attachment to the poor, for even when he writes about the rich, he is more concerned with what they lack than with what they have.

'The Teaching of Literature', publ. in ibid.

## Sinéad O'Connor (b. 1966)
IRISH SINGER AND SONGWRITER

Described by the *New Musical Express* as 'the Johnny Rotten of the Eighties' for her rebellious, publicity conscious antics and voted both Best and Worst Female Artist in a *Rolling Stone* readers' poll in 1990, she had an international hit the same year with the Prince song 'Nothing Compares 2 U'. Her outspoken views on politics, women and the Pope (whose picture she tore up on prime-time television) kept her in the public eye during the 1990s, which ended with her embracing Christianity.

1 [On popular music] I believe our purpose is to inspire and guide the human race.

*Independent* 12 February 1991

2 Loneliness is a crowded room.

Interview in the *Observer* 13 September 1998

## Wendy O'Connor
KURT COBAIN'S MOTHER

1 [On her son's suicide] Now he's gone and joined that stupid club.

Quoted by TONY PARSONS in the *Daily Telegraph* 14 April 1994. Referring to the number of other deaths by young rock stars.

## Cristina Odone (b. 1960)
ITALIAN JOURNALIST AND AUTHOR

Having been Editor of the *Catholic Herald* (1992–6) and television critic for the *Daily Telegraph* (1996–8), she joined the *New Statesman* as Deputy Editor in 1998. She has also written novels, including *The Shrine* (1996) and *A Perfect Wife* (1997).

1 Catholicism is like a bowl of spaghetti, full of different strands. It is only if you eat them all together that it will do you any good.

*Independent* 21 October 1992

## Georgia O'Keeffe (1887–1986)
US ARTIST

A pioneer of American abstract art, she went on to produce more figurative work, often incorporating flowers, bones and rocks inspired by the desert landscape of New Mexico, as in *Black Iris* (1926) and *Cow's Skull, Red, White and Blue* (1931). She was married to photographer Alfred Stieglitz.

1 Marks on paper are free – free speech – press – pictures all go together I suppose.

Letter, 14 January 1916, quoted in *Portrait of an Artist*, ch. 3 (1986) by Laurie Lisle

2 Before I put a brush to canvas, I question, 'Is this mine? . . . Is it influenced by some idea which I have acquired from some man?' . . . I am trying with all my skill to do a painting that is all of women, as well as all of me.

Debate reported in *New York World* 16 March 1930, quoted in ibid. ch. 9

3 When you take a flower in your hand and really look at it, it's your world for the moment. I want to give that world to someone else. Most people in the city rush around so, they have no time to look at a flower. I want them to see it whether they want to or not.

*New York Post* 16 May 1946, quoted in ibid. ch. 6. Flowers were a favourite subject of O'Keeffe's.

4 I hate flowers – I paint them because they're cheaper than models and they don't move.

Quoted in the *New York Herald Tribune* 18 April 1954, repr. in ibid.

O'Keeffe was responding to the remark, 'How perfect to meet you with flowers in your hands!'

5 I don't very much enjoy looking at paintings in general. I know too much about them. I take them apart.

Quoted in the *San Francisco Examiner and Chronicle* 16 March 1971

## Ben Okri (b. 1959)
NIGERIAN AUTHOR

*The New York Times* likened his work to 'a continent dreamed up, in tandem, by Hieronymus Bosch and Jorge Luis Borges', although Okri himself describes it as 'a kind of realism, but a realism with many more dimensions'. Among his novels are the Booker Prize-winning *The Famished Road* (1991) and *Astonishing the Gods* (1995), while *An African Elegy* (1992) is a poetry collection.

1 The sun bared the reality of our lives and everything was so harsh it was a mystery that we could understand and care for one another or for anything at all.

*The Famished Road*, bk 2, ch. 10 (1991)

2 Many people have walked out of life because they stopped seeing it. Many have fallen into the abyss because they were looking for solid ground, for certainties. Happy are those who are still, and to whom things come.

ibid. bk 4, ch. 13

3 I think our childhood goes back thousands of years, farther back than the memory of any race.

*Astonishing the Gods*, bk 4, ch. 17 (1995)

4 Each moment offered us clarity and liberation but we settled for the comforting shapes of legends, no matter how monstrous or useless.

*Infinite Riches*, bk 1, ch. 11 (1998)

5 Suffering is an aspect of the great Promethean will, the thing in us which most makes the spirit wake up. Modern literature is the product of too much false suffering, too much false pain. Real suffering is like the dirt that miners dig up and carry away. It is necessary if we are to find the true gold that writers seek.

Quoted in the *Guardian* 21 August 1999

## Claes Oldenburg (b. 1929)
SWEDISH-BORN US ARTIST

A member of the Pop art movement, he began his 'happenings' in 1962, from which developed his giant soft sculptures of ordinary objects, such as food and light switches. His 'Colossal Monuments' include *Clothespin* in Philadelphia and *Colossal Ashtray with Fagends* at the Pompidou Centre in Paris.

1 I am for an art that is political-erotical-mystical, that does something other than sit on its ass in a museum.

I am for an art that grows up not knowing it is art at all, an art given the chance of having a starting point of zero.

I am for an art that employs itself with everyday crap and still comes out on top.

I am for an art that imitates the human, that is comic, if necessary, or violent, or whatever is necessary.

'I Am For an Art', catalogue for exhibition in New York, June 1961, repr. in *Store Days* (1966)

2 Basically collectors want nudes. So I have supplied for them nude cars, nude telephones, nude electric plugs, nude switches, nude fans, newd electretcetera and sew on.

Quoted in Moderna Museet Gallery catalogue, Stockholm, 1966, repr. in *Icons and Images of the Sixties*, 'Pop Art: Claes Oldenburg's Contented Objects' (1971) by Nicholas and Elena Calas

## (Sir) Laurence Olivier (1907–89)
BRITISH ACTOR AND DIRECTOR

Baron Olivier of Brighton. Often regarded as the greatest actor of his generation, he played all the major Shakespearian roles on the

stage and also starred in the films *Wuthering Heights* (1939), *Henry V* (1944) and *Hamlet* (1948, Academy Award), among many others. Married to actresses Vivien Leigh and Joan Plowright, he was the first director of the National Theatre (1963–73) and the first actor to be made a life peer (1970). An actor-manager of the old school, he famously advised DUSTIN HOFFMAN, his co-star in the film *Marathon Man* (1976) who insisted on staying awake for days on end in order to 'inhabit' his role, 'Why don't you try acting, dear boy – it's so much easier.'

1 Shakespeare – the nearest thing in incarnation to the eye of God.

*Kenneth Harris Talking To*, 'Sir Laurence Olivier' (1971)

2 Acting is a masochistic form of exhibitionism. It is not quite the occupation of an adult.

*Time* magazine 3 July 1978

## Charles Olson (1910–70)
US POET AND CRITIC

Spokesman of the Black Mountain Poets, he published the influential essay 'Projective Verse' (1950) in which he maintained that poetry should be dependent on the rhythms of breathing rather than rhyme and metre. He is also known for *The Maximus Poems* (1953–70) and a study of Herman Melville, *Call Me Ishmael* (1947).

1 I take SPACE to be the central fact to man born in America . . . I spell it large because it comes large here. Large and without mercy.

*Call Me Ishmael*, sect. 1 (1947)

2 Get on with it, keep moving, keep in, speed, the nerves, their speed, the perceptions, theirs, the acts, the split second acts, the whole business, keep it moving as fast as you can, citizen . . . So there we are, fast, there's the dogma.

'Projective Verse', first publ. in *Poetry New York* (1950), repr. in *Selected Writings of Charles Olson* (ed. Robert Creeley, 1951)

## Jacqueline Kennedy Onassis See JACQUELINE KENNEDY.

## Michael Ondaatje (b. 1943)
SRI LANKAN-BORN CANADIAN NOVELIST AND POET

He emigrated first to England and in 1962 to Canada. His poetry collections include *The Collected Works of Billy the Kid* (1970) and *There's a Trick with a Knife I'm Learning to Do* (1979), though he is best known for his novel *The English Patient* (1992, filmed 1996).

1 The first sentence of every novel should be: 'Trust me, this will take time but there is order here, very faint, very human.' Meander if you want to get to town.

*In the Skin of a Lion*, bk 2, 'Palace of Purification' (1987)

2 The past is still, for us, a place that is not safely settled.

*The Faber Book of Contemporary Canadian Short Stories*, Introduction (1990)

3 The desert could not be claimed or owned – it was a piece of cloth carried by winds, never held down by stones, and given a hundred shifting names long before Canterbury existed, long before battles and treaties quilted Europe and the East. Its caravans, those strange rambling feasts and cultures, left nothing behind, not an ember.

*The English Patient*, ch. 4 (1992)

4 A libertine was one who made love before nightfall
Or without darkening the room.

'A Gentleman Compares His Virtue to a Piece of Jade', publ. in *Handwriting* (1994)

# Eugene O'Neill (1888–1953)

US PLAYWRIGHT

The first American dramatist to win the Nobel Prize for Literature (1936), he also won a total of four Pulitzer Prizes, including those for *Beyond the Horizon* (1920), *Strange Interlude* (1928) and the autobiographical *Long Day's Journey Into Night* (1956), generally considered his finest play. On hearing he was giving up drinking, GEORGE BERNARD SHAW remarked: 'He'll probably never write a good play again.'

1  Life is for each man a solitary cell whose walls are mirrors.

Lazarus, in *Lazarus Laughed*, act 2, sc. 1 (1927)

2  When men make gods, there is no God!

ibid. sc. 2

3  Man's loneliness is but his fear of life.

ibid. act 3, sc. 2

4  The old – like children – talk to themselves, for they have reached that hopeless wisdom of experience which knows that though one were to cry it in the streets to multitudes, or whisper it in the kiss to one's beloved, the only ears that can ever hear one's secrets are one's own!

Tiberius, in ibid. act 4, sc. 1

5  Life is perhaps most wisely regarded as a bad dream between two awakenings, and every day is a life in miniature.

Chu-Yin, in *Marco Millions*, act 2, sc. 2 (1928)

6  The only living life is in the past and future – the present is an interlude – strange interlude in which we call on past and future to bear witness we are living.

Nina, in *Strange Interlude*, pt 2, act 8 (1928)

7  The sea hates a coward!

Bryant, in *Mourning Becomes Electra*, pt 2, act 4 (1931)

8  It is like acid always burning in my brain that the stupid butchering of the last war taught men nothing at all, that they sank back listlessly on the warm manure pile of the dead and went to sleep, indifferently bestowing custody of their future, their fate, into the hands of State departments, whose members are trained to be conspirators, card sharps, double-crossers and secret betrayers of their own people; into the hands of greedy capitalist ruling classes so stupid they could not even see when their own greed began devouring itself; into the hands of that most debased type of pimp, the politician, and that most craven of all lice and job-worshippers, the bureaucrats.

Letter to his son, June 1942, publ. in *Selected Letters of Eugene O'Neill* (ed. Travis Bogard and Jackson R. Bryer, 1988)

9  The lie of a pipe dream is what gives life to the whole misbegotten mad lot of us, drunk or sober.

Larry, in *The Iceman Cometh*, act 1 (1946). 'It is a play about pipe dreams,' O'Neill remarked about this work. 'And the philosophy is that there is always one dream left, one final dream, no matter how low you have fallen, down there at the bottom of the bottle. I know, because I saw it.'

10  None of us can help the things life has done to us. They're done before you realize it, and once they're done they make you do other things until at last everything comes between you and what you'd like to be, and you've lost your true self forever.

Mary, in *Long Day's Journey into Night*, act 2, sc. 1 (1956)

11  We fought so long against small things that we became small ourselves.

Quoted by VÁCLAV HAVEL in *Disturbing the Peace*, ch. 3 (1986)

12  I knew it. I knew it. Born in a hotel room – and God damn it – died in a hotel room.

Attributed, shortly before his death in the Shelton Hotel, Boston, 27 November 1953

# Yoko Ono (b. 1933)

JAPANESE-BORN US ARTIST

Full name Yoko Ono Lennon. A painter, sculptor and performance artist who was a prominent member of New York's neo-Dadaist Fluxus group, she emphasized spectator participation in her work of the 1960s. After her marriage to JOHN LENNON in 1969, her performance art developed feminist and pacifist themes. 'Maybe we were naïve,' she commented on the publicity events for peace which she staged with Lennon, 'but still we were very honest about everything we did.'

1  Everybody's an artist. Everybody's God. It's just that they're inhibited. I believe in people so much that if the whole of civilization is burned so we don't have any memory of it, even then people will start to build their own art. It is a necessity – a function. We don't need history.

Interview for Dutch TV, October 1968, publ. in *Imagine* (ed. Andrew Solt and Sam Egan, 1988)

2  Woman is the nigger of the world.

Interview in *Nova* 1968, quoted in *The Lennon Tapes* (1981). The words were used by JOHN LENNON as a song title on the album *Some Time in New York City* (1972), and recall those of ZORA NEALE HURSTON: 'De nigger woman is de mule uh de world so fur as Ah can see' (*Their Eyes Were Watching God*, ch. 2, 1937).

3  The odds of not meeting in this life are so great that every meeting is like a miracle. It's a wonder that we don't make love to every single person we meet.

Sleeve notes on *Feeling the Space* (album, 1973)

4  If all of us just loved and cared for one person each. That is all it takes. Love breeds love. Maybe then we will be able to prevent each other from going insane. Maybe then we will be able to prevent each other from becoming violent, as violence is in our hearts and not in our weapons. Guilt is not in the one who pulls the trigger, but in each of us who allows it.

Letter to the world's press, following the murder of JOHN LENNON in 1980

5  We are living in a very chaotic and confused world, and if we think that we're not in rage it's hypocritical. What we do is maybe suppress our rage and get sick from it; or you may take it out on your spouse or your family or the people around you. And, actually, the rage is not against those people, it's against yourself; I think it's a rage that's there for a good reason, and that we should admit it and share it and use the energy of that anger to do something about it.

Interview in the *Guardian* 20 January 1996

6  In classical music, people were doing very complex things, for the sake of being complex. I learned that rock, with two simple chords, can bring an incredible communication of the spirit.

Interview in the *Wire* April 1996

# Lord Onslow (b. 1938)

BRITISH PEER

Sir Michael Onslow, Baron Cranley. An outspoken Tory maverick with liberal leanings, he is a substantial Surrey landowner and one-time radio presenter. He was one of the ninety-two hereditary peers to keep their seats after reform of the House of Lords in 1999, declaring: 'I'm not a half-wit because I'm a hereditary peer. I may be a half-wit, but it's not because I'm a hereditary peer.'

1  I will be sad if I look up or down after my death and don't see my son asleep on the same benches on which I slept.

Quoted in the *Guardian* 26 October 1998. Speaking against Labour's plans for reforming the House of Lords. He commented that he would 'go out like a football hooligan' if he lost his seat.

## J. Robert Oppenheimer (1904–67)

US PHYSICIST

Full name Julius Robert Oppenheimer. In 1943 he became Director at the Los Alamos laboratory, overseeing the Manhattan Project to develop the atomic bomb. Horrified at the bomb's destructive power, he resigned in 1945, later arguing unsuccessfully for joint US–Soviet control of atomic energy. In 1953 he was suspended from government-sponsored nuclear research on account of his left-wing connections.

1 **In some sort of crude sense, which no vulgarity, no humor, no overstatement can quite extinguish, the physicists have known sin; and this is a knowledge which they cannot lose.**
'Physics in the Contemporary World', lecture at Massachusetts Institute of Technology, 25 November 1947, first publ. in *Technology Review* no. 50, 1948, repr. in *Open Mind* (1955). Oppenheimer's remark became notorious after it was quoted in *Time* magazine 23 February 1948 and 8 November 1948.

2 **When you see something that is technically sweet, you go ahead and do it and you argue about what to do about it only after you have had your technical success. That is the way it was with the atomic bomb.**
*In the Matter of J. Robert Oppenheimer: USAEC Transcript of Hearing Before Personnel Security Board* (1954). Said during hearings investigating allegations of former communist associations, in connection with Oppenheimer's involvement in the Los Alamos project to develop the atomic bomb.

## Martin Oppenheimer (b. 1930)

GERMAN-BORN US SOCIOLOGIST

A frequent contributor to the press and periodicals, he had a wide influence on non-violent protest in the 1960s through his books *A Manual for Direct Action* (1964, with George Lakey) and *The Urban Guerrilla* (1969).

1 **Today's city is the most vulnerable social structure ever conceived by man.**
*The Urban Guerrilla*, ch. 7 (1969)

## Susie Orbach (b. 1946)

BRITISH PSYCHOTHERAPIST AND AUTHOR

Her work is directed to understanding eating disorders, which she has studied in her books *Fat is a Feminist Issue* (1978) and *Hunger Strike: The Anorectic's Struggle as a Metaphor for Our Time* (1985).

1 **Fat is a social disease, and fat is a feminist issue.**
*Fat is a Feminist Issue*, Introduction (1978). 'Fat,' wrote Orbach, 'is a way of saying "no" to powerlessness and self-denial.'

## Tony O'Reilly (b. 1936)

IRISH ENTREPRENEUR

After a career as a rugby international, winning twenty-three caps for Ireland over fifteen years, he went into business, becoming Chairman of Independent Newspapers in 1980, and Chief Executive (1979–98) and Chairman (from 1987) of the Heinz International Corporation.

1 **Truly great brands are far more than just labels for products; they are symbols that encapsulate the desires of consumers; they are standards held aloft under which the masses congregate.**
Speech to British Council of Shopping Centres, 1990, quoted in 'Brand Leader' by Fintan O'Toole, publ. in *Granta* no. 53, spring 1996

## Leoluca Orlando (b. 1947)

SICILIAN POLITICIAN

Christian Democrat Mayor of Palermo from 1985, he was expelled from the party and subsequently formed his own party, La Rete

('network'), dedicated to eradicating Mafia influence and reinvigorating the city's cultural life. He was re-elected Mayor in 1993, since when his party has polled consistently highly in local and regional elections.

1 **In Italy it is not important who you are but whom you belong to.**
Quoted in the *International Herald Tribune* 25 April 1991

## P. J. O'Rourke (b. 1947)

US JOURNALIST

Full name Patrick John O'Rourke. Former Editor-in-chief of *National Lampoon*, later associated with *Rolling Stone*, he is famed for his 'acidic sketches' of contemporary public affairs from a humorous right-wing perspective. His essays are collected in *Holidays in Hell* (1988), *Give War A Chance* (1992) and *The Enemies List* (1996). Jeffrey Abbott of *The Times* called him 'the gunslinger of the eminently respectable school of American right-wing libertarian philosophers', while for Michael Riley of *Time* magazine he is 'an acerbic master of gonzo journalism'.

1 **Name me, if you can, a better feeling than the one you get when you've half a bottle of Chivas in the bag with a gram of coke up your nose and a teenage lovely pulling off her tube top in the next seat over while you're doing a hundred miles an hour in a suburban side street.**
*Republican Party Reptile*, 'How to Drive Fast On Drugs While Getting Your Wing Wang Squeezed and Not Spill Your Drink' (1987)

2 **Western civilization not only provides a bit of life, a pinch of liberty and the occasional pursuance of happiness, it's also the only thing that's ever tried to. Our civilization is the first in history to show even the slightest concern for average, undistinguished, none-too-commendable people like us.**
*Holidays in Hell*, Introduction (1988)

3 **In the end we beat them with Levi 501 jeans. Seventy-two years of Communist indoctrination and propaganda was drowned out by a three-ounce Sony Walkman. A huge totalitarian system ... has been brought to its knees because nobody wants to wear Bulgarian shoes ... Now they're lunch, and we're number one on the planet.**
'The Death of Communism', first publ. in *Rolling Stone* November 1989, repr. in *Give War A Chance* (1992)

4 **[Of the Gulf War] We spend all day broadcasting on the radio and TV telling people back home what's happening here. And we learn what's happening here by spending all day monitoring the radio and TV broadcasts from back home.**
'Gulf Diary' 31 January 1991, first publ. in *Rolling Stone*, repr. in ibid.

5 **Politics are for foreigners with their endless wrongs and paltry rights. Politics are a lousy way to get things done. Politics are, like God's infinite mercy, a last resort.**
*Parliament of Whores*, author's Preface to the British edn (1991)

6 **Maybe a nation that consumes as much booze and dope as we do and has our kind of divorce statistics should pipe down about 'character issues'. Either that or just go ahead and determine the presidency with three-legged races and pie-eating contests. It would make better TV.**
ibid. 'Attack of the Midget Vote Suckers'

7 **Whatever it is that the government does, sensible Americans would prefer that the government do it to somebody else. This is the idea behind foreign policy.**
ibid. 'Very Foreign Policy'

8 **[On ecologists] The neo-hippie-dips, the sentimentality-crazed iguana anthropomorphizers, the Chicken Littles, the three-bong-hit William Blakes – thank God these**

people don't actually go outdoors much, or the environment would be even worse than it is already.

ibid. 'Dirt of The Earth: The Ecologists'

9 Every government is a parliament of whores. The trouble is, in a democracy the whores are us.

ibid. 'At Home In the Parliament of Whores'

10 No drug, not even alcohol, causes the fundamental ills of society. If we're looking for the sources of our troubles, we shouldn't test people for drugs, we should test them for stupidity, ignorance, greed and love of power.

*Give War A Chance*, 'Studying For Our Drug Test' (1992)

11 At forty-seven the things which really matter and the things which are really fun are the dreadful things that our parents really said mattered. Family and work and duty. Crap like that.

Interview in the *Guardian* 25 November 1995

## José Ortega y Gasset (1883–1955)

SPANISH ESSAYIST AND PHILOSOPHER

Called the most influential Spanish author of his time, he played a significant part in introducing Spanish readers to modernist fiction. His major work, *The Revolt of the Masses* (1930), denounced the anti-intellectualism and intolerance of both left and right in the years preceding the Spanish Civil War.

1 I am I plus my surroundings and if I do not preserve the latter, I do not preserve myself.

*Meditations on Quixote*, 'To the Reader' (1914)

2 I do not deny that there may be other well-founded causes for the hatred which various classes feel toward politicians, but the *main one seems to me that politicians are symbols of the fact that every class must take every other class into account.*

*Invertebrate Spain*, ch. 2, 'Direct Action' (1921)

3 Poetry has become the higher algebra of metaphors.

*The Dehumanization of Art*, 'More About the Dehumanization of Art' (1925)

4 The characteristic of the hour is that the commonplace mind, knowing itself to be commonplace, has the assurance to proclaim the rights of the commonplace and to impose them wherever it will.

*The Revolt of the Masses*, ch. 1 (1930)

5 Civilization is nothing else than the attempt to reduce force to being the *ultima ratio*.

ibid. ch. 8

6 Liberalism – it is well to recall this today – is the supreme form of generosity; it is the right which the majority concedes to minorities and hence it is *the noblest cry that has ever resounded in this planet.* It announces the determination to share existence with the enemy; more than that, with an enemy which is weak.

ibid.

7 We have need of history in its entirety, not to fall back into it, but to see if we can escape from it.

ibid. ch. 10

8 A revolution does not last more than fifteen years, the period which coincides with the flourishing of a generation.

ibid.

9 Youth does not require reasons for living, it only needs pretexts.

ibid. ch. 14, sect. 3

10 Biography is: a system in which the contradictions of a human life are unified.

'In Search of Goethe from Within', first publ. in *Partisan Review* December 1949, repr. in *The Dehumanization of Art and Other Essays* (1968)

11 Poetry is adolescence fermented, and thus preserved.

ibid.

## Joe Orton (1933–67)

BRITISH PLAYWRIGHT

Originally named John Kingsley. His 'outrageous farces', notably *Entertaining Mr Sloane* (1964), *Loot* (1966) and *What the Butler Saw* (1969), owed their popularity to their black humour, bad taste and witty dialogue. He was murdered by his lover, failed author Kenneth Halliwell, who then took his own life.

1 I always say to myself that the theatre is the Temple of Dionysus, and not Apollo. You do the Dionysus thing on your typewriter, and then you allow a little Apollo in, just a little to shape and guide it along certain lines you may want to go along. But you can't allow Apollo in completely.

Interview on BBC Radio, 28 July 1964, quoted in *Prick Up Your Ears: the Biography of Joe Orton*, ch. 1 (1978) by John Lahr

2 Every luxury was lavished on you – atheism, breast-feeding, circumcision.

Hal, in *Loot*, act 1 (1966)

3 Reading isn't an occupation we encourage among police officers. We try to keep the paper work down to a minimum.

Truscott, in ibid. act 2

4 I was enraged that there were so many rubbishy novels and rubbishy books. It reminded me of the Bible: 'Of the making of books, there is no end', because there isn't. Libraries might as well not exist; they've got endless shelves of rubbish and hardly any space for good books.

*Evening News* 9 June 1967, quoted in *Prick Up Your Ears: the Biography of Joe Orton*, ch. 3 (1978) by John Lahr. Orton was explaining his defacement of library books, for which he and his lover Halliwell received a six-month jail sentence in 1962.

5 You were born with your legs apart. They'll send you to the grave in a Y-shaped coffin.

Dr Prentice to his wife, in *What the Butler Saw*, act 1 (1969)

6 In an age of declining faith, sir, surely it's enough for the young to hold spiritual convictions. It's an act of pedantry to ask that they should be the right ones.

Notes for dialogue in *What the Butler Saw*, quoted in *Prick Up Your Ears: the Biography of Joe Orton*, ch. 6 (1978) by John Lahr

## George Orwell (1903–50)

BRITISH AUTHOR

After working as an Imperial Police officer in Burma, he travelled and wrote in Europe, often performing menial jobs, as described in *Down and Out in Paris and London* (1933). His socialist sympathies were expressed in *The Road to Wigan Pier* (1937) and *Homage to Catalonia* (1938) and in his many essays. His novels, as he admitted, were mere 'disguises' for his social commentary, though two of them became classics: *Animal Farm* (1945, filmed 1954) and *Nineteen Eighty-Four* (1949, filmed 1956 and 1984). His work was written within a strong moral framework, provoking CYRIL CONNOLLY to remark: 'He could not blow his nose without moralising on conditions in the handkerchief industry.'

1 He was an embittered atheist (the sort of atheist who does not so much disbelieve in God as personally dislike Him).

*Down and Out in Paris and London*, ch. 30 (1933). Referring to Bozo, a London 'screever' or pavement artist. In later years, Bozo was heard to remark that Orwell 'always had £50 in his pocket' during his 'down-and-out' experiences.

2 I sometimes think that the price of liberty is not so much eternal vigilance as eternal dirt.

*The Road to Wigan Pier*, ch. 4 (1937). A reference to John Philpot Curran, 'The condition upon which God hath given liberty to man is eternal vigilance' (1790).

3 As with the Christian religion, the worst advertisement for Socialism is its adherents.

ibid. ch. 11

4 The high-water mark, so to speak, of Socialist literature is W.H. Auden, a sort of gutless Kipling, and the even feebler poets who are associated with him.

ibid. In his essay 'Inside the Whale' (1940), Orwell wrote: 'Some years ago I described Auden as "a sort of gutless Kipling". As criticism this was quite unworthy, indeed it was merely a spiteful remark, but it is a fact that in Auden's work, especially his earlier work, an atmosphere of uplift – something rather like Kipling's *If* or Newbolt's *Play up, Play up, and Play the Game!* – never seems to be very far away.'

5 We of the sinking middle class ... may sink without further struggles into the working class where we belong, and probably when we get there it will not be so dreadful as we feared, for, after all, we have nothing to lose but our aitches.

ibid. ch. 13

6 And then England – southern England, probably the sleekest landscape in the world. It is difficult when you pass that way ... to believe that anything is really happening anywhere. Earthquakes in Japan, famines in China, revolutions in Mexico? Don't worry, the milk will be on the doorstep tomorrow morning, the *New Statesman* will come out on Friday ... And then the huge peaceful wilderness of outer London, the barges on the miry river, the familiar streets, the posters telling of cricket matches and Royal weddings, the men in bowler hats, the pigeons in Trafalgar Square, the red buses, the blue policemen – all sleeping the deep, deep sleep of England, from which I sometimes fear that we shall never wake till we are jerked out of it by the roar of bombs.

*Homage to Catalonia*, ch. 14 (1938). Describing Orwell's return from Spain in closing words of book.

7 I'm fat, but I'm thin inside. Has it ever struck you that there's a thin man inside every fat man, just as they say there's a statue inside every block of stone?

*Coming Up For Air*, pt 1, ch. 3 (1939). See also KINGSLEY AMIS 4, CYRIL CONNOLLY 18.

8 To say 'I accept' in an age like our own is to say that you accept concentration camps, rubber truncheons, Hitler, Stalin, bombs, aeroplanes, tinned food, machine guns, putsches, purges, slogans, Bedaux belts, gas masks, submarines, spies, provocateurs, press-censorship, secret prisons, aspirins, Hollywood films and political murder.

*Inside the Whale and Other Essays*, 'Inside the Whale', sect. 1 (1940)

9 Of course there is much more in *Ulysses* than this ['commonplaceness of material'], because Joyce is a kind of poet and also an elephantine pedant, but his real achievement has been to get the familiar on to paper.

ibid.

10 The 'Communism' of the English intellectual is something explicable enough. It is the patriotism of the deracinated.

ibid. sect. 2

11 So much of left-wing thought is a kind of playing with fire by people who don't even know that fire is hot.

ibid.

12 Good novels are not written by orthodoxy-sniffers, nor by people who are conscience-stricken about their own orthodoxy. Good novels are written by people who are *not frightened*.

ibid.

13 For a creative writer possession of the 'truth' is less important than emotional sincerity.

ibid. sect. 3

14 Progress is not an illusion, it happens, but it is slow and invariably disappointing.

ibid. 'Charles Dickens', sect. 1

15 Men are only as good as their technical development allows them to be.

ibid. sect. 4

16 Most revolutionaries are potential Tories, because they imagine that everything can be put right by altering the *shape* of society; once that change is effected, as it sometimes is, they see no need for any other.

ibid. sect. 6

17 The clatter of clogs in the Lancashire mill towns, the to-and-fro of the lorries on the Great North Road, the queues outside the Labour Exchanges, the rattle of pin-tables in the Soho pubs, the old maids biking to Holy Communion through the mists of the autumn mornings – all these are not only fragments, but *characteristic* fragments, of the English scene. How can one make a pattern out of this muddle?

*The Lion and the Unicorn*, pt 1, 'England Your England', sect. 1 (1941). John Major nostalgically evoked this passage; see JOHN MAJOR 8.

18 England ... resembles a family, a rather stuffy Victorian family, with not many black sheep in it but with all its cupboards bursting with skeletons. It has rich relations who have to be kowtowed to and poor relations who are horribly sat upon, and there is a deep conspiracy of silence about the source of the family income. It is a family in which the young are generally thwarted and most of the power is in the hands of irresponsible uncles and bed-ridden aunts. Still, it is a family. It has its private language and its common memories, and at the approach of an enemy it closes its ranks. A family with the wrong members in control – that, perhaps, is as near as one can come to describing England in a phrase.

ibid. sect. 3

19 Probably the battle of Waterloo *was* won on the playing-fields of Eton, but the opening battles of all subsequent wars have been lost there.

ibid. sect. 4

20 Whatever is funny is subversive, every joke is ultimately a custard pie, and the reason why so large a proportion of jokes centre round obscenity is simply that all societies, as the price of survival, have to insist on a fairly high standard of sexual morality. A dirty joke is not, of course, a serious attack upon morality, but it is a sort of mental rebellion, a momentary wish that things were otherwise.

'The Art of Donald McGill', publ. in *Horizon* September 1941, repr. in *Collected Essays* (1961)

21 The high sentiments always win in the end, the leaders who offer blood, toil, tears and sweat always get more out of their followers than those who offer safety and a good time. When it comes to the pinch, human beings are heroic.

ibid.

22 I know it is the fashion to say that most of recorded history is lies anyway. I am willing to believe that history is for the most part inaccurate and biased, but what is peculiar to our own age is the abandonment of the idea that history *could* be truthfully written.

'Looking Back on the Spanish War', sect. 4, written 1943, publ. in *England Your England* (1953), repr. in *Homage to Catalonia* (1966 edn)

23 To a surprising extent the war-lords in shining armour, the apostles of the martial virtues, tend not to die fighting when the time comes. History is full of ignominious getaways by the great and famous.

'Who Are the War Criminals?', publ. in *Tribune* 22 October 1943, repr. in *The Collected Essays, Journalism and Letters of George Orwell*, vol. 2 (ed. Sonia Orwell and Ian Angus, 1968)

24  Autobiography is only to be trusted when it reveals something disgraceful. A man who gives a good account of himself is probably lying, since any life when viewed from the inside is simply a series of defeats.

'Benefit of Clergy: Some Notes on Salvador Dali' written for *The Saturday Book* (1944), publ. in ibid. vol. 3. The essay was suppressed by the publishers of *The Saturday Book* and appeared in *Dickens, Dali and Others* (ed. George Orwell, 1946).

25  [On the English attitude to food] As a rule they will refuse even to sample a foreign dish, they regard such things as garlic and olive oil with disgust, life is unliveable to them unless they have tea and puddings.

'The English People: England at First Glance', written 1944, publ. in *Britain in Pictures* (1947), repr. in ibid.

26  To write or even speak English is not a science but an art. There are no reliable words . . . Whoever writes English is involved in a struggle that never lets up even for a sentence. He is struggling against vagueness, against obscurity, against the lure of the decorative adjective, against the encroachment of Latin and Greek, and, above all, against the worn-out phrases and dead metaphors with which the language is cluttered up.

'The English People: The English Language', ibid. Consequently, Orwell explained: 'The peculiarities of the English language make it almost impossible for anyone who has left school at fourteen to learn a foreign language after he has grown up.'

27  Language ought to be the joint creation of poets and manual workers.

'The English People: The Future of the English People', ibid.

28  The English are probably more capable than most peoples of making revolutionary change without bloodshed. In England, if anywhere, it would be possible to abolish poverty without destroying liberty.

ibid.

29  For all I know, by the time this book is published my view of the Soviet régime may be the generally accepted one. But what use would that be in itself? To exchange one orthodoxy for another is not necessarily an advance. The enemy is the gramophone mind, whether or not one agrees with the record that is being played at the moment.

'The Freedom of the Press', proposed preface to *Animal Farm* (1945), first publ. in *The Times Literary Supplement* 15 September 1972, repr. in *Animal Farm* fiftieth anniversary edn (1995)

30  If liberty means anything at all it means the right to tell people what they do not want to hear. The common people still vaguely subscribe to that doctrine and act on it. In our country – it is not the same in all countries: it was not so in republican France, and it is not so in the USA today – it is the liberals who fear liberty and the intellectuals who want to do dirt on the intellect.

ibid.

31  Four legs good, two legs bad.

*Animal Farm*, ch. 3 (1945). By the end of the story, the animals' revolutionary maxim has changed to 'Four legs good, two legs *better*' (ch. 10).

32  All animals are equal but some animals are more equal than others.

ibid. ch. 10. The animals' commandment as it appeared at the end of the story, originally 'All animals are equal'.

33  To walk through the ruined cities of Germany is to feel an actual doubt about the continuity of civilization.

*Observer* 8 April 1945

34  Serious sport has nothing to do with fair play. It is bound up with hatred, jealousy, boastfulness, and disregard of

all the rules and sadistic pleasure in witnessing violence: in other words it is war minus the shooting.

'Sporting Spirit', publ. in *Tribune* 14 December 1945, repr. in *Shooting an Elephant* (1950)

35  He is a man of thirty-five, but looks fifty. He is bald, has varicose veins and wears spectacles, or would wear them if his only pair were not chronically lost. If things are normal with him, he will be suffering from malnutrition, but if he has recently had a lucky streak, he will be suffering from a hangover. At present it is half past eleven in the morning, and according to his schedule he should have started work two hours ago; but even if he had made any serious effort to start he would have been frustrated by the almost continuous ringing of the telephone bell, the yells of the baby, the rattle of an electric drill out in the street, and the heavy boots of his creditors clumping up the stairs. The most recent interruption was the arrival of the second post, which brought him two circulars and an income tax demand printed in red. Needless to say this person is a writer.

'Confessions of a Book Reviewer' (1946), repr. in *The Collected Essays, Journalism and Letters of George Orwell*, vol. 4 (ed. Sonia Orwell and Ian Angus, 1968)

36  The Catholic and the Communist are alike in assuming that an opponent cannot be both honest and intelligent.

'The Prevention of Literature', first publ. in *Polemic* January 1946, repr. in *Collected Essays* (1961)

37  In our time, political speech and writing are largely the defence of the indefensible.

'Politics and the English Language', first publ. in *Horizon* April 1946, repr. in *Shooting an Elephant* (1950)

38  The great enemy of clear language is insincerity. When there is a gap between one's real and one's declared aims, one turns as it were instinctively to long words and exhausted idioms, like a cuttlefish squirting out ink.

ibid.

39  The quickest way of ending a war is to lose it.

'Second Thoughts on James Burnham', first publ. in *Polemic* May 1946, repr. in *Shooting an Elephant* (1950)

40  No one can look back on his schooldays and say with truth that they were altogether unhappy.

'Such, Such were the Joys', written 1947, first publ. in *Partisan Review* September/October 1952, repr. in *The Collected Essays, Journalism and Letters of George Orwell*, vol. 4 (ed. Sonia Orwell and Ian Angus, 1968). Orwell himself attended Eton.

41  It was a bright, cold day in April and the clocks were striking thirteen.

*Nineteen Eighty-Four*, pt 1, ch. 1 (1949). Opening words of book.

42  BIG BROTHER IS WATCHING YOU.

Caption to 'Ingsoc' poster, in ibid. The poster is described as 'one of those pictures which are so contrived that the eyes follow you about when you move'.

43  War is peace. Freedom is slavery. Ignorance is strength.

Ingsoc party slogan, in ibid.

44  Who controls the past controls the future: who controls the present controls the past.

Ingsoc party slogan in ibid. ch. 3

45  Don't you see that the whole aim of Newspeak is to narrow the range of thought? In the end we shall make thoughtcrime literally impossible, because there will be no words in which to express it.

Symes, in ibid. ch. 5

46  Freedom is the freedom to say that two plus two make four. If that is granted, all else follows.

Winston Smith writing in his diary, in ibid. pt 2, ch. 7

47  *Doublethink* means the power of holding two contradic-

tory beliefs in one's mind simultaneously, and accepting both of them.

Extract from Goldstein's book, in ibid. ch. 9

48 Power is not a means, it is an end. One does not establish a dictatorship in order to safeguard a revolution; one makes the revolution in order to establish the dictatorship.

O'Brien, in ibid. pt 3, ch. 3

49 If you want a vision of the future, imagine a boot stamping on a human face – forever.

ibid.

50 Saints should always be judged guilty until they are proved innocent.

'Reflections on Gandhi', first publ. in *Partisan Review* January 1949, repr. in *Shooting an Elephant* (1950) Orwell expressed scepticism of all forms of sainthood: 'It is probable,' he wrote, 'that some who achieve or aspire to sainthood have never felt much temptation to be human beings.'

51 One cannot really be a Catholic and grown-up.

Manuscript Notebook (1949), repr. in *The Collected Essays, Journalism and Letters of George Orwell*, vol. 4 (ed. Sonia Orwell and Ian Angus, 1968)

52 At 50, everyone has the face he deserves.

ibid. Last entry in Orwell's notebook, 17 April 1949. ALBERT CAMUS, in *The Fall* (1956), expressed much the same notion: 'After a certain age every man is responsible for his face.'

# John Osborne (1929–94)
## BRITISH PLAYWRIGHT

He developed his career at London's Royal Court Theatre, where Jimmy Porter in *Look Back in Anger* (1956, filmed 1958) became the mouthpiece of a generation of 'angry young men'. Milton Shulman, in the *Evening Standard*, believed that the play 'aims at being a despairing cry but achieves only the stature of a self-pitying snivel', while for others it revitalized British theatre. *The Entertainer* (1957, filmed 1960) was equally successful, although later plays, for example *Luther* (1960), were neither as ground-breaking nor as acclaimed as his earlier work.

1 Why do I do this every Sunday? Even the book reviews seem to be the same as last week's. Different books – same reviews.

Jimmy Porter, in *Look Back in Anger*, act 1 (1956). Opening words of play.

2 Oh heavens, how I long for a little ordinary human enthusiasm. Just enthusiasm – that's all. I want to hear a warm, thrilling voice cry out Hallelujah! Hallelujah! I'm alive!

ibid.

3 I don't think one 'comes down' from Jimmy's university. According to him, it's not even red brick, but white tile.

Alison, in ibid. act 2, sc.1

4 Anyone who's never watched somebody die is suffering from a pretty bad case of virginity.

Jimmy Porter, in ibid.

5 The whole point of a sacrifice is that you give up something you never really wanted in the first place . . . People are doing it around you all the time. They give up their careers, say – or their beliefs – or sex.

ibid. act 3, sc.1

6 There aren't any good, brave causes left. If the big bang does come, and we all get killed off, it won't be in aid of the old-fashioned grand design. It'll just be for the Brave New-nothing-very-much-thank-you. About as pointless and inglorious as stepping in front of a bus. No, there's nothing left for it, me boy, but to let yourself be butchered by the women.

ibid.

7 It's no good trying to fool yourself about love. You can't

fall into it like a soft job, without dirtying up your hands. It takes muscle and guts. And if you can't bear the thought of messing up your nice, clean soul, you'd better give up the whole idea of life, and become a saint. Because you'll never make it as a human being. It's either this world or the next.

ibid. sc.2

8 What are we hoping to get out of it, what's it all in aid of – is it really just for the sake of a gloved hand waving at you from a golden coach?

Jean, in *The Entertainer*, no. 10 (1957)

9 Here we are, we're alone in the universe, there's no God, it just seems that it all began by something as simple as sunlight striking on a piece of rock. And here we are. We've only got ourselves. Somehow, we've just got to make a go of it. *We've only got ourselves.*

ibid. no. 12

10 It's easy to answer the ultimate questions – it saves you bothering with the immediate ones.

George, in *Epitaph for George Dillon*, act 2 (1958, written with Anthony Creighton)

11 Damn you, England. You're rotting now, and quite soon you'll disappear. My hate will outrun you yet if only for a few seconds. I wish it could be eternal.

Letter to *Tribune* 18 August 1961

12 Inside every playwright there is a Falstaff, gathering like a boil to be lanced by his liege employers – fashion and caprice.

*Almost a Gentleman*, ch. 18 (autobiography, 1991)

13 What we remember is what we become. What we have forgotten is more kindly and disturbs only our dreams. We become resemblances of our past.

ibid. ch. 26

14 I have only one regret remaining now in this matter of Adolf. It is simply that I was unable to look down upon her open coffin and, like that bird in the Book of Tobit, drop a good, large mess in her eye.

ibid. ch. 28. 'Adolf' was Osborne's name for his wife, JILL BENNETT. Tobit, a pious Jew in the Apocrypha's Book of Tobit, was blinded by sparrows' droppings.

15 Homophobia may be offensive but the other side of the coin is just as noisome, whatever they may tell you in Euroboy or Zipper.

*Spectator* 17–24 December 1994

# Peter O'Toole (b. 1932)
## IRISH-BORN BRITISH ACTOR

Equally adept in classical drama and modern comedy, he established his reputation at the Royal Shakespeare Company before achieving international recognition in the title role of the film *Lawrence of Arabia* (1962). Later films include *The Ruling Class* (1972), while on stage he memorably played the dissipated Jeffrey Bernard in the 1990s, a part ideally suited to his erratic and often inebriated style.

1 The only exercise I get these days is walking behind the coffins of my friends who take exercise.

Quoted in the *Observer* 1 August 1999

# John Otway (b. 1953)
## BRITISH ROCK MUSICIAN

He achieved short-lived stardom in 1977 when, together with Wild Willy Barrett, he had a hit with the punk-ish 'Really Free'. Never again reaching the same heights, he continued touring as a solo artist, retaining a loyal following for his cheesy antics.

1 There's no point in success if you don't let it go to your head. That's what it's for.

Quoted in the *Sunday Correspondent* 6 May 1990. Otway spent recklessly after signing a record contract with a record company when aged twenty-four, including the purchase of a Bentley, which he was never able to drive.

## Wilfred Owen (1893–1918)
BRITISH POET

Volunteering in 1915 for service in the First World War, he served as an infantry officer and received the Military Cross, although was horrified by the experience of trench warfare. In 1917 he befriended SIEGFRIED SASSOON who encouraged him to write about what Owen called 'the pity of war, the pity war distilled'. After Owen's death in action, a week before the Armistice, Sassoon collected his poems for publication. YEATS characterized him as 'all blood, dirt and sucked sugar stick'.

1 What passing-bells for these who die as cattle?
  Only the monstrous anger of the guns.
  'Anthem for Doomed Youth', written 1917, publ. in *The Poems of Wilfred Owen* (ed. Edmund Blunden, 1931)

2 Red lips are not so red
  As the stained stones kissed by the English dead.
  'Greater Love', written 1917, publ. in ibid. Opening lines of poem.

3 If you could hear, at every jolt, the blood
  Come gargling from the froth-corrupted lungs,
  Bitter as the cud
  Of vile, incurable sores on innocent tongues, –
  My friend, you would not tell with such high zest
  To children ardent for some desperate glory,
  The old Lie: Dulce et decorum est
  Pro patria mori.
  'Dulce et Decorum Est', written 1918, publ. in ibid.

4 Was it for this the clay grew tall?
  O what made fatuous sunbeams toil
  To break earth's sleep at all?
  'Futility', written 1918, publ. in ibid.

5 Courage was mine, and I had mystery,
  Wisdom was mine, and I had mastery,
  'Strange Meeting', written 1918, publ. in ibid.

6 I am the enemy you killed, my friend.
  I knew you in this dark; for so you frowned
  Yesterday through me as you jabbed and killed.
  I parried; but my hands were loath and cold.
  Let us sleep now . . .
  ibid. Closing lines of poem, of which variant versions exist.

7 Above all I am not concerned with Poetry.
  My subject is War, and the pity of War.
  The Poetry is in the pity.
  Draft preface, written 1918, publ. in ibid. The lines were the motto for BENJAMIN BRITTEN's *War Requiem* (1962), which combined Owen's poems with the Latin Mass for the Dead.

8 All a poet can do to-day is warn. That is why the true Poets must be truthful.
  ibid.

## Amos Oz (b. 1939)
ISRAELI NOVELIST

Original name Amos Klausner. Called 'Israel's most persuasive spokesman to the outside world' by the poet D.J. Enright, he is the author of novels and short stories dealing with modern and historical Israel, the best known of which is *My Michael* (1972). Other works include *Elsewhere, Perhaps* (1973), *A Perfect Peace* (1982) and *In the Land of Israel* (1983).

1 It is crystal clear to me that if Arabs put down a draft resolution blaming Israel for the recent earthquake in Iran it would probably have a majority, the US would veto it and Britain and France would abstain.
  *The Times* 24 October 1990. Referring to Israel's refusal to cooperate with UN attempts to carry out an inquiry after Israeli police fired on demonstrators at Temple Mount, Jerusalem.

## Cynthia Ozick (b. 1928)
US NOVELIST AND SHORT-STORY WRITER

Her work, deeply rooted in Jewish culture and folklore, has been praised by A. ALVAREZ for its 'crooked flights of imagination and a poet's perfectionist habit of mind and obsession with language'. Examples of her novels are *Trust* (1966) and *The Messiah of Stockholm* (1987), and her short stories include *The Pagan Rabbi* (1971).

1 Wondrous hole! Magical hole! Dazzlingly influential hole! Noble and effulgent hole! From this hole everything follows logically: first the baby, then the placenta, then, for years and years and years until death, a way of life. It is all logic, and she who lives by the hole will live also by its logic. It is, appropriately, logic with a hole in it.
  'The Hole/Birth Catalog', publ. in *The First Ms Reader* (ed. Francine Klagsbrun, 1972)

2 The usefulness of madmen is famous: they demonstrate society's logic flagrantly carried out down to its last scrimshaw scrap.
  ibid.

## Vance Packard (b. 1914)
US AUTHOR AND JOURNALIST

Described as 'a blend of amateur sociologist and crusading journalist', he addresses anxieties raised by rapid social change. His most influential work, *The Hidden Persuaders* (1957), highlights the incursions of consumer advertising; other books include *The Status Seekers* (1959), and *The People Shapers* (1977).

1 The professional persuaders . . . see us as bundles of day-dreams, misty hidden yearnings, guilt complexes, irrational emotional blockages. We are image lovers given to impulsive and compulsive acts. We annoy them with our seemingly senseless quirks, but we please them with our growing docility in responding to their manipulation of symbols that stir us to action.
   *The Hidden Persuaders*, ch. 1 (1957)

## Reginald Paget (1908–90)
BRITISH POLITICIAN

Baron Paget of Northampton. The scion of five generations of Conservative politicians, he held the Labour seat for Northampton (1945–74). He was outspoken against HAROLD WILSON and was said to be the slowest speaker in the House. His publications include *The Human Journey* (1979), an account of human life.

1 When sexual indulgence has reduced a man to the shape of Lord Hailsham, sexual continence involves no more than a sense of the ridiculous.
   Speech to House of Commons, 17 June 1963, during a debate on the Profumo affair, quoted in *The Fine Art of Political Wit*, ch. 12 (1964) by Leon Harris. Paget was one of the few who spoke up for Profumo during the scandal. BERNARD LEVIN called his words 'of such deadly and elegant cruelty that its like had not been fashioned in England since the death of Pope'.

## Camille Paglia (b. 1947)
US AUTHOR AND CRITIC

In *Sexual Personae* (1990), *Sex, Art, and American Culture* (1992), and *Vamps and Tramps* (1994) she berates orthodox feminist theory for downplaying the role of eroticism in Western culture. Her libertarian outlook and contentious style have caused her to be branded a right-wing publicity-seeker. 'I'm an egomaniac,' she admitted. 'I have no rivals . . . I was born with the killer instinct.'

1 Men know they are sexual exiles. They wander the earth seeking satisfaction, craving and despising, never content. There is nothing in that anguished motion for women to envy.
   *Sexual Personae* ch. 1 (1990)

2 Male urination really *is* a kind of accomplishment, an arc of transcendence. A woman merely waters the ground she stands on.
   ibid.

3 Pornography is human imagination in tense theatrical action; its violations are a protest against the violations of our freedom by nature.
   ibid.

4 Out with stereotypes, feminism proclaims. But stereotypes are the west's stunning sexual personae, the vehicles of art's assault against nature. The moment there is imagination, there is myth.
   ibid.

5 Popular culture is the new Babylon, into which so much art and intellect now flow. It is our imperial sex theater, supreme temple of the western eye. We live in the age of idols. The pagan past, never dead, flames again in our mystic hierarchies of stardom.
   ibid. ch. 4

6 Television is actually closer to reality than anything

in books. The madness of TV is the madness of human life.

*Harper's Magazine* March 1991

7 There is no female Mozart because there is no female Jack the Ripper.

*International Herald Tribune* 26 April 1991

8 Gay men may seek sex without emotion; lesbians often end up in emotion without sex.

'Homosexuality at the Fin de Siècle', publ. in *Esquire* October 1991, repr. in *Sex, Art, and American Culture* (1992)

9 Gay men are guardians of the masculine impulse. To have anonymous sex in a dark alleyway is to pay homage to the dream of male freedom. The unknown stranger is a wandering pagan god. The altar, as in prehistory, is anywhere you kneel.

ibid.

10 If you live in rock and roll, as I do, you see the reality of sex, of male lust and women being aroused by male lust. It attracts women. It doesn't repel them.

Interview in *Playboy* October 1991, repr. in ibid., 'The Rape Debate'

11 When anything goes, it's women who lose.

*Observer* 15 December 1991

12 The prostitute is not, as feminists claim, the victim of men but rather their conqueror, an outlaw who controls the sexual channel between nature and culture.

'Elizabeth Taylor: Hollywood's Pagan Queen', publ. in *Penthouse* March 1992, repr. in *Sex, Art, and American Culture* (1992)

13 We need a new kind of feminism, one that stresses personal responsibility and is open to art and sex in all their dark, unconsoling mysteries.

*Sex, Art, and American Culture*, Introduction (1992)

14 If civilization had been left in female hands we would still be living in grass huts.

Quoting herself in ibid.

## Marcel Pagnol (1895–1974)
FRENCH DRAMATIST AND FILM DIRECTOR

His plays and films are rooted in his upbringing in Marseilles and rural Provence. *Manon des Sources* (film, 1953) was adapted by himself into two novels *Jean de Florette* (1962) and *Manon des Sources* (1963), which were in turn successfully filmed by Claude Berri in 1986 and 1987. He founded *Cahiers du Film* in 1931 and in 1946 was the first film-maker to be elected to the Académie Française.

1 One has to look out for engineers – they begin with sewing machines and end up with the atomic bomb.

*Critique des critiques*, ch. 3 (1949)

## Ian Paisley (b. 1926)
NORTHERN IRISH POLITICIAN

Founder in 1951 of the Free Presbyterian Church of Ulster, he has been an MP in Westminster from 1970 and as leader of the Democratic Unionists was elected to the European Parliament in 1979. His fiercely anti-nationalist political stance and fundamentalist religious beliefs have led him consistently to reject rapprochement with Northern Ireland's Catholic community. His writings include *No Pope Here* (1982), *Understanding Events in Northern Ireland* (1995) and *My Plea for the Old Sword* (1997).

1 I would rather be British than just.

Quoted in *Ulster*, ch. 3 (1972) by the *Sunday Times* Insight Team. The remark was addressed to Bernadette Devlin (see BERNADETTE MCALISKEY) in October 1969.

2 [Of draught Guinness] I would be quite happy to see the Devil's buttermilk banned from society.

Quoted in the *Irish Times* 14 March 1998

3 There are various ways to martyr a man. You can lie about him, and I have been lied about. You can ostracize him, and the fundamentalists have been ostracized. You can defame him. You can seek to destroy him. You can, first of all, kill his character. And my character has been assassinated across the world by the media.

Quoted in the *Guardian* 25 April 1998. 'They're not against me personally,' he continued, 'I recognize that. They're against my preaching, because I won't give in . . . But I am not sacrificing my religious views for anybody. I am a captive to the Bible.'

## Michael Palin (b. 1943)
BRITISH ACTOR, AUTHOR AND TELEVISION PRESENTER

With a reputation as 'the nicest man in show business', he was a member of the MONTY PYTHON'S FLYING CIRCUS team (1969–74). He has subsequently appeared in the film *A Fish Called Wanda* (1988), presented travelogues for BBC TV, such as *Around the World in Eighty Days* (1989), and written the novel *Hemingway's Chair* (1995, televised 1999).

1 Travel, at its best, is a process of continually conquering disbelief.

*Pole to Pole* 'Day 20' (1992)

## Arnold Palmer (b. 1929)
US GOLFER

A popularizer of golf in the 1950s and 1960s, he won the United States amateur championship in 1954 and went on to win all the major professional titles except for the USA PGA championship. He was the first golfer to earn $1 million prize-money.

1 Concentration comes out of a combination of confidence and hunger.

Quoted in 'Stairway to Heaven' (1993) by Timothy O'Grady, repr. as 'Playing Handball with Zeus' in *The Esquire Book of Sports Writing* (ed. Greg Williams, 1995)

## Vance Palmer (1885–1959)
AUSTRALIAN AUTHOR AND POET

Best known for his novel *The Passage* (1930), he came to be regarded as Australia's principal man of letters. He also wrote stories, plays and essays, and with his wife, the critic Nettie Palmer, helped set up the Pioneer Players in Melbourne.

1 It is the business of Art to give things shape. Anyone who takes no delight in the firm outline of an object, or in its essential character, has no artistic sense . . . He cannot even be nourished by Art. Like Ephraim, he feeds upon the East wind, which has no boundaries.

'On Boundaries' (1921), repr. in *Intimate Portraits* (ed. H.P. Heseltine, 1969)

2 The truth is that literature, particularly fiction, is not the pure medium we sometimes assume it to be. Response to it is affected by things other than its own intrinsic quality; by a curiosity or lack of it about the people it deals with, their outlook, their way of life.

'Fragment of Autobiography' (1958), repr. in ibid.

## Emmeline Pankhurst (1857–1928)
BRITISH SUFFRAGETTE

She founded the Women's Franchise League in 1889, and, supported by her daughters Christabel and SYLVIA PANKHURST, the Women's Social and Political Union in 1903. Their tactics aimed at obtaining the vote for women led to her arrest and imprisonment on several occasions. During the First World War she turned her attention to mobilizing women for factory work.

1 We never went to prison in order to be martyrs. We went there in order that we might obtain the rights of

citizenship. We were willing to break laws that we might force men to give us the right to make laws.
*My Own Story*, pt. 2, ch. 8 (1914)

## Sylvia Pankhurst (1882–1968)
BRITISH POLITICAL ACTIVIST

With her mother EMMELINE PANKHURST and sister Christabel she was a founding member of the Women's Social and Political Union, but broke with it to form the East London Federation. In 1914 she established *The Woman's Dreadnought* (later called *The Worker's Dreadnought*). She remained an independent socialist, though was expelled from the Communist Party which she joined after the Russian Revolution.

1 Some people say that the lives of working women are too hard and their education too small for them to become a powerful voice in winning the vote. Such people have forgotten their history.
*The Woman's Dreadnought* 8 March 1914, quoted *in Sylvia Pankhurst: A Life in Radical Politics*, ch. 3 (1999) by Mary Davis

2 International solidarity is a sentiment which only attains a sturdy growth amongst those who are fully convinced that capitalism has had its day.
*India and the Earthly Paradise* (1926), quoted in ibid. ch. 6

## Charlie Parker (1920–55)
US JAZZ MUSICIAN

Nicknamed 'Bird' or 'Yardbird', he was a master alto sax player, composer and bandleader, legendary for his improvisatory technique. Along with trumpeter Dizzy Gillespie he is associated with creating the bebop style of jazz with such recordings as 'Salt Peanuts' and 'Ornithology' (1944–7). His premature death was the result of alcohol and drugs.

1 Music is your own experience, your own thoughts, your wisdom. If you don't live it, it won't come out of your horn. They teach you there's a boundary line to music. But, man, there's no boundary line to art.
Quoted in *Hear Me Talkin' to Ya*, 'Coda' (ed. Nat Shapiro and Nat Hentoff, 1955)

## Dorothy Parker (1893–1967)
US HUMOROUS WRITER

Described by ALEXANDER WOOLLCOTT as 'a combination of Little Nell and Macbeth', she took over from P.G. WODEHOUSE as drama critic at *Vanity Fair* in 1917, moving to *Life* soon after with ROBERT BENCHLEY and playwright ROBERT SHERWOOD. With them, she became a key figure of the Algonquin literary circle. Her popular writings include *Enough Rope* (poetry, 1926) and *Here Lies* (collected short stories, 1939). Legendary for her quick wit and humour, she was a champion of liberal causes. She died a depressed alcoholic.

1 Brevity is the soul of lingerie.
Caption publ. in *Vogue*, 1916, quoted in *While Rome Burns*, 'Our Mrs Parker' (1934) by Alexander Woollcott. An allusion to Shakespeare, 'Brevity is the soul of wit' (*Hamlet* act 2, sc. 2).

2 Where's the man could ease a heart
Like a satin gown?
'The Satin Dress', publ. in *Enough Rope* (1926)

3 Oh, life is a glorious cycle of song,
A medley of extemporanea;
And love is a thing that can never go wrong;
And I am Marie of Roumania.
'Comment', publ. in ibid.

4 Razors pain you;
Rivers are damp;
Acids stain you;
And drugs cause cramp.

Guns aren't lawful;
Nooses give;
Gas smells awful;
You might as well live.
'Résumé', publ. in ibid.

5 Scratch a lover, and find a foe.
'Ballade of a Great Weariness', publ. in ibid.

6 Why is it no one ever sent me yet
One perfect limousine, do you suppose?
Ah no, it's always just my luck to get
One perfect rose.
'One Perfect Rose', publ. in ibid.

7 Men seldom make passes
At girls who wear glasses.
'News Item', publ. in ibid.

8 If, with the literate, I am
Impelled to try an epigram,
I never seek to take the credit;
We all assume that Oscar said it.
'A Pig's-Eye View of Literature', publ. in *Sunset Gun* (1928)

9 Tonstant Weader fwowed up.
*New Yorker* 20 October 1928, repr. in *The Collected Dorothy Parker*, pt 2 (1973). Closing words of review of *The House at Pooh Corner*, in Parker's 'Constant Reader' column.

10 Drink, and dance and laugh and lie,
Love the reeling midnight through,
For tomorrow we shall die!
(But, alas, we never do.)
'The Flaw in Paganism', publ. in *Death and Taxes* (1931)

11 How do they know?
Remark on hearing the announcement that CALVIN COOLIDGE had died (1933), quoted in the *Paris Review* summer 1956, repr. in *Writers at Work* (first series, ed. Malcolm Cowley, 1958)

12 *The House Beautiful* is the play lousy.
*New Yorker*, 1933, quoted in ibid. Review of *The House Beautiful* by Channing Pollock.

13 She [KATHARINE HEPBURN] runs the gamut of emotions from A to B.
Theatre review of *The Lake* (1933), quoted in obituary, *Publishers Weekly* 19 June 1967

14 [Suggested epitaph] Excuse my dust.
Quoted in *While Rome Burns*, 'Our Mrs Parker' (1934) by Alexander Woollcott

15 [Of a departing guest] That woman speaks eighteen languages and can't say No in any of them.
Quoted in ibid.

16 And there was that wholesale libel on a Yale prom. If all the girls attending it were laid end to end, Mrs Parker said, she wouldn't be at all surprised.
ibid.

17 Good work, Mary. We all knew you had it in you.
Quoted in ibid. Telegram to a friend (Mrs Robert Sherwood) who had become a mother after a prolonged pregnancy.

18 Sorrow is tranquility remembered in emotion.
'Sentiment', publ. in *Here Lies* (1939). Adapting Wordsworth, 'Poetry . . . takes its origin from emotion recollected in tranquillity' (*Lyrical Ballads*, Preface to second edn, 1802).

19 All those writers who write about their childhood! Gentle God, if I wrote about mine you wouldn't sit in the same room with me.
Interview in the *Paris Review* summer 1956, repr. in *Writers at Work* (first series, ed. Malcolm Cowley, 1958)

20 [On women writers] As artists they're rot, but as providers they're oil wells; they gush. Norris said she never wrote a story unless it was fun to do. I understand Ferber whistles at her typewriter. And there was that poor sucker Flaubert

rolling around on his floor for three days looking for the right word.

ibid.

21 There's a helluva distance between wisecracking and wit. Wit has truth in it; wisecracking is simply callisthenics with words.

ibid.

22 Hollywood money isn't money. It's congealed snow, melts in your hand, and there you are.

ibid. 'I can't talk about Hollywood,' Parker declared. 'It was a horror to me when I was there and it's a horror to look back on. I can't imagine how I did it. When I got away from it I couldn't even refer to the place by name. "Out there," I called it.'

23 It's not the tragedies that kill us, it's the messes.

ibid.

24 This is not a novel to be tossed aside lightly. It should be thrown with great force.

Book review, quoted in *The Algonquin Wits* (ed. Robert E. Drennan, 1968)

25 Enjoyed it! One more drink and I'd have been under the host.

Quoted in ibid. On being asked whether she had enjoyed a party.

26 You can lead a horticulture, but you can't make her think.

Quoted in *You Might As Well Live* (1970) by John Keats. On being challenged to make a sentence using the word 'horticulture'.

27 [On her abortion] It serves me right for putting all my eggs in one bastard.

Quoted in ibid. pt 2, ch. 3

# Lord Parker (1900–72)

BRITISH JUDGE

Hubert Lister, Baron Parker of Waddington. He was made a Lord Justice of Appeal in 1954 and was Lord Chief Justice of England (1958–71). The harshness of the forty-two-year sentence given to the spy George Blake drew widespread criticism.

1 A judge is not supposed to know anything about the facts of life until they have been presented in evidence and explained to him at least three times.

Quoted in the *Observer* 12 March 1961

# Ross Parker (1914–74) and
# Hugh Charles (1907–95)

BRITISH SONGWRITERS

The two collaborated on songs throughout the Second World War. Hugh Charles also worked with NOEL GAY, among others, and later concentrated on theatrical productions.

1 There'll always be an England
   While there's a country lane,
   Wherever there's a cottage small
   Beside a field of grain.

'There'll Always Be an England' (song, 1939). Originally performed by BILLY COTTON and his Orchestra. See also VERA LYNN 10.

# C. Northcote Parkinson (1909–93)

BRITISH HISTORIAN AND POLITICAL SCIENTIST

Full name Cyril Northcote Parkinson. Modelling himself on 'the sixteenth-century courtier who could do everything', he wrote a number of historical, political and economic works, for instance *The Evolution of Political Thought* (1958), but is better known for *Parkinson's Law* (1957), a tongue-in-cheek look at businesses and bureaucracies.

1 Work expands so as to fill the time available for its completion. General recognition of this fact is shown in the

proverbial phrase 'It is the busiest man who has time to spare'.

*Parkinson's Law or The Pursuit of Progress*, 'Parkinson's Law or the Rising Pyramid' (1958). Opening words of book.

2 A committee is organic rather than mechanical in its nature: it is not a structure but a plant. It takes root and grows, it flowers, wilts, and dies, scattering the seed from which other committees will bloom in their turn.

ibid. 'Directors and Councils or Coefficient of Inefficiency'

3 The Law of Triviality . . . briefly stated, it means that the time spent on any item of the agenda will be in inverse proportion to the sum involved.

ibid. 'High Finance or the Point of Vanishing Interest'

4 The man who is denied the opportunity of taking decisions of importance begins to regard as important the decisions he is allowed to take.

ibid. 'Pension Point or the Age of Retirement'

5 Expenditure rises to meet income.

*The Law and the Profits*, ch. 1 (1960). Opening sentence of book.

6 Expansion means complexity, and complexity decay.

*In-laws and Outlaws*, 'The Third Law' (1962)

# Cecil Parkinson (b. 1931)

BRITISH POLITICIAN

Baron Parkinson of Carnforth. He was elected a Conservative MP in 1970 and rose to become party Chairman (1981–3) and a close confidant of MARGARET THATCHER. His affair with his secretary Sara Keays, who subsequently bore him a child, forced him to resign, although he rejoined the cabinet (1987–90) and was again party Chairman (1997–8).

1 From the days when the miners' leaders thought they owned the Government to the day when every miner owns part of his own mine – that's the British revolution.

*Daily Mail* 13 October 1988

2 It is better to be a has-been than a never-was.

*Guardian* 29 June 1990

3 In politics people give you what they think you deserve and deny you what they think you want.

Television interview, ITV, 19 November 1990

# Michael Parkinson (b. 1935)

BRITISH JOURNALIST AND BROADCASTER

He is best known as host of his own television chat show *Parkinson* (1971–82 and from 1998), and renowned for his smooth style and professional composure. A co-founder and presenter of *TV-am* (1983–4), he has also written widely on sport and was voted British Sports Feature Writer of the Year in 1995.

1 The kind of show I do consists of two consenting adults performing unnatural acts in public.

Quoted in the *Sunday Times* 27 December 1987. On his new chat show.

# Norman Parkinson (1913–90)

BRITISH FASHION PHOTOGRAPHER

Original name Ronald William Parkinson Smith. For fifty years he was one of Britain's most famous fashion and portrait photographers, associated particularly with the magazines *Vogue* and *Queen*. He was also known for his official portraits of the royal family. From 1963 he made his base in Tobago.

1 I could never bear to be buried with people to whom I had not been introduced.

Quoted in obituary in the *Guardian* 16 February 1990

# Matthew Parris (b. 1949)

BRITISH POLITICIAN AND JOURNALIST

After work in the Foreign Office and other government posts, he became a Conservative MP (1979–86) and later presenter of London Weekend Television's *Weekend World* (1986–8). Since 1988 he has been parliamentary sketch-writer for *The Times* and columnist for the *Spectator*. Among his books are *I Couldn't Possibly Comment* (1993) and *Unfrocked: 2000 Years of Church Scandal* (1997).

1 Being an MP feeds your vanity and starves your self-respect.
*The Times* 9 February 1994

2 Since the dawn of man every politician has been torn between a wish to say something memorable, and a terror of saying something which is remembered.
Introduction to *Read My Lips* (1996) by Matthew Parris and Phil Mason

3 As we ridicule the po-faced puritans of the Left, we forget how ripe for ridicule are the sniffy certainties of our own creed ... We too, we who are PS – the politically sound – have our thought police, our pursed lips and our mental phrasebook of sound (and unsound) expressions, sound (and unsound) attitudes, sound (and unsound) belief.
*Spectator* 19 February 2000. Examples he gave include the following: ' "Sexuality" is non-PS, as is "gender" and "ethnicity", the correct expressions (in reverse order) being "race", "sex" and "which team is he playing for?".'

4 The PS mentality combines a secret consciousness of being in the majority with the pseudo-plaintive tone of the put-upon. The PS voice is confident of the sympathy of the pack. It is the whimper-bark of the natural bully, eternally convinced that his victim is picking the fight.
ibid.

# Talcott Parsons (1902–79)

US SOCIOLOGIST

In his principal books *The Structure of Social Action* (1937) and *The Social System* (1951), he argued that, in his own words, 'all societies have a common pulse and a stable and enduring structure' and that social practices had to be studied in terms of their function in maintaining society. This theory of functionalism was prevalent in United States sociology from the 1940s until the 1960s.

1 It is a fact that social existence depends to a large extent on a moral consensus of its members and that the penalty of its too radical breakdown is social extinction. This fact is one which the type of liberal whose theoretical background is essentially utilitarian is all too apt to ignore.
*The Structure of Social Action*, vol. 1, ch. 10 (1937)

2 Science is intimately integrated with the whole social structure and cultural tradition. They mutually support one other – only in certain types of society can science flourish, and conversely without a continuous and healthy development and application of science such a society cannot function properly.
*The Social System*, ch. 8 (1951)

# Tony Parsons (b. 1955)

BRITISH JOURNALIST

A 'street-wise' writer on popular culture, he was, at the age of eighteen, a leader writer on the *New Musical Express* and one of the first champions of punk. Proceeding to the *Daily Telegraph*, the *Daily Mirror* and *GQ*, he was in 1999 reputedly the country's highest paid columnist.

1 The trouble with the working class today is that they are such peasants. Something has died in them – a sense of grace, all feelings of community, their intelligence, de-

cency and wit. Socialism is finished here because it is no longer possible to feel sentimental about the workers.
'The Tattooed Jungle', publ. in *Arena* September/October 1989, repr. in *Dispatches from the Front Line of Popular Culture* (1994)

2 Begging defaces the city, degrades the spirit. It dehumanizes you as well as them; it brutalizes us all. You learn to walk past these people, you have to, and it makes it easier to turn away from the truly needy. These professional leeches, big strapping lads some of them, harden your heart, put callouses on your soul. They make every cry for help seem like junk mail.
'Street Trash', publ. in *Arena* September/October 1991, repr. in ibid.

3 Being middle class means always having to say you're sorry.
'The Polenta Jungle', publ. in *Arena* March/April 1993, repr. in ibid. See also ERICH SEGAL 1.

4 The discreet charms of the bourgeoisie have been underrated for too long. They are the most cultured class. The hardest working. They believe in the welfare state but are aware of its corrupting nature. Yes, there are many things to despise about the middle class. But, unlike the nobs and the riff-raff, they do not know their place. They believe in self-improvement.
ibid.

5 There are few things in this world more reassuring than an unhappy Lottery winner.
*Observer* 8 November 1998

6 Pornography is many things to many men. But it is never adult. Pornography exists in a state of perpetual adolescence ... Planet porn is Disneyland for habitual monkey-spankers.
*GQ* January 2000

# Frances Partridge (b. 1900)

BRITISH TRANSLATOR AND AUTHOR

Born in Bloomsbury, she was for years at the centre of the Bloomsbury literary set whose exploits she portrayed in her memoirs *Love in Bloomsbury* (1981) and *A Bloomsbury Album* (1987). She was a literary translator for much of her life and has also published *A Pacifist's War* (1978) and *Everything to Lose: Diaries, 1945–1960* (1985).

1 It is a purely relative matter where one draws the plimsoll-line of condemnation, and ... if you find the whole of humanity falls below it you have simply made a mistake and drawn it too high. And are probably below it yourself.
Journal entry, 3 September 1959, publ. in *Julia*, ch. 17 (1983)

# Pier Paolo Pasolini (1922–75)

ITALIAN FILM-MAKER AND ESSAYIST

He converted to Marxism after the Second World War though was later expelled from the Communist Party on account of his homosexuality. After writing on slum life in Rome in novels, he turned to directing films, often using violence, depravity and eroticism as vehicles for social comment. 'I do nothing to console, nothing to embellish reality, nothing to sell the goods,' he stated. Among his films are *The Gospel According to St Matthew* (1964), *The Canterbury Tales* (1972) and *Salò* (1975). He was murdered in Ostia, allegedly by a homosexual prostitute.

1 In my desperation there is no more purity, no more innocence ... Now I am a desert completely explored; there is no way to save me. I am all consciousness.
Entry for 21 November 1946, in the second of Pasolini's 'Red Notebooks', publ. in *Pasolini Requiem*, ch. 9 (1992) by David Barth Schwartz

2 Don't think for a moment that the middle-class journalist cares at all for the truth; to be in some way honest; to be

personal. He completely depersonalizes himself, to allow himself to speak to a hypothetical public, one which he naturally considers right-thinking but idiotic, normal but ferocious, uncensored but vile.

'Le belle bandiere', column in *Vie Nuove* 15 October 1960, repr. in ibid. ch. 16

3 Too often a great mistake is made in discussions about censorship: that of putting the debate in the terms proposed by the censors: that is of the moralistic-sexual. Instead it is quite otherwise: one must completely ignore their hypocritical pretext, and see what should be obvious to a child, that censorship is a political issue, with sex as a simple and shameless pretext.

ibid. 17 December 1960

4 The atheism of a militant Communist is the essence of religion compared to the cynicism of a capitalist: in the first, one can always find those moments of idealism, of desperation, of psychological violence, of conscious will, of faith – which are elements, even degraded, of religion – in the second one finds only Mammon.

ibid. 29 October 1964, ch. 18

5 The relationship between a son and his mother is not a historical relationship, it is a purely interior, private relationship which is outside history, indeed it is meta-historical, and therefore ideologically unproductive, whereas what produces history is the relationship of hatred and love between father and son.

'Perché quella di Edipo è una storia', Introduction to *Oedipus Rex* (film, 1967), repr. in *Pasolini Requiem*, ch. 20 (1992) by David Barth Schwartz

6 Death does determine life ... Once life is finished it acquires a sense; up to that point it has not got a sense; its sense is suspended and therefore ambiguous.

*Pasolini On Pasolini: Interviews With Oswald Stack*, ch. 3 (1969)

7 The sexual freedom of today for most people is really only a convention, an obligation, a social duty, a social anxiety, a necessary feature of the consumer's way of life.

'Sono Contro l'Aborto', first publ. in *Il Corriere della Sera* 19 January 1975, repr. in *Scritti Corsari* (1975)

8 Hope? I have none and furthermore I condemn it with everything in my power. Hope is the flag, the special marker of hypocrisy ... I don't believe in it. I believe only in my own vitality.

Quoted in *Pasolini Requiem*, ch. 19 (1992) by David Barth Schwartz

# Boris Pasternak (1890–1960)

RUSSIAN POET, NOVELIST AND TRANSLATOR

He began his literary career as a poet and author of short fiction, publishing *Aerial Ways*, a short story collection, in 1933. His reputation in the West was established with his only novel *Dr Zhivago* (1957, filmed 1965), an epic of the Revolution and its aftermath that was banned in the Soviet Union. Political pressure forced him to refuse the 1958 Nobel Prize for Literature. See also OSIP MANDELSTAM 4.

1 We live in days to come, I tell them firmly,
And share one lot in common now. If crippled,
No matter! Stay. We are in fact run over
By the New Man in the wagon of his Plan.

'When I Grow Weary', publ. in *Second Birth* (1932), repr. in *Poems* (transl. Eugene M. Kayden, 1959)

2 My soul, you are a mourner
Of all where I survive.
You are a mausoleum
Of those tortured alive.

'My Soul' (1957) repr. in *Modern Russian Poetry* (ed. Vladimir Markov and Merrill Sparks, 1966)

3 The snow was falling soft and slow

From land to land.
A candle flamed upon a table;
A candle flamed.

'Winter Night' (1957) repr. in *Poems* (transl. Eugene M. Kayden, 1959)

4 What is history? Its beginning is that of the centuries of systematic work devoted to the solution of the enigma of death, so that death itself may eventually be overcome. That is why people write symphonies, and why they discover mathematical infinity and electromagnetic waves.

Nikolay Nikolayevich, in *Doctor Zhivago* (1957), ch. 1, sect. 5

5 That's metaphysics, my dear fellow. It's forbidden me by my doctor, my stomach won't take it.

Ivan Ivanovich, in ibid.

6 No deep and strong feeling, such as we may come across here and there in the world, is unmixed with compassion. The more we love, the more the object of our love seems to us to be a victim.

ibid. ch. 12, sect. 7

7 I don't like people who have never fallen or stumbled. Their virtue is lifeless and it isn't of much value. Life hasn't revealed its beauty to them.

Zhivago, in ibid. ch. 13, sect. 12

8 [Of life in communist Russia] Everything established, settled, everything to do with home and order and the common round, has crumbled into dust and been swept away in the general upheaval and reorganization of the whole of society. The whole human way of life has been destroyed and ruined. All that's left is the bare, shivering human soul, stripped to the last shred, the naked force of the human psyche for which nothing has changed because it was always cold and shivering and reaching out to its nearest neighbour, as cold and lonely as itself.

Lara, in ibid. sect. 13

9 As far as modern writing is concerned, it is rarely rewarding to translate it, although it might be easy ... Translation is very much like copying paintings.

Interview in *Writers at Work* (second series, ed. George Plimpton, 1963). 'The only interesting sort of translating is that of classics,' Pasternak declared.

10 It is no longer possible for lyric poetry to express the immensity of our experience. Life has grown too cumbersome, too complicated. We have acquired values which are best expressed in prose.

ibid.

# Jan Patocka (1907–77)

CZECH PHILOSOPHER AND ACTIVIST

Specializing in phenomenology, hermeneutics and the philosophy of science, he lectured at Charles University of Prague until 1948 when he was banned as a result of the Communist takeover. He was professor there 1965–70.

1 The real test of a man is not how well he plays the role he has invented for himself, but how well he plays the role that destiny assigned to him.

Quoted in *Disturbing the Peace*, ch. 2 (1986) by Václav Havel. Advice given to HAVEL.

# Brian Patten (b. 1946)

BRITISH POET

One of the 'Liverpool poets', along with Adrian Henri and ROGER MCGOUGH, he shares their commitment to poetry as live performance. His lyrical, observational and accessible poems are published in *Notes to the Hurrying Man* (1969), *Love Poems* (1981) and *Storm Damage* (1988) among other collections. He also writes for children.

1 When in public poetry should take off its clothes and

wave to the nearest person in sight; it should be seen in the company of thieves and lovers rather than that of journalists and publishers.

'Prose Poem Towards a Definition of Itself', publ. in *Little Johnny's Confession* (1967)

2 But the graffiti evokes an image of the crowd,
The lost androgynous animal
That does not die but daily swells,
That longs for kindness then reveals
A different nature on toilet walls.

'Reading Between the Graffiti', publ. in *Vanishing Trick* (1976)

# Chris Patten (b. 1944)
BRITISH POLITICIAN

Before serving as Conservative Party Chairman (1990–92), he was Minister for Overseas Development and as Environment Secretary was responsible for administering the poll tax. After losing his seat he was Governor of Hong Kong (1992–7) and in 1998 headed the commission on the reform of the Royal Ulster Constabulary.

1 Green politics at its worst amounts to a sort of Zen fascism; less extreme, it denounces growth and seeks to stop the world so that we can all get off.

*Independent* 19 April 1989

2 In a democracy everybody has a right to be represented, including the jerks.

*Evening Standard* 2 May 1991

3 There is a sort of exotic preposterousness about a lot of elections, the way arguments are made even cruder.

Quoted in the *Observer* 30 June 1991. Patten managed the electoral campaign of 1992 which led to a fourth successive Conservative victory, although he himself lost his seat.

# Tom Paulin (b. 1949)
BRITISH POET

Although born in Leeds, he is known as an Ulster poet, whose vision of a non-sectarian Ireland is expressed in such works as *A State of Justice* (1977) and *The Liberty Tree* (1983). His poetic style is known for its complexity and use of Ulster vernacular. A founder member of the Field Day Theatre Company, he has edited a volume of political verse and appears on television as a cultural commentator.

1 Puritan metaphor is a form of irony which has a habit of becoming literal: a dynamic millenarian rhetoric can inspire men to place actual dynamite under the status quo.

'Paisley's Progress' (1982), repr. in *Writing to the Moment* (1996)

2 I live in the half-light
of a strange
shivering translation
where the kingdom of letters
is like the postal system
of a frozen state
and your last question
slips through like code.

'What Kind of Formation are B Specials?', publ. in *The Liberty Tree* (1983)

3 Maybe the true taste of it
is knowing the limits of your own fraudulence

'Middle Age', publ. in *Walking a Line* (1994)

4 His [T.S. Eliot's] work seems endlessly subtle and intelligent, many of his cadences are perfect, but there is a malignity in it which is terrifying. It's so firm and so quiet, because like a true politician Eliot never apologizes and he never explains.

'T.S. Eliot and Anti-Semitism' (review of Anthony Julius, *T.S. Eliot, Anti-Semitism and Literary Form*, 1996), publ. in *Writing to the*

*Moment* (1996) 'I can think of no other modern writer whose prejudices have been treated with such tolerance,' wrote Paulin of ELIOT.

# Cesare Pavese (1908–50)
ITALIAN POET, NOVELIST AND TRANSLATOR

His translations, notably that of Herman Melville's *Moby Dick* (1932), helped to popularize modern English and American literature in Italy. His novels include *The Moon and the Bonfires* (1950) and *The House on the Hill* (1961). Regarded by some as an anti-Fascist hero, he considered himself a coward and was later disillusioned with politics. He killed himself in a Turin hotel.

1 Living is like working out a long addition sum, and if you make a mistake in the first two totals you will never find the right answer. It means involving oneself in a complicated chain of circumstances.

Journal entry 5 May 1936, publ. in *This Business of Living: Diary 1935–1950* (1952, transl. 1961)

2 Literature is a defence against the attacks of life. It says to life: 'You can't deceive me. I know your habits, foresee and enjoy watching all your reactions, and steal your secret by involving you in cunning obstructions that halt your normal flow.'

Journal entry 10 November 1938, publ. in ibid.

3 Perfect behaviour is born of complete indifference.

ibid. 21 February 1940

4 Artists are the monks of the bourgeois state.

ibid. 25 July 1940

5 A man is never completely alone in this world. At the worst, he has the company of a boy, a youth, and by and by a grown man – the one he used to be.

ibid. winter 1941–2

6 The richness of life lies in memories we have forgotten.

ibid. 13 February 1944

7 At great periods you have always felt, deep within you, the temptation to commit suicide. *You gave yourself to it*, breached your own defences. You were a child. The idea of suicide was a protest against life; by dying, you would escape this longing for death.

ibid. 1 January 1950. Suicide was a continuing theme in Pavese's diaries. 'No one ever lacks a good reason for suicide,' he wrote in 1938. He took his own life on 27 August 1950, shortly after being awarded the Strega Prize.

8 I have knocked about the world enough to know that one lot of flesh and blood is as good as another. But that's why you get tired and try to put down roots. To find somewhere where you belong so that you are worth more than the usual round of the seasons and last a bit longer.

Narrator (Anguilla), in *The Moon and the Bonfires*, ch. 1 (1950)

9 When they're dealing with the dead, priests are always right.

ibid. ch. 12

# Luciano Pavarotti (b. 1935)
ITALIAN TENOR

Along with José Carreras and Placido Domingo he is one of the 'Three Tenors' who have helped to popularize opera. His recording of 'Nessun Dorma' from Puccini's *Turandot* was adopted as the theme tune for the 1990 football World Cup. He performs frequently to raise funds for Bosnian victims of war and other causes.

1 I am not a musician. I don't go in too deep. If you have the music in your head, and you sing it with your body, then you'll be alright.

Quoted in the *Observer* 27 July 1997

# Jeremy Paxman (b. 1950)

BRITISH TELEVISION PRESENTER AND JOURNALIST

Famous for his abrasive style as an interrogator on BBC2's *Newsnight*, whose victims are said to have been 'Paxmanned', he once asked Conservative Home Secretary Michael Howard the same question thirteen times in succession. He has also worked as a film-maker for *Panorama* and authored studies of the British identity in *Friends in High Places* (1990) and *The English* (1998).

1 The BBC is rather like a cross between the Church of England and the Post Office.

*Friends in High Places*, ch. 4 (1990)

2 It's very difficult to remain calm when you're listening to someone talk complete bollocks.

Quoted in the *Observer* 6 April 1997

3 I hate the word 'sneering'. I can't help the way my face looks.

ibid.

4 It sometimes seems the Church of England thinks God is just the ultimate 'good chap'.

*The English: A Portrait of a People*, ch. 6 (1998)

5 The English approach to ideas is not to kill them, but to let them die of neglect.

*Independent* 24 October 1998

6 Things rush on [to television] at a fantastic speed, get recycled, pushed out and not thought about again. The fight is about controlling what goes through that sausage machine, which is what the spin doctors are about.

Interview in the *Guardian* 24 January 2000

# Cynthia Payne (b. 1934)

BRITISH HOUSEWIFE AND BROTHEL-KEEPER

Revelations about her suburban 'vicarage tea-parties with sex thrown in' led to a court case in 1986, and formed the basis for the film *Personal Services* (1987).

1 [On sex] To me it's just like having a cup of tea. After two abortions I am not particularly interested in sex, but I know it makes other people happy.

*The Times* 4 February 1987. Remark after being acquitted of running a brothel in Streatham, in the 'sex-for-luncheon-vouchers' case.

# Octavio Paz (1914–98)

MEXICAN POET AND ESSAYIST

He is regarded as one of the leading figures of the post-Second World War literature of Latin America. His poetry includes the collections *Eagle or Sun?* (1951) and *Salamandra* (1962), which includes the long poem 'Sal'. His most important prose work is *The Labyrinth of Solitude* (1950), an analysis of Mexican culture and history. He was awarded the Nobel Prize for Literature in 1990.

1 Modern man is loath to pretend that his thinking is wide-awake. But this wide-awake thinking has led us into the mazes of a nightmare in which the torture chambers are endlessly repeated in the mirrors of reason.

*The Labyrinth of Solitude*, ch. 9 (1950)

2 Man, even man debased by the neocapitalism and pseudo-socialism of our time, is a marvellous being because he sometimes *speaks*. Language is the mark, the sign, not of his fall but of his original innocence. Through the Word we may regain the lost kingdom and recover powers we possessed in the far-distant past.

*Alternating Current*, 'André Breton or the Quest of the Beginning' (1967)

3 Art is an invention of aesthetics, which in turn is an invention of philosophers . . . What we call art is a game.

ibid.

4 To read a poem is to hear it with our eyes; to hear it is to see it with our ears.

ibid. 'Recapitulations'

5 Social criticism begins with grammar and the re-establishing of meanings.

*The Other Mexico: Critique of the Pyramid*, 'Development and Other Mirages' (1972)

6 Wisdom lies neither in fixity nor in change, but in the dialectic between the two.

*The Times* 8 June 1989

7 Writers, you know, are the beggars of Western society.

Quoted in the *Independent on Sunday* 30 December 1990

# Mervyn Peake (1911–68)

BRITISH AUTHOR AND ILLUSTRATOR

His fantasy trilogy, *Titus Groan* (1946), *Gormenghast* (1950) and *Titus Alone* (1959), featuring an eccentric cast of characters in the surreal Gothic setting of Gormenghast castle, became a cult classic. He also wrote verse and illustrated *Treasure Island* and *The Ancient Mariner* as well as his own works. His ambition, he declared, was to 'create arabesques, abstracts, of thrilling colour, worlds on their own, landscapes and roofscapes and skyscapes peopled with hierophants and lords'.

1 [Of babies] They resemble rubber, your ladyship, ha, ha, ha. Just a core of india-rubber, with an elastic centre. Oh yes, they are. Very, very much so. Resilience is no word for it – oh dear me, no. Every ounce, a bounce, ha, ha, ha! Every ounce, a bounce.

Doctor Prunesquallor to the Countess of Groan, in *Titus Groan*, 'Titus is Christened' (1946)

2 My memory is so very untrustworthy. It's as fickle as a fox. Ask me to name the third lateral bloodvessel that runs east to west when I lie on my face at sundown, or the percentage of chalk to be found in the knuckles of an average spinster in her fifty-seventh year, ha, ha, ha! – or even ask me, my dear boy, to give details of the pulse rate of frogs two minutes before they die of scabies – these things are no tax upon my memory, ha, ha, ha! but ask me to remember exactly what you said your problems were, a minute ago, and you will find that my memory has forsaken me utterly.

Doctor Prunesquallor to Steerpike, in ibid. 'At the Prunesquallors'

3 There is a kind of laughter that sickens the soul. Laughter when it is out of control: when it screams and stamps its feet, and sets the bells jangling in the next town. Laughter in all its ignorance and cruelty. Laughter with the seed of Satan in it.

*Sometime, Never*, 'Boy in Darkness' (1956)

4 Each day I live in a glass room
Unless I break it with the thrusting
Of my senses and pass through
The splintered walls to the great landscape.

'Each Day I Live in a Glass Room', publ. in *A Reverie of Bone* (1967)

# Norman Vincent Peale (1898–1993)

US CLERGYMAN AND AUTHOR

He helped establish the American Foundation of Religion and Psychiatry next to the church where he was a minister in New York (1932–84), integrating popular religion with pop psychology, as outlined in *The Power of Positive Thinking* (1952) and *The Power of the Positive Factor* (1987). Politically a conservative, he was a close associate of the Nixon family in later years.

1 One of the greatest tragedies of the average person is the tendency to spend our whole lives perfecting our faults.

*The Power of Positive Thinking*, ch. 15 (1952)

## Patrick Henry Pearse (1879–1916)

IRISH NATIONALIST LEADER

He edited the Gaelic League's journal, lectured in Irish at University College, Dublin, and founded a bilingual school. He joined the Irish Republican Brotherhood in 1915, was appointed Commander-in-Chief of the 1916 Easter Rising and was proclaimed President of a provisional Irish government. He was shot after the failure of the Rising.

1 There are in every generation those who shrink from the ultimate sacrifice, but there are in every generation those who make it with joy and laughter and these are the salt of the generations.

Commemoration address, 2 March 1914, Brooklyn, New York. The speech was in honour of Irish patriot Robert Emmet, executed in 1803 for his part in an abortive invasion of Ireland.

2 Life springs from death and from the graves of patriot men and women spring living nations. The Defenders of this Realm have worked well in secret and in the open. They think that they have pacified Ireland. They think that they have pacified half of us and intimidated the other half. They think that they have foreseen everything, think that they have provided against everything; but the fools, the fools, the fools! – they have left us our Fenian dead, and while Ireland holds these graves, Ireland unfree shall never be at peace.

Graveside oration, 1 August 1915, quoted in *Patrick Pearse: The Triumph of Failure*, ch. 6, sect. 3 (1977) by Ruth Dudley Edwards. The last part of this speech was incorporated into SEAN O'CASEY'S *The Plough and the Stars*, act 2 (1926).

## Hesketh Pearson (1887–1964)

BRITISH BIOGRAPHER

Having been a successful actor and theatre director, he turned to biography in 1931. His subjects included Gilbert and Sullivan (1935), GEORGE BERNARD SHAW (1942), ARTHUR CONAN DOYLE (1943), Oscar Wilde (1946) and Benjamin Disraeli (1951).

1 Misquotation is, in fact, the pride and privilege of the learned. A widely-read man never quotes accurately, for the rather obvious reason that he has read too widely.

*Common Misquotations*, Introduction (1934). 'Misquotations,' Pearson wrote, 'are the only quotations that are never misquoted.'

## John Peel (b. 1939)

BRITISH DISC JOCKEY

Original name John Ravenscroft. A consistent trailblazer for new music, he worked as a DJ in America until 1967, then for the pirate Radio London and subsequently the BBC's Radio 1. From the 1990s he has also presented popular family-oriented programmes on TV and radio.

1 I don't want to sound like I'm bragging but I think I've finally managed to play the record at the right speed.

*The John Peel Show*, Radio 1, 20 April 2000. Peel's propensity for playing records at the wrong speed is legendary, often not noticed until the end of the track.

## D.A. Pennebaker (b. 1930)

US FILM-MAKER

Full name Don Alan Pennebaker. Part of a co-operative film-making group since 1959, he has concentrated on documentaries and performance footage. His best known films are linked to rock music, *Don't Look Back* (1967), a record of BOB DYLAN'S 1965 English tour, and *Monterey Pop* (1969).

1 I guess I think that films have to be made totally by fascists – there's no room for democracy in making film.

*Independent* 29 July 1988

## S.J. Perelman (1904–79)

US HUMORIST

Full name Sydney Joseph Perelman. Describing himself as 'button cute, rapier keen, wafer-thin and pauper-poor', he was a prolific journalist and screenwriter. His Hollywood scripts included *Monkey Business* (1931) and *Horse Feathers* (1932) for the MARX brothers. He also wrote a number of plays and film scripts with his wife Laura, sister of novelist Nathanael West.

1 There is nothing like a good, painstaking survey full of decimal points and guarded generalizations to put a glaze like a Sung vase on your eyeball.

*Keep It Crisp* (1946)

2 English life, while very pleasant, is rather bland. I expected kindness and gentility and I found it, but there is such a thing as too much couth.

Quoted in the *Observer* 24 September 1971

## Shimon Peres (b. 1923)

POLISH-BORN ISRAELI POLITICIAN AND PRIME MINISTER

Originally named Shimon Perski. As Foreign Minister, he played a large part in the Palestine Liberation Organization–Israeli peace accord, for which he shared the Nobel Peace Prize with Itzhak Rabin and YASSER ARAFAT in 1994. He has also served as prime minister (1984–6 and 1995–6) and has been leader of the Labour Party since 1997.

1 Television has made dictatorship impossible, but democracy unbearable.

Quoted in the *Financial Times* 31 January 1995

## Gabriel Péri (d. 1942)

FRENCH COMMUNIST DEPUTY

1 I will soon be going out to shape all the singing tomorrows.

Letter written shortly before his execution by the Germans, July 1942, quoted in *The New York Times* 11 April 1943

## Anthony Perkins (1932–92)

US SCREEN ACTOR

He specialized in roles as a troubled young man before achieving international fame in the role of Norman Bates in the film *Psycho* (1960). Among his later films are *The Champagne Murders* (1968) and *Catch-22* (1970).

1 A boy's best friend is his mother.

Norman Bates (Anthony Perkins), in *Psycho* (film, 1960, screenplay by Joseph Stefano based on novel by Robert Bloch, produced and directed by ALFRED HITCHCOCK)

2 We all go a little mad sometimes.

ibid.

3 I have learned more about love, selflessness and human understanding in this great adventure in the world of Aids than I ever did in the cut-throat, competitive world in which I spent my life.

Posthumous statement, publ. in the *Independent on Sunday* 20 September 1992

## Carl Perkins (b. 1932)

US ROCK MUSICIAN

His hit 'Blue Suede Shoes' (1956), a blend of black beat and country, became the 'anthem of rockabilly', although his version was eclipsed by that of ELVIS PRESLEY. Several of his songs were recorded by The Beatles and he made a come-back in the country charts in 1964 and again in a rockabilly revival in 1977.

1 It's one for the money,
   Two for the show,

Three to get ready,
Now go, cat, go!
But don't you step on my Blue Suede Shoes.
You can do anything but lay off my Blue Suede Shoes.

'Blue Suede Shoes' (song, 1956). A million-seller, the song topped both Country and Rhythm 'n' Blues charts, and reached no. 2 in the pop charts.

## Eva Perón (1919–52)
ARGENTINIAN POLITICIAN

An actress before marrying JUAN PERÓN (1945), 'Evita', as she was popularly known, took on the role of his chief adviser when he became President in 1946. She founded the Peronista Feminist Party in 1949 and gained support for her husband through her work for the poor, who idolized her. The musical *Evita* (1979) was based on her life. See also TIM RICE 1.

1 You will all have clothes like these some day . . . Some day you will be able to sit next to any rich woman on a basis of complete equality. What we are fighting for is to destroy the inequality between you and the wives of your bosses.

Presidential campaign speech, 1946, quoted in *The Perón Era*, 'Evita' (1965) by Robert J. Alexander. As wife of the President, Eva Perón reportedly spent 40,000 dollars annually on her dresses alone.

2 Almsgiving tends to perpetuate poverty; aid does away with it once and for all. Almsgiving leaves a man just where he was before. Aid restores him to society as an individual worthy of all respect and not as a man with a grievance. Almsgiving is the generosity of the rich; social aid levels up social inequalities. Charity separates the rich from the poor; aid raises the needy and sets him on the same level with the rich.

'My Labour in the Field of Social Aid', speech to the American Congress of Industrial Medicine, 5 December 194

3 Never abandon the poor – they are the only ones who know how to be loyal.

Quoted in *Evita: An Intimate Portrait of Eva Perón* (1997) by Tomás de Elia and Juan Pablo Queiroz. Spoken to Juan Perón, 25 July 1952, the day before her death.

4 When I die, take off the red varnish and replace it with a plain varnish.

Quoted by her maid, in *Eva Perón*, ch. 13 (1978) by John Barnes. Among her last words.

5 Fanaticism is the wisdom of the spirit. What matter if one is a fanatic, if one is that in the company of martyrs and heroes . . . ? In any case life has its real value not when it is lived in a spirit of egotism, just for oneself, but when one surrenders oneself, completely and fanatically, to an ideal which has more value than life itself.

*Evita: The Real Lives of Eva Perón*, ch. 7 (1996) by Nicholas Fraser and Marysa Navarro

6 I will come again, and I will be millions.

Quoted in ibid. Epilogue

## Juan Perón (1895–1974)
ARGENTINIAN POLITICIAN

Elected President in 1946, he won the support of the masses through a programme of social reforms known as 'justicialismo'. Following the death of his second wife EVA PERÓN, the antagonism of both Church and army and the faltering economy led to his overthrow in 1955 and subsequent exile. He returned to power in 1973.

1 I never killed anybody. Nobody died with his shoes on.

Quoted in *Eva Perón*, Epilogue (1978) by John Barnes

## Laurence J. Peter (1919–90)
US-CANADIAN AUTHOR

Full name Laurence Johnston Peter. His book *The Peter Principle* (1969) argues that people are promoted to positions for which they

are incompetent. He has also published sequels and a collection of quotations, *Peter's Quotations: Ideas For Our Time* (1977).

1 In a hierarchy every employee tends to rise to his level of incompetence.

The 'Peter Principle', in *The Peter Principle*, ch. 1 (1969, written with Raymond Hull). Compare with the 'Paula Principle': 'Women stay below their level of competence, because they hold back from promotion' (Liz Filkin, quoted in the *Observer* 19 October 1986).

## Kim Philby (1912–88)
BRITISH INTELLIGENCE OFFICER AND SOVIET SPY

Full name Harold Adrian Russell Philby. Recruited by the Soviets before being employed by British intelligence in 1940, he was liaison officer between MI6 and the CIA in Washington (1949–51) and was dismissed from the service in 1955 for his Communist sympathies. He defected to the USSR in 1963 and took Russian citizenship.

1 To betray, you must first belong. I never belonged.

*Sunday Times* 17 December 1967

## Philip, Duke of Edinburgh (b. 1921)

After service in the Royal Navy during the Second World War, the Greek-born Philip Mountbatten adopted British nationality in 1947, marrying the future ELIZABETH II the same year. He is notorious for his insensitive remarks, particularly on issues of race.

1 Dentopedalogy is the science of opening your mouth and putting your foot in it. I've been practising it for years.

Address to General Dental Council, quoted in *Time* magazine 21 November 1960

2 I never see any home cooking. All I get is fancy stuff.

Quoted in the *Observer* 28 October 1962

3 All money nowadays seems to be produced with a natural homing instinct for the Treasury.

Quoted in the *Observer* 26 May 1963

4 We live in what virtually amounts to a museum – which does not happen to a lot of people.

Remark, 25 February 1964, quoted in *Anatomy of Britain Today*, pt 1, ch. 2 (1965) by Anthony Sampson

5 When a man opens the car door for his wife, it's either a new car or a new wife.

*Today* 2 March 1988

6 I don't think a prostitute is more moral than a wife, but they are doing the same thing.

Speech 6 December 1988, quoted in the *Daily Mail* 7 December 1988, Prince Philip, discussing claims that those who sell slaughtered meat have greater moral authority than those who participate in blood sports.

## Adam Phillips (b. 1954)
BRITISH PSYCHOANALYST AND AUTHOR

He believes in widening the appeal of his subject, of which he has written in literary and aphoristic vein in *On Kissing, Tickling and Being Bored* (1993). He has also published *Winnicott* (1988), a study of the psychoanalyst D.W. Winnicott.

1 All of us may be surrealists in our dreams, but in our worries we are incorrigibly bourgeois.

'Worrying and its Discontents', first publ. in *Raritan*, vol. 9, no. 9, 1989, repr. in *On Kissing, Tickling and Being Bored* (1993)

## Julia Phillips (b. 1945)
US FILM PRODUCER

She gained the distinction of being the first woman producer to be awarded an Oscar, for *The Sting* (1973), co-produced with her husband Michael Phillips. *Taxi Driver* (1976) and *Close Encounters of the Third Kind* (1977) were other co-productions, before a cocaine habit and a divorce ended her film career, a story she elaborated in the bestseller *You'll Never Eat Lunch in This Town Again* (1990).

1 Hollywood is a place that attracts people with massive holes in their souls.
*The Times* 3 April 1991

## Edith Piaf (1918–63)
FRENCH SINGER

Original name Edith Giovanna Gassion. Helped to a mainstream career by MAURICE CHEVALIER, she was known for her powerful voice and waif-like appearance, to which she owed her name Piaf (Parisian slang for 'little sparrow'). Her funeral brought Paris traffic to a standstill.

1 *Quand il me prend dans ses bras*
*Il me parle tout bas*
*Je vois la vie en rose.*
(When he takes me in his arms
He speaks to me in a low voice
I see *la vie en rose*.)
'La Vie en rose' (song, 1946, written by Louiguy, Piaf and Mal Davis)

2 *Non! Rien de rien . . .*
*Non, je ne regrette rien!*
*Ni le bien qu'on m'a fait,*
*Ni le mal. Tout ça m'est bien égal!*
(No, I regret nothing . . .
Neither the good nor the bad,
It's all the same for me.)
'Non, je ne regrette rien' (song, 1961, written by Charles Dumont and Michael Vaucaire)

## Francis Picabia (1878–1953)
FRENCH PAINTER AND POET

He was associated with all the principal art movements of the early twentieth century, including Neo-Impressionism, Cubism, Dadaism, and Surrealism. With MARCEL DUCHAMP and MAN RAY he introduced Dadaism to New York and edited the anti-art magazine, which he published in different cities and variously titled *291, 391, 491* and *591*.

1 My arse contemplates those who talk behind my back.
*391* 10 July 1921, repr. in *Yes No: Poems and Sayings*, 'Sayings' (ed. Rémy Hall, 1990)

2 Men have always need of god! A god to defend them against other men.
'Trompettes de Jericho', first publ. in *Comoedia* 19 January 1922, repr. in *Écrits*, vol. 2, '1922' (ed. Olivier Revault d'Allones and Dominique Bouissou, 1978)

3 Let us never forget that the greatest man is never more than an animal disguised as a god.
'Jésus dit à ces Juifs', first publ. in *La Vie moderne* 25 February 1923, repr. in ibid. '1923'

4 Wherever art appears, life disappears.
'L'Humour poétique', first publ. in *La Nef* December 1950/January 1951, repr. in ibid.

5 Nature is unfair? So much the better, inequality is the only bearable thing, the monotony of equality can only lead us to boredom.
ibid.

## Pablo Picasso (1881–1973)
SPANISH ARTIST

Between 1909 and 1914 he collaborated with Braque on developing the ideas of Cubism, of which his *Les Demoiselles d'Avignon* (1906–1907) is generally considered the first major example. This and *Guernica* (1937), showing the bombing of a Basque town during the Spanish Civil War, are probably his best known paintings. Recurrent themes in his other works include harlequins, minotaurs and African imagery.

1 We all know that Art is not truth. Art is a lie that makes us realize truth, at least the truth that is given us to understand. The artist must know the manner whereby to convince others of the truthfulness of his lies.
'Picasso Speaks', publ. in *The Arts* May 1923, repr. in *Picasso: Fifty Years of His Art* (1946) by Alfred H. Barr Jr

2 Through art we express our conception of what nature is not.
ibid.

3 Everything is a miracle. It is a miracle that one does not dissolve in one's bath like a lump of sugar.
Quoted in *Opium* (1929) by JEAN COCTEAU

4 They ought to put out the eyes of painters as they do goldfinches in order that they can sing better.
*Intransigeant* 15 June 1932, repr. in *Picasso on Art* (1972) by Dore Ashton

5 When you start with a portrait and search for a pure form, a clear volume, through successive eliminations, you arrive inevitably at the egg. Likewise, starting with the egg and following the same process in reverse, one finishes with the portrait.
ibid.

6 Painting is a *jeu d'esprit*.
*Arts* 29 June 1935, quoted in *Picasso: Fifty Years of His Art* (1946) by Alfred H. Barr Jr

7 Art is not the application of a canon of beauty but what the instinct and the brain can conceive beyond any canon. When we love a woman we don't start measuring her limbs.
'Conversation avec Picasso', publ. in *Cahiers d'art*, vol. 10, no. 10 (1935), repr. in ibid.

8 There ought to be an absolute dictatorship . . . a dictatorship of painters . . . a dictatorship of one painter . . . to suppress all those who have betrayed us, to suppress the cheaters, to suppress the tricks, to suppress mannerisms, to suppress charms, to suppress history, to suppress a heap of other things. But common sense always gets away with it. Above all, let's have a revolution against that!
ibid.

9 To finish a work? To finish a picture? What nonsense! To finish it means to be through with it, to kill it, to rid it of its soul, to give it its final blow . . . the *coup de grâce* for the painter as well as for the picture.
Quoted in *Picasso: portraits et souvenirs*, ch. 7 (1946) by Jaime Sabartés

10 [Of genius] It is personality with a penny's worth of talent. Error which chances to rise above the commonplace.
Quoted in ibid. ch. 9

11 The genius of Einstein leads to Hiroshima.
Remark to Françoise Gilot in 1946, quoted in *Life with Picasso*, pt 2 (1964) by Françoise Gilot and Carlton Lake

12 Youth has no age.
*Arts de France* no. 6, 1946, repr. in *Picasso on Art* (1972) by Dore Ashton

13 Now at least we know everything that painting isn't.
Said in Rome 1949, quoted in *Scritti di Picasso* (1964) by Mario De Micheli. In answer to whether figurative painting was still possible after the advances made by photography and cinema, reported by artist Renato Guttuso in his journals.

14 Painting is a blind man's profession. He paints not what he sees, but what he feels, what he tells himself about what he has seen.
Quoted in *Journals*, pt 1 'War and Peace' (1956) by JEAN COCTEAU

15 One does a whole painting for one peach and people think just the opposite – that that particular peach is but a detail.

*Vogue* 1 November 1956

16 Success is dangerous. One begins to copy oneself, and to copy oneself is more dangerous than to copy others. It leads to sterility.

ibid.

17 Art is never chaste. It ought to be forbidden to ignorant innocents, never allowed into contact with those not sufficiently prepared. Yes, art is dangerous. Where it is chaste, it is not art.

Quoted in *Pablo Picasso*, ch. 11 (1957) by Antonina Vallentin

18 Ah, good taste! What a dreadful thing! Taste is the enemy of creativeness.

Quoted in *Quote Magazine* 24 March 1957

19 If all the ways I have been along were marked on a map and joined up with a line, it might represent a minotaur.

Official catalogue of the Musée d'Antibes, known as the Musée Picasso, quoted in *Picasso in Antibes* (1960) by Dor de la Souchère

20 Today, as you know, I am famous and very rich. But when I am alone with myself, I haven't the courage to consider myself an artist, in the great and ancient sense of that word . . . I am only a public entertainer, who understands his age.

*Le Spectacle du monde* November 1962, repr. in *The Trousered Ape*, ch. 2 (1971) by Duncan Williams

21 One starts to get young at the age of sixty and then it is too late.

*Sunday Times* 20 October 1963

22 God is really only another artist. He invented the giraffe, the elephant, and the cat. He has no real style. He just keeps on trying other things.

Quoted in *Life with Picasso*, pt 1 (1964) by Françoise Gilot and Carlton Lake

23 Is there anything more dangerous than sympathetic understanding?

Quoted in *Picasso Says . . .*, 'Solitude' (1966) by Hélène Parmelin

## Marge Piercy (b. 1936)
US NOVELIST AND POET

Her stated aim 'to be useful' is reflected in her visionary political and feminist fiction and poetry. Novels include *Small Changes* (1973), *Woman on the Edge of Time* (1976), and *City of Darkness, City of Light* (1997), set in the French Revolution. Her poetry is collected in *Hard Loving* (1969) and *To Be of Use* (1973), among other titles.

1 Many of my generation . . . suspect the Age of Greed and Waste to be . . . crudely overdrawn. But to burn your compost! To pour your shit into the water others downstream must drink! That fish must live in! Into rivers whose estuaries and marshes are links in the whole offshore food chain . . . Nobody's going to believe this. It all goes to show you can be too smart to see the middle step and fall on your face leaping!

Luciente, in *Woman on the Edge of Time*, ch. 2 (1976)

2 We have limited resources. We plan co-operatively. We can afford to waste . . . nothing. You might say our – you'd say religion? – ideas make us see ourselves as partners with water, air, birds, fish trees.

ibid. ch. 6

3 I write to change consciousness, to reach those people who don't agree already. Cultural work is one of the most effective ways of reaching people. If you don't support alternate ways of imagining things, people aren't going to be able to imagine a better world.

*Vida*, flyleaf (1979)

## Harold Pinter (b. 1930)
BRITISH PLAYWRIGHT

His work for the theatre explores the illogical below the seemingly rational surfaces of everyday language. Among his best known plays are *The Birthday Party* (1957), *The Caretaker* (1960, filmed 1963) and *The Homecoming* (1965). Later works include the explicitly political *Mountain Language* (1988) and *Ashes to Ashes* (1996). *Various Voices* (1998) is a collection of essays and poems, and he has also written numerous screenplays. When asked what his plays were about, he once answered, 'the weasel under the cocktail cabinet'.

1 If only I could get down to Sidcup! I've been waiting for the weather to break. He's got my papers, this man I left them with, it's got it all down there, I could prove everything.

Davies, in *The Caretaker*, act 1 (1960)

2 You're nothing else but a wild animal, when you come down to it. You're a barbarian. And to put the old tin lid on it, you stink from arse-hole to breakfast time.

Mick, speaking to Davies, in ibid. act 3

3 I have never been loved. From this I derive my strength.

Spooner, in *No Man's Land*, act 1 (1975)

4 You are in no man's land. Which never moves, which never changes, which never grows older, but which remains forever, icy and silent.

Spooner, in ibid. act 2

5 I tend to believe that cricket is the greatest thing that God ever created on earth.

'Pinter on Pinter' in the *Observer* 5 October 1980

6 I hate despair. I find it intolerable. The stink of it gets up my nose. It's a blemish. Despair, old fruit, is a cancer. It should be castrated. Indeed I've often found that that works. Chop the balls off and despair goes out the window.

Nicholas, in *One for the Road* (1985)

7 You have to look very carefully at your motives if you become a public figure. The danger is that you become an exhibitionist, self-important, pompous . . . Before you know where you are you're having make-up put on, your eyelashes are being tinted.

'A Play and its Politics', conversation, February 1985, publ. with play *One for the Road* (1985)

8 Now hear this. You are mountain people. You hear me? Your language is dead. It is forbidden. It is not permitted to speak your mountain language in this place.

Officer, in *Mountain Language*, sc. 1 (1988)

9 The US is without doubt the greatest show on the road. Brutal, indifferent, scornful and ruthless it may be, but it's also very smart. As a salesman it's out on its own. And its most saleable commodity is self-love. The US has actually educated itself to be in love with itself.

'It Never Happened', publ. in the *Guardian* 4 December 1996, repr. in *Various Voices* (1998)

10 That the torturers listen to music and are very kind to their children has been well established throughout twentieth-century history. This is one of the very complex states of affairs in the psychology of our social and political lives.

'Writing, Politics and *Ashes to Ashes*', interview in Barcelona, 6 December 1996, publ. in ibid.

11 It comes easily for the English people to mock. It's a very odd situation indeed in England; you try to address real facts of life that surround you and are treated with great hostility.

ibid. On the public response to his political involvement.

## Luigi Pirandello (1867–1936)

ITALIAN AUTHOR AND PLAYWRIGHT

The Sicilian-born writer of the novel *The Late Mattia Pascal* (1903) and the plays *Six Characters in Search of an Author* (1921) and *Henry IV* (1922) was particularly drawn to the themes of tragic alienation and the illusion of personality. In 1925 he established his own theatre, the Teatro d'Arte, and toured Europe. He received the Nobel Prize for Literature in 1934.

1 Anyone can be heroic from time to time, but a gentleman is something you have to be all the time.

Maurizio, in *The Pleasure of Honesty* act 1 (1918)

2 In bed my real love has always been the sleep that rescued me by allowing me to dream.

Silia, in *The Rules of the Game* act 2 (1919, transl. 1959)

3 But you must play your part, just as I am playing mine. It's all in the game ... Each of us must play his part through to the end.

Leone, in ibid.

4 Six Characters in Search of an Author.

Play title (1921)

5 Nature uses human imagination to lift her work of creation to even higher levels.

The Father, in *Six Characters in Search of an Author*, act 1 (1921)

6 Whoever has the luck to be born a character can laugh even at death. Because a character will never die! A man will die, a writer, the instrument of creation: but what he has created will never die!

ibid.

7 Each of us, face to face with other men, is clothed with some sort of dignity, but we know only too well all the unspeakable things that go on in the heart.

ibid.

8 When the characters are really alive before their author, the latter does nothing but follow them in their action, in their words, in the situations which they suggest to him.

ibid. act 3

9 Every true man, sir, who is a little above the level of the beasts and plants does not live for the sake of living, without knowing how to live; but he lives so as to give a meaning and a value of his own to life.

ibid.

10 You know what it means to be with a madman? To be with someone who shakes the foundations, the logic of the whole structure of everything you've built in and around yourselves.

Henry IV, in *Henry IV*, act 2 (1922)

## Robert M. Pirsig (b. 1928)

US AUTHOR

His stated aim in writing is to relate metaphysics to 'cultural problems of today'. *Zen and the Art of Motorcycle Maintenance* (1974) attempts to do this through an account of a motorcycle journey across America, narrated as both a physical expedition and a psychological quest. *Lila* (1991) is about 'sailing, philosophy, sex and madness'.

1 The Buddha, the Godhead, resides quite as comfortably in the circuits of a digital computer or the gears of a cycle transmission as he does at the top of a mountain or in the petals of a flower.

*Zen and the Art of Motorcycle Maintenance*, pt 1, ch. 1 (1974)

2 A motorcycle functions entirely in accordance with the laws of reason, and a study of the art of motorcycle maintenance is really a miniature study of the art of rationality itself.

ibid. pt 2, ch. 8

3 Traditional scientific method has always been at the very best, 20–20 hindsight. It's good for seeing where you've been. It's good for testing the truth of what you think you know, but it can't tell you where you *ought* to go.

ibid. pt 3, ch. 24

## Brad Pitt (b. 1963)

US SCREEN ACTOR

Full name William Bradley Pitt. Dubbed the 'sexiest man alive', he has appeared in *True Romance* (1993) *Twelve Monkeys* (1995), *Meet Joe Black* (1998) and *Fight Club* (1999). Noted for his dislike of the publicity drawn to his celebrity lifestyle, he was judged 'overrated as a hermit as he is an underrated actor' by *Film Review Magazine*.

1 Celebrity is bestial. It is the worst type of karma because of the huge solitude it brings. You are like a gazelle that finds itself straying from the flock. And soon your path is cut off by lions.

Quoted in the *Daily Telegraph* 24 December 1998

## Walter B. Pitkin (1878–1953)

US AUTHOR, EDITOR AND PSYCHOLOGIST

A prolific writer on psychology, he was on the editorial staff of the New York *Tribune* (1907–1908) and *Evening Post* (1909–1910), and in 1940 designed a $100,000 yacht, which sank in the Hudson River. His books include *The Psychology of Happiness* (1929), *Life Begins at Forty* (1932) and *Let's Get What We Want* (1935).

1 Life begins at forty.

Book title (1932)

## Pius XI (1857–1939)

ITALIAN ECCLESIASTIC AND POPE

Ambrogio Damiano Achille Ratti. Pope from 1922, he was responsible for signing the Lateran Treaty (1929) with MUSSOLINI, a concordat that established the independence of the Vatican State. During his pontificate the number of missionaries doubled, religious instruction for Catholic schoolchildren was made compulsory and the role of the laity was widened.

1 Whether considered as a doctrine, or as an historical fact, or as a movement, socialism, if it really remains socialism, cannot be brought into harmony with the dogmas of the Catholic church ... Religious socialism, Christian socialism, are expressions implying a contradiction in terms.

*Quadragesimo Anno* (encyclical, 1931)

## Pius XII (1876–1958)

ITALIAN ECCLESIASTIC AND POPE

Eugenio Pacelli. He was made Pope in 1939 and is remembered for his conservative approach to doctrine and politics. He strove to relieve the suffering of the Second World War while maintaining diplomatic relations with both Allied and Axis governments, but failed to speak out against Nazi atrocities.

1 The Church welcomes technological progress and receives it with love, for it is an indubitable fact that technological progress comes from God and, therefore, can and must lead to Him.

Christmas message, 1953, publ. in *The Harvest of a Quiet Eye* (ed. Alan L. Mackay, 1977)

## Erin Pizzey (b. 1939)

BRITISH ACTIVIST AND AUTHOR

In 1971 she founded Chiswick Women's Aid, the first shelter in Britain for battered wives and their children. Her book *Scream*

*Quietly or the Neighbours Will Hear* (1974) highlights violence among middle class families. She has also written novels.

1 **To me, a good family is the basis of democracy and is democratic to the core. That's why the feminists had to destroy it.**
Quoted in the *Observer* 11 February 1996

## Max Planck (1858–1947)
GERMAN PHYSICIST

His break with classical physics resulted in his revolutionary quantum theory (1900), the application of which in turn led to EINSTEIN's theory of relativity and NIELS BOHR's atomic theory. He was professor at Berlin (1892–1926) and received the Nobel Prize for Physics in 1918.

1 **A new scientific truth does not triumph by convincing its opponents and making them see the light, but rather because its opponents eventually die, and a new generation grows up that is familiar with it.**
*Scientific Autobiography and Other Papers*, 'Scientific Autobiography' (1948)

## Sylvia Plath (1932–63)
US POET

Her only collection of poems to be published in her own lifetime was *The Colossus* (1960), while her best known works are her partly autobiographical novel *The Bell Jar* (1963) and *Ariel* (1965). Her suicide, a year after separating from her husband TED HUGHES, was the culmination of a series of attempts on her own life. Hughes published her *Collected Poems* (1981) and celebrated her memory in *Birthday Letters* (1998).

1 **How frail the human heart must be –
a mirrored pool of thought . . .**
'I Thought I Could Not Be Hurt', first poem written aged fourteen, quoted in *Letters Home: Correspondence 1950–1963*, Introduction (1975) by Aurelia Schober Plath

2 **Prim, pink-breasted, feminine, she nurses
Chocolate fancies in rose-papered rooms.**
'Female Author', publ. in *Collected Poems*, 'Juvenilia' (ed. Ted Hughes, 1981)

3 **Apparently, the most difficult feat for a Cambridge male is to accept a woman not merely as feeling, not merely as thinking, but as managing a complex, vital interweaving of both.**
*Isis* (Oxford students' magazine) 6 May 1956. Written while Plath was a student at Cambridge.

4 **Overnight, very
Whitely, discreetly,
Very quietly**

**Our toes, our noses
Take hold on the loam,
Acquire the air.**
'Mushrooms' written 1959, publ. in *The Colossus* (1960)

5 **These poems do not live: it's a sad diagnosis.
They grew their toes and fingers well enough,
Their little foreheads bulged with concentration.
If they missed out on walking about like people
It wasn't for any lack of mother-love.**
'Stillborn' written 1960, publ. in *Crossing the Water* (1971)

6 **Love set you going like a fat gold watch.
The midwife slapped your footsoles, and your bald cry
Took its place among the elements.**
'Morning Song', first publ. in the *Observer* 21 May 1961, repr. in *Ariel* (1965)

7 **Widow. The word consumes itself . . .**
'Widow', written 1961, publ. in *Crossing the Water* (1971)

8 **Is there no way out of the mind?**
'Apprehensions', written 1962, publ. in ibid.

9 **If neurotic is wanting two mutually exclusive things at one and the same time, then I'm neurotic as hell. I'll be flying back and forth between one mutually exclusive thing and another for the rest of my days.**
Narrator (Esther Greenwood), in *The Bell Jar*, ch. 8 (1963)

10 **Every woman adores a Fascist,
The boot in the face, the brute
Brute heart of a brute like you.**
'Daddy', first publ. in *Encounter* October 1963, repr. in *Ariel* (1965)

11 **Dying
Is an art, like everything else.
I do it exceptionally well.**

**I do it so it feels like hell.
I do it so it feels real.
I guess you could say I've a call.**
'Lady Lazarus', ibid.

12 **Kindness glides about my house.
Dame Kindness, she is so nice!
The blue and red jewels of her rings smoke
In the windows, the mirrors
Are filling with smiles.**
'Kindness', written 1963, publ. in *Ariel* (1965)

13 **Perfection is terrible, it cannot have children.**
'The Munich Mannequins', ibid.

14 **The woman is perfected.
Her dead**

**Body wears the smile of accomplishment**
'Edge', publ. in *Ariel* (1965). Opening lines of Plath's last poem, written a week before her suicide.

## William Plomer (1903–73)
SOUTH AFRICAN AUTHOR AND POET

He edited the anti-racist magazine *Voorslag* ('Whiplash') in Durban, together with LAURENS VAN DER POST and Roy Campbell, and racism was also the subject of his most famous novel *Turbott Wolfe* (1925). He settled in London in 1929 and later wrote poetry, and also librettos for BENJAMIN BRITTEN. STEPHEN SPENDER described his work as 'wind-blown, sun-saturated, sparkling'.

1 **When her guests were awash with champagne and with gin
She was recklessly sober, as sharp as a pin.
An abstemious man would reel at her look
As she rolled a bright eye and praised his last book.**
'Slightly Foxed, or The Widower of Bayswater', publ. in *Collected Poems* (1960)

2 **Peristalsis calls for roughage,
Haulms and fibres, husks and grit,
Nature's way to open bowels,
Maybe – let them practise it.**
'The Flying Bum', publ. in ibid.

3 **The commonplace needs no defence,
Dullness is in the critic's eye,
Without a licence life evolves
From some dim phase its own surprise.**
'The Bungalows', publ. in ibid.

4 **Everything sings
in snowy stillness
in marble wonder,
in formal myth,
believed because
impossible,
believed as only
a poem can be,**

the anti-fact
of a holy spore
spreading the Word
unsaid before.

'A Church in Bavaria', publ. in ibid.

5 The dead are non-living
the hungry are non-fed:
don't think because you're non-unconscious
that you're alive – you're non-dead.

'Bureaucratic Negatives', publ. in ibid.

## Norman Podhoretz (b. 1930)

US EDITOR, CRITIC AND ESSAYIST

He joined the staff of *Commentary* in 1955 as literary critic and became Editor in 1960. In a style that he admitted 'could be characterized as provocative' he emphasized the 'cultural roots of political developments' in his writings. Two volumes of autobiography (1968 and 1979) were followed by social critique, *The Present Danger: Do We Have the Will to Reverse the Decline of American Power?* (1980).

1 Our culture is ill-equipped to assert the bourgeois values which would be the salvation of the under-class, because we have lost those values ourselves.

*Daily Mail* 10 November 1989

## Political Slogans

See also STOKELY CARMICHAEL 1, DARIO FO 4, JOHN LENNON 4, MALCOLM X 5.

1 Land. Bread. Peace.

Revolutionary slogan of 1917 calling for land reform, access to food and Russian withdrawal from the First World War. Taken up and promoted by the Bolsheviks.

2 Our day will come.
(*Tiocfaidh Ar La.*)

IRA slogan, 1920s

3 We shall not be moved.

Title of labour and civil rights song, 1930s, adapted from an earlier gospel hymn

4 One realm, one people, one leader.
(*Ein Reich, ein Volk, ein Führer.*)

Nazi Party slogan, early 1930s

5 Strength through joy.
(*Kraft durch Freude.*)

German Labour Front slogan from 1933, credited to Robert Ley (1890–1945), German Nazi and head of the Labour Front 1933–45

6 War will cease when men refuse to fight. What are *you* going to do about it?

Pacifist slogan, c. 1936. In May 1940 the Peace Pledge Union was prosecuted under Defence Regulation 39a for a poster with these words. The Editor, Canon Stuart Morris, told the court that the poster was 'two-year-old stock' and 'inappropriate at the present time' as activists were anxious 'not to be thought to be obstructing the war effort'. The slogan is often quoted as 'Wars will cease . . .'.

7 A bayonet is a weapon with a worker at each end.

British pacifist slogan, 1940s

8 Ban the bomb.

US anti-nuclear slogan, from 1953, adopted in Britain by the Campaign for Nuclear Disarmament

9 Hey, hey, LBJ, how many kids did you kill today?

Anti-Vietnam War slogan, opposing LYNDON BAINES JOHNSON's continuation of the war

10 Hell no, we won't go.

Chant of US draft resisters refusing to serve in the Vietnam War

11 Make love not war.

Hippy slogan of the 1960s

12 Burn, baby, burn!

Slogan linked to the race riots in Watts, Los Angeles, August 1965, in *I Hear America Talking*, 'The Blacks' (1976) by Stuart Berg Flexner

13 Black is beautiful.

Slogan of the Black Power movement, 1960s

14 Power to the people.

Slogan of the Black Panther movement, from c. 1968. Also the title of a song by JOHN LENNON in 1971.

15 Every mother a willing mother. Every child a wanted child.

Abortion rights slogan, early 1970s

16 Who governs Britain?

Conservative slogan for 1974 general election. In the wake of the industrial disputes, in particular the long miners' strike, which had characterized the government of EDWARD HEATH and which had precipitated the election, the Conservative Party made the struggle with the unions the central issue of their electoral campaign. The Labour Party under HAROLD WILSON concentrated instead on creating a harmonious 'social contract' with the unions, as highlighted in their manifesto 'Let Us Work Together'. The result of the election was a marginal Labour victory and a government heavily dependent on the unions.

17 Save the whale.

Greenpeace slogan from 1970s

18 It takes up to 40 dumb animals to make a fur coat but only one to wear it.

Slogan of anti-fur trade group Lynx, mid-1980s. The words appeared on a banner in DAVID BAILEY's celebrated video in support of the group.

19 Let Nicaragua live.

Slogan opposing the REAGAN administration's campaign against Nicaragua's Sandinista government, mid-1980s

20 The people united
Will never be defeated.
(*El pueblo unido
Jamás será vencido.*)

Chanted on demonstrations against US intervention in Central America, 1980s. Taken up by a number of other movements including Seattle protesters against the World Trade Organization in 1999.

21 Ulster says no.

Unionist slogan opposing the Anglo-Irish Agreement of 15 November 1985

22 Think globally, act locally.

Friends of the Earth slogan, mid-1980s

23 Better to break the law than break the poor.

Slogan of the British anti-Poll Tax campaign, late 1980s, thought to have been coined by members of Militant Tendency

24 If not us, who? If not now, when?

Slogan by Czech university students in Prague, November 1989

25 Coal not dole.

Slogan early 1990s, protesting plans of the Conservative government to close British coal mines

26 Reclaim the streets.

Slogan used by direct action groups in London, early 1990s, and adopted internationally

27 Freedom to drive or freedom to breathe.

Anti-roads slogan, from early 1990s

28 Keep your rosaries out of our ovaries.

Women's Action Committee against anti-abortionists, 1992

29 Fight for your right to party.

Slogan of the Advance Party, formed to resist the provisions of the Criminal Justice Act of 1994 banning open-air raves. Also the title of a song by the Beastie Boys which charted in 1987.

30 No compromise in defence of the earth.

Slogan of the international direct action movement, Earth First, 1990s

31 Under the tarmac, the trees.

Anti-roads slogan, 1990s

32 **Resistance as global as capital.**

Slogan of 'anti-capitalist' protesters, from late 1990s, directed against policies of the World Trade Organization and the International Monetary Fund. The slogan is sometimes rendered 'Resistance Transnational as Capital'.

## Jackson Pollock (1912–56)

US ARTIST

At first influenced by Surrealists such as Miró, 'Jack the Dripper', as he was nicknamed, became a leading Abstract Expressionist, his action painting characterized by intricate swirling lines from dripped or poured paint. Examples of his work are *Number Ten* (1949) and *Blue Poles* (1952). He was killed in a car accident.

1 When I say artist I don't mean in the narrow sense of the word – but the man who is building things – creating molding the earth – whether it be the plains of the west – or the iron ore of Penn. It's all a big game of construction – some with a brush – some with a shovel – some choose a pen.

Letter to his father, 1932, publ. in *Jackson Pollock: A Catalogue Raisonné of Paintings, Drawings and Other Works*, vol. 4 (ed. Francis V. O'Connor and Eugene V. Thaw, 1978)

2 The method of painting is the natural growth out of a need. I want to express my feelings rather than illustrate them. Technique is just a means of arriving at a statement . . . I *can* control the flow of paint: there is no accident, just as there is no beginning and no end.

Narrative to *Jackson Pollock* (film, 1951, made by Hans Nemuth and Paul Falkenberg), publ. in *Jackson Pollock* (1960) by Bryan Robertson

## Georges Pompidou (1911–74)

FRENCH PRESIDENT

Holding government posts since 1946, he aided the drafting of the constitution of the Gaullist Fifth Republic (1958–9), negotiated the settlement in Algeria (1961) and while Prime Minister (1962–8) dealt with the student riots of 1968. He succeeded De Gaulle as President in 1969.

1 There are three roads to ruin; women, gambling and technicians. The most pleasant is with women, the quickest is with gambling, but the surest is with technicians.

Quoted in the *Sunday Telegraph* 26 May 1968

## Iggy Pop (b. 1947)

US ROCK MUSICIAN

Original name James Newell Osterberg. Founder of the proto-punk band the Stooges in 1967, he gathered a reputation as an anarchic self-mutilator and self-exposer in the band's live sets. His career was revived by DAVID BOWIE in 1977, with whom he recorded two classic albums, *The Idiot* and *Lust for Life* (both 1978).

1 No fun, my babe. No Fun.
No fun to hang around feeling the same old way.
No fun to hang around, freaked out for another day.
No fun to be all alone, walking by myself.
No fun to be alone in love with nobody else.

'No Fun' (song, written by Iggy Pop and Ron Asheton) on the album *The Stooges* (1969) by Iggy Pop and The Stooges

2 Nihilism is best done by professionals.

*Independent* 12 July 1990

3 I spent most of the Eighties, most of my *life*, riding around in somebody else's car, in possession of, or ingested of, something illegal, on my way from something illegal to something illegal with many illegal things happening all around me.

Interview in the *Guardian* 17 February 1996

## (Sir) Karl Popper (1902–94)

AUSTRIAN-BORN BRITISH PHILOSOPHER

His first and major book *The Logic of Scientific Discovery* (1934) posits the doctrine that true scientific theories must pass the test of 'falsifiability'. *The Open Society and its Enemies* (1945), a work he called his war effort, profoundly criticized Plato, Hegel and Marx. He left Austria in 1937 and was professor at the London School of Economics from 1949 to 1969.

1 We may become the makers of our own fate when we have ceased to pose as its prophets.

*The Open Society and its Enemies*, Introduction (1945)

2 All science is cosmology, I believe, and for me the interest of philosophy, no less than that of science, lies solely in the contributions which it has made to it.

Preface (1959) to *The Logic of Scientific Discovery* (1934)

3 For this, indeed, is the true source of our ignorance – the fact that our knowledge can only be finite, while our ignorance must necessarily be infinite.

Lecture to British Academy, 20 January 1960, publ. in *Proceedings of the British Academy*, vol. 4 (1960)

4 Science may be described as the art of systematic over-simplification.

Quoted in the *Observer* 1 August 1982

## Cole Porter (1893–1964)

US COMPOSER AND LYRICIST

The epitome of suave sophistication, he was unequalled for his deft and witty wordplay set to perfectly adapted melodies. Such songs as 'Let's Do It' (1928), 'Night and Day' (1928) and 'Ev'ry Time We Say Goodbye' (1944) were interpreted by a range of artists, and most comprehensively by Ella Fitzgerald. From 1937 he was severely disabled after a riding accident.

1 If you want to buy my wares
Follow me and climb the stairs . . .
Love for sale.

'Love For Sale' (song) in *The New Yorkers* (stage musical, 1930)

2 Night and day, you are the one,
Only you beneath the moon and under the sun.

'Night and Day' (song) in *The Gay Divorce* (stage musical, 1932), filmed as *The Gay Divorcee*, 1934). Originally sung by Fred Astaire.

3 Oh, give me land, lots of land
Under starry skies above
Don't fence me in.

'Don't Fence Me In' (song, 1934). The song, first recorded by Roy Rogers and the Sons of Pioneers, was later a hit for Bing Crosby with the Andrews sisters and revived in *Hollywood Canteen* (film musical, 1944).

4 I've got you under my skin.

'I've Got You Under My Skin' (song, 1934), in *Born to Dance* (film musical, 1936)

5 In olden days a glimpse of stocking
Was looked on as something shocking
But now, God knows,
Anything goes.

'Anything Goes' (song), in *Anything Goes* (stage musical 1934, film 1956). Sung by Ethel Merman in the musical and by Mitzi Gaynor in the film version.

6 Good authors, too, who once knew better words
Now only use four-letter words
Writing prose . . .
Anything goes.

ibid.

7 At words poetic, I'm so pathetic
That I always have found it best
Instead of getting 'em off my chest,
To let 'em rest unexpressed.
'You're the Top' (song), in ibid. Sung by William Gaxton and Ethel Merman in the original show, the song was recorded by Porter himself and later covered by Ella Fitzgerald and Buddy Greco, among others. The lyrics were adapted by P.G. WODEHOUSE for the 1935 London show.

8 You're the Nile,
You're the Tower of Pisa,
You're the smile
On the Mona Lisa . . .
But if, baby, I'm the bottom,
You're the top!
ibid.

9 I get no kick from champagne.
Mere alcohol doesn't thrill me at all,
So tell me why should it be true
That I get a kick out of you.
'I Get a Kick Out of You' (song), in ibid.

10 Miss Otis regrets (she's unable to lunch today).
'Miss Otis Regrets' (song), in Hi Diddle Diddle (stage musical, 1934)

11 There's no love song finer,
But how strange the change from major to minor
Every time we say goodbye.
'Ev'ry Time We Say Goodbye' (song ), in Seven Lively Arts (stage musical, 1944). The song was a hit for Benny Goodman (1945) and recorded by Ella Fitzgerald (1956) in a version described by her biographer Stuart Nicholson as 'a "We'll Meet Again" for the Cold War generation'.

12 He may have hair upon his chest
But, sister, so has Lassie.
'I Hate Men' (song), in Kiss Me Kate (stage musical 1948, filmed 1953)

13 I love Paris in the springtime.
'I Love Paris' (song) in Can-Can (stage musical, 1953, film 1960)

14 Birds do it, bees do it,
Even educated fleas do it.
Let's do it, let's fall in love.
'Let's Do It' (song, 1954). The song was first featured in a 1928 show, Paris, without this verse.

## Katherine Anne Porter (1890–1980)

US AUTHOR

Her first short story collection, Flowering Judas, appeared in 1928, followed by a novel Hacienda (1934) and the three novellas in Pale Horse, Pale Rider (1939). Her best known work, Ship of Fools (1962), stirred public controversy for its allegorical depiction of pre-Second World War Germany.

1 They [Herr Freytag and Mrs Treadwell] had both noticed that a life of dissipation sometimes gave to a face the look of gaunt suffering spirituality that a life of asceticism was supposed to give and quite often did not.
Ship of Fools, pt 3 (1962)

2 The real sin against life is to abuse and destroy beauty, even one's own – even more, one's own, for that has been put in our care and we are responsible for its well-being.
Herr Freytag, in ibid.

3 Human life itself may be almost pure chaos, but the work of the artist – the only thing he's good for – is to take these handfuls of confusion and disparate things, things that seem to be irreconcilable, and put them together in a frame to give them some kind of shape and meaning. Even if it's only his view of a meaning. That's what he's for – to give his view of life.
Interview in Writers at Work (second series, ed. George Plimpton, 1963)

4 A cultivated style would be like a mask. Everybody knows it's a mask, and sooner or later you must show yourself – or at least, you show yourself as someone who could not afford to show himself, and so created something to hide behind.
ibid.

5 If it is not perfect, it is not love, and if it is not love, it is bound to be hate sooner of later. This is perhaps a not too exaggerated statement of the extreme position of Romantic Love, more especially in America, where we are all brought up on it, whether we know it or not
'The Necessary Enemy', publ. in The Collected Essays and Occasional Writings of Katherine Anne Porter (1970)

## Peter Porter (b. 1929)

AUSTRALIAN POET

Since 1951 he has lived outside Australia, mainly in Britain. His poetry, collected in numerous works including Preaching to the Converted (1972), The Cost of Seriousness (1978) and English Subtitles (1981), draws inspiration from a range of subjects from foreign travel to personal loss. CLIVE JAMES once said his poetry was 'so freighted with learned references that I can't even tell if I don't know what they mean'.

1 When I dream of God I see
A Massacre of Cats. Why
should they insist on their own
language and religion, who
needs to purr to make his point?
Death to all cats! The Rule
of Dogs shall last a thousand years!
'Mort aux chats', publ. in Preaching to the Converted (1972)

2 Sparrows acclimatize but I still seek
The permanently upright city where
Speech is nature, and plants conceive in pots,
Where one escapes from what one is and who
One was, where home is just a postmark
And country wisdom clings to calendars,
The opposite of the sunburned truth-teller's
World, haunted by precepts and the Pleiades.
'On First Looking into Chapman's Hesiod', publ. in Living in a Calm Country (1975)

3 The channels of our lives are blocked,
The hand is stopped upon the clock,
No one can say why hearts will break
And marriages are all opaque:
A map of loss, some posted cards,
The living house reduced to shards,
The abstract hell of memory,
The pointlessness of poetry.
'An Exequy', publ. in The Cost of Seriousness (1978)

4 Nobody feels well after his fortieth birthday
But the convalescence is touched by glory.
'Returning', publ. in English Subtitles (1981)

## Dennis Potter (1935–94)

BRITISH DRAMATIST AND SCREENWRITER

The writer of controversial and innovative plays for the BBC for nearly thirty years, he often evoked memories of his own youth in his scripts, as in Pennies from Heaven (1978) and The Singing Detective (1986), both incorporating popular songs, and Blue Remembered Hills (1979), set in the Forest of Dean where he himself grew up and featuring adults playing children's roles.

1 The TV play . . . is not necessarily a miserable compromise between theatre and cinema. It need be neither the photographed stage play nor the thumbnail film. There are strengths and potentialities which belong to television alone, and I think it is an exhilarating medium for the

young writer as well as being the nearest thing we are ever likely to get to a 'theatre of the people'.

*The Nigel Barton Plays*, Introduction (1967)

2 In the last resort, politics don't count for you. Your brave new society will never come because you are incapable of working for it, incapable of telling lies for it, cheating for it, humiliating yourself for it. When you actually talk to real people you cower away from their ignorance and their apathy, don't you? Your condescending Hampstead Socialism collapses at the first belch of wind from a navvy's guts. You can't stand the stink of life, sweetheart!

Nigel Barton, addressing his wife Anne, in *Vote Vote Vote For Nigel Barton*, sc. 20, BBC play, broadcast 15 December 1965

3 To be a candidate is to submit to a personally humiliating experience, in which the set smile freezes on your face like a grin on a corpse. Dead ideas. Dead thoughts. Dead slogans. All of them sicked up on your doorstep. No wonder people are disgusted by this gruesome charade.

Nigel Barton, addressing a council dinner, in ibid. sc. 24

4 Blimey, I can almost taste it! It's looking for the blue, ennit, and the gold. The patch of blue sky. The gold of the, of the bleed'n dawn, or – the light in somebody's eyes – Pennies From Heaven, that's what it is. And we can't see 'em, clinking and clinking, all around, all over the place . . . just bend down and pick 'em up.

Arthur, in *Pennies From Heaven*, episode 2 (BBC television series, 1978)

5 Even in a future land of Muzak, monosodium glutamate and melamined encounters, the old resilient dreams will insist on making metaphors and finding illumination in the midst of surrounding dross. There is, then, no place where 'God' cannot reach.

*Brimstone and Treacle*, Introduction (1987). The play *Brimstone and Treacle* was originally written to be broadcast in 1976 but was banned on grounds of taste and not shown until 1989.

6 There's no way that you, nor any other man, could ever understand what it is that you men make us women think of our bodies.

Jessica, in *Blackeyes* (BBC television series, 1989)

7 The trouble with words is that you never know whose mouths they've been in.

*Guardian* 15 February 1993

8 Things are both more trivial than they ever were, and more important than they ever were, and the difference between the trivial and the important doesn't seem to matter – but the *nowness* of everything is absolutely wondrous . . . The fact is, that if you see the present tense, boy do you see it, and boy can you celebrate it!

Interview with Melvyn Bragg, Channel 4, 5 April 1994. Referring to the terminal stages of his illness.

9 Religion to me has always been the wound, not the bandage.

ibid.

10 I find the word 'British' harder and harder to use as time passes.

ibid.

11 I think we should always look back on our own past with a sort of tender contempt. As long as the tenderness is there but also please let some of the contempt be there, because we know what we're like, we know how we hustle and bustle and shove and push, and you sometimes use grand words to cloak it.

ibid.

12 Cheap songs, so-called, actually do have something of the Psalms of David about them. They do say the world is other than it is. They do illuminate. This is why people say, 'Listen, they're playing our song'. It's not because

that particular song actually expresses the depth of the feelings that they felt when they met each other and heard it. It is that somehow it re-evokes it, but with a different coating of irony and self-knowledge. Those feelings come bubbling back.

ibid.

13 The closer writing approaches to therapy, the worse it becomes.

Quoted in *Dennis Potter: A Life On Screen*, ch. 3 (1995) by John R. Cook

# Ezra Pound (1885–1972)
US POET AND CRITIC

A founder of the Imagist movement while in London (1908–20), he settled in Italy in 1925 where he backed MUSSOLINI and broadcast Fascist propaganda during the Second World War. He was judged insane by a US psychiatric committee after the war and confined to a mental hospital until 1958. His main works are the *Cantos* (1917–70), and he also translated from French, Chinese, Japanese and Italian. GERTRUDE STEIN described him as 'a village explainer, excellent if you were a village, but if you were not, not'.

1 Humanity is the rich effluvium, it is the waste and the manure and the soil, and from it grows the tree of the arts.

*Poetry* October 1914. Objecting to the motto on the cover of the magazine *Poetry*, that 'To have great poets, there must be great audiences too', a quote by Walt Whitman ('Ventures on an Old Theme', 1881). Pound upheld that the arts were dependent on no one.

2 The Image is more than an idea. It is a vortex or cluster of fused ideas and is endowed with energy.

'Affirmations – As for Imagisme', publ. in *New Age* 28 January 1915, repr. in *Selected Prose 1909–1965*, pt 7 (ed. William Cookson, 1973)

3 If a patron buys from an artist who needs money (needs money to buy tools, time, food), the patron then makes himself equal to the artist; he is building art into the world; he creates.

Letter, 8 March 1915, publ. in *The Letters of Ezra Pound 1907–1941* (ed. D.D. Paige, 1951). Pound was urging US collector John Quinn to support the new renaissance of the arts that Pound believed was imminent.

4 There are few things more difficult than to appraise the work of a man suddenly dead in his youth; to disentangle 'promise' from achievement; to save him from that sentimentalizing which confuses the tragedy of the interruption with the merit of the work actually performed.

*Gaudier-Brzeska: a Memoir*, ch. 13 (1916). Of French sculptor and Vorticist Henri Gaudier-Brzeska, killed in action in France, 1915.

5 The apparition of these faces in the crowd;
Petals on a wet, black bough.

'In a Station of the Metro', publ. in *Lustra* (1916)

6 Winter is icummen in,
Lhude sing Goddamm,
Raineth drop and staineth slop,
And how the wind doth ramm!
Sing: Goddamm.

'Ancient Music', publ. in *Lustra* (1917 edn). Pound's pastiche of the medieval song ('Sumer is icumen in,/Lhude sing cuccu!') was originally dropped from the 1916 edition of *Lustra*, having been considered offensive.

7 A great age of literature is perhaps always a great age of translations.

*Egoist* October 1917, quoted in *A Serious Character*, pt 2, ch. 20 (1988) by Humphrey Carpenter

8 A man of genius has a right to any mode of expression.

Letter to the painter J.B. Yeats (father of W.B. YEATS), 4 February 1918, quoted in *A Serious Character*, pt 2, ch. 10 (1988) by Humphrey Carpenter

9  The age demanded an image
   Of its accelerated grimace,
   Something for the modern stage,
   Not, at any rate, an Attic grace;

   Not, not certainly, the obscure reveries
   Of the inward gaze;
   Better mendacities
   Than the classics in paraphrase!

   'E.P. Ode pour l'élection de son sépulcre', pt 2, publ. in *Hugh
   Selwyn Mauberley* (1920)

10  There died a myriad,
    And of the best, among them,
    For an old bitch gone in the teeth,
    For a botched civilization.

    ibid. pt 5

11  The curse of me & my nation is that we always think
    things can be bettered by immediate action of some sort,
    *any* sort rather than no sort.

    Letter to JAMES JOYCE, 7–8 June 1920, publ. in *Pound/Joyce: The
    Letters of Ezra Pound to James Joyce* (ed. Forrest Read, 1968)

12  It is more than likely that the brain itself is, in origin and
    development, only a sort of great clot of genital fluid held
    in suspense or reserved … This hypothesis … would
    explain the enormous content of the brain as a maker or
    presenter of images.

    'Translator's Postscript' to *Physique de l'amour* (1922) by Rémy de
    Gourmont

13  I consider criticism merely a preliminary excitement, a
    statement of things a writer has to clear up in his own
    head sometime or other, probably antecedent to writing;
    of no value unless it come to fruit in the created work
    later.

    'On Criticism in General', publ. in *Criterion* January 1923

14  Great literature is simply language charged with meaning
    to the utmost possible degree.

    *How to Read*, pt 2 (1931)

15  The author's conviction on this day of New Year is that
    music begins to atrophy when it departs too far from the
    dance; that poetry begins to atrophy when it gets too far
    from music; but this must not be taken as implying that
    all good music is dance music or all poetry lyric. Bach and
    Mozart are never too far from physical movement.

    *ABC of Reading*, 'Warning' (1934)

16  Literature is news that STAYS news.

    ibid. ch. 2

17  Good writers are those who keep the language efficient.
    That is to say, keep it accurate, keep it clear.

    ibid. ch. 3

18  [Of Mussolini] AS A MIND, who the hell else is there
    left for me to take an interest IN?

    Letter, 28 August 1934, quoted in *A Serious Character*, pt 3, ch. 13
    (1988) by Humphrey Carpenter. Interviewed in May 1945, Pound
    described MUSSOLINI as 'a very human, imperfect character who
    lost his head', and in the opening lines of canto 74 (first of his *Pisan
    Cantos*, written in 1948 while he was awaiting trial for treason), he
    spoke of 'the enormous tragedy of the dream in the peasant's bent
    shoulders'.

19  [Of Henry Miller's *Tropic of Cancer*] Here is a dirty book
    worth reading … a bawdy which will be very useful to
    put Wyndham and JJ into their proper cubby holes; cause
    Miller is sore and without kinks.

    Letter, 1 December 1934, quoted by Karl Shapiro in 'The Greatest
    Living Author', preface to *Tropic of Cancer* (1960 edn) by HENRY
    MILLER. The book was first published in Paris in 1934, but sup-
    pressed in the US and Britain. 'Wyndham' was WYNDHAM LEWIS,
    'JJ' was JAMES JOYCE.

20  Man is an over-complicated organism. If he is doomed to
    extinction he will die out for want of simplicity.

    *Guide to Kulchur*, pt 3, sect. 5, ch. 19 (1938)

21  In our time, the curse is monetary illiteracy, just as in-
    ability to read plain print was the curse of earlier centuries.

    ibid. pt 4, sect. 8, ch. 31

22  Mass ought to be in Latin, unless you cd. do it in Greek
    or Chinese. In fact, *any* abracadabra that no bloody
    member of the public or half-educated ape of a clargimint
    cd. think he understood.

    Letter, 7 March 1940, publ. in *The Letters of Ezra Pound 1907–1941*
    (ed. D.D. Paige, 1951)

23  Adolf Hitler was a Jeanne d'Arc, a saint. He was a martyr.
    Like many martyrs, he held extreme views.

    Interview in the *Philadelphia Record* and *Chicago Sun* 9 May 1945

24  I guess the definition of a lunatic is a man surrounded by
    them.

    Quoted in *Charles Olson and Ezra Pound*, 'Canto 3, January 24 1946'
    (1975) by Catherine Seelye. Said to CHARLES OLSON in 1945, when
    Olson visited Pound in St Elizabeth's Hospital, Washington, the
    institution for the criminally insane in which Pound was detained
    pending a judgment on his wartime broadcasts from Rome.

25  With one day's reading a man may have the key in his
    hands.

    *Pisan Cantos*, canto 74 (1948)

26  As a lone ant from a broken ant-hill
    from the wreckage of Europe, ego scriptor.

    ibid. canto 76

27  WOT IZZA COMIN'?
    'I'll tell you wot izza comin'
    Sochy-lism is a-comin''

    ibid. canto 77

28  There once was a brainy baboon
    Who always breathed down a bassoon,
    For he said, 'It appears
    That in billions of years
    I shall certainly hit on a tune.'

    Letter, 21 July 1949, quoted in *A Serious Character*, pt 2, ch. 16.
    (1988) by Humphrey Carpenter. Pound himself took up the bassoon
    for a few months in 1921.

29  I have always thought the suicide shd bump off at least
    one swine before taking off for parts unknown.

    Letter to ARCHIBALD MACLEISH, 10 September 1956, quoted in
    ibid. pt 5, ch. 3

30  Technique is the test of sincerity. If a thing isn't worth
    getting the technique to say, it is of inferior value.

    Interview in *Writers at Work* (second series, ed. George Plimpton,
    1963)

31  No verse is *libre* for the man who wants to do a good job.

    ibid.

32  There is natural ignorance and there is artificial ignorance.
    I should say at the present moment the artificial ignorance
    is about eighty-five per cent.

    ibid.

33  If the individual, or heretic, gets hold of some essential
    truth, or sees some error in the system being practised,
    he commits so many marginal errors himself that he is
    worn out before he can establish his point.

    ibid. Pound was obliquely referring to his own 'heresy', which
    resulted in his incarceration in a US mental institution.

34  It is difficult to write a paradiso when all the superficial
    indications are that you ought to write an apocalypse. It
    is obviously much easier to find inhabitants for an inferno
    or even a purgatorio.

    ibid.

35  Somebody said that I am the last American living the
    tragedy of Europe.

    ibid.

36 You let *me* throw the bricks through the front window. You go in at the back door and take the swag.

Remark to poet T.S. ELIOT, reported by Pound acolyte and critic Hugh Kenner, quoted in *A Serious Character*, pt 2, ch. 13 (1988) by Humphrey Carpenter

37 The worst mistake I made was that stupid, suburban prejudice of anti-Semitism.

In conversation with ALLEN GINSBERG in June 1968, quoted in ibid. pt 5, ch. 5

## Anthony Powell (1905–2000)
BRITISH NOVELIST

He is best known for his novel sequence *A Dance to the Music of Time* (twelve volumes, 1951–75) in which he surveys and satirizes the upper middle classes over a period of fifty years. In the words of critic Hillary Spurling: 'There was no more persistent enemy of the bogus or banal.'

1 Slowly, but very deliberately, the brooding edifice of seduction, creaking and incongruous, came into being, a vast Heath Robinson mechanism, dually controlled by them and lumbering gloomily down vistas of triteness. With a sort of heavy-fisted dexterity the mutually adapted emotions of each of them became synchronized, until the unavoidable anti-climax was at hand.

*Afternoon Men*, ch. 9 (1931). Referring to Lola and Atwater.

2 Parents . . . are sometimes a bit of a disappointment to their children. They don't fulfil the promise of their early years.

Stringham, in *A Buyer's Market*, ch. 2 (1952, second book of *A Dance to the Music of Time*)

3 Self-love seems so often unrequited.

Narrator (Nicholas Jenkins), in *The Acceptance World*, ch. 1 (1955, third book of *A Dance to the Music of Time*)

4 Growing old's like being increasingly penalized for a crime you haven't committed.

Dick Umfraville, in *Temporary Kings*, ch. 1 (1973, eleventh book of *A Dance to the Music of Time*)

5 Few persons who have ever sat for a portrait can have felt anything but inferior while the process is going on.

Quoted in the *Observer* 9 January 1983

## Enoch Powell (1912–98)
BRITISH POLITICIAN

A classical scholar, austere intellectual and devotee of High Toryism, he became a Conservative MP in 1950 and served as Minister of Health (1960–63). His outspoken views on immigration caused him to lose his position in the shadow cabinet in 1968. Opposed to Britain's entry to the Common Market, he resigned from the Conservative Party in 1974 and served as an Ulster Unionist MP (1974–87).

1 History is littered with the wars which everybody knew would never happen.

Speech to Conservative Party Conference, Scarborough, 19 October 1967, quoted in *The Times* 20 October 1967

2 Those whom the gods wish to destroy, they first make mad. We must be mad, literally mad, as a nation to be permitting the annual inflow of some fifty thousand dependants, who are for the most part the material of the future growth of the immigrant-descended population. It is like watching a nation busily engaged in heaping up its own funeral pyre.

Speech to West Midlands Conservatives, Birmingham, 20 April 1968, publ. in *The Penguin Book of Twentieth-Century Speeches* (ed. Brian MacArthur, 1999). Powell was dropped from EDWARD HEATH's shadow cabinet the day after making this notorious warning about the consequences of immigration into Britain from Commonwealth countries.

3 As I look ahead, I am filled with foreboding. Like the Roman, I seem to see 'the River Tiber foaming with much blood'.

ibid. Quoting the Sybil's prophesy in Virgil's *Aeneid*, bk 6: 'Et Thybrim multo spumantem sanguine cerno.' The phrase 'rivers of blood' had been used previously in different contexts by Thomas Jefferson and WINSTON CHURCHILL, among others.

4 Remove advertising, disable a person or firm from preconising its wares and their merits, and the whole of society and of the economy is transformed. The enemies of advertising are the enemies of freedom.

*Listener* 31 July 1969

5 I do not keep a diary. Never have. To write a diary every day is like returning to one's own vomit.

*Sunday Times* 6 November 1977

6 All political lives, unless they are cut off in mid-stream at a happy juncture, end in failure, because that is the nature of politics and of human affairs.

*Joseph Chamberlain*, Epilogue (1977)

7 There is one thing you can be sure of with the Conservative Party, before anything else – they have a grand sense for where the votes are.

*Listener* 28 May 1981

8 No battle is worth fighting except the last one.

Quoted in the *Observer* 2 January 1983

9 Command and obedience, Establishment and deference, they're two sides of the same coin. The Establishment is unacknowledged power. It is *the power that need not speak its name*.

Quoted in *Friends in High Places*, Introduction (1990) by JEREMY PAXMAN

## Vince Powell and Harry Driver
BRITISH TV COMEDY SCRIPTWRITERS

Among the numerous series co-scripted by the pair are *Bless this House*, *Love Thy Neighbour* and, their greatest success, *Never Mind the Quality, Feel the Width* (1967–71). Powell is also known for *Mind Your Language* (1977–86).

1 Never mind the quality, feel the width.

Title of comedy series, ITV (1967–71). The series began as a single play for ABC TV's *Armchair Theatre*.

## John Cowper Powys (1872–1963)
BRITISH AUTHOR AND CRITIC

Author of more than fifty works of poetry, essays and fiction, he is best known for his novels *A Glastonbury Romance* (1932), *Weymouth Sands* (1934) and *Maiden Castle* (1936), all drawing on themes from his West Country childhood. Much of his adult life was spent as a lecturer in the US, although he returned to spend his last years in North Wales.

1 The strongest of all psychic forces in the world is unsatisfied desire.

*A Glastonbury Romance*, vol. 1, ch. 4 (1932)

2 If you give up *possession*, if you give up trying to possess what attracts you, a lovely, thrilling happiness flows through you and you feel you're in touch with the secret of everything. There are only two mortal sins in the world; one of these is to be cruel and the other is *to possess*, and they are both destructive of happiness.

Sam Dekker, in ibid. ch. 7

3 Every human creature is a terror to every other human creature. Human minds are like unknown planets, encountering and colliding. Every one of them contains jagged precipices, splintered rock-peaks, ghastly crevasses,

smouldering volcanoes, scorched and scorching deserts, blistering sands, evil dungeons from behind whose barred windows mad and terrible faces peer out.

ibid. ch. 14

4 What's Poetry if it isn't something that has to fight for the unseen against the seen, for the dead against the living, for the mysterious against the obvious? Poetry always takes sides. It's the only Lost Cause we've got left! It fights for the . . . for the . . . for the Impossible!

Lady Rachel Zoyland, in ibid. ch. 17

5 It is an old and bitter experience of the human race that when once a gulf-stream of a particular evil has got started, it is always being whipped forward by some new little breeze, or enlarged by some new little stream emptying itself into it. A magnetic power, it seems, in such a gulf-stream of evil, attracts these casual and accidental encouragements.

ibid. vol. 2, ch. 10

## Elvis Presley (1935–77)

US SINGER

He was the first singer to fuse a country and western sound with rhythm and blues, and the first white singer to introduce overt sexuality into his act. After his early hits, among them 'Heartbreak Hotel', 'Blue Suede Shoes' and 'Love Me Tender', he was drafted into the army in 1958, for many the turning point of his career. In the 1960s he concentrated mainly on films, while his act moved increasingly towards the high kitsch of Las Vegas. He always retained a dedicated fan base, however, and after his death from overdosing on prescription drugs his career was seen as a parable of the times, and his home became a shrine. 'Everything starts and ends with him,' said BRUCE SPRINGSTEEN. 'He wrote the book.' See also ALBERT GOLDMAN 1, THOM GUNN 4, JERRY LEE LEWIS 3.

1 You ain't nothin' but a hound dog,
Cryin' all the time.

'Hound Dog' (song, 1952, written by Jerry Leiber and Mike Stoller). The song was the Leiber/Stoller partnership's first hit when recorded by Big Mama Thornton in 1952, although Presley's 1956 recording was a much bigger success.

2 Now since my baby left me
I've found a new place to dwell
Down at the end of Lonely Street
At Heartbreak Hotel.

'Heartbreak Hotel' (song, 1956, written by Mae Boren Axton, Tommy Durden and Elvis Presley). Presley's first no. 1 hit is mainly credited to Mae Boren Axton, mother of HOYT AXTON.

3 I wish not to be given a title or an appointed position. I can and will do more good if I were made a Federal Agent at Large, and I will help best by doing it my way through my communications with people of all ages. First and Foremost I am an entertainer but all I need is the Federal Credentials.

Letter to President NIXON, 19 December 1970, offering Presley's services as a Federal Agent to work to curb drug abuse by young people. Elvis was made an agent of the Bureau of Narcotics and Dangerous Drugs by Nixon, receiving an enamel shield which, according to biographer Albert Goldman, became one of his most treasured possessions.

4 I don't aim to let this fame business get me. God gave me a voice. If I turned against God, I'd be finished.

Quoted in All You Need is Love, 'Hail! Hail! Rock 'n' Roll!' (1976) by Tony Palmer

## Jacques Prévert (1900–77)

FRENCH POET AND SCREENWRITER

Influenced by Surrealism, he first became popular in the 1920s with humorous 'song poems' about Paris street life. In the 1930s and 1940s he ranked as France's most important film critic and also collaborated extensively with the director Marcel Carné, supplying the screenplay for Les Enfants du Paradis (1944) among other films. His verse collections include Paroles (1946), Spectacle (1951), Imaginaires (1970), and Choses et Autres (1972).

1 Our Father which art in heaven
Stay there
And we will stay on earth
Which is sometimes so pretty.

'Pater Noster', publ. in Paroles (1946, rev. 1949, transl. Lawrence Ferlinghetti, 1958). Opening lines of poem.

2 An orange on the table
Your dress on the rug
And you in my bed
Sweet present of the present
Cool of night
Warmth of my life.

'Alicante', publ. in ibid.

3 Man
You beheld the saddest and dreariest of all the flowers of the earth
And as with other flowers you gave it a name
You called it Thought.

'Flowers and Wreaths', publ. in ibid.

4 When truth is no longer free, freedom is no longer real: the truths of the police are the truths of today.

'Intermède', publ. in Spectacle (1951)

5 Even if happiness forgets you a little bit, never completely forget about it.

ibid.

## Gerald Priestland (1927–91)

BRITISH BROADCASTER

Religious correspondent for BBC TV and radio, in 1983 he hosted Priestland Right and Wrong for Channel 4. He is the author of America (1968), Dilemmas of Journalism (1979) and My Pilgrim Way: Later Writings (ed. Roger Toulmin, 2000).

1 Journalists belong in the gutter because that is where the ruling classes throw their guilty secrets.

Radio London, 19 May 1988

## J.B. Priestley (1894–1984)

BRITISH AUTHOR

Full name John Boynton Priestley. Cambridge educated but always attached to his Yorkshire roots, he was popular as a 'middlebrow' author and entertaining playwright. After publishing numerous works of literary criticism, he had success with his gently humorous novel The Good Companions (1929) and with his plays Time and the Conways (1937) and An Inspector Calls (1947). Essays – Thoughts in the Wilderness was published in 1957.

1 Find a street without a flower, and you may be sure that there the English are in exile, still hoping and planning behind the lace curtain and the aspidistra for a time and place that will break into living blossom.

English Journey, ch. 2, sect. 3 (1934)

2 This is the age, among things, of chocolate.

ibid. ch. 4, sect. 3

3 Men are much better than their ordinary life allows them to be.

ibid. ch. 6, sect. 3. Referring to the contrast between the comradeship of soldiers in war and 'the civilian life to which they returned, a condition of things in which they found their manhood stunted, their generous impulses baffled, their double instinct for leadership and loyalty completely checked'.

4 The Theatre is no place to think in. You can think much better quietly at home. An intelligent book will make

more people think than the most exquisite production of the finest play. But what the dramatist can do ... is to make his audience feel.

*Two Time Plays*, Introduction (1937)

5 Our trouble is that we drink too much tea. I see in this the slow revenge of the Orient, which has diverted the Yellow River down our throats.

Quoted in the *Observer* 15 May 1949

6 Already we Viewers, when not viewing, have begun to whisper to one another that the more we elaborate our means of communication, the less we communicate.

*Thoughts in the Wilderness*, 'Televiewing' (1957)

7 I can't help feeling wary when I hear anything said about the masses. First you take their faces from 'em, calling them the masses, and then you accuse 'em of not having any faces.

Narrator (Henry Sulgrave), in *Saturn Over the Water*, ch. 5 (1961)

8 It is hard to tell where the MCC ends and the Church of England begins.

*New Statesman* 20 July 1962

## J.A. Primo de Rivera (1903–36)

SPANISH POLITICIAN

Full name José Antonio Primo de Rivera. Son of the military dictator who ruled Spain from 1923 until his overthrow in 1930, he founded the Spanish Fascist Party, Falange Española, in 1933. He was executed by the Republicans at the start of the Civil War.

1 Fascism is a European inquietude. It is a way of knowing everything – history, the State, the achievement of the proletarianization of public life, a new way of knowing the phenomena of our epoch.

Quoted in *The Spanish Civil War*, bk 1, ch. 8 (1961) by Hugh Thomas

2 We, who have already borne on the road to Paradise the lives of the best among us, want a difficult, erect, implacable Paradise; a Paradise where one can never rest and which has, beside the threshold of the gates, angels with swords.

Quoted in *Falange*, ch. 7 (1962) by Stanley Payne

## (Sir) V.S. Pritchett (1900–97)

BRITISH AUTHOR AND CRITIC

Full name Victor Sawdon Pritchett. The 'wise, foxy and kindly grandfather of present English letters' began his career as a foreign correspondent and was literary critic with the *New Statesman* for twenty years. His fiction is known for its sympathetic but sceptical view of human illusions, as in his novels *Dead Man Leading* (1937) and *Mr Beluncle* (1951) and his short stories.

1 The principle of procrastinated rape is said to be the ruling one in all the great bestsellers.

*The Living Novel*, 'Clarissa' (1946)

2 The detective novel is the art-for-art's-sake of our yawning Philistinism, the classic example of a specialized form of art removed from contact with the life it pretends to build on.

'The Roots of Detection', publ. in the *New Statesman* 16 June 1951, repr. in *Books in General* (1953)

3 In my family, as far as we are concerned, we were born and what happened before that is myth.

*A Cab at the Door* (1968). Opening words of first volume of autobiography.

4 It is often said that in Ireland there is an excess of genius unsustained by talent; but there is talent in the tongues.

*Midnight Oil*, ch. 6 (second volume of autobiography, 1971)

5 Life – how curious is that habit that makes us think it is not here, but elsewhere.

ibid. 'Life is elsewhere' is a loose translation of Rimbaud's line *La vraie vie est absente. Nous ne sommes pas de monde* from his poem 'Délires'. The words were used by MILAN KUNDERA as the title of his novel (written 1969, publ. 1973) in which he cites André Breton's Surrealist Manifesto (see ANDRÉ BRETON 2) and the adoption of the words as a slogan by students in Paris, May 1968.

6 Well, youth is the period of assumed personalities and disguises. It is the time of the sincerely insincere.

ibid. ch. 8

7 How extraordinary it is that one feels most guilt about the sins one is unable to commit.

ibid. ch. 10

## Gilbert Proesch (b. 1943)

ITALIAN-BORN BRITISH ARTIST

Full name Gilbert Proesch. He made his name in the late 1960s, when he and his partner George Passmore, together known as Gilbert and George, presented themselves as 'singing' and 'living sculptures'. The two usually portray themselves in their own panelled photo-works, which have a strong homoerotic element. They received the Turner Prize in 1986.

1 We try not to have ideas, preferring accidents. To create, you must empty yourself of every artistic thought.

*Independent* 17 April 1989

## Marcel Proust (1871–1922)

FRENCH NOVELIST

After his mother's death in 1905 he became a recluse, devoting his energies to exploring in fictional form the psychology of human memory. *Remembrance of Things Past* (title also transl. *In Search of Lost Time*, 1913–27) was much influenced by Bergson's observations on time. 'After Proust, there are certain things that simply cannot be done again,' FRANCOISE SAGAN declared. 'He marks off for you the boundaries of your talent.'

1 One becomes moral as soon as one is unhappy.

*Within a Budding Grove*, 'Madame Swann at Home' (vol. 1 of *Remembrance of Things Past*, transl. C. K. Scott Moncrieff and Terence Kilmartin, 1981)

2 The charms of the passing stranger are generally in direct ratio to the swiftness of our passage.

ibid. 'Place-Names: The Place'

3 If a little day-dreaming is dangerous, the cure for it is not to dream less but to dream more, to dream all the time.

Elstir, in ibid.

4 Our memory is like one of those shops in the window of which is exposed now one, now another photograph of the same person. And as a rule the most recent exhibit remains for some time the only one to be seen.

Narrator, in ibid.

5 The features of our face are hardly more than gestures which force of habit made permanent. Nature, like the destruction of Pompeii, like the metamorphosis of a nymph, has arrested us in an accustomed movement.

ibid.

6 For one disorder that doctors cure with medicaments (as I am assured they do occasionally succeed in doing) they produce a dozen others in healthy subjects by inoculating them with that pathogenic agent a thousand times more virulent that all the microbes in the world, the idea that one is ill.

Dr. du Boulbon, in *The Guermantes Way*, ch. 1 (vol. 2 of *Remembrance of Things Past*, transl. C. K. Scott Moncrieff and Terence Kilmartin, 1981)

7 Everything we think of as great has come to us from

neurotics. It is they and they alone who found religions and create great works of art.

ibid.

8 We may, indeed, say that the hour of death is uncertain, but when we say this we think of that hour as situated in a vague and remote expanse of time; it does not occur to us that it can have any connexion with the day that has already dawned and can mean that death – or its first assault and partial possession of us, after which it will never leave hold of us again – may occur this very afternoon, so far from uncertain, this afternoon whose time-table, hour by hour, has been settled in advance.

Narrator, in ibid.

9 A change in the weather is sufficient to create the world and ourselves anew.

ibid. ch. 2

10 Illness is the most heeded of doctors: to kindness and wisdom we make promises only; pain we obey.

*Cities of the Plain*, pt 2, ch 1, ibid.

11 The regularity of a habit is generally in proportion to its absurdity.

*The Captive* (vol. 3 of *Remembrance of Things Past*, transl. C. K. Scott Moncrieff and Terence Kilmartin, 1981)

12 No banishment, indeed, to the South Pole, or to the summit of Mont Blanc, can separate us so entirely from our fellow creatures as a pronlonged soujourn in the seclusion of an inner vice.

ibid.

13 That translucent alabaster of our memories.

ibid.

14 When two people part it is the one who is not in love who makes the tender speeches.

ibid.

15 We find a little of everything in our memory; it is a sort of pharmacy, a sort of chemical laboratory, in which our groping hand may come to rest, now on a sedative drug, now on a dangerous poison.

ibid.

16 The human plagiarism which is most difficult to avoid, for individuals . . . is self-plagiarism.

*The Fugitive*, ibid.

17 Let us leave pretty women to men with no imagination.

ibid. The line originally appeared in Proust's early novel *Jean Santeuil* (1899).

18 The true paradises are paradises we have lost.

*Time Regained* (vol. 3 of *Remembrance of Things Past*, transl. C. K. Scott Moncrieff and Terence Kilmartin, 1981)

19 A work in which there are theories is like an object which still has its price-tag on it.

ibid.

20 I understood that all these materials for a work of litera-ture were simply my past life; I understood that they had come to me, in frivolous pleasures, in indolence, in tenderness, in unhappiness, and that I had stored them up without divining the purpose for which they were destined or even their continued existence any more than a seed does when it forms within itself a reserve of all the nutritious substances from which it will feed a plant.

ibid.

21 If unhappiness develops the forces of the mind, happiness alone is salutary to the body.

ibid.

22 As for happiness, that is really useful to us in one way only, by making unhappiness possible.

ibid.

## Mario Puzo (b. 1920)

US NOVELIST

After publishing two little-read novels, he wrote his bestselling novel of the Mafia, *The Godfather* (1969), purely for the money. 'I was forty-five years old and tired of being an artist.' He received an Academy Award for his screenplay for FRANCIS FORD COPPOLA's film adaptation (1972). He also co-scripted *The God-father* Parts II (1974) and III (1990). Another 'Mafia' novel, *The Last Don*, was published in 1996.

1 He's a businessman . . . I'll make him an offer he can't refuse.

Don Vito Corleone, in *The Godfather*, bk 1, ch. 1 (1969). The line also appears in FRANCIS FORD COPPOLA's film version of the book, written in collaboration with Puzo (1972).

2 A lawyer with his briefcase can steal more than a hundred men with guns.

ibid. A favourite saying of the Don, dropped from the screenplay.

3 Like many businessmen of genius he [Don Corleone] learned that free competition was wasteful, monopoly efficient. And so he simply set about achieving that efficient monopoly.

ibid. bk 3, ch. 14

4 He [Jordan Hawley] was . . . a degenerate gambler. That is, a man who gambled simply to gamble and must lose. As a hero who goes to war must die. Show me a gambler and I'll show you a loser, show me a hero and I'll show you a corpse.

*Fools Die*, ch. 2 (1978)

5 What we think of as our sensitivity is only the higher evolution of terror in a poor dumb beast. We suffer for nothing. Our own death wish is our only real tragedy.

Merlyn, in ibid. ch. 55

## Thomas Pynchon (b. 1937)

US NOVELIST

Reading Pynchon's novels has been likened by critic Kenneth Macleish to 'exploring a maze with an opinionated and eccentric guide'. Experimental, esoteric, and crammed with mathematical and scientific information, they include his first book *V* (1963), *The Crying of Lot 49* (1966) and his magnum opus *Gravity's Rainbow* (1973), a darkly farcical anti-war satire.

1 Living inside the System is like riding across the country in a bus driven by a maniac bent on suicide . . .

*Gravity's Rainbow*, pt 3 (1973)

2 If there is something comforting – religious, if you want – about paranoia, there is still also anti-paranoia, where nothing is connected to anything, a condition not many of us can bear for long.

ibid.

3 There's nothing so loathsome as a sentimental surrealist.

ibid. pt 4

## Muhammar Qaddafi (b. 1942)

LIBYAN LEADER

Described in turn as 'the mad dog of the Middle East' by RONALD REAGAN and 'my brother leader' by NELSON MANDELA, he deposed King Idris in 1969 and became Chairman of Libya's new governing body, the Revolutionary Command Council (1969–77) and self-appointed President of Libya in 1977. He expelled foreigners, closed down British and US bases, encouraged a return to Islamic fundamentalism and in 1990 supported Iraq's invasion of Kuwait.

1 Nations whose nationalism is destroyed are subject to ruin.

The Green Book, pt 3, 'The Social Basis of the Third Universal Theory' (1976–9)

## Mary Quant (b. 1934)

BRITISH FASHION DESIGNER

A prime mover in the world of 1960s 'swinging' fashions, she opened one of London's first boutiques, Bazaar, in Chelsea, which sold her 'mod' and affordable designs of vinyl boots, skinny rib sweaters and the mini-skirts that she is credited with inventing.

1 I saw no reason why childhood shouldn't last for ever. I wanted everyone to retain the grace of a child and not to have to become stilted, confined, ugly beings. So I created clothes that worked and moved and allowed people to run, to jump, to leap, to retain their precious freedom.

Interview in Harper's and Queen May 1973

2 Having money is rather like being a blond. It is more fun but not vital.

Quoted in the Observer 2 November 1986

## Dan Quayle (b. 1947)

US POLITICIAN AND VICE-PRESIDENT

He was elected as a Republican to the House of Representatives in 1976 and to the Senate in 1980. Chosen as GEORGE BUSH's running mate in 1988, he was roundly criticized for his draft avoidance in the 1960s and lack of political experience. As Vice-president 1989–93 he was mocked for his gaffes, and called a 'twink' by P.J. O'ROURKE.

1 Space is almost infinite. As a matter of fact, we think it is infinite.

Daily Telegraph 8 March 1989

2 You do the policy, I'll do the politics.

Remark to aide, quoted in the International Herald Tribune 13 January 1992

## Antony Quinn (b. 1915)

MEXICAN-BORN US SCREEN ACTOR

During an acting career spanning sixty years, he was known for his full-blooded performances and won Academy Awards for Viva Zapata (1952) and Lust for Life (1956), although he was more impressive in the title role in Zorba the Greek (1964). As he recalled: 'They said all I was good for was playing Indians.'

1 In Europe an actor is an artist. In Hollywood, if he isn't working, he's a bum.

Quoted in Halliwell's Filmgoer's Companion (ed. Leslie Halliwell, 1984)

## Jonathan Raban (b. 1942)
BRITISH AUTHOR AND CRITIC

Known as 'a master of the quick sketch', he has written extensively on travel, as in *Old Glory* (1981), describing a voyage down the Mississippi, and *Coasting* (1986) and *Passage to Juneau: A Sea and Its Meanings* (1999), on sailing around Britain and off America's Pacific coast respectively. He has also published literary criticism.

1 The city as we imagine it, then, soft city of illusion, myth, aspiration, and nightmare, is as real, maybe more real, than the hard city one can locate on maps in statistics, in monographs on urban sociology and demography and architecture.
*Soft City*, ch. 1 (1974)

2 Life, as the most ancient of all metaphors insists, is a journey; and the travel book, in its deceptive simulation of the journey's fits and starts, rehearses life's own fragmentation. More even than the novel, it embraces the contingency of things.
*For Love and Money*, pt 5 (1987)

## (Sir) Sarvepalli Radhakrishnan (1888–1975)
INDIAN PHILOSOPHER AND PRESIDENT

Professor of Eastern Religions and Ethics at Oxford (1936–52) and Chancellor of the University of Delhi (1953–62), he was Chairman of UNESCO's executive board (1948–9), Indian Ambassador to the Soviet Union (1949–52) and later India's President (1962–7).

1 [Of organized religion] It is not God that is worshipped but the group or authority that claims to speak in His name. Sin becomes disobedience to authority not violation of integrity.
Quoted in *Techniques of Persuasion*, ch. 11 (1965) by J.A.C. Brown

## James Rado (b. 1939) and
## Gerome Ragni (b. 1942)
US SONGWRITERS

Rado and Ragni are remembered principally as lyricists for the first rock musical *Hair* (1967), which prompted the reaction by Brendan Gill of the *New Yorker*: 'One can't not consent to this merry mind-blowing exercise in holy gibberish.'

1 This is the dawning of the age of Aquarius.
'Aquarius' (song, with music by Galt MacDermot) in *Hair* (stage musical 1967, filmed 1979)

## Craig Raine (b. 1944)
BRITISH POET AND CRITIC

He was poetry editor at Faber and Faber (1981–91) and chief exponent of what JAMES FENTON named the 'Martian' school, which treats familiar objects from an alien perspective, as in *A Martian Sends a Postcard Home* (1979). Other collections include *Rich* (1984) and *Whereabouts Unknown* (1996), and he has also written the libretto for Nigel Osborne's opera, *The Electrification of the Soviet Union* (1986), adapted from a novella by BORIS PASTERNAK.

1 The mind is a museum
to be looted at night.
'The Grey Boy', publ. in *Rich* (1984)

2 The task of the artist at any time is uncompromisingly simple – to discover what has not yet been done, and to do it.
*Guardian* 19 August 1988

3 Great writers arrive among us like new diseases – threatening, powerful, impatient for patients to pick up their virus, irresistible.
*Independent on Sunday* 18 November 1990

## Kathleen Raine (b. 1908)

BRITISH POET

Her meditative and lyrical work, much of it inspired from the natural world, includes *Stone and Flower* (1943) and *The Hollow Hill* (1965). She is an authority on William Blake and in 1981 founded the journal *Temenos*.

1 Unwise we feel, but wise we know
  Living in time is but to seem –
  Like green leaves on a tree we grow,
  But each must fall and fade alone.
  'Seen in a Glass', dated 21 June 1941, publ. in *Living in Time* (1946)

2 The ghosts are hungry, the ghosts are divine,
  but the pigs eat the meal, and the priests drink the wine.
  'Maternal Grief', publ. in *Stone and Flower* (1943). Closing lines of poem.

3 Cameras and motor-cars
  Spin on the hub of nothingness
  On which revolve the years and stars.
  'Ex nihilo', publ. in *The Pythoness* (1949)

4 Love mourns its dead
  Not by number, but, one by one, each by name.
  'Statistical Grief', publ. in *The Oracle in the Heart (Poems 1975–1978)* (1980)

5 I couldn't claim that I have never felt the urge to explore evil, but when you descend into hell you have to be very careful.
  *The Times* 18 April 1992

## (Sir) Walter Raleigh (1861–1922)

BRITISH SCHOLAR AND CRITIC

His confessed aim in writing was 'to explain people', as in his studies of William Blake and Samuel Johnson. Other works include *Shakespeare's England* (1916), *The War in the Air* (1922), a history of the RAF, and his collected lighter pieces *Laughter from a Cloud* (1923).

1 I wish I loved the Human Race;
  I wish I loved its silly face;
  I wish I liked the way it walks;
  I wish I liked the way it talks;
  And when I'm introduced to one
  I wish I thought *What Jolly Fun!*
  'Wishes of an Elderly Man', publ. in *Laughter from a Cloud* (1923)

## (Sir) David Ramsbotham (b. 1934)

BRITISH GENERAL AND PRISONS INSPECTOR

After an army career in which he rose to become a general in the Territorial Army (1987–93), he became Inspector of Prisons for England and Wales in 1995. In 1999 he caused controversy when he called for the early release of James Bulger's killers.

1 Prison *is* punishment, it is not *for* punishment.
  Interview on *The World at One*, BBC Radio 4, 14 March 1996. Opposing calls for harsher prison regimes.

## Jeannette Rankin (1880–1973)

US SUFFRAGIST AND POLITICIAN

She was the first woman to be elected to Congress, serving two terms (1917–19 and 1941–3). A Republican and a pacifist, she spent her life campaigning for women's rights and in 1941 was the only member to vote against war with Japan. In 1968 she headed 5,000 women on a march on Capitol Hill in protest against the Vietnam War.

1 The individual woman is required . . . a thousand times a day to choose either to accept her appointed role and thereby rescue her good disposition out of the wreckage of her self-respect, or else follow an independent line of behavior and rescue her self-respect out of the wreckage of her good disposition.
  Quoted in *Jeannette Rankin: First Lady in Congress*, ch. 3 (1974) by Hannah Josephson

2 You can no more win a war than you can win an earthquake.
  Quoted in ibid. ch. 8

## Frederic Raphael (b. 1931)

BRITISH AUTHOR AND CRITIC

A writer of novels and plays which explore contemporary social issues, he is best known for *The Graduate Wife* (1962) and *The Glittering Prizes* (1976). He wrote the film scripts for *Darling* (1965) and *Far From the Madding Crowd* (1967) and has also written widely for television.

1 The great networks are there to prove that ideas can be canned like spaghetti. If everything ends up by tasting like everything else, is that not the evidence that it has been properly cooked?
  'The Language of Television', publ. in *The State of the Language* (ed. Christopher Ricks, 1980)

2 The party of God and the party of Literature have more in common than either will admit; their texts may conflict, but their bigotries coincide. Both insist on being the sole custodians of the true word and its only interpreters.
  *Sunday Times* 12 February 1989

## (Sir) Terence Rattigan (1911–77)

BRITISH PLAYWRIGHT

A versatile dramatic technician, he had numerous West End successes starting with the comedy *French Without Tears* (1936). His more serious plays include *The Winslow Boy* (1946, filmed 1948 and 1999), *The Deep Blue Sea* (1952), *Separate Tables* (1954) and *Ross* (1960), a study of T.E. LAWRENCE.

1 It is easy to do justice – very hard to do right. Unfortunately while the appeal of justice is intellectual, the appeal of right appears for some odd reason to induce tears in court.
  Sir Robert Morton, in *The Winslow Boy*, act 4 (1946)

2 The headmaster said you ruled them with a rod of iron. He called you the Himmler of the lower fifth.
  Peter Gilbert, addressing Andrew Crocker-Harris, in *The Browning Version* (1948)

## (Sir) Simon Rattle (b. 1955)

BRITISH CONDUCTOR

He turned the City of Birmingham Symphony Orchestra into a world-class orchestra during his time as Conductor (1980–91) and Director (1991–8), promoting the twentieth-century repertoire and new music. In 1999 he was appointed Chief Conductor and Artistic Director of the Berlin Philharmonic Orchestra for the 2002 season.

1 If anyone has conducted a Beethoven performance, and then doesn't have to go to an osteopath, then there's something wrong.
  *Guardian* 31 May 1990

## Irina Ratushinskaya (b. 1954)

RUSSIAN POET

As a result of her campaigning for human rights she was arrested in 1982 and sentenced to seven years hard labour and five years in exile. She was released in 1986. Her poems, scratched into soap and committed to memory while she was in prison, are influenced by her Roman Catholicism and are collected in *No, I'm Not Afraid* (1986) and *Grey Is the Colour of Hope* (1988). 'For a poet,' she said, 'it is more important to keep in touch with God than politicians.'

1 In order to understand birds
   You have to be a convict.
   And if you share your bread –
   It means your time is done.

   'The Sparrows of Butyrki' written 1981, publ. in *No, I'm Not Afraid* (1986)

## Man Ray (1890–1976)
US PAINTER AND PHOTOGRAPHER

Original name Emanuel Rudnitsky. He took up photography in 1915 when he met the Surrealist artist MARCEL DUCHAMP and in 1922 invented the rayograph (an image formed on light sensitive paper without a camera), and he also devised the technique of solarization. After moving to Paris in 1921, he made Surrealist films, for example *Anemic Cinema* (1924).

1 It has never been my object to record my dreams, just the determination to realize them.

   Julien Levy exhibition catalogue, April 1945, quoted in *Man Ray*, Introduction (1988) by Neil Baldwin

2 To me, a painter, if not the most useful, is the least harmful member of our society.

   *Self Portrait*, ch. 6 (1963)

3 I paint what cannot be photographed, that which comes from the imagination or from dreams, or from an unconscious drive. I photograph the things that I do not wish to paint, the things which already have an existence.

   Interview, publ. in *Caméra*, repr. in *Man Ray: Photographer* (ed. Philippe Sers, 1981). Man Ray repeated this remark in slightly different forms on various occasions.

4 An original is a creation
   motivated by desire.
   Any reproduction of an original
   is motivated by necessity . . .
   It is marvelous that we are
   the only species that creates
   gratuitous forms.
   To create is divine, to reproduce
   is human.

   'Originals Graphic Multiples', publ. in *Objets de mon affection* (1983), repr. in *Man Ray*, ch. 24 (1988) by Neil Baldwin

## Sam Rayburn (1882–1961)
US LEGISLATOR AND POLITICIAN

Serving as a Democrat in the House of Representatives (1913–61), he was an architect of ROOSEVELT's New Deal programme and Speaker of the House (1940–61). He described himself as 'without prefix, without suffix, and without apology', and his period in office (the longest on record) and political influence resulted in the sobriquet 'Mr Democrat'.

1 If you want to get along, go along.

   Quoted in *Forge of Democracy*, ch. 6 (1963) by Neil MacNeil

## Piers Paul Read (b. 1941)
BRITISH AUTHOR

Described by MALCOLM BRADBURY as 'a realist, a densely social novelist who knows that public and private worlds intersect at every point', he had success with *A Married Man* (1979) and *On the Third Day* (1990). His non-fiction work includes *Alive: The Story of the Andes Survivors* (1974).

1 Sins become more subtle as you grow older: you commit sins of despair rather than lust.

   *Daily Telegraph* 3 October 1990

## Peter Reading (b. 1946)
BRITISH POET

Described by TOM PAULIN as 'the unofficial laureate of a decaying England', he writes of the degradation of life at the end of the twentieth century in uncompromising language. His collections include *Diplopic* (1983), which gives two versions of every event, *Ukulele Music* (1985) and *Eschatological* (1996).

1 This is unclean: to eat turbots on Tuesdays,
   tying the turban unclockwise at cockcrow,
   cutting the beard in a south-facing mirror,
   wearing the mitre while sipping the Bovril,
   chawing the pig and the hen and the ox-tail.

   *Going On* (1985). First lines of untitled poem.

2 Anyone who lives in this time is concerned with grottiness.

   *International Herald Tribune* 10 March 1988

3 Nothing can ever be done;
   things are intractably thus;
   all know the bite of grief, all will be brought to destiny's issue;
   those who have precognition suffer
   sorrow beforehand;
   bodies are bankrupt, the main Expedition has left us behind it.

   Concluding lines of untitled poem publ. in *Perduta Gente* (1989)

## Nancy Reagan (b. 1923)
US SCREEN ACTRESS AND FIRST LADY

Named Nancy Davis before her marriage to RONALD REAGAN in 1952, she appeared in *The Next Voice You Hear* (1950), *Donovan's Brain* (1953) and, opposite her husband, *Hellcats of the Navy* (1957). *Good Housekeeping* voted her one of the Ten Most Admired American Women in 1977.

1 A woman is like a teabag – only in hot water do you realize how strong she is.

   Quoted in the *Observer* 29 March 1981. The quote has also been ascribed to ELEANOR ROOSEVELT, as cited by HILLARY CLINTON.

2 I see the first lady as another means to keep a president from becoming isolated.

   *International Herald Tribune* 26 May 1988

3 Just say no.

   Slogan for campaign to persuade people not to take illegal drugs, 1980s

## Ronald Reagan (b. 1911)
US SCREEN ACTOR, POLITICIAN AND PRESIDENT

The 'Great Communicator' was a sportscaster before signing a Hollywood contract in 1937 and appearing in some fifty films. He was President of the Screen Actors' Guild (1947–52) and politically a liberal Democrat, called 'a real firebrand' by J.K. GALBRAITH, but he switched to the Republican Party in 1962. He was elected Governor of California in 1966 and was US President 1980–89, during which time he initiated arms talks with the USSR, while advocating new weapons technology in space, and presided over armed intervention in Grenada and Libya and the Iran-Contra scandal. See also JACK DEMPSEY 1, RONALD KNOX 4, GORE VIDAL 16, 17.

1 Randy – where's the rest of me?

   Drake McHugh (Ronald Reagan) to Randy Monaghan (Ann Sheridan), in *Kings Row* (film, 1942, screenplay by Casey Robinson, based on the novel by Henry Bellamann, directed by Sam Wood). The words are spoken by McHugh, a war veteran, who wakes to find his legs amputated by a malicious doctor, in what is generally regarded as Reagan's best film performance. They provided him with a title for his 1965 autobiography, *Where's the Rest of Me?*

2 [On Vietnam] We are at war with the most dangerous enemy that has ever faced mankind in his long climb from

the swamp to the stars, and it has been said if we lose that war, and in so doing lose this way of freedom of ours, history will record with the greatest astonishment that those who had the most to lose did the least to prevent its happening.

'A Time for Choosing' television address, 27 October 1964, publ. in *Speaking My Mind* (1989)

3 No government ever voluntarily reduces itself in size. Government programs, once launched, never disappear. Actually, a government bureau is the nearest thing to eternal life we'll ever see on this earth!

ibid.

4 A tree's a tree. How many more do you need to look at?

Speech 12 September 1965, quoted in *Sacramento Bee* 12 March 1966. Reagan later denied having made this statement.

5 Politics is just like show business, you have a hell of an opening, coast for a while, and then have a hell of a close.

Remark in 1966, quoted in *There He Goes Again* (ed. Mark Green and Gail MacColl, 1983)

6 Government does not solve problems; it subsidizes them.

Speech 11 December 1972, publ. in *Speaking My Mind*, 'The Wit and Wisdom of Ronald Reagan' (1989)

7 Inflation is as violent as a mugger, as frightening as an armed robber and as deadly as a hit man.

Speech at Republican Party fund-raising dinner, quoted in the *Los Angeles Times* 20 October 1978

8 Of the four wars in my lifetime, none came about because the US was too strong.

Quoted in the *Observer* 29 June 1980

9 Approximately 80% of our air pollution stems from hydrocarbons released by vegetation, so let's not go overboard in setting and enforcing tough emission standards from man-made sources.

*Sierra* 10 September 1980, quoted in *Reagan's Reign of Error*, 'Killer Trees' (ed. Mark Green and Gail MacColl, 1987). Reagan later amended this figure to 93 per cent.

10 You can tell a lot about a fellow's character by his way of eating jelly beans.

Quoted in *The New York Times* 15 January 1981

11 There is nothing better for the inside of a man than the outside of a horse.

Remark 13 August 1987, North Platte, Nebraska, quoted in *Time* magazine 28 December 1987. Said to be one of Reagan's favourite expressions, uttered on various occasions and probably not original.

12 Well, I learned a lot ... You'd be surprised. They're all individual countries.

Quoted in the *Washington Post* 6 December 1982. Following a tour of South America.

13 We might come closer to balancing the Budget if all of us lived closer to the Commandments and the Golden Rule.

Quoted in the *Observer* 5 February 1983

14 So, in your discussions of the nuclear freeze proposals, I urge you to beware the temptation of pride – the temptation of blithely declaring yourselves above it all and label both sides equally at fault, to ignore the facts of history and the aggressive impulses of an evil empire, to simply call the arms race a giant misunderstanding and thereby remove yourself from the struggle between right and wrong, good and evil.

Speech at Annual Convention of the National Association of Evangelicals, Orlando, Florida, 8 March 1983, publ. in *Speaking My Mind* (1989). In the same speech, Reagan declared, speaking of those who live in 'totalitarian darkness': 'Let us be aware that while they preach the supremacy of the state, declare its omnipotence over individual man, and predict its eventual domination of all peoples of the earth – they are the focus of evil in the modern world.'

15 If the Soviet Union let another political party come into existence, they would still be a one-party state, because everybody would join the other party.

Said to Polish Americans in Chicago, 23 June 1983, publ. in ibid. 'The Wit and Wisdom of Ronald Reagan'

16 My fellow Americans, I am pleased to tell you I just signed legislation which outlaws Russia forever. The bombing begins in five minutes.

Microphone test for radio broadcast, 11 August 1984, quoted in *The New York Times* 13 August 1984

17 [On the Nicaraguan Contras] They are our brothers, these freedom fighters ... They are the moral equal of our Founding Fathers and the brave men and women of the French Resistance. We cannot turn away from them, for the struggle here is not right versus left; it is right versus wrong.

Speech to Conservative Political Action Conference, Washington D.C., 1 March 1985, publ. in *Speaking My Mind* (1989)

18 Freedom-loving people around the world must say: I am a Berliner. I am a Jew in a world still threatened by anti-Semitism. I am an Afghan, and I am a prisoner of the gulag. I am a refugee in a crowded boat foundering off the coast of Vietnam. I am Laotian, a Cambodian, a Cuban, and a Miskito Indian in Nicaragua. I, too, am a potential victim of totalitarianism.

Speech at Bitburg, West Germany, 27 May 1985, publ. in ibid.

19 After seeing *Rambo* last night I know what to do next time this happens.

Following the hijack of an aeroplane carrying US passengers in 1985, quoted in *City Limits* 16 December 1987. *Rambo* star SYLVESTER STALLONE was quoted in the *Sunday Express* 17 July 1988 as saying: 'When President Reagan stood up and said: "Having seen *Rambo* I know what to do with Libya", it was the kiss of death. He made Rambo a Republican.'

20 We know that this mad dog of the Middle East has a goal of a world revolution, Muslim fundamentalist revolution, which is targeted on many of his own Arab compatriots and where we figure in that I don't know.

Of Libyan leader Colonel QADDAFI, at press conference, 9 April 1986, quoted in *The New York Times* 10 April 1986. Six days later, Reagan launched a bombing raid on Tripoli, killing about a hundred civilians.

21 No one can kill Americans and brag about it. No one.

Quoted in the *Observer* 27 April 1986, after the US attack on Libya, 15 April 1986. The attack followed the bombing of a discotheque in West Berlin, where two American servicemen were killed and 200 injured.

22 Surround yourself with the best people you can find, delegate authority, and don't interfere.

*Fortune* September 1986

23 That's the nice thing about this job. You get to quote yourself shamelessly. If you don't, Larry Speakes will.

*Daily Telegraph* 14 April 1988. SPEAKES was then Press Secretary at the White House.

24 Would you go out there and win one for the Gipper?

Speech in San Diego, 7 November 1988, publ. in *Speaking My Mind* (1989). One of Reagan's favourite sayings, this is associated with the football star George Gipp (1895–1931), whom he played in the 1940 film *Knute Rockne – All-American*.

25 Information is the oxygen of the modern age. It seeps through the walls topped by barbed wire, it wafts across the electrified borders.

Quoted in the *Guardian* 14 June 1989

# Helen Reddy (b. 1941)

AUSTRALIAN-BORN US SINGER AND SONGWRITER

Her song 'I am a Woman' (1972) became an anthem for the women's liberation movement of the 1970s. This was followed by her second no. 1 hit, 'Delta Dawn' (1973), and 'Angie Baby' (1974), her only major British chart success. She also appeared in the films *Pete's Dragon* (1977) and *Sgt Pepper's Lonely Hearts Club Band* (1978).

1 Yes, I am wise, but it's wisdom born of pain
   Yes, I've paid the price, but look how much I've gained
   If I have to, I can do anything
   I am strong, I am invincible, I am woman.
   'I am Woman' (song) on the album *I Am Woman* (1972)

## Florence Reece

She was the wife of a rank-and-file organizer for the National Miners' Union in Harlan County, Kentucky, and composer of the workers' anthem, 'Which Side Are You On?' (1931).

1 Come all of you good workers,
   Good news to you I'll tell
   Of how the good old union
   Has come in here to dwell.
   Which side are you on?
   'Which Side Are You On?' (song, 1931). Reece recounted how she wrote the words to this song after a raid of her home by the High Sheriff and his deputies ('they were really company gun thugs') in search of her husband during the year-long coal strike at the Brookside Mine in Harlan. Set to a traditional hymn tune, it was sung by her daughters in the union hall and later became an anthem of diverse left-wing causes. The events of the strike were portrayed in the film *Harlan County, U.S.A.* (1976).

## John Reed (1887–1920)

US JOURNALIST AND AUTHOR

A contributor to *The Masses* (1911–17), he covered the Mexican Revolution in *Insurgent Mexico* (1914) and wrote *The War in Eastern Europe* (1916) and *Ten Days That Shook the World* (1919), an eye-witness account of the Russian Revolution. He helped found the Communist Labor Party in the US and returned to Russia to work in the propaganda bureau. He died of typhus and was buried in the Kremlin. WARREN BEATTY's film *Reds* (1981) is loosely based on his life.

1 In the relations of a weak Government and a rebellious people there comes a time when every act of the authorities exasperates the masses, and every refusal to act excites their contempt.
   *Ten Days That Shook the World*, ch. 3 (1919)

2 The devout Russian people no longer needed priests to pray them into heaven. On earth they were building a kingdom more bright than any heaven had to offer, and for which it was a glory to die.
   ibid. ch. 10

## Lou Reed (b. 1944)

US ROCK MUSICIAN

His often dark and sombre songs were the defining sound for the Velvet Underground, the proto-punk New York art band that he co-founded in 1965. Since 1970 he has had a successful solo career, with hit albums including *Transformer* (1972) and *New York* (1989).

1 I'm waiting for my man
   Twenty-six dollars in my hand
   Up to Lexington 125
   Feeling sick and dirty more dead than alive
   I'm waiting for my man.
   'I'm Waiting for the Man' (song) on the album *The Velvet Underground and Nico* (1967) by the Velvet Underground and Nico

2 I don't know just where I'm going
   But I'm gonna try for the kingdom if I can
   'Cause it makes me feel like I'm a man
   When I put a spike into my vein

   And I'll tell ya, things aren't quite the same.
   'Heroin' (song) on ibid.

3 You're so vicious.
   'Vicious' (song) on the album *Transformer* (1972)

4 It's such a perfect day
   I'm glad I spent it with you.
   'Perfect Day' (song) on ibid.

5 The currents rage deep inside us
   This is the age of video violence.
   'Video Violence' (song) on the album *Mistrial* (1986)

6 I don't like nostalgia unless it's mine.
   *Evening Standard* 8 June 1989

7 When you're growing up in a small town
   You know you'll grow down in a small town
   There is only one good use for a small town
   You hate it and you know you'll have to leave.
   'Small Town' (song) on the album *Songs for Drella* (1990) by Lou Reed and John Cale

8 Life is like Sanskrit read to a pony.
   'What's Good' (song) on the album *Magic and Loss* (1992)

## Oliver Reed (1938–99)

BRITISH ACTOR

A symbol of unreconstructed masculinity, he was regularly in the news for his drunken and violent off-screen behaviour. His films include *The Damned* (1962), *Women in Love* (1969), *The Devils* (1971) and *Castaway* (1987). He died in a Maltese bar.

1 I do not live in the world of sobriety.
   Quoted in the *Sunday Times* 27 December 1987

## William Rees-Mogg (b. 1928)

BRITISH JOURNALIST AND PUBLIC FIGURE

Baron Rees-Mogg of Hinton Blewitt. After editing *The Times* (1967–81), he was made Chairman of the Arts Council (1982–9) and was the first head of the Broadcasting Standards Council (1988–93).

1 In the end you must either allow people liberty or you must shoot them. If a man claims a vote you must either give him a vote or be prepared to take his life.
   Quoted by TONY PARSONS in *Arena* September/October 1989, 'The Tattooed Jungle'

2 As long as Archer remained the candidate the dormant Ethics and Integrity Committee was as much a sign of virtue as an unread Bible in a brothel.
   *The Times* 22 November 1999. JEFFREY ARCHER was forced to withdraw from the London mayoral election following the revelation that he lied in a previous libel case in 1986. WILLIAM HAGUE had earlier endorsed Archer as 'a candidate of probity and integrity'.

## Martha Reeves (b. 1941)

US SINGER

A secretary to Tamla Motown A&R executive William 'Mickey' Stevenson, she recorded with the Vandellas, an earthier version of the Supremes and best remembered for 'Dancing in the Street' (1964). Other hits included 'Heatwave' (1963) and 'Nowhere to Run' (1965).

1 Calling out around the world
   Are you ready for a brand new beat?
   Summer's here and the time is right
   For dancing in the street.
   'Dancing in the Street' (song, 1964, written by William 'Mickey' Stevenson and Marvin Gaye) on the album *Dance Party* (1965) by Martha and the Vandellas

## Wilhelm Reich (1897–1957)
AUSTRIAN-BORN US PSYCHOANALYST AND
BIOPHYSICIST

In his principal work, *The Function of the Orgasm* (1927), he argued that neuroses were a result of sexual repression and could be released through regular orgasm. His combination of Marxism and psychoanalysis led to his expulsion from the Communist Party in 1933 and from the International Psychoanalytical Association in 1934. Emigrating to the USA in 1939, he founded the Orgone Institute but was prosecuted for fraudulent practices and died in gaol.

1 The pleasure of living and the pleasure of the orgasm are identical. Extreme orgasm anxiety forms the basis of the general fear of life.
*The Function of the Orgasm*, ch. 5, sect. 4 (1927, transl. 1942)

## Jamie Reid (b. 1947)
BRITISH ARTIST

He came to notice in the 1970s for his contributions to the iconography of punk, notably his depiction of the Queen pierced with a safety pin. He co-wrote *Up They Rise* (1987) with Jon Savage.

1 Please wash your hands before leaving the twentieth century.
Title of multi-media exhibition, 1970s, quoted in *The Incomplete Works of Jamie Reid*, 'Death' (1987) by Jamie Reid and Jon Savage

## Jimmy Reid
BRITISH TRADE UNION OFFICIAL

He was active in the industrial disputes of the early 1970s, notably at the Upper Clyde Shipyard in 1971.

1 A rat race is for rats. We're not rats. We're human beings. Reject the insidious pressures in society that would blunt your critical faculties to all that is happening around you, that would caution silence in the face of injustice lest you jeopardize your chances of promotion and self-advancement. This is how it starts and, before you know where you are, you're a fully paid-up member of the rat pack. The price is too high.
Rectorial address Glasgow University, April 1972, quoted in *Writings on the Wall*, pt 1 (ed. Tony Benn, 1984)

## Theodor Reik (1888–1969)
US PSYCHOLOGIST

Called by *The New York Times* 'one of the titans of psychoanalysis', he was a lifelong friend of FREUD, although he differed from him in his belief that neuroses developed from a weakness in the ego. His books include *Myth and Guilt* (1957), *Sex in Man and Woman* (1960) and *The Need To Be Loved* (1963).

1 In our civilization, men are afraid that they will not be men enough and women are afraid that they may be considered only women.
*Esquire* November 1958

## Ad Reinhardt (1913–67)
US ARTIST

Full name Adolf Reinhardt. He joined the avant-garde American Abstract Artists association in 1937 and developed a minimal, monochrome style, as typified by *Abstract Painting No. 5* (1962) and *Black Painting No. 34* (1964), one of a series of 'Black Paintings'.

1 Art is too serious to be taken seriously.
Quoted in *Ad Reinhardt*, pt 1 (1981) by Lucy R. Lippard

## June Reinisch (b. 1943)
US PSYCHOLOGIST

A contributor to journals and popular magazines, she was joint editor and contributor to *Masculinity/Femininity* (1987), and *AIDS and Sex* and *Adolescence and Puberty* (both 1990).

1 When people say women can't be trusted because they cycle every month, my response is that men cycle every day, so they should only be allowed to negotiate peace treaties in the evening.
*The Times* 20 January 1992

## Agnes Repplier (1858–1950)
US AUTHOR AND SOCIAL CRITIC

A humorous and popular speaker, essayist and contributor to periodicals on any subject from cats to war, she published numerous works, including *Books and Men* (1888), *Points of Fiction* (1920) and an autobiography, *Eight Decades* (1937).

1 Anyone, however, who has had dealings with dates knows that they are worse than elusive, they are perverse. Events do not happen at the right time, nor in their proper sequence. That sense of harmony with place and season which is so strong in the historian – if he be a readable historian – is lamentably lacking in history, which takes no pains to verify his most convincing statements.
*To Think of Tea!* ch. 1 (1932)

2 Humor brings insight and tolerance. Irony brings a deeper and less friendly understanding.
*In Pursuit of Laughter*, ch. 9 (1936)

## James Reston (1909–95)
SCOTTISH-BORN US JOURNALIST

Known as 'Scotty', he was one of the most influential journalists of his time. His career was closely linked to *The New York Times* as a reporter and columnist, Washington Bureau Chief (1953–64), Executive Editor (1968–9) and Vice-president (1969–74). He won a Pulitzer Prize in 1945 and again in 1957 for national reporting. ALISTAIR COOKE called him 'the most agile filcher of confidential agreements, the most alert, the most probing, the most knowledgeable – the best – of all Washington correspondents'.

1 The conflict between the men who make and the men who report the news is as old as time. News may be true, but it is not truth, and reporters and officials seldom see it the same way . . . In the old days, the reporters or couriers of bad news were often put to the gallows; now they are given the Pulitzer Prize, but the conflict goes on.
*The Artillery of the Press*, 'The Tug of History' (1966)

2 Europe has a press that stresses opinions; America a press, radio, and television that emphasize news.
ibid. 'The President and the Press'

3 All politics . . . are based on the indifference of the majority.
*The New York Times* 12 June 1968

4 In foreign policy you have to wait twenty-five years to see how it comes out.
*International Herald Tribune* 18 November 1991

## David Reuben (b. 1933)
US PSYCHIATRIST

According to GORE VIDAL he is a 'relentlessly cheery, often genuinely funny writer . . . a moralist, expressing the hang-ups of today's middleaged, middle-class American Jews'. His most famous work, *Everything You Always Wanted To Know About Sex, But Were Afraid To Ask* (1969), was followed by *Everything You Always Wanted To*

*Know about Nutrition* (1978), following the same question-and-answer format.

1 **Everything you always wanted to know about sex, but were afraid to ask.**

Book title (1969). Reuben's manual became America's number-one non-fiction bestseller and gave the title to WOODY ALLEN's satirical movie released in 1972.

## Kenneth Rexroth (1905–82)
US POET, CRITIC AND TRANSLATOR

Known as 'Godfather of the Beats', he was described by his friend and former student Thomas Sanchez as 'longtime iconoclast, one-time radical, Roman Catholic, Communist fellow traveller, jazz scholar, I.W.W. anarchist, translator, philosopher, playwright, librettist, orientalist, critical essayist, radio personality, newspaper columnist, painter, poet and longtime Buddhist'. In his forty years as a poet he covered all themes and poetic techniques, as in his collections *The Phoenix and the Tortoise* (1944), *The Signature of All Things* (1950) and *The Morning Star* (1979).

1 **Into the gap between technology and environment, a black and fearsome chasm, man pours himself.**

'The Mirror of Magic', publ. in *New Republic* (1948), repr. in *With Eye and Ear* (1970)

2 **Man thrives where angels die of ecstasy and pigs die of disgust. The contemporary situation is like a long-standing, fatal disease. It is impossible to recall what life was like without it. We seem always to have had cancer of the heart.**

*Bird in the Bush: Obvious Essays* by Kenneth Rexroth, 'Kenneth Patchen, Naturalist of the Public Nightmare' (1959)

3 **Inside, the hideous British
Necrophilia and the rancid
Stink of the Church of England.**

'The Dragon and the Unicorn' pt 1, publ. in *Collected Longer Poems* (1968). Of Salisbury Cathedral.

## Malvina Reynolds See PETE SEEGER.

## Zandra Rhodes (b. 1940)
BRITISH FASHION DESIGNER

After opening the Fulham Road Clothes Shop in 1967, she showed her first collection in 1969 and was British Designer of the Year in 1972, her designs making use of chiffons and silks. In 1975 she branched out into cosmetics and jewellery.

1 **The advantage of being female is that once you're past 65, you can be a dowager empress. After the difficult part in the middle, you're allowed to be eccentric.**

Quoted in the *Guardian* 19 September 1998

## Jean Rhys (c. 1890–1979)
BRITISH AUTHOR

Original name Ella Gwendoline Rhys Williams. She incorporated her experiences during her years in Paris in the company of artists and painters in *The Left Bank and Other Stories* (1927), followed by novels including *Voyage in the Dark* (1934) and *Good Morning, Midnight* (1939). Her best known work, *Wide Sargasso Sea* (1966), published after thirty years' retirement in Cornwall, developed the story of Rochester's mad wife in Charlotte Brontë's *Jane Eyre*.

1 **The feeling of Sunday is the same everywhere, heavy, melancholy, standing still. Like when they say, 'As it was in the beginning, is now, and ever shall be, world without end'.**

Narrator (Anna Morgan), in *Voyage in the Dark*, pt 1, ch. 4 (1934)

2 **She [Audrey] could give herself up to the written word as naturally as a good dancer to music or a fine swimmer to**

water. The only difficulty was that after finishing the last sentence she was left with a feeling at once hollow and uncomfortably full. Exactly like indigestion.

'The Insect World', publ. in *Sleep It Off, Lady* (1976)

## Ruggiero Ricci (b. 1918)
US VIOLINIST

He made his debut at the age of ten and became noted for his command of the nineteenth-century bravura repertoire. He toured widely in North America and Europe and in 1971 introduced Paganini's rediscovered Concerto No. 4.

1 **A specialist is someone who does everything else worse.**

*Daily Telegraph* 25 May 1990

## (Sir) Tim Rice (b. 1944)
BRITISH SONGWRITER

In partnership with the composer Andrew Lloyd Webber he wrote *Joseph and the Amazing Technicolor Dreamcoat* (1968), *Jesus Christ Superstar* (1971) and *Evita* (1978). He was also the lyricist for *Chess* (1984) and *The Lion King* (1994), the latter with music by ELTON JOHN.

1 **Don't cry for me Argentina.**

Title of song (1976, music by Andrew Lloyd Webber) in *Evita* (stage musical 1978, filmed 1996). The song was a hit for Julie Covington in 1976 and 1978 and for MADONNA in 1996.

## Mandy Rice-Davies (b. 1944)
BRITISH MODEL AND CLUB HOSTESS

As a show girl in Murray's Cabaret Club in London, she met Christine Keeler, mistress of both Conservative cabinet minister John Profumo and the Soviet naval attaché in London. In 1963 she gave evidence in subsequent investigations of possible breaches of national security. She later became a night-club owner in Israel.

1 **He would, wouldn't he?**

Remark in court, 29 June 1963, quoted in the *Guardian* 1 July 1963. In response to the statement that Lord Astor, one of her alleged clients, had denied having had sex with her. The exchange took place in the wake of the Profumo affair.

2 **My life has been one long descent into respectability.**

Quoted by LYNN BARBER in the *Independent on Sunday* 31 March 1991. Referring to reports that Rice-Davies was on social terms with Sir Denis Thatcher, husband of MARGARET THATCHER.

## Adrienne Rich (b. 1929)
US POET AND AUTHOR

Described by MARGARET ATWOOD as 'one of America's best poets', she addresses feminist themes in such volumes as *Snapshots of a Daughter-in-Law* (1963) and *The Will to Change* (1971). She later became equally known for her prose writings, which include *Of Woman Born* (1976) and the essays collected in *On Lies, Secrets, and Silence* (1979) and *Blood, Bread, and Poetry* (1986).

1 **We who were loved will never
unlive that crippling fever.**

'After a Sentence in "Malte Laurids Brigge"', publ. in *Snapshots of a Daughter-in-Law* (1963)

2 **Only to have a grief
equal to all these tears!**

'Peeling Onions', publ. in ibid.

3 **The mind's passion is all for singling out.
Obscurity has another tale to tell.**

'Focus', publ. in *Necessities of Life* (1966)

4 **Now, again, poetry
violent, arcane, common,
hewn of the commonest living substance**

into archway, portal, frame
I grasp for you, your bloodstained splinters, your
ancient and stubborn poise
– as the earth trembles –
burning out from the grain

'The Fact of a Doorframe', publ. in *The Fact of a Doorframe* (1974)

5  Every journey into the past is complicated by delusions,
false memories, false namings of real events.

*Of Woman Born*, Foreword (1976)

6  The worker can unionize, go out on strike; mothers are
divided from each other in homes, tied to their children
by compassionate bonds; our wildcat strikes have most
often taken the form of physical or mental breakdown.

ibid. ch. 2

7  No one lives in this room
without confronting the whiteness of the wall
behind the poems, planks of books,
photographs of dead heroines.
Without contemplating last and late
the true nature of poetry. The drive
to connect. The dream of a common language.

'Origins and History of Consciousness', publ. in *The Dream of a Common Language* (1978)

8  They can rule the world while they can persuade us
our pain belongs in some order.
Is death by famine worse than death by suicide,
than a life of famine and suicide . . . ?

'Hunger', publ. in ibid.

9  How we dwelt in two worlds
the daughters and the mothers
in the kingdom of the sons.

'Sibling Mysteries', publ. in ibid.

10  Rape is a part of war; but it may be more accurate to say
that the capacity for dehumanizing another which so
corrodes male sexuality is carried over from sex into war.

'Caryatid', first publ. in *American Poetry Review* May/June 1973, repr. in *On Lies, Secrets, and Silence* (1979)

11  The connections between and among women are the most
feared, the most problematic, and the most potentially
transforming force on the planet.

'Disloyal To Civilization: Feminism, Racism, Gynophobia', first publ. in *Chrysalis*, no. 7 (1979), repr. in ibid.

## (Sir) Cliff Richard (b. 1940)

BRITISH SINGER

Original name Harry Webb. Backed by the Shadows he was promoted as Britain's answer to ELVIS PRESLEY. He followed the success of 'Move It' (1958) and 'Living Doll' (1959) with family films including *The Young Ones* (1961) and *Summer Holiday* (1963). He has had regular chart hits throughout his career, including a no. 1 for his millennium recording of 'Our Father' (1999).

1  The young ones
Darling we're the young ones
And the young ones should never be afraid.

'The Young Ones' (song, written by Sid Tepper and Roy Bennett) on the album *The Young Ones* (1961) by Cliff Richard and the Shadows. The song featured in the film of the same name (1962), and the title was used for the TV comedy *The Young Ones* (1982–4).

2  He said, 'Son, you are a bachelor boy
And that's the way to stay.
Son, you'll be a bachelor boy
Until your dying day.'

'Bachelor Boy' (song, written by Bruce Welch and Cliff Richard, 1962) on the album *More Hits By Cliff* (1965) by Cliff Richard and the Shadows

3  We're all going on a summer holiday,

No more worries for a week or two.

'Summer Holiday' (song, written by Bruce Welch and Brian Bennett) on the album *Summer Holiday* by Cliff Richard and the Shadows and in the eponymous film (both 1963)

4  If you have got the public in the palm of your hand, you
can be sure that is where they want to be.

*Observer* 4 December 1988

## Keith Richards (b. 1943)

BRITISH ROCK MUSICIAN

Originally named Keith Richard. Responsible for the chopped guitar chords that characterized the sound of the Rolling Stones, with MICK JAGGER he wrote most of the band's material and produced their later records. See also PHILIP NORMAN 1.

1  [Of rock 'n' roll] Music for the neck downwards.

Quoted in *Sound Effects: Youth, Leisure and the Politics of Rock*, ch. 7 (1979) by Simon Frith

## Miranda Richardson (b. 1958)

BRITISH ACTRESS

She made her stage debut with *Moving* (1980–81) and starred as Ruth Ellis in the film *Dance With a Stranger* (1985). Often typecast as a neurotic, she was praised for her roles in the films *Damage* (1992) and *Tom and Viv* (1994). She is also known for her part as Elizabeth I ('Queenie') in the TV series *Blackadder*.

1  Insecurity, commonly regarded as a weakness in normal
people, is the basic tool of the actor's trade.

*Guardian* 5 December 1990

## Christopher Ricks (b. 1933)

BRITISH CRITIC

He has edited *English Poetry and Prose 1540–1674* (1970) and the *English Poets* series for Penguin, among other works, and is author of *The Force of Poetry* (1984).

1  When a language creates – as it does – a community within
the present, it does so only by courtesy of a community
between the present and the past.

*The State of the Language*, Preface (1980)

## Laura Riding (1901–91)

US POET

Associated with the Fugitives, a group of Southern writers, she lived abroad 1926–39, much of the time with ROBERT GRAVES, with whom she established the Seizin Press (1927–38). She published numerous volumes of verse as well as the journal *Epilogue* (1935–8), and from 1941 worked on lexicographical studies. PAUL AUSTER described her as 'trying to peel back the skin of the world in order to find some absolute and unassailable place of permanence'.

1  The next world is
As near to this
As time is similar
To truth familiar

'From Later to Earlier', publ. in *The Poems of LR* (1938). Last lines of poem.

2  Art, whose honesty must work through artifice, cannot
avoid cheating truth.

*Selected Poems: In Five Sets*, Preface (1975)

## Anne Ridler (b. 1912)

BRITISH POET

Her work, appearing in such collections as *The Nine Bright Shiners* (1943) and *A Matter of Life and Death* (1959), evokes everyday life from a metaphysical viewpoint. She has also worked on opera librettos and as a translator and editor.

1 And when our baby stirs and struggles to be born
  It compels humility: what we began
  Is now its own.
  'For a Child Expected', publ. in *The Nine Bright Shiners* (1943)

2 To mark time is not to move:
  Only the unkempt hours drip from the clock
  Or pull at the cord coiled in its groove,
  The marker moveless, and the change illusion.
  'To Mark Time', publ. in *The Golden Bird* (1951)

3 Nothing is lost.
  We are too sad to know that, or too blind;
  Only in visited moments do we understand:
  It is not that the dead return –
  They are about us always, though unguessed.
  'Nothing is Lost', publ. in *A Matter of Life and Death* (1959)

4 In every generation
  The young acquire an image of their elders
  Tranquil, assured, with every day mapped out
  From punctual meals to reading by the fire.
  Threescore and ten is not like that at all
  We find on getting there.
  'Threescore and Ten', publ. in *New and Selected Poems* (1988)

5 Immortality
  Is not mere repetition:
  It is a blue flash,
  A kingfisher vision
  It is a new-feathered
  And procreant love,
  Seen where the halcyon
  Nests on the waves.
  'The Halcyons', publ. in ibid.

## Joan Rivers (b. 1935)
US COMIC

Originally Joan Alexandra Molinsky. Starting out as an acid-tongued stand-up comedienne, she gained wider success on television from 1965 on *The Tonight Show*, which she regularly hosted 1971–86. She subsequently hosted *The Late Show* (1986–7) and her own shows on television, including *The Joan Rivers Show* (from 1989), and she has also directed films and recorded albums.

1 I hate housework! You make the beds, you do the dishes – and six months later you have to start all over again.
  Quoted in *Woman Talk*, 'Work' (ed. Michèle Brown and Ann O'Connor, 1984)

2 My routines come out of total unhappiness. My audiences are my group therapy.
  BBC 2 television broadcast 23 February 1990

## Leonard Robbins (1877–1947)
US AUTHOR

Among his works are *Jersey Jingles* (1907), *Mountains and Men* (1931) and *Cure It With a Garden* (1933).

1 How a minority,
  Reaching majority,
  Seizing authority,
  Hates a minority!
  'Minorities'

## Tom Robbins (b. 1936)
US AUTHOR

He describes himself as 'an ordinary, sweet, witty guy who happens to possess a luminous cosmic vision and a passionate appreciation of fine sentences'. His novels, which won a following initially among the counterculture of California, include *Another Roadside*

*Attraction* (1971), *Even Cowgirls Get the Blues* (1976, filmed 1994) and *Jitterbug Perfume* (1984).

1 Life is too small a container for certain individuals.
  *Jitterbug Perfume*, pt 3 (1984)

2 Zippers are primal and modern at the very same time. On the one hand, your zipper is primitive and reptilian, on the other, mechanical and slick. A zipper is where the Industrial Revolution meets the Cobra Cult, don't you think? Ahh. Little alligators of ecstasy, that's what zippers are. Sexy, too. Now your button, a button is slim and persnickety. There's somethin' Victorian about a row o' buttons. But a zipper, why a zipper is the very snake at the gate of Eden, waitin' to escort a true believer into the Garden.
  Dr Dannyboy, in ibid. pt 4

## Paul Robeson (1898–1976)
US SINGER AND ACTOR

Admitted to the bar before pursuing a stage career from 1921, he was famous for both his acting and singing prowess, as in *Show Boat* (1927), in which he sang 'Ol' Man River', and *Othello* in London (1930). He also appeared in numerous films. His left-wing sympathies and opposition to racial discrimination drove him to leave the USA, and he lived in England 1958–63.

1 Songs of liberation – who can lock them up? The spirit of freedom – who can jail it? A people's unity – what lash can beat it down? Civil rights – what doubletalk can satisfy our needs?
  'A Lesson from Our South African Brothers and Sisters', publ. in *Freedom* September 1952

## Bruce Robinson (b. 1946)
BRITISH FILM-MAKER

He wrote the screenplay for *The Killing Fields* (1984) and wrote and directed *Withnail and I* (1987) and *How to Get Ahead in Advertising* (1989), both of which attracted a cult following. Later films include *Jennifer 8* (1992) and *Still Crazy* (1998).

1 We are indeed drifting into the arena of the unwell, making an enemy of our own future.
  Marwood (Paul McGann), in *Withnail and I* (film, 1987, written and directed by Bruce Robinson)

2 All right, this is the plan. We'll get in there and get wrecked. Then we'll eat a pork pie. Then we'll go home and drop a couple of Surmontil 50s each. That means we'll miss out Monday, but come up smiling Tuesday morning.
  Withnail (Richard E. Grant), in ibid.

3 I don't advise a haircut, man. All hairdressers are in the employment of the government. Hairs are your aerials. They pick up signals from the cosmos, and transmit them directly into the brain. This is the reason bald-headed men are uptight.
  Danny (Ralph Brown), in ibid.

4 We've gone on holiday by mistake.
  Withnail (Richard E. Grant), in ibid.

5 We want the finest wines available to humanity. And we want them *here*, and we want them *now*.
  ibid.

6 We're living in a shop. The world is one magnificent fucking shop, and if it hasn't got a price tag, it isn't worth having. There is no greater freedom than freedom of choice.
  Dennis Bagley (Richard E. Grant), in *How to Get Ahead in Advertising* (film, 1989, written and directed by Bruce Robinson)

7 You sit in front of the typewriter and the first thing you

have to deal with is the government of the mind, the super-ego, sitting up there on top of your head.

Interview in *The Idler* November/December 1995

## Edward G. Robinson (1893–1973)

ROMANIAN-BORN US ACTOR

Originally Emmanuel Goldenberg. A prolific stage performer, he gained stardom with his portrayal of the vicious gangster Rico in *Little Caesar* (1930), which led on to similar roles in films such as *Key Largo* (1948). 'Some people have youth,' he once said, 'some have beauty – I have menace.'

1 Mother of Mercy, is this the end of Rico?

Rico Bandello (Edward G. Robinson), in *Little Caesar* (film, 1931, screenplay by Francis E. Faragoh and Robert W. Lee based on novel by W.R. Burnett, directed by Mervyn LeRoy). Dying words, on being gunned down by the police.

2 Murder is never perfect. It always falls apart sooner or later. When two people are involved, it's usually sooner . . . They're stuck with each other and they've got to ride all the way to the end of the line and it's a one-way trip and the last stop is the cemetery.

Barton Keyes (Edward G. Robinson), in *Double Indemnity* (film, 1944, screenplay by BILLY WILDER and RAYMOND CHANDLER based on JAMES M. CAIN's novel, directed by Billy Wilder, 1944)

## Edwin Arlington Robinson (1869–1935)

US POET

Now remembered for a few poems such as 'Miniver Cherry' and 'Richard Cory', he was the first person to be awarded a Pulitzer Prize for poetry for his *Collected Poems* (1922), which he followed with *The Man Who Died Twice* (1924) and the narrative *Tristram* (1927). ROBERT FROST described his life as 'a revel in the facilities of language'.

1 I shall have more to say when I am dead.

'John Brown', publ. in *The Three Taverns* (1920). Last line of poem.

## Mary Robinson (b. 1944)

IRISH POLITICIAN AND PRESIDENT

She served in the Irish Senate (1969–89) and twice ran as a Labour Party candidate for the Dáil, but resigned from the Party in 1985 over the Anglo-Irish Agreement. Campaigning for reform of the laws on contraception, abortion and homosexuality, she became in 1990 Ireland's first woman president and the first president since 1945 not to have been backed by the Fianna Fáil Party. She resigned in 1997 to take up a position as UN Commissioner on Human Rights.

1 [Of Irish women] Instead of rocking the cradle, they rocked the system.

Quoted in *The Times* 10 November 1990. Speech on becoming President, alluding to William Ross Wallace's poem, 'The Hand That Rules the World' (1865): 'The hand that rocks the cradle/Is the hand that rules the world.'

## Gene Roddenberry (1921–91)

US TV PRODUCER AND WRITER

As a police officer in Los Angeles in the 1950s he wrote TV scripts in his spare time for the crime serial *Dragnet*, then full time for shows including *Have Gun Will Travel* and *Dr Kildare*. He is best known as creator of the science fiction series *Star Trek*, launched in 1966, and *Star Trek: the Next Generation* (1987–94). He acted as Executive Consultant on the Star Trek films produced by Paramount.

1 Space – the final frontier. These are the voyages of the starship *Enterprise*. Its five-year mission: to explore strange new worlds, to seek out new life and new civilizations, to boldly go where no man has gone before.

Voiceover in *Star Trek* (TV series 1966–9, created and produced by Gene Roddenberry). This preamble to each episode includes what is probably the most famous split infinitive ever recorded.

2 Beam me up, Scotty.

Attributed to Captain James T. Kirk (William Shatner), in ibid. These words were never actually spoken in the series; the nearest is 'Beam us up, Mr Scott,' said by Captain Kirk to his chief engineer.

3 We are, in many ways . . . two people. As long as the inner person believes and admits that decency is good, the outer person who has to deal with the world – a world that is not always fair – is allowed to slip from time to time. I suppose that I have thought all my life that the only real person was the inner me.

Interview in *The Humanist* March/April 1991, quoted in *Gene Roddenberry: The Man Behind the Myth*, ch. 5 (1994) by Joel Engel

## Anita Roddick (b. 1942)

BRITISH BUSINESSWOMAN

With her husband she opened the first Body Shop in Brighton in 1976 and by 1994 became Chief Executive of the company, which had 800 outlets world-wide, retailing beauty products according to ethical and ecological principles. 'Our products are not the Body and Blood of Jesus Christ,' she has said. 'The Body Shop is important to me for the strings that I can attach to the products.'

1 It is immoral to trade on fear. It is immoral constantly to make women feel dissatisfied with their bodies. It is immoral to deceive a customer by making miracle claims for a product. It is immoral to use a photograph of a glowing sixteen-year-old to sell a cream aimed at preventing wrinkles in a forty-year-old.

*Body and Soul*, ch. 1 (1991)

2 I think that business practices would improve immeasurably if they were guided by 'feminine' principles – qualities like love and care and intuition.

ibid.

3 We will compromise on almost anything, but not on our values, or our aesthetics, or our idealism, or our sense of curiosity.

ibid. ch. 11

4 The most important principle of my life is moving out of the comfort zone. It's not just a junkie fix of experience: this is the majority world; reality.

Quoted in the *Observer* 26 April 1998. On travelling in remote parts.

## Richard Rodriguez (b. 1944)

US AUTHOR AND JOURNALIST

Raised in California but with his roots in Mexico, he describes his writing as a 'marriage of journalism and literature', taking GEORGE ORWELL as a model. He is the author of two volumes of autobiography, *Hunger of Memory* (1982) and *Days of Obligation* (1992), as well as of *Frontiers* (1990), based on a TV series.

1 Mexico is a nineteenth-century country arranged for gaslight. Once brought into the harsh light of the twentieth-century media, Mexico can only seem false. In its male, in its public, in its city aspect, Mexico is an arch-transvestite, a tragic buffoon. Dogs bark and babies cry when Mother Mexico walks abroad in the light of day. The policeman, the Marxist mayor – Mother Mexico doesn't even bother to shave her mustachios. Swords and rifles and spurs and bags of money chink and clatter beneath her skirts. A chain of martyred priests dangles from her waist, for she is an austere, pious lady. Ay, how much – clutching her jangling bosoms; spilling cigars – how much she has suffered.

*Frontiers*, 'Night and Day' (1990)

2 In tragic cultures, the old have something to teach the young. And they are believed.

ibid.

3 In America, the Indian is relegated to the obligatory first chapter – the Once Great Nation chapter – after which the Indian is cleared away as easily as brush, using a very sharp rhetorical tool called an 'alas'.

'Mixed Blood', publ. in *Harper's Magazine* November 1991

## Ginger Rogers (1911–95)
US SCREEN ACTRESS

Originally Virginia Katherine McMath. She starred in ten films as the dancing partner of Fred Astaire, including *The Gay Divorcee* (1934) and *Shall We Dance* (1937), all immensely popular during the Depression era. As KATHARINE HEPBURN remarked: 'He gives her class and she gives him sex.' Altogether Rogers appeared in more than seventy films, winning an Oscar for her part in *Kitty Foyle* (1940), and acted on the stage in *Hello Dolly!* (1965) and *Mame* (1969).

1 Cigarette me, big boy.

*Young Man of Manhattan* (film, 1930, screenplay by Robert Presnell based on story by Katherine Brush, directed by Monta Bell). Rogers's first screen role.

## (Sir) Richard Rogers (b. 1933)
BRITISH ARCHITECT

Baron Rogers of Riverside He was a founder member of Team 4 with Norman Foster. His notable buildings include the Pompidou Centre, Paris (with Renzo Piano, 1979), and in London the Lloyds (1985) and Reuters (1992) buildings.

1 Form follows profit is the aesthetic principle of our times.

*The Times* 13 February 1991

## Will Rogers (1879–1935)
US HUMORIST

Starting out as the lariat-throwing 'Cherokee Kid' in Wild West shows from 1902, he added wise-cracking and homespun philosophy to his act in the *Ziegfeld Follies* (1916–25). He later became a national institution for his aphoristic columns in *The New York Times* from 1922, radio broadcasts and films, such as *Connecticut Yankee* (1931) and *State Fair* (1933).

1 People are getting smarter nowadays; they are letting lawyers, instead of their conscience, be their guide.

*The Illiterate Digest*, 'Helping the Girls with their Income Taxes' (1924)

2 Everything is funny as long as it is happening to somebody else.

ibid. 'Warning to Jokers: Lay Off the Prince'

3 The United States never lost a war or won a conference.

*Wit and Wisdom* (ed. Jack Lait, 1936). Remark following the Versailles Peace Conference, at which President WOODROW WILSON spurned all suggestions that the US should take territory or payment as a result of participating in the First World War.

4 Communism to me is one-third practice and two-thirds explanation.

ibid.

5 There's only one thing that can kill the movies, and that's education.

*The Autobiography of Will Rogers*, ch. 6 (1949)

6 You can't say that civilization don't advance ... for in every war they kill you a new way.

ibid. ch. 14

7 When you put down the good things you ought to have done, and leave out the bad ones you did do – well, that's Memoirs.

ibid. ch. 16

8 I don't know jokes; I just watch the government and report the facts.

Quoted in 'A Rogers Thesaurus' in *Saturday Review* 25 August 1962

## Ernst Röhm (1887–1934)
GERMAN NAZI LEADER

An early supporter of HITLER, he was the leader of the Nazi 'Brownshirts' but was executed, along with 100 others, on the Night of the Long Knives, 29–30 June 1934, for his alleged part in the plot to assassinate Hitler.

1 All revolutions devour their own children.

Remark to HANS FRANK, 30 June 1933, recorded by Frank in his memoirs (1955), quoted in *The Face of the Third Reich*, 'Ernst Röhm and the Lost Generation' (1963, transl. 1970) by Joachim C. Fest

## Katie Roiphe (b. 1968)
US FEMINIST WRITER

She caused controversy with her study of date or acquaintance rape on college campuses, *The Morning After: Sex, Fear and Feminism on Campus* (1993), which rejected views of men as 'sexual beasts' and women as 'delicate vessels' and criticized feminists for being obsessed with sexual victimization. Later publications include *Last Night in Paradise: Sex and Morals at the Century's End* (1997).

1 In this era of Just Say No and No Means No, we don't have many words for embracing experience. Now instead of liberation and libido, the emphasis is on trauma and disease.

*The Morning After*, 'The Blue-Light System' (1993)

2 The idea that men don't know what women mean when women say no stems from something deeper and more complicated than feminist concerns with rape. The conservative thrust of the movement against date rape is that women need to be protected from men who don't share their social background.

ibid. 'The Rape-Crisis, or "Is Dating Dangerous?"'

## Ida Rolf (1896–1979)
US BIOCHEMIST AND PHYSICAL THERAPIST

His deep massage therapy, disseminated through an international network of schools and popularized in the 1960s and 1970s, aimed to counteract the effects of bad posture on the body and mind.

1 An effective human being is a whole that is greater than the sum of its parts.

*Rolfing: The Integration of Human Structures*, Preface (1977)

## Mickey Rooney (b. 1920)
US ACTOR AND ENTERTAINER

Original name Joe Yule. Described by author and critic James Agee as 'a rope-haired, kazoo-voiced kid with a comic strip face', he was a stage performer from the age of two and by the early 1940s was regarded as the most popular American film star. His short stature fitted him for a series of juvenile roles, including in *Boys Town* (1938), *The Human Comedy* (1943) and *National Velvet* (1944).

1 Women liked me because I made them laugh. And what is an orgasm, except laughter of the loins?

*Life is Too Short*, ch. 32 (autobiography, 1991). Rooney was married eight times, first to Ava Gardner.

# Eleanor Roosevelt (1884–1962)

US DIPLOMAT AND FIRST LADY

After her marriage to FRANKLIN D. ROOSEVELT in 1905, she became a public figure in her own right, involved in liberal causes such as civil and women's rights. She acted as her husband's stand-in during his illness and after his death was delegate to the UN Assembly (1946–52) and played a major role in the drafting of the Universal Declaration of Human Rights. See ADLAI STEVENSON 17.

1 No one can make you feel inferior without your consent.
   *This Is My Story* (1937)

2 A trait no other nation seems to possess in quite the same degree that we do – namely, a feeling of almost childish injury and resentment unless the world as a whole recognizes how innocent we are of anything but the most generous and harmless intentions.
   'My Day', syndicated newspaper column, 11 November 1946

3 You always admire what you really don't understand.
   'Meet the Press', on NBC-TV, 16 September 1956

4 You will feel that you are no longer clothing yourself, you are dressing a public monument.
   Quoted in the *New York Herald Tribune* 27 October 1960. Warning to wives of future presidents.

5 I think, at a child's birth, if a mother could ask a fairy godmother to endow it with the most useful gift, that gift would be curiosity.
   Quoted in *Today's Health* 2 October 1966

# Franklin D. Roosevelt (1882–1945)

US POLITICIAN AND PRESIDENT

Full name Franklin Delano Roosevelt. Although paralysed from 1921 as a result of polio, he rose to become the only US president to win four elections (1933–45). A Democrat, he countered the Depression with the New Deal economic programme, resisted US involvement in the Second World War until the Japanese attack on Pearl Harbor (1941) and subsequently led the war effort. He was the first president to broadcast over the radio, using his 'Fireside Chats' to explain issues and policies.

1 These unhappy times call for the building of plans that . . . build from the bottom up and not from the top down, that put their faith once more in the forgotten man at the bottom of the economic pyramid.
   Radio broadcast 7 April 1932, publ. in *Public Papers and Addresses of Franklin D. Roosevelt*, vol. 1 (1938)

2 But while they prate of economic laws, men and women are starving. We must lay hold of the fact that economic laws are not made by nature. They are made by human beings.
   Acceptance speech at Democratic national convention, Chicago, 2 July 1932, publ. in ibid.

3 I pledge you, I pledge myself, to a new deal for the American people.
   ibid. At the height of the economic crisis, Roosevelt's 'New Deal' became the slogan of his successful campaign for the presidency.

4 Let me assert my firm belief that the only thing we have to fear is fear itself – nameless, unreasoning, unjustified terror which paralyzes needed efforts to convert retreat into advance.
   Inaugural address, 4 March 1933, publ. in *The Penguin Book of Twentieth-Century Speeches* (ed. Brian MacArthur, 1999). Roosevelt had used the expression 'the only thing we have to fear is fear itself' on previous occasions, and it has numerous earlier attributions, including the Duke of Wellington, Montaigne, Thoreau and the Bible. WINSTON CHURCHILL in his wartime broadcasts is also associated with the words.

5 In the field of world policy I would dedicate this nation to the policy of the good neighbor.
   ibid.

6 I see one-third of a nation ill-housed, ill-clad, ill-nourished.
   Second inaugural address, 20 January 1937, publ. in *Public Papers and Addresses of Franklin D. Roosevelt*, vol. 6 (1941)

7 War is a contagion.
   Speech in Chicago, 5 October 1937, quoted in *The Wit and Wisdom of Franklin D. Roosevelt*, 'War' (ed. Maxwell Meyersohn, 1950)

8 A radical is a man with both feet firmly planted in the air. A conservative is a man with two perfectly good legs, who, however, has never learned to walk forward. A reactionary is a somnambulist walking backwards. A liberal is a man who uses his legs and his hands at the behest . . . of his head.
   Radio broadcast 26 October 1939, publ. in *Public Papers and Addresses of Franklin D. Roosevelt*, vol. 8 (1941)

9 And while I am talking to you mothers and fathers, I give you one more assurance. I have said this before, but I shall say it again and again and again: Your boys are not going to be sent into any foreign wars.
   Speech in Boston, 30 October 1940, publ. in ibid. vol. 9. Roosevelt made the speech while campaigning for his third term as president. He declared war against Japan just over a year later (see below).

10 We have the men – the skill – the wealth – and above all, the will . . . We must be the great arsenal of democracy.
   'Fireside Chat' radio broadcast, 29 December 1940, publ. in *The Penguin Book of Twentieth-Century Speeches* (ed. Brian MacArthur, 1999)

11 We look forward to a world founded upon four essential human freedoms. The first is freedom of speech and expression – everywhere in the world. The second is freedom of every person to worship God in his own way – everywhere in the world. The third is freedom from want . . . everywhere in the world. The fourth is freedom from fear . . . anywhere in the world.
   Annual Message to Congress, Washington, D.C., 6 January 1941, publ. in ibid.

12 Yesterday, December 7, 1941 – a date which will live in infamy – the United States of America was suddenly and deliberately attacked by naval and air forces of the Empire of Japan.
   Address to Congress, 8 December 1941, publ. in *Public Papers and Addresses of Franklin D. Roosevelt*, vol. 10 (1950). The attack on Pearl Harbor precipitated an immediate declaration of war on Japan by both the US and Britain.

13 It is fun to be in the same decade with you.
   Telegram to WINSTON CHURCHILL, 30 January 1942, in response to sixtieth birthday greetings, quoted in *The Hinge of Fate*, ch. 4 (1950) by Winston Churchill

14 More than an end to war, we want an end to the beginnings of all wars.
   Speech prepared for Jefferson Day broadcast, 13 April 1945, quoted in *The Wit and Wisdom of Franklin D. Roosevelt*, 'War' (ed. Maxwell Meyersohn, 1950). Roosevelt died suddenly the day before the speech was due to be made, at Warm Springs, Georgia.

# Theodore Roosevelt (1858–1919)

US POLITICIAN AND PRESIDENT

He became Republican President (1901–1909) after the assassination of William McKinley and is the youngest US president to date. He is remembered for his Square Deal programme of social reform and regulation of business monopolies. His approach to foreign policy was characterized by his dictum 'Speak softly and carry a big stick', and he was awarded the Nobel Peace Prize in 1906 for his part in ending the Russo-Japanese War. He later formed his own Progressive Party, at the head of which he unsuccessfully stood for president in the 1912 election.

1 There is no room in this country for hyphenated Americanism ... The one absolutely certain way of bringing this nation to ruin, of preventing all possibility of its continuing to be a nation at all, would be to permit it to become a tangle of squabbling nationalities.

Speech in New York, 12 October 1915, publ. in *Works*, vol. 20 (Memorial edn, 1923–6)

2 One of our defects as a nation is a tendency to use what have been called 'weasel words.' When a weasel sucks eggs the meat is sucked out of the egg. If you use a 'weasel word' after another there is nothing left of the other.

Speech in St Louis, Missouri, 31 May 1916, publ. in ibid. vol. 24 (1926). Referring to WOODROW WILSON's proposal for 'universal voluntary military training'.

3 There can be no fifty-fifty Americanism in this country. There is room here for only 100% Americanism, only for those who are Americans and nothing else.

Speech at State Republican Party Convention, Saratoga, New York, 19 July 1918, publ. in *Roosevelt Policy*, vol. 3 (1919)

## Richard Rorty (b. 1931)
US PHILOSOPHER

His work is influenced by John Dewey and Jürgen Habermas and includes *Philosophy and the Mirror of Nature* (1979), an attack on the aims of traditional philosophy, *Contingency, Irony, and Solidarity* (1989) and *Objectivity, Relativism and Truth* (1991), the last two concerning literary criticism and social theory.

1 There is nothing deep down inside us except what we have put there ourselves.

*Consequences of Pragmatism*, 'Pragmatism and Philosophy' (1982). Refuting the notion that there is some innate metaphysical 'truth' about human beings.

2 Openmindedness should not be fostered because, as Scripture teaches, Truth is great and will prevail, nor because, as Milton suggests, Truth will always win in a free and open encounter. It should be fostered for its own sake.

*Contingency, Irony, and Solidarity*, ch. 3 'The Contingency of Community' (1989)

3 Truth is simply a compliment paid to sentences seen to be paying their way.

Quoted in *The New York Times Magazine* 12 February 1990

4 Always strive to excel, but only on weekends.

ibid.

## Richard Dean Rosen (b. 1949)
US JOURNALIST AND CRITIC

He published his first book, *Me and My Friends, We No Longer Profess Any Graces: A Premature Memoir* (1971) while still an undergraduate, and later invented the term 'psychobabble' to describe the idiom which emerged in the Bay area of San Francisco, as described in *Psychobabble: Fast Talk and Quick Cure in the Era of Feeling* (1977). He has also worked as an editor and critic and as R.D. Rosen has published mysteries featuring the baseball player-turned-sleuth Harvey Blissberg.

1 It's apparent that we can't proceed any further without a name for this institutionalized garrulousness, this psychological patter, this need to catalogue the ego's condition. Let's call it psychobabble, this spirit which now tyrannizes conversation in the seventies.

*Psychobabble: Fast Talk and Quick Cure in the Era of Feeling*, 'Psychobabble' (1977). The jargon of 'psychobabble', Rosen explained, 'is now spoken by magazine editors, management consultants, sandal makers, tool and die workers, chiefs of state, Ph.D.s in clinical psychology, and just about everyone else'. It consists of 'a set of repetitive verbal formalities that kills off the very spontaneity, candor, and understanding it pretends to promote. It's an idiom that reduces psychological insight to a collection of standardized

observations, that provides a frozen lexicon to deal with an infinite variety of problems.'

2 Confession, alas, is the new handshake.

ibid.

## Harold Rosenberg (1906–78)
US ART CRITIC AND AUTHOR

In 1952 he coined the phrase 'action painting' to describe his conception of the work of art as embodied in the artistic process rather than in the completed art object, as explained in *The Anxious Object* (1964). He proposed an 'aesthetics of impermanence' in works such as *Artworks and Packages* (1969) and *The De-Definition of Art* (1972). From 1966 he was art critic of the *New Yorker*.

1 Whoever undertakes to create soon finds himself engaged in creating himself. Self-transformation and the transformation of others have constituted the radical interest of our century, whether in painting, psychiatry, or political action.

*The Tradition of the New*, Preface (1960)

2 Revolution in art lies not in the will to destroy but in the revelation of what has already been destroyed. Art kills only the dead.

ibid. ch. 6

3 Kitsch is the daily art of our time, as the vase or the hymn was for earlier generations. For the sensibility it has that arbitrariness and importance which works take on when they are no longer noticeable elements of the environment. In America kitsch is Nature. The Rocky Mountains have resembled fake art for a century.

ibid. ch. 18

4 Only conservatives believe that subversion is still being carried on in the arts and that society is being shaken by it ... Advanced art today is no longer a cause – it contains no moral imperative. There is no virtue in clinging to principles and standards, no vice in selling or in selling out.

'The Cultural Situation Today', first publ. in *Partisan Review* summer 1972, repr. as Introduction to *Discovering the Present* (1973)

5 What better way to prove that you understand a subject than to make money out of it?

ibid.

6 Art is the laboratory for making new men.

*Discovering the Present*, ch. 24 (1973)

7 The story of Americans is the story of arrested metamorphoses. Those who achieve success come to a halt and accept themselves as they are. Those who fail become resigned and accept themselves as they are.

ibid.

## Alan S.C. Ross (1907–80)
BRITISH LINGUISTICS SCHOLAR

Full name Alan Strode Campbell Ross. Author of numerous scholarly studies on German and Scandinavian etymology, he is popularly remembered for works such as *How to Pronounce It* (1970) and *Don't Say It* (1973), and also for his coinage of the expressions 'U' and 'non-U' to denote linguistic usage condoned (or otherwise) by the conventions of class snobbery.

1 There are, it is true, still a few minor points of life which may serve to demarcate the upper class, but they are only minor ones ... When drunk, gentlemen often become amorous or maudlin or vomit in public, but they never become truculent.

'U and Non-U: An Essay in Sociological Linguistics' (1954), repr. in *Noblesse Oblige* (1956) by NANCY MITFORD

2 It must be remembered that, in these matters, U-speakers have ears to hear, so that one single pronunciation, word,

or phrase will suffice to brand an apparent U-speaker as originally non-U (for U-Speakers themselves never make 'mistakes').

ibid.

## Andrew Ross (b. 1956)
BRITISH SOCIAL THEORIST

In works such as *Strange Weather: Culture, Science and Technology in the Age of Limits* (1991) and *The Chicago Gangster Theory of Life* (1995) he extended conventional notions of ecology to explore their relationship to issues of social justice. He has since published *No Sweat* (1997), about the fashion industry and the global exploitation of garment workers, and *Real Love: In Pursuit of Cultural Justice* (1998).

1 The powerful appeal of ecology as a practical politics lies in its capacity to encourage people to make consistent links between the social and emotional shape of everyday actions and a quantitative world-picture of physical causes and effects. Above all, it is a politics of information and knowledge, exceptional among social and political movements in its overriding appeal to science for proof of the justice of ecological claims.

*Strange Weather*, ch. 6 (1991)

## Harold Ross (1892–1951)
US EDITOR

He began his career as a reporter in the American West and after US entry into the First World War edited the army's newspaper, *Stars and Stripes*. As the *New Yorker*'s gifted and eccentric first Editor (from 1925), he set standards of intelligence and sophistication and nurtured such talents as JAMES THURBER, EDMUND WILSON and TRUMAN CAPOTE.

1 The *New Yorker* will be the magazine which is not edited for the old lady from Dubuque.

Attributed, from prospectus for the *New Yorker* (1925), later quoted '. . . little old lady from Dubuque'. The prospectus, however, 'bears neither the stamp of Ross's hand nor, read aloud, the sound of Ross's voice', according to JAMES THURBER. The magazine, he wrote, was 'whatever else, first and foremost the magazine of the young man from Aspen'.

2 Editing is the same as quarreling with writers – same thing exactly.

*Time* magazine 6 March 1950

3 Is Moby Dick the whale or the man?

Quoted in *The Years With Ross*, ch. 4 (1959) by James Thurber

## Jean Rostand (1894–1977)
FRENCH BIOLOGIST AND AUTHOR

Alongside his books for the scientific community, including *Toads* (1934) and *An Introduction to Genetics* (1936), he wrote popular works for a wider audience, such as *Life and Its Problems* (1939) and *A Biologist's View* (1954). He was known for his astute, though often highly critical, insights into the social and psychological context of scientific research.

1 Kill a man, one is a murderer; kill a million, a conqueror; kill them all, a God.

*Pensées d'un biologiste*, (1939), repr. in *The Substance of Man*, ch. 5 (1962)

2 To be adult is to be alone.

ibid. ch. 6

3 I still understand a few words in life, but I no longer think they make a sentence.

ibid.

4 Nothing leads the scientist so astray as a premature truth.

ibid. ch. 7

5 Greatness, in order to gain recognition, must all too often consent to ape greatness.

ibid. ch. 8

6 Beauty in art is often nothing but ugliness subdued.

ibid.

7 To reflect is to disturb one's thoughts.

ibid. ch. 10

8 I should have no use for a paradise in which I should be deprived of the right to prefer hell.

ibid.

9 Hatred, for the man who is not engaged in it, is a little like the odour of garlic for one who hasn't eaten any.

ibid.

10 There are moments when very little truth would be enough to shape opinion. One might be hated at extremely low cost.

ibid.

11 Far too often the choices reality proposes are such as to take away one's taste for choosing.

ibid.

12 To love an idea is to love it a little more than one should.

*Carnets d'un biologiste*, repr. in ibid.

13 Certain brief sentences are peerless in their ability to give one the feeling that nothing remains to be said.

ibid.

14 God, that checkroom of our dreams.

ibid. Other translations give '. . . dumping ground of our dreams'.

15 The ideal, without doubt, varies, but its enemies, alas, are always the same.

ibid.

## Leo Rosten (1908–97)
US AUTHOR

A versatile author who wrote 'as my interests guide and seduce me', he published short fiction, screenplays and biography, but is best known for his humorous sketches about a new immigrant in the US, *The Education of H\*y\*m\*a\*n K\*a\*p\*l\*a\*n* (1937) and its sequels, and for *The Joys of Yiddish* (1968).

1 [Of W.C. Fields] Anybody who hates dogs and babies can't be all bad.

Speech in honour of W.C. FIELDS at Masquers' Club Dinner, Hollywood, 16 February 1939, quoted in the *Saturday Review* 12 June, 1976. Often erroneously ascribed to Fields, with the words: 'Anyone who hates children and dogs can't be all bad.'

## Theodore Roszak (b. 1933)
US SOCIAL CRITIC

His pioneering work, *The Making of a Counter-Culture* (1969), has been described as 'brilliantly hard-headed'. A teacher of interdisciplinary studies at California State University in the 1960s, he remains a powerful critic of industrial capitalism in works such as *Pontifex* (1975), his venture into fiction, and *Personal Planet* (1977). In 1999 he published *The Gendered Atom*, on 'the sexual psychology of science'.

1 There are dragons buried beneath our cities, primordial energies greater than the power of our bombs. Two thousand years of Judeo-Christian soul-shaping and three centuries of crusading scientific intellect have gone into their interment . . . But now they wake and stir.

*Where the Wasteland Ends*, Introduction (1972)

2 Technological optimism is the snake oil of urban-industrialism.

ibid. ch. 2

3 If God has at last died in our culture, he has not been

buried. For the casually religious, he lingers on like a fond old relative who has been so expertly embalmed that we may prop him up in the far corner of the living room and pretend the old fellow is still with us.

ibid. ch. 6

## Philip Roth (b. 1933)
US NOVELIST

An irreverent satirist, fascinated with themes of social constraints as they conflict with personal impulse, he preserves a love-hate relationship with the Jewish faith of his ancestors. His major works include *Portnoy's Complaint* (1969), *Zuckerman Unbound* (1981) and *American Pastoral* (1997). He describes the life of a fiction writer as 'undermining experience, embellishing experience, rearranging and enlarging experience into a species of mythology'.

1 Only in America . . . do these peasants, our mothers, get their hair dyed platinum at the age of sixty, and walk up and down Collins Avenue in Florida in pedalpushers and mink stoles – and with opinions on every subject under the sun. It isn't their fault they were given a gift like speech – look, if cows could talk, they would say things just as idiotic.

*Portnoy's Complaint*, 'Cunt Crazy' (1969)

2 A Jewish man with parents alive is a fifteen-year-old boy, and will remain a fifteen-year-old boy until *they die*!

ibid.

3 My God! The English language is a *form of communication*! Conversation isn't just crossfire where you shoot and get shot at! Where you've got to duck for your life and aim to kill! Words aren't only bombs and bullets – no, they're little gifts, containing *meanings*!

ibid. 'The Most Prevalent Form of Degradation in Erotic Life'

4 To become a celebrity is to become a brand name. There is Ivory Soap, Rice Krispies, and Philip Roth. Ivory is the soap that floats; Rice Krispies the breakfast cereal that goes snap-crackle-pop; Philip Roth the Jew who masturbates with a piece of liver.

'Interview with Le Nouvel Observateur', May 1981, repr. in *Reading Myself and Others* (1975, rev. 1985)

5 When you publish a book, it's the world's book. The world edits it.

*The New York Times Book Review* 2 September 1979

6 Is an intelligent human being likely to be much more than a large-scale manufacturer of misunderstanding?

Nathan Zuckerman, in *The Counterlife*, ch. 5 (1986)

7 All I can tell you with certainty is that I, for one, have no self, and that I am unwilling or unable to perpetrate upon myself the joke of a self . . . What I have instead is a variety of impersonations I can do, and not only of myself – a troupe of players that I have internalized, a permanent company of actors that I can call upon when a self is required . . . I am a theater and nothing more than a theater.

ibid. Zuckerman writing to Maria

8 England's made a Jew of me in only eight weeks, which, on reflection, might be the least painful method. A Jew without Jews, without Judaism, without Zionism, without Jewishness, without a temple or an army or even a pistol, a Jew clearly without a home, just the object itself, like a glass or an apple.

ibid.

9 Obviously the facts are never just coming at you but are incorporated by an imagination that is formed by your previous experience. Memories of the past are not memories of facts but memories of your imaginings of the facts.

*The Facts*, opening letter to Zuckerman (1988)

10 Family indivisibility, the first commandment.

ibid. Prologue

11 I write fiction and I'm told it's autobiography, I write autobiography and I'm told it's fiction, so since I'm so dim and they're so smart, let *them* decide what it is or it isn't.

Philip, in *Deception* (1990)

12 I cannot and do not live in the world of discretion, not as a writer, anyway. I would prefer to, I assure you – it would make life easier. But discretion is, unfortunately, not for novelists.

ibid. Said to his wife.

## Mark Rothko (1903–70)
LATVIAN-BORN US PAINTER

Original name Marcus Rothkovich. From 1938 he began to experiment with 'automatism' and produced increasingly non-representational work. His use of large expanses of colour led to the development of Colour Field painting. From 1958 to 1966 he worked on a series of fourteen immense canvases which were placed in a nondenominational chapel in Houston, Texas, re-named the Rothko Chapel after his death by suicide.

1 Both the sense of community and of security depend on the familiar. Freed of them, transcendental experience becomes possible.

'The Romantics Were Prompted', publ. in *Possibilities* winter 1947–8, repr. in *Theories of Modern Art*, ch. 9 (1968) by Herschel B. Chipp

2 Pictures must be miraculous: the instant one is completed, the intimacy between the creation and the creator is ended. He is an outsider. The picture must be for him, as for anyone experiencing it later, a revelation, an unexpected and unprecedented resolution of an eternally familiar need.

ibid.

## Guy de Rothschild (b. 1909)
FRENCH BANKER

Born into the most famous family in international banking, he was awarded the Croix de Guerre in the Second World War. He was President of the Compagnie du Chemin de Fer du Nord (1949–68) and of the Banque Rothschild (1968–78) and is author of *Mon ombre siamoise* (1993) and *Le Fantôme de Léa* (1998).

1 I have no idea what a poor Rothschild would look like. I suppose he would vanish in anonymity.

*The Whims of Fortune*, ch. 1 (autobiography, 1985)

## Constance Rourke (1885–1941)
US AUTHOR

In 1915 she retired from university teaching to concentrate on her studies of American literature and popular culture. Her *American Humor* (1931) and the posthumously published *The Roots of American Culture* (1942) are now widely regarded as forerunners of contemporary cultural studies.

1 An emotional man may possess no humor, but a humorous man usually has deep pockets of emotion, sometimes tucked away or forgotten.

*American Humor*, ch. 1 (1931)

## Rowan and Martin's Laugh-In

The show started as a one-hour special for TV in 1967 and proved so popular that it was developed into a series (1967–73). Scripted by an extensive and changing roster of writers, its sketches featuring familiar characters were interspersed with routines by its two frontmen, Dan Rowan (1922–87) and Dick Martin (b. 1923).

1 Very interesting . . . but stupid!

Catch-phrase by German soldier (Arte Johnson), in *Rowan and Martin's Laugh-In* (TV comedy series, 1967–73). Arte Johnson was a regular on the show 1968–71.

## Helen Rowland (1875–1950)
US JOURNALIST

She wrote humorous non-fiction on the subject of marriage and the single life. Among her works are *Reflections of a Bachelor Girl* (1903), *The Sayings of Mrs Solomon* (1920) and *A Guide to Men* (1922).

1 A husband is what is left of a lover, after the nerve has been extracted.

*A Guide to Men*, Prelude (1922)

2 Somehow, a bachelor never quite gets over the idea that he is a thing of beauty and a boy for ever!

ibid. 'Bachelors'. An allusion to Keats, 'A thing of beauty is a joy for ever' (*Endymion*, 1818).

3 A fool and her money are soon courted.

ibid. 'First Interlude'

4 Oh yes, there is a vast difference between the savage and the civilized man, but it is never apparent to their wives until after breakfast.

ibid. 'Cymbals and Kettle-drums'

5 A widow is a fascinating being with the flavor of maturity, the spice of experience, the piquancy of novelty, the tang of practised coquetry, and the halo of one man's approval.

ibid. 'Widows'

## Richard Rowland (1880–1947)
US FILM PRODUCER

1 The lunatics have taken charge of the asylum.

Comment in 1920, quoted in *A Million and One Nights*, vol. 2, ch. 79 (1926) by Terry Ramsaye. On the formation of *United Artists* film production company by CHARLIE CHAPLIN, Douglas Fairbanks, D.W. GRIFFITH and Mary Pickford.

## Tiny Rowland (1917–98)
BRITISH BUSINESSMAN

Original name Roland Walter Fuhrhop. Mine owner and newspaper publisher, he joined Lonrho (London and Rhodesian Mining and Land Company) in 1961, becoming its Managing Director and Chief Executive until 1995. From 1983 until 1993 he was Chairman of the *Observer* and in 1985 made an unsuccessful bid for the House of Fraser against Harrods proprietor MOHAMED AL-FAYED, with whom he maintained a public feud.

1 Europe and the U.K. are yesterday's world. Tomorrow is in the United States.

Quoted in the *Observer* 16 January 1983

2 There is no jungle in the whole of Africa like the jungle of the City of London.

Quoted in *My Life With Tiny*, ch. 8 (1987) by Richard Hall

## J.K. Rowling (b. 1966)
BRITISH AUTHOR

Full name Joanne Kathleen Rowling. Having worked as a teacher in Portugal, she returned to Scotland, and as an unemployed single parent started writing the fantasy *Harry Potter and the Philosopher's Stone* (1997). 'Harry just strolled into my head fully formed,' she said. This and subsequent books in the series have since topped the bestseller lists in Britain and America.

1 It is our choices, Harry, that show what we truly are, far more than our abilities.

Albus Dumbledore, in *Harry Potter and the Chamber of Secrets*, ch. 18 (1998)

## A.L. Rowse (1903–97)
BRITISH HISTORIAN AND CRITIC

Full name Alfred Leslie Rowse. A fellow of All Souls College, Oxford, he was known for his studies of sixteenth-century England, *Tudor Cornwall* (1941) and *The England of Elizabeth* (1950), as well as for general works such as *The Use of History* (1946). He wrote biographies of Shakespeare and Marlowe and two volumes of autobiography, *A Cornish Childhood* (1942) and *A Cornishman at Oxford* (1965).

1 In an imperfect world, it seems to me that, of all human institutions, the university of Oxford, and in it the college of All Souls, come nearest to perfection.

*The Saturday Book*, 'All Souls' (1945)

2 This filthy twentieth century. I hate its guts.

*Time* magazine 13 November 1978

## Arundhati Roy (b. 1961)
INDIAN NOVELIST

Her upbringing in the minority Syrian Christian community in the state of Kerala forms the setting for her Booker Prize-winning novel *The God of Small Things* (1997). Shunning public notice, she has nevertheless become a controversial figure in India for her outspoken support of environmental causes. *The Cost of Living* (1999) includes attacks on India's nuclear armament programme and the Narmada dam project.

1 It is curious how sometimes the memory of death lurks on for so much longer than the memory of life that it purloined.

*The God of Small Things*, ch. 1 (1997)

2 Men's bums never grow up. Like school satchels, they evoke in an instant memories of childhood.

ibid. ch. 3

3 It is after all so easy to shatter a story. To break a chain of thought. To ruin a fragment of a dream being carried around carefully like a piece of porcelain.

ibid. ch. 9

4 If there is a nuclear war, our foes will not be China or America or even each other. Our foe will be the earth herself. The very elements – the sky, the air, the land, the wind and water – will all turn against us. Their wrath will be terrible.

'The End of Imagination', publ. in *Outlook* August 1998 and *Frontline* August 1998, repr. in *The Cost of Living* (1999)

5 If protesting against having a nuclear bomb implanted in my brain is anti-Hindu and anti-national, then I secede. I hereby declare myself an independent, mobile republic. I am a citizen of the earth. I own no territory. I have no flag. I'm female, but have nothing against eunuchs. My policies are simple. I'm willing to sign any nuclear non-proliferation treaty or nuclear test ban treaty that's going. Immigrants are welcome. You can help me design our flag.

ibid.

6 If you are religious, then remember that this bomb is Man's challenge to God. It's worded quite simply: *We have the power to destroy everything that You have created.* If you're not (religious), then look at it this way. This world of ours is four thousand, six hundred million years old. It could end in an afternoon.

ibid. Closing words of essay.

7 To slow a beast, you break its limbs. To slow a nation, you break its people. You rob them of volition. You demonstrate your absolute command over their destiny. You make it clear that ultimately it falls to you to decide who lives, who dies, who prospers, who doesn't. To exhibit your capability you show off all that you can do, and how

easily you can do it. How easily you could press a button and annihilate the earth. How you can start a war, or sue for peace. How you can snatch a river away from one and gift it to another. How you can green a desert, or fell a forest and plant one somewhere else. You use caprice to fracture a people's faith in ancient things – earth, forest, water, air.

'The Greater Common Good', publ. in *Outlook* June 1999 and *Frontline* June 1999, repr. in ibid.

8 Big Dams are to a Nation's 'Development' what Nuclear Bombs are to its Military Arsenal. They're both weapons of mass destruction. They're both weapons governments use to control their own people. Both twentieth-century emblems that mark a point in time when human intelligence has outstripped its own instinct for survival.

ibid.

## Jerry Rubin (1938–94)
US ESSAYIST AND RADICAL LEADER

Aiming to marry hippy culture with radical politics, he classified himself as a Yippie, one of 'the anticapitalist comics' of the 1960s, organizing Vietnam War teach-ins and mass direct action. He was tried for allegedly fomenting riot at the 1968 Democratic convention in Chicago, but later acquitted. His *Do It! Scenarios of the Revolution* (1970) was a bestseller.

1 The left demands full employment for all – we demand full unemployment for all. The world owes us a living!

*Do It!* 'Yippie!', Extract 13 (1970)

2 Our message: Don't grow up. Growing up means *giving up your dreams.*

ibid.

3 Our parents are waging a genocidal war against their own kids. The economy has no use or need for youth. Everything is already built. *Our existence is a crime.*

ibid. Extract 14

4 Most men act so tough and strong on the outside because on the inside, we are scared, weak, and fragile. Men, not women, are the weaker sex.

*Chicago Tribune* 16 March 1978

## Volker Ruhe (b. 1942)
GERMAN POLITICIAN AND DEFENCE MINISTER

Nicknamed by his enemies 'Volker Rupel' (Volker the Lout), he is Germany's longest serving Defence Minister (from 1992), responsible for merging West Germany's forces with those of the former Communist East while at the same time reducing overall numbers.

1 I am not willing to risk the lives of German soldiers for countries whose names we cannot spell properly.

*Independent* 28 August 1992. On intervening in the Bosnian conflict.

## Robert Runcie (1921–2000)
BRITISH ECCLESIASTIC

Baron Runcie of Cuddesden. As Archbishop of Canterbury (1980–91), he criticized the THATCHER government's 'pharisaical attitudes' to the poor and the effects of free-market policies on the inner city. He refused to treat the commemorative service at the end of the 1982 Falklands War as a victory celebration and initiated dialogue with the Vatican, setting out his views on ecumenicalism in *The Unity We Seek* (1989).

1 Those who dare to interpret God's will must never claim Him as an asset for one nation or group rather than another. War springs from the love and loyalty which should be offered to God being applied to some God

substitute, one of the most dangerous being nationalism.

Sermon at the Falkland Islands Thanksgiving Service, St Paul's Cathedral, London, 26 July 1982, in *The Times* 27 July 1982

2 Without centuries of Christian anti-Semitism, Hitler's passionate hatred would never have been so fervently echoed.

*Daily Telegraph* 10 November 1988

3 I never liked the prospect of enquiring into what happened in a man's bedroom unless he's prepared to tell me.

*The Purple, the Blue and the Red*, BBC Radio 4, 16 May 1996. Interview with Anthony Howard, who asked him whether he had ever knowingly ordained practising homosexuals.

## Damon Runyon (1884–1946)
US AUTHOR

He began his career as a reporter and became popular for his lively stories of New York life, including *Blue Plate Special* (1934) and *Take it Easy* (1939). His collection *Guys and Dolls* (1931) was adapted as a stage musical (1950, filmed 1955), and with Howard Lindsay he co-authored the Broadway farce *A Slight Case of Murder* (1935). He worked as a film producer from 1941.

1 My boy . . . always try to rub up against money, for if you rub up against money long enough, some of it may rub off on you.

Feet Samuels, in 'A Very Honourable Guy', publ. in *Cosmopolitan* August 1929, repr. in *Guys and Dolls* (1931)

2 I long ago come to the conclusion that all life is six to five against.

Sam the Gonoph, in 'A Nice Price', publ. in *Collier's* 8 September 1934, repr. in *Money from Home* (1935)

## Salman Rushdie (b. 1947)
INDIAN-BORN BRITISH AUTHOR

From *Midnight's Children* (1981) to *The Moor's Last Sigh* (1995) and *The Ground Beneath Her Feet* (1999) he has used allegory, symbolism and verbal ingenuity to depict both Western and Indian society. Publication of *The Satanic Verses* (1988) led to a death sentence for blasphemy issued by Iran's AYATOLLAH KHOMEINI and a life in hiding, although he has gradually re-entered public life since Khomeini's death.

1 Sometimes legends make reality, and become more useful than the facts.

*Midnight's Children*, bk 1, 'Hit-the-spittoon' (1981)

2 Reality is a question of perspective; the further you get from the past, the more concrete and plausible it seems – but as you approach the present, it inevitably seems more and more incredible.

ibid. bk 2, 'All-India Radio'

3 The real risks for any artist are taken . . . in pushing the work to the limits of what is possible, in the attempt to increase the sum of what it is possible to think. Books become good when they go to this edge and risk falling over it – when they endanger the artist by reason of what he has, or has not, *artistically* dared.

'Imaginary Homelands' (1982), repr. in *Imaginary Homelands* (1991)

4 To explain why we become attached to our birthplaces we pretend that we are trees and speak of roots. Look under your feet. You will not find gnarled growths sprouting through the soles. Roots, I sometimes think, are a conservative myth, designed to keep us in our places.

*Shame*, ch. 5 (1983)

5 We who have grown up on a diet of honour and shame can still grasp what must seem unthinkable to peoples living in the aftermath of the death of God and of tragedy: that men will sacrifice their dearest love on the implacable

altars of their pride . . . Between shame and shamelessness lies the axis upon which we turn; meteorological conditions at both these poles are of the most extreme, ferocious type. Shamelessness, shame: the roots of violence.

ibid. ch. 7

6 In this world without quiet corners, there can be no easy escapes from history, from hullabaloo, from terrible, unquiet fuss.

'Outside the Whale' (1984), repr. in *Imaginary Homelands* (1991)

7 I hate admitting that my enemies have a point.

Hamza, in *The Satanic Verses*, 'Mahound' (1988)

8 Such is the miraculous nature of the future of exiles: what is first uttered in the impotence of an overheated apartment becomes the fate of nations.

ibid. 'Ayesha'. Referring to the Imam, exiled in London.

9 Your blasphemy, Salman, can't be forgiven . . . To set your words against the Words of God.

Mahound, in ibid. 'Return to Jahilia'. Addressing Salman the Persian who, despite his crime of pitting 'his Word against mine', is spared the death-sentence.

10 Where there is no belief, there is no blasphemy.

Narrator, in ibid.

11 Whores and writers, Mahound. We are the people you can't forgive.

The 'famous satirist' Baal, in ibid. 'Return to Jahilia'. Mahound, Prophet of Jahilia, replies, 'Writers and whores. I see no difference . . .'

12 If Woody Allen were a Muslim, he'd be dead by now.

Quoted in the *Independent* 18 February 1989. Of the death threats by Muslim extremists following the publication of *The Satanic Verses*.

13 A poet's work is to name the unnameable, to point at frauds, to take sides, start arguments, shape the world, and stop it going to sleep.

ibid.

14 As author of *The Satanic Verses* I recognize that Moslems in many parts of the world are genuinely distressed by the publication of my novel. I profoundly regret the distress that publication has occasioned to sincere followers of Islam. Living as we do in a world of many faiths this experience has served to remind us that we must all be conscious of the sensibilities of others.

Statement following Khomeini's fatwa (see AYATOLLAH RU-HOLLAH KHOMEINI 1), 19 February 1989, quoted in *A Satanic Affair*, ch. 5 (1990) by Malise Ruthven. A statement issued by the Ayatollah's office the following day declared: 'even if Salman Rushdie repents and becomes the most pious person of this age, it is still the duty of all Muslims to use all their efforts, wealth and lives to send him to hell.'

15 Literature is where I go to explore the highest and lowest places in human society and in the human spirit, where I hope to find not absolute truth but the truth of the tale, of the imagination and of the heart.

Quoted in the *Observer* 19 February 1989

16 Writers and politicians are natural rivals. Both groups try to make the world in their own images; they fight for the same territory.

ibid.

17 Doubt, it seems to me, is the central condition of a human being in the twentieth century.

ibid.

18 Books choose their authors; the act of creation is not entirely a rational and conscious one.

*Independent on Sunday* 4 February 1990

19 Throughout human history, the apostles of purity, those who have claimed to possess a total explanation, have wrought havoc among mere mixed-up human beings.

'In Good Faith', publ. in *The Independent on Sunday* 4 February 1990, repr. in *Imaginary Homelands* (1991)

20 The idea of the sacred is quite simply one of the most conservative notions in any culture, because it seeks to turn other ideas – uncertainty, progress, change – into crimes.

'Is Nothing Sacred?', Herbert Read Memorial Lecture, ICA, London, 6 February 1990, publ. in the *Guardian* 7 February 1990, repr. in ibid. In the wake of Khomeini's fatwa, the lecture was read by HAROLD PINTER.

21 Not even the visionary or mystical experience ever lasts very long. It is for art to capture that experience, to offer it to, in the case of literature, its readers; to be, for a secular, materialist culture, some sort of replacement for what the love of god offers in the world of faith.

ibid.

22 Literature is the one place in any society where, within the secrecy of our own heads, we can hear *voices talking about everything in every possible way*. The reason for ensuring that that privileged arena is preserved is not that writers want the absolute freedom to say and do whatever they please. It is that we, all of us, readers and writers and citizens and generals and godmen, need that little, unimportant-looking room. We do not need to call it sacred, but we do need to remember that it is necessary.

ibid.

23 Free speech is the whole thing, the whole ball game. Free speech is life itself.

Interview in the *Guardian* 8 November 1990

24 I used to say: 'there is a God-shaped hole in me.' For a long time I stressed the absence, the hole. Now I find it is the shape which has become more important.

Quoted in the *Independent on Sunday* 30 December 1990. Referring to his conversion to Islam after being branded an 'enemy of Islam'.

25 I have never been to Sarajevo, but I feel that I belong to it, in a way . . . I . . . can claim to be, in some sense, an exile from Sarajevo, even though it is a city I do not know. There is a Sarajevo of the mind, an imagined Sarajevo whose ruination and torment exiles us all.

*Index on Censorship* May/June 1994

26 Mother India with her garishness and her inexhaustible motion, Mother India who loved and betrayed and ate and destroyed and again loved her children, and with whom the children's passionate conjoining and eternal quarrel stretched long beyond the grave; who stretched into great mountains like exclamations of the soul and along vast rivers full of mercy and disease, and across harsh drought-ridden plateaux on which men hacked with pickaxes at the dry infertile soil.

*The Moor's Last Sigh*, ch. 5 (1995)

27 Civilization is the sleight of hand that conceals our natures from ourselves.

ibid. ch. 18

28 In the waking dreams our societies permit, in our myths, our arts, our songs, we celebrate the non-belongers, the different ones, the outlaws, the freaks. What we forbid ourselves we pay good money to watch, in a playhouse or movie theatre, or to read about between the secret covers of a book.

*The Ground Beneath Her Feet*, ch. 3 (1999)

29 In a time of constant transformation, beatitude is the joy that comes with belief, with certainty.

ibid. ch. 12

30 As human knowledge has grown, it has also become plain that every religious story ever told about how we got here

is quite simply wrong. This, finally, is what all religions have in common. They didn't get it right. There was no celestial churning, no maker's dance, no vomiting of galaxies, no snake or kangaroo ancestors, no Valhalla, no Olympus, no six-day conjuring trick followed by a day of rest. Wrong, wrong, wrong.

'Imagine No Heaven', publ. in the *Guardian* 16 October 1999, repr. in *Letters to the Six Billionth World Citizen* (1999)

31 The real wars of religion are the wars religions unleash against ordinary citizens within their 'sphere of influence'.
ibid.

32 To choose unbelief is to choose mind over dogma, to trust in our humanity instead of all these dangerous divinities.
ibid.

## Dean Rusk (1909–94)
US POLITICIAN

A Democrat, he held a succession of foreign affairs posts in the TRUMAN administration (1947–51) and was Secretary of State under JOHN F. KENNEDY, playing a key role during the Cuban missile crisis, and LYNDON JOHNSON. A vehement anticommunist, he was instrumental in escalating the Vietnam War. He retired from office in 1969.

1 One of the best ways to persuade others is with your ears – by listening to them.
*Reader's Digest* July 1961

2 We're eyeball to eyeball, and I think the other fellow just blinked.
Remark 24 October 1962, in *Saturday Evening Post* 8 December 1962. Referring to the Cuban missile crisis.

## Bertrand Russell (1872–1970)
BRITISH PHILOSOPHER AND MATHEMATICIAN

Earl Russell of Kingston. Hugely influential for most of the twentieth century both as a thinker and liberal activist, he co-authored with his former tutor A.N. WHITEHEAD *Principia Mathematica* (1910–13). Among his numerous other publications are *A History of Western Philosophy* (1945) and his *Autobiography* (1967–9). A lifelong pacifist, he was gaoled for his stand against conscription in the First World War and again as an anti-nuclear campaigner when almost ninety. He was awarded the Nobel Prize for Literature in 1950.

1 A hallucination is a fact, not an error; what is erroneous is a judgment based upon it.
'On the Nature of Acquaintance: Neutral Monism' (1914), repr. in *Logic and Knowledge* (1956)

2 And all this madness, all this rage, all this flaming death of our civilization and our hopes, has been brought about because a set of official gentlemen, living luxurious lives, mostly stupid, and all without imagination or heart, have chosen that it should occur rather than that any one of them should suffer some infinitesimal rebuff to his country's pride.
Letter to the *Nation*, 16 August 1914, repr. in *The Autobiography of Bertrand Russell*, vol. 2, ch. 1 (1968). The letter was written on 12 August 1914, eight days after the declaration of war.

3 Organic life, we are told, has developed gradually from the protozoon to the philosopher, and this development, we are assured, is indubitably an advance. Unfortunately it is the philosopher, not the protozoon, who gives us this assurance.
*Mysticism and Logic*, ch. 6 (1917)

4 It is clear that thought is not free if the profession of certain opinions makes it impossible to earn a living. It is clear also that thought is not free if all the arguments on one side of a controversy are perpetually presented as

attractively as possible, while the arguments on the other side can only be discovered by diligent search.
Moncure Conway Lecture, 1922, publ. in *Sceptical Essays*, 'Free Thought and Official Propaganda' (1928)

5 Machines are worshipped because they are beautiful and valued because they confer power; they are hated because they are hideous and loathed because they impose slavery.
*Sceptical Essays*, 'Machines and the Emotions' (1928)

6 It is obvious that 'obscenity' is not a term capable of exact legal definition; in the practice of the Courts, it means 'anything that shocks the magistrate'.
ibid. 'The Recrudescence of Puritanism'

7 Advocates of capitalism are very apt to appeal to the sacred principles of liberty, which are all embodied in one maxim: *The fortunate must not be restrained in the exercise of tyranny over the unfortunate.*
ibid. 'Freedom in Society'

8 The fundamental defect of fathers, in our competitive society, is that they want their children to be a credit to them.
ibid. 'Freedom versus Authority in Education'

9 Marriage is for women the commonest mode of livelihood, and the total amount of undesired sex endured by women is probably greater in marriage than in prostitution.
*Marriage and Morals*, 'Prostitution' (1929)

10 Men who are unhappy, like men who sleep badly, are always proud of the fact.
*The Conquest of Happiness*, ch. 1 (1930)

11 Boredom is . . . a vital problem for the moralist, since at least half the sins of mankind are caused by the fear of it.
ibid. ch. 4

12 Conventional people are roused to fury by departures from convention, largely because they regard such departures as a criticism of themselves.
ibid. ch. 9

13 Many people when they fall in love look for a little haven of refuge from the world, where they can be sure of being admired when they are not admirable, and praised when they are not praiseworthy.
ibid. ch. 12

14 To be able to fill leisure intelligently is the last product of civilization.
ibid. ch. 14. At present, Russell added, 'very few people have reached this level'.

15 The fundamental concept in social science is Power, in the same sense in which Energy is the fundamental concept in physics.
*Power*, ch. 1 (1938)

16 To acquire immunity to eloquence is of the utmost importance to the citizens of a democracy.
ibid. ch. 18, sect. 4

17 Religions, which condemn the pleasures of sense, drive men to seek the pleasures of power. Throughout history power has been the vice of the ascetic.
*New York Herald Tribune Magazine* 6 May 1938

18 The essence of the Liberal outlook lies not in *what* opinions are held, but in *how* they are held: instead of being held dogmatically, they are held tentatively, and with a consciousness that new evidence may at any moment lead to their abandonment.
*Unpopular Essays*, 'Philosophy and Politics' (1950)

19 Admiration of the proletariat, like that of dams, power stations, and aeroplanes, is part of the ideology of the machine age.
ibid. 'The Superior Virtue of the Oppressed'

20 Man is a credulous animal, and must believe *something*;

in the absence of good grounds for belief, he will be satisfied with bad ones.

ibid. 'An Outline of Intellectual Rubbish'

21 For my part I distrust *all* generalizations about women, favourable and unfavourable, masculine and feminine, ancient and modern; all alike, I should say, result from paucity of experience.

ibid.

22 We used to think that Hitler was wicked when he wanted to kill all the Jews, but Kennedy and Macmillan and others both in the East and in the West pursue policies which will probably lead to killing not only all the Jews but all the rest of us too. They are much more wicked than Hitler and this idea of weapons of mass extermination is utterly and absolutely horrible and it is a thing which no man with one spark of humanity can tolerate and I will not pretend to obey a government which is organizing the massacre of the whole of mankind. I will do anything I can to oppose such Governments in any non-violent way that seems likely to be fruitful, and I should exhort all of you to feel the same way. We cannot obey these murderers. They are wicked and abominable. They are the wickedest people that ever lived in the history of man and it is our duty to do what we can.

Extempore comment added to speech at disarmament conference, Birmingham, 15 April 1961, publ. in *The Autobiography of Bertrand Russell*, vol. 3, ch. 3 (1967). The closing words of this speech made headlines in the press in the following days.

23 Three passions, simple but overwhelmingly strong, have governed my life: the longing for love, the search for knowledge, and unbearable pity for the suffering of mankind.

*The Autobiography of Bertrand Russell*, vol. 1, Prologue, 'What I Have Lived For' (1967). Opening words.

24 [Of the First World War] I had supposed until that time that it was quite common for parents to love their children, but the war persuaded me that it is a rare exception. I had supposed that most people liked money better than almost anything else, but I discovered that they liked destruction even better. I had supposed that intellectuals frequently loved truth, but I found here again that not ten per cent of them prefer truth to popularity.

ibid. vol. 2, ch. 1

## Dora Russell (1894–1986)
BRITISH AUTHOR AND ACTIVIST

Founder of the Workers' Birth Control Group (1924), she helped establish the National Council for Civil Liberties (now Liberty), and with her former husband, BERTRAND RUSSELL, was a leading member of the Campaign for Nuclear Disarmament in the 1950s. From 1936 to 1943 she ran Beacon Hill progressive school, an

experience recounted in her autobiography *The Tamarisk Tree* (1975). She also wrote *In Defence of Children* (1932) and *The Religion of the Machine Age* (1983).

1 We want better reasons for having children than not knowing how to prevent them.

*Hypatia*, ch. 4 (1925)

2 All my life I have tried to do too many different things. I wonder if this is not a perpetual dilemma for women. A man enters on a job or profession, needs to stick to it to earn his living, and is unlikely to have to change it on marriage. For a woman marriage presents not only practical problems, but she finds herself emotionally pulled all ways, and tends by tradition and impulse to put the needs of others before her own. What is more, opening her eyes on the world, she feels intensely responsible for setting it to rights.

*The Tamarisk Tree*, ch. 9 (1975)

3 Women must not merely imitate men. Women have more to give than performing any job in society like neutered robots. Those who talk today of rousing the 'consciousness' of women contribute an idea of real importance. It was such a grievous mistake to leave out women. For whence can come love, compassion and understanding if not out of the relations of men and women and of them to their children?

ibid. ch. 14

4 We have never yet had a Labour Government that knew what taking power really means; they always act like second-class citizens.

Quoted in the *Observer* 30 January 1983

5 We do not want our world to perish. But in our quest for knowledge, century by century, we have placed all our trust in a cold, impartial intellect which only brings us nearer to destruction. We have heeded no wisdom offering guidance. Only by learning to love one another can our world be saved. Only love can conquer all.

*Challenge to the Cold War*, ch. 14 (1985). Final words of final volume of autobiography.

## Gilbert Ryle (1900–76)
BRITISH PHILOSOPHER

Known for his work in linguistic philosophy, he helped to establish Oxford as a major centre of philosophy in the years following the Second World War. He was author of *The Concept of Mind* (1949), *Dilemmas* (1954) and *On Thinking* (1979), among other writings.

1 A myth is, of course, not a fairy story. It is the presentation of facts belonging to one category in the idioms appropriate to another. To explode a myth is accordingly not to deny the facts but to re-allocate them.

*The Concept of Mind*, Introduction (1949)

## Charles Saatchi (b. 1943) and
## Maurice Saatchi (b. 1946)
IRAQI-BORN BRITISH ADVERTISERS

The advertising agency the brothers opened in 1970 grew to become the world's largest, noted for its eye-catching style. It was engaged in 1978 to promote the image of the Conservative Party. In 1995 Maurice Saatchi left to form his own company. Charles Saatchi is owner of the Saatchi Gallery, specializing in contemporary British art.

1 **Labour isn't working.**

British Conservative Party slogan, 1978–9. A 1999 survey in *Campaign* ranked the poster on which it appeared as the most memorable of the century. The long dole queue pictured was made up of members of the Young Conservatives, not Saatchi employees, as DENIS HEALEY suggested at the time. The poster was cited as instrumental in the downfall of JAMES CALLAGHAN's Labour administration, partly because he rose to the gibe and complained, and it marked the beginning of a new era of 'aggressive' advertising, aimed at traditional Labour voters who feared for their jobs.

2 **Australians wouldn't give a XXXX for anything else.**

Advertisement for Castlemaine lager, from 1986

3 **Tell Sid.**

Advertising slogan for the privatization of British Gas, 1986

4 **An ace caff with quite a nice museum attached.**

Advertisement for Victoria and Albert Museum, London, 1989. The most visible feature of a marketing drive spearheaded by museum director Elisabeth Esteve-Coll, the advertisement created great negative publicity by suggesting that culture took second place at the museum.

## Rafael Sabatini (1875–1950)
BRITISH AUTHOR

Born in Italy of an English father, he wrote in English as, he asserted, 'all the best stories are written in English'. He achieved international success with *Scaramouche* (1921), set in the French revolution. Other titles include *The Sea Hawk* (1915) and *Captain Blood* (1922), both also in the genre of historical fiction.

1 **He was born with a gift of laughter and a sense that the world was mad. And that was all his patrimony.**

*Scaramouche*, bk 1, ch. 1 (1921). These opening words which describe the book's hero André-Louis Moreau, are inscribed on the gate of the Hall of Graduate Studies, Yale University.

## Ernesto Sábato (b. 1911)
ARGENTINIAN NOVELIST AND ESSAYIST

His criticism of Peronism led to his dismissal from his post as Professor of Theoretical Physics in 1944, following which he took up writing. His novels, such as *The Outsider* (1950) and *On Heroes and Tombs* (1961), address metaphysical and existential issues, as do his essays, including 'Heterodoxia' (1953). He has also published a series of dialogues with JORGE LUIS BORGES (1976).

1 **Just as the office worker dreams of murdering his hated boss and so is saved from really murdering him, so it is with the author; with his great dreams he helps his readers to survive, to avoid their worst intentions. And society, without realizing it . . . respects and even exalts him, albeit with a kind of jealousy, fear and even repulsion, since few people want to discover the horrors that lurk in the depths of their souls. This is the highest mission of great literature, and there is no other.**

Interview in the *Independent* 20 June 1992

## Jonathan Sacks (b. 1948)
BRITISH CHIEF RABBI

He was rabbi of the synagogues at Golders Green (1978–82) and Marble Arch (1983–90). His books include *The Persistence of Faith*

(1991), *Will We Have Jewish Grandchildren?* (1994) and *The Politics of Hope* (1997).

1 Modernity is the transition from fate to choice.

'The Persistence of Faith', 1990 Reith Lecture, publ. in *The Persistence of Faith*, ch. 1, 'Liberation or Privation' (1991)

2 We no longer talk of virtues but of values, and values are tapes we play on the Walkman of the mind: any tune we choose so long as it does not disturb others.

ibid. ch. 2, 'The Eclipse of Morality'

## Oliver Sacks (b. 1933)

BRITISH NEUROLOGIST

His accounts of unusual neurological conditions such as *Awakenings* (1973, filmed 1990), relating the temporary cure of patients afflicted with a sleeping sickness, and *The Man Who Mistook His Wife for a Hat* (1985) have found a wide readership. *An Anthropologist on Mars* (1995) is also a volume of case studies.

1 The man who mistook his wife for a hat.

Title of book (1985)

## Margaret Sackville (1881–1963)

BRITISH POET

The third daughter of the Earl of Warr, her *Poems* were published in 1901 and she continued to publish verse throughout her life, including her last volume, *Quatrains* (1960).

1 When all is said and done, monotony may after all be the best condition for creation.

*The Works of Susan Ferrier*, vol. 1, Introduction (1929)

## Vita Sackville-West (1892–1962)

BRITISH AUTHOR, POET AND GARDENER

Full name Victoria Mary Sackville-West. A prolific writer of poetry, fiction, history and biography, for example the long poem 'The Land' (1926) and the novels *The Edwardians* (1930) and *All Passion Spent* (1931), she was wife of HAROLD NICOLSON with whom she travelled widely before settling at Sissinghurst Castle, whose gardens she made famous. A close friend of VIRGINIA WOOLF, she was the model of the hero/heroine of her *Orlando* (1928).

1 Women ought to have freedom the same as men when they are young. It is a rotten and ridiculous system at present; it's simply cheating one of one's youth. It was alright for Victorians. But this generation is discarding, and the next one will have discarded, the chrysalis. Women, like men, ought to have their youth so glutted with freedom that they hate the very idea of freedom.

Letter to her husband, HAROLD NICOLSON, 1 June 1919, quoted in *Portrait of a Marriage*, pt 4 (1973) by Nigel Nicolson

2 Travel is the most private of pleasures. There is no greater bore than the travel bore. We do not in the least want to hear what he has seen in Hong-Kong.

*Passenger to Teheran*, ch. 1 (1926)

3 It is necessary to write, if the days are not to slip emptily by. How else, indeed, to clap the net over the butterfly of the moment?

*Twelve Days*, ch. 1 (1928)

## William Safire (b. 1929)

US JOURNALIST

He was special assistant to President NIXON (1969–73) and has been a columnist on *The New York Times* from 1973. In 1978 he won the Pulitzer Prize for commentary.

1 To 'know your place' is a good idea in politics. That is not to say 'stay in your place' or 'hang on to your place', because ambition or boredom may dictate upward or downward mobility, but a sense of place – a feel for one's own position in the control room – is useful in gauging what you should try to do.

*Before The Fall*, Prologue (1975)

## Françoise Sagan (b. 1935)

FRENCH NOVELIST

Original name Françoise Quoirez. She became an overnight phenomenon with her first book, written aged eighteen, *Bonjour Tristesse* (1954, filmed 1957), which she followed with *A Certain Smile* (1956, filmed 1958), both testaments of the emotions and disillusions of adolescence. Among her other novels are *Aimez-Vous Brahms?* (1959, filmed 1961) and *La Chamade* (1965).

1 Jazz music is an intensified insouciance.

Dominique, in *A Certain Smile*, pt 1, ch. 7 (1956)

2 Writing is a question of finding a certain rhythm. I compare it to the rhythms of jazz. Much of the time life is a sort of rhythmic progression of three characters. If one tells oneself that life is like that, one feels it less arbitrary.

Interview in *Writers at Work* (first series, ed. Malcolm Cowley, 1958)

3 Of course the illusion of art is to make one believe that great literature is very close to life, but exactly the opposite is true. Life is amorphous, literature is formal.

ibid.

4 To jealousy, nothing is more frightful than laughter.

Lucile, in *La Chamade*, ch. 9 (1965)

## Edward Said (b. 1935)

PALESTINIAN-BORN US SOCIAL AND LITERARY CRITIC

He is one of the foremost Palestinian spokesmen on Middle Eastern issues. His writings include *Orientalism* (1978), *Culture and Imperialism* (1993) and *Peace and Its Discontents: Essays on Palestine* (1995).

1 Taking the late eighteenth century as a very roughly defined starting point Orientalism can be discussed and analyzed as the corporate institution for dealing with the Orient – dealing with it by making statements about it, authorizing views of it, describing it, by teaching it, settling it, ruling over it: in short, Orientalism as a Western style for dominating, restructuring, and having authority over the Orient.

*Orientalism*, Introduction (1978)

2 The web of racism, cultural stereotypes, political imperialism, dehumanizing ideology holding in the Arab or the Muslim is very strong indeed, and it is this web which every Palestinian has come to feel as his uniquely punishing destiny.

ibid.

3 Culture is a sort of theatre where various political and ideological causes engage one another. Far from being a placid realm of Apollonian gentility, culture can even be a battleground on which causes expose themselves to the light of day and contend with one another.

*Culture and Imperialism*, Introduction (1993)

4 There are far too many politicized people on earth today for any nation readily to accept the finality of America's historical mission to lead the world.

ibid. ch. 4, sect. 1

5 Reading and writing texts are never neutral activities: there are interests, powers, pleasures entailed no matter how aesthetic or entertaining the work. Media, political economy, mass institutions – in fine, the tracings of secular power and the influence of the state – are part of what we call literature.

ibid. sect. 2

6 Truly this has been the age of Ayatollahs, in which a

phalanx of guardians (Khomeni, the Pope, Margaret Thatcher) simplify and protect one or another creed, essence, primordial faith. One fundamentalism invidiously attacks the others in the name of sanity, freedom, and goodness.

ibid. sect. 3

7 [On Arab 'powerlessness'] Power, after all, is not just military strength. It is the social power that comes from democracy, the cultural power that comes from freedom of expression and research, the personal power that entitles every Arab citizen to feel that he or she is in fact a citizen, and not just a sheep in some great shepherd's flock.

'A Powerless People', publ. in the *Guardian* 25 April 1996

8 I have no other explanation for our situation, which cannot be extenuated or explained away by appeals to the ravages of imperialism, or to corrupt regimes, or any of the other litanies of self-exculpation. The problem is Arab powerlessness.

ibid.

## Lisa St Aubin de Terán (b. 1953)
BRITISH AUTHOR

Experience of farming in Venezuela (1972–8) forms the material of much of her fiction, notably *Keepers of the House* (1982). She was nominated by *The Times* as one of the best young UK novelists of 1983, the same year she published *The Slow Train to Milan*, which has been adapted for the screen, as has *The Bay of Silence* (1986). Her second husband was the poet George MacBeth.

1 Travelling is like flirting with life. It's like saying, 'I would stay and love you, but I have to go; this is my station'.

*Off the Rails*, ch. 2 (1989)

## Iberico Saint Jean
ARGENTINIAN SOLDIER AND POLITICIAN

As general, he was Governor of the province of Buenos Aires during the military rule in Argentina.

1 First we kill all the subversives; then, their collaborators; later, those who sympathize with them; afterward, those who remain indifferent; and finally, the undecided.

Quoted in the *Boletin de las Madres de Plaza de Mayo* May 1985, repr. in *The Demon Lover*, ch. 4 (1989) by ROBIN MORGAN

## Adela Rogers St Johns (1894–1988)
US AUTHOR AND JOURNALIST

She was the author of a novel, *The Skyrocket* (1925), of *How to Write a Story and Sell It* (1955) and of *First Step Up Toward Heaven* (1959), a book about Forest Lawn Cemetery. *Final Verdict: A Biography of Earl Rogers* appeared in 1963.

1 I think every woman's entitled to a middle husband she can forget.

Quoted in the *Los Angeles Times* 13 October 1974

## Yves Saint Laurent (b. 1936)
FRENCH FASHION DESIGNER

He worked with CHRISTIAN DIOR from 1954 and succeeded him as designer in the Dior house on his death in 1957. He established his own house in 1962, created 'power dressing' and in 1966 sold ready-to-wear clothes through his chain of Rive Gauche boutiques. He has also designed costumes for ballets and films, including *The Pink Panther* (1962) and *Belle de Jour* (1967).

1 Fashions fade, style is eternal.

*Andy Warhol's Interview* 13 April 1975

2 I knew the youthfulness of the sixties: Talitha and Paul Getty lying on a starlit terrace in Marrakesh, beautiful and damned, and a whole generation assembled as if for eternity where the curtain of the past seemed to lift before an extraordinary future.

Interview in *Ritz* no. 85 1984

3 I have often said that I wish I had invented blue jeans: the most spectacular, the most practical, the most relaxed and nonchalant. They have expression, modesty, sex appeal, simplicity – all I hope for in my clothes.

ibid.

4 We must never confuse elegance with snobbery.

ibid.

5 It pains me physically to see a woman victimized, rendered pathetic, by fashion.

ibid.

6 A designer who is not also a couturier, who hasn't learned the most refined mysteries of physically creating his models, is like a sculptor who gives his drawings to another man, an artisan, to accomplish. For him the truncated process of creating will always be an interrupted act of love, and his style will bear the shame of it, the impoverishment.

ibid.

7 A good model can advance fashion by ten years.

ibid.

## Antoine de Saint-Exupéry (1900–44)
FRENCH AVIATOR AND AUTHOR

Called by William Benét the 'prose poet of the new world of the skies', he was the author of the novel *Night Flight* (1931), the autobiographical *Wind, Sand and Stars* (1939) and the allegory *The Little Prince* (1943). He disappeared on a mission over occupied France.

1 Each man must look to himself to teach him the meaning of life. It is not something discovered: it is something moulded.

*Wind, Sand, and Stars*, ch. 2, sect. 1 (publ. in France as *Terre des hommes*, 1939)

2 Only the unknown frightens men. But once a man has faced the unknown, that terror becomes the known.

ibid. ch. 2, sect. 2

3 Perfection is finally attained not when there is no longer anything to add but when there is no longer anything to take away, when a body has been stripped down to its nakedness.

ibid. ch. 3

4 The machine does not isolate man from the great problems of nature but plunges him more deeply into them.

ibid.

5 Transport of the mails, transport of the human voice, transport of flickering pictures – in this century as in others our highest accomplishments still have the single aim of bringing men together.

ibid.

6 The aeroplane has unveiled for us the true face of the earth.

ibid. ch. 5

7 Love does not consist in gazing at each other but in looking together in the same direction.

ibid. ch. 8

8 Night, the beloved. Night, when words fade and things come alive. When the destructive analysis of day is done, and all that is truly important becomes whole and sound again. When man reassembles his fragmentary self and grows with the calm of a tree.

*Flight to Arras*, ch. 1 (1942)

9 War is not a true adventure. It is a mere ersatz. Where ties are established, where problems are set, where creation is stimulated – there you have adventure. But there is no adventure in heads-or-tails, in betting that the toss will come out of life or death. War is not an adventure. It is a disease. It is like typhus.

ibid. ch. 8

10 If France is to be judged, judge her not by the effects of her defeat but by her readiness to sacrifice herself.

ibid. ch. 15

11 When the body sinks into death, the essence of man is revealed. Man is a knot, a web, a mesh into which relationships are tied. Only those relationships matter. The body is an old crock that nobody will miss. I have never known a man to think of himself when dying. Never.

ibid. ch. 19

12 Grown-ups never understand anything for themselves, and it is tiresome for children to be always and forever explaining things to them.

*The Little Prince*, ch. 1 (1943)

13 It is only with the heart that one can see rightly; what is essential is invisible to the eye.

ibid. ch. 21

## J.D. Salinger (b. 1919)
US AUTHOR

Full name Jerome David Salinger. Dubbed by NORMAN MAILER, 'the greatest mind ever to stay in prep school', he is known for his first and only novel *The Catcher in the Rye* (1951), which has become a classic text of adolescent rebellion. He subsequently published stories and 'short fictions', but the novella *Hapworth 16, 1924* (1997) was his first published work in thirty-four years of a life of seclusion.

1 If you really want to hear about it, the first thing you'll probably want to know is where I was born, and what my lousy childhood was like, and how my parents were occupied and all before they had me, and all that David Copperfield kind of crap, but I don't feel like going into it.

Narrator (Holden Caulfield), in *Catcher in the Rye*, ch. 1 (1951). Opening lines of book.

2 What I like best is a book that's at least funny once in a while . . . What really knocks me out is a book that, when you're all done reading it, you wish the author that wrote it was a terrific friend of yours and you could call him up on the phone whenever you felt like it. That doesn't happen much, though.

ibid. ch. 3

3 I don't know about bores. Maybe you shouldn't feel too sorry if you see some swell girl getting married to them. They don't hurt anybody most of them, and maybe they're all terrific whistlers or something. Who the hell knows? Not me.

ibid. ch. 17

4 I don't even like *old* cars. I mean they don't even interest me. I'd rather have a goddam horse. A horse is at least *human*, for God's sake.

ibid.

5 I keep picturing all these little kids playing some game in this big field of rye and all . . . If they're running and they don't look where they're going I have to come out from somewhere and *catch* them. That's all I'd do all day. I'd just be the catcher in the rye and all. I know it's crazy, but that's the only thing I'd really like to be.

ibid. ch. 22

## Anthony Sampson (b. 1926)
BRITISH JOURNALIST AND AUTHOR

After editing *Drum* magazine in South Africa (1951–5) he served on the editorial staff of the *Observer* (1955–66). He is author of, among other works, *The Seven Sisters* (1975), on oil corporations, and *The Arms Bazaar* (1977), but is probably best known for his ongoing guide to British society, *Anatomy of Britain* (first publ. 1962).

1 Once you touch the trappings of monarchy, like opening an Egyptian tomb, the inside is liable to crumble.

*Anatomy of Britain Today*, ch. 2 (1965)

2 In America journalism is apt to be regarded as an extension of history: in Britain, as an extension of conversation.

ibid. ch. 9

3 Members rise from CMG (known sometimes in Whitehall as 'Call Me God') to KCMG ('Kindly Call Me God') to GCMG ('God Calls Me God').

ibid. ch. 18

## Carl Sandburg (1878–1967)
US POET AND AUTHOR

'The great mid-West, that vast region of steel mills and slaughter-houses, of cornfields and prairies, of crowded cities and empty skies, spoke through Carl Sandburg,' eulogized Louis Untermeyer. He established his reputation with his first volumes of poetry, *Chicago Poems* (1916) and *Cornhuskers* (1918), and was awarded a Pulitzer Prize for his *Complete Poems* (1950). He also collected American folksong in *The American Songbag* (1927) and wrote prose works, including a two-part biography of Abraham Lincoln (1926–39), which also won a Pulitzer Prize.

1 Hog Butcher for the World,
Tool Maker, Stacker of Wheat,
Player with Railroads and the Nation's Freight Handler;
Stormy, husky, brawling,
City of the Big Shoulders.

'Chicago', publ. in *Chicago Poems* (1916)

2 The fog comes
on little cat feet.

It sits looking
over harbour and city
on silent haunches
and then moves on.

'Fog', publ. in ibid.

3 I tell you the past is a bucket of ashes.

'Prairie', publ. in *Cornhuskers* (1918)

4 Pile the bodies high at Austerlitz and Waterloo.
Shovel them under and let me work –
I am the grass; I cover all.

'Grass', publ. in ibid.

5 Poetry is the opening and closing of a door, leaving those who look through to guess about what is seen during a moment.

'Poetry Considered', publ. in *Atlantic Monthly* March 1923

6 The sea speaks a language polite people never repeat.
It is a colossal scavenger slang and has no respect.
Is it a terrible thing to be lonely?

'Two Nocturns', publ. in *Good Morning, America* (1928)

7 The girl held still and studied.
'Do you know . . . I know something?'
'Yes, what is it you know?'
'Sometime they'll give a war and nobody will come.'

*The People, Yes*, sect. 23 (1936). Referring to a girl watching a military parade. The words were popularized during the anti-war protests of the 1960s and were adapted for the film *Suppose They Gave a War and Nobody Came?* (1970). See also ALLEN GINSBERG 10.

8  The greatest cunning is to have none at all.
   *ibid.* sect. 94

9  In the darkness with a great bundle of grief the people
       march. In the night, and overhead a shovel of stars
       for keeps, the people march:
             'Where to? What next?'
   *ibid.* sect. 107. Closing lines of book.

10  A baby is God's opinion that life should go on.
    *Remembrance Rock*, ch. 2 (1948)

11  Slang is a language that rolls up its sleeves, spits on its
    hands and goes to work.
    *The New York Times* 13 February 1959

12  In these times you have to be an optimist to open your
    eyes when you wake in the morning.
    *New York Post* 9 September 1960

13  Ordering a man to write a poem is like commanding a
    pregnant woman to give birth to a red-headed child.
    Quoted in *Reader's Digest* February 1978

## George Sanders (1906–72)
BRITISH ACTOR

'I was beastly but never coarse. A high-class sort of heel,' he
commented on his usual roles as cad, crook and bounder for more
than thirty years in Hollywood. He took the lead in *The Saint*
(1939–41) and *The Falcon* (1941–3) series and won an Oscar for *All
About Eve* (1950). Other films include *Rebecca* (1940), *The Picture
of Dorian Gray* (1944) and *Village of the Damned* (1960), and he
featured in many historical romances. Married to ZSA ZSA GABOR
and later to her sister Magda, he took his own life, he said, out of
boredom (see below).

1  Miss Caswell is an actress, a graduate of the Copacabana
   school of dramatic arts.
   Addison De Witt (George Sanders), introducing his protégée Miss
   Caswell (Marilyn Monroe) to Margo Channing (Bette Davis), in
   *All About Eve* (film, 1950, written and directed by Joseph L. Mankiewicz). Sanders won an Oscar as Best Supporting Actor for his
   part as the venomous drama critic, one of six Academy Awards
   accumulated by the film.

2  Dear World, I am leaving because I am bored. I feel I have
   lived long enough. I am leaving you with your worries in
   this sweet cesspool. Good luck.
   Suicide note, publ. in *George Sanders: An Exhausted Life*, ch. 20
   (1991) by Richard Vanderbeets

## Margaret Sanger (1883–1966)
US PIONEER OF BIRTH CONTROL MOVEMENT

Experience as a nurse in working-class communities led her to
publish *The Woman Rebel* (1914), a paper illegally giving information on birth control. In 1916 she set up a New York clinic, for
which she was briefly imprisoned, and in 1921 she founded the
American Birth Control League and served as its President until
1928. Her writings include *What Every Mother Should Know* (1917)
and *My Fight for Birth Control* (1931).

1  A mutual and satisfied sexual act is of great benefit to the
   average woman, the magnetism of it is health giving.
   When it is not desired on the part of the woman and she
   gives no response, it should not take place. The submission
   of her body without love or desire is degrading to the
   woman's finer sensibility, all the marriage certificates on
   earth to the contrary notwithstanding.
   *Family Limitation*, 'Coitus Interruptus' (1914)

2  No woman can call herself free who does not own and
   control her body. No woman can call herself free until she
   can choose consciously whether she will or will not be a
   mother.
   *Parade* 1 December 1963

## George Santayana (1863–1952)
SPANISH-BORN US PHILOSOPHER, POET AND NOVELIST

Originally Jorge de Santayana. He was Professor of Philosophy at
Harvard (1907–12) where he counted T.S. ELIOT among his stu-
dents. He retained his Spanish citizenship and in 1912 returned to
Europe, settling in Rome in 1924. His reputation rests mainly on
his work as a materialist sceptic philosopher, for example *The Sense
of Beauty* (1896), *Scepticism and Animal Faith* (1923), and *Realms of
Being* (1927–40). He also published poetry and the novel *The Last
Puritan* (1935).

1  Oxford, the paradise of dead philosophies.
   *Egotism in German Philosophy* (1916). Santayana lived in Oxford
   during the First World War.

2  [On the Englishman] He carries his English weather in
   his heart wherever he goes, and it becomes a cool spot in
   the desert, and a steady and sane oracle amongst all the
   delirium of mankind.
   *Soliloquies in England*, 'The British Character' (1922)

3  There is no cure for birth and death save to enjoy the
   interval.
   *ibid.* 'War Shrines'

4  Scepticism is the chastity of the intellect, and it is shameful
   to surrender it too soon or to the first comer; there is
   nobility in preserving it coolly and proudly through a
   long youth, until at last, in the ripeness of instinct and
   discretion, it can be safely exchanged for fidelity and
   happiness.
   *Scepticism and Animal Faith*, ch. 9 (1923)

5  The young man who has not wept is a savage, and the old
   man who will not laugh is a fool.
   *Dialogues in Limbo*, ch. 3 (1925)

6  Chaos is a name for any order that produces confusion in
   our minds.
   *Dominations and Powers*, bk 1, pt 1, ch. 1 (1951)

## Sapphire (b. 1950)
US AUTHOR AND POET

An unsentimental chronicler of the raw experiences of black
American women, she is author of the poetry collection *American
Dreams* (1994) and a novel, *Push* (1998).

1  The farmer takes Jill down the well
   & all the king's horses
   & all the king's men
   can't put that baby together again.
   *crooked man*
   *crooked man*
   *pumpkin eater*
   *childhood stealer.*
   'Mickey Mouse Was A Scorpio', publ. in *American Dreams* (1994).
   Sapphire recalled that it was the writing of this poem that first made
   her suspect she had been abused as a child.

2  death is where
   jimi hendrix is,
   where our revolution
   ended up.
   'where jimi is', publ. in ibid.

## Susan Sarandon (b. 1946)
US SCREEN ACTRESS

Early in her career she made an impact for her role as Janet in the
film of the cult classic *The Rocky Horror Picture Show* (1975) and
co-starred with BURT LANCASTER in French director Louis Malle's
*Atlantic City* (1980), before going on to star in numerous Hollywood films, such as *Thelma and Louise* (1991), *The Client* (1994)
and *Dead Man Walking* (1995), for which she won an Oscar.

1 Do you really have to be the ice queen intellectual or the slut whore? Isn't there some way to be both?
*Observer* 14 September 1991

## Ken Saro-Wiwa (1941–95)
NIGERIAN AUTHOR AND ACTIVIST

Full name Kenule Saro-Wiwa. He was the author of several novels, including *Sozaboy* (1985), written in pidgin English, and of radio and television drama, notably the comedy TV series *Basi and Company*, which ran for 150 episodes in the 1980s, satirizing Nigerian corruption. As leader of the Movement for the Survival of the Ogoni People he campaigned against the dispossession and damage to the environment wrought by the oil industry, for which cause he was arrested in 1994 and, despite world-wide protest, executed by hanging.

1 Lord take my soul, but the struggle continues.
Quoted in the *Daily Telegraph* 13 November 1995. Among his last words before being hanged.

## May Sarton (b. 1912)
US POET AND NOVELIST

Her fiction, poetry and several autobiographies have been praised for their truth, insight, and sensitive handling of feminist and lesbian themes. *Collected Poems* (1974), containing material from her first publications in the 1930s, consolidated her reputation as a poet. *A World of Light: Portraits and Celebrations* (1989) has been adapted for film, with Sarton portraying herself.

1 May we agree that private life is irrelevant? Multiple, mixed, ambiguous at best – out of it we try to fashion the crystal clear, the singular, the absolute, and that is what *is* relevant; that is what matters.
Hilary Stevens, in *Mrs Stevens Hears the Mermaids Singing*, pt 2 (1965)

2 The creative person, the person who moves from an irrational source of power, has to face the fact that this power antagonizes. Under all the superficial praise of the 'creative' is the desire to kill. It is the old war between the mystic and the nonmystic, a war to the death.
Narrator, in ibid.

3 Self-respect is nothing to hide behind. When you need it most it isn't there.
Hilary Stevens, in ibid. 'Epilogue: Mar'

## Jean-Paul Sartre (1905–80)
FRENCH PHILOSOPHER AND AUTHOR

The leading exponent of Existentialism, notably in *Being and Nothingness* (1943), he was active in the French Resistance in the 1940s, an experience that informs much subsequent work. In 1945 he co-founded with SIMONE DE BEAUVOIR the journal *Les Temps modernes*. His fiction includes *Nausea* (1938) and *Roads to Freedom* (1945–9) and the plays *The Flies* (1943) and *No Exit* (1944). He refused the Nobel Prize for Literature in 1964, actively protested against the Vietnam War and supported the student movement in 1968. See also CHARLES DE GAULLE 13.

1 I am condemned to be free.
*Being and Nothingness*, pt 4, ch. 1, sect. 1 (1943, transl. 1956)

2 Existence precedes and rules essence.
ibid. Sartre ascribes the notion to HEIDEGGER, although the latter specifically repudiated Sartre's reading of his maxim.

3 I am responsible for everything . . . except for my very responsibility, for I am not the foundation of my being. Therefore everything takes place as if I were compelled to be responsible. I am *abandoned* in the world . . . in the sense that I find myself suddenly alone and without help, engaged in a world for which I bear the whole responsi-

bility without being able, whatever I do, to tear myself away from this responsibility for an instant.
ibid. pt 4, ch. 1, sect. 3

4 Man is a useless passion.
ibid. pt 4, ch. 2, sect. 2

5 All human actions are equivalent . . . and . . . all are on principle doomed to failure.
ibid. 'Conclusion', sect. 2

6 Human life begins on the far side of despair.
Orestes, in *The Flies*, act 3, sc. 2 (*Les Mouches*, 1943)

7 Hell is other people.
(*L'enfer, c'est les autres.*)
Garcin, in *No Exit*, sc. 5 (*Huis Clos*, 1944)

8 What then did you expect when you unbound the gag that muted those black mouths? That they would chant your praises? Did you think that when those heads that our fathers had forcibly bowed down to the ground were raised again, you would find adoration in their eyes?
'Orphée Noir', Preface to *Anthologie de la nouvelle poésie nègre et malgache* (1948)

9 Every age has its own poetry; in every age the circumstances of history choose a nation, a race, a class to take up the torch by creating situations that can be expressed or transcended only through poetry.
ibid.

10 One is still what one is going to cease to be and already what one is going to become. One lives one's death, one dies one's life.
*Saint Genet: Actor and Martyr*, bk 2, 'The Melodious Child Dead in Me . . .' (1952, transl. 1963)

11 The French bourgeois doesn't dislike shit, provided it is served up to him at the right time.
ibid. 'To Succeed in Being All, Strive to be Nothing in Anything'

12 Fascism is not defined by the number of its victims, but by the way it kills them.
*Libération* 22 June 1953. Referring to the execution of Julius and Ethel Rosenberg.

13 Communism I like, but Communist intellectuals are savages.
Quoted in the *Observer* 25 March 1956

14 I hate victims who respect their executioners.
Leni, in *The Condemned of Altona*, act 1, sc. 1 (1960)

15 You can see it's the end; Europe is springing leaks everywhere. What then has happened? It simply is that in the past we made history and now it is being made of us. The ratio of forces has been inverted.
*The Wretched of the Earth*, Preface (1961)

16 She [my grandmother] believed in nothing; only her scepticism kept her from being an atheist.
*Les Mots*, 'Lire' (1964)

17 I confused things with their names: that is belief.
ibid. 'Écrire'

18 One does not *adopt* an idea, one slips into it.
*Notebooks for an Ethics*, Notebook 1 (1983)

## Siegfried Sassoon (1886–1967)
BRITISH POET

Remembered above all for his powerfully outspoken anti-war poems of the First World War, published in *Counter-Attack* (1918) and *Satirical Poems* (1926), he wrote a semi-fictionalized autobiography, *The Complete Memoirs of George Sherston*, consisting of *Memoirs of a Fox-Hunting Man* (1928), *Memoirs of an Infantry Officer* (1930) and *Sherston's Progress* (1936).

1 I am making this statement as an act of wilful defiance of military authority, because I believe that the War is being

deliberately prolonged by those who have the power to end it.

'A Soldier's Declaration' (1917), widely publ. in the press and repr. in *Memoirs of an Infantry Officer*, pt 10, ch. 2 (1930). ROBERT GRAVES, who thought Sassoon 'quite right in his views but absolutely wrong in his action', persuaded the medical board of the War Office that Sassoon was in a state of mental collapse and thus averted a court martial, although Sassoon himself actually desired one.

2 Soldiers are citizens of death's grey land,
  Drawing no dividend from time's tomorrows.
  'Dreamers', publ. in *Counter-Attack and Other Poems* (1918)

3 Soldiers are sworn to action; they must win
  Some flaming, fatal climax with their lives.
  Soldiers are dreamers; when the guns begin
  They think of firelit homes, clean beds and wives.
  ibid.

4 'Good-morning; good morning!' the General said
  When we met him last week on our way to the line.
  Now the soldiers he smiled at are most of 'em dead,
  And we're cursing his staff for incompetent swine.
  'He's a cheery old card,' grunted Harry to Jack
  As they slogged up to Arras with rifle and pack.

  But he did for them both by his plan of attack.
  'The General', publ. in ibid.

5 But the past is just the same, – and War's a bloody
          game . . .
  Have you forgotten yet? . . .
  Look down, and swear by the slain of the War that you'll
          never forget.
  'Aftermath', publ. in *The War Poems of Siegfried Sassoon* (1919)

6 Everyone suddenly burst out singing;
  And I was filled with such delight
  As prisoned birds must find in freedom.
  'Everyone Sang', publ. in ibid.

7 The song was wordless; the singing will never be done.
  ibid.

8 In me the tiger sniffs the rose.
  *The Heart's Journey*, no. 7 (1928)

9 Who will remember, passing through this Gate,
  The unheroic Dead who fed the guns?
  Who shall absolve the foulness of their fate, –
  Those doomed, conscripted, unvictorious ones?
  'On Passing the New Menin Gate', publ. in ibid. no. 21

10 Here was the world's worst wound. And here with pride
  'Their name liveth for ever' the Gateway claims.
  Was ever an immolation so belied
  As these intolerably nameless names?
  ibid.

## Erik Satie (1866–1925)
FRENCH COMPOSER AND PIANIST

Mentor of the group of composers known as Les Six, he pioneered the break with nineteenth-century French Romanticism. His music, which had links with the Dada and Surrealist movements, is characterized by parody (with such instructions to the pianist as 'as light as an egg'), novel harmony, as in *Trois Gymnopédies* (1888), and an aesthetic of simplicity, as in *Trois Gnossiennes* (1890) and *The People's Mass* (1895). *Parade* (1917) made use of a typewriter.

1 The brain of the critic is like a shop, a big shop. Everything is to be found there: orthopaedics, science, bedding, arts, travelling rugs . . . The critic knows all, sees all, says all, hears all, touches all, stirs all, eats all, confuses all, and still keeps on thinking. What a man!!!
  'In Praise of Critics', lecture February 1918, publ. in *The Writings of Erik Satie* (ed. Nigel Wilkins, 1980)

## Salvatore Satta (1902–75)
ITALIAN LAWYER AND NOVELIST

He was known as one of Italy's foremost jurists, responsible for rewriting the Italian Penal Code after the Second World War to rid it of its Fascist aspects. Found among his papers after his death was the novel that he had worked on for more than thirty years, *The Day of Judgment* (1979), which has been compared to GIUSEPPE TOMASI DI LAMPEDUSA's *The Leopard*.

1 If we really think about it, God exists for any single individual who puts his trust in Him, not for the whole of humanity, with its laws, its organizations, and its violence. Humanity is the demon which God does not succeed in destroying.
  *The Day of Judgment*, ch. 15 (1979)

2 The most important thing in their lives . . . was to have a lawsuit going. It was not a question of winning or losing it, and indeed it was vital to do neither, for otherwise the suit would be over and done with. A lawsuit was part of the personality, if not the only visible sign of it, to such an extent that there was often no real animosity between the litigants, because they both needed each other.
  ibid. ch. 20. The novel recounts the lives of the inhabitants of an inland mountain town in Sardinia around the turn of the twentieth century.

## Jennifer Saunders (b. 1957)
BRITISH COMEDIAN

With Dawn French, she scripted and acted in *Girls on Top* (1985–6) for BBC2 and was a member of the television team that developed *The Comic Strip Presents . . .* in the 1980s. She later developed her own series, *Absolutely Fabulous* (1992–5), a satire on the world of fashion and the media that was a hit on both sides of the Atlantic.

1 Not instant, darling. Grind some beans. That's not proper coffee . . . that's just beans that have been cremated. I want them entire with life force.
  Edina (Jennifer Saunders), in *Absolutely Fabulous*, first series, 'Fashion', first broadcast 12 November 1992

2 Mum, you've absolved yourself of responsibility. You live from self-induced-crisis to self-induced-crisis. Someone chooses what you wear. Someone does your brain. Someone tells you what to eat, and, three times a week, someone sticks a hose up your bum and flushes it all out for you.
  Saffron (Julia Sawalha), in ibid. Edina replies: 'It's called colonic irrigation, darling, and it's not to be sniffed at.'

## Dorothy L. Sayers (1893–1957)
BRITISH AUTHOR

Full name Dorothy Leigh Sayers. She is best known for her popular detective novels featuring the elegant and erudite Lord Peter Wimsey, such as *Whose Body?* (1923), *Clouds of Witness* (1926) and *Murder Must Advertise* (1933). As a Christian apologist she wrote *The Man Born to Be King* (1941–2), a controversial sequence of radio plays about the life of Christ, as well as theological essays. She was also a translator of note.

1 Lawyers enjoy a little mystery, you know. Why, if everybody came forward and told the truth, the whole truth, and nothing but the truth straight out, we should all retire to the workhouse.
  Sir Impey Biggs, in *Clouds of Witness*, ch. 3 (1926)

2 She always says, my lord, that facts are like cows. If you look them in the face hard enough they generally run away.
  Bunter, in ibid. ch. 4

3 Death seems to provide the minds of the Anglo-Saxon

race with a greater fund of amusement than any other single subject.

*The Third Omnibus of Crime*, Introduction (1935)

4  If it were not for the war,
   This war
   Would suit me down to the ground.
   'London Calling: Lord I Thank Thee'

5  Except ye become as little children, except you can wake on your fiftieth birthday with the same forward-looking excitement and interest in life that you enjoyed when you were five, 'ye cannot enter the kingdom of God'. One must not only die daily, but every day we must be born again.
   *Creed or Chaos? and Other Essays in Popular Mythology*, 'Strong Meat' (1947)

## Alexei Sayle (b. 1952)

BRITISH COMEDIAN, ACTOR AND PRESENTER

In the late 1970s he performed in the Comedy Store and went on to appear on television in *The Young Ones* (1982) and *Alexei Sayle's Stuff* (1988). He has also written the short stories *Barcelona Plates* (2000).

1  'Ullo John Got a New Motor?
   Song title (1984)

## Arthur Scargill (b. 1938)

BRITISH TRADE UNION LEADER

A coal miner from the age of eighteen, he joined the Young Communist League (1955), the Co-operative Party (1963) and the Labour Party (1966), while active in the National Union of Miners. Elected NUM national President in 1981, he led the 1984–5 national protest strike against pit closures. In 1996, disenchanted with New Labour, he founded the Socialist Labour Party.

1  If the church to which you went decided to stop worshipping God and started worshipping the devil, you would have second thoughts. The leadership of New Labour has abandoned their socialist faith and embraced capitalism which is tantamount to embracing the devil!
   Interview in the *Guardian* 4 May 1996

## Simon Schama (b. 1945)

BRITISH HISTORIAN AND AUTHOR

After lecturing at Oxford and Cambridge, he has been Professor of History at Harvard since 1980. Both praised and criticized for his evocative descriptions and racy narrative style, he has published, among other works, *Patriots and Liberators* (about the forming of the modern Dutch republic), *Citizens: A Chronicle of the French Revolution* (1989) and *Rembrandt's Eyes* (1999).

1  Historians are left forever chasing shadows, painfully aware of their inability ever to reconstruct a dead world in its completeness however thorough or revealing their documentation . . . We are doomed to be forever hailing someone who has just gone around the corner and out of earshot.
   *Dead Certainties*, 'Afterword' (1991)

2  Landscapes are culture before they are nature; constructs of the imagination projected onto wood and water and rock.
   *Landscape and Memory*, ch. 1, sect. 3 (1995)

3  [Of Amsterdam] A ticktock city, ruled by the unforgiving government of timepieces.
   *Rembrandt's Eyes*, pt 4, ch. 7, sect. 1 (1999)

4  Never confuse a genius with a Saint.
   ibid. pt 5, ch. 10, sect. 3

## Felix E. Schelling (1858–1935)

US ACADEMIC

A professor at the University of Pennsylvania, he wrote extensively on English Renaissance literature. His chief publications include *English Literature During the Lifetime of Shakespeare* (1910), *A History of English Drama* (1914), and *Foreign Influences in Elizabethan Plays* (1923).

1  True education makes for inequality; the inequality of individuality, the inequality of success, the glorious inequality of talent, of genius; for inequality, not mediocrity, individual superiority, not standardization, is the measure of the progress of the world.
   *Pedagogically Speaking*, ch. 8 (1929)

## Elsa Schiaparelli (1890–1973)

ITALIAN-BORN FRENCH FASHION DESIGNER

She moved to Paris in 1920, where she began designing clothes and opened a workshop in 1927 and salon in 1928. She quickly became famed for her striking use of bright colours, particularly shocking pink, shoulder pads and flamboyant hats. In 1949 she opened a salon in New York and was the first couturier to use synthetic fabrics and zips.

1  Fashion is born by small facts, trends, or even politics, never by trying to make little pleats and furbelows, by trinkets, by clothes easy to copy, or by the shortening or lengthening of a skirt.
   *Shocking Life*, ch. 9 (1954)

## Arthur M. Schlesinger Jr (b. 1917)

US HISTORIAN AND ACADEMIC

Full name Arthur Meier Schlesinger. He became adviser to President KENNEDY (1961–3) and to Kennedy's successor, JOHNSON, whose administration he left over its aggressive policy in Vietnam. His works include *The Age of Jackson* (1945, Pulitzer Prize), *A Thousand Days: John F. Kennedy in the White House* (1965, Pulitzer Prize) and the monumental three-volume *The Age of Roosevelt* (1957–60). Professor of Humanities at the City University, New York (1966–95), he has called politics 'the most entertaining diversion in a democracy'.

1  The choice we face is not between progress with conflict and progress without conflict. The choice is between conflict and stagnation. You cannot expel conflict from society any more than you can from the human mind. When you attempt it, the psychic costs in schizophrenia or torpor are the same.
   The totalitarians regard the toleration of conflict as our central weakness. So it may appear to be in an age of anxiety. But we know it to be basically our central strength.
   *The Vital Center: The Politics of Freedom* (1949)

2  I trust that a graduate student some day will write a doctoral essay on the influence of the Munich analogy on the subsequent history of the twentieth century. Perhaps in the end he will conclude that the multitude of errors committed in the name of 'Munich' may exceed the original error of 1938.
   *The Bitter Heritage: Vietnam and American Democracy*, 'The Inscrutability of History' (1967)

3  Science and Technology revolutionize our lives, but memory, tradition and myth frame our response. Expelled from individual consciousness by the rush of change, history finds its revenge by stamping the collective unconscious with habits, values, expectations, dreams. The dialectic between past and future will continue to form our lives.
   'The Challenge of Change', publ. in *The New York Times Magazine* 27 July 1986

4 Only a cad tells the truth about his love affairs.
   *Sunday Times Review* 27 September 1998. Referring to the CLINTON and MONICA LEWINSKY affair.

## Artur Schnabel (1882–1951)
GERMAN-BORN US PIANIST

Making his concert début at the age of eight, he became an international celebrity, specializing in Beethoven, Mozart and Schubert. He became a household name for his 1931 recording of the complete Beethoven sonatas and concertos, and he also composed extensively for the piano. Fleeing the rise of Nazism in Germany, he moved to Switzerland, finally settling in the USA in 1939.

1 Applause is a receipt, not a bill.
   Quoted in *The Musical Life*, 'Ovation and Triumph' (1958) by Irving Kolodin. Explaining why he did not render applause the tribute of encores.

2 The notes I handle no better than many pianists. But the pauses between the notes – ah, that is where the art resides.
   Quoted in the *Chicago Daily News* 11 June 1958

## Paul Schrader (b. 1946)
US FILM-MAKER

Raised as a strict Calvinist, in his film work he often addresses themes of violence and redemption. He wrote the screenplays of *Taxi Driver* (1976), *The Mosquito Coast* (1986) and *The Last Temptation of Christ* (1988) and also scripted and directed *Blue Collar* (1978) and *American Gigolo* (1979) among others.

1 Movies are about people who *do* things. The number one fantasy of the cinema is that we can do something – we are relatively impotent in our own lives so we go to movies to watch people who are in control of their lives.
   Interview in *Schrader on Schrader*, ch. 5 (ed. Kevin Jackson, 1990)

2 I could be just a writer very easily. I am not a writer. I am a *screen*writer, which is half a film-maker . . . But it is *not* an art form, because screenplays are not works of art. They are invitations to others to collaborate on a work of art.
   Quoted in *Writers in Hollywood 1915–1951*, Preface (1990) by Ian Hamilton

3 Saving someone's life is like falling in love, the best drug in the world. You wonder if you've become immortal. It's as if God has passed through you. Why deny it? God *was* you.
   Frank Pierce (Nicholas Cage), in *Bringing Out the Dead* (film, 1999, screenplay by Paul Schrader based on novel by Joe Connolly, directed by Martin Scorsese)

## Charles Schulz (1922–2000)
US CARTOONIST

The creator of Charlie Brown and Snoopy learned his cartooning through a correspondence course and worked freelance for the *Saturday Evening Post*. His internationally popular series (originally called *Li'l Folks*) was repeatedly rejected before, in 1950, United Features bought it and re-named it *Peanuts*. Having announced his retirement, he died the night before his last strip was to appear.

1 Big sisters are the crab grass in the lawn of life.
   Linus, in *Peanuts* (strip cartoon, 1952)

## E.F. Schumacher (1911–77)
GERMAN-BORN BRITISH ECONOMIST

Full name Ernst Friedrich Schumacher. A consultant on the Beveridge report that established the post-war British welfare state, he continued to advise government on energy policy in the 1950s. In 1966 he founded the Intermediate Technology Development Group, which set out to develop the ideal of sustainable communities based on intermediate technology. He set out his theories in the bestselling *Small is Beautiful* (1973).

1 Call a thing immoral or ugly, soul-destroying or a degradation of man, a peril to the peace of the world or to the well-being of future generations; as long as you have not shown it to be 'uneconomic' you have not really questioned its right to exist, grow, and prosper.
   *Small is Beautiful*, pt 1, ch. 3 (1973)

2 I have no doubt that it is possible to give a new direction to technological development, a direction that shall lead it back to the real needs of man, and that also means: *to the actual size of man*. Man is small, and, therefore, small is beautiful. To go for giantism is to go for self-destruction.
   ibid. pt 2, ch. 10

## Joseph Schumpeter (1883–1950)
MORAVIAN-BORN US ECONOMIST

Briefly Minister of Finance in Austria's first Republican government (1919), he moved to the United States in 1932. In *The Theory of Economic Development* (1934) he viewed economic growth as driven by the activity of a few creative entrepreneurs. Other works include *Business Cycles* (1939), *Capitalism, Socialism and Democracy* (1942) and *A History of Economic Analysis* (1954), which was edited by his widow.

1 For the duration of its collective life, or the time during which its identity may be assumed, each class resembles a hotel or an omnibus, always full, but always of different people.
   *Social Classes*, ch. 3, no. 7 (1927)

2 Entrepreneurial profit . . . is the expression of the value of what the entrepreneur contributes to production.
   *The Theory of Economic Development*, ch. 4 (1934)

3 Marxism is essentially a product of the bourgeois mind.
   *Capitalism, Socialism and Democracy*, ch. 1 (1942)

4 Economic progress, in capitalist society, means turmoil.
   ibid. ch. 3

5 The evolution of the capitalist style of life could be easily – and perhaps most tellingly – described in terms of the genesis of the modern Lounge Suit.
   ibid. ch. 11

6 Capitalism inevitably and by virtue of the very logic of its civilization creates, educates and subsidizes a vested interest in social unrest.
   ibid. ch. 13, sect. 2

7 Bureaucracy is not an obstacle to democracy but an inevitable complement to it.
   ibid. ch. 18

8 Democracy is a political *method*, that is to say, a certain type of institutional arrangement for arriving at political – legislative and administrative – decisions and hence incapable of being an end in itself.
   ibid. ch. 20, sect. 3

## Arnold Schwarzenegger (b. 1947)
AUSTRIAN-BORN US SCREEN ACTOR

As a body builder who called himself 'the Austrian Oak', he was five times Mr Universe and seven times Mr Olympia. His appearance in the documentary *Pumping Iron* (1977) led to film roles in *Conan the Barbarian* (1982) and *The Terminator* (1984), the film that established him as a superstar. He became a US citizen in 1983.

1 I'll be back.
   The Terminator (Arnold Schwarzenegger), in *The Terminator* (film, 1984, written and directed by James Cameron)

2 Hasta la vista, baby.
   The Terminator (Arnold Schwarzenegger), in *Terminator 2: Judg-*

*ment Day* (film, 1991, written, directed and produced by James Cameron)

3 Money doesn't make you happy. I now have $50 million but I was just as happy when I had $48 million.
Quoted in *Brewer's Cinema* (1995)

## Norman Schwarzkopf (b. 1934)
US SOLDIER

He joined the US army in 1956 and commanded forces in Vietnam, where he was critical of American strategy. He directed Operation Desert Storm against Iraq (1990–91), earning him the nickname 'Stormin' Norman'.

1 A very great man once said you should love your enemies, and that's not a bad piece of advice. We can love them, but, by God, that doesn't mean we're not going to fight them.
*Daily Telegraph* 1 February 1991

## Albert Schweitzer (1875–1965)
GERMAN THEOLOGIAN, MISSIONARY AND MUSICIAN

In 1896 he decided to live for science and art until the age of thirty, then devote his life to social service. He resigned as Principal of Strasbourg theological college in 1905 and began studying medicine, and in 1913, in a spirit 'not of benevolence but of atonement', he founded the leprosy hospital at Lambaréné in French-occupied Equatorial Africa where he spent the rest of his life. As well as a study of J.S. Bach and works on theology, he wrote *The Philosophy of Civilization* (1923) and a number of autobiographical works. He was awarded the Nobel Peace Prize in 1952 for his teaching of 'reverence of life'.

1 Pessimism is depreciated will-to-live.
*The Philosophy of Civilization*, vol. 2: *Civilization and Ethics*, ch. 2 (1923)

2 True ethics begin where the use of language ceases.
ibid. ch. 21

3 The African is my brother – but he is my younger brother by several centuries.
Quoted in the *Observer* 23 October 1955

## Martin Scorsese (b. 1942)
US FILM-MAKER

Described by critic DAVID THOMSON as a 'devotee of intelligence, visual beauty, and verbal style', he returns frequently in his work to the themes of masculinity and alienation. Among the many films he has directed, *Mean Streets* (1973), *Raging Bull* (1980) and *Goodfellas* (1990) are his acknowledged masterpieces.

1 You don't make up for your sins in church. You do it on the streets. You do it at home. The rest is bullshit and you know it.
Voiceover, in *Mean Streets* (film, 1973, screenplay by Martin Scorsese and Mardik Martin, directed by Martin Scorsese)

2 I saw beauty in movies, usually westerns – I loved the landscape, I loved the colour of the horses and I wished I could be there. But I wasn't. So I dealt with the beauty on the streets, and the beauty was extraordinary.
Interview in the *Guardian* 11 December 1999

## C.P. Scott (1846–1932)
BRITISH AUTHOR AND JOURNALIST

Full name Charles Prestwich Scott. When he was twenty-five, he became Editor of the *Manchester Guardian*, a position he held for fifty-nine years (until 1929), the longest editorship of a national newspaper anywhere in the world. He established the paper as a liberal rival of *The Times*, taking up such controversial causes as

opposition to the Boer War and campaigns for civil liberties. From 1895 to 1906 he was a Liberal Member of Parliament.

1 Neither in what it gives, nor in what it does not give, nor in the mode of presentation, must the unclouded face of truth suffer wrong. Comment is free, but facts are sacred.
*Manchester Guardian* 5 May 1921. Editorial marking the paper's first hundred years. TOM STOPPARD in *Night and Day* (1978) adapted the aphorism: 'Comment is free, but facts are on expenses.'

## George C. Scott (b. 1926)
US SCREEN ACTOR

He has specialized in tough, authoritative roles as in *The Hustler* (1962), *The List of Adrian Messenger* (1963) *Dr. Strangelove* (1963) and *Dick Tracy* (1989). He has also pursued a parallel career as a theatre producer and director, and directed two of his own films, *Rage* (1973) and *The Savage is Loose* (1974). He was the first actor ever to refuse an Oscar (for his role in *Patton: Lust for Glory*, 1970), denouncing the award selection process as a 'meat parade'.

1 [On nuclear war] I'm not saying we wouldn't get our hair mussed, Mister President, but I do say not more than ten to twenty million dead depending on the breaks.
General 'Buck' Turgidson (George C. Scott), in *Dr. Strangelove: Or How I Learned To Stop Worrying And Love The Bomb* (film, 1963, screenplay by STANLEY KUBRICK, Terry Southern and Peter George, based on Peter George's novel *Red Alert*, produced and directed by Stanley Kubrick)

2 All this stuff you heard about America not wanting to fight, wanting to stay out of the war, is a lot of horse dung. Americans, traditionally, love to fight. All real Americans love the sting of battle . . . Americans play to win all the time. I wouldn't give a hoot in hell for a man who lost and laughed. That's why Americans have never lost – and will never lose – a war, because the very thought of losing is hateful to Americans.
General George S. Patton Jr (George C. Scott), in *Patton* (film, 1970, screenplay by Francis Ford Coppola and Edmund H. North, directed by Franklin J. Schaffner). In the film's opening speech, Patton addresses the audience as though they were his troops. The screenplay was based on Ladislas Farago's *Patton: Ordeal and Triumph* (1966) and *A Soldier's Story* (1951) by General OMAR BRADLEY.

3 No bastard ever won a war by dying for his country. He won it by making the other poor dumb bastard die for his country.
ibid.

## Paul Scott (1920–78)
BRITISH AUTHOR

He was a publisher and literary agent before turning to writing, which was chiefly about India and Malaya. His best known work is his tetralogy *The Raj Quartet* (1966–75), a chronicle of life among the British and Anglo-Indians in the last years of the Raj. The books were adapted for Granada television as *The Jewel in the Crown* (1982).

1 Ah, well, the truth is always one thing, but in a way it's the other thing, the gossip, that counts. It shows where people's hearts lie.
Count Bronowsky, in *The Day of the Scorpion*, bk 1, pt 3, ch. 3 (1968)

## Gil Scott Heron (b. 1949)
US MUSICIAN AND AUTHOR

A novelist and poet, he set his work to music and composed political songs in a jazz-soul idiom, as on the albums *Pieces of a Man* (1971) and *Free Will* (1972). Writing on a range of issues including South Africa and nuclear power, he had later success with the album *Reflections* (1981) and the 1982 rap 'B Movie'. Called 'the Godfather of Rap', he is quoted: 'I hope there's a godmother, 'cos I want to talk to her about these kids.'

1 The revolution will not go better with Coke.
The revolution will not fight the germs that may cause
    bad breath,
The revolution will put you in the driver's seat.

The revolution will not be televised, will not be
    televised,
Will not be televised, will not be televised,
The revolution will be no rerun, brother,
The revolution will be live.

'The Revolution Will Not Be Televised' (song, written with Brian Jackson) on the album *Pieces of a Man* (1971). The song was covered by Patti LaBelle.

2 What's the word?
Tell me brother, have you heard
from Johannesburg?

'Johannesburg' (song) on the album *From South Africa to South California* (1976)

## Roger Scruton (b. 1944)
BRITISH PHILOSOPHER AND AUTHOR

A conservative thinker, but critical of free-market capitalism, he considers philosophy to be valuable only when, he says, 'connected to critical intelligence in the fields of human value'. Among his works are *The Meaning of Conservatism* (1980), *Sexual Desire* (1986), *A Dictionary of Political Thought* (1982) and *An Intelligent Person's Guide to Philosophy* (1996), as well as two novels.

1 Government is the primary need of every man subject to
the discipline of social intercourse, and freedom the name
of at least one of his anxieties.

*The Meaning of Conservatism*, ch. 1 (1980)

2 Once in parliament, a member, rightly subject to the
discipline of party, ceases to represent his constituents in
any matter of state. He is a part of the apparatus of state.
What he does is determined by the established interests
that seek expression through his party, and not by any
'promises' that he once made at the hustings. Democracy
is simply one means of gaining power, and so of freeing
oneself from the immediate demands of the multitude.

ibid. ch. 3

3 We yearn, in fact, to *justify* the human body, to give
grounds for our feeling that this is God's image. And in
this yearning is expressed our real knowledge that we are
our bodies and that they are we.

*Sexual Desire: A Philosophical Investigation*, ch. 9 (1986)

## John Sebastian (b. 1944)
US ROCK MUSICIAN

He formed the folk-rock band the Lovin' Spoonful, for which he was both lead singer and composer, in 1965, and later performed solo at the Woodstock Festival. His *John B. Sebastian* album was a bestseller in 1970, and in 1976 'Welcome Back' became a no. 1 hit. *Tar Beach* (1993) was his first album since the 1970s.

1 Hot town,
Summer in the city,
Back o' my neck gettin' dirty and gritty.

'Summer in the City' (song, written by John Sebastian, Mark Sebastian and Steve Boone) on the album *Hums of The Lovin' Spoonful* (1966) by the Lovin' Spoonful

## Alan Seeger (1888–1916)
US POET

After a Harvard education he travelled to Paris in 1912 seeking to establish himself as a poet. On the outbreak of the First World

War, he joined the French Foreign Legion and was killed in the Somme offensive. His popular poems 'I Have a Rendezvous with Death' and 'Ode in Memory of the American Volunteers' were published in *Poems* (1916), followed by *The Letters and Diary of Alan Seeger* (1917). A war memorial to American volunteers in Paris is sculpted with his features.

1 I have a rendezvous with Death
At some disputed barricade.

'I Have a Rendezvous with Death', publ. in *North American Review* October 1916, repr. in *Poems* (1916)

2 And I to my pledged word am true,
I shall not fail that rendezvous.

ibid.

## Pete Seeger (b. 1919)
US FOLK SINGER AND SONGWRITER

A Communist Party member until 1951, he co-founded the Almanac Singers (1940–41), a campaigning folk band which included WOODIE GUTHRIE, and the Weavers (1948–58). In the 1950s he was a victim of the McCarthyite witch-hunt, although he continued to appear at protests and fund-raising events, and his songs have been widely covered.

1 If I had a hammer, I'd hammer in the morning,
I'd hammer in the evening all over this land.

'The Hammer Song' (song, 1949, written by Pete Seeger and Lee Hays) on the album *Sing Out With Pete* (1961). The song was successfully recorded by Peter, Paul and Mary in 1962 as 'If I Had a Hammer', becoming a staple at protests in the 1960s. 'We wrought better than we thought,' commented Seeger years later, 'the song has grown with time.'

2 Where have all the flowers gone?

'Where Have All the Flowers Gone?' (song, c. 1956) on the album *The Bitter and the Sweet* by Pete Seeger (1963). The song, which was covered by the Kingston Trio as well as by Peter, Paul and Mary in 1962, was inspired by a passage in the novel *And Quiet Flows the Don* (1934) by Mikhail Sholokhov, quoting a Ukrainian folk song: 'Where are the flowers, the girls have plucked them. Where are the girls, they've all taken husbands. Where are the men, they're all in the army.' BOB DYLAN, apparently, had spent a fruitless year searching for this song.

3 Little boxes on the hillside,
Little boxes made of ticky tacky;
Little boxes on the hillside
Little boxes all the same.

There's a green one, and a pink one,
And a blue one, and a yellow one
And they're all made out of ticky tacky,
and they all look just the same.

'Little Boxes' (song, 1962, written by Malvina Reynolds) on the album *We Shall Overcome* (1963)

4 I had thought that folk music was something old, back in
the library, and pop music was new – it was something
you could hear on the radio. All of a sudden I realized
that was a phony distinction. Millions of people were
making music which grew out of the old traditions, mostly
making up new words to fit old tunes. New words to fit
new circumstances. This is what I call the folk process.

Quoted in *All You Need is Love*, 'Go Down Moses!' (1976) by Tony Palmer

## Erich Segal (b. 1937)
US AUTHOR

A Yale professor who has published scholarly works on Greco-Roman comedy, he also wrote film scripts and was one of the writers for the Beatles film *Yellow Submarine* (1968). It was his screenplay for *Love Story* (1970), however, that made him a household name. His accompanying novel, slated by critics for clichéd writing, nevertheless sold 11 million copies; his later *Doctors* (1987) was better received.

1 **Love means never having to say you're sorry.**

Jenny Cavilleri (Ali MacGraw), in *Love Story* (film, 1970, screenplay by Erich Segal, directed by Arthur Hiller). The words, which appear in ch. 13 of Segal's novelization of the film as 'Love means not ever having to say you're sorry', were used as a publicity slogan for the film, subsequently spawning numerous variations on the theme. See also TONY PARSONS 3.

## E.C. Segar (1894–1938)

US CARTOONIST

Full name Elzie Crisler Segar. He joined the *Chicago American* and began the strip *Looping the Loop* in 1918 and, in 1919, *The Thimble Theatre* for the New York *Evening Journal*, which recounted the trials and tribulations of the Oyl Family, later joined by Popeye the sailor.

1 **I yam what I yam.**

Catch-phrase of Popeye from 1929. Originally created for *The Thimble Theatre* syndicated strip, Popeye's character took over from Olive and Castor Oyl, making his first official appearance 17 January 1929 and first film appearance in 1933 for the Fleischer Studio's *Talkartoon* series, opposite Betty Boop. After Segar's death, the strip was drawn by different animators in various TV cartoons, and his character was fleshed out in ROBERT ALTMAN's *Popeye* (1980) with ROBIN WILLIAMS in the title role.

2 **I likes to eat my spinach.**

ibid.

## Will Self (b. 1961)

BRITISH AUTHOR

Known for his dark humour and exploration of unusual states of mind, he has drawn on his own experience of heroin addiction for his short stories *The Quantity Theory of Insanity* (1991) and his novel *My Idea of Fun* (1994). *Junk Mail* appeared in 1995 and *How the Dead Live* in 2000. He has also drawn cartoons for *City Limits* and the *New Statesman*.

1 *Wake up.* The avant-garde is dead. It's been marketed.

Interview in *The Idler* November/December 1993

2 **Some people are born slack – others have slacking thrust upon them.**

'Slack Attack', publ. in the *Observer* 2 January 1994, repr. in *Junk Mail* (1995)

3 **As far as I can see, the history of experimental art in the twentieth century is intimately bound up with the experience of intoxification.**

Quoted in *The Face* November 1994

## W.C. Sellar (1898–1951) and
## R.J. Yeatman (1897–1968)

BRITISH AUTHORS

Full names Walter Carruthers Sellar and Robert Julian Yeatman. Sellar, a schoolteacher, and Yeatman, a copywriter and advertising manager, collaborated on *1066 and All That* (1930), a classic compendium of schoolroom howlers, followed by *And Now All This* (1932), *Horse Nonsense* (1933) and *Garden Rubbish* (1936).

1 **History is not what you thought. *It is what you can remember.* All other history defeats itself.**

*1066 and All That*, 'Compulsory Preface' (1930)

2 **The Roman Conquest was, however, a Good Thing, since the Britons were only natives at the time.**

ibid. ch. 1, 'Culture Among the Ancient Britons'

3 **We come at last to the Central Period of British History . . . consisting in the *utterly memorable Struggle between***

the Cavaliers (*Wrong but Wromantic*) and the Roundheads (*Right but Repulsive*).

ibid. ch. 35, 'Charles I and the Civil War'

4 **King Edward's new policy of peace was very successful and culminated in the Great War to End War. This pacific and inevitable struggle was undertaken in the reign of His Good and memorable Majesty King George V and it was the cause of nowadays and the end of History.**

ibid. ch. 61, 'The Great War'

5 **Do not on any account attempt to write on both sides of the paper at once.**

ibid. 'Test Paper V'. Closing words of book.

## Peter Sellers (1925–80)

BRITISH COMEDIAN AND ACTOR

Beginning his career as a stand-up comedian, he took part in the radio *Goon Show* (1951–60) after meeting with SPIKE MILLIGAN. Recognized as a brilliantly versatile actor, he played three separate roles in KUBRICK's film *Dr. Strangelove* (1963), and from 1963 he was the bumbling Inspector Clouseau in the *Pink Panther* films. He was also acclaimed for his performance in *Being There* (1979).

1 **You silly twisted boy!**

Favourite expression of Lance Brigadier Grytpype-Thynne (Peter Sellers), in *The Goon Show* (BBC radio comedy series, 1951–60, written by Spike Milligan), publ. in *The Goon Show Scripts*, ed. Spike Milligan, 1972)

2 **There is no me. I do not exist. There used to be a me but I had it surgically removed,**

*Time* magazine 3 March 1980. Remark four months before his death.

## David O. Selznick (1902–65)

US FILM PRODUCER

Full name David Oliver Selznick. After working for Paramount, RKO and MGM, he founded Selznick International Pictures in 1936. His films include *Dinner at Eight* (1933) and the Oscar-winning *Gone with the Wind* (1939) and *Rebecca* (1940). He was known as a hard taskmaster – 'The way I see it, my function is to be responsible for everything' – and for the legendary length of his memos.

1 **Hollywood's like Egypt, full of crumbled pyramids. It'll never come back. It'll just keep on crumbling until finally the wind blows the last studio prop across the sands.**

Said in 1951 to journalist and author Ben Hecht, quoted in *A Child of the Century*, bk 5, 'Enter, the Movies' (1954) by Ben Hecht

## Rod Serling (1924–75)

US WRITER AND PRODUCER FOR TELEVISION

Full name Edwin Rodman Serling. He was the creator and host of the science fiction *The Twilight Zone* (1959–64) and fantasy *Night Gallery* (1970–73) TV series, as well as the author of more than 200 plays for television. Many of these were controversial, among them *A Town Has Turned to Dust* (1958), about lynching, and *The Rank and File* (1959), about labour-union corruption. His screenplays were often based on his television scripts, such as *Patterns of Power* (1956) and *Seven Days in May* (1964), and he co-wrote *The Planet of the Apes* (1967).

1 **There is a fifth dimension beyond those known to man. It is a dimension vast as space and timeless as infinity. It is the middle ground between light and shadow, between the pit of his fears and the summit of his knowledge. This is the dimension of imagination. It is an area called the Twilight Zone.**

*The Twilight Zone*, Preamble (TV series, created, written and narrated by Rod Serling, 1959–64)

## Andres Serrano (b. 1950)

US PHOTOGRAPHER

He achieved notoriety with his 1987 work, 'Piss Christ' and also used bodily fluids in his photographs 'Milk' and 'Blood and Milk'. Other subjects include corpses, the Ku Klux Klan and the homeless.

1 **What the nuns told us in school when I was going to religious instruction was that we worship not the crucifix but Christ . . . We aren't supposed to worship the symbol or give it the same level of reverence that we give Christ because it's only a representation.**
On the depiction of the crucifix in his 1987 work, *Piss Christ*, in the *Boston Globe* 20 August 1989, quoted in *Body and Soul*, 'Andres Serrano: Invisible Power' (ed. Brian Wallis, 1995). Serrano's image aroused enormous controversy in the United States and Britain.

2 **I've always believed there was no such thing as the sacred without the profane – and in some cases it's hard to tell the difference.**
Quoted in *Contemporary Photographers* (3rd edn, ed. Martin Marix Evans, 1995)

## Vikram Seth (b. 1952)

INDIAN AUTHOR

His travel writing includes *From Heaven Lake* (1983), his poetry is collected in *Mappings* (1980) and *Beastly Tales From Here to There* (1992), but he is most famous for his 1,300-page novel *A Suitable Boy* (1993), which recounts the post-independence 'India of the drawing room'. *The Golden Gate* (1986), termed by GORE VIDAL 'the great California novel', is written entirely in sonnets.

1 **Music is not a cheap spectacle – not the entertainment of the brothel. It is like prayer.**
Ustad Majeed Khan, in *A Suitable Boy*, ch. 6, sect. 2 (1993)

2 **Making music and making love – it's a bit too easy an equation.**
Julia, in *An Equal Music*, pt 3, sect. 16 (1999)

3 **Strange to be a man and never grow big with child. To feel a part of you opening, and a part of you leaving, and howling as if it were not a part of you. Then it puts on a green cap and a grey suit and has friends.**
Narrator (Michael), in ibid. pt 8, sect 13. Observation while watching schoolchildren.

## Brian Sewell

BRITISH ART CRITIC

Art critic for the *Evening Standard* from the 1980s, he was arts journalist of the year in 1994 and alternately revered and reviled for his traditionalist stance, though he himself states: 'I try to stand apart.'

1 **There is now a universal belief that the far side of a fallen barrier is always preferable . . . and we are into new generations of artists who have never known the art of the past and have no skills or traditions by which to return to it. Time and again in the history of art, artists have broken a barrier into a cul-de-sac, and it is those who have stepped back into the past who have then, fully armed, leaped into the future.**
'Gravity and Grace', first publ. in the *Evening Standard* (1993), repr, in *The Reviews That Caused the Rumpus*, ch. 5 (1994)

2 **[Of the Queen] She deserves better than to be perpetuated as an old-age pensioner about to lose her bungalow.**
Quoted in the *Independent on Sunday* 12 May 1996. On the portrait by Anthony Williams to mark the Queen's seventieth birthday.

## Anne Sexton (1928–74)

US POET

Advised to write seriously by her psychiatrist after the birth of her second child, she produced numerous collections, including *Bedlam and Back* (1960) and *Live or Die* (1966, Pulitzer Prize). Her confessional style of poetry drew comparisons with SYLVIA PLATH and was also criticized for addressing such topics as menstruation, abortion and addiction. Plagued with emotional breakdowns and depression all her adult life, she committed suicide.

1 **Everyone has left me**
**except my muse,**
*that good nurse.*
**She stays in my hand,**
**a mild white mouse.**
'Flee on Your Donkey', publ. in *Live or Die* (1966). The title quotes Rimbaud's *Fêtes de la faim* (1872).

2 **But suicides have a special language.**
**Like carpenters they want to know** *which tools.*
**They never ask** *why build.*
'Wanting to Die', publ. in ibid.

3 **The sea is mother-death and she is a mighty female, the one who wins, the one who sucks us all up.**
Entry 19 November 1971 in 'A Small Journal', publ. in *The Poet's Story* (ed. Howard Moss, 1974)

4 **It doesn't matter who my father was; it matters who I remember he was.**
ibid. 1 January 1972

5 **God owns heaven**
**but He craves the earth.**
'The Earth', publ. in *The Awful Rowing Toward God* (1975). In his essay 'A Visionary' (1891) YEATS recalls G.W. Russell (here referred to as 'X–') (see Æ) meeting an old peasant who 'dumb to most men, poured out his cares for him . . . Once he burst out with, "God possesses the heavens – God possesses the heavens – but He covets the world".'

6 **My faith**
**is a great weight**
**hung on a small wire,**
**as doth the spider**
**hang her baby on a thin web.**
'Small Wire', publ. in ibid.

7 **My ideas are a curse.**
**They spring from a radical discontent**
**With the awful order of things.**
'February 3rd', publ. in *Scorpio, Bad Spider, Die: the Horoscope Poems* (1978)

## Yitzhak Shamir (b. 1915)

POLISH-BORN ISRAELI POLITICIAN AND PRIME MINISTER

Originally Yitzhak Jazernicki. In his twenties he became a founder member of the Israel Freedom Fighters (later known as the Stern Gang) and, arrested by the British in 1941, was given asylum in France. Returning to Israel in 1948 he eventually entered the Knesset in 1973, was Foreign Minister (1980–83 and 1984–6) and subsequently took over the leadership of the right-wing Likud Party. He was Prime Minister 1983–4 and 1986–92.

1 **[On Palestinian self-government] Should there be maniacs who raise the idea, they will encounter an iron fist which will leave no trace of such attempts.**
Quoted in *The Times* 11 August 1988

2 **Our image has undergone change from David fighting Goliath to being Goliath.**
Quoted in the *Daily Telegraph* 25 January 1989

## The Shangri-Las (1964–77)

US VOCAL GROUP

The all-girl vocal group created by George 'Shadow' Morton in 1964 consisted of the Weiss sisters, Mary and Betty, and the twins Mary Ann and Marge Ganser. They peaked in the mid-1960s with such hits as 'Remember (Walking in the Sand)' (1964), with atmospheric seagull cries, and the dramatic 'Leader of the Pack' (1964), with its revving motorbike.

1 I met him at the candy store,
He turned around and smiled at me,
You get the picture?
('Yes we see')
That's when I fell for the leader of the pack.
'The Leader of The Pack' (song, 1964, written by George Morton, Jeff Barry and Ellie Greenwich) on the album *Golden Hits of the Shangi-Las* (1966)

## Omar Sharif (b. 1932)
EGYPTIAN SCREEN ACTOR

Original name Michel Shalhouz. He made his film debut in 1953, became Egypt's top male star and subsequently attracted international attention for his role in *Lawrence of Arabia* (1962). He starred in *Doctor Zhivago* (1965), and his other films include *Funny Girl* (1968), and *The Mirror has Two Faces* (1996). He is also a renowned international bridge-player.

1 Making love? It's a communion with a woman. The bed is the holy table. There I find passion – and purification.
Quoted in *City Limits* 18 December 1986

## Helen Sharman (b. 1963)
BRITISH SCIENTIST AND ASTRONAUT

Selected from 13,000 applicants to be the British member of the Russian scientific space mission, Project Juno (May 1991), she spent six days aboard the *Mir* space station, becoming Britain's first astronaut. Since then she has become a lecturer and broadcaster in science education and published *The Space Place* (1997).

1 There is very little difference between men and women in space.
*Independent on Sunday* 9 June 1991

## Al Sharpton (b. 1954)
US CIVIL RIGHTS CAMPAIGNER

After becoming an ordained minister when he was ten years old, he became director of the National Youth Movement (later renamed United African Movement) in 1970. A fiery polemicist and a believer in direct action to end racial discrimination, he once said: 'I am a man of faith but not that much faith.'

1 What I profess to do is help the oppressed and if I cause a load of discomfort in the white community and the black community, that in my opinion means I'm being effective, because I'm not trying to make them comfortable. The job of an activist is to make people tense and cause social change.
*Independent on Sunday* 21 April 1991

## George Bernard Shaw (1856–1950)
IRISH PLAYWRIGHT AND CRITIC

Moving from Dublin to London in 1876, he established himself as a music and drama critic before beginning to write plays in 1885. As an active member of the Fabian Society he combined a passion for social reform with fierce wit in his numerous writings. His plays include *Arms and the Man* (1894), *Candida* (1897), *The Devil's Disciple* (1897), *Man and Superman* (1905), *The Doctor's Dilemma* (1906) and *Pygmalion* (1913, adapted as musical *My Fair Lady*, 1956, filmed 1964). He was awarded the Nobel Prize for Literature in 1935. LENIN famously lamented, 'He is a good man fallen among Fabians', while HAROLD NICOLSON opined in 1950, 'I do not think Shaw will be a great literary figure in 2000 AD'. See also JAMES AGATE 2, MRS PATRICK CAMPBELL 1, BERT LESTON TAYLOR 2, W. B. YEATS 12.

1 The secret of being miserable is to have leisure to bother

about whether you are happy or not. The cure for it is occupation.
*Parents and Children*, 'Children's Happiness' (1914)

2 A perpetual holiday is a good working definition of hell.
ibid.

3 When our relatives are at home, we have to think of all their good points or it would be impossible to endure them. But when they are away, we console ourselves for their absence by dwelling on their vices.
Captain Shotover, in *Heartbreak House*, act 1 (1920)

4 Cruelty would be delicious if one could only find some sort of cruelty that didn't really hurt.
Mrs Hushabye, in ibid.

5 It is a curious sensation: the sort of pain that goes mercifully beyond our powers of feeling. When your heart is broken, your boats are burned: nothing matters any more. It is the end of happiness and the beginning of peace.
Ellie, in ibid.

6 We know now that the soul is the body, and the body the soul. They tell us they are different because they want to persuade us that we can keep our souls if we let them make slaves of our bodies.
Ellie, in ibid.

7 Old men are dangerous: it doesn't matter to them what is going to happen to the world.
Captain Shotover, in ibid. Ellie responds: 'I should have thought nothing else mattered to old men. They can't be very interested in what is going to happen to themselves.'

8 I feel nothing but the accursed happiness I have dreaded all my life long: the happiness that comes as life goes, the happiness of yielding and dreaming instead of resisting and doing, the sweetness of the fruit that is going rotten.
ibid.

9 A man's interest in the world is only the overflow from his interest in himself. When you are a child your vessel is not yet full; so you care for nothing but your own affairs. When you grow up, your vessel overflows; and you are a politician, a philosopher, or an explorer and adventurer. In old age the vessel dries up: there is no overflow: you are a child again.
ibid.

10 Never waste jealousy on a real man: it is the imaginary man that supplants us all in the long run.
Hector Hushabye, in ibid.

11 Go anywhere in England where there are natural, wholesome, contented, and really nice English people; and what do you always find? That the stables are the real centre of the household ... There are only two classes in good society in England: the equestrian classes and the neurotic classes.
Lady Utterword, in ibid. act 3

12 [Of *Ulysses*] In Ireland they try to make a cat cleanly by rubbing its nose in its own filth. Mr Joyce has tried the same treatment on the human subject. I hope it may prove successful.
Letter to JAMES JOYCE's publisher Sylvia Beach, 10 October 1921, publ. in *Letters of James Joyce*, vol. 3 (ed. Richard Ellman, 1966). Shaw called *Ulysses* a 'revolting record of a disgusting phase of civilization; but it is a truthful one', although he refused the invitation to purchase a copy. In *The Table Talk of GBS* (1924), Shaw is quoted: 'I could not write the words Mr Joyce used: my prudish hand would refuse to form the letters.'

13 All the sweetness of religion is conveyed to the world by the hands of story-tellers and image-makers. Without their fictions the truths of religion would for the multitude be neither intelligible nor even apprehensible; and the prophets would prophesy and the teachers teach in vain.
*Back to Methuselah*, Preface, 'What to Do with the Legends' (1922)

14 You see things; and you say 'Why?' But I dream things that never were; and I say 'Why not?'

The Serpent, in ibid., 'In the Beginning', act 1. These words are often associated with ROBERT KENNEDY after they were quoted by him in an address to the Irish Parliament in Dublin, June 1963, and attributed to him by Edward Kennedy at Robert's funeral service in 1968.

15 Life is too short for men to take it seriously.

Franklyn, in ibid. 'The Gospel of the Brothers Barnabas'

16 Life is a disease; and the only difference between one man and another is the stage of the disease at which he lives. You are always at the crisis: I am always in the convalescent stage. I enjoy convalescence. It is the part that makes illness worth while.

Lubin, in ibid. Addressing his political rival Burge.

17 A nap, my friend, is a brief period of sleep which overtakes superannuated persons when they endeavour to entertain unwelcome visitors or to listen to scientific lectures.

The Elderly Gentleman, in ibid. 'Tragedy of an Elderly Gentleman', act 1

18 It is difficult, if not impossible, for most people to think otherwise than in the fashion of their own period.

*Saint Joan*, Preface (1923)

19 We want a few mad people now. See where the sane ones have landed us!

Poulengey, in ibid. sc.1

20 A miracle is an event which creates faith. That is the purpose and nature of miracles ... Frauds deceive. An event which creates faith does not deceive: therefore it is not a fraud, but a miracle.

The Archbishop, in ibid. sc. 2

21 What Englishman will give his mind to politics as long as he can afford to keep a motor car?

Balbus, in *The Apple Cart*, act 1 (1929)

22 A king is not allowed the luxury of a good character. Our country has produced millions of blameless greengrocers, but not one blameless monarch.

King Magnus, in ibid.

23 The national anthem belongs to the eighteenth century. In it you find us ordering God about to do our political dirty work.

A member of the Caravan of the Curious, in *The Adventures of the Black Girl in Her Search for God* (1932)

24 When Satan makes impure verses, Allah sends a divine tune to cleanse them.

The Arab, in ibid.

25 Newspapers are unable, seemingly, to discriminate between a bicycle accident and the collapse of civilization.

Preface (1933) to *Too True to be Good* (1931)

26 The trouble, Mr Goldwyn, is that you are only interested in art and I am only interested in money.

Quoted in *The Great Goldwyn*, ch. 3 (1937) by Alva Johnson. Addressed to SAMUEL GOLDWYN, according to publicity chief HOWARD DIETZ, during talks to engage Shaw as a writer for Hollywood. The words, released as a statement for the press, are probably an approximation of the original dialogue.

27 A government which robs Peter to pay Paul can always depend on the support of Paul.

*Everybody's Political What's What*, ch. 30 (1944)

28 [Dancing is] a perpendicular expression of a horizontal desire.

Attributed in the *New Statesman* 23 March 1962

## Irwin Shaw (1913–84)

US AUTHOR

He wrote the first of his twelve plays, the anti-war *Bury the Dead*

(1936), in the same year as his first screenplay, *The Big Game*. After publishing successful short stories in the *New Yorker*, he turned to novels, the first of which, *The Young Lions* (1948), prompted by his experiences in the Second World War, became a bestseller. This was followed by *Two Weeks in Another Town* (1960) and *Rich Man, Poor Man* (1969).

1 I cringe when critics say I'm a master of the popular novel. What's an unpopular novel?

*Observer* 6 March 1983

## Sandie Shaw (b. 1947)

BRITISH SINGER

Original name Sandra Goodrich. Famous for her bare feet and miniskirt, she made her name with such hits as 'There's Always Something There to Remind Me' and 'Girl Don't Come' (both 1964). In 1967 she was Britain's first winner of the Eurovision Song Contest with 'Puppet on a String'.

1 I'm just a normal everyday kind of goddess.

Said in 1988, quoted in the *New Musical Express* 4 February 1995

## William Shawcross (b. 1902)

BRITISH LAWYER

Baron Shawcross of Friston. He served as Attorney-General 1945–51 and was chief British prosecutor at the Nuremberg Trials (1945–6), later leading the investigations of the Lynskey Tribunal (1948) and the Klaus Fuchs 'atomic spy' case (1950).

1 You cannot do justice to the dead. When we talk about doing justice to the dead we are talking about retribution for the harm done to them. But retribution and justice are two different things.

Quoted in the *Daily Telegraph* 1 May 1991. Discussing the War Crimes Bill and the prosecution of ex-Nazis living in Britain.

## Gail Sheehy (b. 1937)

US AUTHOR AND CRITIC

She has established herself as a guide to the ageing process and the transition into what she calls the 'Flaming Fifties' and 'Serene Sixties'. Among her titles are *Passages: Predictable Crises of Adult Life* (1976), *The Silent Passage* (1993), concerning the menopause, and *Passages in Men's Lives* (1998). She has also written on politics and social issues.

1 There is no more defiant denial of one man's ability to possess one woman exclusively than the prostitute who refuses to be redeemed.

*Hustling*, ch. 1 (1971)

2 Democratization is not democracy; it is a slogan for the temporary liberalization handed down from an autocrat. Glasnost is not free speech; only free speech, constitutionally guaranteed, is free speech.

Gorbachev, 'Looking for Mikhail Gorbachev' (1991)

3 The secret of a leader lies in the tests he has faced over the whole course of his life and the *habit of action* he develops in meeting those tests.

ibid.

## Gilbert Shelton (b. 1940)

US CARTOONIST

He created the Fabulous Furry Freak Brothers in International Underground Comix in 1968, and with three partners set up the Rip Off Press a year later. The original partners dispersed in 1986, but the Freak Brothers made sporadic appearances subsequently.

1 We have plenty of grass, and as we all know, dope will get

you through times of no money better than money will get you through times of no dope.

Freewheelin' Franklin, in 'The Freaks Pull a Heist' (1971), publ. in *Fabulous Furry Freak Brothers* (strip cartoon, from 1968). The line became a motto for the Freak Brothers and their following.

## Ron Shelton (b. 1945)

US FILM-MAKER

His films include *Bull Durham* (1988), *Blaze* (1989) and *White Men Can't Jump* (1992). He appeared as himself in *Looking for Oscar* (1999).

1 I believe in the Church of Baseball. I tried all the major religions and most of the minor ones. I've worshipped Buddha, Allah, Brahma, Vishnu, Siva, trees, mushrooms and Isadora Duncan. I know things. For instance: there are 108 beads in a Catholic rosary and there are 108 stitches in a baseball. When I learned that, I gave Jesus a chance.

Opening monologue in *Bull Durham* (film, 1988, written and directed by Ron Shelton)

2 Nobody on this planet ever really chooses each other. I mean, it's all a question of quantum physics, molecular attraction and timing.

Anne Savoy (Susan Sarandon), in ibid.

3 The world is made for people who aren't cursed with self-awareness.

Anne Savoy (Susan Sarandon), in ibid.

## Sam Shepard (b. 1943)

US PLAYWRIGHT, SCREENWRITER AND ACTOR

Original name Samuel Shepard Rogers. In 1974 he became playwright-in-residence at the Magic Theatre, San Francisco, where most of his subsequent work has been first produced. His plays, often concerning spiritual vacuity and the mythology of the American West, include *Killer's Head* (1975), *Buried Child* (1978, Pulitzer Prize) and *Simpatico* (1994). He has acted in *Days of Heaven* (1978), among other films, and he wrote the screenplay for *Paris Texas* (1984).

1 A concert audience has a face. It looks worked upon. Wild eyed. Stimulated from a distant source like a laboratory experiment. As though the stage event, the action being watched and heard, is only a mirror image of some unseen phenomenon.

*Rolling Thunder Logbook*, 'Audience' (1977)

2 Fans are more dangerous than a man with a weapon because they're after something invisible. Some imagined 'something'. At least with a gun you know what you're facing.

ibid. 'Fans'

3 All the land has been discovered. Some parts of hidden South America maybe still lie out of sight, but this land here has been discovered. Every inch. Now the move is inner space. New religions. est. Gurus. Meditation. Outer space is too expensive and only lies within the reach of the government or corporate industry.

ibid. 'Explore'

4 In this business we make movies, American movies. Leave the films to the French.

Saul, in *True West*, act 2, sc. 5 (1980)

5 Ideas emerge from plays, not the other way round.

'Language, Visualization and the Inner Library', publ. in *American Dreams* (ed. Bonnie Marranca, 1981)

6 I feel there are territories within us that are totally unknown. Huge, mysterious, and dangerous territories . . . And if we don't enter those in art of one kind or another, whether it's playwriting, or painting, or music, or what-

ever, then I don't understand the point of doing anything. It's the reason I write. I try to go into parts of myself that are unknown.

Quoted in *The Other American Drama*, ch. 3 (1994) by Marc Robinson

## Norman Sherry (b. 1925)

BRITISH ACADEMIC AND AUTHOR

He wrote on GRAHAM GREENE and Jane Austen, but his special interest has been Joseph Conrad, on whom he has published numerous works, for instance *Conrad and His World* (1972).

1 The facts of a person's life will, like murder, come out.

*International Herald Tribune* 15 September 1989. Referring to his biography *Life of Graham Greene 1904–39* (1989).

## Robert E. Sherwood (1896–1955)

US PLAYWRIGHT

Full name Robert Emmet Sherwood. Editor of *Life* (1924–8) and a member of DOROTHY PARKER's Algonquin Round table, he was awarded three Pulitzer Prizes for his plays *Idiot's Delight*, (1936), *Abe Lincoln in Illinois* (1939), and *There Shall be No Night* (1941), and one for his biographical *Roosevelt and Hopkins* (1949). He was also chief speech-writer for FRANKLIN D. ROOSEVELT.

1 All Coolidge had to do in 1924 was to keep his mean trap shut, to be elected. All Harding had to do in 1920 was repeat 'Avoid foreign entanglements.' All Hoover had to do in 1928 was to endorse Coolidge. All Roosevelt had to do in 1932 was to point to Hoover.

Quoted in *Wit's End* (ed. Robert E Drennan 1968)

## Carol Shields (b. 1935)

US-BORN CANADIAN AUTHOR

Coming to notice with *The Republic of Love* (1992), she won wide acclaim for *The Stone Diaries* (1993), a chronicle of the life of an 'ordinary' Canadian woman. *Larry's Party* (1996) is written from the male point of view.

1 Canada is a country where nothing seems ever to happen. A country always dressed in its Sunday go-to-meeting clothes. A country you wouldn't ask to dance a second waltz. Clean. Christian. Dull. Quiescent. But growing. Yes, it must be admitted, the Dominion is growing.

*The Stone Diaries*, ch. 3 (1993)

## Clare Short (b. 1946)

BRITISH POLITICIAN

A popular and outspoken Labour MP for Birmingham Ladywood since 1983, she was opposition spokesperson for women (1993–5), campaigning against nudity in the tabloids. She joined the shadow cabinet in 1995 and was appointed Secretary of State for International Development in the Labour government of 1997.

1 Political correctness is a concept invented by hardrightwing forces to defend their right to be racist, to treat women in a degrading way and to be truly vile about gay people. They invent this idea of people who are politically correct, with a rigid, monstrous attitude to life so they can attack them. But we have all had to learn to modify our language. That's all part of being a decent human being.

Interview in the *Guardian* 18 February 1995

2 It will be golden elephants next.

Quoted in the *Observer* 24 August 1997. Referring to calls to increase aid to Montserrat following the eruption there.

3 Lloyd George and Roosevelt had mistresses, no one dwelt

on it. Now we have to discuss oral sex. It's not just dumbing down, it's a sort of crassness.

Interview in the *Daily Telegraph* 31 January 1998

4 Hubris is, certainly, the disease of politics. The health and safety commission should send everyone a warning.

Interview in the *Independent* 28 September 1998

## Nigel Short (b. 1965)
BRITISH CHESS PLAYER

An international master from 1980, he became the youngest ever grandmaster from Britain in 1984. He resigned from the international chess federation FIDE in 1993 to form the Professional Chess Association with GARY KASPAROV.

1 Chess is ruthless: you've got to be prepared to kill people.

Quoted in the *Observer* 11 August 1991

## Jerry Siegel (1914–96)
US CARTOONIST
and
## Joe Shuster (1914–92)
CANADIAN-BORN US CARTOONIST

Schoolmates Siegel and Shuster devised their Man of Steel, Superman, as a prototype in a fanzine in 1933, and the hero was taken up by Action Comics in 1938, later appearing on radio and TV and in films. Siegel wrote the adventures of Superman until 1948 and then again 1959–65, in the interim scripting several newspaper strips such as Funnyman and Ken Winston. Shuster drew Superman until 1947 and later collaborated with Siegel in creating Funnyman.

1 Is it a bird? Is it a plane? No, it's SUPERMAN!

Voices in the crowd in *Superman* (cartoon, from 1933). Sometimes rendered as 'It's a bird . . . It's a plane . . .'

2 Faster than a speeding bullet! More powerful than a locomotive! Able to leap tall buildings at a single bound! . . . Strange visitor from another planet, who came to earth with powers and abilities far beyond those of mortal men. Superman! Who can change the course of mighty rivers, bend steel in his bare hands, and who . . . fights a never ending battle for truth, justice and the American way!

Voiceover in *Superman* (radio adaptation, from 1940). Spoken at the start of each radio (and later TV) broadcast.

## Alan Sillitoe (b. 1928)
BRITISH AUTHOR

A factory worker who left school at the age of fourteen, he has been called one of the most articulate 'angry young men' for his stories of working-class heroes, as in his first book *Saturday Night and Sunday Morning* (1958, filmed 1960) and the novella *The Loneliness of the Long-Distance Runner* (1959, filmed 1962).

1 The loneliness of the long-distance runner.

Title of novel (1959)

## Ignazio Silone (1900–78)
ITALIAN NOVELIST AND JOURNALIST

Original name Secondo Tranquilli. One of the founder members of the Italian Communist Party, he began to write when forced into exile in 1930. Such novels as his first, *Fontamara* (1930), and *Bread and Wine* (1937), portray socialist heroes and ideological clashes. After the Second World War he returned to Italy and political life as a leader of the Democratic Socialist Party but retired in 1950. In a symposium with ARTHUR KOESTLER in 1968 he called himself 'a socialist without a party, a Christian without a church'.

1 Fascism was a counter-revolution against a revolution that never took place.

*The School for Dictators*, ch. 4 (1938)

2 The final conflict will be between the Communists and the ex-Communists.

Quoted in *The Unfinished Country*, pt 4, 'The Hero as Ex-Communist' (1959) by MAX LERNER. Remark to Communist leader Palmiro Togliatti.

## Georges Simenon (1903–85)
BELGIAN CRIME WRITER

The prodigious author of over 500 novels, he made his name with the Maigret detective series (from 1931), known the world over through film and television adaptations. 'I have no imagination,' he once admitted, 'I take everything from life.'

1 Writing is not a profession, but a vocation of unhappiness.

Interview in the *Paris Review* summer 1955, repr. in *Writers at Work* (first series, ed. Malcolm Cowley, 1958)

## Paul Simon (b. 1941)
US SINGER AND SONGWRITER

Principal songwriter in a long-standing folksinging partnership with Art Garfunkel, he was responsible for 'The Sound of Silence' (1964) and 'Bridge Over Troubled Water' (1970) among many other songs. He pursued a solo career from 1971, using music from around the world for the albums *Graceland* (1986) and *Rhythm of the Saints* (1990).

1 Hello darkness, my old friend,
I've come to talk with you again.

'The Sound of Silence' (song) on the album *Wednesday Morning 3 a.m.* (1964) by Simon and Garfunkel. Given an electric backing, the song was a hit single in 1965 and reappeared on the album *Sounds of Silence* (1966).

2 And the sign said, 'The words of the prophets
Are written on the subway walls
And tenement halls'
And whispered in the sounds of silence.

ibid.

3 Hiding in my room, safe within my womb,
I touch no one and no one touches me.
I am a rock,
I am an island.

'I Am a Rock' (song) on the album *The Paul Simon Songbook* (1965)

4 And here's to you, Mrs Robinson
Jesus loves you more than you will know.
God bless you please, Mrs Robinson
Heaven holds a place for those who pray.

'Mrs Robinson' (song) in the film *The Graduate* (1967), released on the soundtrack and, in a different version, on the album *Bookends* (1968) by Simon and Garfunkel

5 They've all gone to look for America.

'America' (song) on the album *Bookends* (1968) by Simon and Garfunkel

6 When times get rough,
And friends just can't be found
Like a bridge over troubled water
I will lay me down.

'Bridge Over Troubled Water' (song) on the album *Bridge Over Troubled Water* (1970) by Simon and Garfunkel. The words are said to have been inspired by 'Mary Don't You Weep', a song by the gospel group the Swan Silvertones, which includes the line 'I'll be a bridge over deep water if you trust in my name'.

7 One man's ceiling is another man's floor.

'One Man's Ceiling is Another Man's Floor' (song) on the album *There Goes Rhymin' Simon* (1973)

8 Medicine is magical and magical is art
The Boy in the Bubble

And the baby with the baboon heart
And I believe
These are the days of lasers in the jungle
Lasers in the jungle somewhere
Staccato signals of constant information
A loose affiliation of millionaires.

'The Boy in the Bubble' (song, with music by Paul Simon and Forere Motloheloa) on the album *Graceland* (1986)

9 The Mississippi Delta was shining
Like a National guitar.

'Graceland' (song) on ibid.

10 Improvisation is too good to leave to chance.

*International Herald Tribune* 12 October 1990

## Nina Simone (b. 1933)

US SINGER, SONGWRITER AND PIANIST

Original name Eunice Kathleen Waymon. Her career in jazz and soul music spans four decades, starting with the double release of 'I Love You Porgy' and 'My Baby Just Cares for Me' in 1959. In the 1960s she was the 'poet laureate of the civil rights movement' with protest songs such as 'Mississippi Goddam' (1964) and 'Why? (The King of Love is Dead)' (1968). She later lived in Africa and Europe.

1 Hey! Do you see it, can't you feel it
It's all in the air
I can't stand oppression much longer
Somebody say a prayer.

Alabama's got me so upset
Tennessee made me lose my rest
And everybody knows about Mississippi – Goddam.

'Mississippi Goddam' (song) on album *Nina Simone in Concert* (1964). Inspired by the murder of Medgar Evers, one of a series of racist murders of children.

2 To be young, gifted and black
Is where it's at!

'Young, Gifted and Black' (song, written by Weldon J. Irvine Jr, 1969) on the album *Black Gold* (1970)

## O.J. Simpson (b. 1947)

US FOOTBALLER AND COMMENTATOR

Full name Orenthal James Simpson. One of the greatest running backs in the history of American football, he played for the Buffalo Bills (1969–78) and was National Football Player of the Decade in 1979, retiring the same year to pursue a broadcasting career. In 1994 he was charged with the murder of his estranged wife and her friend but was acquitted after a sensational televised trial, only to be found guilty in a civil suit in 1997 when damages were awarded against him.

1 The only thing that endures is character. Fame and wealth – all that is illusion. All that endures is character.

Remark in November 1995, quoted in the *Guardian* 30 December 1995

## Frank Sinatra (1915–98)

US SINGER AND SCREEN ACTOR

An idol in the 1940s with such hits as 'Without a Song' and the film *Anchors Away* (1945), he suffered a slump in popularity until his role in *From Here to Eternity* (film, 1953) won him an Oscar. The albums *Songs for Swinging Lovers* (1956) and *Come Fly With Me* (1959) helped to make him a top-selling artist in the 1950s and 1960s. His reputation later suffered from rumours of Mafia involvement. The singer and politician Sonny Bono commented: 'Frank walks like America. Cocksure.'

1 Show me a guy who has feelings, and I'll show you a sucker.

Johnny Baron (Frank Sinatra), in *Suddenly* (film, 1954, screenplay by Richard Sale, directed by Lewis Allen)

2 Strangers in the night, exchanging glances
Wond'ring in the night, what were the chances
We'd be sharing love before the night was through.

'Strangers in the Night' (song, written by Charles Singleton and Eddie Snyder with music by Bert Kaempfert) on album *Strangers in the Night* (1966)

3 And now the end is near
And so I face the final curtain,
I'll state my case of which I'm certain.
I've lived a life that's full, I traveled each and ev'ry
highway,
And more, much more than this. I did it my way.

'My Way' (song, 1969, written by Claude François, Jacques Revaux and Paul Anka) on the album *My Way* (1969). The Canadian songwriter Paul Anka adapted the song from a French original, 'Comme d'habitude', for Sinatra, whose signature tune it became.

4 Ol' blue eyes is back.

Title of album (1973). Referring to a decision made in 1970 to retire.

5 [On rock 'n' roll] The most brutal, ugly, desperate, vicious form of expression it has been my misfortune to hear.

Quoted in *Sound Effects: Youth, Leisure and the Politics of Rock*, ch. 5 (1979) by Simon Frith

6 I could go on stage and make a pizza and they'd still come to see me.

Quoted in the *Independent on Sunday* 31 May 1992

## Nancy Sinatra (b. 1940)

US SINGER

The daughter of FRANK SINATRA, she launched her career as a pop singer in 1965 and had six hits in 1966–7 under the tutelage of Lee Hazlewood, including 'These Boots are Made for Walkin'' (1966) and, duetting with her father, 'Somethin' Stupid' (1967).

1 These boots are made for walkin'
And that's just what they'll do
One of these days these boots are going to walk all over
you.

'These Boots are Made for Walkin'' (song, 1966, written by Lee Hazlewood)

## Iain Sinclair (b. 1943)

BRITISH AUTHOR

Described by writer Peter Ackroyd as 'the De Quincey of contemporary English letters', he has published, among other works, the poetry collection *Flesh Eggs and Scalp Metal* (1983), the novel *White Chappell, Scarlet Tracings* (1989) and *Lights Out for the Territory* (1997), a description of journeys in London.

1 An involuntary return to the point of departure is, without doubt, the most disturbing of all journeys.

*Downriver*, 'Riverside Opportunities', sect. 9 (1991)

## Upton Sinclair (1878–1968)

US NOVELIST AND SOCIAL REFORMER

Regarding his writing mainly as the expression of his political beliefs, he published more than eighty titles, of which the best known is *The Jungle* (1906), a novel about immigrant workers in the Chicago meat industry. Other works include *Oil!* (1927) and *Dragon's Teeth* (1942), for which he won a Pulitzer Prize. He ran for election to political office several times, without success.

1 It is up to you to prove that human beings do not have to be prowling wolves or sly lynxes, but can be rational, just, and kindly members of a commonwealth.

*I, Governor of California and How I Ended Poverty in California* (Democratic Party campaign pamphlet, 1934)

2 Co-operation is the coming idea.

*Co-op: A Novel of Living Together*, ch. 14 (1936)

3 Concerning *The Jungle* I wrote that 'I aimed at the public's heart, and by accident I hit it in the stomach'. I helped to clean up the yards and improve the country's meat supply. Now the workers have strong unions and, I hope, are able to look out for themselves.

*The Autobiography*, ch. 5, sect. 14 (1963)

## (Sir) Donald Sinden (b. 1923)
BRITISH ACTOR

A thespian of the old school, he has varied his work on stage from the classical, notably in Shakespearian roles, to modern comedies, for example *There's a Girl in My Soup* (1966) and *Present Laughter* (1981). His films include *The Cruel Sea* (1953) and *The Day of the Jackal* (1973) and he has also appeared frequently on television.

1 Actors ought to be larger than life. You come across quite enough ordinary, nondescript people in daily life and I don't see why you should be subjected to them on the stage too.

*Observer* 12 February 1989

## Peter Singer (b. 1946)
AUSTRALIAN PHILOSOPHER

A utilitarian philosopher who has been denounced as 'professor Death' in the *Wall Street Journal* for his views on the value of human life, he is the author of *Animal Liberation* (1975), in which he coined the word 'speciesism', and *Practical Ethics* (1979). He stood as a Green candidate in the 1996 Australian election and was appointed Professor of Bioethics at Princeton in 1999.

1 Ethics is not an ideal system which is all very noble in theory but no good in practice. The reverse of this is closer to the truth: an ethical judgement that is no good in practice must suffer from a theoretical defect as well, for the whole point of ethical judgement is to guide practice.

*Practical Ethics*, ch. 1 (1979)

2 Killing them [infants], therefore, cannot be equated with killing normal human beings, or any other self-conscious beings. No infant – disabled or not – has as strong a claim to life as beings capable of seeing themselves as distinct entities, existing over time.

ibid. ch. 7

3 The difficult issue is not whether the end can ever justify the means, but which means are justified by which ends.

ibid. ch. 11

4 The tyranny of human over nonhuman animals . . . has caused and today is still causing an amount of pain and suffering that can only be compared with that which resulted from the centuries of tyranny by white humans over black humans. The struggle against this tyranny is a struggle as important as any of the moral and social issues that have been fought over in recent years.

*Animal Liberation: Towards an End to Man's Inhumanity*, Preface (1975)

5 If possessing a higher degree of intelligence does not entitle one human to use another for his own ends, how can it entitle humans to exploit nonhumans for the same purpose?

ibid. ch. 1

6 The belief that human life, and only human life, is sacrosanct is a form of speciesism.

ibid.

## (Dame) Edith Sitwell (1887–1964)
BRITISH POET AND CRITIC

Her striking, eccentric appearance, which she herself called 'the ordinary carried to a high degree of pictorial perfection', was made famous by the photographs of Cecil Beaton, for whom she possessed 'the mad moonstruck ethereality of a ghost'. Her experimental poetry eschewed traditional rhythms and imagery in favour of dance and jazz rhythms, for example in *Façade* (1923), which she recited through a microphone to the accompaniment of music by William Walton. She also wrote prose works.

1 Jane, Jane,
Tall as a crane,
The morning light creaks down again.

'Aubade', publ. in *Façade* (1923). Opening lines of poem.

2 Still falls the Rain–
Dark as the world of man, black as our loss –
Blind as the nineteen hundred and forty nails
Upon the Cross.

'The Raids, 1940. Night and Dawn', publ. in *Street Songs* (1942). Opening lines of poem later set to music by BENJAMIN BRITTEN.

3 I have often wished I had time to cultivate modesty . . . But I am too busy thinking about myself.

Quoted in the *Observer* 30 April 1950

4 Eccentricity is *not*, as dull people would have us believe, a form of madness. It is often a kind of innocent pride, and the man of genius and the aristocrat are frequently regarded as eccentrics because genius and aristocrat are entirely unafraid of and uninfluenced by the opinions and vagaries of the crowd.

*Taken Care Of*, ch. 15 (1965)

5 Vulgarity is, in reality, nothing but a modern, chic, pert descendant of the goddess Dullness.

ibid. ch. 19

## Robert Skidelsky (b. 1939)
BRITISH HISTORIAN AND ACADEMIC

Baron Skidelsky of Tilton. An eminent historian, he has been Professor of Political Economy at Warwick since 1990 and was House of Lords opposition spokesman on culture, media and sport (1997–8) and on treasury affairs (1998–9). His books include *Oswald Mosley* (1975) and *The World After Communism* (1994).

1 Historians are pessimistic by nature, because the only future they can imagine is the past.

Said at Cheltenham Festival of Literature 6–15 October 1995, quoted in the *Daily Telegraph* 21 October 1995

## Cornelia Otis Skinner (1901–79)
US AUTHOR AND ACTRESS

Famous for her stage monologues and plays, such as *The Pleasure of His Company* (1958), she is also known for her humorous books, notably *Excuse It, Please!* (1936), and the collections *Nuts in May* (1950) and *The Ape in Me* (1959).

1 It's not that I don't want to be a beauty, that I don't yearn to be dripping with glamor. It's just that I can't see how any woman can find time to do to herself all the things that must apparently be done to make herself beautiful and, having once done them, how anyone without the strength of mind of a foreign missionary can keep up such a regime.

*Dithers and Jitters*, 'The Skin-Game' (1937)

2 That food has always been, and will continue to be, the basis for one of our greater snobbisms does not explain the fact that the attitude toward the food choice of others is becoming more and more heatedly exclusive until it may well turn into one of those forms of bigotry against which gallant little committees are constantly planning campaigns in the cause of justice and decency.

*Bottoms Up!*, 'Your Very Good Health' (1950)

3 It is disturbing to discover in oneself these curious revelations of the validity of the Darwinian theory. If it is true

that we have sprung from the ape, there are occasions when my own spring appears not to have been very far.

*The Ape in Me*, 'The Ape in Me' (1959)

## Wayne Sleep (b. 1948)

BRITISH DANCER AND CHOREOGRAPHER

Small of stature and extrovert in character, he was principal dancer with the Royal Ballet (1973–83) and performed in the original production of *Cats* (1981). He formed his own company, Dash, in 1980, and adapted his TV series *The Hot Shoe Show* (1983–4) for the stage, fusing classical, jazz, tap and disco.

1 I am the chip on my own shoulder.

Interview in *In the Psychiatrist's Chair*, BBC Radio 4, 13 September 1998

## Grace Slick (b. 1939)

US ROCK MUSICIAN

Starting out with the San Francisco band the Great Society in 1965, she joined Jefferson Airplane as lead singer and songwriter in 1966. After such successful albums as *Surrealistic Pillow* (1967) and *Volunteers* (1969) Airplane mutated into Jefferson Starship in 1974, which had a top-selling album in *Red Octopus* (1975).

1 One pill makes you larger
And one pill makes you small.
And the ones that mother gives you
Don't do anything at all.
Go ask Alice
When she's ten feet tall.

'White Rabbit' (song) on the album *Surrealistic Pillow* (1967) by Jefferson Airplane. The song was originally written for Slick's band the Great Society.

2 Remember what the dormouse said:
'Feed your head'.

ibid. In an interview in 1977, Slick explained: ' "Feed your head" doesn't mean take every fucking drug that comes along, "Feed your head" means read . . . listen and read' (quoted in *Shaman Woman, Mainline Lady*, ed. Cynthia Palmer and Michael Horowitz, 1982).

## Joe Slovo (1926–95)

LITHUANIAN-BORN SOUTH AFRICAN ACTIVIST

Although he was white and in exile for twenty-seven years, he was one of the most influential figures in the African National Congress, and on his return to South Africa in 1990 a key negotiator between the nationalist parties and the government. Chief of Staff of the ANC's military wing (1985–7) and general secretary of the South African Communist Party (1987–91), he was Minister of Housing in MANDELA's government (1994–5). He was married to the assassinated anti-apartheid activist Ruth First. 'In most families it is the children who leave home,' their daughter Gillian Slovo wrote in her memoirs. 'In mine it was the parents.'

1 There are only two sorts of people in life you can trust – good Christians and good Communists.

*Independent* 4 November 1988

2 Let us look at the capitalist roots of the racial miseries of our own country, South Africa. The real question is not whether a system works, but for whom it works.

Quoted in obituary in the *Guardian* 7 January 1995. Criticizing the notion that capitalism works and socialism has failed.

## Elizabeth Smart (1913–86)

CANADIAN NOVELIST AND POET

Her greatest work *By Grand Central Station I Sat Down and Wept* (1945) was inspired by her own affair with poet George Barker, narrated in highly charged language. In 1977 she published *The*

*Assumption of the Rogues and the Rascals*, which dealt with her experiences in England.

1 Vanity is a vital aid to nature: completely and absolutely necessary to life. It is one of nature's ways to bind you to the earth.

Journal entry 25 June 1933, publ. in *Necessary Secrets*, pt 1, ch. 2 (ed. Alice Van Wart, 1991)

2 O I know they make war because they want peace; they hate so that they may live; and they destroy the present to make the world safe for the future. When have they not done and said they did it for that?

ibid. 18 February 1941

3 By Grand Central Station I sat down and wept.

Title of book (1945)

4 I am over-run, jungled in my bed, I am infested with a menagerie of desires: my heart is eaten by a dove, a cat scrambles in the cave of my sex, hounds in my bed obey a whipmaster who cries nothing but havoc as the hours test my endurance with an accumulation of tortures. Who, if I cried, would hear me among the angelic orders?

*By Grand Central Station I Sat Down and Wept*, pt 1 (1945)

## Alfred E. Smith (1873–1944)

US POLITICIAN

Full name Alfred Emanuel Smith, known as Al Smith. He was four times Democratic Governor of New York (1918–26) and in 1928 the first Roman Catholic to run for the presidency. Nicknamed the 'Happy Warrior', he stood as a champion of urban America but was defeated by HERBERT HOOVER.

1 All the ills of democracy can be cured by more democracy.

Speech in Albany, 27 June 1933, quoted in *The New York Times* 28 June 1933

2 No sane local official who has hung up an empty stocking over the municipal fireplace, is going to shoot Santa Claus just before a hard Christmas.

*New Outlook* December 1933. The phrase 'Nobody shoots at Santa Claus' was used repeatedly by Smith in campaign speeches in 1936, attacking FRANKLIN D. ROOSEVELT and what were claimed to be the spendthrift policies of the New Deal.

## (Sir) Cyril Smith (b. 1928)

BRITISH POLITICIAN

Conspicuous for his twenty-seven-stone figure, he was the Liberal (1972–88) and Liberal Democrat (1988–92) MP for Rochdale, and Liberal Chief Whip (1975–6).

1 [Of the House of Commons] This place is the longest running farce in the West End.

Said in July 1973, quoted in *Big Cyril*, ch. 8 (autobiography, 1977) by Cyril Smith

## Delia Smith (b. 1941)

BRITISH COOKERY WRITER AND BROADCASTER

Cookery writer for the London *Evening Standard* (1972–85) among other publications and host of a TV show, she is a household name in Britain. Her books consistently top the bestseller lists. She was criticized for the 'back-to-basics' approach of her *How to Cook* (1998) but retains a devotional following.

1 A hen's egg is, quite simply, a work of art, a masterpiece of design and construction with, it has to be said, brilliant packaging!

*How to Cook* bk 1, ch. 1 (1998)

2 If you sometimes feel depressed or let down, if you're suffering from the pressures of life, or simply having a plain old grey day, my advice is to roast a chicken.

*How to Cook*, bk 2, ch. 4 (1999)

## Ebbe Roe Smith

US SCREENWRITER

1 I've never liked you. You wanna know why? You don't curse. I don't trust the man who doesn't curse. Not a fuck or a shit in all these years. Real men curse, Prendergast.

Capt. Yardley (Raymond J. Barry), in *Falling Down* (film, 1993, screenplay by Ebbe Roe Smith, directed by Joel Schumacher). Bidding farewell to Prendergast (Robert Duvall) on his last day in the Los Angeles police department.

## F.E. Smith (1872–1930)

BRITISH LAWYER AND POLITICIAN

Full name Frederick Edwin Smith, First Earl of Birkenhead. A renowned speaker and wit, he was elected a Conservative MP in 1906 and became Attorney-General (1915–19) and Lord Chancellor (1919–22). He played a key role in the Irish Settlement (1921) and was Secretary of State for India (1924–8). MARGOT ASQUITH thought him 'very clever, but his brains go to his head'.

1 The world continues to offer glittering prizes to those who have stout hearts and sharp swords.

Rectorial Address, Glasgow University, 7 November 1923, publ. in *The Times* 8 November 1923. Smith, whose whole life was seen as a quest for 'glittering prizes', provided the title of FREDERIC RAPHAEL's novel about Cambridge graduates, *The Glittering Prizes* (1976).

## Ian Smith (b. 1919)

RHODESIAN POLITICIAN AND PRIME MINISTER

He founded the Rhodesian Front (later Republican Front) in 1962, became Prime Minister of a white minority government in 1964 and unilaterally declared Rhodesian independence in 1965. He conceded majority rule in 1979 but remained active in the Republican Front until 1987.

1 We have the happiest Africans in the world.

Quoted in the *Observer* 20 November 1971

2 Let me say again, I don't believe in black majority rule in Rhodesia – not in a thousand years. I believe in blacks and whites working together.

Speech broadcast 20 March 1976, quoted in the *Sunday Times* 21 March 1976

## Joan Smith (b. 1953)

BRITISH JOURNALIST AND AUTHOR

Known as a commentator on women in society, she wrote for the *Sunday Times* (1979–84) and has published *Mysogynies* (1989), *What Men Say* (1994) and *Different for Girls* (1997).

1 What Diana seemed to have forgotten, and most people were too dazzled by her performance to recall, was the traditional fate of the women with whom she had chosen to bracket herself . . . they all wind up young, beautiful and dead.

*Different for Girls: How Culture Creates Women*, pt 1 (1997)

## Lillian Smith (1897–1966)

US AUTHOR

Challenging the attitudes of America's Old South, her fiction describes segregation and its dehumanizing effects. Her novel *Strange Fruit* (1944) was a bestseller and sold more than 3 million copies in her lifetime. Other work includes *Killers of the Dream* (1949). She also worked for the Congress on Racial Equality (1946–66), but resigned when she could not countenance militancy.

1 To find the point where hypothesis and fact meet; the delicate equilibrium between dream and reality; the place where fantasy and earthly things are metamorphosed into a work of art; the hour when faith in the future becomes knowledge of the past; to lay down one's power for others in need; to shake off the old ordeal and get ready for the new; to question, knowing that never can the full answer be found; to accept uncertainties quietly, even our incomplete knowledge of God; this is what man's journey is about, I think.

*The Journey*, ch. 15 (1954)

2 The human heart dares not stay away too long from that which hurt it most. There is a return journey to anguish that few of us are released from making.

*Killers of the Dream*, pt 1, ch. 1 (1949, rev. 1961)

3 Man, born of woman, has found it a hard thing to forgive her for giving him birth. The patriarchal protest against the ancient matriarch has borne strange fruit through the years.

ibid. pt 2, ch. 4

## Liz Smith (b. 1923)

US COLUMNIST

Known for decades as a gossip queen, she is famous for her column in the *New York Daily News* (from 1976), syndicated to more than sixty newspapers. She has also contributed articles to *Cosmopolitan*, *Vogue*, *Good Housekeeping* and *Esquire*, among other publications.

1 Gossip is news running ahead of itself in a red satin dress.

*American Way* syndicated column 3 September 1985

2 Most good gossip columnists have a touch of Savonarola in them.

*International Herald Tribune* 4 April 1991

## Logan Pearsall Smith (1865–1946)

US-BORN BRITISH ESSAYIST AND APHORIST

He settled in England and took British citizenship in 1913, earning his living as a lexicographer, bibliographer and essayist. His works of criticism include *Milton and His Modern Critics* (1940), but he is chiefly remembered for his collection of aphorisms collected in *Afterthoughts* (1931) and *All Trivia* (1933, rev. 1945).

1 Happiness is a wine of the rarest vintage, and seems insipid to a vulgar taste.

*Afterthoughts*, 'Life and Human Nature' (1931)

2 How awful to reflect that what people say of us is true!

ibid.

3 There are few sorrows, however poignant, in which a good income is of no avail.

ibid.

4 Growing old is not a gradual decline, but a series of drops, full of sorrow, from one ledge to another below it. But when we pick ourselves up we find our bones are, after all, not broken; while level enough and not unpleasing is the new terrace which lies unexplored before us.

ibid. 'Age and Death'

5 There is more felicity on the far side of baldness than young men can possibly imagine.

ibid.

6 The old know what they want; the young are sad and bewildered.

ibid.

7 What music is more enchanting than the voices of young people, when you can't hear what they say?

ibid.

8 There are people who are beautiful in dilapidation, like old houses that were hideous when new.

ibid.

9 The denunciation of the young is a necessary part of

the hygiene of older people, and greatly assists in the circulation of their blood.

ibid.

10 The mere process of growing old together will make the slightest acquaintance seem like bosom friends.

ibid.

11 I can't forgive my friends for dying; I don't find these vanishing acts of theirs at all amusing.

ibid.

12 Those who set out to serve both God and Mammon soon discover that there isn't a God.

ibid. 'Other People'

13 Most people sell their souls, and live with a good conscience on the proceeds.

ibid.

14 When they come downstairs from their Ivory Towers, Idealists are very apt to walk straight into the gutter.

ibid.

15 It is the wretchedness of being rich that you live with rich people.

ibid. 'In the World'

16 To suppose, as we all suppose, that we could be rich and not behave as the rich behave, is like supposing that we could drink all day and keep absolutely sober.

ibid.

17 The test of a vocation is the love of the drudgery it involves.

ibid. 'Art and Letters'

18 A bestseller is the gilded tomb of a mediocre talent.

ibid. See also CYRIL CONNOLLY 2.

19 The notion of making money by popular work, and then retiring to do good work, is the most familiar of all the devil's traps for artists.

ibid.

20 Aphorisms are salted and not sugared almonds at Reason's feast.

ibid. 'Myself'

21 People say that life is the thing, but I prefer reading.

ibid.

22 We need two kinds of acquaintances, one to complain to, while to the others we boast.

*All Trivia*, 'In the World' (1933)

23 What I like in a good Author isn't what he says, but what he whispers.

ibid. 'Art and Letters'

24 There is one thing that matters – to set a chime of words tinkling in the minds of a few fastidious people.

Quoted by CYRIL CONNOLLY in obituary, the *New Statesman* 9 March 1946. In answer to the question, two weeks before his death, whether he had discovered any meaning in life.

## Mark E. Smith (b. 1957)
BRITISH ROCK MUSICIAN

The driving force behind the industrial punk band the Fall since 1977 and its only constant member, he contributes scathing, often surreal lyrics delivered in a hectoring rant. The group's numerous recordings include their debut single 'Bingo Master's Break Out' (1978) and the album *This Nation's Saving Grace* (1985).

1 The media overestimates its own importance. I was on the cover of everything for three years but I still only had half a bottle of milk in the fridge.

Said in 1990, quoted in the *New Musical Express* 4 February 1995

## Patti Smith (b. 1946)
US ROCK MUSICIAN AND POET

A close associate of photographer Robert Mapplethorpe, she wrote avant-garde poetry, for instance *Seventh Heaven* (1971), and co-wrote the play *Cowboy Mouth* with SAM SHEPARD (1971). She performed her verse to a musical backing and created the Patti Smith Group in 1974, whose album *Horses* (1975) was one of the key records of the US punk movement.

1 Jesus died for somebody's sins but not mine.

Preamble to 'Gloria' (song, written by VAN MORRISON) on the album *Horses* (1975)

2 There's no bullshit going down with rock and roll. It's an honest form and one of the most open. It encompasses poetry, jazz and just about anything you can imagine . . . it is the highest form. It goes beyond color, gender – anything.

*Cashbox* 24 January 1976

## Stevie Smith (1902–71)
BRITISH POET AND NOVELIST

Original name Florence Margaret Smith, she was nicknamed 'Stevie' after the jockey Steve Donoghue, on account of her small stature. Her unconventional poetry, in turn humorous and serious, was illustrated with her own whimsical line drawings. She achieved success with her first fiction publication, *Novel on Yellow Paper* (1936), and with such verse collections as *Mother, What Is Man?* (1942) and *Not Waving But Drowning* (1957). 'She looks at the world with a mental squint,' remarked SEAMUS HEANEY, 'there is a discouraging wobble in the mirror she holds up to nature.'

1 If you cannot have your dear husband for a comfort and a delight, for a breadwinner and a crosspatch, for a sofa, chair or a hot-water bottle, one can use him as a Cross to be Borne.

Narrator (Pompey Casmilus) in *Novel on Yellow Paper* (1936)

2 A good time was had by all.

Title of collection of verse (1937). Given as the original source of this expression in *A Dictionary of Catch Phrases* by Eric Partridge (ed. Paul Beale, 1985).

3 This Englishwoman is so refined
She has no bosom and no behind.

'This Englishwoman', publ. in *A Good Time Was Had By All* (1937)

4 I'm sorry to say my dear wife is a dreamer,
And as she dreams she gets paler and leaner.
'Then be off to your Dream, with his fly-away hat,
I'll stay with the girls who are happy and fat.'

'*BE OFF!*' publ. in *Mother, What is Man?* (1942)

5 Fourteen-year-old, why must you giggle and dote,
Fourteen-year-old, why are you such a goat?
I'm fourteen years old, that is the reason,
I giggle and dote in season.

'The Conventionalist', publ. in ibid.

6 I may be smelly, and I may be old,
Rough in my pebbles, reedy in my pools,
But where my fish float by I bless their swimming
And I like people to bathe in me, especially women.

'The River God', publ. in *Harold's Leap* (1950)

7 Oh, no no no, it was too cold always
(Still the dead one lay moaning)
I was much too far out all my life
And not waving but drowning.

'Not Waving But Drowning', publ. in *Not Waving But Drowning* (1957)

8 Marred pleasure's best, shadow makes the sun strong.

'The Queen and the Young Princess', publ. in ibid.

9 People who are always praising the past
And especially the times of faith as best

Ought to go and live in the Middle Ages
And be burnt at the stake as witches and sages.

'The Past', publ. in ibid.

10 All Poetry has to do is to make a strong communication.
All the poet has to do is to listen. The poet is not an
important fellow. There will always be another poet.

'My Muse' (1960), publ. in *Me Again: Uncollected Writings* (ed. Jack
Barbera and William McBrien, 1981)

11 Why does my Muse only speak when she is unhappy?
She does not, I only listen when I am unhappy
When I am happy I live and despise writing
For my Muse this cannot but be dispiriting.

'My Muse', publ. in *Selected Poems* (1962)

12 Oh these illegitimate babies!
Oh girls, girls,
Silly little valuable things,
You should have said, No, I am valuable,
And again, It is because I am valuable
I say, No.

'Valuable', publ. in *The Frog Prince and Other Poems* (1966)

# (Dame) Ethel Smyth (1858–1944)

BRITISH COMPOSER AND FEMINIST

Recognized as the first significant British woman composer, she
is known for her operas, such as *The Wreckers* (1906) and *The
Boatswain's Mate* (1916), as well as for songs and choral pieces. 'The
March of the Women' (1911) became the anthem for the suffragette
movement, of which she was an active supporter and for which
she suffered a three-month imprisonment.

1 The habit some writers indulge in of perpetual quotation
is one it behoves lovers of good literature to protest
against, for it is an insidious habit which in the end must
cloud the stream of thought, or at least check spontaneity.
If it be true that *le style c'est l'homme*, what is likely to
happen if *l'homme* is for ever eking out his own personality
with that of some other individual?

*Streaks of Life*, 'The Quotation-Fiend' (1924)

2 Because I have conducted my own operas and love sheep-
dogs; because I generally dress in tweeds, and sometimes,
at winter afternoon concerts, have even conducted in
them; because I was a militant suffragette and seized a
chance of beating time to 'The March of the Women'
from the window of my cell in Holloway Prison with a
tooth-brush; because I have written books, spoken
speeches, broadcast, and don't always make sure that my
hat is on straight; for these and other equally pertinent
reasons, in a certain sense I am well known.

*As Time Went On*, Epilogue (1936)

# Steven Soderbergh (b. 1963)

US FILM-MAKER

An overnight success with his quirky take on adultery, *sex, lies, and
videotape* (1989), he was criticized for his 'sophomoric' second film,
*Kafka* (1991) but returned to form with *King of the Hill* (1993) and
*Out of Sight* (1998).

1 I think men get more and more in love with the person
they're . . . and women get more and more attracted to
the person they love.

Graham Dalton ( James Spader), in *sex, lies, and videotape* (film,
1989, written and directed by Steven Soderbergh). The rapt Anne
(Andy MacDowell) replies, 'That's beautiful . . .'

2 Lying is like alcoholism. You are always recovering.

ibid.

# Bienvenida Sokolow (b. 1958)

SPANISH-BORN SOCIETY FIGURE

The former-wife of Sir Antony Buck, as which she was nicknamed
'Lady Buck' in the tabloids, she calls herself a 'working celebrity'.
She has featured in the gossip columns since being revealed as the
mistress of Sir Peter Harding, Chief of Defence Staff and later
Deputy Chairman of GEC-Marconi. 'I deserve to have a degree of
limelight, more than most people, because I work at it,' she states.
'I didn't just sit back and enjoy the benefits.'

1 For me affection was more visible in terms of finance than
in terms of words. People can talk and not mean what
they say, but with money, you know it will not let you
down.

Interview in *The Times* 4 March 1995

# Valerie Solanas (1936–88)

US FEMINIST

Having appeared as an actress in ANDY WARHOL's film *I, a Man*
(1967), she achieved notoriety for shooting Warhol in 1968, and
was judged schizophrenic in the ensuing trial, where she was
defended by FLORYNCE KENNEDY. Her intended victim had originally been MAURICE GIRODIAS, whose Olympia Press eventually
published her extremist *SCUM Manifesto* (1968). The film *I Shot
Andy Warhol* (1996) was made about her life.

1 Life in this society being, at best, an utter bore and no
aspect of society being at all relevant to women, there
remains to civic-minded, responsible, thrill-seeking
females only to overthrow the government, eliminate the
money system, institute complete automation and destroy
the male sex.

*The SCUM Manifesto* (1968), repr. in *Sisterhood is Powerful* (ed.
Robin Morgan, 1970). The acronym *SCUM* stood for 'Society for
Cutting Up Men'.

2 To call a man an animal is to flatter him; he's a machine,
a walking dildo.

ibid.

3 Our society is not a community, but merely a collection
of isolated family units.

ibid.

4 To be sure he's a 'Man', the male must see to it that the
female be clearly a 'Woman', the opposite of a 'Man', that
is, the female must act like a faggot.

ibid.

5 Just as humans have a prior right to existence over dogs
by virtue of being more highly evolved and having a
superior consciousness, so women have a prior right to
existence over men. The elimination of any male is, therefore, a righteous and good act, an act highly beneficial to
women as well as an act of mercy.

ibid. Her grounds for female evolutionary pre-eminence was her
assertion that, on account of his chromosomes, 'the male is an
incomplete female'.

# Philippe Sollers (b. 1936)

FRENCH AUTHOR AND CRITIC

Original name Philippe Joyaux. An exponent of the *nouveau roman*
or 'new novel' in the 1960s, he was described by PHILIP ROTH as
'the sort of intellectual clown we don't breed in America – urbane,
bestial, candid, effervescent, an irrepressible ejaculator of farcical
wisdom, a master of good-natured malice'. He is the author of
works on Francis Bacon, PICASSO and Fragonard, as well as *Women*
(1983), *Watteau in Venice* (1994) and the novels *Le Fête à Venise*
(1991) and *Le Secret* (1992).

1 Writing is the continuation of politics by other means.

*Tel quel: théorie d'ensemble*, 'Écriture et révolution' (1968). An adaptation of Karl von Clausewitz's aphorism, 'War is . . . nothing but the continuation of politics by other means' (from *On War*, 1832).

## Ted Solotaroff (b. 1928)
US EDITOR

Associated with the *New American Review* since 1966, he rose to become Senior Editor (1977–9) and remained open to all good new writing 'by virtue of catholicity'. Among those he encouraged were PHILIP ROTH, E.L. DOCTOROW and DON BARTHELME. His own writing was published in *The Red Hot Vacuum and Other Pieces on the Writing of the Sixties* (1970).

1 Aggression, the writer's main source of energy.

'Writing in the Cold', publ. in *Granta* no. 15, 1985

## Alexander Solzhenitsyn (b. 1918)
RUSSIAN NOVELIST

Called 'a bearer of light' by ANNA AKHMATOVA, he published his first book *One Day in the Life of Ivan Denisovich* (1962) after eight years in prison for criticizing STALIN. The political nature of his writing brought him repeatedly into official disfavour and from 1964 he published abroad. He was awarded the Nobel Prize for Literature in 1970 and was finally exiled in 1974 following the publication of *The Gulag Archipelago* (1973). He returned to Russia in 1994. 'I can say without affectation that I belong to the Russian convict world no less . . . than I do to Russian literature,' he is quoted. 'I got my education there, and it will last forever.'

1 Here, lads, we live by the law of the *taiga*. But even here people manage to live. D'you know who are the ones the camps finish off? Those who lick other men's left-overs, those who set store by the doctors, and those who peach on their mates.

Kuziomin, in *One Day in the Life of Ivan Denisovich* (1962)

2 Literature that is not the breath of contemporary society, that dares not transmit the pains and fears of that society, that does not warn in time against threatening moral and social dangers – such literature does not deserve the name of literature; it is only a façade. Such literature loses the confidence of its own people, and its published works are used as wastepaper instead of being read.

Open letter to the Fourth Soviet Writers' Congress, 16 May 1967, repr. in *Solzhenitsyn: A Documentary Record*, 'The Struggle Intensifies' (ed. Leopold Labedz, 1970, rev. 1974)

3 Justice *is* conscience, not a personal conscience but the conscience of the whole of humanity. Those who clearly recognize the voice of their own conscience usually recognize also the voice of justice.

Letter to three students, October 1967, publ. in ibid.

4 One should never direct people towards happiness, because happiness too is an idol of the market-place. One should direct them towards mutual affection. A beast gnawing at its prey can be happy too, but only human beings can feel affection for each other, and this is the highest achievement they can aspire to.

Shulubin, in *Cancer Ward*, pt 2, ch. 10 (1968)

5 You only have power over people so long as you don't take *everything* away from them. But when you've robbed a man of *everything* he's no longer in your power – he's free again.

Bobynin, in *The First Circle*, ch. 17 (1968)

6 For a country to have a great writer . . . is like having another government. That's why no régime has ever loved great writers, only minor ones.

Innokenty, in ibid. ch. 57

7 Blow the dust off the clock. Your watches are behind the times. Throw open the heavy curtains which are so dear to you – you do not even suspect that the day has already dawned outside.

Letter to the Secretariat of the Soviet Writers' Union, 12 November 1969, publ. in *Solzhenitsyn: A Documentary Record*, 'Expulsion' (ed. Leopold Labedz, 1970, rev. 1974)

8 Violence finds its only refuge in falsehood, falsehood its only support in violence. Any man who has once acclaimed violence as his METHOD must inexorably choose falsehood as his PRINCIPLE.

Nobel Prize lecture, 1970, publ. in ibid., 'The Struggle Continues'

9 People can live through hardship, but from hard feelings they perish.

'Asphyxiation', written 1971, publ. in *The Oak and the Calf*, 'Second Supplement' (1980)

10 There are many ways of killing a poet.

ibid.

11 It is not because the truth is too difficult to see that we make mistakes. It may even lie on the surface; but we make mistakes because the easiest and most comfortable course for us is to seek insight where it accords with our emotions – especially selfish ones.

'Peace and Violence', sect. 2, first publ. in *Index* no. 4, 1973, repr. in *Solzhenitsyn: A Documentary Record*, 'Trials in Détente' (ed. Leopold Labedz, 1970, rev. 1974)

12 In our country the lie has become not just a moral category but a pillar of the State.

*Time* magazine 19 January 1974, repr. in *The Oak and the Calf*, appendix (1975)

13 Woe to that nation whose literature is cut short by the intrusion of force. This is not merely interference with freedom of the press but the sealing up of a nation's heart, the excision of its memory.

*Time* magazine 25 February 1974

14 For us in Russia, communism is a dead dog, while, for many people in the West, it is still a living lion.

Radio broadcast on BBC Russian service, publ. in the *Listener* 15 February 1979

15 The clock of communism has stopped striking. But its concrete building has not yet come crashing down. For that reason, instead of freeing ourselves, we must try to save ourselves from being crushed by its rubble.

'How We Must Rebuild Russia', publ. in *Komsomolskaya Pravda* 18 September 1990. Opening sentence of essay.

## Anastasio Somoza (1925–80)
NICARAGUAN DICTATOR

Full name Anastasio Somoza García. He initiated a military coup while Commander-in-Chief of the army in 1936 and assumed dictatorial powers, exiling his political opponents and amassing a personal fortune. He was assassinated and succeeded by his sons.

1 Indeed, you won the elections, but I won the count.

Quoted in the *Guardian* 17 June 1977. Addressed to an opponent who accused him of rigging the election. See also TOM STOPPARD 8.

## Stephen Sondheim (b. 1930)
US SONGWRITER AND COMPOSER

Judged one of the greatest Broadway wordsmiths, he was responsible for the lyrics in BERNSTEIN's *West Side Story* (1957) and wrote both words and music for such shows as *A Funny Thing Happened on the Way to the Forum* (1962), *A Little Night Music* (1973) and *Sunday in the Park with George* (1984), a Pulitzer Prizewinner.

1 I like to be in America!
OK by me in America!
Ev'rything free in America
For a small fee in America!

'America' (song, with music by Leonard Bernstein) in *West Side Story* (stage musical 1957, film 1961)

2 The concerts you enjoy together
Neighbors you annoy together
Children you destroy together
That make marriage a joy.

'The Little Things You Do Together' (song) in *Company* (stage musical, 1970)

3 A toast to that invincible bunch
The dinosaurs surviving the crunch
Let's hear it for the ladies who lunch.

'The Ladies Who Lunch' (song) in ibid. Performed in the original cast by Elaine Stritch.

4 Ev'ry day a little death
On the lips and in the eyes,
In the murmurs, in the pauses,
In the gestures, in the sighs.
Ev'ry day a little dies.

'Every Day a Little Death' (song) in *A Little Night Music* (stage musical 1973, filmed 1977)

5 Send in the clowns.

Song title in ibid. The song was a hit for Judy Collins in 1975 and performed by Elizabeth Taylor in the film version. In circus or vaudeville the words are the traditional desperate summons for some distraction for the audience when something goes badly wrong.

6 The fact is popular art dates. It grows quaint. How many people feel strongly about Gilbert and Sullivan today compared to those who felt strongly in 1890?

*International Herald Tribune* 20 June 1989

# Susan Sontag (b. 1933)
US AUTHOR AND CRITIC

Famously described as 'probably the most intelligent woman in America' by JONATHAN MILLER and called 'a foraging pluralist' by ELIZABETH HARDWICK, she is a perceptive and original voice in modern cultural criticism and author of *Against Interpretation* (1966), *On Photography* (1976) and *Illness as a Metaphor* (1979). She has also written novels and made films, including *Duet for Cannibals* (1964) and *Unguided Tour* (1983).

1 The truth is always something that is told, not something that is known. If there were no speaking or writing, there would be no truth about anything. There would only be what is.

*The Benefactor*, ch. 1 (1963)

2 The truth is balance, but the opposite of truth, which is unbalance, may not be a lie.

'Simone Weil', publ. in *New York Review of Books* (1963), repr. in *Against Interpretation* (1966)

3 Interpretation is the revenge of the intellect upon art. Even more. It is the revenge of the intellect upon the world. To interpret is to impoverish, to deplete the world – in order to set up a shadow world of 'meanings'.

'Against Interpretation', sect. 4, publ. in *Evergreen Review* December 1964, repr. in ibid.

4 Any critic is entitled to wrong judgments, of course. But certain lapses of judgment indicate the radical failure of an entire sensibility.

'The Literary Criticism of George Lukács', first publ. in *Bookweek* (1964) repr. in ibid.

5 Intelligence . . . is really a kind of taste: taste in ideas.

'Notes on "Camp"' (1964), repr. in ibid.

6 Camp is a vision of the world in terms of style – but a particular kind of style. It is the love of the exaggerated, the 'off', of things-being-what-they-are-not.

ibid. Note 8

7 What is most beautiful in virile men is something feminine; what is most beautiful in feminine women is something masculine.

ibid. Note 9

8 As the dandy is the nineteenth century's surrogate for the aristocrat in matters of culture, so Camp is the modern dandyism. Camp is the answer to the problem: how to be a dandy in the age of mass culture.

ibid. Note 45

9 Jews and homosexuals are the outstanding creative minorities in contemporary urban culture. Creative, that is in the truest sense: they are creators of sensibilities. The two pioneering forces of modern sensibility are Jewish moral seriousness and homosexual aestheticism and irony.

ibid. Note 51

10 Art is seduction, not rape.

'On Style', first publ. in *Partisan Review* (1965), repr. in ibid.

11 The truth is that Mozart, Pascal, Boolean algebra, Shakespeare, parliamentary government, baroque churches, Newton, the emancipation of women, Kant, Marx, and Balanchine ballets don't redeem what this particular civilization has wrought upon the world. The white race *is* the cancer of human history.

'What's Happening in America', publ. in *Partisan Review* spring 1967, repr. in *Styles of Radical Will* (1969)

12 Cogito ergo boom.

*Styles of Radical Will* (1969) ' "Thinking Against Oneself": Reflections on Cioran'. Parenthetical comment on our sense that we stand 'in the ruins of thought, and on the verge of the ruins of history and of man himself'. From Descartes' formula *Cogito, ergo sum*, 'I think therefore I am' (*Discours de la méthode*, 1637).

13 [On Nazi symbolism in sado-masochism] Now there is a master scenario available to everyone. The color is black, the material is leather, the seduction is beauty, the justification is honesty, the aim is ecstasy, the fantasy is death.

'Fascinating Fascism' (1974), repr. in *Under the Sign of Saturn* (1980)

14 Photography is the inventory of mortality. A touch of the finger now suffices to invest a moment with posthumous irony.

*On Photography*, 'Melancholy Objects' (1977)

15 The taste for quotations (and for the juxtaposition of incongruous quotations) is a Surrealist taste.

ibid.

16 It is not altogether wrong to say that there is no such thing as a bad photograph – only less interesting, less relevant, less mysterious ones.

ibid. 'The Heroism of Vision'

17 The painter constructs, the photographer discloses.

ibid.

18 Illness is the night-side of life, a more onerous citizenship. Everyone who is born holds dual citizenship, in the kingdom of the well and in the kingdom of the sick. Although we all prefer to use only the good passport, sooner or later each of us is obliged, at least for a spell, to identify ourselves as citizens of that other place.

*Illness As Metaphor*, Preface (1978). Opening words.

19 Depression is melancholy minus its charms – the animation, the fits.

ibid. ch. 7

20 Any important disease whose causality is murky, and

for which treatment is ineffectual, tends to be awash in significance.

ibid. ch. 8

21 The writer is either a practising recluse or a delinquent, guilt-ridden one; or both. Usually both.

'When Writers Talk among Themselves', publ. in *The New York Times* 5 January 1986

22 Victims suggest innocence. And innocence, by the inexorable logic that governs all relational terms, suggests guilt.

*AIDS and Its Metaphors*, ch. 1 (1989)

23 Societies need to have one illness which becomes identified with evil, and attaches blame to its 'victims.'

ibid.

24 Authoritarian political ideologies have a vested interest in promoting fear, a sense of the imminence of takeover by aliens – and real diseases are useful material.

ibid. ch. 6

25 Fear of sexuality is the new, disease-sponsored register of the universe of fear in which everyone now lives.

ibid. ch. 7

26 The ideology of capitalism makes us all into connoisseurs of liberty – of the indefinite expansion of possibility.

ibid.

27 AIDS occupies such a large part in our awareness because of what it has been taken to represent. It seems the very model of all the catastrophes privileged populations feel await them.

ibid. ch. 8

28 In a woman, beauty is something total. It is what stands, in a woman, for character. It is also, of course, a performance; something willed, designed, obtained.

Introduction to *Women* (1999) by Annie Leibovitz

# Wole Soyinka (b. 1934)
NIGERIAN AUTHOR

After studies in Nigeria, Britain and the USA, he became Director of the School of Drama at the University of Ibadan. Most of his numerous plays concern the adaptation of his native Yoruba culture to modern westernized society, as in *A Dance of the Forests* (1963), and the conflicts with colonial culture, as in *Death and the King's Horseman* (1975). He wrote about his imprisonment (1967–9) during the Nigerian Civil War in *The Man Died* (1972) and in books of verse, for example *A Shuttle in the Crypt* (1972). He was awarded the Nobel Prize for Literature in 1986.

1 The man dies in all who keep silent in the face of tyranny.

*The Man Died* (1972), ch. 1

2 Prison is only a new stage from which the struggle must be waged . . . prison, especially political prison is an artificial erection in more senses than one whose bluff must be called and whose impotence must be demonstrated.

ibid. ch. 8

3 *I do not seek; I find.* Let actions alone be the manifestations of the authentic being in defence of its authentic visions. History is too full of failed prometheans bathing their wounded spirits in the tragic stream.

ibid. ch. 12

4 For me, justice is the first condition of humanity.

ibid.

5 Life has an end. A life that will outlive
Fame and friendship begs another name.

Elesin, in *Death and the King's Horseman*, sc. 1 (1975)

# (Dame) Muriel Spark (b. 1918)
BRITISH NOVELIST

A former editor of *Poetry Review* who has also published volumes of verse, she is best known for her novels, notably *The Prime of Miss Joan Brodie* (1961, filmed 1969), which she herself described as 'more progressive than I realized'. Her other works of fiction include *The Ballad of Peckham Rye* (1960), *The Girls of Slender Means* (1963), *The Mandelbaum Gate* (1965) and *The Driver's Seat* (1970, filmed 1974), and in 1992 she published her autobiography, *Curriculum Vitae*.

1 Being over seventy is like being engaged in a war. All our friends are going or gone and we survive amongst the dead and the dying as on a battlefield.

Miss Taylor, in *Memento Mori*, ch. 4 (1959)

2 If I had my life over again I should form the habit of nightly composing myself to thoughts of death. I would practise, as it were, the remembrance of death. There is no other practice which so intensifies life. Death, when it approaches, ought not to take one by surprise. It should be part of the full expectancy of life. Without an ever-present sense of death life is insipid. You might as well live on the whites of eggs.

Henry Mortimer, in ibid. ch. 11

3 I am putting old heads on your young shoulders; all my pupils are the crème de la crème.

Miss Brodie, in *The Prime of Miss Jean Brodie*, ch. 1 (1961)

4 Give me a girl at an impressionable age, and she is mine for life!

Miss Brodie, in ibid. The words echo a Jesuit maxim: 'Give me a child for the first seven years, and you may do what you like with him afterwards.'

5 One's prime is elusive. You little girls, when you grow up, must be on the alert to recognize your prime at whatever time of your life it may occur. You must then live it to the full.

Miss Brodie, in ibid.

6 Art and religion first; then philosophy; lastly science. That is the order of the great subjects of life, that's their order of importance.

Miss Brodie, in ibid. ch. 2

7 To me education is a leading out of what is already there in the pupil's soul. To Miss Mackay it is a putting in of something that is not there, and that is not what I call education, I call it intrusion.

Miss Brodie, in ibid.

8 New York, home of the vivisectors of the mind, and of the mentally vivisected still to be reassembled, of those who live intact, habitually wondering about their states of sanity, and home of those whose minds have been dead, bearing the scars of resurrection.

*The Hothouse by the East River*, ch. 1 (1973)

9 I wouldn't take the Pope too seriously. He's a Pole first, a pope second, and maybe a Christian third.

*International Herald Tribune* 29 May 1989

10 If you're going to do a thing, you should do it thoroughly. If you're going to be a Christian, you may as well be a Catholic.

*Independent* 2 August 1989

# Larry Speakes (b. 1939)
US EXECUTIVE AND WHITE HOUSE OFFICIAL

He was Press Secretary under Presidents FORD (1977) and REAGAN (1981–7).

1 I would dodge, not lie, in the national interest.

*The New York Times* 10 October 1986

## Phil Spector (b. 1940)

US POP PRODUCER AND SONGWRITER

With the vocal group the Teddy Bears he had a hit with his song 'To Know Him Is To Love Him' (1958), inspired by the words on his father's tombstone. As a record producer he specialized in recording relatively unknown singers and groups backed by a 'wall of sound', pioneering the use of over-dubbing, echo effects and other studio techniques. His biggest hits were with the Ronettes, whose lead singer he married, and he later worked with the Beatles.

1 I always went in for that Wagnerian approach to rock and roll.

Quoted in *Out of His Head*, ch. 5 (1974) by Richard Williams

## Albert Speer (1905–81)

GERMAN ARCHITECT AND NAZI MINISTER

As HITLER's architect he built the New Reich Chancellery in Berlin (1939, now demolished), though his more visionary and grandiose designs were not realized. He was Armaments Minister from 1942 and after the war was the only leader at the Nuremberg trials to admit responsibility for the Nazi regime. He was sentenced to twenty years for employing slave labour.

1 Today, almost forty years later, I grow dizzy when I recall that the number of manufactured tanks seems to have been more important to me than the vanished victims of racism.

*The Slave State*, ch. 21 (1981)

## Charles Spencer (b. 1964)

BRITISH JOURNALIST AND BUSINESSMAN

Earl Spencer, Viscount Althorp. He was page of honour to the Queen (1977–9), NBC correspondent and presenter (1987–91 and 1993–6) and a reporter for Granada Television (1991–3). As brother to Princess DIANA, he was vehemently outspoken against the press and the royal family after her death and set up a permanent exhibition commemorating her at Althorp, where she is buried.

1 [Of Princess Diana] I . . . always believed the press would kill her in the end. But not even I could believe they would take such a direct hand in her death as seems to be the case.

Speech to press outside his home, Cape Town, 31 August 97, publ. in *The Times* 1 September 1997

2 It would appear that every proprietor and every editor of every publication that had paid for intrusive and exploitative photographs of her, encouraging greedy and ruthless individuals to risk everything in pursuit of Diana's image, has blood on his hands today.

ibid.

3 It is a point to remember that, of all the ironies about Diana, perhaps the greatest was this: a girl given the name of the ancient goddess was, in the end, the most hunted person of the modern age.

Funeral oration at Westminster Abbey, 6 September 1997, quoted in the *Observer* 7 September 1997

## Dale Spender (b. 1943)

AUSTRALIAN FEMINIST AUTHOR

Formerly a lecturer, she has edited anthologies of literature as well as the journal *Women's Studies International Forum*. Her books include *Man Made Language* (1980), *Invisible Women* (1982), on the disadvantages of co-education, and *There's Always Been a Women's Movement This Century* (1983).

1 Paradoxically, the most constructive thing women can do . . . is to write, for in the *act* of writing we deny our mutedness and begin to eliminate some of the difficulties that have been put upon us.

*Man Made Language*, ch. 7 (1980)

## (Sir) Stephen Spender (1909–95)

BRITISH POET

Described by Robert Craft as 'the least insular writer of his generation', he co-founded with CYRIL CONNOLLY the magazine *Horizon* of which he was editor (1939–41) and he was co-editor of *Encounter* (1953–67). His poetry collections, such as *Poems from Spain* (1939) and *The Edge of Darkness* (1949), are influenced by his experiences in the Spanish Civil War and the Second World War. He also published criticism and translations. See also AUDEN 48.

1 My parents kept me from children who were rough
And who threw words like stones and who wore torn clothes.

'My parents kept me from children who were rough', publ. in *Poems*, no. 12 (1933). Opening lines of poem.

2 I think continually of those who were truly great.
Who, from the womb, remembered the soul's history
Through corridors of light where the hours are suns,
Endless and singing.

'I Think Continually', publ. in ibid. no. 23. Opening lines of poem.

3 The names of those who in their lives fought for life,
Who wore at their hearts the fire's centre.
Born of the sun they travelled a short while toward the sun
And left the vivid air signed with their honour.

ibid. Closing lines of poem.

4 After the first powerful plain manifesto
The black statement of pistons, without more fuss
But gliding like a queen, she leaves the station.

'The Express', publ. in ibid. no. 26

5 Steaming through metal landscape on her lines,
She plunges new eras of white happiness,
Where speed throws up strange shapes, broad curves
And parallels clean like the steel of guns.

ibid. Spender later amended the last line to read, 'like trajectories from guns'.

6 Now over these small hills they have built the concrete
That trails black wire:
Pylons, those pillars
Bare like nude, giant girls that have no secret.

'The Pylons', publ. in ibid. no. 28. The poem provided a label, 'the Pylon Poets', for the 1930s poets who wrote about the modern industrialized landscape, including also AUDEN and DAY LEWIS.

7 Finally, they cease to hate: for although hate
Bursts from the air and whips the earth like hail
Or pours it up in fountains to marvel at,
And although hundreds fell, who can connect
The inexhaustible anger of the guns
With the dumb patience of these tormented animals?

'Two Armies', publ. in *The Still Centre* (1939)

8 The guns spell money's ultimate reason
In letters of lead on the spring hillside.

'Ultima Ratio Regum', publ. in *Poems for Spain* (ed. Stephen Spender and John Lehmann, 1939). Opening lines of poem.

## Oswald Spengler (1880–1936)

GERMAN HISTORIAN

He is noted for his work *The Decline of the West* (two volumes, 1918 and 1922), which argues, through what he termed a 'morphological method', a cyclical theory of human development in accordance with 'historical destiny'. Sceptical and pessimistic about the future, he predicted a phase of 'Caesarism'.

1 In place of a world, there is a *city*, a *point*, in which the

whole life of broad regions is collecting while the rest dries up. In place of a type-true people, born of and grown on the soil, there is a new sort of nomad, cohering unstably in fluid masses, the parasitical city dweller, traditionless, utterly matter-of-fact, religionless, clever, unfruitful, deeply contemptuous of the countryman and especially that highest form of countryman, the country gentleman.

*The Decline of the West*, vol. 1, ch. 1, sect. 12 (1918)

2 The last man of the world-city no longer *wants* to live – he may cling to life as an individual, but as a type, as an aggregate, no, for it is a characteristic of this collective existence that it eliminates the terror of death.

ibid. vol. 2, ch. 4, sect. 5 (1922)

3 Formerly no one was allowed to think freely; now it is permitted, but no one is capable of it any more. Now people want to think only what they are supposed to want to think, and this they consider freedom.

ibid. ch. 12, sect. 4

## The Spice Girls

BRITISH POP GROUP

Britain's most successful female vocal group shot to fame in 1996 with their international hit 'Wannabe'. The group consists of Melanie Chisholm ('Mel C', 'Sporty Spice'), Emma Bunton ('Baby Spice'), Victoria Adams (later Beckham, 'Posh Spice'), Geri Halliwell ('Ginger Spice') and Melanie Brown ('Mel B', 'Scary Spice'). Geri Halliwell left the group in 1998 to become a UN 'goodwill ambassador' and pursue a successful solo career.

1 I'll tell you what I want what I really really want
(So tell me what you want, what you really really want)
If you wanna be my lover
Gotta get with my friends
Make it last forever
Friendship never ends!

'Wannabe' (song, written by Matthew Rowbottom and Richard Stannard) on the album *Spice* (1996)

## Steven Spielberg (b. 1947)

US FILM-MAKER

J.G. BALLARD once called him 'the Puccini of the cinema, a little too sweet for some tastes, but what melodies, what orchestrations, what cathedrals of emotion'. The most commercially successful director to date, whose hits include *Jaws* (1975), *E.T.* (1982) *Back to the Future* (1985), *Empire of the Sun* (1988) and *Jurassic Park* (1993), he was awarded an Oscar for *Schindler's List* (1993). In 1994 he co-founded the studio DreamWorks SKG.

1 Close encounters of the third kind.

Title of film (written and directed by Steven Spielberg, 1977)

2 The most expensive habit in the world is celluloid, not heroin, and I need a fix every few years.

Interview in *Time* magazine 16 April 1979

## Gayatri Chakravorty Spivak (b. 1942)

INDIAN-BORN US EDUCATOR, AUTHOR AND TRANSLATOR

After studies in India and at Cornell University she published *Myself, I Must Remake* on YEATS (1974), but it was her 1976 translation of DERRIDA's *Of Grammatology* that established her reputation. It was followed by *In Other Worlds* (1987) and *A Critique of Post-Colonial Reason* (1999).

1 The fall into the abyss of deconstruction inspires us with as much pleasure as fear. We are intoxicated with the prospect of never hitting bottom.

Translator's Preface (1976) to *Of Grammatology* (1967) by Jacques Derrida

2 The subaltern cannot speak. There is no virtue in global laundry lists with 'woman' as a pious item. Representation has not withered away. The female intellectual as intellectual has a circumscribed task which she must not disown with a flourish.

'Can the Subaltern Speak?' publ. in *Colonial Discourse and Post-Colonial Theory: A Reader* (ed. Patrick Williams and Laura Chrisman, 1994)

## Benjamin Spock (1903–98)

US PAEDIATRICIAN AND AUTHOR

His seminal work *The Common Sense Book of Baby and Child Care* (1946) advocated a more relaxed attitude to child-rearing. He was later outspoken against the Vietnam War and rebutted criticism of being responsible for a permissive new generation, stressing that his approach had not dismissed discipline out of hand.

1 I think that more of our children would grow up happier and more stable if they were acquiring a conviction, all through childhood, that the most important thing that human beings can do is serve humanity in some function and to live by their ideals.

*Baby and Child Care*, 'The Parents' Part', sect. 11 (1946, rev. 1968)

2 It is fascinating to realize that what distinguishes man so sharply from other creatures are those attitudes he develops soon after the age of 5: his inhibition and sublimation of sexuality, his interest in symbols, abstractions, systems and rules, his capacity for being inspired by heroes, God and spiritual ideals.

ibid. sect. 13

3 Man can build a magnificent reality in adulthood out of what was only an illusion in early childhood – his loving, joyous, trusting, ingenuous, unrealistic over-idealization of his two parents.

ibid.

4 A child loves his play, not because it's easy, but because it's hard.

ibid. 'Managing Young Children', sect. 457

5 I was proud of the youths who opposed the war in Vietnam because they were my babies.

*The Times* 2 May 1988

## Viola Spolin (b. 1911)

US THEATRICAL DIRECTOR AND PRODUCER

Based in Chicago, she became known as the 'high priestess of improvisational theatre' and as a pioneer of games as a basis for theatre training. She has worked extensively with children and within the community.

1 We learn through experience and experiencing, and no one teaches anyone anything. This is as true for the infant moving from kicking to crawling to walking as it is for the scientist with his equations. If the environment permits it, anyone can learn whatever he chooses to learn; and if the individual permits it, the environment will teach him everything it has to teach.

*Improvisation for the Theater*, ch. 1 (1963)

2 Through spontaneity we are re-formed into ourselves. It creates an explosion that for the moment frees us from handed-down frames of reference, memory choked with old facts and information and undigested theories and techniques of other people's findings. Spontaneity is the moment of personal freedom when we are faced with reality, and see it, explore it and act accordingly. In this reality the bits and pieces of ourselves function as an organic whole. It is the time of discovery, of experiencing, of creative expression.

ibid.

3 The audience is the most revered member of the theater. Without an audience there is no theater. Every technique learned by the actor, every curtain, every flat on the stage, every careful analysis by the director, every coordinated scene, is for the enjoyment of the audience. They are our guests, our evaluators, and the last spoke in the wheel which can then begin to roll. They make the performance meaningful.

ibid.

## John Spong (b. 1931)
US ECCLESIASTIC

Ordained an Episcopalian minister in 1955, he has stated his mission to 'write as a believing skeptic inside the structures of the church for those who have drifted outside these structures'. His books include *Honest Prayer* (1973) and *The Living Commandments* (1977).

1 I learned early in life that you get places by having the right enemies.

*Guardian* 20 July 1988

2 The priesthood in many ways is the ultimate closet in Western civilization, where gay people particularly have hidden for the past two thousand years.

*Daily Telegraph* 12 July 1990

## Jerry Springer (b. 1944)
US TELEVISION HOST

Child of refugees from Nazi Germany, born in wartime London, he went to the US as a boy where he aspired to a career in politics and served as Mayor of Cincinatti until the day his personal cheque was found in a Kentucky brothel. In 1982 he began a career in political reporting and was Cincinnati's foremost news anchor until 1993. His confessional *Jerry Springer Show*, with which he boasts he is 'proud to set a new low', began in 1991 and has since been seen globally.

1 My show is the stupidest show on TV. If you are watching it, get a life. I would not watch my show. My show is a circus. That's all it is.

*Independent on Sunday* 7 March 1999

## Bruce Springsteen (b. 1949)
US ROCK MUSICIAN

Nicknamed 'The Boss', after years as an icon of blue-collar rock and roll he became a major star with the album *Born to Run* (1975), and found a huge international audience with 1984's *Born in the USA*. Lower key acoustic material can be found on *The Ghost of Tom Joad* (1995). Although GREIL MARCUS commended Springsteen's 'ability to make his music bleed', the singer Chris Rea judged him 'the Walt Disney of street poets – as useful a social commentator as Donald Duck'.

1 In the day we sweat it out in the streets of a runaway
     American dream
   At night we ride through mansions of glory in suicide
     machines.

'Born to Run' (song) on the album *Born to Run* (1975) by Bruce Springsteen and the E Street Band

2 Baby this town rips the bones from your back,
   It's a death trap, it's a suicide rap,
   We gotta get out while we're young
   'Cause tramps like us baby we were born to run.

ibid.

3 Born down in a dead man's town
   The first kick I took was when I hit the ground
   You end up like a dog that's been beat too much
   Till you spend half your life just covering up.
   Born in the USA

I was born in the USA.

'Born in the USA' (song) on the album *Born in the USA (1984) by Bruce Springsteen and the E Street Band*. When REAGAN attempted to enlist the support of Springsteen for the 'message of hope' in this and other songs, Springsteen repudiated any connection with the President on stage a few days later, causing WALTER MONDALE to quip: 'Bruce may have been born to run, but he wasn't born yesterday.'

4 People want to forget. There was Vietnam, there was Watergate, there was Iran. We were beaten, we were hustled, and then we were humiliated. And I think people got a need to feel good about the country they live in ... And you see the Reagan reelection ads on TV. You know: 'It's morning in America'. And you say, well, it's not morning in Pittsburgh. It's not morning above 125th Street in New York. It's midnight, and, like, there's a bad moon risin'.

Interview in *Rolling Stone* December 1984

5 Your success story is a bigger story than whatever you're trying to say on stage.

*Q* August 1992

## Josef Stalin (1879–1953)
SOVIET LEADER

Original name Josef Vissarionovich Dzhugashvili. He joined the Bolsheviks in 1903 and co-founded the party's paper *Pravda* in 1912. After the 1917 revolution he became Commissar for Nationalities and by 1924 he had manoeuvred to become General Secretary of the Central Committee and have his main rival TROTSKY banished. He presided over the building of a modern industrial state at the price of the deaths of millions, ruthlessly eliminating all critics of his regime. Trotsky called him 'Our party's most outstanding mediocrity.' See also JOHN KENNEDY 25, NIKITA KHRUSHCHEV 2 and 3, OSIP MANDELSTAM 7, LEON TROTSKY 8, 21, 22, YEVGENY YEVTUSHENKO 5.

1 He who wants to lead a movement, and at the same time keep in touch with the masses, must wage a war on two fronts – against those who lag behind and against those who rush on ahead.

*Pravda* 2 March 1930, repr. in *Parallel Lives*, ch. 8, sect. 2 (1998) by Alan Bullock

2 The Pope? How many divisions has he got?

Said 13 May 1935, quoted in *The Second World War*, vol. 1, 'The Gathering Storm', ch. 8 (1948) by WINSTON CHURCHILL. Addressed to French Foreign Minister Pierre Laval in reply to a suggestion that the Soviet Union should encourage Catholicism in order to propitiate the Pope.

3 Gratitude . . . is a sickness suffered by dogs.

Quoted in *Stalin's Secret War*, ch. 2 (1981) by Nikolai Tolstoy

4 Cadres determine everything.

One of his favourite watchwords, quoted in *Parallel Lives*, ch. 4, sect. 3 (1998) by Alan Bullock

5 A single death is a tragedy, a million deaths is a statistic.

Attributed

## Sylvester Stallone (b. 1946)
US ACTOR AND FILM-MAKER

For DAVID THOMSON, 'Stallone may be the most self-conscious noble savage since Mussolini'. After parts in WOODY ALLEN's *Bananas* (1971) and in *The Lords of Flatbush* (1974), he was inspired by watching MUHAMMAD ALI to write the film *Rocky* (1976), which established him as a major Hollywood star. Usually cast as action hero, as in the Rocky sequels, *Rambo* (1985) and *Cliffhanger* (1993), which he co-wrote, he describes himself as the 'manifestation of his own fantasy' with 'the voice of a Mafioso pall bearer'.

1 Rambo isn't violent. I see Rambo as a philanthropist.

*Today* 27 May 1988. See RONALD REAGAN 19.

# Konstantin Stanislavsky (1863–1938)

RUSSIAN THEATRICAL DIRECTOR, ACTOR AND
THEORIST

He is known for his pioneering approach to acting in which actors aim, through minute study, to 'become' the characters they play. As co-founder in 1897 of the Moscow Art Theatre, he directed the first productions of Chekhov and works by Gorky, Andreyev and Maeterlinck. His book *An Actor Prepares* (1936) was a great influence on the 'method' school in the USA.

1 In the creative process there is the father, the author of the play; the mother, the actor pregnant with the part; and the child, the role to be born.

*An Actor Prepares*, ch. 16 (1936)

2 Talent is nothing but a prolonged period of attention and a shortened period of mental assimilation.

*The Art of the Stage*, ch. 22 (1950)

# Vivian Stanshall (1943–95)

BRITISH MUSICIAN AND ENTERTAINER

A full-time English eccentric, he was a member of the 1920s-inspired Bonzo Dog Doo-Dah Band, which appeared in the Beatles' film *Magical Mystery Tour* (1967) and recorded the album *Gorilla* (1967) and the hit single 'I'm the Urban Spaceman' (1968). After breaking with the band, he narrated Mike Oldfield's *Tubular Bells* (1973) and created the bufferish 'Sir Henry at Rawlinson End' on radio, record and film.

1 Cool Britannia
Britannia take a trip
Britons ever ever ever will be hip.

'Cool Britannia' (song) on the album *Gorilla* (1967) by the Bonzo Dog Doo-Dah Band. Thought to be the first use of 'Cool Britannia', subsequently used on a *Newsweek* cover and associated with Britain under TONY BLAIR.

# (Dame) Freya Stark (1893–1993)

BRITISH TRAVEL WRITER

A diminutive but self-assured figure, she spent most of her adult life travelling in the Middle East, and worked for the British Ministry of Information in Aden, Egypt and Iraq during the Second World War. Her writings include *Valley of the Assassins* (1934), *West is East* (1945) and *A Peak in Darien* (1976). For the last forty years of her life she based herself in Asolo, Italy, but continued to travel into her eighties.

1 The great and almost only comfort about being a woman is that one can always pretend to be more stupid than one is and no one is surprised.

*Valley of the Assassins*, ch. 2 (1934)

2 Of the general inadequacy of intellect in the conduct of life Britain is the most majestic exponent. She is instinctively disliked by such people as French, Persians, Hindus, who are clever by nature, and think that *intellect can rule . . .* With the intellectual, it is not our stupidity, but the fact that we prove it possible to live by non-intellectual standards, which makes us disliked.

*Perseus in the Wind*, ch. 4 (1948)

3 The slightest living thing answers a deeper need than all the works of man because it is *transitory*. It has an evanescence of life, or growth, or change: it passes, as we do, from one stage to another, from darkness to darkness, into a distance where we, too, vanish out of sight. A work of art is static; and its value and its weakness lie in being so: but the tuft of grass and the clouds above it belong to our own travelling brotherhood.

ibid. ch. 14

4 Pain and fear and hunger are effects of causes which can be foreseen and known: but sorrow is a debt which someone else makes for us.

ibid. ch. 16

5 Perhaps the best function of parenthood is to teach the young creature to love with *safety*, so that it may be able to venture unafraid when later emotion comes; the thwarting of the instinct to love is the root of all sorrow and not sex only but divinity itself is insulted when it is repressed. To disapprove, to condemn – the human soul shrivels under barren righteousness.

*Traveller's Prelude*, ch. 10 (1950)

# Edwin Starr (b. 1942)

US SOUL SINGER

A soul-shouter in the style of JAMES BROWN, he is best known for his song 'War' and the albums *Soulmaster* (1968) and *War and Peace* (1970).

1 War . . .
What is it good for?
Absolutely nothing.

'War' (song, written by Norman Whitfield and Barrett Strong) on the album *War and Peace* (1970)

# Ringo Starr (b. 1940)

BRITISH DRUMMER

Original name Richard Starkey. He was drummer and occasional singer with the Beatles from 1962. As a solo artist he had hits with 'It Don't Come Easy' (1971) and 'Back Off Boogaloo' (1972) and as an actor appeared in the films *Candy* (1968), *The Magic Christian* (1970) and *That'll Be the Day* (1973). 'I don't like talking,' he is quoted. 'Some people gab all day and some people play it smogo. I haven't got a smiling face or a talking mouth.'

1 I've never really done anything to create what has happened. It creates itself. I'm here because it happened. But I didn't do anything to make it happen apart from saying 'Yes'.

Quoted in *The Beatles Illustrated Lyrics*, vol. 1 (ed. Alan Aldridge, 1969)

2 [On India] It was just like Butlins.

ibid. On returning from meditating at Rishikesh.

# Tommy Steele (b. 1936)

BRITISH ACTOR AND SINGER

Original name Thomas Hicks. Starting out as Britain's first rock 'n' roll star with the hit song 'Rock With the Cavemen' (1956), he later acted in *She Stoops to Conquer* (1960) at the Old Vic, demonstrated his Cockney pizzazz in the musical *Half a Sixpence* (1963, filmed 1967) and starred in the film *Finian's Rainbow* (1968) and the stage musical *Singin' in the Rain* (1983).

1 Show business is really 90 per cent luck and 10 per cent being able to handle it when it gets offered to you.

*Listener* 10 October 1974

# Lincoln Steffens (1866–1936)

US AUTHOR AND EDITOR

One of the chief 'muckraker' journalists of the early twentieth century who set out to expose corruption in business and politics, he was a reporter on the New York *Evening Post* (1892–8) before becoming Editor of *McClure's, American* and *Everybody's* magazines (1902–11). His books include *The Shame of the Cities* (1904), *The Struggle for Self-Government* (1906) and his *Autobiography* (1931).

1 We Americans can't seem to get it that you can't commit rape a little.

Quoted in *Lincoln Steffens*, ch. 11, sect. 3 (1974) by Justin Kaplan. Referring to US intervention in Mexico in 1914.

2 I have been over into the future, and it works.

*Autobiography*, ch. 18 (1931). Remark on his return from the Soviet Union in 1919 to financier BERNARD BARUCH.

# Gertrude Stein (1874–1946)

US AUTHOR

An experimental writer described by CLIFTON FADIMAN as 'a past master in making nothing happen very slowly', she is famous for her obscure repetitive word play in works such as *Three Lives* (1909) and *Tender Buttons* (1914). *The Autobiography of Alice B. Toklas* (1933) is actually a biography of Stein herself, using the name of her lifelong companion. She also wrote librettos for operas with music by Virgil Thompson, among them *Four Saints in Three Acts* (1929) and *The Mother of Us All* (1947). See also CLIFTON FADIMAN 1.

1 One does not get better but different and older and that is always a pleasure.

Letter to author F. SCOTT FITZGERALD, 22 May 1925, publ. in *The Crack-Up* (ed. Edmund Wilson, 1945)

2 All of you young people who served in the war. You are a lost generation . . . You have no respect for anything. You drink yourselves to death.

Remark to ERNEST HEMINGWAY, quoted as epigraph to *The Sun Also Rises* (1926). Hemingway's novel describes the lives of expatriates in Paris in the 1920s. The words are also quoted in his memoir of his own time in Paris, *A Moveable Feast*, ch. 3 (1964). In Stein's *Everybody's Autobiography*, ch. 2 (1937), she recalls the origin of the expression 'lost generation': 'It was this hotel-keeper who said what it is said I said that the war generation was a lost generation. And he said it in this way. He said that every man becomes civilized between the ages of eighteen and twenty-five. If he does not go through a civilizing experience at that time in his life he will not be a civilized man. And the men who went to war at eighteen missed the period of civilizing, and they could never be civilized. They were a lost generation.'

3 The United States is just now the oldest country in the world, there always is an oldest country and she is it, it is she who is the mother of the twentieth century civilization. She began to feel herself as it just after the Civil War. And so it is a country the right age to have been born in and the wrong age to live in.

'Why I Do Not Live In America', publ. in *Transition* fall 1928, repr. in *How Writing Is Written* (ed. Robert Bartlett Haas, 1974)

4 Pigeons on the grass alas.
Pigeons on the grass alas.
Short longer grass short longer longer shorter yellow grass Pigeons large pigeons on the shorter longer yellow
    grass
alas pigeons on the grass.

*Four Saints in Three Acts*, act 3, sc. 2 (1929), publ. in *Operas and Plays* (1932)

5 [Of Ezra Pound] He was a village explainer, excellent if you were a village, but if you were not, not.

*The Autobiography of Alice B. Toklas*, ch. 7 (1933). When asked later what she meant by calling POUND (whom she 'liked . . . but did not find amusing') 'a village explainer', Stein told THORNTON WILDER, 'Ezra Pound still lives in a village and his world is a kind of village and people keep explaining things when they live in a village . . . I have come not to mind if certain people live in villages and some of my friends still appear to live in villages and a village can be cozy as well as intuitive but must one really keep perpetually explaining and elucidating?' (quoted by Frederic Prokosch in *Voices: A Memoir*, 'The Evil Corner', 1983).

6 Hemingway, remarks are not literature.

ibid. Referring to the inclusion by HEMINGWAY of a comment he had made about E.E. CUMMINGS's autobiographical novel *The*

*Enormous Room* ('the greatest book he had ever read') in a manuscript of short stories that he showed to Stein.

7 The contemporary thing in art and literature is the thing which doesn't make enough difference to the people of that generation so that they can accept it or reject it.

'How Writing Is Written', publ. in *Choate Literary Magazine* February 1935, repr. in *How Writing Is Written* (ed. Robert Bartlett Haas, 1974)

8 The unreal is natural, so natural that it makes of unreality the most natural of anything natural. That is what America does, and that is what America is.

'I Came and Here I Am', publ. in *Cosmopolitan* February 1936, repr. in ibid.

9 In the United States there is more space where nobody is than where anybody is. That is what makes America what it is.

*The Geographical History of America* (1936)

10 Native always means people who belong somewhere else, because they had once belonged somewhere. That shows that the white race does not really think they belong anywhere because they think of everybody else as native.

*Everybody's Autobiography*, ch. 1 (1937)

11 It is funny that men are proudest of is the thing that any man can do and doing does in the same way, that is being drunk and being the father of their son.

ibid. ch. 2

12 It takes a lot of time to be a genius, you have to sit around so much doing nothing, really doing nothing.

ibid.

13 The minute you or anybody else knows what you are you are not it, you are what you or anybody else knows you are and as everything in living is made up of finding out what you are it is extraordinarily difficult really not to know what you are and yet to be that thing.

ibid. ch. 3

14 Counting is the religion of this generation it is its hope and its salvation.

ibid.

15 There is no there there.

ibid. ch. 4. Referring to Oakland, California, where Stein spent her childhood.

16 Just before she died she asked, 'What *is* the answer?' No answer came. She laughed and said, 'In that case, what is the question?' Then she died.

Quoted in *Gertrude Stein, A Biography of Her Work*, ch. 6 (1951) by Donald Sutherland. The biography concludes: 'Those were her last words, but they say what she had always been saying.'

17 Oh, I wish I were a miser; being a miser must be so occupying.

Quoted by THORNTON WILDER in interview in *Writers at Work* (first series, ed. Malcolm Cowley, 1958)

18 Nature is commonplace. Imitation is more interesting.

Quoted in *My Autobiography*, ch. 20 (1964) by CHARLIE CHAPLIN

19 In France one must adapt oneself to the fragrance of a urinal.

Quoted in *Voices: A Memoir*, 'Style' (1983) by Frederic Prokosch. The author and poet Prokosch had paid a visit to Stein in Paris, asking her opinion of the city. 'Alice deplores the public urinals,' Stein explained, addressing herself in the third person, 'I keep explaining to Alice that the Parisians are all wine-drinkers and for a gentleman the bladder is more restless than for a lady.'

20 A writer must always try to have a philosophy and he should also have a psychology and a philology and many other things. Without a philosophy and a psychology and all these various other things he is not really worthy of being called a writer. I agree with Kant and Schopenhauer and Plato and Spinoza and that is quite enough to be

called a philosophy. But then of course a philosophy is not the same thing as a style.

Quoted in ibid.

## John Steinbeck (1902–68)

US AUTHOR

His first novel, *Tortilla Flat* (1935), a humorous study of the farmers of Monterey, anticipates *In Dubious Battle* (1936) and *Of Mice and Men* (1937) in its solidarity with the proletariat. *The Grapes of Wrath* (1939, filmed 1940), a Pulitzer Prize-winner, raised awareness about the plight of migrant workers. Later novels include *East of Eden* (1952) and *Winter of Our Discontent* (1961). In 1962 he won the Nobel Prize for Literature.

1 Aw, I'm looking ahead too much. Our job's just to push along our little baby strike, if we can. But God damn it, Jim, if we could get the National Guard called out, now with the crops coming ready, we'd have the whole district organized by spring.

Mac, in *In Dubious Battle*, ch. 3 (1936). Mac, a Communist Party labour organizer, is discussing plans to strike among California's apple pickers with Jim, a new recruit. The novel's title alludes to the claim of Satan in Milton's *Paradise Lost* that he challenged God 'in dubious battle' (with an uncertain outcome) and 'shook his throne', and suggests Steinbeck's own ambivalent attitude to the methods employed by the communist organizers.

2 Man, unlike anything organic or inorganic in the universe, grows beyond his work, walks up the stairs of his concepts, emerges ahead of his accomplishments.

*The Grapes of Wrath*, ch. 14 (1939)

3 Fear the time when the strikes stop while the great owners live – for every little beaten strike is proof that the step is being taken . . . fear the time when Manself will not suffer and die for a concept, for this one quality is the foundation of Manself, and this one quality is man, distinctive in the universe.

ibid.

4 Is a tractor bad? Is the power that turns the long furrows wrong? If this tractor were ours it would be good – not mine, but ours. We could love that tractor then as we have loved this land when it was ours. But this tractor does two things – it turns the land and turns us off the land. There is little difference between this tractor and a tank. The people are driven, intimidated, hurt by both. We must think about this.

ibid.

5 Wherever they's a fight so hungry people can eat, I'll be there. Wherever they's a cop beatin' up a guy, I'll be there . . . I'll be in the way guys yell when they're mad an' – I'll be in the way kids laugh when they're hungry an' they know supper's ready. An' when our folks eat the stuff they raise an' live in the houses they build – why, I'll be there.

Tom Joad, in ibid. ch. 28. Farewell speech to his mother, in which he articulates union-organizer Jim Casy's belief that human beings make up 'one big soul ever'body's a part of '.

6 A journey is like marriage. The certain way to be wrong is to think you control it.

*Travels With Charley: in Search of America*, pt 1 (1961)

7 Even while I protest the assembly-line production of our food, our songs, our language, and eventually our souls, I know that it was a rare home that baked good bread in the old days. Mother's cooking was with rare exceptions poor, that good unpasteurized milk touched only by flies and bits of manure crawled with bacteria, the healthy old-time life was riddled with aches, sudden death from unknown causes, and that sweet local speech I mourn was the child of illiteracy and ignorance. It is the nature of a man as he grows older, a small bridge in time, to protest against change, particularly change for the better.

ibid. pt 2

8 This monster of a land, this mightiest of nations, this spawn of the future, turns out to be the macrocosm of microcosm me.

ibid. pt 3

9 It is true that we are weak and sick and ugly and quarrelsome but if that is all we ever were, we would millenniums ago have disappeared from the face of the earth.

'On Intent', publ. in *Writers at Work* (fourth series, ed. George Plimpton, 1977)

10 Time is the only critic without ambition.

'On Critics', publ. in ibid.

11 Give a critic an inch, he'll write a play.

ibid.

## Gloria Steinem (b. 1934)

US FEMINIST WRITER AND EDITOR

She co-founded the Women's Action Alliance in 1970 and the National Women's Political Caucus in 1971, and was founding editor of the feminist *Ms.* magazine (1981–7). Active in civil rights and peace campaigns, she is author of *Marilyn* (1986), *Revolution from Within* (1992) and *Moving Beyond Words* (1994).

1 No man can call himself liberal, or radical, or even a conservative advocate of fair play, if his work depends in any way on the unpaid or underpaid labor of women at home, or in the office.

*The New York Times* 26 August 1971

2 Any woman who chooses to behave like a full human being should be warned that the armies of the status quo will treat her as something of a dirty joke. That's their natural and first weapon. She will *need* her sisterhood.

'Sisterhood', publ. in *Ms.* spring 1972, repr. in *Outrageous Acts and Everyday Rebellions* (1983)

3 Pornography is about dominance. Erotica is about mutuality.

'Erotica vs. Pornography' adapted from articles in *Ms.* August 1977 and November 1978, repr. in ibid.

4 Power can be taken, but not given. The process of the taking is empowerment in itself.

'Far From the Opposite Shore' adapted from articles in *Ms.* July 1978 and July/August 1982, repr. in ibid.

5 If men could menstruate . . . clearly, menstruation would become an enviable, boast-worthy, masculine event: Men would brag about how long and how much . . . Sanitary supplies would be federally funded and free. Of course, some men would still pay for the prestige of such commercial brands as Paul Newman Tampons, Muhammed Ali's Rope-a-Dope Pads, John Wayne Maxi Pads, and Joe Namath Jock Shields – 'For Those Light Bachelor Days'.

'If Men Could Menstruate', publ. in *Ms.* October 1978, repr. in ibid.

6 The authority of any governing institution must stop at its citizen's skin.

'Night Thoughts of a Media-Watcher', publ. in *Ms.* November 1981

7 We are becoming the men we wanted to marry.

*Ms.* July/August 1982

8 I have yet to hear a man ask for advice on how to combine marriage and a career.

Radio interview 2 April 1984, LBC

9 A woman without a man is like a fish without a bicycle.

Attributed. Although the quote is generally attributed to Steinem, the words were current as graffiti in the 1970s, in the form: 'A woman needs a man like a fish needs a bicycle.'

## George Steiner (b. 1929)

FRENCH-BORN US CRITIC AND NOVELIST

A leading figure in the study of comparative literature and of language, he is internationally known for *Tolstoy or Dostoevsky* (1958), *The Death of Tragedy* (1960), and *Language and Silence* (1967). *After Babel* (1975) was adapted for television as *The Tongues of Men* (1977) and his novel *The Portage to San Cristobal of A.H.* (1981) was adapted for the stage in 1983.

1 We know that a man can read Goethe or Rilke in the evening, that he can play Bach and Schubert, and go to his day's work at Auschwitz in the morning.
*Language and Silence*, Preface (1967)

2 Language can only deal meaningfully with a special, re-stricted segment of reality. The rest, and it is presumably the much larger part, is silence.
ibid. 'The Retreat from the Word'

3 Pornographers subvert this last, vital privacy; they do our imagining for us. They take away the words that were of the night and shout them over the roof-tops, making them hollow.
ibid. 'Nightworks'

4 To shoot a man because one disagrees with his interpret-ation of Darwin or Hegel is a sinister tribute to the supremacy of ideas in human affairs – but a tribute never-theless.
ibid. 'Marxism and the Literary Critic'

5 It is not the literal past that rules us, save, possibly, in a biological sense. It is images of the past . . . Each new historical era mirrors itself in the picture and active myth-ology of its past or of a past borrowed from other cultures. It tests its sense of identity, of regress or new achievement, against that past.
*In Bluebeard's Castle*, ch. 1 (1971). Opening passage of book.

6 The immense majority of human biographies are a gray transit between domestic spasm and oblivion.
ibid. ch. 3

7 To many men . . . the miasma of peace seems more suffo-cating than the bracing air of war.
'Has Truth a Future?', Bronowski Memorial Lecture, 1978

8 The age of the book is almost gone.
*Daily Mail* 27 June 1988

9 There is something terribly wrong with a culture inebri-ated by noise and gregariousness.
*Daily Telegraph* 23 May 1989

10 Almost overwhelmingly, European culture, at the close of this millennium, is that of the museum. Who among us believes that we shall witness a new Dante, a Shakespeare of the 21st Century, a Mozart to come?
'Modernity, Mythology and Magic', lecture at the Salzburg Festival, 1994, publ. in the *Guardian* 6 August 1994

11 Nothing is more symptomatic of the enervation, of the decompression of the Western imagination, than our in-capacity to respond to the landings on the Moon. Not a single great poem, picture, metaphor has come of this breathtaking act, of Prometheus's rescue of Icarus or of Phaeton in flight towards the stars.
ibid.

12 We Jews walk closer to our children than other men . . . because to have children is possibly to condemn them.
Interview in the *Guardian* 6 January 1996

## Bruce Sterling (b. 1954)

US SCIENCE FICTION AUTHOR

His novels *Involution Ocean* (1977) and *Islands in the Net* (1988) established him as the 'standard bearer of the cyberpunks'. These

were followed by his short story collection, *Globalhead*, the non-fiction *The Hacker Crackdown* (both 1992) and the novels *Heavy Weather* (1995) and *Holy Fire* (1997).

1 If poets are the unacknowledged legislators of the world, science-fiction writers are its court jesters. We are Wise Fools who can leap, caper, utter prophecies, and scratch ourselves in public. We can play with Big Ideas because the garish motley of our pulp origins makes us seem harmless.
Preface to *Burning Chrome* (1986) by WILLIAM GIBSON

2 Technology itself has changed. Not for us the giant steam snorting wonders of the past: the Hoover Dam, the Empire State Building, the nuclear power plant. Eighties tech sticks to the skin, responds to the touch: the personal computer, the Sony Walkman, the portable telephone, the soft contact lens.
*Mirrorshades*, Preface (ed. Bruce Sterling, 1986). Sterling went on: 'The Eighties are an era of reassessment, of integration, of hybridized influences, of old notions shaken loose and reinterpreted with a new sophistication, a broader perspective.'

3 The hacker and the rocker are this decade's pop-culture idols, and cyberpunk is very much a pop phenomenon: spontaneous, energetic, close to its roots. Cyberpunk comes from the realm where the computer hacker and the rocker overlap, a cultural Petri dish where writhing gene lines splice.
ibid.

## Wallace Stevens (1879–1955)

US POET

He worked most of his life in law and insurance while establishing a reputation as a poet. His work, which explores the transformational power of poetic language, includes the verse collections *Har-monium* (1923), *The Man with the Blue Guitar* (1937), and *The Auroras of Autumn* (1950). A number of his verses have been set to music. 'Life is not people and scene, but thought and feeling,' he said. 'The world is myself. Life is myself.'

1 The day of the sun is like the day of a king. It is a prom-enade in the morning, a sitting on the throne at noon, a pageant in the evening.
Journal entry 20 April 1920, publ. in *Souvenirs and Prophecies: the Young Wallace Stevens*, ch. 6 (ed. Holly Stevens, 1966)

2 Poetry is the supreme fiction, madame.
Take the moral law and make a nave of it
And from the nave build haunted heaven.
'A High-Toned Old Christian Woman', publ. in *Harmonium* (1923)

3 The only emperor is the emperor of ice-cream.
'The Emperor of Ice-Cream', publ. in ibid.

4 Civilization must be destroyed. The hairy saints
Of the North have earned this crumb by their
complaints.
'Land of Pine and Marble', publ. in ibid. 'New England Verses'

5 Everything is complicated; if that were not so, life and poetry and everything else would be a bore.
Letter, 19 December 1935, publ. in *Letters of Wallace Stevens* (ed. Holly Stevens, 1967)

6 Union of the weakest develops strength
Not wisdom. Can all men, together, avenge
One of the leaves that have fallen in autumn?
But the wise man avenges by building his city in snow.
'Like Decorations in a Nigger Cemetery', sect. 50, publ. in *Ideas of Order* (1936)

7 They said, 'You have a blue guitar,
You do not play things as they are.'
The man replied, 'Things as they are

Are changed upon the blue guitar.'
'The Man with the Blue Guitar', publ. in *The Man with the Blue Guitar* (1937)

8 It is the unknown that excites the ardor of scholars, who, in the known alone, would shrivel up with boredom.
'The Irrational Element in Poetry', lecture (c. 1937), publ. in *Opus Posthumous* (1957)

9 The squirming facts exceed the squamous mind, If one may say so.
'Connoisseur of Chaos', publ. in *Parts of a World* (1942)

10 The reason can give nothing at all
Like the response to desire.
'Dezembrum', publ. in ibid. Last lines of poem.

11 All the great things have been denied and we live in an intricacy of new and local mythologies, political, economic, poetic, which are asserted with an ever-enlarging incoherence.
'The Noble Rider and the Sound of Words', lecture (1942), repr. in *The Necessary Angel* (1951)

12 We have been a little insane about the truth. We have had an obsession.
ibid.

13 The philosopher proves that the philosopher exists. The poet merely enjoys existence.
'The Figure of the Youth as Virile Poet', lecture August 1943, publ. 1944, repr. in ibid.

14 The greatest poverty is not to live
In a physical world, to feel that one's desire
Is too difficult to tell from despair.
'Esthétique du mal', sect. 15, publ. in *Transport to Summer* (1947)

15 The whole race is a poet that writes down
The eccentric propositions of its fate.
'Men Made Out of Words', publ. in ibid. Last lines of poem.

16 So, too, if, to our surprise, we should meet one of these morons whose remarks are so conspicuous a part of the folklore of the world of the radio – remarks made without using either the tongue or the brain, spouted much like the spoutings of small whales – we should recognize him as below the level of nature but not as below the level of the imagination.
'Three Academic Pieces', no. 1 (1947), repr. in *The Necessary Angel* (1951)

17 What our eyes behold may well be the text of life but one's meditations on the text and the disclosures of these meditations are no less a part of the structure of reality.
ibid.

18 To regard the imagination as metaphysics is to think of it as part of life, and to think of it as part of life is to realize the extent of artifice. We live in the mind.
'Imagination as Value', lecture at Columbia University, 1948, publ. 1949, repr. in ibid.

19 If poetry should address itself to the same needs and aspirations, the same hopes and fears, to which the Bible addresses itself, it might rival it in distribution.
ibid.

20 Style is not something applied. It is something that permeates. It is of the nature of that in which it is found, whether the poem, the manner of a god, the bearing of a man. It is not a dress.
'Two or Three Ideas' (1951), repr. in *Opus Posthumous* (1957)

21 Thought is an infection. In the case of certain thoughts, it becomes an epidemic.
*Opus Posthumous*, 'Adagia' (1957)

22 As life grows more terrible, its literature grows more terrible.
ibid.

23 Intolerance respecting other people's religion is toleration itself in comparison with intolerance respecting other people's art.
ibid.

24 Perhaps it is of more value to infuriate philosophers than to go along with them.
ibid.

25 One cannot spend one's time in being modern when there are so many more important things to be.
ibid.

26 Most modern reproducers of life, even including the camera, really repudiate it. We gulp down evil, choke at good.
ibid.

27 A poem need not have a meaning and like most things in nature often does not have.
ibid.

28 One's ignorance is one's chief asset.
ibid.

29 The imagination is man's power over nature.
ibid.

# Adlai Stevenson (1900–65)

US POLITICIAN

As a Democrat, he held several advisory and executive positions, including that of Governor of Illinois (1948–52). In the 1940s he helped establish the United Nations, and was US ambassador there (1960–65). Credited with making politics 'intellectually respectable once again', he stood unsuccessfully as the Democratic presidential candidate against EISENHOWER in 1952 and 1956.

1 Let's face it. Let's talk sense to the American people. Let's tell them the truth, that there are no gains without pains, that we are now on the eve of great decisions, not easy decisions.
Acceptance speech at Democratic National Convention, Chicago, 26 July 1952, publ. in *Speeches* (1953)

2 What do we mean by patriotism in the context of our times? I venture to suggest that what we mean is a sense of national responsibility . . . a patriotism which is not short, frenzied outbursts of emotion, but the tranquil and steady dedication of a lifetime.
'The Nature of Patriotism', speech to American Legion Convention, New York, 27 August 1952, publ. in ibid.

3 The sound of tireless voices is the price we pay for the right to hear the music of our own opinions. But there is also, it seems to me, a moment at which democracy must prove its capacity to act. Every man has a right to be heard; but no man has the right to strangle democracy with a single set of vocal chords.
Speech in New York, 28 August 1952, publ. in *The Papers of Adlai E. Stevenson*, vol. 4 (1974). See also ADLAI STEVENSON 16.

4 A hungry man is not a free man.
'Farm Policy', speech at Kasson, Minnesota, 6 September 1952, publ. in *The Speeches of Adlai Stevenson* (1952)

5 I have been thinking that I would make a proposition to my Republican friends. That if they will stop telling lies about Democrats, we will stop telling the truth about them.
Campaign speech, 10 September 1952, Fresno, California, quoted in *Adlai Stevenson of Illinois*, ch. 8 (1976) by John Bartlow Martin. The remark has been earlier attributed to Republican Chauncey Depew (senator 1899–1911), though with the party names reversed.

6 There is no evil in the atom; only in men's souls.
'The Atomic Future', speech at Hartford, Connecticut, 18 September 1952, publ. in *Speeches* (1953)

7 In America any boy may become President, and I suppose it's just one of the risks he takes!

Speech in Indianapolis, 26 September 1952, publ. in *Major Campaign Speeches of Adlai E. Stevenson: 1952* (1953)

8 Nothing so dates a man as to decry the younger generation.

Speech at University of Wisconsin, Madison, 8 October 1952, publ. in *Speeches* (1953)

9 The Republican Vice Presidential Candidate . . . asks you to place him a heartbeat from the Presidency.

Referring to Richard Nixon, in 'The Hiss Case', speech in Cleveland, Ohio, 23 October 1952, publ. in *Speeches* (1953). NIXON became Vice-president under EISENHOWER in the November election and was re-elected 1956. This is thought to be the first use of the phrase 'heartbeat from the presidency' to describe the position of Vice-president.

10 The Republican party makes even its young men seem old; the Democratic Party makes even its old men seem young.

Quoted in *Richard Nixon: A Political and Personal Portrait*, ch. 7 (1959) by Earl Mazo. Comparing RICHARD NIXON to the septuagenarian Democratic Vice-president Alben Barkley, during the 1952 presidential race.

11 A funny thing happened to me on the way to the White House.

Speech in Washington, D.C., 13 December 1952, quoted in *Portrait: Adlai E. Stevenson*, ch. 1 (1965) by Alden Whitman. Said after his landslide defeat in the presidential election against EISENHOWER.

12 We cannot be any stronger in our foreign policy – for all the bombs and guns we may heap up in our arsenals – than we are in the spirit which rules inside the country. Foreign policy, like a river, cannot rise above its source.

Speech in New Orleans, 4 December 1954, publ. in *What I Think* (1956)

13 We hear the Secretary of State [John Foster Dulles] boasting of his brinkmanship – the art of bringing us to the edge of the abyss.

Speech at Hartford, Connecticut, 25 February 1956, quoted in *The New York Times* 26 February 1956. See also JOHN FOSTER DULLES 1.

14 Freedom is not an ideal, it is not even a protection, if it means nothing more than freedom to stagnate, to live without dreams, to have no greater aim than a second car and another television set.

'Putting First Things First', publ. in *Foreign Affairs* January 1960

15 With the supermarket as our temple and the singing commercial as our litany, are we likely to fire the world with an irresistible vision of America's exalted purpose and inspiring way of life?

*Wall Street Journal* 1 June 1960

16 The first principle of a free society is an untrammeled flow of words in an open forum.

*The New York Times* 19 January 1962

17 She [Eleanor Roosevelt] would rather light a candle than curse the darkness, and her glow has warmed the world.

Quoted in *The New York Times* 8 November 1962. Comment on learning of the death of ELEANOR ROOSEVELT, echoing the motto of the Christopher Society: 'It is better to light one candle than curse the darkness.'

18 A politician is a statesman who approaches every question with an open mouth.

Quoted in *The Fine Art of Political Wit*, ch. 10 (1964) by Leon Harris

19 The General [President EISENHOWER] has dedicated himself so many times, he must feel like the cornerstone of a public building.

ibid.

20 Nixon is the kind of politician who would cut down a redwood tree, then mount the stump for a speech on conservation.

ibid.

21 An editor is someone who separates the wheat from the chaff and then prints the chaff.

Quoted in *The Stevenson Wit* (1966). The aphorism has also been attributed to writer Elbert Hubbard.

## Stephen Stills (b. 1945)
US ROCK MUSICIAN

A founder member of LA folk-rock band Buffalo Springfield (1966–8), he wrote many of their songs. He was later part of the close harmony group Crosby, Stills and Nash (later Crosby, Stills, Nash and Young), recorded solo albums including *Stephen Stills* (1970), and formed the band Manassas.

1 You better stop, hey,
What's that sound?
Everybody look what's goin' down.

'For What it's Worth' (song, 1967) on the album *Retrospective* (1969) by Buffalo Springfield. The song, written after the 1967 riots in Los Angeles, became a protest anthem about police brutality.

2 If you can't be with the one you love,
Love the one you're with.

'Love the One You're With' (song) on the album *Stephen Stills* (1970). The lyrics of the song, which was also a hit for the Isley Brothers, recall the 1947 song by YIP HARBURG, 'When I'm Not Near the Girl I Love': 'When I'm not near the girl I love,/I love the girl I'm near.'

## Sting (b. 1951)
BRITISH ROCK MUSICIAN

Original name Gordon Sumner. The singer, bassist and principal songwriter with the new wave group the Police until 1986, he has pursued a successful solo career with such records as *The Dream of the Blue Turtles* (1985) and *Soul Cages* (1991), drawing on classical, jazz and world music. He has also campaigned for Amnesty International and the Brazilian rain forest. See also MARK KNOPFLER 1.

1 Music has ceased to belong to the young . . . The rock rebel is defunct. He's meaningless.

Interview in *Smash Hits* 19 August 1982

2 Humans make the mistake of believing that it's their right to survive. Species die out on this planet all the time without anybody noticing. The planet will still be here, and we must lose this attitude of divine right, that something will save us, which we've developed over the centuries. The Martians aren't going to come down and save us. God isn't going to save us.

Interview in *Rolling Stone* September 1983

3 If you love somebody set them free.

Song title on the album *The Dream of the Blue Turtles* (1985)

4 If I were a Brazilian without land or money or the means to feed my children, I would be burning the rain forest too.

*International Herald Tribune* 14 April 1989

5 Celebrity is good for kick-starting ideas, but often celebrity is a lead weight around your neck. It's like you pointing at the moon, but people are looking at your finger.

Interview in *Mojo* February 95

## Karlheinz Stockhausen (b. 1928)
GERMAN COMPOSER

He was a member of the Paris-based 'Musique Concrète' group and in 1953 helped found the electronic music studio at Cologne, becoming its director (1963–77). His work combines electronic and orchestral sounds, as in *Kontakte* (1960) and his operatic cycle *Licht*, begun in 1977.

1 Think NOTHING
Wait until it is absolutely still within you
When you have attained this
Begin to play
As soon as you start to think stop
And try to retain
The state of NON-THINKING
Then continue playing.

*The New York Times* 30 December 1973. Instructions to performers of his work, 'Es'.

## Matt Stone (b. 1971) and
## Trey Parker (b. 1972)
US ANIMATORS

Set in Boulder, Colorado, where the two met at university, their controversial cartoon series *South Park*, featuring the eight-year-olds Kyle, Stan, Kenny and Cartman, became a global hit from its debut in 1997, followed by the movie *South Park: Bigger, Longer and Uncut* (1999). Asked whether he worried about offending any individual groups, Parker (full name Donald McKay Parker) answered: 'You can't worry about one group. You just have to offend everyone equally, and I think we do that pretty well.'

1 Oh my God, they've killed Kenny!

*South Park* (cartoon series, from 1997, written by Matt Stone and Trey Parker). The exclamation, or a variation of it, is made by one of the characters towards the end of most episodes.

## Oliver Stone (b. 1946)
US FILM-MAKER

Examining America's recent past, he was acclaimed for his films *Platoon* (1986) and *Born on the Fourth of July* (1989), both inspired by his time as an infantryman in the Vietnam War and both Oscar-winners. Other films raised controversy: *JFK* (1991) for its version of the KENNEDY assassination, and the ultra-violent *Natural Born Killers* (1994).

1 Excuses are like assholes, Taylor – everybody got one.

Sgt O'Neill (John McGinley), in *Platoon* (film, 1986, written and directed by Oliver Stone).

2 One of the joys of going to the movies was that it was trashy, and we should never lose that.

*International Herald Tribune* 15 February 1988

## Robert Stone (b. 1937)
US NOVELIST

Explorer of society's margins, war zones and the criminal underworld, he lived a bohemian life with JACK KEROUAC in the 1950s before turning to writing full-time. Best known for his fictionalized study of US imperialism, *A Flag for Sunrise* (1981), he has also published *A Hall of Mirrors* (1967), *Dog Soldiers* (1974, filmed 1978) and *Damascus Gate* (1999), and has written screenplays.

1 Life is a means of extracting fiction.

Interview in *Writers at Work* (eighth series, ed. George Plimpton, 1988)

## Sharon Stone (b. 1958)
US SCREEN ACTRESS

Although appearing in films since 1980, she made her breakthrough with *Basic Instinct* (1992) in which she is chiefly remembered for revealing her lack of underwear. Later films include *Casino* (1995) and *The Muse* (1999). The actor Richard E. Grant has described her as 'incredibly stylish . . . as if she has watched a catalogue of Grace Kelly movies a little too closely'.

1 [Of Hollywood] If you have a vagina *and* an attitude in this town, then that's a lethal combination.

*Empire* June 1992

2 With women, it's dog years when you are 40. It's as if you are a thousand years old. It's over.

Quoted in the *Observer* 7 February 1999

## Marie Carmichael Stopes (1880–1958)
BRITISH SCIENTIST AND PIONEER OF BIRTH CONTROL

In 1904 she became the first female science lecturer at the University of Manchester and in 1918 published the controversial and influential *Married Love* (1918), which advocated birth control. She founded the first British birth control clinic in London in 1921 and was the author of more than seventy books, including *Contraception: its Theory, History and Practice* (1923) and *Sex and Religion* (1929).

1 An impersonal and scientific knowledge of the structure of our bodies is the surest safeguard against prurient curiosity and lascivious gloating.

*Married Love*, ch. 5 (1918)

## (Sir) Tom Stoppard (b. 1937)
CZECH-BORN BRITISH PLAYWRIGHT

Original name Thomas Straussler. 'A dazzling high-wire performer', according to critic Michael Billington, Stoppard states his aim as 'a perfect marriage between the play of ideas and farce'. He became established with *Rosencrantz and Guildenstern are Dead* (1966, filmed 1991), followed by *The Real Inspector Hound* (1968), *Jumpers* (1972) and *Travesties* (1974). He has also written the novel *Lord Malquist and Mr Moon* (1966) and the screenplays *Empire of the Sun* (1987) and *The Russia House* (1990).

1 Nothing is the history of the world viewed from a suitable distance. Revolution is a trivial shift in the emphasis of suffering; the capacity for self-indulgence changes hands. But the world does not alter its shape or its course. The seasons are inexorable, the elements constant. Against such vast immutability the human struggles take place on the same scale as the insect movement in the grass, and carnage in the streets is no more than the spider-sucked husk of a fly on a dusty window-sill.

Lord Malquist, in *Lord Malquist and Mr Moon*, pt 1, ch. 1 (1966)

2 My problem is that I am not frightfully interested in anything, except myself. And of all forms of fiction autobiography is the most gratuitous.

Lord Malquist, in ibid. pt 2, ch. 3

3 Let it be said of me that I was born appalled, lived disaffected, and died in the height of fashion.

Lord Malquist, in ibid. pt 6, ch. 2

4 We do on stage things that are supposed to happen off. Which is a kind of integrity, if you look on every exit as being an entrance somewhere else.

Player, in *Rosencrantz and Guildenstern are Dead*, act 1 (1966)

5 Eternity is a terrible thought. I mean, where's it going to end?

Rosencrantz, in ibid. act 2

6 The bad end unhappily, the good unluckily. That is what tragedy means.

Player, in ibid. The line is an adaptation of one by Oscar Wilde: 'The good ended happily, and the bad unhappily. That is what fiction means' (*The Importance of Being Earnest*, 1895).

7 Life is a gamble at terrible odds – if it was a bet, you wouldn't take it.

Player, in ibid. act 3

8 It's not the voting that's democracy, it's the counting.

Dotty, in *Jumpers*, act 1 (1972). See also ANASTASIO SOMOZA 1.

9 It's better to be quotable than honest.

Quoted in the *Guardian* 21 March 1973

10 War is capitalism with the gloves off and many who go to war know it but they go to war because they don't want to be a hero.

Tzara, in *Travesties*, act 1 (1974)

11 I'm with you on the free press. It's the newspapers I can't stand.

Ruth, in *Night and Day*, act 1 (1978)

12 [On baseball] I don't think I can be expected to take seriously any game which takes less than three days to reach its conclusion.

Quoted in the *Guardian* 24 December 1984. Stoppard is known to be a fanatical cricket fan.

13 I still believe that if your aim is to change the world, journalism is a more immediate short-term weapon.

*Guardian* 18 March 1988

## (Sir) Richard Storey (b. 1937)
BRITISH NEWSPAPER PUBLISHER

He was for more than twenty-five years Chairman of, and investor in, Portsmouth and Sunderland Newspapers, resigning as Chairman shortly before PSN was bought out by the Johnston Press in May 1999.

1 The first rule of venture capitalism should be Shoot the Inventor.

Quoted in *Eddy Shah: Today and the Newspaper Revolution*, ch. 21 (1988) by Brian MacArthur. Referring to entrepreneur Eddie Shah. Storey was one of Shah's backers.

## Anthony Storr (b. 1920)
BRITISH PSYCHIATRIST

His work has been called 'psychology made properly and truly popular', as in the influential manual *The Art of Psychotherapy* (1980). Among his other titles are *C.G. Jung* (1973), *Freud* (1989), *Churchill's Black Dog* (1988) and *Feet of Clay: A Study of Gurus* (1997).

1 Self-realization is not an anti-social principle; it is firmly based on the fact that men need each other in order to be themselves.

*The Integrity of the Personality*, ch. 2 (1960)

2 A happy marriage perhaps represents the ideal of human relationship – a setting in which each partner, while acknowledging the need of the other, feels free to be what he or she by nature is: a relationship in which instinct as well as intellect can find expression; in which giving and taking are equal; in which each accepts the other, and I confronts Thou.

ibid. ch. 9

3 The professional must learn to be moved and touched emotionally, yet at the same time stand back objectively: I've seen a lot of damage done by tea and sympathy.

*The Times* 22 October 1992

## Lytton Strachey (1880–1932)
BRITISH BIOGRAPHER AND HISTORIAN

A literary critic who turned to biography, he was a member of the Bloomsbury group of writers and artists and author of *Eminent Victorians* (1918), described by CYRIL CONNOLLY as 'the work of a great anarch'. Other titles include *Queen Victoria* (1921), and *Elizabeth and Essex* (1928). He was remembered by T.E. LAWRENCE as 'an outraged wet mackerel of a man', and by EDITH SITWELL to have been 'cut out of very thin cardboard'.

1 The history of the Victorian Age will never be written: we know too much about it.

*Eminent Victorians*, Preface (1918). Opening words of book.

2 Ignorance is the first requisite of the historian – ignorance, which simplifies and clarifies, which selects and omits, with a placid perfection unattainable by the highest art.

ibid.

## Igor Stravinsky (1882–1971)
RUSSIAN-BORN US COMPOSER

A seminal figure in twentieth-century music, he was a composer of ballets, operas, religious pieces and works for piano and orchestra. *The Firebird* (1910), *Petrushka* (1911) and *The Rite of Spring*, which provoked a theatre riot at its first performance in 1913, were all written for Diaghilev ballets. Other well-known works include the choral-orchestral *Symphony of Psalms* (1930), the operas *Oedipus Rex* (1927) and *The Rake's Progress* (1951), and *Canticum Sacrum* (1955). 'We have a duty towards music,' he asserted, 'namely to invent it.'

1 Film music should have the same relationship to the film drama that somebody's piano playing in my living room has to the book I am reading.

*Music Digest* September 1946

2 My music is best understood by children and animals.

Quoted in the *Observer* 8 October 1961

## Jack Straw (b. 1946)
BRITISH POLITICIAN

He was president of the National Union of Students (1969–71) and elected a Labour MP in 1979. After holding various posts in the shadow cabinet, he was appointed Home Secretary in the 1997 BLAIR government.

1 Parents are responsible for their children. That is the key belief and assertion.

Quoted in the *Daily Telegraph* 27 December 1997. Outlining the government's policy after he had escorted his seventeen-year-old son to a police station to be charged with trying to sell cannabis to a reporter from the *Daily Mirror*.

## Galen Strawson (b. 1952)
BRITISH PHILOSOPHER AND LITERARY CRITIC

In his works on the nature of mind, the Oxford-based thinker addresses problems of causality and human responsibility. His publications include *Freedom and Belief* (1986), *Realism and Causation: A Study of Hume* (1989), and *Secret Connexion: Causation, Realism and David Hume* (1992).

1 It is an insult to God to believe in God. For on the one hand it is to suppose that he has perpetrated acts of incalculable cruelty. On the other hand, it is to suppose that he has perversely given his human creatures an instrument – their intellect – which must inevitably lead them, if they are dispassionate and honest, to deny his existence. It is tempting to conclude that if he exists, it is the atheists and agnostics that he loves best, among those with any pretensions to education. For they are the ones who have taken him most seriously.

*Independent* 24 June 1990

## Janet Street-Porter (b. 1946)
BRITISH BROADCASTER AND JOURNALIST

Winning a reputation as a 'mouthy' presenter and producer for the under 25s, she became the BBC's first Commissioning Editor for youth programmes in 1988 and head of youth and entertainment in 1991. In 1999 she was appointed Editor of the *Independent on Sunday*.

1 I'm not bothered by the provenance of things – to use a painter's analogy. I just think, 'Is it hot?'

Interview in the *Independent on Sunday* 20 December 1992

2 TV is not where truly innovative ideas end up any more. Why? Because TV isn't fun any more and fun is where ideas breed. A terminal blight has hit the TV industry, nipping fun in the bud and stunting our growth. This blight is management – the dreaded Four Ms: male, middle class, middle-aged and mediocre.

*MacTaggart Lecture, Edinburgh Television Festival, 25 August 1995, publ. in the* Guardian *26 August 1995*

3 I'm proud to say I've made a career out of being trivial. I think it's an art form.

Observer *12 November 1995. Referring to her new column.*

4 We've now invented the ultimate tool for keeping the sads busy: the internet. But behind all the techno-babble about cyberspace and hyper-text and virtual worlds, behind all the promises of total immersion in a parallel universe, there's a boring reality: a bunch of screeching modems, lost jobs, and boring computer-nerds getting all excited over a glorified telephone exchange. I'm sick of the spurious claims devotees make for the internet, and I'm particularly sick of the internerds.

*Without Walls: J'Accuse – Technonerds, Channel 4, 19 March 1996*

## (Sir) Roy Strong (b. 1935)

BRITISH HISTORIAN AND MUSEUM DIRECTOR

Flamboyant director of the National Portrait Gallery from 1967 and the Victoria and Albert Museum (1974–87) he is also a broadcaster, writer, garden expert and art historian. Among his many publications are *The English Renaissance Miniature* (1983), *Royal Gardens* (1992) and *The Tudor and Stuart Monarchy* (1995)

1 Art history and museology have got such a death-grip that any form of educational attachment is howled down as spoon-feeding! SPOON-FEEDING, when 90% of the population still think that Botticelli is a brand of Chianti!

*Journal entry, 20 September 1975 in* The Roy Strong Diaries 1967– 1987 *(1997)*

2 Good design is good housekeeping.

Creating Small Gardens, *Introduction (1986)*

## Nadine Strossen (b. 1950)

US HUMAN RIGHTS LAWYER AND AUTHOR

Describing herself as 'a free-speech absolutist' she is a member of the National Board of Directors of the American Civil Liberties Union, and author of *Regulating Campus Hate Speech: A Modest Proposal?* (1990) and *Defending Pornography* (1995).

1 The MacDworkinite idea that pornography is violence against women insults the many women who experience actual, brutal, three-dimensional violence in their real lives . . . I certainly would like nothing better than to find a simple, fast route to equality and safety for women. But censoring sexual speech is really a detour or, worse, a dead end.

Defending Pornography, *ch. 13 (1995). On the anti-pornography stance of* CATHARINE MACKINNON *and* ANDREA DWORKIN.

2 Women are not little children. Women are not weak, not victims. Pleasure and danger go together, of course they do. We want the pleasure, and we can cope with danger.

*Interview in the* Observer *28 January 1996. Referring to calls to censor negative images of women.*

## Joe Strummer (b. 1952) and
## Mick Jones (b. 1955)

BRITISH ROCK MUSICIANS

Chief songwriters of the most politicized of the punk groups of 1977, the Clash, they became icons of inner-city revolt. After Jones left the band in 1983 he had hits with Big Audio Dynamite, while Strummer (original name John Graham Mellor) went on to form the Mescaleros.

1 White riot! I wanna riot!
White riot! a riot of my own.

*'White Riot' (song) on the album* The Clash *(1977) by the Clash*

2 Career opportunities, the ones that never knock,
Every job they offer you is to keep you out the dock.

*'Career Opportunities' (song) on ibid. The song was re-recorded sung by children on the Clash album* Sandinista *(1980).*

3 Every gimmick-hungry yob digging gold from rock 'n' roll
Grabs the mike to tell us he'll die before he's sold
But I believe in this – and it's been tested by research –
That he who fucks nuns will later join the church.

*'Death or Glory' (song) on the album* London Calling *(1979) by the Clash*

## Arthur Hays Sulzberger (1891–1968)

US NEWSPAPER PROPRIETOR

Publisher of *The New York Times* from 1935, he was also Chairman of the Board (1957–61). He expanded the sales of 'the good grey *Times*', as he called it, and launched an international edition in 1949. He wrote letters to the paper published under the pseudonym A. Aitchess (A.H.S.).

1 We [journalists] tell the public which way the cat is jumping. The public will take care of the cat.

*Quoted in* Time *magazine 8 May 1950*

## Edith Summerskill (1901–80)

BRITISH POLITICIAN

Baroness Summerskill of Ken Wood. A Labour MP (1938–55) and Chairman of the Party (1954–5), she was responsible for administering food rationing in ATTLEE's government. She campaigned for hygiene in food, good health care and women's rights, regarding as her highest achievement the law passed in 1949 requiring milk to be pasteurized.

1 Nagging is the repetition of unpalatable truths.

*Speech to Married Women's Association, House of Commons, 14 July 1960, quoted in* The Times *15 July 1960*

## The Sun

1 Crisis? What crisis?

*Headline, 11 January 1979. On James Callaghan's blithe denial of 'mounting chaos' in the economy. See also* JAMES CALLAGHAN 1.

2 Stick it up your junta!

*Headline, 20 April 1982. Referring to a boycott of Argentine corned beef during the Falklands conflict.*

3 GOTCHA!

*Headline, 4 May 1982. On the sinking of the Argentinian cruiser,* General Belgrano. *The headline appeared in the first edition only; subsequent editions were toned down, with the replacement: 'Did 1200 Argies drown?'*

4 Freddie Starr ate my hamster.

*Headline, 13 March 1986*

5 Up yours, Delors.

*Headline, 1 November 1990. On Jacques Delors, President of the European Commission, seen to be attempting to increase EU powers at the expense of British sovereignty.*

6 If Kinnock wins today, will the last person to leave Britain please turn out the lights.

*Headline, 9 April 1992. On election day, in which* NEIL KINNOCK *was the Labour challenger to* JOHN MAJOR.

7 It was the Sun wot won it.

*Headline, 10 April 1992. Following the unexpected Conservative victory in the general election, maintaining* JOHN MAJOR *in power* and giving the Conservatives their fourth successive term in office.

8 **One's bum year.**

Headline, 25 November 1992. Reporting the Queen's speech of the preceding day, in which she had referred to her 'annus horribilis'. See also ELIZABETH II 5.

9 **Is THIS the most dangerous man in Britain?**

Headline, 24 June 1998. Of Prime Minister TONY BLAIR, suspected of favouring Britain's membership of the Single European Currency.

## Gloria Swanson (1897–1983)
US SCREEN ACTRESS

Original name Gloria Svensson. The highest paid star of the silent era, she started out as one of producer Mack Sennett's 'Bathing Beauties' before appearing as a leading sophisticate in CECIL B. DE MILLE's films ('I acquired my expensive tastes from Mr De Mille,' she said). *Sadie Thompson* (1928) was made by her own production company and *Sunset Boulevard* revived her career in 1950. She married six times.

1 **I *am* big. It's the pictures that got small.**

Norma Desmond (Gloria Swanson), in *Sunset Boulevard* (film, 1950, screenplay by Billy Wilder, Charles Brackett and D.M. Marsham Jr, directed by BILLY WILDER). Riposte to Joe Gillis (William Holden), in one of their opening scenes together: 'You're Norma Desmond! You used to be in silent pictures. Used to be big.'

2 **I hate that word. It's *return* – a return to the millions of people who've never forgiven me for deserting the screen.**

ibid. On her 'comeback'.

3 **I just want to tell you all how happy I am to be back in the studio, making a picture again! You don't know much I've missed all of you . . . You see, this is my life. It always will be! There's nothing else. Just us, and the cameras, and those wonderful people out there in the dark. All right, Mr De Mille. I'm ready for my closeup.**

ibid. Last lines of the film, spoken while descending staircase.

4 **When I die, my epitaph should read: *She Paid the Bills*. That's the story of my private life.**

Quoted in the *Saturday Evening Post* 22 July 1950

## Graham Swift (b. 1949)
BRITISH AUTHOR

His novels and short stories concern ordinary characters at critical points of their lives and explore themes of memory, history and landscape. His first novel, *The Sweet-Shop Owner* (1980), was followed by *Shuttlecock* (1981), *Waterland* (1983), *Ever After* (1992) and *Last Orders* (1996), which won the Booker Prize.

1 **I am struck by the way people behave on the Tube. They look at each other beadily and inquisitively, and something goes on in their thoughts which must be equivalent to the way dogs and other animals, when they meet, sniff each other's arses and nuzzle each other's fur.**

*Shuttlecock*, ch. 3 (1981)

2 **All nature's creatures join to express nature's purpose. Somewhere in their mounting and mating, rutting and butting is the very secret of nature itself.**

ibid. ch. 11

3 **Life is one tenth Here and Now, nine-tenths a history lesson. For most of the time the Here and Now is neither now nor here.**

*Waterland*, ch. 8 (1983)

4 **People die when curiosity goes. People have to find out, people have to know. How can there be any true revolution till we know what we are made of?**

ibid. ch. 27

5 **[On the car] It's the best thing that's ever been invented. If it hadn't been invented we'd've had to invent it. And it**

aint just a seat on wheels. It's a workmate. It's a mate. It won't ask no questions, it won't tell no lies. It's somewhere you can be and be who you are. If you aint got no place to call your own, you're okay in a motor.

Narrator (Ray), in *Last Orders*, 'Vince' (1996)

6 **Crying's like pissing. You don't want to get caught short.**

Narrator (Ray), in ibid. 'Rochester'

## Meera Syal (b. 1963)
BRITISH ACTRESS AND AUTHOR

She has appeared on television for BBC2 in the play *Sister Wife* (1992) and in the comedy series *The Real McCoy* (1991–3) and *Goodness Gracious Me* (1998–9). She is also the author of the novels *Anita and Me* (1996) and *Life Isn't All Ha Ha Hee Hee* (1999).

1 **My Aunties did not rage against fate or England when they swapped misery tales, they put everything down to the will of Bhagwan, their karma, their just deserts inherited from their last reincarnation which they had to live through with grace and dignity. In the end, they knew God was on their side. I got the feeling that most of the Tollington women assumed that He had simply forgotten them.**

Meena, in *Anita and Me*, ch. 3 (1996)

2 **We were born here. We haven't got another world that we carry around in our heads. We have to compete. We had to take on a lot of the battles that they couldn't or wouldn't engage in. We had to redefine the image they'd given of Indians as these ethereal, exotic people, clannish, never quite involved.**

Interview in the *Guardian* 6 April 1996. Contrasting the experience of British-born Asians with the attitudes of her parents' generation.

## Thomas Szasz (b. 1920)
HUNGARIAN-BORN US PSYCHIATRIST

His arguments that mental illness does not exist, that psychiatry is 'neither a science nor a healing art' and that psychiatrists act as social police are set out in *The Myth of Mental Illness* (1961) and *The Manufacture of Madness* (1971). As for psychoanalysis, 'the poor need jobs and money, not psychoanalysis. The uneducated need knowledge and skills, not psychoanalysis.'

1 **In the past, men created witches; now they create mental patients.**

*The Manufacture of Madness*, Introduction (1971). 'Institutional psychiatry is a continuation of the Inquisition,' Szasz wrote. 'All that has really changed is the vocabulary and the social style.'

2 **Permissiveness is the principle of treating children as if they were adults; and the tactic of making sure they never reach that stage.**

*The Second Sin*, 'Social Relations' (1973)

3 **A child becomes an adult when he realizes that he has a right not only to be right but also to be wrong.**

ibid. 'Childhood'

4 **Masturbation: the primary sexual activity of mankind. In the nineteenth century, it was a disease; in the twentieth, it's a cure.**

ibid. 'Sex'

5 **A teacher should have maximal authority, and minimal power.**

ibid. 'Education'

6 **Happiness is an imaginary condition, formerly often attributed by the living to the dead, now usually attributed by adults to children, and by children to adults.**

ibid. 'Emotions'

7 **The proverb warns that 'You should not bite the hand**

that feeds you.' But maybe you should, if it prevents you from feeding yourself.

ibid. 'Control and Self-control'

8 People often say that this or that person has not yet found himself. But the self is not something one finds; it is something one creates.

ibid. 'Personal Conduct'

9 The stupid neither forgive nor forget; the naïve forgive and forget; the wise forgive but do not forget.

ibid.

10 Adulthood is the ever-shrinking period between childhood and old age. It is the apparent aim of modern industrial societies to reduce this period to a minimum.

ibid. 'Social Relations'

11 Two wrongs don't make a right, but they make a good excuse.

ibid.

12 The greatest analgesic, soporific, stimulant, tranquilizer, narcotic, and to some extent even antibiotic – in short, the closest thing to a genuine panacea – known to medical science is work.

ibid. 'Medicine'

13 He who does not accept and respect those who want to reject life does not truly accept and respect life itself.

ibid. 'Suicide'

14 Psychoanalysis is an attempt to examine a person's self-justifications. Hence it can be undertaken only with the patient's cooperation and can succeed only when the patient has something to gain by abandoning or modifying his system of self-justification.

ibid. 'Psychoanalysis'

15 Narcissist: psychoanalytic term for the person who loves himself more than his analyst; considered to be the manifestation of a dire mental disease whose successful treatment depends on the patient learning to love the analyst more and himself less.

ibid.

16 Aided and abetted by corrupt analysts, patients who have nothing better to do with their lives often use the psychoanalytic situation to transform insignificant childhood hurts into private shrines at which they worship unceasingly the enormity of the offenses committed against them.

ibid. 'Psychoanalysis'. Szasz continues: 'This solution is immensely flattering to the patients – as are all forms of unmerited self-aggrandizement; it is immensely profitable for the analysts – as are all forms pandering to people's vanity; and it is often immensely unpleasant for nearly everyone else in the patient's life.'

17 Doubt is to certainty as neurosis is to psychosis. The neurotic is in doubt and has fears about persons and things; the psychotic has convictions and makes claims about them. In short, the neurotic has problems, the psychotic has solutions.

ibid. 'Mental Illness'

18 If you talk to God, you are praying; if God talks to you, you have schizophrenia. If the dead talk to you, you are a spiritualist; if God talks to you, you are a schizophrenic.

ibid. 'Schizophrenia'

19 There is no psychology; there is only biography and autobiography.

ibid. 'Psychology'

## Katharine Tait (b. 1923)

The daughter of BERTRAND and DORA RUSSELL, she spent most of the Second World War in America. She briefly worked for the British Ministry of Information and in the Episcopalian church. She was the author of the memoir *My Father, Bertrand Russell* (1975).

1 Reason, progress, unselfishness, a wide historical perspective, expansiveness, generosity, enlightened self-interest. I had heard it all my life, and it filled me with despair.

Quoted in *Bertrand Russell*, Afterword (1992) by Caroline Moorehead. Referring to her life with BERTRAND RUSSELL.

## Quentin Tarantino (b. 1963)

US FILM-MAKER

After a brief acting career, he made his debut as a director with *Reservoir Dogs* (1992), controversial for its violence and savage, ironic humour. He continued acting, taking cameo parts in his own and others' films. His direction of *Pulp Fiction* (1994) won the Golden Palm at Cannes, and he wrote the screenplays for *True Romance* and *Natural Born Killers* (both 1995).

1 Somebody's stickin' a red hot poker up our asses and we gotta find out whose name is on the handle.

Mr Pink (Steve Buscemi), in *Reservoir Dogs* (film, 1992, written and directed by Quentin Tarantino)

2 Why am I Mr Pink? . . . Why can't we pick our own color? . . . Mr Pink sounds like Mr Pussy. Tell you what, let me be Mr Purple. That sounds good to me.

ibid. Mr Pink argues over the choice of alias in the run up to a heist. Tarantino's character also objects: 'Mr Brown, that's a little too close to Mr Shit.'

3 Let's go to work.

Joe Cabot (Lawrence Tierney), in ibid. The words featured on posters advertising the film.

4 I don't really give a fuck what you know or don't know, but I'm going to torture you anyway, regardless.

Mr Blonde (Michael Madsen), in ibid. Addressed to a captured policeman, whose ear he is about to slice off.

5 The worst thing about movies is, no matter how far you can go, when it comes to violence you are wearing a pair of handcuffs that novelists . . . don't wear.

Interview, May 1993, quoted in *Reservoir Dogs*, Introduction (screenplay, 1995)

6 I'm gonna git medieval on your ass.

Marsellus Wallace (Ving Rhames), in *Pulp Fiction* (film, 1994, written and directed by Quentin Tarantino). Speaking to Zed as he prepares to sodomize him.

7 Zed's dead, baby, Zed's dead.

Butch Coolidge (Bruce Willis), in ibid.

8 Violence is one of the most fun things to watch.

Quoted in *Quentin Tarantino: The Man and His Movies*, ch. 11 (1995) by Jami Bernard. Said at the screening of *Pulp Fiction* in Cannes, March 1994.

9 I steal from every single movie ever made. I love it – if my work has anything it's that I'm taking this from this and that from that and mixing them together. If people don't like that, then tough titty, don't go and see it, all right? I steal from everything. Great artists steal, they don't do homages.

Interview in *Empire* November 1994, quoted in ibid.

10 The minute any word has that much power, everyone on the planet should scream it.

Quoted in ibid. On the frequent use of the word 'nigger' in the script of *Pulp Fiction*.

11 Everybody thought I'd gone crazy . . . I wasn't crazy. But when I was holding the shotgun, it all became clear. I

realized for the first time my one true calling in life. I'm a natural born killer.

Mickey Knox (Woody Harrelson), in *Natural Born Killers* (film, 1995, screenplay by Quentin Tarantino, directed by Oliver Stone). In a dispute with Stone, Tarantino later disowned the film.

12 Killing you and what you represent is a statement. I'm not exactly sure what it's saying.

Mickey Knox (Woody Harrelson) to a TV show host, in ibid. During their interview earlier from prison, Mickey explains: 'It's just murder. All creatures and species do it. I know a lot of people who deserve to die. That's where I come in, fate's messenger.'

## Booth Tarkington (1869–1946)
US AUTHOR

As one of the most popular authors of the early twentieth century, he wrote prolifically, for example on childhood and adolescence in *Penrod* (1914) and *Seventeen* (1917), and such novels as *The Magnificent Ambersons* (1918, filmed 1942) and *Alice Adams* (1921, filmed 1935), both Pulitzer Prize-winners. He also wrote numerous plays and works for children.

1 There are two things that will be believed of any man whatsoever, and one of them is that he has taken to drink.

*Penrod*, ch. 10 (1914)

2 An ideal wife is any woman who has an ideal husband.

Gallup, in 'The Hopeful Pessimist', publ. in *Looking Forward and Others* (1926)

## Andrey Tarkovsky (1932–86)
RUSSIAN FILM-MAKER

His films combine an epic style and spirituality, most notably in *Andrei Rublev* (1966), which was banned by the Soviet authorities until 1971, the science fiction *Solaris* (1972) and *The Sacrifice* (1986), made two years after he had defected to Italy. 'My purpose,' he said, 'is to make films that will help people to live, even if they sometimes cause unhappiness.'

1 Of course life has no point. If it had man would not be free, he'd become a slave to that point and his life would be governed by completely new criteria: the criteria of slavery.

Journal entry, 5 September 1970, publ. in *Time Within Time: The Diaries 1970–1986* (1989)

2 Talent is not given to man by God; rather man is doomed to carry the cross of talent. For the artist is a being who strives (but not in secret or in hiding, nor moving in circles, nor in the spaciousness of some kind of ecological niche) to master ultimate truth. The artist masters that truth every time he creates something perfect, something whole.

ibid. 5 December 1973

3 Time is such a simple, almost primitive idea. It is just a means of material differentiation, a way of uniting us all; for in our external, material lives we value the synchronized efforts of individual people.

ibid. 12 December 1979

4 A person fulfils his duty to society in the name of an idea, always doing violence to someone or something.

ibid. 22 January 1981

5 Perhaps I am an agnostic, in the sense that I reject everything that humanity presents as new to the world, on the grounds that the methods used were inappropriate. The formula $E = mc^2$ cannot be right, because there can be no such thing as positive knowledge.

ibid. 15 July 1981

## Jeffrey Tate (b. 1943)
BRITISH CONDUCTOR

He made his operatic debut in 1980 with Berg's *Lulu* at the New York Metropolitan Opera, was Principal Conductor of the Royal Opera House, Covent Garden (1986–91), and Chief Conductor of the Rotterdam Philharmonic Orchestra (1991–5). His specialisms are the Mozart symphonies and piano concertos.

1 The most perfect expression of human behaviour is a string quartet.

*New Yorker* 30 April 1990

## A.J.P. Taylor (1906–90)
BRITISH HISTORIAN

Full name Alan John Percivale Taylor. A prolific author, likened to Macaulay for his breadth and accessibility, he also reached a wide audience as a broadcaster. He was an authority on the Habsburg monarchy and on Bismarck, and his major works include *The Struggle for Mastery in Europe, 1848–1918* (1954), *The Origins of the Second World War* (1961) and *English History, 1914–1945* (1965).

1 There is nothing more agreeable in life than to make peace with the Establishment – and nothing more corrupting.

*New Statesman* 29 August 1953

2 We are apt to say that a foreign policy is successful only when the country, or at any rate the governing class, is united behind it. In reality, every line of policy is repudiated by a section, often by an influential section, of the country concerned.

*The Trouble Makers*, ch. 1 (1957)

3 The crusade against Communism was even more imaginary than the spectre of Communism.

*The Origins of the Second World War*, ch. 2 (1961)

4 [Of Lord Northcliffe] He aspired to power instead of influence, and as a result forfeited both.

*English History, 1914–1945*, ch. 1 (1965). The press magnate Lord Northcliffe was accused of making *The Times* and his other newspapers mouthpieces for his political ambitions.

5 [Of Field Marshal Alexander] Perfect soldier, perfect gentleman . . . never gave offence to anyone not even the enemy.

Letter, 16 March 1973, publ. in *Letters to Eva* (ed. Eva Haraszti Talyor, 1991)

6 In my opinion, most of the great men of the past were only there for the beer – the wealth, prestige and grandeur that went with the power.

Quoted in *Voices 1870–1914*, Introduction (1984) by Peter Vansittart (see ADVERTISING SLOGANS 10)

## Bert Leston Taylor (1866–1921)
US HUMORIST AND COLUMNIST

From 1900 he worked for the *Chicago Tribune*, where his column 'A Line-o'-Type or Two' appeared for twenty years. His books include *Line-O-Type Lyrics* (1902), *A Line-O-Verse Or Two* (1911) and *The So-Called Human Race* (1922).

1 A bore is a man who, when you ask him how he is, tells you.

*The So-Called Human Race* (1922)

2 All we can get out of a Shaw play is two hours and a half of mental exhilaration. We are, inscrutably, denied the pleasure of wondering what Shaw means, or whether he is sincere.

ibid.

## D.J. Taylor (b. 1960)
BRITISH AUTHOR

Full name David John Taylor. His works on English literature include *A Vain Conceit: British Fiction in the 1980s* (1989) and *After the War: The Novel and English Society Since 1945* (1993). He has also written the novel *English Settlement* (1996) and the biography *Thackeray* (1999).

1 Always in England if you had the type of brain that was capable of understanding T.S. Eliot's poetry or Kant's logic, you could be sure of finding large numbers of people who would hate you violently.
*Guardian* 14 September 1989

## Derek Taylor (1934–97)
BRITISH JOURNALIST

A journalist in Liverpool and London, he became known at the *Daily Express* as 'the Beatles man' for his enthusiasm for, and close connections with, what he called 'the gay quartet of grammar-school boys'. He became press officer at Apple Corps in 1968, and remained close to the ex-Beatles after he left in 1970.

1 [On working for the Beatles] A poached egg on the Underground on the Bakerloo Line between Trafalgar Square and Charing Cross? Yes, Paul. A sock full of elephant shit on Otterspool Promenade? Give me 10 minutes, Ringo. Two Turkish dwarfs dancing the Charleston on a sideboard? Male or female, John? Pubic hair from Sonny Liston? It's early closing, George (gulp), but give me until noon tomorrow. The only gig I would do after this is the Queen. Their staff are terrified of them, and not without reason. They have fired more people than any comparable employer unit in the world. They make Lord Beaverbrook look like Jesus.
Quoted in *Shout! The True Story of the Beatles*, pt 4, 'May 1970' (1981) by Philip Norman

## Norman Tebbit (b. 1931)
BRITISH POLITICIAN

Baron Tebbit of Chingford. Elected a Conservative MP in 1970, he held Cabinet posts in employment and in trade and industry in the early 1980s, and was Party Chairman (1985–7). He was the architect of anti-trade union and privatization legislation and has always remained a loyal supporter of MARGARET THATCHER, despite a cooling of relations in 1987 when he returned to the back benches. Possessed with what Austin Mitchell called 'a nasty instinct for the exposed groin', he was labelled 'the Chingford skinhead' for his confrontational style. See also MICHAEL FOOT 1

1 He didn't riot. He got on his bike and looked for work.
Speech to Conservative Party Conference, Blackpool, 15 October 1981, quoted in the *Daily Telegraph* 16 October 1981. Tebbit's speech, which contrasted his unemployed father's self-help approach during the Depression with the attitude of rioters in Britain, was given a rousing ovation by the conference but drew criticism elsewhere in the country at a time when unemployment stood at three million.

2 It is certainly safe, in view of the movement to the right of intellectuals and political thinkers, to pronounce the brain death of socialism.
*The Times* 26 April 1988

3 [On Margaret Thatcher] Gradually it was becoming clear that she was a Prime Minister unlike any since Churchill. Nonetheless, the 'wets', the weaker willed, the craven-hearted and the embittered failures amongst the Conservative Party still hoped she would go away and let them go back to their old ways.
*Upwardly Mobile*, ch. 8 (memoirs, 1988). On MARGARET THATCHER's record by the summer of 1981.

4 For me the British Broadcasting Corporation might have

better called itself the Stateless Persons Broadcasting Corporation for it certainly did not reflect the mood of the British people who finance it.
ibid. ch. 8. Referring to the BBC's coverage of the Falklands War.

5 The word 'conservative' is used by the BBC as a portmanteau word of abuse for anyone whose views differ from the insufferable, smug, sanctimonious, naive, guilt-ridden, wet, pink orthodoxy of that sunset home of the third-rate minds of that third-rate decade, the nineteen-sixties.
Quoted in the *Independent* 24 February 1990

6 Parliament must not be told a direct untruth, but it's quite possible to allow them to mislead themselves.
Quoted in the *Observer* 17 March 1991

## Mother Teresa (1910–97)
ALBANIAN-BORN ROMAN CATHOLIC MISSIONARY

Original name Agnes Gonxha Bojaxhin. In India since 1928, she left the Irish Order of Loreto Sisters in 1948 and, assuming Indian citizenship, devoted her life to alleviating the plight of Calcutta's slum-dwellers. She founded the Congregation of the Missionaries of Charity in 1950, established a leper colony in West Bengal in 1957 and by the time of her death had extended her 'missionary multinational' to eighty-seven countries and 160 cities. Popularly regarded as a saint, she was awarded the Nobel Peace Prize in 1979. See also MARK TULLY 1.

1 The biggest disease today is not leprosy or tuberculosis, but rather the feeling of being unwanted.
Quoted in the *Observer* 3 October 1971

2 To keep a lamp burning we have to keep putting oil in it.
Quoted in *Time* magazine 29 December 1975

3 Our life of poverty is as necessary as the work itself. Only in heaven will we see how much we owe to the poor for helping us to love God better because of them.
*A Gift for God*, 'Carriers of Christ's Love' (1975)

4 We ourselves feel that what we are doing is just a drop in the ocean. But if that drop was not in the ocean, I think the ocean would be less because of that missing drop. I do not agree with the big way of doing things.
ibid.

5 There must be a reason why some people can afford to live well. They must have worked for it. I only feel angry when I see waste. When I see people throwing away things that we could use.
ibid. 'Riches'

6 I try to give to the poor people for love what the rich could get for money. No, I wouldn't touch a leper for a thousand pounds; yet I willingly cure him for the love of God.
ibid.

7 We must have a real living determination to reach holiness. 'I will be a saint' means I will despoil myself of all that is not God; I will strip my heart of all created things; I will live in poverty and detachment; I will renounce my will, my inclinations, my whims and fancies, and make myself a willing slave to the will of God.
ibid. 'Willing Slaves to the Will of God'

8 Many people mistake our work for our vocation. Our vocation is the love of Jesus.
From documentary film *Mother Teresa*, quoted in *The New York Times* 28 November 1986

9 So many signatures for such a small heart.
Quoted in the *Evening Standard* 3 January 1992. Referring to form-filling in a California hospital.

## Studs Terkel (b. 1912)

US AUTHOR AND BROADCASTER

Called 'a national resource' by J.K. GALBRAITH, he acted in radio soap operas and worked as a disc jockey, sports commentator and TV compère before establishing himself as a recorder of oral history. His books include *The Good War* (1984, Pulitzer Prize), *American Dreams* (1980) and *Coming of Age* (1995).

1 Something was still there, that something that distinguishes an artist from a performer: the revealing of self. Here I be. Not for long, but here I be. In sensing her mortality, we sensed our own.

*Talking to Myself*, bk 4, ch. 4 (1977). On seeing BILLIE HOLIDAY perform in Chicago, 1956.

2 At a time when pimpery, lick-spittlery, and picking the public's pocket are the order of the day – indeed, officially proclaimed as virtue – the poet must play the madcap to keep his balance. And ours.

ibid.

## Mary Church Terrell (1863–1954)

US CIVIL RIGHTS ACTIVIST

She lectured against discrimination, disenfranchisement and racial violence throughout the USA. In 1901 she became Honorary Life President of the National Association of Colored Women, and she was also a charter member of the National Association for the Advancement of Colored People.

1 Please stop using the word 'Negro' . . . We are the only human beings in the world with fifty-seven variety of complexions who are classed together as a single racial unit. Therefore, we are really truly colored people, and that is the only name in the English language which accurately describes us.

Letter to the editor, in the *Washington Post* 14 May 1949

## Quinlan Terry (b. 1937)

BRITISH ARCHITECT

Considered one of Britain's leading exponents of classical architecture, he created the New Common Room at Gray's Inn, was responsible for buildings at Downing College, Cambridge (1992), and restored the State Room at 10 Downing Street (1988). His book *The Revival of Architecture* (1986) questions modernist orthodoxy.

1 I don't think we can ignore the Modern Movement. But I wouldn't have minded at all if it hadn't happened. I think the world would be a much nicer place.

*International Herald Tribune* 25 April 1988

## Margaret Thatcher (b. 1925)

BRITISH POLITICIAN AND PRIME MINISTER

Baroness Thatcher of Kesteven. Called 'the best man in England' by RONALD REAGAN, she became Conservative Party leader in 1975 and subsequently Britain's first woman prime minister (1979–90), and the longest serving holder of that office since 1820. She championed monetarist economics, privatization, share ownership and the curbing of trade-union power, and retained her popularity despite high unemployment and the 'poll tax', eventually coming to grief on European policy. See also KINGSLEY AMIS 10, ALAN BENNETT 4, JULIAN CRITCHLEY 2, ARIEL DORFMAN 4, NORMAN FOWLER 1, NEIL KINNOCK 1, NORMAN TEBBIT 3.

1 No woman in my time will be Prime Minister or Chancellor or Foreign Secretary – not the top jobs. Anyway I wouldn't want to be Prime Minister. You have to give yourself 100%.

Interview in the *Sunday Telegraph* 26 October 1969. Mrs Thatcher was then Shadow Education Spokesman.

2 Most of us have stopped using silver for everyday.

Quoted in the *Observer* 2 August 1970

3 One of the things being in politics has taught is that men are not a reasoned or reasonable sex.

Television interview, 14 January 1972, BBC

4 I owe nothing to Women's Lib.

Quoted in the *Observer* 1 December 1974

5 We must have an ideology. The other side have got an ideology they can test their policies against. We must have one as well.

Speech to the Conservative Philosophy Group, 1975, quoted in *One of Us*, ch. 18 (1989) by Hugo Young. The speech was made shortly after Thatcher was elected Conservative Party leader in February.

6 In politics if you want anything said, ask a man. If you want anything done, ask a woman.

*People* 15 September 1975

7 When the next Conservative government comes to power, many trade unionists will have put it there. Millions of them vote for us at every election. I want to say this to them and to all our supporters in industry: go out and join in the work of your unions; go to their meetings and stay to the end, and learn the union rules as well as the far Left knows them. Remember that if parliamentary democracy dies, free trades unions die with it.

Speech to Conservative Party Conference, Blackpool, 10 October 1975, publ. in *The Revival of Britain; Speeches on Home and European Affairs 1975–1988* (ed. Alistair B. Cooke, 1989)

8 Ladies and gentlemen, I stand before you tonight in my red chiffon evening gown, my face softly made up, my fair hair gently waved . . . the Iron Lady of the Western World! Me? A cold war warrior? Well, yes – if that is how they wish to interpret my defence of values and freedoms fundamental to our way of life.

Speech at Finchley, 31 January 1976, quoted in the *Sunday Times* 1 February 1976. A week earlier, an article in the Soviet newspaper *Red Star* had branded her an 'Iron Lady'.

9 We have to get our production and our earnings into balance. There's no easy popularity in what we are proposing, but it is fundamentally sound. Yet I believe people accept there is no real alternative.

Speech at Conservative Women's Conference, 21 May 1980, quoted in the *Daily Telegraph* 22 May 1980. Thatcher's repetition of the formula 'There is no alternative' led to her being given the acronym 'Tina'.

10 To those waiting with bated breath for that favourite media catch-phrase, the U-turn, I have only this to say. You turn, if you want; the lady's Not for turning.

Speech to the Conservative Party Conference, Brighton, 10 October 1980, publ. in *The Times* 11 October 1980. On her determination to persist in monetarist policies. The punning reference is to the play by CHRISTOPHER FRY, *The Lady's Not for Burning* (1946).

11 Just rejoice at that news and congratulate our forces and the marines.

Quoted in *The Times* 26 April 1982. Said to journalists on the recapture of South Georgia during the Falklands conflict, 25 April 1982, and usually remembered as 'Rejoice, rejoice . . .'

12 [On the Falklands campaign] When you've spent half your political life dealing with humdrum issues like the environment, it's exciting to have a real crisis on your hands.

Speech to Scottish Conservative Party Conference, 14 May 1982, quoted in *One of Us*, ch. 13 (1989) by Hugo Young

13 We have to see that the spirit of the South Atlantic – the real spirit of Britain – is kindled not only by war but can now be fired by peace. We have the first prerequisite. We know we can do it – we haven't lost the ability. That is the Falklands Factor. We have proved ourselves to ourselves. It is a lesson we must not now forget.

Speech to Conservative women, Cheltenham, 3 July 1982, publ.

in *The Penguin Book of Twentieth-Century Speeches* (ed. Brian MacArthur, 1999). The 'Falklands Factor' was widely seen as crucial in securing the Conservative Party's election win in 1983.

14 **I am extraordinarily patient provided I get my own way in the end.**

Quoted in the *Observer* 2 January 1983

15 **It was then that the iron entered my soul.**

On her time in EDWARD HEATH's cabinet, quoted in the *Observer* 27 March 1983. Thatcher and Heath were to become irreconcilable political opponents.

16 **I was asked whether I was trying to restore Victorian values. I said straight out I was. And I am.**

Speech to British Jewish Community, 21 July 1983, quoted in *Thatcher's Reign*, 'Let Our Children Grow Tall – The Family' (1984) by Melanie McFadyean and Margaret Renn. Referring to interview by Brian Walden on 'Weekend World' 17 January 1983, when she stated that Victorian values 'were the values when our country became great ... As our people prospered, so they used their independence and initiative to prosper others, not compulsion by the state.'

17 **[Of Mikhail Gorbachev] We can do business together.**

Quoted in *The Times* 18 December 1984. After a meeting at which GORBACHEV had declared Soviet willingness to discuss nuclear arms reductions. He became First Secretary of the Soviet Communist Party three months later.

18 **We must try to find ways to starve the terrorist and the hijacker of the oxygen of publicity on which they depend.**

Speech to American Bar Association, London, 15 July 1985, quoted in *The Times* 16 July 1985

19 **No one would remember the Good Samaritan if he'd only had good intentions – he had money as well.**

Television interview, 6 January 1986, quoted in *The Times* 12 January 1986

20 **I hope to go on and on.**

Television interview, 11 May 1987, quoted in the *Independent* 12 May 1987

21 **There is no such thing as society: there are individual men and women, and there are families.**

Interview in *Woman's Own* 31 October 1987

22 **We have not successfully rolled back the frontiers of the State in Britain only to see them reimposed at a European level, with a European super-State exercising a new dominance from Brussels.**

'The Bruges Speech', 20 September 1988, publ. in *The Penguin Book of Twentieth-Century Speeches* (ed. Brian MacArthur, 1999). The speech was drafted by Sir Charles Powell, Thatcher's adviser on foreign affairs.

23 **People think that at the top there isn't much room. They tend to think of it as an Everest. My message is that there is tons of room at the top.**

*Daily Telegraph* 30 September 1988. Thatcher's words recall those attributed to Daniel Webster c. 1801, rejecting advice that he stay out of the crowded legal profession: 'There is always room at the top.'

24 **We have become a grandmother.**

Quoted in *The Times* 4 March 1989

25 **The cocks may crow, but it's the hen that lays the egg.**

Quoted in the *Sunday Times* 9 April 1989

26 **Most women defend themselves. It is the female of the species – it is the tigress and lioness in you – which tends to defend when attacked.**

*Daily Mail* 4 May 1989

27 **I think perhaps we manage our revolutions much more quietly in this country.**

*Daily Telegraph* 12 July 1989. Said in the wake of the bicentenary celebrations of the French Revolution in Paris.

28 **If it is once again one against forty-eight, then I am very sorry for the forty-eight.**

Quoted in the *Daily Telegraph* 25 October 1989. Referring to the pending 1989 Commonwealth Conference.

29 **I am in favour of agreement but against consensus.**

Quoted in *One of Us*, ch. 18 (1989) by Hugo Young. On one occasion Thatcher had the word 'consensus' removed from a Commonwealth conference communiqué in favour of 'agreement'. 'To me, consensus seems to be the process of abandoning all beliefs, principles, values and policies,' she explained. 'So it is something in which no one believes and to which no one objects.'

30 **I am in politics because of the conflict between good and evil, and I believe that in the end good will triumph.**

Quoted in the *Guardian* 23 October 1990

31 **The President of the Commission, M. Delors, said at this conference the other day that he wanted the European Parliament to be the democratic body of the Community, he wanted the Commission to be the Executive, and he wanted the Council of Ministers to be the Senate. No. No. No.**

Speech to House of Commons, 30 October 1990, publ. in *Hansard*. Referring to talks at the EU summit in Rome.

32 **[On the Gulf crisis] I seem to smell the stench of appeasement in the air.**

Quoted in the *Independent* 31 October 1990

33 **I shan't be pulling the levers there but I shall be a very good back-seat driver.**

Quoted in the *Independent* 27 November 1990. On the appointment of JOHN MAJOR as the next prime minister.

34 **Home is where you come to when you have nothing better to do.**

Interview in *Vanity Fair* June 1991

35 **The lesson of the century has been that the people feel far more comfortable and more stable with a nation state. It is the nation state which is the unit of loyalty. Ours is the United Kingdom.**

*Sunday Telegraph* 13 December 1992

36 **Idleness, selfishness, fecklessness, envy and irresponsibility are the vices upon which socialism in any form flourishes and which it in turn encourages. But socialism's devilishly clever tactic is to play up to all those human failings, while making those who practise them feel good about it.**

Nicholas Ridley Memorial Lecture 22 August 1996, publ. in *Margaret Thatcher: The Collected Speeches* (ed. Robin Harris, 1997)

37 **In my lifetime Europe has been the source of our problems, not the source of our solutions. It's America and Britain that saved the world.**

Interview in *Saga Magazine* September 1998

38 **Is he one of us?**

Attributed, referring to candidates for office. The words gave Hugo Young the title for his biography, *One of Us* (1989)

## Paul Theroux (b. 1941)

US NOVELIST AND TRAVEL WRITER

He has written extensively of the expatriate experience, as in his novels *Jungle Lovers* (1971) and *The Mosquito Coast* (1981, filmed 1986) and in short stories and essays. His travel writings include chronicles of railway journeys, notably *The Great Railway Bazaar* (1975) and *The Old Patagonian Express* (1979). His thriller *Doctor Slaughter* (1984) was filmed as *Half Moon Street* (1987).

1 **The expatriate does not have to think; he has long since decided that nothing should change, the jungle should not alter. In Africa he is superior and should remain so. Most agree with him; all the people he works with agree with him; Africans with money and position are the most convinced of all that change means upsetting the nature of society.**

'Tarzan Is an Expatriate' (1967), repr. in *Sunrise with Seamonsters* (1985)

2 **I have seldom heard a train go by and not wished I**

was on it. Those whistles sing bewitchment: railways are irresistible bazaars, snaking along perfectly level no matter what the landscape, improving your mood with speed, and never upsetting your drink.

*The Great Railway Bazaar*, ch. 1 (1975)

3 Extensive traveling induces a feeling of encapsulation, and travel, so broadening at first, contracts the mind.

ibid. ch. 21

4 What interests me is the waking in the morning, the progress from the familiar to the slightly odd, to the rather strange, to the totally foreign, and finally to the outlandish. The journey, not the arrival, matters; the voyage, not the landing.

*The Old Patagonian Express*, ch. 1 (1979)

5 Travel is glamorous only in retrospect.

Quoted in the *Observer* 7 October 1979

6 People do not become writers out of healthy literary impulse, but out of a deep loneliness, a deficiency, a kind of dysfunction . . . and on the positive side, they turn to books for solace. It's all sorts of things. It's conceit. It's signalling for attention. People who are normal don't become writers.

Interview in *Guardian* 11 November 1995

7 The notion of a literary quarrel – or anything that looks like a quarrel – is like catnip to literary philistines and lazy intellects.

*Daily Telegraph* 21 November 1998. Referring to the end of his friendship with V.S. NAIPAUL as related in Theroux's book *Sir Vidia's Shadow* (1998).

8 The man who is tired of London is tired of looking for a parking space.

Interview in the *Daily Telegraph* 30 November 1998. A twist on Dr Johnson's saying, 'When a man is tired of London, he is tired of life' (in Boswell's *Life*, 1791). Theroux, who moved to Hawaii after years in London, made a similar observation in *The Kingdom By the Sea*, ch. 1 (1983).

# Dylan Thomas (1914–53)

WELSH POET

Having, as he put it, 'fallen in love with words', especially the cadences of Wales, he published *18 Poems* in 1934 and gained further recognition with *Deaths and Entrances* (1946). He narrated his 'play for voices', *Under Milk Wood*, on radio in New York shortly before his death from alcohol poisoning. His verdict on himself was: 'I am in the path of Blake, but so far behind that only the wings of his heels are in sight.'

1 Never be lucid, never state,
If you would be regarded great,
The simplest thought or sentiment
(For thought, we know, is decadent).

'A Letter to My Aunt Discussing the Correct Approach to Modern Poetry', written 1933, publ. in *The Poems* (ed. Daniel Jones, 1971)

2 The force that through the green fuse drives the flower
Drives my green age; that blasts the roots of trees
Is my destroyer.

'The force that through the green fuse drives the flower' publ. in the *Sunday Referee* 29 October 1933, reprinted in *18 Poems* (1934)

3 The hand that signed the treaty bred a fever,
And famine grew, and locusts came;
Great is the hand that holds dominion over
Man by a scribbled name.

'The hand that signed the paper felled a city', publ. in *New Verse* December 1935, repr. in *25 Poems* (1936)

4 Though lovers be lost love shall not;
And death shall have no dominion.

'And death shall have no dominion', publ. in *25 Poems* (1936). St Paul used these words in Romans 6:9: 'Christ being raised from

the dead dieth no more; death hath no more dominion over him.' An earlier version of Thomas's poem was published in *New English Weekly* 18 May 1933, the first of his poems to be accepted by a London literary magazine.

5 I know we're not saints or virgins or lunatics; we know all the lust and lavatory jokes, and most of the dirty people; we can catch buses and count our change and cross the roads and talk real sentences. But our innocence goes awfully deep, and our discreditable secret is that we don't know anything at all, and our horrid inner secret is that we don't care that we don't.

Letter to Caitlin, later his wife, end of 1936, publ. in *The Collected Letters of Dylan Thomas* (ed. Paul Ferris, 1985)

6 The hunchback in the park
A solitary mister
Propped between trees and water.

'The hunchback in the park', publ. in *Life and Letters Today* October 1941, repr. in *New Poems 1942* (1942)

7 A poet writing a poem is at peace with everything except words, which are eternal actions; only in the lulls between the warring work on words can he be at war with men.

Letter, 30 July 1945, publ. in *The Collected Letters of Dylan Thomas* (ed. Paul Ferris, 1985)

8 Deep with the first dead lies London's daughter,
Robed in the long friends,
The grains beyond age, the dark veins of her mother,
Secret by the unmourning water
Of the riding Thames.
After the first death, there is no other.

'A Refusal to Mourn the Death, by Fire, of a Child in London', publ. in *Horizon* October 1945, repr. in *Deaths and Entrances* (1946)

9 In my craft or sullen art
Exercised in the still night
When only the moon rages
And the lovers lie abed
With all their griefs in their arms,
I labour by singing light.

'In my craft or sullen art', ibid.

10 Now as I was young and easy under the apple boughs
About the lilting house and happy as the grass was
green.

'Fern Hill', in ibid.

11 Do not go gentle into that good night,
Old age should burn and rage at close of day;
Rage, rage, against the dying of the light.

'Do not go gentle into that good night', publ. in *Botteghe Oscure* November 1951, repr. in *Collected Poems* (1952)

12 These poems, with all their crudities, doubts, and confusions, are written for the love of Man and in praise of God, and I'd be a damn' fool if they weren't.

*Collected Poems*, 'Author's note' (1952)

13 [Of Wales] The land of my fathers. My fathers can have it.

*Adam* December 1953. 'Land of my Fathers' is the Welsh national anthem.

14 Too many of the artists of Wales spend too much time talking about the position of the artists of Wales. There is only one position for an artist anywhere: and that is, upright.

*Quite Early One Morning*, 'Wales and the Artist' (1954)

15 To begin at the beginning: It is spring, moonless night in the small town, starless and bible-black, the cobblestreets silent and the hunched courters'-and-rabbits' wood limping invisible down to the sloeblack, slow, black, crow-black, fishingboat-bobbing sea.

*Under Milk Wood* (1954). Opening words.

16 I must put my pyjamas in the drawer marked pyjamas.

Mr Ogmore, in ibid.

17 And before you let the sun in, mind it wipes its shoes.

Mrs Ogmore-Pritchard, in ibid. The same character utters an almost identical line in an untitled poem in *Quite Early One Morning* (1954), which included earlier versions of *Under Milk Wood*.

18 Oh, I'm a martyr to music.

Mrs Organ Morgan, in ibid.

19 You just wait. I'll sin till I blow up!

Mae Rose Cottage, in ibid.

20 We are not wholly bad or good
Who live our lives under Milk Wood.

First Voice, in ibid.

21 I've had eighteen straight whiskies. I think that's the record.

Quoted in *Dylan Thomas in America*, ch. 8 (1956) by John Malcolm Brinnin. On the day after he spoke these words in a New York hotel, Thomas fell into a coma from which he never recovered.

22 [An alcoholic is] a man you don't like who drinks as much as you do.

Quoted in *The Life of Dylan Thomas*, ch. 6 (1965) by Constantine Fitzgibbon

## Edward Thomas (1878–1917)
BRITISH POET AND AUTHOR

Original name Edward Eastaway. He wrote walking tours and essays on the countryside as well as critical studies before being encouraged by ROBERT FROST to turn to poetry in 1914. The bulk of his verse was produced during the last two years of his life and published posthumously in *Poems* (1917) and *Last Poems* (1918) after his death at the battle of Arras.

1 The past is the only dead thing that smells sweet.

'Early One Morning', publ. in *Poems* (1917)

2 The steam hissed. Someone cleared his throat.
No one left and no one came
On the bare platform. What I saw
Was Adlestrop – only the name.

'Adlestrop', publ. in ibid.

3 There's none less free than who
Does nothing and has nothing else to do,
Being free only for what is not to his mind,
And nothing is to his mind.

'Liberty', publ. in ibid.

4 I have come to the borders of sleep,
The unfathomable deep
Forest where all must lose
Their way, however straight,
Or winding, soon or late;
They cannot choose.

'Lights Out', publ. in ibid.

5 As for myself,
Where first I met the bitter scent is lost.
I, too, often shrivel the grey shreds,
Sniff them and think and sniff again and try
Once more to think what it is I am remembering,
Always in vain. I cannot like the scent,
Yet I would gather up others more sweet,
With no meaning, than this bitter one.

'Old Man', publ. in *Last Poems* (1918)

6 This is no case of petty right or wrong
That politicians or philosophers
Can judge. I hate not Germans, nor grow hot
With love of Englishmen, to please newspapers.
Beside my hate for one fat patriot
My hatred of the Kaiser is love true.

'This is no case of petty right or wrong', publ. in ibid. Opening lines.

## Lewis Thomas (1913–93)
US PHYSICIAN AND ACADEMIC

Dean of the Yale School of Medicine (1971–3), he achieved recognition for his popular essays, chiefly reflections on biology and medicine, such as *The Lives of a Cell* (1974), *The Medusa and the Snail* (1979) and *The Fragile Species* (1992).

1 It hurts the spirit, somehow, to read the word *environments*, when the plural means that there are so many alternatives there to be sorted through, as in a market, and voted on.

*The Lives of a Cell*, 'Natural Man' (1974)

2 We are designed, coded, it seems, to place the highest priority on being individuals, and we must do this first, at whatever cost, even if it means disability for the group.

*The Medusa and the Snail*, 'On Committees' (1979)

3 We are built to make mistakes, coded for error.

ibid. 'To Err is Human'

4 Sometimes you get a glimpse of a semicolon coming, a few lines farther on, and it is like climbing a steep path through woods and seeing a wooden bench just at a bend in the road ahead, a place where you can expect to sit for a moment, catching your breath.

ibid. 'Notes on Punctuation'

5 If you want to use a cliché you must take full responsibility for it yourself and not try to job it off on anon., or on society.

ibid.

6 Music is the effort we make to explain to ourselves how our brains work. We listen to Bach transfixed because this is listening to a human mind.

ibid. 'On Thinking About Thinking'

## R.S. Thomas (b. 1913)
WELSH POET AND CLERGYMAN

Full name Ronald Stuart Thomas. A self-taught Welsh speaker and committed Welsh nationalist, he was ordained an Anglican vicar in 1936, a post he called a 'lonely and often barren predicament'. His poems deal with the Welsh landscape and the hardships of his parishioners, as in *The Stones of the Field* (1946) and *Song at the Year's Turning* (1955). For poet Anne Stevenson, he is 'a religious poet who sees the tragedy, not the pathos, in the human condition'.

1 There is no present in Wales,
And no future;
There is only the past,
Brittle with relics,
Wind-bitten towers and castles
With sham ghost;
Mouldering quarries and mines;
And an impotent people,
Sick with inbreeding,
Worrying the carcase of an old song.

'Welsh Landscape', publ. in *An Acre of Land* (1952). Closing lines.

2 They chose their pastors as they chose their horses
For their hard work

Narrator, in *The Minister* (1953), reprinted in *Song at the Year's Turning* (1955)

3 There is always the thin pane of glass set up between us
And our desires.
We stare and stare and stare, until the night comes
And the glass is superfluous.

The minister, in ibid.

4 The pulpit is a kind of block-house
From which to fire the random shot
Of innuendo; but woe betide the man
Who leaves the pulpit for the individual

Assault.

The minister, in ibid.

5 Stay, then, village, for round you spins
On slow axis a world as vast
And meaningful as any poised
By great Plato's solitary mind.

'The Village', publ. in *Song at the Year's Turning* (1955)

6 There stood the ladies from the council houses:
Blue eyes and Birmingham yellow
Hair, and the ritual murder of vowels.

'Border Blues', publ. in *Poetry for Supper* (1958)

7 But what to do? Doctors in verse
Being scarce now, most poets
Are their own patients, compelled to treat
Themselves first, their complaint being
Peculiar always.

'The Cure', publ. in ibid. Opening lines.

8 Sunlight's a thing that needs a window
Before it enter a dark room.
Windows don't happen.

'Poetry for Supper', publ. in ibid.

9 Live large, man, and dream small.

'Lore', publ. in *Tares* (1961)

10 It was the mind's weight
Kept me bent, as I grew tall.

'Sorry' publ. in *The Bread of Truth* (1963)

11 Those who crowd
A small window dirty it
With their breathing, though sublime
And inexhaustible the view.

'The Small Window', publ. in *Not That He Brought Flowers* (1968)

12 I never thought other than
That God is that great absence
In our lives, the empty silence
Within, the place where we go
Seeking, not in hope to
Arrive or find.

'Via Negativa', publ. in *H'm* (1972)

# Hunter S. Thompson (b. 1939)
US JOURNALIST

Full name Hunter Stockton Thompson. A 'New Journalist' of the 1960s, he invented the 'gonzo' genre of reporting, offering highly subjective accounts of the world with himself as protagonist. His books, including *Hell's Angels* (1966), *Fear and Loathing in Las Vegas* (1972, filmed 1998) and *Fear and Loathing on the Campaign Trail '72* (1973), were searing but witty indictments of American corruption and decadence.

1 Richard Nixon has never been one of my favourite people, anyway. For years I've regarded his very existence as a monument to all the rancid genes and broken chromosomes that corrupt the possibilities of the American Dream; he was a foul caricature of himself, a man with no soul, no inner convictions, with the integrity of a hyena and the style of a poison toad.

'Presenting: the Richard Nixon Doll (Overhauled 1968 Model)', publ. in *Pageant* July 1968, repr. in *The Great Shark Hunt*, pt 2 (1979)

2 Myths and legends die hard in America. We love them for the extra dimension they provide, the illusion of near-infinite possibility to erase the narrow confines of most men's reality. Weird heroes and mould-breaking champions exist as living proof to those who need it that the tyranny of 'the rat race' is not yet final.

'Those Daring Young Men in their Flying Machines . . . Ain't What They Used to Be!' publ. in *Pageant* September 1969, repr. in ibid. pt 3

3 Fear and loathing in Las Vegas

Book title (1972). The core of the book, whose title was frequently adapted for other publications by Thompson, originally appeared in articles in *Rollling Stone* in November 1971 under his pseudonym Raoul Duke.

4 History is hard to know, because of all the hired bullshit, but even without being sure of 'history' it seems entirely reasonable to think that every now and then the energy of a whole generation comes to a head in a long fine flash, for reasons that nobody really understands at the time – and which never explain, in retrospect, what actually happened.

*Fear and Loathing in Las Vegas*, ch. 8 (1972)

5 If I'd written all the truth I knew for the past ten years, about 600 people – including me – would be rotting in prison cells from Rio to Seattle today. Absolute truth is a very rare and dangerous commodity in the context of professional journalism.

'Fear and Loathing at the Superbowl', publ. in *Rolling Stone* 15 February 1973, repr. in *The Great Shark Hunt*, pt 1 (1979)

6 *Gonzo* journalism . . . is a style of 'reporting' based on William Faulkner's idea that the best fiction is far more *true* than any kind of journalism – and the best journalists have always known this . . . True *gonzo* reporting needs the talents of a master journalist, the eye of an artist/photographer and the heavy balls of an actor. Because the writer *must* be a participant in the scene, while he's writing it – or at least taping it, or even sketching it. Or all three. Probably the closest analogy to the ideal would be a film director/producer who writes his own scripts, does his own camera work and somehow manages to film himself in action, as the protagonist or at least a main character.

*The Great Shark Hunt*, 'Jacket Copy for Fear and Loathing in Las Vegas' (1979)

7 In a nation ruled by swine, all pigs are upward-mobile – and the rest of us are fucked until we can put our acts together: not necessarily to win, but mainly to keep from losing completely. We owe that to ourselves and our crippled self-image as something better than a nation of panicked sheep.

ibid.

8 Going to trial with a lawyer who considers your whole life-style a Crime in Progress is not a happy prospect.

'A Letter to *The Champion*: a publication of the National Assoc. of Criminal Defense Lawyers', July 1990, publ. in *Songs Of The Doomed* (1991)

# Jim Thompson (1906–77)
US AUTHOR

As a pulp novelist he published some thirty thrillers, among them *The Killer Inside Me* (1952, filmed 1975), which STANLEY KUBRICK called 'probably the most chilling and believable first-person story of a criminally warped mind I have ever encountered'. Other titles include *The Grifters* (1959, filmed 1990) and *The Getaway* (1963, filmed 1972).

1 We're living in a funny world, kid, a peculiar civilization. The police are playing crooks in it, and the crooks are doing police duty. The politicians are preachers, and the preachers are politicians. The tax collectors collect for themselves. The Bad People want us to have more dough, and the Good People are fighting to keep it from us.

Lou Ford, in *The Killer Inside Me*, ch. 12 (1952)

# David Thomson (b. 1941)
BRITISH FILM CRITIC AND AUTHOR

He has written widely on the film industry and its personalities as in *Movie Man* (1967), *A Biographical Dictionary of the Cinema* (1975, revised as *A Biographical Dictionary of Film* in 1994) and *America in the Dark* (1977). His reviews appear regularly in British and US publications.

1 [On television] It is on – like the light. The ordinary viewer, the average citizen, would delight the movie business if he or she saw one movie every six weeks. But he, she, we, the moblike broken family, goes back and forth, like leopards in our cage, while TV is 'on', six or seven hours a day. The world works by way of TV: that is where marketing occurs; that is how politicians play at running the country; and that is where news is defined and focused. It is lamentable, if you want to take that view. Though I suspect a greater damage to our culture and our ideas came earlier, in permitting photography. That was the first great drug, and it trained us for the others.

*A Biographical Dictionary of Film*, 'Dennis Potter' (1994)

## John Thorne (b. 1943)
US COOKERY WRITER

In 1980 he started writing culinary pamphlets and newsletters that presented a holistic approach to eating and cooking and are collected in *Simple Cooking* (1987), *Outlaw Cook* (1992) and *Serious Pig* (1996).

1 All recipes are built on the belief that somewhere at the beginning of the chain there is a cook who does not use them. This is the great nostalgia of our cuisine, ever invoking an absent mother-cook who once laid her hands on the body of the world for us and worked it into food. The promise of every cookbook is that it offers a way back onto her lap.

'Cuisine Mécanique', publ. in *The Journal of Gastronomy* spring 1990

## Adam Thorpe (b. 1956)
BRITISH POET AND NOVELIST

Brought up in India, Cameroon and England, he published two collections of poetry, *Mornings in the Baltic* (1988) and *Meeting Montaigne* (1990), before his award-winning first novel *Ulverton* (1992), followed by *Pieces of Light* (1998).

1 The tesserae of the past – Bronze-Age, Roman, mediaeval – thrown up by the coulter are as infant toys to the booming venerableness of the chalk that cradles them. And we – who are we to flail and clamour, to batter and slay, when all that surrounds us tells us of our insignificance, of our infinitesimal capacities, of our inevitable anonymity in the eternal reaches of Time?

*Ulverton*, ch. 10 (1992)

## Jeremy Thorpe (b. 1929)
BRITISH POLITICIAN

He served as Liberal MP for North Devon (1959–79) and was a popular leader of the Party (1967–76). He was forced to resign by a scandal in which he was acquitted of charges of conspiracy to murder a male lover and lost his seat at the next general election.

1 Greater love hath no man than this, that he lay down his friends for his life.

Remark, 1962, quoted in *The General Election of 1964*, ch. 1 (1965) by D.E. Butler and Anthony King. The quip, made following a Cabinet 'reorganization' by Prime Minister HAROLD MACMILLAN in which several members of the Cabinet were sacked, is an adaptation of the words of Christ in John 15:13: 'Greater love hath no man than this, that a man lay down his life for his friends.'

## Colin Thubron (b. 1919)
BRITISH TRAVEL WRITER AND NOVELIST

A descendant of John Dryden, he has based such books as *Among the Russians* (1983) and *Behind the Wall* (1987) on his travels in Asia. His novels include *Falling* (1989) and *Turning Back the Sun* (1991).

1 Rudeness in old men is considered a sign of vitality. In fact it is quite the opposite. It springs from shrunken sympathies.

Synesius, in *Emperor*, pt 2, ch. 13 (1978)

2 I imagine integrity as a quality of light: a kind of grey translucence, sunless. It is not at all beautiful. But it makes other lights seem disfiguring.

Constantine, in ibid.

3 If a man would be happy for a week (ran a saying), he could take a wife; if he planned happiness for a month, he must kill a pig; but if he desired happiness for ever, he should plant a garden.

*Behind the Wall: a Journey Through China*, ch. 4 (1987)

## James Thurber (1894–1961)
US HUMORIST AND ILLUSTRATOR

Praised by ALISTAIR COOKE as 'one of the world's greatest humorists', he was Managing Editor of the *New Yorker* (1927–33), to which he contributed wry sketches, cartoons and stories until his death. His short story 'The Secret Life of Walter Mitty' (1932, filmed 1947) prompted Larry Adler to comment: 'Freud discovered the Id, and Thurber named it Walter Mitty.'

1 A drawing is always dragged down to the level of its caption.

*New Yorker* 2 August 1930

2 It takes that *je ne sais quoi* which we call sophistication for a woman to be magnificent in a drawing-room when her faculties have departed but she herself has not yet gone home.

ibid.

3 All right, have it your way – you heard a seal bark.

Cartoon caption in the *New Yorker* 30 January 1932, repr. in *The Thurber Carnival*, pt 8 (1945). Spoken by wife to husband in bed.

4 In an extensive reading of recent books by psychologists, psychoanalysts, psychiatrists, and inspirationalists, I have discovered that they all suffer from one or more of these expression-complexes: italicizing, capitalizing, exclamation-pointing, multiple-interrogating, and itemizing. These are all forms of what the psychos themselves would call, if they faced their condition frankly, Rhetorical-Over-Compensation.

'Peace, It's Wonderful', publ. in the *Saturday Review* 21 November 1936, repr. in *James Thurber Collecting Himself* (ed. Michael J. Rosen, 1989)

5 It's a naïve domestic Burgundy without any breeding, but I think you'll be amused by its presumption.

Cartoon caption, in the *New Yorker* 27 March 1937, repr. in *The Thurber Carnival*, pt 9 (1945). Spoken by a pleased-looking host, to the consternation of his guests at dinner.

6 Well, if I called the wrong number, why did you answer the phone?

Woman on phone, in cartoon caption, in the *New Yorker* 5 June 1937, repr. in ibid.

7 Every man is occasionally visited by the suspicion that the planet on which he is riding is not really going anywhere; that the Force which controls its measured eccentricities hasn't got anything special in mind. If he broods on this somber theme long enough he gets the doleful idea that the laughing children on a merry-go-round or

the thin, fine hands of a lady's watch are revolving more purposely than he is.

'Thinking Ourselves Into Trouble', pt 1, publ. in *Forum and Century* June 1939, repr. in *James Thurber Collecting Himself* (ed. Michael J. Rosen, 1989)

8 Philosophy offers the rather cold consolation that perhaps we and our planet do not actually exist; religion presents the contradictory and scarcely more comforting thought that we exist but that we cannot hope to get anywhere until we cease to exist. Alcohol, in attempting to resolve the contradiction, produces vivid patterns of Truth which vanish like snow in the morning sun and cannot be recalled; the revelations of poetry are as wonderful as a comet in the skies – and as mysterious. Love, which was once believed to contain the Answer, we now know to be nothing more than an inherited behavior pattern.

ibid.

9 Next to reasoning, the greatest handicap to the optimum development of Man lies in the fact that this planet is just barely habitable. Its mimimum temperatures are too low, and its maximum temperatures too high. Its day is not long enough, and its night is too long. The disposition of its water and earth is distinctly unfortunate (the existence of the Mediterranean Sea in the place where we find it is perhaps the unhappiest accident in the whole firmament). These factors encourage depression, fear, war, and lack of vitality. They describe a planet, which is by no means perfectly devised for the nurturing or for the perpetuation of a higher intelligence.

ibid. pt 2

10 Early to rise and early to bed makes a male healthy and wealthy and dead.

*Fables for our Time*, 'The Shrike and the Chipmunks' (1940)

11 You might as well fall flat on your face as lean over too far backward.

ibid. 'The Bear who Let it Alone'

12 It is better to have loafed and lost than never to have loafed at all.

ibid. 'The Courtship of Arthur and Al'

13 Somebody once said that I am incapable of drawing a man, but that I draw abstract things like despair, disillusion, despondency, sorrow, lapse of memory, exile, and that these things are sometimes in a shape that might be called Man or Woman.

Interview with Jack Sher in the *Detroit Free Press* 25 February 1940

14 The only rules comedy can tolerate are those of taste, and the only limitations those of libel.

'The Duchess and the Bugs' (c. 1953), repr. in *Lanterns and Lances* (1961)

15 Discussion in America means dissent.

ibid.

16 Humor does not include sarcasm, invalid irony, sardonicism, innuendo, or any other form of cruelty. When these things are raised to a high point they can become wit, but unlike the French and the English, we have not been much good at wit since the days of Benjamin Franklin.

Letter, 25 June 1954, publ. in *Horn Book Magazine* April 1962

17 Speed is scarcely the noblest virtue of graphic composition, but it has its curious rewards. There is a sense of getting somewhere fast, which satisfies a native American urge.

*A Thurber Garland*, Preface (1955)

18 With sixty staring me in the face, I have developed inflammation of the sentence structure and definite hardening of the paragraphs.

Quoted in the *New York Post* 30 June 1955

19 The laughter of man is more terrible than his tears, and takes more forms – hollow, heartless, mirthless, maniacal.

*The New York Times Magazine* 7 December 1958

20 I consider that that 'that' that worries us so much should be forgotten. Rats desert a sinking ship. Thats infest a sinking magazine.

Memo to the *New Yorker* in 1959, first publ. in *The New York Times Book Review* 4 December 1988

21 I always begin at the left with the opening word of the sentence and read toward the right and I recommend this method.

ibid. On his editorial technique.

22 When all things are equal, translucence in writing is more effective than transparency, just as glow is more revealing than glare.

ibid.

23 We are a nation that has always gone in for the loud laugh, the wow, the yak, the belly laugh, the dozen other labels for the roll-'em-in-the-aisles gagerissimo. This is the kind of laugh that delights actors, directors, and producers, but dismays writers of comedy because it is the laugh that often dies in the lobby. The appreciative smile, the chuckle, the soundless mirth, so important to the success of comedy, cannot be understood unless one sits among the audience and feels the warmth created by the quality of laughter that the audience takes home with it.

*The New York Times* 21 February 1960

24 Humor is emotional chaos remembered in tranquility.

*New York Post* 29 February 1960. An earlier version of Thurber's quip was attributed to him by Max Eastman in *Enjoyment of Laughter* (1936): 'Humor is a kind of emotional chaos told about calmly and quietly in retrospect. There is always a laugh in the utterly familiar.' The words are adapted from Wordsworth's dictum: 'Poetry . . . takes its origin from emotion recollected in tranquillity' (Preface to *Lyrical Ballads*, 2nd edn, 1801).

25 I'm 65 and I guess that puts me in with the geriatrics. But if there were fifteen months in every year, I'd only be 48. That's the trouble with us. We number everything. Take women, for example. I think they deserve to have more than twelve years between the ages of 28 and 40.

*Time* magazine 15 August 1960

26 From now on, I think it is safe to predict, neither the Democratic nor the Republican Party will ever nominate for President a candidate without good looks, stage presence, theatrical delivery, and a sense of timing.

Unpublished manuscript, 20 March 1961, publ. in *James Thurber Collecting Himself* (ed. Michael J. Rosen, 1989). Referring to the Kennedy-Nixon TV debates.

27 My opposition [to interviews] lies in the fact that offhand answers have little value or grace of expression, and that such oral give and take helps to perpetuate the decline of the English language.

Letter to Henry Brandon, quoted in *As We Are* (1961) by Henry Brandon. Written following a lengthy interview with him.

## Paul Tillich (1886–1965)

GERMAN-BORN US THEOLOGIAN

An influential Protestant thinker, he formulated a theology that incorporated existentialist themes, as set out in his major work, *Systematic Theology* (three volumes, 1951–63). He also wrote *The Religious Situation* (1926), *The Courage to Be* (1952), and *The Eternal Now* (1963). He was one of the first non-Jewish academics to be expelled by the Nazis for his opposition to their regime, fleeing to the US in 1933.

1 Religion is the state of being grasped by an ultimate

concern, a concern which qualifies all other concerns as preliminary and which itself contains the answer to the question of a meaning of our life.

*Christianity and the Encounter of the World Religions*, ch. 1 (1963)

## Alvin Toffler (b. 1928)
US AUTHOR

Writing as a 'futurologist', he regards the advent of information technology as the beginning of a 'Third Wave' of civilization, after agriculture and the industrial revolution. His books include *Future Shock* (1970), *The Third Wave* (1980) and *Powershift* (1990).

1 Future shock is the dizzying disorientation brought on by the premature arrival of the future. It may well be the most important disease of tomorrow.

   *Future Shock*, pt 1, ch. 1, 'The Unprepared Visitor' (1970)

2 Knowledge is the most democratic source of power.

   *Powershift: Knowledge, Wealth, and Violence at the Edge of the 21st Century*, pt 1, ch. 2, 'The Democratic Difference' (1990)

## J.R.R. Tolkien (1892–1973)
BRITISH NOVELIST AND SCHOLAR

Full name John Ronal Reuel Tolkien. An Oxford professor and leading philologist, he was author of many scholarly publications, for instance *Beowulf* (1937) and *Chaucer as a Philologist* (1943), but is best remembered for his fantasies *The Hobbit* (1937) and *The Lord of the Rings* (1954–5, filmed 1978).

1 Curse it! Curse it! Curse it! Curse the Baggins! It's gone! What has it got in its pocketses? Oh we guess, we guess, my precious. He's found it, yes he must have. My birthday-present.

   Gollum, in *The Hobbit*, ch. 5 (1937). Referring to the Ring, which Gollum has guessed Bilbo Baggins has in his pocket, in a game of riddles played for Bilbo's life.

2 Gandalf looked at him. 'My dear Bilbo!' he said. 'Something is the matter with you! You are not the hobbit that you were.'

   ibid. ch. 19. On Bilbo's new poetical and adventurous spirit at the end of the tale.

3 The Road goes ever on and on
   Down from the door where it began
   Now far ahead the Road has gone,
   And I must follow, if I can,
   Pursuing it with eager feet,
   Until it joins some larger way
   Where many paths and errands meet.
   And whither then? I cannot say.

   Bilbo Baggins, in *The Lord of the Rings*, pt 1: *The Fellowship of the Ring*, bk 1, ch. 1 (1954). The rhyme recurs with variations elsewhere in the work, and a version appears at the end of *The Hobbit*.

4 Many that live deserve death. And some that die deserve life. Can you give it to them? Then do not be too eager to deal out death in judgement. For even the very wise cannot see all ends.

   Gandalf, in ibid. ch. 2. Responding to Frodo's remark that Gollum's wicked actions deserve death.

5 Faithless is he that says farewell when the road darkens.

   The dwarf Gimli, in ibid. bk 2, ch. 3

6 Rising swiftly up, far above the Towers of the Black Gate, high above the mountains, a vast soaring darkness sprang into the sky, flickering with fire. The earth groaned and quaked. The Towers of the Teeth swayed, tottered, and fell down; the mighty rampart crumbled; the Black Gate was hurled in ruin; and from far away, now dim, now growing, now mounting to the clouds, there came a drumming rumble, a roar, a long echoing roll of ruinous noise.

'The realm of Sauron is ended!' said Gandalf. 'The Ring-bearer has fulfilled his Quest.'

   ibid. pt 3: *The Return of the King*, bk 6, ch. 4 (1955). Referring to the outcome of the struggle between Frodo and Gollum on the edge of the Cracks of Doom, as Gollum topples into the abyss, taking the Ring with him to destruction.

## Tatyana Tolstaya (b. 1951)
RUSSIAN AUTHOR

The great-grandniece of Leo Tolstoy, she was called by JOSEPH BRODSKY 'the most original, tactile, luminous voice in Russian prose today'. She is the author of the short stories *On the Golden Porch* (1989) and *Sleepwalker in a Fog* (1991).

1 [On Russian writers] Already the writers are complaining that there is too much freedom. They need some pressure. The worse your daily life, the better your art. If you have to be careful because of oppression and censorship, this pressure produces diamonds.

   *Independent* 31 May 1990

2 In Russia, people suffer from the stillness of time.

   ibid.

## Lily Tomlin (b. 1939)
US COMEDIENNE

She became known on the cast of the TV show ROWAN AND MARTIN'S LAUGH-IN (1969–72) and has since acted in numerous films, among them *Nashville* (1975), *The Late Show* (1977) and *Tea with Mussolini* (1999). She is also known for her one-woman stage shows *Appearing Nightly* (1977) and *The Search for Signs of Intelligent Life in the Universe* (1985–6).

1 The Fifties was the most sexually frustrated decade ever: ten years of foreplay. And the Sixties, well, the Sixties was like coitus interruptus. The only thing we didn't pull out of was Vietnam.

   Routine on Broadway show, *Appearing Nightly* (1977), recorded on *Lily Tomlin on Stage*, 'Glenna – A Child of the Sixties' (album, 1977, material written by Lily Tomlin and Jane Wagner)

2 There will be sex after death; we just won't be able to feel it.

   Quoted in *Hammer and Tongues* (ed. Michèle Brown and Ann O'Connor, 1986)

3 If love is the answer, could you rephrase the question?

   Quoted in *Funny Business* (1992) by David Housham and John Frank-Keyes

## Michael Torke (b. 1961)
US COMPOSER

Called by *The New York Times* 'the Ravel of his generation', he is one of the most widely choreographed contemporary composers and regarded as a rhythmic and melodic minimalist. His works include *Javelin* (1994), commissioned for the Olympics, *Book of Proverbs* (1996) and *Brick Symphony* (1997). In 1997 he was appointed First Associate Composer of the Royal Scottish National Orchestra.

1 Why waste money on psychotherapy when you can listen to the B Minor Mass?

   *Independent* 21 September 1990

## Peter Tosh (1944–87)
JAMAICAN REGGAE MUSICIAN

Original name Winston McIntosh. With his childhood friends BOB MARLEY and Bunny Livingston, he was one of the original Wailin' Wailers in the early 1960s, leaving the band in 1974 to pursue a solo career. A committed Rastafarian, he was murdered by burglars at his home in Kingston, Jamaica. See also BOB MARLEY.

1 Legalize it
And we will advertise it.
'Legalize It' (song) on the album *Legalize It* (1976)

## Michel Tournier (b. 1924)
FRENCH AUTHOR

His symbolist and intellectual novels, such as *Friday and Robinson* (1967), *The Erl King* (1970, Prix Goncourt) and *Gemini* (1975), have won him an international reputation. He has been a member of the Académie Goncourt since 1972.

1 The writer who labours on a book for four years becomes that book and assimilates all its alien elements, which add up to a structure far more impressive, vast, complex, and learned than their author . . . The work is all-consuming, a pious labour, a parasite. And when it has fed on me and sucked my blood, when it begins to make its own way in the world, I lie wan, drained, disgusted and exhausted, and obsessed with thoughts of death.
*The Wind Spirit: An Autobiography*, ch. 3 (1977, transl. 1988)

2 A myth is first of all a multistoreyed structure, each story being built according to an identical plan but at a different level of abstraction . . . The child's tale that is the myth's ground floor, as it were, is just as essential as its metaphysical summit.
ibid.

3 A writer is a cottage industry. Some craftsmen make tortoiseshell combs, others make leather wallets. I make Michel Tournier manuscripts.
*Independent on Sunday* 17 February 1991

## Sue Townsend (b. 1946)
BRITISH AUTHOR

Although she has written plays, including *The Great Celestial Cow* (1984), she is best known for her satirical works *The Secret Diary of Adrian Mole aged 13½* (1982), its sequel *Adrian Mole: The Cappuccino Years* (1999) and the novel *The Queen and I* (1992).

1 My brain is hurting. I have just had two pages of *Macbeth* to translate into English.
Adrian Mole's journal entry for 21 January, in *The Secret Diary of Adrian Mole aged 13½* (1982)

2 Marriage is nothing like being in prison! Women are let out every day to go to the shops and stuff, and quite a lot go to work.
ibid. 2 March

3 Offal is the new black.
Adrian Mole's journal entry for 18 May, in *Adrian Mole: The Cappuccino Years* (1999). On culinary trends.

## Pete Townshend (b. 1945)
BRITISH ROCK MUSICIAN

He was the guitarist and chief songwriter of the leading 'mod' band the High Numbers, renamed the Who in 1964. His guitar-smashing antics on stage epitomized the group's nihilistic and rebellious image, although he was also regarded as one of rock's 'intellectuals' and was composer of the first 'rock opera', *Tommy*, in 1969. He later worked in publishing and released solo records.

1 People try to put us down
(Talkin' 'bout my generation)
Just because we get around
(Talkin' 'bout my generation)
Things they do look awful c-c-cold
(Talkin' 'bout my generation)
Hope I die before I get old.
'My Generation' (song) on the album *My Generation* (1965) by the Who

2 I was born with a plastic spoon in my mouth.
'Substitute' (song) on ibid.

3 I . . . know what it's like to be a mod among 2 million mods, and it's incredible. It's like being the only white man at the Apollo. Someone comes up and touches you, and you become black . . . It covered everybody, everybody looked the same, and everybody acted the same, and everybody wanted to be the same . . . It was the closest to patriotism that I've ever felt.
Interview in *Rolling Stone* September 1968

4 It's an ordinary day for Brian. Like, he died every day, you know.
Comment to press, July 1969, quoted in *The Life and Good Times of the Rolling Stones* by Philip Norman (1989). On the drowning of Rolling Stones guitarist Brian Jones. Stung by criticism of his off-the-cuff remark, Townshend wrote a song called 'A Normal Day for Brian, the Man Who Died Everyday', never released.

5 I'll tip my hat to the new constitution
Take a bow for the new revolution
Smile and grin at the change all around
Pick up my guitar and play
Just like yesterday.
Then I'll get on my knees and pray
We don't get fooled again.
'Won't Get Fooled Again' (song) on the album *Who's Next* (1971) by the Who

6 When I'm onstage, I feel this incredible, almost spiritual experience . . . lost in a naturally induced high. Those great rock-'n'-roll experiences are getting harder and harder to come by, because they have to transcend a lot of drug-induced stupor. But when they occur, they are sacred.
Interview in *Playboy* June 1974

7 So much of what I am I got from you. I had no idea how much of it was secondhand.
Quoted in *Rolling Stone* 8 February 1990. Addressed to the Rolling Stones at the Rock and Roll Hall of Fame induction ceremony, January 1989.

8 It is amorphous, but basically it always has the same job, which is to get you through the day. And that seems to me to be a profoundly important job; it is like fresh bread.
Interview in the *Observer* 25 February 1996. In reply to the question: 'What is pop music anyway?'

## A.J. Toynbee (1889–1975)
BRITISH HISTORIAN

Full name Arnold Joseph Toynbee. The scion of a family of historians, he was Director and Research Professor of the Royal Institute of International Affairs (1925–55) and a prolific author. His monumental *A Study of History* (twelve volumes, 1934–61), written on the theory of 'challenge and response', made him a household name. His other works include *Hellenism: The History of a Civilization* (1959) and *Some Problems of Greek History* (1966).

1 History not used is nothing, for all intellectual life is action, like practical life, and if you don't use the stuff – well, it might as well be dead.
Television broadcast 17 April 1955 NBC-TV

2 Civilization is a movement and not a condition, a voyage and not a harbour.
*Reader's Digest* October 1958

3 We human beings do have some genuine freedom of choice and therefore some effective control over our own destinies. I am not a determinist. But I also believe that the decisive choice is seldom the latest choice in the series. More often than not, it will turn out to be some choice made relatively far back in the past.
'Some Great "If's" Of History', publ. in *The New York Times* 5 March 1961

4 We have been God-like in our planned breeding of our domesticated plants and animals, but we have been rabbit-like in our unplanned breeding of ourselves.
Speech to World Food Congress, Washington, D.C., quoted in the *National Observer* 10 June 1963.

## Polly Toynbee (b. 1946)
BRITISH JOURNALIST

Granddaughter of A.J. TOYNBEE, she has been writer and editor for various newspapers, including the *Observer*, the *Guardian* and the *Independent*, and was Columnist of the Year in 1986. She was Social Affairs Editor for the BBC 1988–95.

1 [On the Millennium Dome] There never could have been message or meaning in an exhibition of this kind. In the end only art transcends the platitudes of politicians, the empty exhortations and the hollow Christian attempts to impose a banality of its own. The lesson is that only those elements created by artists have meaning.
*Guardian*, 5 January 2000

## Violet Trefusis (1894–1972)
BRITISH NOVELIST

The daughter of Alice Keppel, mistress of Edward VII, she divided her time between France and Italy and wrote in both English and French. Her novels include *Sortie de secours* (1929), *Tandem* (1933) and *Pirates at Play* (1950), and she also wrote two volumes of reminiscences, *Prelude to Misadventure* (1942) and *Don't Look Round* (1952).

1 You are my lover and I am your mistress and kingdoms and empires and governments have tottered and suc-cumbed before now to that mighty combination.
Letter to VITA SACKVILLE-WEST, March 1919, publ. in *Letters to Vita Sackville-West* (1989). Closing words of letter. The two had a passionate affair between 1918 and 1921.

2 I hate men. They fill me with revulsion, even quite small boys. Marriage is an institution that ought to be confined to temperamental old maids, weary prostitutes, and royalty.
Letter to Vita Sackville-West, May/June 1919, quoted in *Portrait of a Marriage*, pt 4 (1973) by Nigel Nicolson. Violet married Denys Trefusis on 16 June 1919.

## G.M. Trevelyan (1876–1962)
BRITISH HISTORIAN

Full name George Macaulay Trevelyan. A popular and imaginative social historian, he was the author of studies of Garibaldi (1907–11) and later of *History of England* (1926) and *English Social History* (1942). He was Professor of Modern History at Cambridge from 1927 to 1951.

1 Socrates gave no diplomas or degrees, and would have subjected any disciple who demanded one to a discon-certing catechism on the nature of true knowledge.
*History of England*, bk 2 ch. 4 (1926)

2 Social history might be defined negatively as the history of a people with the politics left out.
*English Social History*, Introduction (1942)

3 Disinterested intellectual curiosity is the life blood of real civilization.
ibid.

4 In those days, before it became scientific, cricket was the best game in the world to watch, with its rapid sequence of amusing incidents, each ball a potential crisis! Squire, farmer, blacksmith, and labourer, with their women and children came to see the fun, were at ease together and happy all the summer afternoon. If the French *noblesse*

had been capable of playing cricket with their peasants, their chateaux would never have been burnt.
ibid. ch. 8. Referring to England in the eighteenth century.

5 Education . . . has produced a vast population able to read but unable to distinguish what is worth reading, an easy prey to sensations and cheap appeals.
ibid. ch. 18

## Calvin Trillin (b. 1935)
US JOURNALIST AND AUTHOR

A debunker of pomposity, he was a commentator on regional stories across the United States, as in *Uncivil Liberties* (1982), a collection of his magazine pieces. His understated humour is evident in his books written as a roving gourmand, including *Alice, Let's Eat* (1978) and *Third Helpings* (1983).

1 As far as I'm concerned, 'whom' is a word that was invented to make everyone sound like a butler.
'Whom Says So?', publ. in *Nation* 8 June 1985

2 The talk shows are stuffed full of sufferers who have regained their health – congressmen who suffered through a serious spell of boozing and skirt-chasing, White House aides who were stricken cruelly with overweening am-bition, movie stars and baseball players who came down with acute cases of wanting to trash hotel rooms while under the influence of recreational drugs. Most of them have found God, or at least a publisher.
'Diseases of the Mighty', publ. in *Nation* 19 October 1985

3 Everything was blamed on Castro. Mudslides in Cali-fornia. The fact that you can't buy a decent tomato any-more. Was there an exceptionally high pollen count in Massapequa, Long Island, one day? It was Castro, ex-porting sneezes.
'Castro Forgotten, Alas', syndicated column, 18 May 1986

## Lionel Trilling (1905–75)
US CRITIC

His critical works, such as *The Liberal Imagination* (1950), *The Opposing Self* (1955) and *Sincerity and Authenticity* (1972), empha-size a moral dimension within a social context in the liberal tra-dition of Matthew Arnold, on whom he wrote a standard text (1939). He was associated with Columbia University for more than forty years.

1 Probably it is impossible for humor to be ever a revolu-tionary weapon. Candide can do little more than generate irony.
Notebook entry c. 1931–2, publ. in *Partisan Review 50th Anniversary Edition* (ed. William Philips, 1985)

2 We are all ill: but even a universal sickness implies an idea of health.
'Art and Neurosis', publ. in *Partisan Review* winter 1945, repr. in *The Liberal Imagination* (1950)

3 In the American metaphysic, reality is always material reality, hard, resistant, unformed, impenetrable, and un-pleasant.
'Reality in America', first publ. in *Nation* 20 April 1946, repr. in ibid.

4 Every neurosis is a primitive form of legal proceeding in which the accused carries on the prosecution, imposes judgment and executes the sentence: all to the end that someone else should not perform the same process.
Notebook entry, 1946, publ. in *Partisan Review 50th Anniversary Edition* (ed. William Philips, 1985)

5 We are at heart so profoundly anarchistic that the only form of state we can imagine living in is Utopian; and so

cynical that the only Utopia we can believe in is authoritarian.

*ibid.* 1948

6 We who are liberal and progressive know that the poor are our equals in every sense except that of being equal to us.

'The Princess Casamassima', first publ. as Introduction to *The Princess Casamassima* (1948) by Henry James, repr. in *The Liberal Imagination* (1950)

7 If one defends the bourgeois, philistine virtues, one does not defend them merely from the demonism or bohemianism of the artist but from the present bourgeoisie itself.

Notebook entry, c. 1951, publ. in *Partisan Review 50th Anniversary Edition* (ed. William Philips, 1985)

8 Immature artists imitate. Mature artists steal.

*Esquire* September 1962

9 A primary function of art and thought is to liberate the individual from the tyranny of his culture in the environmental sense and to permit him to stand beyond it in an autonomy of perception and judgment.

*Beyond Culture*, Preface (1965)

# David Trimble (b. 1944)
NORTHERN IRISH POLITICIAN

MP for Upper Bann since 1990, he has been leader of the Ulster Unionist Party since 1995 and was a key figure in the Good Friday agreement in 1998, following which he became First Minister of the Northern Ireland Assembly. Together with John Hume, he was awarded the Nobel Peace Prize in 1998.

1 We are not saying that, simply because someone has a past, they can't have a future. We always acknowledge that people have to change.

Quoted in the *Daily Telegraph* 2 July 1998. Accepting his election as First Minister of the Northern Ireland Assembly.

2 Peace is not the absence of war. Lasting peace is rooted in justice. It is rooted in a democratic culture which cherishes the rule of law and scorns the summary justice, social terrorism and gangsterism which are a fact of life for too many people in Northern Ireland.

Quoted in the *Observer* 18 October 1998. On being awarded the Nobel Peace Prize.

# Alexander Trocchi (1925–83)
SCOTTISH AUTHOR

He co-founded the literary quarterly *Merlin* in Paris in 1950 and was instrumental in publishing SAMUEL BECKETT's early work *Watt* (1952). A pivotal figure of the London Underground in the early 1960s, he is remembered chiefly for his autobiographical novel *Cain's Book* (1960). LEONARD COHEN called him 'a public junkie' after he injected himself with heroin on live TV in America.

1 No doubt I shall go on writing, stumbling across tundras of unmeaning, planting words like bloody flags in my wake. Loose ends, things unrelated, shifts, nightmare journeys, cities arrived at and left, meetings, desertions, betrayals, all manner of unions, adulteries, triumphs, defeats . . . these are the facts.

*Cain's Book* (1960)

2 All great art, and today all great artlessness, must appear extreme to the mass of men, as we know them today. It springs from the anguish of great souls. From the souls of men not formed, but deformed in factories whose inspiration is pelf.

*ibid.*

# Leon Trotsky (1879–1940)
RUSSIAN REVOLUTIONARY

Original name Lev Davidovich Bronstein. Until the death of LENIN he was the second most powerful man in the Soviet Union, responsible for modernizing the Red Army as Commissar for Military Affairs (1918–24). However his emphasis on world revolution alienated him from STALIN, and he was exiled in 1929, and eventually assassinated in Mexico. His works include *History of the Russian Revolution* (1932–3) and *The Revolution Betrayed* (1937).

1 The Federated Republic of Europe – the United States of Europe – that is what must be. National autonomy no longer suffices. Economic evolution demands the abolition of national frontiers. If Europe is to remain split into national groups, then Imperialism will recommence its work. Only a Federated Republic of Europe can give peace to the world.

Conversation at Smolny, 30 October 1917, quoted in *Ten Days That Shook the World*, ch. 3 (1926) by JOHN REED

2 The literary 'fellow travellers' of the Revolution.

*Literature and Revolution*, ch. 2 (1923). By 'fellow travellers' (*paputchiki*), a term originally used by the 'old Socialists', Trotsky was referring to writers who sympathized with the Bolshevik Revolution but had no 'revolutionary past' and to whom 'the Communist ideal is foreign'. It later came to be used to mean any uncommitted sympathizers of a cause. The phrase appeared in English in an article by MAX LERNER, 'Mr Roosevelt and his Fellow-Travelers' (1936).

3 Technique is noticed most markedly in the case of those who have not mastered it.

*ibid.* ch. 6. Referring to the 'breathless literary schools that followed the revolution'.

4 Learning carries within itself certain dangers because out of necessity one has to learn from one's enemies.

*ibid.*

5 If the Revolution has the right to destroy bridges and art monuments whenever necessary, it will stop still less from laying its hand on any tendency in art which, no matter how great its achievement in form, threatens to disintegrate the revolutionary environment or to arouse the internal forces of the Revolution, that is, the proletariat, the peasantry and the intelligentsia, to a hostile opposition to one another. Our standard is, clearly, political, imperative and intolerant.

*ibid.* ch. 7

6 Ideas that enter the mind under fire remain there securely and for ever.

*My Life*, ch. 35 (1930)

7 If we had had more time for discussion we should probably have made a great many more mistakes.

*ibid.* ch. 36. Referring to discussions in the Central Committee of the Soviet Communist Party about the proposed development of the Red Army.

8 It was the supreme expression of the mediocrity of the apparatus that Stalin himself rose to his position.

*ibid.* ch. 40. In his last book, *Stalin* (1947), drafted while in exile in Mexico, Trotsky wrote of his feelings towards STALIN: 'Our paths diverged so long ago and so far, and in my eyes he is so much the instrument of historical forces that are alien and hostile to me, that my feelings towards him differ little from those I have towards Hitler or the Mikado. The personal element burned out long ago.' Trotsky was assassinated on Stalin's orders, before the book could be finished.

9 Where force is necessary, there it must be applied boldly, decisively and completely. But one must know the limitations of force; one must know when to blend force with a manoeuvre, a blow with an agreement.

*What Next?* ch. 14 (1932)

10 The slanders poured down like Niagara. If you take into consideration the setting – the war and the revolution –

and the character of the accused – revolutionary leaders of millions who were conducting their party to the sovereign power – you can say without exaggeration that July 1917 was the month of the most gigantic slander in world history.

*History of the Russian Revolution*, vol. 2, ch. 4 (1933)

11 There is no example in history of a revolutionary movement involving such gigantic masses being so bloodless.

ibid. vol. 2, ch. 7. Referring to the initial stages of the Russian Revolution, which included the storming of Moscow's Winter Palace.

12 Revolutions are always verbose.

ibid. ch. 12

13 There is a limit to the application of democratic methods. You can inquire of all the passengers as to what type of car they like to ride in, but it is impossible to question them as to whether to apply the brakes when the train is at full speed and accident threatens.

ibid. vol. 3, ch. 6

14 Insurrection is an art, and like all arts has its own laws.

ibid.

15 From being a patriotic myth, the Russian people have become an awful reality.

ibid. ch. 7. Referring to the chaotic aftermath of the October Revolution, 1917.

16 [On the Mensheviks] You are pitiful isolated individuals; you are bankrupts; your role is played out. Go where you belong from now on – into the dustbin of history!

ibid. vol. 3, ch. 10. The Mensheviks, who participated in Kerensky's provisional government in 1917, were overthrown by the Bolsheviks and suppressed.

17 The historic ascent of humanity, taken as a whole, may be summarized as a succession of victories of consciousness over blind forces – in nature, in society, in man himself.

ibid. vol. 3, 'Conclusions'

18 The depth and strength of a human character are defined by its moral *reserves*. People reveal themselves completely only when they are thrown out of the customary conditions of their life, for only then do they have to fall back on their reserves.

Journal entry, 5 April 1935, publ. in *Diary in Exile* (1959)

19 England is nothing but the last ward of the European madhouse, and quite possibly it will prove to be the ward for particularly violent cases.

ibid. 11 April 1935

20 Old age is the most unexpected of all things that happen to a man.

ibid. 8 May 1935

21 In Stalin each [Soviet bureaucrat] easily finds himself. But Stalin also finds in each one a small part of his own spirit. Stalin is the personification of the bureaucracy. That is the substance of his political personality.

*The Revolution Betrayed*, ch. 11 (1937)

22 Under all conditions well-organized violence seems to him [Stalin] the shortest distance between two points.

*Stalin*, ch. 3 (1947)

23 The end may justify the means as long as there is something that justifies the end.

Quoted in *Antonio Gramsci: an Introduction to his Thought*, Preface (1970) by Alberto Pozzolini

## Bobby Troup (1918–99)

US SONGWRITER AND ACTOR

He wrote songs for his wife, the singer and actress Julie London, as well as for FRANK SINATRA, LITTLE RICHARD and Tommy

Dorsey, whom he played in *The Gene Krupa Story* (film, 1959). He starred with London in the TV series, *Emergency* (1971–6).

1 If you ever plan to motor west,
  Travel my way, take the highway that's the best –
  Get your kicks on Route 66.

'Route 66' (song, 1946). The song was a hit for the Nat Cole Trio.

## François Truffaut (1932–84)

FRENCH FILM-MAKER

A critic before turning director, he was a pioneer of New Wave cinema, gaining an international reputation with *The Four Hundred Blows* (1959). Other films include *Jules and Jim* (1961) and *Day for Night* (1973), for which he received an Oscar. 'I make films,' he stated, 'that I would like to have seen when I was a young man.' He also acted, appearing in SPIELBERG's *Close Encounters of the Third Kind* (1978).

1 I've always had the impression that real militants are like cleaning women, doing a thankless, daily but necessary job.

Letter to JEAN-LUC GODARD, May–June 1973, publ. in *Letters* (1988)

2 When humour can be made to alternate with melancholy, one has a success, but when the *same* things are funny and melancholic at the same time, it's just wonderful.

Letter, 15 January 1980, publ. in ibid.

3 All film directors, whether famous or obscure, regard themselves as misunderstood or underrated. Because of that, they all lie. They're obliged to overstate their own importance.

Letter, 8 January 1981, publ. in ibid.

## Harry S. Truman (1884–1972)

US POLITICIAN AND PRESIDENT

A Democrat, he became President in 1945 on the death of FRANKLIN D. ROOSEVELT and was re-elected in 1948. He issued the order to drop the atom bomb on Japan in 1945, initiated the Marshall Plan for European aid and helped found NATO. His 'Truman Doctrine', which promised US support for those threatened by the Soviets, exacerbated the Cold War. 'I never gave them hell,' he said, 'I just tell the truth and they think it's hell.'

1 The human animal cannot be trusted for anything *good* except en masse. The combined thought and action of the whole people of any race, creed or nationality, will always point in the right direction.

Memorandum, 22 May 1945, publ. in *Mr President*, pt 3 (1952) by William Hillman

2 There is nothing new in the world except the history you do not know.

Quoted in ibid. pt 2, ch. 1

3 Study men, not historians.

Letter, 19 July 1950, publ. in *Off the Record* (ed. Robert H. Ferrell, 1980)

4 A politician is a man who understands government and it takes a politician to run a government. A statesman is a politician who's been dead ten or fifteen years.

Speech to Reciprocity Club, Washington, D.C., 11 April 1958, quoted in the *New York World-Telegram and Sun* 12 April 1958

5 If you can't stand the heat, get out of the kitchen.

Favourite saying of Truman's, quoted in *Mr Citizen*, ch. 15 (1960)

6 The buck stops here.

Motto on Truman's desk at the White House, quoted in *The Man from Missouri* (1962) by Alfred Steinberg

7 Washington is a very easy city for you to forget where you came from and why you got there in the first place.

*Plain Speaking: Conversations with Harry S. Truman*, ch. 11 (1973) by Merle Miller

8 When you get to be President, there are all those things, the honors, the twenty-one gun salutes, all those things. You have to remember it isn't for you. It's for the Presidency.

ibid. ch. 15

## Dalton Trumbo (1905–76)

US SCREENWRITER AND AUTHOR

A member of the Hollywood Ten who refused to testify before the House Committee on Un-American Activities, he served a year in prison and was blacklisted in 1947–60. His novel *Johnny Got His Gun* (1939) was filmed in 1971, and he wrote the screenplays for *Kitty Foyle* (1940), *Roman Holiday* (1953, under the name Ian McKellan Hunter) and *The Brave One* (1956), for which he won an Oscar as Robert Rich.

1 Bankers, nepotists, contracts and talkies: on four fingers one may count the leeches which have sucked a young and vigorous industry into paresis.

'The Fall of Hollywood', publ. in *North American Review* August 1933, quoted in *Writers in Hollywood 1915–1951*, ch. 6 (1990) by Ian Hamilton

2 Nothing is bigger than life. There's nothing noble in death. What's noble about lying in the ground and rotting? What's noble about never seeing the sunshine again? What's noble about having your arms and legs blown off? What's noble about being an idiot? What's noble about being blind and deaf and dumb? What's noble about being dead?

Joe Bonham, in *Johnny Got His Gun*, bk 1, ch.10 (1939)

## Donald Trump (b. 1946)

US BUSINESSMAN

A high-profile property tycoon, he was in the late 1980s the owner of Trump Parc, Trump Shuttle airline, New York's Trump Tower and casinos in Atlantic City, including Trump's Castle. He recovered from near bankruptcy in 1990.

1 Deals are my art form. Other people paint beautifully on canvas or write wonderful poetry. I like making deals, preferably big deals. That's how I get my kicks.

*Trump: The Art of the Deal*, ch. 1 (written with Tony Schwartz, 1987)

2 The point is that you can't be too greedy.

ibid. ch. 2

3 I'm a bit of a P.T. Barnum. I make stars out of everyone.

Quoted in the *Observer* 7 July 1991. Referring to the women in his life.

## Marina Tsvetaeva (1892–1941)

RUSSIAN POET AND PLAYWRIGHT

Praised by PASTERNAK for 'the intense lyrical power of her poetic form', she is best known for *The Encampment of Swans* (1917–22), written in praise of counter-revolutionaries, *Craft* (1923) and *After Russia* (1928). She left Russia in 1922, but returned in 1939 when her husband was shot and her daughter arrested. She later committed suicide.

1 Freedom! A wanton slut on a profligate's breast!

'Verses About Sonechka' (1917), reprinted in *The Heritage of Russian Verse* (ed. Dimitri Obolensky, 1965)

2 Love is a stepmother, and no mother.
Then expect no justice and mercy from her.

'Two Songs: 2' (1920) repr. in *Twentieth-Century Russian Poetry* (ed. Albert C. Todd, Max Hayward and Daniel Weissbort, 1993)

3 What is the main thing in love? to know and to hide. To know about the one you love and to hide that you love. At times the hiding (shame) overpowers the knowing

(passion). The passion for the hidden – the passion for the revealed.

*The House at Old Pimen*, ch. 2 (1934), repr. in *A Captive Spirit: Selected Prose* (ed. and transl. J. Marin King, 1980). Referring to her youthful love for a girl.

4 My desk, most loyal friend
thank you. You've been with me on
every road I've taken.
My scar and my protection.

'Desk', written 1933–5, publ. in *Selected Poems* (1971, transl. Elaine Feinstein)

5 It crawls, the underground snake,
crawls, with its load of people.
And each one has his
newspaper, his skin
disease; a twitch of chewing;
newspaper *caries*.
Masticators of gum,
readers of newspapers.

'Readers of Newspapers', written 1935, publ. in ibid.

6 There are books so alive that you're always afraid that while you weren't reading, the book has gone and changed, has shifted like a river; while you went on living, it went on living too, and like a river moved on and moved away. No one has stepped twice into the same river. But did anyone ever step twice into the same book?

*Pushkin and Pugachev* (1937), repr. in *A Captive Spirit: Selected Prose* (ed. and transl. J. Marin King, 1980). A reference to Heraclitus: 'You cannot step twice into the same river.'

7 A deception that elevates us is dearer than a host of low truths.

ibid.

## Barbara W. Tuchman (1912–89)

US HISTORIAN

Her bestselling books, which combine a literary and narrative approach, include *The Guns of August* (1962) and *Stilwell and the American Experience in China: 1911–1945* (1970), both of which won Pulitzer Prizes.

1 Dead battles, like dead generals, hold the military mind in their dead grip.

*The Guns of August*, ch. 2 (1962)

2 No more distressing moment can ever face a British government than that which requires it to come to a hard, fast and specific decision.

ibid. ch. 9

3 In April 1917 the illusion of isolation was destroyed, America came to the end of innocence, and of the exuberant freedom of bachelor independence. That the responsibilities of world power have not made us happier is no surprise. To help ourselves manage them, we have replaced the illusion of isolation with a new illusion of omnipotence.

'How We Entered World War I', publ. in *The New York Times Magazine* 5 May 1967

4 Reasonable orders are easy enough to obey; it is capricious, bureaucratic or plain idiotic demands that form the habit of discipline.

*Stilwell and the American Experience in China: 1911–1945*, pt 1, ch. 1 (1970)

5 Diplomacy means all the wicked devices of the Old World, spheres of influence, balances of power, secret treaties, triple alliances, and, during the interwar period, appeasement of Fascism.

'If Mao Had Come to Washington in 1945', publ. in *Foreign Affairs* October 1972. Referring to 'the deep-seated American distrust . . . of diplomacy and diplomats'.

# Sophie Tucker (1884–1966)

RUSSIAN-BORN US SINGER

Originally named Sophie Abuza. With a career spanning more than sixty years, she appeared in vaudeville, burlesque, nightclubs and music halls and became known as 'the last of the red-hot mamas' for her blues and jazz singing style. Among her best known songs are 'Some of These Days' (1911) and 'My Yiddisher Mama' (1925).

1 I've been rich and I've been poor. Believe me, honey, rich is better.

*Some of These Days* (1945)

2 From birth to 18 a girl needs good parents. From 18 to 35, she needs good looks. From 35 to 55, good personality. From 55 on, she needs good cash. I'm saving my money.

Remark 1953, quoted in *Sophie*, 'When They Get Too Wild For Everyone Else' (1978) by Michael Freedland

# Mark Tully (b. 1935)

BRITISH JOURNALIST AND BROADCASTER

Associated with the BBC since 1964, he was chief of the Delhi bureau (1972–93) and Southeast Asia correspondent (1993–4). Among his publications are *No Full Stops in India* (1991) and *The Lives of Jesus* (1996). From 1995 he has presented 'Something Understood' for BBC Radio 4.

1 [Of Mother Teresa] She somehow managed to combine poverty and glamour, and in that too she was like the Mahatma. They both knew that embracing poverty could be as glamorous as exhibiting wealth. It's only the middle road which is dull.

Appreciation of MOTHER TERESA in the *Observer* 7 September 1997

# Stephen Tumim (b. 1930)

BRITISH JUDGE

He was a circuit judge (1978–96) and Chief Inspector of Prisons for England and Wales (1987–95). His book *Crime and Punishment* (1997) was an indictment of the penal system.

1 How you deal with crime depends on what sort of people you send to prison. We tend to send men, under 25, who come from broken homes and did very badly at school because they didn't try very hard and played truant, what one might call yobs . . . These boys will come out bitter, not trained and not fit for work in the community we live in. And they're going to be with us for another 50 years.

Interview in the *Guardian* 13 April 1996. Referring to the typical prison population.

# Ed Turner (b. 1935)

US TELEVISION EXECUTIVE

Managing Editor of Cable News Network, he was appointed Vice-president in 1984.

1 If we had had the right technology back then, you would have seen Eva Braun on the Donahue show and Adolf Hitler on Meet the Press.

Quoted in the *Daily Telegraph* 5 September 1990

# Kathleen Turner (b. 1954)

US ACTRESS

She won success with her debut, the film noir *Body Heat* (1981), and later with the comedy *Romancing the Stone* (1984). She provided the husky voice of Jessica in *Who Framed Roger Rabbit?* (1988) and took the lead in the thriller *V.I. Warshawski* (1991).

1 You're not too smart, are you? I like that in a man.

Matty Walker (Kathleen Turner), in *Body Heat* (film, 1981, written and directed by Lawrence Kasdan)

2 Being a sex symbol has to do with an attitude, not looks. Most men think it's looks, most women know otherwise.

Quoted in the *Observer* 27 April 1986

# Ted Turner (b. 1938)

US BROADCASTING AND SPORTS EXECUTIVE

Full name Robert Edward Turner. Called by *Time* magazine 'the most openly ambitious man in America', he is Chairman of the Board and President of Turner Broadcasting Systems (merged with Time Warner, 1996), parent company of the news channel CNN. His marriage to JANE FONDA in 1991 ended in separation in 2000.

1 Life is like a B-movie. You don't want to leave in the middle of it but you don't want to see it again.

*International Herald Tribune* 2 March 1990

# Scott Turow (b. 1949)

US LAWYER AND AUTHOR

His bestselling suspense novels, including *Presumed Innocent* (1987, filmed 1990), *The Burden of Proof* (1990) and *The Laws of Our Fathers* (1996), are drawn from his inside experience as an attorney. *The New York Times Magazine* praised his 'brash, backroom sensibility'.

1 Ladies and gentlemen, let me tell you again what you are to presume. [The defendant] is innocent. I am the judge. I am telling you that. Presume he is innocent. When you sit there, I want you to look and say to yourself, There sits an innocent man.

Judge Larren Lyttle addressing the jury, in *Presumed Innocent*, ch. 26 (1987). Judge Lyttle begins the selection of the jury by asking one member whether the defendant committed the crime, and, on receiving the answer, 'I wouldn't know, Judge,' dismissed the juror.

# Desmond Tutu (b. 1931)

SOUTH AFRICAN CHURCHMAN

He was the first black bishop of Johannesburg (1985–6) and Archbishop of Cape Town (1986–96). Dedicated to the struggle for a democratic, just and non-racial South Africa, he advocated economic sanctions but deplored the use of violence. He was awarded the Nobel Peace Prize in 1984 and appointed Chairman of the Truth and Reconciliation Commission in 1995.

1 I am fifty-two years of age. I am a bishop in the Anglican Church, and a few people might be constrained to say that I was reasonably responsible. In the land of my birth I cannot vote, whereas a young person of eighteen can vote. And why? Because he or she possesses that wonderful biological attribute – a white skin.

Quoted in the *Guardian Weekly* 8 April 1984

2 Be nice to the whites, they need you to rediscover their humanity.

Quoted in *The New York Times* 19 October 1984

3 I am a leader by default, only because nature does not allow a vacuum.

*Christian Science Monitor* 20 December 1984

4 Having looked the past in the eye, having asked for forgiveness and having made amends, let us shut the door on the past – not in order to forget it but in order not to allow it to imprison us.

Report of South Africa's Truth and Reconciliation Committee, Foreword, quoted in the *Daily Telegraph* 30 October 1998

## Jill Tweedie (1936–93)
BRITISH AUTHOR AND JOURNALIST

She was a broadcaster, columnist for the *Guardian* and Journalist of the Year in 1971. Among her novels are *It's Only Me* (1980), *Bliss* (1984) and *Internal Affairs* (1986).

1 It is easy and dismally enervating to think of opposition as merely perverse or actually evil – far more invigorating to see it as essential for honing the mind, and as a positive good in itself. For the day that moral issues cease to be fought over is the day the word 'human' disappears from the race.

*Independent* May 1989

## Anne Tyler (b. 1941)
US AUTHOR

Her tales, mainly of the everyday life of the South related with sympathy and ironic humour, include *Morgan's Passing* (1980), *The Accidental Tourist* (1985, filmed 1988) and *Breathing Lessons* (1988), winner of a Pulitzer Prize.

1 I've always thought a hotel ought to offer optional small animals . . . I mean a cat to sleep on your bed at night, or a dog of some kind to act pleased when you come in. You ever notice how a hotel room feels so lifeless?

Macon Leary, in *The Accidental Tourist*, ch. 9 (1985)

## Kenneth Tynan (1927–80)
BRITISH THEATRE CRITIC

He was drama critic of the *Observer* (1954–63) and literary manager of London's National Theatre (1963–9) under LAURENCE OLIVIER. He championed the work of JOHN OSBORNE, vigorously opposed censorship and was the author of the revue *Oh! Calcutta!* (1969), one of the most notorious successes of the 1960s. For HAROLD CLURMAN, 'he possesses in regard to the theatre something like absolute pitch', while for GEORGE STEINER he was 'an anti-intellectual to the tip of his brilliant, histrionic fingers'.

1 What, when drunk, one sees in other women, one sees in Garbo sober . . . Most actresses in action live only to look at men, but Garbo looks at flowers, clouds and furniture with the same admiring compassion, like Eve on the morning of creation.

*Sight and Sound* April 1954, repr. in *Curtains*, 'The American Theatre' (1961)

2 A play . . . is basically a means of spending two hours in the dark without being bored.

*Observer* 7 August 1955, repr. in *The Life of Kenneth Tynan*, ch. 11 (1987) by Kathleen Tynan. After seeing *Waiting For Godot* by SAMUEL BECKETT. Tynan, who called himself a 'godotista', was, according to Kathleen Tynan, one of only two major British critics of the time to praise Beckett's work (the other was Harold Hobson).

3 The theatre's press-agent, asked for a description of the iconoclastic young gate-crasher, said that he was first and foremost 'an angry young man'. Before long the phrase, in itself not particularly striking, had snowballed into a cult. It did so because it defined a phenomenon that was nationally recognizable. It gave a name to a generation of young intellectuals who disliked being called intellectuals, since they thought the word phony, affected, and 'wet'. There is nothing new in young men being angry: in fact, it would be news if they were anything else.

'The Angry Young Movement' (1958), repr. in *Tynan on Theatre* (1964). Referring to George Fearon, press agent at the Royal Court Theatre, which first staged JOHN OSBORNE's *Look Back in Anger* in 1956.

4 Art is parasitic on life, just as criticism is parasitic on art.

'Ionesco and the Phantom', publ. in the *Observer* 6 July 1958, repr. in *Notes and Counter-Notes* by Eugène Ionesco (1962)

5 A neurosis is a secret you don't know you're keeping.

Journal entry, 9 July 1961, publ. in *The Life of Kenneth Tynan*, ch. 18 (1987) by Kathleen Tynan

6 Satire is protest, couched in wit, against the notion that there is anything more important than the fact that all men must die.

*Observer* 29 April 1962, repr. in ibid.

7 A good drama critic is one who perceives what is happening in the theatre of his time. A great drama critic also perceives what is not happening.

*Tynan Right and Left*, Foreword (1967)

8 One of the things that I promised myself that we might see at this theatre was that drama should be re-established to the same level of eminence that it attained with the Greeks; that the theatre should be a place where great matters of public concern were presented . . . In these days, when the churches are empty, there is nowhere except the theatre where such matters can be properly debated as the Greeks debated them: matters of supreme conscience, of the highest level of importance, moral concern with great events and the motives behind them. That is what theatre is for.

Board Meeting at the National Theatre, 24 April 1967, as remembered by LAURENCE OLIVIER in *Confessions of an Actor*, appendix (1982)

## Mike Tyson (b. 1966)
US BOXER

He became the youngest heavyweight champion in 1986 and was world champion 1987–90. Convicted of rape, he was sentenced to prison in 1992 and released on probation in 1995. His championship fight against Evander Holyfield in 1997 was stopped after he bit off part of his opponent's ear.

1 My objective is to be the ultimate professional. Regardless of whatever happens, the job has to be done. That's what being a professional is.

Quoted in *The New York Times* 28 June 1988

2 [On Hemingway] He uses those short, sharp words just like hooks and upper cuts. You always know what he's saying 'cause he says it very clearly.

Quoted in the *Independent on Sunday* 13 February 1994. Referring to his discovery of a liking for the works of ERNEST HEMINGWAY while in prison.

3 A lot of people get the misconception that by being free that you're *free*. That's not necessarily true. There's more people on the outside who are in prison than I'll ever be in here.

Quoted in 'The Education of Mike Tyson' (1994) by Pete Hamill, repr. in *The Esquire Book of Sports Writing* (ed. Greg Williams 1995)

4 I have no self-esteem, but the biggest ego in the world.

*Independent on Sunday* 18 October 1998

## Tristan Tzara (1896–1963)
ROMANIAN POET

Original name Sami Rosenstock. After launching the Dada movement in Zurich in 1916 he moved to Paris where he took part in the movement's 'happenings'. He published *Vingt-cinq poèmes* (1918) and *Sept manifestes dada* (1920), and later more conventional lyrical poetry such as *Mouchoir de nuages* (1925) and *L'Homme approximatif* (1930). He wrote a study of the Surrealist movement in 1948.

1 Art is a private thing, the artist makes it for himself; a comprehensible work is the product of a journalist . . .

We need works that are strong, straight, precise, and forever beyond understanding.

'Dada Manifesto', publ. in *Dada* 3, 1918, repr. in *The Dada Painters and Poets* (ed. Robert Motherwell, 1951)

2 The rest, called *literature*, is a dossier of human imbecility for the guidance of future professors.

'Note on Poetry', publ. in *Dada* 4/5, May 1919, repr. in *Lampisteries* (1963)

3 DADA doubts everything. Dada is an armadillo. Everything is Dada, too. Beware of Dada. Anti-dadaism is a disease: selfkleptomania, man's normal condition, is DADA. But the real dadas are against DADA.

'Dada Manifesto on Feeble Love and Bitter Love' sect. 7, publ. in *La Vie des lettres* no. 4, 1921, repr. in *The Dada Painters and Poets* (ed. Robert Motherwell, 1951)

# UNESCO

1 Since wars begin in the minds of men, it is in the minds of men that the defences of peace must be constructed.

Preamble to constitution (1945). The wording is said to have been drafted by both CLEMENT ATTLEE and ARCHIBALD MACLEISH, who was then Chairman of the US delegation to the London conference responsible for drawing up the constitution, which was adopted on 16 November 1945.

## John Updike (b. 1932)
US AUTHOR AND CRITIC

His many novels of adultery and middle-class alienation include *Couples* (1968) and the sequences following the fortunes of car salesman 'Rabbit' Angstrom and the novelist Henry Bech. 'I like middles,' he stated, 'it is in the middles that extremes clash, where ambiguity restlessly rules.' *Rabbit is Rich* (1981) and *Rabbit at Rest* (1990) both won Pulitzer Prizes.

1 The difficulty with humorists is that they will mix what they believe with what they don't; whichever seems likelier to win an effect.

*Rabbit, Run* (1960)

2 The Founding Fathers in their wisdom decided that children were an unnatural strain on parents. So they provided jails called schools, equipped with tortures called an education. School is where you go between when your parents can't take you and industry can't take you.

George Caldwell, in *The Centaur*, ch. 4 (1963)

3 A healthy male adult bore consumes each year one and a half times his own weight in other people's patience.

*Assorted Prose*, 'Confessions of a Wild Bore' (1965)

4 If men do not keep on speaking terms with children, they cease to be men, and become merely machines for eating and for earning money.

ibid. 'A Foreword for Younger Readers'

5 Every marriage tends to consist of an aristocrat and a peasant. Of a teacher and a learner.

*Couples*, ch. 1 (1968)

6 It is not difficult to deceive the first time, for the deceived possesses no antibodies; unvaccinated by suspicion, she overlooks latenesses, accepts absurd excuses, permits the flimsiest patchings to repair great rents in the quotidian.

ibid. ch. 2

7 An affair wants to spill, to share its glory with the world. No act is so private it does not seek applause.

ibid.

8 Sex is like money; only too much is enough.

Piet Hanema, in ibid. ch. 5

9 The first breath of adultery is the freest; after it, constraints aping marriage develop.

Narrator, in ibid.

10 Things go bad. Food goes bad, people go bad, maybe a whole country goes bad. The blacks now have more than ever, but it feels like less, maybe. We were all brought up to want things and maybe the world isn't big enough for all that wanting. I don't know. I don't know anything.

Harry 'Rabbit' Angstrom, in *Rabbit Redux* (1971)

11 Confusion is just a local view of things working out in general.

ibid.

12 Government is either organized benevolence or organized madness; its peculiar magnitude permits no shading.

Buchanan, in *Buchanan Dying*, act 1 (1974)

13 Morality . . . is a child of life, moral indignation a tool of

survival. Once death has equalized all men, worth flies from their deeds as utility flies from their artifacts.

Buchanan, in ibid. act 3

14 To be President of the United States, sir, is to act as advocate for a blind, venomous, and ungrateful client; still, one must make the best of the case, for the purposes of Providence.

President James Polk, in ibid. act 2

15 I think 'taste' is a social concept and not an artistic one. I'm willing to show good taste, if I can, in somebody else's living room, but our reading life is too short for a writer to be in any way polite. Since his words enter into another's brain in silence and intimacy, he should be as honest and explicit as we are with ourselves.

Interview in *The New York Times Book Review* 10 April 1977, repr. in *Hugging the Shore*, Appendix (1983)

16 I would rather have as my patron a host of anonymous citizens digging into their own pockets for the price of a book or a magazine than a small body of enlightened and responsible men administering public funds. I would rather chance my personal vision of truth striking home here and there in the chaos of publication that exists than attempt to filter it through a few sets of official, honorably public-spirited scruples.

Testimony given before the House of Representatives Committee on Education and Labor, 30 January 1978, Boston, publ. in ibid.

17 That a marriage ends is less than ideal; but all things end under heaven, and if temporality is held to be invalidating, then nothing real succeeds.

*Too Far To Go*, Foreword (1979)

18 America is a vast conspiracy to make you happy.

*Problems*, 'How to Love America and Leave it at the Same Time' (1980)

19 Writing criticism is to writing fiction and poetry as hugging the shore is to sailing in the open sea.

*Hugging the Shore*, Foreword (1983)

20 We must lighten ourselves to survive. We must not cling. Safety lies in lessening, in becoming random and thin enough for the new to enter.

*The Witches of Eastwick*, pt 1 (1984, filmed 1987). Referring to the 'natural principle of divestment'.

21 [On the literary interview] It rots a writer's brain, it cretinizes you. You say the same thing again and again, and when you do that happily you're well on the way to being a cretin. Or a politician.

Interviewed by MARTIN AMIS in the *Observer* 30 August 1987, repr. in *Visiting Mrs Nabokov*, 'John Updike' (1993) by Martin Amis

22 Peace is not something we are entitled to but an illusory respite we earn. On both the personal and national level, islands of truce created by balances of terror and potential violence are the best we can hope for.

*Self-Consciousness*, ch. 2 (1989)

23 Dreams come true; without that possibility, nature would not incite us to have them.

ibid. ch. 3

24 To say that war is madness is like saying that sex is madness: true enough, from the standpoint of a stateless eunuch, but merely a provocative epigram for those who must make their arrangements in the world as given.

ibid. ch. 4

25 Among the repulsions of atheism for me has been its drastic uninterestingness as an intellectual position. Where was the ingenuity, the ambiguity, the humanity (in the Harvard sense) of saying that the universe just happened to happen and that when we're dead we're dead?

ibid.

26 Our brains are no longer conditioned for reverence and

awe. We cannot imagine a Second Coming that would not be cut down to size by the televised evening news, or a Last Judgment not subject to pages of holier-than-Thou second-guessing in *The New York Review of Books*.

ibid. ch. 6

27 The yearning for an afterlife is the opposite of selfish: it is love and praise for the world that we are privileged, in this complex interval of light, to witness and experience.

ibid.

28 God is a word, however problematical, we do not have to look up in the dictionary. We seem to have its acquaintance from birth.

ibid.

29 Religion enables us to ignore nothingness and get on with the jobs of life.

ibid.

30 Looking foolish does the spirit good. The need not to look foolish is one of youth's many burdens; as we get older we are exempted from more and more, and float upward in our heedlessness, singing *Gratia Dei sum quod sum*.

ibid. *Gratia Dei sum quod sum* ('Thanks be to God that I am what I am') is one of the epigraphs of Updike's volume of memoirs, taken from an inscription on the tomb of Bishop West in Ely Cathedral.

31 Celebrity is a mask that eats into the face. As soon as one is aware of being 'somebody,' to be watched and listened to with extra interest, input ceases, and the performer goes blind and deaf in his overanimation. One can either see or be seen.

ibid.

32 Customs and convictions change; respectable people are the last to know, or to admit, the change, and the ones most offended by fresh reflections of the facts in the mirror of art.

*New Yorker* 30 July 1990

33 In asking forgiveness of women for our mythologizing of their bodies, for being *unreal* about them, we can only appeal to their own sexuality, which is different but not basically different, perhaps, from our own. For women, too, there seems to be that tangle of supplication and possessiveness, that descent toward infantile undifferentiation, that omnipotent helplessness, that merger with the cosmic mother-warmth, that flushed pulse-quickened leap into overestimation, projection, general mix-up.

'The Female Body', publ. in the *Michigan Quarterly Review* (1990), repr. in *The Best American Essays, 1991* (ed. Joyce Carol Oates, 1991)

34 Now that I am sixty, I see why the idea of elder wisdom has passed from currency.

*New Yorker* November 1992

35 Life robs us of ourselves, piece by small piece. What is eventually left is someone else.

*Brazil*, ch. 23 (1994)

36 For a Jew to move through post-war Europe is to move through hordes of ghosts, vast animated crowds that, since 1945, are not there at all – up in smoke. The feathery touch of the mysteriously absent is felt on all sides.

*Bech at Bay*, 'Bech in Czech' (1998)

## Zdeněk Urbánek (b. 1917)
CZECH AUTHOR AND TRANSLATOR

Between 1948 and 1989 many of his works circulated as *samizdat* in Czechoslovakia. His novels include *The Story of the Pale Dominic* (1940) and *Following Don Quixote* (1949), and he has published collections of short stories, for example *Lives and Consciences* (1944), and essays, *Uncommon Cases* (1993).

1 You in the West have a problem. You are unsure when

you are being lied to, when you are being tricked. We do not suffer from this; and unlike you, we have acquired the skill of reading between the lines.

Interview with John Pilger, August 1977, quoted by him in the *Guardian* 12 February 1990

## (Sir) Peter Ustinov (b. 1921)
BRITISH ACTOR, WRITER AND DIRECTOR

Esteemed as a raconteur and broadcaster, he was once described by the *New Statesman* as 'a tubby character with the affable, slouchy, sulky exterior of a Giant Panda'. His plays include *Romanoff and Juliet* (1956, filmed 1961), *Halfway Up the Tree* (1967) and *Beethoven's Tenth* (1983), and he has acted in numerous films.

1 Laughter would be bereaved if snobbery died.

Quoted in the *Observer* 13 March 1955

2 A diplomat these days is nothing but a head-waiter who's allowed to sit down occasionally.

The General, in *Romanoff and Juliet*, act 1 (1956). Ustinov himself played the General in the first production of the play.

3 Love is an act of endless forgiveness, a tender look which becomes a habit.

*Christian Science Monitor* 9 December 1958

4 If Botticelli were alive today he'd be working for *Vogue*.

Quoted in the *Observer* 21 October 1962

5 To refuse awards . . . is another way of accepting them with more noise than is normal.

Quoted in *Marlon Brando*, ch. 13 (1974, rev. 1989) by David Shipman. Of the refusal of Oscars by MARLON BRANDO and GEORGE C. SCOTT.

6 What is a more irrefutable proof of madness than an inability to have a doubt?

*Dear Me*, ch. 1 (1977)

7 I do not believe that friends are necessarily the people you like best, they are merely the people who got there first.

ibid. ch. 5

8 Sex is a conversation carried out by other means. If you get on well out of bed, half the problems of bed are solved.

Interview in *Speaking Frankly* (1978) by Wendy Leigh

9 [Of the USA] Unfortunately, the balance of nature decrees that a super-abundance of dreams is paid for by a growing potential for nightmares.

*Independent* 25 February 1989

10 The truth is really an ambition which is beyond us.

*International Herald Tribune* 12 March 1990

11 Critics search for ages for the wrong word which, to give them credit, they eventually find.

Interview in the *Sunday Telegraph* 15 November 1998

## Roger Vadim (1928–2000)
FRENCH FILM-MAKER

Better known for the impetus he gave to the careers of his female stars than for the quality of his glossily erotic films, he made an international sex icon of his first wife BRIGITTE BARDOT in *And God Created Woman* (1956), secured a part for his second wife Annette Stroyberg in *Les Liaisons Dangereuses* (1959), generally regarded as his best film, and later gave starring roles to CATHERINE DENEUVE and his third wife JANE FONDA. He later made films in Hollywood, without matching his earlier success.

1 [Of BRIGITTE BARDOT] She was a wanton woman who had sacrificed her body to the god of success, perpetuating the myth of the film world in which depravity pays better than talent.

*Memoirs of the Devil*, ch. 8 (1975). 'From the moment I liberated Brigitte,' Vadim was earlier quoted as saying, 'the moment I showed her how to be truly herself, our marriage was all downhill' (*Sunday Express*, 2 July 1972).

## Paul Valéry (1871–1945)
FRENCH POET AND ESSAYIST

After abandoning poetry for almost twenty years in favour of scientific studies, he established himself as France's leading poet with *The Young Fate* (1917) and *Enchantments* (1922), which included the major poem 'The Graveyard by the Sea'. He also wrote numerous essays and notebooks.

1 Science means simply the aggregate of all the recipes that are always successful. All the rest is literature.

*Moralités* (1932), repr. in *Collected Works*, vol. 14, 'Analects' (ed. J. Matthews, 1970). The last words echo Verlaine, 'All the rest is mere fine writing' ('L'Art poétique', 1882).

2 God created man and, finding him not sufficiently alone, gave him a companion to make him feel his solitude more keenly.

*Tel Quel* 1, 'Moralités' (1941)

3 Politics is the art of preventing people from taking part in affairs which properly concern them.

*Tel Quel* 2, 'Rhumbs' (1943)

## Laurens van der Post (1906–96)
SOUTH AFRICAN WRITER AND PHILOSOPHER

Described by author Jan Morris as 'a mystic, disguised as a novelist and man of action', he became a mentor to PRINCE CHARLES. His philosophical reflections, in which he wrote on ecology from a holistic viewpoint, include *The Lost World of the Kalahari* (1958) and *The Heart of the Hunter* (1961), while he recreated his wartime experience as prisoner of the Japanese in *The Seed and the Sower* (1963, filmed as *Merry Christmas, Mr. Lawrence* 1983).

1 Life was only possible for all of us because, in our past, there had been those who had put the claims of life itself before all else. Did it really matter whether the end came from the crab within or the hyaena without? We will have the courage to meet it and give meaning to the manner of our dying provided we, like these humble, wrinkled old Bushmen, have not set a part of ourselves above the wholeness of life.

*The Lost World of the Kalahari*, ch. 10 (1958)

2 We suffer from a hubris of the mind. We have abolished superstition of the heart only to install a superstition of the intellect in its place.

*The Heart of the Hunter* (1961)

3 The educating of the parents is really the education of the child: children tend to live what is unlived in the parents, so it is vital that parents should be aware of their inferior,

their dark side, and should press on getting to know themselves.

*A Walk with a White Bushman* (1986)

4 What is most threatening and destructive in human society today is the human being who is split in his own nucleus: it is the fission in the modern soul which makes nuclear fission so dangerous – he is a split atom. He has got to heal himself, make himself whole.

ibid.

5 Somehow we should learn to know that our problems are our most precious possessions. They are the raw materials of our salvation: no problem, no redemption.

ibid.

6 I feel that Buddhism is a religion of the high mountains. It is a religion of altitude. Christianity is a religion of serving creation in the here and now; it is very much of the earth, where man does his ploughing and sowing, his begetting and his suffering, seeking to find the great in the small, infinity in a grain of sand.

ibid. The last words allude to William Blake: 'To see a world in a grain of sand/And a heaven in a wild flower' ('Auguries of Innocence', c. 1803).

7 The man of the Kalahari is Esau and we are Jacob, and there is a great gulf between us. This sense of property, of possession that we have is utterly foreign to the Esaus of the world. We have, he is.

ibid.

8 The people who want sanctions remind me a lot of missionaries, who are anchored off an island full of prancing savages and cannibals whom they say they want to convert, but refuse to disembark and go among them, shouting instead, 'If you stop being cannibals, we will bring you the Bible!' This is metaphorically what they are trying to do with sanctions in South Africa.

ibid.

## Carl Van Doren (1885–1950)
US MAN OF LETTERS

Editor of the *Cambridge History of American Literature* (1917–21), he helped to establish the study of American letters on university curricula. He is also noted for his biographies, including of Jonathan Swift (1930), Sinclair Lewis (1933) and Benjamin Franklin (1938, Pulitzer Prize).

1 A classic is a book that doesn't have to be written again.

Quoted by JAMES THURBER in the *Bermudian* November 1950

## Raoul Vaneigem (b. 1934)
BELGIAN PHILOSOPHER

Associated with the Situationists, he challenged what he considered the puritanism of the traditional Left with his conception of playfully subversive activism. His book *The Revolution of Everyday Life* (1967) was a major influence on the New Left of the late 1960s, and he published *The Movement of the Free Spirit* in 1986.

1 The organization controlling the material equipment of our everyday life is such that what in itself would enable us to construct it richly plunges us instead into a poverty of abundance, making alienation all the more intolerable as each convenience promises liberation and turns out to be only one more burden. We are condemned to slavery to the means of liberation.

'Basic Banalities II', publ. in *Internationale Situationiste* January 1963, repr. in *Situationist International Anthology* (ed. Ken Knabb, 1981)

2 Who wants a world in which the guarantee that we shall not die of starvation entails the risk of dying of boredom?

*The Revolution of Everyday Life*, Introduction (1967, transl. 1983)

3 There are more truths in twenty-four hours of a man's life than in all the philosophies.

ibid. ch. 1, sect. 1

4 People who talk about revolution and class struggle without referring explicitly to everyday life, without understanding what is subversive about love and what is positive in the refusal of constraints, such people have a corpse in their mouth.

ibid. ch. 1, sect. 4. The final words were graffitied onto walls in Paris during the 1968 revolt.

5 Never before has a civilization reached such a degree of a contempt for life; never before has a generation, drowned in mortification, felt such a rage to live.

ibid. ch. 5

6 To be rich nowadays merely means to possess a large number of poor objects.

ibid. ch. 7, sect. 2

7 In the kingdom of consumption the citizen is king. A democratic monarchy: equality before consumption, fraternity in consumption, and freedom through consumption. The dictatorship of consumer goods has finally destroyed the barriers of blood, lineage and race.

ibid.

8 The eruption of lived pleasure is such that in losing myself I find myself; forgetting that I exist, I realize myself.

ibid. ch. 20, sect. 2

## Nicholas Van Hoogstraten (b. 1945)
BRITISH BUSINESSMAN

An outspoken property tycoon, he was named Britain's youngest millionaire at the age of twenty-three and has since become a figure of controversy for his conflict with walkers claiming right of way across his property in Sussex.

1 The Ramblers are just a bunch of the dirty mac brigade. The great unwashed. Would you have a lot of Herberts in your garden?

Quoted in the *Independent on Sunday* 6 December 1998. Referring to protesters demanding access to footpaths on his Uckfield estate. After being taken to court by the Ramblers Association, he was obliged to allow right of way in 2000.

## Bartolomeo Vanzetti (1888–1927)
ITALIAN-BORN US POLITICAL ACTIVIST

Having emigrated to the United States in 1908, he was with Nicola Sacco convicted of murder in 1921, the cause of a vociferous campaign alleging the two were being prosecuted for their anarchist beliefs. The death sentences were carried out despite an international outcry.

1 My conviction is that I have suffered for things that I am guilty of. I am suffering because I am a radical, and indeed I am a radical; I have suffered because I was an Italian, and indeed I am an Italian; I have suffered more for my family and for my beloved than for myself; but I am so convinced to be right that if you would execute me two times, and if I could be reborn two other times, I would live again to do what I have done already.

Last speech to court, Dedham, Massachusetts, 19 April 1927, publ. in *The Penguin Book of Twentieth-Century Speeches* (ed. Brian MacArthur, 1999)

## Mario Vargas Llosa (b. 1936)
PERUVIAN NOVELIST

Believing in the 'moral obligation of a writer in Latin America to be involved in civic activities', he stood unsuccessfully for president in Peru in 1990. His fiction frequently describes hypocrisy and corruption in domestic politics, and his first novel, *The Time of the Hero* (1962), was publicly burned. Other titles include *Conversation in the Cathedral* (1969) and *Aunt Julia and the Scriptwriter* (1977).

1 Since it is impossible to know what's really happening, we Peruvians lie, invent, dream and take refuge in illusion. Because of these strange circumstances, Peruvian life, a life in which so few actually do read, has become literary.
Narrator, in *The Real Life of Alejandro Mayta*, ch. 9 (1984)

2 There is an incompatibility between literary creation and political activity.
*International Herald Tribune* 1 April 1988

3 Eroticism has its own moral justification because it says that pleasure is enough for me; it is a statement of the individual's sovereignty.
*International Herald Tribune* 23 October 1990

4 Prosperity or egalitarianism – you have to choose. I favour freedom – you never achieve real equality anyway: you simply sacrifice prosperity for an illusion.
*Independent on Sunday* 5 May 1991

## Gianni Versace (1946–97)
ITALIAN FASHION DESIGNER

Considering himself a tailor rather than designer, he introduced his collections of men's and women's wear in 1978 and was famed for his gaudy colours and sexy cut. His clients included ELTON JOHN, MICHAEL JACKSON and PRINCESS DIANA. He was shot dead outside his home in Florida.

1 I like to dress egos. If you haven't got an ego today, you can forget it.
Quoted in obituary in the *Guardian* 16 July 1997

## Hendrik Verwoerd (1901–66)
SOUTH AFRICAN POLITICIAN AND PRIME MINISTER

He was responsible for much of the apartheid legislation as Minister for Native Affairs (1950–58) and as Prime Minister (1958–66). In 1961 he withdrew South Africa from the Commonwealth and declared a republic. He was assassinated in the House of Assembly in Cape Town.

1 Is not our role to stand for the one thing which means our own salvation here but with which it will also be possible to save the world, and with which Europe will be able to save itself, namely the preservation of the white man and his state?
Speech in 1964, quoted in *The Oxford History of South Africa*, vol. 2, ch. 10 (ed. M. Wilson and L. Thompson, 1971)

## Sid Vicious (1957–79)
BRITISH PUNK ROCKER

Original name John Ritchie. He played with the group the Flowers of Romance before joining the Sex Pistols on bass in 1977, and he became the band's vocalist after Johnny Rotten (see JOHN LYDON) left the following year. He was arrested in New York charged with murdering his girlfriend and died of a drugs overdose while awaiting trial. A film of the affair, *Sid and Nancy*, was made in 1986.

1 I've only been in love with a beer bottle and a mirror.
*Sounds* 9 October 1976

2 I don't understand why people think it's so difficult to learn to play guitar. I found it incredibly easy. You just pick a chord, go twang, and you've got music.
ibid.

## Gore Vidal (b. 1925)
US NOVELIST AND CRITIC

An urbane and sardonic social commentator, he was raised in a political environment and in 1960 ran unsuccessfully for Congress as a Democrat. He caused scandal for his treatment of homosexuality and transsexuality in his novels *The City and the Pillar* (1948) and *Myra Breckinridge* (1968), while works such as *Julian* (1964), *Burr* (1973) and *Lincoln* (1984) fictionally explore the lives of historical figures. The writer FREDERIC RAPHAEL called him 'a tribune who has little use for the plebs but no deference towards the patricians'.

1 It is difficult to find a reputable American historian who will acknowledge the crude fact that a Franklin Roosevelt, say, wanted to be President merely to wield power, to be famed and to be feared. To learn this simple fact one must wade through a sea of evasions: history as sociology, leaders as teachers, bland benevolence as a motive force, when, finally, power *is* an end to itself, and the instinctive urge to prevail the most important single human trait, the necessary force without which no city was built, no city destroyed.
'Robert Graves and the Twelve Caesars', written 1952, publ. in the *Nation* 1959, repr. in *Rocking the Boat* (1963)

2 A talent for drama is not a talent for writing, but is an ability to articulate human relationships.
*The New York Times* 17 June 1956

3 Laughing at someone else is an excellent way of learning how to laugh at oneself; and questioning what seem to be the absurd beliefs of another group is a good way of recognizing the potential absurdity of many of one's own cherished beliefs.
'Satire in the 1950's', publ. in the *Nation* 26 April 1958, repr. in *Collected Essays 1952–1972* (1974)

4 Sex is. There is nothing more to be done about it. Sex builds no roads, writes no novels and sex certainly gives no meaning to anything in life but itself.
'Norman Mailer's Self-Advertisements', publ. in the *Nation* 2 January 1960, repr. in ibid.

5 If most men and women were forced to rely upon physical charm to attract lovers, their sexual lives would be not only meager but in a youth-worshiping country like America painfully brief.
'Notes on Pornography', publ. in *The New York Review of Books* 31 March 1966, repr. in ibid.

6 It is the spirit of the age to believe that any fact, no matter how suspect, is superior to any imaginative exercise, no matter how true.
'French Letters: Theories of the New Novel', publ. in *Encounter* December 1967, repr. in ibid.

7 Always a godfather, never a god.
Quoted in *The Life of Kenneth Tynan*, ch. 27 (1987) by Kathleen Tynan. On being asked to be godfather to Kenneth and Kathleen Tynan's daughter Roxana in 1967.

8 There is something about a bureaucrat that does not like a poem.
*Sex, Death and Money*, Preface (1968)

9 The theater needs continual reminders that there is nothing more debasing than the work of those who do well what is not worth doing at all.
*Newsweek* 25 March 1968

10 I'm all for bringing back the birch, but only between consenting adults.
Television interview with DAVID FROST, quoted in the *Sunday Times* 16 September 1973

11 Whenever a friend succeeds, a little something in me dies.
ibid.

12 Each writer is born with a repertory company in his head. Shakespeare has perhaps 20 players, and Tennessee Williams has about 5, and Samuel Beckett one – and maybe a clone of that one. I have 10 or so, and that's a

lot. As you get older, you become more skillful at casting them.

*Times Herald* 18 June 1978

13 In America, the race goes to the loud, the solemn, the hustler. If you think you're a great writer, you must say that you are.

Interview in *Writers at Work* (fifth series, ed. George Plimpton, 1981)

14 Some writers take to drink, others take to audiences.

ibid.

15 A narcissist is someone better looking than you are.

*The New York Times* 12 March 1981

16 [Of Ronald Reagan] A triumph of the embalmer's art.

Quoted in the *Observer* 26 April 1981

17 As the age of television progresses the Reagans will be the rule, not the exception. To be perfect for television is all a President has to be these days.

Quoted in the *Observer* 7 February 1982

18 There is no such thing as a homosexual or a heterosexual person. There are only homo- or heterosexual acts. Most people are a mixture of impulses if not practises.

*Armageddon? Essays 1983–1987*, 'Tennessee Williams: Someone to Laugh at the Squares With', sect. 1 (1987). Vidal has reiterated this remark on various occasions.

19 On 16 September 1985, when the Commerce Department announced that the United States had become a debtor nation, the American Empire died.

ibid. 'The Day the American Empire Ran Out of Gas'

20 Writing fiction has become a priestly business in countries that have lost their faith.

*Independent* 16 August 1989

21 Think of the earth as a living organism that is being attacked by billions of bacteria whose numbers double every forty years. Either the host dies, or the virus dies, or both die.

'Gods and Greens', publ. in the *Observer* 27 August 1989, repr. in *A View from the Diner's Club* (1991)

22 I find in most novels no imagination at all. They seem to think the highest form of the novel is to write about marriage, because that's the most important thing there is for middle-class people.

*Guardian* 2 November 1989

23 The only thing pornography has been known to cause is solitary masturbation; as for corruption, the only immediate victim is English prose.

Quoted in the *Observer* 28 January 1996

24 What is real politics? Who collects what money from whom to spend on whom for what. That's all there is to it, but no politician in the United States dares address that subject for fear we'll discover who bought him and for how much – not to mention how the military got us $5 trillion into debt.

Interview in the *Independent* 19 August 1998

25 It is not enough to succeed. Others must fail.

Attributed

26 He will lie even when it is inconvenient, the sign of a true artist.

Attributed

27 Never miss a chance to have sex or appear on television.

Attributed

## King Vidor (1894–1982)

US FILM-MAKER

Originally King Wallis Vidor. A key figure of Hollywood's silent era, he established a reputation for his films emphasizing social

issues, notably *The Big Parade* (1925) and *The Crowd* (1928). Later films include *Our Daily Bread* (1934) and *Duel in the Sun* (1946). Several times nominated, in 1979 he received his first Academy Award in recognition of his 'incomparable achievements as a cinematic creator and innovator'.

1 Marriage isn't a word – it's a *sentence*!

Caption in *The Crowd* (silent film, 1928)

## Judith Viorst (b. 1935)

US POET AND JOURNALIST

'Married life is the rock on which I sit,' she states, and it is a recurrent theme of her light humorous verse, which has been compared to that of OGDEN NASH, published in *The Village Square* (1965), *It's Hard to Be Hip Over Thirty* (1968), and *Forever Fifty* (1989). Her essays appeared in *Yes, Married: A Saga of Love and Complaint* (1972), and she has also written for children, including *I'll Fix Anthony* (1988) and *Earrings* (1990).

1 With four walk-in closets to walk in,
Three bushes, two shrubs, and one tree,
The suburbs are good for the children,
But no place for grown-ups to be.

'The Suburbs Are Good For The Children', publ. in *It's Hard to Be Hip Over Thirty and Other Tragedies of Married Life* (1968)

2 But it's hard to be hip over thirty
When everyone else is nineteen,
When the last dance we learned was the Lindy,
And the last we heard, girls who looked like Barbra Streisand
Were trying to do something about it.

'It's Hard to Be Hip Over Thirty', publ. in ibid.

3 It's true love because
If he said quit drinking martinis but I kept on drinking them and the next morning I couldn't get out of bed,
He wouldn't tell me he told me.

'True Love', publ. in ibid.

## Viz

BRITISH COMIC

The comic started in Newcastle as an enthusiasm of Chris Donald and his friends, sold at punk gigs in the early 1980s. Adopted by Virgin in 1984, its growth made it the publishing phenomenon of the decade. It features characters such as Sid the Sexist, Johnny Fartpants and the Fat Slags.

1 Buster Gonad and his Unfeasibly Large Testicles.

Comic character, inspired by 'Claude Hopper and his unfeasibly large feet'

2 Oooh-errr.

Finbarr Saunders (and his Double Entendres)

## Stephen Vizinczey (b. 1933)

HUNGARIAN NOVELIST AND CRITIC

After participating in the 1956 Hungarian uprising he fled to Canada where he edited *Exchange* magazine (1960–61) and became a producer in Canadian broadcasting. His bestselling novel *In Praise of Older Women* (1965) was followed by his collections of essays, *The Rules of Chaos* (1968) and *Truth and Lies in Literature* (1986).

1 The truth is that our race survived ignorance; it is our scientific genius that will do us in.

Book review in *The Times* 21 September 1970, repr. in *Truth and Lies in Literature*, 'Leonardo's Regret' (1986)

2 Consistency is a virtue for trains: what we want from a philosopher is insights, whether he comes by them consistently or not.

Book review in the *Sunday Telegraph* 21 April 1974, repr. in ibid. 'Good Faith and Bad'

3 Strange as it may seem, no amount of learning can cure stupidity, and formal education positively fortifies it.
Book review in the *Sunday Telegraph* 2 March 1975, repr. in ibid. 'Europe's Inner Demons'

4 When you close your eyes to tragedy, you close your eyes to greatness.
Book review in the *Sunday Telegraph* 5 January 1984, repr. in ibid. 'Who Killed Kleist?'

5 We now have a whole culture based on the assumption that people know nothing and so anything can be said to them.
Book review in the *Observer* 24 June 1990

## V.N. Volosinov (1905–60)

RUSSIAN LINGUIST

Full name Valentin Nikolaevic Volosinov. Associated with M.M. Bakhtin and his school of criticism which sought to strip away the preconceptions about literature that previous critical traditions had thrown up, he was author of a Marxist critique of Freud and *Marxism and the Philosophy of Language* (1929), among other works. 'The word is a two-sided act,' he wrote. 'I give myself verbal shape from another's point of view. The word is a bridge between myself and the other.'

1 The domain of ideology coincides with the domain of signs. They equate with one another. Wherever a sign is present, ideology is present, too. *Everything ideological possesses semiotic value.*
*Marxism and the Philosophy of Language*, ch. 1 (1929)

## Kurt Vonnegut (b. 1922)

US NOVELIST

He blends science fiction and fantasy with social comment in his novels, such as his first, *Piano Player* (1952), and subsequently *Cat's Cradle* (1963) and *Breakfast of Champions* (1973). His best known, *Slaughterhouse Five* (1969), is based on his experience as a prisoner of war in Germany, where he survived the fire-bombing of Dresden.

1 I have been a soreheaded occupant of a file drawer labeled 'Science Fiction' . . . and I would like out, particularly since so many serious critics regularly mistake the drawer for a urinal.
*Wampeters, Foma and Granfalloons*, 'Science Fiction' (1974)

2 We would be a lot safer if the Government would take its money out of science and put it into astrology and the reading of palms . . . Only in superstition is there hope. If you want to become a friend of civilization, then become an enemy of the truth and a fanatic for harmless balderdash.
ibid. 'When I Was Twenty-One'

3 The two real political parties in America are the *Winners* and the *Losers*. The people don't acknowledge this. They claim membership in two imaginary parties, the *Republicans* and the *Democrats*, instead.
ibid. 'In a Manner that Must Shame God Himself'

4 Being American is to eat a lot of beef steak, and boy, we've got a lot more beef steak than any other country, and that's why you ought to be glad you're an American. And people have started looking at these big hunks of bloody meat on their plates, you know, and wondering what on earth they think they're doing.
Interview in *City Limits* 11 March 1983

5 What war has always been is a puberty ceremony. It's a very rough one, but you went away a boy and came back a man, maybe with an eye missing or whatever but godammit you were a man and people had to call you a man thereafter.
ibid.

6 The feeling about a soldier is, when all is said and done, he wasn't really going to do very much with his life anyway. The example usually is: 'he wasn't going to compose Beethoven's Fifth.'
ibid.

7 I was taught that the human brain was the crowning glory of evolution so far, but I think it's a very poor scheme for survival.
Quoted in the *Observer* 27 December 1987

8 The world has been ruined by appeasement. Appeasement of whom? Of the Communists? Of the Neo-Nazis? No! Appeasement of the compulsive war-preparers. I can scarcely name a nation that has not lost most of its freedom and wealth in attempts to appease its own addicts to preparations for war.
*Fates Worse than Death*, ch. 14 (1991)

## John Vorster (1915–83)

SOUTH AFRICAN POLITICIAN AND PRIME MINISTER

Originally named Balthazar Johannes Vorster. He was elected a National Party MP in 1953 and appointed Justice Minister in 1961, presiding over some of the worst repression of the apartheid years. As Prime Minister from 1966, he pursued a dialogue with black African states and instigated military intervention in Angola in 1975. He resigned in 1978 over a scandal over the misdirection of government funds.

1 As far as criticism is concerned, we don't resent that unless it is absolutely biased, as it is in most cases.
Quoted in the *Observer* 9 November 1969

## Andrei Voznesensky (b. 1933)

RUSSIAN POET

Vice-president of the Russian branch of PEN, he attracted thousands to his poetry readings until a clamp-down by the Soviet authorities in 1963. His experimental verse, known for its use of metaphor, 'the engine of form' as he put it, has been published in *Parabola* (1960), *Heart of Achilles* (1966) and *Nostalgia for the Present* (1978), among other collections.

1 I am Goya
of the bare field, by the enemy's beak gouged
till the craters of my eyes gape
I am grief

I am the tongue
of war, the embers of cities
on the snows of the year 1941
I am hunger
'I am Goya' (1960, transl. Stanley Kunitz), repr. in *Antiworlds and the Fifth Ace* (ed. Patricia Blake and Max Hayward, 1966)

2 Along a parabola life like a rocket flies,
Mainly in darkness, now and then on a rainbow.
'Parabolic Ballad' (1960, transl. W.H. AUDEN), publ. in *Encounter* April 1963, repr. in ibid. Opening lines of poem.

3 The urge to kill, like the urge to beget,
Is blind and sinister. Its craving is set
Today on the flesh of a hare: tomorrow it can
Howl the same way for the flesh of a man.
'Hunting a Hare' (1964, transl. W.H. Auden), repr. in ibid.

## Terry Waite (b. 1939)

BRITISH ECCLESIASTIC AND NEGOTIATOR

As special adviser to the Archbishop of Canterbury, ROBERT RUNCIE, he negotiated for the release of British and US hostages held in Beirut by the Islamic Jihad but in 1987 was himself taken hostage and held until 1991, an experience described in *Taken on Trust* (1993).

1 Freeing hostages is like putting up a stage set, which you do with the captors, agreeing on each piece as you slowly put it together; then you leave an exit through which both the captor and the captive can walk with sincerity and dignity.

Television broadcast, ABC TV, 3 November 1986. On his trips to Lebanon as special envoy of the Archbishop of Canterbury to negotiate the release of hostages held by terrorists, eleven weeks before his own abduction.

2 The terrible thing about terrorism is that ultimately it destroys those who practise it. Slowly but surely, as they try to extinguish life in others, the light within them dies.

*Guardian* 20 February 1992

## Derek Walcott (b. 1930)

WEST INDIAN POET AND PLAYWRIGHT

Born in Santa Lucia, he has spent most of his life in Trinidad where he founded (1959), and for twenty-five years ran, the Trinidad Theatre Workshop. He is best known for his verse collections in which he makes frequent use of 'chants, jokes and fables', such as *The Castaway* (1965), *The Gulf* (1969), *The Fortunate Traveller* (1981) and the epic *Omeros* (1990). In 1992 he was the first native Caribbean to be awarded the Nobel Prize for Literature.

1 I who have cursed
The drunken officer of British rule, how choose
Between this Africa and the English tongue I love?
Betray them both, or give back what they give?

'A Far Cry From Africa', publ. in *In a Green Night* (1962)

2 The peace of white horses,
The pastures of ports,
The litany of islands,
The rosary of archipelagoes.

'A Sea-Chantey', publ. in ibid.

3 Irascibility, muse of middle age.

'The Estranging Sea', ch. 18, sect. 3, publ. in *Another Life* (1973)

4 Adam had an idea.
He and the snake would share
the loss of Eden for a profit.
So both made the New World. And it looked good.

'New World', publ. in *Sea Grapes* (1976)

5 I try to forget what happiness was,
and when that don't work, I study the stars.

'The Schooner *Flight*', sect. 11, publ. in *The Star-Apple Kingdom* (1980)

6 *I going to bite them young ladies, partner,
like a hot dog or a hamburger
and if you thin, don't be in a fright
is only big fat women I going to bite.*

'The Spoiler's Return', publ. in *The Fortunate Traveller*, pt 2 (1981)

7 Famine sighs like a scythe
across the field of statistics and the desert
is a moving mouth. In the hold of this earth
10,000,000 shoreless souls are drifting.
Somalia: 765,000, their skeletons will go under the tidal sand.

'The Fortunate Traveller', sect. 1, publ. in ibid. pt 3

8 To curse your birthplace is the final evil.

*Midsummer*, 'Poem 29', sect. 1 (1984)

9 Any serious attempt to try to do something worthwhile is ritualistic.

Interview in *Writers at Work* (eighth series, ed. George Plimpton, 1988)

10 I come from a place that likes grandeur; it likes large gestures; it is not inhibited by flourish; it is a rhetorical society; it is a society of physical performance; it is a society of style.

ibid.

11 The English language is nobody's special property. It is the property of the imagination: it is the property of the language itself.

ibid.

12 Poetry, which is perfection's sweat but which must seem as fresh as the raindrops on a statue's brow, combines the natural and the marmoreal; it conjugates both tenses simultaneously: the past and the present, if the past is the sculpture and the present the beads of dew or rain on the forehead of the past.

Nobel Lecture, 1992, publ. in *The Antilles, Fragments of Epic Memory* (1993)

13 Break a vase, and the love that reassembles the fragments is stronger than that love which took its symmetry for granted when it was whole.

'Dissolving the Sigh of History', publ. in the *Guardian* 16 December 1992

## George Wald (1906–97)

US BIOCHEMIST

After research work in Berlin, he was based at Harvard (1932–77), where he worked on the biochemistry of vision. In 1933 he discovered vitamin A in the eye's retina, and later its role in the composition of rhodopsin, the light-sensitive pigment in the eye. He shared the 1967 Nobel Prize for Physiology or Medicine with Ragnar Granit and Haldan Hartline.

1 We are the products of editing, rather than of authorship.

'The Origin of Optical Activity', publ. in *Annals of the New York Academy of Sciences*, vol. 69 (1957)

2 It would be a poor thing to be an atom in a universe without physicists, and physicists are made of atoms. A physicist is an atom's way of knowing about atoms.

Foreword to *The Fitness of the Environment* (1959) by L.J. Henderson

## George Walden (b. 1939)

BRITISH POLITICIAN

He held diplomatic posts from 1967 before being elected a Conservative MP in 1983, becoming Under-secretary of State at the Department of Education and Science (1985–7). He is the author of *Ethics and Foreign Policy* (1990) and *We All Should Know Better: Solving the Education Crisis* (1996).

1 A country losing touch with its own history is like an old man losing his glasses, a distressing sight, at once vulnerable, unsure, and easily disoriented.

*The Times* 20 December 1986

## Kurt Waldheim (b. 1918)

AUSTRIAN DIPLOMAT AND PRESIDENT

He was Secretary-General of the United Nations (1972–81) and in 1986 was elected President of Austria, but was defeated in 1992 after allegations of complicity with the Nazi regime before and during the Second World War.

1 There is no such thing as collective guilt.

Quoted in the *International Herald Tribune* 11 March 1988. Referring to Austria's Nazi past.

## Lech Walesa (b. 1943)

POLISH TRADE UNION LEADER AND PRESIDENT

In 1980 he founded the 'free trade union' Solidarity at the Gdansk shipyards, winning economic and political concessions from the government. He was imprisoned after the banning of the union in 1981, but released in 1982, and awarded the Nobel Peace Prize in 1983. He led Solidarity to victory in the democratic elections of 1989, and served as Poland's President (1990–95).

1 You have riches and freedom here but I feel no sense of faith or direction. You have so many computers, why don't you use them in the search for love?

Quoted in the *Daily Telegraph* 14 December 1988. Said in Paris on his first visit outside the Soviet bloc.

2 The supply of words in the world market is plentiful but the demand is falling. Let deeds follow words now.

*Newsweek* 27 November 1989

## Alice Walker (b. 1944)

US AUTHOR AND CRITIC

Her particular preoccupation is the racial and sexual oppression of black women. Her early novels, *The Third Life of Grange Copeland* (1970) and *Meridian* (1976), were followed by *The Color Purple* (1982, filmed 1985), which won a Pulitzer Prize. She has also published several volumes of verse and essays and an indictment of female circumcision, *Possessing the Secret of Joy* (1992).

1 The sight of a Black nun strikes their sentimentality; and, as I am unalterably rooted in native ground, they consider me a work of primitive art, housed in a magical color; the incarnation of civilized, anti-heathenism, and the fruit of a triumphing idea.

'The Diary of an African Nun', publ. in *Freedomways* summer 1968

2 The gift of loneliness is sometimes a radical vision of society or one's people that has not previously been taken into account.

Interview, publ. in *Interviews with Black Writers* (ed. John O'Brien, 1973)

3 It seems our fate to be incorrect ... and in our incorrectness stand.

ibid.

4 And so our mothers and grandmothers have, more often than not anonymously, handed on the creative spark, the seed of the flower they themselves never hoped to see ... Guided by my heritage of a love of beauty and a respect for strength – in search of my mother's garden, I found my own.

'In Search of Our Mothers' Gardens', publ. in *Ms.* May 1974, repr. in *In Search of Our Mothers' Gardens* (1983)

5 All partisan movements add to the fullness of our understanding of society as a whole. They never detract; or, in any case, one must not allow them to do so. Experience adds to experience.

'Can I Be My Brother's Sister?' publ. in *Ms.* October 1975, repr. in ibid. 'Brothers and Sisters'

6 It is healthier, in any case, to write for the adults one's children will become than for the children one's 'mature' critics often are.

'A Writer Because of, Not in Spite of, Her Children', publ. in *Ms.* January 1976, repr. in ibid.

7 Writing saved me from the sin and inconvenience of violence.

'One Child of One's Own', publ. in *Ms.* August 1979, repr. in ibid.

8 The original 'crime' of 'niggers' and lesbians is that they prefer themselves.

'Breaking Chains and Encouraging Life', publ. in *Ms.* April 1980, repr. in ibid.

9 The good news may be that Nature is phasing out the white man, but the bad news is that's who She thinks we all are.

'Nuclear Madness: What You Can Do', publ. in *Black Scholar* spring 1982, repr. in ibid.

10 To me, the black black woman is our essential mother – the blacker she is the more us she is – and to see the hatred that is turned on her is enough to make me despair, almost entirely, of our future as a people.

'If the Present Looks Like the Past, What Does the Future Look Like?' publ. in *Essence* July 1982, repr. in ibid.

11 The trouble with our people is as soon as they got out of slavery they didn't want to give the white man nothing else. But the fact is, you got to give 'em something. Either your money, your land, your woman or your ass.

Pa, in *The Color Purple* (1982)

12 She say, Celie, tell the truth, have you ever found God in church? I never did. I just found a bunch of folks hoping for him to show. Any God I ever felt in church I brought in with me. And I think all the other folks did too. They come to church to *share* God, not find God.

Shug, in ibid.

13 Somewhere in the bible it say Jesus' hair was like lamb's wool, I say. Well, say Shug, if he came to any of these churches we talking bout he'd have to have it conked before anybody paid him any attention. The last thing niggers want to think about they God is that his hair kinky.

Narrator (Celie), in ibid.

14 I think it pisses God off if you walk by the color purple in a field somewhere and don't notice it.

Shug, in ibid.

15 Womanist is to feminist as purple is to lavender.

*In Search of Our Mothers' Gardens*, epigraph (1983)

16 Anybody can observe the Sabbath, but making it holy surely takes the rest of the week.

ibid. 'To the Editors of *Ms.* Magazine'

17 There are those who believe Black people possess the secret of joy and that it is this that will sustain them through any spiritual or moral or physical devastation.

*Possessing the Secret of Joy*, Epigraph (1992)

18 They circumcised women, little girls, in Jesus's time. Did he know? Did the subject anger or embarrass him? Did the early church erase the record? Jesus himself was circumcised; perhaps he thought only the cutting done to him was done to women, and therefore, since he survived, it was all right.

ibid. pt 21, 'Tashi – Evelyn – Mrs Johnson'

## Derek Wall see PENNY KEMP and DEREK WALL

## George Wallace (1919–98)
US POLITICIAN

As a circuit judge in Alabama (1953–9) he made segregationist rulings in defiance of the US Civil Rights Commission, and as state Governor (1963–7) he attempted to block desegregation in Alabama schools. He was shot and paralysed while running for nomination as the Democratic Party presidential candidate in 1972. In subsequent terms as Governor (1971–9, 1983–7) he modified his segregationist views.

1 Segregation now, segregation tomorrow and segregation forever!

Inaugural address as Governor of Alabama, January 1963, publ. in the *Birmingham World* 19 January 1963. Wallace's speechwriter, Asa Carter (1926–79), was a Ku Klux Klansman who went on to have literary success under the name of Forrest Carter, with, for example,

*Gone to Texas*, filmed by CLINT EASTWOOD as *The Outlaw Josey Wales* (1976).

## Mark Wallinger (b. 1959)
BRITISH ARTIST

His work, a satirical commentary on divisions in contemporary British society, varies from paintings to mixed-media installations. In 1992 he painted *Race, Class, Sex*, four life-size paintings of thoroughbred stallions in the manner of George Stubbs, and in 1994 he entitled a living race horse *A Real Work of Art*.

1 This century has needed witnesses more than it has needed artists. The camera asserts what it has seen. The artists are just looking.

*Guardian* 13 January 1996

## Michelene Wandor (b. 1940)
BRITISH POET, PLAYWRIGHT AND CRITIC

Her verse and plays, which include *Spilt Milk* (1972), *Scissors* (1978), *Whose Greenham?* (1986) and *The Pankhursts* (1990), chiefly address themes of women's relations to a patriarchal culture. Her *Collected Poems* appeared in 1990. She is a regular broadcaster and scriptwriter with the BBC.

1 Stupid word, that. Period. In America it means 'full stop', like in punctuation. That's stupid as well. A period isn't a full stop. It's a new beginning. I don't mean all that creativity, life-giving force, earth-mother stuff, I mean it's a new beginning to the month, relief that you're not pregnant, when you don't have to have a child.

*Guests in the Body*, 'Mother's Pride' (1986)

2 I have decided to give up heterosexuality. I have decided that, while the project of altering the balance of power within heterosexual relationships is still a valid one, it is no longer one I can espouse – so to speak. There is no revolutionary hope for the heterosexual, and I have therefore decided to love myself and become a lesbian.

In conversation with her mother, in 'Meet My Mother', publ. in *Close Company: Stories of Mothers and Daughters* (ed. Christine Park and Caroline Heaton, 1987)

## (Dame) Barbara Ward (1914–81)
BRITISH ECONOMIST AND JOURNALIST

Baroness Jackson of Lodsworth. She and her husband, UN official Robert Jackson, worked as advisers on development planning in India and Pakistan, and she was later Schweitzer Professor of International Economic Development at Columbia University (1963–73). Her popular writings on conservation and ecology include *The Rich Nations and the Poor Nations* (1962), *Spaceship Earth* (1966) and *Only One Earth* (1972, written with René Dubos).

1 There is no human failure greater than to launch a profoundly important endeavour and then leave it half done. This is what the West has done with its colonial system. It shook all the societies in the world loose from their old moorings. But it seems indifferent whether or not they reach safe harbour in the end.

*The Rich Nations and the Poor Nations*, ch. 2 (1962)

2 We cannot cheat on DNA. We cannot get round photosynthesis. We cannot say I am not going to give a damn about phytoplankton. All these tiny mechanisms provide the preconditions of our planetary life. To say we do not care is to say in the most literal sense that 'we choose death'.

'Only One Earth', publ. in *Who Speaks for Earth?* (ed. Maurice F. Strong, 1973)

## Andy Warhol (c. 1928–87)

US ARTIST AND FILM-MAKER

Originally named Andrew Warhola. A leading figure in the Pop art of the 1960s, he produced deliberately impersonal and surface-oriented work, presenting images of popular icons and soup cans alike as mass-produced commodities. He was director-producer of *Chelsea Girls* (1966) and producer of numerous other films including *Empire* (1965) and *Flesh* (1968). GORE VIDAL called him 'a genius with the IQ of a moron', while for EDMUND WHITE he was 'the man whose heart is as warm as a hanky soaked in ethyl chloride'. See also TOM WOLFE 9.

1 My image is a statement of the symbols of the harsh, impersonal products and brash materialistic objects on which America is built today. It is a projection of everything that can be bought and sold, the practical but impermanent symbols that sustain us.
'New Talent U.S.A.', publ. in *Art in America*, vol. 50, no. 1, 1962

2 Those who talk about individuality the most are the ones who most object to deviation, and in a few years it may be the other way around. Some day everybody will just think what they want to think, and then everybody will probably be thinking alike; that seems to be what is happening.
Interview in *Art News* November 1963, repr. in *Pop Art Redefined* (1969) by John Russell and Suzi Gablik

3 I think somebody should be able to do all my paintings for me.
ibid.

4 If you want to know all about Andy Warhol, just look at the surface: of my paintings and films and me, and there I am. There's nothing behind it.
'Warhol in his Own Words', publ. in the *Los Angeles Free Press* 17 March 1967, repr. in *Andy Warhol: A Retrospective* (1986)

5 [On The Velvet Underground] There are beautiful sounds in rock. Very lazy, dreamlike noises. You can forget about the lyrics in most songs. Just dig the noise, and you've got our sound . . . We're musical primitives.
Quoted in the *New York Magazine*, 1967, repr. in *The Faber Book of Pop*, pt 5, '1966: A Quiet Evening at the Balloon Farm' (ed. Hanif Kureishi and Jon Savage, 1995). Warhol supported The Velvet Underground from 1965, and nominally produced their first album (1967).

6 In the future everybody will be world famous for fifteen minutes.
*Andy Warhol* (exhibition catalogue, 1968). Ten years later, in *Andy Warhol's Exposures*, 'Studio 54' (1979), he wrote: 'I'm bored with that line. I never use it any more. My new line is, "In fifteen minutes everybody will be famous."'

7 I used to think that everything was just being funny but now I don't know. I mean, how can you tell?
Quoted in *Vogue* 1 March 1970

8 Sex is more exciting on the screen and between the pages than between the sheets.
*From A to B and Back Again*, ch. 3 (1975)

9 Fantasy love is much better than reality love. Never doing it is very exciting. The most exciting attractions are between two opposites that never meet.
ibid.

10 Among other things, drag queens are living testimony to the way women used to want to be, the way some people still want them to be, and the way some women still actually want to be. Drags are ambulatory archives of ideal moviestar womanhood. They perform a documentary service, usually consecrating their lives to keeping the glittering alternative alive and available for (not-too-close) inspection.
ibid.

11 I'm confused about who the news belongs to. I always

have it in my head that if your name's in the news, then the news should be paying you. Because it's *your news* and they're taking it and selling it as their product . . . If people didn't give the news their news, and if everybody kept their news to themselves, the news wouldn't have any news.
ibid. ch. 5

12 Before I was shot, I always thought that I was more half-there than all-there – I always suspected that I was watching TV instead of living life . . . Right when I was being shot and ever since, I knew that I was watching television. The channels switch, but it's all television.
ibid. ch. 6. Referring to the attempt on his life by VALERIE SOLANAS in 1968.

13 Being good in business is the most fascinating kind of art . . . Making money is art and working is art and good business is the best art.
ibid.

14 I suppose I have a really loose interpretation of 'work', because I think that just being alive is so much work at something you don't always want to do. Being born is like being kidnapped. And then sold into slavery. People are working every minute. The machinery is always going. Even when you sleep.
ibid.

15 Since people are going to be living longer and getting older, they'll just have to learn how to be babies longer.
ibid. ch. 7

16 Isn't life a series of images that change as they repeat themselves?
Quoted in *Warhol*, 'Too Much Work 1980–84' (1989) by Victor Bokris

17 Dying is the most embarrassing thing that can ever happen to you, because someone's got to take care of all your details.
ibid. 'Goodbye 1986–7'. On being admitted to hospital two days before his death, Warhol was said by a member of staff to be the only person in her experience who remembered his Blue Cross and health insurance ID numbers by heart.

## Jack L. Warner (1892–1978)

US FILM PRODUCER

Original name Jack Leonard Eichelbaum. He joined his brothers, Albert, Harry and Sam, in Warner Brothers, which in 1927 was the first production company to introduce sound and by the 1930s was releasing about 100 films a year. He was President in 1956–72, personally produced *My Fair Lady* (1964) and presided over the sale of the studio to Seven Arts in 1967.

1 I would rather take a twenty-mile hike than crawl through a book.
Attributed in *Writers in Hollywood 1915–1951*, ch. 5, sect. 2 (1990) by Ian Hamilton

## Jack Warner (1895–1981)

BRITISH ACTOR

He became a film actor after work as a variety comedian. Among his screen appearances are *The Captive Heart* (1946), *Valley of the Eagles* (1951), *The Ladykillers* (1955) and, most famously, *The Blue Lamp* (1950), in which he appeared as PC Dixon, a role he extended in the TV series *Dixon of Dock Green*.

1 Evenin' all.
George Dixon (Jack Warner), in *Dixon of Dock Green* (BBC TV series, 1955–76, created by Ted Willis). Each episode of the series started and ended with Sergeant Dixon's familiar salute and 'Evenin' all'.

# Marina Warner (b. 1946)

BRITISH AUTHOR AND CRITIC

She explores the themes of sexuality and myth in works such as *Alone of All Her Sex* (1976) and *Monuments and Maidens* (1985) and in her novels including *In a Dark Wood* (1977) and *The Lost Father* (1988). *The Mermaids in the Basement* (1993) is a collection of her short stories.

1 Although Mary cannot be a model for the New Woman, a goddess is better than no goddess at all, for the sombre-suited masculine world of the Protestant religion is altogether too much like a gentleman's club to which the ladies are only admitted on special days.

*Alone of All Her Sex*, Epilogue (1976)

2 I've noticed that the sign of a screen villain these days is fondling. Whenever anyone intends harm, they announce it by squeezing someone by the shoulder or the upper arm . . . Movements of affection betoken insincerity: only the deadliest villain would reach out softly to touch an innocent face. So lethal is such a gesture that you expect him to leave a burnmark, like napalm. Sincere people never touch each other. . . . Kissers nowadays are invariably Judases.

*Anna Collouthar, in The Lost Father, ch. 22 (1988)*

3 All the soppy talk about the inner child has not laid to rest deep fantasies about the inner ogre.

*No Go the Bogeyman*, ch. 6 (1998)

4 Children imitate their elders: they cannot generate moral standards independently of the adults who surround them. Some will be Red Guards and denounce their grand-mothers if their schoolteachers expect it of them; some will see visions of the Virgin Mary. They are not the keepers of our good conscience, and their aberrations reflect, and, in some shocking instances, magnify our own.

ibid.

5 Fears trace a map of a society's values; we need fear to know who we are and what we do not want to be.

ibid. Epilogue

# Sylvia Townsend Warner (1893–1978)

BRITISH AUTHOR

Praised by JOHN UPDIKE for her 'brilliantly varied and superbly self-possessed literary production', she blended fantasy and reality in her fiction and poems. Her novels include *Lolly Willowes* (1926), and *A Garland of Straw* (1943) and *Kingdoms of Elfin* (1977) are short story collections. She was also an expert on Tudor music and took part in the Spanish Civil War.

1 There are some women . . . in whom conscience is so strongly developed that it leaves little room for anything else. Love is scarcely felt before duty rushes to encase it, anger impossible because one must always be calm and see both sides, pity evaporates in expedients, even grief is felt as a sort of bruised sense of injury, a resentment that one should have grief forced upon one when one has always acted for the best.

*Autumn River*, 'Total Loss' (1966)

2 When other helpers fail and comforts flee, when the senses decay and the mind moves in a narrower and narrower circle, when the grasshopper is a burden and the postman brings no letters, and even the Royal Family is no longer quite what it was, an obituary column stands fast.

ibid. 'Their Quiet Lives'

# Mary Warnock (b. 1924)

BRITISH PHILOSOPHER

Baroness Warnock of Weeke. A fellow and tutor in philosophy at St Hugh's, Oxford (1949–66, 1976–84) and Mistress of Girton College, Cambridge (1985–91), she has advised and chaired committees on education, animal experiments and medical ethics. Her publications include *The Uses of Philosophy* (1992), *Imagination and Time* (1994) and *An Intelligent Person's Guide to Ethics* (1998)

1 Oxford is, and always has been, full of cliques, full of factions, and full of a particular non-social snobbiness.

*Observer* 2 November 1980

# Charles Marquis Warren (1917–90)

US WRITER, DIRECTOR AND PRODUCER

He specialized in writing and directing westerns, helping to shape the popular stereotype of the West during the 1950s and 1960s in the TV series *Gunsmoke*, *The Virginian* and *Rawhide* and the films *Little Big Horn* (1951), *Arrowhead* (1953), *Seven Angry Men* (1955) and *Charro!* (1969).

1 Head 'em up, move 'em out, rope 'em in, head 'em off, pull 'em down, move 'em on.

Preamble to *Rawhide* (TV series, 1959–66, created by Charles Marquis Warren). The series, which ran for 217 episodes and included CLINT EASTWOOD among its stars, was based on the 1866 diary of drover and pioneer cowboy George Duffield.

# James Warren (b. 1936)

US SCREEN ACTOR

1 Maybe I'm gonna die. You've got even bigger problems – you're gonna live.

Johnny Rico ( James Warren) to his brother, in *The Brothers Rico* (film, 1957, screenplay by Lewis Meltzer and Ben Perry adapted from Georges Simenon's novelette, directed by Phil Karlson)

# Robert Penn Warren (1905–89)

US POET AND NOVELIST

Described by *The New York Times Book Review* as 'a man of letters on the old-fashioned, outsize scale', he won three Pulitzer Prizes for the poetry collections *Promises* (1957) and *Now and Then: Poems 1976–78* (1978) and the novel *All the King's Men* (1946, filmed 1949) based on the life of Governor Huey Long. He was a leading exponent of the New Criticism, and became the USA's first Poet Laureate in 1986.

1 Storytelling and copulation are the two chief forms of amusement in the South. They're inexpensive and easy to procure.

*Newsweek* 25 August 1980

# Robert Warshow (1917–55)

US AUTHOR

1 In ways that we do not easily or willingly define, the gangster speaks for us, expressing that part of the American psyche which rejects the qualities and the demands of modern life, which rejects 'Americanism' itself.

'The Gangster as Tragic Hero', publ. in *Partisan Review* 1948, repr. in *The Immediate Experience* (1970)

2 In the deeper layers of the modern consciousness . . . every attempt to succeed is an act of aggression, leaving one alone and guilty and defenseless among enemies: one is *punished* for success. This is our intolerable dilemma: that failure is a kind of death and success is evil and dangerous, is – ultimately – impossible.

ibid.

# Denzel Washington (b. 1954)

US SCREEN ACTOR

He gained notice in the TV series *St Elsewhere* (1982–8) and made his film debut in *Carbon Copy* (1981). He has since played leading roles in *Cry Freedom* (1987) as STEVE BIKO, *Glory* (1989), for which he received an Academy Award, and *Malcolm X* (1992).

1 I don't want to be in bed with anybody who's stronger than me or that has more hair on their chest than I do. Now you can call me old-fashioned, you can call me conservative . . . just call me a man.

Joe Miller (Denzel Washington), in *Philadelphia*, (film, 1993, screenplay by Ron Nyswaner, directed by Jonathan Demme)

## Michio Watanabe (1923–95)
JAPANESE POLITICIAN

Elected to the national House of Representatives in 1963 as a Liberal Democrat, he rose to become Deputy Prime Minister (1991) but failed in three attempts to become Prime Minister.

1 People with high ideals don't necessarily make good politicians. If clean politics is so important, we should leave the job to scientists and the clergy.

Quoted in *Newsweek* 12 June 1989

## Keith Waterhouse (b. 1929)
BRITISH AUTHOR

Calling himself a 'journeyman writer', he drew on his Yorkshire working-class background for his whimsical novel *Billy Liar* (1959), which he adapted for the stage the following year with Willis Hall. With Hall he wrote the screenplays for *Whistle Down the Wind* (1961) and *A Kind of Loving* (1962), and he later had success with the stage show *Jeffrey Bernard is Unwell* (1989).

1 Lying in bed, I abandoned the facts again and was back in Ambrosia.

Narrator (Billy Fisher), in *Billy Liar*, ch. 1 (1959). Opening sentence of book.

2 Jeffrey Bernard is unwell.

Title of stage adaptation of Jeffrey Bernard's *Spectator* columns (1989). Referring to the *Spectator*'s customary notice of the non-appearance of the column written by Bernard (1932–97), whose notoriously dissolute lifestyle frequently resulted in missed editorial deadlines. The show, starring PETER O'TOOLE, ran in London's West End 1989 and 1999.

3 We are . . . entering an era of nuisance politics, where the kind of political obsessives and hyper-activists who in the old Cold War days had no more chance of influencing events than a cabbage white has of changing back into a caterpillar, now see to their great joy a golden opportunity for bossing people about and stopping them from doing things. Put that cigarette out – the times they are a-changing.

*Daily Mail* 29 August 1991, repr. in *Sharon and Tracy and the Rest*, 'Joy for the Joiners' (1992)

## Alan Watts (1915–73)
BRITISH-BORN US PHILOSOPHER AND AUTHOR

Living in America from 1938, he was ordained an Episcopalian priest in 1944 and became known as a lecturer and broadcaster on comparative philosophy and religion. His interpretations of Eastern thought, for example *The Spirit of Zen* (1936) and *The Meaning of Happiness* (1953), gave him a reputation as 'the brain and Buddha of American Zen'.

1 Zen . . . does not confuse spirituality with thinking about God while one is peeling potatoes. Zen spirituality is just to peel the potatoes.

*The Way of Zen*, pt 2, ch. 2 (1957)

2 Trying to define yourself is like trying to bite your own teeth.

*Life* 21 April 1961

## Auberon Waugh (b. 1939)
BRITISH JOURNALIST AND NOVELIST

The eldest son of EVELYN WAUGH, he has contributed to most national papers and major periodicals, including the *Telegraph*, the *New Statesman* and *Private Eye*, and has been Editor of the *Literary Review* since 1986. His novels include *The Foxglove Saga* (1960). The writer Anne Fremantle called him 'a latterday Swift, as savage, as sincere, as almost unbearably iconoclastic'.

1 Religion was inevitably going to contract into a small nucleus of enthusiasts, and all they've achieved is to change the enthusiasts; the new enthusiasts happen to be the ones who like clapping their hands and looking soppy. They repel me.

Interview in *Singular Encounters* (1990) by Naim Attallah. Referring to new trends within the Catholic Church.

2 Anyone wishing to communicate with Americans should do so by e-mail, which has been specially invented for the purpose, involving neither physical proximity nor speech.

'Way of the World', column in the *Daily Telegraph* 1 November 1995

3 The seven million impotent American males who emerged as customers for Viagra were almost certainly the product of a changing relationship between the sexes, whereby the woman is nowadays accepted as the more important member of a partnership, being more intelligent, more opinionated and the better judge of moral or political correctness.

*Sunday Telegraph* 27 September 1998

4 Novels have gone, novels are over. We don't want novels any more in this country. It's all been written. Nothing left to say. There's not a 'smart' set to emulate now, or to write about. If there's anything to say it's better done these days in newspapers or magazines.

Quoted in the *Observer* 21 November 1999

## Evelyn Waugh (1903–66)
BRITISH NOVELIST

His experiences as teacher in a private school and reporter in Fleet Street were recycled in two of his most successful social satires, *Decline and Fall* (1928) and *Scoop* (1938), while in the 1930s he also established a reputation as a travel writer. *Brideshead Revisited* (1945) marked a more serious, elegiac style. His wartime experiences were fictionalized in the *Sword of Honour* trilogy, which appeared between 1952 and 1961. He regarded his conversion to Catholicism in 1928 the most important event of his life, once commenting: 'You don't know how much nastier I would be if I hadn't become a Catholic.'

1 I expect you'll be becoming a schoolmaster, sir. That's what most of the gentlemen does, sir, that gets sent down for indecent behaviour.

The porter, in *Decline and Fall*, 'Prelude' (1928)

2 We schoolmasters must temper discretion with deceit.

Dr Fagan, in ibid. pt 1, ch. 2

3 That's the public-school system all over. They may kick you out, but they never let you down.

Captain Grimes, in ibid. pt 1, ch. 3. Paul Pennyfeather, to whom these words are addressed, had been given a letter of recommendation by his housemaster after being expelled from school.

4 We can trace almost all the disasters of English history to the influence of Wales.

Dr Fagan, in ibid. pt 1, ch. 8

5 I came to the conclusion many years ago that almost all crime is due to the repressed desire for aesthetic expression.

Prison Governor Sir Wilfred Lucas-Dockery, in ibid. pt 3, ch. 1. Spoken to Paul Pennyfeather, who has just been informed that he is to be put to work in the Arts and Crafts Workshop.

6 Anyone who has been to an English public school will always feel comparatively at home in prison. It is the people brought up in the gay intimacy of the slums . . . who find prison so soul-destroying.

ibid. pt 3, ch. 4. See also JONATHAN AITKEN 2.

7 If we can't stamp out literature in the country, we can at least stop its being brought in from outside.

Customs officer, in *Vile Bodies*, ch. 2 (1930)

8 All this fuss about sleeping together. For physical pleasure I'd sooner go to my dentist any day.

Nina Blount, in ibid. ch. 6. Spoken to her fiancé Adam Fenwick-Symes.

9 *Feather-footed through the plashy fen passes the questing vole.*

William Boot's 'Lush Places' column, in *Scoop*, bk 1, ch. 1, sect. 4 (1938). Considered an example of 'good style' by the staff of *The Beast*.

10 News is what a chap who doesn't care much about anything wants to read. And it's only news until he's read it. After that it's dead.

Corker, in ibid. bk 1, ch. 5, sect. 1

11 You should ask me whether I have any message for the British public. I have. It is this: *Might must find a way.* Not '*Force*', remember; other nations use 'force'; we Britons alone use 'Might'.

Mr Baldwin, in ibid. bk 2, ch. 5, sect. 1

12 [On journalists] If, for instance, they have heard something from the postman, they attribute it to 'a semi-official statement;' if they have fallen into conversation with a stranger at a bar, they can conscientiously describe him as 'a source that has hitherto proved umimpeachable'. It is only when the journalist is reporting a whim of his own, and one to which he attaches minor importance, that he defines it as the opinion of 'well-informed circles'.

'Well-Informed Circles and How to Move In Them' (1939), repr. in *The Essays, Articles and Reviews of Evelyn Waugh* (ed. Donat Gallagher, 1983)

13 It is a curious thing that every creed promises a paradise which will be absolutely uninhabitable for anyone of civilized taste.

Ambrose, in *Put Out More Flags*, ch. 1 sect. 7 (1942)

14 The human mind is inspired enough when it comes to inventing horrors; it is when it tries to invent a Heaven that it shows itself cloddish. But Limbo is the place. In Limbo one has natural happiness without the beatific vision; no harps; no communal order; but wine and conversation and imperfect, various humanity. Limbo for the unbaptized, for the pious heathen, the sincere sceptic.

Ambrose, in ibid.

15 His courtesy was somewhat extravagant. He would write and thank people who wrote to thank him for wedding presents and when he encountered anyone as punctilious as himself the correspondence ended only with death.

*Life* 8 April 1946

16 [Of California] They are a very decent generous lot of people out here and *they don't expect you to listen* . . . It's the secret of social ease in this country. They talk entirely for their own pleasure. Nothing they say is designed to be heard.

Sir Francis Hinsley, in *The Loved One* (1948). Hinsley is a British expatriate in California.

17 You never find an Englishman among the under-dogs – except in England, of course.

Sir Ambrose Abercrombie, in ibid.

18 That impersonal insensitive friendliness which takes the place of ceremony in that land of waifs and strays.

ibid. Referring to Aimée Thanatogenos, an American.

19 In the dying world I come from quotation is a national vice. It used to be the classics, now it's lyric verse.

Dennis Barlow, in ibid.

20 Impotence and sodomy are socially O.K. but birth control is flagrantly middle-class.

'An Open Letter . . . On a Very Serious Subject', publ. in *Encounter*, repr. in *Noblesse Oblige*, pt 3 (ed. Nancy Mitford, 1956)

21 We are American at puberty. We die French.

Journal entry, 18 July 1961, publ. in *The Diaries of Evelyn Waugh* (ed. Michael Davie, 1976)

22 Punctuality is the virtue of the bored.

ibid. 26 March 1962

23 Manners are especially the need of the plain. The pretty can get away with anything.

Quoted in the *Observer* 15 April 1962

24 One forgets words as one forgets names. One's vocabulary needs constant fertilizing or it will die.

Journal entry, 25 December 1962, publ. in *The Diaries of Evelyn Waugh* (ed. Michael Davie, 1976)

25 It was announced that the trouble was not 'malignant' . . . It was a typical triumph of modern science to find the only part of Randolph that was not malignant and remove it.

ibid. March 1964. Waugh was referring to Randolph Churchill, son of WINSTON CHURCHILL and an old friend of Waugh's, with whom relations became increasingly acrimonious.

26 An artist must be a reactionary. He has to stand out against the tenor of the age and not go flopping along.

Interview in *Writers at Work* (third series, ed. George Plimpton, 1967)

# Ruby Wax (b. 1953)
US TELEVISION PRESENTER

After moving to Britain in the 1970s, she worked as a script editor for the show *Absolutely Fabulous* and with French and SAUNDERS for *Girls on Top* (1985–6), but is best known for her own shows, in her own words 'a roller coaster ride of talk', in which her angle is 'I don't kiss anyone's butt'.

1 My whole career has been an act of revenge.

*Guardian* 18 April 1991

# John Wayne (1907–79)
US SCREEN ACTOR

Original name Marion Michael Morrison. Known as 'The Duke', he played a succession of macho but honourable roles in Westerns and war films, including *Red River* (1948), *True Grit* (1969, Academy Award) and *The Shootist* (1976). 'I play John Wayne in every picture regardless of the character,' he once remarked, 'and I've been doing all right, haven't I?'

1 A man oughta do what he thinks is right.

Hondo Lane ( John Wayne), in *Hondo* (film, 1953, screenplay by James Edward Grant, directed by John Farrow)

2 Out here, due process is a bullet.

Col. Mike Kirby ( John Wayne), in *The Green Berets* (film, 1968, screenplay by James Lee Barrett, directed by John Wayne and Ray Kellogg)

3 I'm just an ordinary goddamn American and I talk for all the ordinary goddamn Americans, the butchers and bakers and plumbers. I know these people; I know what they think.

Quoted in *The Film Greats*, 'John Wayne' (1985) by Barry Norman

4 Nobody should come to the movies unless he believes in heroes.

Quoted in *The Official John Wayne Reference Book* (1985, rev. 1993) by Charles John Kieskalt

## Sigourney Weaver (b. 1949)
US SCREEN ACTRESS

The daughter of Sylvester Weaver, President of NBC, she has had leading roles in *Alien* (1979) and its sequels, *The Year of Living Dangerously* (1983) and *Gorillas in the Mist* (1988), among other films. She was co-producer of *Alien* (1992).

1 Never burn bridges. Today's junior prick, tomorrow's senior partner.

Katharine Parker (Sigourney Weaver), in *Working Girl* (film, 1988, screenplay by Kevin Wade, directed by Mike Nichols)

## Jack Webb (1920–87)
US ACTOR AND PRODUCER

He starred in the *Dragnet* police series on radio and TV and also in the films *Pete Kelly's Blues* (1955) and *The Last Time I Saw Archie* (1961), all of which he also produced. His first wife was the singer and actress Julie London.

1 This is the city. Los Angeles, California. I work here. I carry a badge. My name's Friday. The story you are about to see is true; the names have been changed to protect the innocent.

Sgt Joe Friday (Jack Webb), introducing *Dragnet* (radio and TV series, 1949–71, created by Jack Webb and Richard L. Breen, written, produced, directed and starring Jack Webb). Originally produced for radio, then successfully on TV for another eighteen years, the crime series *Dragnet* started every episode with this monologue. Friday's speech was also characterized by such expressions as, 'Just the facts, ma'am' and 'That's my job'.

## Mary Webb (1881–1927)
BRITISH AUTHOR

Her romantic fiction describes the Shropshire countryside in a melodramatic style that was later satirized by STELLA GIBBONS in *Cold Comfort Farm* (1932). She became popular after her novel *Precious Bane* (1924) was praised by Prime Minister STANLEY BALDWIN.

1 To many women marriage is . . . merely a physical change impinging on their ordinary nature, leaving their mentality untouched, their self-possession intact. They are not burnt by even the red fire of physical passion – far less by the white fire of love.

*The Golden Arrow*, ch. 18 (1916)

2 The past is only the present become invisible and mute; and because it is invisible and mute, its memoried glances and its murmurs are infinitely precious. We are to-morrow's past.

*Precious Bane*, Foreword (1924)

3 'Saddle your dreams afore you ride 'em.'

ibid. bk 1, title of ch. 6

## Sidney Webb (1859–1947)
BRITISH SOCIALIST

Baron Passfield. Founder of the Fabian Society (1884), and of the London School of Economics (1895), he was elected in 1915 to the Labour Party's NEC and was instrumental in drafting Labour's constitution (see LABOUR PARTY CONSTITUTION). He entered parliament as a Labour MP in 1922. With his wife Beatrice he also founded the *New Statesman* (1913) and published *English Local Government* (nine volumes, 1906–29), *The Decay of Capitalist Civilization* (1921) and *Soviet Communism* (1935).

1 Let me insist on what our opponents habitually ignore, and indeed, what they seem intellectually incapable of understanding, namely the inevitable gradualness of our scheme of change.

Speech to Labour Party Conference, London, 26 June 1923, publ. in *The Labour Party on the Threshold* (Fabian Tract no. 207, 1923). Referring to the programme of the Labour Party, then in opposition.

2 Marriage is the waste-paper basket of the emotions.

Quoted in *Autobiography*, vol. 1, ch. 4 (1967) by BERTRAND RUSSELL. This was his habitual saying, according to his wife Beatrice Webb, although Russell denied ever hearing it. The Webbs were, he wrote, 'the most completely married couple that I have ever known. They were, however, very averse from any romantic view of love or marriage. Marriage was a social institution designed to fit instinct into a legal framework.'

## Max Weber (1864–1920)
GERMAN SOCIOLOGIST

Regarded as the founder of modern sociology, he is best known for *The Protestant Ethic and the Spirit of Capitalism* (1904), in which he equated the rise of capitalism with the Protestant work ethic, and *Economy and Society* (1922).

1 One can say that three pre-eminent qualities are decisive for the politician: passion, a feeling of responsibility, and a sense of proportion.

'Politics as a Vocation' (1919), repr. in *Essays in Sociology* (ed. H.H. Gerth and C. WRIGHT MILLS, 1946)

2 Only he has the calling for politics who is sure that he will not crumble when the world from his point of view is too stupid or base for what he wants to offer. Only he who in the face of all this can say 'In spite of all!' has the calling for politics.

ibid.

3 A really definitive and good accomplishment is today always a specialized accomplishment. And whoever lacks the capacity to put on blinders, so to speak, and to come up to the idea that the fate of his soul depends upon whether or not he makes the correct conjecture at this passage of this manuscript may as well stay away from science. He will never have what one may call the 'personal experience' of science. Without this strange intoxication, ridiculed by every outsider; without this passion . . . you have *no* calling for science and you should do something else. For nothing is worthy of man as man unless he can pursue it with passionate devotion.

'Science as a Vocation' (1919), repr. in ibid.

## Jeffrey Weeks (b. 1945)
BRITISH SEXOLOGIST

His published works on sex, gender and society include *Coming Out* (1977), *Sex, Politics and Society* (1981), *Invented Moralities* (1995) and *Making Sexual History* (1999).

1 It is only possible to express the feelings of the body through the lacework of meanings that envelop it. Sexuality is as much about language as it is about sexual organs.

*Against Nature*, Introduction (1991)

## Simone Weil (1909–43)
FRENCH PHILOSOPHER AND MYSTIC

Although she officially embraced no religion, she was passionately concerned with religious matters as well as social equality and pacifism. She interspersed teaching philosophy with periods of manual work, and died from pleurisy after restricting herself to the same diet as those in Nazi labour camps. Her works, mostly published posthumously, include *Gravity and Grace* (1947), *Waiting for God* (1950) and *Notebooks* (1951, 1955, 1956).

1 I am not a Catholic; but I consider the Christian idea, which has its roots in Greek thought and in the course of the centuries has nourished all of our European civilization, as something that one cannot renounce without becoming degraded.

Letter, March 1937, publ. in *Vie de Simone Weil*, vol. 2, ch. 3 (1976) by Simone Pétrement

2 What a country calls its vital economic interests are not the things which enable its citizens to live, but the things which enable it to make war. Petrol is more likely than wheat to be a cause of international conflict.

'The Power of Words', publ. in *Nouveaux Cahiers* 1 and 15 April 1937, repr. in *Selected Essays* (ed. Richard Rees, 1962)

3 I suffer more from the humiliations inflicted by my country than from those inflicted on her.

Letter to GEORGES BERNANOS, c. 1938, publ. in ibid.

4 Who were the fools who spread the story that brute force cannot kill ideas? Nothing is easier. And once they are dead they are no more than corpses.

'Three Letters on History: Théophile de Viau' (1938 or 1939), publ. in ibid.

5 The real stumbling-block of totalitarian régimes is not the spiritual need of men for freedom of thought; it is men's inability to stand the physical and nervous strain of a permanent state of excitement, except during a few years of their youth.

'Cold War Policy in 1939' (1939), publ. in ibid.

6 If Germany, thanks to Hitler and his successors, were to enslave the European nations and destroy most of the treasures of their past, future historians would certainly pronounce that she had civilized Europe.

'The Great Beast', pt 3 (1939–40), publ. in ibid.

7 It is not the cause for which men took up arms that makes a victory more just or less, it is the order that is established when arms have been laid down.

ibid. 'Conclusion'

8 I would suggest that barbarism be considered as a permanent and universal human characteristic which becomes more or less pronounced according to the play of circumstances.

'Hitler and Roman Foreign Policy', publ. in *Nouveaux Cahiers* 1 January 1940

9 Force is as pitiless to the man who possesses it, or thinks he does, as it is to its victims; the second it crushes, the first it intoxicates. The truth is, nobody really possesses it.

'The *Iliad* or the Poem of Force', publ. in *Cahiers du Sud* December 1940/January 1941, repr. in *Simone Weil: An Anthology* (ed. Sian Miles, 1986). Translation by MARY MCCARTHY.

10 Humanism was not wrong in thinking that truth, beauty, liberty, and equality are of infinite value, but in thinking that man can get them for himself without grace.

'The Romanesque Renaissance', publ. in *Cahiers du Sud* 1941 or 1942, repr. in *Selected Essays* (ed. Richard Rees, 1962)

11 When a contradiction is impossible to resolve except by a lie, then we know that it is really a door.

*New York Notebook*, written 1942, publ. 1950, repr. in *First and Last Notebooks*, pt 3 (ed. Richard Rees, 1970)

12 Equality is the public recognition, effectively expressed in institutions and manners, of the principle that an equal degree of attention is due to the needs of all human beings.

'Draft for a Statement of Human Obligation' (1943), publ. in *Selected Essays* (ed. Richard Rees, 1962)

13 One cannot imagine St Francis of Assisi talking about rights.

'Human Personality' (1943), publ. in *La Table Ronde* December 1950, repr. in ibid.

14 Real genius is nothing else but the supernatural virtue of humility in the domain of thought.

ibid.

15 Beauty always promises, but never gives anything.

ibid.

16 There is one, and only one, thing in modern society more hideous than crime – namely, repressive justice.

ibid.

17 It is only the impossible that is possible for God. He has given over the possible to the mechanics of matter and the autonomy of his creatures.

'A War of Religions' (1943), publ. in ibid.

18 We must prefer real hell to an imaginary paradise.

ibid.

19 A test of what is real is that it is hard and rough. Joys are found in it, not pleasure. What is pleasant belongs to dreams.

*Gravity and Grace*, 'Illusions' (1947)

20 Purity is the power to contemplate defilement.

ibid. 'Attention and Will'

21 A work of art has an author and yet, when it is perfect, it has something which is essentially anonymous about it.

ibid. 'Beauty'

22 Culture is an instrument wielded by teachers to manufacture teachers, who, in their turn, will manufacture still more teachers.

*The Need For Roots*, pt 2, 'Uprootedness in the Towns' (1949)

23 Every time that I think of the crucifixion of Christ, I commit the sin of envy.

*Waiting on God*, 'Letter 4' (1950)

24 Those who are unhappy have no need for anything in this world but people capable of giving them their attention.

ibid. 'Reflections on the Right Use of School Studies'

25 A doctrine serves no purpose in itself, but it is indispensable to have one if only to avoid being deceived by false doctrines.

*Écrits de Londres*, 'Fragments et Notes' (1957)

26 It would seem that man was born a slave, and that slavery is his natural condition. At the same time nothing on earth can stop man from feeling himself born for liberty. Never, whatever may happen, can he accept servitude; for he is a thinking creature.

*Oppression and Liberty*, ch. 4 (1958)

27 In the Church, considered as a social organism, the mysteries inevitably degenerate into beliefs.

Quoted in *Simone Weil: Utopian Pessimist*, ch. 9 (1989) by David McLellan

# Steven Weinberg (b. 1933)

US THEORETICAL PHYSICIST

In 1967 he developed a theory applicable to both electromagnetic and weak nuclear forces, and from it evolved a model of particle interaction potentially capable of providing a unifying account of all the forces of nature. His publications include *The First Three Minutes* (1977), *Dreams of a Final Theory* (1993) and *The Quantum Theory of Fields* (two volumes, 1995 and 1996). He shared the 1979 Nobel Prize for Physics with Abdus Salam and Sheldon Glashow.

1 The more the universe seems comprehensible, the more it also seems pointless.

*The First Three Minutes*, ch. 8 (1977)

2 The effort to understand the universe is one of the very

few things that lifts human life a little above the level of farce, and gives it some of the grace of tragedy.

ibid. Closing sentence of book.

## George Weiss (b. 1940)
BRITISH ECCENTRIC

A feature of the London satire scene since the 1960s, he also goes under the name 'Captain Rainbow'.

1 Most idealistic people are skint. I have discovered that people with money have no imagination, and people with imagination have no money.

*Guardian* 3 November 1984

## Colin Welch (b. 1924)
BRITISH JOURNALIST

As parliamentary sketch writer, columnist and editor he was long associated with the *Daily Telegraph* (1950–83) and has also contributed to the *Spectator*, the *Daily Mail* and the *Independent*.

1 To be conservative requires no brains whatsoever. Cabbages, cows and conifers are conservatives, and are so stupid they don't even know it. All that is basically required is acceptance of what exists.

*Spectator* 21 July 1967

## Fay Weldon (b. 1933)
BRITISH NOVELIST AND TELEVISION PLAYWRIGHT

Formerly an advertising copywriter, she writes with astute irony of women and their struggles with men. Among her many novels are *Praxis* (1978), *The Life and Loves of a She-Devil* (1983, televised 1985, filmed 1989) and *The Hearts and Lives of Men* (1987). She has also written numerous plays, scripts and adaptations for television, including Jane Austen's *Pride and Prejudice* (1980). See also ADVERTISING SLOGANS 6.

1 The New Women! I could barely recognize them as being of the same sex as myself, their buttocks arrogant in tight jeans, openly inviting, breasts falling free and shameless and feeling no apparent obligation to smile, look pleasant or keep their voices low. And how they live! Just look at them to know how! If a man doesn't bring them to orgasm, they look for another who does. If by mistake they fall pregnant, they abort by vacuum aspiration. If they don't like the food, they push the plate away. If the job doesn't suit them, they hand in their notice. They are satiated by everything, hungry for nothing. They are what I wanted to be; they are what I worked for them to be: and now I see them, I hate them.

Narrator (Praxis Duveen), in *Praxis*, ch. 2 (1978)

2 We shelter children for a time; we live side by side with men; and that is all. We owe them nothing, and are owed nothing. I think we owe our friends more, especially our female friends.

Narrator (Praxis Duveen), in ibid. ch. 19

3 You end up as you deserve. In old age you must put up with the face, the friends, the health, and the children you have earned.

Narrator (Praxis Duveen), in ibid. ch. 21

4 Writers were never meant to be professionals. Writing is not a profession, it is an activity, an essentially amateur occupation. It is what you do when you are not living. It is something you do with your hands, like knitting.

Auntie Fay, in *Letters to Alice*, Letter 5 (1984)

5 That to be good is to be happy is not something particu-

larly evident in any of our experiences of real life, yet how badly we want it, and need it, to be true.

ibid. On Jane Austen's promise, 'If you are good . . . you will be happy.'

6 Young women especially have something invested in being *nice people*, and it's only when you have children that you realize you're not a nice person at all, but generally a selfish bully.

*Independent on Sunday* 5 May 1991

7 Your generation does too much sharing. To share grief is to double grief, not halve it.

Christabel, in 'A Good Sound Marriage' (1991), publ. in *Wicked Women* (1995)

8 Push, rend, slither, pop, baby's here. Baby cries.

'Pains' (1994), publ. in ibid.

9 Therapists, New Agers and Born Again Christians seldom blink. A blink marks the mind's registration of a new idea. Converts have no intention of receiving new ideas. They know already all they want to know.

Elaine Desmond, in 'End of the Line', publ. in ibid.

10 Experts are never in real danger. Everyone needs them. The chambermaid always survives the palace revolution. Someone has to make the beds.

Defoe Desmond, in ibid.

11 We are all one-syllable people now, two at the most. So we mumble and stumble into our futures. But it is still our task and our reward to scavenge through the universe, picking up the detritus of lost concepts, dusting them down, making them shine. Latin was the best polishing cloth of all, but we threw it away.

Elaine Desmond, in ibid.

12 Rape isn't actually the worst thing that can happen to a woman if you're safe and alive.

*Independent on Sunday* 5 July 1998

## Orson Welles (1915–85)
US FILM-MAKER AND ACTOR

'A bravura personality', according to KENNETH TYNAN, he founded the Mercury Theatre in 1937 and went on to make what many consider the greatest film ever made, *Citizen Kane* (1941, Academy Award), a tour de force in which he was producer, director, screenwriter and leading actor. He produced and directed *The Magnificent Ambersons* (1942) and *The Lady From Shanghai* (1948), both praised by critics but commercial failures. Most agreed that he never fulfilled his potential. 'Everybody denies I am a genius,' he once said, 'but nobody ever called me one!' See also MICHEÁL MACLIAMMÓIR 2.

1 Ladies and gentlemen, I have a grave announcement to make. Incredible as it may seem, strange beings who landed in New Jersey tonight are the vanguard of an invading army from Mars.

Radio broadcast, Hallowe'en, 1938, CBS, from a reading of *The War of the Worlds* (1898, audio cassette 1995) by H.G. WELLS. According to the later reports, despite clear warnings that the broadcast was science fiction, listeners jammed switchboards and roads as they abandoned their homes in large numbers, with some people claiming they had actually seen the Martians.

2 In Italy for thirty years under the Borgias they had warfare, terror, murder, bloodshed – they produced Michelangelo, Leonardo da Vinci and the Renaissance. In Switzerland they had brotherly love, five hundred years of democracy and peace, and what did they produce? The cuckoo clock!

Harry Lime, in *The Third Man*, (film, 1949, screenplay by GRAHAM GREENE, directed by Carol Reed). Welles starred in the film and contributed the speech to Greene's screenplay; he later claimed that his words were based on a fragment of an old Hungarian play. Welles played the role of Cesare Borgia in the film *Prince of Foxes*, also released in 1949.

3 The essential is to excite the spectators. If that means playing *Hamlet* on a flying trapeze or in an aquarium, you do it.

*Les Nouvelles littéraires*, 1953, quoted in *Citizen Welles*, ch. 16 (1989) by Frank Brady

4 [Of RKO studios] The biggest electric train set any boy ever had!

Quoted in *The Fabulous Orson Welles*, ch. 7 (1956) by Peter Noble

5 I hate television. I hate it as much as peanuts. But I can't stop eating peanuts.

*New York Herald Tribune* 12 October 1956

6 When you are down and out something always turns up – and it is usually the noses of your friends.

*The New York Times* 1 April 1962

7 I hate it when people pray on the screen. It's not because I hate praying, but whenever I see an actor fold his hands and look up in the spotlight, I'm lost. There's only one other thing in the movies I hate as much, and that's sex. You just can't get in bed or pray to God and convince me on the screen.

Interview in *The Americans*, 'Can a Martian Survive by Pretending to be a Leading American Actor?' (1970) by David Frost

8 [On men] I think we're a kind of desperation. We're sort of a maddening luxury. The basic and essential human is the woman, and all that we're doing is trying to brighten up the place.

ibid.

9 The ideal American type is perfectly expressed by the Protestant, individualist, anti-conformist, and this is the type that is in the process of disappearing. In reality there are few left.

Interview in *Hollywood Voices* (ed. Andrew Sarris, 1971)

10 A good artist should be isolated. If he isn't isolated, something is wrong.

ibid.

11 The director is simply the audience. So the terrible burden of the director is to take the place of that yawning vacuum, to *be* the audience and to select from what happens during the day which movement shall be a disaster and which a gala night. His job is to preside over accidents.

Speech to the Hollywood Foreign Press Association, broadcast at the memorial service for Welles in Los Angeles, 4 November 1985, publ. in *Citizen Welles*, ch. 21 (1989) by Frank Brady

12 We're born alone, we live alone, we die alone. Only through our love and friendship can we create the illusion for the moment that we're not alone.

Danny's friend (Welles), in *Someone to Love* (film, 1987, written and directed by Henry Jaglom). Contributed to screenplay by Welles, who appeared in the film as Henry Jaglom's unnamed mentor.

13 I want to give the audience a *hint* of a scene. No more than that. Give them too much and they won't contribute anything themselves. Give them just a suggestion and you get them working with you. That's what gives the theater meaning: when it becomes a social act.

Quoted in *Citizen Welles*, ch. 8 (1989) by Frank Brady

## H.G. Wells (1866–1946)

BRITISH AUTHOR

Full name Herbert George Wells. A prolific author and member of the Fabian Society, he was a pioneer of science fiction with such works as *The Time Machine* (1895) and *The War of the Worlds* (1898), and the author of comic novels, including *Kipps* (1905) and *The History of Mr. Polly* (1910), both social commentaries on lower-middle class life. His non-fiction works include *The Outline of History* (1920) and *The Science of Life* (1931). His lover REBECCA WEST described him as 'the old maid among novelists', but BRIAN

ALDISS considered him 'the Shakespeare of science fiction'. See also HENRY JAMES 2.

1 Moral indignation is jealousy with a halo. It is the peculiar snare of the perplexed orthodox.

*The Wife of Sir Isaac Harman*, ch. 9, sect. 2 (1914)

2 Nothing could have been more obvious to the people of the early twentieth century than the rapidity with which war was becoming impossible. And as certainly they did not see it. They did not see it until the atomic bombs burst in their fumbling hands.

*The World Set Free: A Story of Mankind*, ch. 2, sect. 5 (1914). In his fantasy, Wells predicted an age of atomic energy starting with a war commencing in 1956.

3 I had rather be called a journalist than an artist.

Letter to HENRY JAMES, 8 July 1915, publ. in *Henry James and H.G. Wells* (ed. Leon Edel and Gordon N. Ray, 1958)

4 Beauty isn't a special inserted sort of thing. It is just life, pure life, life nascent, running clear and strong.

Quoted by REBECCA WEST in book review, the *Daily News* 14 August 1915, repr. in *The History of Mr Wells*, ch. 5 (1995) by Michael Foot

5 He [Mr Britling] was inordinately proud of England and he abused her incessantly.

*Mr Britling Sees It Through* bk 1, ch. 2, sect. 2 (1916)

6 We English are everlasting children in an everlasting nursery.

ibid. ch. 2 sect. 5

7 Human history becomes more and more a race between education and catastrophe.

*The Outline of History*, vol. 2, ch. 41 (1920)

8 In England we have come to rely upon a comfortable time-lag of fifty years or a century intervening between the perception that something ought to be done and a serious attempt to do it.

*The Work, Wealth and Happiness of Mankind*, ch. 2 (1931)

9 Mankind which began in a cave and behind a windbreak will end in the disease-soaked ruins of a slum.

*The Fate of Homo Sapiens*, ch. 26 (1939)

10 There comes a moment in the day when you have written your pages in the morning, attended to your correspondence in the afternoon, and have nothing further to do. Then comes that hour when you are bored; that's the time for sex.

Quoted in *My Autobiography*, ch. 16 (1964) by CHARLIE CHAPLIN

## John Wells (1936–98)

BRITISH AUTHOR, ACTOR AND DIRECTOR

He was co-editor of *Private Eye* (1964–7) and author of the satirical diaries of Mary Wilson and Denis Thatcher that appeared there. Among the plays he has written are *Listen to the Knocking Bird* (1965), *Mrs. Wilson's Diary* (1968) and *Anyone for Denis?* (1981), in which he took the part of Denis Thatcher.

1 Infantilism is possibly the hallmark of our generation.

Quoted in *Beyond the Fringe . . . and Beyond*, pt 4 (1989) by Ronald Bergan

## Irvine Welsh (b. 1958)

SCOTTISH AUTHOR

His novel *Trainspotting* (1993, filmed 1996) accorded him cult status for its unsentimental portrayal of the subculture of heroin addicts. *The Acid House* (1994) and *Ecstasy* (1996) are collections of short stories inspired by the dance culture, while the novel *Filth* (1998) was adapted for the stage.

1 Take yir best orgasm, multiply the feeling by twenty, and you're still fuckin miles off the pace. Ma dry, cracking

bones are soothed and liquefied by ma beautiful heroine's tender caresses. The earth moved, and it's still moving.

Renton, in *Trainspotting*, 'Kicking' (1993)

2 They'd rather gie a merchant school old boy with severe brain damage a job in nuclear engineering than gie a schemie wi a Ph.D. a post as a cleaner in an abbatoir.

Renton, in ibid.

3 Ah don't hate the English. They're just wankers. We are colonized by wankers. We can't even pick a decent, healthy culture to be colonized by. No. We're ruled by effete arseholes. What does that make us?

Renton, in ibid. 'Relapsing'

4 Choose us. Choose life. Choose mortgage payments; choose washing machines; choose cars; choose sitting oan a couch watching mind-numbing and spirit-crushing game shows, stuffing fuckin junk food intae yir mooth. Choose rotting away, pishing and shiteing yersel in a home, a total fuckin embarrassment tae the selfish, fucked-up brats ye've produced. Choose life.

Well, ah choose no tae choose life.

Renton, in ibid. 'Blowing It: Searching for the Inner Man'

5 People are a wee bit fed up with the lack of substance in middle class postmodern writing. You know, that somehow the Oxbridge writer goes into this kind of super-market and justs picks whatever style or voices that they like . . . You can't do subcultures as an Oxford twat hanging around the fucking streets, sitting in pubs and listening in on people.

Interview in *Dazed and Confused* February 1996

## Wim Wenders (b. 1945)
GERMAN FILM-MAKER

Brought up on American movies, he was a key figure in the German cinema of the 1970s with such films as *Summer in the City* (1970) and *Kings of the Road* (1976). In the US he established himself with the critically and commercially popular *Paris, Texas* (1984), followed by *Wings of Desire* (1987) and *Faraway, So Close!* (1993). Themes of isolation, alienation and wandering recur in his work.

1 The Yanks have colonized our subconscious.

Robert Lander (Hans Zischler), in *Kings of the Road* (film, 1976, written and directed by Wim Wenders)

2 Stories give people the feeling that there is meaning, that there is ultimately an order lurking behind the incredible confusion of appearances and phenomena that surrounds them . . . Stories are substitutes for God. Or maybe the other way round.

'Impossible Stories', talk given at a colloquium on narrative technique, 1982, publ. in *The Logic of Images* (1988)

3 A lot of my films start off with roadmaps instead of scripts. Sometimes it feels like flying blind without instruments. You fly all night and in the morning you arrive some-where. That is: you have to try to make a landing some-where so the film can end.

'Like flying blind without instruments' (1984), publ. in ibid.

4 The camera is a weapon against the tragedy of things, against their disappearing.

'Why do you make films?', reply to questionnaire April 1987, repr. in ibid.

5 The more opinions you have, the less you see.

*Evening Standard* 25 April 1990

6 What I fear most is an overdose of images. I fear losing the ability to discriminate between the good and the ugly.

Interview in the *Independent on Sunday* 19 April 1992

## Arnold Wesker (b. 1932)
BRITISH PLAYWRIGHT

He once claimed his role to be 'that of a propagandist, direct or indirect, for world socialism', as expressed through his plays such as *Roots* (1959), *Chips with Everything* (1962) and *Caritas* (1981). With trade union support, he founded and ran (1962–70) Centre 42, a gallery, theatre and studio in London.

1 I was never an angry young man, none of us was. On the contrary, we were all very happy young men and women. Who would not have been happy? Discovered, applauded, paid, made internationally famous overnight? But I am an angry old man.

Quoted in the *Independent on Sunday* 23 October 1994

## Mae West (1892–1980)
US ACTRESS

After appearances in vaudeville, she wrote and produced a play, *Sex* (1926), for which she spent a week in prison for 'corrupting the morals of youth'. She transferred her vampish persona to the screen in a series of successful films including *I'm No Angel* (1933), *Klondike Annie* (1936) and *Every Day's a Holiday* (1937). Mistress of the double entendre, she claimed to have written all her own lines.

1 Goodness had nothing to do with it.

*Night After Night* (film, 1932, screenplay by Vincent Laurence, directed by Archie Mayo). Response to checkroom girl's exclamation, 'Goodness, what beautiful diamonds!', also the title of West's autobiography (1960).

2 Is that a gun in your pocket, or are you just glad to see me?

Lady Lou (Mae West), in *She Done Him Wrong* (film, 1933, screenplay by Harvey Thew and John Bright based on Mae West's play *Diamond Lil*, directed by Lowell Sherman)

3 Am I making myself clear, boys?

ibid.

4 Why don't you come up sometime 'n see me? I'm home every evening . . . come on up, I'll tell your fortune.

ibid.

5 When women go wrong, men go right after them.

ibid.

6 I've been things and seen places.

ibid.

7 It's not the men in my life, but the life in my men.

Tira (Mae West), in *I'm No Angel* (film, 1933, screenplay by Mae West and Harlan Thompson, directed by Wesley Ruggles). Rephrasing a reporter's remarks.

8 Beulah, peel me a grape.

ibid.

9 She's the kind of girl who climbed the ladder of success, wrong by wrong.

ibid.

10 When I'm good, I'm very, very good, but when I'm bad, I'm better.

ibid.

11 I believe that it's better to be looked over than it is to be overlooked.

Belle, in *Belle of the Nineties* (film, 1934, screenplay by Mae West, directed by Leo McCarey)

12 When choosing between two evils, I always like to pick the one I never tried before.

Frisco Doll (Mae West), in *Klondike Annie* (film, 1936, screenplay by Mae West, directed by Raoul Walsh)

13 Give a man a free hand and he'll try to put it all over you.

ibid.

14 I always say, keep a diary and some day it'll keep you.

Peaches O'Day, in *Every Day's a Holiday* (film, 1937, screenplay by Mae West, directed by A. Edward Sutherland)

15 You ought to get out of those wet clothes and into a dry Martini.

ibid. The line is said to have been borrowed by West, originally coined in the 1920s by ROBERT BENCHLEY's press agent.

16 Too much of a good thing can be wonderful.

*Goodness Had Nothing To Do With It*, ch. 21 (1960)

17 I think censorship is necessary; the things they're doing and saying in films right now just shouldn't be allowed. There's no dignity anymore and I think that's very important.

Interview in *Take One* 22 January 1974, quoted in *Writers in Hollywood 1915–1951*, ch. 4, sect. 2 (1990) by Ian Hamilton

18 There are no good girls gone wrong, just bad girls found out.

*On Sex, Health and ESP*, 'Last Word' (1975)

19 My advice to those who think they have to take off their clothes to be a star is, once you're boned, what's left to create the illusion? Let 'em wonder. I never believed in givin' them too much of me.

Quoted by David Ray Johnson in 'Biographical Study', appendix to *On Sex, Health and ESP* (1975)

20 I used to be Snow White – but I drifted.

Attributed

21 A hard man's good to find.

Attributed. Sometimes quoted with the added '. . . but you'll mostly find him asleep'.

## (Dame) Rebecca West (1892–1983)

BRITISH AUTHOR

Original name Cicily Isabel Fairfield. An ardent feminist, she was the author of psychological novels, for instance *The Thinking Reed* (1936) and *The Birds Fall Down* (1966), but is best known for her reports of the Nuremberg trials and for her study of the Balkans, *Black Lamb and Grey Falcon* (1942). In 1913 she began a long association with H.G. WELLS.

1 I wonder if we are all wrong about each other, if we are just composing unwritten novels about the people we meet?

Letter 1917, quoted as epigraph to *Rebecca West: A Life* (1987) by Victoria Glendinning

2 Most works of art, like most wines, ought to be consumed in the district of their fabrication.

*Ending in Earnest*, 'Journey's End Again' (1931)

3 There is no such thing as conversation. It is an illusion. There are intersecting monologues, that is all.

*The Harsh Voice*, 'There Is No Conversation' (1935)

4 It is queer how it is always one's virtues and not one's vices that precipitate one into disaster.

*There Is No Conversation*, ch. 1 (1935)

5 She [Isabelle] saw she had fallen into the hands of one of those doctors who have strayed too far from aperients in the direction of the soul.

*The Thinking Reed* (1936) ch. 10

6 All good biography, as all good fiction, comes down to the study of original sin, of our inherent disposition to choose death when we ought to choose life.

*Time and Tide* (1941)

7 There is no wider gulf in the universe than yawns between those on the hither and thither side of vital experience.

*Black Lamb and Grey Falcon*, vol. 1, 'Serbia' (1942)

8 All men should have a drop of treason in their veins, if nations are not to go soft like so many sleepy pears.

*The Meaning of Treason*, pt 4, 'Conclusion' (1949)

9 Just how difficult it is to write biography can be reckoned

by anybody who sits down and considers just how many people know the real truth about his or her love affairs.

'The Art of Skepticism', publ. in *Vogue* 1 November 1952

10 Any authentic work of art must start an argument between the artist and his audience.

*The Court and the Castle*, pt 1, ch. 1 (1957)

11 Motherhood is the strangest thing, it can be like being one's own Trojan horse.

Letter, 20 August 1959, quoted in *Rebecca West: A Life*, pt 5, ch. 8 (1987) by Victoria Glendinning

12 He is every other inch a gentleman.

Quoted in ibid. pt 3, ch. 5. Referring to novelist Michael Arlen. ALEXANDER WOOLLCOTT is also credited with this remark about Arlen in *Wit's End* (ed. Robert E. Drennan, 1968).

## Edward Weston (1886–1958)

US PHOTOGRAPHER

With Ansel Adams, who regarded him as having 'recreated the mother-forms and forces of nature', he founded the 'f/64' school of photography, which rejected soft focus in favour of clear definition. He is known for his studies of landscapes, clouds, vegetables and nudes, and was the first photographer to receive a Guggenheim fellowship.

1 I have been photographing our toilet, that glossy enameled receptacle of extraordinary beauty . . . Here was every sensuous curve of the 'human figure divine' but minus the imperfections. Never did the Greeks reach a more significant consummation to their culture, and it somehow reminded me, in the glory of its chaste convulsions and in its swelling, sweeping, forward movement of finely progressing contours, of the Victory of Samothrace.

Journal entry, 21 October 1925, publ. in *The Daybooks of Edward Weston*, vol. 1, pt 4, ch. 1 (ed. Nancy Newhall, 1961)

2 Photography suits the temper of this age – of active bodies and minds. It is a perfect medium for one whose mind is teeming with ideas, imagery, for a prolific worker would be slowed down by painting or sculpting, for one who sees quickly and acts decisively, accurately.

Journal entry, June 1934, publ. in ibid. vol. 2, pt 3, ch. 10 (ed. Nancy Newhall, 1966)

## Vivienne Westwood (b. 1941)

BRITISH FASHION DESIGNER

From selling punk fashions in the 1970s with MALCOLM MCLAREN she helped create the New Romantic look of the 1980s and in her 1990–91 Portrait collection showed her long-standing interest in 'innerwear as outerwear'. Influential on the designers GAULTIER, Galliano and Lang, she has been twice named Designer of the Year (1990 and 1991).

1 Every time I hear that word, I cringe. Fun! I think it's disgusting; it's just running around. It's not my idea of pleasure.

*Independent on Sunday* 18 February 1990

2 It is not possible for a man to be elegant without a touch of femininity.

*Independent* 12 July 1990

3 The catwalk is theatre. It's about provocation and outrage.

Quoted in *Fashion and Perversity*, pt 1 by Fred Vermorel (1996)

4 What is sex after all? It's self-expression.

Quoted in ibid.

5 Fashion is really about being naked.

Quoted in ibid.

6 It is elegance that is potent and subversive. Elegance in a world of vulgarity.

Quoted in ibid.

7 The English aristocracy is now only the middle class with knobs on.
*Guardian* 22 February 1997

8 The only possible effect one can have on the world is through unpopular ideas. They are the only subversion.
Quoted in *Westwood* (1999) by Catherine McDermott

9 You can say everything you want to say through tailoring – I believe that everything resides in technique. You can't teach creativity and it is from technique that one is able to be creative. This is the terrible mistake of this century – to put creativity first.
Quoted in ibid.

10 The last people with any ideas are young people. The age in which we live, this non-stop distraction, is making it more impossible for the young generation to ever have the curiosity or discipline ... because you need to be alone to find out anything.
Interview in the *Independent on Sunday* 8 November 1998

## Tina Weymouth (b. 1950) and Chris Frantz (b. 1951)
US ROCK MUSICIANS

Married in 1977, they were members of the new wave/funk/pop group Talking Heads (see also DAVID BYRNE) and in 1980 formed the spin-off Tom Tom Club (referred to as 'Talking Heads on vacation') with Weymouth's sisters on vocals.

1 What are words worth?
Words in papers
Words in books
Words on TV
Words are crooks
Words of comfort
Words of peace
Words to make the fighting cease
Words to tell you what to do
Words are working hard for you.
'Wordy Rappinghood' (song) on the album *The Tom Tom Club* (1980)

## Edith Wharton (1862–1937)
US AUTHOR

Encouraged by HENRY JAMES, she established her reputation as a novelist of manners and a satirist of her own aristocratic class with *The House of Mirth* (1905). Much of her work compared American and European society, but *Ethan Frome* (1911) was set in New England and *The Age of Innocence* (1920), with which she became the first woman to win a Pulitzer Prize, in New York.

1 Mrs Ballinger is one of the ladies who pursue Culture in bands, as though it were dangerous to meet it alone.
*Xingu and Other Stories*, 'Xingu' (1916)

2 How much longer are we going to think it necessary to be 'American' before (or in contradistinction to) being cultivated, being enlightened, being humane, and having the same intellectual discipline as other civilized countries? It is really too easy a disguise for our shortcomings to dress them up as a form of patriotism!
Letter 19 July 1919, publ. in *The Letters of Edith Wharton* (ed. R.W.B. Leavis and Nancy Lewis, 1988)

3 I have never known a novel that was good enough to be good in spite of its being adapted to the author's political views.
Letter to UPTON SINCLAIR, 19 August 1927, publ. in ibid.

4 There's no such thing as old age, there is only sorrow.
*A Backward Glance*, 'A First Word' (1934)

## Charles Wheeler (b. 1923)
BRITISH JOURNALIST AND BROADCASTER

He joined the BBC in 1946 and was Chief Foreign Correspondent for America (1965–73) and Europe (1973–6) and subsequently a presenter of *Panorama* and *Newsweek*. He was Journalist of the Year in 1988.

1 He smiled rather too much. He smiled at breakfast, you know.
Remembering the spy George Blake on *Inside Story* BBC 1, quoted in the *Independent* 20 September 1990

## Francis Wheen (b. 1957)
BRITISH JOURNALIST AND BROADCASTER

A contributor to numerous newspapers and periodicals, including the *Independent*, the *Guardian* and *Private Eye*, he has also presented *News-Stand* and other programmes for BBC radio. His books include *Television: a History* (1985) and *Karl Marx* (1999).

1 The only fetters binding the working class today are mock-Rolex watches.
*Karl Marx*, Introduction (1999)

## E.B. White (1899–1985)
US AUTHOR AND EDITOR

Full name Elwyn Brooks White. He began a long association with the *New Yorker* in 1925 where he wrote the 'Talk of the Town' column. His books include *Is Sex Necessary?* (1929), co-authored with his friend and colleague JAMES THURBER, and his children's classic of poetry and humorous stories *Charlotte's Web* (1952).

1 I say it's spinach, and I say the hell with it.
Cartoon caption, in the *New Yorker* 8 December 1928. Little girl in reply to her mother's remark, 'It's broccoli, dear' (drawing by Carl Rose).

2 Democracy is the recurrent suspicion that more than half of the people are right more than half of the time.
*New Yorker* 3 July 1944

3 The so-called science of poll-taking is not a science at all but mere necromancy. People are unpredictable by nature, and although you can take a nation's pulse, you can't be sure that the nation hasn't just run up a flight of stairs.
'Polling', publ. in the *New Yorker* 13 November 1948, repr. in *Writings from the New Yorker 1927–1976* (ed. Rebecca M. Dale, 1991)

4 Television hangs on the questionable theory that whatever happens anywhere should be sensed everywhere. If everyone is going to be able to see everything, in the long run all sights may lose whatever rarity value they once possessed, and it may well turn out that people, be able to see and hear practically everything, will be specially interested in almost nothing.
'Television', publ. in the *New Yorker* 4 December 1948, repr. in ibid.

5 Commuters give the city its tidal restlessness; natives give it solidity and continuity; but the settlers give it passion.
'Here is New York', publ. in *Holiday* April 1949

6 The terror of the atom age is not the violence of the new power but the speed of man's adjustment to it – the speed of his acceptance.
*The Second Tree From the Corner*, 'Notes on Our Time' (1954)

7 Commuter – one who spends his life
In riding to and from his wife;
A man who shaves and takes a train,
And then rides back to shave again.
'The Commuter', publ. in *Poems and Sketches* (1982)

8 Shocking writing is like murder: the questions the jury must decide are the questions of motive and intent.
Interview in *Writers at Work* (eighth series, ed. George Plimpton, 1988)

# Edmund White (b. 1940)

US AUTHOR

He is best known for his essays, collected in *States of Desire: Travels in Gay America* (1980) and *The Burning Library* (1994), and the novel *A Boy's Own Story* (1982), describing an adolescent coming to terms with his homosexuality.

1 In the lifelong romance each man has with himself, he should know which vows he's sworn.

'The Gay Philosopher', written 1969, publ. in *The Burning Library* (1994)

2 Perhaps sex and sentiment *should* be separated. Isn't sex, shadowed as it always is by jealousy and ruled by caprice, a rather risky basis for a sustained, important relationship?

'Fantasia on the Seventies' (1977), repr. in ibid.

3 Sado-masochism is a futile effort to reduce ubiquitous cruelty to the comprehensible scope of sex.

'Sado Machismo', publ. in *New Times* 8 January 1979, repr. in ibid.

4 When 'morality' is discussed I invariably discover, halfway into the conversation, that what is meant are not the great ethical questions ... but the rather dreary business of sexual habit, which to my mind is an aesthetic rather than an ethical issue.

*States of Desire: Travels in Gay America*, ch. 2 (1980)

5 I feel sorry for a man who never wanted to go to bed with his father; when the father dies, how can his ghost get warm except in a posthumous embrace? For that matter, how does the survivor get warm?

*A Boy's Own Story*, ch. 1 (1982)

6 For my father ... manliness was not discussable, but had it been, it would have included a good business suit, ambition, paying one's bills on time, enough knowledge of baseball to hand out like tips at the barbershop, a residual but never foolhardy degree of courage, and an unbreachable reserve; to the headmaster manliness ... entailed tweeds, trust funds, graciousness to servants, a polite but slightly chilly relationship to God, a pretended interest in knowledge and an obsessive interest in sports, especially muddy, dangerous ones.

ibid. ch. 6

7 I have no contempt for that time of life when our friendships are most passionate and our passions are incorrigible and none of our sentiments yet compromised by greed or cowardice or disappointment. The volatility and intensity of adolescence are qualities we should aspire to preserve.

'Paradise Found', publ. in *Mother Jones* June 1983, repr. in *The Burning Library* (1994)

8 We treat the failure of marriage as though it were the failure of individuals to achieve it – a decline in grit or maturity or commitment or stamina rather than the unraveling of a poorly tied knot. Bourgeois marriage was meant to concentrate friendship, romance, and sex into an institution at once familial and economic. Only the most intense surveillance could keep such a bulky, ill-assorted load from bursting at the seams.

'Sexual Culture', publ. in *Vanity Fair*, 1983, repr. in ibid.

9 The right to have sex, even to look for it, has been so stringently denied to gays for so many centuries that the drive toward sexual freedom remains a bright, throbbing banner in the fierce winds whipping over the ghetto.

ibid.

10 All men want quick, uncomplicated sexual adventure (as well as sustained romantic passion); in a world of all men, that desire is granted.

ibid.

11 The AIDS epidemic has rolled back a big rotting log and revealed all the squirming life underneath it, since it involves, all at once, the main themes of our existence: sex, death, power, money, love, hate, disease and panic. No American phenomenon has been so compelling since the Vietnam War.

*States of Desire: Travels in Gay America* (1980) 'Afterword – AIDS: An American Epidemic' (added to 1986 edn)

# T.H. White (1906–64)

BRITISH AUTHOR

Full name Terence Hanbury White. Writing mostly for children, he is best known for his tetralogy based on Arthurian legend, *The Once and Future King* (1939–58), and his other works also mix medievalism, fantasy and science fiction.

1 The once and future king.

Book title (1958). The words, which refer to King Arthur, are derived from the inscription supposed to be on his tomb, according to Sir Thomas Malory's *Le Morte d'Arthur*, bk 21, ch. 7 (1485): 'Hic iacet Arthurus, rex quondam rexque futurus.'

# Alfred North Whitehead (1861–1947)

BRITISH PHILOSOPHER

He established his reputation with his work on mathematical logic and collaborated with his former pupil BERTRAND RUSSELL to produce *Principia Mathematica* (three volumes, 1910–13). His metaphysical theory was published in *Process and Reality* (1929) and he also wrote popular works, including *The Aims of Education* (1929), *Adventures of Ideas* (1933) and *Modes of Thought* (1938).

1 Uneducated clever women, who have seen much of the world, are in middle life so much the most cultured part of the community. They have been saved from this horrible burden of inert ideas.

'The Aims of Education', publ. in *The Organization of Thought* (1917), repr. in *The Aims of Education and Other Essays* (1929)

2 Style is the ultimate morality of mind.

ibid.

3 Every philosophy is tinged with the colouring of some secret imaginative background, which never emerges explicitly into its train of reasoning.

*Science and the Modern World*, ch. 1 (1926)

4 The safest general characterization of the European philosophical tradition is that it consists of a series of footnotes to Plato.

*Process and Reality*, pt 2, ch. 1, sect. 1 (1929)

5 In a general way the whole period of education is dominated by this threefold rhythm. Till the age of thirteen or fourteen there is the romantic stage, from fourteen to eighteen the stage of precision, and from eighteen to two and twenty the stage of generalization.

*The Aims of Education and Other Essays*, 'The Rhythmic Claims of Freedom and Discipline' (1929)

6 Life is an offensive, directed against the repetitive mechanism of the Universe.

*Adventures of Ideas*, pt 1, ch. 5 (1933)

7 It is more important that a proposition be interesting than that it be true. This statement is almost a tautology. For the energy of operation of a proposition in an occasion of experience is its interest, and is its importance. But of course a true proposition is more apt to be interesting than a false one.

ibid. pt 4, ch. 16

8 Art is the imposing of a pattern on experience, and our aesthetic enjoyment is recognition of the pattern.

*Dialogues of Alfred North Whitehead*, '10 June 1943' (ed. Lucien Price, 1954)

9 There are no whole truths; all truths are half-truths. It is trying to treat them as whole truths that plays the devil.

ibid. Prologue

## Katharine Whitehorn (b. 1926)

BRITISH JOURNALIST

She became a columnist for the *Observer* in 1960 and Assistant Editor (1980–88). Her witty articles and essays on daily life are collected in *Only on Sundays* (1966) and *View from a Column* (1981), among other books, and she also wrote the series *How to Survive in Hospital* (1972) and *How to Survive in the Kitchen* (1979).

1 When it comes to housework the one thing no book of household management can ever tell you is how to begin. Or maybe I mean *why*.

*Roundabout*, 'Nought for Homework' (1962)

2 From a commercial point of view, if Christmas did not exist it would be necessary to invent it.

ibid. 'The Office Party'

3 An office party is not, as is sometimes supposed, the Managing Director's chance to kiss the tea-girl. It is the tea-girl's chance to kiss the Managing Director (however bizarre an ambition this may seem to anyone who has seen the Managing Director face on). Bringing down the mighty from their seats is an agreeable and necessary pastime, but no one supposes that the mighty, having struggled so hard to get seated, will enjoy the de-thronement.

ibid.

4 Hats divide generally into three classes: offensive hats, defensive hats, and shrapnel.

*Shouts and Murmurs*, 'Hats' (1963)

5 [Of the English climate] People get a bad impression of it by continually trying to treat it as if it was a bank clerk, who ought to be on time on Tuesday next, instead of philosophically seeing it as a painter, who may do anything so long as you don't try to predict what.

*Observer* 7 August 1966

6 Any committee that is the slightest use is composed of people who are too busy to want to sit on it for a second longer than they have to.

*Observations*, 'Are You Sitting Comfortably?' (1970)

7 I wouldn't say when you've seen one Western you've seen the lot; but when you've seen the lot you get the feeling you've seen one.

*Sunday Best*, 'Decoding the West' (1976)

8 The thing has been blown up out of all proportion. PC language is *not* enjoined on one and all – there are a lot more places where you can say 'spic' and 'bitch' with impunity than places where you can smoke a cigarette.

*Observer* 25 August 1991

## Gough Whitlam (b. 1916)

AUSTRALIAN POLITICIAN AND PRIME MINISTER

Elected a Labor MP in 1952, he became the first Australian Labor Prime Minister for twenty-three years in 1972. He was dismissed by the Governor General amid controversial circumstances in 1975 after the opposition had blocked his finance bills, and he retired from politics in 1977 to serve with UNESCO.

1 The punters know that the horse named Morality rarely gets past the post, whereas the nag named Self-Interest always runs a good race.

*Daily Telegraph* 19 October 1989

## Anne Widdecombe (b. 1947)

BRITISH POLITICIAN

An outspoken Conservative MP since 1987, she was a junior minister in the Home Office (1995–7) and became Shadow Home Secretary in 1999, the same year she converted to Roman Catholicism. Both reviled and adored, she elicited the tribute by JEREMY PAXMAN: 'She is a goddess. I am in love with her.'

1 [Of Michael Howard] He has something of the night in him.

Quoted in the *Sunday Times* 11 May 1997. The remark was said to have seriously damaged former Home Secretary Michael Howard's candidature for the Conservative Party leadership election, which was won by WILLIAM HAGUE.

2 Being English means, to me, tea on vicarage lawns, roses in a summer twilight, people keeping themselves to themselves, well-fed cats purring on hearthrugs, the bottom right-hand column of the 'Times' correspondence column.

Quoted in the *Big Issue* 10–16 August 1998

## Norbert Wiener (1894–1964)

US MATHEMATICIAN

He taught at the Massachusetts Institute of Technology (1919–60), where he worked on stochastic processes and, during the Second World War, guided missiles. He later became interested in the 'science of control and communication in the animal and machine' for which he coined the word 'cybernetics', as described in his book *Cybernetics* (1948). Other works include *The Human Use of Human Beings* (1950).

1 A painter like Picasso, who runs through many periods and phases, ends up by saying all those things which are on the tip of the tongue of the age to say, and finally sterilizes the originality of his contemporaries and juniors.

*The Human Use of Human Beings*, ch. 7 (1950)

2 The idea that information can be stored in a changing world without an overwhelming depreciation of its value is false. It is scarcely less false than the more plausible claim that after a war we may take our existing weapons, fill their barrels with cylinder oil, and coat their outsides with sprayed rubber film, and let them statically await the next emergency.

ibid.

## Elie Wiesel (b. 1928)

ROMANIAN-BORN US AUTHOR

A survivor of Auschwitz, he worked in journalism in Israel and the United States. Much of his work is based on his traumatic personal experiences, including three novels, *Night* (1958), *Dawn* (1961) and *The Accident* (1961), among numerous other works. He was awarded the Nobel Peace Prize in 1986.

1 The opposite of love is not hate, it's indifference. The opposite of art is not ugliness, it's indifference. The opposite of faith is not heresy, it's indifference. And the opposite of life is not death, it's indifference.

*U.S. News and World Report* 27 October 1986

2 How do you describe the sorting out on arriving at Auschwitz, the separation of children who see a father or mother going away, never to be seen again? How do you express the dumb grief of a little girl and the endless lines of women, children and rabbis being driven across the Polish or Ukrainian landscapes to their deaths? No, I can't do it. And because I'm a writer and teacher, I don't understand how Europe's most cultured nation could have done that. For these men who killed with submachine-guns in the

Ukraine were university graduates. Afterwards they would go home and read a poem by Heine. So what happened?

Testifying at the trial of Klaus Barbie in Lyons, 2 June 1987, quoted in *Le Monde* 4 June 1987

3 Once you bring life into the world, you must protect it. We must protect it by changing the world.

Interview in *Writers at Work* (eighth series, ed. George Plimpton, 1988)

4 Nobody is stronger, nobody is weaker than someone who came back. There is nothing you can do to such a person because whatever you could do is less than what has already been done to him. We have already paid the price.

ibid.

5 What does mysticism really mean? It means the way to attain knowledge. It's close to philosophy, except in philosophy you go horizontally while in mysticism you go vertically.

ibid.

6 We are heading towards catastrophe. I think the world is going to pieces. I am very pessimistic. Why? Because the world hasn't been punished yet, and the only punishment that could be adequate is the nuclear destruction of the world.

ibid.

7 When you see the abyss, and we have looked into it, then what? There isn't much room at the edge – one person, another, not many. If you are there, others cannot be there. If you are there, you become a protective wall. What happens? You become part of the abyss.

ibid.

8 I marvel at the resilience of the Jewish people. Their best characteristic is their desire to remember. No other people has such an obsession with memory.

*Daily Mail* 15 July 1988. Wiesel's 'major preoccupation', he said on a previous occasion, is 'the kingdom of memory. I want to protect and enrich that kingdom, glorify that kingdom and serve it.'

9 In this place of darkness and malediction we can but stand in awe and remember its stateless, faceless and nameless victims. Close your eyes and look: endless nocturnal processions are converging here, and here it is always night. Here heaven and earth are on fire.

Address at fiftieth anniversary of liberation of Auschwitz, 27 January 1995, publ. in *The Penguin Book of Twentieth-Century Speeches* (ed. Brian MacArthur, 1999)

10 It is true that not all the victims were Jews. But all the Jews were victims.

ibid.

## Billy Wilder (b. 1906)

AUSTRIAN-BORN US FILM-MAKER

Originally Samuel Wilder. Working in Hollywood from 1934, he enjoyed a long association with co-writers Charles Brackett and later I.A.L. Diamond on films such as *Double Indemnity* (1944), *Sunset Boulevard* (1950), *The Seven Year Itch* (1955) and *The Apartment* (1960), for which he won an Oscar. 'I have ten commandments,' he once said, 'The first nine are, thou shalt not bore. The tenth is, thou shalt have right of final cut.'

1 One's too many, and a hundred's not enough.

Nat the bartender (Howard Da Silva), in *The Lost Weekend* (film, 1945, screenplay by Charles Brackett and Billy Wilder based on novel by Charles Jackson, directed by Billy Wilder). Spoken to regular customer Don Birnam (Ray Milland), whose descent into alcoholic breakdown the film graphically portrays.

2 I don't go to church. Kneeling bags my nylons.

Lorraine (Jan Sterling), in *The Big Carnival* (film, 1951, screenplay by Billy Wilder, Lesser Samuel and Walter Newman, produced and directed by Billy Wilder). The movie was originally released under the title *Ace in the Hole*.

3 Well, nobody's perfect.

Osgood E. Fielding III (Joe E. Brown), in *Some Like It Hot* (film, 1959, screenplay by Billy Wilder and I.A.L. Diamond, produced and directed by Billy Wilder, 1959). On discovering that his fiancée (JACK LEMMON) is a man, in final words of film.

4 A woman without a man is like a trailer without a car; it ain't going nowhere.

Polly the Pistol (Kim Novak), in *Kiss Me, Stupid* (film, 1964, written and directed by Billy Wilder)

5 Ah, Marilyn, Hollywood's Joan of Arc, our Ultimate Sacrificial Lamb. Well, let me tell you, she was mean, terribly mean. The meanest woman I have ever known in this town. I am appalled by this Marilyn Monroe cult. Perhaps it's getting to be an act of courage to say the truth about her. Well, let me be courageous. I have never met anyone as utterly mean as Marilyn Monroe. Nor as utterly fabulous on the screen.

Interview in the *Los Angeles Times*, 1968, quoted in *Billy Wilder in Hollywood*, ch. 19 (1977) by Maurice Zolotow

6 [France is] a country where the money falls apart but you can't tear the toilet paper.

Quoted in ibid. ch. 18

7 Hindsight is always twenty-twenty.

Quoted in *Wit and Wisdom of the Moviemakers*, ch. 7 (ed. John Robert Columbo, 1979)

8 An audience is never wrong. An individual member of it may be an imbecile, but a thousand imbeciles together in the dark – that is critical genius.

*Arena* TV profile, 24 January 1992, BBC2

## Thornton Wilder (1897–1975)

US NOVELIST AND PLAYWRIGHT

He achieved status as a bestselling writer through his treatment of universal themes, 'those things which repeat and repeat and repeat in the lives of millions', as he once put it. His novel *The Bridge of San Luis Rey* (1927, filmed 1929) won the Pulitzer Prize, as did his plays, the innovative *Our Town* (1938, filmed 1940), acted on a bare stage, and *The Skin of Our Teeth* (1942).

1 I've never forgotten for long at a time that living is struggle. I know that every good and excellent thing in the world stands moment by moment on the razor-edge of danger and must be fought for – whether it's a field, or a home, or a country.

Antrobus, in *The Skin of Our Teeth*, act 3 (1942)

2 Literature is the orchestration of platitudes.

*Time* magazine 12 January 1953

3 Marriage is a bribe to make a housekeeper think she's a householder.

Vendergelder, in *The Matchmaker*, act 1 (1954). The play, which was adapted from a previous work, *The Merchant of Yonkers* (1939), was later the basis for the Broadway musical *Hello Dolly!* (1963).

4 Never support two weaknesses at the same time. It's your combination sinners – your lecherous liars and your miserly drunkards – who dishonor the vices and bring them into bad repute.

Malachi, in ibid. act 3

5 The test of an adventure is that when you're in the middle of it, you say to yourself, 'Oh, now I've got myself into an awful mess; I wish I were sitting quietly at home.' And the sign that something's wrong with you is when you sit quietly at home wishing you were out having lots of adventure.

Barnaby, in ibid. act 4

6 I am convinced that, except in a few extraordinary cases, one form or another of an unhappy childhood is essential to the formation of exceptional gifts.

Interview in *Writers at Work* (first series, ed. Malcolm Cowley, 1958)

7 A dramatist is one who believes that the pure event, an action involving human beings, is more arresting than any comment that can be made upon it.

ibid.

## Paul Wilkinson (b. 1937)

BRITISH SCHOLAR

Professor of International Relations from 1990 and appointed Director of the Centre for the Study of Political Violence at St Andrew's University, Scotland, in 1999, he is the author of *Political Terrorism* (1974), *The New Fascists* (1981) and *Northern Ireland* (1991).

1 Fighting terrorism is like being a goalkeeper. You can make a hundred brilliant saves but the only shot that people remember is the one that gets past you.

*Daily Telegraph* 1 September 1992

## George F. Will (b. 1941)

US POLITICAL COLUMNIST

Widely known as a journalist and broadcaster, he has written columns for *Newsweek* and the *Washington Post* and was Washington Editor for the *National Review* (1972–6). Among his publications are *The Pursuit of Virtue, and Other Tory Notions* (1982), *Statecraft as Soulcraft: What Government Does* (1983), and *The Leveling Wind* (1994).

1 It is no longer enough to be lusty. One must be a sexual gourmet.

'The Ploy of Sex' (1974), repr. in *The Pursuit of Happiness, and Other Sobering Thoughts* (1978)

2 A politician's words reveal less about what he thinks about his subject than what he thinks about his audience.

Quoted in *A Ford, Not a Lincoln*, ch. 1 (1975) by Richard Reeves

3 Voters don't decide issues, they decide *who* will decide issues.

*Newsweek* 8 March 1976

4 Statecraft is soulcraft. Just as all education is moral education because learning conditions conduct, much legislation is moral legislation because it conditions the action and the thought of the nation in broad and important spheres of life.

*Statecraft as Soulcraft: What Government Does*, ch. 1 (1984)

5 Politics should share one purpose with religion: the steady emancipation of the individual through the education of his passions.

ibid. ch. 2

6 Americans are overreaching; overreaching is the most admirable and most American of the many American excesses.

ibid. ch. 4

7 To be an intelligent fan is to participate in something. It is an activity, a form of appreciating that is good for the individual's soul, and hence for society.

*Men at Work: The Craft of Baseball*, Introduction (1990)

8 Football combines the two worst things about America: it is violence punctuated by committee meetings.

*International Herald Tribune* 7 May 1990

## Hank Williams (1923–53)

US COUNTRY MUSICIAN

Performing at southern honky-tonks in his teens, he made his first recordings in 1946 and rose to become country music's biggest star, characterized by his melancholy lyrics and strong melodies. Backed by his band the Drifting Cowboys, he had hits with 'Lovesick Blues', 'I'm So Lonesome I Could Cry' (both 1949) and the more upbeat

'Hey, Good-Lookin'' (1951). Addicted to drink and drugs, he died young of alcohol-related heart disease.

1 Your cheatin' heart.

Title of song (1953), film biopic (1964) and biography by Chet Flippo (1981). Recorded on Williams's last session in Nashville, the song posthumously topped both *Billboard* and *Cashbox* country charts for months and came to be covered by more than 300 other artists.

2 You've got to have smelled a lot of mule manure before you can sing like a hillbilly.

Quoted in *All You Need is Love*, 'Making Moonshine' by Tony Palmer (1976)

## Raymond Williams (1921–88)

WELSH NOVELIST AND CRITIC

Credited with the founding of cultural materialism as an approach to literature, he was author of *Culture and Society* (1958) and *The Long Revolution* (1961). He was active in the New Left and published the *May Day Manifesto* of 1968 and *Marxism and Literature* (1977), while his Welsh affiliations are apparent in his novels, including *Border Country* (1960) and *The Volunteers* (1978).

1 What breaks capitalism, all that will ever break capitalism, is capitalists. The faster they run the more strain on their heart.

Monkey Pitter, in *Loyalties*, pt 3, ch. 2 (1985)

2 It wasn't idealism that made me, from the beginning, want a more secure and rational society. It was an intellectual judgement, to which I still hold. When I was young its name was socialism. We can be deflected by names. But the need was absolute, and is still absolute.

Norman Braose, in ibid. pt 5, ch. 5

## Robbie Williams (b. 1974)

BRITISH POP MUSICIAN

After leaving one of the first 1990s boy bands, Take That, in 1995, he quickly became a major solo star with the hits 'Freedom' (1996), 'Angels' (1997) and 'Let Me Entertain You' (1998) and the album *Life Thru a Lens* (1997).

1 Some say that we are players, some say that we are pawns.
   But we've been making money since the day that we were born.

'Millennium' (song, co-written with Guy Chambers) on the album *I've Been Expecting You* (1998)

## Robin Williams (b. 1951)

US ACTOR AND COMEDIAN

He began his career in stand-up comedy, followed by TV appearances in *Happy Days* and *Mork and Mindy* (1978–82). A versatile comedian, he also shows his serious and occasionally sentimental sides in his film roles, which include *Good Morning, Vietnam* (1987), *Dead Poets Society* (1989), *Mrs. Doubtfire* (1993) and *Good Will Hunting* (1997), for which he won an Academy Award.

1 Come on now! You kick out the gooks, the next thing you know, you have to kick out the chinks, the spicks, the spooks, the kikes and all that's going to be left is a couple of brain-dead rednecks.

Adrian Cronauer (Robin Williams), in *Good Morning, Vietnam* (film, 1987, screenplay by Mitch Markowitz, directed by Barry Levinson)

2 You're only given a little spark of madness. You mustn't lose it.

Quoted in *Funny Business* (1992) by David Housham and John Frank-Keyes

## Shirley Williams (b. 1930)

BRITISH LIBERAL DEMOCRAT POLITICIAN

Baroness Williams of Crosby. Daughter of the novelist VERA BRITTAIN, she became a Labour MP in 1964 and served in ministerial positions. In 1981 she was the first elected MP of the new Social Democratic Party and its President (1982–3). She moved to the United States in 1998 and was appointed Professor of Politics at Harvard.

1 The Catholic Church has never really come to terms with women. What I object to is being treated either as Madonnas or Mary Magdalenes.

*Observer* 22 March 1981

## Tennessee Williams (1911–83)

US PLAYWRIGHT

His background of growing up in genteel poverty in the deep South is relayed in most of his plays, not least in his first success *The Glass Menagerie* (1944). He won Pulitzer Prizes for *A Streetcar Named Desire* (1947, filmed 1951) and *Cat on a Hot Tin Roof* (1955, filmed 1958), but his experimental drama, such as *Camino Real* (1953), was less well received. He also wrote fiction and verse.

1 In memory everything seems to happen to music.

Tom, in *The Glass Menagerie*, sc. 1 (1944)

2 Time is the longest distance between two places.

Tom, in ibid. sc. 7

3 I can't stand a naked light bulb, any more than I can a rude remark or a vulgar action.

Blanche DuBois, in *A Streetcar Named Desire*, sc. 3 (1947)

4 I have always depended on the kindness of strangers.

Blanche DuBois, in ibid. sc. 11. Her final words.

5 Time rushes toward us with its hospital tray of infinitely varied narcotics, even while it is preparing us for its inevitably fatal operation.

*The Rose Tattoo*, 'The Timeless World of a Play' (1951)

6 When so many are lonely as seem to be lonely, it would be inexcusably selfish to be lonely alone.

Don Quixote, in *Camino Real*, Prologue (1953)

7 You said 'They're harmless dreamers and they're loved by the people.' – 'What,' I asked you, 'is harmless about a dreamer, and what,' I asked you, 'is harmless about the love of the people? – Revolution only needs good dreamers who remember their dreams.'

Gutman to the Generalissimo, in ibid. Block 2

8 The most dangerous word in any human tongue is the word for brother. It's inflammatory.

Gutman, in ibid.

9 We have to distrust each other. It is our only defence against betrayal.

Marguerite Gautier, in ibid. Block 10

10 Oh, Jacques, we're used to each other, we're a pair of captive hawks caught in the same cage, and so we've grown used to each other. That's what passes for love at this dim, shadowy end of the Camino Real . . .

Marguerite Gautier to Jacques Casanova, in ibid.

11 We're all of us guinea pigs in the laboratory of God. Humanity is just a work in progress.

The Gipsy, in ibid. Block 12

12 Everyone says he's sincere, but everyone isn't sincere. If everyone was sincere who says he's sincere there wouldn't be half so many insincere ones in the world and there would be lots, lots, lots more really sincere ones!

Esmeralda, in ibid.

13 Mendacity is a system that we live in. Liquor is one way out an' death's the other.

Brick, in *Cat on a Hot Tin Roof*, act 2 (1955)

14 You've got many refinements. I don't think you need to worry about your failure at long division. I mean, after all, you got through short division, and short division is all that a lady ought to be called on to cope with . . .

Silva (Karl Malden) speaking to Baby Doll (Carroll Baker), in *Baby Doll* (film, 1956, screenplay by Tennessee Williams, directed by Elia Kazan)

15 We're all of us sentenced to solitary confinement inside our own skins, for life!

Val Xavier, in *Orpheus Descending*, act 2, sc. 1 (1957)

16 I don't believe in villains or heroes, only in right or wrong ways that individuals are taken, not by choice, but by necessity or by certain still uncomprehended influences in themselves, their circumstances and their antecedents.

*New York Post* 17 March 1957

17 The world is a funny paper read backwards. And that way it isn't so funny.

Self-interview, in the *Observer* 7 April 1957

18 Don't look forward to the day you stop suffering, because when it comes you'll *know* you're dead.

Quoted in the *Observer* 26 January 1958

19 It haunts me, the passage of time. I think time is a merciless thing. I think life is a process of burning oneself out and time is the fire that burns you. But I think the spirit of man is a good adversary.

*New York Post* 30 April 1958

20 We all live in a house on fire, no fire department to call; no way out, just the upstairs window to look out of while the fire burns the house down with us trapped, locked in it.

Chris, in *The Milk Train Doesn't Stop Here Anymore*, sc. 6 (1963)

## William Carlos Williams (1883–1963)

US POET

A practising physician, he is known for celebrating the everyday in his verse, often in unconventional rhythm and metre. Early volumes include *The Tempers* (1913) and *Sour Grapes* (1921). His major work, *Paterson* (1946–58), was based on themes of the city of that name in New Jersey, and his final verse collection *Pictures from Breughel* (1962) won a Pulitzer Prize. He also wrote fiction, plays and essays.

1 The pure products of America
go crazy –
mountain folk from Kentucky

or the ribbed north end of
Jersey
with its isolate lakes and

valleys, its deaf-mutes, thieves.

'To Elsie', publ. in *Spring and All* (1923)

2 Afraid lest he be caught up in a net of words, tripped up, bewildered and so defeated – thrown aside – a man hesitates to write down his innermost convictions.

Journal entry, 7 July 1929, publ. in *The Embodiment Of Knowledge* (1974)

3 It's the anarchy of poverty
delights me.

'The Poor', publ. in *Recent Verse* (1938)

4 Say it! No ideas but in things.

*Paterson*, bk 1, 'The Delineaments of the Giants', sect. 1 (1946, rev. 1963). Williams's poetic dictum – to present the subject concretely, without literary artifice – was influential on the Beat writers, notably ALLEN GINSBERG.

5 It is dangerous to leave written that which is badly written. A chance word, upon paper, may destroy the world. Watch carefully and erase, while the power is still yours, I say to myself, for all that is put down, once it escapes, may rot

its way into a thousand minds, the corn become a black smut, and all libraries, of necessity, be burned to the ground as a consequence.

Only one answer: write carelessly so that nothing that is not green will survive.

ibid. bk 3, 'The Library', sect. 3

6 It is difficult
to get the news from poems
yet men die miserably every day
for lack
of what is found there.

'Asphodel, That Greeny Flower', publ. in *Journey to Love* (1955)

## Roy Williamson (1937–90)
SCOTTISH FOLK MUSICIAN

He was a founding member of the Corrie Folk Trio, which formed in the 1960s and continued with Ronnie Brown as a duo, the Corries, until 1990. He is best known for the song 'Flower of Scotland'.

1 O Flower of Scotland,
When will we see
Your like again,
That fought and died for,
Your wee bit hill and glen,
And stood against him,
Proud Edward's Army,
And sent him homeward,
Tae think again.

'Flower of Scotland' (song, 1968) on the album *The Corries in Concert* (1969) by the Corries. The song has come to be regarded as Scotland's unofficial national anthem.

## Wendell Willkie (1892–1944)
US LAWYER AND POLITICIAN

An outspoken opponent of the New Deal, he ran as Republican candidate for the presidency in 1940 but was narrowly defeated by F.D. ROOSEVELT. Committed to international cooperation and civil rights, he undertook a round-the-world trip and published *One World* (1943) on his return. HAROLD L. ICKES called him: 'The rich man's Roosevelt; the simple barefoot boy from Wall Street.'

1 The constitution does not provide for first and second class citizens.

*An American Programme*, ch. 2 (1944)

## A.N. Wilson (b. 1950)
BRITISH AUTHOR

Full name Andrew Norman Wilson. Known for his novels satirizing British society, such as *The Sweets of Pimlico* (1977), *The Healing Art* (1980) and *Love Unknown* (1986), he has also written biographies of Walter Scott (1980), Milton (1985), and Hilaire Belloc (1984). *How Can We Know?* (1985) and *Paul: The Mind of the Apostle* (1997) are works of Christian apologia. He is regarded as a High Church Conservative.

1 In universities and intellectual circles, academics can guarantee themselves popularity – or, which is just as satisfying, unpopularity – by being opinionated rather than by being learned.

Book review in the *Guardian* 30 September 1989

2 The fact that logic cannot satisfy us awakens an almost insatiable hunger for the irrational.

ibid.

3 If you know somebody is going to be awfully annoyed by

something you write, that's obviously very satisfying, and if they howl with rage or cry, that's honey.

Quoted in the *Independent on Sunday* 13 September 1992

4 The cult of a year ago has dwindled and become, as religions tend to, the preserve of children, homosexuals and lonely housewives.

Interview with ANTHONY CLARE in *In the Psychiatrist's Chair* 13 September 1998, Radio 4. Referring to the reaction to the death of PRINCESS DIANA.

## (Sir) Angus Wilson (1913–91)
BRITISH AUTHOR

On the staff of the British Museum Library until 1955, he had success with his stories satirizing the middle class and the novels *Hemlock and After* (1952) and *Anglo-Saxon Attitudes* (1956).

1 The opportunities for heroism are limited in this kind of world: the most people can do is sometimes not to be as weak as they've been at other times.

Interview in *Writers at Work* (first series, ed. Malcolm Cowley, 1958)

## Charles E. Wilson (1890–1961)
US INDUSTRIALIST AND POLITICIAN

As President of General Motors (1941–52) he contributed substantially to US munitions production during the Second World War. He served as Secretary of Defense under Eisenhower (1953–7) but proved controversial for his tactless remarks (he habitually addressed Congress as 'you men') and his refusal to sell off his shares in GM while holding public office.

1 For years I thought what was good for our country was good for General Motors and vice versa. The difference did not exist. Our company is too big. It goes with the welfare of the country.

Statement to US Senate committee, January 1953, quoted in *The New York Times* 24 February 1953. The words – usually quoted 'What's good for the country is good for General Motors, and *vice versa*' – were pounced upon by the Democrats on the committee, who were in a majority, to question his true loyalties.

## Harold Wilson (1916–95)
BRITISH POLITICIAN AND PRIME MINISTER

Baron Wilson of Rievaulx. Variously regarded as adroit, devious, Machiavellian and paranoid, he delighted in his 'common touch', expressed in his Gannex raincoat, constant pipe-smoking and fondness for HP sauce. He was Labour Prime Minister 1964–70 and 1974–6, during which time he faced successive sterling crises and inflation. He introduced economic sanctions against Rhodesia in 1965 and renegotiated Britain's terms of entry into the EEC in 1974.

1 This Party is a moral crusade or it is nothing.

Speech to Labour Party Conference, 1 October 1962, quoted in *The Times* 2 October 1962. The words were recalled by TONY BLAIR on Wilson's death.

2 If I had the choice between smoked salmon and tinned salmon, I'd have it tinned. With vinegar.

Quoted in the *Observer* 11 November 1962

3 We are redefining and we are restating our Socialism in terms of the scientific revolution. But that revolution cannot become a reality unless we are prepared to make far-reaching changes in economic and social attitudes which permeate our whole system of society. The Britain that is going to be forged in the white heat of this revolution will be no place for restrictive practices or for outdated methods on either side of industry.

Speech to Labour Party Conference, Scarborough, 1 October 1963, publ. in *The Penguin Book of Twentieth-Century Speeches* (ed. Brian MacArthur, 1999). In his first conference speech as party leader,

Wilson attempted to associate Labour with what became known as the 'white heat of the technological revolution', in contrast to the perceived old-fashioned ideas of ALEC DOUGLAS-HOME's Conservative Party.

4 **A week is a long time in politics.**

Attributed, c. 1964. In *Sayings of the Century*, 'Prime Ministers: A Word from No. 10' (1984) by Nigel Rees, it is reported that in 1977 Wilson was unable to remember when or even if he had uttered this aphorism always associated with him. The words were probably said off the record to lobby correspondents.

5 **From now the pound abroad is worth fourteen per cent or so less in terms of other currencies. It does not mean, of course, that the pound here in Britain, in your pocket or purse, or in your bank, has been devalued.**

Broadcast 19 November 1967, BBC TV, quoted in *The Times* 20 November 1967

6 **One man's wage rise is another man's price increase.**

Speech at Blackburn, 8 January 1970, quoted in the *Observer* 11 January 1970

## Robert Wilson (b. 1941)
US THEATRE DIRECTOR AND DESIGNER

An avant-garde director, he makes use of deliberately slow pacing and patterned repetition in his pieces, which can last up to twelve hours. He has worked with composers such as Philip Glass in *Einstein on the Beach* (1976) and Tom Waits in *The Black Rider* (1990).

1 **Once something becomes discernible, or understandable, we no longer need to repeat it. We can destroy it.**

Quoted in the *Sunday Times* 17 November 1991

## Woodrow Wilson (1856–1924)
US POLITICIAN AND PRESIDEN

Full name Thomas Woodrow Wilson. As Democratic President (1913–21), he reluctantly entered the First World War in 1917, contributed to the armistice with his 'Fourteen Points' plan and championed the League of Nations. He was awarded the Nobel Peace Prize in 1919. 'In Wilson, the whole of mankind breaks camp, sets out from home and wrestles with the universe and its gods,' WILLIAM BOLITHO eulogized.

1 **It is like writing history with lightning and my only regret is that it is all so terribly true.**

Attributed remark at the White House, 18 February 1915, quoted in *The Image*, ch. 4 (1962) by DANIEL J. BOORSTIN. On seeing D.W. GRIFFITH's epic of the Civil War, *The Birth of a Nation*.

2 **No nation is fit to sit in judgement upon any other nation.**

Speech in New York, 20 April 1915, publ. in *Selected Addresses* (1918)

3 **Once lead this people into war and they will forget there ever was such a thing as tolerance.**

Quoted in *Mr Wilson's War*, pt 3, ch. 12 (1917) by JOHN DOS PASSOS

4 **A little group of wilful men reflecting no opinion but their own have rendered the great Government of the United States helpless and contemptible.**

Statement 4 March 1917, quoted in *The New York Times* 5 March 1917. Referring to a successful filibuster against Wilson's bill to arm US merchant ships against German submarine attacks.

5 **The world must be made safe for democracy. Its peace must be planted upon the tested foundations of political liberty.**

Speech to Congress, 2 April 1917, publ. in *The Penguin Book of Twentieth-Century Speeches* (ed. Brian MacArthur, 1999). Proposing a state of war against Germany, which was almost unanimously voted four days later. A year earlier, Wilson had run his re-election campaign on the boast of having 'kept us out of war', having pursued a policy of remaining 'studiously neutral'. See also THOMAS WOLFE 1.

6 **Sometimes people call me an idealist. Well, that is the way**

I know I am an American . . . America is the only idealistic nation in the world.

Speech at Sioux Falls, North Dakota, 8 September 1919, publ. in *The Messages and Papers of Woodrow Wilson*, vol. 2 (ed. Albert Shaw, 1924)

## R. Foster Winans (b. 1948)
US JOURNALIST

A *Wall Street Journal* reporter, he was tried and convicted for 'insider dealing'.

1 **The only reason to invest in the market is because you think you know something others don't.**

*Newsweek* 1 December 1986

## Oprah Winfrey (b. 1954)
US CHAT SHOW HOST

Her daytime talk show *The Oprah Winfrey Show* (from 1985), on which controversial problems are aired, led to her becoming in 1997 the highest paid entertainer in the United States. She has also appeared in the film *The Color Purple* (1985) and the TV series *The Women of Brewster Place* (1989).

1 **I am those women. I am every one of them. And they are me. That's why we get along so well.**

Quoted in *Oprah!*, 'A Day with Oprah' (1987) by Robert Waldron. Referring to the victims and survivors who appear on her show.

2 **What I've learned about being angry with people is that it generally hurts you more than it hurts them.**

Quoted in ibid. ch. 2

3 **I've been guilty of misusing TV. It's a dangerous medium and is misused all the time.**

*Radio Times* 23 February 1999

## Michael Winner (b. 1935)
BRITISH FILM-MAKER

He is associated with films of revenge and vigilante violence, particularly the three *Death Wish* films he directed (1974, 1981, 1985). Other films include *The Jokers* (1967), *The Big Sleep* (1978) and *Dirty Weekend* (1992).

1 **The truth of the matter is that muggers are very interesting people.**

*Daily Express* 11 May 1989

## Shelley Winters (b. 1922)
US ACTRESS

Original name Shirley Schrift. In many of her early films she was typecast playing murder victims and vulnerable characters, although she extended her roles in *The Diary of Anne Frank* (1959) and *A Patch of Blue* (1965), both winning her Oscars, and in *The Poseidon Adventure* (1972).

1 **Every now and then, when you're on stage, you hear the best sound a player can hear. It's a sound you can't get in movies or in television. It is the sound of a wonderful, deep silence that means you've hit them where they live.**

*Theatre Arts* June 1956

## Yvor Winters (1900–68)
US LITERARY CRITIC AND POET

He was associated with New Criticism but maintained the view that literature should be evaluated for its moral content. His main critical works were *In Defense of Reason* (1947) and *The Function of Criticism* (1957). *To the Holy Spirit* (1947) was his last volume of poetry.

1 **Professors of literature, who for the most part are genteel**

but mediocre men, can make but a poor defense of their profession, and the professors of science, who are frequently men of great intelligence but of limited interests and education, feel a politely disguised contempt for it; and thus the study of one of the most pervasive and powerful influences on human life is traduced and neglected.

*In Defense of Reason*, Foreword (1947)

## Jeanette Winterson (b. 1959)

BRITISH AUTHOR

She came to notice with her first novel, the autobiographical *Oranges Are Not the Only Fruit* (1985), in which she recounts her upbringing in an Evangelist household and her self-fulfilment as a lesbian. This was followed by *Written on the Body* (1992) and *Art and Lies* (1994), among others.

1 Oranges are not the only fruit.
   Title of novel (1985)

2 However it is debased or misinterpreted, love is a redemptive feature. To focus on one individual so that their desires become superior to yours is a very cleansing experience.
   *The Times* 26 August 1992

3 Why is it that the most unoriginal thing we can say to one another is still the thing we long to hear? 'I love you' is always a quotation. You did not say it first and neither did I, yet when you say it and when I say it we speak like savages who have found three words and worship them.
   *Written on the Body* (1992)

4 Why do human beings need answers? Partly I suppose because without one, almost any one, the question itself soon sounds silly.
   ibid.

5 It's awkward, in a society where the cult of the individual has never been preached with greater force, and where many of our collective ills are a result of that force, to say that it is the Self to which one must attend. But the Self is not a random collection of stray desires striving to be satisfied, nor is it only by suppressing such desires, as women are encouraged to do, that any social cohesion is possible. Our broken society is not born out of the triumph of the individual, but out of his effacement.
   *Art and Lies*, 'Handel' (1994)

6 There's no such thing as autobiography there's only art and lies.
   ibid. 'Sappho'

7 The masses are fobbed off with gadgets, while the real science takes place behind closed doors, the preserve of the pharmaceuticals and the military. Genetic control will be the weapon of the future. Doctors will fill the ranks of the New Model Army. . . . The white coat will replace the khaki fatigues as the gun gives way to the syringe.
   ibid. 'Handel'

8 No one working in the English language now comes close to my exuberance, my passion, my fidelity to words.
   *Sunday Times* 13 March 1994. On naming herself the best living author writing in English.

## Ludwig Wittgenstein (1889–1951)

AUSTRIAN-BORN BRITISH PHILOSOPHER

Having trained as an engineer at Berlin and Manchester, he studied mathematics and logic under BERTRAND RUSSELL at Cambridge (1912–13). He served in the Austrian army during the First World War and wrote his seminal work on logical positivism, *Tractatus Logico-Philosophicus* (1921), in an Italian prison camp. He later returned to Cambridge, became a naturalized British citizen in 1938

and wrote *Philosophical Investigations* (1953), examining the uses and inherent logic of language.

1 Logic takes care of itself; all we have to do is to look and see how it does it.
   Entry, 13 October 1914, publ. in *Notebooks 1914–1916* (ed. G.E.M. Anscombe, 1961). Also in *Tractatus Logico-Philosophicus*, sect. 5:473 (1921).

2 When one is frightened of the truth . . . then it is never the *whole* truth that one has an inkling of.
   Entry, 15 October 1914, publ. in ibid.

3 The logic of the world is prior to all truth and falsehood.
   Entry, 18 October 1914, publ. in ibid. Reformulated in *Tractatus Logico-Philosophicus*, sect. 5:552 (1921): 'Logic is *prior* to every experience – that something *is so*.'

4 Don't get involved in partial problems, but always take flight to where there is a free view over the whole *single* great problem, even if this view is still not a clear one.
   Entry, 1 November 1914, publ. in ibid.

5 It is one of the chief skills of the philosopher not to occupy himself with questions which do not concern him.
   Entry, 1 May 1915, publ. in ibid.

6 Language is a part of our organism and no less complicated than it.
   Entry, 14 May 1915, publ. in ibid. Also in *Tractatus Logico-Philosophicus*, sect. 4:002 (1921): 'Everyday language is a part of the human organism and is no less complicated than it.'

7 The philosophical I is not the human being, not the human body or the human soul with the psychological properties, but the metaphysical subject, the boundary (not a part) of the world.
   Entry, 2 September 1915, publ. in ibid. Also in *Tractatus Logico-Philosophicus*, sect. 5:641 (1921).

8 In order to be able to set a limit to thought, we should have to find both sides of the limit thinkable (i.e. we should have to be able to think what cannot be thought).
   *Tractatus Logico-Philosophicus*, Preface (1921)

9 I am my world. (The microcosm.)
   ibid. sect. 5:63

10 Death is not an event in life: we do not live to experience death. If we take eternity to mean not infinite temporal duration but timelessness, then eternal life belongs to those who live in the present.
   ibid. sect. 6:4311

11 Whereof one cannot speak, thereof one must be silent. (*Wovon man nicht sprechen kann, darüber muss man schweigen.*)
   ibid. sect. 7. Wittgenstein had elaborated in the book's Preface: 'What can be said at all can be said clearly, and what we cannot talk about we must pass over in silence.' KARL POPPER, in his *Conjectures and Refutations* (1963), reported Franz Urbach's rejoinder to this: 'But it is only here that speaking becomes worthwhile.'

12 You get tragedy where the tree, instead of bending, breaks.
   Journal entry, 1929, publ. in *Culture and Value* (ed. G.H. von Wright with Heikki Nyman, 1980). 'For a truly religious man nothing is tragic,' Wittgenstein is recorded as saying in 1930.

13 Philosophy is like trying to open a safe with a combination lock: each little adjustment of the dials seems to achieve nothing, only when everything is in place does the door open.
   Conversation in 1930, publ. in *Personal Recollections*, ch. 6 (ed. Rush Rhees, 1981)

14 A philosopher who is not taking part in discussions is like a boxer who never goes into the ring.
   ibid.

15 The face is the soul of the body.
   Journal entry, 1932–4, publ. in *Culture and Value* (ed. G.H. von Wright with Heikki Nyman, 1980)

16 Resting on your laurels is as dangerous as resting when you are walking in the snow. You doze off and die in your sleep.

Journal entry, 1939–40, publ. in ibid.

17 I sit astride life like a bad rider on a horse. I only owe it to the horse's good nature that I am not thrown off at this very moment.

ibid.

18 Someone who knows too much finds it hard not to lie.

Journal entry, 1947, publ. in ibid.

19 Never stay up on the barren heights of cleverness, but come down into the green valleys of silliness.

Journal entry, 1948, publ. in ibid.

20 Humour is not a mood but a way of looking at the world. So if it is correct to say that humour was stamped out in Nazi Germany, that does not mean that people were not in good spirits, or anything of that sort, but something much deeper and more important.

ibid.

21 For a *large* class of cases – though not for all – in which we employ the word 'meaning' it can be defined thus: the meaning of a word is its use in the language.

*Philosophical Investigations*, pt 1, sect. 43 (1953)

22 Philosophy is a battle against the bewitchment of our intelligence by means of language.

ibid. pt 1, sect. 109. Wittgenstein argued that most philosophical problems arose from the systematic misuse of language, and could be solved by a new critical method of linguistic analysis.

23 The real discovery is the one which enables me to stop doing philosophy when I want to. – The one that gives philosophy peace, so that it is no longer tormented by questions which bring *itself* into question.

ibid. pt 1, sect. 133

24 Like everything metaphysical the harmony between thought and reality is to be found in the grammar of the language.

*Zettel*, sect. 55 (1967)

25 If you do know that *here is one hand*, we'll grant you all the rest.

*On Certainty*, sect. 1 (ed. G.E.M. Anscombe and G.H. von Wright, 1969). Opening sentence of response to a lecture by the philosopher G.E. Moore, which countered Hegelianism on the grounds of common sense. Moore famously declared, as he raised his hand, 'I *know* this is a hand.'

26 It would strike me as ridiculous to want to doubt the existence of Napoleon; but if someone doubted the existence of the earth 150 years ago, perhaps I should be more willing to listen, for now he is doubting our whole system of evidence.

ibid. sect. 185

27 Knowledge is in the end based on acknowledgement.

ibid. sect. 378

# (Sir) P.G. Wodehouse (1881–1975)

BRITISH NOVELIST

Full name Pelham Grenville Wodehouse. Called 'English literature's performing flea' by SEAN O'CASEY, he was the author of bestselling humorous novels which centred on the upper-class world of Bertie Wooster and his valet Jeeves. After internment by the Germans in the Second World War, he made a series of radio broadcasts from Berlin which led to accusations of Nazi collusion. He subsequently lived in America, taking US citizenship in 1955.

1 It is a good rule in life never to apologize. The right sort of people do not want apologies, and the wrong sort take a mean advantage of them.

The narrator in *The Man Upstairs*, 'The Man Upstairs' (1914)

2 'What ho!' I said.
'What ho!' said Motty.
'What ho! What ho!'
'What ho! What ho! What ho!'
After that it seemed rather difficult to go on with the conversation.

Exchange between Motty (Lord Pershore) and Wooster, in *My Man Jeeves*, 'Jeeves and the Unbidden Guest' (1919)

3 In this matter of shimmering into rooms the chappie is rummy to a degree . . . He moves from point to point with as little uproar as a jellyfish.

Bertie Wooster of Jeeves, in ibid., 'Jeeves and the Hard-Boiled Egg'

4 What a queer thing Life is! So unlike anything else, don't you know, if you see what I mean.

Bertie Wooster, in ibid. 'Rallying Round Old George'

5 Chumps always make the best husbands. When you marry, Sally, grab a chump. Tap his forehead first, and if it rings solid, don't hesitate. All the unhappy marriages come from the husbands having brains. What good are brains to a man? They only unsettle him.

Miss Winch, in *The Adventures of Sally*, ch. 10 (1922)

6 [He] was a tubby little chap who looked as if he had been poured into his clothes and had forgotten to say 'When!'

*Very Good, Jeeves!*, 'Jeeves and the Impending Doom' (1930)

# Terry Wogan (b. 1938)

IRISH BROADCASTER

Associated with the BBC since 1965, he is known for his cosily irreverent humour in such radio programmes as *The Terry Wogan Show* (1969–72) and *The Breakfast Show* (1972–84) and for hosting on television the annual *Eurovision Song Contest* and the *Children in Need* telethon.

1 Television contracts the imagination and radio expands it.

Quoted in the *Observer* 30 December 1984

2 All popular radio is based on repetition and familiarity. It's almost that the listener knows what you're going to say before you say it . . . If you did it for long enough, you wouldn't have to say anything at all.

*Independent on Sunday* 15 March 1998

# Christa Wolf (b. 1929)

GERMAN NOVELIST

With the publication of *Moscow Novella* (1961) and *The Divided Heaven* (1963) she came to be regarded as one of East Germany's foremost writers. Her fiction frequently depicted the effects of life in a totalitarian regime and her best known book *The Quest for Christa T.* (1968) was originally banned in her country.

1 The ingenuous open heart preserves one's ability to say 'I' to a stranger, until a moment comes when this strange 'I' returns and enters into 'me' again. Then at one blow the heart is captive, one is pre-possessed; that much can be foretold.

*The Quest for Christa T.*, ch. 1 (1968, transl. 1982)

2 *To become oneself, with all one's strength.* Difficult. A bomb, a speech, a rifle shot – and the world can look a different place. And then where is this 'self'?

ibid. ch. 17

3 The most beautiful thing under the sun is being under the sun.

*A Model Childhood*, ch. 8 (1976)

# Naomi Wolf (b. 1962)

US AUTHOR

Her critique of the stereotypes imposed on women *The Beauty Myth* (1990) inspired FAY WELDON to hail her as an 'early heroine of Woman's World, Nineties Style', while her second book *Fire With Fire* (1993) argued in favour of 'power feminism' over 'victim feminism'.

1 'Beauty' is a currency system like the gold standard. Like any economy, it is determined by politics, and in the modern age in the West it is the last, best belief system that keeps male dominance intact.
*The Beauty Myth*, 'The Beauty Myth' (1990)

2 To ask women to become unnaturally thin is to ask them to relinquish their sexuality.
ibid. 'Hunger'

3 Pain is real when you get other people to believe in it. If no one believes in it but you, your pain is madness or hysteria or your own unfeminine inadequacy. Women have learned to submit to pain by hearing authority figures – doctors, priests, psychiatrists – tell us that what we feel is not pain.
ibid. 'Violence'

# Humbert Wolfe (1885–1940)

BRITISH POET AND AUTHOR

As a civil servant he rose to become Deputy Secretary at the Ministry of Labour (1938–40). His writings include *London Sonnets* (1919), *Lampoons* (1925) and *Requiem* (1927) as well as studies of Tennyson, Shelley and George Moore.

1 You cannot hope
   to bribe or twist
   (thank God!) the
   British journalist.

   But, seeing what
   the man will do
   unbribed, there's
   no occasion to.
*The Uncelestial City*, bk 1, 'Over the Fire' (1930)

# Thomas Wolfe (1900–38)

US AUTHOR

His small output includes *Look Homeward, Angel* (1929), its sequel *Of Time and the River* (1935) and the semi-autobiographical *The Web and The Rock* (1939), edited and published posthumously. According to WILLIAM FAULKNER, 'He tried to do the greatest of the impossible – to reduce all human experience to literature.'

1 Making the world safe for hypocrisy.
Luke, in *Look Homeward, Angel*, pt 3, ch. 36 (1929). Referring to the naval base at Norfolk. See also WOODROW WILSON 5.

2 If a man has a talent and cannot use it, he has failed. If he has a talent and uses only half of it, he has partly failed. If he has a talent and learns somehow to use the whole of it, he has gloriously succeeded, and won a satisfaction and a triumph few men ever know.
*The Web and the Rock*, ch. 29 (1939)

3 [Of New York] It was a cruel city, but it was a lovely one, a savage city, yet it had such tenderness, a bitter, harsh, and violent catacomb of stone and steel and tunneled rock, slashed savagely with light, and roaring, fighting a constant ceaseless warfare of men and of machinery; and yet it was so sweetly and so delicately pulsed, as full of warmth, of passion, and of love, as it was full of hate.
ibid. ch. 30. Monk's vision of New York.

4 There had been a time on earth when poets had been young and dead and famous – and were men. But now the poet as the tragic child of grandeur and destiny had changed. The child of genius was a woman, now, and the man was gone.
ibid. Referring to the poetess Rosalind Bailey.

# Tom Wolfe (b. 1931)

US AUTHOR AND JOURNALIST

A writer on the *Washington Post* and *New York Herald Tribune* (1959–66), he was a major figure in the New Journalism with his portrait of 1960s counter-culture, *The Electric Kool-Aid Acid Test* (1968) and such essays as 'Radical Chic and Mau-Mauing the Flak-Catchers' (1970), in which he coined the phrase 'radical chic'. His biggest success was his fable of New York in the 1980s, *The Bonfire of the Vanities* (1987, filmed 1990).

1 [On the hippy stereotype] His hair has the long jesuschrist look. He is wearing the costume clothes. But most of all, he now has a very tolerant and therefore withering attitude toward all those who are still struggling in the old activist political ways ... while he, with the help of psychedelic chemicals, is exploring the infinite regions of human consciousness.
*The Electric Kool-Aid Acid Test* (1968), ch. 26

2 Radical Chic, after all, is only radical in Style; in its heart it is part of Society and its traditions – Politics, like Rock, Pop, and Camp, has its uses.
*Radical Chic and Mau-Mauing the Flak-Catchers* (1970). Originally publ. as essay in *New York* 8 June 1970.

3 All these years, in short, I had assumed that in art, if nowhere else, seeing is believing. Well – how very short-sighted! ... I had gotten it backward all along. Not 'seeing is believing', you ninny, but 'believing is seeing', for *Modern Art has become completely literary: the paintings and other works exist only to illustrate the text.*
*The Painted Word*, Introduction (1975)

4 The notion that the public accepts or rejects anything in Modern Art, the notion that the public scorns, ignores, fails to comprehend, allows to wither, crushes the spirit of, or commits any other crime against Art or any individual artist is merely a romantic fiction, a bittersweet Trilby sentiment. The game is completed and the trophies distributed long before the public knows what has happened.
ibid. ch. 2

5 We are now in the Me Decade – seeing the upward roll of ... the third great religious wave in American history.
*Mauve Gloves and Madmen, Clutter and Vine*, 'The Me Decade and the Third Great Awakening' (1976)

6 The idea was to prove at every foot of the way up that you were one of the elected and anointed ones who had *the right stuff* and could move higher and higher and even – ultimately, God willing, one day – that you might be able to join that special few at the very top, that elite who had the capacity to bring tears to men's eyes, the very Brotherhood of the Right Stuff itself.
*The Right Stuff*, ch. 2 (1979). Of pilots and astronauts on the NASA training programme.

7 A cult is a religion with no political power.
*In Our Time*, ch. 2, 'Jonestown' (1980)

8 It is very comforting to believe that leaders who do terrible things are, in fact, mad. That way, all we have to do is make sure we don't put psychotics in high places and we've got the problem solved.
ibid.

9 [Of Andy Warhol] He was the person who created Attitude. Before Warhol, in artistic circles, there was Ideology – you took a stance against the crassness of American life. Andy Warhol turned that on its head, and created an

attitude. And that attitude was 'It's so awful, it's wonderful. It's so tacky, let's wallow in it.'

Quoted in *Rolling Stone* 9 April 1987. Comment made a few days after WARHOL's death.

10 On Wall Street he and a few others – how many? – three hundred, four hundred, five hundred? – had become precisely that . . . Masters of the Universe.

*The Bonfire of the Vanities*, ch. 1 (1987). Referring to bond dealer Sherman McCoy and his colleagues.

11 The phrase pops into his head at that very instant: *social X-rays* . . . They keep themselves so thin, they look like X-ray pictures . . . You can see lamplight through their bones . . . while they're chattering about *interiors* and *landscape gardening* . . . and encasing their scrawny shanks in metallic Lycra tubular tights for their Sports Training classes.

ibid.

12 A liberal is a conservative who has been arrested.

ibid. ch. 24

13 Pornography was the great vice of the Seventies; plutography – the graphic depiction of the acts of the rich – is the great vice of the Eighties.

Interview in the *Sunday Times* 10 January 1988

14 To a man of sixty . . . one of the grimmest reminders of the Reaper's approach comes when his doctors, the people who have attended to his body for decades, begin retiring on him . . . or dying on him . . . or both.

*A Man in Full*, ch. 10 (1998)

15 You don't need to worry about what an incalculable luxury literature is. Entire civilizations are founded without any literature at all and without anybody missing it. It's only later on when there's a big enough class of indolent drones to write the stuff and read the stuff that you have literature.

Lewis Gardner, in ibid. ch. 28

## Kenneth Wolstenholme (b. 1920)

BRITISH SPORTS COMMENTATOR

Having joined the BBC in 1946, he became the channel's leading football commentator during the 1950s and 1960s, notably for *Match of the Day*.

1 They think it's all over – it is now.

Television broadcast from Wembley, 30 July 1966, BBC. Commentary in closing seconds of World Cup Final, at which England beat West Germany 4–2 in extra time.

## Virginia Woolf (1882–1941)

BRITISH NOVELIST, CRITIC AND ESSAYIST

A central figure of the Bloomsbury Group, she founded the Hogarth Press in 1917 with her husband Leonard Woolf. Her own writings were often ground-breaking, for example *To the Lighthouse* (1927) and *The Waves* (1931), which use stream of consciousness, and *Orlando* (1928), whose androgynous protagonist is portrayed over four centuries. EDITH SITWELL considered her 'a beautiful little knitter', while Harold Laski accused her of organizing her own immortality: 'Every phrase and gesture was studied . . . when she said something a little out of the ordinary, she wrote it down herself in a notebook.' Plagued by mental illness all her life, she committed suicide.

1 Life is not a series of gig lamps symmetrically arranged; life is a luminous halo, a semi-transparent envelope surrounding us from the beginning of consciousness to the end.

'Modern Fiction', publ. as 'Modern Novels' in *The Times Literary Supplement* 10 April 1919, repr. in *The Common Reader* (1925)

2 The good diarist writes either for himself alone or for a posterity so distant that it can safely hear every secret and justly weigh every motive. For such an audience there is need neither of affectation nor of restraint. Sincerity is what they ask, detail, and volume; skill with the pen comes in conveniently, but brilliance is not necessary; genius is a hindrance even; and should you know your business and do it manfully, posterity will let you off mixing with great men, reporting famous affairs, or having lain with the first ladies in the land.

'Rambling Round Evelyn', publ. in *The Times Literary Supplement* 28 October 1920 as review of *The Early Life and Education of John Evelyn 1620–1641*, repr. in ibid.

3 The eyes of others our prisons; their thoughts our cages.

*Monday or Tuesday*, 'An Unwritten Novel' (1921)

4 But when the self speaks to the self, who is speaking? – the entombed soul, the spirit driven in, in, in to the central catacomb; the self that took the veil and left the world – a coward perhaps, yet somehow beautiful, as it flits with its lantern restlessly up and down the dark corridors.

ibid.

5 One likes people much better when they're battered down by a prodigious siege of misfortune than when they triumph.

Journal entry, 13 August 1921, publ. in *The Diary of Virginia Woolf*, vol. 1 (ed. Anne O. Bell, 1978)

6 Each had his past shut in him like the leaves of a book known to him by heart; and his friends could only read the title, James Spalding, or Charles Budgeon, and the passengers going the opposite way could read nothing at all – save 'a man with a red moustache', 'a young man in grey smoking a pipe'.

*Jacob's Room*, ch. 5 (1922). Referring to passengers on an omnibus.

7 It's not catastrophes, murders, deaths, diseases, that age and kill us; it's the way people look and laugh, and run up the steps of omnibuses.

ibid. ch. 9

8 Never did I read such tosh. As for the first two chapters we will let them pass, but the 3rd 4th 5th 6th – merely the scratching of pimples on the body of the bootboy at Claridges.

Letter to LYTTON STRACHEY, 24 August 1922, publ. in *Letters*, vol. 2 (ed. Nigel Nicolson, 1976). Referring to *Ulysses* by JAMES JOYCE.

9 We are nauseated by the sight of trivial personalities decomposing in the eternity of print.

'The Modern Essay', publ. in *The Times Literary Supplement* 30 November 1922 as 'Modern Essays', repr. in *The Common Reader* (1925). Referring to inferior essayists.

10 A good essay must have this permanent quality about it; it must draw its curtain round us, but it must be a curtain that shuts us in not out.

ibid.

11 We all indulge in the strange, pleasant process called thinking, but when it comes to saying, even to someone opposite, what we think, then how little we are able to convey! The phantom is through the mind and out of the window before we can lay salt on its tail, or slowly sinking and returning to the profound darkness which it has lit up momentarily with a wandering light.

'Montaigne', publ. in *The Times Literary Supplement* 31 January 1924 as review of *Essays of Montaigne*, repr. in ibid.

12 The man who is aware of himself is henceforward independent; and he is never bored, and life is only too short, and he is steeped through and through with a profound yet temperate happiness. He alone lives, while other people, slaves of ceremony, let life slip past them in a kind of dream.

ibid.

13 Once conform, once do what other people do because

they do it, and a lethargy steals over all the finer nerves and faculties of the soul. She becomes all outer show and inward emptiness; dull, callous, and indifferent.

ibid.

14  If we didn't live venturously, plucking the wild goat by the beard, and trembling over precipices, we should never be depressed, I've no doubt; but already should be faded, fatalistic and aged.

Journal entry, 2 August 1924, publ. in *The Diary of Virginia Woolf*, vol. 2 (ed. Anne O. Bell, 1978)

15  [On poetry] I want the concentration and the romance, and the words all glued together, fused, glowing: have no time to waste any more on prose.

ibid. 15 August 1924

16  Humour is the first of the gifts to perish in a foreign tongue.

*The Common Reader*, 'On Not Knowing Greek' (1925)

17  Those comfortably padded lunatic asylums which are known, euphemistically, as the stately homes of England.

ibid. 'Lady Dorothy Nevill'

18  *Middlemarch*, the magnificent book which with all its imperfections is one of the few English novels for grown-up people.

ibid. 'George Eliot'

19  The word-coining genius, as if thought plunged into a sea of words and came up dripping.

'Notes on an Elizabethan Play', publ. in *The Times Literary Supplement* 5 March 1925, repr. in ibid. Referring to the merits of Elizabethan drama.

20  Really I don't like human nature unless all candied over with art.

Journal entry, 13 May 1926, publ. in *The Diary of Virginia Woolf*, vol. 3 (ed. Anne O. Bell, 1980)

21  [On cinema] A strange thing has happened – while all the other arts were born naked, this, the youngest, has been born fully-clothed. It can say everything before it has anything to say. It is as if the savage tribe, instead of finding two bars of iron to play with, had found scattering the seashore fiddles, flutes, saxophones, trumpets, grand pianos by Erhard and Bechstein, and had begun with incredible energy, but without knowing a note of music, to hammer and thump upon them all at the same time.

'The Cinema', publ. in *Nation and Athenaeum* 3 July 1926, repr. in *The Captain's Death Bed* (1950)

22  Arnold Bennett says that the horror of marriage lies in its 'dailiness.' All acuteness of relationship is rubbed away by this. The truth is more like this: life – say 4 days out of 7 – becomes automatic; but on the 5th day a bead of sensation (between husband and wife) forms which is all the fuller and more sensitive because of the automatic customary unconscious days on either side. That is to say the year is marked by moments of great intensity. Hardy's 'moments of vision.' How can a relationship endure for any length of time except under these conditions?

Journal entry, 2 August 1926, publ. in *The Diary of Virginia Woolf*, vol. 3 (ed. Anne O. Bell, 1980)

23  For love . . . has two faces; one white, the other black; two bodies; one smooth, the other hairy. It has two hands, two feet, two tails, two, indeed, of every member and each one is the exact opposite of the other. Yet, so strictly are they joined together that you cannot separate them.

*Orlando*, ch. 2 (1928)

24  Different though the sexes are, they inter-mix. In every human being a vacillation from one sex to the other takes place, and often it is only the clothes that keep the male or female likeness, while underneath the sex is the very opposite of what it is above.

ibid. ch. 4

25  Every secret of a writer's soul, every experience of his life, every quality of his mind is written large in his works.

ibid.

26  Where the Mind is biggest, the Heart, the Senses, Magnanimity, Charity, Tolerance, Kindliness, and the rest of them scarcely have room to breathe.

ibid.

27  At 46 one must be a miser; only have time for essentials.

Journal entry, 22 March 1928, publ. in *The Diary of Virginia Woolf*, vol. 3 (ed. Anne O. Bell, 1980)

28  The first duty of a lecturer – to hand you after an hour's discourse a nugget of pure truth to wrap up between the pages of your notebooks and keep on the mantelpiece for ever.

*A Room of One's Own*, ch. 1 (1929). The book was originally a paper read to women students at Cambridge University.

29  A woman must have money and a room of her own if she is to write fiction.

ibid.

30  One cannot think well, love well, sleep well, if one has not dined well.

ibid.

31  Why are women . . . so much more interesting to men than men are to women?

ibid. ch. 2

32  Women have served all these centuries as looking-glasses possessing the magic and delicious power of reflecting the figure of man at twice its natural size.

ibid.

33  Fiction is like a spider's web, attached ever so lightly perhaps, but still attached to life at all four corners. Often the attachment is scarcely perceptible.

ibid. ch. 3

34  Publicity in women is detestable. Anonymity runs in their blood. The desire to be veiled still possesses them. They are not even now as concerned about the health of their fame as men are, and, speaking generally, will pass a tombstone or a signpost without feeling an irresistible desire to cut their names on it.

ibid.

35  Who shall measure the heat and violence of the poet's heart when caught and tangled in a woman's body?

ibid.

36  The history of men's opposition to women's emancipation is more interesting perhaps than the story of that emancipation itself.

ibid.

37  It is the nature of the artist to mind excessively what is said about him. Literature is strewn with the wreckage of men who have minded beyond reason the opinions of others.

ibid.

38  Masterpieces are not single and solitary births; they are the outcome of many years of thinking in common, of thinking by the body of the people, so that the experience of the mass is behind the single voice.

ibid. ch. 4

39  Some collaboration has to take place in the mind between the woman and the man before the art of creation can be accomplished. Some marriage of opposites has to be consummated. The whole of the mind must lie wide open if we are to get the sense that the writer is communicating his experience with perfect fullness.

ibid. ch. 6

40  [Of Queen Victoria] Knew her own mind. But the mind

radically commonplace, only its inherited force, and cumulative sense of power, making it remarkable.

Journal entry, 27 December 1930, publ. in *The Diary of Virginia Woolf*, vol. 3 (ed. Anne O. Bell, 1980)

41 On the outskirts of every agony sits some observant fellow who points.

Bernard, in *The Waves* (1931)

42 Things have dropped from me. I have outlived certain desires; I have lost friends, some by death ... others through sheer inability to cross the street.

Bernard, in ibid.

43 Against you I will fling myself, unvanquished and un-yielding, O Death!

Bernard, in ibid. Final words of the novel, chosen by Leonard Woolf as Virginia's epitaph at her burial-place and former home, Monk's House, Rodmell, Sussex.

44 Now, aged 50, I'm just poised to shoot forth quite free straight and undeflected my bolts whatever they are.

Journal entry, 2 October 1932, publ. in *The Diary of Virginia Woolf*, vol. 4 (ed. Anne O. Bell, 1982)

45 One has to secrete a jelly in which to slip quotations down people's throats – and one always secretes too much jelly.

Letter 4 July 1938, publ. in *Leave the Letters Till We're Dead: Letters*, vol. 6 (ed. Nigel Nicolson, 1980)

46 We can best help you to prevent war not by repeating your words and following your methods but by finding new words and creating new methods.

*Three Guineas* (1938)

47 If you insist upon fighting to protect me, or 'our' country, let it be understood soberly and rationally between us that you are fighting to gratify a sex instinct which I cannot share; to procure benefits which I have not shared and probably will not share.

ibid.

48 That great Cathedral space which was childhood.

'A Sketch of the Past', written 1939–40, publ. in *Moments of Being* (ed. Jeanne Schulkind, 1976)

49 There can be no two opinions as to what a highbrow is. He is the man or woman of thoroughbred intelligence who rides his mind at a gallop across country in pursuit of an idea.

*The Death of the Moth*, 'Middlebrow' (1942)

50 The middlebrow is the man, or woman, of middlebred intelligence who ambles and saunters now on this side of the hedge, now on that, in pursuit of no single object, neither art itself nor life itself, but both mixed indistinguishably, and rather nastily, with money, fame, power, or prestige.

ibid.

## Alexander Woollcott (1887–1943)
US COLUMNIST AND CRITIC

A flamboyant personality, described by *Life* magazine as 'testy as a wasp and much more poisonous', he was theatre critic of *The New York Times* (1914–22) and the *New York World* (1925–8) and a broadcaster in his show *Town Crier* (1929–42). He was a prominent figure of the Algonquin Round Table.

1 All the things I really like to do are either immoral, illegal, or fattening.

*The Knock at the Stage Door* (1933)

## Derek Worlock (1920–96)
BRITISH ROMAN CATHOLIC CLERIC

He became Archbishop of Liverpool in 1976 and worked in close cooperation with his Anglican counterpart David Sheppard, with whom he wrote *Better Together* (1988) and *Christ in the Wilderness* (1990).

1 [On the homeless] I am my brother's keeper, and he's sleeping pretty rough these days.

*Observer* 16 December 1990

## (Sir) Peregrine Worsthorne (b. 1923)
BRITISH JOURNALIST

He had a long association with the *Daily Telegraph* (1953–89) becoming Assistant Editor from 1961. His publications include *Peregrinations* (1980) and *By the Right* (1987).

1 The principal purpose of politics [is] the evolution and maintenance of a securely established ruling class with a justified sense of its own honourable superiority.

Quoted in *New Socialist* November 1985, repr. in *We, the Nation*, ch. 3 (1995) by A.J. Davies

## Frank Lloyd Wright (1869–1959)
US ARCHITECT

At first designing simple prairie houses such as his own home Taleisin East (1925), he specialized in geometric forms utilizing modern engineering technology. Among his best known buildings are the Imperial Hotel in Tokyo (1920, now demolished) and the Guggenheim Museum, New York (1959), based on a spiral ramp.

1 The physician can bury his mistakes, but the architect can only advise his client to plant vines – so they should go as far as possible from home to build their first buildings.

*The New York Times Magazine* 4 October 1953

2 The screech and mechanical uproar of the big city turns the citified head, fills citified ears – as the song of birds, wind in the trees, animal cries, or as the voices and songs of his loved ones once filled his heart. He is sidewalk-happy.

*The Living City*, pt 1, 'Earth' (1958)

3 All fine architectural values are human values, else not valuable.

ibid. pt 3, 'Recapitulation'

4 I find it hard to believe that the machine would go into the creative artist's hand even were that magic hand in true place. It has been too far exploited by industrialism and science at expense to art and true religion.

ibid. pt 5, 'Night is but a Shadow Cast by the Sun'

## Allie Wrubel (1905–73)
US COMPOSER

Active from the 1920s to the 1950s, he wrote both music and lyrics, contributing to many films and collaborating with MORT DIXON. His numerous songs include 'The Lady in Red' (1935), 'Music, Maestro Please' (1938) and 'Zip A Dee Doo Dah' (1946). During the late 1940s he worked for Walt Disney studios.

1 Zip a dee doo dah,
Zip a dee ay,
My, oh my, what a wonderful day.

'Zip A Dee Doo Dah' (song, with music by Ray Gilbert), in *Song of the South* (film musical, 1946). The song received an Academy Award.

## Woodrow Wyatt (1918–97)
BRITISH JOURNALIST

Baron Wyatt of Weeford. Known as a bon vivant, raconteur and 'Wodehousian eccentric', he was associated with the *Daily Mirror* (1965–73) and the *Sunday Mirror* (1973–83) and later wrote for *The Times*. He was also a Labour MP (1945–55, 1959–70) but later became an ardent supporter of MARGARET THATCHER.

1 **A man falls in love through his eyes, a woman through her ears.**

*To the Point*, 'The Ears Have It' (1981).Wyatt elaborated, apropos of women, 'what is said to them and what they believe about a man's status is usually more important than the superficiality of good looks.'

# Tammy Wynette (1942–98)
US COUNTRY SINGER

Originally named Virginia Wynette Pugh. From 1966, her partnership with producer Billy Sherrill, co-writer of her massive hit 'Stand By Your Man', made her country music's most successful female singer. In 1969 she married and made records with country superstar George Jones, but his drinking and abuse led to divorce and provided more material for her plaintive ballads.

1 **Our D-I-V-O-R-C-E becomes final today**
   **Me and Little Joe will be going away**
   **I love you both and this will be pure H-E double L for me.**
   **Oh, I wish that we could stop this D-I-V-O-R-C-E.**
   'D-I-V-O-R-C-E' (song, 1968, written with Bobby Braddock and Curly Putman) on the album *Greatest Hits* (1969)

2 **Sometimes it's hard to be a woman**
   **Giving all your love to just one man.**
   'Stand by Your Man' (song, 1968, written with Billy Sherrill) on ibid. Opening lines of song.

3 **Stand by your man.**
   **Give him two arms to cling to**
   **And something warm to come to.**
   ibid.

# Stefan Wyszynski (1901–81)
POLISH ECCLESIASTIC

He was from 1948 Archbishop of Warsaw and Gniezno and Primate of Poland, and was appointed a cardinal in 1952. After being imprisoned (1953–6) he concluded an agreement with the communist government allowing religious instruction in state schools. During the 1970s he lent his support to opposition movements such as Solidarity.

1 **The Poles do not know how to hate, thank God.**
   Quoted in the *Observer* 8 June 1986

## R.J. Yeatman see W.C. SELLAR and R.J. YEATMAN

# William Butler Yeats (1865–1939)
IRISH POET AND PLAYWRIGHT

In the forefront of Ireland's cultural and literary revival, he was the author of plays such as *The Land of Heart's Desire* (1894) and others written for Dublin's Abbey Theatre, which he helped to found in 1904. His poems, often steeped in symbolism and mysticism, include the collections *Wild Swans at Coole* (1919) and *The Tower* (1928). He was a senator of the Irish Free State (1922–8) and in 1923 was awarded the Nobel Prize for Literature. See also W.H. AUDEN 16.

1   In dreams begins responsibility.
    *Responsibilities*, Epigraph (1914)

2   I think it better that in times like these
    A poet's mouth be silent, for in truth
    We have no gift to set a statesman right.
    'On Being Asked for a War Poem', written 1915, publ. in *The Wild Swans at Coole* (1919). Opening lines of poem.

3   Too long a sacrifice
    Can make a stone of the heart.
    O when may it suffice?
    'Easter 1916', written 1916, publ. in *Michael Robartes and the Dancer* (1921)

4   I write it out in a verse –
    MacDonagh and MacBride
    And Connolly and Pearse
    Now and in time to be,
    Wherever green is worn,
    Are changed, changed utterly:
    A terrible beauty is born.
    ibid. The names are of leaders of the Easter Rising who were executed by the British.

5   Some burn damp faggots, others may consume
    The entire combustible world in one small room
    As though dried straw, and if we turn about
    The bare chimney is gone black out
    Because the work had finished in that flare.
    'In Memory of Major Robert Gregory', st. 11, written 1918, publ. in *The Wild Swans at Coole* (1919)

6   I know that I shall meet my fate
    Somewhere among the clouds above;
    Those that I fight I do not hate,
    Those that I guard I do not love.
    'An Irish Airman Foresees His Death', written 1918, publ. in ibid. Opening lines of poem.

7   My country is Kiltartan Cross;
    My countrymen Kiltartan's poor.
    ibid.

8   I balanced all, brought all to mind,
    The years to come seemed waste of breath,
    A waste of breath the years behind
    In balance with this life, this death.
    ibid.

9   Things fall apart; the centre cannot hold;
    Mere anarchy is loosed upon the world,
    The blood-dimmed tide is loosed, and everywhere
    The ceremony of innocence is drowned;
    The best lack all conviction, while the worst
    Are full of passionate intensity.
    'The Second Coming', written 1919, publ. in *Michael Robartes and the Dancer* (1921)

10  Now I know
    That twenty centuries of stony sleep
    Were vexed to nightmare by a rocking cradle,
    And what rough beast, its hour come round at last,

Slouches towards Bethlehem to be born?

ibid. Closing lines of poem.

11 An intellectual hatred is the worst.

'A Prayer for My Daughter', written 1919, publ. in ibid.

12 I agree about Shaw – he is haunted by the mystery he flouts. He is an atheist who trembles in the haunted corridor.

Letter to George Russell (AE), 1 July 1921, publ. in *The Letters of W.B. Yeats* (ed. Allan Wade, 1954). Yeats expressed ambiguous views towards SHAW in his *Autobiography* (1938): 'We all hated him with the left side of our heads, while admiring him immensely with the right side.'

13 A shudder in the loins engenders there
The broken wall, the burning roof and tower
And Agamemnon dead.

'Leda and the Swan', written 1923, publ. in *The Tower* (1928)

14 We make out of the quarrel with others, rhetoric, but of the quarrel with ourselves, poetry.

'Anima Hominis', sect. 5, publ. in *Essays* (1924)

15 An aged man is but a paltry thing,
A tattered coat upon a stick, unless
Soul clap its hands and sing, and louder sing
For every tatter in its mortal dress.

'Sailing to Byzantium', written 1926, publ. in *The Tower* (1928)

16 After Stéphane Mallarmé, after Paul Verlaine, after Gustave Moreau, after Puvis de Chavannes, after our own verse, after all our subtle colour and nervous rhythm, after the faint mixed tints of Conder, what more is possible? After us the Savage God.

*Autobiographies*, 'The Trembling of the Veil', bk 4, sect. 20 (1926). A. ALVAREZ took from these lines the title for his study on suicide, *The Savage God* (1971).

17 Englishmen are babes in philosophy and so prefer faction-fighting to the labour of its unfamiliar thought.

Letter, 24 March 1927, publ. in *The Letters of W.B. Yeats* (ed. Allan Wade, 1954)

18 Nor dread nor hope attend
A dying animal;
A man awaits his end
Dreading and hoping all.

'Death', written 1927, publ. in *The Winding Stair and Other Poems* (1933). Opening lines of poem.

19 The innocent and the beautiful
Have no enemy but time.

'In Memory of Eva Gore-Booth and Con Markiewicz', written 1927, publ. in ibid.

20 Swift has sailed into his rest;
Savage indignation there
Cannot lacerate his breast.
Imitate him if you dare,
World-besotted traveller; he
Served human liberty.

'Swift's Epitaph', written 1930, publ. in ibid.

21 The intellect of man is forced to choose
Perfection of the life, or of the work,
And if it take the second must refuse
A heavenly mansion, raging in the dark.

'The Choice', written 1931, publ. in ibid.

22 Out of Ireland have we come,
Great hatred, little room,
Maimed us at the start.
I carry from my mother's womb
A fanatic heart.

'Remorse for Intemperate Speech', written 1931, publ. in ibid.

23 A woman can be proud and stiff
When on love intent;
But love has pitched his mansion in

The place of excrement;
For nothing can be sole or whole
That has not been rent.

'Crazy Jane Talks with the Bishop', written 1931, publ. in *Words for Music Perhaps* (1932) and in ibid.

24 The ghost of Roger Casement
Is beating on the door.

'The Ghost of Roger Casement', written 1936, publ. in *New Poems* (1938)

25 You that would judge me, do not judge alone
This book or that, come to this hallowed place
Where my friends' portraits hang and look thereon;
Ireland's history in their lineaments trace;
Think where man's glory most begins and ends
And say my glory was I had such friends.

'The Municipal Gallery Re-visited', written 1937, publ. in ibid.

26 Irish poets, learn your trade,
Sing whatever is well made,
Scorn the sort now growing up
All out of shape from toe to top.

'Under Ben Bulben', sect. 5, written 1938, publ. in *Last Poems* (1939)

27 Cast your mind on other days
That we in coming days may be
Still the indomitable Irishry.

ibid.

28 Under bare Ben Bulben's head
In Drumcliff churchyard Yeats is laid.
An ancestor was rector there
Long years ago, a church stands near,
By the road an ancient cross.
No marble, no conventional phrase;
On limestone quarried near the spot
By his command these words are cut:
*Cast a cold eye*
*On life, on death*
*Horseman pass by!*

ibid. sect. 6. The last three lines are engraved on Yeats's gravestone at Drumcliff, north of Sligo.

29 Man can embody truth but he cannot know it.

Letter, 4 January 1939, publ. in *The Letters of W.B. Yeats* (ed. Allan Wade, 1954). Written three weeks before his death.

30 You know what the Englishman's idea of compromise is? He says, Some people say there is a God. Some people say there is no God. The truth probably lies somewhere between these two statements.

Quoted by Wilfred Whitten in *John O'London's Weekly* 24 June 1949

31 Accursed who brings to light of day
The writings I have cast away.

'Untitled', publ. in *The Variorum Edition of the Poems of W.B. Yeats*, 'Poems Not Included in the Definitive Edition' (ed. Peter Allt and Russell K. Alspach, 1957)

# Jack Yellen (1892–1991)
POLISH-BORN US LYRICIST

His songs were used in Broadway revues of the 1920s and musical films, such as *The King of Jazz* (1930). Among his numerous successes are 'All Aboard for Dixieland' (1913) and 'Ain't She Sweet' (1927). He also co-wrote songs for SOPHIE TUCKER, notably 'My Yiddisher Mama' (1925) and her signature tune 'I'm the Last of the Red-Hot Mamas' (1928).

1 Happy days are here again!
The skies above are clear again.
Let us sing a song of cheer again,
Happy days are here again!

'Happy Days Are Here Again' (song, 1929, with music by Milton Ager)

## Boris Yeltsin (b. 1931)

RUSSIAN POLITICIAN AND PRESIDENT

He was elected President of the Russian Federation in 1991 and supported GORBACHEV after the attempted coup two months later. He was re-elected in 1996 but resigned in 1999, after criticism over his handling of the Chechnya conflict and recurring ill health.

1 Let's not talk about Communism. Communism was just an idea, just pie in the sky.

Remark during a visit to the United States, quoted in the *Independent* 13 September 1989

2 Oh, where is the poet or bard who will compose an ode to Russian rumours? Thanks to the chronic shortage of truthful (or even false) information, our people live on rumours.

*Against the Grain*, ch. 9 (1990)

## Sergei Yesenin (1895–1925)

RUSSIAN POET

Calling himself the 'last poet of wooden Russia', his simple lyric poetry contrasted with his wild and dissolute lifestyle. He was the leading figure of the Russian Imagist group of poets and published his verse in *Confessions of a Hooligan* (1921) and *Moscow of the Taverns* (1924) among other works. He was briefly married (1922–3) to ISADORA DUNCAN and hanged himself after writing a suicide note in his own blood.

1 Have you seen it
Through the steppeland roaring
In misty lakeland rain
With its iron nostril snoring
On iron paws – the train?

'The Colt and the Train', sect. 3, publ. in *Prayers for the Dead* (1920, transl. Peter Tempest)

## Yevgeny Yevtushenko (b. 1933)

RUSSIAN POET

A spokesman for the post-Stalinist generation and for greater artistic freedom, he aroused controversy with the poems 'Babii Yar' (1961) and 'Stalin's Heirs' (1962). He travelled widely and gave his support to ALEXANDER SOLZHENITSYN on his arrest in 1974. His later works include *Love Poems* (1977) and the novel *Wild Berries* (1982).

1 Great twentieth century: sputnik century:
what an angst is in you, what wide perplexity!
You are a good century and a century of the pit,
cannibal century to the ideas you beget,
century of the angry young men's target.

'The Angries'(1959), publ. in *Collected Translations* (1996) by Edwin Morgan

2 Give me a mystery – just a plain and simple one – a mystery which is diffidence and silence, a slim little, barefoot mystery: give me a mystery – just one!

'Mysteries', st. 10 (1960), repr. in *The Heritage of Russian Verse* (ed. Dimitri Obolensky, 1965)

3 In my blood there is no Jewish blood.
In their callous rage,
All anti-Semites must hate me now as a Jew.
For that reason
I am a true Russian.

'Babii Yar' (1961), publ. in *The Poetry of Yevgeny Yevtushenko 1953 to 1965* (1966, transl. George Reavey). Last lines of poem describing the massacre of 96,000 Jews in the Ukraine by the Nazis. The poem, which caused controversy by implying that the Soviet régime was anti-Semitic, was used by Shostokovich as the centrepoint of his Thirteenth Symphony.

4 In any man who dies there dies with him
his first snow and kiss and fight . . .

Not people die but worlds die in them.

'People', publ. in *Selected Poems* (1962, transl. Robin Milner-Gulland and Peter Levi)

5 No, Stalin did not die.
He thinks that death can be fixed.
We removed
him
from the mausoleum.
But how do we remove Stalin
from Stalin's heirs?

'Stalin's Heirs', publ. in ibid.

6 Why is it that right-wing bastards always stand shoulder to shoulder in solidarity, while liberals fall out among themselves?

Quoted in the *Observer* 15 December 1991

## Anzia Yezierska (c. 1885–1970)

POLISH AUTHOR

After emigrating to the United States, she wrote short story collections, including *Hungry Hearts* (1920), and passionate books about Russian Jewish immigrants such as *Salome of the Tenements* (1922). Her autobiography, *Red Ribbon on a White Horse*, appeared in 1950.

1 Without comprehension, the immigrant would forever remain shut out – a stranger in America. Until America can release the heart as well as train the hand of the immigrant, he would forever remain driven back upon himself, corroded by the very richness of the unused gifts within his soul.

*Hungry Hearts and Other Stories*, pt 3 'How I Found America' (1920)

2 [Of Poland] Poverty was an ornament on a learned man like a red ribbon on a white horse.

Letter from Boruch Shlomoe Mayer to Anzia Yezierska, in *Red Ribbon on a White Horse*, ch. 9 (1950)

## Peter York (b. 1950)

BRITISH JOURNALIST

A 'style guru' regularly consulted for his views on social trends, he invented, together with Ann Barr, his colleague at *Harper's & Queen*, the label 'Sloane Ranger' to describe the typical younger readers of that magazine. *Peter York's The Eighties* (1996) similarly dissected the prevalent fashions of the 1980s. See also ANN BARR and PETER YORK.

1 You will not get anyone to admit belonging to the Sloanes. Some have even adopted mufti (jeans). But nobody need feel ashamed of being a Sloane Ranger.

'The Sloane Rangers', publ. in *Harpers & Queen* October 1975, repr. in *Style Wars* (1980)

2 If beauty isn't genius it usually signals at least a high level of animal cunning.

'Discontinued Models', publ. in *London Collection Magazine* April 1978, repr. in ibid.

3 In the Golden Age, that is the 1970s, the Phoney Wars were . . . style wars . . . Style became a weapon to forge your own legend. Style started to be accessible in a quite unprecedented way.

*Style Wars*, 'Style Wars' (1980)

4 NQOCD (not quite our class, darling) is an American joke. You might say 'He's a bit ordinaire . . .'

*The Official Sloane Ranger's Handbook*, 'The First Social Steps' (1982, written with ANN BARR)

5 Hooray Henries are aged between 18 and 30; main interest, getting drunk together; ambition, if ambitious: to get drunk enough to do some crazy thing which will go down in the Hooray annals as a Historic Act of Hilarity.

ibid. 'Hooray Henry'

6　One of the less agreeable aspects of the communications age was the message T-shirt. Lacking in charisma? Get a message, get a T-shirt, get a brand. We became a nation of sandwich boards.

*Interview in the Sunday Telegraph* 31 December 1995

7　The eighties are a long story about fun, greed and money. The eighties are what happened when what looked like the majority went out and took what the minority had previously thought of as its own. It was a bloodless revolution.

*Peter York's The Eighties*, ch. 1 (1996, written with Charles Jennings)

## Andrew Young (b. 1932)
US POLITICIAN AND DIPLOMAT

Ordained a Protestant minister, he was a close associate of MARTIN LUTHER KING and campaigned for desegregation and civil rights. He was elected to Congress as a Democrat (1973–7), the first African-American to represent Georgia for a century, and was subsequently US representative to the United Nations (1977–9) and Mayor of Atlanta (1981–9).

1　Once the Xerox copier was invented, diplomacy died.

*Playboy* July 1977

2　Moral power is probably best when it is not used. The less you use it the more you have.

*Observer* 8 September 1979

## Neil Young (b. 1945)
CANADIAN ROCK MUSICIAN

He has been a maverick in rock since the 1960s, both as an introspective singer/songwriter and high-octane guitarist. He played with Buffalo Springfield, as part of Crosby, Stills, Nash and Young, and subsequently with his 'house-band' Crazy Horse. *After the Goldrush* (1970), *Harvest* (1972) and *Harvest Moon* (1992) are among his most successful albums.

1　My my, hey hey
　Rock and roll is here to stay
　It's better to burn out
　Than to fade away
　My my, hey hey.

'My My, Hey Hey (Out of the Blue)' (song, written with Jeff Blackburn) on the album *Rust Never Sleeps* (1979). The words were quoted by KURT COBAIN in his suicide note.

## Marguerite Yourcenar (1903–87)
BELGIAN-BORN FRENCH NOVELIST

Original name Marguerite de Crayencour. She is known for her historical novels, for example *The New Eurydice* (1931) and *Memoirs of Hadrian* (1941), and for the long prose poem *Fires* (1939). In 1980 she became she first woman to be elected to the Académie Française.

1　Men who care passionately for women attach themselves at least as much to the temple and to the accessories of the cult as to their goddess herself.

*Memoirs of Hadrian*, 'Varius Multiplex Multi Formis' (1941, transl. 1954)

## Darryl Zanuck (1902–79)

US FILM PRODUCER

He was co-founder of Twentieth-Century Pictures in 1933 and became Vice-president when it merged with Fox to become Twentieth-Century Fox (1935–52). Among his film productions are *The Grapes of Wrath* (1940), *How Green Was My Valley* (1942) and *The Sound of Music* (1965). 'Success in movies boils down to three things,' he asserted, 'stories, stories, stories.'

1 If two men on the same job agree all the time, then one is unnecessary. If they disagree all the time, then both are useless.
Quoted in the *Observer* 23 October 1949

## Frank Zappa (1940–93)

US ROCK MUSICIAN

Known for his eclectic influences and caustically ironic style, he operated outside the mainstream using a variety of genres to satirize the modern era. *Freak Out* (1966) was the first of more than fifty albums he recorded, many with his band The Mothers of Invention, others with full orchestras. His film *200 Motels* (1971) was a sequence of surreal and irreverent sketches.

1 Most rock journalism is people who can't write, interviewing people who can't talk, for people who can't read.
*Chicago Tribune* 18 January 1978

2 Music, in performance, is a type of sculpture. The air in the performance is sculpted into something.
*The Real Frank Zappa Book*, ch. 8 (1989, written with Peter Occhiogrosso)

3 No change in musical style will survive unless it is accompanied by a change in clothing style. Rock is to dress up to.
ibid. ch. 9

4 The sad thing about the Sixties was the weak-mindedness of the so-called radicals and the way that they managed to get co-opted. I think one of the things that helped that happen was LSD. It's the only chemical known to mankind that will convert a hippy to a yuppie.
Quoted in the *Independent on Sunday* 26 January 1992

## Franco Zeffirelli (b. 1923)

ITALIAN THEATRE, OPERA AND FILM DIRECTOR

He has worked in all the major opera houses of the world and is noted for, among other productions, *Lucia di Lammermoor* at Covent Garden (1959) and *Falstaff* at the New York Metropolitan Opera House (1964). His films are characterized by a visual richness and include *The Taming of the Shrew* (1966) and *Romeo and Juliet* (1968).

1 I know that theatre people often have a very simplistic view of politics and tend to express very black and white patriotic sentiments but perhaps that is because we know the value of illusion, how it can help strengthen the weak, and stimulate the weary.
*Zeffirelli*, ch. 12 (1986)

2 It's hard for other people to realize just how easily we Florentines live with that past in our hearts and minds because it surrounds us in a very real way. To most people, the Renaissance is a few paintings on a gallery wall; to us it is more than an environment – it's an entire culture, a way of life.
ibid. ch. 14

## Zhang Jie (b. 1937)

CHINESE AUTHOR

He is known for his short stories, such as *As Long as Nothing Happens, Nothing Will* (1988), novellas, including *The Ark* (1984), and the novel, *Only One Sun* (1988).

1 What do a few lies on TV matter? They can be swallowed, digested and excreted, or follow people when they doze off to sink into oblivion.

Teacher Li, in 'What's Wrong with Him?' publ. in *As Long as Nothing Happens, Nothing Will* (1988)

# Fred Zinnemann (1907–97)

AUSTRIAN-BORN US FILM-MAKER

After directing shorts, he scored a success with *High Noon* in 1952 and went on to win Academy Awards for *From Here to Eternity* (1953) and *A Man for All Seasons* (1966). According to critic DAVID THOMSON, 'He had all the disposable qualities: diligence instead of imagination; more care than instinct; solemnity, but no wit.'

1 Dialogue is a necessary evil.

Interview in the *Independent on Sunday* 31 May 1992

# Alexander Zinoviev (b. 1922)

SOVIET PHILOSOPHER

He is known for *Yawning Heights* (1976), a surrealist work which looks forward to a 'great Future' of Soviet society. Later titles include *The Reality of Communism* (1981).

1 They were right. The Soviet régime is not the embodiment of evil as you think in the West. They have laws and I broke them. I hate tea and they love tea. Who is wrong?

*Sunday Times* 3 May 1981. Referring to his forced exile from the Soviet Union.

# Indexes

# List of Themes

# Achievement and Failure

| | | |
|---|---|---|
| Achievement | Losing | Reward |
| Adversity, hardship | Luck | Solutions |
| Awards | Misfortune | Struggle |
| Dissipation | Mistakes | Success |
| Failure | Motivation | Surrender |
| Fame, celebrity, stardom | Obscurity | Survival |
| Fans | Opportunity | Tragedy |
| Faults and fault-finding | Perfection | Trouble |
| Gaffes | Popularity | Victims |
| Glory | Potential | Villains |
| Greatness | Problems | Weakness |
| Hero-worship | Progress | Winning |
| Heroes | Reputation | |

# Actions, Circumstances, Events

| | | |
|---|---|---|
| Accidents | Circumstances | Disasters |
| Action | Coincidence | Events |
| Adventure | Consequences | Necessity |
| Change | Crises | |

# Belief and Opinion

| | | |
|---|---|---|
| Afterlife | Evil | Nihilism |
| Agnostics | Fairies | Opinion |
| Astrology | Faith | Pope |
| Atheism | Fanaticism | Prayer |
| Belief | Free will | Principles |
| Bias and prejudice | Fundamentalism | Preaching |
| Bible | Ghosts | Prophecy |
| Buddhism | God | Protestantism |
| Catholicism | Gods and goddesses | Puritans |
| Causes | Heaven, paradise | Religion |
| Certainty | Hell | Ritual |
| Christianity | Heresy | Sacred and profane |
| Church | Hypocrisy | Sacrifice |
| Church and society | Idealism | Saints |
| Churches and churchgoing | Immortality | Salvation |
| Credulity | Islam | Scepticism |
| Creeds | Jesus Christ | Sin |
| Cults | Judaism and the Jews | Soul |
| Cynicism | Judgment Day | Spirituality |
| Denial | Magic | Superstition |
| Destiny, fate | Martyrdom | Taboo |
| Devil | Miracles | Theology |
| Doctrine | Missionaries | Truth |
| Dogmatism | Morality | Uncertainty |
| Doubt | Mysticism | Visionaries |
| Ethics, values | Myth | |

# Body

| | | |
|---|---|---|
| Ability | Fertility | Obesity |
| Abortion | Genes | Orgasm |
| AIDS | Hair, baldness | Pain |
| Bodily functions | Health | Pornography |
| Body | Homoeopathy | Sleep |
| Breasts | Hygiene | Smells |
| Cancer | Illness | Teeth |
| Circumcision | Illness: convalescence | Thinness |
| Disability | Masturbation | Touch |
| Disease | Medicine | Virginity |
| Doctors | Menopause | Vision |
| Drugs | Menstruation | Voice |
| Drugs: addiction | Noses | |
| Faces | Nudity | |

# Business and Economics

| | | |
|---|---|---|
| Banking | Economy | Miserliness, thrift |
| Business | Free enterprise | Money |
| Business: women in business | Great Depression | Partnership |

Corporations
Contracts
Debt
Economics
Economists

Inflation
Insurance
Investment
Management
Marketing

Profit
Property
Selling
Stock market
Taxation

## Cosmos, Earth and Space

Aliens
Cosmos
Creation

Moon
Space
Universe

World
World: the end

## Culture and Media

Advertising
Aesthetics
Angry young men
Anthologies and dictionaries
Aphorisms and epigrams
Architects
Architecture
Art
Art: and commerce
Art: modern art
Art: and nature
Art: political art
Art: and society
Artists
Arts
Arts: and women
Auden, W. H.
Authenticity
Authorship
Autobiography
Avant-garde
Bach, J. S.
Bauhaus
BBC
Beatles
Beats
Biography
Books
Books: bestsellers
Books: classics
Cartoons and drawing
Censorship
Cinema
Cinema: film-makers
Cinema: Hollywood
Cinema: horror and suspense
Cinema: screenwriting
Cinema: sex and violence
Conductors
Crafts
Creativity
Criticism
Critics
Culture
Dada
Dance
Deconstruction
Design

Diaries
Disc-jockeys
Disney, Walt
Drama
Dylan, Bob
Editing
Editors
Eliot, T. S.
Fiction
Fiction: crime and thrillers
Fitzgerald, F. Scott
Hellman, Lillian
Hemingway, Ernest
Historians
Humanities
Imagery
Interviews
Jagger, Mick
James, Henry
Journalism, journalists
Joyce, James
Lawrence, D. H.
Lennon, John
Listening
Literary criticism
Literature
Literature: modern
Literature: and society
Media
McCartney, Paul
Miller, Henry
Minimalism
Modernism
Museums
Music
Music: blues
Music: composition
Music: country
Music: folk
Music: groups
Music: jazz
Music: pop and popular
Music: punk
Music: rap
Music: reggae
Music: rock, rock 'n' roll
Music: soul
Musical instruments

Muzak
Narrative, story-telling
News
Noise
Opera
Presley, Elvis
Press
Press barons
Painting
Patronage
Photography
Picasso, Pablo
Plagiarism
Poetry
Poets
Pop culture
Popular culture
Portraits
Post-modernism
Pottery
Pound, Ezra
Psychedelia
Publishing and publishers
Radio
Reading
Realism
Rushdie affair
Satire
Science fiction
Shakespeare, William
Shaw, George Bernard
Silence
Sitwells
Song
Stein, Gertrude
Stravinsky, Igor
Surrealism
Swift, Jonathan
Symbols, signs
Technique
Television
Theatre
Warhol, Andy
Wilde, Oscar
Writers
Writing
Yeats, W. B.

## Dress and Appearance

Appearance
Beauty
Colour
Cross-dressing
Dress

Elegance
Fashion, haute couture
Glamour
Hats
Jewellery

Make-up, cosmetics
Models and modelling
Shoes
Ugliness
Vanity

## Existence and Reality

Absurdity
Chaos, confusion

Futility
Illusion

Obvious
Possibility

Commonplace          Interpretation          Reality
Existence            Meaning
Facts                Mystery

## Food and Drink

Alcohol              Cocktails               Hunger
Alcohol: alcoholism  Coffee                  Lunch
Alcohol: drunkenness Cooking                 Restaurants
Bars, pubs and cafés Dinner parties          Tea
Beer                 Famine                  Toast
Breakfast            Food and eating         Wine

## Gifts and Giving

Aid                  Fundraising             Gratitude
Benefactors          Generosity              Ingratitude
Charity              Gifts and giving

## Humanity

Acceptance                          Experience                       Perseverance, obstinacy, resolve
Aggression                          Extroverts                       Personality
Altruism                            Favours                          Pessimism
Ambition                            Fear                             Posing, pretentiousness
Anger                               Foolishness                      Primitive life
Angst                               Gender                           Promises
Apathy, indifference, resignation   Girls                            Purity
Awareness                           Good deeds, goodness             Resentment
Banality                            Greed                            Respectability
Barbarism                           Grief                            Responsibility
Behaviour                           Guilt                            Role-playing
Blame                               Habit, routine                   Secrets
Boredom                             Happiness                        Self
Bores                               Honesty, integrity               Self-assertion, self-expression
Boys                                Honour                           Self-confidence
Candour                             Hope                             Self-deception
Caprice                             Horror, wonder, surprise         Self-destructiveness
Carelessness                        Human nature                     Self-fulfilment
Character                           Human race                       Self-image, self-portraits
Charisma                            Humiliation                      Self-improvement
Charm                               Humility                         Self-interest
Confession                          Hypocrisy                        Self-knowledge
Conservatism                        Identity                         Self-pity
Consistency                         Idleness, slacking               Self-promotion
Courage                             Imitation                        Self-respect
Cowardice                           Impulse                          Self-restraint
Cruelty                             Inertia                          Self-sacrifice
Crying                              Innocence, loss of innocence     Self-sufficiency
Cunning                             Introspection, self-absorption   Selfishness
Curiosity                           Laughter                         Sensitivity
Depression                          Mediocrity                       Sentimentality
Destructiveness                     Melancholy and despair           Shyness
Dignity                             Men                              Sincerity
Disappointment                      Men: masculinity                 Single-mindedness
Discipline                          Men: the new man                 Smiling
Dissatisfaction                     Men: and women                   Sorrow, unhappiness
Duty                                Misery                           Suffering
Eccentricity                        Modesty                          Virtue and vice
Effort                              Naïvete                          Vitality
Emotion                             Narcissism                       Wisdom
Enthusiasm                          Normality                        Wishing
Envy                                Optimism                         Women
Excellence                          Passion                          Women: and men
Excess                              Passivity
Excuses                             Patience

## Human Relations

Abuse, rudeness      Fellowship              Marriage: failed
Admiration           Flirting                Marriage: and love
Adultery             Seduction               Mothers
Advice               Forgiveness             Negotiation
Affection            Friends, friendship     Neighbours
Agreement            Frigidity               Opposition

Alienation
Ancestry
Apologies
Argument
Authority
Betrayal
Bisexuality
Chastity
Chivalry
Cliques
Communication
Competition
Compromise
Consensus
Conspiracy
Contradiction
Correspondence
Couples
Courtesy, manners, tact
Criticism
Defiance
Desire
Disagreement
Divorce
Eroticism
Families
Fathers

Godparents
Gossip
Guests
Hate
Heart, heartbreak
Homosexuality
Husbands
Infatuation
Inferiority
Influence
Intimacy
Involvement
Isolation
Jealousy
Kindness
Kissing
Lesbianism
Loneliness
Love
Love: ended
Love: and sex
Love affairs
Lovers
Loyalty
Lust
Malice, misanthropy
Marriage

Other people
Paranoia
Parents
Persuasion
Pity, compassion
Promiscuity
Prostitution
Quarrels
Relationships
Respect
Revenge
Romance
Sadism, masochism
Sex
Sexism
Sexual abuse, child abuse, incest
Sexual deviation
Sexuality
Singles
Solitude
Sons
Strangers
Sympathy
Tolerance, intolerance
Weddings
Widows
Wives

## Knowledge and Education

Academia
Cambridge University
Education
Examinations
Experts
Ignorance
Information
Knowledge

Learning
Libraries
Oxford University
Pedantry
Research
Scholars and scholarship
School
School: private schools

Students
Teachers
Training
Triviality
Unknown
University

## Law and Disorder

Capital punishment
Corporal punishment
Corruption
Crime and criminals
Delinquency
Detectives

Drugs: dealers and smugglers
Judges
Justice
Law and lawyers
Litigation
Murder

Police
Prison
Rape
Riots
Trials

## Life and Death

Adolescence, teens
Adulthood and maturity
Age
Age: the twenties
Age: the thirties
Age: the forties
Age: the fifties
Age: the sixties
Age: the seventies
Babies
Bereavement

Birth
Birth control
Birthdays and anniversaries
Childbirth
Childhood
Children
Dead
Death
Epitaphs
Funerals, burials, graves
Generation gap

Last words
Life
Life: purpose of life
Life and death
Live fast, die young
Middle age
Old age
Pregnancy
Retirement
Suicide
Youth

## Mind

Behaviourism
Brain
Concentration
Conscience
Consciousness and the
  subconscious
Daydreams
Dreams
Freud, Sigmund
Genius
Humanism

Inspiration
Intellect, intellectuals
Intelligence
Logic
Memory
Mental illness, madness
Metaphysics
Mind
Neurosis
Obsession
Openmindedness

Pressure and stress
Psyche
Psychiatric institutions
Psychiatry, pyschotherapy
Psychoanalysis
Psychology
Reason
Russell, Bertrand
Structuralism, post-structuralism
Stupidity
Theory

Ideas | Philosophers | Thinking and thought
Imagination, fantasy | Philosophy | Understanding

## Nature and Environment

Animals | Flowers, gardens, gardening | Rivers
Birds | Grass | Sea
Cats | Holism | Seasons
Clouds | Hurricanes | Seasons: spring
Desert | Horses | Seasons: summer
Dogs | Insects | Seasons: winter
Dolphins and whales | Land | Snow
Earth | Mountains | Sun
Ecology | Mud | Trees
Environment | Nature | Water
Evolution | Pets | Weather
Farming | Pollution | Wind
Fish | Rain | Zoos

## Peoples and Places

Africa | Germany | Third World
Asia | Germany: Berlin | United States
Australia | Germany: East Germany | United States: African-Americans
Bosnia | Greece | United States: Americans
Britain | Holland | United States: Boston
Britain: the British | India | United States: California and the
Canada | Ireland |    West
Caribbean | Ireland: the Irish | United States: Chicago
China | Ireland: Northern Ireland | United States: Los Angeles
Cuba | Israel | United States: the Midwest
Czechoslovakia | Italy | United States: Native Americans
East | Italy: Rome | United States: New England and
England | Italy: Venice |    the East
England: the English | Latin America | United States: New York
England: Essex | Middle East | United States: the South
England: London | Nicaragua | United States: US Constitution
England: Manchester | Palestine | United States: Washington, DC
England: Norfolk | Poland | USSR
Europe | Rhodesia | USSR: glasnost and perestroika
Europe: and America | Russia | Wales
Europe: Eastern Europe | Scotland | West
France | South Africa
France: Paris | Switzerland

## Performance, Entertainment and Humour

Acting | Dean, James | Performance
Actors and actresses | Entertainment | Publicity
Applause | Garbo, Greta | Sex symbols
Audiences | Humour | Show business
Bakewell, Joan | Humour: sense of humour | Soap opera
Bardot, Brigitte | Irony | Stereotypes
Brando, Marlon | Jokes and jokers | Taylor, Elizabeth
Chat shows | Mockery | Welles, Orson
Comedy | Monroe, Marilyn | Westerns
Comedians | Parody | Wit

## Politics and International Relations

Activism and protest | Gorbachev, Mikhail | Commons
Alliances | Government | Parliament: the House of Lords
Animal liberation | Guevara, Che | Policy
Appeasement | Hoover, J. Edgar | Political correctness
Attlee, Clement | Howard, Michael | Political parties
Baldwin, Stanley | Ideology | Politicians and statesmen
Blair, Tony | Imperialism, colonialism and | Politics
British Empire |    decolonization | Politics: and women
Bush, George | Internationalism | Polls, surveys
Callaghan, James | Johnson, Lyndon B. | Power
Capitalism | Kennedys | President
Casement, Roger | Kinnock, Neil | President: the First Lady
Chamberlain, Neville | Labour Party | President: the Vice-President
Churchill, Winston | Law, Bonar | Propaganda
Clinton, Bill | Leadership, accountability | Qadaffi, Muhammar

Communism
Conservative Party
Coolidge, Calvin
Demagogues
Democracy
Democratic Party
Dictatorship
Diplomacy
Eden, Anthony
Eisenhower, Dwight D.
Elections, voting
European Union
Extremism
Fascism
Feminism
Ford, Gerald
Foreign policy
Freedom, liberty
Freedom of speech
Gandhi, Mohandas K.
Globalization

Liberals
Lloyd George, David
Macdonald, Ramsay
Macmillan, Harold
Major, John
Majority
Marxism
McCarthyism
Moderation
Mosley, Oswald
Mussolini, Benito
Nationalization
Nationalism
Nations
Nazism
New World Order
Nixon, Richard
Official Secrets Acts
Oppression
Parliament
Parliament: the House of

Radicals
Reactionaries
Reagan, Ronald
Reform
Repression
Republican Party
Sanctions
Socialism
Spin doctors
Stalin, Josef
State
Suez affair
Suffragists, suffragettes
Superpowers
Tebbit, Norman
Thatcher, Margaret
Totalitarianism
Tyranny
United Nations
Watergate affair

## Science and Technology

Anthropology
Archaeology
Astronomy
Chemistry
Computers
Einstein, Albert
Engineering

Internet
Machinery
Mathematics
Physics
Robots
Science
Science: and society

Scientists
Social sciences
Statistics
Technology
Telephone

## Society

Aristocracy
Beggars
Black consciousness, black power
Black culture
Bourgeoisie
Bureaucracy
Ceremony and etiquette
Cities and towns
Cities: suburbs
Civil rights, human rights
Civilization
Class
Clubs
Community
Consumer society
Decadence
Dissent
Elitism
Equality and inequality
Establishment
Hermits
Hippies
Homeless
Houses and homes

Housework, housewives
Illegitimacy
Immigration
Institutions
Ladies and gentlemen
Luxury
Masses
Materialism
Middle class
Millennium Dome
Minorities
Mods
Multiculturalism, pluralism
Obscenity
Outcasts and outlaws
Patriotism
People
Permissive society
Population
Poverty and the poor
Privacy
Public
Public life
Race

Racism
Rat race
Rebellion, civil unrest
Rebels
Rich
Royal Family
Royal Family: Princess Diana
Scandal
Scapegoats
Segregation
Slavery
Sloane Rangers
Slums
Snobbery
Society
Underclass
Upper class
Utopia, dystopia
Villages
Wealth
Whites
Working class
Yuppies

## Speech and Language

Accent
Clichés
Conversation
Eloquence
Euphemisms
Graffiti
Greetings
Innuendo
Intelligibility
Labels

Language
Language: English
Lies and lying
Loquacity
Mottos and maxims
Nagging
Names
Nonsense
Platitudes, generalizations
Questions and answers

Quotations, soundbites
Slander
Slang
Speech
Speeches and speechmaking
Spelling, grammar, punctuation
Swearing
Translation
Words

## Sport and Recreation

| | | |
|---|---|---|
| Abstinence | Exercise | Parties |
| Athletics | Fans | Pleasure |
| Baseball | Festivals | Sailing |
| Boxing | Football | Sport |
| Bullfighting | Football: American football | Smoking |
| Cards | Gambling | Tennis |
| Chess | Golf | Tourism |
| Cricket | Holiday | Weekends |
| Enjoyment, fun | Leisure | |

## Style, Individuality and Choice

| | | |
|---|---|---|
| Camp | Indecision | Provincialism |
| Choice | Individualism | Simplicity |
| Complexity | Individuality | Sophistication |
| Conformity | Innovation, novelty | Style |
| Control | Kitsch | Talent |
| Decisions | Modernity | Taste |
| Ends and means | Nonconformity | Temptation |
| Improvisation, spontaneity | Originality | Vulgarity |

## Time: Past, Present, Future

| | | |
|---|---|---|
| Antiquity | New Year | Sundays |
| Christmas | Night | Time |
| Days | Nostalgia | Tradition |
| Days: morning | Nineteenth century | Twentieth century |
| Days: afternoon | Past | Twentieth century: 1920s |
| Days: evening | Planning | Twentieth century: 1930s |
| Easter | Posterity | Twentieth century: 1940s |
| Eternity | Prediction | Twentieth century: 1950s |
| Future | Present | Twentieth century: 1960s |
| Heritage | Procrastination | Twentieth century: 1970s |
| History | Punctuality | Twentieth century: 1980s |
| Millennium | Reminiscence and regret | Twentieth century: 1990s |
| Modern times | Romans | |
| New age | Roots | |

## Travel, Transport

| | | |
|---|---|---|
| Aeroplanes | Exploration | Speed |
| Bicycles | Foreign countries | Submarines |
| Bikers | Foreigners | Tourism |
| Buses | Hotels | Trains |
| Cars | Journeys | Travel |
| Departures, farewells | Roads | Walking |
| Emigration, exile, refugees | Roads: on the road | |
| Expatriates | Ships | |

## War and Peace

| | | |
|---|---|---|
| Air Force | Genocide | Revolution |
| Arms Industry | Guerrilla warfare | Revolutionaries |
| Arms Race | Gulf conflict | Russian Revolution |
| Army | Guns | Sabotage |
| Assassination | Hitler, Adolf | Second World War |
| Battles | Holocaust | Spanish Civil War |
| Cold War | Hostages | Spies |
| Concentration camps | Killing | Terrorism |
| Defeat | Korean War | Torture |
| Defence | Navy | Vietnam War |
| Disarmament | Nonviolence | Victory |
| Enemies | Nuclear age | Violence |
| English Civil War | Nuclear protest | War |
| Falklands conflict | Nuclear testing | War correspondents |
| First World War | Nuclear war | War crimes |
| Force | Pacifism | War and peace |
| French Revolution | Peace | |
| Generals | Resistance | |

## Work

# Achievement and Failure

## Actions, Circumstances, Events

## Belief and Opinion

## Body

## Business and Economics

## Human Relations

John Lydon [2]
Anna Magnani [1]
Johnny Mercer [1]
Iris Murdoch [8]
Ann Oakley [3]
Edna O'Brien [5]
Yoko Ono [4]
John Osborne [7]
Harold Pinter [3]
Political slogans [11]
Cole Porter [2, 14]
Katherine Anne Porter [5]
Bertrand Russell [13]
Antoine Saint-Exupéry [7]
Erich Segal [1]
Sting [3]
Mother Teresa [6]
Lily Tomlin [3]
Marina Tsvetaeva [2, 3]
Peter Ustinov [3]
Sid Vicious [1]
Judith Viorst [3]
Andy Warhol [9]
Tennessee Williams [10]
Jeanette Winterson [2, 3]
Virginia Woolf [23]
Woodrow Wyatt [1]
William Butler Yeats [23]

**Love: ended**
Brigitte Bardot [1]
Otto Harbach [1]
Lorenz Hart [2]Vladimir
    Mayakovsky [6]
Edna St. Vincent Millay [6]
Margaret Mitchell [8]
Iris Murdoch [4]
Edna O'Brien [6]
Elvis Presley [2]
Marcel Proust [14]
Adrienne Rich [1]

**Love: and sex**
Steven Soderbergh [1]

**Love affairs**
Arthur M. Schlesinger Jr. [4]
John Updike [7]

**Lovers**
W.H. Auden [21]
Elizabeth Bowen [5]
Robert Graves [11]
Dorothy Parker [5]
Jacques Prévert [2]
Violet Trefusis [1]
Donald Trump [3]

**Loyalty**
Oscar Hammerstein II [6]
Lyndon B. Johnson [8]
Henry Kissinger [5]
Tammy Wynette [3]

**Lust**
Jimmy Carter [1]
Robert Graves [4]
Aldous Huxley [16]
Camille Paglia [10]
Mae West [2]
George F. Will [1]

**Malice, misanthropy**
Eric Hoffer [19]
Patrick Kavanagh [3]
Lou Reed [3]
John Steinbeck [9]

**Marriage**
Vicki Baum [2]
Julie Burchill [9]
Anthony Burgess [8]
Mrs Patrick Campbell [2]

Pauline Collins [1]
Richard Curtis [1]
Simone de Beauvoir [6]
Diana, Princess of Wales [7]
Isadora Duncan [3]
Andrea Dworkin [5]
Edna Ferber [1]
Richard Ford [1]
Michael Frayn [2]
Robert Frost [18]
Carolyn Heilbrun [4]
Gabriel García Márquez [6]
Zsa Zsa Gabor [2]
Robert Graves [9]
Germaine Greer [4]
Jane Harrison [2]
A.P. Herbert [2]
Bianca Jagger [1]
Erica Jong [11]
Ann Landers [1]
Philip Larkin [11, 16]
Denise Levertov [1]
C.S. Lewis [10]
Phyllis McGinley [3]
André Maurois [2]
H.L. Mencken [21]
Iris Murdoch [1, 2]
Mike Myers [2]
Bertrand Russell [9]
Stephen Sondheim [2]
Anthony Storr [2]
Sue Townsend [1]
Violet Trefusis [2]
John Updike [5]
King Vidor [1]
Mary Webb [1]
Sidney Webb [2]
Thornton Wilder [3]
Virginia Woolf [22]

**Marriage: failed**
Erica Jong [13]
John Updike [17]
Edmund White [8]

**Marriage: and love**
Sammy Cahn [2]

**Mothers**
Marguerite Duras [4]
James Joyce [9]
Phyllis McGinley [6]
Vladimir Nabokov [4]
Ann Oakley [1]
Anthony Perkins [1]
Adrienne Rich [6]
Philip Roth [1]
Fay Weldon [6]
Rebecca West [11]

**Negotiation**
Winston Churchill [45]
Robert Holmes à Court [1]
John F. Kennedy [7]
Nelson Mandela [4]

**Neighbours**
G.K. Chesterton [13]
Quentin Crisp [2]
Robert Frost [2]
Irving Layton [6]
Paul Simon [7]

**Opposition**
Charles De Gaulle [10]
Jill Tweedie [1]

**Other people**
Charles Bukowski [8]
E.M. Cioran [9]
Yoko Ono [3]
Jean-Paul Sartre [7]
Rebecca West [1]

Virginia Woolf [3, 5]

**Paranoia**
Advertising slogans [4]
Luis Buñuel [6]
Bob Dylan [24]
Henry Kissinger [7]
Thomas Pynchon [2]

**Parents**
Ama Ata Aidoo [2]
Samuel Beckett [14]
Bill Clinton [5]
Bill Cosby [1]
Edward VIII [3]
Robert Frost [29]
Elizabeth Jennings [3]
Jacqueline Kennedy [1]
Philip Larkin [20]
Jim Morrison [3, 9]
Pier Paolo Pasolini [5]
Anthony Powell [2]
Benjamin Spock [3]
Freya Stark [5]
Jack Straw [1]
Laurens van der Post [3]

**Persuasion**
Steve Biko [5]
Janet Frame [1]
Harper Lee [3]
Dean Rusk [1]

**Pity, compassion**
John Berger [13]
William Faulkner [1]
James Joyce [5]
Milan Kundera [5]
Boris Pasternak [6]

**Promiscuity**
Joe Orton [5]
Reginald Paget [1]
Dorothy Parker [15]
Stephen Stills [2]
Edmund White [9]

**Prostitution**
Polly Adler [1, 2]
Marlene Dietrich [3]
Tama Janowitz [1]
Camille Paglia [12]
Cole Porter [1]
Mandy Rice-Davies [1]
Gail Sheehy [1]

**Quarrels**
Walter Benjamin [4]
William Ralph Inge [1]
Derek Walcott [13]

**Relationships**
Anna Akhmatova [3]
Woody Allen [22]
Julian Barnes [10]
Bill Clinton [3]
Quentin Crisp [12, 18]
Marianne Faithfull [1]
Betty Friedan [4]
Jerry Hall [1]
Barbara Grizzuti Harrison [2]
Al Hoffman and Dick Manning [1]
Ron Shelton [2]

**Respect**
Aretha Franklin [1]

**Revenge**
Dashiell Hammett [1]
Seamus Heaney [4]
Ronald Reagan [21]
Quentin Tarantino [1]
Ruby Wax [1]

**Romance**
Alan Ayckbourn [2]
Beverly Jones [1]
Kate Millett [3]

**Sadism, masochism**
Tom Lehrer [2]
Susan Sontag [13]
Edmund White [3]

**Sex**
James Agate [1]
Woody Allen [3, 23]
Enid Bagnold [3]
Beryl Bainbridge [3]
Tallulah Bankhead [5]
Julian Barnes [15]
Boy George [1]
Charles Bukowski [6]
Julie Burchill [2]
Angela Carter [4]
Billy Crystal [1]
Geena Davis [1]
Simone de Beauvoir [4]
Midge Decter [1]
Don DeLillo [11]
Marlene Dietrich [6]
Andrea Dworkin [4]
Oriana Fallaci [1]
Oliver Flanagan [2]
Nancy Friday [4]
Betty Friedan [2]
Bob Guccione [2]
Thom Gunn [1]
Piet Hein [1]
Lillian Hellman [8]
Ernest Hemingway [17]
Nick Hornby [9, 10]
Erica Jong [3]
Philip Larkin [18]
D.H. Lawrence [16]
John Lydon [8]
Anita Loos [4]
Jay McInerney [3]
Norman Mailer [15]
Anthony Marriott and Alistair
    Foot [1]
George Mikes [2]
Henry Miller [8, 18]
Blake Morrison [7]
Malcolm Muggeridge [5]
Les Murray [6]
Mike Myers [3]
Cynthia Payne [1]
David Reuben [1]
Margaret Sanger [1]
Omar Sharif [1]
Graham Swift [2]
John Updike [8]
Peter Ustinov [8]
Gore Vidal [4]
Andy Warhol [8]
Evelyn Waugh [8]
H.G. Wells [10]
Vivienne Westwood [4]
Edmund White [2, 4]

**Sexism**
Florynce R. Kennedy [3]
Kate Millett [1]
Gloria Steinem [1, 2]

**Sexual abuse, child abuse, incest**
Woody Allen [28]
Martin Amis [14]
Beatrix Campbell [1]
Elizabeth Janeway [2]
Sapphire [1]

**Sexual deviation**
Quentin Tarantino [6]

Simone Weil [10]

## Ideas
Alain [2]
Isaiah Berlin [3]
Penelope Fitzgerald [1]
E.M. Forster [3]
Jean Genet [5]
Ellen Glasgow [2]
Damien Hirst [2]
Randall Jarrell [6]
John Maynard Keynes [18]
Wyndham Lewis [3]
Sean O'Casey [1]
Jean Rostand [12]
Jean-Paul Sartre [18]
Anne Sexton [7]
George Steiner [4]
Andrey Tarkovsky [4]
Leon Trotsky [6]
Vivienne Westwood [8]
William Carlos Williams [4]

## Imagination, fantasy
Richard Ellmann [1]
Graffiti [2]
Elizabeth Jennings [6]
Barbara Grizzuti Harrison [1]
Ursula Le Guin [9]
Iris Murdoch [23]
Malcolm Muggeridge [8]
Vladimir Nabokov [8]
Luigi Pirandello [5]
Ezra Pound [12]
Rod Serling [1]
Wallace Stevens [18, 29]

## Inspiration
Robert Bresson [4]
Samuel Goldwyn [5]
A.E. Housman [1]
Philip Larkin [24]
Henry Miller [19]
Anne Sexton [1]
Stevie Smith [11]

## Intellect, intellectuals
James Agate [4]
Spiro T. Agnew [2]
W.H. Auden [32]
Louise Bogan [3]
Charles Bukowski [7]
Albert Camus [1]
Noam Chomsky [5]
Albert Einstein [8]
Stephen Jay Gould [4]
Václav Havel [8]
Lillian Hellman [6]
Harold L. Ickes [2]
John Milton Keynes [11]
Milan Kundera [17]
Bernard-Henri Lévy [2]
Laurens van der Post [2]
Ludwig Wittgenstein [19]
Virginia Woolf [49]

## Intelligence
Douglas Adams [4]
Lisa Alther [1]
Agatha Christie [1]
Ian Dury [5]
F. Scott Fitzgerald [19]
John Fowles [6]
Erich Fromm [4]
Aldous Huxley [21]
Henry Kissinger [3]
Peter Singer [5]
Susan Sontag [5]

## Logic
E.M. Forster [10]
A.N. Wilson [2]
Ludwig Wittgenstein [1, 3]

## Memory
Julian Barnes [8]
J.M. Barrie [1]
Augusto Roa Bastos [1]
Elizabeth Bowen [7]
Luis Buñuel [2]
Cyril Connolly [21]
Douglas Coupland [6]
Eugène Ionesco [8]
Milan Kundera [3]
Blake Morrison [1]
John Osborne [13]
Cesare Pavese [6]
Mervyn Peake [2]
Marcel Proust [4, 13, 15]
Tennessee Williams [1]

## Mental illness, madness
Samuel Beckett [10]
Hermann Broch [4]
Jean Cocteau [10]
Salvador Dali [2]
Isadora Duncan [2]
T.S. Eliot [37]
Martha Graham [3]
Joseph Heller [7]
R.D. Laing [2, 8, 9, 10]
Cynthia Ozick [2]
Anthony Perkins [2]
Luigi Pirandello [10]
Ezra Pound [24]
G.B. Shaw [19]
Thomas Szasz [1]
Peter Ustinov [6]
Robin Williams [2]

## Metaphysics
Woody Allen [19]
Boris Pasternak [5]

## Mind
René Magritte [2]
Sylvia Plath [8]
John Cooper Powys [3]
Craig Raine [1]
R.S. Thomas [10]
Virginia Woolf [26]

## Neurosis
Sigmund Freud [17]
Carl Jung [10]
Arthur Miller [13]
Sylvia Plath [9]
Marcel Proust [7]
Wayne Sleep [1]
Thomas Szasz [17]
Lionel Trilling [4]
Kenneth Tynan [5]

## Obsession
Dustin Hoffman [4]
Nick Hornby [3]

## Openmindedness
Richard Rorty [2]

## Philosophers
A.J. Ayer [1]
Wallace Stevens [13, 24]
Katharine Tait [1]
Ludwig Wittgenstein [5, 14]

## Philosophy
Louis-Ferdinand Céline [3]
Timothy Leary [5]
Iris Murdoch [15, 20]
Alfred North Whitehead [3, 4]
Gertrude Stein [20]
Ludwig Wittgenstein [13, 22, 23]

## Pressure and stress
John Belushi [1]
Stephen Early [1]

Harry S. Truman [5]

## Psyche
Carl Jung [7]
Marina Warner [3]

## Psychiatric institutions
Janet Frame [1]
Ken Kesey [1]

## Psychiatry, psychotherapy
Samuel Goldwyn [8]
Marshall McLuhan [7]
Anthony Storr [3]
Michael Torke [1]

## Psychoanalysis
Woody Allen [18]
Saul Bellow [5]
Sigmund Freud [3, 14]
Germaine Greer [2]
Peter Medawar [2]
Thomas Szasz [14, 16]

## Psychology
Thomas Szasz [19]
James Thurber [4]

## Reason
Louis Aragon [2]
E.M. Cioran [2]
Erich Fromm [4]

## Russell, Bertrand
Bertrand Russell [23]

## Structuralism, post-structuralism
Terry Eagleton [3]
Ihab Hassan [1]

## Stupidity
John Fowles [6]
Tom Hanks [2]
Yip Harburg [6]
Eric Hoffer [17]
Primo Levi [8]
Kathleen Turner [1]
Stephen Vizinczey [3]

## Theory
A.J. Ayer [3]
J.B.S. Haldane [3]
Ruth Hubbard [1]

## Thinking and thought
Theodor W. Adorno [2]
Edward De Bono [1]
T.S. Eliot [44]
Michael Frayn [3]
Robert Frost [30]
Northrop Frye [1]
J.K. Galbraith [4]
William Golding [2]
Eric Hoffer [11]
Aldous Huxley [3]
Arthur Koestler [6]
Octavio Paz [1]
Jacques Prévert [3]
Jean Rostand [7]
Bertrand Russell [4]
G.B. Shaw [18]
Oswald Spengler [3]
Wallace Stevens [21]
Stockhausen [1]
Ludwig Wittgenstein [8]
Virginia Woolf [11]

## Understanding
J. William Fulbright [1]
Franz Kafka [3]
Martin Luther King [10]
Peter Høeg [2]

Jean Rostand [3]
Philip Roth [6]
Robert Wilson [1]

## Peoples and Places

### Africa
Maya Angelou [7]
Isak Dinesen [2]
W.E.B. Du Bois [1]
Marcus Garvey [3]
Jean Genet [4]
Doris Lessing [1]
Albert Schweitzer [3]
Ian Smith [1]

### Asia
Advertising slogans [5]
Joseph Brodsky [3]
Alexander Cockburn [1]
Carl Jung [18]

### Australia
Peter Carey [1]
Germaine Greer [10]
Robert Hughes [1]
Barry Humphries [3, 4]
Thomas Keneally [1, 2]
Les Murray [1, 5]

### Bosnia
Zlata Filipovic [1]
Volker Ruhe [1]
Salman Rushdie [25]

### Britain
Dean Acheson [1]
Tony Benn [2]
Bill Bryson [3]
William Hague [1]
Lord Harlech [1]
Halvard Lange [1]
John Major [6, 8]
George Mikes [3]
Jawarharlal Nehru [1]
Dennis Potter [10]
Vivian Stanshall [1]
Freya Stark [2]
Barbara Tuchman [2]

### Britain: the British
John Betjeman [8]
Melvyn Bragg [1]
Steven Berkoff [3]
Hugh, Sir Casson [1]
Winston Churchill [21]
Douglas Dunn [1]
Paul Gallico [1]
Henry James [1]
James Joyce [22]
Anthony Marriott and Alistair
  Foot [1]
Robert Morley [1]
G.B. Shaw [23]

### Canada
Margaret Atwood [2]
Leonard Cohen [2]
Robertson Davies [2]
Charles De Gaulle [11]
Michael Ondaatje [2]
Carol Shields [1]

### Caribbean
Michael Manley [1]
Derek Walcott [10]

### China
James Fenton [6]
Kaixi Wuer [1]
Mao Zedong [16]

### Cuba
Federico García Lorca [5]
Nikita Khrushchev [7]

Richard Nixon [16]
Calvin Trillin [3]

### Czechoslovakia
Winston Churchill [12]

### East
Edward Said [1]

### England
James Baldwin [10]
John Betjeman [3, 9, 14]
Anthony Burgess [5]
William Burroughs [12]
Martin Carthy [1]
Raymond Chandler [8]
G.K. Chesterton [5, 12]
Winston Churchill [38]
Alistair Cooke [1]
Noël Coward [6]
Cecil Day Lewis [4]
Norman Douglas [4]
Margaret Drabble [6]
Farouk I [1]
E.M. Forster [1, 2]
Germaine Greer [16]
Ivor Gurney [4]
Margaret Halsey [1]
David Hare [4]
A.P. Herbert [3]
Linton Kwesi Johnson [2]
Jackie Mason [1]
Roger Miller [1]
Marianne Moore [2]
George Orwell [6]
John Osborne [11]
Ross Parker and Hugh Charles [1]
Jeremy Paxman [5]
S.J. Perelman [2]
Harold Pinter [11]
George Santayana [2]
D.J. Taylor [1]
Leon Trotsky [19]
H.G. Wells [6, 8]
Anne Widdecombe [2]

### England: the English
James Agate [1]
Thomas Beecham [4]
Brendan Behan [1]
G.K. Chesterton [12]
Germaine Greer [3]
Margaret Halsey [3]
James Joyce [14]
Miles Kington [1]
Kathy Lette [2]
Jackie Mason [2]
George Mikes [1]
Alice Duer Miller [1, 2]
Ogden Nash [11]
George Orwell [17, 18, 25, 28]
J.B. Priestley [1]
Stevie Smith [3]
Evelyn Waugh [17]
Irvine Welsh [3]
William Butler Yeats [17, 30]

### England: Essex
Damon Albarn [1]
Ian Dury [2]

### England: London
T.S. Eliot [19]
Noel Gay [2]
George VI [1]
Ira Gershwin [4]
Hubert Gregg [1]
Charles, Prince of Wales [4]
Mick Jagger and Keith Richards [5]
Paul Theroux [8]

### England: Manchester
William Bolitho [1]

### England: Norfolk
Noël Coward [2]

### Europe
Marlene Dietrich [6]
H.A.L. Fisher [2]
Hugh Gaitskell [3]
Misha Glenny [1]
 Nadine Gordimer [2]
Helmut Kohl [2]
Milan Kundera [16]
Mary McCarthy [1]
Jean-Paul Sartre [2]
George Steiner [10]
Margaret Thatcher [37]
Leon Trotsky [1]

### Europe: and America
Don DeLillo [2]
Federico García Lorca [4]
Stuart Gorrell [1]
Woody Guthrie [1]
Randall Jarrell [7]
Mary McCarthy [4]

### Europe: Eastern Europe
Gerald Ford [4]
Misha Glenny [1]
Václav Havel [15]
John F. Kennedy [21]

### France
Jean Anouilh [7]
Barbara Cartland [3]
Willa Cather [5]
Charles De Gaulle [2, 3, 6, 9]
Maurice Girodias [1]
Graffiti [8]
Texas Guinan [1]
Antony Jay [1]
Henry Miller [22]
Robert Morley [2]
Ivor Novello [1]
Jean-Paul Sartre [11]
Gertrude Stein [19]
Evelyn Waugh [21]
Billy Wilder [6]

### France: Paris
Fred Allen [2]
John Berger [11]
Marguerite Duras [1]
Oscar Hammerstein II [2]
Ernest Hemingway [36]
Adolf Hitler [19]
Cole Porter [13]

### Germany
Willa Cather [5]
John Cleese [1]
Matt Frei [1]
Graffiti [10]
Robert Harris [1]
Martin Heidegger [2]
Adolf Hitler [8]
William Joyce [1]
Helmut Kohl [1]
Thomas Mann [8]
François Mauriac [1]
Edward Thomas [6]

### Germany: Berlin
Bertolt Brecht [18]
Hans Magnus Enzensberger [7]
John F. Kennedy [21]

### Germany: East Germany
Lothar de Maizière [1]

### Greece
Louis de Bernières [4]

### Holland
Alan Coren [1]
Simon Schama [3]

### India
E.M. Forster [5]
André Malraux [3]
Jawarharlal Nehru [1, 2]
Salman Rushdie [26]
Ringo Starr [2]
Winston Churchill [9]

### Ireland
W.H. Auden [16]
James Connolly [2]
J.P. Donleavy [1]
Roddy Doyle [1]
Oliver Flanagan [1, 2]
Bob Geldof [4]
Charles Haughey [1]
Seamus Heaney [7]
Frank McCourt [1]
Conor Cruise O'Brien [1]
Edna O'Brien [4]
Sean O'Casey [13]
V.S. Pritchett [4]
William Butler Yeats [4, 7, 26, 27]

### Ireland: the Irish
Brendan Behan [2]
James Joyce [3, 4, 16]
Patrick Henry Pearse [2]
Political slogans [2]
Mary Robinson [1]
William Butler Yeats [22]

### Ireland: Northern Ireland
Gerry Adams [1, 2]
Anonymous [8]
Tony Blair [5, 6]
Brian Friel [3]
Seamus Heaney [5, 11]
Jack Holland [1]
Ian Paisley [1]
Political slogans [21]
David Trimble [2]

### Israel
David Ben-Gurion [1]
Golda Meir [2]
Yitzhak Shamir [2]

### Italy
Gesualdo Bufalino [1]
Luciano De Crescenzo [1]
Hans Magnus Enzensberger [4]
Carlo Levi [1, 3]
George Mikes [4]
Leoluca Orlando [1]
Franco Zeffirelli [2]

### Italy: Rome
Cecil Day Lewis [7]

### Italy: Venice
Robert Benchley [5]
Truman Capote [2]

### Latin America
Salvador Allende [1]
Mario Vargas Llosa [2]
Pablo Neruda [3, 11]
Ronald Reagan [12]
Tim Rice [1]
Richard Rodriguez [1]

### Middle East
Yasser Arafat [1]
Gertrude Bell [3]
Patrick Buchanan [3]
Ramsey Clark [3]
Robert Fisk [2]
Muhammad Heikal [1]

# Society

## Aristocracy
Robert Bolt [2]
G.K. Chesterton [17]
Noël Coward [12]
Isak Dinesen [3]
Vivienne Westwood [7]
Virginia Woolf [17]

## Beggars
Bertolt Brecht [2]
Tony Parsons [2]

## Black consciousness, black power
Amiri Baraka [3]
Steve Biko [4]
Stokely Carmichael [1, 2]
Sam Cooke [1]
Marcus Garvey [1]
Malcolm X [5]
Political slogans [13]
Paul Robeson [1]
Jean-Paul Sartre [8]
Nina Simone [2]
Alice Walker [17]

## Black culture
James Baldwin [2]
James Brown [2]
Frantz Fanon [2]
Marcus Garvey [2]
Nikki Giovanni [3]
Dick Gregory [1]
Langston Hughes [2, 8]
Jesse Jackson [4]

## Bourgeoisie
Alexander Blok [2]
Cyril Connolly [4]
Hermann Hesse [7]
D.H. Lawrence [19]
Tony Parsons [2]
Norman Podhoretz [1]
Lionel Trilling [7]

## Bureaucracy
G.K. Chesterton [11]
Aldous Huxley [15]
Eugene J. McCarthy [1]
Osip Mandelstam [5]
Eugene O'Neill [8]
Ronald Reagan [3]
Joseph Schumpeter [7]
Mother Teresa [9]
Gore Vidal [8]

## Ceremony and etiquette
F. Gonzalez-Crussi [1]
George Gurdjieff [5]
Cesare Pavese [3]

## Cities and towns
Advertising slogans [25]
Anonymous [13]
John Berger [11]
John Betjeman [5, 11]
Italo Calvino [3]
John Cooper Clarke [4]
Cyril Connolly [15]
Federico García Lorca [4]
Grandmaster Flash [1]
Mark Hellinger [2]
Edward Hoagland [3]
Ewan MacColl [1]
Margaret Mead [9]
Desmond Morris [3]
Toni Morrison [6]
Lewis Mumford [6]
Martin Oppenheimer [1]

Peter Porter [2]
Jonathan Raban [1]
Theodore Roszak [1]
John Sebastian [1]
Oswald Spengler [1]
E.B. White [5]
Frank Lloyd Wright [2]

## Cities: suburbs
Cyril Connolly [14]
Arthur Kroker [1]
Judith Viorst [1]

## Civil rights, human rights
Ramsey Clark [1]
Dick Gregory [1]
Suzanne LaFollette [2]
Bob Marley [1]
Political slogans [3]
Simone Weil [13]

## Civilization
Georges Bernanos [5]
Allan Bloom [3]
Kenneth Clark [1, 3]
Cyril Connolly [16]
Louis de Bernières [6]
Will Durant [1]
Havelock Ellis [1]
Sigmund Freud [2, 12]
Mahatma Gandhi [6]
Malcolm Muggeridge [12]
José Ortega y Gasset [5]
Salman Rushdie [27]
Wallace Stevens [4]
A.J. Toynbee [2]
Simone Weil [6]

## Class
Martin Amis [8]
George Bush [4]
Jarvis Cocker [1]
Lord Curzon [1]
Mao Zedong [13]
Herbert Marcuse [1]
Joseph Schumpeter [1]
Peter York [4]

## Clubs
Groucho Marx [12]

## Community
Bill Clinton [2]
Sigmund Freud [11]
Paul Goodman [2]
Upton Sinclair [2]

## Consumer society
Douglas Coupland [4]
Bob Dylan [16]
Erich Fromm [5]
J.K. Galbraith [3]
Eric Hoffer [1]
Janis Joplin [2]
Tony O'Reilly [1]
Bruce Robinson [6]
Adlai Stevenson [1]
Raoul Vaneigem [7]

## Decadence
Cyril Connolly [17]

## Dissent
Jacob Bronowski [2]
Charles De Gaulle [13]
Antonio Gramsci [1]
Archibald MacLeish [3]
James Thurber [15]
Alice Walker [8]

## Elitism
John Carey [1]
Jonathan Miller [6]

Margaret Thatcher [38]

## Equality and inequality
Erich Fromm [7]
Jacquetta Hawkes [1]
D.H. Lawrence [5]
Herbert Marcuse [1]
George Orwell [32]
Mario Vargas Llosa [5]
Simone Weil [12]
Wendell Willkie [1]

## Establishment
Art Buchwald [1]
Noel Gallagher [4]
James Goldsmith [1]
Lewis H. Lapham [5]
Andrew Neil [1]
Enoch Powell [9]
J.B. Priestley [8]
A.J.P. Taylor [1]

## Hermits
Roger Miller [1]
Harold Pinter [2]
Dylan Thomas [6]

## Hippies
Robert Crumb [1]
Ben Elton [1]
Joni Mitchell [2]
Tom Wolfe [1]

## Homeless
Bob Dylan [23]
T.S. Eliot [32]
Ogden Nash [18]
Derek Worlock [1]

## Houses and homes
John Betjeman [16]
Bill Bryson [1]
Norman Douglas [3]
James Fenton [1]
Richard Ford [2]
Robert Frost [4]
Kahlil Gibran [4]
Richard Hamilton [2]
Hermann Hesse [4]
Philip Larkin [10]
Le Corbusier [1]
Cesare Pavese [8]
Pete Seeger [3]
Margaret Thatcher [34]
Edward Weston [1]

## Housework, housewives
Roseanne Barr [1]
Shirley Conran [2]
Quentin Crisp [7]
Erica Jong [1]
Vladimir Ilyich Lenin [10]
Mary McCarthy [9]
Ann Oakley [2]
Joan Rivers [1]
Katharine Whitehorn [1]

## Illegitimacy
Edna Gladney [1]
Stevie Smith [12]

## Immigration
Roy Hattersley [4]
Walter Lippmann [1]
Enoch Powell [2, 3]
Theodore Roosevelt [3]
Meera Syal [2]
Anzia Yezierska [1]

## Institutions
J.K. Galbraith [12]
William Ralph Inge [4]
C. Wright Mills [4]

## Ladies and gentlemen
Edward Fox [1]
Russell Lynes [3]
Luigi Pirandello [1]
Rebecca West [12]

## Luxury
Charlie Chaplin [3]
Joe Orton [2]

## Masses
Georges Bernanos [5]
Václav Havel [7]
Adolf Hitler [2]
Carl Jung [13]
Mao Zedong [10]
J.B. Priestley [7]
Josef Stalin [1]
Harry S. Truman [1]

## Materialism
Guy Debord [3]
Malcolm de Chazal [1]
Erich Fromm [5]
John Maynard Keynes [8]
Madonna [1]
Raoul Vaneigem [1]

## Middle class
Hermann Hesse [6]
George Orwell [5]
Tony Parsons [3]

## Millennium Dome
Polly Toynbee [1]

## Minorities
Leonard Robbins [1]
Susan Sontag [9]

## Mods
Pete Townshend [3]

## Multiculturalism, pluralism
Jesse Jackson [1, 6]
Toni Morrison [5]

## Obscenity
Mervyn Griffith-Jones [1]
Anaïs Nin [3]
Bertrand Russell [6]
E.B. White [8]

## Outcasts and outlaws
Quentin Crisp [1]
Bob Dylan [27]
Ralph Ellison [1]
John Lennon [19]
Salman Rushdie [28]
Bruce Springsteen [2]

## Patriotism
Julian Barnes [4]
Luis Buñuel [5]
Johnny Cash [1]
Edith Cavell [1]
G.K. Chesterton [14]
Lawrence Durrell [1]
Eric Hobsbawm [3]
John F. Kennedy [9]
H.L. Mencken [19]
Adlai Stevenson [2]
H.G. Wells [5]
Edith Wharton [2]

## People
Political slogans [20]
Carl Sandburg [9]

## Permissive society
Roger McGough [2]
Camille Paglia [11]
Pier Paolo Pasolini [7]

## Sport and Recreation

*– I don't see A. as a mainland*
Maritain [1]
*– A. . . . as prematurely old*
Miller, H. [16]
*– A.'s . . . mission to lead the world*
Said [4]
*– They've all gone to look for A.*
Simon [5]
*– I like to be in A.*
Sondheim [1]
*– A. is a vast conspiracy*
Updike [18]
*– In A., the race goes to the loud*
Vidal [13]
*– pure products of A.*
Williams, W.C. [1]
*– A. is the only idealistic nation*
Wilson, W. [6]

**American**
*– A. arrives in Paris*
Allen, F. [2]
*– A. history is longer, larger*
Baldwin, J. [5]
*– chief business of the A. people*
Coolidge [3]
*– A. type can never be a ballet dancer*
Duncan [4]
*– constant in the average A. imagination*
Eco [1]
*– To be an A.*
Fiedler [2]
*– no second acts in A. lives*
Fitzgerald, F.S. [22]
*– as A. as lynch mobs*
Garcia [2]
*– All modern A. literature comes from*
Hemingway [15]
*– A. patriotism measures itself*
Hobsbawm [3]
*– A. . . . is a permanent revolutionary*
Hoffer [1]
*– In every A. . . . an air of incorrigible innocence*
Housman [2]
*– A. boys 9 or 10,000 miles away*
Johnson, L.B. [7]
*– A. professors*
Lewis, S. [3]
*– A. character looks always as if*
McCarthy, M. [2]
*– doesn't make you an A.*
Malcolm X [4]
*– A. means white*
Morrison, T. [7]
*– last A. living the tragedy of Europe*
Pound [35]
*– A. Empire died*
Vidal [19]
*– Being A. is to eat a lot of beef steak*
Vonnegut [4]
*– A. at puberty*
Waugh, E. [21]
*– just an ordinary goddamn A.*
Wayne [3]
*– ideal A. type is . . . Protestant*
Welles [9]
*– necessary to be 'A.'*
Wharton [2]

**Americanism**
*– no room in this country for hyphenated A.*
Roosevelt, T. [1]
*– no fifty-fifty A. in this country*
Roosevelt, T. [3]

**Americanization**
*– Modernization is A.*
Murdoch, R. [3]

**Americans**
*– nothing the matter with A. except their ideals*
Chesterton [18]
*– A. . . . a huge rescue squad*
Cleaver [2]
*– A. who . . . always speak of sex*
Fallaci [1]
*– I don't see much future for the A.*
Hitler [17]
*– A. are overcome not by the sense*
Lasch [1]
*– A.are the loneliest of all*
McCullers [1]
*– A. with a capital A*
Murray, B. [1]
*– A. want action for their money*
Nelson, P. [1]
*– A. don't like sexual movies*
Nicholson [3]
*– No one can kill A.*
Reagan, R. [21]
*– story of A.*
Rosenberg [7]
*– A. . . . love to fight*
Scott, G.C. [2]
*– A. are overreaching*
Will [6]

**ammunition**
*– pass the a.!*
Forgy [1]

**amnesia**
*– a. is the most wished-for state*
Guare [2]

**amorphous**
*– a., but like fresh bread*
Townshend [8]

**amusement**
*– I'm not here for your a.*
Lydon [5]

**anarchist**
*– Accidental Death of an A.*
Fo [1]

**ancestry**
*– A. has never counted much in England*
Mitford [2]

**anchor**
*– ones we choose to love become our a.*
Harrison, T. [3]

**angle**
*– never miss an a.*
Disney [2]

**Anglo-Irishman**
*– A. . . . a Protestant with a horse*
Behan [2]

**angry**
*– young men being a.*
Tynan [3]
*– I was never an a. young man*
Wesker [1]
*– What I've learned about being a.*
Winfrey [2]

**angst**
*– Teenage a. has paid off well*
Cobain [2]

**anguish**
*– return journey to a.*
Smith, L. [2]

**animal**
*– nothing else but a wild a.*
Pinter [2]

**animals**
*– I'll stick to the a.*
Bardot [3]
*– A. . . . a lowlife way to kill*
Hoagland [1]
*– Nothing to be done . . . about a.*
Hoban [6]
*– attitude towards . . . a.*
Kundera [8]

*– tyranny of human over nonhuman a.*
Singer [4]

**annihilate**
*– press a button and a. the earth*
Roy [7]

**annihilation**
*– attracted/ by . . . my own a.*
Gunn [5]

**anniversaries**
*– Our a. go by*
Dunn [9]

**Annus horribilis**
*– turned out to be an A. h.*
Elizabeth II [5]

**anointed**
*– considers himself the Lord's a.*
Nash [13]

**answers**
*– Why do human beings need a.?*
Winterson [4]

**ant**
*– As a lone a. from a broken ant-hill*
Pound [26]

**anthem**
*– national a. belongs to the eighteenth century*
Shaw, G.B. [23]

**anthologies**
*– a. will undoubtedly continue in favor*
Janeway [1]

**anthropologists**
*– a. are busy*
Hamilton, E. [1]

**Anti-Catholicism**
*– A. is the anti-semitism*
Buchanan [1]

**Anti-Christ**
*– I am an A.*
Lydon [1]

**Anti-paranoia**
*– a., where nothing is connected to anything*
Pynchon [2]

**Anti-semitism**
*– Without centuries of Christian a.*
Runcie [2]
*– suburban prejudice of a.*
Pound [37]

**anything**
*– A. goes*
Porter, C. [6]

**apartheid**
*– closed the book on a.*
de Klerk [1]

**apathy**
*– a. of human beings*
Keller [2]

**aphorism**
*– A. should be/ like a burr*
Layton [7]

**aphorisms**
*– a. that, like airplanes*
Nabokov [1]
*– A. are salted and not sugared*
Smith L.P. [20]

**apologize**
*– I'm not here to a.*
Botha [1]
*– good rule in life never to a.*
Wodehouse [1]

**apology**
*– stiff a. is a second insult*
Chesterton [22]

**appalled**
*– I was born a.*
Stoppard [3]

**appearance**
*– at work upon the façade of his a.*
Murdoch, I. [10]

**appeasement**
*– world has been ruined by a.*
Vonnegut [8]
*– stench of a. in the air*
Thatcher [32]

**applause**
*– bouquets and storms of a.*
Markova [1]
*– A. is a receipt, not a bill*
Schnabel [1]

**apple**
*– never eat a windfall a.*
Carter, A. [2]

**appraisal**
*– a. seems chiefly useful*
Moore, M. [6]

**apprentices**
*– all a. in a craft*
Hemingway [32]

**April**
*– A. is the cruellest month*
Eliot [17]

**aquarium**
*– A. is gone*
Lowell, R. [7]

**Aquarius**
*– dawning of the age of A.*
Rado & Ragni [1]

**Arabs**
*– in our war with the A.*
Meir [2]
*– if A. put down a draft resolution*
Oz [1]

**Arbeit**
*– A. macht frei*
Anonymous [1]

**archaeologist**
*– a. is the best husband*
Christie [5]

**archbishop**
*– A. – A Christian ecclesiastic*
Mencken [24]

**Archer**
*– As long as A. remained the candidate*
Rees-Mogg [2]

**arches**
*– Underneath the A.*
Flanagan, B. [1]

**archipelagoes**
*– rosary of a.*
Walcott [2]

**architect**
*– Great A. of the Universe*
Jeans [1]
*– a. can only advise his client to plant vines*
Wright [1]

**architectonic**
*– imbued with the a. spirit*
Gropius [1]

**architects**
*– a. want to live beyond their deaths*
Johnson, Philip [3]

**architectural**
*– a. values are human values*
Wright [3]

**architecture**
*– it's modern a.*
Banks-Smith [1]
*– extrahuman a. and furious rhythm*
García Lorca [4]
*– A. is to make us know . . . who we are*
Jellicoe [1]
*– A. is . . . how to waste space*
Johnson, Philip [2]

**Argentina**
*– Don't cry for me A.*
Rice [1]

**esthete**
– *e. stands in the same relation to beauty*
Kraus [5]

**eternity**
– *E. is a terrible thought*
Stoppard [5]

**ethical**
– *point of e. judgement is to guide practice*
Singer [1]

**ethics**
– *True e. begins where . . . language ceases*
Schweitzer [2]

**Eton**
– *I lived at E. in the 1950s*
Aitken [2]
– *my feelings on leaving E.*
Connolly, C. [11]

**euphemism**
– *where we keep the . . . e.*
Albee [4]

**euphemisms**
– *E. are unpleasant truths*
Crisp [16]

**Europe**
– *All the dogs of E. bark*
Auden [19]
– *think of E. as a hardcover book*
DeLillo [2]
– *E. is a continent of . . . mongrels*
Fisher, H.A.L. [2]
– *E. has become the most unstable continent*
Glenny [1]
– *If you live in E.*
Gordimer [2]
– *lamps are going out all over E.*
Grey, Lord [1]
– *two poles of E.*
Kundera [16]
– *E. is the unfinished negative*
McCarthy, M. [4]
– *Does this boat go to E., France*
Monroe [2]
– *E. is springing leaks everywhere*
Sartre [15]
– *Federated Republic of E.*
Trotsky [1]
– *gifts of E. civilization*
Du Bois [1]
– *E. culture . . . is that of the museum*
Steiner [10]

**europeanised**
– *They sort of E. us all*
Hoffman, D. [3]

**Europeanism**
– *E. is nothing but imperialism*
Healey [1]
– *E. and Americans are like men and women*
Jarrell [7]

**Europeans**
– *only really materialistic people . . . E.*
McCarthy, M. [1]

**evangelicals**
– *Educated clerics don't like e.*
Hare [5]

**evenin'**
– *E. all*
Warner, J. [1]

**evening**
– *When the e. is spread out against the sky*
Eliot [1]
– *Some enchanted e.*
Hammerstein II [7]

**events**
– *force of e. wakes slumberous talents*
Hoagland [6]

**ever**
– *decided to live for e.*
Heller [2]

**everyone**
– *Now she's like e. else*
De Gaulle [4]

**everything**
– *we cannot do e. for everyone*
Clinton, B. [6]

**evil**
– *fearsome banality of e.*
Arendt [3]
– *Those to whom e. is done*
Auden [23]
– *face of 'e.' is . . . the face of total need*
Burroughs, W. [7]
– *all means are permitted to fight an e.*
Dawson, C. [1]
– *better . . . to do e. than to do nothing*
Eliot [29]
– *E. is not a mystical principle*
Levinas [3]
– *what is the greatest e.*
McGoohan [2]
– *E. is something you recognise*
Masters [1]
– *no explanation for e.*
Maugham [11]
– *gulf-stream of e.*
Powys [5]
– *never felt the urge to explore e.*
Raine, K. [5]
– *aggressive impulses of an e. empire*
Reagan, R. [14]

**evils**
– *e. . . . have the ability to survive*
Bellow [4]
– *men do not live only by fighting e.*
Berlin, Isaiah [1]
– *choosing between two e.*
West, M. [12]

**evolution**
– *E. is nothing but/ . . . false steps*
Holub [3]
– *E. is to allegory as statues are to birdshit*
Jones, S. [1]
– *E. is . . . a race to stay in the same place*
Jones, S. [2]

**evolutionary**
– *do not make e. sense*
Dawkins [1]

**excel**
– *Always strive to e.*
Rorty [4]

**excess**
– *champion of e.*
Bankhead [3]

**excluded**
– *E. . . . from the social order*
Genet [2]

**excruciated**
– *you were e.*
Joyce, J. [28]

**excuses**
– *E. are like assholes*
Stone, O. [1]

**executed**
– *to be e. on schedule*
Gilmore [1]

**executives**
– *Damn the great e.*
Lewis, S. [2]

**exercise**
– *E. is the yuppie version of bulimia*
Ehrenreich [1]
– *my friends who take e.*
O'Toole [1]

**exhilaration**
– *All we can get out of a Shaw play . . . mental e.*
Taylor, B.L. [2]

**exiles**
– *miraculous nature of the future of e.*
Rushdie [8]

**exist**
– *give us the impression we e.*
Beckett [9]

**existence**
– *E. is elsewhere*
Breton [2]
– *e. is a problem*
Fromm [1]
– *real tragedy of human e.*
Gould [6]
– *e. is meaningful*
Hammarskjöld [5]
– *terrible lurking thing in e.*
Hoban [5]
– *justify his e.*
Hoffer [13]
– *purpose of human e.*
Jung [4]
– *improvisation of human e.*
McCullers [2]
– *E. precedes and commands essence*
Sartre [2]

**exit**
– *every e. as being an entrance*
Stoppard [4]

**expansion**
– *E. means complexity*
Parkinson, C.N. [6]

**expatriate**
– *You're an e.*
Hemingway [4]
– *e. does not have to think*
Theroux [1]

**expectations**
– *revolution of rising e.*
Cleveland [1]

**expediency**
– *go by the e. of the moment*
Eastwood [2]

**expedition**
– *the main E. has/left us behind*
Reading [3]

**expenditure**
– *E. rises to meet income*
Parkinson, C.N. [5]

**experience**
– *one year's e.*
Carr, J. [2]
– *E. is a dim lamp*
Céline [7]
– *No matter how vital e. might be*
Glasgow [3]
– *E. is not . . . having actually swum*
Huxley, A. [14]
– *learn through e.*
Spolin [1]
– *hither and thither side of vital e.*
West, R. [7]

**experiment**
– *for the sake of an unsuccessful e.*
Konrád [1]

**expert**
– *e. is a man who has made all the mistakes*
Bohr [1]
– *responsibility of the e.*
Kissinger [11]

**experts**
– *E. are never in real danger*
Weldon [10]

**expletive**
– *E. deleted*
Nixon [11]

**exploitation**
– *e. of the young*
Janeway [2]

**exploration**
– *We shall not cease from e.*
Eliot [52]

**explorer**
– *e. of psychic areas*
Burroughs, W. [9]

**express**
– *I will try to e. myself*
Joyce, J. [10]
– *E. yourself*
Madonna [2]

**exterminate**
– *E.! Exterminate*
Nation [1]

**extremism**
– *e. in the defense of liberty*
Goldwater [1]

**extremist**
– *what kind of e. will we be*
King, M.L. [14]

**extremists**
– *What is objectionable . . . about e.*
Kennedy, R. [2]

**extroversion**
– *My e. is a way of managing*
Fisher, C. [1]

**exuberance**
– *No one . . . comes close to my e.*
Winterson [8]

**eye**
– *less in this than meets the e.*
Bankhead [1]
– *handful of e. people*
Hirst [4]
– *One e. sees, the other feels*
Klee [2]

**eyeball**
– *e. to eyeball*
Rusk [2]

**eyebrow**
– *left e. raised*
Moore, R. [1]

**eyebrows**
– *Nobody is born with perfect e.*
Evangelista [2]

**eyes**
– *I have the e. of a dead pig*
Brando [8]
– *Ol' blue e. is back*
Sinatra, F. [4]
– *What our e. behold*
Stevens [17]
– *e. of others our prisons*
Woolf [3]

**Fabians**
– *good man fallen among F.*
Lenin [9]

**face**
– *My f. looks like a wedding-cake*
Auden [49]
– *whole life shows in your f.*
Bacall [3]
– *f. of Garbo is an Idea*
Barthes [3]
– *pretty f. is a passport*
Burchill [3]
– *blank helpless sort of f.*
Carey, J [1]
– *f. is only the serial number*
Kundera [13]
– *f. that she keeps in a jar*
Lennon & McCartney [7]

**fear**
– We must travel in the direction of our f.
Berryman [1]
– prefect f. casteth out love
Connolly, C. [12]
– f. in a handful of dust
Eliot [18]
– only thing we have to f. is fear itself
Roosevelt, F. [4]

**fears**
– F. trace a map of a society's values
Warner, M. [5]

**February**
– not Puritanism but F.
Krutch [2]

**fecundator**
– Woman does not forget she needs the f.
Nin [1]

**fecundity**
– what it is about f.
Dillard [1]
– excessive national f.
Keynes [1]

**feeling**
– f. is bad form
Forster [1]
– deepest f. always shows itself in silence
Moore, M. [4]
– Name me . . . a better f.
O'Rourke [1]
– No deep and strong f.
Pasternak [6]

**female**
– f. of the species
Kipling [4]
– no f. Mozart
Paglia [7]

**feminine**
– Prim, pink-breasted, f.
Plath [2]
– beautiful in virile men is something f.
Sontag [7]

**feminism**
– Real f. is spinsterhood
King, F. [1]
– do not regard f. with an uplifting sense
Lewis, W. [1]
– We need a new kind of f.
Paglia [13]

**feminist**
– good part . . . of being a f.
Burchill [4]
– happily married to an eloquent f.
Clarke [4]
– F. a woman, usually ill-favoured
Humphries [2]
– I became a f. as an alternative
Kempton [1]

**fences**
– 'Good f. make good neighbors.'
Frost, R. [2]

**fervour**
– F. is the weapon of choice
Fanon [1]

**fetters**
– only f. binding the working class today
Wheen [1]

**fever**
– will never/unlive that crippling f.
Rich [1]

**fiction**
– If you write f. you are . . . corrupted
Burgess, A. [3]

– predilection for genre f.
Disch [1]
– modern f. has only one subject
Fowles [5]
– F. . . . is no longer necessary
Handke [1]
– f. has become a priestly business
Vidal [20]

**fifties**
– f. seem to have taken place
Hardwick [2]
– tranquilized F.,
Lowell, R. [3]
– F. was the most sexually frustrated decade
Tomlin [1]

**fiftieth**
– wake on your f. birthday
Sayers [5]

**fifty**
– By the time we hit f.
Dressler [1]
– years between f. and seventy
Eliot [57
– real sadness of f.
Lerner, M. [4]
– When you're 50 you start thinking
Oates [6]

**fifty-two**
– When you get to f.
Leith [1]

**fight**
– Pale Ebenezer thought it wrong to f.
Belloc [8]
– we shall f. on the beaches
Churchill, W. [16]
– I'll f. to the end
Diana, Princess of Wales [6]

**fighters**
– All f. are prostitutes
Holmes, L. [1]

**fighting**
– I want to keep f.
Foreman [1]
– not fifty ways of f.
Malraux [1]
– F. is like champagne
Mitchell, M. [5]
– If you insist upon f.
Woolf [47]

**film**
– f. is a petrified fountain of thought
Cocteau [12]
– centre of a f. is a burden
Day Lewis, D. [1]
– f. is just a reflection
Dunn [3]
– You should look straight at a f.
Herzog [1]
– Making a f. means . . . to tell a story
Hitchcock [2]
– no room for democracy in making f.
Pennebaker [1]
– F. music should have the same relationship
Stravinsky [1]

**films**
– F. can only be made by by-passing the will
Bresson [5]
– my f. start off with roadmaps
Wenders [3]

**filth**
– rubbing its nose in its own f.
Shaw, G.B. [12]

**finger**
– f. lickin' good
Advertising slogans [12]

– play the electric piano with more than one f.
McCartney [9]

**fingers**
– Let your f. do the walking
Advertising slogans [15]

**finish**
– To f. a work
Picasso [9]

**fire**
– duty is to hire and f.
Maxwell [3]
– Come on baby light my f.
Morrison, J. [1]
– left-wing thought is . . . playing with f.
Orwell [11]
– wore at their hearts the f.'s centre
Spender, S. [3]
– We all live in a house on f.
Williams, T. [20]

**fired**
– sooner or later they're going to get f.
Goldman, W. [2]

**fires**
– Keep the home f. burning
Ford, L. G. [1]

**first**
– F. things first
Conran, S. [3]

**first lady**
– f. l. is . . . an unpaid public servant
Johnson, Lady B. [2]
– see the f. l. as another means
Reagan, N. [2]

**first-born**
– a massacre of the f.
Abbott [1]

**fish**
– thanks for all the f.
Adams. D. [6]
– F. fuck in it
Fields, W.C. [6]
– like a f. without a bicycle
Steinem [9]

**fish-knives**
– Phone for the f., Norman
Betjeman [13]

**fission**
– f. in the modern soul
van der Post [4]

**fist**
– encounter an iron f.
Shamir [1]

**five-year plan**
– what's left/of the f.
Mayakovsky [5]

**flag**
– right to burn the f.
Cash [1]

**flat**
– very f., Norfolk
Coward [2]

**flattery**
– f. of posterity . . . is worth nothing
Borges [11]

**Fleet Street**
– how bad F. really is
Livingstone [1]

**fleshpots**
– f. of Euston
Joyce, J. [29]

**flexible**
– your f. friend
Advertising slogans [1]

**fling**
– Against you I will f. myself
Woolf [43]

**flooded**
– Streets f.. Please advise
Benchley [5]

**Florentines**
– we F. live with that past
Zeffirelli [2]

**flower**
– take a f. in your hand
O'Keeffe [3]
– Find a street without a f.
Priestley [1]

**flowers**
– strange f. of reason
Aragon [2]
– giving f. to the cops
Burroughs, W. [11]
– I hate f.
O'Keeffe [4]
– Where have all the f. gone
Seeger, P. [2]

**flying**
– men in their f. machines
Davies, J. [1]

**foaming**
– River Tiber f. with much blood
Powell, E. [3]

**fog**
– f. comes/on little cat feet
Sandburg [2]

**foggy**
– f. day in London Town
Gershwin [4]

**fogies**
– world is burdened with young f.
Davies, R. [3]

**folk**
– All music is f. music
Armstrong, L. [4]
– whole trouble with a f. song
Lambert [1]
– f. music was something old
Seeger, P. [4]

**folks**
– Th-th-th-th-that's all, f.
Avery [1]

**follow**
– F. me if I advance!
Ngo Dinh Diem [1]

**fond**
– You have to be very f. of men
Duras [5]

**food**
– F. first, then morality
Brecht [3]
– Sharing f. with another human
Fisher, M.F.K. [3]
– f. is more dangerous than sex
Mason [1]
– attitude toward the f. choice of others
Skinner [2]

**fool**
– f. all of the people all of the time
Adams, F.P. [3]
– f. who proclaims the general folly first
Jung [16]
– You can f. all the people
Levine [1]
– f. and her money are soon courted
Rowland, H. [3]

**fooled**
– don't get f. again
Townshend [5]

**foolish**
– Looking f. does the spirit good
Updike [30]

**fools**
– determination to banish f. foundered
Bunting [6]

– *Southern trees bear a strange f.*
  Holiday [1]
**fruit tree**
– *Fame is but a f. t.*
  Drake [1]
**fruitful**
– *'Be f., and multiply'*
  Allen, W. [1]
**fuck**
– *zipless f. is absolutely pure*
  Jong [3]
– *They f. you up, your mum and dad*
  Larkin [20]
**Führer**
– *will of the F.*
  Frank, H. [1]
**fun**
– *most f. I've ever had*
  Allen, W. [23]
– *People must not do things for f.*
  Herbert [1]
– *No f., my babe. No Fun*
  Pop [1]
– *F.! I think it's disgusting*
  Westwood [1]
**funeral**
– *only reason I might go to the f.*
  Anonymous [14]
**funny**
– *F. is funny is funny*
  Connolly, B. [3]
– *only man . . . can be f.*
  Knox [2]
– *Surely nothing could be that f.*
  Melly [3]
– *Everything is f.*
  Rogers, W. [2]
– *f. thing happened to me*
  Stevenson [11]
– *everything was just being f.*
  Warhol [7]
**fur**
– *40 dumb animals to make a f. coat*
  Political slogans [18]
**future**
– *f. a . . . suburb of the soul*
  Ballard [6]
– *I have a Vision of the F.*
  Betjeman [11]
– *I don't try to describe the f.*
  Bradbury, R. [1]
– *danger of the f.*
  Fromm [6]
– *turning away from the f.*
  Gates [1]
– *f. is already in place*
  Grass [5]
– *f.'s no calamitous change*
  Hughes, T. [4]
– *Nobody 'as a f.*
  Leigh [3]
– *first men of a F.*
  Lewis. W. [4]
– *When there's no f.*
  Lydon [3]
– *fixed image of the f.*
  Mitchell, Juliet [1]
– *better prepared for the f.*
  Murdoch, I. [22]
– *vision of the f.*
  Orwell [49]
– *been over into the f.*
  Steffens [2]
– *F. shock is . . . the premature arrival of the future*
  Toffler [1]
**futures**
– *old f. have a way of hanging around*
  Gibson [2]
**fuzzy**
– *f. end of the lollipop*
  Monroe [4]

**gadfly**
– *be a g. in the conscience*
  Coggan [1]
**gaffe**
– *g. is when a politician tells the truth*
  Kinsley [2]
**gag**
– *g. that muted those black mouths*
  Sartre [8]
**gain**
– *To g. that which is worth having*
  McAliskey [1]
**galaxies**
– *all these g. inside of us*
  Shepard [6]
**galleon**
– *Stately as a g.*
  Grenfell [2]
**gambler**
– *Show me a g.*
  Puzo [4]
**game**
– *g. with a lot of waiting*
  Irving, J. [2]
– *g. which takes less than three days*
  Stoppard [12]
**games**
– *greatest dread of all, the dread of g.*
  Betjeman [15]
**Gandhi**
– *G., a seditious Middle Temple lawyer*
  Churchill, W. [8]
**gang**
– *with a g. like that*
  Kerouac [5]
**gangster**
– *g. speaks for us*
  Warshow [1]
**gangsterism**
– *g. is a very important avenue*
  Doctorow [5]
**garbage**
– *chosen the g. disposal unit*
  Debord [3]
**Garbo**
– *one sees in G. sober*
  Tynan [1]
**garden**
– *in search of my mother's g.*
  Walker [4]
**gardening**
– *G. is not a rational act*
  Atwood [3]
**gardens**
– *Paradise haunts g.*
  Jarman [8]
**gastronomic**
– *complete g. satisfaction*
  Fisher, M.F.K. [2]
**gastronomical**
– *G. perfection can be reached*
  Fisher, M.F.K. [5]
**gay**
– *condition that is now called g.*
  Baldwin, J. [11]
– *we must also create a g. life*
  Foucault [4]
– *g. people . . . get into right-wing politics*
  Maupin [3]
– *If you don't want people to think you're g.*
  Michael [1]
– *G. men are guardians of the masculine*
  Paglia [9]
**geezers**
– *Old g. don't jump*
  Barnes, J. [13]

**general**
– *best service a retired g. can perform*
  Bradley [3]
– *G. has dedicated himself*
  Stevenson [19]
**General Motors**
– *good for G. M.*
  Wilson, C.E. [1]
**general strike**
– *G. S. has taught the working classes more*
  Balfour [2]
**generalizations**
– *g. work to protect the mind*
  Nemerov [3]
– *distrust all g. about women*
  Russell, B. [21]
**generation**
– *Let us not then speak ill of our g.*
  Beckett [6]
– *Ours was a gentle g.*
  Dunn [7]
– *Every g. revolts against its fathers*
  Mumford [1]
– *energy of a whole g.*
  Thompson, H.S. [4]
– *Talkin' 'bout my g.*
  Townshend [1]
– *g. drowned in mortification*
  Vaneigem [5]
**generosity**
– *G. is a part of my character*
  Lever [1]
**generous**
– *a g. man defined*
  Greer [10]
– *g. to a fault*
  Harris, S. [1]
– *cynic is . . . prematurely disappointed*
  Harris, S. [2]
**genes**
– *go by the name of g.*
  Dawkins [2]
**genetic**
– *G. control . . . weapon of the future*
  Winterson [7]
**Genetic manipulation**
– *g. m. seeks to transform a process*
  Charles, Prince of Wales [10]
**genial**
– *more g. human traits are assigned to the underclass*
  Millett [4]
**genital**
– *great clot of g. fluid*
  Pound [12]
**genius**
– *nature of g. is to provide idiots with ideas*
  Aragon [3]
– *Almost everybody is born a g.*
  Bukowski [4]
– *I'm not a g.*
  Hirst [5]
– *man of g. makes no mistakes*
  Joyce, J. [19]
– *man of g. has a right*
  Pound [8]
– *Never confuse a g. with a Saint*
  Schama [4]
– *takes a lot of time to be a g.*
  Stein [12]
– *Real g. is nothing else*
  Weil [14]
**genocide**
– *G. . . . is an exercise in community building*
  Gourevitch [1]

**gentleman**
– *g. doesn't pounce . . . he glides*
  Crisp [17]
– *Being a g. is the number one priority*
  Fox [1]
– *g. is something you have to be*
  Pirandello [1]
**genuineness**
– *G. only thrives in the dark*
  Huxley, A. [6]
**George**
– *G. – don't do that*
  Grenfell [1]
**Georgia**
– *G. on my mind*
  Gorrell [1]
– *Being a G. author*
  O'Connor, F. [5]
**geriatrics**
– *65 . . . puts me in with the g.*
  Thurber [25]
**German**
– *common G. soldier*
  Hitler [16]
– *Unhappy G. nation*
  Mann, T. [8]
**Germans**
– *Gracious Lord, oh bomb the G.*
  Betjeman [6]
– *G. classify*
  Cather [5]
– *G. are called brutal*
  Forster [2]
**Germany**
– *death is a master from G.*
  Celan [1]
– *from G. to Downing Street*
  Chamberlain [2]
– *this country is at war with G.*
  Chamberlain [3]
– *G. has an inferiority complex*
  Harris, Robert [1]
– *G. will either be a world power*
  Hitler [8]
– *G. calling*
  Joyce, W. [1]
– *I love G. so dearly*
  Mauriac [1]
– *walk through the ruined cities of G.*
  Orwell [33]
– *If G. . . . were to enslave the European nations*
  Weil [6]
**Gestapo**
– *milkman and not the G.*
  Bidault [2]
**getaways**
– *History is full of ignominious g.*
  Orwell [23]
**Gettysburg**
– *G. address was so short*
  Hemingway [22]
**ghost**
– *if a g. exists*
  Kubrick [3]
**ghosts**
– *only g. in the making*
  Barker, P. [2]
– *g. you chase you never catch*
  Malkovich [1]
– *g. are hungry*
  Raine, K. [2]
**giants**
– *world of nuclear g. and ethical infants*
  Bradley [1]
**gift**
– *When God hands you a g.*
  Capote [6]

– *something boring about somebody else's h.*
Huxley, A. [1]
– *Here is a possibility of perfect h.*
Kafka [4]
– *perfect h. is unrealizable*
Levi, P. [2]
– *how poor is the language of h.*
Mandelstam [2]
– *lamentable phrase 'the pursuit of h.'*
Muggeridge [4]
– *H. is . . . everyday mode of consciousness*
Murdoch, I. [7]
– *most exciting h.*
Nash, O. [9]
– *if h. forgets you a little bit*
Prévert [5]
– *h. alone is salutary to the body*
Proust [21]
– *h. . . . is really useful to us in one way*
Proust [22]
– *accursed h. I have dreaded*
Shaw, G.B. [3]
– *H. is a wine of the rarest vintage*
Smith, L.P. [1]
– *never direct people towards h.*
Solzhenitsyn [4]
– *H. is an imaginary condition*
Szasz [6]

**happy**
– *We all want to be h.*
Boyd [1]
– *They seldom looked h.*
Holleran [1]
– *If a man would be h. for a week*
Thubron [3]
– *H. days are here again*
Yellen [1]

**hard-nosed**
– *h., small-eyed, sparse of hair*
Neruda [8]

**hard-sell**
– *no/h. or soft-sell TV push*
Nash, O. [22]

**hardship**
– *People can live through h.*
Solzhenitsyn [9]

**harlot**
– *woman hasn't got a tiny streak of a h.*
Lawrence, D.H. [22]

**Harlow**
– *The t is silent, as in H.*
Asquith, M. [3]
– *H. the house of the dead*
Auden [2]
– *At H., you could have any boy*
Mortimer [6]

**has-been**
– *better to be a h.*
Parkinson, C. [2]

**hasta**
– *H. la vista, baby*
Schwarzenegger [2]

**hat**
– *leopard-skin pill-box h.*
Dylan [25]
– *man who mistook his wife for a h.*
Sacks, O. [1]

**hatchet**
– *fergits where he buried a h.*
Hubbard [2]

**hate**
– *I cannot love anyone if I h. myself*
Jung [9]
– *H. traps us by binding us*
Kundera [14]

**hated**
– *Never h. a man enough to give him diamonds*
Gabor [1]
– *might be h. at extremely low cost*
Rostand [10]

**hatred**
– *h. only perceives the topmost surface*
Broch [3]
– *I must have no h.*
Cavell [1]
– *What we need is h.*
Genet [3]
– *h. . . . is a little like the odour of garlic*
Rostand [9]
– *intellectual h. is the worst*
Yeats [11]

**hats**
– *H. divide generally into three classes*
Whitehorn [4]

**having**
– *I'll have what she's h.*
Ephron [4]

**head**
– *if you can keep your h.*
Kerr, J. [1]
– *Feed your h.*
Slick [2]
– *H. 'em up*
Warren, J. [1]

**healing**
– *H./ . . . is not a science*
Auden [44]
– *hour of a white h.*
Jennings [4]

**health**
– *he's a h. fanatic*
Clarke [3]

**heard**
– *right to be h.*
Humphrey [2]

**heart**
– *desires of the h. are as crooked as corkscrews*
Auden [7]
– *When your h. is broken*
Shaw, G.B. [5]
– *I aimed at the country's h.*
Sinclair, U. [3]
– *Your cheatin' h.*
Williams, H. [1]
– *fanatic h.*
Yeats [22]

**heartbeat**
– *h. from the Presidency*
Stevenson [9]

**heartbreak**
– *H. Hotel*
Presley [2]

**heat**
– *I want the h.*
Amis, M. [5]
– *If you can't stand the h.*
Truman [5]
– *white h. of the technological revolution*
Wilson, H. [3]

**heaven**
– *H. – I'm in Heaven*
Berlin, Irving [4]
– *kingdom of h. suffers violence*
Joyce, J. [13]
– *trouble with kingdoms of h. on earth*
Muggeridge [11]
– *Pennies From H.*
Potter [4]

**hell**
– *Let me go to h.*
Beckett [14]

– *H. is not to love any more*
Bernanos [3]
– *H. and damnation,/life is such fun*
Blok [1]
– *H. is oneself*
Eliot [56]
– *the h. which we see*
Golding [3]
– *safest road to H.*
Lewis, C.S. [2]
– *prevent you from going to h.*
Lodge Jr. [1]
– *H. is other people*
Sartre [7]
– *prefer real h. to an imaginary paradise*
Weil [18]

**hello**
– *H., good evening, and welcome*
Frost, D. [1]

**hells**
– *strange h. within the minds war made*
Gurney [1]

**help**
– *not helpful to h. a friend*
Hurd [1]
– *with a little h. from my friends*
Lennon & McCartney [10]

**helper**
– *mother's little h.*
Jagger/Richards [3]

**hen**
– *better take a wet h.*
Khrushchev [5]

**here**
– *We're h./Because/We're here*
Anonymous [20]
– *how did I get h.*
Byrne [2]

**Here and Now**
– *H. and N. is neither now nor here*
Swift [3]

**heretic**
– *oppressor or a h.*
Camus [11]

**heritage**
– *'h.' as a term of obligation*
Ascherson [1]

**hero**
– *show me a h.*
Fitzgerald, F.S. [23]
– *business of a h.*
Lenin [7]
– *h. is a man who would argue*
Mailer [9]

**hero**
– *I'm a hero wid coward's legs*
Milligan [2]

**heroes**
– *We can be h./Just for one day*
Bowie [4]
– *Unhappy the land that is in need of h.*
Brecht [12]
– *doesn't make any h. anymore*
Greene [12]
– *H. are created by popular demand*
Johnson, G. [1]
– *country for h. to live in*
Lloyd George [3]
– *individuals who don't want to be h.*
Moore, B. [2]
– *unless he believes in h.*
Wayne [4]

**heroic**
– *human beings are h.*
Orwell [21]

**heroism**
– *opportunities for h. are limited*
Wilson, A. [1]

**heterosexuality**
– *failed to convert me to h.*
McKellen [1]
– *I have decided to give up h.*
Wandor [2]

**hiding**
– *h. is dangerous adventure*
Frank, A. [5]

**hierarchy**
– *In a h. every employee tends to rise*
Peter [1]

**high**
– *how low you go to get h.*
Lennon [18]
– *Eight miles h.*
McGuinn [1]
– *lost in a naturally induced h.*
Townshend [6]

**highbrow**
– *no two opinions as to what a h. is*
Woolf [49]

**hilarity**
– *h. was like a scream from a crevasse*
Greene [10]

**hillbilly**
– *before you can sing like a h.*
Williams, H. [2]

**him**
– *It is either h. or us*
Eden, A [2]
– *I'm with h.*
Fisher, C. [2]

**Himmler**
– *H. of the lower fifth*
Rattigan [2]

**hindsight**
– *H. is always twenty-twenty*
Wilder, B. [7]

**hip**
– *H. is the sophistication*
Mailer [2]
– *hard to be h. over thirty*
Viorst [2]

**hippies**
– *lazy, self-obsessed h.*
Elton [1]

**Hiroshima**
– *memory of what happened at H.*
Hersey [1]

**historian**
– *one safe rule for the h.*
Fisher, H.A.L. [1]

**historians**
– *H. are left forever chasing shadows*
Schama [1]
– *H. are pessimistic by nature*
Skidelsky [1]
– *Study men, not h.*
Truman [3]

**history**
– *bugle note of h.*
Bevan [4]
– *hand of h. upon our shoulders*
Blair [5]
– *H. begins when men begin to think*
Carr, E.H. [1]
– *H. will absolve me*
Castro [1]
– *Don't know much about h.*
Cooke, S. [2]
– *once you have confronted H.?*
De Gaulle [7]
– *H. teaches us that men . . . behave wisely*
Eban [1]

**job**
– Gizza j.
Bleasdale [1]
– no-future j. in the service sector
Coupland [1]
– out of a j. makes you passive
Doyle [3]
**job**
– Everyone sees life through their j.
Gray, A. [2]
**jobs**
– j. should be open to everybody
Kennedy, F. [3]
**Joe**
– Hey J.
Hendrix [1]
**Johannesburg**
– What's the word/ . . . /From J.
Scott-Heron [2]
**John Thomas**
– J. T. says good-night to lady Jane
Lawrence, D.H. [16]
**Johnny**
– Go J. go
Berry [3]
– Here's J.!
Carson, J. [1]
**joke**
– life has been one great big j.
Angelou [6]
– j. with a double meaning
Barker, R. [1]
– j. is a hired object
Miller, J. [2]
– every j. is ultimately a custard pie
Orwell [20]
**jokes**
– Family j. . . . are the bond
Benson [1]
– Forgive, O Lord, my little j.
Frost, R. [28]
– woman makes herself laugh at
her husband's . . . j.
Greer [4]
**Joneses**
– Keeping up with the J.
Crisp [2]
**journalism**
– J. . . . turning one's enemies into
money
Brown, C. [1]
– J. . . . consists in saying
Chesterton [8]
– honest j. is essential
Gellhorn [1]
– In America j. is regarded as
Sampson [2]
– j. is a more immediate short-term
weapon
Stoppard [13]
– Most rock j. is people who can't
write
Zappa [1]
– Every j. . . . is a kind of
confidence man
Malcolm [1]
– middle-class j.
Pasolini [2]
**journalist**
– j. is reporting a whim of his own
Waugh, E. [12]
– rather be called a j. than an
artist
Wells. H.G. [3]
– bribe . . . the/British journalist
Wolfe, H. [1]
**journalists**
– J. say a thing that . . . isn't true
Bennett, Arnold [4]
– j. . . . are ignorant
Black [1]
– j. sit at the edge of history
Fisk [1]

– J. belong in the gutter
Priestland [1]
**journey**
– Life . . . is a j.
Raban [2]
– this is what man's j. is about
Smith, L. [1]
– j. is like marriage
Steinbeck [6]
– j., not the arrival, matters
Theroux [4]
– J. . . . are born and not made
Durrell [2]
**journeys**
– J., those magic caskets
Lévi-Strauss [7]
– j. . . . occasion for pleasant
encounters
McEwan [4]
**joy**
– little j. into your humdrum lives
Hagen [1]
– City of Dreadful J.
Huxley, A. [8]
– Black people possess the secret
of j.
Walker [17]
**Joyce**
– J. is a kind of poet
Orwell [9]
**Judas**
– boyhood of J./Christ was betrayed
[1]
**judge**
– bringing the j. . . . into the dock
Algren [5]
– j. is not supposed to know . . .
facts of life
Parker, Lord [1]
**judgement**
– deal out death in j.
Tolkien [4]
**judges**
– judges don't age
Bagnold [1]
– Let judges secretly despair of
justice
Cohen [1]
**judgment**
– Don't wait for the Last J.
Camus [17]
**judgments**
– public has an interest only in j.
Benjamin [9]
**judicial**
– J. judgment must take deep
account
Frankfurter [2]
**June**
– J. is bustin' out all over
Hammerstein II [5]
**jungle**
– It's like a j. sometimes
Grandmaster Flash [1]
– law of the j. has broken down
Jumblatt [1]
**jungled**
– over-run, j. in my bed
Smart [4]
**junk**
– J. is the ideal product
Burroughs, W. [3]
– J. is just another nine to five gig
Carroll [1]
**junky**
– j. runs on junk time
Burroughs, W. [1]
**junta**
– Stick it up your j.
Sun [2]
**justice**
– price of j. is eternal publicity
Bennett, Arnold [7]

– J. should not only be done
Hewart [1]
– what stings is j.
Mencken [13]
– It is easy to do j.
Rattigan [1]
– cannot do j. to the dead
Shawcross [1]
– J. is conscience
Solzhenitsyn [3]
– j. is the first condition of
humanity
Soyinka [4]
– repressive j.
Weil [16]
**Kaiser**
– hatred of the K. is love true
Thomas, E. [6]
**Kalahari**
– man of the K. is Esau
van der Post [7]
**kangaroo**
– Tie me k. down, sport
Harris, Rolf [1]
**Kansas**
– I've a feeling we're not in K.
anymore
Garland, J. [2]
**karma**
– k. is working from another
lifetime
Hoddle [1]
**Kate**
– And some, alas, with K.
Auden [26]
**Kennedy**
– In the lead car were President
and Mrs K.
Johnson, Lady B. [1]
– man who accompanied
Jacqueline K.
Kennedy, J.F. [10]
**Kennedys**
– Who killed the K.
Jagger/Richards [4]
**Kenny**
– they've killed K.
Stone & Parker [1]
**Kerouac**
– K. opened a million coffee bars
Burroughs, W. [15]
**Keyhole**
– Every age has a k.
McCarthy, M. [7]
**Keynesians**
– We are all K. now
Friedman [2]
**kick**
– I get a k. out of you
Porter, C. [9]
**kill**
– you may have to k. me
Biko [8]
– k. yourself too late
Cioran [10]
– gift designed to k.
Douglas, K. [2]
– commandment Do not k.
John Paul II [5]
– how many kids did you k.
today
Political slogans [9]
– K. a man, one is a murderer
Rostand [1]
– urge to k., like the urge to
beget
Voznesensky [3]
**killed**
– everyone can be k.
Coppola [1]
**killer**
– I'm a natural born k.
Tarantino [11]

**killing**
– K. you and what you
represent
Tarantino [12]
**Kilroy**
– I helped K. write it.
Ferlinghetti [3]
– K. was here
Graffiti [1]
**Kiltartan**
– My country is K. Cross
Yeats [7]
**kinder**
– I want a k., gentler nation
Bush, G. [6]
**kindness**
– When k. has left people
Cather [4]
– k. that gazes upon itself
Gibran [6]
– terrible thing, this k.
Le Guin [2]
– Dame K. glides about my house
Plath [12]
**King**
– the K.'s life
Dawson, Lord [1]
– k. for a night
De Niro [2]
– once and future k.
White, T.H. [1]
**kingdoms**
– k. . . . have tottered
Trefusis [1]
**kings**
– k. in golden suits
Cheever [4]
– only five k. left
Farouk [1]
**kiss**
– euthanasia of a k.
de la Mare [5]
– k. is still a kiss
Hupfeld [1]
– What did that mean, to k.
Joyce, J. [2]
– K. Kiss Bang Bang
Kael [5]
– When women k.
Mencken [18]
– k. can be a comma
Mistinguett [1]
– k. all the fellows
Murray, L. [4]
**Kitchener**
– K. is a great poster
Asquith, E. [1]
**kitsch**
– k. . . . integral part of the human
condition
Kundera [7]
– K. is the daily art of our time
Rosenberg [3]
**knack**
– we've lost the k.
Day Lewis, C. [5]
**knees**
– We have gone on our k.
de Klerk [2]
**know**
– Not many people k. that
Caine [1]
– To k. all is not to forgive all
Crisp [6]
– To really k. someone
Jouhandeau [1]
– How do they k.
Parker, D. [11]
– not to k. what you are
Stein [13]
**knowin'**
– k. more than they do
Lee, H. [3]

*– L. is an offensive*
Whitehead [6]
*– Once you bring l. into the world*
Wiesel [3]
*– What a queer thing L. is*
Wodehouse [4]
**life-fate**
*– l. of the modern individual*
Mills [3]
**life-sentence**
*– l. in the dungeon of self*
Connolly, C. [20]
**light**
*– thousand points of l.*
Bush, G. [7]
*– l. of the oncoming train*
Lowell, R. [8]
**light bulb**
*– can't stand a naked l. b.*
Williams, T. [3]
**lightning**
*– I'd rather be a l. rod*
Kesey [2]
*– like writing history with l.*
Wilson, W. [1]
**liked**
*– I'm so universally l.*
De Vries [4]
*– He's l., but he's not well liked*
Miller, A. [1]
**Limbo**
*– L. is the place*
Waugh, E. [14]
**limit**
*– no l. to what a man can do*
Montague [1]
**limousine**
*– One perfect l.*
Parker, D. [6]
**Linda Tripp**
*– I hate L. T.*
Lewis, C.S. [1]
**line**
*– draw a l. without blurring it*
Churchill, W. [38]
*– An active l. on a walk*
Klee [8]
**lingerie**
*– vast variety of l.*
Izzard [2]
**lion**
*– nation . . . that had the l.'s heart*
Churchill, W. [49]
**lips**
*– Read my l.*
Bush, G. [5]
*– Red l. are not so red*
Owen [2]
**lipstick**
*– L. is power*
Follett [1]
**liquidity**
*– purpose in l.*
Brooke [3]
**listen**
*– they don't expect you to l.*
Waugh, E. [16]
**listening**
*– l. implies an inborn talent*
Copland [2]
**literary**
*– L. works cannot be taken over like factories*
Brecht [10]
*– England has the most sordid l. scene*
Burroughs, W. [12]
*– L. experience heals the wound*
Lewis, C.S. [6]
*– incompatibility between l. creation*
Vargas Llosa [2]

**literature**
*– L. is without proofs*
Barthes [11]
*– L. is not exhaustible*
Borges [6]
*– English l. is a kind of training*
Butler [1]
*– L. is the art of writing*
Connolly, C. [6]
*– L. . . . is condemned (or privileged)*
de Man [3]
*– test of l.*
Drew [1]
*– moral duty of l.*
Fischer [3]
*– l. goes as freight*
García Márquez [3]
*– attempt to devote oneself to l. alone*
Havel [6]
*– Scott took L. so solemnly*
Hemingway [23]
*– How simple the writing of l.*
Hemingway [30]
*– l. flourishes best*
Inge [5]
*– l. cannot grow from a neglected . . . soil*
James, P.D. [2]
*– L. is mostly about having sex*
Lodge [1]
*– crown of l. is poetry*
Maugham [15]
*– What is not in the open street is . . . l.*
Miller, H. [5]
*– What makes l. interesting*
Miller, J. [3]
*– human in language is l.*
Newman, B. [1]
*– l. . . . is not the pure medium*
Palmer, V. [2]
*– L. is a defence against the attacks of life*
Pavese [2]
*– materials for a work of l. were simply my past life*
Proust [20]
*– L. is where I go to explore the highest*
Rushdie [1]
*– L. is the one place in any society*
Rushdie [22]
*– highest mission of great l.*
Sábato [1]
*– Life is amorphous, l. is formal*
Sagan [3]
*– L. that is not the breath of contemporary*
Solzhenitsyn [2]
*– Woe to that nation whose l. is cut short*
Solzhenitsyn [13]
*– l. grows more terrible*
Stevens [22]
*– All the rest is l.*
Valéry [1]
*– If we can't stamp out l. in the country*
Waugh, E. [7]
*– L. is the orchestration of platitudes*
Wilder, T. [2]
*– incalculable luxury l.*
Wolfe, Tom [15]
*– L. is strewn with the wreckage of men*
Woolf [37]
**live**
*– easier to l. through someone else*
Friedan [4]

*– does not l. for the sake of living*
Pirandello [9]
*– l. large*
Thomas, R.S. [9]
**lives**
*– If men's l. are worth giving*
Ewart [4]
*– many l. are needed to make just one*
Montale [1]
**living**
*– as you go on l. with someone*
Barnes, J. [10]
*– L. and partly living*
Eliot [32]
*– I want to go on l.*
Frank, A. [3]
*– no longer praise the l.*
Hoffer [19]
*– Living is like . . . a long addition sum*
Pavese [1]
*– world owes us a l.*
Rubin [1]
*– slightest l. thing answers a deeper need*
Stark [3]
**lizard**
*– I am the L. King*
Morrison, J. [5]
**loafed**
*– better to have l. and lost*
Thurber [12]
**lodge**
*– flee to my l. in the hills*
Marx, G. [4]
**logic**
*– L.! What rubbish*
Forster [10]
*– L. takes care of itself*
Wittgenstein [1]
*– l. of the world is prior to all truth*
Wittgenstein [3]
**Lolita**
*– L., light of my life*
Nabokov [2]
**London**
*– man who is tired of L.*
Theroux [8]
**Londoner**
*– spirit of the L. stands resolute*
George VI [1]
*– Maybe it's because I'm a L.*
Gregg [1]
**loneliness**
*– No one ever discovers . . . his own l.*
Bernanos [4]
*– L. is a crowded room*
O'Connor, S. [2]
*– l. is but his fear of life*
O'Neill [3]
*– l. of the long-distance runner*
Sillitoe [1]
*– gift of l. is sometimes a radical vision*
Walker [2]
**lonely**
*– drinking and making love . . . two most l. pastimes*
Du Maurier [4]
*– When so many are l.*
Williams, T. [6]
**long**
*– best to live as l. as possible*
Mishima [2]
**long division**
*– worry about your failure at l. d.*
Williams, T. [14]
**Long Island**
*– L. I. represents . . . what God would have done*
Fleming, P. [1]

**long run**
*– L. r. is a misleading guide*
Keynes [4]
**longer**
*– people are going to be living l.*
Warhol [15]
**look**
*– L. at me, Ma, look at me*
Bruce [2]
**looked over**
*– better to be l. o.*
West, M. [11]
**looking**
*– Here's looking at you*
Bogart [2]
**looking-glasses**
*– Women have served . . . as l.*
Woolf [32]
**Lords**
*– L. without anger and honour*
Chesterton [11]
**Los Angeles**
*– L.A. was just a big dry sunny place*
Chandler [11]
*– Everybody in L.A. lives miles away*
Gray, S. [1]
*– Call L. A. any dirty name you like*
James [1]
*– If L. A. is not the one authentic rectum*
Mencken [17]
**loser**
*– world loves a good l.*
Hubbard [5]
**losers**
*– Why join a bunch of l.*
Neil [1]
**losing**
*– art of l. isn't hard to master*
Bishop [5]
**lost**
*– Nothing is l.*
Ridler [3]
*– You are a l. generation*
Stein [2]
**lottery**
*– unhappy L. winner*
Parsons, Tony [5]
**lounge suit**
*– genesis of the modern L. S.*
Schumpeter [5]
**Louvre**
*– L. is like the morgue*
Cocteau [6]
**love**
*– We men have got l. well weighed up*
Amis, K. [1]
*– There is l. of course*
Anouilh [5]
*– l. one another or die*
Auden [24]
*– Women are programmed to l. completely*
Bainbridge [6]
*– L. is only what people agree exists*
Barnes, J. [11]
*– To fall in l. is to create a religion*
Borges [7]
*– And all the little emptiness of l.*
Brooke [6]
*– l. and marriage*
Cahn [2]
*– Make thy l. sure*
Crane [3]
*– L. is the extra effort we make*
Crisp [19]
*– Falling in l. again*
Dietrich [1]

– *P. is a battle against the
    bewitchment*
  Wittgenstein [22]
– *stop doing p. when I want to*
  Wittgenstein [23]
– *p. proves that the philosopher
    exists*
  Stevens [13]

**phone**
– *Death invented the p.*
  Hughes, T. [11]
– *happy . . . that the p. is for
    you*
  Lebowitz [8]
– *why did you answer the p.*
  Thurber [6]

**photograph**
– *p. is a secret*
  Arbus [2]
– *We must p. it!*
  Calvino [1]
– *no such thing as a bad p.*
  Sontag [16]

**photographs**
– *P. deceive time*
  Allende, I. [3]

**photography**
– *in p. everything is so ordinary*
  Bailey [2]
– *magic of p. is metaphysical*
  Donovan [1]
– *p. is truth*
  Godard [3]
– *p. . . . creates the illusion of
    innocence*
  McEwan [7]
– *P. is the inventory of mortality*
  Sontag [14]
– *P. suits the temper of this
    age*
  Weston [2]

**physicists**
– *p. have known sin*
  Oppenheimer, J. R. [1]
– *p. are made of atoms*
  Wald [2]

**physics**
– *p. should represent a reality*
  Einstein [12]
– *People . . . who believe in p.*
  Einstein [15]

**Picasso**
– *P. is a communist*
  Dali [1]
– *painter like P.*
  Wiener [1]

**picture**
– *what a p. can be worth*
  De Mille [1]
– *If it's a good p.*
  Goldwyn [6]
– *destroy a person's p. of himself*
  Lessing [2]

**pictures**
– *P. are for entertainment*
  Goldwyn [10]
– *P. must be miraculous*
  Rothko [2]

**pig**
– *peasant becomes fond of his p.*
  Berger [5]

**pigeon**
– *instructions for being a p.*
  Bryson [5]

**pigeons**
– *P. on the grass alas*
  Stein [4]

**pigs**
– *all p. are upward-mobile*
  Thompson, H.S. [7]

**pike**
– *P., three inches long*
  Hughes, T. [7]

**pilgrimage**
– *life cannot be lived without p.*
  Hamilton-Paterson [2]

**pill**
– *One p. makes you larger*
  Slick [1]

**pimp**
– *you're a gastronomic p.*
  Bevan [17]

**pimples**
– *scratching of p.*
  Woolf [8]

**pink**
– *Why am I Mr P.?*
  Tarantino [2]

**Pinochet**
– *P. brought democracy to Chile*
  Dorfman [4]

**pint**
– *p. . . . very nearly an armful*
  Hancock [2]

**pips**
– *until the p. squeak*
  Geddes [1]

**piss**
– *pitcher of warm p.*
  Garner [1]

**pissing**
– *like p. in your father's beer*
  Hemingway [35]
– *inside the tent p.*
  Johnson, L.B. [9]

**pistons**
– *black statement of p.*
  Spender, S. [4]

**pity**
– *Don't p. me now*
  Agate [3]
– *P. is the feeling which arrests the
    mind*
  Joyce, J. [5]
– *Poetry is in the p.*
  Wilfred Owen [7]

**pizza**
– *go on stage and make a p.*
  Sinatra, F. [6]

**place**
– *'know your p.' is a good idea in
    politics*
  Safire, W. [1]

**places**
– *we could go p.*
  Garfield [1]

**plagiarism**
– *distinguish between tradition
    and p.*
  Bayley [1]
– *If you steal from one author,
    it's p.*
  Mizner [3]
– *human p. which is most difficult
    to avoid*
  Proust [16]

**plain**
– *no p. women on television*
  Ford, A. [1]
– *p. people know about love*
  Hepburn [2]
– *PINT OF P. IS YOUR ONLY
    MAN*
  O'Brien, F. [1]

**planet**
– *p. . . . is not really going
    anywhere*
  Thurber [7]
– *this p. is just barely habitable*
  Thurber [9]

**planning**
– *p. is indispensable*
  Eisenhower [6]
– *P. and competition can be
    combined*
  Hayek [1]

**plantation**
– *still be working on a p.*
  Holiday [4]

**plants**
– *I just come and talk to the p.*
  Charles, Prince of Wales [3]

**platitude**
– *a p. is simply a truth repeated*
  Baldwin, S. [1]

**Plato**
– *series of footnotes to P.*
  Whitehead [4]

**play**
– *prime business of a p.*
  Miller, A. [5]
– *House Beautiful is the p. lousy*
  Parker, D. [12]
– *child loves his p.*
  Spock [4]
– *play . . . a means of spending two
    hours in the dark*
  Tynan [5]

***Playboy***
– *what P. is really all about*
  Hefner [1]

**plays**
– *If you want to see your p.
    performed*
  Havel [14]
– *I write p. for people*
  Keeffe [1]
– *I do not see p. because I can nap
    at home*
  Maclaine [1]

**playwright**
– *p. . . . the litmus paper*
  Miller, A. [8]
– *Inside every p. there is a Falstaff*
  Osborne [12]

**pleasure**
– *Why can I not get some p. for
    myself*
  Belushi [3]
– *Give yourself to absolute p.*
  Curry, T. [1]
– *P. that isn't paid for*
  Loos [2]
– *Marred p.'s best*
  Smith, S. [8]
– *eruption of lived p.*
  Vaneigem [8]

**plots**
– *good supply of tragic p.*
  Cope [1]
– *We inherit p.*
  Hospital [1]

**plutography**
– *p. . . . great vice of the Eighties*
  Wolfe, Tom [13]

**poem**
– *p. . . . begins as a lump*
  Frost, R. [10]
– *p. is a momentary defeat of
    pessimism*
  Harrison, T. [2]
– *When you begin to read a p.*
  Jarrell [2]
– *p. is usually a highly professional*
  Larkin [15]
– *p. should not mean*
  MacLeish [1]
– *To read a p. is to hear it*
  Paz [4]
– *Ordering a man to write a p.*
  Sandburg [13]
– *p. need not have a meaning*
  Stevens [27]

**poems**
– *May your p. run away from
    home*
  McGough [3]
– *These p. do not live*
  Plath [5]

– *p. . . . written for the love of Man*
  Thomas, D. [12]
– *It is difficult/to get the news
    from p.*
  Williams, W.C. [6]

**poet**
– *Never trust a p. who can drive*
  Amis, M. [12]
– *p. can earn much more money*
  Auden [33]
– *No p. or novelist wishes*
  Auden [36]
– *As a p. there is only one political
    duty*
  Auden [47]
– *know at least one p. from cover*
  Brodsky [2]
– *worst tragedy for a p.*
  Cocteau [3]
– *earnings of a p.*
  Dahlberg [1]
– *p. like an acrobat*
  Ferlinghetti [1]
– *Is encouragement what the p.
    needs?*
  Fitzgerald, R. [1]
– *To be a p. is a condition*
  Graves [6]
– *war p. . . . cuts falsehood like a
    knife*
  Gurney [3]
– *p. should express the emotion*
  Hardy [2]
– *primed favourite continental p.*
  Joyce, J. [32]
– *p.'s work is to name the
    unnameable*
  Rushdie [13]
– *many ways of killing a p.*
  Solzhenitsyn [10]
– *p. must play the madcap*
  Terkel [2]
– *p. writing a poem is at peace*
  Thomas, D. [7]
– *heat and violence of the p.'s
    heart*
  Woolf [35]
– *p.'s mouth be silent*
  Yeats [2]

**poetic**
– *I would define the p. effect*
  Eco [7]
– *At words p., I'm so pathetic*
  Porter, C. [7]

**poetmen**
– *I HATE OLD P.*
  Corso [1]

**poetry**
– *p. makes nothing happen*
  Auden [17]
– *p. teaches us how to talk to
    ourselves*
  Bloom, H. [2]
– *nothing to say/ . . . and that is/p.*
  Cage [1]
– *P. is indispensable*
  Cocteau [11]
– *P. is . . . an escape from
    emotion*
  Eliot [11]
– *poem is not p.*
  Eliot [47]
– *P. is/powerless as grass*
  Feinstein [2]
– *sheep of p.*
  Fenton [2]
– *P. is a way of taking life*
  Frost, R. [27]
– *P. is what is lost in translation*
  Frost, R. [32]
– *P. is the language in which man
    explores*
  Fry, C. [6]

**punk**
– *P. . . . was just another English spectacle*
  Burchill [5]
– *P. to me was a form of free speech*
  Marcus [7]

**punks**
– *P. in their silly leather jackets*
  Lydon [7]

**purchase**
– *world of potential p.*
  Fisher, C. [3]

**pure**
– *p. as the driven slush*
  Bankhead [2]

**puritan**
– *p. is a person*
  Chesterton [16]
– *To the P., all things are impure*
  Lawrence, D.H. [13]
– *P. metaphor is a form of irony*
  Paulin [1]

**puritanism**
– *new p.*
  McInerney [4]
– *P. . . . fear that someone . . . may be happy*
  Mencken [8]

**purity**
– *apostles of p.*
  Rushdie [19]
– *P. is the power to contemplate defilement*
  Weil [20]

**purple**
– *P. haze all in my brain*
  Hendrix [2]
– *walk by the color p.*
  Walker [14]

**Purple Cow**
– *yes, I wrote the 'P. C.'*
  Burgess, G. [1]

**purpose**
– *Here is God's p.*
  Fuller [1]

**pursued**
– *only the p., the pursuing*
  Fitzgerald, F.S. [8]

**pusher**
– *God damn the p. man*
  Axton [1]

**pussy**
– *persian p. from over the sea*
  Marquis [3]

**pyjamas**
– *in the drawer marked p.*
  Thomas, D. [16]

**pylons**
– *P., those pillars*
  Spender, S. [6]

**pyramid**
– *forgotten man at the bottom of the economic p.*
  Roosevelt, F. [1]

**pyre**
– *heaping up its own funeral p.*
  Powell, E. [2]

**quality**
– *Never mind the q.*
  Powell, V./Driver, Harry. [8]

**Quantum mechanics**
– *Q. m. is certainly imposing*
  Einstein [3]

**quarks**
– *Three q. for Muster Mark*
  Joyce, J. [31]

**quarrel**
– *q. . . . between people*
  Chamberlain [1]
– *lover's q. with the world*
  Frost, R. [25]
– *takes . . . one to make a q.*
  Inge [1]

– *of the q. with ourselves, poetry*
  Yeats [14]

**quarrels**
– *Books and harlots have their q. in public*
  Benjamin [4]

**Quebec**
– *Long live Free Q!*
  De Gaulle [11]

**queen**
– *q. of people's hearts*
  Diana, Princess of Wales [5]

**queer**
– *modern q. was invented*
  Jarman [5]

**quest**
– *The Ring-bearer has fulfilled his Q.*
  Tolkien [6]

**question**
– *need to q.*
  Coupland [12]
– *what is the q.*
  Stein [16]

**questions**
– *All nonsense q. are unanswerable*
  Lewis, C.S. [12]
– *easy to answer the ultimate q.*
  Osborne [10]

**quit**
– *I now q. altogether public affairs*
  Edward VIII [2]
– *try again. Then q.*
  Fields, W.C. [5]

**quotable**
– *better to be q. than honest*
  Stoppard [9]

**quotation**
– *Fidelity . . . is the sine qua non of journalistic q.*
  Malcolm [2]
– *q. is not an excerpt*
  Mandelstam [8]
– *q. marks tend to be blotted out*
  Miller, A. [10]
– *indulge in of perpetual q.*
  Smyth [1]
– *q. is a national vice*
  Waugh, E. [19]

**quotations**
– *Q. . . . are like wayside robbers*
  Benjamin [6]
– *read books of q.*
  Churchill, W. [5]
– *Q. are useful*
  Debord [4]
– *pretentious q. . . . the surest road to tedium*
  Fowler, H.W. [1]
– *taste for q. . . . is a Surrealist taste*
  Sontag [15]

**quote**
– *get to q. yourself shamelessly*
  Reagan, R. [23]

**rabbit**
– *We are the white r.*
  Gaarder [1]
– *Run, r.*
  Gay [3]

**race**
– *R. prejudice is not only a shadow over the colored*
  Buck [1]
– *No r. has the last word on culture*
  Garvey [2]
– *whole r. is a poet that writes down*
  Stevens [15]

**races**
– *only two r. on this planet*
  Fowles [6]

**racism**
– *R. is an ism*
  Benedict [2]
– *R.? But isn't it . . . misanthropy?*
  Brodsky [4]
– *R. as a form of skin worship*
  Jackson, J. [3]
– *vanished victims of r.*
  Speer [1]

**rackets**
– *r. are run on strictly A. lines*
  Capone [1]

**radical**
– *I never dared be r.*
  Frost, R. [21]
– *r. is a man with both feet firmly planted in the air*
  Roosevelt, F. [8]

**radio**
– *folklore of the world of the r.*
  Stevens [16]
– *popular r. is based on repetition*
  Wogan[2]

**radio-active**
– *left a r. and not radiant land*
  Houston [1]

**rage**
– *R. is the only quality*
  Breslin [1]
– *r. . . . against yourself*
  Ono [5]
– *r., against the dying of the light*
  Thomas, D. [11]

**railways**
– *r. are irresistible bazaars*
  Theroux [2]

**rain**
– *r. in Spain*
  Lerner, A.J. [2]
– *sound of the r. is like the voices*
  Mishima [1]
– *Still falls the R.*
  Sitwell [2]

**rainbow**
– *Somewhere over the r.*
  Garland, J. [1]
– *our nation is a r.*
  Jackson, J. [6]

**ramblers**
– *R. are just a . . . dirty mac brigade*
  Van Hoogstraten [1]

**Rambo**
– *After seeing R. last night*
  Reagan, R. [19]
– *I see R. as a philanthropist*
  Stallone [1]

**rape**
– *Politically, I call it r.*
  MacKinnon [1]

**rape**
– *principle of procrastinated r.*
  Pritchett [1]
– *R. is a part of war*
  Rich [10]
– *movement against date r.*
  Roiphe [2
– *you can't commit r. a little*
  Steffens [1]
– *R. isn't actually the worst thing*
  Weldon [12]

**raped**
– *it is like being r.*
  Diana, Princess of Wales [4]

**rapists**
– *all men are r.*
  French [2]

**rapper**
– *influence to your son as a r.*
  Ice Cube [2]

**rapping**
– *r. for people*
  Ice-T [3]

**rat**
– *You dirty, double-crossing r.*
  Cagney [1]
– *Anyone can r.*
  Churchill, W. [3]

**rat race**
– *r. is for rats*
  Reid, Jimmy [1]

**Razors**
– *R. pain you*
  Parker, D. [4]

**reactionaries**
– *I thank God for r.*
  Collingwood [1]

**read**
– *conventional good r. is usually a bad read*
  Bradbury, M. [3]
– *nobody ought to r. while he was talking*
  Brittain [3]
– *r part of it all the way through*
  Goldwyn [11]
– *your wife or your servants to r.*
  Griffith-Jones [1]
– *I never loved to r.*
  Lee, H. [1]
– *r. toward the right*
  Thurber [21]

**reader**
– *ideal r. suffering from an ideal insomnia*
  Joyce, J. [26]

***Reader's Digest***
– *R. D. is a tourist guidebook*
  Dorfman [1]

**reading**
– *R. isn't an occupation we encourage*
  Orton [3]
– *With one day's r.*
  Pound [25]
– *I prefer r.*
  Smith L.P. [21]
– *unable to distinguish what is worth r.*
  Trevelyan [5]

**Reagan**
– *R. was a flesh and blood version*
  Hoggart [3]
– *battle for the mind of Ronald R.*
  Noonan [3]

**Reagans**
– *R. will be the rule*
  Vidal [17]

**real**
– *One wants glimpses of the r.*
  Brodkey [2]
– *r. is hard and rough*
  Weil [19]

**realist**
– *to be a r. you must believe in miracles*
  Ben-Gurion [1]

**reality**
– *R. is r–ather like a r–abbit*
  Barnes, J. [16]
– *accidental encounter with r.*
  Daney [1]
– *R. . . . doesn't go away*
  Dick [1]
– *Cannot bear very much r.*
  Eliot [36]
– *I'd like to take part in a change of r.*
  Hendrix [4]
– *R. is a question of perspective*
  Rushdie [2]
– *r. is always material reality*
  Trilling [3]

**reason**
– *R. is a whore*
  Cioran [2]

– *R. is man's instrument for arriving at the truth*
Fromm [4]

**reasons**
– *Men are never convinced of your r.*
Camus [15]

**rebel**
– *what is a r.?*
Camus [9]
– *No one can go on being a r. too long*
Durrell [4]
– *R. Without a Cause*
Linder [1]
– *To be a r. is not to be a revolutionary*
Millett [6]

**rebellion**
– *Poor Siegfried's r. hadn't counted*
Barker, P. [1]

**rebellious**
– *In the relations of . . . a r. people*
Reed, J. [1]

**recipes**
– *All r. are built on the belief*
Thorne [1]

**recollection**
– *Imagine the organ of r.*
Barnes, J. [8]

**record**
– *r. of one's life*
Kenny [1]
– *play the r. at the right speed*
Peel [1]

**recovery**
– *r. is brought about not by the physician*
Groddeck [1]

**red**
– *make a right turn on a r. light*
Allen, W. [17]

**red brick**
– *not even r. b.*
Osborne [3]

**Redford**
– *Robert R. . . . has turned almost alarmingly blond*
Kael [9]

**reflect**
– *To r. is to disturb one's thoughts*
Rostand [7]

**reflection**
– *r. as on the surface of a mirror*
Charles, Prince of Wales [2]

**reforms**
– *political and social r.*
Haldane [1]

**refuge**
– *haven of r. from the world*
Russell, B. [13]

**refugee**
– *I am a r. in a crowded boat*
Reagan, R. [18]

**refugees**
– *judge politicians by how they treat r.*
Livingstone [5]

**refuse**
– *when men r. to fight*
Political slogans[6]

**refuses**
– *man . . . r. to be what he is*
Camus [8]

**reggae**
– *R. music is simple*
Marley [4]

**regime**
– *gummy, eat-and-let-eat r.*
Chinua Achebe [1]

**regrets**
– *end up with the right r.*
Miller, A. [14]

**regrette**
– *Non, je ne r. rien*
Piaf [2]

**Reich**
– *no restless R.*
Kohl [1]

**reinvent**
– *you have to r. yourself*
Hirst [3]

**reject**
– *those who want to r. life*
Szasz [13]

**rejoice**
– *Just r. at that news*
Thatcher [11]

**relationship**
– *r. . . . is like a shark*
Allen, W. [22]
– *formula for achieving a successful r.*
Crisp [18]

**relationships**
– *take the danger out of human r.*
Harrison, B [2]

**relatives**
– *Every man sees in his r.*
Mencken [7]
– *When our r. are at home*
Shaw, G.B. [3]

**relativity**
– *theory of r.*
Einstein [1]
– *That's r.*
Einstein [13]

**relaxation**
– *sunk from a riot of r.*
Nash, O. [20]

**released**
– *I shall be r.*
Dylan [29]

**religion**
– *R. and art*
Cather [8]
– *r. without science is blind*
Einstein [7]
– *To know a person's r.*
Hoffer [7]
– *consolations of r.*
Lewis, C.S. [1]
– *no reason to bring r. into it*
O'Casey [4]
– *R. to me has always been the wound*
Potter [9]
– *All the sweetness of r. is conveyed*
Shaw, G.B. [13]
– *R. is the state of being grasped*
Tillich [1]
– *R. enables us to ignore nothingness*
Updike [29]

**religions**
– *impertinent to great r.*
Le Carré [7]
– *All r. of the only God*
Montale [2]

**religious**
– *hope I never get so old I get r.*
Bergman, Ingmar [4]
– *I am a passionately r. man*
Lawrence, D.H. [1]

**remarks**
– *r. are not literature*
Stein [6]

**remedy**
– *Auntie Maggie's R.*
Formby [5]

**remember**
– *We will r. them*
Binyon [1]
– *What we r. is what we become*
Osborne [13]

**remorse**
– *r. ought to stop biting*
Nash, O. [10]

**rendezvous**
– *shall not fail that r.*
Seeger, A. [2]

**repetition**
– *humiliated r.*
Barthes [9]

**reporter**
– *become a royal r.*
Hastings [1]
– *If the r. has killed our imagination*
Kraus [4]

**reprieve**
– *been granted a r.*
Kapuciski [4]

**reproducers**
– *Most modern r. of life*
Stevens [26]

**Republican**
– *R. party makes even its young men*
Stevenson [10]

**reputation**
– *One makes one's r.*
Frayn [1]
– *Until you've lost your r.*
Mitchell, M. [3]

**research**
– *r. is surely the art of the soluble*
Medawar [1]
– *R. is usually a policeman*
Moore, B. [3]

**reserves**
– *defined by its moral r.*
Trotsky [18]

**resistance**
– *R. as global as capital*
Political slogans [32]

**resources**
– *We have limited r.*
Piercy [2]

**respect**
– *R. Find out what it means to me*
Franklin [1]

**respectability**
– *long descent into r.*
Rice-Davies [2]

**respectable**
– *eventually you get r.*
Garcia [3]

**responds**
– *moment that a man no longer r.*
Mishima [2]

**responsibility**
– *R. is what awaits outside . . .*
Creativity
Gordimer [4]
– *bear the whole r.*
Sartre [3]
– *you've absolved yourself of r.*
Saunders [2]

**rest**
– *where's the r. of me*
Reagan, R. [1]

**restaurant**
– *get anything you want at Alice's R.*
Guthrie, A. [1]

**retire**
– *r. into a fungus basement*
Mitchell, A. [2]

**retraint**
– *Why are we so full of r.*
Miller, H. [10]

**retreat**
– *r. ahead of it*
Barthes [8]

**return**
– *I came through and I shall r.*
MacArthur [1]

– *I hate that word. It's r.*
Swanson [2]

**revenge**
– *understand the exact/ . . . r.*
Heaney [4]
– *career has been an act of r.*
Wax [1]

**reverence**
– *no longer conditioned for r. and awe*
Updike [26]

**reverie**
– *R. is not a mind vacuum*
Bachelard [2]

**review**
– *bad r. is even less important*
Murdoch, I. [26]

**reviewers**
– *r. are powerful*
Clurman [1]

**reviews**
– *When the r. are bad*
Liberace [1]

**revolt**
– *interested in anything about r.*
Morrison, J. [7]

**revolution**
– *logic of r.*
Ali, T. [1]
– *idea that a r. in the West*
Ali, T. [2]
– *I began r. with 82 men*
Castro [3]
– *R. is the festival of the oppressed*
Greer [8]
– *make peaceful r. impossible*
Kennedy, J.F. [15]
– *nothing better than only r.*
Khrushchev [11]
– *children of the r. are always ungrateful*
Le Guin [5]
– *cannot make a r. in white gloves*
Lenin [8]
– *r. is not a dinner party*
Mao Zedong [1]
– *r. does not last more than fifteen years*
Ortega y Gasset [8]
– *r. will not be televised*
Scott-Heron [1]
– *If the R. has the right to destroy bridges*
Trotsky [5]

**revolutionaries**
– *Most r. are potential Tories*
Orwell [16]

**revolutionary**
– *radical r. will become a conservative*
Arendt [5]
– *cannot sustain r. attitudes*
Djilas [3]
– *I am a r. woman*
Fonda [1]
– *r. is guided by strong feelings of love*
Guevara [3]
– *If today I stand here as a r.*
Hitler [3]
– *first duty of a r.*
Hoffman, A. [1]

**revolutionist**
– *r. ought to be careful*
Dos Passos [2]

**revolutions**
– *History is a relay of r.*
Alinsky [1]
– *R. are celebrated when . . . no longer dangerous*
Boulez [1]
– *violence of r.*
Galbraith [10]

– r. have to be successful
  Gilliatt [3]
– R. are brought about by men
  Nkrumah [2]
– All r. devour their own children
  Röhm [1]
– manage our r. much more
  quietly
  Thatcher [27]
– R. are always verbose
  Trotsky [12]

**rhetorical-over-compensation**
– psychos themselves would call
  . . . R.
  Thurber [4]

**Rhine**
– you think of the R.
  Baldwin, S. [4]

**Rhythm**
– Hit me with your r. stick
  Dury [4]
– I got r.
  Gershwin [1]
– All God's chillun got r.
  Gus Kahn [1]

**rhythms**
– r. of women's lives
  Mead [3]

**rich**
– being r. is about acting
  Amis, M. [3]
– Poor little r. girl
  Coward [1]
– the r. . . . are different
  Fitzgerald, F. S. [14]
– r. is better
  Grahame [2]
– r. were dull
  Hemingway [16]
– I don't care how r. he is
  Monroe [3]
– most obnoxious . . . are those who
  serve the r.
  O'Brien, E. [2]
– wretchedness of being r.
  Smith L.P. [15]
– not behave as the r. behave
  Smith L.P. [16]
– r. is better
  Tucker [1]
– To be r. . . . means to possess
  Vaneigem [6]

**riches**
– r. and freedom here
  Walesa [1]

**Rico**
– is this the end of R.
  Robinson, E.G. [1]

**ridiculous**
– fine sense of the r.
  Albee [3]

**right**
– Where did I go r.
  Brooks, M. [2]
– r. is not what someone gives
  you
  Clark, R. [1]
– nothing . . . gives us the r. to
  stop time
  Gellhorn [2]
– believe that they are exclusively
  in the r.
  Huxley, A. [9]
– I am not . . . a man of the r.
  Mosley [5]
– man oughta do what he thinks
  is r.
  Wayne [1]
– r. more than half of the time
  White, E.B. [2]

**rights**
– embattled gates to equal r.
  Deutsch [2]

– Civil R.: What black folks are
  given
  Gregory [1]

**riot**
– r. is at bottom
  King, M.L. [20]
– White r.! I wanna riot!
  Strummer & Jones [1]

**rip**
– You r.! Boom! Boom
  Lee, T. [1]

**rise**
– still, like dust, I'll r.
  Angelou [9]

**ritualistic**
– something worthwhile is r.
  Walcott [9]

**river**
– watch the r. flow
  Dylan [31]
– r./Is a strong brown god
  Eliot [45]
– Ol' man r.
  Hammerstein II [1]
– r. is a god
  Hughes, T. [11]

**riverrun**
– r., past Eve and Adam's
  Joyce, J. [25]

**road**
– people who stay in the middle of
  the r.
  Bevan [9]
– rolling English r.
  Chesterton [5]
– old r. is rapidly agin'
  Dylan [3]
– Follow the yellow brick r.
  Harburg [4]
– r. must . . . lead to the whole
  world
  Kerouac [7]
– King of the r.
  Miller, R. [1]
– R. goes ever on and on
  Tolkien [3]

**roads**
– Two r. diverged
  Frost, R. [8]
– They're busy making bigger r.
  Hein [2]

**Robinson**
– Mrs R., you're trying to seduce
  me
  Hoffman, D. [1]
– God bless you please, Mrs R.
  Simon [4]

**robot**
– like a watchful r.
  Kesey [1]

**robotics**
– three fundamental Rules of R.
  Asimov [1]

**rock**
– r. around the clock tonight
  Haley, B. [1]
– r., with two simple chords
  Ono [6]
– I am a r.
  Simon [3]
– r. rebel is defunct
  Sting [1]
– beautiful sounds in r.
  Warhol [5]
– R. is to dress up to
  Zappa [3]

**rock 'n' roll**
– Hail, hail r.
  Berry [2]
– sing for a r. band
  Jagger/Richards [5]
– r. . . . is the highest form
  Smith, P. [2]

– I know it's only r.
  Jagger/Richards [7]
– R. doesn't necessarily mean a
  band
  McLaren [2]
– R. is a combination of good
  ideas
  Marcus [4]

**role**
– any artist or poet's r.
  Lennon [17]
– no longer play the r.
  Moore, B. [1]

**rolling**
– Like a r. stone?
  Dylan [23]

**Roman**
– R. Conquest was . . . a Good
  Thing
  Sellar & Yeatman [2]

**romance**
– Where's the r. gone
  Ayckbourn [2]
– R. . . . the elusive, fake
  Jones, B. [1]

**romantic**
– reading r. novels
  Cooper, J. [1]
– extreme position of R. Love
  Porter, K.A. [5]

**Rome**
– keep home to keep R. Rome
  Corso [2]
– We burn/For R. so near us
  Day Lewis, C. [7]

**roots**
– ultimately without r.
  Levin [3]
– try to put down r.
  Pavese [8]
– R. . . . are a conservative myth
  Rushdie [4]

**rosaries**
– Keep your r. out of our ovaries
  Political slogans [28]

**rose**
– I never promised you a r.
  garden
  Green, Hannah [1]
– Goodbye English r.
  John [4]
– nothing more difficult . . . than to
  paint a r.
  Matisse [2]
– I see la vie en r.
  Piaf [1]

**roses**
– r. in December
  Barrie [1]
– with r. and locomotives
  Cummings, E.E. [2]

**Rothschild**
– what a poor R. would look like
  Rothschild [1]

**Roubles**
– My verse/has brought me/no r.
  Mayakovsky [4]

**rough**
– sleeping pretty r. these days
  Worlock [1]

**Roumania**
– I am Marie of R.
  Parker, D. [3]

**Route 66**
– Get your kicks on R.
  Troup [1]

**routine**
– R. . . . is a sign of ambition
  Auden [31]

**routines**
– My r. come out of total
  unhappiness
  Rivers [2]

**rude**
– let's talk r.
  Flanders & Swann [6]
– No one can be as . . . r. as the
  British
  Gallico [1]

**rudeness**
– strongest motives for r.
  Crisp [14]
– r. in old men
  Thubron [1]

**ruin**
– always somebody about to r. your
  day
  Bukowski [8]
– three roads to r.
  Pompidou [1]

**ruins**
– Of all r.
  Doyle, A.C.[5]

**rulers**
– R./Asleep to all things
  Aidoo [1]

**rules**
– She simply waives the bloody r.
  Berkoff [1]
– not wise to violate r.
  Eliot [58]

**rumours**
– our people live on r.
  Yeltsin [2]

**rump**
– To shake your r.
  Byrne [3]

**run**
– He can r. But he can't hide
  Louis [1]
– born to r.
  Springsteen [2]

**Russia**
– action of R.
  Churchill, W. [13]
– In R., the past carries razors
  Harris, Robert [3]
– R. and America circle each
  other
  Hughes, T. [3]
– In R., people suffer from the
  stillness
  Tolstaya [2]

**Russian**
– so-called new R. man
  Kapuciski [9]
– devout R. people no longer
  needed priests
  Reed, J. [3]
– R. people have become an
  awful reality]
  Trotsky [15

**Russians**
– R. have always been . . .
  concerned with ethics
  Gilliatt [4]

**Rwanda**
– R. had presented the
  world
  Gourevitch [2]

**Sabbath**
– Anybody can observe the S.
  Walker [16]

**sabotage**
– most effective forms of . . . s.
  Dick [2]

**sacred**
– not much is really s.
  Dylan [16]
– S. cows make the best
  hamburgers
  Hoffman, A. [3]
– idea of the s.
  Rushdie [20]
– no such thing as the s.
  Serrano [2]

– *s. is mother-death*
Sexton [3]

**seagulls**
– *When the s. follow the trawler*
Cantona [1]

**seal**
– *you heard a s. bark*
Thurber [3]

**seals**
– *calmer than the s. in the Arctic Ocean*
Fields, D. [2]

**season**
– *every s. is a kind/Of rich nostalgia*
Jennings [1]

**seat belts**
– *Fasten your s. b.*
Davis, B. [3]

**second**
– *Finishing s.*
Nixon [18]

**secondhand**
– *how much of it was s.*
Townshend [7]

**seconds**
– *s., snatched from eternity*
Doisneau [1]

**secret**
– *S. sits in the middle*
Frost, R. [26]

**secrets**
– *Men with s. tend to be drawn*
DeLillo [4]

**sectarian**
– *cat out of the s. bag*
Heaney [11]

**seduction**
– *S. is often difficult to distinguish*
Dworkin [3]
– *brooding edifice of s.*
Powell, A. [1]

**see**
– *come up sometime 'n s. me*
West, M. [4]

**seed**
– *s. never explains the flower*
Hamilton, E. [1]

**seeing**
– *the politics of s. and being seen*
Campbell, B. [3]
– *S. is the function of memory*
Hockney [5]
– *s. is believing*
Wolfe, Tom [3]

**seek**
– *I do not s.; I find*
Soyinka [3]

**segregate**
– *In America, you can s. the people*
Jordan [6]

**segregation**
– *S. now, segregation tomorrow*
Wallace [1]

**selection**
– *natural s. determined the evolution*
Lorenz [2]

**self**
– *s. is now the sacred cow*
Hughes, Robert [3]
– *choose the s. you want*
McCarthy, M. [11]
– *s. . . . is something one creates*
Szasz [8]
– *when the s. speaks to the self*
Woolf [4]

**self-analysis**
– *What is interesting about s.*
Brookner [7]

**self-awareness**
– *cursed with s.*
Shelton [3]

**self-deception**
– *s. remains the most difficult*
Didion [1]

**self-destruction**
– *When the beginnings of s. enter*
Cheever [1]

**self-determination**
– *S., the autonomy of the individual*
Marcuse [3]

**self-interest**
– *S. always runs a good race*
Whitlam [1]

**selfishness**
– *S. is like listening to good jazz*
Larkin [14]

**self-love**
– *S. seems so often unrequited*
Powell, A. [3]

**self-made**
– *He was a s. man*
Heller [3]

**self-parody**
– *S. is the first portent of age*
McMurtry [1]

**Self-pity**
– *S. comes so naturally*
Maurois [1]

**self-realization**
– *S. is not an anti-social principle*
Storr [1]

**Self-respect**
– *S. – feeling that no one . . . is suspicious*
Mencken [20]
– *S. is nothing to hide behind*
Sarton [3]

**sell**
– *delinquent and insatiable need to s.*
Berger [14]

**semicolon**
– *glimpse of a s. coming*
Thomas [4]

**sense**
– *Make s. who may*
Beckett [22]

**sensibility**
– *dissociation of s. set in*
Eliot [15]

**sentences**
– *Certain brief s. are peerless*
Rostand [13]

**sentiment**
– *healthy to enjoy s.*
Chesterton [15]

**sentimental**
– *What's wrong with s.*
McCartney [3]

**sentimentality**
– *no place for s.*
Burroughs, W. [16]
– *S. is . . . erected upon brutality*
Jung [4]
– *S. is the emotional promiscuity*
Mailer [11]
– *S. is only sentiment*
Maugham [12]

**September**
– *days grow short/When you reach S.*
Anderson, M. [1]

**serenity**
– *God, give us s. to accept*
Niebuhr [4]

**servant**
– *public servant doing my best*
Jackson, J. [5]

**servants**
– *best s. of the people*
Lippmann [2]

**service**
– *devoted to your s.*
Elizabeth II [1]
– *Pressed into s.*
Frost, R. [7]

**sessions**
– *pay for the s. you miss*
Allen, W. [18]

**settlers**
– *When old s. say*
Lessing [1]

**seventies**
– *sure I remember the S.*
Hopper [3]

**seventy**
– *good for s. years*
Graves [15]
– *Oh, to be s. again!*
Holmes Jr. [2]
– *Being over s. is like*
Spark [1]

**sewer**
– *I used to live in a s.*
Darnell [1]
– *trip through a s.*
Mizner [2]

**sex**
– *Is s. dirty?*
Allen, W. [3]
– *S. – the great inequality*
Bagnold [3]
– *I've tried several varieties of s.*
Bankhead [5]
– *English weren't famous for s.*
Barnes, J. [15]
– *categories of s. . . . are cosmic categories*
Berdyaev [1]
– *S. has never been an obsession*
Boy George [1]
– *S. . . . was meant to be short, nasty and brutish*
Burchill [2]
– *we've made mistakes, we've had s.*
Bush, G. [3]
– *S. pleasure in woman*
de Beauvoir [4]
– *S. is what you can get*
DeLillo [11]
– *S. and drugs and rock and roll*
Dury [1]
– *S. is antithetical to material greed*
Friday [4]
– *s. in the America of the feminine*
Friedan [2]
– *healthy s. life mitigates*
Hein [1]
– *S. is about the only grown-up thing*
Hornby [9]
– *it's a whole different s.*
Lemmon [1]
– *art forms have become so obsessed with s.*
Loos [4]
– *S. appeal is fifty percent*
Loren [1]
– *S. is two minutes of squelching*
Lydon [8]
– *nothing safe about s.*
Mailer [15]
– *No s. please*
Marriott & Foot [1]
– *Continental people have s. lives*
Mikes [2]
– *I swim in a perpetual sea of s.*
Miller, H. [1]
– *S. is one of the . . . reasons for reincarnation*
Miller, H. [18]
– *S. is the mysticism of materialism*
Muggeridge [5]

– *S. is a Nazi*
Murray, L. [6]
– *wanted to know about s.*
Reuben [1]
– *undesired s. endured by women*
Russell, B. [9]
– *There will be s. after death*
Tomlin [2]
– *s. symbol has to do with an attitude*
Turner, K. [2]
– *S. is like money*
Updike [8]
– *S. builds no roads*
Vidal [4]
– *S. is more exciting on the screen*
Warhol [3]
– *that's the time for s.*
Wells. H.G. [10]
– *What is s. after all*
Westwood [4]
– *s. and sentiment should be separated*
White, E. [2]
– *right to have s.*
White, E. [9]

**sexes**
– *Different though the s. are*
Woolf [24]

**sexism**
– *virulent s. is beyond question*
Millett [5]

**sexist**
– *bonds of community seem 's.'*
Gilder [1]

**sex-typed**
– *mind is not s.*
Mead [8]

**sexual**
– *world of s. abuse*
Campbell, B. [1]
– *truth about the s. revolution*
Decter [1]
– *s. life of adult women*
Freud [8]
– *s. dominion obtains*
Millett [1]
– *s. freedom of today*
Pasolini [7]
– *dreary business of s. habit*
White, E. [4]
– *One must be a s. gourmet*
Will [1]

**sexual act**
– *mutual and satisfied s. a.*
Sanger [1]

**sexualité**
– *Liberté! Fraternité! S.!*
graffito [8]

**sexuality**
– *s. . . . puts us on an even footing*
Cioran [3]
– *s. in movies*
Deneuve [1]
– *S. is a part of our behaviour*
Foucault [4]
– *s. is as wide as the sea*
Jarman [2]
– *Fear of s. is the new disease*
Sontag [25]
– *S. is as much about language*
Weeks [1]

**shadow**
– *s. still stands over all of us*
Alliluyeva [2]
– *Falls the S.*
Eliot [26]

**shag**
– *Shall we s. now*
Myers [3]

**shake**
– *S., rattle and roll*
Haley, B. [2]

**soundbites**
– *not a time for s.*
Blair [5]

**South**
– *While the S. is . . . Christ-haunted*
O'Connor, F. [4]
– *chief forms of amusement in the S.*
Warren, R.P. [1]

**Southerner**
– *average S. has the speech patterns*
Bryson [2]

**Southerners**
– *S. can never resist a losing cause*
Mitchell, M. [6]

**Soviet**
– *half a century of S. rule*
Alliluyeva [3]

**Soviet**
– *no S. domination of Eastern Europe*
Ford, G. [4]
– *S. régime is not the embodiment of evil*
Zinoviev [1]

**Soviet Union**
– *If the S. U. can give up*
Fuentes [3]

**space**
– *artifact designed for s. travel*
Burroughs, W. [14]
– *S. isn't remote at all*
Hoyle [1]
– *s. was the uncontrollable mystery*
McLuhan [3]
– *S. to be the central fact*
Olson [1]
– *S. is almost infinite*
Quayle [1]
– *S. – the final frontier*
Roddenberry [1]
– *very little difference . . . in s.*
Sharman [1]
– *there is more s. where nobody is*
Stein [9]

**spaces**
– *s. between the houses*
Fenton [1]

**space-ships**
– *S. . . . are no escape*
Koestler [4]

**Spanish Inquisition**
– *Nobody expects the S. I.*
Monty Python's Flying Circus [5]

**speak**
– *learn to speak properly*
Bainbridge [8]
– *teach kids to s. badly*
Elton [5]
– *Whereof one cannot s.*
Wittgenstein [11]

**special relationship**
– *this means a s.*
Churchill, W. [35]

**specialist**
– *s. is someone who does everything else worse*
Ricci [1]

**specialists**
– *All other men are s.*
Doyle, A.C. [4]

**speciesism**
– *form of s.*
Singer [6]

**spectacles**
– *immense accumulation of s.*
Debord [2]

**speech**
– *s. is itself a critique of life*
Mann, T. [7]

– *s. is poetry*
Noonan [2]

**speed**
– *S. provides the one . . . modern pleasure*
Huxley, A. [20]
– *S. is scarcely the noblest virtue*
Thurber [17]

**spell**
– *I put a s. on you*
Hawkins [1]
– *countries whose names we cannot s. properly.*
Ruhe [1]

**spender**
– *Hey! Big S.*
Fields, D. [3]

**spiders**
– *s. marching through the air*
Lowell, R. [1]

**spider's web**
– *Fiction is like a s. w.*
Woolf [33]

**spies**
– *What do you think s. are*
Le Carré [1]

**spike**
– *When I put a s. into my vein*
Reed, L. [2]

**spin doctor**
– *rather . . . a s. d. than a hidden persuader*
Bell, T. [1]

**spinach**
– *likes to eat mys.*
Popeye [2]
– *I say it's s.*
White, E.B. [1]

**spirit**
– *Pure S., one hundred degrees proof*
Huxley, A. [23]

**spirits**
– *evil s. of the past*
Kohl [2]

**spiritual**
– *young to hold s. convictions*
Orton [6]

**spirituality**
– *furtively prurient s.*
Jung [2]

**split infinitive**
– *neither know nor care what a s. i. is*
Fowler, H.W. [2]

**spontaneity**
– *Through s. we are re-formed*
Spolin [2]

**spoon**
– *born with a plastic s. in my mouth*
Townshend [2]

**spoon-feeding**
– *educational attachment is howled down as s.*
Strong [1]

**sport**
– *in s. you have to have a narrow tunnel vision*
Botham [2]
– *I'm fanatical about s.*
Gray, S. [4]
– *take politics out of s.*
Hain [1]
– *Serious s. has nothing to do with fair play*
Orwell [34]

**sporting**
– *What. . . . governed the British s. event?*
Buford [1]
– *s. moment as their best ever*
Hornby [7]

**springtime**
– *S. for Hitler and Germany*
Brooks, M. [1]

**spy**
– *s. world will . . . be the collective couch*
Le Carré [4]

**squamous**
– *squirming facts exceed the s. mind*
Stevens [9]

**St Francis**
– *S. F. of Assisi talking about rights*
Weil [13]

**stables**
– *s. are the real centre of the household*
Shaw, G.B. [11]

**stage**
– *don't put your daughter on the s.*
Coward [11]
– *s. is like a cage of light*
Depardieu [1]
– *my room was a s.*
Hendrix [3]

**stain**
– *s. upon the silence*
Beckett [19]

**stake**
– *not burning people at the s.*
Beatty [1]

**Stalin**
– *S. . . . is the most alarming figure*
Harris, Robert [2]
– *S. considered that he never erred*
Khrushchev [3]
– *S. is the personification of the bureaucracy*
Trotsky [21]
– *how do we remove S.*
Yevtushenko [5]

**stammer**
– *What has influenced my life . . . my s.*
Maugham [16]

**stand**
– *Get up, s. up*
Marley [1]

**standardization**
– *s. is called equality*
Fromm [7]

**star**
– *not a s. until they can spell your name*
Bogart [7]
– *Once you're a s. you're dead*
Hoffman, D. [2]
– *If you want to be a s.*
Horne [1]
– *S. Wars*
Lucas, G. [1]

**stardust**
– *We are s.*
Mitchell, Joni [2]

**stare**
– *singleness of that wide s.*
Larkin [19]

**stars**
– *S. of death*
Akhmatova [2]
– *s. are dead*
Auden [10]
– *seven s. go squawking*
Auden [11]
– *road to a knowledge of the s.*
Eddington [2]
– *s. are essentially worthless*
Goldman, W. [1]
– *God makes s.*
Goldwyn [7]
– *s. which shone over Babylon*
Goodman, Linda [1]

– *I study the s.*
Walcott [5]

**start**
– *s. life all over again*
Fellini [1]

**started**
– *I've s., so I'll finish*
Magnusson [1]

**starter**
– *Few thought he was even a s.*
Attlee [1]

**starvation**
– *go through the kingdoms of s.*
Long [1]

**state**
– *reinforcement of the power of the s.*
Camus [10]
– *s. is a state of Slavery*
Gill [1]

**statecraft**
– *S. is soulcraft*
Will [4]

**stately**
– *s. Homes of England*
Coward [12]

**Stately park**
– *wandering round and round a s. p.*
Maugham [9]

**statement**
– *sweeping s.*
Kavanagh [2]

**statesman**
– *s. is a politician who's been dead*
Truman [4]

**statisticians**
– *Thou shalt not sit/With s.*
Auden [27]

**stay**
– *Makin' a long s. short*
Hubbard [6]

**steal**
– *Great artists s.*
Tarantino [9]

**steaming**
– *S. through metal landscape*
Spender, S. [5]

**steel**
– *pangs of dust and s.*
Crane [4]

**Stein**
– *I don't like the family S.*
Anonymous [4]

**stench**
– *s. in the nostrils of the gods*
De Forest [1]

**step**
– *one more s. along the world*
Carter, Sydney [2]

**steppeland**
– *Through the s. roaring*
Yesenin [1]

**steps**
– *Perhaps I am doomed to retrace my s.*
Breton [3]

**stereotypes**
– *Out with s., feminism proclaims*
Paglia [4]

**sterilization**
– *s. . . . is one method of birth control*
Gandhi, I. [1]

**stigma**
– *s. . . . will serve to beat a dogma*
Guedalla [3]

**still**
– *be wholly s. and alone*
Kafka [6]
– *Happy are those who are s.*
Okri [2]

**Stock Exchange**
– make a fortune on the S. E.
Mortimer [4]

**stocking**
– glimpse of s.
Porter, C. [5]

**stomach**
– pit of my burning, nauseous s.
Cobain [3]

**stone**
– they'll stone you
Dylan [26]

**stories**
– precisely the disappointing s.
Frisch [1]
– s. – in the good sense
Gould [3]
– all s. . . . end in death
Hemingway [12]
– We make the oldest s. new
Marcus [1]
– S. are substitutes for God
Wenders [1]

**stormy**
– S. weather
Koestler [1]

**story**
– I'll tell you a s.
Fitzgerald, F.S. [26]
– Every age has its own s.
Morrison, B. [2]

**story-teller**
– Death is the sanction of . . . the s.
Benjamin [11]
– The secret of the s.
Crace [2]

**storytellers**
– If a nation loses its s.
Handke [2]

**straight**
– I want to be s.
Dury [7]

**Strand**
– never alone with a S.
Advertising slogans [25]

**stranger**
– You may see a s.
Hammerstein II [7]

**strangers**
– S. in the night
Sinatra, F. [2]
– depended on the kindness of s.
Williams, T. [4]

**stream**
– When I heard the word 's.'
Joyce, J. [33]

**streets**
– Down these mean s.
Chandler [7]
– Reclaim the s.
Political slogans [26]

**strength**
– s. lined with tenderness
Angelou [3]
– S. through joy
Political slogans[5]

**strife**
– in place of s.
Castle [1]

**strike**
– no right to s.
Coolidge [1]
– push along our little baby s.
Steinbeck [1]

**string quartet**
– perfect expression . . . is a s. q.
Tate [1]

**striven**
– To have s. so hard
Kissinger [12]

**striving**
– salvation is in s. to achieve
Kapuciski [2]

**struggle**
– S. is the father of all things
Hitler [9]
– s. of man against power
Kundera [3]
– s. is my life
Mandela, N. [1]
– s. to set oneself free
Marcus [2]
– s. continues
Saro-Wiwa [1]
– living is s.
Wilder, T. [1]

**stuff**
– Brotherhood of the Right S.
Wolfe, Tom [6]

**stupid**
– s. believe that to be truthful is
easy
Cather [1]
– S. is as stupid does
Hanks [2]
– considered s. . . . is more painful
Levi, P. [8]

**stupidity**
– no amount of learning can cure s.
Vizinczey [3]

**style**
– s. is just the outside of content
Godard [7]
– Our own epoch is determining
. . . its own s.
Le Corbusier [2]
– S. [is] the hallmark of a
temperament
Maurois [5]
– S. and Structure are the essence
Nabokov [12]
– This is s.
Neruda [10]
– cultivated s. would be like a mask
Porter, K.A. [4]
– s. is eternal
Saint Laurent [1]
– S. is not something applied
Stevens [20]
– S. is the ultimate morality of
mind
Whitehead [2]
– Phoney Wars were . . . s. wars
York [3]

**subconscious**
– Yanks have colonized our s.
Wenders [1]

**subjects**
– order of the great s. of life
Spark [6]

**submarine**
– We all live in a yellow s
Lennon & McCartney [8]

**suburban**
– Faces, they have, those s. people
Drabble [3]
– always will have a s. President
Kroker [1]

**suburbs**
– s. are incubators of apathy
Connolly, C. [14]
– s. are good for the children
Viorst [1]

**subversives**
– First we kill all the s.
Saint Jean [1]

**succeed**
– It is not enough to s.
Vidal [25]

**success**
– penalty of s.
Astor [2]
– got to keep on being a s.
Berlin, Irving [9]
– A (S.) = X (Work)
Einstein [16]

– S. is a lousy teacher
Gates [2]
– S. is more dangerous than failure
Greene [23]
– idea that s. spoils people
Maugham [10]
– logic of worldly s.
Merton [2]
– no point in s.
Otway [1]
– S. is dangerous
Picasso [16]
– S. makes life easier
Springsteen [5]
– one is punished for s.
Warshow [2]

**successful**
– cannot bear s. people
John [3]

**sucker**
– never give a s.
Fields, W.C. [2]
– I'll show you a s.
Sinatra, F. [1]

**Suez**
– S. Canal was flowing through my
drawing room
Eden, C [1]

**suffer**
– If we must s.
Ellman [2]
– I s. very eloquently
Mitchell, Joni [6]

**suffered**
– have s. for things that I am guilty
of
Vanzetti [1]

**suffering**
– Is s. so very serious?
Colette [2]
– the marks of s.
Fitzgerald, F.S. [18]
– will not give up his s.
Gurdjieff [4]
– Passive/S. makes the world go
round
Heaney [10]
– Human life is reduced to real s.
Hesse [5]
– s. must become Love
Mansfield [4]
– not true that s. ennobles the
character
Maugham [4]
– s. of either sex
Mead [4]
– S. is an aspect of the great
Promethean will
Okri [5]
– day you stop s.
Williams, T. [18]

**sugar**
– spoonful of s. helps the
medicine
Andrews [1]

**suicide**
– If I commit s.
Artaud [1]
– s. is not worth the trouble
Benjamin [8]
– prevalence of s.
Ellis, H. [4]
– s. remains the courageous act
Greene [16]
– longest s. note in history
Kaufman, Gerald [1]
– contemplation of s.
Lebowitz [3]
– s. kills two people
Miller, A. [7]
– committing s. through lack of
intelligence
O'Brien, E. [1]

– temptation to commit s.
Pavese [7]
– s. shd bump off . . . one
swine
Pound [29]

**suicides**
– s. have a special language
Sexton [2]

**suitablility**
– criterion of s. and convenience
Moore, M. [2]

**suits**
– My s. are not white
Bell, M. [1]
– s. you sir
Fast Show [2]

**summer**
– an invincible s.
Camus [12]
– but s. to your heart
Millay [7]

**summertime**
– no cure for the s. blues
Cochran [1]
– S. and the living is easy
Gershwin [2]

**sun**
– see the s. the other way around
Bishop [4]
– s. has got its hat on
Gay [1]
– black s. has appeared
Kaixi Wuer [1]
– s. bared the reality of our lives
Okri [1]
– day of the s. is like the day of a
king
Stevens [1]
– It Was The S. Wot Won It
Sun [7]
– before you let the s. in
Thomas, D. [17]
– most beautiful thing under the s.
Wolf, C. [3]

**sunbonnet**
– s. as well as the sombrero
Ferber [2]

**Sunday**
– boredom of S. afternoon
Connolly, C. [22]
– Why do I do this every S.
Osborne [1]
– S. is the same everywhere
Rhys [1]

**Sunday Times**
– uncontainable
communicativeness
Amis, M. [13]

**Sundays**
– nothing but S. for weeks
Hoban [3]

**sunflower**
– perfect beauty of a s.
Ginsberg [4]

**Sung**
– glaze like a S. vase on your
eyeball
Perelman [1]

**sunlight**
– s. on the garden
MacNeice [2]

**sunny**
– s. side of the street
Fields, D. [1]

**supercalifragilisticexpialidocious!**
– S.!
Andrews [2]

**superiority**
– s. has been accorded
de Beauvoir [1]

**supermarket**
– with the s. as our temple
Stevenson [15]

*– cannot have both t. and . . .
civilisation*
Murdoch, I. [3]
*– T. is sui generis*
Murdoch, I. [18]
*– For the t., we are silent*
Murray, L. [7]
*– committing ourselves to the t.*
Nixon [8]
*– only one t.*
O'Connor, F. [1]
*– possession of the 't.' is less
important*
Orwell [13]
*– When t. is no longer free*
Prévert [4]
*– T. is simply a compliment*
Rorty [3]
*– unclouded face of t.*
Scott, C.P. [1]
*– t. is always something*
Sontag [1]
*– t. is balance*
Sontag [2]
*– little insane about the t.*
Stevens [1]
*– Absolute t. is a very rare . . .
commodity*
Thompson, H.S. [5]
*– t. is really an ambition*
Ustinov [10]
*– frightened of the t.*
Wittgenstein [2]
*– Man can embody t.*
Yeats [29]
**truths**
*– t. being in and out of favor*
Frost, R. [5]
*– no new t.*
McCarthy, M. [8]
*– more t. in twenty-four hours*
Vaneigem [3]
**truth-telling**
*– T. . . . key to responsible
citizenship*
Hoover, J.E. [1]
**T-Shirt**
*– Get a message, get a T.*
York [6]
**tubby**
*– Grows t. without exercise*
Milne [3]
**Tube**
*– way people behave on the T.*
Swift [1]
**tulips**
*– T. through the t.*
Dubin [1]
**tunes**
*– t. the chauffeurs . . . can whistle*
Beecham [3]
**Turgenev**
*– I beat Mr T.*
Hemingway [24]
**turn**
*– I'd love to t. you on*
Lennon & McCartney [14]
**turning**
*– lady's not for t.*
Thatcher [10]
**turnip**
*– candle in that great t.*
Churchill, W. [42]
**TV**
*– British T. . . . trivializes the
serious*
Ballard [7]
*– madness of TV is the madness of
human life*
Paglia [6]
*– The T. play . . . a 'theatre of the
people'*
Potter [1]

*– T. isn't fun any more*
Street-Porter [2]
*– world works by way of T.*
Thomson [1]
*– guilty of misusing T.*
Winfrey [3]
**twang**
*– go t., and you've got
music*
Vicious [2]
**twat**
*– dead t.*
graffito [12]
**twenties**
*– the early t.*
Fitzgerald, F.S. [16]
**Twentieth Century**
*– horror of the T. C.*
Mailer [13]
*– filthy t.*
Rowse [2]
*– Great t. c.*
Yevtushenko [1]
**twenty-one**
*– acute limited excellence at t.*
Fitzgerald, F.S. [6]
**twilight**
*– dreamcrossed t.*
Eliot [28]
**Twilight Zone**
*– area called the T. Z.*
Serling [1]
**twiminds**
*– You have become of twosome t.*
Joyce, J. [27]
**twinkle**
*– our right to t.*
Monroe [5]
**typewriter**
*– hope to go with my head on
that t.*
Bukowski [9]
*– sit in front of the t.*
Robinson, B. [7]
**typing**
*– that isn't writing . . . it's t.*
Capote [1]
**tyrannise**
*– t. over his bank balance*
Keynes [16]
**tyranny**
*– Under conditions of t.*
Arendt [6]
*– silent in the face of t.*
Soyinka [1]
**U.S.A.**
*– God bless the U., so large*
Auden [42]
*– turned the U. into a nation of
hobbledehoys*
Loos [4]
*– Born in the U.*
Springsteen [3]
**ugliness**
*– I seated u. on my knee*
Dali [4]
*– u. lasts*
Gainsbourg [2]
**ukelele**
*– my little u.*
Formby [1]
*– Little U. In My Hand*
Formby [2]
**ulcer**
*– I am an 8 U. man*
Early, S. [1]
**Ulster**
*– U. says no*
Political slogans [21]
**ultraliberalism**
*– U. today translates into . . .
isolationism*
Agnew [3]

**Ulysses**
*– U. . . . is a dogged attempt to
cover*
Forster [11]
**unbearable**
*– in victory u.*
Churchill, W. [52]
**unbelief**
*– comprehend me in my u.*
Kersh [2]
*– To choose u.*
Rushdie [32]
**unbloody**
*– heads are heroically u.*
Nash, O. [3]
**unborn**
*– cemetery . . . of the u.*
John Paul II [3]
**unclean**
*– This is u.*
Reading [1]
**unconscious**
*– nature of the u.*
Clare [1]
*– images of the u.*
Jung [1]
*– My u. knows more*
Kraus [7]
**uncouth**
*– Too much Truth/Is u.*
Adams, F.P. [2]
**under-belly**
*– exposure of the u. of the Axis*
Churchill, W. [30]
**under-class**
*– salvation of the u.*
Podhoretz [1]
**understand**
*– The liberals can u. everything*
Bruce [6]
*– People who u. your thought*
Fulbright [1]
*– desire to u. has a built-in
brutality*
Høeg [2]
*– What better way to prove that
you u.*
Rosenberg [5]
*– u. a few words in life*
Rostand [3]
**understanding**
*– sign of the beginning of u.*
Kafka [3]
*– Shallow u. from people of good
will*
King, M.L. [10]
*– more dangerous than
sympathetic u.*
Picasso [23]
**understood**
*– I have u. you.*
De Gaulle [5]
**uneconomic**
*– not shown it to be 'u.'*
Schumacher [1]
**unemployed**
*– When we're u.*
Jackson, J. [2]
**unemployment**
*– I know what u. is like*
Archer [1]
**unfeasibly**
*– U. Large testicles*
Viz [1]
**unhappiness**
*– Nothing is funnier than u.*
Beckett [12]
*– u. is best defined*
De Bono [2]
*– loyalty we feel to u.*
Greene [9]
*– what you wish was that makes u.*
Joplin [3]

**unhappy**
*– Men who are u.*
Russell, B. [10]
*– u. have no need for anything*
Weil [24]
**uniform**
*– got a u. and a gun*
Baldwin, J. [9]
**Union**
*– power of the Industrial U.*
Connolly, J [1]
**unions**
*– join in the work of your u.*
Thatcher [7]
**united**
*– The People u.*
Political slogans [20]
**United Nations**
*– U.N. is not . . . a product of do-
gooders*
Hammarskjöld [2]
*– U. N. cannot do anything*
O'Brien, C. [2]
**United States**
*– What the U. S. does best*
Fuentes [1]
*– U.S. has now achieved . . . a
socialist state*
Kael [1]
*– U.S. has to move very fast*
Kennedy [22]
*– most at home in the U. S.*
Lewis, W. [5]
*– U. S. never lost a war*
Rogers, W. [3]
*– Tomorrow is in the U.S.*
Rowland, T. [1]
*– U. S. is just now the oldest
country*
Stein [3]
**universe**
*– u. will express itself*
Calvino [4]
*– good u. next door*
Cummings, E.E. [8]
*– Disturb the u.*
Eliot [3]
*– u. is an orchard*
Gray, A. [3]
*– u. is . . . queerer than we can
suppose*
Haldane [4]
*– u. is not hostile*
Holmes, J. [1]
*– more the u. seems comprehensible*
Weinberg [1]
*– effort to understand the u.*
Weinberg [2]
**universities**
*– u. . . . they are élitist*
Lodge [2]
**university**
*– most important function of the u.*
Bloom, A. [4]
*– U. is a Mecca*
Bronowski [7]
**unjust**
*– u. law is itself a species of
violence*
Gandhi, M. [5]
**unknown**
*– U. Prime Minister*
Asquith, H. [2]
*– mind loves the u.*
Magritte [2]
*– Only the u. frightens men*
Saint-Exupéry [2]
*– u. that excites the ardor of
scholars*
Stevens [8]
**unlikeness**
*– realization of u.*
Leavis [2]